HANDBOOK OF
U.S. LABOR
STATISTICS

Handbook of
U.S. Labor
Statistics

Employment, Earnings, Prices, Productivity, and Other Labor Data

17th Edition
2014

Edited by Mary Meghan Ryan

Bernan Press

Lanham • Boulder • New York • London

Published by Bernan Press

An imprint of The Rowman & Littlefield Publishing Group, Inc.

4501 Forbes Boulevard, Suite 200, Lanham, Maryland 20706

www.rowman.com

800-865-3457; info@bernan.com

16 Carlisle Street, London W1D 3BT, United Kingdom

ISBN-13: 978-1-59888-700-6
eISBN-13: 978-1-59888-701-3

ISSN: 1526-2553

CONTENTS

LIST OF TABLES

CHAPTER 1: POPULATION, LABOR FORCE, AND EMPLOYMENT STATUS

POPULATION, LABOR FORCE, AND EMPLOYMENT STATUS

EMPLOYMENT

UNEMPLOYMENT

PERSONS WITH A DISABILITY: LABOR FORCE CHARACTERISTICS

EMPLOYMENT SITUATION OF VETERANS

VOLUNTEERING IN THE UNITED STATES

CHAPTER 2: EMPLOYMENT, HOURS, AND EARNINGS

EMPLOYMENT AND HOURS

CHAPTER 5: PRODUCTIVITY AND COSTS

CHAPTER 6: COMPENSATION OF EMPLOYEES

EMPLOYMENT COST INDEX (ECI)

EMPLOYER COSTS FOR EMPLOYEE COMPENSATION (ECEC)

EMPLOYEE BENEFITS SURVEY

CHAPTER 7: RECENT TRENDS IN THE LABOR MARKET

MASS LAYOFFS

CHAPTER 11: CONSUMER EXPENDITURES

CHAPTER 12: AMERICAN TIME USE SURVEY

CHAPTER 13: INCOME DATA IN THE UNITED STATES (CENSUS BUREAU)

CHAPTER 14: OCCUPATIONAL SAFETY AND HEALTH

LIST OF FIGURES

PREFACE

Bernan Press is pleased to present a compilation of Bureau of Labor Statistics (BLS) data in this 17th edition of its award-winning *Handbook of U.S Labor Statistics: Employment, Earnings, Prices, Productivity, and Other Labor Data.* BLS and the U.S. Census Bureau provide a treasure trove of historical information about all aspects of labor and employment in the United States. The current edition maintains the content of previous editions and updates the text with additional data and new features. The data in this *Handbook* are excellent sources of information for analysts in both government and the private sector.

The *Handbook* addresses many of the issues that are being discussed across the United States, such as high unemployment, employment projections for the future, the decline in income, the rapidly increasing costs of health care services, and the dramatic aging of the labor force. In addition, this publication provides an abundance of data on topics such as prices, productivity, consumer expenditures, occupational safety and health, international labor comparisons, and much more.

The comprehensive and historical data presented in the *Handbook* allow the user to understand the background of current events and compare today's economy with previous years. Select data in this publication go back to 1913 and several tables have data going back to the 1940s.

FEATURES OF THIS PUBLICATION

- Over 225 tables that present authoritative data on labor market statistics, including employment and unemployment, mass layoffs, prices, productivity, and data from the American Time Use Survey (ATUS).

- Each chapter is preceded by a figure that calls attention to noteworthy trends in the data.

- In addition to the figures, the introductory material for to each chapter also contains highlights of other salient data.

- The tables in each section are also preceded by notes and definitions, which contain concise descriptions of the data sources, concepts, definitions, and methodology from which the data are derived.

- The introductory notes also include references to more comprehensive reports. These reports provide additional data and more extensive descriptions of estimation methods, sampling, and reliability measures.

NEW IN THIS EDITION

The 17th edition includes the latest employment projections released by BLS. In addition, a section in Chapter 1 on volunteering in the United States has been added, along with additional benefit tables in Chapter 6 and new tables on international labor comparisons in Chapter 10. Finally, figures on a variety of topics, including the labor force, household income, eldercare, labor productivity, and employment, have been added throughout the book

SOURCES OF ADDITIONAL INFORMATION

BLS data are primarily derived from surveys conducted by the federal government or through federal-state cooperative arrangements. The comparability of data over time can be affected by changes in the surveys, which are essential for keeping pace with the current structure of economic institutions and for taking advantage of improved survey techniques. Revisions of current data are also periodically made as a result of the availability of new information. In addition, some tables in this *Handbook* were dropped due to the data being from a one-time survey that is now outdated or due to the survey being entirely restructured. Introductory notes to each chapter summarize specific factors that may affect the data. In the tables, the ellipsis character ("…") indicates that data are not available.

More extensive methodological information, including further discussion of the sampling and estimation procedures used for each BLS program, is contained in the *BLS Handbook of Methods*. This publication is in the process of being updated, and completed chapters are available on the BLS Web site at http://www.bls.gov. Other sources of current data and analytical include the *Monthly Labor Review* and a daily Internet publication, *The Editor's Desk* (TED). All of these publications can be found on the BLS Web site as well. Other relevant publications, including those from the Census Bureau, are noted in the notes and definitions in each chapter.

OTHER PUBLICATIONS BY BERNAN PRESS

The *Handbook of U.S. Labor Statistics: Employment, Earnings, Prices, Productivity, and Other Labor Data* is just one of a number of publications in Bernan Press's award-winning U.S. DataBook Series. Other titles include *The Almanac of American Education*; *Business Statistics of the United States: Patterns of Economic Change*; *Crime in the United States*; *Housing Statistics of the United States*; *State*

Profiles: The Population and Economy of Each U.S. State; and *Vital Statistics of the United States: Births, Life Expectancy, Deaths, and Selected Health Data*. In addition, Bernan Press publishes *Employment, Hours, and Earnings: States and Areas* as a special edition of this *Handbook*. Each of these titles provides statistical information from official government sources.

CHAPTER 1: POPULATION, LABOR FORCE, AND EMPLOYMENT STATUS

POPULATION, LABOR FORCE, AND EMPLOYMENT STATUS

HIGHLIGHTS

This chapter presents the detailed historical information collected in the Current Population Survey (CPS), a monthly survey of households that gathers data on the employment status of the population. Basic data on labor force, employment, and unemployment are shown for various characteristics of the population, including age, sex, race, Hispanic origin, and marital status.

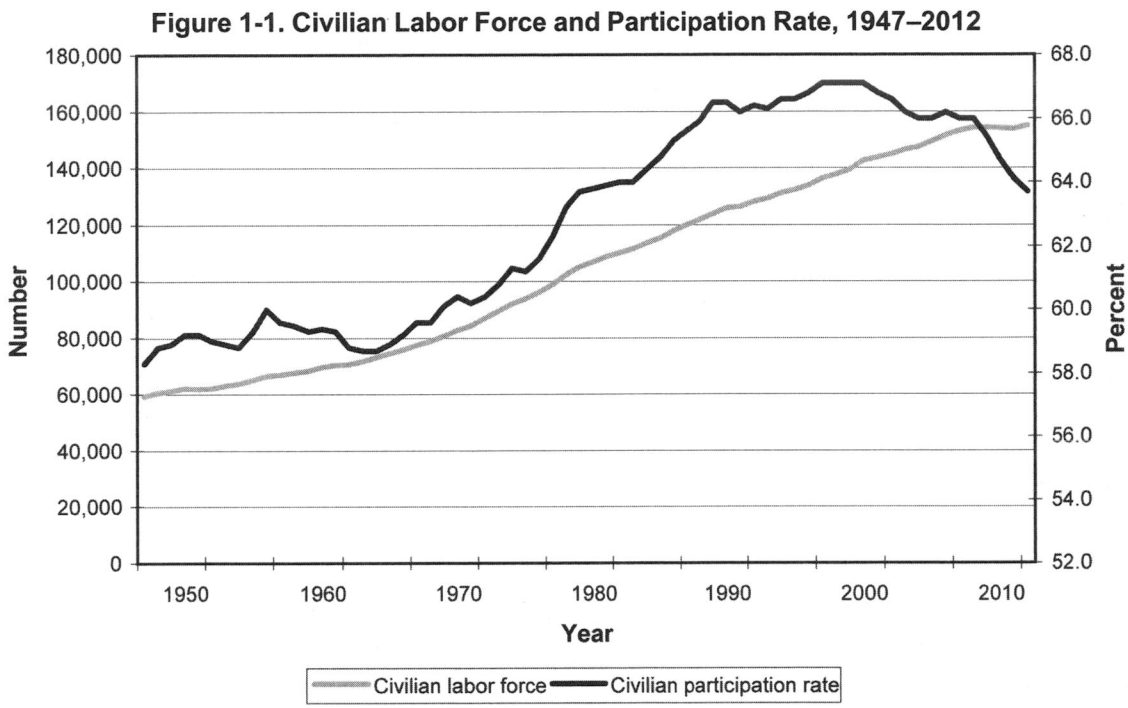

Figure 1-1. Civilian Labor Force and Participation Rate, 1947–2012

Nearly 155 million people were in the labor force in 2012 compared with less than 60 million people in 1947. While the labor force has grown considerably, the labor force participation rate has grown much slower increasing from 58.3 percent in 1947 to 63.7 percent in 2012. In fact, the labor force participation rate declined in 2012 for the fourth consecutive year. (See Table 1-1.)

OTHER HIGHLIGHTS

- Although the civilian labor force participation rate for the total population declined in 2012 to 63.7 percent, the labor force participation rate for those 65 years and over continued to increase. In 2012, it was 18.5 percent—the highest it has been since 1962. (See Table 1-8.)

- In 2012, employment increased 1.9 percent after rising 0.6 percent in 2011. From 2008 through 2010, employment declined each year. The drop in employment was the steepest between 2008 and 2009, when it fell 3.8 percent. (See Table 1-1.)

- While the proportion of white men in the labor force declined from 1980 to 2012, the proportion of black women in the labor force increased from 4.9 percent to 6.3 percent. Hispanic representation in the labor force rose significantly, increasing from 5.7 percent in 1980 to 15.7 percent in 2012. (See Table 1-7.)

NOTES AND DEFINITIONS

CURRENT POPULATION SURVEY OF HOUSEHOLDS

COLLECTION AND COVERAGE

The Current Population Survey (CPS) is a monthly survey that analyzes and publishes statistics on the labor force, employment, and unemployment, classified by a variety of demographic, social, and economic characteristics. This survey is conducted by the Census Bureau for the Bureau of Labor Statistics (BLS). The information is collected from a probability sample of approximately 60,000 households. Respondents are interviewed to obtain information about the employment status of each household member age 16 years and over. Persons under 16 years of age are excluded from the official estimates because child labor laws, compulsory school attendance, and general social custom in the United States severely limit the types and amount of work that these children can do.

The inquiry relates to the household member's employment status during the calendar week, Sunday through Saturday that includes the 12th day of the month. This is known as the "reference week." Actual field interviewing is conducted during the following week (the week that contains the 19th day of the month).

CONCEPTS AND DEFINITIONS

The concepts and definitions underlying the labor force data have been modified—but not substantially altered—since the inception of the survey in 1940 when it began as a Work Projects Administration program. Current definitions of some of the major concepts used in the CPS are described below.

The *civilian noninstitutional population* includes persons 16 years of age and over who reside in the 50 states and the District of Columbia who are not inmates of institutions (such as penal and mental facilities and homes for the aged) and who are not on active duty in the armed forces.

An *employed* person is any person who, during the reference week: (1) did any work at all (at least one hour) as a paid employees in their own business, profession, or on their own farm, or who worked 15 hours or more as an unpaid worker in an enterprise operated by a member of the family; and (2) any person who was not working but who had a job or business from which he or she was temporarily absent due to vacation, illness, bad weather, childcare problems, maternity or paternity leave, labor-management disputes, job training, or other family or personal reasons, despite whether the employee was being paid for the time off or was seeking other jobs.

Each employed person is counted only once, even if he or she holds more than one job. For purposes of occupation and industry classification, multiple jobholders are counted as being in the job at which they worked the greatest number of hours during the reference week.

Included in the total are employed citizens of foreign countries who were temporarily in the United States but not living on the premises of an embassy. Excluded are persons whose only activity during the reference week consisted of work around their own house (painting, repairing, or own home housework) or volunteer work for religious, charitable, and similar organizations.

Unemployed persons are all persons who had no employment during the reference week, but who were available for work (except for temporary illness) and had made specific efforts to find employment some time during the four-week period ending with the reference week. Persons who were waiting to be recalled to a job from which they had been laid off need not have been looking for work to be classified as unemployed.

Reasons for unemployment are divided into four major groups: (1) job losers, defined as (a) persons on temporary layoff, who have been given a date to return to work or who expect to return to work within six months; (b) permanent job losers, whose employment ended involuntarily and who began looking for work; and (c) persons who completed a temporary job and began looking for work after the job ended; (2) job leavers, defined as persons who quit or otherwise terminated their employment voluntarily and immediately began looking for work; (3) reentrants, defined as persons who previously worked but were out of the labor force prior to beginning their job search; and (4) new entrants, defined as persons who had never worked but were currently searching for work.

Duration of unemployment represents the length of time (through the current reference week) that persons classified as unemployed had been looking for work. For persons on layoff, duration of unemployment represents the number of full weeks they had been on layoff. Mean duration of unemployment is the arithmetic average computed from single weeks of unemployment; median duration of unemployment is the midpoint of a distribution of weeks of unemployment.

A *spell of unemployment* is a continuous period of unemployment of at least one week's duration and is terminated by either employment or withdrawal from the labor force.

Extent of unemployment refers to the number of workers and proportion of the labor force that were unemployed at some time during the year. The number of weeks unemployed is the total number of weeks accumulated during the entire calendar year.

The unemployment rate is the number of unemployed persons as a percentage of the civilian labor force.

The *civilian labor force* comprises all civilians classified as employed or unemployed.

The *participation rate* represents the proportion of the civilian noninstitutional population currently in the labor force.

The *employment-population ratio* represents the proportion of the population that is currently employed.

Persons not in the labor force are all persons in the civilian noninstitutional population who are neither employed nor unemployed. Information is collected about their desire for and availability to take a job at the time of the CPS interview, job search activity during the prior year, and reason for not looking for work during the four-week period ending with the reference week. Persons not in the labor force who want and are available for a job and who have looked for work within the past 12 months (or since the end of their last job, if they had held one within the past 12 months), but who are not currently looking, are designated as marginally attached to the labor force. The marginally attached are divided into those not currently looking because they believe their search would be futile—so-called discouraged workers—and those not currently looking for other reasons, such as family responsibilities, ill health, or lack of transportation.

Discouraged workers are defined as persons not in the labor force who want and are available for a job and who have looked for work sometime in the past 12 months (or since the end of their last job, if they held one within the past 12 months), but who are not currently looking because they believe that there are no jobs available or there are none for which they would qualify. The reasons for not currently looking for work include a person's belief that no work is available in his or her line of work or area; he or she could not find any work; he or she lacks necessary schooling, training, skills, or experience; employers would think he or she is too young or too old; or he or she would encounter hiring discrimination.

Usual full- or part-time status refers to hours usually worked per week. Full-time workers are those who usually work 35 hours or more (at all jobs). This group includes some individuals who worked less than 35 hours during the reference week for economic or noneconomic reasons. Part-time workers are those who usually work less than 35 hours per week (at all jobs), regardless of the number of hours worked during the reference week. These concepts are used to differentiate a person's normal schedule from his or her specific activity during the reference week. Unemployed persons who are looking for full-time work or who are on layoff from full-time jobs are counted as part of the full-time labor force; unemployed persons who are seeking part-time work or who are on layoff from part-time jobs are counted as part of the part-time labor force.

Year-round, full-time workers are workers who primarily worked at full-time jobs for 50 weeks or more during the preceding calendar year. Part-year workers worked either full- or part-time for 1 to 49 weeks.

At work part-time for economic reasons, sometimes called involuntary part-time, refers to individuals who gave an economic reason for working 1 to 34 hours during the reference week. Economic reasons include slack work or unfavorable business conditions, inability to find full-time work, and seasonal declines in demand. Those who usually work part-time must also indicate that they want and are available to work full-time to be classified as working part-time for economic reasons.

At work part-time for noneconomic reasons refers to persons who usually work part-time and were at work 1 to 34 hours during the reference week for a noneconomic reason. Noneconomic reasons include illness or other medical limitations, childcare problems or other family or personal obligations, school or training, retirement or Social Security limits on earnings, and being in a job where full-time work is less than 35 hours. This also includes workers who gave an economic reason for usually working 1 to 34 hours but said they do not want to work full-time or were unavailable for full-time work.

Absences are defined as instances in which persons who usually work 35 or more hours a week worked less than that during the reference period for reasons of illness or family obligations. Excluded are situations in which work was missed for vacation, holidays, or other reasons. The estimates are based on one fourth of the sample only.

Earnings are a remuneration of a worker or group of workers for services performed during a specific period of time.

Usual weekly earnings for wage and salary workers include any overtime pay, commissions, or tips usually received (at the main job in the case of multiple jobholders). Earnings reported on a basis other than weekly (such as annual, monthly, or hourly) are converted to weekly. The term "usual" is as perceived by the respondent. If the respondent asks for a definition of usual, interviewers are instructed to define the term as more than half the weeks worked during the past 4 or 5 months.

Minimum wage refers to the prevailing federal minimum wage which was $7.25 in 2012. It increased from $6.55 per hour to $7.25 per hour on July 24, 2009, and has remained at that level since. Data are for wage and salary workers who were paid hourly rates and refer to a person's earnings at the sole or principal job.

A *multiple jobholder* is an employed person who, during the reference week, had two or more jobs as a wage and salary worker, was self-employed and also held a wage and salary job, or worked as an unpaid family worker and also held a wage and salary job. Self-employed persons with multiple businesses and persons with multiple jobs as unpaid family workers are excluded.

Occupation, industry, and class of worker for members of the employed population are determined by the job held during the reference week. Persons with two or more jobs are classified as being in the job at which they worked the greatest number of hours. The unemployed are classified according to their last job. Beginning with data published in 2003, the systems used to classify occupational and industry data changed. They are currently based on the Standard Occupational Classification (SOC) system and the North American Industry Classification System (NAICS). (See the following section on historical comparability for a discussion of previous classification systems used in the CPS.) The class-of-worker breakdown assigns workers to one of the following categories: private and government wage and salary workers, self-employed workers, and unpaid family workers. Wage and salary workers receive wages, salaries, commissions, tips, or pay in kind from a private employer or from a government unit. Self-employed workers are those who work for profit or fees in their own businesses, professions, trades, or on their own farms. Only the unincorporated self-employed are included in the self-employed category in the class-of-worker typology. Self-employed workers who respond that their businesses are incorporated are included among wage and salary workers, because they are technically paid employees of a corporation. An unpaid family worker is a person working without pay for 15 hours or more per week on a farm or in a business operated by a member of the household to whom he or she is related by birth or marriage.

Educational attainment refers to years of school completed in regular schools, which include graded public, private, and parochial elementary, and high schools, whether day or night

school. Colleges, universities, and professional schools are also included.

Tenure refers to length of time a worker has been continuously employed by his or her current employer. These data are collected through a supplement to the CPS. All employed persons were asked how long they had been working continuously for their present employer and, if the length of time was one or two years, a follow-up question was asked about the exact number of months. The follow-up question was included for the first time in the February 1996 supplement to the CPS. CPS supplements that obtained information on tenure in the January of 1983, 1987, and 1991 did not include the follow-up question. Prior to 1983, the question on tenure was asked differently. Data prior to 1983 are thus not strictly comparable to data for subsequent years.

White, Black, and Asian are terms used to describe the race of persons. Persons in these categories are those who selected that race only. Persons falling in the remaining race categories—American Indian or Alaskan Native, Native Hawaiian or Other Pacific Islander, and persons who selected more than one race category—are included in the estimates of total employment and unemployment but are not shown separately because the number of survey respondents is too small to develop estimates of sufficient quality for monthly publication.

Hispanic origin refers to persons who identified themselves in the enumeration process as being Spanish, Hispanic, or Latino. Persons of Hispanic or Latino origin may be of any race.

Single, never married; married, spouse present; and other marital status are the terms used to define the marital status of individuals at the time of the CPS interview. Married, spouse present, applies to a husband and wife if both were living in the same household, even though one may be temporarily absent on business, vacation, in a hospital, etc. Other marital status applies to persons who are married, spouse absent; widowed; or divorced. Married, spouse absent relates to persons who are separated due to marital problems, as well as husbands and wives living apart because one was employed elsewhere, on duty with the armed forces, or any other reason.

A *household* consists of all persons—related family members and all unrelated persons—who occupy a housing unit and have no other usual address. A house, an apartment, a group of rooms, or a single room is regarded as a housing unit when occupied or intended for occupancy as separate living quarters.

A *householder* is the person (or one of the persons) in whose name the housing unit is owned or rented. The term is not applied to either husbands or wives in married-couple families; it refers only to persons in families maintained by either men or women without a spouse.

A *family* is defined as a group of two or more persons residing together who are related by birth, marriage, or adoption. All such persons are considered as members of one family. Families are classified as either married-couple families or families maintained by women or men without spouses.

Children refer to "own" children of the husband, wife, or person maintaining the family, including sons and daughters, stepchildren, and adopted children. Excluded are other related children, such as grandchildren, nieces, nephews, cousins, and unrelated children.

Persons are referred to as disabled if they answer yes to the following questions: 1) Are you deaf or do you have serious difficulty hearing? 2) Are you blind or do you serious difficulty seeing even when wearing glasses? 3) Because of a physical, mental, or emotional condition, do you have serious difficulty concentrating, remembering, or making decisions? 4) Do you have serious difficulty walking or climbing stairs? 5) Do you have difficulty dressing or bathing? 6) Because of a physical, mental, or emotional condition, do you have difficulty doing errands alone such as visiting a doctor's office or shopping? Labor force measures are only tabulated for persons 16 years and over.

Veterans are men and women who previously served on active duty in the U.S. Armed Forces and who were civilians at the time they were surveyed.

Nonveterans are men and women who never served on active duty in the U.S. Armed Forces.

World War II, Korean War, Vietnam-era, and Gulf War-era veterans are men and women who served in the Armed Forces during these periods, regardless of where they served.

Veterans of other service periods are men and women who served in the Armed Forces at any time other than World War II, the Korean War, the Vietnam era, or the Gulf War era.

Veteran status is obtained from responses to the question, "Did you ever serve on active duty in the U.S. Armed Forces?"

Period of service is obtained from answers to the question asked of veterans, "When did you serve on active duty in the U.S. Armed Forces?" The following service periods are identified:

Gulf War era II — September 2001–present

Gulf War era I — August 1990–August 2001

Vietnam era — August 1964–April 1975

Korean War — July 1950–January 1955

World War II — December 1941–December 1946

Other service periods — All other time periods

Veterans who served in Iraq, Afghanistan, or both are individuals who served in Iraq at any time since March 2003, in Afghanistan at any time since October 2001, or in both locations.

Presence of service-connected disability is determined by answers to the question, "Has the Department of Veterans Affairs (VA) or Department of Defense (DoD) determined that you have a service-connected disability, that is, a health condition or impairment caused or made worse by any of your military service?"

Service-connected disability rating is based on answers to the question, "What is your current service connected disability rating?" Answers can range from 0 to 100 percent, in increments of 10 percentage points.

Volunteers are persons who performed unpaid volunteer activities at any point during the survey reference year.

Organizations are associations, societies, or groups of people who share a common interest. Examples include churches, youth groups, and civic organizations.

Activities are the specific tasks the volunteer did for an organization. Examples include tutoring, fundraising, and serving food

HISTORICAL COMPARABILITY

While the concepts and methods are very similar to those used for the inaugural survey in 1940, a number of changes have been made over the years to improve the accuracy and usefulness of the data. Only recent major changes are described here.

Major changes to the CPS, such as the complete redesign of the questionnaire and the use of computer-assisted interviewing for the entire survey, were introduced in 1994. In addition, there were revisions to some of the labor force concepts and definitions, including the implementation of changes recommended in 1979 by the National Commission on Employment and Unemployment Statistics (NCEUS, also known as the Levitan Commission). Some of the major changes to the survey at this time were:

1) The introduction of a redesigned and automated questionnaire. The CPS questionnaire was totally redesigned in order to obtain more accurate, comprehensive, and relevant information, and also to take advantage of state-of-the-art computer interviewing techniques. Computer-assisted interviewing has important benefits most notably that it facilitates the use of a relatively complex questionnaire that incorporates complicated skip patterns and standardized follow-up questions. Additionally, certain questions are automatically tailored to the individual's situation to make them more understandable.

2) Official labor force measures were defined more precisely. While the labor force status of most people is straightforward, some persons are more difficult to classify correctly, especially if they are engaged in activities that are relatively informal or intermittent. Many of the changes to the questionnaire were made to deal with such cases. This was accomplished by rewording and adding questions to conform more precisely to the official definitions, making the questions easier to understand and answer, minimizing reliance on volunteered responses, revising response categories, and taking advantage of the benefits of an automated interview.

3) The amount of data available was expanded. The questionnaire redesign also made it possible to collect several types of data on topics such as multiple job holding and usual hours regularly for the first time.

4) Several labor definitions were modified. The most important definitional changes concerned discouraged workers. The Levitan Commission had criticized the former definition because it was based on a subjective desire for work and on somewhat arbitrary assumptions about an individual's availability to take a job. As a result of the redesign, two requirements were added: in order for persons to qualify as discouraged, they must have engaged in some job search within the past year (or since they last worked, if they worked within the past year), and they must be currently available to take a job. (Formerly, availability was inferred from responses to other questions; now there is a direct question.) Also, beginning in January 1994, questions on this subject are asked of the full CPS sample, permitting estimates of the number of discouraged workers to be published monthly (rather than quarterly).

Beginning in January 2003, several other changes were introduced into the CPS. These changes included the following:

1) Population controls that reflected the results of the 2000 census were introduced into the monthly CPS estimation process. The new controls increased the size of the civilian noninstitutional population by about 3.5 million in May 2002. As a result, they also increased the estimated numbers of people unemployed and employed. Because the increases were roughly proportional, however, the overall unemployment rate did not change significantly. Data from January 2000 through December 2002 were revised to reflect these new controls. Over and above these revisions, the U.S. Census Bureau introduced another large upward adjustment to the controls as part of its annual update of population estimates for 2003. These updated population estimates were not available in time to incorporate them into the revised population controls for January 2000 to December 2002. Thus, the data on employment and unemployment levels for January 2003 (and beyond) are not strictly comparable with those for earlier months. The unemployment rate and other ratios, however, were not substantially affected by the 2003 population control revisions.

2) Questions on race and Hispanic origin were modified to comply with the new standards for maintaining, collecting, and presenting federal data on race and ethnicity for federal statistical agencies. The questions were reworded to indicate that individuals could select more than once race category and to convey more clearly that individuals should report their own perception of what race is. These changes had no impact on the overall civilian noninstitutional population and civilian labor force. However, they did reduce the population and labor force levels of Whites, Blacks, and Asians beginning in January 2003.

3) Improvements were introduced to both the second stage and composite weighting procedures. These changes adapted the weighting procedures to the new race/ethnic classification system and enhanced the stability over time for demographic groups. The second-stage weighting procedure substantially reduced the variability of estimates and corrected, to some extent, for CPS underreporting.

CHANGES IN THE OCCUPATIONAL AND INDUSTRIAL CLASSIFICATION SYSTEM

In January 2003, the CPS adopted the 2002 census industry and occupational classification systems, which were derived, respectively, from the 2002 North American Industry Classification System (NAICS) and the 2000 Standard Occupational Classification (SOC) system. The 1990 Census occupational and industry classifications were replaced. The introduction of the new industry and occupational classification systems in 2003 created a complete break in comparability at all levels of industry and occupation aggregation. The composition of detailed occupations and industries changed substantially in the 2002 systems compared with the 1990 systems, as did the structure for aggregating them into major groups. Therefore, any comparisons of data on the different classifications are not possible without major adjustments.

Historical employment series on the 2002 Census classifications are available at broad levels of occupational and industry aggregation back to 1983. However, historical employment series at the detailed occupational and industry levels on the 2002 classifications are available back to 2000 only.

In 2009, BLS began using the 2007 Census industry classification system, which was derived from the 2007 NAICS series, and still uses it currently. The 2010 Census occupational classification was introduced with data for January 2011 and replaced an earlier version that was based on the 2000 SOC. As a result of the classification change, occupational data beginning with January 2011 are not strictly comparable with earlier years. Although the names of the broad- and intermediate-level occupational groups in the 2010 Census occupational classification remained the same, some detailed occupations were re-classified between the broader groups, affecting comparability over time.

SOURCES OF ADDITIONAL INFORMATION

A complete description of sampling and estimation procedures and further information on the impact of historical changes in the surveys can be found in the updated version of Chapter 1 of the *BLS Handbook of Methods*. This can be found on the BLS Web site at http://www.bls.gov/opub/hom/.

Table 1-1. Employment Status of the Civilian Noninstitutional Population, 1947–2012

(Thousands of people, percent.)

Year	Civilian noninstitutional population	Civilian labor force								Not in labor force
		Total	Participation rate	Employed				Unemployed		
				Total	Percent of population	Agriculture	Nonagricultural industries	Number	Unemploy-ment rate	
1947	101 827	59 350	58.3	57 038	56.0	7 890	49 148	2 311	3.9	42 477
1948	103 068	60 621	58.8	58 343	56.6	7 629	50 714	2 276	3.8	42 447
1949	103 994	61 286	58.9	57 651	55.4	7 658	49 993	3 637	5.9	42 708
1950	104 995	62 208	59.2	58 918	56.1	7 160	51 758	3 288	5.3	42 787
1951	104 621	62 017	59.2	59 961	57.3	6 726	53 235	2 055	3.3	42 604
1952	105 231	62 138	59.0	60 250	57.3	6 500	53 749	1 883	3.0	43 093
1953	107 056	63 015	58.9	61 179	57.1	6 260	54 919	1 834	2.9	44 041
1954	108 321	63 643	58.8	60 109	55.5	6 205	53 904	3 532	5.5	44 678
1955	109 683	65 023	59.3	62 170	56.7	6 450	55 722	2 852	4.4	44 660
1956	110 954	66 552	60.0	63 799	57.5	6 283	57 514	2 750	4.1	44 402
1957	112 265	66 929	59.6	64 071	57.1	5 947	58 123	2 859	4.3	45 336
1958	113 727	67 639	59.5	63 036	55.4	5 586	57 450	4 602	6.8	46 088
1959	115 329	68 369	59.3	64 630	56.0	5 565	59 065	3 740	5.5	46 960
1960	117 245	69 628	59.4	65 778	56.1	5 458	60 318	3 852	5.5	47 617
1961	118 771	70 459	59.3	65 746	55.4	5 200	60 546	4 714	6.7	48 312
1962	120 153	70 614	58.8	66 702	55.5	4 944	61 759	3 911	5.5	49 539
1963	122 416	71 833	58.7	67 762	55.4	4 687	63 076	4 070	5.7	50 583
1964	124 485	73 091	58.7	69 305	55.7	4 523	64 782	3 786	5.2	51 394
1965	126 513	74 455	58.9	71 088	56.2	4 361	66 726	3 366	4.5	52 058
1966	128 058	75 770	59.2	72 895	56.9	3 979	68 915	2 875	3.8	52 288
1967	129 874	77 347	59.6	74 372	57.3	3 844	70 527	2 975	3.8	52 527
1968	132 028	78 737	59.6	75 920	57.5	3 817	72 103	2 817	3.6	53 291
1969	134 335	80 734	60.1	77 902	58.0	3 606	74 296	2 832	3.5	53 602
1970	137 085	82 771	60.4	78 678	57.4	3 463	75 215	4 093	4.9	54 315
1971	140 216	84 382	60.2	79 367	56.6	3 394	75 972	5 016	5.9	55 834
1972	144 126	87 034	60.4	82 153	57.0	3 484	78 669	4 882	5.6	57 091
1973	147 096	89 429	60.8	85 064	57.8	3 470	81 594	4 365	4.9	57 667
1974	150 120	91 949	61.3	86 794	57.8	3 515	83 279	5 156	5.6	58 171
1975	153 153	93 775	61.2	85 846	56.1	3 408	82 438	7 929	8.5	59 377
1976	156 150	96 158	61.6	88 752	56.8	3 331	85 421	7 406	7.7	59 991
1977	159 033	99 009	62.3	92 017	57.9	3 283	88 734	6 991	7.1	60 025
1978	161 910	102 251	63.2	96 048	59.3	3 387	92 661	6 202	6.1	59 659
1979	164 863	104 962	63.7	98 824	59.9	3 347	95 477	6 137	5.8	59 900
1980	167 745	106 940	63.8	99 303	59.2	3 364	95 938	7 637	7.1	60 806
1981	170 130	108 670	63.9	100 397	59.0	3 368	97 030	8 273	7.6	61 460
1982	172 271	110 204	64.0	99 526	57.8	3 401	96 125	10 678	9.7	62 067
1983	174 215	111 550	64.0	100 834	57.9	3 383	97 450	10 717	9.6	62 665
1984	176 383	113 544	64.4	105 005	59.5	3 321	101 685	8 539	7.5	62 839
1985	178 206	115 461	64.8	107 150	60.1	3 179	103 971	8 312	7.2	62 744
1986	180 587	117 834	65.3	109 597	60.7	3 163	106 434	8 237	7.0	62 752
1987	182 753	119 865	65.6	112 440	61.5	3 208	109 232	7 425	6.2	62 888
1988	184 613	121 669	65.9	114 968	62.3	3 169	111 800	6 701	5.5	62 944
1989	186 393	123 869	66.5	117 342	63.0	3 199	114 142	6 528	5.3	62 523
1990	189 164	125 840	66.5	118 793	62.8	3 223	115 570	7 047	5.6	63 324
1991	190 925	126 346	66.2	117 718	61.7	3 269	114 449	8 628	6.8	64 578
1992	192 805	128 105	66.4	118 492	61.5	3 247	115 245	9 613	7.5	64 700
1993	194 838	129 200	66.3	120 259	61.7	3 115	117 144	8 940	6.9	65 638
1994	196 814	131 056	66.6	123 060	62.5	3 409	119 651	7 996	6.1	65 758
1995	198 584	132 304	66.6	124 900	62.9	3 440	121 460	7 404	5.6	66 280
1996	200 591	133 943	66.8	126 708	63.2	3 443	123 264	7 236	5.4	66 647
1997	203 133	136 297	67.1	129 558	63.8	3 399	126 159	6 739	4.9	66 837
1998	205 220	137 673	67.1	131 463	64.1	3 378	128 085	6 210	4.5	67 547
1999	207 753	139 368	67.1	133 488	64.3	3 281	130 207	5 880	4.2	68 385
2000	212 577	142 583	67.1	136 891	64.4	2 464	134 427	5 692	4.0	69 994
2001	215 092	143 734	66.8	136 933	63.7	2 299	134 635	6 801	4.7	71 359
2002	217 570	144 863	66.6	136 485	62.7	2 311	134 174	8 378	5.8	72 707
2003	221 168	146 510	66.2	137 736	62.3	2 275	135 461	8 774	6.0	74 658
2004	223 357	147 401	66.0	139 252	62.3	2 232	137 020	8 149	5.5	75 956
2005	226 082	149 320	66.0	141 730	62.7	2 197	139 532	7 591	5.1	76 762
2006	228 815	151 428	66.2	144 427	63.1	2 206	142 221	7 001	4.6	77 387
2007	231 867	153 124	66.0	146 047	63.0	2 095	143 952	7 078	4.6	78 743
2008	233 788	154 287	66.0	145 362	62.2	2 168	143 194	8 924	5.8	79 501
2009	235 801	154 142	65.4	139 877	59.3	2 103	137 775	14 265	9.3	81 659
2010	237 830	153 889	64.7	139 064	58.5	2 206	136 858	14 825	9.6	83 941
2011	239 618	153 617	64.1	139 869	58.4	2 254	137 615	13 747	8.9	86 001
2012	243 284	154 975	63.7	142 469	58.6	2 186	140 283	12 506	8.1	88 310

Table 1-2. Employment Status of the Civilian Noninstitutional Population, by Sex, 1975–2012

(Thousands of people, percent.)

Sex and year	Civilian noninstitutional population	Civilian labor force								Not in labor force
		Total	Participation rate	Employed				Unemployed		
				Total	Percent of population	Agriculture	Non-agricultural industries	Number	Unemployment rate	
Men										
1975	72 291	56 299	77.9	51 857	71.7	2 824	49 032	4 442	7.9	15 993
1976	73 759	57 174	77.5	53 138	72.0	2 744	50 394	4 036	7.1	16 585
1977	75 193	58 396	77.7	54 728	72.8	2 671	52 057	3 667	6.3	16 797
1978	76 576	59 620	77.9	56 479	73.8	2 718	53 761	3 142	5.3	16 956
1979	78 020	60 726	77.8	57 607	73.8	2 686	54 921	3 120	5.1	17 293
1980	79 398	61 453	77.4	57 186	72.0	2 709	54 477	4 267	6.9	17 945
1981	80 511	61 974	77.0	57 397	71.3	2 700	54 697	4 577	7.4	18 537
1982	81 523	62 450	76.6	56 271	69.0	2 736	53 534	6 179	9.9	19 073
1983	82 531	63 047	76.4	56 787	68.8	2 704	54 083	6 260	9.9	19 484
1984	83 605	63 835	76.4	59 091	70.7	2 668	56 423	4 744	7.4	19 771
1985	84 469	64 411	76.3	59 891	70.9	2 535	57 356	4 521	7.0	20 058
1986	85 798	65 422	76.3	60 892	71.0	2 511	58 381	4 530	6.9	20 376
1987	86 899	66 207	76.2	62 107	71.5	2 543	59 564	4 101	6.2	20 692
1988	87 857	66 927	76.2	63 273	72.0	2 493	60 780	3 655	5.5	20 930
1989	88 762	67 840	76.4	64 315	72.5	2 513	61 802	3 525	5.2	20 923
1990	90 377	69 011	76.4	65 104	72.0	2 546	62 559	3 906	5.7	21 367
1991	91 278	69 168	75.8	64 223	70.4	2 589	61 634	4 946	7.2	22 110
1992	92 270	69 964	75.8	64 440	69.8	2 575	61 866	5 523	7.9	22 306
1993	93 332	70 404	75.4	65 349	70.0	2 478	62 871	5 055	7.2	22 927
1994	94 355	70 817	75.1	66 450	70.4	2 554	63 896	4 367	6.2	23 538
1995	95 178	71 360	75.0	67 377	70.8	2 559	64 818	3 983	5.6	23 818
1996	96 206	72 087	74.9	68 207	70.9	2 573	65 634	3 880	5.4	24 119
1997	97 715	73 261	75.0	69 685	71.3	2 552	67 133	3 577	4.9	24 454
1998	98 758	73 959	74.9	70 693	71.6	2 553	68 140	3 266	4.4	24 799
1999	99 722	74 512	74.7	71 446	71.6	2 432	69 014	3 066	4.1	25 210
2000	101 964	76 280	74.8	73 305	71.9	1 861	71 444	2 975	3.9	25 684
2001	103 282	76 886	74.4	73 196	70.9	1 708	71 488	3 690	4.8	26 396
2002	104 585	77 500	74.1	72 903	69.7	1 724	71 179	4 597	5.9	27 085
2003	106 435	78 238	73.5	73 332	68.9	1 695	71 636	4 906	6.3	28 197
2004	107 710	78 980	73.3	74 524	69.2	1 687	72 838	4 456	5.6	28 730
2005	109 151	80 033	73.3	75 973	69.6	1 654	74 319	4 059	5.1	29 119
2006	110 605	81 255	73.5	77 502	70.1	1 663	75 838	3 753	4.6	29 350
2007	112 173	82 136	73.2	78 254	69.8	1 604	76 650	3 882	4.7	30 036
2008	113 113	82 520	73.0	77 486	68.5	1 650	75 836	5 033	6.1	30 593
2009	114 136	82 123	72.0	73 670	64.5	1 607	72 062	8 453	10.3	32 013
2010	115 174	81 985	71.2	73 359	63.7	1 665	71 694	8 626	10.5	33 189
2011	116 317	81 975	70.5	74 290	63.9	1 698	72 592	7 684	9.4	34 343
2012	117 343	82 327	70.2	75 555	64.4	1 626	73 930	6 771	8.2	35 017
Women										
1975	80 860	37 475	46.3	33 989	42.0	584	33 404	3 486	9.3	43 386
1976	82 390	38 983	47.3	35 615	43.2	588	35 027	3 369	8.6	43 406
1977	83 840	40 613	48.4	37 289	44.5	612	36 677	3 324	8.2	43 227
1978	85 334	42 631	50.0	39 569	46.4	669	38 900	3 061	7.2	42 703
1979	86 843	44 235	50.9	41 217	47.5	661	40 556	3 018	6.8	42 608
1980	88 348	45 487	51.5	42 117	47.7	656	41 461	3 370	7.4	42 861
1981	89 618	46 696	52.1	43 000	48.0	667	42 333	3 696	7.9	42 922
1982	90 748	47 755	52.6	43 256	47.7	665	42 591	4 499	9.4	42 993
1983	91 684	48 503	52.9	44 047	48.0	680	43 367	4 457	9.2	43 181
1984	92 778	49 709	53.6	45 915	49.5	653	45 262	3 794	7.6	43 068
1985	93 736	51 050	54.5	47 259	50.4	644	46 615	3 791	7.4	42 686
1986	94 789	52 413	55.3	48 706	51.4	652	48 054	3 707	7.1	42 376
1987	95 853	53 658	56.0	50 334	52.5	666	49 668	3 324	6.2	42 195
1988	96 756	54 742	56.6	51 696	53.4	676	51 020	3 046	5.6	42 014
1989	97 630	56 030	57.4	53 027	54.3	687	52 341	3 003	5.4	41 601
1990	98 787	56 829	57.5	53 689	54.3	678	53 011	3 140	5.5	41 957
1991	99 646	57 178	57.4	53 496	53.7	680	52 815	3 683	6.4	42 468
1992	100 535	58 141	57.8	54 052	53.8	672	53 380	4 090	7.0	42 394
1993	101 506	58 795	57.9	54 910	54.1	637	54 273	3 885	6.6	42 711
1994	102 460	60 239	58.8	56 610	55.3	855	55 755	3 629	6.0	42 221
1995	103 406	60 944	58.9	57 523	55.6	881	56 642	3 421	5.6	42 462
1996	104 385	61 857	59.3	58 501	56.0	871	57 630	3 356	5.4	42 528
1997	105 418	63 036	59.8	59 873	56.8	847	59 026	3 162	5.0	42 382
1998	106 462	63 714	59.8	60 771	57.1	825	59 945	2 944	4.6	42 748
1999	108 031	64 855	60.0	62 042	57.4	849	61 193	2 814	4.3	43 175
2000	110 613	66 303	59.9	63 586	57.5	602	62 983	2 717	4.1	44 310
2001	111 811	66 848	59.8	63 737	57.0	591	63 147	3 111	4.7	44 962
2002	112 985	67 363	59.6	63 582	56.3	587	62 995	3 781	5.6	45 621
2003	114 733	68 272	59.5	64 404	56.1	500	63 904	3 868	5.7	46 461
2004	115 647	68 421	59.2	64 728	56.0	546	64 182	3 694	5.4	47 225
2005	116 931	69 288	59.3	65 757	56.2	544	65 213	3 531	5.1	47 643
2006	118 210	70 173	59.4	66 925	56.6	543	66 382	3 247	4.6	48 037
2007	119 694	70 988	59.3	67 792	56.6	490	67 302	3 196	4.5	48 707
2008	120 675	71 767	59.5	67 876	56.2	518	67 358	3 891	5.4	48 908
2009	121 665	72 019	59.2	66 208	54.4	496	65 712	5 811	8.1	49 646
2010	122 656	71 904	58.6	65 705	53.6	541	65 164	6 199	8.6	50 752
2011	123 300	71 642	58.1	65 579	53.2	556	65 023	6 063	8.5	51 658
2012	125 941	72 648	57.7	66 914	53.1	560	66 353	5 734	7.9	53 293

Table 1-3. Employment Status of the Civilian Noninstitutional Population, by Sex, Age, Race, and Hispanic Origin, 1990–2012

(Thousands of people.)

Characteristic	1990	1991	1992	1993	1994	1995	1996	1997	1998	1999	2000	2001
ALL RACES												
Both Sexes												
Civilian noninstitutional population	189 164	190 925	192 805	194 838	196 814	198 584	200 591	203 133	205 220	207 753	212 577	215 092
Civilian labor force	125 840	126 346	128 105	129 200	131 056	132 304	133 943	136 297	137 673	139 368	142 583	143 734
Employed	118 793	117 718	118 492	120 259	123 060	124 900	126 708	129 558	131 463	133 488	136 891	136 933
Agriculture	3 223	3 269	3 247	3 115	3 409	3 440	3 443	3 399	3 378	3 281	2 464	2 299
Nonagricultural industries	115 570	114 449	115 245	117 144	119 651	121 460	123 264	126 159	128 085	130 207	134 427	134 635
Unemployed	7 047	8 628	9 613	8 940	7 996	7 404	7 236	6 739	6 210	5 880	5 692	6 801
Not in labor force	63 324	64 578	64 700	65 638	65 758	66 280	66 647	66 837	67 547	68 385	69 994	71 359
Men, 16 Years and Over												
Civilian noninstitutional population	90 377	91 278	92 270	93 332	94 355	95 178	96 206	97 715	98 758	99 722	101 964	103 282
Civilian labor force	69 011	69 168	69 964	70 404	70 817	71 360	72 087	73 261	73 959	74 512	76 280	76 886
Employed	65 104	64 223	64 440	65 349	66 450	67 377	68 207	69 685	70 693	71 446	73 305	73 196
Agriculture	2 546	2 589	2 575	2 478	2 554	2 559	2 573	2 552	2 553	2 432	1 861	1 708
Nonagricultural industries	62 559	61 634	61 866	62 871	63 896	64 818	65 634	67 133	68 140	69 014	71 444	71 488
Unemployed	3 906	4 946	5 523	5 055	4 367	3 983	3 880	3 577	3 266	3 066	2 975	3 690
Not in labor force	21 367	22 110	22 306	22 927	23 538	23 818	24 119	24 454	24 799	25 210	25 684	26 396
Men, 20 Years and Over												
Civilian noninstitutional population	83 030	84 144	85 247	86 256	87 151	87 811	88 606	89 879	90 790	91 555	93 875	95 181
Civilian labor force	64 916	65 374	66 213	66 642	66 921	67 324	68 044	69 166	69 715	70 194	72 010	72 816
Employed	61 678	61 178	61 496	62 355	63 294	64 085	64 897	66 284	67 135	67 761	69 634	69 776
Agriculture	2 329	2 383	2 385	2 293	2 351	2 335	2 356	2 356	2 350	2 244	1 756	1 613
Nonagricultural industries	59 349	58 795	59 111	60 063	60 943	61 750	62 541	63 927	64 785	65 517	67 878	68 163
Unemployed	3 239	4 195	4 717	4 287	3 627	3 239	3 146	2 882	2 580	2 433	2 376	3 040
Not in labor force	18 114	18 770	19 034	19 613	20 230	20 487	20 563	20 713	21 075	21 362	21 864	22 365
Women, 16 Years and Over												
Civilian noninstitutional population	98 787	99 646	100 535	101 506	102 460	103 406	104 385	105 418	106 462	108 031	110 613	111 811
Civilian labor force	56 829	57 178	58 141	58 795	60 239	60 944	61 857	63 036	63 714	64 855	66 303	66 848
Employed	53 689	53 496	54 052	54 910	56 610	57 523	58 501	59 873	60 771	62 042	63 586	63 737
Agriculture	678	680	672	637	855	881	871	847	825	849	602	591
Nonagricultural industries	53 011	52 815	53 380	54 273	55 755	56 642	57 630	59 026	59 945	61 193	62 983	63 147
Unemployed	3 140	3 683	4 090	3 885	3 629	3 421	3 356	3 162	2 944	2 814	2 717	3 111
Not in labor force	41 957	42 468	42 394	42 711	42 221	42 462	42 528	42 382	42 748	43 175	44 310	44 962
Women, 20 Years and Over												
Civilian noninstitutional population	91 614	92 708	93 718	94 647	95 467	96 262	97 050	97 889	98 786	100 158	102 790	103 983
Civilian labor force	53 131	53 708	54 796	55 388	56 655	57 215	58 094	59 198	59 702	60 840	62 301	63 016
Employed	50 535	50 634	51 328	52 099	53 606	54 396	55 311	56 613	57 278	58 555	60 067	60 417
Agriculture	631	639	625	598	809	830	827	798	768	803	567	558
Nonagricultural industries	49 904	49 995	50 702	51 501	52 796	53 566	54 484	55 815	56 510	57 752	59 500	59 860
Unemployed	2 596	3 074	3 469	3 288	3 049	2 819	2 783	2 585	2 424	2 285	2 235	2 599
Not in labor force	38 483	39 000	38 922	39 260	38 813	39 047	38 956	38 691	39 084	39 318	40 488	40 967
Both Sexes, 16 to 19 Years												
Civilian noninstitutional population	14 520	14 073	13 840	13 935	14 196	14 511	14 934	15 365	15 644	16 040	15 912	15 929
Civilian labor force	7 792	7 265	7 096	7 170	7 481	7 765	7 806	7 932	8 256	8 333	8 271	7 902
Employed	6 581	5 906	5 669	5 805	6 161	6 419	6 500	6 661	7 051	7 172	7 189	6 740
Agriculture	264	247	237	224	249	275	261	244	261	234	141	128
Nonagricultural industries	6 317	5 659	5 432	5 580	5 912	6 144	6 239	6 417	6 790	6 938	7 049	6 611
Unemployed	1 212	1 359	1 427	1 365	1 320	1 346	1 306	1 271	1 205	1 162	1 081	1 162
Not in labor force	6 727	6 808	6 745	6 765	6 715	6 746	7 128	7 433	7 388	7 706	7 642	8 027
WHITE[1]												
Both Sexes												
Civilian noninstitutional population	160 625	161 759	162 972	164 289	165 555	166 914	168 317	169 993	171 478	173 085	176 220	178 111
Civilian labor force	107 447	107 743	108 837	109 700	111 082	111 950	113 108	114 693	115 415	116 509	118 545	119 399
Employed	102 261	101 182	101 669	103 045	105 190	106 490	107 808	109 856	110 931	112 235	114 424	114 430
Agriculture	2 998	3 026	3 018	2 895	3 162	3 194	3 276	3 208	3 160	3 083	2 320	2 174
Nonagricultural industries	99 263	98 157	98 650	100 150	102 027	103 296	104 532	106 648	107 770	109 152	112 104	112 256
Unemployed	5 186	6 560	7 169	6 655	5 892	5 459	5 300	4 836	4 484	4 273	4 121	4 969
Not in labor force	53 178	54 061	54 135	54 589	54 473	54 965	55 209	55 301	56 064	56 577	57 675	58 713
Men, 16 Years and Over												
Civilian noninstitutional population	77 369	77 977	78 651	79 371	80 059	80 733	81 489	82 577	83 352	83 930	85 370	86 452
Civilian labor force	59 638	59 656	60 168	60 484	60 727	61 146	61 783	62 639	63 034	63 413	64 466	64 966
Employed	56 703	55 797	55 959	56 656	57 452	58 146	58 888	59 998	60 604	61 139	62 289	62 212
Agriculture	2 353	2 384	2 378	2 286	2 347	2 347	2 436	2 389	2 376	2 273	1 743	1 606
Nonagricultural industries	54 350	53 413	53 580	54 370	55 104	55 800	56 452	57 608	58 228	58 866	60 546	60 606
Unemployed	2 935	3 859	4 209	3 828	3 275	2 999	2 896	2 641	2 431	2 274	2 177	2 754
Not in labor force	17 731	18 321	18 484	18 887	19 332	19 587	19 706	19 938	20 317	20 517	20 905	21 486
Men, 20 Years and Over												
Civilian noninstitutional population	71 457	72 274	73 040	73 721	74 311	74 879	75 454	76 320	76 966	77 432	78 966	80 029
Civilian labor force	56 116	56 387	56 976	57 284	57 411	57 719	58 340	59 126	59 421	59 747	60 850	61 519
Employed	53 685	53 103	53 357	54 021	54 676	55 254	55 977	56 986	57 500	57 934	59 119	59 245
Agriculture	2 148	2 192	2 197	2 114	2 151	2 132	2 224	2 201	2 182	2 094	1 640	1 512
Nonagricultural industries	51 537	50 912	51 160	51 907	52 525	53 122	53 753	54 785	55 319	55 839	57 479	57 733
Unemployed	2 431	3 284	3 620	3 263	2 735	2 465	2 363	2 140	1 920	1 813	1 731	2 275
Not in labor force	15 340	15 887	16 064	16 436	16 900	17 161	17 114	17 194	17 545	17 685	18 116	18 510

[1]Beginning in 2003, persons who selected this race group only; persons who selected more than one race group are not included. Prior to 2003, persons who reported more than one race group were included in the group they identified as the main race.

Table 1-3. Employment Status of the Civilian Noninstitutional Population, by Sex, Age, Race, and Hispanic Origin, 1990–2012—*Continued*

(Thousands of people.)

Characteristic	2002	2003	2004	2005	2006	2007	2008	2009	2010	2011	2012
ALL RACES											
Both Sexes											
Civilian noninstitutional population	217 570	221 168	223 357	226 082	228 815	231 867	233 788	235 801	237 830	239 618	243 284
Civilian labor force	144 863	146 510	147 401	149 320	151 428	153 124	154 287	154 142	153 889	153 617	154 975
Employed	136 485	137 736	139 252	141 730	144 427	146 047	145 362	139 877	139 064	139 869	142 469
Agriculture	2 311	2 275	2 232	2 197	2 206	2 095	2 168	2 103	2 206	2 254	2 186
Nonagricultural industries	134 174	135 461	137 020	139 532	142 221	143 952	143 194	137 775	136 858	137 615	140 283
Unemployed	8 378	8 774	8 149	7 591	7 001	7 078	8 924	14 265	14 825	13 747	12 506
Not in labor force	72 707	74 658	75 956	76 762	77 387	78 743	79 501	81 659	83 941	86 001	88 310
Men, 16 Years and Over											
Civilian noninstitutional population	104 585	106 435	107 710	109 151	110 605	112 173	113 113	114 136	115 174	116 317	117 343
Civilian labor force	77 500	78 238	78 980	80 033	81 255	82 136	82 520	82 123	81 985	81 975	82 327
Employed	72 903	73 332	74 524	75 973	77 502	78 254	77 486	73 670	73 359	74 290	75 555
Agriculture	1 724	1 695	1 688	1 654	1 663	1 604	1 650	1 607	1 665	1 698	1 626
Nonagricultural industries	71 179	71 636	72 836	74 319	75 838	76 650	75 836	72 062	71 694	72 592	73 930
Unemployed	4 597	4 906	4 456	4 059	3 753	3 882	5 033	8 453	8 626	7 684	6 771
Not in labor force	27 085	28 197	28 730	29 119	29 350	30 036	30 593	32 013	33 189	34 343	35 017
Men, 20 Years and Over											
Civilian noninstitutional population	96 439	98 272	99 476	100 835	102 145	103 555	104 453	105 493	106 596	107 736	108 686
Civilian labor force	73 630	74 623	75 364	76 443	77 562	78 596	79 047	78 897	78 994	79 080	79 387
Employed	69 734	70 415	71 572	73 050	74 431	75 337	74 750	71 341	71 230	72 182	73 403
Agriculture	1 629	1 614	1 596	1 577	1 579	1 514	1 552	1 514	1 589	1 611	1 547
Nonagricultural industries	68 104	68 801	69 976	71 473	72 852	73 823	73 198	69 828	69 641	70 571	71 856
Unemployed	3 896	4 209	3 791	3 392	3 131	3 259	4 297	7 555	7 763	6 898	5 984
Not in labor force	22 809	23 649	24 113	24 392	24 584	24 959	25 406	26 596	27 603	28 656	29 299
Women, 16 Years and Over											
Civilian noninstitutional population	112 985	114 733	115 647	116 931	118 210	119 694	120 675	121 665	122 656	123 300	125 941
Civilian labor force	67 363	68 272	68 421	69 288	70 173	70 988	71 767	72 019	71 904	71 642	72 648
Employed	63 582	64 404	64 728	65 757	66 925	67 792	67 876	66 208	65 705	65 579	66 914
Agriculture	587	580	547	544	543	490	518	496	541	556	560
Nonagricultural industries	62 995	63 824	64 181	65 213	66 382	67 302	67 358	65 712	65 164	65 023	66 353
Unemployed	3 781	3 868	3 694	3 531	3 247	3 196	3 891	5 811	6 199	6 063	5 734
Not in labor force	45 621	46 461	47 225	47 643	48 037	48 707	48 908	49 646	50 752	51 658	53 293
Women, 20 Years and Over											
Civilian noninstitutional population	105 136	106 800	107 658	108 850	109 992	111 330	112 260	113 265	114 333	115 107	117 614
Civilian labor force	63 648	64 716	64 923	65 714	66 585	67 516	68 382	68 856	68 990	68 810	69 765
Employed	60 420	61 402	61 773	62 702	63 834	64 799	65 039	63 699	63 456	63 360	64 640
Agriculture	557	550	515	519	520	460	491	471	519	534	534
Nonagricultural industries	59 863	60 852	61 258	62 182	63 315	64 339	64 548	63 228	62 936	62 826	64 106
Unemployed	3 228	3 314	3 150	3 013	2 751	2 718	3 342	5 157	5 534	5 450	5 125
Not in labor force	41 488	42 083	42 735	43 136	43 407	43 814	43 878	44 409	45 343	46 297	47 849
Both Sexes, 16 to 19 Years											
Civilian noninstitutional population	15 994	16 096	16 222	16 398	16 678	16 982	17 075	17 043	16 901	16 774	16 984
Civilian labor force	7 585	7 170	7 114	7 164	7 281	7 012	6 858	6 390	5 906	5 727	5 823
Employed	6 332	5 919	5 907	5 978	6 162	5 911	5 573	4 837	4 378	4 327	4 426
Agriculture	124	111	121	100	108	121	125	119	98	109	105
Nonagricultural industries	6 207	5 808	5 786	5 877	6 054	5 790	5 448	4 719	4 281	4 218	4 321
Unemployed	1 253	1 251	1 208	1 186	1 119	1 101	1 285	1 552	1 528	1 400	1 397
Not in labor force	8 409	8 926	9 108	9 234	9 397	9 970	10 218	10 654	10 995	11 048	11 162
WHITE[1]											
Both Sexes											
Civilian noninstitutional population	179 783	181 292	182 643	184 446	186 264	188 253	189 540	190 902	192 075	193 077	193 204
Civilian labor force	120 150	120 546	121 086	122 299	123 834	124 935	125 635	125 644	125 084	124 579	123 684
Employed	114 013	114 235	115 239	116 949	118 833	119 792	119 126	114 996	114 168	114 690	114 769
Agriculture	2 171	2 148	2 103	2 077	2 063	1 953	2 021	1 968	2 071	2 134	2 033
Nonagricultural industries	111 841	112 087	113 136	114 872	116 769	117 839	117 104	113 028	112 098	112 556	112 735
Unemployed	6 137	6 311	5 847	5 350	5 002	5 143	6 509	10 648	10 916	9 889	8 915
Not in labor force	59 633	60 746	61 558	62 148	62 429	63 319	63 905	65 258	66 991	68 498	69 520
Men, 16 Years and Over											
Civilian noninstitutional population	87 361	88 249	89 044	90 027	91 021	92 073	92 725	93 433	94 082	94 801	94 266
Civilian labor force	65 308	65 509	65 994	66 694	67 613	68 158	68 351	68 051	67 728	67 551	66 921
Employed	61 849	61 866	62 712	63 763	64 883	65 289	64 624	61 630	61 252	71	61 990
Agriculture	1 611	1 597	1 583	1 562	1 554	1 501	1 539	1 499	1 557	1 602	1 515
Nonagricultural industries	60 238	60 269	61 129	62 201	63 330	63 788	63 085	60 131	59 695	60 318	60 476
Unemployed	3 459	3 643	3 282	2 931	2 730	2 869	3 727	6 421	6 476	5 631	4 931
Not in labor force	22 053	22 740	23 050	23 334	23 408	23 915	24 374	25 382	26 353	27 249	27 345
Men, 20 Years and Over											
Civilian noninstitutional population	80 922	81 860	82 615	83 556	84 466	85 420	86 056	86 789	87 502	88 191	87 780
Civilian labor force	62 067	62 473	62 944	63 705	64 540	65 214	65 483	65 372	65 265	65 165	64 540
Employed	59 124	59 348	60 159	61 255	62 259	62 806	62 304	59 626	59 438	60 118	60 193
Agriculture	1 519	1 517	1 495	1 488	1 473	1 417	1 447	1 410	1 483	1 518	1 438
Nonagricultural industries	57 605	57 831	58 664	59 767	60 785	61 389	60 857	58 216	57 955	58 600	58 755
Unemployed	2 943	3 125	2 785	2 450	2 281	2 408	3 179	5 746	5 828	5 046	4 347
Not in labor force	18 855	19 386	19 671	19 851	19 927	20 206	20 573	21 417	22 236	23 026	23 241

[1]Beginning in 2003, persons who selected this race group only; persons who selected more than one race group are not included. Prior to 2003, persons who reported more than one race group were included in the group they identified as the main race.

Table 1-3. Employment Status of the Civilian Noninstitutional Population, by Sex, Age, Race, and Hispanic Origin, 1990–2012—*Continued*

(Thousands of people.)

Characteristic	1990	1991	1992	1993	1994	1995	1996	1997	1998	1999	2000	2001
WHITE[1]												
Women, 16 Years and Over												
Civilian noninstitutional population	83 256	83 781	84 321	84 918	85 496	86 181	86 828	87 417	88 126	89 156	90 850	91 660
Civilian labor force	47 809	48 087	48 669	49 216	50 356	50 804	51 325	52 054	52 380	53 096	54 079	54 433
Employed	45 558	45 385	45 710	46 390	47 738	48 344	48 920	49 859	50 327	51 096	52 136	52 218
Agriculture	645	641	640	609	815	847	840	819	784	810	578	568
Nonagricultural industries	44 913	44 744	45 070	45 780	46 923	47 497	48 080	49 040	49 543	50 286	51 558	51 650
Unemployed	2 251	2 701	2 959	2 827	2 617	2 460	2 404	2 195	2 053	1 999	1 944	2 215
Not in labor force	35 447	35 695	35 651	35 702	35 141	35 377	35 503	35 363	35 746	36 060	36 770	37 227
Women, 20 Years and Over												
Civilian noninstitutional population	77 539	78 285	78 928	79 490	79 980	80 567	81 041	81 492	82 073	82 953	84 718	85 526
Civilian labor force	44 648	45 111	45 839	46 311	47 314	47 686	48 162	48 847	49 029	49 714	50 740	51 218
Employed	42 796	42 862	43 327	43 910	45 116	45 643	46 164	47 063	47 342	48 098	49 145	49 369
Agriculture	598	601	594	572	772	799	798	771	729	765	546	537
Nonagricultural industries	42 198	42 261	42 733	43 339	44 344	44 844	45 366	46 292	46 612	47 333	48 599	48 831
Unemployed	1 852	2 248	2 512	2 400	2 197	2 042	1 998	1 784	1 688	1 616	1 595	1 849
Not in labor force	32 891	33 174	33 089	33 179	32 666	32 881	32 879	32 645	33 044	33 239	33 978	34 308
Both Sexes, 16 to 19 Years												
Civilian noninstitutional population	11 630	11 200	11 004	11 078	11 264	11 468	11 822	12 181	12 439	12 700	12 535	12 556
Civilian labor force	6 683	6 245	6 022	6 105	6 357	6 545	6 607	6 720	6 965	7 048	6 955	6 661
Employed	5 779	5 216	4 985	5 113	5 398	5 593	5 667	5 807	6 089	6 204	6 160	5 817
Agriculture	252	233	228	209	239	262	254	236	250	224	135	125
Nonagricultural industries	5 528	4 984	4 757	4 904	5 158	5 331	5 413	5 571	5 839	5 980	6 025	5 692
Unemployed	903	1 029	1 037	992	960	952	939	912	876	844	795	845
Not in labor force	4 947	4 955	4 982	4 973	4 907	4 923	5 215	5 462	5 475	5 652	5 581	5 894
BLACK[1]												
Both Sexes												
Civilian noninstitutional population	21 477	21 799	22 147	22 521	22 879	23 246	23 604	24 003	24 373	24 855	24 902	25 138
Civilian labor force	13 740	13 797	14 162	14 225	14 502	14 817	15 134	15 529	15 982	16 365	16 397	16 421
Employed	12 175	12 074	12 151	12 382	12 835	13 279	13 542	13 969	14 556	15 056	15 156	15 006
Agriculture	142	160	153	143	136	101	98	117	138	117	77	62
Nonagricultural industries	12 034	11 914	11 997	12 239	12 699	13 178	13 444	13 852	14 417	14 939	15 079	14 944
Unemployed	1 565	1 723	2 011	1 844	1 666	1 538	1 592	1 560	1 426	1 309	1 241	1 416
Not in labor force	7 737	8 002	7 985	8 296	8 377	8 429	8 470	8 474	8 391	8 490	8 505	8 717
Men, 16 Years and Over												
Civilian noninstitutional population	9 573	9 725	9 896	10 083	10 258	10 411	10 575	10 763	10 927	11 143	11 129	11 172
Civilian labor force	6 802	6 851	6 997	7 019	7 089	7 183	7 264	7 354	7 542	7 652	7 702	7 647
Employed	5 995	5 961	5 930	6 047	6 241	6 422	6 456	6 607	6 871	7 027	7 082	6 938
Agriculture	124	139	138	128	118	93	86	103	118	99	67	56
Nonagricultural industries	5 872	5 822	5 791	5 919	6 122	6 329	6 371	6 504	6 752	6 952	7 015	6 882
Unemployed	806	890	1 067	971	848	762	808	747	671	671	620	709
Not in labor force	2 772	2 874	2 899	3 064	3 169	3 228	3 311	3 409	3 386	3 386	3 427	3 525
Men, 20 Years and Over												
Civilian noninstitutional population	8 364	8 479	8 652	8 840	9 171	9 280	9 414	9 575	9 727	9 926	9 952	9 993
Civilian labor force	6 221	6 357	6 451	6 568	6 646	6 730	6 806	6 910	7 053	7 182	7 240	7 200
Employed	5 602	5 692	5 706	5 681	5 964	6 137	6 167	6 325	6 530	6 702	6 741	6 627
Agriculture	119	117	131	131	115	89	83	101	112	96	67	55
Nonagricultural industries	5 483	5 576	5 575	5 550	5 849	6 048	6 084	6 224	6 418	6 606	6 675	55
Unemployed	619	664	745	886	682	593	639	585	524	480	499	573
Not in labor force	2 143	2 122	2 202	801	2 525	2 550	2 608	2 665	2 673	2 743	2 711	2 792
Women, 16 Years and Over												
Civilian noninstitutional population	11 904	12 074	12 251	12 438	12 621	12 835	13 029	13 241	13 446	13 711	13 772	13 966
Civilian labor force	6 938	6 946	7 166	7 206	7 413	7 634	7 869	8 175	8 441	8 713	8 695	8 774
Employed	6 180	6 113	6 221	6 334	6 595	6 857	7 086	7 362	7 685	8 029	8 073	8 068
Agriculture	18	21	15	15	18	8	13	14	20	18	10	6
Nonagricultural industries	6 162	6 092	6 206	6 320	6 577	6 849	7 073	7 348	7 665	8 011	8 064	8 062
Unemployed	758	833	944	872	818	777	784	813	756	684	621	706
Not in labor force	4 965	5 129	5 086	5 231	5 208	5 201	5 159	5 066	5 005	4 999	5 078	5 192
Women, 20 Years and Over												
Civilian noninstitutional population	10 760	10 959	11 152	11 332	11 496	11 682	11 833	12 016	12 023	12 451	12 561	12 758
Civilian labor force	6 517	6 572	6 778	6 824	7 004	7 175	7 405	7 686	7 912	8 224	8 215	8 323
Employed	5 884	5 874	5 978	6 095	6 320	6 556	6 762	7 013	7 290	7 663	7 703	7 741
Agriculture	18	20	15	14	17	7	12	13	19	17	9	6
Nonagricultural industries	5 867	5 853	5 963	6 081	6 303	6 548	6 749	7 000	7 272	7 646	7 694	7 735
Unemployed	633	698	800	729	685	620	643	673	622	561	512	582
Not in labor force	4 243	4 388	4 374	4 508	4 492	4 507	4 428	4 330	4 291	4 226	4 346	4 434
Both Sexes, 16 to 19 Years												
Civilian noninstitutional population	2 238	2 187	2 155	2 181	2 211	2 284	2 356	2 412	2 443	2 479	2 389	2 388
Civilian labor force	866	774	816	807	852	911	923	933	1 017	959	941	898
Employed	598	494	492	494	552	586	613	631	736	691	711	637
Agriculture	7	8	7	9	1	5	3	3	8	4	1	1
Nonagricultural industries	591	486	485	485	547	581	611	611	728	687	710	637
Unemployed	268	280	324	313	300	325	310	310	281	268	230	260
Not in labor force	1 372	1 413	1 339	1 374	1 360	1 372	1 434	1 434	1 427	1 520	1 448	1 490

[1]Beginning in 2003, persons who selected this race group only; persons who selected more than one race group are not included. Prior to 2003, persons who reported more than one race group were included in the group they identified as the main race.

Table 1-3. Employment Status of the Civilian Noninstitutional Population, by Sex, Age, Race, and Hispanic Origin, 1990–2012—*Continued*

(Thousands of people.)

Characteristic	2002	2003	2004	2005	2006	2007	2008	2009	2010	2011	2012
WHITE[1]											
Women, 16 Years and Over											
Civilian noninstitutional population	92 422	93 043	93 599	94 419	95 242	96 180	96 814	97 469	97 993	98 276	98 938
Civilian labor force	54 842	55 037	55 092	55 605	56 221	56 777	57 284	57 593	57 356	57 028	56 763
Employed	52 164	52 369	52 527	53 186	53 950	54 503	54 501	53 366	52 916	52 770	52 779
Agriculture	560	551	520	515	510	452	482	469	513	532	519
Nonagricultural industries	51 604	51 818	52 007	52 672	53 440	54 050	54 019	52 897	52 402	52 238	52 260
Unemployed	2 678	2 668	2 565	2 419	2 271	2 274	2 782	4 227	4 440	4 257	3 985
Not in labor force	37 581	38 006	38 508	38 814	39 021	39 403	39 531	39 876	40 638	41 248	42 175
Women, 20 Years and Over											
Civilian noninstitutional population	86 266	86 905	87 430	88 200	88 942	89 790	90 400	91 078	91 683	92 068	92 766
Civilian labor force	51 717	52 099	52 212	52 643	53 286	53 925	54 508	54 976	54 957	54 700	54 475
Employed	49 448	49 823	50 040	50 589	51 359	51 996	52 124	51 231	50 997	50 881	50 911
Agriculture	532	522	488	492	488	423	457	444	492	511	493
Nonagricultural industries	48 916	49 301	49 552	50 097	50 871	51 572	51 667	50 787	50 505	50 371	50 418
Unemployed	2 269	2 276	2 172	2 054	1 927	1 930	2 384	3 745	3 960	3 818	3 564
Not in labor force	34 548	34 806	35 218	35 557	35 656	35 864	35 892	36 101	36 725	37 368	38 291
Both Sexes, 16 to 19 Years											
Civilian noninstitutional population	12 596	12 527	12 599	12 690	12 856	13 043	13 084	13 035	12 891	12 818	12 658
Civilian labor force	6 366	5 973	5 929	5 950	6 009	5 795	5 644	5 295	4 861	4 714	4 669
Employed	5 441	5 064	5 039	5 105	5 215	4 990	4 697	4 138	3 733	3 691	3 665
Agriculture	121	109	116	97	102	113	118	114	96	105	103
Nonagricultural industries	5 320	4 955	4 923	5 008	5 113	4 877	4 580	4 025	3 637	3 585	3 563
Unemployed	925	909	890	845	794	805	947	1 157	1 128	1 024	1 004
Not in labor force	6 230	6 554	6 669	6 739	6 847	7 248	7 440	7 740	8 030	8 103	7 988
BLACK[1]											
Both Sexes											
Civilian noninstitutional population	25 578	25 686	26 065	26 517	27 007	27 485	27 843	28 241	28 708	29 114	29 907
Civilian labor force	16 565	16 526	16 638	17 013	17 314	17 496	17 740	17 632	17 862	17 881	18 400
Employed	14 872	14 739	14 909	15 313	15 765	16 051	15 953	15 025	15 010	15 051	15 856
Agriculture	69	63	50	51	60	53	55	66	59	52	61
Nonagricultural industries	14 804	14 676	14 859	15 261	15 705	15 998	15 898	14 959	14 951	14 999	15 795
Unemployed	1 693	1 787	1 729	1 700	1 549	1 445	1 788	2 606	2 852	2 831	2 544
Not in labor force	9 013	9 161	9 428	9 504	9 693	9 989	10 103	10 609	10 846	11 233	11 508
Men, 16 Years and Over											
Civilian noninstitutional population	11 391	11 454	11 656	11 882	12 130	12 361	12 516	12 705	12 939	13 164	13 508
Civilian labor force	7 794	7 711	7 773	7 998	8 128	8 252	8 347	8 265	8 415	8 454	8 594
Employed	6 959	6 820	6 912	7 155	7 354	7 500	7 398	6 817	6 865	6 953	7 302
Agriculture	63	52	43	43	51	46	49	56	53	47	51
Nonagricultural industries	6 896	6 768	6 869	7 111	7 303	7 454	7 350	6 761	6 812	6 905	7 252
Unemployed	835	891	860	844	774	752	949	1 448	1 550	1 502	1 292
Not in labor force	3 597	3 743	3 884	3 884	4 002	4 110	4 169	4 441	4 524	4 710	4 913
Men, 20 Years and Over											
Civilian noninstitutional population	10 196	10 278	11 656	10 659	10 864	11 057	11 194	11 379	11 626	11 882	12 189
Civilian labor force	7 347	7 346	7 773	7 600	7 720	7 867	7 962	7 914	8 076	8 125	8 256
Employed	6 652	6 586	6 912	6 901	7 079	7 245	7 151	6 628	6 680	6 765	7 104
Agriculture	62	51	274	43	49	45	47	55	52	46	50
Nonagricultural industries	6 591	6 535	6 638	6 858	7 030	7 201	7 104	6 573	6 628	6 719	7 053
Unemployed	695	760	860	699	640	622	811	1 286	1 396	1 360	1 152
Not in labor force	2 848	2 932	3 884	3 060	3 144	3 189	3 232	3 465	3 550	17	3 932
Women, 16 Years and Over											
Civilian noninstitutional population	14 187	14 232	14 409	14 635	14 877	15 124	15 328	15 536	15 769	15 950	16 400
Civilian labor force	8 772	8 815	8 865	9 014	9 186	9 244	9 393	9 367	9 447	9 427	9 805
Employed	7 914	7 919	7 997	8 158	8 410	8 551	8 554	8 208	8 145	8 098	8 553
Agriculture	6	11	7	8	9	7	6	10	6	5	10
Nonagricultural industries	7 907	7 908	7 990	8 150	8 402	8 544	8 548	8 198	8 139	8 093	8 543
Unemployed	858	895	868	856	775	693	839	1 159	1 302	1 329	1 252
Not in labor force	5 415	5 418	5 544	5 621	5 691	5 879	5 934	6 169	6 322	6 523	6 595
Women, 20 Years and Over											
Civilian noninstitutional population	12 966	13 026	14 409	13 377	13 578	13 788	13 974	14 178	14 425	14 638	15 076
Civilian labor force	8 348	8 409	8 865	8 610	8 723	8 828	8 991	8 988	9 110	9 110	9 433
Employed	7 610	7 636	7 997	7 876	8 068	8 240	8 260	7 956	7 944	7 906	8 313
Agriculture	5	10	7	7	7	7	6	10	6	5	10
Nonagricultural industries	7 604	7 626	7 701	7 868	8 060	8 233	8 254	7 946	7 938	7 901	8 303
Unemployed	738	772	868	734	656	588	732	1 032	1 165	1 204	1 119
Not in labor force	4 618	4 618	5 544	4 768	4 854	4 960	4 982	5 190	5 315	5 529	5 643
Both Sexes, 16 to 19 Years											
Civilian noninstitutional population	2 416	2 382	2 423	2 481	2 565	2 640	2 676	2 684	2 657	2 594	2 643
Civilian labor force	870	771	762	803	871	801	787	729	677	647	711
Employed	611	516	520	536	618	566	541	442	386	380	438
Agriculture	2	1	0	1	3	1	1	1	1	1	0
Nonagricultural industries	609	515	520	535	614	564	540	440	385	379	438
Unemployed	260	255	241	267	253	235	246	288	291	267	272
Not in labor force	1 546	1 611	1 661	1 677	1 694	1 839	1 889	1 954	1 980	1 947	1 932

[1]Beginning in 2003, persons who selected this race group only; persons who selected more than one race group are not included. Prior to 2003, persons who reported more than one race group were included in the group they identified as the main race.

Table 1-3. Employment Status of the Civilian Noninstitutional Population, by Sex, Age, Race, and Hispanic Origin, 1990–2012—*Continued*

(Thousands of people.)

Characteristic	1990	1991	1992	1993	1994	1995	1996	1997	1998	1999	2000	2001
HISPANIC[2]												
Both Sexes												
Civilian noninstitutional population	15 904	16 425	16 961	17 532	18 117	18 629	19 213	20 321	21 070	21 650	23 938	24 942
Civilian labor force	10 720	10 920	11 338	11 610	11 975	12 267	12 774	13 796	14 317	14 665	16 689	17 328
Employed	9 845	9 828	10 027	10 361	10 788	11 127	11 642	12 726	13 291	13 720	15 735	16 190
Agriculture	517	512	524	523	560	604	609	660	742	734	536	423
Nonagricultural industries	9 328	9 315	9 503	9 838	10 227	10 524	11 033	12 067	12 549	12 986	15 199	15 767
Unemployed	876	1 092	1 311	1 248	1 187	1 140	1 132	1 069	1 026	945	954	1 138
Not in labor force	5 184	5 506	5 623	5 922	6 142	6 362	6 439	6 526	6 753	6 985	7 249	7 614
Men, 16 Years and Over												
Civilian noninstitutional population	8 041	8 296	8 553	8 824	9 104	9 329	9 604	10 368	10 734	10 713	12 174	12 695
Civilian labor force	6 546	6 664	6 900	7 076	7 210	7 376	7 646	8 309	8 571	8 546	9 923	10 279
Employed	6 021	5 979	6 093	6 328	6 530	6 725	7 039	7 728	8 018	8 067	9 428	9 668
Agriculture	449	453	468	469	494	527	537	571	651	642	449	345
Nonagricultural industries	5 572	5 526	5 625	5 860	6 036	6 198	6 502	7 157	7 367	7 425	8 979	9 323
Unemployed	524	685	807	747	680	651	607	582	552	480	494	611
Not in labor force	1 495	1 632	1 654	1 749	1 894	1 952	1 957	2 059	2 164	2 167	2 252	2 416
Men, 20 Years and Over												
Civilian noninstitutional population	7 126	7 392	7 655	7 930	8 178	8 375	8 611	9 250	9 573	9 523	10 841	11 386
Civilian labor force	6 034	6 198	6 432	6 621	6 747	6 898	7 150	7 779	8 005	7 950	9 247	9 595
Employed	5 609	5 623	5 757	5 992	6 189	6 367	6 655	7 307	7 570	7 576	8 859	9 100
Agriculture	415	419	437	441	466	501	510	544	621	602	423	328
Nonagricultural industries	5 195	5 204	5 320	5 551	5 722	5 866	6 145	6 763	6 949	6 974	8 435	8 773
Unemployed	425	575	675	629	558	530	495	471	436	374	388	495
Not in labor force	1 092	1 194	1 223	1 309	1 431	1 477	1 461	1 471	1 568	1 573	1 595	1 791
Women, 16 Years and Over												
Civilian noninstitutional population	7 863	8 130	8 408	8 708	9 014	9 300	9 610	9 953	10 335	10 937	11 764	12 247
Civilian labor force	4 174	4 256	4 439	4 534	4 765	4 891	5 128	5 486	5 746	6 119	6 767	7 049
Employed	3 823	3 848	3 934	4 033	4 258	4 403	4 602	4 999	5 273	5 653	6 307	6 522
Agriculture	68	59	57	55	66	76	72	89	91	92	87	77
Nonagricultural industries	3 755	3 789	3 877	3 978	4 191	4 326	4 531	4 910	5 182	5 561	6 220	6 445
Unemployed	351	407	504	501	508	488	525	488	473	466	460	527
Not in labor force	3 689	3 874	3 969	4 174	4 248	4 409	4 482	4 466	4 589	4 819	4 997	5 198
Women, 20 Years and Over												
Civilian noninstitutional population	7 041	7 301	7 569	7 846	8 122	8 382	8 654	8 950	9 292	9 821	10 574	11 049
Civilian labor force	3 941	4 110	4 218	4 421	4 520	4 779	5 106	5 304	5 666	6 275	6 557	6 863
Employed	3 567	3 603	3 693	3 800	3 989	4 116	4 341	4 705	4 928	5 290	5 903	6 121
Agriculture	62	53	51	49	61	72	69	83	85	88	81	73
Nonagricultural industries	3 505	3 549	3 642	3 751	3 928	4 044	4 272	4 622	4 843	5 202	5 822	6 048
Unemployed	289	339	418	418	431	404	438	401	376	376	371	436
Not in labor force	3 184	3 360	3 459	3 628	3 701	3 863	3 875	3 845	3 988	4 155	4 299	4 492
Both Sexes, 16 to 19 Years												
Civilian noninstitutional population	1 737	1 732	1 737	1 756	1 818	1 872	1 948	2 121	2 204	2 307	2 523	2 508
Civilian labor force	829	781	796	771	807	850	845	911	1 007	1 049	1 168	1 176
Employed	668	602	577	570	609	645	646	714	793	854	973	969
Agriculture	40	41	36	33	32	31	29	33	36	45	31	22
Nonagricultural industries	628	562	541	537	577	614	617	682	757	809	942	947
Unemployed	161	179	219	201	198	205	199	197	214	196	194	208
Not in labor force	907	951	941	985	1 010	1 022	1 103	1 210	1 197	1 257	1 355	1 331

[2]May be of any race.

Table 1-3. Employment Status of the Civilian Noninstitutional Population, by Sex, Age, Race, and Hispanic Origin, 1990–2012—*Continued*

(Thousands of people.)

Characteristic	2002	2003	2004	2005	2006	2007	2008	2009	2010	2011	2012
HISPANIC[2]											
Both Sexes											
Civilian noninstitutional population	25 963	27 551	28 109	29 133	30 103	31 383	32 141	32 891	33 713	34 438	36 759
Civilian labor force	17 943	18 813	19 272	19 824	20 694	21 602	22 024	22 352	22 748	22 898	24 391
Employed	16 590	17 372	17 930	18 632	19 613	20 382	20 346	19 647	19 906	20 269	21 878
Agriculture	448	446	441	423	428	426	441	426	480	523	491
Nonagricultural industries	16 141	16 927	17 489	18 209	19 185	19 956	19 904	19 221	19 426	19 746	21 387
Unemployed	1 353	1 441	1 342	1 191	1 081	1 220	1 678	2 706	2 843	2 629	2 514
Not in labor force	8 020	8 738	8 837	9 310	9 409	9 781	10 116	10 539	10 964	11 540	12 368
Men, 16 Years and Over											
Civilian noninstitutional population	13 221	14 098	14 417	14 962	15 473	16 154	16 524	16 897	17 359	17 753	18 434
Civilian labor force	10 609	11 288	11 587	11 985	12 488	13 005	13 255	13 310	13 511	13 576	14 026
Employed	9 845	10 479	10 832	11 337	11 887	12 310	12 248	11 640	11 800	12 049	12 643
Agriculture	361	350	356	350	347	352	364	344	377	418	388
Nonagricultural industries	9 484	10 129	10 476	10 987	11 540	11 958	11 884	11 296	11 423	11 631	12 255
Unemployed	764	809	755	647	601	695	1 007	1 670	1 711	1 527	1 383
Not in labor force	2 613	2 810	2 831	2 977	2 985	3 149	3 270	3 588	3 849	4 177	4 408
Men, 20 Years and Over											
Civilian noninstitutional population	11 928	12 797	13 082	13 586	14 046	14 649	14 971	15 305	15 693	15 941	16 555
Civilian labor force	9 977	10 756	11 020	11 408	11 888	12 403	12 629	12 730	12 958	13 030	13 407
Employed	9 341	10 063	10 385	10 872	11 391	11 827	11 769	11 256	11 438	11 685	12 212
Agriculture	345	336	335	341	337	337	351	332	367	405	374
Nonagricultural industries	8 996	9 727	10 050	10 532	11 054	11 490	11 418	10 924	11 071	11 281	11 838
Unemployed	636	693	635	536	497	576	860	1 474	1 519	1 345	1 195
Not in labor force	1 951	2 041	2 061	2 177	2 157	2 246	2 342	2 575	2 735	2 911	3 149
Women, 16 Years and Over											
Civilian noninstitutional population	12 742	13 452	13 692	14 172	14 630	15 229	15 616	15 993	16 353	16 685	18 324
Civilian labor force	7 334	7 525	7 685	7 839	8 206	8 597	8 769	9 043	9 238	9 322	10 365
Employed	6 744	6 894	7 098	7 295	7 725	8 072	8 098	8 007	8 106	8 220	9 235
Agriculture	87	96	85	73	80	74	77	82	103	105	103
Nonagricultural industries	6 657	6 798	7 013	7 222	7 645	7 999	8 021	7 925	8 003	8 115	9 131
Unemployed	590	631	587	544	480	525	672	1 036	1 132	1 102	1 130
Not in labor force	5 408	5 928	6 007	6 333	6 424	6 632	6 847	6 951	7 116	7 363	7 959
Women, 20 Years and Over											
Civilian noninstitutional population	11 528	12 211	12 420	12 858	13 262	13 791	14 127	14 463	14 776	15 090	16 548
Civilian labor force	7 096	7 096	7 257	7 377	7 735	8 108	8 274	8 560	8 789	8 902	9 853
Employed	6 367	6 541	6 752	6 913	7 321	7 662	7 707	7 707	7 788	8 902	8 858
Agriculture	84	91	78	70	77	69	75	78	101	104	100
Nonagricultural industries	6 283	6 450	6 674	6 843	7 244	7 593	7 632	7 570	7 687	7 814	8 758
Unemployed	496	555	504	464	414	446	567	911	1 001	984	995
Not in labor force	4 666	5 114	5 163	5 481	5 527	5 682	5 853	5 903	5 987	6 187	6 695
Both Sexes, 16 to 19 Years											
Civilian noninstitutional population	2 507	2 543	2 608	2 689	2 796	2 944	3 042	3 123	3 243	3 407	3 656
Civilian labor force	1 103	960	995	1 038	1 071	1 091	1 121	1 063	1 002	965	1 131
Employed	882	768	792	847	900	894	870	742	680	665	808
Agriculture	19	19	25	13	14	20	15	16	12	14	17
Nonagricultural industries	863	749	767	834	887	874	855	726	668	651	791
Unemployed	221	192	203	191	170	197	251	321	322	300	324
Not in labor force	1 404	1 583	1 612	1 651	1 725	1 853	1 921	2 061	2 242	2 442	2 524

[2]May be of any race.

Table 1-4. Employment Status of the Civilian Noninstitutional Population, by Sex, Race, and Marital Status, 1990–2012

(Thousands of people.)

Race, marital status, and year	Men				Women			
	Civilian noninstitutional population	Civilian labor force			Civilian noninstitutional population	Civilian labor force		
		Total	Employed	Unemployed		Total	Employed	Unemployed
ALL RACES								
Single								
1990	25 870	19 357	17 405	1 952	21 901	14 612	13 336	1 276
1991	26 197	19 411	17 011	2 400	22 173	14 681	13 198	1 482
1992	26 436	19 709	17 098	2 611	22 475	14 872	13 263	1 609
1993	26 570	19 706	17 261	2 445	22 713	15 031	13 484	1 547
1994	26 786	19 786	17 604	2 181	23 000	15 333	13 847	1 486
1995	26 918	19 841	17 833	2 007	23 151	15 467	14 053	1 413
1996	27 387	20 071	18 055	2 016	23 623	15 842	14 403	1 439
1997	28 311	20 689	18 783	1 906	24 285	16 492	15 037	1 455
1998	28 693	21 037	19 240	1 798	24 941	17 087	15 755	1 332
1999	29 104	21 351	19 686	1 665	25 576	17 575	16 267	1 308
2000	29 887	22 002	20 339	1 663	25 920	17 849	16 628	1 221
2001	30 646	22 285	20 298	1 988	26 462	18 021	16 635	1 386
2002	31 072	22 289	19 983	2 306	26 999	18 203	16 583	1 621
2003	31 691	22 297	19 841	2 457	27 802	18 397	16 723	1 674
2004	32 422	22 776	20 395	2 381	28 228	18 616	16 995	1 621
2005	33 125	23 214	21 006	2 209	29 046	19 183	17 588	1 595
2006	33 931	23 974	21 907	2 067	29 624	19 474	17 978	1 496
2007	34 650	24 276	22 143	2 132	30 219	19 745	18 322	1 422
2008	35 274	24 643	21 938	2 705	30 980	20 231	18 513	1 717
2009	36 087	24 640	20 628	4 011	31 500	20 224	17 800	2 424
2010	37 137	24 985	20 850	4 135	32 548	20 592	17 950	2 642
2011	37 782	25 301	21 474	3 827	33 266	20 878	18 266	2 612
2012	38 180	25 494	22 002	3 492	34 267	21 506	18 973	2 533
Married, Spouse Present								
1990	53 793	42 275	40 829	1 446	52 917	30 901	29 714	1 188
1991	54 158	42 303	40 429	1 875	53 169	31 112	29 698	1 415
1992	54 509	42 491	40 341	2 150	53 501	31 700	30 100	1 600
1993	55 178	42 834	40 935	1 899	53 838	31 980	30 499	1 482
1994	55 560	43 005	41 414	1 592	54 155	32 888	31 536	1 352
1995	56 100	43 472	42 048	1 424	54 716	33 359	32 063	1 296
1996	56 363	43 739	42 417	1 322	54 970	33 618	32 406	1 211
1997	56 396	43 808	42 642	1 167	54 915	33 802	32 755	1 047
1998	56 670	43 957	42 923	1 034	55 331	33 857	32 872	985
1999	57 089	44 244	43 254	990	56 178	34 372	33 450	921
2000	58 167	44 987	44 078	908	57 557	35 146	34 209	937
2001	58 448	45 233	44 007	1 226	57 610	35 236	34 153	1 083
2002	59 102	45 766	44 116	1 650	58 165	35 477	34 153	1 323
2003	60 063	46 404	44 653	1 751	59 069	36 046	34 695	1 352
2004	60 412	46 550	45 084	1 466	59 278	35 845	34 600	1 244
2005	60 545	46 771	45 483	1 287	59 205	35 941	34 773	1 168
2006	60 751	46 842	45 700	1 142	59 576	36 314	35 272	1 042
2007	61 760	47 520	46 314	1 206	60 474	36 881	35 832	1 049
2008	61 794	47 450	45 860	1 590	60 554	37 194	35 869	1 325
2009	61 773	47 114	43 998	3 115	60 675	37 264	35 207	2 057
2010	61 254	46 430	43 292	3 138	60 257	36 742	34 582	2 160
2011	61 358	45 954	43 283	2 671	60 061	36 141	34 110	2 031
2012	61 757	46 094	43 820	2 274	61 219	36 436	34 521	1 915
Divorced, Widowed, or Separated								
1990	10 714	7 378	6 871	508	23 968	11 315	10 639	676
1991	10 924	7 454	6 783	671	24 304	11 385	10 600	786
1992	11 325	7 763	7 001	762	24 559	11 570	10 689	881
1993	11 584	7 864	7 153	711	24 955	11 784	10 927	856
1994	12 008	8 026	7 432	594	25 304	12 018	11 227	791
1995	12 160	8 048	7 496	551	25 539	12 118	11 407	712
1996	12 456	8 276	7 735	541	25 791	12 397	11 691	706
1997	13 009	8 764	8 260	504	26 218	12 742	12 082	660
1998	13 394	8 965	8 530	435	26 190	12 771	12 143	628
1999	13 528	8 918	8 507	411	26 276	12 909	12 324	585
2000	13 910	9 291	8 888	403	27 135	13 308	12 748	559
2001	14 188	9 367	8 892	476	27 738	13 592	12 949	642
2002	14 411	9 445	8 804	641	27 821	13 683	12 846	837
2003	14 680	9 537	8 838	699	27 862	13 828	12 986	842
2004	14 875	9 654	9 045	608	28 141	13 961	13 133	828
2005	15 481	10 048	9 484	563	28 680	14 163	13 396	768
2006	15 923	10 440	9 895	545	29 010	14 385	13 675	709
2007	15 763	10 341	9 797	544	29 001	14 362	13 638	724
2008	16 044	10 427	9 688	739	29 141	14 342	13 494	849
2009	16 275	10 370	9 043	1 326	29 490	14 531	13 201	1 330
2010	16 783	10 570	9 217	1 352	29 851	14 570	13 173	1 397
2011	17 177	10 719	9 533	1 186	29 974	14 623	13 203	1 420
2012	17 406	10 738	9 734	1 005	30 454	14 706	13 420	1 286

Note: See notes and definitions for information on historical comparability.

Table 1-4. Employment Status of the Civilian Noninstitutional Population, by Sex, Race, and Marital Status, 1990–2012—*Continued*

(Thousands of people.)

Race, marital status, and year	Men				Women			
	Civilian noninstitutional population	Civilian labor force			Civilian noninstitutional population	Civilian labor force		
		Total	Employed	Unemployed		Total	Employed	Unemployed
WHITE[1]								
Single								
1990	20 746	15 993	14 617	1 376	16 555	11 522	10 729	794
1991	20 899	15 989	14 233	1 756	16 569	11 497	10 557	939
1992	21 025	16 129	14 285	1 844	16 684	11 502	10 526	976
1993	20 974	16 033	14 303	1 730	16 768	11 613	10 633	980
1994	21 071	16 074	14 539	1 535	16 936	11 805	10 885	920
1995	21 132	16 080	14 674	1 406	17 046	11 830	10 967	864
1996	21 454	16 285	14 891	1 394	17 282	11 977	11 099	878
1997	22 236	16 810	15 507	1 303	17 728	12 322	11 443	879
1998	22 513	17 007	15 746	1 261	18 247	12 742	11 945	797
1999	22 788	17 272	16 116	1 157	18 635	13 029	12 206	823
2000	23 266	17 659	16 504	1 154	18 808	13 215	12 449	766
2001	23 979	17 970	16 561	1 409	19 253	13 368	12 491	877
2002	24 289	17 924	16 289	1 635	19 625	13 556	12 550	1 006
2003	24 419	17 755	16 031	1 723	19 924	13 462	12 461	1 001
2004	24 929	18 090	16 435	1 655	20 210	13 597	12 628	969
2005	25 436	18 338	16 833	1 505	20 702	13 906	12 957	949
2006	26 012	18 928	17 500	1 428	21 085	14 109	13 199	909
2007	26 431	19 063	17 580	1 483	21 408	14 255	13 357	897
2008	27 023	19 395	17 474	1 920	22 064	14 648	13 578	1 070
2009	27 559	19 392	16 528	2 864	22 371	14 733	13 193	1 540
2010	28 250	19 582	16 653	2 929	23 000	14 803	13 171	1 632
2011	28 707	19 823	17 175	2 648	23 455	14 988	13 421	1 567
2012	28 338	19 601	17 202	2 399	23 662	15 067	13 568	1 499
Married, Spouse Present								
1990	47 841	37 515	36 338	1 177	47 240	27 271	26 285	986
1991	48 137	37 507	35 923	1 585	47 456	27 479	26 290	1 189
1992	48 416	37 671	35 886	1 785	47 705	27 951	26 623	1 329
1993	48 937	37 953	36 396	1 557	47 944	28 221	26 993	1 228
1994	49 169	38 008	36 719	1 288	48 120	29 017	27 888	1 129
1995	49 597	38 376	37 211	1 165	48 497	29 360	28 290	1 070
1996	49 800	38 616	37 522	1 094	48 684	29 517	28 496	1 020
1997	49 719	38 593	37 636	957	48 542	29 664	28 809	855
1998	49 901	38 629	37 793	836	48 722	29 534	28 727	808
1999	50 091	38 765	37 968	797	49 296	29 806	29 056	749
2000	50 775	39 169	38 451	717	50 194	30 344	29 582	762
2001	50 850	39 246	38 265	981	50 077	30 336	29 472	864
2002	51 284	39 580	38 261	1 319	50 489	30 511	29 463	1 048
2003	51 859	39 908	38 529	1 379	50 957	30 805	29 740	1 065
2004	51 992	39 935	38 774	1 161	50 939	30 544	29 549	996
2005	52 034	40 141	39 130	1 011	50 865	30 599	29 676	922
2006	52 035	40 103	39 207	896	51 200	30 950	30 111	839
2007	52 775	40 559	39 594	965	51 868	31 363	30 533	830
2008	52 708	40 404	39 157	1 247	51 637	31 456	30 367	1 089
2009	52 693	40 142	37 644	2 498	51 786	31 584	29 891	1 694
2010	52 211	39 489	36 999	2 490	51 364	31 161	29 412	1 748
2011	52 142	38 951	36 870	2 081	51 074	30 555	28 925	1 630
2012	51 904	38 569	36 805	1 764	51 414	30 332	28 793	1 539
Divorced, Widowed, or Separated								
1990	8 782	6 131	5 748	382	19 461	9 016	8 544	471
1991	8 941	6 159	5 641	518	19 757	9 111	8 538	573
1992	9 210	6 368	5 788	580	19 931	9 216	8 561	654
1993	9 459	6 498	5 957	541	20 206	9 382	8 764	618
1994	9 819	6 644	6 193	451	20 439	9 533	8 965	569
1995	10 005	6 689	6 261	428	20 638	9 613	9 087	526
1996	10 234	6 883	6 474	408	20 862	9 831	9 325	506
1997	10 622	7 236	6 855	382	21 147	10 068	9 607	461
1998	10 937	7 398	7 064	334	21 157	10 104	9 656	449
1999	11 050	7 375	7 056	320	21 225	10 261	9 834	427
2000	11 329	7 638	7 333	305	21 847	10 521	10 105	416
2001	11 623	7 750	7 386	364	22 330	10 729	10 255	474
2002	11 789	7 804	7 299	505	22 308	10 775	10 151	624
2003	11 971	7 846	7 305	541	22 162	10 769	10 168	602
2004	12 124	7 969	7 503	466	22 450	10 950	10 350	600
2005	12 558	8 215	7 800	415	22 853	11 101	10 552	548
2006	12 974	8 583	8 176	407	22 957	11 162	10 640	523
2007	12 867	8 536	8 115	421	22 904	11 159	10 613	547
2008	12 995	8 552	7 992	560	23 112	11 180	10 556	624
2009	13 181	8 517	7 459	1 058	23 312	11 275	10 282	993
2010	13 620	8 657	7 601	1 056	23 630	11 392	10 333	1 059
2011	13 952	8 777	7 875	903	23 747	11 484	10 424	1 060
2012	14 024	8 751	7 983	767	23 861	11 364	10 418	947

Note: See notes and definitions for information on historical comparability.

[1]Beginning in 2003, persons who selected this race group only; persons who selected more than one race group are not included. Prior to 2003, persons who reported more than one race group were included in the group they identified as their main race.

Table 1-4. Employment Status of the Civilian Noninstitutional Population, by Sex, Race, and Marital Status, 1990–2012—*Continued*

(Thousands of people.)

Race, marital status, and year	Men				Women			
	Civilian noninstitutional population	Civilian labor force			Civilian noninstitutional population	Civilian labor force		
		Total	Employed	Unemployed		Total	Employed	Unemployed
ALL OTHER RACES								
Single								
1990	5 124	3 364	2 788	576	5 346	3 090	2 607	482
1991	5 298	3 422	2 778	644	5 604	3 184	2 641	543
1992	5 411	3 580	2 813	767	5 791	3 370	2 737	633
1993	5 596	3 673	2 958	715	5 945	3 418	2 851	567
1994	5 715	3 712	3 065	646	6 064	3 528	2 962	566
1995	5 786	3 761	3 159	601	6 105	3 637	3 086	549
1996	5 933	3 786	3 164	622	6 341	3 865	3 304	561
1997	6 075	3 879	3 276	603	6 557	4 170	3 594	576
1998	6 180	4 030	3 494	537	6 694	4 345	3 810	535
1999	6 316	4 079	3 570	508	6 941	4 546	4 061	485
2000	6 621	4 343	3 835	509	7 112	4 634	4 179	455
2001	6 667	4 315	3 737	579	7 209	4 653	4 144	509
2002	6 783	4 365	3 694	671	7 374	4 647	4 033	615
2003	7 272	4 542	3 810	734	7 878	4 935	4 262	673
2004	7 493	4 686	3 960	726	8 018	5 019	4 367	652
2005	7 689	4 876	4 173	704	8 344	5 277	4 631	646
2006	7 919	5 046	4 407	639	8 539	5 365	4 779	587
2007	8 219	5 213	4 563	649	8 811	5 490	4 965	525
2008	8 251	5 248	4 464	785	8 916	5 583	4 935	647
2009	8 528	5 248	4 100	1 147	9 129	5 491	4 607	884
2010	8 887	5 403	4 197	1 206	9 548	5 789	4 779	1 010
2011	9 075	5 478	4 299	1 179	9 811	5 890	4 845	1 045
2012	9 842	5 893	4 800	1 093	10 605	6 439	5 405	1 034
Married, Spouse Present								
1990	5 952	4 760	4 491	269	5 677	3 630	3 429	202
1991	6 021	4 796	4 506	290	5 713	3 633	3 408	226
1992	6 093	4 820	4 455	365	5 796	3 749	3 477	271
1993	6 241	4 881	4 539	342	5 894	3 759	3 506	254
1994	6 391	4 997	4 695	304	6 035	3 871	3 648	223
1995	6 503	5 096	4 837	259	6 219	3 999	3 773	226
1996	6 563	5 123	4 895	228	6 286	4 101	3 910	191
1997	6 677	5 215	5 006	210	6 373	4 138	3 946	192
1998	6 769	5 328	5 130	198	6 609	4 323	4 145	177
1999	6 998	5 479	5 286	193	6 882	4 566	4 394	172
2000	7 392	5 818	5 627	191	7 363	4 802	4 627	175
2001	7 598	5 987	5 742	245	7 533	4 900	4 681	219
2002	7 818	6 186	5 855	331	7 676	4 966	4 690	275
2003	8 204	6 496	6 124	372	8 112	5 241	4 955	287
2004	8 420	6 615	6 310	305	8 339	5 301	5 051	248
2005	8 511	6 630	6 353	276	8 340	5 342	5 097	246
2006	8 716	6 739	6 493	246	8 376	5 364	5 161	203
2007	8 985	6 961	6 720	241	8 606	5 518	5 299	219
2008	9 086	7 046	6 703	343	8 917	5 738	5 502	236
2009	9 080	6 972	6 354	617	8 889	5 680	5 316	363
2010	9 043	6 941	6 293	648	8 893	5 581	5 170	412
2011	9 216	7 003	6 413	590	8 987	5 586	5 185	401
2012	9 853	7 525	7 015	510	9 805	6 104	5 728	376
Divorced, Widowed, or Separated								
1990	1 932	1 247	1 123	126	4 507	2 299	2 095	205
1991	1 983	1 295	1 142	153	4 547	2 274	2 062	213
1992	2 115	1 395	1 213	182	4 628	2 354	2 128	227
1993	2 125	1 366	1 196	170	4 749	2 402	2 163	238
1994	2 189	1 382	1 239	143	4 865	2 485	2 262	222
1995	2 155	1 359	1 235	123	4 901	2 505	2 320	186
1996	2 222	1 393	1 261	133	4 929	2 566	2 366	200
1997	2 387	1 528	1 405	122	5 071	2 674	2 475	199
1998	2 457	1 567	1 466	101	5 033	2 667	2 487	179
1999	2 478	1 543	1 451	91	5 051	2 648	2 490	158
2000	2 581	1 653	1 555	98	5 288	2 787	2 643	143
2001	2 565	1 617	1 506	112	5 408	2 863	2 694	168
2002	2 622	1 641	1 505	136	5 513	2 908	2 695	213
2003	2 709	1 691	1 533	158	5 700	3 059	2 818	240
2004	2 751	1 685	1 542	142	5 691	3 011	2 783	228
2005	2 923	1 833	1 684	148	5 827	3 062	2 844	220
2006	2 949	1 857	1 719	138	6 053	3 223	3 035	186
2007	2 896	1 805	1 682	123	6 097	3 203	3 025	177
2008	3 049	1 875	1 696	179	6 029	3 162	2 938	225
2009	3 094	1 853	1 584	268	6 178	3 256	2 919	337
2010	3 163	1 913	1 616	296	6 221	3 178	2 840	338
2011	3 225	1 942	1 658	283	6 227	3 139	2 779	360
2012	3 382	1 987	1 751	238	6 593	3 342	3 002	339

Note: See notes and definitions for information on historical comparability.

Table 1-5. Employment Status of the Civilian Noninstitutional Population, by Region, Division, State, and Selected Territory, 2011–2012

(Thousands of people, percent.)

Region, division, and state	2011						2012					
	Civilian noninstitutional population	Civilian labor force					Civilian noninstitutional population	Civilian labor force				
		Total	Participation rate	Employed	Unemployed	Unemployment rate		Total	Participation rate	Employed	Unemployed	Unemployment rate
UNITED STATES[1]	239 618	153 617	64.1	139 869	13 747	8.9	243 284	154 975	63.7	142 469	12 506	8.1
Northeast	44 127	28 208	63.9	25 887	2 321	8.2	44 378	28 389	64.0	26 066	2 324	8.2
New England	11 605	7 735	66.7	7 134	601	7.8	11 683	7 720	66.1	7 161	560	7.2
Connecticut	2 826	1 902	67.3	1 733	169	8.9	2 842	1 879	66.1	1 722	157	8.4
Maine	1 079	704	65.2	649	54	7.7	1 083	706	65.2	655	52	7.3
Massachusetts	5 289	3 470	65.6	3 216	254	7.3	5 335	3 475	65.1	3 242	234	6.7
New Hampshire	1 059	738	69.7	697	41	5.5	1 067	742	69.5	701	41	5.5
Rhode Island	842	563	66.9	499	63	11.2	845	560	66.3	502	58	10.4
Vermont	510	359	70.4	339	20	5.6	512	356	69.5	339	18	5.0
Middle Atlantic	32 522	20 473	63.0	18 753	1 720	8.4	32 695	20 669	63.2	18 905	1 764	8.5
New Jersey	6 926	4 545	65.6	4 120	425	9.4	6 970	4 595	65.9	4 159	436	9.5
New York	15 477	9 528	61.6	8 741	788	8.3	15 567	9 587	61.6	8 773	815	8.5
Pennsylvania	10 118	6 400	63.3	5 893	507	7.9	10 158	6 487	63.9	5 973	513	7.9
Midwest	52 053	34 265	65.8	31 405	2 860	8.3	52 318	34 149	65.3	31 631	2 518	7.4
East North Central	36 152	23 282	64.4	21 144	2 139	9.2	36 306	23 200	63.9	21 300	1 899	8.2
Illinois	9 942	6 580	66.2	5 943	637	9.7	9 984	6 593	66.0	6 008	585	8.9
Indiana	5 001	3 158	63.1	2 875	283	9.0	5 030	3 150	62.6	2 886	264	8.4
Michigan	7 752	4 676	60.3	4 190	486	10.4	7 784	4 657	59.8	4 232	426	9.1
Ohio	8 995	5 805	64.5	5 304	502	8.6	9 022	5 748	63.7	5 335	413	7.2
Wisconsin	4 462	3 064	68.7	2 833	231	7.5	4 486	3 052	68.0	2 840	211	6.9
West North Central	15 901	10 982	69.1	10 261	721	6.6	16 013	10 949	68.4	10 330	618	5.6
Iowa	2 377	1 659	69.8	1 562	97	5.9	2 389	1 639	68.6	1 553	86	5.2
Kansas	2 164	1 499	69.3	1 401	98	6.5	2 177	1 489	68.4	1 404	85	5.7
Minnesota	4 153	2 970	71.5	2 777	192	6.5	4 187	2 969	70.9	2 802	168	5.6
Missouri	4 648	3 022	65.0	2 767	255	8.4	4 669	2 993	64.1	2 785	207	6.9
Nebraska	1 401	1 007	71.9	962	45	4.4	1 412	1 021	72.3	981	40	3.9
North Dakota	533	382	71.7	369	13	3.5	545	392	71.9	380	12	3.1
South Dakota	625	444	71.0	423	21	4.8	633	446	70.5	426	20	4.4
South	89 012	56 160	63.1	51 237	4 923	8.8	90 105	56 525	62.7	52 174	4 351	7.7
South Atlantic	47 146	29 753	63.1	26 999	2 754	9.3	47 740	30 008	62.9	27 538	2 469	8.2
Delaware	712	441	61.9	408	33	7.4	720	444	61.7	412	32	7.1
District of Columbia	515	348	67.6	313	35	10.1	524	362	69.1	329	32	8.9
Florida	15 235	9 275	60.9	8 322	953	10.3	15 457	9 369	60.6	8 562	807	8.6
Georgia	7 383	4 768	64.6	4 295	473	9.9	7 481	4 806	64.2	4 372	434	9.0
Maryland	4 554	3 093	67.9	2 868	225	7.3	4 601	3 123	67.9	2 910	213	6.8
North Carolina	7 403	4 660	62.9	4 183	477	10.2	7 492	4 723	63.0	4 275	448	9.5
South Carolina	3 615	2 167	59.9	1 942	226	10.4	3 658	2 167	59.2	1 970	197	9.1
Virginia	6 245	4 198	67.2	3 928	270	6.4	6 321	4 210	66.6	3 962	247	5.9
West Virginia	1 485	803	54.1	740	63	7.8	1 487	805	54.1	746	59	7.3
East South Central	14 312	8 709	60.9	7 894	814	9.4	14 405	8 678	60.2	7 978	700	8.1
Alabama	3 729	2 182	58.5	1 993	189	8.7	3 748	2 156	57.5	1 999	157	7.3
Kentucky	3 366	2 072	61.6	1 875	196	9.5	3 379	2 075	61.4	1 904	171	8.2
Mississippi	2 244	1 338	59.6	1 198	141	10.5	2 254	1 333	59.1	1 211	122	9.2
Tennessee	4 974	3 117	62.7	2 829	288	9.3	5 024	3 114	62.0	2 864	249	8.0
West South Central	27 553	17 698	64.2	16 343	1 354	7.7	27 961	17 840	63.8	16 658	1 182	6.6
Arkansas	2 252	1 360	60.4	1 252	108	7.9	2 263	1 356	59.9	1 257	99	7.3
Louisiana	3 474	2 070	59.6	1 919	151	7.3	3 498	2 084	59.6	1 949	134	6.4
Oklahoma	2 867	1 784	62.2	1 679	105	5.9	2 893	1 803	62.3	1 709	94	5.2
Texas	18 960	12 484	65.8	11 494	991	7.9	19 307	12 597	65.2	11 743	855	6.8
West	55 861	35 897	64.3	32 167	3 730	10.4	56 598	35 986	63.6	32 665	3 321	9.2
Mountain	16 920	11 011	65.1	10 030	981	8.9	17 168	11 029	64.2	10 161	867	7.9
Arizona	4 921	3 049	62.0	2 762	287	9.4	4 998	3 030	60.6	2 779	252	8.3
Colorado	3 924	2 723	69.4	2 490	233	8.6	3 990	2 743	68.7	2 524	220	8.0
Idaho	1 180	767	65.0	703	64	8.3	1 194	773	64.7	719	55	7.1
Montana	786	499	63.5	466	33	6.6	793	508	64.1	477	31	6.0
Nevada	2 097	1 392	66.4	1 208	184	13.2	2 131	1 379	64.7	1 226	152	11.1
New Mexico	1 582	932	58.9	862	70	7.5	1 590	936	58.9	871	65	6.9
Utah	1 993	1 347	67.6	1 254	93	6.9	2 028	1 354	66.8	1 276	77	5.7
Wyoming	438	303	69.2	285	18	6.1	445	306	68.8	290	16	5.4
Pacific	38 941	24 885	63.9	22 137	2 748	11.0	39 430	24 957	63.3	22 504	2 453	9.8
Alaska	529	366	69.2	338	28	7.6	537	366	68.2	341	26	7.0
California	28 070	18 404	63.5	16 237	2 167	11.8	29 040	10 495	63.0	10 560	1 935	10.5
Hawaii	1 055	658	62.4	615	43	6.5	1 066	652	61.2	614	38	5.8
Oregon	3 065	1 975	64.4	1 785	190	9.6	3 097	1 963	63.4	1 792	171	8.7
Washington	5 312	3 482	65.5	3 162	320	9.2	5 382	3 481	64.7	3 197	284	8.2

Note: Data refer to place of residence. Region and division data are derived from summing the component states. Sub-national data reflect revised population controls and model reestimation.

[1]Due to separate processing and weighing procedures, totals for the United States differ from the results obtained by aggregating data for regions, divisions, or states.

Table 1-6. Civilian Noninstitutional Population, by Age, Race, Sex, and Hispanic Origin, 1948–2012

(Thousands of people.)

Race, Hispanic origin, sex, and year	16 years and over	16 to 19 years			20 years and over						
		Total	16 to 17 years	18 to 19 years	Total	20 to 24 years	25 to 34 years	35 to 44 years	45 to 54 years	55 to 64 years	65 years and over
ALL RACES											
Both Sexes											
1948	103 068	8 449	4 265	4 185	94 618	11 530	22 610	20 097	16 771	12 885	10 720
1949	103 994	8 215	4 139	4 079	95 778	11 312	22 822	20 401	17 002	13 201	11 035
1950	104 995	8 143	4 076	4 068	96 851	11 080	23 013	20 681	17 240	13 469	11 363
1951	104 621	7 865	4 096	3 771	96 755	10 167	22 843	20 863	17 464	13 692	11 724
1952	105 231	7 922	4 234	3 689	97 305	9 389	23 044	21 137	17 716	13 889	12 126
1953	107 056	8 014	4 241	3 773	99 041	8 960	23 266	21 922	17 991	13 830	13 075
1954	108 321	8 224	4 336	3 889	100 095	8 885	23 304	22 135	18 305	14 085	13 375
1955	109 683	8 364	4 440	3 925	101 318	9 036	23 249	22 348	18 643	14 309	13 728
1956	110 954	8 434	4 482	3 953	102 518	9 271	23 072	22 567	19 012	14 516	14 075
1957	112 265	8 612	4 587	4 026	103 653	9 486	22 849	22 786	19 424	14 727	14 376
1958	113 727	8 986	4 872	4 114	104 737	9 733	22 563	23 025	19 832	14 923	14 657
1959	115 329	9 618	5 337	4 282	105 711	9 975	22 201	23 207	20 203	15 134	14 985
1960	117 245	10 187	5 573	4 615	107 056	10 273	21 998	23 437	20 601	15 409	15 336
1961	118 771	10 513	5 462	5 052	108 255	10 583	21 829	23 585	20 893	15 675	15 685
1962	120 153	10 652	5 503	5 150	109 500	10 852	21 503	23 797	20 916	15 874	16 554
1963	122 416	11 370	6 301	5 070	111 045	11 464	21 400	23 948	21 144	16 138	16 945
1964	124 485	12 111	6 974	5 139	112 372	12 017	21 367	23 940	21 452	16 442	17 150
1965	126 513	12 930	6 936	5 995	113 582	12 442	21 417	23 832	21 728	16 727	17 432
1966	128 058	13 592	6 914	6 679	114 463	12 638	21 543	23 579	21 977	17 007	17 715
1967	129 874	13 480	7 003	6 480	116 391	13 421	22 057	23 313	22 256	17 310	18 029
1968	132 028	13 698	7 200	6 499	118 328	13 891	22 912	23 036	22 534	17 614	18 338
1969	134 335	14 095	7 422	6 673	120 238	14 488	23 645	22 709	22 806	17 930	18 657
1970	137 085	14 519	7 643	6 876	122 566	15 323	24 435	22 489	23 059	18 250	19 007
1971	140 216	15 022	7 849	7 173	125 193	16 345	25 337	22 274	23 244	18 581	19 406
1972	144 126	15 510	8 076	7 435	128 614	17 143	26 740	22 358	23 338	19 007	20 023
1973	147 096	15 840	8 227	7 613	131 253	17 692	28 172	22 287	23 431	19 281	20 389
1974	150 120	16 180	8 373	7 809	133 938	17 994	29 439	22 461	23 578	19 517	20 945
1975	153 153	16 418	8 419	7 999	136 733	18 595	30 710	22 526	23 535	19 844	21 525
1976	156 150	16 614	8 442	8 171	139 536	19 109	31 953	22 796	23 409	20 185	22 083
1977	159 033	16 688	8 482	8 206	142 345	19 582	33 117	23 296	23 197	20 557	22 597
1978	161 910	16 695	8 484	8 211	145 216	20 007	34 091	24 099	22 977	20 875	23 166
1979	164 863	16 657	8 389	8 268	148 205	20 353	35 261	24 861	22 752	21 210	23 767
1980	167 745	16 543	8 279	8 264	151 202	20 635	36 558	25 578	22 563	21 520	24 350
1981	170 130	16 214	8 068	8 145	153 916	20 820	37 777	26 291	22 422	21 756	24 850
1982	172 271	15 763	7 714	8 049	156 508	20 845	38 492	27 611	22 264	21 909	25 387
1983	174 215	15 274	7 385	7 889	158 941	20 799	39 147	28 932	22 167	22 003	25 892
1984	176 383	14 735	7 196	7 538	161 648	20 688	39 999	30 251	22 226	22 052	26 433
1985	178 206	14 506	7 232	7 274	163 700	20 097	40 670	31 379	22 418	22 140	26 997
1986	180 587	14 496	7 386	7 110	166 091	19 569	41 731	32 550	22 732	22 011	27 497
1987	182 753	14 606	7 501	7 104	168 147	18 970	42 297	33 755	23 183	21 835	28 108
1988	184 613	14 527	7 284	7 243	170 085	18 434	42 611	34 784	24 004	21 641	28 612
1989	186 393	14 223	6 886	7 338	172 169	18 025	42 845	35 977	24 744	21 406	29 173
1990	189 164	14 520	6 893	7 626	174 644	18 902	42 976	37 719	25 081	20 719	29 247
1991	190 925	14 073	6 901	7 173	176 852	18 963	42 688	39 116	25 709	20 675	29 700
1992	192 805	13 840	6 907	6 933	178 965	18 846	42 278	39 852	27 206	20 604	30 179
1993	194 838	13 935	7 010	6 925	180 903	18 642	41 771	40 733	28 549	20 574	30 634
1994	196 814	14 196	7 245	6 951	182 619	18 353	41 306	41 534	29 778	20 635	31 012
1995	198 584	14 511	7 407	7 104	184 073	17 864	40 798	42 254	30 974	20 735	31 448
1996	200 591	14 934	7 678	7 256	185 656	17 409	40 252	43 086	32 167	20 990	31 751
1997	203 133	15 365	7 861	7 504	187 769	17 442	39 559	43 883	33 391	21 505	31 989
1998	205 220	15 644	7 895	7 749	189 576	17 593	38 778	44 299	34 373	22 296	32 237
1999	207 753	16 040	8 060	7 979	191 713	17 968	37 976	44 635	35 587	23 064	32 484
2000	212 577	15 912	7 978	7 934	196 664	18 311	38 703	44 312	37 642	24 230	33 466
2001	215 092	15 929	8 020	7 909	199 164	18 877	38 505	44 195	38 904	25 011	33 672
2002	217 570	15 994	8 099	7 895	201 576	19 348	38 472	43 894	39 711	26 343	33 808
2003	221 168	16 096	8 561	7 535	205 072	19 801	39 021	43 746	40 522	27 728	34 253
2004	223 357	16 222	8 574	7 648	207 134	20 197	38 939	43 226	41 245	28 919	34 609
2005	226 082	16 398	8 778	7 619	209 685	20 276	39 064	43 005	42 107	30 165	35 068
2006	228 815	16 678	9 089	7 589	212 137	20 265	39 230	42 753	42 901	31 375	35 613
2007	231 867	16 982	9 222	7 760	214 885	20 427	39 751	42 401	43 544	32 533	36 228
2008	233 788	17 075	9 133	7 942	216 713	20 409	39 993	41 699	43 960	33 491	37 161
2009	235 801	17 043	8 944	8 100	218 757	20 524	40 280	40 919	44 365	34 671	37 998
2010	237 830	16 901	8 943	7 957	220 929	21 047	40 903	40 090	44 297	35 885	38 706
2011	239 618	16 774	8 727	8 048	222 843	21 423	41 364	39 499	43 842	36 987	39 729
2012	243 284	16 984	8 891	8 093	226 300	21 799	40 975	39 642	43 697	38 318	41 869

Table 1-6. Civilian Noninstitutional Population, by Age, Race, Sex, and Hispanic Origin, 1948–2012—*Continued*

(Thousands of people.)

Race, Hispanic origin, sex, and year	16 years and over	16 to 19 years			20 years and over						
		Total	16 to 17 years	18 to 19 years	Total	20 to 24 years	25 to 34 years	35 to 44 years	45 to 54 years	55 to 64 years	65 years and over
ALL RACES											
Men											
1948	49 996	4 078	2 128	1 951	45 918	5 527	10 767	9 798	8 290	6 441	5 093
1949	50 321	3 946	2 062	1 884	46 378	5 405	10 871	9 926	8 379	6 568	5 226
1950	50 725	3 962	2 043	1 920	46 763	5 270	10 963	10 034	8 472	6 664	5 357
1951	49 727	3 725	2 039	1 687	46 001	4 451	10 709	10 049	8 551	6 737	5 503
1952	49 700	3 767	2 121	1 647	45 932	3 788	10 855	10 164	8 655	6 798	5 670
1953	50 750	3 823	2 122	1 701	46 927	3 482	11 020	10 632	8 878	6 798	6 119
1954	51 395	3 953	2 174	1 780	47 441	3 509	11 067	10 718	9 018	6 885	6 241
1955	52 109	4 022	2 225	1 798	48 086	3 708	11 068	10 804	9 164	6 960	6 380
1956	52 723	4 020	2 238	1 783	48 704	3 970	10 983	10 889	9 322	7 032	6 505
1957	53 315	4 083	2 284	1 800	49 231	4 166	10 889	10 965	9 499	7 109	6 602
1958	54 033	4 293	2 435	1 858	49 740	4 339	10 787	11 076	9 675	7 179	6 683
1959	54 793	4 652	2 681	1 971	50 140	4 488	10 625	11 149	9 832	7 259	6 785
1960	55 662	4 963	2 805	2 159	50 698	4 679	10 514	11 230	10 000	7 373	6 901
1961	56 286	5 112	2 742	2 371	51 173	4 844	10 440	11 286	10 112	7 483	7 006
1962	56 831	5 150	2 764	2 386	51 681	4 925	10 207	11 389	10 162	7 610	7 386
1963	57 921	5 496	3 162	2 334	52 425	5 240	10 165	11 476	10 274	7 740	7 526
1964	58 847	5 866	3 503	2 364	52 981	5 520	10 144	11 466	10 402	7 873	7 574
1965	59 782	6 318	3 488	2 831	53 463	5 701	10 182	11 427	10 512	7 990	7 649
1966	60 262	6 658	3 478	3 180	53 603	5 663	10 224	11 294	10 598	8 099	7 723
1967	60 905	6 537	3 528	3 010	54 367	5 977	10 495	11 161	10 705	8 218	7 809
1968	61 847	6 683	3 634	3 049	55 165	6 127	10 944	11 040	10 819	8 336	7 897
1969	62 898	6 928	3 741	3 187	55 969	6 379	11 309	10 890	10 935	8 464	7 990
1970	64 304	7 145	3 848	3 299	57 157	6 861	11 750	10 810	11 052	8 590	8 093
1971	65 942	7 430	3 954	3 477	58 511	7 511	12 227	10 721	11 129	8 711	8 208
1972	67 835	7 705	4 081	3 624	60 130	8 061	12 911	10 762	11 167	8 895	8 330
1973	69 292	7 855	4 152	3 703	61 436	8 429	13 641	10 746	11 202	8 990	8 426
1974	70 808	8 012	4 231	3 781	62 796	8 600	14 262	10 834	11 315	9 140	8 641
1975	72 291	8 134	4 252	3 882	64 158	8 950	14 899	10 874	11 298	9 286	8 852
1976	73 759	8 244	4 266	3 978	65 515	9 237	15 528	11 010	11 243	9 444	9 053
1977	75 193	8 288	4 290	4 000	66 904	9 477	16 108	11 260	11 144	9 616	9 297
1978	76 576	8 309	4 295	4 014	68 268	9 693	16 598	11 665	11 045	9 758	9 509
1979	78 020	8 310	4 251	4 060	69 709	9 873	17 193	12 046	10 944	9 907	9 746
1980	79 398	8 260	4 195	4 064	71 138	10 023	17 833	12 400	10 861	10 042	9 979
1981	80 511	8 092	4 087	4 005	72 419	10 116	18 427	12 758	10 797	10 151	10 170
1982	81 523	7 879	3 911	3 968	73 644	10 136	18 787	13 410	10 726	10 215	10 371
1983	82 531	7 659	3 750	3 908	74 872	10 140	19 143	14 067	10 689	10 261	10 573
1984	83 605	7 386	3 655	3 731	76 219	10 108	19 596	14 719	10 724	10 285	10 788
1985	84 469	7 275	3 689	3 586	77 195	9 746	19 864	15 265	10 844	10 392	11 084
1986	85 798	7 275	3 768	3 507	78 523	9 498	20 498	15 858	10 986	10 336	11 347
1987	86 899	7 335	3 824	3 510	79 565	9 195	20 781	16 475	11 215	10 267	11 632
1988	87 857	7 304	3 715	3 588	80 553	8 931	20 937	17 008	11 625	10 193	11 859
1989	88 762	7 143	3 524	3 619	81 619	8 743	21 080	17 550	11 981	10 092	12 134
1990	90 377	7 347	3 534	3 813	83 030	9 320	21 117	18 529	12 238	9 778	12 049
1991	91 278	7 134	3 548	3 586	84 144	9 367	20 977	19 213	12 554	9 780	12 254
1992	92 270	7 023	3 542	3 481	85 247	9 326	20 792	19 585	13 271	9 776	12 496
1993	93 332	7 076	3 595	3 481	86 256	9 216	20 569	20 037	13 944	9 773	12 717
1994	94 355	7 203	3 718	3 486	87 151	9 074	20 361	20 443	14 545	9 810	12 918
1995	95 178	7 367	3 794	3 573	87 811	8 835	20 079	20 800	15 111	9 856	13 130
1996	96 206	7 600	3 955	3 645	88 606	8 611	19 775	21 222	15 674	9 997	13 327
1997	97 715	7 836	4 053	3 783	89 879	8 706	19 478	21 669	16 276	10 282	13 469
1998	98 758	7 968	4 059	3 909	90 790	8 804	19 094	21 857	16 773	10 649	13 613
1999	99 722	8 167	4 143	4 024	91 555	8 899	18 565	21 969	17 335	11 008	13 779
2000	101 964	8 089	4 096	3 993	93 875	9 101	19 106	21 683	18 365	11 583	14 037
2001	103 282	8 101	4 102	3 999	95 181	9 368	19 056	21 643	18 987	11 972	14 155
2002	104 585	8 146	4 140	4 006	96 439	9 627	19 037	21 523	19 379	12 641	14 233
2003	106 435	8 163	4 365	3 797	98 272	9 878	19 347	21 463	19 784	13 305	14 496
2004	107 710	8 234	4 318	3 916	99 476	10 125	19 358	21 255	20 160	13 894	14 684
2005	109 151	8 317	4 481	3 836	100 835	10 181	19 446	21 177	20 585	14 502	14 944
2006	110 605	8 459	4 613	3 846	102 145	10 191	19 568	21 082	20 991	15 095	15 219
2007	112 173	8 618	4 658	3 960	103 555	10 291	19 858	20 910	21 313	15 658	15 525
2008	113 113	8 660	4 625	4 035	104 453	10 249	19 999	20 567	21 512	16 123	16 002
2009	114 136	8 643	4 548	4 095	105 493	10 284	20 167	20 199	21 731	16 698	16 414
2010	115 174	8 578	4 540	4 038	106 596	10 550	20 465	19 807	21 713	17 291	16 769
2011	116 317	8 582	4 486	4 095	107 736	10 844	20 711	19 446	21 451	17 810	17 474
2012	117 343	8 657	4 550	4 107	108 686	10 889	20 205	19 416	21 339	18 416	18 422

Table 1-6. Civilian Noninstitutional Population, by Age, Race, Sex, and Hispanic Origin, 1948–2012—*Continued*

(Thousands of people.)

Race, Hispanic origin, sex, and year	16 years and over	16 to 19 years			20 years and over						
		Total	16 to 17 years	18 to 19 years	Total	20 to 24 years	25 to 34 years	35 to 44 years	45 to 54 years	55 to 64 years	65 years and over
ALL RACES											
Women											
1948	53 071	4 371	2 137	2 234	48 700	6 003	11 843	10 299	8 481	6 444	5 627
1949	53 670	4 269	2 077	2 195	49 400	5 907	11 951	10 475	8 623	6 633	5 809
1950	54 270	4 181	2 033	2 148	50 088	5 810	12 050	10 647	8 768	6 805	6 006
1951	54 895	4 140	2 057	2 084	50 754	5 716	12 134	10 814	8 913	6 955	6 221
1952	55 529	4 155	2 113	2 042	51 373	5 601	12 189	10 973	9 061	7 091	6 456
1953	56 305	4 191	2 119	2 072	52 114	5 478	12 246	11 290	9 113	7 032	6 956
1954	56 925	4 271	2 162	2 109	52 654	5 376	12 237	11 417	9 287	7 200	7 134
1955	57 574	4 342	2 215	2 127	53 232	5 328	12 181	11 544	9 479	7 349	7 348
1956	58 228	4 414	2 244	2 170	53 814	5 301	12 089	11 678	9 690	7 484	7 570
1957	58 951	4 529	2 303	2 226	54 421	5 320	11 960	11 821	9 925	7 618	7 774
1958	59 690	4 693	2 437	2 256	54 997	5 394	11 776	11 949	10 157	7 744	7 974
1959	60 534	4 966	2 656	2 311	55 570	5 487	11 576	12 058	10 371	7 875	8 200
1960	61 582	5 224	2 768	2 456	56 358	5 594	11 484	12 207	10 601	8 036	8 435
1961	62 484	5 401	2 720	2 681	57 082	5 739	11 389	12 299	10 781	8 192	8 679
1962	63 321	5 502	2 739	2 764	57 819	5 927	11 296	12 408	10 754	8 264	9 168
1963	64 494	5 874	3 139	2 736	58 620	6 224	11 235	12 472	10 870	8 398	9 419
1964	65 637	6 245	3 471	2 775	59 391	6 497	11 223	12 474	11 050	8 569	9 576
1965	66 731	6 612	3 448	3 164	60 119	6 741	11 235	12 405	11 216	8 737	9 783
1966	67 795	6 934	3 436	3 499	60 860	6 975	11 319	12 285	11 379	8 908	9 992
1967	68 968	6 943	3 475	3 470	62 026	7 445	11 562	12 152	11 551	9 092	10 220
1968	70 179	7 015	3 566	3 450	63 164	7 764	11 968	11 996	11 715	9 278	10 441
1969	71 436	7 167	3 681	3 486	64 269	8 109	12 336	11 819	11 871	9 466	10 667
1970	72 782	7 373	3 796	3 578	65 408	8 462	12 684	11 679	12 008	9 659	10 914
1971	74 274	7 591	3 895	3 697	66 682	8 834	13 110	11 553	12 115	9 870	11 198
1972	76 290	7 805	3 994	3 811	68 484	9 082	13 829	11 597	12 171	10 113	11 693
1973	77 804	7 985	4 076	3 909	69 819	9 263	14 531	11 541	12 229	10 290	11 963
1974	79 312	8 168	4 142	4 028	71 144	9 393	15 177	11 627	12 263	10 377	12 304
1975	80 860	8 285	4 168	4 117	72 576	9 645	15 811	11 652	12 237	10 558	12 673
1976	82 390	8 370	4 176	4 194	74 020	9 872	16 425	11 786	12 166	10 742	13 030
1977	83 840	8 400	4 193	4 206	75 441	10 103	17 008	12 036	12 053	10 940	13 300
1978	85 334	8 386	4 189	4 197	76 948	10 315	17 493	12 435	11 932	11 118	13 658
1979	86 843	8 347	4 139	4 208	78 496	10 480	18 070	12 815	11 808	11 303	14 021
1980	88 348	8 283	4 083	4 200	80 065	10 612	18 725	13 177	11 701	11 478	14 372
1981	89 618	8 121	3 981	4 140	81 497	10 705	19 350	13 533	11 625	11 605	14 680
1982	90 748	7 884	3 804	4 081	82 864	10 709	19 705	14 201	11 538	11 694	15 017
1983	91 684	7 616	3 635	3 981	84 069	10 660	20 004	14 865	11 478	11 742	15 319
1984	92 778	7 349	3 542	3 807	85 429	10 580	20 403	15 532	11 501	11 768	15 645
1985	93 736	7 231	3 543	3 688	86 506	10 351	20 805	16 114	11 574	11 748	15 913
1986	94 789	7 221	3 618	3 603	87 567	10 072	21 233	16 692	11 746	11 675	16 150
1987	95 853	7 271	3 677	3 594	88 583	9 776	21 516	17 279	11 968	11 567	16 476
1988	96 756	7 224	3 569	3 655	89 532	9 503	21 674	17 776	12 378	11 448	16 753
1989	97 630	7 080	3 361	3 719	90 550	9 282	21 765	18 387	12 763	11 314	17 039
1990	98 787	7 173	3 359	3 813	91 614	9 582	21 859	19 190	12 843	10 941	17 198
1991	99 646	6 939	3 353	3 586	92 708	9 597	21 711	19 903	13 155	10 895	17 446
1992	100 535	6 818	3 366	3 452	93 718	9 520	21 486	20 267	13 935	10 828	17 682
1993	101 506	6 859	3 415	3 444	94 647	9 426	21 202	20 696	14 605	10 801	17 917
1994	102 460	6 993	3 528	3 465	95 467	9 279	20 945	21 091	15 233	10 825	18 094
1995	103 406	7 144	3 613	3 531	96 262	9 029	20 719	21 454	15 862	10 879	18 318
1996	104 385	7 335	3 723	3 612	97 050	8 798	20 477	21 865	16 493	10 993	18 424
1997	105 418	7 528	3 808	3 721	97 889	8 736	20 081	22 214	17 115	11 224	18 520
1998	106 462	7 676	3 835	3 840	98 786	8 790	19 683	22 442	17 600	11 646	18 625
1999	108 031	7 873	3 917	3 955	100 158	9 069	19 411	22 666	18 251	12 056	18 705
2000	110 613	7 823	3 882	3 941	102 790	9 211	19 597	22 628	19 276	12 647	19 430
2001	111 811	7 828	3 917	3 910	103 983	9 509	19 449	22 552	19 917	13 039	19 517
2002	112 985	7 848	3 959	3 889	105 136	9 721	19 435	22 371	20 332	13 703	19 575
2003	114 733	7 934	4 195	3 738	106 800	9 924	19 674	22 283	20 738	14 423	19 758
2004	115 647	7 989	4 257	3 732	107 658	10 072	19 581	21 970	21 085	15 025	19 925
2005	116 931	8 081	4 297	3 784	108 850	10 095	19 618	21 828	21 521	15 663	20 125
2006	118 210	8 218	4 476	3 742	109 992	10 074	19 662	21 671	21 910	16 280	20 394
2007	119 694	8 364	4 564	3 800	111 330	10 137	19 893	21 491	22 231	16 876	20 703
2008	120 675	8 415	4 508	3 907	112 260	10 160	19 994	21 132	22 448	17 367	21 160
2009	121 665	8 401	4 396	4 004	113 265	10 240	20 113	20 721	22 633	17 973	21 584
2010	122 656	8 323	4 403	3 919	114 333	10 497	20 438	20 283	22 584	18 594	21 937
2011	123 300	8 193	4 241	3 952	115 107	10 579	20 653	20 053	22 391	19 177	22 255
2012	125 941	8 327	4 341	3 986	117 614	10 910	20 770	20 226	22 358	19 902	23 447

Table 1-6. Civilian Noninstitutional Population, by Age, Race, Sex, and Hispanic Origin, 1948–2012—*Continued*

(Thousands of people.)

Race, Hispanic origin, sex, and year	16 years and over	16 to 19 years			20 years and over						
		Total	16 to 17 years	18 to 19 years	Total	20 to 24 years	25 to 34 years	35 to 44 years	45 to 54 years	55 to 64 years	65 years and over
WHITE											
Both Sexes											
1954	97 705	7 180	3 786	3 394	90 524	7 794	20 818	19 915	16 569	12 993	12 438
1955	98 880	7 292	3 874	3 419	91 586	7 912	20 742	20 110	16 869	13 169	12 785
1956	99 976	7 346	3 908	3 438	92 629	8 106	20 564	20 314	17 198	13 341	13 105
1957	101 119	7 505	4 007	3 498	93 612	8 293	20 342	20 514	17 562	13 518	13 383
1958	102 392	7 843	4 271	3 573	94 547	8 498	20 063	20 734	17 924	13 681	13 645
1959	103 803	8 430	4 707	3 725	95 370	8 697	19 715	20 893	18 257	13 858	13 951
1960	105 282	8 924	4 909	4 016	96 355	8 927	19 470	21 049	18 578	14 070	14 260
1961	106 604	9 211	4 785	4 427	97 390	9 203	19 289	21 169	18 845	14 304	14 581
1962	107 715	9 343	4 818	4 526	98 371	9 484	18 974	21 293	18 872	14 450	15 297
1963	109 705	9 978	5 549	4 430	99 725	10 069	18 867	21 398	19 082	14 681	15 629
1964	111 534	10 616	6 137	4 481	100 916	10 568	18 838	21 375	19 360	14 957	15 816
1965	113 284	11 319	6 049	5 271	101 963	10 935	18 882	21 258	19 604	15 215	16 070
1966	114 566	11 862	5 993	5 870	102 702	11 094	18 989	21 005	19 822	15 469	16 322
1967	116 100	11 682	6 051	5 632	104 417	11 797	19 464	20 745	20 067	15 745	16 602
1968	117 948	11 840	6 225	5 616	106 107	12 184	20 245	20 474	20 310	16 018	16 875
1969	119 913	12 179	6 418	5 761	107 733	12 677	20 892	20 156	20 546	16 305	17 156
1970	122 174	12 521	6 591	5 931	109 652	13 359	21 546	19 929	20 760	16 591	17 469
1971	124 758	12 937	6 750	6 189	111 821	14 208	22 295	19 694	20 907	16 884	17 833
1972	127 906	13 301	6 910	6 392	114 603	14 897	23 555	19 673	20 950	17 250	18 278
1973	130 097	13 533	7 021	6 512	116 563	15 264	24 685	19 532	20 991	17 484	18 607
1974	132 417	13 784	7 114	6 671	118 632	15 502	25 711	19 628	21 061	17 645	19 085
1975	134 790	13 941	7 132	6 808	120 849	15 980	26 746	19 641	20 981	17 918	19 587
1976	137 106	14 055	7 125	6 930	123 050	16 368	27 757	19 827	20 816	18 220	20 064
1977	139 380	14 095	7 150	6 944	125 285	16 728	28 703	20 231	20 575	18 540	20 508
1978	141 612	14 060	7 132	6 928	127 552	17 038	29 453	20 932	20 322	18 799	21 007
1979	143 894	13 994	7 029	6 964	129 900	17 284	30 371	21 579	20 058	19 071	21 538
1980	146 122	13 854	6 912	6 943	132 268	17 484	31 407	22 174	19 837	19 316	22 050
1981	147 908	13 516	6 704	6 813	134 392	17 609	32 367	22 778	19 666	19 485	22 487
1982	149 441	13 076	6 383	6 693	136 366	17 579	32 863	23 910	19 478	19 591	22 945
1983	150 805	12 623	6 089	6 534	138 183	17 492	33 286	25 027	19 349	19 625	23 403
1984	152 347	12 147	5 918	6 228	140 200	17 304	33 889	26 124	19 348	19 629	23 906
1985	153 679	11 900	5 922	5 978	141 780	16 853	34 450	27 100	19 405	19 620	24 352
1986	155 432	11 879	6 036	5 843	143 553	16 353	35 293	28 062	19 587	19 477	24 780
1987	156 958	11 939	6 110	5 829	145 020	15 808	35 667	29 036	19 965	19 242	25 301
1988	158 194	11 838	5 893	5 945	146 357	15 276	35 876	29 818	20 652	18 996	25 739
1989	159 338	11 530	5 506	6 023	147 809	14 879	35 951	30 774	21 287	18 743	26 175
1990	160 625	11 630	5 464	6 166	148 996	15 538	35 661	31 739	21 535	18 204	26 319
1991	161 759	11 200	5 451	5 749	150 558	15 516	35 342	32 854	22 052	18 074	26 721
1992	162 972	11 004	5 478	5 526	151 968	15 354	34 885	33 305	23 364	17 951	27 108
1993	164 289	11 078	5 562	5 516	153 210	15 087	34 365	33 919	24 456	17 892	27 493
1994	165 555	11 264	5 710	5 554	154 291	14 708	33 865	34 582	25 435	17 924	27 776
1995	166 914	11 468	5 822	5 646	155 446	14 313	33 355	35 222	26 418	17 986	28 153
1996	168 317	11 822	6 026	5 796	156 495	13 907	32 852	35 810	27 403	18 136	28 387
1997	169 993	12 181	6 213	5 968	157 812	13 983	32 091	36 325	28 388	18 511	28 514
1998	171 478	12 439	6 264	6 176	159 039	14 138	31 286	36 610	29 132	19 231	28 642
1999	173 085	12 700	6 342	6 358	160 385	14 394	30 516	36 755	30 048	19 855	28 818
2000	176 220	12 535	6 264	6 271	163 685	14 552	30 948	36 261	31 550	20 757	29 617
2001	178 111	12 556	6 291	6 265	165 556	15 001	30 770	36 113	32 475	21 434	29 762
2002	179 783	12 596	6 346	6 250	167 187	15 360	30 676	35 750	33 012	22 540	29 849
2003	181 292	12 527	6 629	5 898	168 765	15 536	30 789	35 352	33 466	23 589	30 033
2004	182 643	12 599	6 561	6 038	170 045	15 817	30 585	34 845	34 005	24 549	30 245
2005	184 446	12 690	6 768	5 921	171 757	15 871	30 592	34 554	34 649	25 534	30 556
2006	186 264	12 856	6 981	5 875	173 408	15 848	30 661	34 217	35 228	26 486	30 968
2007	188 253	13 043	7 026	6 018	175 210	15 945	31 011	33 770	35 665	27 392	31 426
2008	189 540	13 084	6 962	6 122	176 456	15 914	31 234	33 093	35 941	28 109	32 165
2009	190 902	13 035	6 775	6 261	177 867	15 963	31 471	32 378	36 166	29 022	32 867
2010	192 075	12 891	6 799	6 091	179 184	16 280	31 813	31 647	36 064	29 983	33 396
2011	193 077	12 818	6 673	6 145	180 259	16 562	32 136	31 030	35 526	30 799	34 206
2012	193 204	12 658	6 617	6 040	180 547	16 289	31 242	30 597	34 935	31 511	35 973

Table 1-6. Civilian Noninstitutional Population, by Age, Race, Sex, and Hispanic Origin, 1948–2012—*Continued*

(Thousands of people.)

Race, Hispanic origin, sex, and year	16 years and over	16 to 19 years			20 years and over						
		Total	16 to 17 years	18 to 19 years	Total	20 to 24 years	25 to 34 years	35 to 44 years	45 to 54 years	55 to 64 years	65 years and over
WHITE											
Men											
1954	46 462	3 455	1 902	1 553	43 007	3 074	9 948	9 688	8 172	6 341	5 787
1955	47 076	3 507	1 945	1 563	43 569	3 241	9 936	9 768	8 303	6 398	5 923
1956	47 602	3 500	1 955	1 546	44 102	3 464	9 851	9 848	8 446	6 455	6 038
1957	48 119	3 556	2 000	1 557	44 563	3 638	9 758	9 917	8 605	6 518	6 127
1958	48 745	3 747	2 140	1 607	44 998	3 783	9 656	10 018	8 765	6 574	6 203
1959	49 408	4 079	2 370	1 710	45 329	3 903	9 499	10 081	8 909	6 639	6 298
1960	50 065	4 349	2 476	1 874	45 716	4 054	9 373	10 131	9 042	6 721	6 395
1961	50 608	4 479	2 407	2 073	46 129	4 204	9 290	10 178	9 148	6 819	6 490
1962	51 054	4 520	2 426	2 094	46 534	4 306	9 080	10 239	9 191	6 917	6 801
1963	52 031	4 827	2 792	2 036	47 204	4 610	9 039	10 309	9 297	7 031	6 919
1964	52 869	5 148	3 090	2 059	47 721	4 862	9 024	10 301	9 417	7 153	6 963
1965	53 681	5 541	3 050	2 492	48 140	5 017	9 056	10 262	9 516	7 261	7 028
1966	54 061	5 820	3 023	2 798	48 241	4 974	9 085	10 136	9 592	7 362	7 092
1967	54 608	5 671	3 058	2 613	48 937	5 257	9 339	10 013	9 688	7 474	7 167
1968	55 434	5 787	3 153	2 635	49 647	5 376	9 752	9 902	9 790	7 585	7 242
1969	56 348	6 005	3 246	2 759	50 343	5 589	10 074	9 760	9 895	7 705	7 320
1970	57 516	6 179	3 329	2 851	51 336	5 988	10 441	9 678	9 999	7 822	7 409
1971	58 900	6 420	3 412	3 008	52 481	6 546	10 841	9 578	10 066	7 933	7 517
1972	60 473	6 627	3 503	3 125	53 845	7 042	11 495	9 568	10 078	8 089	7 573
1973	61 577	6 737	3 555	3 182	54 842	7 312	12 075	9 514	10 099	8 178	7 664
1974	62 791	6 851	3 604	3 247	55 942	7 476	12 599	9 564	10 165	8 288	7 849
1975	63 981	6 929	3 609	3 320	57 052	7 766	13 131	9 578	10 134	8 413	8 031
1976	65 132	6 993	3 609	3 384	58 138	7 987	13 655	9 674	10 063	8 556	8 203
1977	66 301	7 024	3 625	3 399	59 278	8 175	14 139	9 880	9 957	8 708	8 420
1978	67 401	7 022	3 619	3 404	60 378	8 335	14 528	10 236	9 845	8 826	8 608
1979	68 547	7 007	3 568	3 439	61 540	8 470	15 008	10 563	9 730	8 949	8 820
1980	69 634	6 941	3 508	3 433	62 694	8 581	15 529	10 863	9 636	9 059	9 027
1981	70 480	6 764	3 401	3 363	63 715	8 644	16 005	11 171	9 560	9 139	9 195
1982	71 211	6 556	3 249	3 307	64 655	8 621	16 260	11 756	9 463	9 188	9 367
1983	71 922	6 340	3 098	3 242	65 581	8 597	16 499	12 314	9 408	9 208	9 556
1984	72 723	6 113	3 019	3 094	66 610	8 522	16 816	12 853	9 434	9 217	9 768
1985	73 373	5 987	3 026	2 961	67 386	8 246	17 042	13 337	9 488	9 262	10 010
1986	74 390	5 977	3 084	2 894	68 413	8 002	17 564	13 840	9 578	9 201	10 229
1987	75 189	6 015	3 125	2 890	69 175	7 729	17 754	14 338	9 771	9 101	10 481
1988	75 855	5 968	3 015	2 953	69 887	7 473	17 867	14 743	10 114	9 001	10 688
1989	76 468	5 813	2 817	2 996	70 654	7 279	17 908	15 237	10 434	8 900	10 897
1990	77 369	5 913	2 809	3 103	71 457	7 764	17 766	15 770	10 598	8 680	10 879
1991	77 977	5 704	2 805	2 899	72 274	7 748	17 615	16 340	10 856	8 640	11 074
1992	78 651	5 611	2 819	2 792	73 040	7 676	17 403	16 579	11 513	8 602	11 268
1993	79 371	5 650	2 862	2 788	73 721	7 545	17 158	16 900	12 058	8 590	11 470
1994	80 059	5 748	2 938	2 810	74 311	7 357	16 915	17 247	12 545	8 618	11 629
1995	80 733	5 854	2 995	2 859	74 879	7 163	16 653	17 567	13 028	8 653	11 815
1996	81 489	6 035	3 099	2 936	75 454	6 971	16 395	17 868	13 518	8 734	11 968
1997	82 577	6 257	3 209	3 048	76 320	7 087	16 043	18 163	14 030	8 929	12 067
1998	83 352	6 386	3 233	3 153	76 966	7 170	15 644	18 310	14 400	9 286	12 155
1999	83 930	6 498	3 266	3 232	77 432	7 244	15 150	18 340	14 834	9 581	12 283
2000	85 370	6 404	3 224	3 181	78 966	7 329	15 528	18 003	15 578	10 028	12 501
2001	86 452	6 422	3 229	3 194	80 029	7 564	15 486	17 960	16 047	10 369	12 604
2002	87 361	6 439	3 251	3 189	80 922	7 750	15 470	17 792	16 317	10 918	12 676
2003	88 249	6 390	3 378	3 012	81 860	7 856	15 569	17 620	16 555	11 442	12 818
2004	89 044	6 429	3 301	3 129	82 615	8 024	15 486	17 404	16 834	11 922	12 946
2005	90 027	6 471	3 464	3 006	83 556	8 057	15 507	17 286	17 169	12 415	13 123
2006	91 021	6 555	3 551	3 004	84 466	8 052	15 567	17 143	17 467	12 891	13 346
2007	92 073	6 653	3 567	3 086	85 420	8 113	15 762	16 927	17 686	13 341	13 591
2008	92 725	6 669	3 550	3 120	86 056	8 072	15 884	16 599	17 830	13 698	13 972
2009	93 433	6 644	3 469	3 175	86 789	8 076	16 011	16 260	17 956	14 154	14 332
2010	94 082	6 580	3 473	3 107	87 502	8 240	16 174	15 920	17 919	14 634	14 615
2011	94 801	6 610	3 496	3 114	88 191	8 485	16 332	15 540	17 602	15 018	15 213
2012	94 266	6 486	3 387	3 099	87 780	8 211	15 691	15 263	17 287	15 333	15 995

Table 1-6. Civilian Noninstitutional Population, by Age, Race, Sex, and Hispanic Origin, 1948–2012—*Continued*

(Thousands of people.)

Race, Hispanic origin, sex, and year	16 years and over	16 to 19 years			20 years and over						
		Total	16 to 17 years	18 to 19 years	Total	20 to 24 years	25 to 34 years	35 to 44 years	45 to 54 years	55 to 64 years	65 years and over
WHITE											
Women											
1954	51 242	3 725	1 884	1 841	47 517	4 720	10 870	10 227	8 397	6 652	6 651
1955	51 802	3 785	1 929	1 856	48 017	4 671	10 806	10 342	8 566	6 771	6 862
1956	52 373	3 846	1 953	1 892	48 527	4 642	10 713	10 466	8 752	6 886	7 067
1957	52 998	3 949	2 007	1 941	49 049	4 655	10 584	10 597	8 957	7 000	7 256
1958	53 645	4 096	2 131	1 966	49 549	4 715	10 407	10 716	9 159	7 107	7 442
1959	54 392	4 351	2 337	2 015	50 041	4 794	10 216	10 812	9 348	7 219	7 653
1960	55 214	4 575	2 433	2 142	50 639	4 873	10 097	10 918	9 536	7 349	7 865
1961	55 993	4 732	2 378	2 354	51 261	4 999	9 999	10 991	9 697	7 485	8 091
1962	56 660	4 823	2 392	2 432	51 837	5 178	9 894	11 054	9 681	7 533	8 496
1963	57 672	5 151	2 757	2 394	52 521	5 459	9 828	11 089	9 785	7 650	8 710
1964	58 663	5 468	3 047	2 422	53 195	5 706	9 814	11 074	9 943	7 804	8 853
1965	59 601	5 778	2 999	2 779	53 823	5 918	9 826	10 996	10 088	7 954	9 042
1966	60 503	6 042	2 970	3 072	54 461	6 120	9 904	10 869	10 230	8 107	9 230
1967	61 491	6 011	2 993	3 019	55 480	6 540	10 125	10 732	10 379	8 271	9 435
1968	62 512	6 053	3 072	2 981	56 460	6 809	10 493	10 572	10 520	8 433	9 633
1969	63 563	6 174	3 172	3 002	57 390	7 089	10 818	10 396	10 651	8 600	9 836
1970	64 656	6 342	3 262	3 080	58 315	7 370	11 105	10 251	10 761	8 769	10 060
1971	65 857	6 518	3 338	3 180	59 340	7 662	11 454	10 117	10 841	8 951	10 315
1972	67 431	6 673	3 407	3 267	60 758	7 855	12 060	10 105	10 872	9 161	10 705
1973	68 517	6 796	3 466	3 331	61 721	7 951	12 610	10 018	10 891	9 306	10 943
1974	69 623	6 933	3 510	3 424	62 690	8 026	13 112	10 064	10 896	9 356	11 236
1975	70 810	7 011	3 523	3 488	63 798	8 214	13 615	10 063	10 847	9 505	11 556
1976	71 974	7 062	3 516	3 546	64 912	8 381	14 102	10 153	10 752	9 664	11 860
1977	73 077	7 071	3 525	3 545	66 007	8 553	14 564	10 351	10 618	9 832	12 088
1978	74 213	7 038	3 513	3 524	67 174	8 704	14 926	10 696	10 476	9 974	12 399
1979	75 347	6 987	3 460	3 527	68 360	8 815	15 363	11 017	10 327	10 122	12 717
1980	76 489	6 914	3 403	3 511	69 575	8 904	15 878	11 313	10 201	10 256	13 022
1981	77 428	6 752	3 303	3 449	70 677	8 965	16 362	11 606	10 106	10 346	13 292
1982	78 230	6 519	3 134	3 385	71 711	8 959	16 603	12 154	10 015	10 402	13 579
1983	78 884	6 282	2 991	3 292	72 601	8 895	16 788	12 714	9 941	10 418	13 847
1984	79 624	6 034	2 899	3 135	73 590	8 782	17 073	13 271	9 914	10 412	14 138
1985	80 306	5 912	2 895	3 017	74 394	8 607	17 409	13 762	9 917	10 358	14 342
1986	81 042	5 902	2 953	2 949	75 140	8 351	17 728	14 223	10 009	10 277	14 551
1987	81 769	5 924	2 985	2 939	75 845	8 079	17 913	14 698	10 194	10 141	14 820
1988	82 340	5 869	2 878	2 991	76 470	7 804	18 009	15 074	10 537	9 994	15 052
1989	82 871	5 716	2 690	3 027	77 154	7 600	18 043	15 537	10 853	9 843	15 278
1990	83 256	5 717	2 654	3 063	77 539	7 774	17 895	15 969	10 937	9 524	15 440
1991	83 781	5 497	2 646	2 850	78 285	7 768	17 726	16 514	11 196	9 435	15 647
1992	84 321	5 393	2 659	2 734	78 928	7 678	17 482	16 727	11 851	9 350	15 841
1993	84 918	5 428	2 700	2 728	79 490	7 542	17 206	17 019	12 398	9 302	16 023
1994	85 496	5 516	2 772	2 744	79 980	7 351	16 950	17 335	12 890	9 306	16 148
1995	86 181	5 614	2 827	2 787	80 567	7 150	16 702	17 654	13 390	9 333	16 337
1996	86 828	5 787	2 927	2 860	81 041	6 936	16 457	17 943	13 884	9 402	16 419
1997	87 417	5 924	3 004	2 920	81 492	6 896	16 047	18 162	14 357	9 582	16 447
1998	88 126	6 053	3 031	3 023	82 073	6 969	15 642	18 300	14 732	9 944	16 486
1999	89 156	6 202	3 076	3 127	82 953	7 150	15 366	18 415	15 214	10 274	16 536
2000	90 850	6 131	3 041	3 090	84 718	7 223	15 420	18 258	15 972	10 729	17 116
2001	91 660	6 134	3 062	3 071	85 526	7 438	15 284	18 153	16 428	11 065	17 158
2002	92 422	6 157	3 096	3 061	86 266	7 611	15 207	17 958	16 695	11 622	17 173
2003	93 043	6 137	3 251	2 886	86 905	7 680	15 220	17 731	16 911	12 147	17 216
2004	93 599	6 169	3 260	2 909	87 430	7 794	15 099	17 441	17 170	12 627	17 299
2005	94 419	6 219	3 304	2 915	88 200	7 814	15 086	17 268	17 480	13 119	17 433
2006	95 242	6 301	3 429	2 871	88 942	7 796	15 094	17 074	17 760	13 596	17 623
2007	96 180	6 390	3 458	2 932	89 790	7 832	15 249	16 843	17 979	14 051	17 835
2008	96 814	6 414	3 412	3 003	90 400	7 042	15 349	16 493	18 111	14 411	18 193
2009	97 469	6 391	3 306	3 086	91 078	7 887	15 460	16 118	18 210	14 868	18 535
2010	97 993	6 311	3 327	2 984	91 683	8 040	15 640	15 727	18 146	15 349	18 781
2011	98 276	6 208	3 177	3 031	92 068	8 077	15 803	15 490	17 925	15 781	18 992
2012	98 938	6 172	3 230	2 942	92 766	8 078	15 550	15 334	17 648	16 179	19 978

Table 1-6. Civilian Noninstitutional Population, by Age, Race, Sex, and Hispanic Origin, 1948–2012—*Continued*

(Thousands of people.)

Race, Hispanic origin, sex, and year	16 years and over	16 to 19 years			20 years and over						
		Total	16 to 17 years	18 to 19 years	Total	20 to 24 years	25 to 34 years	35 to 44 years	45 to 54 years	55 to 64 years	65 years and over
BLACK											
Both Sexes											
1974	15 329	2 137	1 122	1 014	13 192	2 137	3 103	2 382	2 202	1 679	1 689
1975	15 751	2 191	1 146	1 046	13 560	2 228	3 258	2 395	2 211	1 717	1 755
1976	16 196	2 264	1 165	1 098	13 932	2 303	3 412	2 435	2 220	1 736	1 826
1977	16 605	2 273	1 175	1 097	14 332	2 400	3 566	2 493	2 225	1 765	1 883
1978	16 970	2 270	1 169	1 101	14 701	2 483	3 717	2 547	2 226	1 794	1 932
1979	17 397	2 276	1 167	1 109	15 121	2 556	3 899	2 615	2 240	1 831	1 980
1980	17 824	2 289	1 171	1 119	15 535	2 606	4 095	2 687	2 249	1 870	2 030
1981	18 219	2 288	1 161	1 127	15 931	2 642	4 290	2 758	2 260	1 913	2 069
1982	18 584	2 252	1 119	1 134	16 332	2 697	4 438	2 887	2 263	1 935	2 113
1983	18 925	2 225	1 092	1 133	16 700	2 734	4 607	2 999	2 260	1 964	2 135
1984	19 348	2 161	1 056	1 105	17 187	2 783	4 789	3 167	2 288	1 977	2 183
1985	19 664	2 160	1 083	1 077	17 504	2 649	4 873	3 290	2 372	2 060	2 259
1986	19 989	2 137	1 090	1 048	17 852	2 625	5 026	3 410	2 413	2 079	2 298
1987	20 352	2 163	1 123	1 040	18 189	2 578	5 139	3 563	2 460	2 097	2 352
1988	20 692	2 179	1 130	1 049	18 513	2 527	5 234	3 716	2 524	2 110	2 402
1989	21 021	2 176	1 116	1 060	18 846	2 479	5 308	3 900	2 587	2 118	2 454
1990	21 477	2 238	1 101	1 138	19 239	2 554	5 407	4 328	2 618	1 970	2 362
1991	21 799	2 187	1 085	1 102	19 612	2 585	5 419	4 538	2 682	1 985	2 403
1992	22 147	2 155	1 086	1 069	19 992	2 615	5 404	4 722	2 809	1 996	2 446
1993	22 521	2 181	1 113	1 069	20 339	2 600	5 409	4 886	2 941	2 016	2 487
1994	22 879	2 211	1 168	1 044	20 668	2 616	5 362	5 038	3 084	2 045	2 524
1995	23 246	2 284	1 198	1 086	20 962	2 554	5 337	5 178	3 244	2 079	2 571
1996	23 604	2 356	1 238	1 118	21 248	2 519	5 311	5 290	3 408	2 110	2 609
1997	24 003	2 412	1 255	1 158	21 591	2 515	5 279	5 410	3 571	2 164	2 653
1998	24 373	2 443	1 241	1 202	21 930	2 546	5 221	5 510	3 735	2 224	2 695
1999	24 855	2 479	1 250	1 229	22 376	2 615	5 197	5 609	3 919	2 295	2 741
2000	24 902	2 389	1 205	1 183	22 513	2 611	5 089	5 488	4 168	2 407	2 750
2001	25 138	2 388	1 212	1 176	22 750	2 686	5 003	5 467	4 343	2 478	2 775
2002	25 578	2 416	1 235	1 181	23 162	2 779	5 015	5 460	4 513	2 571	2 823
2003	25 686	2 382	1 309	1 074	23 304	2 773	4 978	5 387	4 628	2 692	2 846
2004	26 065	2 423	1 350	1 072	23 643	2 821	5 020	5 335	4 739	2 827	2 899
2005	26 517	2 481	1 341	1 140	24 036	2 835	5 075	5 311	4 869	2 980	2 967
2006	27 007	2 565	1 408	1 157	24 442	2 851	5 133	5 302	4 992	3 137	3 027
2007	27 485	2 640	1 497	1 143	24 845	2 891	5 210	5 271	5 110	3 284	3 080
2008	27 843	2 676	1 459	1 217	25 168	2 914	5 262	5 198	5 183	3 429	3 182
2009	28 241	2 684	1 462	1 221	25 557	2 973	5 349	5 109	5 290	3 596	3 239
2010	28 708	2 657	1 438	1 219	26 051	3 097	5 491	5 031	5 322	3 773	3 337
2011	29 114	2 594	1 353	1 240	26 520	3 168	5 606	4 995	5 357	3 955	3 440
2012	29 907	2 643	1 381	1 262	27 265	3 326	5 455	5 107	5 446	4 281	3 650
BLACK											
Men											
1974	6 875	1 027	554	471	5 848	956	1 381	1 055	997	753	707
1975	7 060	1 051	565	486	6 009	1 002	1 452	1 060	997	769	730
1976	7 265	1 099	579	518	6 167	1 036	1 521	1 077	999	774	756
1977	7 431	1 102	586	516	6 329	1 080	1 589	1 102	998	786	774
1978	7 577	1 093	579	514	6 484	1 120	1 657	1 128	995	794	789
1979	7 761	1 100	581	519	6 661	1 151	1 738	1 159	998	809	804
1980	7 944	1 110	583	526	6 834	1 171	1 828	1 191	999	825	822
1981	8 117	1 110	577	534	7 007	1 189	1 914	1 224	1 003	844	835
1982	8 283	1 097	556	542	7 186	1 225	1 983	1 282	1 003	848	846
1983	8 447	1 087	542	545	7 360	1 254	2 068	1 333	1 000	857	847
1984	8 654	1 055	524	531	7 599	1 292	2 164	1 411	1 012	858	861
1985	8 790	1 059	543	517	7 731	1 202	2 180	1 462	1 060	924	902
1986	8 956	1 049	548	503	7 907	1 195	2 264	1 517	1 072	934	924
1987	9 128	1 065	566	499	8 063	1 173	2 320	1 587	1 092	944	947
1988	9 289	1 074	569	505	8 215	1 151	2 367	1 656	1 121	951	970
1989	9 439	1 075	575	501	8 364	1 128	2 403	1 741	1 145	956	989
1990	9 573	1 094	555	540	8 479	1 144	2 412	1 968	1 183	855	917
1991	9 725	1 072	546	526	8 652	1 168	2 417	2 060	1 211	864	933
1992	9 896	1 056	544	512	8 840	1 194	2 409	2 150	1 268	868	951
1993	10 083	1 075	559	516	9 008	1 181	2 425	2 228	1 330	874	969
1994	10 258	1 087	586	501	9 171	1 207	2 399	2 300	1 392	889	985
1995	10 411	1 131	601	530	9 280	1 161	2 388	2 362	1 462	901	1 006
1996	10 575	1 161	623	538	9 414	1 154	2 373	2 413	1 534	914	1 025
1997	10 763	1 188	634	553	9 575	1 153	2 363	2 471	1 607	936	1 045
1998	10 927	1 201	623	578	9 727	1 166	2 335	2 520	1 682	956	1 068
1999	11 143	1 218	628	589	9 926	1 197	2 321	2 566	1 765	986	1 091
2000	11 129	1 178	605	572	9 952	1 195	2 277	2 471	1 889	1 067	1 053
2001	11 172	1 179	606	573	9 993	1 224	2 212	2 440	1 960	1 096	1 060
2002	11 391	1 195	615	580	10 196	1 281	2 223	2 437	2 042	1 137	1 075
2003	11 454	1 176	661	515	10 278	1 291	2 210	2 401	2 094	1 189	1 093
2004	11 656	1 195	680	516	10 461	1 326	2 242	2 382	2 150	1 250	1 111
2005	11 882	1 223	682	541	10 659	1 341	2 277	2 372	2 202	1 319	1 148
2006	12 130	1 266	713	552	10 864	1 355	2 318	2 369	2 261	1 390	1 170
2007	12 361	1 305	742	563	11 057	1 380	2 366	2 352	2 318	1 454	1 186
2008	12 516	1 322	718	604	11 194	1 384	2 398	2 313	2 335	1 519	1 245
2009	12 705	1 326	736	590	11 379	1 410	2 454	2 271	2 392	1 592	1 260
2010	12 939	1 313	715	598	11 626	1 474	2 540	2 234	2 406	1 673	1 299
2011	13 164	1 282	642	640	11 882	1 510	2 612	2 222	2 435	1 759	1 344
2012	13 508	1 319	707	612	12 189	1 586	2 461	2 286	2 484	1 923	1 449

Table 1-6. Civilian Noninstitutional Population, by Age, Race, Sex, and Hispanic Origin, 1948–2012—*Continued*

(Thousands of people.)

Race, Hispanic origin, sex, and year	16 years and over	16 to 19 years			20 years and over						
		Total	16 to 17 years	18 to 19 years	Total	20 to 24 years	25 to 34 years	35 to 44 years	45 to 54 years	55 to 64 years	65 years and over
BLACK											
Women											
1974	8 454	1 110	567	542	7 344	1 181	1 723	1 327	1 206	926	981
1975	8 691	1 141	581	560	7 550	1 226	1 806	1 334	1 213	948	1 025
1976	8 931	1 165	585	580	7 765	1 266	1 890	1 357	1 220	962	1 070
1977	9 174	1 171	590	581	8 003	1 320	1 978	1 390	1 228	979	1 108
1978	9 394	1 177	589	588	8 217	1 363	2 061	1 419	1 231	999	1 143
1979	9 636	1 176	586	589	8 460	1 405	2 160	1 455	1 242	1 022	1 176
1980	9 880	1 180	587	593	8 700	1 435	2 267	1 496	1 250	1 045	1 208
1981	10 102	1 178	584	593	8 924	1 453	2 376	1 534	1 257	1 069	1 234
1982	10 300	1 155	563	592	9 146	1 472	2 455	1 605	1 260	1 087	1 267
1983	10 477	1 138	550	588	9 340	1 480	2 539	1 666	1 260	1 107	1 288
1984	10 694	1 106	532	574	9 588	1 491	2 625	1 756	1 276	1 119	1 322
1985	10 873	1 101	540	560	9 773	1 447	2 693	1 828	1 312	1 136	1 357
1986	11 033	1 088	542	545	9 945	1 430	2 762	1 893	1 341	1 145	1 374
1987	11 224	1 098	557	541	10 126	1 405	2 819	1 976	1 368	1 153	1 405
1988	11 402	1 105	561	544	10 298	1 376	2 867	2 060	1 403	1 159	1 432
1989	11 582	1 100	541	559	10 482	1 351	2 905	2 159	1 441	1 162	1 464
1990	11 904	1 144	546	598	10 760	1 410	2 995	2 360	1 435	1 114	1 446
1991	12 074	1 115	539	576	10 959	1 417	3 003	2 478	1 471	1 121	1 470
1992	12 251	1 099	542	557	11 152	1 421	2 995	2 573	1 542	1 127	1 495
1993	12 438	1 106	554	552	11 332	1 419	2 983	2 659	1 611	1 142	1 518
1994	12 621	1 125	582	543	11 496	1 410	2 963	2 738	1 692	1 156	1 538
1995	12 835	1 153	597	556	11 682	1 392	2 948	2 816	1 782	1 178	1 565
1996	13 029	1 195	615	580	11 833	1 364	2 938	2 877	1 874	1 196	1 584
1997	13 241	1 225	620	604	12 016	1 362	2 916	2 939	1 964	1 228	1 608
1998	13 446	1 243	618	624	12 203	1 380	2 886	2 991	2 053	1 268	1 626
1999	13 711	1 261	621	640	12 451	1 418	2 876	3 043	2 153	1 310	1 650
2000	13 772	1 211	600	611	12 561	1 416	2 812	3 017	2 279	1 340	1 697
2001	13 966	1 209	606	603	12 758	1 462	2 790	3 026	2 383	1 382	1 714
2002	14 187	1 221	620	601	12 966	1 498	2 792	3 023	2 471	1 434	1 747
2003	14 232	1 206	648	558	13 026	1 482	2 768	2 986	2 534	1 504	1 753
2004	14 409	1 227	670	557	13 182	1 495	2 778	2 954	2 590	1 577	1 789
2005	14 635	1 258	659	598	13 377	1 494	2 797	2 939	2 666	1 661	1 819
2006	14 877	1 299	694	605	13 578	1 495	2 815	2 933	2 731	1 747	1 857
2007	15 124	1 336	755	581	13 788	1 511	2 844	2 918	2 792	1 830	1 893
2008	15 328	1 354	741	613	13 974	1 530	2 864	2 885	2 848	1 910	1 937
2009	15 536	1 357	726	631	14 178	1 563	2 895	2 839	2 898	2 004	1 979
2010	15 769	1 344	723	621	14 425	1 623	2 951	2 796	2 916	2 101	2 038
2011	15 950	1 312	712	600	14 638	1 657	2 994	2 773	2 922	2 196	2 096
2012	16 400	1 324	674	650	15 076	1 740	2 994	2 821	2 963	2 358	2 201
HISPANIC											
Both Sexes											
1975	6 862	962	. . .	. . .	5 900	. . .	. . .	. . .	. . .	. . .	. . .
1976	6 910	953	494	480	6 075	1 053	1 775	1 261	936	570	479
1977	7 362	1 024	513	508	6 376	1 163	1 869	1 283	989	587	485
1978	7 912	1 076	561	515	6 836	1 265	2 004	1 378	1 033	627	529
1979	8 207	1 095	544	551	7 113	1 296	2 117	1 458	1 015	659	566
1980	9 598	1 281	638	643	8 317	1 564	2 508	1 575	1 190	782	698
1981	10 120	1 301	641	660	8 819	1 650	2 698	1 680	1 231	832	728
1982	10 580	1 307	639	668	9 273	1 724	2 871	1 779	1 264	880	755
1983	11 029	1 304	635	670	9 725	1 790	3 045	1 883	1 298	928	781
1984	11 478	1 300	633	667	10 178	1 839	3 224	1 996	1 336	973	810
1985	11 915	1 298	638	661	10 617	1 864	3 401	2 117	1 377	1 015	843
1986	12 344	1 302	658	644	11 042	1 899	3 510	2 239	1 496	1 023	875
1987	12 867	1 332	651	681	11 536	1 910	3 714	2 464	1 492	1 061	895
1988	13 325	1 354	662	692	11 970	1 940	3 807	2 565	1 571	1 159	920
1989	13 791	1 399	672	727	12 392	1 950	3 953	2 658	1 649	1 182	1 001
1990	15 904	1 737	821	915	14 167	2 428	4 589	3 001	1 817	1 247	1 084
1991	16 425	1 732	819	913	14 693	2 481	4 674	3 243	1 879	1 283	1 134
1992	16 961	1 737	836	901	15 224	2 444	4 806	3 458	1 980	1 321	1 216
1993	17 532	1 756	855	901	15 776	2 487	4 887	3 632	2 094	1 324	1 353
1994	18 117	1 818	902	916	16 300	2 518	5 000	3 756	2 223	1 401	1 401
1995	18 629	1 872	903	969	16 757	2 528	5 050	3 965	2 294	1 483	1 437
1996	19 213	1 948	962	986	17 265	2 524	5 181	4 227	2 275	1 546	1 512
1997	20 321	2 121	1 088	1 033	18 200	2 623	5 405	4 453	2 581	1 580	1 558
1998	21 070	2 204	1 070	1 135	18 865	2 731	5 447	4 636	2 775	1 615	1 662
1999	21 650	2 307	1 113	1 194	19 344	2 700	5 512	4 833	2 868	1 713	1 718
2000	23 938	2 523	1 214	1 309	21 415	3 255	6 466	5 189	3 061	1 736	1 708
2001	24 942	2 508	1 173	1 334	22 435	3 417	6 726	5 346	3 339	1 816	1 792
2002	25 963	2 507	1 216	1 291	23 456	3 508	7 010	5 606	3 494	1 953	1 885
2003	27 551	2 543	1 346	1 197	25 008	3 533	7 506	6 003	3 845	2 093	2 027
2004	28 109	2 608	1 337	1 270	25 502	3 666	7 470	6 055	3 987	2 208	2 115
2005	29 133	2 689	1 415	1 274	26 444	3 647	7 684	6 293	4 217	2 361	2 242
2006	30 103	2 796	1 518	1 277	27 307	3 603	7 856	6 519	4 466	2 516	2 347
2007	31 383	2 944	1 559	1 385	28 440	3 648	8 129	6 785	4 720	2 685	2 473
2008	32 141	3 042	1 620	1 422	29 098	3 620	8 147	6 946	4 937	2 840	2 609
2009	32 891	3 123	1 602	1 522	29 768	3 623	8 099	7 078	5 192	3 017	2 759
2010	33 713	3 243	1 673	1 570	30 469	3 880	8 084	7 123	5 351	3 167	2 864
2011	34 438	3 407	1 808	1 598	31 031	4 193	8 107	7 103	5 414	3 311	2 903
2012	36 759	3 656	1 906	1 750	33 103	4 502	8 512	7 551	5 831	3 613	3 094

. . . = Not available.

Table 1-6. Civilian Noninstitutional Population, by Age, Race, Sex, and Hispanic Origin, 1948–2012—*Continued*

(Thousands of people.)

Race, Hispanic origin, sex, and year	16 years and over	16 to 19 years			20 years and over						
		Total	16 to 17 years	18 to 19 years	Total	20 to 24 years	25 to 34 years	35 to 44 years	45 to 54 years	55 to 64 years	65 years and over
HISPANIC											
Men											
1975	3 219	...	...	...	2 741	...	...	...	...	...	...
1976	3 241	...	...	...	2 764	...	...	...	...	...	...
1977	3 483	...	...	...	2 982	...	...	...	...	...	...
1978	3 750	...	...	...	3 228	...	...	...	...	...	...
1979	3 917	...	...	...	3 362	...	...	...	...	...	...
1980	4 689	...	...	...	4 036	...	...	...	...	...	...
1981	4 968	...	...	...	4 306	...	...	...	...	...	...
1982	5 203	...	...	...	4 539	...	...	...	...	...	...
1983	5 432	...	...	...	4 771	...	...	...	...	...	...
1984	5 661	...	...	...	5 005	...	...	...	...	...	...
1985	5 885	...	...	...	5 232	...	...	...	...	...	...
1986	6 106	...	...	...	5 451	...	...	...	...	...	...
1987	6 371	...	...	...	5 700	...	...	...	...	...	...
1988	6 604	...	...	...	5 921	...	...	...	...	...	...
1989	6 825	...	...	...	6 114	...	...	...	...	...	...
1990	8 041	...	...	...	7 126	...	...	...	...	...	...
1991	8 296	...	...	...	7 392	...	...	...	...	...	...
1992	8 553	...	...	...	7 655	...	...	...	...	...	...
1993	8 824	...	...	...	7 930	...	...	...	...	...	...
1994	9 104	926	472	454	8 178	1 346	2 627	1 871	1 076	644	614
1995	9 329	954	481	473	8 375	1 337	2 657	1 966	1 127	668	619
1996	9 604	992	485	507	8 611	1 321	2 692	2 144	1 111	712	630
1997	10 368	1 119	585	534	9 250	1 439	2 872	2 275	1 266	747	651
1998	10 734	1 161	586	575	9 573	1 462	2 907	2 377	1 342	771	714
1999	10 713	1 190	571	619	9 523	1 398	2 805	2 407	1 397	767	749
2000	12 174	1 333	640	693	10 841	1 784	3 380	2 626	1 527	799	725
2001	12 695	1 310	619	690	11 386	1 846	3 529	2 765	1 650	848	749
2002	13 221	1 293	615	678	11 928	1 890	3 727	2 875	1 716	902	817
2003	14 098	1 301	674	627	12 797	1 905	4 033	3 098	1 910	989	862
2004	14 417	1 336	664	672	13 082	1 981	4 024	3 147	1 990	1 046	894
2005	14 962	1 376	730	646	13 586	1 956	4 155	3 284	2 114	1 123	953
2006	15 473	1 428	763	664	14 046	1 916	4 266	3 414	2 251	1 204	996
2007	16 154	1 505	790	714	14 649	1 928	4 430	3 563	2 384	1 287	1 058
2008	16 524	1 553	838	716	14 971	1 890	4 438	3 655	2 502	1 365	1 121
2009	16 897	1 593	818	774	15 305	1 875	4 405	3 735	2 647	1 459	1 184
2010	17 359	1 666	847	819	15 693	2 016	4 381	3 783	2 741	1 538	1 234
2011	17 753	1 812	951	861	15 941	2 278	4 379	3 702	2 717	1 604	1 260
2012	18 434	1 879	970	909	16 555	2 341	4 424	3 822	2 911	1 729	1 329
HISPANIC											
Women											
1975	3 644	...	...	...	3 161	...	...	...	...	...	...
1976	3 669	...	...	...	3 263	...	...	...	...	...	...
1977	3 879	...	...	...	3 377	...	...	...	...	...	...
1978	4 159	...	...	...	3 608	...	...	...	...	...	...
1979	4 291	...	...	...	3 751	...	...	...	...	...	...
1980	4 909	...	...	...	4 281	...	...	...	...	...	...
1981	5 151	...	...	...	4 513	...	...	...	...	...	...
1982	5 377	...	...	...	4 734	...	...	...	...	...	...
1983	5 597	...	...	...	4 954	...	...	...	...	...	...
1984	5 816	...	...	...	5 173	...	...	...	...	...	...
1985	6 029	...	...	...	5 385	...	...	...	...	...	...
1986	6 238	...	...	...	5 591	...	...	...	...	...	...
1987	6 496	...	...	...	5 835	...	...	...	...	...	...
1988	6 721	...	...	...	6 050	...	...	...	...	...	...
1989	6 965	...	...	...	6 278	...	...	...	...	...	...
1990	7 863	...	...	...	7 041	...	...	...	...	...	...
1991	8 130	...	...	...	7 301	...	...	...	...	...	...
1992	8 408	...	...	...	7 569	...	...	...	...	...	...
1993	8 708	...	...	...	7 846	...	...	...	...	...	...
1994	9 014	892	430	462	8 122	1 173	2 373	1 885	1 147	757	787
1995	9 300	918	422	496	8 382	1 191	2 393	1 999	1 167	815	818
1996	9 610	956	477	479	8 654	1 203	2 489	2 082	1 164	834	882
1997	9 953	1 003	503	500	8 950	1 184	2 533	2 178	1 315	833	907
1998	10 335	1 044	483	560	9 292	1 269	2 539	2 259	1 433	844	948
1999	10 937	1 116	542	575	9 821	1 302	2 707	2 425	1 470	947	969
2000	11 764	1 190	574	616	10 574	1 471	3 086	2 564	1 534	937	982
2001	12 247	1 198	554	644	11 049	1 571	3 198	2 581	1 689	968	1 043
2002	12 742	1 214	601	613	11 528	1 617	3 283	2 732	1 777	1 051	1 068
2003	13 452	1 242	672	570	12 211	1 628	3 473	2 905	1 935	1 105	1 166
2004	13 692	1 272	674	598	12 420	1 685	3 447	2 908	1 997	1 162	1 221
2005	14 172	1 313	685	628	12 858	1 692	3 529	3 009	2 103	1 237	1 289
2006	14 630	1 368	755	613	13 262	1 688	3 590	3 105	2 215	1 313	1 351
2007	15 229	1 439	769	670	13 791	1 720	3 698	3 222	2 336	1 398	1 416
2008	15 616	1 489	782	706	14 127	1 730	3 710	3 291	2 435	1 475	1 488
2009	15 993	1 531	783	748	14 463	1 748	3 694	3 343	2 545	1 558	1 576
2010	16 354	1 578	826	752	14 776	1 864	3 703	3 340	2 610	1 628	1 630
2011	16 685	1 595	857	738	15 090	1 915	3 727	3 401	2 696	1 707	1 643
2012	18 324	1 776	936	841	16 548	2 161	4 088	3 729	2 920	1 884	1 765

. . . = Not available.

Table 1-7. Civilian Labor Force, by Age, Sex, Race, and Hispanic Origin, 1948–2012

(Thousands of people.)

Race, Hispanic origin, sex, and year	16 years and over	16 to 19 years			20 years and over						
		Total	16 to 17 years	18 to 19 years	Total	20 to 24 years	25 to 34 years	35 to 44 years	45 to 54 years	55 to 64 years	65 years and over
ALL RACES											
Both Sexes											
1948	60 621	4 435	1 780	2 654	56 187	7 392	14 258	13 397	10 914	7 329	2 897
1949	61 286	4 288	1 704	2 583	57 000	7 340	14 415	13 711	11 107	7 426	3 010
1950	62 208	4 216	1 659	2 557	57 994	7 307	14 619	13 954	11 444	7 633	3 036
1951	62 017	4 103	1 743	2 360	57 914	6 594	14 668	14 100	11 739	7 796	3 020
1952	62 138	4 064	1 806	2 257	58 075	5 840	14 904	14 383	11 961	7 980	3 005
1953	63 015	4 027	1 727	2 299	58 989	5 481	14 898	15 099	12 249	8 024	3 236
1954	63 643	3 976	1 643	2 300	59 666	5 475	14 983	15 221	12 524	8 269	3 192
1955	65 023	4 092	1 711	2 382	60 931	5 666	15 058	15 400	12 992	8 513	3 305
1956	66 552	4 296	1 878	2 418	62 257	5 940	14 961	15 694	13 407	8 830	3 423
1957	66 929	4 275	1 843	2 433	62 653	6 071	14 826	15 847	13 768	8 853	3 290
1958	67 639	4 260	1 818	2 442	63 377	6 272	14 668	16 028	14 179	9 031	3 199
1959	68 369	4 492	1 971	2 522	63 876	6 413	14 435	16 127	14 518	9 227	3 158
1960	69 628	4 841	2 095	2 747	64 788	6 702	14 382	16 269	14 852	9 385	3 195
1961	70 459	4 936	1 984	2 951	65 524	6 950	14 319	16 402	15 071	9 636	3 146
1962	70 614	4 916	1 919	2 997	65 699	7 082	14 023	16 589	15 096	9 757	3 154
1963	71 833	5 139	2 171	2 966	66 695	7 473	14 050	16 788	15 338	10 006	3 041
1964	73 091	5 388	2 449	2 940	67 702	7 963	14 056	16 771	15 637	10 182	3 090
1965	74 455	5 910	2 486	3 425	68 543	8 259	14 233	16 840	15 756	10 350	3 108
1966	75 770	6 558	2 664	3 893	69 219	8 410	14 458	16 738	15 984	10 575	3 053
1967	77 347	6 521	2 734	3 786	70 825	9 010	15 055	16 703	16 172	10 792	3 097
1968	78 737	6 619	2 817	3 803	72 118	9 305	15 708	16 591	16 397	10 964	3 153
1969	80 734	6 970	3 009	3 959	73 763	9 879	16 336	16 458	16 730	11 135	3 227
1970	82 771	7 249	3 135	4 115	75 521	10 597	17 036	16 437	16 949	11 283	3 222
1971	84 382	7 470	3 192	4 278	76 913	11 331	17 714	16 305	17 024	11 390	3 149
1972	87 034	8 054	3 420	4 636	78 980	12 130	18 960	16 398	16 967	11 412	3 114
1973	89 429	8 507	3 665	4 839	80 924	12 846	20 376	16 492	16 983	11 256	2 974
1974	91 949	8 871	3 810	5 059	83 080	13 314	21 654	16 763	17 131	11 284	2 934
1975	93 775	8 870	3 740	5 131	84 904	13 750	22 864	16 903	17 084	11 346	2 956
1976	96 158	9 056	3 767	5 288	87 103	14 284	24 203	17 317	16 982	11 422	2 895
1977	99 009	9 351	3 919	5 431	89 658	14 825	25 500	17 943	16 878	11 577	2 934
1978	102 251	9 652	4 127	5 526	92 598	15 370	26 703	18 821	16 891	11 744	3 070
1979	104 962	9 638	4 079	5 559	95 325	15 769	27 938	19 685	16 897	11 931	3 104
1980	106 940	9 378	3 883	5 496	97 561	15 922	29 227	20 463	16 910	11 985	3 054
1981	108 670	8 988	3 647	5 340	99 682	16 099	30 392	21 211	16 970	11 969	3 042
1982	110 204	8 526	3 336	5 189	101 679	16 082	31 186	22 431	16 889	12 062	3 030
1983	111 550	8 171	3 073	5 098	103 379	16 052	31 834	23 611	16 851	11 992	3 040
1984	113 544	7 943	3 050	4 894	105 601	16 046	32 723	24 933	17 006	11 961	2 933
1985	115 461	7 901	3 154	4 747	107 560	15 718	33 550	26 073	17 322	11 991	2 907
1986	117 834	7 926	3 287	4 639	109 908	15 441	34 591	27 232	17 739	11 894	3 010
1987	119 865	7 988	3 384	4 604	111 878	14 977	35 233	28 460	18 210	11 877	3 119
1988	121 669	8 031	3 286	4 745	113 638	14 505	35 503	29 435	19 104	11 808	3 284
1989	123 869	7 954	3 125	4 828	115 916	14 180	35 896	30 601	19 916	11 877	3 446
1990	125 840	7 792	2 937	4 856	118 047	14 700	35 929	32 145	20 248	11 575	3 451
1991	126 346	7 265	2 789	4 476	119 082	14 548	35 507	33 312	20 828	11 473	3 413
1992	128 105	7 096	2 769	4 327	121 009	14 521	35 369	33 899	22 160	11 587	3 473
1993	129 200	7 170	2 831	4 338	122 030	14 354	34 780	34 562	23 296	11 599	3 439
1994	131 056	7 481	3 134	4 347	123 576	14 131	34 353	35 226	24 318	11 713	3 834
1995	132 304	7 765	3 225	4 540	124 539	13 688	34 198	35 751	25 223	11 860	3 819
1996	133 943	7 806	3 263	4 543	126 137	13 377	33 833	36 556	26 397	12 146	3 828
1997	136 297	7 932	3 237	4 695	128 365	13 532	33 380	37 326	27 574	12 665	3 887
1998	137 673	8 256	3 335	4 921	129 417	13 638	32 813	37 536	28 368	13 215	3 847
1999	139 368	8 333	3 337	4 996	131 034	13 933	32 143	37 882	29 388	13 682	4 005
2000	142 583	8 271	3 261	5 010	134 312	14 250	32 755	37 567	31 071	14 356	4 312
2001	143 734	7 902	3 088	4 814	135 832	14 557	32 361	37 404	32 025	15 104	4 382
2002	144 863	7 585	2 870	4 715	137 278	14 781	32 196	36 926	32 597	16 309	4 469
2003	146 510	7 170	2 857	4 313	139 340	14 928	32 343	36 695	33 270	17 312	4 792
2004	147 401	7 114	2 747	4 367	140 287	15 154	32 207	36 158	33 758	18 013	4 998
2005	149 320	7 164	2 825	4 339	142 157	15 127	32 341	36 030	34 402	18 979	5 278
2006	151 428	7 281	2 952	4 329	144 147	15 113	32 573	35 848	35 146	19 984	5 484
2007	153 124	7 012	2 771	4 242	146 112	15 205	33 130	35 527	35 697	20 750	5 804
2008	154 287	6 858	2 552	4 306	147 429	15 174	33 332	35 061	36 003	21 615	6 243
2009	154 142	6 390	2 227	4 163	147 752	14 971	33 298	34 239	36 205	22 505	6 534
2010	153 889	5 906	2 000	3 905	147 983	15 028	33 614	33 366	35 960	23 297	6 718
2011	153 617	5 727	1 873	3 853	147 890	15 270	33 724	32 660	35 360	23 765	7 112
2012	154 975	5 823	1 952	3 870	149 152	15 462	33 465	32 734	35 054	24 710	7 727

Table 1-7. Civilian Labor Force, by Age, Sex, Race, and Hispanic Origin, 1948–2012—*Continued*

(Thousands of people.)

Race, Hispanic origin, sex, and year	16 years and over	16 to 19 years			20 years and over						
		Total	16 to 17 years	18 to 19 years	Total	20 to 24 years	25 to 34 years	35 to 44 years	45 to 54 years	55 to 64 years	65 years and over
ALL RACES											
Men											
1948	43 286	2 600	1 109	1 490	40 687	4 673	10 327	9 596	7 943	5 764	2 384
1949	43 498	2 477	1 056	1 420	41 022	4 682	10 418	9 722	8 008	5 748	2 454
1950	43 819	2 504	1 048	1 456	41 316	4 632	10 527	9 793	8 117	5 794	2 453
1951	43 001	2 347	1 081	1 266	40 655	3 935	10 375	9 799	8 205	5 873	2 469
1952	42 869	2 312	1 101	1 210	40 558	3 338	10 585	9 945	8 326	5 949	2 416
1953	43 633	2 320	1 070	1 249	41 315	3 053	10 736	10 437	8 570	5 975	2 543
1954	43 965	2 295	1 023	1 272	41 669	3 051	10 771	10 513	8 702	6 105	2 526
1955	44 475	2 369	1 070	1 299	42 106	3 221	10 806	10 595	8 838	6 122	2 526
1956	45 091	2 433	1 142	1 291	42 658	3 485	10 685	10 663	9 002	6 220	2 602
1957	45 197	2 415	1 127	1 289	42 780	3 629	10 571	10 731	9 153	6 222	2 477
1958	45 521	2 428	1 133	1 295	43 092	3 771	10 475	10 843	9 320	6 304	2 378
1959	45 886	2 596	1 206	1 390	43 289	3 940	10 346	10 899	9 438	6 345	2 322
1960	46 388	2 787	1 290	1 496	43 603	4 123	10 251	10 967	9 574	6 399	2 287
1961	46 653	2 794	1 210	1 583	43 860	4 253	10 176	11 012	9 668	6 530	2 220
1962	46 600	2 770	1 178	1 592	43 831	4 279	9 920	11 115	9 715	6 560	2 241
1963	47 129	2 907	1 321	1 586	44 222	4 514	9 876	11 187	9 836	6 675	2 135
1964	47 679	3 074	1 499	1 575	44 604	4 754	9 876	11 156	9 956	6 741	2 124
1965	48 255	3 397	1 532	1 866	44 857	4 894	9 903	11 120	10 045	6 763	2 132
1966	48 471	3 685	1 609	2 075	44 788	4 820	9 948	10 983	10 100	6 847	2 089
1967	48 987	3 634	1 658	1 976	45 354	5 043	10 207	10 859	10 189	6 937	2 118
1968	49 533	3 681	1 687	1 995	45 852	5 070	10 610	10 725	10 267	7 025	2 154
1969	50 221	3 870	1 770	2 100	46 351	5 282	10 941	10 556	10 344	7 058	2 170
1970	51 228	4 008	1 810	2 199	47 220	5 717	11 327	10 469	10 417	7 126	2 165
1971	52 180	4 172	1 856	2 315	48 009	6 233	11 731	10 347	10 451	7 155	2 090
1972	53 555	4 476	1 955	2 522	49 079	6 766	12 350	10 372	10 412	7 155	2 026
1973	54 624	4 693	2 073	2 618	49 932	7 183	13 056	10 338	10 416	7 028	1 913
1974	55 739	4 861	2 138	2 721	50 879	7 387	13 665	10 401	10 431	7 063	1 932
1975	56 299	4 805	2 065	2 740	51 494	7 565	14 192	10 398	10 401	7 023	1 914
1976	57 174	4 886	2 069	2 817	52 288	7 866	14 784	10 500	10 293	7 020	1 826
1977	58 396	5 048	2 155	2 893	53 348	8 109	15 353	10 771	10 158	7 100	1 857
1978	59 620	5 149	2 227	2 923	54 471	8 327	15 814	11 159	10 083	7 151	1 936
1979	60 726	5 111	2 192	2 919	55 615	8 535	16 387	11 531	10 008	7 212	1 943
1980	61 453	4 999	2 102	2 897	56 455	8 607	16 971	11 836	9 905	7 242	1 893
1981	61 974	4 777	1 957	2 820	57 197	8 648	17 479	12 166	9 868	7 170	1 866
1982	62 450	4 470	1 776	2 694	57 980	8 604	17 793	12 781	9 784	7 174	1 845
1983	63 047	4 303	1 621	2 682	58 744	8 601	18 038	13 398	9 746	7 119	1 842
1984	63 835	4 134	1 591	2 542	59 701	8 594	18 488	14 037	9 776	7 050	1 755
1985	64 411	4 134	1 663	2 471	60 277	8 283	18 808	14 506	9 870	7 060	1 750
1986	65 422	4 102	1 707	2 395	61 320	8 148	19 383	15 029	9 994	6 954	1 811
1987	66 207	4 112	1 745	2 367	62 095	7 837	19 656	15 587	10 176	6 940	1 899
1988	66 927	4 159	1 714	2 445	62 768	7 594	19 742	16 074	10 566	6 831	1 960
1989	67 840	4 136	1 630	2 505	63 704	7 458	19 905	16 622	10 919	6 783	2 017
1990	69 011	4 094	1 537	2 557	64 916	7 866	19 872	17 481	11 103	6 627	1 967
1991	69 168	3 795	1 452	2 343	65 374	7 820	19 641	18 077	11 362	6 550	1 924
1992	69 964	3 751	1 453	2 297	66 213	7 770	19 495	18 347	12 040	6 551	2 010
1993	70 404	3 762	1 497	2 265	66 642	7 671	19 214	18 713	12 562	6 502	1 980
1994	70 817	3 896	1 630	2 266	66 921	7 540	18 854	18 966	12 962	6 423	2 176
1995	71 360	4 036	1 668	2 368	67 324	7 338	18 670	19 189	13 421	6 504	2 201
1996	72 087	4 043	1 665	2 378	68 044	7 104	18 430	19 602	13 967	6 693	2 247
1997	73 261	4 095	1 676	2 419	69 166	7 184	18 110	20 058	14 564	6 952	2 298
1998	73 959	4 244	1 728	2 516	69 715	7 221	17 796	20 242	14 963	7 253	2 240
1999	74 512	4 318	1 732	2 587	70 194	7 291	17 318	20 382	15 394	7 477	2 333
2000	76 280	4 269	1 676	2 594	72 010	7 521	17 844	20 093	16 269	7 795	2 488
2001	76 886	4 070	1 568	2 501	72 816	7 640	17 671	20 018	16 804	8 171	2 511
2002	77 500	3 870	1 431	2 439	73 630	7 769	17 596	19 828	17 143	8 751	2 542
2003	78 238	3 614	1 405	2 209	74 623	7 906	17 767	19 762	17 352	9 144	2 692
2004	78 980	3 616	1 329	2 288	75 364	8 057	17 798	19 539	17 635	9 547	2 787
2005	80 033	3 590	1 368	2 222	76 443	8 054	17 837	19 495	18 053	10 045	2 959
2006	81 255	3 693	1 453	2 240	77 562	8 116	17 944	19 407	18 489	10 509	3 096
2007	82 136	3 541	1 354	2 187	78 596	8 095	18 308	19 299	18 801	10 904	3 188
2008	82 520	3 472	1 238	2 235	79 047	8 065	18 302	18 972	18 928	11 345	3 436
2009	82 123	3 226	1 103	2 123	78 897	7 839	18 211	18 518	19 001	11 730	3 598
2010	81 985	2 991	990	2 002	78 994	7 864	18 352	18 119	18 856	12 103	3 701
2011	81 975	2 895	917	1 978	79 080	8 101	18 469	17 686	18 483	12 350	3 990
2012	82 327	2 940	950	1 990	79 387	8 110	18 083	17 607	18 363	12 879	4 345

Table 1-7. Civilian Labor Force, by Age, Sex, Race, and Hispanic Origin, 1948–2012—*Continued*

(Thousands of people.)

Race, Hispanic origin, sex, and year	16 years and over	16 to 19 years			20 years and over						
		Total	16 to 17 years	18 to 19 years	Total	20 to 24 years	25 to 34 years	35 to 44 years	45 to 54 years	55 to 64 years	65 years and over
ALL RACES											
Women											
1948	17 335	1 835	671	1 164	15 500	2 719	3 931	3 801	2 971	1 565	513
1949	17 788	1 811	648	1 163	15 978	2 658	3 997	3 989	3 099	1 678	556
1950	18 389	1 712	611	1 101	16 678	2 675	4 092	4 161	3 327	1 839	583
1951	19 016	1 756	662	1 094	17 259	2 659	4 293	4 301	3 534	1 923	551
1952	19 269	1 752	705	1 047	17 517	2 502	4 319	4 438	3 635	2 031	589
1953	19 382	1 707	657	1 050	17 674	2 428	4 162	4 662	3 679	2 049	693
1954	19 678	1 681	620	1 028	17 997	2 424	4 212	4 708	3 822	2 164	666
1955	20 548	1 723	641	1 083	18 825	2 445	4 252	4 805	4 154	2 391	779
1956	21 461	1 863	736	1 127	19 599	2 455	4 276	5 031	4 405	2 610	821
1957	21 732	1 860	716	1 144	19 873	2 442	4 255	5 116	4 615	2 631	813
1958	22 118	1 832	685	1 147	20 285	2 501	4 193	5 185	4 859	2 727	821
1959	22 483	1 896	765	1 132	20 587	2 473	4 089	5 228	5 080	2 882	836
1960	23 240	2 054	805	1 251	21 185	2 579	4 131	5 302	5 278	2 986	908
1961	23 806	2 142	774	1 368	21 664	2 697	4 143	5 390	5 403	3 106	926
1962	24 014	2 146	741	1 405	21 868	2 803	4 103	5 474	5 381	3 197	913
1963	24 704	2 232	850	1 380	22 473	2 959	4 174	5 601	5 502	3 331	906
1964	25 412	2 314	950	1 365	23 098	3 209	4 180	5 615	5 681	3 441	966
1965	26 200	2 513	954	1 559	23 686	3 365	4 330	5 720	5 711	3 587	976
1966	27 299	2 873	1 055	1 818	24 431	3 590	4 510	5 755	5 884	3 728	964
1967	28 360	2 887	1 076	1 810	25 475	3 966	4 848	5 844	5 983	3 855	979
1968	29 204	2 938	1 130	1 808	26 266	4 235	5 098	5 866	6 130	3 939	999
1969	30 513	3 100	1 239	1 859	27 413	4 597	5 395	5 902	6 386	4 077	1 057
1970	31 543	3 241	1 325	1 916	28 301	4 880	5 708	5 968	6 532	4 157	1 056
1971	32 202	3 298	1 336	1 963	28 904	5 098	5 983	5 957	6 573	4 234	1 059
1972	33 479	3 578	1 464	2 114	29 901	5 364	6 610	6 027	6 555	4 257	1 089
1973	34 804	3 814	1 592	2 221	30 991	5 663	7 320	6 154	6 567	4 228	1 061
1974	36 211	4 010	1 672	2 338	32 201	5 926	7 989	6 362	6 699	4 221	1 002
1975	37 475	4 065	1 674	2 391	33 410	6 185	8 673	6 505	6 683	4 323	1 042
1976	38 983	4 170	1 698	2 470	34 814	6 418	9 419	6 817	6 689	4 402	1 069
1977	40 613	4 303	1 765	2 538	36 310	6 717	10 149	7 171	6 720	4 477	1 078
1978	42 631	4 503	1 900	2 603	38 128	7 043	10 888	7 662	6 807	4 593	1 134
1979	44 235	4 527	1 887	2 639	39 708	7 234	11 551	8 154	6 889	4 719	1 161
1980	45 487	4 381	1 781	2 599	41 106	7 315	12 257	8 627	7 004	4 742	1 161
1981	46 696	4 211	1 691	2 520	42 485	7 451	12 912	9 045	7 101	4 799	1 176
1982	47 755	4 056	1 561	2 495	43 699	7 477	13 393	9 651	7 105	4 888	1 185
1983	48 503	3 868	1 452	2 416	44 636	7 451	13 796	10 213	7 105	4 873	1 198
1984	49 709	3 810	1 458	2 351	45 900	7 451	14 234	10 896	7 230	4 911	1 177
1985	51 050	3 767	1 491	2 276	47 283	7 434	14 742	11 567	7 452	4 932	1 156
1986	52 413	3 824	1 580	2 244	48 589	7 293	15 208	12 204	7 746	4 940	1 199
1987	53 658	3 875	1 638	2 237	49 783	7 140	15 577	12 873	8 034	4 937	1 221
1988	54 742	3 872	1 572	2 300	50 870	6 910	15 761	13 361	8 537	4 977	1 324
1989	56 030	3 818	1 495	2 323	52 212	6 721	15 990	13 980	8 997	5 095	1 429
1990	56 829	3 698	1 400	2 298	53 131	6 834	16 058	14 663	9 145	4 948	1 483
1991	57 178	3 470	1 337	2 133	53 708	6 728	15 867	15 235	9 465	4 924	1 489
1992	58 141	3 345	1 316	2 030	54 796	6 750	15 875	15 552	10 120	5 035	1 464
1993	58 795	3 408	1 335	2 073	55 388	6 683	15 566	15 849	10 733	5 097	1 459
1994	60 239	3 585	1 504	2 081	56 655	6 592	15 499	16 259	11 357	5 289	1 658
1995	60 944	3 729	1 557	2 172	57 215	6 349	15 528	16 562	11 801	5 356	1 618
1996	61 857	3 763	1 599	2 164	58 094	6 273	15 403	16 954	12 430	5 452	1 581
1997	63 036	3 837	1 561	2 277	59 198	6 348	15 271	17 268	13 010	5 713	1 590
1998	63 714	4 012	1 607	2 405	59 702	6 418	15 017	17 294	13 405	5 962	1 607
1999	64 855	4 015	1 606	2 410	60 840	6 643	14 826	17 501	13 994	6 204	1 673
2000	66 303	4 002	1 585	2 416	62 301	6 730	14 912	17 473	14 802	6 561	1 823
2001	66 848	3 832	1 520	2 313	63 016	6 917	14 690	17 386	15 221	6 932	1 870
2002	67 363	3 715	1 439	2 277	63 648	7 012	14 600	17 098	15 454	7 559	1 926
2003	68 272	3 556	1 452	2 104	64 716	7 021	14 576	16 933	15 919	8 168	2 099
2004	68 421	3 498	1 418	2 080	64 923	7 097	14 409	16 619	16 123	8 466	2 211
2005	69 288	3 574	1 457	2 117	65 714	7 073	14 503	16 535	16 349	8 934	2 319
2006	70 173	3 588	1 499	2 089	66 585	6 997	14 628	16 441	16 656	9 475	2 388
2007	70 988	3 471	1 417	2 055	67 516	7 110	14 822	16 227	16 896	9 846	2 615
2008	71 767	3 385	1 314	2 071	68 382	7 109	15 030	16 089	17 075	10 270	2 808
2009	72 019	3 163	1 124	2 039	68 856	7 132	15 087	15 720	17 204	10 776	2 937
2010	71 904	2 914	1 011	1 904	68 990	7 164	15 263	15 247	17 104	11 194	3 017
2011	71 642	2 832	957	1 875	68 810	7 169	15 255	14 973	16 876	11 414	3 121
2012	72 648	2 883	1 003	1 880	69 765	7 352	15 382	15 127	16 692	11 830	3 383

Table 1-7. Civilian Labor Force, by Age, Sex, Race, and Hispanic Origin, 1948–2012—*Continued*

(Thousands of people.)

Race, Hispanic origin, sex, and year	16 years and over	16 to 19 years			20 years and over						
		Total	16 to 17 years	18 to 19 years	Total	20 to 24 years	25 to 34 years	35 to 44 years	45 to 54 years	55 to 64 years	65 years and over
WHITE											
Both Sexes											
1954	56 816	3 501	1 448	2 054	53 315	4 752	13 226	13 540	11 258	7 591	2 946
1955	58 085	3 598	1 511	2 087	54 487	4 941	13 267	13 729	11 680	7 810	3 062
1956	59 428	3 771	1 656	2 113	55 657	5 194	13 154	14 000	12 061	8 080	3 166
1957	59 754	3 775	1 637	2 135	55 979	5 283	13 044	14 117	12 382	8 091	3 049
1958	60 293	3 757	1 615	2 144	56 536	5 449	12 884	14 257	12 727	8 254	2 964
1959	60 952	4 000	1 775	2 225	56 952	5 544	12 670	14 355	13 048	8 411	2 925
1960	61 915	4 275	1 871	2 405	57 640	5 787	12 594	14 450	13 322	8 522	2 964
1961	62 656	4 362	1 767	2 594	58 294	6 026	12 503	14 557	13 517	8 773	2 917
1962	62 750	4 354	1 709	2 645	58 396	6 164	12 218	14 695	13 551	8 856	2 912
1963	63 830	4 559	1 950	2 608	59 271	6 537	12 229	14 859	13 789	9 067	2 790
1964	64 921	4 784	2 211	2 572	60 137	6 952	12 235	14 852	14 043	9 239	2 817
1965	66 137	5 267	2 221	3 044	60 870	7 189	12 391	14 900	14 162	9 392	2 839
1966	67 276	5 827	2 367	3 460	61 449	7 324	12 591	14 785	14 370	9 583	2 793
1967	68 699	5 749	2 432	3 318	62 950	7 886	13 123	14 765	14 545	9 817	2 821
1968	69 976	5 839	2 519	3 320	64 137	8 109	13 740	14 683	14 756	9 968	2 884
1969	71 778	6 168	2 698	3 470	65 611	8 614	14 289	14 564	15 057	10 132	2 954
1970	73 556	6 442	2 824	3 617	67 113	9 238	14 896	14 525	15 269	10 255	2 930
1971	74 963	6 681	2 894	3 787	68 282	9 889	15 445	14 374	15 343	10 351	2 880
1972	77 275	7 193	3 096	4 098	70 082	10 605	16 584	14 399	15 283	10 402	2 809
1973	79 151	7 579	3 320	4 260	71 572	11 182	17 764	14 440	15 256	10 240	2 687
1974	81 281	7 899	3 441	4 459	73 381	11 600	18 862	14 644	15 375	10 241	2 656
1975	82 831	7 899	3 375	4 525	74 932	12 019	19 897	14 753	15 308	10 287	2 668
1976	84 767	8 088	3 410	4 679	76 678	12 444	20 990	15 088	15 187	10 371	2 599
1977	87 141	8 352	3 562	4 790	78 789	12 892	22 099	15 604	15 053	10 495	2 647
1978	89 634	8 555	3 715	4 839	81 079	13 309	23 067	16 353	15 004	10 602	2 745
1979	91 923	8 548	3 668	4 881	83 375	13 632	24 101	17 123	14 965	10 767	2 787
1980	93 600	8 312	3 485	4 827	85 286	13 769	25 181	17 811	14 956	10 812	2 759
1981	95 052	7 962	3 274	4 688	87 089	13 926	26 208	18 445	14 993	10 764	2 753
1982	96 143	7 518	3 001	4 518	88 625	13 866	26 814	19 491	14 879	10 832	2 742
1983	97 021	7 186	2 765	4 421	89 835	13 816	27 237	20 488	14 798	10 732	2 766
1984	98 492	6 952	2 720	4 232	91 540	13 733	27 958	21 588	14 899	10 701	2 660
1985	99 926	6 841	2 777	4 065	93 085	13 469	28 640	22 591	15 101	10 679	2 605
1986	101 801	6 862	2 895	3 967	94 939	13 176	29 497	23 571	15 379	10 583	2 732
1987	103 290	6 893	2 963	3 931	96 396	12 764	29 956	24 581	15 792	10 497	2 806
1988	104 756	6 940	2 861	4 079	97 815	12 311	30 167	25 358	16 573	10 462	2 943
1989	106 355	6 809	2 685	4 124	99 546	11 940	30 388	26 312	17 278	10 533	3 094
1990	107 447	6 683	2 543	4 140	100 764	12 397	30 174	27 265	17 515	10 290	3 123
1991	107 743	6 245	2 432	3 813	101 498	12 248	29 794	28 213	18 028	10 129	3 086
1992	108 837	6 022	2 388	3 633	102 815	12 187	29 518	28 580	19 200	10 196	3 135
1993	109 700	6 105	2 458	3 647	103 595	11 987	29 027	29 056	20 181	10 215	3 129
1994	111 082	6 357	2 681	3 677	104 725	11 688	28 580	29 626	21 026	10 319	3 486
1995	111 950	6 545	2 749	3 796	105 404	11 266	28 325	30 112	21 804	10 432	3 466
1996	113 108	6 607	2 780	3 826	106 502	11 003	27 901	30 683	22 781	10 648	3 485
1997	114 693	6 720	2 779	3 941	107 973	11 127	27 362	31 171	23 709	11 086	3 517
1998	115 415	6 965	2 860	4 105	108 450	11 244	26 707	31 221	24 282	11 548	3 448
1999	116 509	7 048	2 849	4 199	109 461	11 436	25 978	31 391	25 102	11 960	3 595
2000	118 545	6 955	2 768	4 186	111 590	11 626	26 336	30 968	26 353	12 463	3 846
2001	119 399	6 661	2 626	4 035	112 737	11 883	26 010	30 778	27 062	13 121	3 883
2002	120 150	6 366	2 445	3 921	113 784	12 073	25 908	30 286	27 405	14 148	3 965
2003	120 546	5 973	2 414	3 560	114 572	12 064	25 752	29 788	27 786	14 944	4 238
2004	121 086	5 929	2 309	3 620	115 156	12 192	25 548	29 305	28 181	15 522	4 408
2005	122 299	5 950	2 390	3 560	116 349	12 109	25 548	29 107	28 685	16 275	4 624
2006	123 834	6 009	2 473	3 536	117 825	12 128	25 681	28 849	29 231	17 132	4 805
2007	124 935	5 795	2 326	3 470	119 139	12 176	26 076	28 394	29 627	17 782	5 085
2008	125 635	5 644	2 126	3 518	119 990	12 142	26 210	27 932	29 780	18 464	5 463
2009	125 644	5 295	1 883	3 413	120 349	11 995	26 277	27 263	29 903	19 199	5 711
2010	125 084	4 861	1 693	3 168	120 223	11 948	26 455	26 510	29 632	19 808	5 869
2011	124 579	4 714	1 581	3 134	119 865	12 120	26 511	25 834	29 036	20 188	6 175
2012	123 684	4 669	1 605	3 065	119 015	11 914	25 806	25 445	28 384	20 752	6 714

Table 1-7. Civilian Labor Force, by Age, Sex, Race, and Hispanic Origin, 1948–2012—*Continued*

(Thousands of people.)

Race, Hispanic origin, sex, and year	16 years and over	16 to 19 years			20 years and over						
		Total	16 to 17 years	18 to 19 years	Total	20 to 24 years	25 to 34 years	35 to 44 years	45 to 54 years	55 to 64 years	65 years and over
WHITE											
Men											
1954	39 759	1 989	896	1 095	37 770	2 654	9 695	9 516	7 913	5 653	2 339
1955	40 197	2 056	935	1 121	38 141	2 803	9 721	9 597	8 025	5 654	2 343
1956	40 734	2 114	1 002	1 110	38 620	3 036	9 595	9 661	8 175	5 736	2 417
1957	40 826	2 108	992	1 114	38 718	3 152	9 483	9 719	8 317	5 735	2 307
1958	41 080	2 116	1 001	1 116	38 964	3 278	9 386	9 822	8 465	5 800	2 213
1959	41 397	2 279	1 077	1 202	39 118	3 409	9 261	9 876	8 581	5 833	2 158
1960	41 743	2 433	1 140	1 293	39 310	3 559	9 153	9 919	8 689	5 861	2 129
1961	41 986	2 439	1 067	1 372	39 547	3 681	9 072	9 961	8 776	5 988	2 068
1962	41 931	2 432	1 041	1 391	39 499	3 726	8 846	10 029	8 820	5 995	2 082
1963	42 404	2 563	1 183	1 380	39 841	3 955	8 805	10 079	8 944	6 090	1 967
1964	42 894	2 716	1 345	1 371	40 178	4 166	8 800	10 055	9 053	6 161	1 942
1965	43 400	2 999	1 359	1 639	40 401	4 279	8 824	10 023	9 130	6 188	1 959
1966	43 572	3 253	1 423	1 830	40 319	4 200	8 859	9 892	9 189	6 250	1 928
1967	44 041	3 191	1 464	1 727	40 851	4 416	9 102	9 785	9 260	6 348	1 944
1968	44 553	3 236	1 504	1 732	41 318	4 432	9 477	9 662	9 340	6 427	1 981
1969	45 185	3 413	1 583	1 830	41 772	4 615	9 773	9 509	9 413	6 467	1 996
1970	46 035	3 551	1 629	1 922	42 483	4 988	10 099	9 414	9 487	6 517	1 978
1971	46 904	3 719	1 681	2 039	43 185	5 448	10 444	9 294	9 528	6 550	1 922
1972	48 118	3 980	1 758	2 223	44 138	5 937	11 039	9 278	9 473	6 562	1 846
1973	48 920	4 174	1 875	2 300	44 747	6 274	11 621	9 212	9 445	6 452	1 740
1974	49 843	4 312	1 922	2 391	45 532	6 470	12 135	9 246	9 455	6 464	1 759
1975	50 324	4 290	1 871	2 418	46 034	6 642	12 579	9 231	9 415	6 425	1 742
1976	51 033	4 357	1 869	2 489	46 675	6 890	13 092	9 289	9 310	6 437	1 657
1977	52 033	4 496	1 949	2 548	47 537	7 097	13 555	9 509	9 175	6 492	1 688
1978	52 955	4 565	2 002	2 563	48 390	7 274	13 939	9 858	9 068	6 508	1 744
1979	53 856	4 537	1 974	2 563	49 320	7 421	14 415	10 183	8 968	6 571	1 761
1980	54 473	4 424	1 881	2 543	50 049	7 479	14 893	10 455	8 877	6 618	1 727
1981	54 895	4 224	1 751	2 473	50 671	7 521	15 340	10 740	8 836	6 530	1 704
1982	55 133	3 933	1 602	2 331	51 200	7 438	15 549	11 289	8 727	6 520	1 677
1983	55 480	3 764	1 452	2 312	51 716	7 406	15 707	11 817	8 649	6 446	1 691
1984	56 062	3 609	1 420	2 189	52 453	7 370	16 037	12 348	8 683	6 410	1 606
1985	56 472	3 576	1 467	2 109	52 895	7 122	16 306	12 767	8 730	6 376	1 595
1986	57 217	3 542	1 502	2 040	53 675	6 986	16 769	13 207	8 791	6 260	1 663
1987	57 779	3 547	1 524	2 023	54 232	6 717	16 963	13 674	8 945	6 200	1 733
1988	58 317	3 583	1 487	2 095	54 734	6 468	17 018	14 068	9 285	6 108	1 787
1989	58 988	3 546	1 401	2 146	55 441	6 316	17 077	14 516	9 615	6 082	1 835
1990	59 638	3 522	1 333	2 189	56 116	6 688	16 920	15 026	9 713	5 957	1 811
1991	59 656	3 269	1 266	2 003	56 387	6 619	16 709	15 523	9 926	5 847	1 763
1992	60 168	3 192	1 260	1 932	56 976	6 542	16 512	15 701	10 570	5 821	1 830
1993	60 484	3 200	1 292	1 908	57 284	6 449	16 244	15 971	11 010	5 784	1 825
1994	60 727	3 315	1 403	1 912	57 411	6 294	15 879	16 188	11 327	5 726	1 998
1995	61 146	3 427	1 429	1 998	57 719	6 096	15 669	16 414	11 730	5 809	2 000
1996	61 783	3 444	1 421	2 023	58 340	5 922	15 475	16 728	12 217	5 943	2 054
1997	62 639	3 513	1 440	2 073	59 126	6 029	15 120	17 019	12 710	6 154	2 094
1998	63 034	3 614	1 487	2 127	59 421	6 063	14 770	17 157	13 003	6 415	2 013
1999	63 413	3 666	1 478	2 188	59 747	6 151	14 292	17 201	13 368	6 618	2 117
2000	64 466	3 615	1 422	2 193	60 850	6 244	14 666	16 880	13 977	6 840	2 243
2001	64 966	3 446	1 334	2 112	61 519	6 363	14 536	16 809	14 400	7 169	2 241
2002	65 308	3 241	1 215	2 026	62 067	6 444	14 499	16 583	14 615	7 665	2 261
2003	65 509	3 036	1 193	1 843	62 473	6 479	14 529	16 398	14 708	7 973	2 386
2004	65 994	3 050	1 127	1 923	62 944	6 586	14 429	16 192	14 934	8 326	2 478
2005	66 694	2 988	1 162	1 826	63 705	6 562	14 426	16 080	15 273	8 734	2 631
2006	67 613	3 074	1 222	1 852	64 540	6 597	14 469	15 962	15 606	9 152	2 753
2007	68 158	2 944	1 147	1 798	65 214	6 567	14 715	15 765	15 846	9 500	2 821
2008	68 351	2 868	1 040	1 829	65 483	6 526	14 715	15 436	15 905	9 855	3 046
2009	68 051	2 679	933	1 746	65 372	6 348	14 669	15 066	15 943	10 160	3 186
2010	67 728	2 463	844	1 619	65 265	6 342	14 734	14 713	15 791	10 422	3 263
2011	67 551	2 386	780	1 606	65 165	6 539	14 785	14 317	15 400	10 629	3 494
2012	66 921	2 382	785	1 596	64 540	6 339	14 256	14 018	15 121	10 970	3 835

Table 1-7. Civilian Labor Force, by Age, Sex, Race, and Hispanic Origin, 1948–2012—*Continued*

(Thousands of people.)

Race, Hispanic origin, sex, and year	16 years and over	16 to 19 years			20 years and over						
		Total	16 to 17 years	18 to 19 years	Total	20 to 24 years	25 to 34 years	35 to 44 years	45 to 54 years	55 to 64 years	65 years and over
WHITE											
Women											
1954	17 057	1 512	552	959	15 545	2 098	3 531	4 024	3 345	1 938	607
1955	17 888	1 542	576	966	16 346	2 138	3 546	4 132	3 655	2 156	719
1956	18 694	1 657	654	1 003	17 037	2 158	3 559	4 339	3 886	2 344	749
1957	18 928	1 667	645	1 021	17 261	2 131	3 561	4 398	4 065	2 356	742
1958	19 213	1 641	614	1 028	17 572	2 171	3 498	4 435	4 262	2 454	751
1959	19 555	1 721	698	1 023	17 834	2 135	3 409	4 479	4 467	2 578	767
1960	20 172	1 842	731	1 112	18 330	2 228	3 441	4 531	4 633	2 661	835
1961	20 670	1 923	700	1 222	18 747	2 345	3 431	4 596	4 741	2 785	849
1962	20 819	1 922	668	1 254	18 897	2 438	3 372	4 666	4 731	2 861	830
1963	21 426	1 996	767	1 228	19 430	2 582	3 424	4 780	4 845	2 977	823
1964	22 027	2 068	866	1 201	19 959	2 786	3 435	4 797	4 990	3 078	875
1965	22 737	2 268	862	1 405	20 469	2 910	3 567	4 877	5 032	3 204	880
1966	23 704	2 574	944	1 630	21 130	3 124	3 732	4 893	5 181	3 333	865
1967	24 658	2 558	968	1 591	22 100	3 471	4 021	4 980	5 285	3 469	877
1968	25 423	2 603	1 015	1 588	22 821	3 677	4 263	5 021	5 416	3 541	903
1969	26 593	2 755	1 115	1 640	23 839	3 999	4 516	5 055	5 644	3 665	958
1970	27 521	2 891	1 195	1 695	24 630	4 250	4 797	5 111	5 781	3 738	952
1971	28 060	2 962	1 213	1 748	25 097	4 441	5 001	5 080	5 816	3 801	958
1972	29 157	3 213	1 338	1 875	25 945	4 668	5 544	5 121	5 810	3 839	963
1973	30 231	3 405	1 445	1 960	26 825	4 908	6 143	5 228	5 811	3 788	947
1974	31 437	3 588	1 520	2 068	27 850	5 131	6 727	5 399	5 920	3 777	897
1975	32 508	3 610	1 504	2 107	28 898	5 378	7 318	5 522	5 892	3 862	926
1976	33 735	3 731	1 541	2 189	30 004	5 554	7 898	5 799	5 877	3 935	940
1977	35 108	3 856	1 614	2 243	31 253	5 795	8 523	6 095	5 877	4 003	959
1978	36 679	3 990	1 713	2 276	32 689	6 035	9 128	6 495	5 936	4 094	1 001
1979	38 067	4 011	1 694	2 318	34 056	6 211	9 687	6 940	5 997	4 196	1 024
1980	39 127	3 888	1 605	2 284	35 239	6 290	10 289	7 356	6 079	4 194	1 032
1981	40 157	3 739	1 523	2 216	36 418	6 406	10 868	7 704	6 157	4 235	1 049
1982	41 010	3 585	1 399	2 186	37 425	6 428	11 264	8 202	6 152	4 313	1 065
1983	41 541	3 422	1 314	2 109	38 119	6 410	11 530	8 670	6 149	4 285	1 074
1984	42 431	3 343	1 300	2 043	39 087	6 363	11 922	9 240	6 217	4 292	1 054
1985	43 455	3 265	1 310	1 955	40 190	6 348	12 334	9 824	6 371	4 303	1 010
1986	44 584	3 320	1 393	1 927	41 264	6 191	12 729	10 364	6 588	4 323	1 069
1987	45 510	3 347	1 439	1 908	42 164	6 047	12 993	10 907	6 847	4 297	1 073
1988	46 439	3 358	1 374	1 984	43 081	5 844	13 149	11 291	7 288	4 354	1 156
1989	47 367	3 262	1 284	1 978	44 105	5 625	13 311	11 796	7 663	4 451	1 259
1990	47 809	3 161	1 210	1 951	44 648	5 709	13 254	12 239	7 802	4 333	1 312
1991	48 087	2 976	1 166	1 810	45 111	5 629	13 085	12 689	8 101	4 282	1 324
1992	48 669	2 830	1 128	1 702	45 839	5 645	13 006	12 879	8 630	4 375	1 305
1993	49 216	2 905	1 167	1 739	46 311	5 539	12 783	13 085	9 171	4 430	1 304
1994	50 356	3 042	1 278	1 764	47 314	5 394	12 702	13 439	9 699	4 593	1 487
1995	50 804	3 118	1 320	1 798	47 686	5 170	12 656	13 697	10 074	4 622	1 466
1996	51 325	3 163	1 360	1 803	48 162	5 081	12 426	13 955	10 563	4 706	1 431
1997	52 054	3 207	1 339	1 867	48 847	5 099	12 242	14 153	10 999	4 932	1 422
1998	52 380	3 351	1 373	1 977	49 029	5 180	11 937	14 064	11 279	5 133	1 435
1999	53 096	3 382	1 371	2 010	49 714	5 285	11 685	14 190	11 734	5 342	1 478
2000	54 079	3 339	1 346	1 993	50 740	5 381	11 669	14 088	12 376	5 623	1 602
2001	54 433	3 215	1 292	1 923	51 218	5 519	11 474	13 969	12 662	5 952	1 642
2002	54 842	3 125	1 229	1 895	51 717	5 628	11 409	13 703	12 790	6 482	1 704
2003	55 037	2 937	1 221	1 716	52 099	5 584	11 223	13 390	13 078	6 970	1 852
2004	55 092	2 879	1 182	1 697	52 212	5 606	11 119	13 114	13 247	7 197	1 930
2005	55 605	2 962	1 228	1 733	52 643	5 546	11 123	13 027	13 413	7 542	1 993
2006	56 221	2 935	1 251	1 684	53 286	5 530	11 212	12 886	13 625	7 980	2 052
2007	56 777	2 851	1 179	1 672	53 925	5 609	11 360	12 629	13 781	8 282	2 264
2008	57 284	2 776	1 086	1 690	54 508	5 616	11 495	12 495	13 875	8 609	2 417
2009	57 593	2 616	950	1 667	54 976	5 647	11 608	12 197	13 960	9 039	2 525
2010	57 356	2 398	849	1 549	54 957	5 607	11 721	11 796	13 841	9 386	2 607
2011	57 028	2 328	800	1 528	54 700	5 581	11 726	11 517	13 636	9 559	2 681
2012	56 763	2 288	819	1 469	54 475	5 575	11 550	11 428	13 263	9 782	2 879

Table 1-7. Civilian Labor Force, by Age, Sex, Race, and Hispanic Origin, 1948–2012—*Continued*

(Thousands of people.)

Race, Hispanic origin, sex, and year	16 years and over	16 to 19 years			20 years and over						
		Total	16 to 17 years	18 to 19 years	Total	20 to 24 years	25 to 34 years	35 to 44 years	45 to 54 years	55 to 64 years	65 years and over
BLACK											
Both Sexes											
1974	9 167	851	317	534	8 317	1 492	2 358	1 777	1 517	917	253
1975	9 263	838	312	524	8 426	1 477	2 466	1 775	1 519	929	258
1976	9 561	837	304	532	8 724	1 544	2 646	1 824	1 518	925	268
1977	9 932	861	304	557	9 072	1 641	2 798	1 894	1 530	943	267
1978	10 432	930	341	589	9 501	1 739	2 961	1 975	1 560	978	289
1979	10 678	912	340	572	9 766	1 793	3 094	2 039	1 584	974	281
1980	10 865	891	326	565	9 975	1 802	3 259	2 081	1 596	978	257
1981	11 086	862	308	554	10 224	1 828	3 365	2 164	1 608	1 009	249
1982	11 331	824	268	556	10 507	1 849	3 492	2 303	1 610	1 012	243
1983	11 647	809	248	561	10 838	1 871	3 675	2 406	1 630	1 032	224
1984	12 033	827	268	558	11 206	1 926	3 800	2 565	1 671	1 020	224
1985	12 364	889	311	578	11 476	1 854	3 888	2 681	1 742	1 059	252
1986	12 654	883	322	562	11 770	1 881	4 028	2 793	1 793	1 051	224
1987	12 993	899	336	563	12 094	1 818	4 147	2 942	1 838	1 098	251
1988	13 205	889	344	545	12 316	1 782	4 226	3 069	1 894	1 069	276
1989	13 497	925	353	572	12 573	1 789	4 295	3 227	1 954	1 023	285
1990	13 740	866	306	560	12 874	1 758	4 307	3 566	2 003	977	262
1991	13 797	774	266	508	13 023	1 750	4 254	3 719	2 042	1 001	256
1992	14 162	816	285	532	13 346	1 763	4 309	3 843	2 142	1 029	259
1993	14 225	807	283	524	13 418	1 764	4 232	3 960	2 212	1 013	237
1994	14 502	852	351	501	13 650	1 800	4 199	4 068	2 308	1 007	267
1995	14 817	911	366	545	13 906	1 754	4 267	4 165	2 404	1 046	271
1996	15 134	923	366	556	14 211	1 738	4 305	4 287	2 553	1 073	255
1997	15 529	933	352	580	14 596	1 783	4 329	4 401	2 724	1 093	265
1998	15 982	1 017	370	646	14 966	1 797	4 332	4 531	2 863	1 163	278
1999	16 365	959	352	607	15 406	1 866	4 430	4 653	2 992	1 180	285
2000	16 397	941	356	585	15 456	1 873	4 281	4 515	3 203	1 264	320
2001	16 421	898	332	565	15 524	1 878	4 180	4 483	3 298	1 335	350
2002	16 565	870	297	574	15 695	1 908	4 134	4 458	3 435	1 407	353
2003	16 526	771	289	482	15 755	1 892	4 060	4 465	3 506	1 466	366
2004	16 638	762	272	489	15 876	1 926	4 076	4 380	3 578	1 538	380
2005	17 013	803	279	525	16 209	1 957	4 145	4 370	3 686	1 647	403
2006	17 314	871	318	553	16 443	1 960	4 197	4 348	3 785	1 739	414
2007	17 496	801	300	501	16 695	1 974	4 254	4 357	3 866	1 811	432
2008	17 740	787	270	517	16 953	1 981	4 328	4 316	3 945	1 908	476
2009	17 632	729	231	499	16 902	1 961	4 300	4 175	3 976	1 995	495
2010	17 862	677	203	473	17 186	2 072	4 418	4 095	3 991	2 104	506
2011	17 881	647	188	459	17 234	2 105	4 434	4 029	3 957	2 155	555
2012	18 400	711	213	498	17 689	2 210	4 333	4 120	4 057	2 369	599
BLACK											
Men											
1974	5 020	480	189	291	4 540	798	1 279	953	838	519	152
1975	5 016	447	168	279	4 569	790	1 328	948	833	520	150
1976	5 101	454	168	285	4 648	820	1 383	969	824	504	149
1977	5 263	476	178	299	4 787	856	1 441	1 003	818	515	154
1978	5 435	491	186	306	4 943	883	1 504	1 022	829	540	166
1979	5 559	480	179	301	5 079	928	1 577	1 049	844	524	156
1980	5 612	479	181	298	5 134	935	1 659	1 061	830	509	138
1981	5 685	462	169	293	5 223	940	1 702	1 093	829	524	134
1982	5 804	436	137	300	5 368	964	1 769	1 152	824	525	135
1983	5 966	433	134	300	5 533	997	1 840	1 196	845	536	119
1984	6 126	440	141	299	5 686	1 022	1 924	1 270	847	505	118
1985	6 220	471	162	310	5 749	950	1 937	1 313	879	544	125
1986	6 373	458	164	294	5 915	957	2 029	1 359	901	552	116
1987	6 486	463	179	284	6 023	914	2 074	1 406	915	586	130
1988	6 596	469	186	283	6 127	913	2 114	1 459	936	565	139
1989	6 701	480	190	291	6 221	904	2 157	1 544	945	530	141
1990	6 802	445	161	284	6 357	879	2 142	1 733	988	496	119
1991	6 851	400	140	260	6 451	896	2 111	1 806	1 010	507	122
1992	6 997	429	149	280	6 568	900	2 121	1 859	1 037	521	130
1993	7 019	425	154	270	6 594	875	2 118	1 918	1 065	506	112
1994	7 089	443	176	266	6 646	891	2 068	1 975	1 102	484	125
1995	7 183	453	184	269	6 730	866	2 089	1 987	1 148	490	150
1996	7 264	458	182	276	6 806	848	2 077	2 036	1 204	509	132
1997	7 354	444	178	266	6 910	832	2 052	2 096	1 287	508	134
1998	7 542	488	181	307	7 053	837	2 034	2 142	1 343	548	150
1999	7 652	470	180	291	7 182	835	2 069	2 206	1 387	547	138
2000	7 702	462	181	281	7 240	875	1 999	2 105	1 497	612	151
2001	7 647	447	166	281	7 200	853	1 915	2 073	1 537	645	177
2002	7 794	446	149	297	7 347	906	1 909	2 064	1 623	664	181
2003	7 711	365	138	228	7 346	918	1 872	2 058	1 627	685	186
2004	7 773	359	128	231	7 414	927	1 931	2 000	1 654	714	188
2005	7 998	399	139	260	7 600	940	1 948	2 028	1 732	756	196
2006	8 128	409	152	256	7 720	971	1 986	1 999	1 792	777	195
2007	8 252	384	137	247	7 867	981	2 037	2 030	1 822	791	206
2008	8 347	385	174	261	7 962	984	2 047	2 008	1 846	852	225
2009	8 265	350	111	239	7 914	954	2 041	1 932	1 852	904	231
2010	8 415	339	96	244	8 076	986	2 118	1 924	1 862	950	236
2011	8 454	329	89	241	8 125	1 012	2 159	1 860	1 854	983	257
2012	8 594	338	99	239	8 256	1 054	2 030	1 908	1 884	1 099	281

Table 1-7. Civilian Labor Force, by Age, Sex, Race, and Hispanic Origin, 1948–2012—*Continued*

(Thousands of people.)

Race, Hispanic origin, sex, and year	16 years and over	16 to 19 years			20 years and over						
		Total	16 to 17 years	18 to 19 years	Total	20 to 24 years	25 to 34 years	35 to 44 years	45 to 54 years	55 to 64 years	65 years and over
BLACK											
Women											
1974	4 148	371	128	243	3 777	694	1 079	824	679	398	100
1975	4 247	391	144	245	3 857	687	1 138	827	686	409	108
1976	4 460	384	136	247	4 076	723	1 264	855	694	421	119
1977	4 670	385	127	258	4 286	785	1 357	891	712	429	113
1978	4 997	439	155	283	4 558	856	1 456	953	731	439	124
1979	5 119	432	161	271	4 687	865	1 517	990	740	451	124
1980	5 253	412	144	267	4 841	867	1 600	1 020	767	469	119
1981	5 401	400	139	261	5 001	888	1 663	1 071	779	485	115
1982	5 527	387	131	256	5 140	885	1 723	1 151	786	487	108
1983	5 681	375	114	261	5 306	874	1 835	1 210	785	496	105
1984	5 907	387	127	260	5 520	904	1 876	1 294	823	515	106
1985	6 144	417	149	268	5 727	904	1 951	1 368	862	515	127
1986	6 281	425	157	268	5 855	924	1 999	1 434	892	499	107
1987	6 507	435	157	278	6 071	904	2 073	1 537	924	512	121
1988	6 609	419	158	262	6 190	869	2 112	1 610	958	504	137
1989	6 796	445	163	281	6 352	885	2 138	1 683	1 009	493	144
1990	6 938	421	145	276	6 517	879	2 165	1 833	1 015	481	143
1991	6 946	374	126	248	6 572	854	2 143	1 913	1 032	494	135
1992	7 166	387	135	252	6 778	863	2 188	1 985	1 105	508	129
1993	7 206	383	129	254	6 824	889	2 115	2 042	1 147	506	125
1994	7 413	409	174	235	7 004	909	2 131	2 093	1 206	523	142
1995	7 634	458	182	276	7 175	887	2 177	2 178	1 256	556	121
1996	7 869	464	184	280	7 405	890	2 228	2 251	1 349	565	122
1997	8 175	489	175	314	7 686	951	2 277	2 305	1 437	585	131
1998	8 441	528	189	339	7 912	960	2 298	2 390	1 520	615	128
1999	8 713	489	172	316	8 224	1 031	2 360	2 447	1 606	633	147
2000	8 695	479	175	305	8 215	998	2 282	2 409	1 706	652	168
2001	8 774	451	166	284	8 323	1 025	2 265	2 410	1 762	690	173
2002	8 772	424	148	276	8 348	1 002	2 225	2 394	1 812	743	171
2003	8 815	406	151	255	8 409	973	2 188	2 407	1 879	781	180
2004	8 865	403	144	259	8 462	999	2 144	2 380	1 924	824	192
2005	9 014	405	140	265	8 610	1 017	2 197	2 342	1 954	891	207
2006	9 186	462	166	297	8 723	989	2 211	2 349	1 993	963	218
2007	9 244	417	163	254	8 828	993	2 218	2 328	2 044	1 019	227
2008	9 393	402	146	256	8 991	997	2 281	2 308	2 099	1 056	251
2009	9 367	379	119	260	8 988	1 008	2 258	2 243	2 124	1 091	264
2010	9 447	337	108	230	9 110	1 086	2 299	2 171	2 129	1 153	270
2011	9 427	318	99	219	9 110	1 093	2 275	2 168	2 104	1 172	298
2012	9 805	373	114	258	9 433	1 157	2 303	2 212	2 173	1 271	317
HISPANIC											
Both Sexes											
1975	4 171	444	. . .	. . .	. . .	. . .	. . .	. . .	. . .	. . .	. . .
1976	4 205	447	176	285	3 820	729	1 248	875	625	294	48
1977	4 536	493	184	305	4 059	813	1 325	916	656	293	55
1978	4 979	533	221	312	4 446	901	1 446	1 008	701	323	67
1979	5 219	551	207	343	4 668	960	1 532	1 062	704	339	72
1980	6 146	645	241	404	5 502	1 136	1 843	1 163	860	414	85
1981	6 492	603	215	388	5 888	1 231	2 015	1 239	886	430	87
1982	6 734	585	192	393	6 148	1 251	2 163	1 313	891	444	85
1983	7 033	590	189	401	6 442	1 282	2 267	1 380	931	495	86
1984	7 451	618	209	409	6 833	1 325	2 436	1 509	954	524	84
1985	7 698	579	199	379	7 119	1 358	2 571	1 595	985	527	82
1986	8 076	571	203	368	7 505	1 414	2 685	1 713	1 097	511	84
1987	8 541	610	206	404	7 931	1 425	2 890	1 904	1 086	545	81
1988	8 982	671	234	437	8 311	1 486	2 957	1 996	1 147	621	103
1989	9 323	680	224	456	8 643	1 483	3 118	2 092	1 205	625	120
1990	10 720	829	276	554	9 891	1 839	3 590	2 386	1 320	647	110
1991	10 920	781	249	532	10 139	1 835	3 596	2 539	1 376	681	111
1992	11 338	796	263	533	10 542	1 815	3 740	2 735	1 442	687	122
1993	11 610	771	246	525	10 839	1 811	3 800	2 865	1 534	684	145
1994	11 975	807	285	522	11 168	1 863	3 865	2 965	1 626	698	151
1995	12 267	850	291	559	11 417	1 818	3 943	3 113	1 671	720	152
1996	12 774	845	284	561	11 929	1 845	4 054	3 361	1 697	806	166
1997	13 796	911	315	596	12 884	2 004	4 298	3 601	1 945	850	186
1998	14 317	1 007	320	688	13 310	2 077	4 372	3 707	2 090	894	169
1999	14 665	1 049	333	717	13 616	2 052	4 330	3 929	2 178	927	199
2000	16 689	1 168	368	800	15 521	2 546	5 197	4 241	2 387	940	209
2001	17 328	1 176	352	824	16 152	2 616	5 380	4 377	2 583	1 000	195
2002	17 943	1 103	335	769	16 840	2 678	5 645	4 545	2 657	1 091	224
2003	18 813	960	322	638	17 853	2 672	5 960	4 867	2 894	1 201	259
2004	19 272	995	297	698	18 277	2 732	5 931	4 931	3 093	1 284	306
2005	19 824	1 038	331	708	18 785	2 651	6 080	5 110	3 256	1 378	311
2006	20 694	1 071	360	710	19 623	2 681	6 295	5 337	3 452	1 490	369
2007	21 602	1 091	347	744	20 511	2 728	6 559	5 552	3 707	1 569	395
2008	22 024	1 121	353	768	20 903	2 668	6 557	5 698	3 862	1 701	417
2009	22 352	1 063	301	762	21 290	2 647	6 435	5 752	4 116	1 866	472
2010	22 748	1 002	264	738	21 747	2 760	6 517	5 783	4 238	1 936	513
2011	22 898	965	251	713	21 933	3 017	6 416	5 702	4 272	2 015	511
2012	24 391	1 131	315	817	23 260	3 205	6 736	6 053	4 569	2 185	512

. . . = Not available.

Table 1-7. Civilian Labor Force, by Age, Sex, Race, and Hispanic Origin, 1948–2012—*Continued*

(Thousands of people.)

Race, Hispanic origin, sex, and year	16 years and over	16 to 19 years			20 years and over						
		Total	16 to 17 years	18 to 19 years	Total	20 to 24 years	25 to 34 years	35 to 44 years	45 to 54 years	55 to 64 years	65 years and over
HISPANIC											
Men											
1975	2 597	. . .	. . .	. . .	2 343	. . .	. . .	. . .	. . .	. . .	. . .
1976	2 580	260	104	155	2 326	433	771	541	398	189	34
1977	2 817	285	105	179	2 530	485	828	567	416	197	42
1978	3 041	299	129	171	2 742	546	882	620	425	217	52
1979	3 184	315	121	194	2 869	562	941	648	445	216	56
1980	3 818	392	147	245	3 426	697	1 161	713	522	270	62
1981	4 005	359	130	229	3 647	747	1 269	756	535	278	61
1982	4 148	333	111	221	3 815	759	1 361	808	539	290	58
1983	4 362	348	109	239	4 014	789	1 447	852	557	311	58
1984	4 563	345	113	232	4 218	822	1 540	910	570	325	51
1985	4 729	334	116	218	4 395	835	1 629	957	591	331	53
1986	4 948	336	114	222	4 612	888	1 669	1 015	661	323	56
1987	5 163	345	112	233	4 818	865	1 801	1 121	652	325	55
1988	5 409	378	123	255	5 031	897	1 834	1 189	686	355	69
1989	5 595	400	129	271	5 195	909	1 899	1 221	719	375	71
1990	6 546	512	165	346	6 034	1 182	2 230	1 403	775	380	65
1991	6 664	466	141	325	6 198	1 202	2 260	1 487	780	401	67
1992	6 900	468	154	314	6 432	1 141	2 366	1 593	844	414	74
1993	7 076	455	145	310	6 621	1 147	2 417	1 675	900	394	88
1994	7 210	463	163	300	6 747	1 184	2 430	1 713	922	410	89
1995	7 376	479	168	311	6 898	1 153	2 469	1 795	965	417	98
1996	7 646	496	156	340	7 150	1 132	2 510	1 966	967	469	105
1997	8 309	531	177	354	7 779	1 267	2 684	2 091	1 112	511	113
1998	8 571	565	188	377	8 005	1 288	2 733	2 173	1 164	541	106
1999	8 546	596	181	415	7 950	1 231	2 633	2 219	1 205	526	136
2000	9 923	676	204	471	9 247	1 590	3 181	2 451	1 337	555	134
2001	10 279	684	200	484	9 595	1 602	3 294	2 562	1 430	582	125
2002	10 609	632	183	449	9 977	1 627	3 484	2 647	1 478	607	134
2003	11 288	532	164	368	10 756	1 642	3 776	2 877	1 630	680	150
2004	11 587	567	156	410	11 020	1 671	3 765	2 934	1 736	728	186
2005	11 985	577	179	398	11 408	1 645	3 879	3 058	1 855	779	192
2006	12 488	600	189	411	11 888	1 646	4 014	3 203	1 960	838	228
2007	13 005	602	189	412	12 403	1 645	4 170	3 346	2 104	904	233
2008	13 255	626	202	424	12 629	1 594	4 172	3 425	2 216	979	243
2009	13 310	580	160	420	12 730	1 542	4 046	3 472	2 350	1 046	273
2010	13 511	553	132	420	12 958	1 612	4 061	3 515	2 407	1 061	302
2011	13 576	545	129	416	13 030	1 811	4 011	3 421	2 372	1 122	293
2012	14 026	620	162	457	13 407	1 837	4 053	3 480	2 542	1 215	280
HISPANIC											
Women											
1975	1 574	. . .	. . .	. . .	1 384	. . .	. . .	. . .	. . .	. . .	. . .
1976	1 625	201	71	130	1 454	295	479	334	227	105	13
1977	1 720	204	80	125	1 523	327	497	349	240	96	13
1978	1 938	233	93	142	1 704	354	564	388	275	106	16
1979	2 035	235	86	149	1 800	397	590	413	258	124	15
1980	2 328	252	93	159	2 076	439	682	450	337	144	22
1981	2 486	244	85	159	2 242	484	745	483	351	152	27
1982	2 586	252	81	172	2 333	492	802	504	352	155	28
1983	2 671	242	80	162	2 429	493	820	529	374	184	29
1984	2 888	273	96	177	2 615	503	896	599	384	199	34
1985	2 970	245	84	161	2 725	524	943	639	394	196	29
1986	3 128	236	89	147	2 893	526	1 016	698	436	189	28
1987	3 377	265	94	171	3 112	559	1 090	783	434	220	27
1988	3 573	293	111	182	3 281	589	1 123	806	461	267	34
1989	3 728	280	95	185	3 448	574	1 219	871	486	251	49
1990	4 174	318	110	207	3 857	657	1 360	983	545	268	45
1991	4 256	315	107	207	3 941	633	1 336	1 052	596	279	44
1992	4 439	328	110	219	4 110	674	1 374	1 142	599	273	48
1993	4 534	316	101	215	4 218	664	1 383	1 190	633	290	57
1994	4 765	345	122	222	4 421	679	1 435	1 252	704	288	62
1995	4 891	371	123	249	4 520	666	1 473	1 318	706	303	54
1996	5 128	349	128	221	4 779	713	1 544	1 395	729	338	61
1997	5 486	381	138	242	5 106	737	1 614	1 510	833	338	73
1998	5 746	442	132	310	5 304	789	1 639	1 533	927	353	62
1999	6 119	453	151	302	5 666	821	1 698	1 710	973	401	63
2000	6 767	492	164	328	6 275	956	2 016	1 791	1 051	386	75
2001	7 049	492	152	340	6 557	1 014	2 086	1 815	1 153	418	70
2002	7 334	471	152	320	6 863	1 051	2 161	1 897	1 179	484	90
2003	7 525	428	158	271	7 096	1 030	2 183	1 990	1 264	520	109
2004	7 685	429	141	288	7 257	1 060	2 166	1 998	1 357	556	119
2005	7 839	462	152	310	7 377	1 005	2 201	2 052	1 401	599	119
2006	8 206	471	171	300	7 735	1 035	2 280	2 134	1 492	652	141
2007	8 597	489	158	332	8 108	1 083	2 389	2 205	1 604	665	162
2008	8 769	495	151	344	8 274	1 074	2 384	2 274	1 646	722	174
2009	9 043	483	141	342	8 560	1 105	2 388	2 280	1 767	820	200
2010	9 238	449	132	317	8 789	1 147	2 456	2 268	1 831	875	211
2011	9 322	419	122	297	8 902	1 206	2 406	2 282	1 899	893	217
2012	10 365	512	152	360	9 853	1 368	2 683	2 574	2 027	969	232

. . . = Not available.

Table 1-8. Civilian Labor Force Participation Rates, by Age, Sex, Race, and Hispanic Origin, 1948–2012

(Percent.)

Race, Hispanic origin, sex, and year	16 years and over	16 to 19 years	20 years and over						
			Total	20 to 24 years	25 to 34 years	35 to 44 years	45 to 54 years	55 to 64 years	65 years and over
ALL RACES									
Both Sexes									
1948	58.8	52.5	59.4	64.1	63.1	66.7	65.1	56.9	27.0
1949	58.9	52.2	59.5	64.9	63.2	67.2	65.3	56.2	27.3
1950	59.2	51.8	59.9	65.9	63.5	67.5	66.4	56.7	26.7
1951	59.2	52.2	59.8	64.8	64.2	67.6	67.2	56.9	25.8
1952	59.0	51.3	59.7	62.2	64.7	68.0	67.5	57.5	24.8
1953	58.9	50.2	59.6	61.2	64.0	68.9	68.1	58.0	24.8
1954	58.8	48.3	59.6	61.6	64.3	68.8	68.4	58.7	23.9
1955	59.3	48.9	60.1	62.7	64.8	68.9	69.7	59.5	24.1
1956	60.0	50.9	60.7	64.1	64.8	69.5	70.5	60.8	24.3
1957	59.6	49.6	60.4	64.0	64.9	69.5	70.9	60.1	22.9
1958	59.5	47.4	60.5	64.4	65.0	69.6	71.5	60.5	21.8
1959	59.3	46.7	60.4	64.3	65.0	69.5	71.9	61.0	21.1
1960	59.4	47.5	60.5	65.2	65.4	69.4	72.2	60.9	20.8
1961	59.3	46.9	60.5	65.7	65.6	69.5	72.1	61.5	20.1
1962	58.8	46.1	60.0	65.3	65.2	69.7	72.2	61.5	19.1
1963	58.7	45.2	60.1	65.1	65.6	70.1	72.5	62.0	17.9
1964	58.7	44.5	60.2	66.3	65.8	70.0	72.9	61.9	18.0
1965	58.9	45.7	60.3	66.4	66.4	70.7	72.5	61.9	17.8
1966	59.2	48.2	60.5	66.5	67.1	71.0	72.7	62.2	17.2
1967	59.6	48.4	60.9	67.1	68.2	71.6	72.7	62.3	17.2
1968	59.6	48.3	60.9	67.0	68.6	72.0	72.8	62.2	17.2
1969	60.1	49.4	61.3	68.2	69.1	72.5	73.4	62.1	17.3
1970	60.4	49.9	61.6	69.2	69.7	73.1	73.5	61.8	17.0
1971	60.2	49.7	61.4	69.3	69.9	73.2	73.2	61.3	16.2
1972	60.4	51.9	61.4	70.8	70.9	73.3	72.7	60.0	15.6
1973	60.8	53.7	61.7	72.6	72.3	74.0	72.5	58.4	14.6
1974	61.3	54.8	62.0	74.0	73.6	74.6	72.7	57.8	14.0
1975	61.2	54.0	62.1	73.9	74.4	75.0	72.6	57.2	13.7
1976	61.6	54.5	62.4	74.7	75.7	76.0	72.5	56.6	13.1
1977	62.3	56.0	63.0	75.7	77.0	77.0	72.8	56.3	13.0
1978	63.2	57.8	63.8	76.8	78.3	78.1	73.5	56.3	13.3
1979	63.7	57.9	64.3	77.5	79.2	79.2	74.3	56.2	13.1
1980	63.8	56.7	64.5	77.2	79.9	80.0	74.9	55.7	12.5
1981	63.9	55.4	64.8	77.3	80.5	80.7	75.7	55.0	12.2
1982	64.0	54.1	65.0	77.1	81.0	81.2	75.9	55.1	11.9
1983	64.0	53.5	65.0	77.2	81.3	81.6	76.0	54.5	11.7
1984	64.4	53.9	65.3	77.6	81.8	82.4	76.5	54.2	11.1
1985	64.8	54.5	65.7	78.2	82.5	83.1	77.3	54.2	10.8
1986	65.3	54.7	66.2	78.9	82.9	83.7	78.0	54.0	10.9
1987	65.6	54.7	66.5	78.9	83.3	84.3	78.6	54.4	11.1
1988	65.9	55.3	66.8	78.7	83.3	84.6	79.6	54.6	11.5
1989	66.5	55.9	67.3	78.7	83.8	85.1	80.5	55.5	11.8
1990	66.5	53.7	67.6	77.8	83.6	85.2	80.7	55.9	11.8
1991	66.2	51.6	67.3	76.7	83.2	85.2	81.0	55.5	11.5
1992	66.4	51.3	67.6	77.0	83.7	85.1	81.5	56.2	11.5
1993	66.3	51.5	67.5	77.0	83.3	84.9	81.6	56.4	11.2
1994	66.6	52.7	67.7	77.0	83.2	84.8	81.7	56.8	12.4
1995	66.6	53.5	67.7	76.6	83.8	84.6	81.4	57.2	12.1
1996	66.8	52.3	67.9	76.8	84.1	84.8	82.1	57.9	12.1
1997	67.1	51.6	68.4	77.6	84.4	85.1	82.6	58.9	12.2
1998	67.1	52.8	68.3	77.5	84.6	84.7	82.5	59.3	11.9
1999	67.1	52.0	68.3	77.5	84.6	84.9	82.6	59.3	12.3
2000	67.1	52.0	68.3	77.8	84.6	84.8	82.5	59.2	12.9
2001	66.8	49.6	68.2	77.1	84.0	84.6	82.3	60.4	13.0
2002	66.6	47.4	68.1	76.4	83.7	84.1	82.1	61.9	13.2
2003	66.2	44.5	67.9	75.4	82.9	83.9	82.1	62.4	14.0
2004	66.0	43.9	67.7	75.0	82.7	83.6	81.8	62.3	14.4
2005	66.0	43.7	67.8	74.6	82.8	83.8	81.7	62.9	15.1
2006	66.2	43.7	67.9	74.6	83.0	83.8	81.9	63.7	15.4
2007	66.0	41.3	68.0	74.4	83.3	83.8	82.0	63.8	16.0
2008	66.0	40.2	68.0	74.4	83.3	84.1	81.9	64.5	16.8
2009	65.4	37.5	67.5	72.9	82.7	83.7	81.6	64.9	17.2
2010	64.7	34.9	67.0	71.4	82.2	83.2	81.2	64.9	17.4
2011	64.1	34.1	66.4	71.3	81.5	82.7	80.7	64.3	17.9
2012	63.7	34.3	65.9	70.9	81.7	82.6	80.2	64.5	18.5

Table 1-8. Civilian Labor Force Participation Rates, by Age, Sex, Race, and Hispanic Origin, 1948–2012—*Continued*

(Percent.)

Race, Hispanic origin, sex, and year	16 years and over	16 to 19 years	20 years and over						
			Total	20 to 24 years	25 to 34 years	35 to 44 years	45 to 54 years	55 to 64 years	65 years and over
ALL RACES									
Men									
1948	86.6	63.7	88.6	84.6	95.9	97.9	95.8	89.5	46.8
1949	86.4	62.8	88.5	86.6	95.8	97.9	95.6	87.5	47.0
1950	86.4	63.2	88.4	87.9	96.0	97.6	95.8	86.9	45.8
1951	86.3	63.0	88.2	88.4	96.9	97.5	95.9	87.2	44.9
1952	86.3	61.3	88.3	88.1	97.5	97.8	96.2	87.5	42.6
1953	86.0	60.7	88.0	87.7	97.4	98.2	96.5	87.9	41.6
1954	85.5	58.0	87.8	86.9	97.3	98.1	96.5	88.7	40.5
1955	85.4	58.9	87.6	86.9	97.6	98.1	96.4	87.9	39.6
1956	85.5	60.5	87.6	87.8	97.3	97.9	96.6	88.5	40.0
1957	84.8	59.1	86.9	87.1	97.1	97.9	96.3	87.5	37.5
1958	84.2	56.6	86.6	86.9	97.1	97.9	96.3	87.8	35.6
1959	83.7	55.8	86.3	87.8	97.4	97.8	96.0	87.4	34.2
1960	83.3	56.1	86.0	88.1	97.5	97.7	95.7	86.8	33.1
1961	82.9	54.6	85.7	87.8	97.5	97.6	95.6	87.3	31.7
1962	82.0	53.8	84.8	86.9	97.2	97.6	95.6	86.2	30.3
1963	81.4	52.9	84.4	86.1	97.1	97.5	95.7	86.2	28.4
1964	81.0	52.4	84.2	86.1	97.3	97.3	95.7	85.6	28.0
1965	80.7	53.8	83.9	85.8	97.2	97.3	95.6	84.6	27.9
1966	80.4	55.3	83.6	85.1	97.3	97.2	95.3	84.5	27.1
1967	80.4	55.6	83.4	84.4	97.2	97.3	95.2	84.4	27.1
1968	80.1	55.1	83.1	82.8	96.9	97.1	94.9	84.3	27.3
1969	79.8	55.9	82.8	82.8	96.7	96.9	94.6	83.4	27.2
1970	79.7	56.1	82.6	83.3	96.4	96.9	94.3	83.0	26.8
1971	79.1	56.1	82.1	83.0	95.9	96.5	93.9	82.1	25.5
1972	78.9	58.1	81.6	83.9	95.7	96.4	93.2	80.4	24.3
1973	78.8	59.7	81.3	85.2	95.7	96.2	93.0	78.2	22.7
1974	78.7	60.7	81.0	85.9	95.8	96.0	92.2	77.3	22.4
1975	77.9	59.1	80.3	84.5	95.2	95.6	92.1	75.6	21.6
1976	77.5	59.3	79.8	85.2	95.2	95.4	91.6	74.3	20.2
1977	77.7	60.9	79.7	85.6	95.3	95.7	91.1	73.8	20.0
1978	77.9	62.0	79.8	85.9	95.3	95.7	91.3	73.3	20.4
1979	77.8	61.5	79.8	86.4	95.3	95.7	91.4	72.8	19.9
1980	77.4	60.5	79.4	85.9	95.2	95.5	91.2	72.1	19.0
1981	77.0	59.0	79.0	85.5	94.9	95.4	91.4	70.6	18.4
1982	76.6	56.7	78.7	84.9	94.7	95.3	91.2	70.2	17.8
1983	76.4	56.2	78.5	84.8	94.2	95.2	91.2	69.4	17.4
1984	76.4	56.0	78.3	85.0	94.4	95.4	91.2	68.5	16.3
1985	76.3	56.8	78.1	85.0	94.7	95.0	91.0	67.9	15.8
1986	76.3	56.4	78.1	85.8	94.6	94.8	91.0	67.3	16.0
1987	76.2	56.1	78.0	85.2	94.6	94.6	90.7	67.6	16.3
1988	76.2	56.9	77.9	85.0	94.3	94.5	90.9	67.0	16.5
1989	76.4	57.9	78.1	85.3	94.4	94.5	91.1	67.2	16.6
1990	76.4	55.7	78.2	84.4	94.1	94.3	90.7	67.8	16.3
1991	75.8	53.2	77.7	83.5	93.6	94.1	90.5	67.0	15.7
1992	75.8	53.4	77.7	83.3	93.8	93.7	90.7	67.0	16.1
1993	75.4	53.2	77.3	83.2	93.4	93.4	90.1	66.5	15.6
1994	75.1	54.1	76.8	83.1	92.6	92.8	89.1	65.5	16.8
1995	75.0	54.8	76.7	83.1	93.0	92.3	88.8	66.0	16.8
1996	74.9	53.2	76.8	82.5	93.2	92.4	89.1	67.0	16.9
1997	75.0	52.3	77.0	82.5	93.0	92.6	89.5	67.6	17.1
1998	74.9	53.3	76.8	82.0	93.2	92.6	89.2	68.1	16.5
1999	74.7	52.9	76.7	81.9	93.3	92.8	88.8	67.9	16.9
2000	74.8	52.8	76.7	82.6	93.4	92.7	88.6	67.3	17.7
2001	74.4	50.2	76.5	01.6	92.7	92.5	00.5	00.3	17.7
2002	74.1	47.5	76.3	80.7	92.4	92.1	88.5	69.2	17.9
2003	73.5	44.3	75.9	80.0	91.8	92.1	87.7	68.7	18.6
2004	73.3	43.9	75.8	79.6	91.9	91.9	87.5	68.7	19.0
2005	73.3	43.2	75.8	79.1	91.7	92.1	87.7	69.3	19.8
2006	73.5	43.7	75.9	79.6	91.7	92.1	88.1	69.6	20.3
2007	73.2	41.1	75.9	78.7	92.2	92.3	88.2	69.6	20.5
2008	73.0	40.1	75.7	78.7	91.5	92.2	88.0	70.4	21.5
2009	72.0	37.3	74.8	76.2	90.3	91.7	87.4	70.2	21.9
2010	71.2	34.9	74.1	74.5	89.7	91.5	86.8	70.0	22.1
2011	70.5	33.7	73.4	74.7	89.2	90.9	86.2	69.3	22.8
2012	70.2	34.0	73.0	74.5	89.5	90.7	86.1	69.9	23.6

Table 1-8. Civilian Labor Force Participation Rates, by Age, Sex, Race, and Hispanic Origin, 1948–2012—*Continued*

(Percent.)

Race, Hispanic origin, sex, and year	16 years and over	16 to 19 years	20 years and over						
			Total	20 to 24 years	25 to 34 years	35 to 44 years	45 to 54 years	55 to 64 years	65 years and over
ALL RACES									
Women									
1948	32.7	42.0	31.8	45.3	33.2	36.9	35.0	24.3	9.1
1949	33.1	42.4	32.3	45.0	33.4	38.1	35.9	25.3	9.6
1950	33.9	41.0	33.3	46.0	34.0	39.1	37.9	27.0	9.7
1951	34.6	42.4	34.0	46.5	35.4	39.8	39.7	27.6	8.9
1952	34.7	42.2	34.1	44.7	35.4	40.4	40.1	28.7	9.1
1953	34.4	40.7	33.9	44.3	34.0	41.3	40.4	29.1	10.0
1954	34.6	39.4	34.2	45.1	34.4	41.2	41.2	30.0	9.3
1955	35.7	39.7	35.4	45.9	34.9	41.6	43.8	32.5	10.6
1956	36.9	42.2	36.4	46.3	35.4	43.1	45.5	34.9	10.8
1957	36.9	41.1	36.5	45.9	35.6	43.3	46.5	34.5	10.5
1958	37.1	39.0	36.9	46.3	35.6	43.4	47.8	35.2	10.3
1959	37.1	38.2	37.1	45.1	35.3	43.4	49.0	36.6	10.2
1960	37.7	39.3	37.6	46.1	36.0	43.4	49.9	37.2	10.8
1961	38.1	39.7	38.0	47.0	36.4	43.8	50.1	37.9	10.7
1962	37.9	39.0	37.8	47.3	36.3	44.1	50.0	38.7	10.0
1963	38.3	38.0	38.3	47.5	37.2	44.9	50.6	39.7	9.6
1964	38.7	37.0	38.9	49.4	37.2	45.0	51.4	40.2	10.1
1965	39.3	38.0	39.4	49.9	38.5	46.1	50.9	41.1	10.0
1966	40.3	41.4	40.1	51.5	39.8	46.8	51.7	41.8	9.6
1967	41.1	41.6	41.1	53.3	41.9	48.1	51.8	42.4	9.6
1968	41.6	41.9	41.6	54.5	42.6	48.9	52.3	42.4	9.6
1969	42.7	43.2	42.7	56.7	43.7	49.9	53.8	43.1	9.9
1970	43.3	44.0	43.3	57.7	45.0	51.1	54.4	43.0	9.7
1971	43.4	43.4	43.3	57.7	45.6	51.6	54.3	42.9	9.5
1972	43.9	45.8	43.7	59.1	47.8	52.0	53.9	42.1	9.3
1973	44.7	47.8	44.4	61.1	50.4	53.3	53.7	41.1	8.9
1974	45.7	49.1	45.3	63.1	52.6	54.7	54.6	40.7	8.1
1975	46.3	49.1	46.0	64.1	54.9	55.8	54.6	40.9	8.2
1976	47.3	49.8	47.0	65.0	57.3	57.8	55.0	41.0	8.2
1977	48.4	51.2	48.1	66.5	59.7	59.6	55.8	40.9	8.1
1978	50.0	53.7	49.6	68.3	62.2	61.6	57.1	41.3	8.3
1979	50.9	54.2	50.6	69.0	63.9	63.6	58.3	41.7	8.3
1980	51.5	52.9	51.3	68.9	65.5	65.5	59.9	41.3	8.1
1981	52.1	51.8	52.1	69.6	66.7	66.8	61.1	41.4	8.0
1982	52.6	51.4	52.7	69.8	68.0	68.0	61.6	41.8	7.9
1983	52.9	50.8	53.1	69.9	69.0	68.7	61.9	41.5	7.8
1984	53.6	51.8	53.7	70.4	69.8	70.1	62.9	41.7	7.5
1985	54.5	52.1	54.7	71.8	70.9	71.8	64.4	42.0	7.3
1986	55.3	53.0	55.5	72.4	71.6	73.1	65.9	42.3	7.4
1987	56.0	53.3	56.2	73.0	72.4	74.5	67.1	42.7	7.4
1988	56.6	53.6	56.8	72.7	72.7	75.2	69.0	43.5	7.9
1989	57.4	53.9	57.7	72.4	73.5	76.0	70.5	45.0	8.4
1990	57.5	51.6	58.0	71.3	73.5	76.4	71.2	45.2	8.6
1991	57.4	50.0	57.9	70.1	73.1	76.5	72.0	45.2	8.5
1992	57.8	49.1	58.5	70.9	73.9	76.7	72.6	46.5	8.3
1993	57.9	49.7	58.5	70.9	73.4	76.6	73.5	47.2	8.1
1994	58.8	51.3	59.3	71.0	74.0	77.1	74.6	48.9	9.2
1995	58.9	52.2	59.4	70.3	74.9	77.2	74.4	49.2	8.8
1996	59.3	51.3	59.9	71.3	75.2	77.5	75.4	49.6	8.6
1997	59.8	51.0	60.5	72.7	76.0	77.7	76.0	50.9	8.6
1998	59.8	52.3	60.4	73.0	76.3	77.1	76.2	51.2	8.6
1999	60.0	51.0	60.7	73.2	76.4	77.2	76.7	51.5	8.9
2000	59.9	51.2	60.6	73.1	76.1	77.2	76.8	51.9	9.4
2001	59.8	49.0	60.6	72.7	75.5	77.1	76.4	53.2	9.6
2002	59.6	47.3	60.5	72.1	75.1	76.4	76.0	55.2	9.8
2003	59.5	44.8	60.6	70.8	74.1	76.0	76.8	56.6	10.6
2004	59.2	43.8	60.3	70.5	73.6	75.6	76.5	56.3	11.1
2005	59.3	44.2	60.4	70.1	73.9	75.8	76.0	57.0	11.5
2006	59.4	43.7	60.5	69.5	74.4	75.9	76.0	58.2	11.7
2007	59.3	41.5	60.6	70.1	74.5	75.5	76.0	58.3	12.6
2008	59.5	40.2	60.9	70.0	75.2	76.1	76.1	59.1	13.3
2009	59.2	37.7	60.8	69.6	75.0	75.9	76.0	60.0	13.6
2010	58.6	35.0	60.3	68.3	74.7	75.2	75.7	60.2	13.8
2011	58.1	34.6	59.8	67.8	73.9	74.7	75.4	59.5	14.0
2012	57.7	34.6	59.3	67.4	74.1	74.8	74.7	59.4	14.4

Table 1-8. Civilian Labor Force Participation Rates, by Age, Sex, Race, and Hispanic Origin, 1948–2012—*Continued*

(Percent.)

Race, Hispanic origin, sex, and year	16 years and over	16 to 19 years	20 years and over						
			Total	20 to 24 years	25 to 34 years	35 to 44 years	45 to 54 years	55 to 64 years	65 years and over
WHITE									
Both Sexes									
1954	58.2	48.8	58.9	61.0	63.5	68.0	67.9	58.4	23.7
1955	58.7	49.3	59.5	62.4	64.0	68.3	69.2	59.3	23.9
1956	59.4	51.3	60.1	64.1	64.0	68.9	70.1	60.6	24.2
1957	59.1	50.3	59.8	63.7	64.1	68.8	70.5	59.9	22.8
1958	58.9	47.9	59.8	64.1	64.2	68.8	71.0	60.3	21.7
1959	58.7	47.4	59.7	63.7	64.3	68.7	71.5	60.7	21.0
1960	58.8	47.9	59.8	64.8	64.7	68.6	71.7	60.6	20.8
1961	58.8	47.4	59.9	65.5	64.8	68.8	71.7	61.3	20.0
1962	58.3	46.6	59.4	65.0	64.4	69.0	71.8	61.3	19.0
1963	58.2	45.7	59.4	64.9	64.8	69.4	72.3	61.8	17.9
1964	58.2	45.1	59.6	65.8	64.9	69.5	72.5	61.8	17.8
1965	58.4	46.5	59.7	65.7	65.6	70.1	72.2	61.7	17.7
1966	58.7	49.1	59.8	66.0	66.3	70.4	72.5	61.9	17.1
1967	59.2	49.2	60.3	66.8	67.4	71.2	72.5	62.3	17.0
1968	59.3	49.3	60.4	66.6	67.9	71.7	72.7	62.2	17.1
1969	59.9	50.6	60.9	67.9	68.4	72.3	73.3	62.1	17.2
1970	60.2	51.4	61.2	69.2	69.1	72.9	73.5	61.8	16.8
1971	60.1	51.6	61.1	69.6	69.3	73.0	73.4	61.3	16.1
1972	60.4	54.1	61.2	71.2	70.4	73.2	72.9	60.3	15.4
1973	60.8	56.0	61.4	73.3	72.0	73.9	72.7	58.6	14.4
1974	61.4	57.3	61.9	74.8	73.4	74.6	73.0	58.0	13.9
1975	61.5	56.7	62.0	75.2	74.4	75.1	73.0	57.4	13.6
1976	61.8	57.5	62.3	76.0	75.6	76.1	73.0	56.9	13.0
1977	62.5	59.3	62.9	77.1	77.0	77.1	73.2	56.6	12.9
1978	63.3	60.8	63.6	78.1	78.3	78.1	73.8	56.4	13.1
1979	63.9	61.1	64.2	78.9	79.4	79.3	74.6	56.5	12.9
1980	64.1	60.0	64.5	78.7	80.2	80.3	75.4	56.0	12.5
1981	64.3	58.9	64.8	79.1	81.0	81.0	76.2	55.2	12.2
1982	64.3	57.5	65.0	78.9	81.6	81.5	76.4	55.3	12.0
1983	64.3	56.9	65.0	79.0	81.8	81.9	76.5	54.7	11.8
1984	64.6	57.2	65.3	79.4	82.5	82.6	77.0	54.5	11.1
1985	65.0	57.5	65.7	79.9	83.1	83.4	77.8	54.4	10.7
1986	65.5	57.8	66.1	80.6	83.6	84.0	78.5	54.3	11.0
1987	65.8	57.7	66.5	80.7	84.0	84.7	79.1	54.6	11.1
1988	66.2	58.6	66.8	80.6	84.1	85.0	80.3	55.1	11.4
1989	66.7	59.1	67.3	80.2	84.5	85.5	81.2	56.2	11.8
1990	66.9	57.5	67.6	79.8	84.6	85.9	81.3	56.5	11.9
1991	66.6	55.8	67.4	78.9	84.3	85.9	81.8	56.0	11.6
1992	66.8	54.7	67.7	79.4	84.6	85.8	82.2	56.8	11.6
1993	66.8	55.1	67.6	79.5	84.5	85.7	82.5	57.1	11.4
1994	67.1	56.4	67.9	79.5	84.4	85.7	82.7	57.6	12.5
1995	67.1	57.1	67.8	78.7	84.9	85.5	82.5	58.0	12.3
1996	67.2	55.9	68.1	79.1	84.9	85.7	83.1	58.7	12.3
1997	67.5	55.2	68.4	79.6	85.3	85.8	83.5	59.9	12.3
1998	67.3	56.0	68.2	79.5	85.4	85.3	83.4	60.1	12.0
1999	67.3	55.5	68.2	79.5	85.1	85.4	83.5	60.2	12.5
2000	67.3	55.5	68.2	79.9	85.1	85.4	83.5	60.0	13.0
2001	67.0	53.1	68.1	79.2	84.5	85.2	83.3	61.2	13.0
2002	66.8	50.5	68.1	78.6	84.5	84.7	83.0	62.8	13.3
2003	66.5	47.7	67.9	77.7	83.6	84.3	83.0	63.3	14.1
2004	66.3	47.1	67.7	77.1	83.5	84.1	82.9	63.2	14.6
2005	66.3	46.9	67.7	76.3	83.5	84.2	82.8	63.7	15.1
2006	66.5	46.7	67.9	76.5	83.8	84.3	83.0	64.7	15.5
2007	66.4	44.4	68.0	76.4	84.1	84.1	83.1	64.9	16.2
2008	66.3	43.1	68.0	76.3	83.9	84.4	82.9	65.7	17.0
2009	65.8	40.6	67.7	75.1	83.5	84.2	82.7	66.2	17.4
2010	65.1	37.7	67.1	73.4	83.2	83.8	82.2	66.1	17.6
2011	64.5	36.8	66.5	73.2	82.5	83.3	81.7	65.5	18.1
2012	64.0	36.9	65.9	73.1	82.6	83.2	81.2	65.9	18.7

Table 1-8. Civilian Labor Force Participation Rates, by Age, Sex, Race, and Hispanic Origin, 1948–2012—*Continued*

(Percent.)

Race, Hispanic origin, sex, and year	16 years and over	16 to 19 years	20 years and over						
			Total	20 to 24 years	25 to 34 years	35 to 44 years	45 to 54 years	55 to 64 years	65 years and over
WHITE									
Men									
1954	85.6	57.6	87.8	86.3	97.5	98.2	96.8	89.1	40.4
1955	85.4	58.6	87.5	86.5	97.8	98.2	96.7	88.4	39.6
1956	85.6	60.4	87.6	87.6	97.4	98.1	96.8	88.9	40.0
1957	84.8	59.2	86.9	86.6	97.2	98.0	96.7	88.0	37.7
1958	84.3	56.5	86.6	86.7	97.2	98.0	96.6	88.2	35.7
1959	83.8	55.9	86.3	87.3	97.5	98.0	96.3	87.9	34.3
1960	83.4	55.9	86.0	87.8	97.7	97.9	96.1	87.2	33.3
1961	83.0	54.5	85.7	87.6	97.7	97.9	95.9	87.8	31.9
1962	82.1	53.8	84.9	86.5	97.4	97.9	96.0	86.7	30.6
1963	81.5	53.1	84.4	85.8	97.4	97.8	96.2	86.6	28.4
1964	81.1	52.7	84.2	85.7	97.5	97.6	96.1	86.1	27.9
1965	80.8	54.1	83.9	85.3	97.4	97.7	95.9	85.2	27.9
1966	80.6	55.9	83.6	84.4	97.5	97.6	95.8	84.9	27.2
1967	80.6	56.3	83.5	84.0	97.5	97.7	95.6	84.9	27.1
1968	80.4	55.9	83.2	82.4	97.2	97.6	95.4	84.7	27.4
1969	80.2	56.8	83.0	82.6	97.0	97.4	95.1	83.9	27.3
1970	80.0	57.5	82.8	83.3	96.7	97.3	94.9	83.3	26.7
1971	79.6	57.9	82.3	83.2	96.3	97.0	94.7	82.6	25.6
1972	79.6	60.1	82.0	84.3	96.0	97.0	94.0	81.1	24.4
1973	79.4	62.0	81.6	85.8	96.2	96.8	93.5	78.9	22.7
1974	79.4	62.9	81.4	86.6	96.3	96.7	93.0	78.0	22.4
1975	78.7	61.9	80.7	85.5	95.8	96.4	92.9	76.4	21.7
1976	78.4	62.3	80.3	86.3	95.9	96.0	92.5	75.2	20.2
1977	78.5	64.0	80.2	86.8	96.0	96.2	92.1	74.6	20.0
1978	78.6	65.0	80.1	87.3	95.9	96.3	92.1	73.7	20.3
1979	78.6	64.8	80.1	87.6	96.0	96.4	92.2	73.4	20.0
1980	78.2	63.7	79.8	87.2	95.9	96.2	92.1	73.1	19.1
1981	77.9	62.4	79.5	87.0	95.8	96.1	92.4	71.5	18.5
1982	77.4	60.0	79.2	86.3	95.6	96.0	92.2	71.0	17.9
1983	77.1	59.4	78.9	86.1	95.2	96.0	91.9	70.0	17.7
1984	77.1	59.0	78.7	86.5	95.4	96.1	92.0	69.5	16.4
1985	77.0	59.7	78.5	86.4	95.7	95.7	92.0	68.8	15.9
1986	76.9	59.3	78.5	87.3	95.5	95.4	91.8	68.0	16.3
1987	76.8	59.0	78.4	86.9	95.5	95.4	91.6	68.1	16.5
1988	76.9	60.0	78.3	86.6	95.2	95.4	91.8	67.9	16.7
1989	77.1	61.0	78.5	86.8	95.4	95.3	92.2	68.3	16.8
1990	77.1	59.6	78.5	86.2	95.2	95.3	91.7	68.6	16.6
1991	76.5	57.3	78.0	85.4	94.9	95.0	91.4	67.7	15.9
1992	76.5	56.9	78.0	85.2	94.9	94.7	91.8	67.7	16.2
1993	76.2	56.6	77.7	85.5	94.7	94.5	91.3	67.3	15.9
1994	75.9	57.7	77.3	85.5	93.9	93.9	90.3	66.4	17.2
1995	75.7	58.5	77.1	85.1	94.1	93.4	90.0	67.1	16.9
1996	75.8	57.1	77.3	85.0	94.4	93.6	90.4	68.0	17.2
1997	75.9	56.1	77.5	85.1	94.2	93.7	90.6	68.9	17.4
1998	75.6	56.6	77.2	84.6	94.4	93.7	90.3	69.1	16.6
1999	75.6	56.4	77.2	84.9	94.3	93.8	90.1	69.1	17.2
2000	75.5	56.5	77.1	85.2	94.5	93.8	89.7	68.2	17.9
2001	75.1	53.7	76.9	84.1	93.9	93.6	89.7	69.1	17.8
2002	74.8	50.3	76.7	83.2	93.7	93.2	89.6	70.2	17.8
2003	74.2	47.5	76.3	82.5	93.3	93.1	88.8	69.7	18.6
2004	74.1	47.4	76.2	82.1	93.2	93.0	88.7	69.8	19.1
2005	74.1	46.2	76.2	81.4	93.0	93.0	89.0	70.4	20.0
2006	74.3	46.9	76.4	81.9	92.9	93.1	89.3	71.0	20.6
2007	74.0	44.3	76.3	80.9	93.4	93.1	89.6	71.2	20.8
2008	73.7	43.0	76.1	80.8	92.6	93.0	89.2	71.9	21.8
2009	72.8	40.3	75.3	78.6	91.6	92.7	88.8	71.8	22.2
2010	72.0	37.4	74.6	77.0	91.1	92.4	88.1	71.2	22.3
2011	71.3	36.1	73.9	77.1	90.5	92.1	87.5	70.8	23.0
2012	71.0	36.7	73.5	77.2	90.9	91.8	87.5	71.6	24.0

Table 1-8. Civilian Labor Force Participation Rates, by Age, Sex, Race, and Hispanic Origin, 1948–2012—*Continued*

(Percent.)

Race, Hispanic origin, sex, and year	16 years and over	16 to 19 years	20 years and over						
			Total	20 to 24 years	25 to 34 years	35 to 44 years	45 to 54 years	55 to 64 years	65 years and over
WHITE									
Women									
1954	33.3	40.6	32.7	44.4	32.5	39.3	39.8	29.1	9.1
1955	34.5	40.7	34.0	45.8	32.8	40.0	42.7	31.8	10.5
1956	35.7	43.1	35.1	46.5	33.2	41.5	44.4	34.0	10.6
1957	35.7	42.2	35.2	45.8	33.6	41.5	45.4	33.7	10.2
1958	35.8	40.1	35.5	46.0	33.6	41.4	46.5	34.5	10.1
1959	36.0	39.6	35.6	44.5	33.4	41.4	47.8	35.7	10.0
1960	36.5	40.3	36.2	45.7	34.1	41.5	48.6	36.2	10.6
1961	36.9	40.6	36.6	46.9	34.3	41.8	48.9	37.2	10.5
1962	36.7	39.8	36.5	47.1	34.1	42.2	48.9	38.0	9.8
1963	37.2	38.7	37.0	47.3	34.8	43.1	49.5	38.9	9.4
1964	37.5	37.8	37.5	48.8	35.0	43.3	50.2	39.4	9.9
1965	38.1	39.2	38.0	49.2	36.3	44.4	49.9	40.3	9.7
1966	39.2	42.6	38.8	51.0	37.7	45.0	50.6	41.1	9.4
1967	40.1	42.5	39.8	53.1	39.7	46.4	50.9	41.9	9.3
1968	40.7	43.0	40.4	54.0	40.6	47.5	51.5	42.0	9.4
1969	41.8	44.6	41.5	56.4	41.7	48.6	53.0	42.6	9.7
1970	42.6	45.6	42.2	57.7	43.2	49.9	53.7	42.6	9.5
1971	42.6	45.4	42.3	58.0	43.7	50.2	53.6	42.5	9.3
1972	43.2	48.1	42.7	59.4	46.0	50.7	53.4	41.9	9.0
1973	44.1	50.1	43.5	61.7	48.7	52.2	53.4	40.7	8.7
1974	45.2	51.7	44.4	63.9	51.3	53.6	54.3	40.4	8.0
1975	45.9	51.5	45.3	65.5	53.8	54.9	54.3	40.6	8.0
1976	46.9	52.8	46.2	66.3	56.0	57.1	54.7	40.7	7.9
1977	48.0	54.5	47.3	67.8	58.5	58.9	55.3	40.7	7.9
1978	49.4	56.7	48.7	69.3	61.2	60.7	56.7	41.1	8.1
1979	50.5	57.4	49.8	70.5	63.1	63.0	58.1	41.5	8.1
1980	51.2	56.2	50.6	70.6	64.8	65.0	59.6	40.9	7.9
1981	51.9	55.4	51.5	71.5	66.4	66.4	60.9	40.9	7.9
1982	52.4	55.0	52.2	71.8	67.8	67.5	61.4	41.5	7.8
1983	52.7	54.5	52.5	72.1	68.7	68.2	61.9	41.1	7.8
1984	53.3	55.4	53.1	72.5	69.8	69.6	62.7	41.2	7.5
1985	54.1	55.2	54.0	73.8	70.9	71.4	64.2	41.5	7.0
1986	55.0	56.3	54.9	74.1	71.8	72.9	65.8	42.1	7.3
1987	55.7	56.5	55.6	74.8	72.5	74.2	67.2	42.4	7.2
1988	56.4	57.2	56.3	74.9	73.0	74.9	69.2	43.6	7.7
1989	57.2	57.1	57.2	74.0	73.8	75.9	70.6	45.2	8.2
1990	57.4	55.3	57.6	73.4	74.1	76.6	71.3	45.5	8.5
1991	57.4	54.1	57.6	72.5	73.8	76.8	72.4	45.4	8.5
1992	57.7	52.5	58.1	73.5	74.4	77.0	72.8	46.8	8.2
1993	58.0	53.5	58.3	73.4	74.3	76.9	74.0	47.6	8.1
1994	58.9	55.1	59.2	73.4	74.9	77.5	75.2	49.4	9.2
1995	59.0	55.5	59.2	72.3	75.8	77.6	75.2	49.5	9.0
1996	59.1	54.7	59.4	73.3	75.5	77.8	76.1	50.1	8.7
1997	59.5	54.1	59.9	73.9	76.3	77.9	76.6	51.5	8.6
1998	59.4	55.4	59.7	74.3	76.3	76.9	76.6	51.6	8.7
1999	59.6	54.5	59.9	73.9	76.0	77.1	77.1	52.0	8.9
2000	59.5	54.5	59.9	74.5	75.7	77.2	77.5	52.4	9.4
2001	59.4	52.4	59.9	74.2	75.1	77.0	77.1	53.8	9.6
2002	59.3	50.8	60.0	74.0	75.0	76.3	76.6	55.8	9.9
2003	59.2	47.9	59.9	72.7	73.7	75.5	77.3	57.4	10.8
2004	58.9	46.7	59.7	71.9	73.6	75.2	77.1	57.0	11.2
2005	50.9	47.6	59.7	71.0	73.7	75.4	76.7	57.5	11.4
2006	59.0	46.6	59.9	70.9	74.3	75.5	76.7	58.7	11.6
2007	59.0	44.6	60.1	71.6	74.5	75.0	76.6	58.9	12.7
2008	59.2	43.3	60.3	71.6	74.9	75.8	76.6	59.7	13.3
2009	59.1	40.9	60.4	71.6	75.1	75.7	76.7	60.8	13.6
2010	58.5	38.0	59.9	69.7	74.9	75.0	76.3	61.1	13.9
2011	58.0	37.5	59.4	69.1	74.2	74.4	76.1	60.6	14.1
2012	57.4	37.1	58.7	69.0	74.3	74.5	75.2	60.5	14.4

Table 1-8. Civilian Labor Force Participation Rates, by Age, Sex, Race, and Hispanic Origin, 1948–2012—*Continued*

(Percent.)

Race, Hispanic origin, sex, and year	16 years and over	16 to 19 years	20 years and over						
			Total	20 to 24 years	25 to 34 years	35 to 44 years	45 to 54 years	55 to 64 years	65 years and over
BLACK									
Both Sexes									
1974	59.8	39.8	63.0	69.8	75.8	74.6	69.1	54.7	15.1
1975	58.8	38.2	62.0	66.1	75.6	74.1	69.0	54.3	14.9
1976	59.0	37.0	62.5	66.8	77.4	74.9	68.6	53.4	14.9
1977	59.8	37.9	63.2	68.2	78.3	75.9	69.0	53.7	14.5
1978	61.5	41.0	64.5	69.9	79.6	77.4	70.4	54.8	15.3
1979	61.4	40.1	64.5	70.0	79.2	77.9	71.1	53.5	14.5
1980	61.0	38.9	64.1	69.0	79.5	77.4	71.4	52.6	13.0
1981	60.8	37.7	64.2	69.2	78.5	78.4	71.2	52.8	12.0
1982	61.0	36.6	64.3	68.6	78.7	79.8	71.1	52.3	11.5
1983	61.5	36.4	64.9	68.4	79.8	80.2	72.1	52.5	10.5
1984	62.2	38.3	65.2	69.2	79.3	81.0	73.0	51.6	10.3
1985	62.9	41.2	65.6	70.0	79.8	81.5	73.4	51.4	11.2
1986	63.3	41.3	65.9	71.7	80.1	81.9	74.3	50.6	9.7
1987	63.8	41.6	66.5	70.5	80.7	82.6	74.7	52.4	10.7
1988	63.8	40.8	66.5	70.5	80.8	82.6	75.0	50.6	11.5
1989	64.2	42.5	66.7	72.2	80.9	82.7	75.5	48.3	11.6
1990	64.0	38.7	66.9	68.8	79.7	82.4	76.5	49.6	11.1
1991	63.3	35.4	66.4	67.7	78.5	82.0	76.2	50.4	10.7
1992	63.9	37.9	66.8	67.4	79.7	81.4	76.2	51.6	10.6
1993	63.2	37.0	66.0	67.8	78.3	81.0	75.2	50.2	9.5
1994	63.4	38.5	66.0	68.8	78.3	80.8	74.8	49.3	10.6
1995	63.7	39.9	66.3	68.7	80.0	80.4	74.1	50.3	10.5
1996	64.1	39.2	66.9	69.0	81.1	81.0	74.9	50.9	9.8
1997	64.7	38.7	67.6	70.9	82.0	81.4	76.3	50.5	10.0
1998	65.6	41.6	68.2	70.6	83.0	82.2	76.7	52.3	10.3
1999	65.8	38.7	68.9	71.4	85.2	83.0	76.4	51.4	10.4
2000	65.8	39.4	68.7	71.8	84.1	82.3	76.9	52.5	11.6
2001	65.3	37.6	68.2	69.9	83.6	82.0	75.9	53.9	12.6
2002	64.8	36.0	67.8	68.6	82.4	81.6	76.1	54.7	12.5
2003	64.3	32.4	67.6	68.2	81.6	82.9	75.8	54.4	12.9
2004	63.8	31.4	67.2	68.3	81.2	82.1	75.5	54.4	13.1
2005	64.2	32.4	67.4	69.0	81.7	82.3	75.7	55.3	13.6
2006	64.1	34.0	67.3	68.8	81.8	82.0	75.8	55.4	13.7
2007	63.7	30.3	67.2	68.3	81.7	82.7	75.7	55.1	14.0
2008	63.7	29.4	67.4	68.0	82.2	83.0	76.1	55.6	15.0
2009	62.4	27.2	66.1	66.0	80.4	81.7	75.2	55.5	15.3
2010	62.2	25.5	66.0	66.9	80.5	81.4	75.0	55.7	15.2
2011	61.4	24.9	65.0	66.5	79.1	80.6	73.9	54.5	16.1
2012	61.5	26.9	64.9	66.5	79.4	80.7	74.5	55.3	16.4
BLACK									
Men									
1974	72.9	46.7	77.6	83.6	92.8	90.4	84.0	76.5	21.6
1975	70.9	42.6	76.0	78.7	91.6	89.4	83.5	76.0	20.7
1976	70.0	41.3	75.4	79.0	90.9	89.9	82.4	73.3	19.8
1977	70.6	43.2	75.6	79.2	90.7	91.0	82.0	74.2	20.0
1978	71.5	44.9	76.2	78.8	90.9	90.5	83.2	75.3	21.1
1979	71.3	43.6	76.3	80.7	90.8	90.4	84.5	72.2	19.5
1980	70.3	43.2	75.1	79.9	90.9	89.1	83.0	70.2	16.9
1981	70.0	41.6	74.5	79.2	88.9	89.3	82.7	70.8	16.0
1982	70.1	39.8	74.7	78.7	89.2	89.8	82.2	72.7	15.9
1983	70.6	39.9	75.2	79.4	89.0	89.7	84.5	72.4	14.0
1984	70.8	41.7	74.8	79.1	88.9	90.0	83.7	68.3	13.7
1985	70.8	44.6	74.4	79.0	88.8	89.8	83.0	68.6	13.9
1986	71.2	43.7	74.8	80.1	89.6	89.6	84.1	70.8	12.6
1987	71.1	43.6	74.7	77.8	89.4	88.6	83.7	72.4	13.7
1988	71.0	43.8	74.6	79.3	89.3	88.2	83.5	68.8	14.3
1989	71.0	44.6	74.4	80.2	89.7	88.7	82.5	66.4	14.3
1990	71.0	40.7	75.0	76.8	88.8	88.1	83.5	67.3	13.0
1991	70.4	37.3	74.6	76.7	87.3	87.7	83.4	66.4	13.0
1992	70.7	40.6	74.3	75.4	88.0	86.5	81.8	67.8	13.7
1993	69.6	39.5	73.2	74.1	87.3	86.1	80.0	67.0	11.6
1994	69.1	40.8	72.5	73.9	86.2	85.9	79.1	65.2	12.7
1995	69.0	40.1	72.5	74.6	87.5	84.1	78.5	66.1	14.9
1996	68.7	39.5	72.3	73.4	87.5	84.4	78.5	66.4	12.9
1997	68.3	37.4	72.2	72.1	86.8	84.8	80.1	65.6	12.9
1998	69.0	40.7	72.5	71.8	87.1	85.0	79.9	66.1	14.0
1999	68.7	38.6	72.4	69.8	89.2	86.0	78.5	65.9	12.7
2000	69.2	39.2	72.8	73.3	87.8	85.2	79.2	67.7	14.4
2001	68.4	37.9	72.1	69.7	86.6	84.9	78.4	66.4	16.7
2002	68.4	37.3	72.1	70.7	85.9	84.7	79.5	66.8	16.9
2003	67.3	31.1	71.5	71.1	84.7	85.7	77.7	67.5	17.0
2004	66.7	30.0	70.9	69.9	86.1	84.0	76.9	66.7	17.0
2005	67.3	32.6	71.3	70.1	85.5	85.5	78.6	65.7	17.1
2006	67.0	32.3	71.1	71.6	85.7	84.4	79.2	63.9	16.7
2007	66.8	29.4	71.2	71.1	86.1	86.3	78.6	63.0	17.3
2008	66.7	29.1	71.1	71.1	85.3	86.8	79.1	65.7	18.1
2009	65.0	26.4	69.6	67.6	83.2	85.1	77.4	64.0	18.3
2010	65.0	25.8	69.5	66.9	83.4	86.1	77.4	65.2	18.1
2011	64.2	25.7	68.4	67.0	82.6	83.7	76.1	63.0	19.1
2012	63.6	25.6	67.7	66.4	82.5	83.5	75.9	63.3	19.4

Table 1-8. Civilian Labor Force Participation Rates, by Age, Sex, Race, and Hispanic Origin, 1948–2012—*Continued*

(Percent.)

Race, Hispanic origin, sex, and year	16 years and over	16 to 19 years	20 years and over						
			Total	20 to 24 years	25 to 34 years	35 to 44 years	45 to 54 years	55 to 64 years	65 years and over
BLACK									
Women									
1974	49.0	33.4	51.4	58.8	62.4	62.2	56.4	42.8	10.4
1975	48.8	34.2	51.1	55.9	62.8	62.0	56.6	43.1	10.7
1976	49.8	32.9	52.5	56.9	66.7	63.0	56.8	43.7	11.3
1977	50.8	32.9	53.6	59.3	68.5	64.1	57.9	43.7	10.5
1978	53.1	37.3	55.5	62.7	70.6	67.2	59.4	43.8	11.1
1979	53.1	36.8	55.4	61.5	70.1	68.0	59.6	44.0	10.9
1980	53.1	34.9	55.6	60.2	70.5	68.1	61.4	44.8	10.2
1981	53.5	34.0	56.0	61.1	70.0	69.8	62.0	45.4	9.3
1982	53.7	33.5	56.2	60.1	70.2	71.7	62.4	44.8	8.5
1983	54.2	33.0	56.8	59.1	72.3	72.6	62.3	44.8	8.2
1984	55.2	35.0	57.6	60.7	71.5	73.7	64.5	46.1	8.0
1985	56.5	37.9	58.6	62.5	72.4	74.8	65.7	45.3	9.4
1986	56.9	39.1	58.9	64.6	72.4	75.8	66.5	43.6	7.8
1987	58.0	39.6	60.0	64.4	73.5	77.8	67.5	44.4	8.6
1988	58.0	37.9	60.1	63.2	73.7	78.1	68.3	43.4	9.6
1989	58.7	40.4	60.6	65.5	73.6	78.0	70.0	42.4	9.8
1990	58.3	36.8	60.6	62.4	72.3	77.7	70.7	43.2	9.9
1991	57.5	33.5	60.0	60.3	71.4	77.2	70.2	44.1	9.2
1992	58.5	35.2	60.8	60.8	73.1	77.1	71.7	45.1	8.6
1993	57.9	34.6	60.2	62.6	70.9	76.8	71.2	44.4	8.3
1994	58.7	36.3	60.9	64.5	71.9	76.4	71.3	45.3	9.2
1995	59.5	39.8	61.4	63.7	73.9	77.3	70.5	47.2	7.7
1996	60.4	38.9	62.6	65.2	75.9	78.2	72.0	47.2	7.7
1997	61.7	39.9	64.0	69.9	78.1	78.4	73.2	47.6	8.2
1998	62.8	42.5	64.8	69.6	79.6	79.9	74.0	48.5	7.9
1999	63.5	38.8	66.1	72.7	82.1	80.4	74.6	48.4	8.9
2000	63.1	39.6	65.4	70.5	81.1	79.9	74.9	48.6	9.9
2001	62.8	37.3	65.2	70.1	81.2	79.6	73.9	49.9	10.1
2002	61.8	34.7	64.4	66.9	79.7	79.2	73.3	51.8	9.8
2003	61.9	33.7	64.6	65.7	79.1	80.6	74.2	51.9	10.3
2004	61.5	32.8	64.2	66.8	77.2	80.6	74.3	52.3	10.7
2005	61.6	32.2	64.4	68.1	78.5	79.7	73.3	53.7	11.4
2006	61.7	35.6	64.2	66.2	78.6	80.1	73.0	55.1	11.8
2007	61.1	31.2	64.0	65.7	78.0	79.8	73.2	55.7	12.0
2008	61.3	29.7	64.3	65.2	79.6	80.0	73.7	55.3	13.0
2009	60.3	27.9	63.4	64.5	78.0	79.0	73.3	54.4	13.3
2010	59.9	25.1	63.2	66.9	77.9	77.7	73.0	54.9	13.3
2011	59.1	24.2	62.2	65.9	76.0	78.2	72.0	53.4	14.2
2012	59.8	28.2	62.6	66.5	76.9	78.4	73.3	53.9	14.4
HISPANIC									
Both Sexes									
1975	60.8	46.2	. . .	. . .	. . .	. . .	. . .	. . .	. . .
1976	60.8	46.9	62.9	. . .	. . .	. . .	. . .	. . .	. . .
1977	61.6	48.2	63.7	. . .	. . .	. . .	. . .	. . .	. . .
1978	62.9	49.6	65.0	. . .	. . .	. . .	. . .	. . .	. . .
1979	63.6	50.3	65.6	. . .	. . .	. . .	. . .	. . .	. . .
1980	64.0	50.3	66.2	. . .	. . .	. . .	. . .	. . .	. . .
1981	64.1	46.4	66.8	. . .	. . .	. . .	. . .	. . .	. . .
1982	63.6	44.8	66.3	. . .	. . .	. . .	. . .	. . .	. . .
1983	63.8	45.3	66.2	. . .	. . .	. . .	. . .	. . .	. . .
1984	64.9	47.5	67.1	. . .	. . .	. . .	. . .	. . .	. . .
1985	64.6	44.6	67.1	. . .	. . .	. . .	. . .	. . .	. . .
1986	65.4	43.9	68.0	. . .	. . .	. . .	. . .	. . .	. . .
1987	66.4	45.8	68.8	. . .	. . .	. . .	. . .	. . .	. . .
1988	67.4	49.6	69.4	. . .	. . .	. . .	. . .	. . .	. . .
1989	67.6	48.6	69.7	. . .	. . .	. . .	. . .	. . .	. . .
1990	67.4	47.8	69.8	. . .	. . .	. . .	. . .	. . .	. . .
1991	66.5	45.1	69.0	. . .	. . .	. . .	. . .	. . .	. . .
1992	66.8	45.8	69.2	. . .	. . .	. . .	. . .	. . .	. . .
1993	66.2	43.9	68.7	. . .	. . .	. . .	. . .	. . .	. . .
1994	66.1	44.4	68.5	74.0	77.3	78.9	73.1	49.8	10.7
1995	65.8	45.4	68.1	71.9	78.1	78.5	72.8	48.6	10.5
1996	66.5	43.4	69.1	73.1	78.2	79.5	74.6	52.2	11.0
1997	67.9	43.0	70.8	76.4	79.5	80.9	75.4	53.8	11.9
1998	67.9	45.7	70.6	76.1	80.3	80.0	75.3	55.4	10.1
1999	67.7	45.5	70.4	76.0	78.6	81.3	75.9	54.1	11.6
2000	69.7	46.3	72.5	78.2	80.4	81.7	78.0	54.2	12.3
2001	69.5	46.9	72.0	76.6	80.0	81.9	77.4	55.1	10.9
2002	69.1	44.0	71.8	76.3	80.5	81.1	76.1	55.8	11.9
2003	68.3	37.7	71.4	75.6	79.4	81.1	75.3	57.4	12.8
2004	68.6	38.2	71.7	74.5	79.4	81.4	77.6	58.1	14.5
2005	68.0	38.6	71.0	72.7	79.1	81.2	77.2	58.4	13.9
2006	68.7	38.3	71.9	74.4	80.1	81.9	77.3	59.2	15.7
2007	68.8	37.1	72.1	74.8	80.7	81.8	78.6	58.5	16.0
2008	68.5	36.9	71.8	73.7	80.5	82.0	78.2	59.9	16.0
2009	68.0	34.0	71.5	73.1	79.5	81.3	79.3	61.9	17.1
2010	67.5	30.9	71.4	71.1	80.6	81.2	79.2	61.1	17.9
2011	66.5	28.3	70.7	72.0	79.1	80.3	78.9	60.8	17.6
2012	66.4	30.9	70.3	71.2	79.1	80.2	78.4	60.5	16.5

. . . = Not available.

Table 1-8. Civilian Labor Force Participation Rates, by Age, Sex, Race, and Hispanic Origin, 1948–2012—*Continued*

(Percent.)

Race, Hispanic origin, sex, and year	16 years and over	16 to 19 years	20 years and over						
			Total	20 to 24 years	25 to 34 years	35 to 44 years	45 to 54 years	55 to 64 years	65 years and over
HISPANIC									
Men									
1975	80.7	. . .	85.5	85.5	. . .	. . .	. . .	. . .	. . .
1976	79.6	. . .	84.2	84.2	. . .	. . .	. . .	. . .	. . .
1977	80.9	. . .	84.8	84.8	. . .	. . .	. . .	. . .	. . .
1978	81.1	. . .	84.9	84.9	. . .	. . .	. . .	. . .	. . .
1979	81.3	. . .	85.3	85.3	. . .	. . .	. . .	. . .	. . .
1980	81.4	. . .	84.9	84.9	. . .	. . .	. . .	. . .	. . .
1981	80.6	. . .	84.7	84.7	. . .	. . .	. . .	. . .	. . .
1982	79.7	. . .	84.0	84.0	. . .	. . .	. . .	. . .	. . .
1983	80.3	. . .	84.1	84.1	. . .	. . .	. . .	. . .	. . .
1984	80.6	. . .	84.3	84.3	. . .	. . .	. . .	. . .	. . .
1985	80.3	. . .	84.0	84.0	. . .	. . .	. . .	. . .	. . .
1986	81.0	. . .	84.6	84.6	. . .	. . .	. . .	. . .	. . .
1987	81.0	. . .	84.5	84.5	. . .	. . .	. . .	. . .	. . .
1988	81.9	. . .	85.0	85.0	. . .	. . .	. . .	. . .	. . .
1989	82.0	. . .	85.0	85.0	. . .	. . .	. . .	. . .	. . .
1990	81.4	. . .	84.7	84.7	. . .	. . .	. . .	. . .	. . .
1991	80.3	. . .	83.8	83.8	. . .	. . .	. . .	. . .	. . .
1992	80.7	. . .	84.0	84.0	. . .	. . .	. . .	. . .	. . .
1993	80.2	. . .	83.5	83.5	. . .	. . .	. . .	. . .	. . .
1994	79.2	50.0	82.5	82.5	92.5	91.5	85.7	63.6	14.4
1995	79.1	50.2	82.4	82.4	92.9	91.3	85.6	62.4	15.8
1996	79.6	50.0	83.0	83.0	93.2	91.7	87.0	65.9	16.7
1997	80.1	47.4	84.1	84.1	93.5	91.9	87.8	68.4	17.3
1998	79.8	48.7	83.6	83.6	94.0	91.4	86.7	70.2	14.9
1999	79.8	50.1	83.5	83.5	93.9	92.2	86.2	68.6	18.2
2000	81.5	50.7	85.3	85.3	94.1	93.3	87.6	69.4	18.5
2001	81.0	52.2	84.3	84.3	93.4	92.7	86.7	68.6	16.8
2002	80.2	48.8	83.6	83.6	93.5	92.1	86.1	67.3	16.3
2003	80.1	40.9	84.1	84.1	93.6	92.9	85.4	68.8	17.4
2004	80.4	42.4	84.2	84.2	93.6	93.2	87.2	69.6	20.8
2005	80.1	41.9	84.0	84.0	93.3	93.1	87.7	69.3	20.1
2006	80.7	42.0	84.6	84.6	94.1	93.8	87.1	69.6	22.9
2007	80.5	40.0	84.7	84.7	94.1	93.9	88.3	70.3	22.0
2008	80.2	40.3	84.4	84.4	94.0	93.7	88.6	71.7	21.7
2009	78.8	36.4	83.2	83.2	91.9	93.0	88.8	71.7	23.0
2010	77.8	33.2	82.6	82.6	92.7	92.9	87.8	69.0	24.5
2011	76.5	30.1	81.7	81.7	91.6	92.4	87.3	69.9	23.3
2012	76.1	33.0	81.0	81.0	91.6	91.1	87.3	70.3	21.1
HISPANIC									
Women									
1975	43.2	. . .	43.8	. . .	. . .	. . .	. . .	. . .	. . .
1976	44.3	. . .	44.6	. . .	. . .	. . .	. . .	. . .	. . .
1977	44.3	. . .	45.1	. . .	. . .	. . .	. . .	. . .	. . .
1978	46.6	. . .	47.2	. . .	. . .	. . .	. . .	. . .	. . .
1979	47.4	. . .	48.0	. . .	. . .	. . .	. . .	. . .	. . .
1980	47.4	. . .	48.5	. . .	. . .	. . .	. . .	. . .	. . .
1981	48.3	. . .	49.7	. . .	. . .	. . .	. . .	. . .	. . .
1982	48.1	. . .	49.3	. . .	. . .	. . .	. . .	. . .	. . .
1983	47.7	. . .	49.0	. . .	. . .	. . .	. . .	. . .	. . .
1984	49.6	. . .	50.5	. . .	. . .	. . .	. . .	. . .	. . .
1985	49.3	. . .	50.6	. . .	. . .	. . .	. . .	. . .	. . .
1986	50.1	. . .	51.7	. . .	. . .	. . .	. . .	. . .	. . .
1987	52.0	. . .	53.3	. . .	. . .	. . .	. . .	. . .	. . .
1988	53.2	. . .	54.2	. . .	. . .	. . .	. . .	. . .	. . .
1989	53.5	. . .	54.9	. . .	. . .	. . .	. . .	. . .	. . .
1990	53.1	. . .	54.8	. . .	. . .	. . .	. . .	. . .	. . .
1991	52.4	. . .	54.0	. . .	. . .	. . .	. . .	. . .	. . .
1992	52.8	. . .	54.3	. . .	. . .	. . .	. . .	. . .	. . .
1993	52.1	. . .	53.8	. . .	. . .	. . .	. . .	. . .	. . .
1994	52.9	38.7	54.4	57.9	60.5	66.4	61.4	38.1	7.9
1995	52.6	40.4	53.9	55.9	61.6	65.9	60.5	37.2	6.6
1996	53.4	36.5	55.2	59.2	62.0	67.0	62.7	40.5	6.9
1997	55.1	38.0	57.0	62.3	63.7	69.3	63.3	40.6	8.1
1998	55.6	42.4	57.1	62.2	64.5	67.9	64.7	41.9	6.6
1999	55.9	40.6	57.7	63.0	62.7	70.5	66.2	42.4	6.5
2000	57.5	41.4	59.3	65.0	65.3	69.9	68.5	41.2	7.7
2001	57.6	41.1	59.3	64.6	65.2	70.3	68.3	43.2	6.7
2002	57.6	38.8	59.5	65.0	65.8	69.5	66.3	46.1	8.5
2003	55.9	34.5	58.1	63.3	62.9	68.5	65.3	47.1	9.4
2004	56.1	33.7	58.4	62.9	62.9	68.7	67.9	47.8	9.8
2005	55.3	35.2	57.4	59.4	62.4	68.2	66.6	48.4	9.3
2006	56.1	34.4	58.3	61.3	63.5	68.7	67.4	49.7	10.4
2007	56.5	34.0	58.8	62.9	64.6	68.4	68.7	47.6	11.4
2008	56.2	33.3	58.6	62.1	64.3	69.1	67.6	48.9	11.7
2009	56.5	31.6	59.2	63.2	64.7	68.2	69.4	52.6	12.7
2010	56.5	28.5	59.5	61.6	66.3	67.9	70.2	53.7	13.0
2011	55.9	26.3	59.0	63.0	64.5	67.1	70.4	52.3	13.2
2012	56.6	28.8	59.5	63.3	65.6	69.0	69.4	51.4	13.2

. . . = Not available.

Table 1-9. Employed and Unemployed Full- and Part-Time Workers, by Age, Sex, and Race, 2000–2012

(Thousands of people.)

Race, sex, age, and year	Employed[1]								Unemployed	
	Full-time workers				Part-time workers					
		At work				At work[2]				
	Total	35 hours or more	1 to 34 hours for economic or noneconomic reasons	Not at work	Total	For economic reasons	For noneconomic reasons	Not at work	Looking for full-time work	Looking for part-time work
ALL RACES										
Both Sexes, 16 Years and Over										
2000	113 846	100 533	9 125	4 188	23 044	2 003	19 548	1 493	4 538	1 154
2001	113 573	99 047	10 464	4 061	23 361	2 297	19 494	1 570	5 546	1 254
2002	112 700	99 042	9 746	3 912	23 785	2 755	19 549	1 481	7 063	1 314
2003	113 324	99 539	9 841	3 944	24 412	3 184	19 702	1 525	7 361	1 413
2004	114 518	100 496	10 053	3 969	24 734	3 113	20 109	1 513	6 762	1 388
2005	117 016	103 044	9 983	3 990	24 714	2 963	20 229	1 522	6 175	1 415
2006	119 688	105 328	10 223	4 137	24 739	2 774	20 356	1 609	5 675	1 326
2007	121 091	106 990	9 976	4 125	24 956	2 851	20 511	1 594	5 789	1 289
2008	120 030	105 575	10 426	4 030	25 332	3 814	20 009	1 509	7 446	1 478
2009	112 634	95 911	12 853	3 870	27 244	6 353	19 327	1 563	12 523	1 741
2010	111 714	97 946	10 217	3 551	27 350	6 965	18 876	1 509	12 970	1 854
2011	112 556	98 976	10 047	3 534	27 313	6 872	18 984	1 525	11 914	1 833
2012	114 809	101 877	9 324	3 607	27 661	6 626	19 509	1 525	10 699	1 807
Both Sexes, 20 Years and Over										
2000	111 353	98 439	8 787	4 127	18 348	1 747	15 297	1 304	3 978	632
2001	111 323	97 161	10 156	4 006	18 870	2 013	15 486	1 371	4 956	682
2002	110 679	97 342	9 474	3 862	19 475	2 448	15 704	1 322	6 395	730
2003	111 578	98 087	9 587	3 904	20 239	2 875	16 001	1 363	6 705	818
2004	112 747	99 034	9 789	3 924	20 598	2 817	16 436	1 345	6 178	764
2005	115 206	101 534	9 729	3 942	20 546	2 698	16 489	1 359	5 619	786
2006	117 844	103 779	9 974	4 090	20 421	2 510	16 478	1 433	5 117	765
2007	119 317	105 499	9 738	4 080	20 819	2 587	16 819	1 413	5 234	742
2008	118 404	104 212	10 204	3 989	21 385	3 492	16 543	1 350	6 790	849
2009	111 414	94 928	12 647	3 839	23 626	5 934	16 286	1 406	11 651	1 061
2010	110 622	97 037	10 057	3 528	24 064	6 552	16 138	1 373	12 155	1 142
2011	111 500	98 103	9 888	3 508	24 043	6 457	16 259	1 327	11 180	1 167
2012	113 667	100 919	9 167	3 582	24 376	6 240	16 750	1 385	9 968	1 141
Men, 16 Years and Over										
2000	65 930	59 345	4 555	2 030	7 375	856	6 105	414	2 486	488
2001	65 623	58 386	5 241	1 996	7 573	1 021	6 129	424	3 144	546
2002	65 205	58 318	4 971	1 916	7 697	1 246	6 050	401	4 029	568
2003	65 379	58 428	5 023	1 927	7 953	1 473	6 056	423	4 291	615
2004	66 444	59 363	5 148	1 933	8 080	1 405	6 258	417	3 843	613
2005	67 858	60 825	5 096	1 937	8 115	1 316	6 370	429	3 444	616
2006	69 307	62 087	5 237	1 984	8 194	1 232	6 510	452	3 192	561
2007	70 035	62 965	5 095	1 975	8 220	1 319	6 424	477	3 326	556
2008	68 853	61 436	5 443	1 974	8 634	1 842	6 349	442	4 396	637
2009	63 951	55 317	6 772	1 862	9 719	3 035	6 170	514	7 696	757
2010	63 501	56 425	5 352	1 723	9 858	3 316	6 066	476	7 827	799
2011	64 333	57 413	5 189	1 731	9 957	3 262	6 216	479	6 903	781
2012	65 477	58 956	4 803	1 719	10 070	3 089	6 491	498	5 988	784
Men, 20 Years and Over										
2000	64 464	58 095	4 370	2 000	5 170	733	4 109	328	2 162	214
2001	64 311	57 273	5 072	1 966	5 465	881	4 253	331	2 801	239
2002	64 006	57 302	4 815	1 889	5 728	1 093	4 299	336	3 642	254
2003	64 364	57 580	4 879	1 905	6 051	1 314	4 388	348	3 906	302
2004	65 377	58 471	5 000	1 906	6 196	1 251	4 600	345	3 511	281
2005	66 803	59 934	4 955	1 914	6 247	1 182	4 705	360	3 118	274
2006	68 193	61 140	5 095	1 958	6 238	1 100	4 762	376	2 861	270
2007	68 968	62 057	4 959	1 952	6 369	1 190	4 782	397	2 990	268
2008	67 895	60 625	5 315	1 955	6 855	1 675	4 802	378	3 994	303
2009	63 242	54 738	6 659	1 845	8 099	2 827	4 828	445	7 151	404
2010	62 854	55 887	5 258	1 710	8 376	3 102	4 857	417	7 336	427
2011	63 690	56 870	5 104	1 715	8 492	3 059	5 010	423	6 461	437
2012	64 810	58 386	4 719	1 705	8 593	2 883	5 271	439	5 547	437

Note: Beginning in January 2004, data reflect revised population controls used in the household survey. See notes and definitions for information on historical comparability.

[1]Employed persons are classified as full- or part-time workers based on their usual weekly hours at all jobs, regardless of the number of hours they were at work during the reference week. Persons absent from work are also classified according to their usual status.
[2]Includes some persons at work 35 hours or more classified by their reason for working part time.

Table 1-9. Employed and Unemployed Full- and Part-Time Workers, by Age, Sex, and Race, 2000–2012—*Continued*

(Thousands of people.)

Race, sex, age, and year	Employed[1]								Unemployed	
	Full-time workers				Part-time workers					
		At work				At work[2]				
	Total	35 hours or more	1 to 34 hours for economic or noneconomic reasons	Not at work	Total	For economic reasons	For noneconomic reasons	Not at work	Looking for full-time work	Looking for part-time work
ALL RACES—*Continued*										
Women, 16 Years and Over										
2000	47 916	41 188	4 570	2 158	15 670	1 147	13 443	1 080	2 052	666
2001	47 950	40 661	5 223	2 065	15 788	1 276	13 365	1 146	2 402	709
2002	47 494	40 723	4 775	1 996	16 088	1 509	13 498	1 080	3 034	747
2003	47 946	41 111	4 818	2 017	16 459	1 711	13 646	1 102	3 070	798
2004	48 073	41 133	4 905	2 036	16 654	1 708	13 851	1 096	2 919	775
2005	49 158	42 219	4 887	2 052	16 598	1 647	13 859	1 092	2 732	799
2006	50 380	43 241	4 986	2 153	16 545	1 542	13 846	1 157	2 483	764
2007	51 056	44 025	4 881	2 150	16 736	1 532	14 087	1 117	2 463	732
2008	51 178	44 139	4 983	2 056	16 698	1 972	13 660	1 067	3 050	841
2009	48 683	40 594	6 080	2 009	17 525	3 318	13 157	1 050	4 827	984
2010	48 214	41 521	4 865	1 828	17 491	3 648	12 810	1 033	5 144	1 055
2011	48 224	41 563	4 858	1 802	17 355	3 610	12 767	977	5 011	1 052
2012	49 331	42 921	4 521	1 888	17 583	3 538	13 018	1 026	4 711	1 023
Women, 20 Years and Over										
2000	46 889	40 344	4 417	2 128	13 178	1 013	11 188	976	1 816	419
2001	47 012	39 889	5 083	2 040	13 405	1 132	11 233	1 040	2 155	444
2002	46 673	40 040	4 660	1 973	13 747	1 355	11 406	986	2 752	476
2003	47 215	40 507	4 708	2 000	14 188	1 560	11 613	1 015	2 799	515
2004	47 371	40 563	4 790	2 017	14 402	1 567	11 836	1 000	2 667	483
2005	48 403	41 600	4 774	2 028	14 299	1 516	11 784	999	2 501	512
2006	49 651	42 639	4 880	2 132	14 183	1 410	11 716	1 057	2 256	495
2007	50 349	43 442	4 779	2 128	14 450	1 397	12 037	1 016	2 244	474
2008	50 509	43 587	4 888	2 034	14 530	1 817	11 740	973	2 796	546
2009	48 171	40 190	5 988	1 994	15 527	3 107	11 459	961	4 500	657
2010	47 767	41 150	4 799	1 818	15 688	3 450	11 282	956	4 819	715
2011	47 810	41 233	4 784	1 792	15 551	3 398	11 249	904	4 719	730
2012	48 857	42 533	4 448	1 877	15 783	3 358	11 480	946	4 420	704
WHITE[3]										
Men, 16 Years and Over										
2000	56 068	50 434	3 896	1 738	6 221	656	5 213	351	1 798	379
2001	55 830	49 625	4 504	1 701	6 381	793	5 225	364	2 323	431
2002	55 369	49 459	4 267	1 644	6 480	980	5 150	350	3 017	443
2003	55 216	49 323	4 266	1 628	6 650	1 146	5 148	357	3 164	479
2004	55 926	49 891	4 396	1 638	6 786	1 092	5 331	363	2 805	477
2005	56 955	50 965	4 334	1 656	6 808	1 014	5 424	370	2 459	471
2006	58 063	51 894	4 484	1 685	6 820	947	5 481	393	2 299	432
2007	58 494	52 460	4 359	1 676	6 795	1 022	5 368	406	2 444	425
2008	57 432	51 104	4 653	1 675	7 192	1 433	5 379	379	3 235	492
2009	53 506	46 153	5 770	1 583	8 124	2 438	5 240	446	5 819	602
2010	53 086	47 055	4 554	1 477	8 166	2 662	5 102	402	5 832	644
2011	53 727	47 865	4 397	1 465	8 193	2 560	5 227	405	5 020	611
2012	53 857	48 409	4 009	1 439	8 133	2 383	5 334	416	4 330	600
Men, 20 Years and Over										
2000	54 778	49 335	3 733	1 710	4 341	558	3 505	278	1 566	165
2001	54 666	48 636	4 354	1 676	4 579	677	3 616	285	2 080	195
2002	54 333	48 581	4 133	1 619	4 790	857	3 640	293	2 743	200
2003	54 339	48 585	4 145	1 609	5 010	1 016	3 703	291	2 893	231
2004	55 005	49 124	4 267	1 614	5 154	961	3 895	299	2 567	217
2005	56 050	50 203	4 213	1 634	5 205	905	3 990	310	2 242	209
2006	57 108	51 081	4 365	1 662	5 150	840	3 987	324	2 074	208
2007	57 591	51 691	4 243	1 656	5 216	915	3 967	334	2 204	204
2008	56 623	50 421	4 542	1 660	5 681	1 302	4 055	324	2 944	235
2009	52 899	45 654	5 676	1 569	6 728	2 269	4 075	384	5 421	325
2010	52 530	46 592	4 472	1 466	6 907	2 484	4 071	352	5 481	347
2011	53 186	47 406	4 328	1 451	6 933	2 392	4 184	357	4 702	344
2012	53 302	47 934	3 941	1 427	6 891	2 218	4 306	367	4 014	333

Note: Beginning in January 2004, data reflect revised population controls used in the household survey. See notes and definitions for information on historical comparability.

[1]Employed persons are classified as full- or part-time workers based on their usual weekly hours at all jobs, regardless of the number of hours they were at work during the reference week. Persons absent from work are also classified according to their usual status.
[2]Includes some persons at work 35 hours or more classified by their reason for working part time.
[3]Beginning in 2003, persons who selected this race group only; persons who selected more than one race group are not included. Prior to 2003, persons who reported more than one race group were included in the group they identified as their main race.

Table 1-9. Employed and Unemployed Full- and Part-Time Workers, by Age, Sex, and Race, 2000–2012—*Continued*

(Thousands of people.)

Race, sex, age, and year	Employed[1]								Unemployed	
	Full-time workers				Part-time workers					
		At work				At work[2]				
	Total	35 hours or more	1 to 34 hours for economic or noneconomic reasons	Not at work	Total	For economic reasons	For noneconomic reasons	Not at work	Looking for full-time work	Looking for part-time work
WHITE[3]—*Continued*										
Women, 16 Years and Over										
2000	38 438	32 942	3 729	1 767	13 698	867	11 870	961	1 422	521
2001	38 445	32 491	4 252	1 702	13 773	971	11 787	1 015	1 664	551
2002	38 152	32 623	3 896	1 633	14 011	1 152	11 903	956	2 084	595
2003	38 249	32 659	3 939	1 652	14 120	1 304	11 860	956	2 038	629
2004	38 240	32 555	4 018	1 667	14 287	1 280	12 038	969	1 968	597
2005	38 973	33 325	3 976	1 672	14 213	1 207	12 043	963	1 807	612
2006	39 813	33 980	4 082	1 751	14 137	1 157	11 967	1 013	1 670	601
2007	40 238	34 486	4 014	1 738	14 265	1 143	12 148	973	1 694	579
2008	40 292	34 569	4 076	1 647	14 209	1 518	11 761	931	2 119	664
2009	38 456	31 885	4 946	1 626	14 910	2 579	11 418	913	3 442	785
2010	38 158	32 710	3 958	1 490	14 758	2 846	11 029	883	3 612	828
2011	38 152	32 731	3 944	1 477	14 618	2 775	10 994	850	3 450	807
2012	38 362	33 244	3 614	1 504	14 416	2 674	10 875	867	3 191	794
Women, 20 Years and Over										
2000	37 585	32 242	3 600	1 743	11 560	754	9 935	872	1 256	339
2001	37 658	31 839	4 139	1 680	11 711	853	9 933	924	1 492	357
2002	37 467	32 049	3 803	1 615	11 981	1 029	10 079	873	1 888	381
2003	37 640	32 158	3 845	1 637	12 183	1 180	10 124	879	1 866	411
2004	37 663	32 085	3 927	1 652	12 377	1 166	10 326	885	1 795	377
2005	38 354	32 820	3 882	1 652	12 235	1 108	10 248	879	1 653	401
2006	39 232	33 500	3 998	1 733	12 128	1 050	10 151	927	1 524	402
2007	39 670	34 015	3 932	1 722	12 326	1 037	10 402	887	1 547	383
2008	39 765	34 128	4 005	1 632	12 359	1 392	10 116	851	1 949	435
2009	38 033	31 547	4 872	1 614	13 198	2 411	9 952	835	3 216	529
2010	37 789	32 404	3 904	1 481	13 208	2 684	9 705	818	3 389	571
2011	37 816	32 466	3 882	1 468	13 065	2 597	9 683	785	3 255	563
2012	50 911	32 936	3 556	1 497	12 923	2 533	9 591	799	3 009	555
BLACK[3]										
Men, 16 Years and Over										
2000	6 350	5 704	445	202	732	144	548	41	542	78
2001	6 178	5 509	468	200	761	165	557	39	626	83
2002	6 194	5 541	480	173	765	188	546	30	749	86
2003	6 055	5 414	453	188	765	221	505	39	804	87
2004	6 177	5 538	460	179	736	205	499	32	763	98
2005	6 381	5 745	463	174	773	207	533	33	742	102
2006	6 529	5 907	446	176	825	201	590	34	681	93
2007	6 673	6 068	429	176	826	195	589	42	660	92
2008	6 548	5 935	440	173	850	276	542	32	849	100
2009	5 871	5 166	556	150	946	379	530	36	1 348	100
2010	5 856	5 279	446	130	1 009	419	550	41	1 448	102
2011	5 892	5 293	445	154	1 060	452	566	43	1 393	108
2012	6 185	5 579	453	153	1 117	442	629	46	1 169	123
Men, 20 Years and Over										
2000	6 222	5 594	429	199	520	125	363	32	468	31
2001	6 069	5 417	455	197	558	145	382	31	542	31
2002	6 073	5 437	465	171	579	166	387	26	660	35
2003	5 980	5 355	439	185	607	201	372	34	717	43
2004	6 089	5 463	449	177	592	189	376	27	689	44
2005	6 287	5 662	452	174	614	189	397	28	655	44
2006	6 424	5 816	433	175	655	185	441	30	596	44
2007	6 574	5 983	417	174	671	181	452	37	580	43
2008	6 461	5 860	430	171	690	252	409	29	764	46
2009	5 811	5 119	544	148	817	355	428	34	1 238	49
2010	5 803	5 235	439	129	877	392	447	37	1 344	52
2011	5 830	5 242	435	153	935	428	470	38	1 299	61
2012	6 117	5 522	443	152	987	421	526	40	1 081	71

Note: Beginning in January 2004, data reflect revised population controls used in the household survey. See notes and definitions for information on historical comparability.

[1]Employed persons are classified as full- or part-time workers based on their usual weekly hours at all jobs, regardless of the number of hours they were at work during the reference week. Persons absent from work are also classified according to their usual status.
[2]Includes some persons at work 35 hours or more classified by their reason for working part time.
[3]Beginning in 2003, persons who selected this race group only; persons who selected more than one race group are not included. Prior to 2003, persons who reported more than one race group were included in the group they identified as their main race.

Table 1-9. Employed and Unemployed Full- and Part-Time Workers, by Age, Sex, and Race, 2000–2012—*Continued*

(Thousands of people.)

Race, sex, age, and year	Employed[1]								Unemployed	
	Full-time workers				Part-time workers				Looking for full-time work	Looking for part-time work
		At work				At work[2]				
	Total	35 hours or more	1 to 34 hours for economic or noneconomic reasons	Not at work	Total	For economic reasons	For noneconomic reasons	Not at work		
BLACK[3]—*Continued*										
Women, 16 Years and Over										
2000	6 780	5 862	632	287	1 293	211	1 005	77	515	106
2001	6 761	5 777	715	270	1 307	223	998	85	584	122
2002	6 588	5 685	640	263	1 326	259	991	76	744	114
2003	6 552	5 709	595	247	1 367	274	1 017	76	774	121
2004	6 597	5 740	611	246	1 399	306	1 022	71	744	124
2005	6 750	5 871	619	260	1 407	320	1 018	70	723	133
2006	7 001	6 131	605	265	1 410	274	1 054	82	655	120
2007	7 119	6 272	584	263	1 432	273	1 085	75	589	104
2008	7 105	6 238	596	272	1 449	302	1 070	77	717	122
2009	6 666	5 696	718	252	1 542	480	984	78	1 027	132
2010	6 525	5 727	582	215	1 621	528	1 010	82	1 142	160
2011	6 450	5 651	592	207	1 648	573	1 004	72	1 165	164
2012	6 750	5 956	557	236	1 803	559	1 157	88	1 099	153
Women, 20 Years and Over										
2000	6 651	5 753	615	283	1 052	197	788	67	456	56
2001	6 647	5 684	695	268	1 094	203	816	75	521	61
2002	6 492	5 605	626	261	1 117	234	816	68	671	67
2003	6 468	5 639	583	246	1 168	257	842	69	698	75
2004	6 512	5 674	595	243	1 195	287	844	64	679	76
2005	6 653	5 789	606	258	1 222	298	861	63	660	74
2006	6 893	6 042	588	263	1 175	255	848	72	588	67
2007	7 024	6 194	570	260	1 216	254	897	65	527	61
2008	7 006	6 160	580	267	1 254	283	902	68	654	78
2009	6 600	5 644	705	250	1 356	449	837	71	951	82
2010	6 471	5 681	575	215	1 473	504	894	75	1 063	103
2011	6 402	5 610	586	207	1 504	549	888	67	1 095	108
2012	6 682	5 901	547	235	1 631	531	1 021	79	1 021	98

Note: Beginning in January 2004, data reflect revised population controls used in the household survey. See notes and definitions for information on historical comparability.

[1]Employed persons are classified as full- or part-time workers based on their usual weekly hours at all jobs, regardless of the number of hours they were at work during the reference week. Persons absent from work are also classified according to their usual status.
[2]Includes some persons at work 35 hours or more classified by their reason for working part time.
[3]Beginning in 2003, persons who selected this race group only; persons who selected more than one race group are not included. Prior to 2003, persons who reported more than one race group were included in the group they identified as their main race.

Table 1-10. Persons Not in the Labor Force, by Age, Sex, and Desire and Availability for Work, 2009–2012

(Thousands of people.)

Category	Total		Age						Sex			
			16 to 24 years		25 to 54 years		55 years and over		Men		Women	
	2009	2010	2009	2010	2009	2010	2009	2010	2009	2010	2009	2010
TOTAL, NOT IN THE LABOR FORCE	81 659	83 941	16 207	17 014	21 823	22 350	43 629	44 577	32 013	33 189	49 646	50 752
Do Not Want a Job Now[1]	75 765	77 882	14 263	14 990	19 199	19 659	42 303	43 233	29 234	30 309	46 531	47 573
Want a Job[1]	5 894	6 059	1 944	2 024	2 624	2 691	1 325	1 344	2 779	2 880	3 115	3 179
Did not search for work in the previous year	3 075	2 948	960	968	1 241	1 189	874	791	1 344	1 279	1 731	1 669
Searched for work in the previous year[2]	2 818	3 111	983	1 056	1 383	1 502	452	553	1 435	1 601	1 384	1 510
Not available to work now	592	623	275	274	256	284	61	65	251	264	341	359
Available to work now	2 226	2 487	708	782	1 127	1 218	391	487	1 184	1 337	1 043	1 151
Reason not currently looking:												
Discouragement over job prospects[3]	778	1 173	200	291	427	595	151	287	485	731	293	442
Reasons other than discouragement	1 449	1 315	509	491	699	623	240	200	699	606	749	709
Family responsibilities	209	286	38	49	131	171	41	66	50	83	159	203
In school or training	306	350	234	262	65	81	7	7	163	191	144	158
Ill health or disability	136	50	19	4	68	21	49	25	70	21	66	29
Other[4]	798	629	219	176	435	350	144	102	417	311	381	318

Category	Total		Age						Sex			
			16 to 24 years		25 to 54 years		55 years and over		Men		Women	
	2011	2012	2011	2012	2011	2012	2011	2012	2011	2012	2011	2012
TOTAL, NOT IN THE LABOR FORCE	86 001	88 310	17 201	17 499	22 961	23 061	45 839	47 750	34 343	35 017	51 658	53 293
Do Not Want a Job Now[1]	79 564	81 752	15 177	15 383	20 107	20 248	44 280	46 120	34 343	35 017	48 266	49 763
Want a Job[1]	6 437	6 558	2 023	2 115	2 854	2 813	1 560	1 630	3 045	3 028	3 392	3 530
Did not search for work in the previous year	3 268	3 390	1 010	1 064	1 303	1 328	955	998	1 463	1 490	1 804	1 900
Searched for work in the previous year[2]	3 169	3 168	1 014	1 052	1 551	1 484	605	632	1 582	1 537	1 587	1 630
Not available to work now	597	651	262	282	262	288	73	82	236	253	361	399
Available to work now	2 573	2 516	752	770	1 289	1 196	532	550	1 346	1 285	1 227	1 232
Reason not currently looking:												
Discouragement over job prospects[3]	989	909	222	217	519	451	248	241	579	541	410	368
Reasons other than discouragement	1 584	1 608	530	553	770	746	284	309	767	743	817	864
Family responsibilities	215	229	30	33	139	147	45	49	48	61	166	168
In school or training	323	339	245	257	75	73	4	9	183	175	140	164
Ill health or disability	169	168	18	18	93	83	58	66	86	80	83	87
Other[4]	877	871	238	245	463	442	177	185	449	427	428	444

[1]Includes some persons who were not asked if they wanted a job.
[2]Persons who had a job during the prior 12 months must have searched since the end of that job.
[3]Includes believes no work available, could not find work, lacks necessary schooling or training, employer thinks too young or old, and other types of discrimination.
[4]Includes those who did not actively look for work in the prior four weeks for reasons such as childcare and transportation problems, as well as a small number for whom reason for nonparticipation was not ascertained.

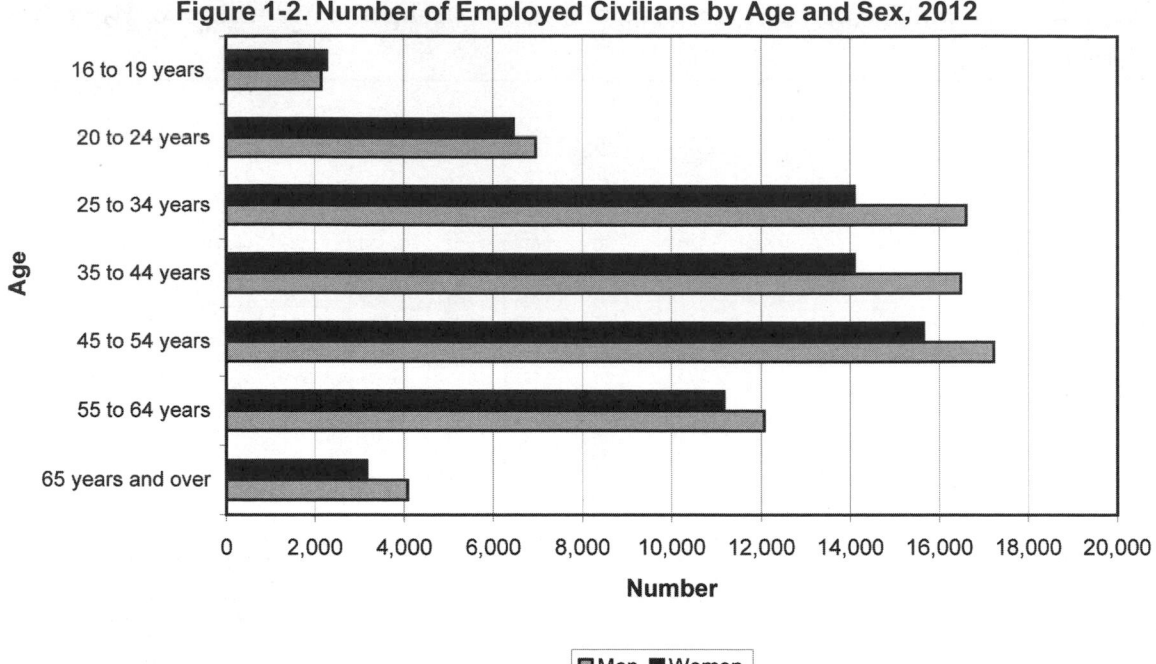

Figure 1-2. Number of Employed Civilians by Age and Sex, 2012

☐ Men ■ Women

There were nearly 142.5 million employed civilians in the labor force in 2012, an increase of 1.9 percent from 2011 but a decline of 2.4 percent from 2007. Men outnumbered women in every age group except among the 16–19 year olds. In 2012, nearly 47 percent of employed civilians were women. (See Table 1-11.)

OTHER HIGHLIGHTS

- While men made up 53.0 percent of employed civilians, they only made up 12.4 percent of employees in healthcare support occupations, 26.4 percent of employees in education, training, and library occupations and 26.7 percent of employees in office and administrative support occupations. (See Table 1-13.)

- Among persons 25 years of age and over, employment declined for those without any college. In 2012, employment increased 1.1 for those with some college, 4.5 percent for those with an associate's degree, 3.7 percent for those with only a bachelor's degree only, and 3.3 percent for those with a bachelor's degree or higher. (See Table 1-16.)

- The multiple jobholding rate declined in May 2013 for the third consecutive year after remaining steady at 5.2 percent from 2008 through 2010. It was significantly higher for women (5.2 percent) than for men (4.7 percent). (See Table 1-17.)

- In 2012, slightly more than 8.4 million families had an unemployed member—a decline from 9.0 million in 2011 and nearly 9.7 million in 2010. (See Table 1-20.)

Table 1-11. Employed Civilians, by Age, Sex, Race, and Hispanic Origin, 1948–2012

(Thousands of people.)

Race, Hispanic origin, sex, and year	16 years and over	16 to 19 years			20 years and over						
		Total	16 to 17 years	18 to 19 years	Total	20 to 24 years	25 to 34 years	35 to 44 years	45 to 54 years	55 to 64 years	65 years and over
ALL RACES											
Both Sexes											
1948	58 343	4 026	1 600	2 426	54 318	6 937	13 801	13 050	10 624	7 103	2 804
1949	57 651	3 712	1 466	2 246	53 940	6 660	13 639	13 108	10 636	7 042	2 864
1950	58 918	3 703	1 433	2 270	55 218	6 746	13 917	13 424	10 966	7 265	2 899
1951	59 961	3 767	1 575	2 192	56 196	6 321	14 233	13 746	11 421	7 558	2 917
1952	60 250	3 719	1 626	2 092	56 536	5 572	14 515	14 058	11 687	7 785	2 919
1953	61 179	3 720	1 577	2 142	57 460	5 225	14 519	14 774	11 969	7 806	3 166
1954	60 109	3 475	1 422	2 053	56 634	4 971	14 190	14 541	11 976	7 895	3 060
1955	62 170	3 642	1 500	2 143	58 528	5 270	14 481	14 879	12 556	8 158	3 185
1956	63 799	3 818	1 647	2 171	59 983	5 545	14 407	15 218	12 978	8 519	3 314
1957	64 071	3 778	1 613	2 167	60 291	5 641	14 253	15 348	13 320	8 553	3 179
1958	63 036	3 582	1 519	2 063	59 454	5 571	13 675	15 157	13 448	8 559	3 045
1959	64 630	3 838	1 670	2 168	60 791	5 870	13 709	15 454	13 915	8 822	3 023
1960	65 778	4 129	1 770	2 360	61 648	6 119	13 630	15 598	14 238	8 989	3 073
1961	65 746	4 108	1 621	2 486	61 638	6 227	13 429	15 552	14 320	9 120	2 987
1962	66 702	4 195	1 607	2 588	62 508	6 446	13 311	15 901	14 491	9 346	3 013
1963	67 762	4 255	1 751	2 504	63 508	6 815	13 318	16 114	14 749	9 596	2 915
1964	69 305	4 516	2 013	2 503	64 789	7 303	13 449	16 166	15 094	9 804	2 973
1965	71 088	5 036	2 075	2 962	66 052	7 702	13 704	16 294	15 320	10 028	3 005
1966	72 895	5 721	2 269	3 452	67 178	7 964	14 017	16 312	15 615	10 310	2 961
1967	74 372	5 682	2 334	3 348	68 690	8 499	14 575	16 281	15 789	10 536	3 011
1968	75 920	5 781	2 403	3 377	70 141	8 762	15 265	16 220	16 083	10 745	3 065
1969	77 902	6 117	2 573	3 543	71 785	9 319	15 883	16 100	16 410	10 919	3 155
1970	78 678	6 144	2 598	3 546	72 534	9 731	16 318	15 922	16 473	10 974	3 118
1971	79 367	6 208	2 596	3 613	73 158	10 201	16 781	15 675	16 451	11 009	3 040
1972	82 153	6 746	2 787	3 959	75 407	10 999	18 082	15 822	16 457	11 044	3 003
1973	85 064	7 271	3 032	4 239	77 793	11 839	19 509	16 041	16 553	10 966	2 886
1974	86 794	7 448	3 111	4 338	79 347	12 101	20 610	16 203	16 633	10 964	2 835
1975	85 846	7 104	2 941	4 162	78 744	11 885	21 087	15 953	16 190	10 827	2 801
1976	88 752	7 336	2 972	4 363	81 416	12 570	22 493	16 468	16 224	10 912	2 747
1977	92 017	7 688	3 138	4 550	84 329	13 196	23 850	17 157	16 212	11 126	2 787
1978	96 048	8 070	3 330	4 739	87 979	13 887	25 281	18 128	16 338	11 400	2 946
1979	98 824	8 083	3 340	4 743	90 741	14 327	26 492	18 981	16 357	11 585	2 999
1980	99 303	7 710	3 106	4 605	91 593	14 087	27 204	19 523	16 234	11 586	2 960
1981	100 397	7 225	2 866	4 359	93 172	14 122	28 180	20 145	16 255	11 525	2 945
1982	99 526	6 549	2 505	4 044	92 978	13 690	28 149	20 879	15 923	11 414	2 923
1983	100 834	6 342	2 320	4 022	94 491	13 722	28 756	21 960	15 812	11 315	2 927
1984	105 005	6 444	2 404	4 040	98 562	14 207	30 348	23 598	16 178	11 395	2 835
1985	107 150	6 434	2 492	3 941	100 716	13 980	31 208	24 732	16 509	11 474	2 813
1986	109 597	6 472	2 622	3 850	103 125	13 790	32 201	25 861	16 949	11 405	2 919
1987	112 440	6 640	2 736	3 905	105 800	13 524	33 105	27 179	17 487	11 465	3 041
1988	114 968	6 805	2 713	4 092	108 164	13 244	33 574	28 269	18 447	11 433	3 197
1989	117 342	6 759	2 588	4 172	110 582	12 962	34 045	29 443	19 279	11 499	3 355
1990	118 793	6 581	2 410	4 171	112 213	13 401	33 935	30 817	19 525	11 189	3 346
1991	117 718	5 906	2 202	3 704	111 812	12 975	33 061	31 593	19 882	11 001	3 300
1992	118 492	5 669	2 128	3 540	112 824	12 872	32 667	31 923	21 022	10 998	3 341
1993	120 259	5 805	2 226	3 579	114 455	12 840	32 385	32 666	22 175	11 058	3 331
1994	123 060	6 161	2 510	3 651	116 899	12 758	32 286	33 599	23 348	11 228	3 681
1995	124 900	6 419	2 573	3 846	118 481	12 443	32 356	34 202	24 378	11 435	3 666
1996	126 708	6 500	2 646	3 853	120 208	12 138	32 077	35 051	25 514	11 739	3 690
1997	129 558	6 661	2 648	4 012	122 897	12 380	31 809	35 908	26 744	12 296	3 761
1998	131 463	7 051	2 762	4 289	124 413	12 557	31 394	36 278	27 587	12 872	3 725
1999	133 488	7 172	2 793	4 379	126 316	12 891	30 865	36 728	28 635	13 315	3 882
2000	136 891	7 189	2 759	4 431	129 701	13 229	31 549	36 433	30 310	14 002	4 179
2001	136 933	6 740	2 558	4 182	130 194	13 348	30 863	36 049	31 036	14 645	4 253
2002	136 485	6 332	2 330	4 002	130 154	13 351	30 306	35 235	31 201	15 674	4 306
2003	137 736	5 919	2 312	3 607	131 817	13 433	30 383	34 881	31 914	16 598	4 608
2004	139 252	5 907	2 193	3 714	133 345	13 723	30 423	34 580	32 469	17 331	4 819
2005	141 730	5 978	2 284	3 694	135 752	13 792	30 680	34 630	33 207	18 349	5 094
2006	144 427	6 162	2 444	3 719	138 265	13 878	31 051	34 569	34 052	19 389	5 325
2007	146 047	5 911	2 286	3 625	140 136	13 964	31 586	34 302	34 563	20 108	5 614
2008	145 362	5 573	1 989	3 584	139 790	13 629	31 383	33 457	34 529	20 812	5 979
2009	139 877	4 837	1 651	3 187	135 040	12 764	30 014	31 517	33 613	21 019	6 114
2010	139 064	4 378	1 418	2 960	134 686	12 699	30 229	30 663	33 191	21 636	6 268
2011	139 869	4 327	1 355	2 972	135 542	13 036	30 537	30 270	32 867	22 186	6 647
2012	142 469	4 426	1 419	3 007	138 043	13 408	30 701	30 576	32 874	23 239	7 245

Table 1-11. Employed Civilians, by Age, Sex, Race, and Hispanic Origin, 1948–2012—*Continued*

(Thousands of people.)

Race, Hispanic origin, sex, and year	16 years and over	16 to 19 years			20 years and over						
		Total	16 to 17 years	18 to 19 years	Total	20 to 24 years	25 to 34 years	35 to 44 years	45 to 54 years	55 to 64 years	65 years and over
ALL RACES											
Men											
1948	41 725	2 344	996	1 348	39 382	4 349	10 038	9 363	7 742	5 587	2 303
1949	40 925	2 124	911	1 213	38 803	4 197	9 879	9 308	7 661	5 438	2 329
1950	41 578	2 186	909	1 277	39 394	4 255	10 060	9 445	7 790	5 508	2 336
1951	41 780	2 156	979	1 177	39 626	3 780	10 134	9 607	8 012	5 711	2 382
1952	41 682	2 107	985	1 121	39 578	3 183	10 352	9 753	8 144	5 804	2 343
1953	42 430	2 136	976	1 159	40 296	2 901	10 500	10 229	8 374	5 808	2 483
1954	41 619	1 985	881	1 104	39 634	2 724	10 254	10 082	8 330	5 830	2 414
1955	42 621	2 095	936	1 159	40 526	2 973	10 453	10 267	8 553	5 857	2 424
1956	43 379	2 164	1 008	1 156	41 216	3 245	10 337	10 385	8 732	6 004	2 512
1957	43 357	2 115	987	1 130	41 239	3 346	10 222	10 427	8 851	6 002	2 394
1958	42 423	2 012	948	1 064	40 411	3 293	9 790	10 291	8 828	5 955	2 254
1959	43 466	2 198	1 015	1 183	41 267	3 597	9 862	10 492	9 048	6 058	2 210
1960	43 904	2 361	1 090	1 271	41 543	3 754	9 759	10 552	9 182	6 105	2 191
1961	43 656	2 315	989	1 325	41 342	3 795	9 591	10 505	9 195	6 155	2 098
1962	44 177	2 362	990	1 372	41 815	3 898	9 475	10 711	9 333	6 260	2 138
1963	44 657	2 406	1 073	1 334	42 251	4 118	9 431	10 801	9 478	6 385	2 038
1964	45 474	2 587	1 242	1 345	42 886	4 370	9 531	10 832	9 637	6 478	2 039
1965	46 340	2 918	1 285	1 634	43 422	4 583	9 611	10 837	9 792	6 542	2 057
1966	46 919	3 253	1 389	1 863	43 668	4 599	9 709	10 764	9 904	6 668	2 024
1967	47 479	3 186	1 417	1 769	44 294	4 809	9 988	10 674	9 990	6 774	2 058
1968	48 114	3 255	1 453	1 802	44 859	4 812	10 405	10 554	10 102	6 893	2 093
1969	48 818	3 430	1 526	1 904	45 388	5 012	10 736	10 401	10 187	6 931	2 122
1970	48 990	3 409	1 504	1 905	45 581	5 237	10 936	10 216	10 170	6 928	2 094
1971	49 390	3 478	1 510	1 968	45 912	5 593	11 218	10 028	10 139	6 916	2 019
1972	50 896	3 765	1 598	2 167	47 130	6 138	11 884	10 088	10 139	6 929	1 953
1973	52 349	4 039	1 721	2 318	48 310	6 655	12 617	10 126	10 197	6 857	1 856
1974	53 024	4 103	1 744	2 359	48 922	6 739	13 119	10 135	10 181	6 880	1 869
1975	51 857	3 839	1 621	2 219	48 018	6 484	13 205	9 891	9 902	6 722	1 811
1976	53 138	3 947	1 626	2 321	49 190	6 915	13 869	10 069	9 881	6 724	1 732
1977	54 728	4 174	1 733	2 441	50 555	7 232	14 483	10 399	9 832	6 848	1 761
1978	56 479	4 336	1 800	2 535	52 143	7 559	15 124	10 845	9 806	6 954	1 855
1979	57 607	4 300	1 799	2 501	53 308	7 791	15 688	11 202	9 735	7 015	1 876
1980	57 186	4 085	1 672	2 412	53 101	7 532	15 832	11 355	9 548	6 999	1 835
1981	57 397	3 815	1 526	2 289	53 582	7 504	16 266	11 613	9 478	6 909	1 812
1982	56 271	3 379	1 307	2 072	52 891	7 197	16 002	11 902	9 234	6 781	1 776
1983	56 787	3 300	1 213	2 087	53 487	7 232	16 216	12 450	9 133	6 686	1 770
1984	59 091	3 322	1 244	2 078	55 769	7 571	17 166	13 309	9 326	6 694	1 703
1985	59 891	3 328	1 300	2 029	56 562	7 339	17 564	13 800	9 411	6 753	1 695
1986	60 892	3 323	1 352	1 971	57 569	7 250	18 092	14 266	9 554	6 654	1 753
1987	62 107	3 381	1 393	1 988	58 726	7 058	18 487	14 898	9 750	6 682	1 850
1988	63 273	3 492	1 403	2 089	59 781	6 918	18 702	15 457	10 201	6 591	1 911
1989	64 315	3 477	1 327	2 150	60 837	6 799	18 952	16 002	10 569	6 548	1 968
1990	65 104	3 427	1 254	2 173	61 678	7 151	18 779	16 771	10 690	6 378	1 909
1991	64 223	3 044	1 135	1 909	61 178	6 909	18 265	17 086	10 813	6 245	1 860
1992	64 440	2 944	1 096	1 848	61 496	6 819	17 966	17 230	11 365	6 173	1 943
1993	65 349	2 994	1 155	1 839	62 355	6 805	17 877	17 665	11 927	6 166	1 916
1994	66 450	3 156	1 288	1 868	63 294	6 771	17 741	18 111	12 439	6 142	2 089
1995	67 377	3 292	1 316	1 977	64 085	6 665	17 709	18 374	12 958	6 272	2 108
1996	68 207	3 310	1 318	1 992	64 897	6 429	17 527	18 816	13 483	6 470	2 172
1997	69 685	3 401	1 355	2 045	66 284	6 548	17 338	19 327	14 107	6 735	2 229
1998	70 693	3 558	1 398	2 161	67 135	6 638	17 097	19 634	14 544	7 052	2 171
1999	71 446	3 685	1 437	2 249	67 761	6 729	16 694	19 811	14 991	7 274	2 263
2000	73 305	3 671	1 394	2 276	69 634	6 974	17 241	19 537	15 871	7 606	2 406
2001	73 196	3 420	1 268	2 151	69 776	6 952	16 915	19 305	16 268	7 900	2 437
2002	72 903	3 169	1 130	2 040	69 734	6 978	16 573	18 932	16 419	8 378	2 455
2003	73 332	2 917	1 115	1 802	70 415	7 065	16 670	18 774	16 588	8 733	2 585
2004	74 524	2 952	1 037	1 915	71 572	7 246	16 818	18 700	16 951	9 174	2 683
2005	75 973	2 923	1 067	1 855	73 050	7 279	16 993	18 780	17 429	9 714	2 857
2006	77 502	3 071	1 182	1 888	74 431	7 412	17 134	18 765	17 920	10 192	3 008
2007	78 254	2 917	1 091	1 827	75 337	7 374	17 452	18 666	18 210	10 556	3 080
2008	77 486	2 736	926	1 810	74 750	7 145	17 183	18 097	18 124	10 919	3 282
2009	73 670	2 328	786	1 543	71 341	6 510	16 223	16 918	17 443	10 890	3 357
2010	73 359	2 129	675	1 454	71 230	6 466	16 358	16 585	17 242	11 140	3 439
2011	74 290	2 108	650	1 459	72 182	6 826	16 674	16 370	17 113	11 469	3 730
2012	75 555	2 152	659	1 493	73 403	6 948	16 607	16 483	17 221	12 068	4 077

Table 1-11. Employed Civilians, by Age, Sex, Race, and Hispanic Origin, 1948–2012—*Continued*

(Thousands of people.)

Race, Hispanic origin, sex, and year	16 years and over	16 to 19 years			20 years and over						
		Total	16 to 17 years	18 to 19 years	Total	20 to 24 years	25 to 34 years	35 to 44 years	45 to 54 years	55 to 64 years	65 years and over
ALL RACES											
Women											
1948	16 617	1 682	604	1 078	14 936	2 588	3 763	3 687	2 882	1 516	501
1949	16 723	1 588	555	1 033	15 137	2 463	3 760	3 800	2 975	1 604	535
1950	17 340	1 517	524	993	15 824	2 491	3 857	3 979	3 176	1 757	563
1951	18 181	1 611	596	1 015	16 570	2 541	4 099	4 139	3 409	1 847	535
1952	18 568	1 612	641	971	16 958	2 389	4 163	4 305	3 543	1 981	576
1953	18 749	1 584	601	983	17 164	2 324	4 019	4 545	3 595	1 998	683
1954	18 490	1 490	541	949	17 000	2 247	3 936	4 459	3 646	2 065	646
1955	19 551	1 547	564	984	18 002	2 297	4 028	4 612	4 003	2 301	761
1956	20 419	1 654	639	1 015	18 767	2 300	4 070	4 833	4 246	2 515	802
1957	20 714	1 663	626	1 037	19 052	2 295	4 031	4 921	4 469	2 551	785
1958	20 613	1 570	571	999	19 043	2 278	3 885	4 866	4 620	2 604	791
1959	21 164	1 640	655	985	19 524	2 273	3 847	4 962	4 867	2 764	813
1960	21 874	1 768	680	1 089	20 105	2 365	3 871	5 046	5 056	2 884	882
1961	22 090	1 793	632	1 161	20 296	2 432	3 838	5 047	5 125	2 965	889
1962	22 525	1 833	617	1 216	20 693	2 548	3 836	5 190	5 158	3 086	875
1963	23 105	1 849	678	1 170	21 257	2 697	3 887	5 313	5 271	3 211	877
1964	23 831	1 929	771	1 158	21 903	2 933	3 918	5 334	5 457	3 326	934
1965	24 748	2 118	790	1 328	22 630	3 119	4 093	5 457	5 528	3 486	948
1966	25 976	2 468	880	1 589	23 510	3 365	4 308	5 548	5 711	3 642	937
1967	26 893	2 496	917	1 579	24 397	3 690	4 587	5 607	5 799	3 762	953
1968	27 807	2 526	950	1 575	25 281	3 950	4 860	5 666	5 981	3 852	972
1969	29 084	2 687	1 047	1 639	26 397	4 307	5 147	5 699	6 223	3 988	1 033
1970	29 688	2 735	1 094	1 641	26 952	4 494	5 382	5 706	6 303	4 046	1 023
1971	29 976	2 730	1 086	1 645	27 246	4 609	5 563	5 647	6 313	4 093	1 021
1972	31 257	2 980	1 188	1 792	28 276	4 861	6 197	5 734	6 318	4 115	1 051
1973	32 715	3 231	1 310	1 920	29 484	5 184	6 893	5 915	6 356	4 109	1 029
1974	33 769	3 345	1 367	1 978	30 424	5 363	7 492	6 068	6 451	4 084	966
1975	33 989	3 263	1 320	1 943	30 726	5 401	7 882	6 061	6 288	4 105	989
1976	35 615	3 389	1 346	2 043	32 226	5 655	8 624	6 400	6 343	4 188	1 017
1977	37 289	3 514	1 403	2 110	33 775	5 965	9 367	6 758	6 380	4 279	1 027
1978	39 569	3 734	1 530	2 204	35 836	6 328	10 157	7 282	6 532	4 446	1 091
1979	41 217	3 783	1 541	2 242	37 434	6 538	10 802	7 779	6 622	4 569	1 124
1980	42 117	3 625	1 433	2 192	38 492	6 555	11 370	8 168	6 686	4 587	1 125
1981	43 000	3 411	1 340	2 070	39 590	6 618	11 914	8 532	6 777	4 616	1 133
1982	43 256	3 170	1 198	1 972	40 086	6 492	12 147	8 977	6 689	4 634	1 147
1983	44 047	3 043	1 107	1 935	41 004	6 490	12 540	9 510	6 678	4 629	1 157
1984	45 915	3 122	1 161	1 962	42 793	6 636	13 182	10 289	6 852	4 700	1 133
1985	47 259	3 105	1 193	1 913	44 154	6 640	13 644	10 933	7 097	4 721	1 118
1986	48 706	3 149	1 270	1 879	45 556	6 540	14 109	11 595	7 395	4 751	1 165
1987	50 334	3 260	1 343	1 917	47 074	6 466	14 617	12 281	7 737	4 783	1 191
1988	51 696	3 313	1 310	2 003	48 383	6 326	14 872	12 811	8 246	4 841	1 286
1989	53 027	3 282	1 261	2 021	49 745	6 163	15 093	13 440	8 711	4 950	1 388
1990	53 689	3 154	1 156	1 998	50 535	6 250	15 155	14 046	8 835	4 811	1 437
1991	53 496	2 862	1 067	1 794	50 634	6 066	14 796	14 507	9 069	4 756	1 440
1992	54 052	2 724	1 032	1 692	51 328	6 053	14 701	14 693	9 657	4 825	1 398
1993	54 910	2 811	1 071	1 740	52 099	6 035	14 508	15 002	10 248	4 892	1 414
1994	56 610	3 005	1 222	1 783	53 606	5 987	14 545	15 488	10 908	5 085	1 592
1995	57 523	3 127	1 258	1 869	54 396	5 779	14 647	15 828	11 421	5 163	1 558
1996	58 501	3 190	1 328	1 862	55 311	5 709	14 549	16 235	12 031	5 269	1 518
1997	59 873	3 260	1 293	1 967	56 613	5 831	14 471	16 581	12 637	5 561	1 532
1998	60 771	3 493	1 364	2 128	57 278	5 919	14 298	16 644	13 043	5 820	1 554
1999	62 042	3 487	1 357	2 130	58 555	6 163	14 171	16 917	13 644	6 041	1 619
2000	63 586	3 519	1 364	2 154	60 067	6 255	14 308	16 897	14 438	6 396	1 773
2001	63 737	3 320	1 289	2 031	60 417	6 396	13 948	16 744	14 768	6 745	1 815
2002	63 582	3 162	1 200	1 962	60 420	6 374	13 733	16 303	14 863	7 296	1 851
2003	64 404	3 002	1 197	1 805	61 402	6 367	13 714	16 106	15 326	7 866	2 023
2004	64 728	2 955	1 156	1 799	61 773	6 477	13 605	15 880	15 518	8 157	2 135
2005	65 757	3 055	1 217	1 838	62 702	6 513	13 687	15 850	15 779	8 635	2 238
2006	66 925	3 091	1 261	1 830	63 834	6 467	13 917	15 804	16 132	9 198	2 316
2007	67 792	2 994	1 195	1 798	64 799	6 590	14 133	15 636	16 353	9 553	2 534
2008	67 876	2 837	1 063	1 774	65 039	6 484	14 200	15 360	16 406	9 893	2 697
2009	66 208	2 509	865	1 644	63 699	6 254	13 791	14 599	16 170	10 128	2 757
2010	65 705	2 249	743	1 506	63 456	6 233	13 870	14 078	15 949	10 496	2 830
2011	65 579	2 219	705	1 514	63 360	6 209	13 863	13 900	15 753	10 717	2 917
2012	66 914	2 274	760	1 514	64 640	6 460	14 094	14 093	15 653	11 171	3 168

Table 1-11. Employed Civilians, by Age, Sex, Race, and Hispanic Origin, 1948–2012—*Continued*

(Thousands of people.)

Race, Hispanic origin, sex, and year	16 years and over	16 to 19 years			20 years and over						
		Total	16 to 17 years	18 to 19 years	Total	20 to 24 years	25 to 34 years	35 to 44 years	45 to 54 years	55 to 64 years	65 years and over
WHITE											
Both Sexes											
1954	53 957	3 078	1 257	1 822	50 879	4 358	12 616	13 000	10 811	7 262	2 831
1955	55 833	3 225	1 330	1 896	52 608	4 637	12 855	13 327	11 322	7 510	2 957
1956	57 269	3 389	1 465	1 922	53 880	4 897	12 748	13 637	11 706	7 822	3 068
1957	57 465	3 374	1 442	1 931	54 091	4 952	12 619	13 716	12 009	7 829	2 951
1958	56 613	3 216	1 370	1 847	53 397	4 908	12 128	13 571	12 113	7 849	2 828
1959	58 006	3 475	1 520	1 955	54 531	5 138	12 144	13 830	12 552	8 063	2 805
1960	58 850	3 700	1 598	2 103	55 150	5 331	12 021	13 930	12 820	8 192	2 855
1961	58 913	3 693	1 472	2 220	55 220	5 460	11 835	13 905	12 906	8 335	2 778
1962	59 698	3 774	1 447	2 327	55 924	5 676	11 703	14 173	13 066	8 511	2 795
1963	60 622	3 851	1 600	2 250	56 771	6 036	11 689	14 341	13 304	8 718	2 683
1964	61 922	4 076	1 846	2 230	57 846	6 444	11 794	14 380	13 596	8 916	2 717
1965	63 446	4 562	1 892	2 670	58 884	6 752	11 992	14 473	13 804	9 116	2 748
1966	65 021	5 176	2 052	3 124	59 845	6 986	12 268	14 449	14 072	9 356	2 713
1967	66 361	5 114	2 121	2 993	61 247	7 493	12 763	14 429	14 224	9 596	2 746
1968	67 750	5 195	2 193	3 002	62 555	7 687	13 410	14 386	14 487	9 781	2 804
1969	69 518	5 508	2 347	3 161	64 010	8 182	13 935	14 270	14 788	9 947	2 888
1970	70 217	5 571	2 386	3 185	64 645	8 559	14 326	14 092	14 854	9 979	2 835
1971	70 878	5 670	2 404	3 266	65 208	9 000	14 713	13 858	14 843	10 014	2 780
1972	73 370	6 173	2 581	3 592	67 197	9 718	15 904	13 940	14 845	10 077	2 714
1973	75 708	6 623	2 806	3 816	69 086	10 424	17 099	14 083	14 886	9 983	2 610
1974	77 184	6 796	2 881	3 916	70 388	10 676	18 040	14 196	14 948	9 958	2 568
1975	76 411	6 487	2 721	3 770	69 924	10 546	18 485	13 979	14 555	9 827	2 533
1976	78 853	6 724	2 762	3 962	72 129	11 119	19 662	14 407	14 549	9 923	2 470
1977	81 700	7 068	2 926	4 142	74 632	11 696	20 844	14 984	14 483	10 107	2 518
1978	84 936	7 367	3 085	4 282	77 569	12 251	22 008	15 809	14 550	10 311	2 642
1979	87 259	7 356	3 079	4 278	79 904	12 594	23 033	16 578	14 522	10 477	2 699
1980	87 715	7 021	2 861	4 161	80 694	12 405	23 653	17 071	14 405	10 475	2 684
1981	88 709	6 588	2 645	3 943	82 121	12 477	24 551	17 617	14 414	10 386	2 676
1982	87 903	5 984	2 317	3 667	81 918	12 097	24 531	18 268	14 083	10 283	2 656
1983	88 893	5 799	2 156	3 643	83 094	12 138	24 955	19 194	13 961	10 169	2 678
1984	92 120	5 836	2 209	3 627	86 284	12 451	26 235	20 552	14 239	10 227	2 580
1985	93 736	5 768	2 270	3 498	87 968	12 235	26 945	21 552	14 459	10 247	2 530
1986	95 660	5 792	2 386	3 406	89 869	12 027	27 746	22 515	14 750	10 176	2 654
1987	97 789	5 898	2 468	3 431	91 890	11 748	28 429	23 596	15 216	10 164	2 738
1988	99 812	6 030	2 424	3 606	93 782	11 438	28 796	24 468	16 054	10 153	2 874
1989	101 584	5 946	2 278	3 668	95 638	11 084	29 091	25 442	16 775	10 223	3 024
1990	102 261	5 779	2 141	3 638	96 481	11 498	28 773	26 282	16 933	9 960	3 035
1991	101 182	5 216	1 971	3 246	95 966	11 116	27 989	26 883	17 269	9 719	2 990
1992	101 669	4 985	1 904	3 081	96 684	11 031	27 552	27 097	18 285	9 701	3 019
1993	103 045	5 113	1 990	3 123	97 932	10 931	27 274	27 645	19 273	9 772	3 037
1994	105 190	5 398	2 210	3 188	99 792	10 736	27 101	28 442	20 247	9 912	3 354
1995	106 490	5 593	2 273	3 320	100 897	10 400	27 014	28 951	21 127	10 070	3 335
1996	107 808	5 667	2 325	3 343	102 141	10 149	26 678	29 566	22 071	10 313	3 364
1997	109 856	5 807	2 341	3 466	104 049	10 362	26 294	30 137	23 061	10 785	3 411
1998	110 931	6 089	2 436	3 653	104 842	10 512	25 729	30 320	23 662	11 272	3 347
1999	112 235	6 204	2 435	3 769	106 032	10 716	25 113	30 548	24 507	11 657	3 491
2000	114 424	6 160	2 383	3 777	108 264	10 944	25 500	30 151	25 762	12 169	3 738
2001	114 430	5 817	2 224	3 593	108 613	11 054	24 948	29 793	26 301	12 743	3 774
2002	114 013	5 441	2 037	3 404	108 572	11 096	24 568	29 049	26 401	13 630	3 828
2003	114 235	5 064	1 999	3 065	109 171	11 052	24 399	28 501	26 762	14 375	4 083
2004	115 239	5 039	1 895	3 145	110 199	11 233	24 337	28 176	27 228	14 965	4 260
2005	116 949	5 105	1 999	3 106	111 844	11 231	24 443	28 102	27 801	15 788	4 480
2006	118 833	5 215	2 099	3 117	113 618	11 296	24 652	27 929	28 419	16 652	4 670
2007	119 792	4 990	1 965	3 026	114 802	11 325	25 024	27 492	28 779	17 262	4 921
2008	119 126	4 697	1 703	2 994	114 428	11 055	24 875	26 736	28 686	17 829	5 247
2009	114 996	4 138	1 443	2 696	110 858	10 438	23 957	25 237	27 891	17 978	5 357
2010	114 168	3 733	1 248	2 485	110 435	10 334	24 097	24 540	27 502	18 464	5 496
2011	114 690	3 691	1 189	2 501	111 000	10 574	24 376	24 156	27 176	18 937	5 780
2012	114 769	3 665	1 207	2 458	111 104	10 561	23 925	23 931	26 769	19 608	6 309

Table 1-11. Employed Civilians, by Age, Sex, Race, and Hispanic Origin, 1948–2012—*Continued*

(Thousands of people.)

Race, Hispanic origin, sex, and year	16 years and over	16 to 19 years			20 years and over						
		Total	16 to 17 years	18 to 19 years	Total	20 to 24 years	25 to 34 years	35 to 44 years	45 to 54 years	55 to 64 years	65 years and over
WHITE											
Men											
1954	37 846	1 723	771	953	36 123	2 394	9 287	9 175	7 614	5 412	2 241
1955	38 719	1 824	821	1 004	36 895	2 607	9 461	9 351	7 792	5 431	2 254
1956	39 368	1 893	890	1 002	37 475	2 850	9 330	9 449	7 950	5 559	2 336
1957	39 349	1 865	874	990	37 484	2 930	9 226	9 480	8 067	5 542	2 234
1958	38 591	1 783	852	932	36 808	2 896	8 861	9 386	8 061	5 501	2 103
1959	39 494	1 961	915	1 046	37 533	3 153	8 911	9 560	8 261	5 588	2 060
1960	39 755	2 092	973	1 119	37 663	3 264	8 777	9 589	8 372	5 618	2 043
1961	39 588	2 055	891	1 164	37 533	3 311	8 630	9 566	8 394	5 670	1 961
1962	40 016	2 098	883	1 215	37 918	3 426	8 514	9 718	8 512	5 749	1 998
1963	40 428	2 156	972	1 184	38 272	3 646	8 463	9 782	8 650	5 844	1 887
1964	41 115	2 316	1 128	1 188	38 799	3 856	8 538	9 800	8 787	5 945	1 872
1965	41 844	2 612	1 159	1 453	39 232	4 025	8 598	9 795	8 924	5 998	1 892
1966	42 331	2 913	1 245	1 668	39 418	4 028	8 674	9 719	9 029	6 096	1 871
1967	42 833	2 849	1 278	1 571	39 985	4 231	8 931	9 632	9 093	6 208	1 892
1968	43 411	2 908	1 319	1 589	40 503	4 226	9 315	9 522	9 198	6 316	1 926
1969	44 048	3 070	1 385	1 685	40 978	4 401	9 608	9 379	9 279	6 359	1 953
1970	44 178	3 066	1 374	1 692	41 112	4 601	9 784	9 202	9 271	6 340	1 914
1971	44 595	3 157	1 393	1 764	41 438	4 935	10 026	9 026	9 256	6 339	1 856
1972	45 944	3 416	1 470	1 947	42 528	5 431	10 664	9 047	9 236	6 363	1 786
1973	47 085	3 660	1 590	2 071	43 424	5 863	11 268	9 046	9 257	6 299	1 689
1974	47 674	3 728	1 611	2 117	43 946	5 965	11 701	9 027	9 242	6 304	1 706
1975	46 697	3 505	1 502	2 002	43 192	5 770	11 783	8 818	9 005	6 160	1 656
1976	47 775	3 604	1 501	2 103	44 171	6 140	12 362	8 944	8 968	6 176	1 579
1977	49 150	3 824	1 607	2 217	45 326	6 437	12 893	9 212	8 898	6 279	1 605
1978	50 544	3 950	1 664	2 286	46 594	6 717	13 413	9 608	8 840	6 339	1 677
1979	51 452	3 904	1 654	2 250	47 546	6 868	13 888	9 930	8 748	6 406	1 707
1980	51 127	3 708	1 534	2 174	47 419	6 652	14 009	10 077	8 586	6 412	1 684
1981	51 315	3 469	1 402	2 066	47 846	6 652	14 398	10 307	8 518	6 309	1 662
1982	50 287	3 079	1 214	1 865	47 209	6 372	14 164	10 593	8 267	6 188	1 624
1983	50 621	3 003	1 124	1 879	47 618	6 386	14 297	11 062	8 152	6 084	1 637
1984	52 462	3 001	1 140	1 861	49 461	6 647	15 045	11 776	8 320	6 108	1 564
1985	53 046	2 985	1 185	1 800	50 061	6 428	15 374	12 214	8 374	6 118	1 552
1986	53 785	2 966	1 225	1 741	50 818	6 340	15 790	12 620	8 442	6 012	1 612
1987	54 647	2 999	1 252	1 747	51 649	6 150	16 084	13 138	8 596	5 991	1 690
1988	55 550	3 084	1 248	1 836	52 466	5 987	16 241	13 590	8 992	5 909	1 748
1989	56 352	3 060	1 171	1 889	53 292	5 839	16 383	14 046	9 335	5 891	1 797
1990	56 703	3 018	1 119	1 899	53 685	6 179	16 124	14 496	9 383	5 744	1 760
1991	55 797	2 694	1 017	1 677	53 103	5 942	15 644	14 743	9 488	5 578	1 707
1992	55 959	2 602	990	1 612	53 357	5 855	15 357	14 842	10 027	5 503	1 772
1993	56 656	2 634	1 031	1 603	54 021	5 830	15 230	15 178	10 497	5 514	1 772
1994	57 452	2 776	1 144	1 632	54 676	5 738	15 052	15 562	10 910	5 490	1 925
1995	58 146	2 892	1 169	1 723	55 254	5 613	14 958	15 793	11 359	5 609	1 921
1996	58 888	2 911	1 161	1 750	55 977	5 444	14 820	16 136	11 834	5 755	1 987
1997	59 998	3 011	1 206	1 806	56 986	5 590	14 567	16 470	12 352	5 972	2 037
1998	60 604	3 103	1 233	1 870	57 500	5 659	14 259	16 715	12 661	6 251	1 955
1999	61 139	3 205	1 254	1 951	57 934	5 753	13 851	16 781	13 046	6 447	2 056
2000	62 289	3 169	1 205	1 965	59 119	5 876	14 238	16 477	13 675	6 678	2 175
2001	62 212	2 967	1 102	1 865	59 245	5 870	13 989	16 280	13 987	6 941	2 178
2002	61 849	2 725	987	1 738	59 124	5 882	13 727	15 910	14 060	7 360	2 184
2003	61 866	2 518	972	1 546	59 348	5 890	13 731	15 675	14 117	7 640	2 295
2004	62 712	2 553	903	1 650	60 159	6 026	13 735	15 572	14 418	8 018	2 390
2005	63 763	2 508	942	1 566	61 255	6 041	13 840	15 544	14 810	8 471	2 550
2006	64 883	2 625	1 020	1 605	62 259	6 114	13 903	15 480	15 189	8 893	2 680
2007	65 289	2 483	951	1 531	62 806	6 066	14 112	15 287	15 399	9 215	2 727
2008	64 624	2 320	808	1 512	62 304	5 858	13 931	14 775	15 300	9 518	2 922
2009	61 630	2 004	692	1 312	59 626	5 379	13 230	13 858	14 710	9 465	2 984
2010	61 252	1 815	598	1 217	59 438	5 347	13 282	13 583	14 542	9 637	3 047
2011	61 920	1 802	573	1 229	60 118	5 630	13 548	13 366	14 370	9 932	3 271
2012	61 990	1 797	563	1 234	60 193	5 547	13 212	13 224	14 264	10 334	3 611

Table 1-11. Employed Civilians, by Age, Sex, Race, and Hispanic Origin, 1948–2012—*Continued*

(Thousands of people.)

Race, Hispanic origin, sex, and year	16 years and over	16 to 19 years			20 years and over						
		Total	16 to 17 years	18 to 19 years	Total	20 to 24 years	25 to 34 years	35 to 44 years	45 to 54 years	55 to 64 years	65 years and over
WHITE											
Women											
1954	16 111	1 355	486	869	14 756	1 964	3 329	3 825	3 197	1 850	590
1955	17 114	1 401	509	892	15 713	2 030	3 394	3 976	3 530	2 079	703
1956	17 901	1 496	575	920	16 405	2 047	3 418	4 188	3 756	2 263	732
1957	18 116	1 509	568	941	16 607	2 022	3 393	4 236	3 942	2 287	717
1958	18 022	1 433	518	915	16 589	2 012	3 267	4 185	4 052	2 348	725
1959	18 512	1 514	605	909	16 998	1 985	3 233	4 270	4 291	2 475	745
1960	19 095	1 608	625	984	17 487	2 067	3 244	4 341	4 448	2 574	812
1961	19 325	1 638	581	1 056	17 687	2 149	3 205	4 339	4 512	2 665	817
1962	19 682	1 676	564	1 112	18 006	2 250	3 189	4 455	4 554	2 762	797
1963	20 194	1 695	628	1 066	18 499	2 390	3 226	4 559	4 654	2 874	796
1964	20 807	1 760	718	1 042	19 047	2 588	3 256	4 580	4 809	2 971	845
1965	21 602	1 950	733	1 217	19 652	2 727	3 394	4 678	4 880	3 118	856
1966	22 690	2 263	807	1 456	20 427	2 958	3 594	4 730	5 043	3 260	842
1967	23 528	2 265	843	1 422	21 263	3 262	3 832	4 797	5 131	3 388	854
1968	24 339	2 287	874	1 413	22 052	3 461	4 095	4 864	5 289	3 465	878
1969	25 470	2 438	962	1 476	23 032	3 781	4 327	4 891	5 509	3 588	935
1970	26 039	2 505	1 012	1 493	23 534	3 959	4 542	4 890	5 582	3 640	921
1971	26 283	2 513	1 011	1 502	23 770	4 065	4 687	4 831	5 588	3 675	924
1972	27 426	2 755	1 111	1 645	24 669	4 286	5 240	4 893	5 608	3 714	928
1973	28 623	2 962	1 217	1 746	25 661	4 562	5 831	5 036	5 628	3 684	920
1974	29 511	3 069	1 269	1 799	26 442	4 711	6 340	5 169	5 706	3 654	862
1975	29 714	2 983	1 215	1 767	26 731	4 775	6 701	5 161	5 550	3 667	877
1976	31 078	3 120	1 260	1 860	27 958	4 978	7 300	5 462	5 580	3 746	891
1977	32 550	3 244	1 319	1 923	29 306	5 259	7 950	5 772	5 585	3 829	912
1978	34 392	3 416	1 420	1 996	30 975	5 535	8 595	6 201	5 710	3 972	964
1979	35 807	3 451	1 423	2 027	32 357	5 726	9 145	6 648	5 773	4 071	993
1980	36 587	3 314	1 327	1 986	33 275	5 753	9 644	6 994	5 818	4 064	1 001
1981	37 394	3 119	1 242	1 877	34 275	5 826	10 153	7 311	5 896	4 077	1 013
1982	37 615	2 905	1 103	1 802	34 710	5 724	10 367	7 675	5 816	4 095	1 032
1983	38 272	2 796	1 032	1 764	35 476	5 751	10 659	8 132	5 809	4 084	1 041
1984	39 659	2 835	1 069	1 766	36 823	5 804	11 190	8 776	5 920	4 118	1 015
1985	40 690	2 783	1 085	1 698	37 907	5 807	11 571	9 338	6 084	4 128	978
1986	41 876	2 825	1 160	1 665	39 050	5 687	11 956	9 895	6 307	4 164	1 042
1987	43 142	2 900	1 216	1 684	40 242	5 598	12 345	10 459	6 620	4 172	1 047
1988	44 262	2 946	1 176	1 770	41 316	5 450	12 555	10 878	7 062	4 244	1 126
1989	45 232	2 886	1 107	1 779	42 346	5 245	12 708	11 395	7 440	4 332	1 227
1990	45 558	2 762	1 023	1 739	42 796	5 319	12 649	11 785	7 551	4 217	1 275
1991	45 385	2 523	954	1 569	42 862	5 174	12 344	12 139	7 781	4 141	1 283
1992	45 710	2 383	915	1 468	43 327	5 176	12 195	12 254	8 258	4 198	1 246
1993	46 390	2 479	959	1 520	43 910	5 101	12 044	12 467	8 776	4 258	1 265
1994	47 738	2 622	1 066	1 556	45 116	4 997	12 049	12 880	9 338	4 423	1 429
1995	48 344	2 701	1 104	1 597	45 643	4 787	12 056	13 157	9 768	4 461	1 415
1996	48 920	2 756	1 164	1 592	46 164	4 705	11 858	13 430	10 237	4 558	1 376
1997	49 859	2 796	1 136	1 660	47 063	4 773	11 727	13 667	10 709	4 813	1 374
1998	50 327	2 986	1 203	1 783	47 342	4 853	11 470	13 604	11 001	5 021	1 392
1999	51 096	2 999	1 181	1 817	48 098	4 963	11 262	13 767	11 461	5 211	1 435
2000	52 136	2 991	1 178	1 813	49 145	5 068	11 262	13 674	12 087	5 490	1 564
2001	52 218	2 850	1 122	1 727	49 369	5 184	10 959	13 513	12 314	5 802	1 597
2002	52 164	2 716	1 050	1 665	49 448	5 214	10 842	13 138	12 341	6 269	1 644
2003	52 369	2 546	1 027	1 519	49 823	5 161	10 668	12 826	12 645	6 735	1 788
2004	52 527	2 486	991	1 495	50 040	5 207	10 602	12 604	12 810	6 947	1 870
2005	53 186	2 597	1 057	1 540	50 589	5 190	10 603	12 558	12 991	7 317	1 930
2006	53 950	2 590	1 079	1 512	51 359	5 182	10 750	12 449	13 230	7 758	1 991
2007	54 503	2 507	1 013	1 494	51 996	5 259	10 912	12 205	13 380	8 047	2 193
2008	54 501	2 377	895	1 482	52 124	5 197	10 943	11 961	13 386	8 312	2 325
2009	53 366	2 134	751	1 383	51 231	5 060	10 727	11 379	13 181	8 513	2 373
2010	52 916	1 918	650	1 268	50 997	4 988	10 815	10 958	12 960	8 827	2 450
2011	52 770	1 889	617	1 272	50 881	4 943	10 828	10 789	12 806	9 005	2 509
2012	52 779	1 868	644	1 224	50 911	5 014	10 713	10 708	12 505	9 274	2 698

Table 1-11. Employed Civilians, by Age, Sex, Race, and Hispanic Origin, 1948–2012—*Continued*

(Thousands of people.)

Race, Hispanic origin, sex, and year	16 years and over	16 to 19 years			20 years and over						
		Total	16 to 17 years	18 to 19 years	Total	20 to 24 years	25 to 34 years	35 to 44 years	45 to 54 years	55 to 64 years	65 years and over
BLACK											
Both Sexes											
1974	8 203	554	190	364	7 649	1 231	2 157	1 682	1 452	884	243
1975	7 894	507	183	325	7 386	1 115	2 145	1 617	1 393	874	241
1976	8 227	508	170	338	7 719	1 193	2 309	1 679	1 416	870	252
1977	8 540	508	169	339	8 031	1 244	2 443	1 754	1 448	892	251
1978	9 102	571	191	380	8 531	1 359	2 641	1 848	1 479	932	273
1979	9 359	579	204	376	8 780	1 424	2 759	1 902	1 502	927	266
1980	9 313	547	192	356	8 765	1 376	2 827	1 910	1 487	925	239
1981	9 355	505	170	335	8 849	1 346	2 872	1 957	1 489	954	231
1982	9 189	428	138	290	8 761	1 283	2 830	2 025	1 469	928	225
1983	9 375	416	123	294	8 959	1 280	2 976	2 107	1 456	937	204
1984	10 119	474	146	328	9 645	1 423	3 223	2 311	1 533	945	209
1985	10 501	532	175	356	9 969	1 399	3 325	2 427	1 598	985	235
1986	10 814	536	183	353	10 278	1 429	3 464	2 524	1 666	982	214
1987	11 309	587	203	385	10 722	1 421	3 614	2 695	1 714	1 036	241
1988	11 658	601	223	378	11 057	1 433	3 725	2 839	1 783	1 018	261
1989	11 953	625	237	388	11 328	1 467	3 801	2 981	1 844	970	265
1990	12 175	598	194	404	11 577	1 409	3 803	3 287	1 897	933	248
1991	12 074	494	161	334	11 580	1 373	3 714	3 401	1 892	957	243
1992	12 151	492	157	335	11 659	1 343	3 699	3 441	1 964	965	246
1993	12 382	494	171	323	11 888	1 377	3 700	3 584	2 059	941	226
1994	12 835	552	224	328	12 284	1 449	3 732	3 722	2 178	953	251
1995	13 279	586	223	363	12 693	1 443	3 844	3 861	2 288	1 004	253
1996	13 542	613	233	380	12 929	1 411	3 851	3 974	2 426	1 025	241
1997	13 969	631	229	401	13 339	1 456	3 903	4 094	2 588	1 048	249
1998	14 556	736	246	490	13 820	1 496	3 967	4 238	2 739	1 118	262
1999	15 056	691	243	448	14 365	1 594	4 091	4 404	2 872	1 134	271
2000	15 156	711	260	451	14 444	1 593	3 993	4 261	3 073	1 226	300
2001	15 006	637	230	408	14 368	1 571	3 840	4 200	3 139	1 283	335
2002	14 872	611	193	417	14 262	1 543	3 726	4 109	3 220	1 332	332
2003	14 739	516	196	320	14 222	1 516	3 618	4 080	3 289	1 373	346
2004	14 909	520	169	351	14 389	1 572	3 635	4 039	3 332	1 452	359
2005	15 313	536	164	372	14 776	1 599	3 722	4 060	3 464	1 555	375
2006	15 765	618	215	402	15 147	1 643	3 809	4 072	3 570	1 659	394
2007	16 051	566	202	364	15 485	1 674	3 888	4 120	3 658	1 732	413
2008	15 953	541	172	369	15 411	1 625	3 870	4 015	3 670	1 791	440
2009	15 025	442	131	310	14 584	1 474	3 582	3 686	3 562	1 827	453
2010	15 010	386	106	280	14 624	1 532	3 641	3 561	3 531	1 899	460
2011	15 051	380	99	281	14 671	1 574	3 632	3 499	3 513	1 943	508
2012	15 856	438	119	319	15 417	1 700	3 693	3 662	3 660	2 161	540
BLACK											
Men											
1974	4 527	322	114	209	4 204	668	1 176	912	803	500	145
1975	4 275	276	98	179	3 998	595	1 159	865	755	487	137
1976	4 404	283	100	184	4 120	635	1 217	897	763	472	137
1977	4 565	291	105	186	4 273	659	1 271	940	777	484	143
1978	4 796	312	106	206	4 483	697	1 357	969	788	516	155
1979	4 923	316	111	205	4 606	754	1 425	983	801	498	147
1980	4 798	299	109	191	4 498	713	1 438	975	770	478	126
1981	4 794	273	95	178	4 520	693	1 457	991	764	492	123
1982	4 637	223	65	158	4 414	660	1 414	997	750	471	122
1983	4 753	222	64	158	4 531	684	1 483	1 034	749	477	105
1984	5 124	252	79	173	4 871	750	1 635	1 138	780	460	108
1985	5 270	278	92	186	4 992	726	1 669	1 187	795	501	114
1986	5 428	278	96	182	5 150	732	1 756	1 211	831	507	112
1987	5 661	304	109	195	5 357	728	1 821	1 283	853	547	124
1988	5 824	316	122	193	5 509	736	1 881	1 348	878	536	131
1989	5 928	327	124	202	5 602	742	1 931	1 415	886	498	131
1990	5 995	303	99	204	5 692	702	1 895	1 586	926	469	114
1991	5 961	255	85	170	5 706	695	1 859	1 634	923	481	114
1992	5 930	249	78	170	5 681	679	1 819	1 650	930	478	124
1993	6 047	254	88	166	5 793	674	1 858	1 717	978	461	106
1994	6 241	276	107	169	5 964	718	1 850	1 795	1 030	455	115
1995	6 422	285	111	174	6 137	714	1 895	1 836	1 085	468	138
1996	6 456	289	109	180	6 167	685	1 867	1 878	1 129	482	126
1997	6 607	282	108	174	6 325	668	1 874	1 955	1 215	487	127
1998	6 871	341	120	221	6 530	686	1 886	2 008	1 284	524	142
1999	7 027	325	120	205	6 702	700	1 926	2 092	1 327	525	131
2000	7 082	341	129	211	6 741	730	1 865	1 984	1 425	596	142
2001	6 938	311	115	196	6 627	703	1 757	1 931	1 452	614	170
2002	6 959	306	95	212	6 652	725	1 729	1 899	1 503	624	172
2003	6 820	234	89	145	6 586	726	1 660	1 868	1 518	638	176
2004	6 912	231	76	155	6 681	739	1 720	1 840	1 534	668	180
2005	7 155	254	76	178	6 901	748	1 759	1 886	1 616	711	182
2006	7 354	275	99	175	7 079	804	1 797	1 882	1 680	734	184
2007	7 500	254	82	172	7 245	816	1 851	1 916	1 717	750	195
2008	7 398	247	70	177	7 151	794	1 805	1 854	1 703	792	204
2009	6 817	189	56	133	6 628	689	1 635	1 662	1 622	813	206
2010	6 865	185	48	137	6 680	692	1 710	1 638	1 594	834	211
2011	6 953	187	49	138	6 765	734	1 733	1 583	1 621	858	236
2012	7 302	198	52	146	7 104	784	1 723	1 667	1 693	988	249

Table 1-11. Employed Civilians, by Age, Sex, Race, and Hispanic Origin, 1948–2012—*Continued*

(Thousands of people.)

Race, Hispanic origin, sex, and year	16 years and over	16 to 19 years			20 years and over						
		Total	16 to 17 years	18 to 19 years	Total	20 to 24 years	25 to 34 years	35 to 44 years	45 to 54 years	55 to 64 years	65 years and over
BLACK											
Women											
1974	3 677	232	77	155	3 445	562	981	770	649	383	98
1975	3 618	231	85	146	3 388	520	985	752	638	387	104
1976	3 823	224	70	154	3 599	558	1 092	782	653	398	115
1977	3 975	217	64	153	3 758	585	1 172	814	671	408	109
1978	4 307	260	85	175	4 047	662	1 283	879	691	416	118
1979	4 436	263	92	171	4 174	670	1 333	919	702	428	119
1980	4 515	248	82	165	4 267	663	1 389	936	717	448	113
1981	4 561	232	75	157	4 329	653	1 415	966	725	462	108
1982	4 552	205	73	132	4 347	623	1 416	1 028	719	457	103
1983	4 622	194	59	136	4 428	596	1 493	1 073	707	460	99
1984	4 995	222	67	155	4 773	673	1 588	1 173	753	485	101
1985	5 231	254	83	171	4 977	673	1 656	1 240	804	484	121
1986	5 386	259	87	171	5 128	696	1 708	1 313	835	475	102
1987	5 648	283	93	190	5 365	693	1 793	1 412	860	489	117
1988	5 834	285	101	184	5 548	697	1 844	1 491	905	482	129
1989	6 025	298	113	185	5 727	725	1 870	1 566	959	472	134
1990	6 180	296	96	200	5 884	707	1 907	1 701	971	464	135
1991	6 113	239	76	164	5 874	677	1 855	1 768	969	476	129
1992	6 221	243	79	164	5 978	664	1 880	1 791	1 034	487	123
1993	6 334	239	82	157	6 095	703	1 842	1 867	1 081	480	121
1994	6 595	275	117	158	6 320	731	1 882	1 926	1 147	497	136
1995	6 857	301	112	189	6 556	729	1 949	2 025	1 202	536	114
1996	7 086	324	124	200	6 762	726	1 984	2 096	1 297	543	115
1997	7 362	349	122	227	7 013	789	2 029	2 139	1 373	561	122
1998	7 685	395	126	268	7 290	810	2 081	2 230	1 455	594	120
1999	8 029	366	123	243	7 663	893	2 165	2 312	1 545	609	139
2000	8 073	370	131	240	7 703	862	2 128	2 277	1 647	630	158
2001	8 068	327	115	212	7 741	868	2 084	2 269	1 686	668	165
2002	7 914	304	99	205	7 610	819	1 997	2 209	1 717	708	160
2003	7 919	283	107	175	7 636	790	1 959	2 211	1 770	735	171
2004	7 997	289	93	196	7 707	833	1 914	2 199	1 798	784	179
2005	8 158	282	88	194	7 876	852	1 964	2 175	1 848	844	193
2006	8 410	343	116	227	8 068	839	2 012	2 191	1 890	925	210
2007	8 551	311	120	191	8 240	858	2 037	2 205	1 941	982	218
2008	8 554	294	102	192	8 260	831	2 065	2 161	1 967	1 000	236
2009	8 208	252	75	178	7 956	784	1 947	2 024	1 939	1 014	246
2010	8 145	201	58	143	7 944	841	1 931	1 923	1 936	1 065	248
2011	8 098	193	50	142	7 906	840	1 899	1 916	1 892	1 086	272
2012	8 553	240	67	173	8 313	916	1 970	1 995	1 968	1 173	291
HISPANIC											
Both Sexes											
1975	3 663	322	. . .	. . .	. . .	. . .	. . .	. . .	. . .	. . .	. . .
1976	3 720	341	124	230	3 436	614	1 135	803	573	269	42
1977	4 079	381	135	245	3 715	715	1 212	860	608	269	50
1978	4 527	423	159	264	4 104	803	1 330	942	661	307	62
1979	4 785	445	152	292	4 340	860	1 430	996	666	319	69
1980	5 527	500	174	325	5 028	998	1 675	1 074	811	389	80
1981	5 813	459	155	304	5 354	1 060	1 837	1 147	829	399	82
1982	5 805	410	119	291	5 394	1 030	1 896	1 173	816	399	80
1983	6 072	423	125	297	5 649	1 068	1 997	1 224	837	441	81
1984	6 651	468	148	320	6 182	1 160	2 201	1 385	883	474	79
1985	6 888	438	144	294	6 449	1 187	2 316	1 473	913	486	75
1986	7 219	430	146	284	6 789	1 231	2 427	1 570	1 011	474	76
1987	7 790	474	149	325	7 316	1 273	2 668	1 775	1 010	512	76
1988	8 250	523	171	353	7 727	1 341	2 749	1 876	1 078	585	97
1989	8 573	548	165	383	8 025	1 325	2 900	1 968	1 129	589	114
1990	9 845	668	208	460	9 177	1 672	3 327	2 229	1 235	611	103
1991	9 828	602	169	433	9 225	1 622	3 264	2 333	1 266	637	103
1992	10 027	577	169	408	9 450	1 575	3 350	2 468	1 316	628	112
1993	10 361	570	160	410	9 792	1 574	3 446	2 605	1 402	630	135
1994	10 788	609	195	415	10 178	1 643	3 517	2 737	1 495	647	139
1995	11 127	645	194	450	10 483	1 609	3 618	2 889	1 565	666	135
1996	11 642	646	199	447	10 996	1 628	3 758	3 115	1 595	748	152
1997	12 726	714	228	487	12 012	1 798	4 029	3 371	1 846	794	173
1998	13 291	793	230	563	12 498	1 883	4 113	3 504	1 994	846	158
1999	13 720	854	254	600	12 866	1 881	4 097	3 738	2 074	886	190
2000	15 735	973	285	688	14 762	2 356	4 950	4 052	2 308	898	197
2001	16 190	969	268	701	15 221	2 404	5 065	4 149	2 472	944	187
2002	16 590	882	254	628	15 708	2 413	5 272	4 273	2 511	1 029	209
2003	17 372	768	242	525	16 604	2 399	5 541	4 573	2 711	1 132	249
2004	17 930	792	211	581	17 138	2 477	5 560	4 671	2 932	1 210	288
2005	18 632	847	253	595	17 785	2 423	5 756	4 879	3 114	1 317	296
2006	19 613	900	287	614	18 712	2 487	6 001	5 106	3 324	1 441	354
2007	20 382	894	269	625	19 488	2 516	6 237	5 314	3 547	1 499	376
2008	20 346	870	248	622	19 476	2 361	6 119	5 371	3 620	1 619	385
2009	19 647	742	192	550	18 905	2 218	5 704	5 168	3 700	1 680	435
2010	19 906	680	165	515	19 226	2 281	5 781	5 185	3 779	1 737	464
2011	20 269	665	155	510	19 604	2 544	5 747	5 179	3 848	1 820	465
2012	21 878	808	204	604	21 070	2 761	6 119	5 552	4 188	1 983	467

. . . = Not available.

Table 1-11. Employed Civilians, by Age, Sex, Race, and Hispanic Origin, 1948–2012—*Continued*

(Thousands of people.)

Race, Hispanic origin, sex, and year	16 years and over	16 to 19 years			20 years and over						
		Total	16 to 17 years	18 to 19 years	Total	20 to 24 years	25 to 34 years	35 to 44 years	45 to 54 years	55 to 64 years	65 years and over
HISPANIC											
Men											
1975	2 301	. . .	. . .	. . .	2 117	. . .	. . .	. . .	. . .	. . .	. . .
1976	2 303	199	74	125	2 109	364	708	504	369	173	. . .
1977	2 564	225	78	147	2 335	427	763	540	394	184	. . .
1978	2 808	241	93	147	2 568	494	824	590	405	207	. . .
1979	2 962	260	93	168	2 701	511	891	615	427	205	. . .
1980	3 448	306	109	198	3 142	611	1 065	662	491	254	. . .
1981	3 597	272	90	182	3 325	642	1 157	707	504	259	. . .
1982	3 583	229	66	162	3 354	621	1 192	729	498	261	. . .
1983	3 771	248	71	177	3 523	655	1 280	760	499	275	. . .
1984	4 083	258	78	180	3 825	718	1 398	841	530	292	. . .
1985	4 245	251	82	169	3 994	727	1 473	888	550	308	. . .
1986	4 428	254	82	172	4 174	773	1 510	929	614	297	. . .
1987	4 713	268	81	188	4 444	777	1 664	1 044	606	303	. . .
1988	4 972	292	87	205	4 680	815	1 706	1 120	645	331	. . .
1989	5 172	319	94	225	4 853	821	1 787	1 152	676	350	. . .
1990	6 021	412	126	286	5 609	1 083	2 076	1 312	722	355	. . .
1991	5 979	356	94	263	5 623	1 063	2 050	1 360	719	369	. . .
1992	6 093	336	97	238	5 757	985	2 127	1 437	768	372	. . .
1993	6 328	337	95	242	5 992	1 003	2 200	1 527	822	360	. . .
1994	6 530	341	109	233	6 189	1 056	2 227	1 600	847	379	79
1995	6 725	358	110	248	6 367	1 030	2 284	1 675	908	384	85
1996	7 039	384	107	277	6 655	1 015	2 345	1 842	918	438	96
1997	7 728	420	130	290	7 307	1 142	2 547	1 978	1 059	477	105
1998	8 018	449	133	315	7 570	1 173	2 592	2 077	1 115	512	101
1999	8 067	491	139	352	7 576	1 135	2 524	2 135	1 151	502	130
2000	9 428	570	159	411	8 859	1 486	3 063	2 358	1 295	532	126
2001	9 668	568	149	419	9 100	1 473	3 142	2 446	1 375	545	119
2002	9 845	504	141	363	9 341	1 476	3 271	2 503	1 396	569	125
2003	10 479	415	121	294	10 063	1 485	3 537	2 724	1 533	639	144
2004	10 832	446	108	338	10 385	1 514	3 557	2 801	1 654	687	174
2005	11 337	465	137	328	10 872	1 511	3 711	2 939	1 781	748	183
2006	11 887	496	146	350	11 391	1 535	3 845	3 088	1 894	809	220
2007	12 310	483	145	338	11 827	1 524	3 982	3 220	2 012	869	220
2008	12 248	479	140	340	11 769	1 406	3 897	3 233	2 080	929	224
2009	11 640	383	94	289	11 256	1 287	3 576	3 108	2 104	930	251
2010	11 800	361	78	283	11 438	1 319	3 591	3 169	2 137	949	273
2011	12 049	364	76	287	11 685	1 535	3 615	3 124	2 141	1 006	266
2012	12 643	431	97	334	12 212	1 584	3 714	3 229	2 334	1 097	256
HISPANIC											
Women											
1975	1 362	. . .	. . .	. . .	1 224	. . .	. . .	. . .	. . .	. . .	. . .
1976	1 417	155	50	106	1 288	249	427	300	204	96	. . .
1977	1 516	155	57	98	1 370	288	449	320	214	86	. . .
1978	1 719	182	65	117	1 537	308	506	352	256	99	. . .
1979	1 824	185	60	125	1 638	349	539	381	241	115	. . .
1980	2 079	193	65	128	1 886	387	610	412	320	136	. . .
1981	2 216	187	65	122	2 029	418	680	440	326	139	. . .
1982	2 222	181	52	129	2 040	409	704	444	318	139	. . .
1983	2 301	175	54	120	2 127	413	717	464	338	166	. . .
1984	2 568	211	71	140	2 357	442	804	544	354	181	. . .
1985	2 642	187	62	125	2 456	460	843	585	362	178	. . .
1986	2 791	176	64	112	2 615	458	917	641	397	177	. . .
1987	3 077	206	69	137	2 872	496	1 004	732	405	209	. . .
1988	3 278	231	84	147	3 047	526	1 042	756	434	254	. . .
1989	3 401	229	71	158	3 172	504	1 114	816	453	239	. . .
1990	3 823	256	82	174	3 567	588	1 251	917	513	256	. . .
1991	3 848	246	76	170	3 603	559	1 214	972	548	268	. . .
1992	3 934	242	72	170	3 693	591	1 223	1 031	548	256	. . .
1993	4 033	233	65	168	3 800	571	1 246	1 077	581	269	. . .
1994	4 258	268	86	182	3 989	587	1 290	1 137	648	268	59
1995	4 403	287	85	202	4 116	579	1 334	1 213	657	282	50
1996	4 602	261	92	169	4 341	612	1 412	1 273	677	310	56
1997	4 999	294	98	196	4 705	656	1 482	1 393	787	318	69
1998	5 273	345	97	247	4 928	710	1 521	1 428	879	334	57
1999	5 653	363	115	248	5 290	746	1 574	1 603	923	384	60
2000	6 307	404	127	277	5 903	870	1 887	1 695	1 013	366	72
2001	6 522	401	119	282	6 121	931	1 923	1 703	1 097	398	67
2002	6 744	378	113	265	6 367	937	2 001	1 770	1 114	460	84
2003	6 894	353	121	231	6 541	914	2 004	1 849	1 178	493	105
2004	7 098	346	103	243	6 752	964	2 003	1 870	1 279	523	114
2005	7 295	382	116	266	6 913	912	2 045	1 940	1 333	569	113
2006	7 725	404	140	264	7 321	951	2 155	2 018	1 430	632	135
2007	8 072	410	124	287	7 662	991	2 255	2 094	1 535	631	155
2008	8 098	391	108	282	7 707	955	2 222	2 138	1 541	690	161
2009	8 007	358	98	261	7 649	931	2 128	2 060	1 596	751	183
2010	8 106	318	87	231	7 788	962	2 189	2 016	1 642	788	191
2011	8 220	301	79	223	7 918	1 010	2 132	2 055	1 707	814	200
2012	9 235	377	107	269	8 858	1 178	2 405	2 323	1 854	887	212

. . . = Not available.

Table 1-12. Civilian Employment-Population Ratios, by Sex, Age, Race, and Hispanic Origin, 1948–2012
(Percent.)

Race, Hispanic origin, and year	Both sexes			Men			Women		
	16 years and over	16 to 19 years	20 years and over	16 years and over	16 to 19 years	20 years and over	16 years and over	16 to 19 years	20 years and over
ALL RACES									
1948	56.6	47.7	57.4	83.5	57.5	85.8	31.3	38.5	30.7
1949	55.4	45.2	56.3	81.3	53.8	83.7	31.2	37.2	30.6
1950	56.1	45.5	57.0	82.0	55.2	84.2	32.0	36.3	31.6
1951	57.3	47.9	58.1	84.0	57.9	86.1	33.1	38.9	32.6
1952	57.3	46.9	58.1	83.9	55.9	86.2	33.4	38.8	33.0
1953	57.1	46.4	58.0	83.6	55.9	85.9	33.3	37.8	32.9
1954	55.5	42.3	56.6	81.0	50.2	83.5	32.5	34.9	32.3
1955	56.7	43.5	57.8	81.8	52.1	84.3	34.0	35.6	33.8
1956	57.5	45.3	58.5	82.3	53.8	84.6	35.1	37.5	34.9
1957	57.1	43.9	58.2	81.3	51.8	83.8	35.1	36.7	35.0
1958	55.4	39.9	56.8	78.5	46.9	81.2	34.5	33.5	34.6
1959	56.0	39.9	57.5	79.3	47.2	82.3	35.0	33.0	35.1
1960	56.1	40.5	57.6	78.9	47.6	81.9	35.5	33.8	35.7
1961	55.4	39.1	56.9	77.6	45.3	80.8	35.4	33.2	35.6
1962	55.5	39.4	57.1	77.7	45.9	80.9	35.6	33.3	35.8
1963	55.4	37.4	57.2	77.1	43.8	80.6	35.8	31.5	36.3
1964	55.7	37.3	57.7	77.3	44.1	80.9	36.3	30.9	36.9
1965	56.2	38.9	58.2	77.5	46.2	81.2	37.1	32.0	37.6
1966	56.9	42.1	58.7	77.9	48.9	81.5	38.3	35.6	38.6
1967	57.3	42.2	59.0	78.0	48.7	81.5	39.0	35.9	39.3
1968	57.5	42.2	59.3	77.8	48.7	81.3	39.6	36.0	40.0
1969	58.0	43.4	59.7	77.6	49.5	81.1	40.7	37.5	41.1
1970	57.4	42.3	59.2	76.2	47.7	79.7	40.8	37.1	41.2
1971	56.6	41.3	58.4	74.9	46.8	78.5	40.4	36.0	40.9
1972	57.0	43.5	58.6	75.0	48.9	78.4	41.0	38.2	41.3
1973	57.8	45.9	59.3	75.5	51.4	78.6	42.0	40.5	42.2
1974	57.8	46.0	59.2	74.9	51.2	77.9	42.6	41.0	42.8
1975	56.1	43.3	57.6	71.7	47.2	74.8	42.0	39.4	42.3
1976	56.8	44.2	58.3	72.0	47.9	75.1	43.2	40.5	43.5
1977	57.9	46.1	59.2	72.8	50.4	75.6	44.5	41.8	44.8
1978	59.3	48.3	60.6	73.8	52.2	76.4	46.4	44.5	46.6
1979	59.9	48.5	61.2	73.8	51.7	76.5	47.5	45.3	47.7
1980	59.2	46.6	60.6	72.0	49.5	74.6	47.7	43.8	48.1
1981	59.0	44.6	60.5	71.3	47.1	74.0	48.0	42.0	48.6
1982	57.8	41.5	59.4	69.0	42.9	71.8	47.7	40.2	48.4
1983	57.9	41.5	59.5	68.8	43.1	71.4	48.0	40.0	48.8
1984	59.5	43.7	61.0	70.7	45.0	73.2	49.5	42.5	50.1
1985	60.1	44.4	61.5	70.9	45.7	73.3	50.4	42.9	51.0
1986	60.7	44.6	62.1	71.0	45.7	73.3	51.4	43.6	52.0
1987	61.5	45.5	62.9	71.5	46.1	73.8	52.5	44.8	53.1
1988	62.3	46.8	63.6	72.0	47.8	74.2	53.4	45.9	54.0
1989	63.0	47.5	64.2	72.5	48.7	74.5	54.3	46.4	54.9
1990	62.8	45.3	64.3	72.0	46.6	74.3	54.3	44.0	55.2
1991	61.7	42.0	63.2	70.4	42.7	72.7	53.7	41.2	54.6
1992	61.5	41.0	63.0	69.8	41.9	72.1	53.8	40.0	54.8
1993	61.7	41.7	63.3	70.0	42.3	72.3	54.1	41.0	55.0
1994	62.5	43.4	64.0	70.4	43.8	72.6	55.3	43.0	56.2
1995	62.9	44.2	64.4	70.8	44.7	73.0	55.6	43.8	56.5
1996	63.2	43.5	64.7	70.9	43.6	73.2	56.0	43.5	57.0
1997	63.8	43.4	65.5	71.3	43.4	73.7	56.8	43.3	57.8
1998	64.1	45.1	65.6	71.6	44.7	73.9	57.1	45.5	58.0
1999	64.3	44.7	65.9	71.6	45.1	74.0	57.4	44.3	58.5
2000	64.4	45.2	66.0	71.9	45.4	74.2	57.5	45.0	58.4
2001	63.7	42.3	65.4	70.9	42.2	73.3	57.0	42.4	58.1
2002	62.7	39.6	64.6	69.7	38.9	72.3	56.3	40.3	57.5
2003	62.3	36.8	64.3	68.9	35.7	71.7	56.1	37.8	57.5
2004	62.3	36.4	64.4	69.2	35.9	71.9	56.0	37.0	57.4
2005	62.7	36.5	64.7	69.6	35.1	72.4	56.2	37.8	57.6
2006	63.1	36.9	65.2	70.1	36.3	72.9	56.6	37.6	58.0
2007	63.0	34.8	65.2	69.8	33.9	72.8	56.6	35.8	58.2
2008	62.2	32.6	64.5	68.5	31.6	71.6	56.2	33.7	57.9
2009	59.3	28.4	61.7	64.5	26.9	67.6	54.4	29.9	56.2
2010	58.5	25.9	61.0	63.7	24.8	66.8	53.6	27.0	55.5
2011	58.4	25.8	60.8	63.9	24.6	67.0	53.2	27.1	55.0
2012	58.6	26.1	61.0	64.4	24.9	67.5	53.1	27.3	55.0

Table 1-12. Civilian Employment-Population Ratios, by Sex, Age, Race, and Hispanic Origin, 1948–2012—*Continued*

(Percent.)

Race, Hispanic origin, and year	Both sexes			Men			Women		
	16 years and over	16 to 19 years	20 years and over	16 years and over	16 to 19 years	20 years and over	16 years and over	16 to 19 years	20 years and over
WHITE									
1954	55.2	42.9	56.2	81.5	49.9	84.0	32.5	31.4	31.1
1955	56.5	44.2	57.4	82.2	52.0	84.7	34.0	33.0	32.7
1956	57.3	46.1	58.2	82.7	54.1	85.0	35.1	34.2	33.8
1957	56.8	45.0	57.8	81.8	52.4	84.1	35.1	34.2	33.9
1958	55.3	41.0	56.5	79.2	47.6	81.8	34.5	33.6	33.5
1959	55.9	41.2	57.2	79.9	48.1	82.8	35.0	34.0	34.0
1960	55.9	41.5	57.2	79.4	48.1	82.4	35.5	34.6	34.5
1961	55.3	40.1	56.7	78.2	45.9	81.4	35.4	34.5	34.5
1962	55.4	40.4	56.9	78.4	46.4	81.5	35.6	34.7	34.7
1963	55.3	38.6	56.9	77.7	44.7	81.1	35.8	35.0	35.2
1964	55.5	38.4	57.3	77.8	45.0	81.3	36.3	35.5	35.8
1965	56.0	40.3	57.8	77.9	47.1	81.5	37.1	36.2	36.5
1966	56.8	43.6	58.3	78.3	50.1	81.7	38.3	37.5	37.5
1967	57.2	43.8	58.7	78.4	50.2	81.7	39.0	38.3	38.3
1968	57.4	43.9	59.0	78.3	50.3	81.6	39.6	38.9	39.1
1969	58.0	45.2	59.4	78.2	51.1	81.4	40.7	40.1	40.1
1970	57.5	44.5	59.0	76.8	49.6	80.1	40.8	40.3	40.4
1971	56.8	43.8	58.3	75.7	49.2	79.0	40.4	39.9	40.1
1972	57.4	46.4	58.6	76.0	51.5	79.0	41.0	40.7	40.6
1973	58.2	48.9	59.3	76.5	54.3	79.2	42.0	41.8	41.6
1974	58.3	49.3	59.3	75.9	54.4	78.6	42.6	42.4	42.2
1975	56.7	46.5	57.9	73.0	50.6	75.7	42.0	42.0	41.9
1976	57.5	47.8	58.6	73.4	51.5	76.0	43.2	43.2	43.1
1977	58.6	50.1	59.6	74.1	54.4	76.5	44.5	44.5	44.4
1978	60.0	52.4	60.8	75.0	56.3	77.2	46.4	46.3	46.1
1979	60.6	52.6	61.5	75.1	55.7	77.3	47.5	47.5	47.3
1980	60.0	50.7	61.0	73.4	53.4	75.6	47.7	47.8	47.8
1981	60.0	48.7	61.1	72.8	51.3	75.1	48.0	48.3	48.5
1982	58.8	45.8	60.1	70.6	47.0	73.0	47.7	48.1	48.4
1983	58.9	45.9	60.1	70.4	47.4	72.6	48.0	48.5	48.9
1984	60.5	48.0	61.5	72.1	49.1	74.3	49.5	49.8	50.0
1985	61.0	48.5	62.0	72.3	49.9	74.3	50.4	50.7	51.0
1986	61.5	48.8	62.6	72.3	49.6	74.3	51.4	51.7	52.0
1987	62.3	49.4	63.4	72.7	49.9	74.7	52.5	52.8	53.1
1988	63.1	50.9	64.1	73.2	51.7	75.1	53.4	53.8	54.0
1989	63.8	51.6	64.7	73.7	52.6	75.4	54.3	54.6	54.9
1990	63.7	49.7	64.8	73.3	51.0	75.1	54.3	54.7	55.2
1991	62.6	46.6	63.7	71.6	47.2	73.5	53.7	54.2	54.8
1992	62.4	45.3	63.6	71.1	46.4	73.1	53.8	54.2	54.9
1993	62.7	46.2	63.9	71.4	46.6	73.3	54.1	54.6	55.2
1994	63.5	47.9	64.7	71.8	48.3	73.6	55.3	55.8	56.4
1995	63.8	48.8	64.9	72.0	49.4	73.8	55.6	56.1	56.7
1996	64.1	47.9	65.3	72.3	48.2	74.2	56.0	56.3	57.0
1997	64.6	47.7	65.9	72.7	48.1	74.7	56.8	57.0	57.8
1998	64.7	48.9	65.9	72.7	48.6	74.7	57.1	57.1	57.7
1999	64.8	48.8	66.1	72.8	49.3	74.8	57.4	57.3	58.0
2000	64.9	49.1	66.1	73.0	49.5	74.9	57.5	57.4	58.0
2001	64.2	46.3	65.6	72.0	46.2	74.0	57.0	57.0	57.7
2002	63.4	43.2	64.9	70.8	42.3	73.1	56.3	56.4	57.3
2003	63.0	40.4	64.7	70.1	39.4	72.5	56.1	56.3	57.3
2004	63.1	40.0	64.8	70.4	39.7	72.8	56.0	56.1	57.2
2005	63.4	40.2	65.1	70.8	38.8	73.3	56.2	56.3	57.4
2006	63.8	40.6	65.5	71.3	40.0	73.7	56.6	56.6	57.7
2007	63.6	38.3	65.5	70.9	37.3	73.5	56.6	56.7	57.9
2008	62.8	35.9	64.8	69.7	34.8	72.4	56.2	56.3	57.7
2009	60.2	31.7	62.3	66.0	30.2	68.7	54.4	54.8	56.3
2010	59.4	29.0	61.6	65.1	27.6	67.9	53.6	54.0	55.6
2011	59.4	28.8	61.6	65.3	27.3	68.2	53.2	53.7	55.3
2012	59.4	29.0	61.5	65.8	27.7	68.6	53.1	53.3	54.9

Table 1-12. Civilian Employment-Population Ratios, by Sex, Age, Race, and Hispanic Origin, 1948–2012—*Continued*

(Percent.)

Race, Hispanic origin, and year	Both sexes			Men			Women		
	16 years and over	16 to 19 years	20 years and over	16 years and over	16 to 19 years	20 years and over	16 years and over	16 to 19 years	20 years and over
BLACK									
1975	50.1	23.1	54.5	60.6	26.3	66.5	41.6	20.2	44.9
1976	50.8	22.4	55.4	60.6	25.8	66.8	42.8	19.2	46.4
1977	51.4	22.3	56.0	61.4	26.4	67.5	43.3	18.5	47.0
1978	53.6	25.2	58.0	63.3	28.5	69.1	45.8	22.1	49.3
1979	53.8	25.4	58.1	63.4	28.7	69.1	46.0	22.4	49.3
1980	52.3	23.9	56.4	60.4	27.0	65.8	45.7	21.0	49.1
1981	51.3	22.1	55.5	59.1	24.6	64.5	45.1	19.7	48.5
1982	49.4	19.0	53.6	56.0	20.3	61.4	44.2	17.7	47.5
1983	49.5	18.7	53.6	56.3	20.4	61.6	44.1	17.0	47.4
1984	52.3	21.9	56.1	59.2	23.9	64.1	46.7	20.1	49.8
1985	53.4	24.6	57.0	60.0	26.3	64.6	48.1	23.1	50.9
1986	54.1	25.1	57.6	60.6	26.5	65.1	48.8	23.8	51.6
1987	55.6	27.1	58.9	62.0	28.5	66.4	50.3	25.8	53.0
1988	56.3	27.6	59.7	62.7	29.4	67.1	51.2	25.8	53.9
1989	56.9	28.7	60.1	62.8	30.4	67.0	52.0	27.1	54.6
1990	56.7	26.7	60.2	62.6	27.7	67.1	51.9	25.8	54.7
1991	55.4	22.6	59.0	61.3	23.8	65.9	50.6	21.5	53.6
1992	54.9	22.8	58.3	59.9	23.6	64.3	50.8	22.1	53.6
1993	55.0	22.6	58.4	60.0	23.6	64.3	50.9	21.6	53.8
1994	56.1	24.9	59.4	60.8	25.4	65.0	52.3	24.5	55.0
1995	57.1	25.7	60.5	61.7	25.2	66.1	53.4	26.1	56.1
1996	57.4	26.0	60.8	61.1	24.9	65.5	54.4	27.1	57.1
1997	58.2	26.1	61.8	61.4	23.7	66.1	55.6	28.5	58.4
1998	59.7	30.1	63.0	62.9	28.4	67.1	57.2	31.8	59.7
1999	60.6	27.9	64.2	63.1	26.7	67.5	58.6	29.0	61.5
2000	60.9	29.8	64.2	63.6	28.9	67.7	58.6	30.6	61.3
2001	59.7	26.7	63.2	62.1	26.4	66.3	57.8	27.0	60.7
2002	58.1	25.3	61.6	61.1	25.6	65.2	55.8	24.9	58.7
2003	57.4	21.7	61.0	59.5	19.9	64.1	55.6	23.4	58.6
2004	57.2	21.5	60.9	59.3	19.3	63.9	55.5	23.6	58.5
2005	57.7	21.6	61.5	60.2	20.8	64.7	55.7	22.4	58.9
2006	58.4	24.1	62.0	60.6	21.7	65.2	56.5	26.4	59.4
2007	58.4	21.4	62.3	60.7	19.5	65.5	56.5	23.3	59.8
2008	57.3	20.2	61.2	59.1	18.7	63.9	55.8	21.7	59.1
2009	53.2	16.5	57.1	53.7	14.3	58.2	52.8	18.6	56.1
2010	52.3	14.5	56.1	53.1	14.1	57.5	51.7	14.9	55.1
2011	51.7	14.7	55.3	52.8	14.6	56.9	50.8	14.7	54.0
2012	53.0	16.6	56.5	54.1	15.1	58.3	52.2	18.1	55.1
HISPANIC									
1975	53.4	. . .	. . .	. . .	. . .	. . .	. . .	. . .	. . .
1976	53.8	. . .	56.6	. . .	. . .	. . .	. . .	. . .	. . .
1977	55.4	. . .	58.3	. . .	. . .	. . .	. . .	. . .	. . .
1978	57.2	. . .	60.0	. . .	. . .	. . .	. . .	. . .	. . .
1979	58.3	. . .	61.0	. . .	. . .	. . .	. . .	. . .	. . .
1980	57.6	. . .	60.5	. . .	. . .	. . .	. . .	. . .	. . .
1981	57.4	. . .	60.7	. . .	. . .	. . .	. . .	. . .	. . .
1982	54.9	. . .	58.2	. . .	. . .	. . .	. . .	. . .	. . .
1983	55.1	. . .	58.1	. . .	. . .	. . .	. . .	. . .	. . .
1984	57.9	. . .	60.7	. . .	. . .	. . .	. . .	. . .	. . .
1985	57.8	. . .	60.7	. . .	. . .	. . .	. . .	. . .	. . .
1986	58.5	. . .	61.5	. . .	. . .	. . .	. . .	. . .	. . .
1987	60.5	. . .	63.4	. . .	. . .	. . .	. . .	. . .	. . .
1988	61.9	. . .	64.6	. . .	. . .	. . .	. . .	. . .	. . .
1989	62.2	. . .	64.8	. . .	. . .	. . .	. . .	. . .	. . .
1990	61.9	. . .	64.8	. . .	. . .	. . .	. . .	. . .	. . .
1991	59.8	. . .	62.8	. . .	. . .	. . .	. . .	. . .	. . .
1992	59.1	. . .	62.1	. . .	. . .	. . .	. . .	. . .	. . .
1993	59.1	. . .	62.1	. . .	. . .	. . .	. . .	. . .	. . .
1994	59.5	33.5	62.4	71.7	36.8	. . .	47.2	30.1	. . .
1995	59.7	34.4	62.6	72.1	37.5	. . .	47.3	31.3	. . .
1996	60.6	33.1	63.7	73.3	38.8	. . .	47.9	27.3	. . .
1997	62.6	33.7	66.0	74.5	37.6	. . .	50.2	29.3	. . .
1998	63.1	36.0	66.2	74.7	38.6	. . .	51.0	33.0	. . .
1999	63.4	37.0	66.5	75.3	41.2	. . .	51.7	32.5	. . .
2000	65.7	38.6	68.9	77.4	42.8	81.7	53.6	33.9	55.8
2001	64.9	38.6	67.8	76.2	43.3	79.9	53.3	33.5	55.4
2002	63.9	35.2	67.0	74.5	39.0	78.3	52.9	31.1	55.2
2003	63.1	30.2	66.4	74.3	31.9	78.6	51.2	28.4	53.6
2004	63.8	30.4	67.2	75.1	33.4	79.4	51.8	27.2	54.4
2005	64.0	31.5	67.3	75.8	33.8	80.0	51.5	29.1	53.8
2006	65.2	32.2	68.5	76.8	34.8	81.1	52.8	29.5	55.2
2007	64.9	30.4	68.5	76.2	32.1	80.7	53.0	28.5	55.6
2008	63.3	28.6	66.9	74.1	30.9	78.6	51.9	26.2	54.6
2009	59.7	23.7	63.5	68.9	24.1	73.5	50.1	23.4	52.9
2010	59.0	21.0	63.1	68.0	21.7	72.9	49.6	20.2	52.7
2011	58.9	19.5	63.2	67.9	20.1	73.3	49.3	18.9	52.5
2012	59.5	22.1	63.6	68.6	22.9	73.8	50.4	21.2	53.5

. . . = Not available.

Table 1-13. Employed Civilians, by Sex, Race, Hispanic Origin, and Occupation, 2010–2012

(Thousands of people.)

Year and occupation	Total	Men	Women	White	Black	Hispanic[1]
2010						
All Occupations	139 064	73 359	65 705	114 168	15 010	19 906
Management, professional, and related occupations	51 743	25 070	26 673	43 268	4 363	3 755
Management, business, and financial operations occupations	20 938	11 945	8 993	18 043	1 537	1 562
Computer and mathematical occupations	3 531	2 620	911	2 663	237	194
Architecture and engineering occupations	2 619	2 282	337	2 205	135	177
Life, physical and social science occupations	1 409	755	655	1 139	88	85
Community and social service occupations	2 337	836	1 500	1 750	451	229
Legal occupations	1 716	878	838	1 510	111	94
Education, training, and library occupations	8 628	2 261	6 367	7 325	810	686
Arts, design, entertainment, sports, and media occupations	2 759	1 484	1 276	2 430	152	244
Healthcare practitioner and technical occupations	7 805	2 009	5 796	6 204	842	484
Healthcare support occupations	3 332	370	2 962	2 252	849	506
Protective service occupations	3 289	2 587	703	2 530	585	437
Food preparation and serving related occupations	7 660	3 439	4 221	6 110	866	1 703
Building and grounds cleaning and maintenance occupations	5 328	3 164	2 164	4 290	722	1 877
Personal care and service occupations	5 024	1 092	3 932	3 756	741	734
Sales and related occupations	33 433	12 419	21 015	27 470	1 503	1 814
Office and administrative support occupations	18 047	4 716	13 331	14 685	2 259	2 413
Farming, fishing, and forestry occupations	987	755	231	889	51	412
Construction and extraction occupations	7 175	6 990	185	6 449	441	2 090
Installation, maintenance, and repair occupations	4 911	4 721	190	4 281	384	769
Production occupations	16 180	12 751	3 429	12 873	2 247	1 755
Transportation and material moving occupations	8 182	6 959	1 224	6 405	1 339	1 640
2011						
All Occupations	139 869	74 290	65 579	114 690	15 051	20 269
Management, professional, and related occupations	52 547	25 552	26 995	43 923	4 398	3 952
Management, business, and financial operations occupations	21 589	12 275	9 314	18 495	1 579	1 662
Computer and mathematical occupations	3 608	2 705	903	2 695	250	205
Architecture and engineering occupations	2 785	2 406	379	2 353	145	2 785
Life, physical and social science occupations	1 303	687	616	1 059	96	1 303
Community and social service occupations	2 352	835	1 518	1 794	427	2 352
Legal occupations	1 770	889	881	1 540	129	1 770
Education, training, and library occupations	8 619	2 274	6 345	7 319	834	8 619
Arts, design, entertainment, sports, and media occupations	2 779	1 499	1 281	2 442	166	2 779
Healthcare practitioner and technical occupations	7 740	1 982	5 758	6 227	773	518
Healthcare support occupations	3 359	413	2 945	2 290	826	466
Protective service occupations	3 210	2 546	664	2 478	560	404
Food preparation and serving related occupations	7 747	3 534	4 213	6 086	973	1 692
Building and grounds cleaning and maintenance occupations	5 492	3 359	2 133	4 423	755	1 909
Personal care and service occupations	4 979	1 077	3 902	3 750	702	730
Sales and related occupations	15 330	7 733	7 597	12 751	1 503	1 935
Office and administrative support occupations	17 736	4 717	13 019	14 328	2 239	2 435
Farming, fishing, and forestry occupations	1 001	785	216	919	43	430
Construction and extraction occupations	7 125	6 962	163	6 419	417	2 095
Installation, maintenance, and repair occupations	4 883	4 710	173	4 233	387	771
Production occupations	8 142	5 826	2 316	6 580	892	1 761
Transportation and material moving occupations	8 318	7 076	1 242	6 510	1 356	1 689
2012						
All Occupations	142 469	75 555	66 914	114 769	15 856	21 878
Management, professional, and related occupations	54 043	26 208	27 834	44 375	4 678	4 516
Management, business, and financial operations occupations	22 678	12 779	9 899	19 095	1 766	1 940
Computer and mathematical occupations	3 016	2 041	976	2 773	284	234
Architecture and engineering occupations	2 846	2 457	390	2 339	159	212
Life, physical and social science occupations	1 316	720	596	1 077	85	88
Community and social service occupations	2 265	819	1 446	1 711	425	251
Legal occupations	1 786	885	901	1 552	127	133
Education, training, and library occupations	8 543	2 253	6 290	7 161	814	829
Arts, design, entertainment, sports, and media occupations	2 814	1 456	1 358	2 395	170	250
Healthcare practitioner and technical occupations	7 977	1 998	5 979	6 273	847	579
Healthcare support occupations	3 496	434	3 062	2 294	925	536
Protective service occupations	3 096	2 449	647	2 350	532	425
Food preparation and serving related occupations	8 018	3 648	4 370	6 209	968	1 911
Building and grounds cleaning and maintenance occupations	5 591	3 430	2 160	4 365	839	2 020
Personal care and service occupations	5 258	1 173	4 085	3 783	774	862
Sales and related occupations	15 457	7 922	7 535	12 563	1 627	2 091
Office and administrative support occupations	17 695	4 730	12 965	14 169	2 280	2 559
Farming, fishing, and forestry occupations	994	768	226	889	53	440
Construction and extraction occupations	7 005	6 832	173	6 253	434	2 027
Installation, maintenance, and repair occupations	4 821	4 666	156	4 130	405	801
Production occupations	8 455	6 109	2 346	6 702	6 702	1 838
Transportation and material moving occupations	8 540	7 185	1 355	6 686	1 356	1 852

Note: Beginning with data for January 2011, the Current Population Survey (CPS) uses the 2010 Census Occupational Classification system derived from the 2010 Standard Occupational Classification (SOC) system. The 2010 classification system replaces an earlier version that was based on the 2000 SOC. As a result of the classification change, CPS occupational data beginning with January 2011 data are not strictly comparable with earlier years.

[1] May be of any race.

Table 1-14. Employed Civilians, by Selected Occupation and Industry, 2010–2012

(Thousands of people.)

Year and occupation	Total employed	Agriculture, forestry, fishing, and hunting	Mining	Construction	Manufacturing Total	Manufacturing Durable goods	Manufacturing Nondurable goods	Wholesale trade
2010								
All Occupations	139 064	2 206	731	9 077	14 081	8 789	5 293	3 805
Management, professional, and related occupations	51 743	1 022	195	1 825	4 274	2 942	1 332	698
Management, business, and financial operations occupations	20 938	982	121	1 610	2 317	1 515	802	538
Computer and mathematical occupations	3 531	6	6	18	434	349	85	61
Architecture and engineering occupations	2 619	3	44	140	995	850	144	27
Life, physical and social science occupations	1 409	24	21	6	215	41	175	21
Community and social service occupations	2 337	1	0	0	1	0	1	X
Legal occupations	1 716	1	0	6	29	16	13	5
Education, training, and library occupations	8 628	3	2	3	26	21	5	4
Arts, design, entertainment, sports, and media occupations	2 759	1	2	39	214	124	90	25
Healthcare practitioner and technical occupations	7 805	3	1	2	43	25	18	17
Healthcare support occupations	3 332	1	X	0	5	4	1	1
Protective service occupations	3 289	19	3	8	31	23	8	4
Food preparation and serving related occupations	7 660	6	1	6	38	8	29	11
Building and grounds cleaning and maintenance occupations	5 328	21	2	37	124	61	63	29
Personal care and service occupations	5 024	54	0	3	9	4	4	2
Sales and related occupations	15 386	20	7	86	630	320	311	1 368
Office and administrative support occupations	18 047	90	57	462	1 323	833	490	639
Farming, fishing, and forestry occupations	987	813	1	1	59	5	54	53
Construction and extraction occupations	7 175	14	269	5 786	296	232	64	31
Installation, maintenance, and repair occupations	4 911	29	61	510	662	431	231	136
Production occupations	7 998	24	40	131	5 539	3 410	2 130	133
Transportation and material moving occupations	8 182	94	93	222	1 092	516	575	700
2011								
All Occupations	139 869	2 254	817	9 039	14 336	9 007	5 329	3 798
Management, professional, and related occupations	52 547	1 066	202	1 780	4 390	3 002	1 388	699
Management, business, and financial operations occupations	21 589	1 017	115	1 552	2 435	1 563	872	541
Computer and mathematical occupations	3 608	5	6	16	412	335	77	69
Architecture and engineering occupations	2 785	5	49	168	1 059	898	161	22
Life, physical and social science occupations	1 303	31	26	7	209	23	186	9
Community and social service occupations	2 352	2	0	1	2	0	2	0
Legal occupations	1 770	X	0	7	24	15	8	6
Education, training, and library occupations	8 619	1	X	3	27	22	5	7
Arts, design, entertainment, sports, and media occupations	2 779	2	3	26	182	124	58	27
Healthcare practitioner and technical occupations	7 740	3	2	1	41	21	19	18
Healthcare support occupations	3 359	1	X	0	8	5	3	1
Protective service occupations	3 210	14	2	18	38	22	16	8
Food preparation and serving related occupations	7 747	2	1	4	40	8	32	10
Building and grounds cleaning and maintenance occupations	5 492	35	3	45	134	70	64	24
Personal care and service occupations	4 979	43	0	4	9	4	4	4
Sales and related occupations	33 066	111	73	602	1 925	1 131	794	1 974
Office and administrative support occupations	17 736	93	59	491	1 298	789	509	673
Farming, fishing, and forestry occupations	1 001	836	1	2	51	5	46	49
Construction and extraction occupations	7 125	9	334	5 733	285	232	53	31
Installation, maintenance, and repair occupations	4 883	22	60	465	676	435	242	142
Production occupations	8 142	28	53	124	5 684	3 538	2 147	133
Transportation and material moving occupations	8 318	87	89	262	1 094	555	540	723
2012								
All Occupations	142 469	2 186	957	8 964	14 686	9 244	5 443	3 694
Management, professional, and related occupations	54 043	1 024	281	1 895	4 446	3 074	1 372	702
Management, business, and financial operations occupations	22 678	978	165	1 633	2 441	1 598	843	547
Computer and mathematical occupations	3 816	2	10	20	431	431	89	70
Architecture and engineering occupations	2 846	3	56	192	1 099	915	184	24
Life, physical and social science occupations	1 316	34	35	12	201	38	163	9
Community and social service occupations	2 265	1	0	2	X	X	X	0
Legal occupations	1 786	0	8	4	24	14	10	6
Education, training, and library occupations	8 543	2	2	2	29	22	7	9
Arts, design, entertainment, sports, and media occupations	2 814	0	4	25	180	121	59	28
Healthcare practitioner and technical occupations	7 977	2	3	3	42	25	17	9
Healthcare support occupations	3 496	3	1	1	6	3	3	3
Protective service occupations	3 096	13	1	17	38	24	14	6
Food preparation and serving related occupations	8 018	2	2	5	45	8	37	10
Building and grounds cleaning and maintenance occupations	5 591	36	36	27	141	67	74	27
Personal care and service occupations	5 258	46	0	2	11	7	4	4
Sales and related occupations	15 457	109	19	85	650	344	307	1 284
Office and administrative support occupations	17 695	92	67	453	1 321	814	507	633
Farming, fishing, and forestry occupations	994	812	1	4	65	6	59	49
Construction and extraction occupations	7 005	7	321	5 620	301	253	48	30
Installation, maintenance, and repair occupations	4 821	33	78	451	676	445	231	129
Production occupations	8 455	30	69	157	5 859	3 630	2 229	126
Transportation and material moving occupations	8 540	71	112	247	1 128	570	558	690

Note: Beginning with data for January 2011, the Current Population Survey (CPS) uses the 2010 Census Occupational Classification system derived from the 2010 Standard Occupational Classification (SOC) system. The 2010 classification system replaces an earlier version that was based on the 2000 SOC. As a result of the classification change, CPS occupational data beginning with January 2011 data are not strictly comparable with earlier years.

X = Not applicable.

Table 1-14. Employed Civilians, by Selected Occupation and Industry, 2010–2012—*Continued*

(Thousands of people.)

Year and occupation	Retail trade	Transportation and warehousing	Utilities	Information	Finance and insurance	Real estate and rental and leasing	Professional and technical services
2010							
All Occupations	15 934	5 880	1 253	3 149	6 605	2 745	9 115
Management, professional, and related occupations	1 722	643	396	1 647	3 384	894	7 073
Management, business, and financial operations occupations	904	525	195	613	2 853	823	2 534
Computer and mathematical occupations	117	41	37	270	328	11	1 349
Architecture and engineering occupations	21	53	112	88	13	10	814
Life, physical and social science occupations	14	5	25	15	21	7	373
Community and social service occupations	2	X	0	1	11	2	9
Legal occupations	20	5	3	11	80	21	1 147
Education, training, and library occupations	22	7	2	122	22	6	50
Arts, design, entertainment, sports, and media occupations	186	5	12	526	28	12	620
Healthcare practitioner and technical occupations	436	2	8	1	28	3	178
Healthcare support occupations	36	1	0	1	7	4	53
Protective service occupations	66	43	15	5	39	22	29
Food preparation and serving related occupations	362	4	0	32	6	21	7
Building and grounds cleaning and maintenance occupations	177	51	16	18	21	201	30
Personal care and service occupations	42	157	0	44	7	28	24
Sales and related occupations	8 704	94	24	403	1 066	1 011	275
Office and administrative support occupations	2 430	1 418	217	562	2 003	298	1 282
Farming, fishing, and forestry occupations	14	8	0	1	0	0	2
Construction and extraction occupations	78	75	119	15	5	42	70
Installation, maintenance, and repair occupations	605	322	216	304	24	115	96
Production occupations	504	89	205	65	35	20	126
Transportation and material moving occupations	1 195	2 974	44	53	7	88	47
2011							
All Occupations	15 927	5 957	1 243	3 150	6 613	2 773	9 461
Management, professional, and related occupations	1 567	665	411	1 685	3 422	907	7 476
Management, business, and financial operations occupations	754	544	204	644	2 848	844	2 808
Computer and mathematical occupations	140	47	37	282	379	16	1 377
Architecture and engineering occupations	22	41	105	97	16	5	874
Life, physical and social science occupations	4	0	26	2	5	1	316
Community and social service occupations	2	0	0	1	18	4	10
Legal occupations	11	5	8	9	81	17	1 213
Education, training, and library occupations	29	16	10	117	22	4	45
Arts, design, entertainment, sports, and media occupations	173	8	15	530	25	12	643
Healthcare practitioner and technical occupations	432	4	5	4	29	4	190
Healthcare support occupations	46	5	X	0	7	6	41
Protective service occupations	62	39	20	11	27	22	21
Food preparation and serving related occupations	379	8	0	19	8	18	7
Building and grounds cleaning and maintenance occupations	165	61	18	20	24	233	32
Personal care and service occupations	51	44	1	34	5	37	33
Sales and related occupations	11 260	1 499	229	916	3 071	1 271	1 531
Office and administrative support occupations	2 518	1 380	208	536	2 009	335	1 223
Farming, fishing, and forestry occupations	11	4	4	0	0	X	4
Construction and extraction occupations	81	74	99	17	5	43	53
Installation, maintenance, and repair occupations	639	332	195	324	24	121	85
Production occupations	532	88	230	68	17	28	127
Transportation and material moving occupations	1 135	3 137	37	54	4	88	52
2012							
All Occupations	16 182	6 082	1 190	2 971	6 786	2 804	9 913
Management, professional, and related occupations	1 723	730	386	1 609	3 695	991	7 833
Management, business, and financial operations occupations	868	580	190	605	3 077	905	3 103
Computer and mathematical occupations	150	48	39	274	404	20	1 429
Architecture and engineering occupations	20	53	104	88	15	7	875
Life, physical and social science occupations	8	6	26	7	12	1	288
Community and social service occupations	1	0	1	2	22	4	15
Legal occupations	14	5	9	12	71	28	1 206
Education, training, and library occupations	28	21	4	112	33	4	35
Arts, design, entertainment, sports, and media occupations	170	8	8	507	25	11	680
Healthcare practitioner and technical occupations	464	8	5	4	35	11	201
Healthcare support occupations	49	0	0	0	3	9	49
Protective service occupations	66	39	14	5	38	24	18
Food preparation and serving related occupations	408	10	1	24	11	25	4
Building and grounds cleaning and maintenance occupations	151	67	14	18	17	217	22
Personal care and service occupations	56	37	1	27	8	30	28
Sales and related occupations	8 860	114	24	357	1 076	891	270
Office and administrative support occupations	2 458	1 384	201	493	1 875	299	1 300
Farming, fishing, and forestry occupations	10	4	1	X	1	X	4
Construction and extraction occupations	71	72	90	10	7	43	80
Installation, maintenance, and repair occupations	627	335	179	302	27	141	85
Production occupations	490	116	224	68	19	33	140
Transportation and material moving occupations	1 213	3 175	47	51	10	102	79

Note: Beginning with data for January 2011, the Current Population Survey (CPS) uses the 2010 Census Occupational Classification system derived from the 2010 Standard Occupational Classification (SOC) system. The 2010 classification system replaces an earlier version that was based on the 2000 SOC. As a result of the classification change, CPS occupational data beginning with January 2011 data are not strictly comparable with earlier years.

X = Not applicable.

Table 1-14. Employed Civilians, by Selected Occupation and Industry, 2010–2012—*Continued*

(Thousands of people.)

Year and occupation	Management, administrative, and waste services	Educational services	Health care and social assistance	Arts, entertainment, and recreation	Accommodation and food services	Other services (except public administration)	Public administration
2010							
All Occupations	6 138	13 155	18 907	2 966	9 564	6 769	6 983
Management, professional, and related occupations	1 086	10 049	10 150	1 007	1 384	1 502	2 790
Management, business, and financial operations occupations	765	1 283	1 522	289	1 305	606	1 153
Computer and mathematical occupations	86	204	192	20	8	45	299
Architecture and engineering occupations	34	36	24	9	2	16	179
Life, physical and social science occupations	22	189	230	13	2	17	188
Community and social service occupations	10	356	980	9	4	608	342
Legal occupations	26	16	30	2	1	20	293
Education, training, and library occupations	13	7 450	656	80	24	50	86
Arts, design, entertainment, sports, and media occupations	36	218	50	577	33	108	68
Healthcare practitioner and technical occupations	93	297	6 467	8	5	31	183
Healthcare support occupations	57	33	2 926	21	11	135	41
Protective service occupations	563	130	73	176	53	18	1 992
Food preparation and serving related occupations	17	402	374	246	6 045	44	39
Building and grounds cleaning and maintenance occupations	2 166	575	493	237	486	530	115
Personal care and service occupations	25	243	1 771	734	89	1 707	85
Sales and related occupations	280	75	69	146	745	351	32
Office and administrative support occupations	939	1 085	2 597	225	392	604	1 424
Farming, fishing, and forestry occupations	7	1	0	2	0	2	20
Construction and extraction occupations	93	61	43	20	13	27	117
Installation, maintenance, and repair occupations	186	149	113	80	49	1 100	152
Production occupations	237	52	158	16	94	445	82
Transportation and material moving occupations	480	300	140	56	201	303	95
2011							
All Occupations	6 358	12 965	18 902	2 922	9 775	6 724	6 853
Management, professional, and related occupations	1 173	10 050	10 185	1 043	1 471	1 498	2 856
Management, business, and financial operations occupations	862	1 303	1 585	293	1 393	632	1 216
Computer and mathematical occupations	84	209	176	18	14	37	286
Architecture and engineering occupations	36	48	17	13	6	17	185
Life, physical and social science occupations	21	207	217	10	2	12	200
Community and social service occupations	10	338	989	10	2	595	367
Legal occupations	42	16	34	2	1	14	279
Education, training, and library occupations	18	7 430	653	82	30	56	68
Arts, design, entertainment, sports, and media occupations	43	239	58	611	18	107	58
Healthcare practitioner and technical occupations	57	260	6 455	5	5	28	198
Healthcare support occupations	63	28	2 966	19	10	115	43
Protective service occupations	555	114	83	176	43	15	1 942
Food preparation and serving related occupations	28	396	408	233	6 106	47	32
Building and grounds cleaning and maintenance occupations	2 258	576	522	259	456	515	112
Personal care and service occupations	24	227	1 771	699	90	1 794	112
Sales and related occupations	268	68	55	146	796	318	40
Office and administrative support occupations	975	1 011	2 489	190	401	572	1 276
Farming, fishing, and forestry occupations	7	4	1	1	1	3	21
Construction and extraction occupations	106	59	43	24	13	25	92
Installation, maintenance, and repair occupations	194	123	104	62	49	1 107	159
Production occupations	240	37	141	21	95	427	68
Transportation and material moving occupations	465	273	136	50	243	290	101
2012							
All Occupations	6 626	12 945	19 405	3 022	10 171	7 168	6 717
Management, professional, and related occupations	1 280	9 960	10 458	1 047	1 563	1 569	2 850
Management, business, and financial operations occupations	974	1 225	1 708	288	1 471	658	1 261
Computer and mathematical occupations	95	227	217	22	9	61	289
Architecture and engineering occupations	39	46	34	12	1	20	159
Life, physical and social science occupations	18	217	211	11	2	12	207
Community and social service occupations	8	313	975	3	4	578	334
Legal occupations	37	15	42	3	0	13	290
Education, training, and library occupations	19	7 351	649	70	43	65	66
Arts, design, entertainment, sports, and media occupations	38	242	66	623	22	129	48
Healthcare practitioner and technical occupations	52	324	6 555	15	11	34	198
Healthcare support occupations	55	32	3 074	20	11	131	50
Protective service occupations	526	115	81	167	42	19	1 866
Food preparation and serving related occupations	31	429	396	237	6 298	50	32
Building and grounds cleaning and maintenance occupations	2 380	586	486	288	509	488	112
Personal care and service occupations	22	245	1 857	744	82	1 962	97
Sales and related occupations	265	60	62	148	857	384	32
Office and administrative support occupations	985	1 046	2 548	207	389	644	1 303
Farming, fishing, and forestry occupations	11	4	2	7	1	3	16
Construction and extraction occupations	94	59	43	17	12	31	80
Installation, maintenance, and repair occupations	195	122	101	60	53	1 094	134
Production occupations	267	31	142	25	111	489	58
Transportation and material moving occupations	515	256	155	54	244	305	87

Note: Beginning with data for January 2011, the Current Population Survey (CPS) uses the 2010 Census Occupational Classification system derived from the 2010 Standard Occupational Classification (SOC) system. The 2010 classification system replaces an earlier version that was based on the 2000 SOC. As a result of the classification change, CPS occupational data beginning with January 2011 data are not strictly comparable with earlier years.

Table 1-15. Employed Civilians in Agriculture and Nonagricultural Industries, by Class of Worker and Sex, 1990–2012

(Thousands of people.)

Sex and year	Total employed	Agriculture				Nonagricultural industries						
		Total	Wage and salary workers	Self-employed workers	Unpaid family workers	Total employed	Wage and salary workers				Self-employed workers	Unpaid family workers
							Total	Government	Private household	Other industries except private households		
Both Sexes												
1990	118 793	3 223	1 740	1 378	105	115 570	106 598	17 769	1 027	87 802	8 719	253
1991	117 718	3 269	1 729	1 423	118	114 449	105 373	17 934	1 010	86 429	8 851	226
1992	118 492	3 247	1 750	1 385	112	115 245	106 437	18 136	1 135	87 166	8 575	233
1993	120 259	3 115	1 689	1 320	106	117 144	107 966	18 579	1 126	88 261	8 959	218
1994	123 060	3 409	1 715	1 645	49	119 651	110 517	18 293	966	91 258	9 003	131
1995	124 900	3 440	1 814	1 580	45	121 460	112 448	18 362	963	93 123	8 902	110
1996	126 707	3 443	1 869	1 518	56	123 264	114 171	18 217	928	95 026	8 971	122
1997	129 558	3 399	1 890	1 457	51	126 159	116 983	18 131	915	97 937	9 056	120
1998	131 463	3 378	2 000	1 341	38	128 085	119 019	18 383	962	99 674	8 962	103
1999	133 488	3 281	1 944	1 297	40	130 207	121 323	18 903	933	101 487	8 790	95
2000	136 891	2 464	1 421	1 010	33	134 427	125 114	19 248	718	105 148	9 205	108
2001	136 933	2 299	1 283	988	28	134 635	125 407	19 335	694	105 378	9 121	107
2002	136 485	2 311	1 282	1 003	26	134 174	125 156	19 636	757	104 764	8 923	95
2003	137 736	2 275	1 299	951	25	135 461	126 015	19 634	764	105 616	9 344	101
2004	139 252	2 232	1 242	964	27	137 020	127 463	19 983	779	106 701	9 467	90
2005	141 730	2 197	1 212	955	30	139 532	129 931	20 357	812	108 761	9 509	93
2006	144 427	2 206	1 287	901	18	142 221	132 449	20 337	803	111 309	9 685	87
2007	146 047	2 095	1 220	856	19	143 952	134 283	21 003	813	112 467	9 557	112
2008	145 362	2 168	1 279	860	28	143 194	133 882	21 258	805	111 819	9 219	93
2009	139 877	2 103	1 242	836	25	137 775	128 713	21 178	783	106 752	836	25
2010	139 064	2 206	1 353	821	33	136 858	127 914	21 003	667	106 244	8 860	84
2011	139 869	2 254	1 380	846	28	137 615	128 934	20 536	722	107 676	8 603	78
2012	142 469	2 186	1 377	780	29	140 283	131 452	20 360	738	110 355	8 749	81
Men												
1990	65 105	2 546	1 355	1 151	39	62 559	56 913	8 245	149	48 519	5 597	48
1991	64 223	2 589	1 359	1 185	45	61 634	55 899	8 300	143	47 456	5 700	35
1992	64 441	2 575	1 371	1 164	40	61 866	56 212	8 348	156	47 708	5 613	41
1993	65 349	2 478	1 323	1 117	39	62 871	56 926	8 435	146	48 345	5 894	50
1994	66 450	2 554	1 330	1 197	27	63 896	58 300	8 327	99	49 874	5 560	37
1995	67 377	2 559	1 395	1 138	26	64 818	59 332	8 267	96	50 969	5 461	25
1996	68 207	2 573	1 418	1 124	31	65 634	60 133	8 110	99	51 924	5 465	36
1997	69 685	2 552	1 439	1 084	29	67 133	61 595	8 015	81	53 499	5 506	31
1998	70 693	2 553	1 526	1 005	23	68 140	62 630	8 178	86	54 366	5 480	29
1999	71 446	2 432	1 450	962	20	69 014	63 624	8 278	74	55 272	5 366	25
2000	73 305	1 861	1 116	725	20	71 444	65 838	8 309	71	57 458	5 573	33
2001	73 196	1 708	990	703	15	71 488	65 930	8 342	63	57 524	5 527	31
2002	72 903	1 724	979	731	14	71 179	65 726	8 437	76	57 212	5 425	29
2003	73 332	1 695	991	694	11	71 636	65 871	8 368	59	57 444	5 736	30
2004	74 525	1 687	970	702	15	72 838	66 951	8 616	60	58 275	5 860	27
2005	75 973	1 654	949	688	17	74 319	68 345	8 760	67	59 518	5 944	30
2006	77 502	1 663	989	664	10	75 838	69 811	8 696	60	61 055	6 004	23
2007	78 254	1 604	973	623	8	76 650	70 697	9 022	76	61 599	5 920	32
2008	77 486	1 650	997	637	16	75 836	70 072	9 089	70	60 912	5 736	29
2009	73 670	1 607	977	613	17	72 062	66 517	9 013	74	57 430	5 527	19
2010	73 359	1 665	1 051	598	17	71 694	66 189	9 059	60	57 070	5 472	33
2011	74 290	1 698	1 050	632	16	72 592	67 306	8 922	78	58 307	5 262	24
2012	75 555	1 626	1 048	562	16	73 930	68 629	8 760	82	59 786	5 266	34
Women												
1990	53 689	678	385	227	66	53 011	49 685	9 524	879	39 282	3 122	205
1991	53 495	680	369	237	73	52 815	49 474	9 635	867	38 972	3 150	191
1992	54 052	672	379	221	73	53 380	50 225	9 788	979	39 458	2 963	192
1993	54 910	637	367	204	67	54 273	51 040	10 144	980	39 916	3 065	168
1994	56 610	855	384	448	23	55 755	52 217	9 965	867	41 385	3 443	95
1995	57 523	881	419	442	20	56 642	53 115	10 095	867	42 153	3 440	86
1996	58 501	871	452	394	25	57 630	54 037	10 107	830	43 100	3 506	87
1997	59 873	847	451	373	23	59 026	55 388	10 116	834	44 438	3 550	89
1998	60 770	825	474	336	15	59 945	56 389	10 205	876	45 308	3 482	74
1999	62 042	849	494	335	20	61 193	57 699	10 625	859	46 215	3 424	70
2000	63 586	602	305	285	12	62 983	59 277	10 939	647	47 690	3 631	76
2001	63 737	591	293	284	13	63 147	59 477	10 993	630	47 853	3 594	75
2002	63 582	587	303	272	12	62 995	59 431	11 199	600	47 552	3 499	66
2003	64 404	580	309	257	14	63 824	60 144	11 267	705	48 172	3 609	72
2004	64 728	546	271	262	12	64 182	60 512	11 367	719	48 426	3 607	63
2005	65 757	544	263	267	13	65 213	61 586	11 598	745	49 243	3 565	63
2006	66 925	543	298	237	8	66 382	62 638	11 641	742	50 254	3 681	64
2007	67 792	490	247	233	11	67 302	63 586	11 981	737	50 868	3 637	80
2008	67 876	518	282	224	12	67 358	63 810	12 169	735	50 907	3 483	65
2009	66 208	496	265	223	8	65 712	62 197	12 165	709	49 322	3 468	47
2010	65 705	541	302	223	16	65 164	61 725	11 944	607	49 174	3 388	51
2011	65 579	556	330	214	12	65 023	61 628	11 614	644	49 370	3 341	54
2012	66 914	560	329	218	13	66 353	62 824	11 600	656	50 568	3 483	47

Table 1-16. Number of Employed Persons Age 25 Years and Over, by Educational Attainment, Sex, Race, and Hispanic Origin, 2001–2012

(Thousands of people.)

Race, Hispanic origin, sex, and year	Total	Less than a high school diploma	High school graduate, no college	Some college, no degree	Associate's degree	College graduate or higher	
						Total	Bachelor's degree only
Both Sexes							
2001	116 846	11 669	36 078	21 459	11 127	36 514	23 907
2002	116 802	11 535	35 779	20 928	11 166	37 395	24 570
2003	118 385	11 537	35 857	21 107	11 313	38 570	25 188
2004	119 622	11 408	35 944	21 284	11 693	39 293	25 484
2005	121 960	11 712	36 398	21 380	12 245	40 225	26 027
2006	124 386	11 892	36 702	21 630	12 514	41 649	26 960
2007	126 172	11 521	36 857	22 076	12 535	43 182	28 055
2008	126 161	11 073	36 097	22 092	12 948	43 951	28 460
2009	122 277	10 371	34 487	21 016	12 872	43 531	27 964
2010	121 987	10 115	34 293	20 838	12 910	43 832	27 977
2011	122 507	9 967	33 823	20 712	13 182	44 822	28 333
2012	124 635	9 923	33 718	20 936	13 770	46 288	29 371
Men							
2001	62 824	7 188	19 274	11 076	5 226	20 060	12 872
2002	62 756	7 220	19 154	10 811	5 221	20 350	13 076
2003	63 349	7 290	19 200	10 858	5 231	20 770	13 354
2004	64 326	7 276	19 535	10 896	5 426	21 192	13 575
2005	65 772	7 487	20 127	10 993	5 739	21 427	13 687
2006	67 019	7 614	20 345	11 110	5 835	22 114	14 138
2007	67 963	7 450	20 434	11 382	5 862	22 835	14 680
2008	67 605	7 108	20 093	11 356	6 021	23 027	14 845
2009	64 831	6 569	19 085	10 772	5 864	22 541	14 368
2010	64 765	6 434	19 159	10 737	5 829	22 606	14 359
2011	65 356	6 388	19 059	10 741	6 029	23 138	14 637
2012	66 455	6 309	19 192	10 862	6 364	23 729	15 024
Women							
2001	54 021	4 480	16 804	10 383	5 901	16 453	11 035
2002	54 046	4 315	16 624	10 117	5 945	17 045	11 493
2003	55 035	4 248	16 657	10 249	6 081	17 800	11 834
2004	55 296	4 132	16 409	10 387	6 267	18 101	11 908
2005	56 188	4 226	16 271	10 388	6 506	18 798	12 340
2006	57 367	4 278	16 357	10 520	6 678	19 535	12 822
2007	58 209	4 071	16 423	10 695	6 674	20 346	13 375
2008	58 555	3 965	16 004	10 737	6 926	20 924	13 614
2009	57 445	3 802	15 402	10 244	7 008	20 990	13 597
2010	57 222	3 681	15 134	10 101	7 080	21 226	13 618
2011	57 151	3 579	14 764	9 971	7 153	21 684	13 697
2012	58 180	3 614	14 527	10 074	7 405	22 559	14 347
White[1]							
2001	97 560	9 550	30 126	17 671	9 393	30 821	20 136
2002	97 476	9 394	29 836	17 209	9 440	31 597	20 670
2003	98 120	9 437	29 645	17 227	9 476	32 335	21 103
2004	98 967	9 335	29 571	17 445	9 817	32 799	21 299
2005	100 613	9 579	29 911	17 515	10 256	33 352	21 550
2006	102 322	9 720	30 188	17 632	10 424	34 357	22 272
2007	103 477	9 446	30 140	17 936	10 419	35 535	23 138
2008	103 373	9 036	29 495	17 873	10 742	36 228	23 511
2009	100 419	8 497	28 372	16 983	10 714	35 854	23 109
2010	100 100	8 290	28 128	16 800	10 707	36 176	23 179
2011	100 426	8 248	27 568	16 713	10 922	36 975	23 533
2012	100 543	8 100	27 112	16 594	11 260	37 476	23 942
Black[1]							
2001	12 797	1 492	4 492	2 871	1 216	2 727	1 921
2002	12 719	1 498	4 453	2 843	1 210	2 715	1 955
2003	12 706	1 376	4 465	2 780	1 199	2 887	2 056
2004	12 817	1 326	4 606	2 717	1 195	2 973	2 097
2005	13 177	1 369	4 742	2 720	1 288	3 057	2 106
2006	13 504	1 389	4 697	2 816	1 338	3 263	2 243
2007	13 811	1 293	4 783	2 912	1 389	3 435	2 362
2008	13 786	1 234	4 719	2 972	1 439	3 423	2 354
2009	13 110	1 096	4 375	2 855	1 422	3 363	2 253
2010	13 092	1 103	4 234	2 864	1 482	3 409	2 260
2011	13 097	1 013	4 298	2 792	1 519	3 474	2 257
2012	13 717	1 016	4 397	2 919	1 584	3 801	2 479
Hispanic[2]							
2001	12 817	4 601	3 796	1 916	781	1 723	1 223
2002	13 294	4 744	3 921	1 900	823	1 906	1 370
2003	14 205	5 073	4 169	2 037	889	2 039	1 468
2004	14 661	5 135	4 330	2 137	931	2 127	1 538
2005	15 362	5 367	4 535	2 230	997	2 232	1 595
2006	16 225	5 620	4 801	2 282	1 095	2 428	1 698
2007	16 973	5 677	5 110	2 382	1 160	2 644	1 898
2008	17 115	5 426	5 232	2 484	1 236	2 736	1 930
2009	18 642	6 064	5 658	2 670	1 357	2 894	2 063
2010	16 946	5 183	5 175	2 474	1 252	2 862	2 025
2011	17 059	5 156	5 216	2 513	1 317	2 857	1 982
2012	18 309	5 269	5 613	2 734	1 482	3 210	2 221

[1]Beginning in 2003, persons who selected this race group only; persons who selected more than one race group are not included. Prior to 2003, persons who reported more than one race group were included in the group they identified as their main race.
[2]May be of any race.

Table 1-16. Number of Employed Persons Age 25 Years and Over, by Educational Attainment, Sex, Race, and Hispanic Origin, 2001–2012—*Continued*

(Thousands of people.)

Race, Hispanic origin, sex, and year	Total	Less than a high school diploma	High school graduate, no college	Some college, no degree	Associate's degree	College graduate or higher	
						Total	Bachelor's degree only
White Men[1]							
2001	53 375	6 080	16 292	9 344	4 501	17 158	11 060
2002	53 242	6 072	16 148	9 102	4 497	17 423	11 217
2003	53 458	6 192	16 068	9 042	4 431	17 725	11 461
2004	54 133	6 188	16 297	9 125	4 613	17 910	11 555
2005	55 214	6 368	16 750	9 225	4 851	18 021	11 551
2006	56 145	6 448	17 018	9 244	4 952	18 483	11 881
2007	56 740	6 364	17 039	9 409	4 964	18 964	12 260
2008	56 446	6 066	16 741	9 397	5 070	19 171	12 482
2009	54 248	5 583	15 966	8 937	4 948	18 813	12 112
2010	54 091	5 461	15 952	8 846	4 922	18 910	12 128
2011	54 488	5 450	15 776	8 878	5 082	19 303	12 344
2012	54 646	5 339	15 711	8 809	5 273	19 513	12 495
White Women[1]							
2001	44 184	3 469	13 834	8 327	4 891	13 663	9 075
2002	44 234	3 322	13 688	8 107	4 944	14 173	9 453
2003	44 662	3 245	13 576	8 185	5 045	14 610	9 643
2004	44 834	3 146	13 275	8 320	5 203	14 888	9 744
2005	45 399	3 211	13 162	8 290	5 405	15 331	9 999
2006	46 177	3 272	13 171	8 388	5 473	15 874	10 391
2007	46 737	3 082	13 102	8 527	5 455	16 571	10 878
2008	46 928	2 970	12 753	8 477	5 672	17 056	11 029
2009	46 172	2 913	12 406	8 046	5 766	17 040	10 997
2010	46 010	2 829	12 176	7 953	5 785	17 266	11 051
2011	45 938	2 798	11 792	7 835	5 840	17 672	11 189
2012	45 897	2 761	11 402	7 784	5 987	17 963	11 447
Black Men[1]							
2001	5 924	762	2 232	1 258	486	1 186	834
2002	5 928	785	2 212	1 264	482	1 185	855
2003	5 860	693	2 190	1 256	492	1 230	890
2004	5 942	676	2 287	1 172	503	1 305	931
2005	6 153	697	2 417	1 171	558	1 310	938
2006	6 276	720	2 338	1 249	535	1 433	1 002
2007	6 429	653	2 340	1 320	570	1 547	1 076
2008	6 357	616	2 358	1 296	579	1 508	1 036
2009	5 939	551	2 199	1 225	544	1 419	958
2010	5 988	561	2 164	1 270	567	1 426	960
2011	6 031	532	2 225	1 235	591	1 449	968
2012	6 320	530	2 281	1 328	639	1 541	1 024
Black Women[1]							
2001	6 873	730	2 260	1 612	729	1 541	1 087
2002	6 791	713	2 241	1 579	729	1 530	1 101
2003	6 846	683	2 275	1 524	707	1 657	1 166
2004	6 874	650	2 319	1 545	691	1 668	1 166
2005	7 024	672	2 325	1 549	730	1 748	1 169
2006	7 228	669	2 359	1 567	803	1 830	1 241
2007	7 382	641	2 443	1 592	819	1 888	1 286
2008	7 429	617	2 361	1 676	859	1 915	1 318
2009	7 171	544	2 176	1 631	877	1 943	1 295
2010	7 104	542	2 070	1 594	915	1 983	1 300
2011	7 066	481	2 073	1 558	928	2 026	1 289
2012	7 397	487	2 115	1 591	945	2 260	1 455
Hispanic Men[2]							
2001	7 628	3 041	2 174	1 082	386	945	669
2002	7 865	3 141	2 244	1 029	415	1 035	732
2003	8 578	3 424	2 461	1 105	451	1 137	806
2004	8 872	3 508	2 583	1 158	468	1 155	837
2005	9 361	3 639	2 775	1 251	503	1 193	847
2006	9 856	3 823	2 932	1 260	547	1 293	891
2007	10 303	3 947	3 100	1 285	567	1 403	1 000
2008	10 363	3 714	3 231	1 371	607	1 439	1 008
2009	9 969	3 508	3 114	1 321	595	1 431	992
2010	10 120	3 517	3 176	1 341	595	1 491	1 045
2011	10 151	3 487	3 158	1 377	636	1 492	1 044
2012	10 629	3 512	3 391	1 420	693	1 612	1 115
Hispanic Women[2]							
2001	5 190	1 560	1 622	834	395	778	553
2002	5 429	1 604	1 676	871	408	871	638
2003	5 627	1 649	1 708	932	438	901	661
2004	5 789	1 628	1 746	980	463	972	701
2005	6 000	1 728	1 759	979	495	1 039	748
2006	6 370	1 797	1 868	1 021	548	1 135	807
2007	6 670	1 730	2 010	1 097	593	1 241	898
2008	6 752	1 712	2 001	1 113	629	1 297	922
2009	6 718	1 724	1 955	1 093	647	1 298	941
2010	6 826	1 666	1 999	1 133	656	1 371	979
2011	6 908	1 669	2 058	1 136	681	1 365	938
2012	7 680	1 757	2 222	1 315	788	1 598	1 106

[1]Beginning in 2003, persons who selected this race group only; persons who selected more than one race group are not included. Prior to 2003, persons who reported more than one race group were included in the group they identified as their main race.
[2]May be of any race.

Table 1-17. Multiple Jobholders and Multiple Jobholding Rates, by Selected Characteristics, May of Selected Years, 1970–2013

(Thousands of people, percent, not seasonally adjusted.)

Year	Total employed	Multiple jobholders				Multiple jobholding rate[1]						
		Total	Men	Women		Total	Men	Women	White	Black[2]	Asian	Hispanic[3]
				Number	Percent of all multiple jobholders							
1970	78 358	4 048	3 412	636	15.7	5.2	7.0	2.2	5.3	4.4	...	...
1971	78 708	4 035	3 270	765	19.0	5.1	6.7	2.6	5.3	3.8	...	...
1972	81 224	3 770	3 035	735	19.5	4.6	6.0	2.4	4.8	3.7	...	...
1973	83 758	4 262	3 393	869	20.4	5.1	6.6	2.7	5.1	4.7	...	...
1974	85 786	3 889	3 022	867	22.3	4.5	5.8	2.6	4.6	3.8	...	...
1975	84 146	3 918	2 962	956	24.4	4.7	5.8	2.9	4.8	3.7	...	...
1976	87 278	3 948	3 037	911	23.1	4.5	5.8	2.6	4.7	2.8	...	...
1977	90 482	4 558	3 317	1 241	27.2	5.0	6.2	3.4	5.3	2.6	...	...
1978	93 904	4 493	3 212	1 281	28.5	4.8	5.8	3.3	5.0	3.1	...	...
1979	96 327	4 724	3 317	1 407	29.8	4.9	5.9	3.5	5.1	3.0	...	...
1980	96 809	4 759	3 210	1 549	32.5	4.9	5.8	3.8	5.1	3.2	...	...
1985	106 878	5 730	3 537	2 192	38.3	5.4	5.9	4.7	5.7	3.2	...	...
1989	117 084	7 225	4 115	3 109	43.0	6.2	6.4	5.9	6.5	4.3	...	...
1991	116 626	7 183	4 054	3 129	43.6	6.2	6.4	5.9	6.4	4.9	...	...
1994	122 946	7 316	3 973	3 343	45.7	6.0	6.0	5.9	6.1	4.9	...	3.8
1995	124 554	7 952	4 225	3 727	46.9	6.4	6.3	6.5	6.6	5.2	...	3.6
1996	126 391	7 846	4 352	3 494	44.5	6.2	6.4	6.0	6.4	5.1	...	4.0
1997	129 565	8 197	4 398	3 800	46.4	6.3	6.3	6.4	6.5	5.7	...	4.1
1998	131 476	8 126	4 438	3 688	45.4	6.2	6.3	6.1	6.3	5.5	...	4.4
1999	133 411	7 895	4 117	3 778	47.9	5.9	5.8	6.1	6.0	5.5	...	3.6
2000	136 685	7 751	4 084	3 667	47.3	5.7	5.6	5.8	5.9	4.9	3.4	3.2
2001	137 121	7 540	3 914	3 626	48.1	5.5	5.3	5.7	5.6	5.3	3.7	3.4
2002	136 559	7 247	3 736	3 511	48.4	5.3	5.1	5.5	5.5	4.7	4.0	3.8
2003	137 567	7 338	3 841	3 498	47.7	5.3	5.3	5.4	5.5	4.3	4.2	3.4
2004	138 867	7 258	3 653	3 605	49.7	5.2	4.9	5.6	5.3	5.1	3.7	3.4
2005	141 591	7 348	3 741	3 607	49.1	5.2	4.9	5.5	5.4	4.4	3.5	2.8
2006	144 041	7 641	3 863	3 778	49.4	5.3	5.0	5.7	5.3	5.4	3.7	3.1
2007	145 864	7 693	3 835	3 858	50.1	5.3	4.9	5.7	5.5	4.4	3.7	3.0
2008	145 927	7 653	3 842	3 812	49.8	5.2	4.9	5.6	5.4	4.9	3.8	2.9
2009	140 363	7 265	3 540	3 725	51.3	5.2	4.8	5.6	5.3	4.8	3.9	3.0
2010	139 497	7 261	3 559	3 702	51.0	5.2	4.8	5.6	5.4	4.6	3.1	3.1
2011	140 028	7 084	3 491	3 593	50.7	5.1	4.7	5.5	5.3	4.5	3.1	3.3
2012	142 727	7 174	3 605	3 569	49.7	5.0	4.8	5.3	5.2	4.9	3.3	3.1
2013	144 432	7 123	3 570	3 553	49.9	4.9	4.7	5.2	5.1	4.4	3.7	3.3

Note: Data prior to 1985 reflect 1970 census–based population controls; years 1985–1991 reflect 1980 census–based controls; years 1994–1999 reflect 1990 census–based controls adjusted for the estimated undercount; and data for years 2000–2002 have been revised to incorporate population controls from the 2000 census. Prior to 1994, data on multiple jobholders were collected only through special periodic supplements to the Current Population Survey (CPS) in May of various years; these supplemental surveys were not conducted in 1981–1984, 1986–1988, 1990, or 1992–1993. Beginning in 1994, data reflect the introduction of a major redesign of the CPS, including the collection of monthly data on multiple jobholders.

[1]Multiple jobholders as a percent of all employed persons in specified group.
[2]Data for years prior to 1977 refer to the Black-and-Other population group.
[3]May be of any race.
. . . = Not available.

Table 1-18. Multiple Jobholders, by Sex, Age, Marital Status, Race, Hispanic Origin, and Job Status, 2009–2012

(Thousands of people, percent.)

Characteristic	Both sexes				Men				Women			
	Number		Rate[1]		Number		Rate[1]		Number		Rate[1]	
	2009	2010	2009	2010	2009	2010	2009	2010	2009	2010	2009	2010
Age												
Total, 16 years and over[2]	7 271	6 878	5.2	4.9	3 530	3 326	4.8	4.5	3 741	3 552	5.6	5.4
16 to 19 years	186	167	3.8	3.8	71	61	3.1	2.9	115	106	4.6	4.7
20 to 24 years	710	695	5.6	5.5	307	289	4.7	4.5	403	406	6.4	6.5
25 to 34 years	1 546	1 519	5.1	5.0	795	768	4.9	4.7	750	751	5.4	5.4
35 to 44 years	1 675	1 554	5.3	5.1	822	798	4.9	4.8	853	756	5.8	5.4
45 to 54 years	1 903	1 724	5.7	5.2	907	809	5.2	4.7	996	916	6.2	5.7
55 to 64 years	1 039	1 021	4.9	4.7	507	490	4.7	4.4	532	531	5.2	5.1
65 years and over	212	197	3.5	3.1	120	112	3.6	3.2	92	86	3.3	3.0
Marital Status												
Single	1 989	2 000	5.2	5.2	890	895	4.3	4.3	1 099	1 105	6.2	6.2
Married, spouse present	3 993	3 644	5.0	4.7	2 212	2 015	5.0	4.7	1 781	1 629	5.1	4.7
Widowed, divorced, or separated	1 289	1 233	5.8	5.2	429	416	4.7	4.5	861	817	6.5	6.2
Race and Hispanic Origin												
White	6 166	5 857	5.4	5.1	3 016	2 861	4.9	4.7	3 150	5 857	5.9	5.7
Black	714	653	4.8	4.3	319	298	4.7	4.3	395	653	4.8	4.3
Hispanic[3]	643	638	3.3	3.2	354	360	3.0	3.1	289	638	3.6	3.4
Full- or Part-Time Status												
Primary job full time, secondary job part time	3 868	3 591	...	...	2 042	211	...	...	1 825	352	...	...
Primary and secondary jobs, both part time	1 821	1 805	...	...	599	67	...	...	1 222	152	...	...
Primary and secondary jobs, both full time	249	263	...	...	157	33	...	...	92	47	...	...
Hours vary on primary or secondary job	1 287	1 182	...	...	704	48	...	...	583	83	...	...

Characteristic	Both sexes				Men				Women			
	Number		Rate[1]		Number		Rate[1]		Number		Rate[1]	
	2011	2012	2011	2012	2011	2012	2011	2012	2011	2012	2011	2012
Age												
Total, 16 years and over[2]	6 880	6 943	4.9	4.9	3 384	3 448	4.6	4.6	3 496	3 495	5.3	5.2
16 to 19 years	183	178	4.2	4.0	78	73	3.7	3.4	104	105	4.7	4.6
20 to 24 years	697	725	5.3	5.4	294	298	4.3	4.3	403	427	6.5	6.6
25 to 34 years	1 496	1 488	4.9	4.8	802	772	4.8	4.6	694	716	5.0	5.1
35 to 44 years	1 483	1 474	4.9	4.8	736	786	4.5	4.8	747	688	5.4	4.9
45 to 54 years	1 697	1 678	5.2	5.1	804	802	4.7	4.7	894	875	5.7	5.6
55 to 64 years	1 083	1 136	4.9	4.9	523	550	4.6	4.6	561	586	5.2	5.2
65 years and over	241	264	3.6	3.6	148	168	4.0	4.1	93	96	3.2	3.0
Marital Status												
Single	2 026	2 031	5.1	5.0	939	917	4.4	4.2	1 087	1 114	6.0	5.9
Married, spouse present	3 646	3 683	4.7	4.7	2 044	2 108	4.7	4.8	1 602	1 575	4.7	4.6
Widowed, divorced, or separated	1 209	1 229	5.3	5.3	402	422	4.2	4.3	806	806	6.1	6.0
Race and Hispanic Origin												
White	5 812	5 756	5.1	5.0	2 883	2 879	4.7	4.6	2 929	2 877	5.6	5.5
Black	679	709	4.5	4.5	328	337	4.7	4.6	351	371	4.3	4.3
Hispanic[3]	611	668	3.0	3.1	358	373	3.0	3.0	253	295	3.1	3.2
Full- or Part-Time Status												
Primary job full time, secondary job part time	3 620	3 590	...	...	1 979	2 003	...	...	1 640	1 587	...	...
Primary and secondary jobs, both part time	1 811	1 906	...	...	619	640	...	...	1 193	1 265	...	...
Primary and secondary jobs, both full time	234	252	...	...	147	157	...	...	88	95	...	...
Hours vary on primary or secondary job	1 172	1 146	...	...	619	621	...	...	552	525	...	...

Note: Estimates for the above race groups (White or Black) do not sum to totals because data are not presented for all races. Beginning in January 2003, data reflect the revised population controls used in the household survey.

[1] Multiple jobholders as a percent of all employed persons in specified group.
[2] Includes a small number of persons who work part time at their primary job and full time at their secondary job(s), not shown separately.
[3] May be of any race.
... = Not available.

Table 1-19. Multiple Jobholders, by Sex and Industry of Principal Secondary Job, Annual Averages, 2010–2012

(Thousands of people.)

Year and industry of secondary job	Both sexes	Men	Women
2010			
All Nonagricultural Industries, Wage and Salary Workers	4 885	2 210	2 675
Mining, quarrying, and oil and gas extraction	8	8	...
Construction	188	158	30
Manufacturing	160	95	65
Durable goods	89	60	29
Nondurable goods	71	35	36
Wholesale and retail trade	902	392	511
Wholesale trade	58	37	21
Retail trade	844	354	490
Transportation and utilities	178	129	50
Transportation and warehousing	156	115	41
Utilities	22	14	8
Information	129	80	49
Financial activities	287	163	125
Professional and business services	713	399	314
Education and health services	1 640	542	1 097
Leisure and hospitality	1 040	489	551
Other services	499	208	291
Other services, except private households	449	204	245
Other services, private households	50	4	46
Public administration	196	128	68
2011			
All Nonagricultural Industries, Wage and Salary Workers	4 940	2 291	2 648
Mining, quarrying, and oil and gas extraction	6	5	0
Construction	201	161	40
Manufacturing	148	93	55
Durable goods	80	60	19
Nondurable goods	69	33	36
Wholesale and retail trade	1 003	409	594
Wholesale trade	97	61	36
Retail trade	907	349	558
Transportation and utilities	162	122	39
Transportation and warehousing	156	119	37
Utilities	6	4	2
Information	113	68	45
Financial activities	314	179	134
Professional and business services	777	443	334
Education and health services	1 605	543	1 062
Leisure and hospitality	1 058	518	540
Other services	509	252	258
Other services, except private households	455	245	210
Other services, private households	55	7	48
Public administration	178	116	62
2012			
All Nonagricultural Industries, Wage and Salary Workers	5 051	2 391	2 660
Mining, quarrying, and oil and gas extraction	5	3	2
Construction	174	142	33
Manufacturing	160	97	63
Durable goods	86	56	30
Nondurable goods	74	41	34
Wholesale and retail trade	938	414	525
Wholesale trade	71	53	18
Retail trade	868	361	507
Transportation and utilities	149	114	35
Transportation and warehousing	137	107	31
Utilities	12	8	4
Information	129	75	54
Financial activities	298	159	139
Professional and business services	783	453	330
Education and health services	1 609	537	1 072
Leisure and hospitality	1 099	561	538
Other services	530	229	301
Other services, except private households	461	222	239
Other services, private households	69	8	61
Public administration	163	112	51

Table 1-20. Employment and Unemployment in Families, by Race and Hispanic Origin, Annual Averages, 2000–2012

(Thousands of people, percent.)

Characteristic	2000	2001	2002	2003	2004	2005	2006	2007	2008	2009	2010	2011	2012
ALL RACES													
Total Families	71 680	73 306	74 169	75 301	75 872	76 443	77 017	77 894	77 943	78 361	78 246	78 362	80 141
With employed member(s)	59 626	60 707	61 121	61 761	62 424	62 933	63 492	64 330	64 058	63 010	62 560	62 529	64 091
As percent of total families	83.2	82.8	82.4	82.0	82.3	82.3	82.4	82.6	82.2	80.4	80.0	79.8	80.0
Some usually work full time[1]	55 683	56 519	56 742	57 229	57 813	58 276	58 918	59 616	59 116	57 037	56 471	56 498	58 007
With no employed member	12 054	12 600	13 048	13 540	13 447	13 509	13 525	13 564	13 884	15 351	15 686	15 833	16 050
As percent of total families	16.8	17.2	17.6	18.0	17.7	17.7	17.6	17.4	17.8	19.6	20.0	20.2	20.0
With unemployed member(s)	4 110	4 847	5 809	6 079	5 593	5 318	4 913	4 914	6 104	9 381	9 695	9 043	8 444
As percent of total families	5.7	6.6	7.8	8.1	7.4	7.0	6.4	6.3	7.8	12.0	12.4	11.5	10.5
Some member(s) employed	2 973	3 494	4 126	4 285	3 915	3 717	3 419	3 497	4 319	6 438	6 566	6 079	5 702
As percent of families with unemployed member(s)	72.3	72.1	71.0	70.5	70.0	69.9	69.6	71.2	70.8	68.6	67.7	67.2	67.5
Some usually work full time[1]	2 675	3 122	3 668	3 790	3 494	3 310	3 049	3 096	3 830	5 460	5 572	5 211	4 902
As percent of families with unemployed member(s)	65.1	64.4	63.1	62.3	62.5	62.2	62.1	63.0	62.7	58.2	57.5	57.6	58.1
WHITE[2]													
Total Families	59 918	60 921	61 494	61 995	62 250	62 567	62 977	63 667	63 490	63 774	63 551	63 635	64 246
With employed member(s)	49 877	50 505	50 785	51 002	51 350	51 645	52 054	52 669	52 273	51 494	51 048	51 030	51 491
As percent of total families	83.2	83.0	82.6	82.3	82.5	82.5	82.7	82.7	82.3	80.7	80.3	80.2	80.1
Some usually work full time[1]	46 639	47 060	47 193	47 356	47 620	47 883	48 395	48 879	48 271	46 629	46 150	46 203	46 710
With no employed member	10 042	10 416	10 709	10 993	10 900	10 922	10 923	10 997	11 217	12 280	12 502	12 605	12 755
As percent of total families	16.8	17.0	17.4	17.7	17.5	17.5	17.3	17.3	17.7	19.3	19.7	19.8	19.9
With unemployed member(s)	3 010	3 553	4 275	4 411	4 078	3 801	3 556	3 587	4 506	7 089	7 202	6 608	6 133
As percent of total families	5.0	5.8	7.0	7.1	6.6	6.1	5.6	5.6	7.1	11.1	11.3	10.4	9.5
Some member(s) employed	2 276	2 661	3 164	3 245	3 000	2 782	2 582	2 653	3 332	5 072	5 069	4 627	4 321
As percent of families with unemployed member(s)	75.6	74.9	74.0	73.6	73.6	73.2	72.6	73.9	74.0	71.5	70.4	70.0	70.5
Some usually work full time[1]	2 052	2 379	2 808	2 873	2 677	2 477	2 306	2 350	2 955	4 294	4 289	3 964	3 719
As percent of families with unemployed member(s)	68.2	67.0	65.7	65.1	65.7	65.2	64.8	65.5	65.6	60.6	59.6	60.0	60.6
BLACK[2]													
Total Families	8 600	8 674	8 845	8 869	8 860	8 952	9 058	9 184	9 297	9 318	9 404	9 370	9 671
With employed member(s)	6 964	6 933	6 987	6 906	6 920	6 986	7 078	7 249	7 290	7 022	7 030	6 954	7 290
As percent of total families	81.0	80.0	79.0	77.9	78.1	78.0	78.1	78.9	78.4	75.4	74.8	74.2	75.4
Some usually work full time[1]	6 401	6 373	6 390	6 270	6 292	6 353	6 437	6 608	6 622	6 265	6 222	6 105	6 419
With no employed member	1 636	1 742	1 858	1 963	1 940	1 966	1 980	1 935	2 006	2 296	2 374	2 416	2 380
As percent of total families	19.0	20.1	21.0	22.1	21.9	22.0	21.9	21.1	21.6	24.6	25.2	25.8	24.6
With unemployed member(s)	881	990	1 162	1 213	1 127	1 140	1 036	990	1 188	1 624	1 807	1 767	1 629
As percent of total families	10.2	11.4	13.1	13.7	12.7	12.7	11.4	10.8	12.8	17.4	19.2	18.9	16.8
Some member(s) employed	535	596	689	695	625	657	596	591	686	886	1 009	985	885
As percent of families with unemployed member(s)	60.8	60.2	59.3	57.3	55.5	57.7	57.6	59.7	57.8	54.5	55.8	55.7	54.3
Some usually work full time[1]	476	533	611	612	556	583	526	519	605	748	862	835	752
As percent of families with unemployed member(s)	54.1	53.8	52.6	50.5	49.3	51.1	50.8	52.4	50.9	46.0	47.7	47.3	46.1
HISPANIC[3]													
Total Families	7 581	8 140	8 650	9 185	9 305	9 603	9 905	10 332	10 500	10 489	10 561	10 902	11 769
With employed member(s)	6 633	7 100	7 485	7 907	8 071	8 312	8 641	9 048	9 135	8 852	8 897	9 178	9 962
As percent of total families	87.5	87.2	86.5	86.1	86.7	86.6	87.2	87.6	87.0	84.4	84.2	84.2	84.6
Some usually work full time[1]	6 255	6 692	6 989	7 383	7 566	7 786	8 129	8 492	8 466	7 923	7 934	8 201	8 978
With no employed member	947	1 040	1 165	1 277	1 235	1 291	1 264	1 285	1 365	1 637	1 664	1 724	1 808
As percent of total families	12.5	12.8	13.5	13.9	13.3	13.4	12.8	12.4	13.0	15.6	15.8	15.8	15.4
With unemployed member(s)	679	809	965	1 020	950	860	793	876	1 159	1 770	1 841	1 781	1 707
As percent of total families	9.0	9.9	11.2	11.1	10.2	9.0	8.0	8.5	11.0	16.9	17.4	16.3	14.5
Some member(s) employed	493	592	686	715	664	606	544	619	846	1 228	1 262	1 226	1 197
As percent of families with unemployed member(s)	72.7	73.2	71.1	70.1	69.9	70.5	68.6	70.6	73.0	69.3	68.6	68.8	70.1
Some usually work full time[1]	446	537	615	640	594	544	491	554	743	1 021	1 060	1 030	1 020
As percent of families with unemployed member(s)	65.8	66.4	63.7	62.7	62.5	63.2	61.9	63.2	64.1	57.7	57.6	57.8	59.7

Note: The race or ethnicity of the family is determined by the race of the householder. Estimates for the above race groups (White or Black) do not sum to totals because data are not presented for all races.

[1]Usually work 35 hours or more a week at all jobs.
[2]Beginning in 2003, families where the householder selected this race group only; families where the householder selected more than one race group are excluded. Prior to 2003, families where the householder selected more than one race group were included in the group that the householder identified as the main race.
[3]May be of any race.

Table 1-21. Families, by Presence and Relationship of Employed Members and Family Type, Annual Averages, 2000–2012

(Thousands of people, percent.)

Characteristic	Number of families												
	2000	2001	2002	2003	2004	2005	2006	2007	2008	2009	2010	2011	2012
MARRIED-COUPLE FAMILIES													
Total	54 704	55 749	56 280	57 074	57 188	57 167	57 509	58 145	58 125	58 124	57 524	57 290	58 431
Member(s) employed, total	45 967	46 680	46 976	47 535	47 767	47 895	48 196	48 676	48 541	47 876	47 238	46 910	47 830
Husband only	10 500	10 833	11 174	11 403	11 712	11 562	11 399	11 509	11 351	11 371	11 311	11 426	11 815
Wife only	2 946	3 257	3 613	3 863	3 843	3 715	3 754	3 858	4 036	4 909	4 937	4 764	4 696
Husband and wife	29 128	29 241	28 873	29 077	28 991	29 330	29 799	30 055	29 854	28 211	27 501	27 229	27 708
Other employment combinations	3 394	3 350	3 317	3 193	3 222	3 288	3 244	3 254	3 300	3 384	3 489	3 491	3 612
No member(s) employed	8 737	9 068	9 303	9 539	9 420	9 272	9 313	9 469	9 585	10 248	10 286	10 379	10 601
FAMILIES MAINTAINED BY WOMEN[1]													
Total	12 775	13 037	13 215	13 450	13 614	14 035	14 208	14 423	14 383	14 610	14 913	15 147	15 517
Member(s) employed, total	10 026	10 131	10 169	10 187	10 358	10 609	10 796	11 087	10 929	10 642	10 715	10 867	11 236
Householder only	5 581	5 667	5 944	5 987	6 021	6 052	6 103	6 307	6 250	6 135	6 189	6 248	6 403
Householder and other member(s)	2 806	2 778	2 559	2 539	2 701	2 830	2 955	2 994	2 870	2 642	2 603	2 683	2 896
Other member(s), not householder	1 639	1 686	1 666	1 660	1 636	1 727	1 738	1 785	1 809	1 866	1 923	1 937	1 937
No member(s) employed	2 749	2 906	3 047	3 263	3 255	3 426	3 412	3 336	3 454	3 968	4 198	4 280	4 281
FAMILIES MAINTAINED BY MEN[1]													
Total	4 200	4 521	4 674	4 777	5 071	5 242	5 300	5 327	5 435	5 627	5 809	5 926	6 192
Member(s) employed, total	3 632	3 895	3 976	4 039	4 299	4 430	4 500	4 568	4 589	4 492	4 607	4 752	5 025
Householder only	1 761	1 875	1 939	1 954	2 060	2 093	2 089	2 170	2 178	2 104	2 215	2 399	2 514
Householder and other member(s)	1 358	1 450	1 440	1 427	1 557	1 639	1 715	1 696	1 659	1 557	1 525	1 506	1 622
Other member(s), not householder	514	570	598	658	682	698	696	701	752	831	867	847	889
No member(s) employed	567	625	698	739	772	812	800	759	845	1 135	1 202	1 174	1 168

Characteristic	Percent distribution												
	2000	2001	2002	2003	2004	2005	2006	2007	2008	2009	2010	2011	2012
MARRIED-COUPLE FAMILIES													
Total	100.0	100.0	100.0	100.0	100.0	100.0	100.0	100.0	100.0	100.0	100.0	100.0	100.0
Member(s) employed, total	84.0	83.7	83.5	83.3	83.5	83.8	83.8	83.7	83.5	82.4	82.1	81.9	81.9
Husband only	19.2	19.4	19.9	20.0	20.5	20.2	19.8	19.8	19.5	19.6	19.7	19.9	20.2
Wife only	5.4	5.8	6.4	6.8	6.7	6.5	6.5	6.6	6.9	8.4	8.6	8.3	8.0
Husband and wife	53.2	52.5	51.3	50.9	50.7	51.3	51.8	51.7	51.4	48.5	47.8	47.5	47.4
Other employment combinations	6.2	6.0	5.9	5.6	5.6	5.8	5.6	5.6	5.7	5.8	6.1	6.1	6.2
No member(s) employed	16.0	16.3	16.5	16.7	16.5	16.2	16.2	16.3	16.5	17.6	17.9	18.1	18.1
FAMILIES MAINTAINED BY WOMEN[1]													
Total	100.0	100.0	100.0	100.0	100.0	100.0	100.0	100.0	100.0	100.0	100.0	100.0	100.0
Member(s) employed, total	78.5	77.7	77.0	75.7	76.1	75.6	76.0	76.9	76.0	72.8	71.9	71.7	72.4
Householder only	43.7	43.5	45.0	44.5	44.2	43.1	43.0	43.7	43.5	42.0	41.5	41.2	41.3
Householder and other member(s)	22.0	21.3	19.4	18.9	19.8	20.2	20.8	20.8	20.0	18.1	17.5	17.7	18.7
Other member(s), not householder	12.8	12.9	12.6	12.3	12.0	12.3	12.2	12.4	12.6	12.8	12.9	12.8	12.5
No member(s) employed	21.5	22.3	23.1	24.3	23.9	24.4	24.0	23.1	24.0	27.2	28.1	28.3	27.6
FAMILIES MAINTAINED BY MEN[1]													
Total	100.0	100.0	100.0	100.0	100.0	100.0	100.0	100.0	100.0	100.0	100.0	100.0	100.0
Member(s) employed, total	86.5	86.2	85.1	84.6	84.8	84.5	84.9	85.7	84.4	79.8	79.3	80.2	81.1
Householder only	41.9	41.5	41.5	40.9	40.6	39.9	39.4	40.7	40.1	37.4	38.1	40.5	40.6
Householder and other member(s)	32.3	32.1	30.8	29.9	30.7	31.3	32.4	31.8	30.5	27.7	26.2	25.4	26.2
Other member(s), not householder	12.2	12.6	12.8	13.8	13.5	13.3	13.1	13.2	13.8	14.8	14.9	14.3	14.4
No member(s) employed	13.5	13.8	14.9	15.5	15.2	15.5	15.1	14.3	15.6	20.2	20.7	19.8	18.9

Note: Detail may not sum to total due to rounding.

[1] No spouse present.

Table 1-22. Unemployment in Families, by Presence and Relationship of Employed Members and Family Type, Annual Averages, 2000–2012

(Thousands of people, percent.)

Characteristic	Number												
	2000	2001	2002	2003	2004	2005	2006	2007	2008	2009	2010	2011	2012
MARRIED-COUPLE FAMILIES													
With Unemployed Member(s), Total	2 584	3 081	3 772	3 857	3 521	3 243	2 968	2 978	3 796	6 056	6 147	5 576	5 140
No member employed	411	531	676	713	615	580	526	512	663	1 218	4 884	4 413	4 123
Some member(s) employed	2 174	2 550	3 096	3 144	2 906	2 664	2 442	2 467	3 133	4 838	1 263	1 162	1 017
Husband unemployed	836	1 160	1 523	1 600	1 333	1 190	1 061	1 110	1 439	2 808	2 813	2 387	2 066
Wife employed	531	736	993	1 023	850	753	679	725	927	1 799	1 783	1 497	1 307
Wife unemployed	789	918	1 117	1 129	1 041	1 004	898	902	1 114	1 630	1 697	1 610	1 567
Husband employed	694	809	969	991	913	873	772	783	975	1 397	1 455	1 350	1 328
Other family member unemployed	959	1 003	1 133	1 129	1 147	1 049	1 010	966	1 243	1 618	1 637	1 579	1 507
FAMILIES MAINTAINED BY WOMEN[1]													
With Unemployed Member(s), Total	1 194	1 324	1 504	1 612	1 521	1 539	1 429	1 416	1 666	2 309	2 446	2 498	2 372
No member employed	587	643	787	842	829	797	753	701	849	1 244	1 094	1 146	1 081
Some member(s) employed	607	681	717	770	692	743	675	714	817	1 065	1 351	1 352	1 290
Householder unemployed	522	593	737	791	758	746	688	650	796	1 141	1 227	1 268	1 191
Other member(s) employed	102	129	147	162	146	161	132	144	181	225	254	275	250
Other member(s) unemployed	672	731	767	821	764	793	740	766	870	1 168	1 218	1 229	1 180
FAMILIES MAINTAINED BY MEN[1]													
With Unemployed Member(s), Total	331	442	533	610	551	536	516	520	642	1 016	1 102	970	932
No member employed	139	178	220	239	234	225	215	205	274	482	587	520	497
Some member(s) employed	192	264	313	371	316	310	301	316	368	535	515	450	435
Householder unemployed	173	234	303	340	296	301	284	294	385	626	680	575	535
Other member(s) employed	67	96	129	158	117	122	118	137	164	239	259	231	209
Other member(s) unemployed	158	208	230	270	255	235	232	226	257	391	422	394	397

Characteristic	Percent distribution												
	2000	2001	2002	2003	2004	2005	2006	2007	2008	2009	2010	2011	2012
MARRIED-COUPLE FAMILIES													
With Unemployed Member(s), Total	100.0	100.0	100.0	100.0	100.0	100.0	100.0	100.0	100.0	100.0	100.0	100.0	100.0
No member employed	15.9	17.2	17.9	18.5	17.5	17.9	17.7	17.2	17.5	20.1	79.4	79.2	80.2
Some member(s) employed	84.1	82.8	82.1	81.5	82.5	82.1	82.3	82.8	82.5	79.9	20.6	20.8	19.8
Husband unemployed	32.3	37.7	40.4	41.5	37.9	36.7	35.7	37.3	37.9	46.4	45.8	42.8	40.2
Wife employed	20.5	23.9	26.3	26.5	24.2	23.2	22.9	24.3	24.4	29.7	29.0	26.9	25.4
Wife unemployed	30.5	29.8	29.6	29.3	29.6	31.0	30.3	30.3	29.3	26.9	27.6	28.9	30.5
Husband employed	26.8	26.3	25.7	25.7	25.9	26.9	26.0	26.3	25.7	23.1	23.7	24.2	25.8
Other family member unemployed	37.1	32.6	30.0	29.3	32.6	32.4	34.0	32.4	32.7	26.7	26.6	28.3	29.3
FAMILIES MAINTAINED BY WOMEN[1]													
With Unemployed Member(s), Total	100.0	100.0	100.0	100.0	100.0	100.0	100.0	100.0	100.0	100.0	100.0	100.0	100.0
No member employed	49.1	48.6	52.3	52.3	54.5	51.8	52.7	49.5	50.9	53.9	44.7	45.9	45.6
Some member(s) employed	50.9	51.4	47.7	47.8	45.5	48.2	47.3	50.5	49.1	46.1	55.3	54.1	54.4
Householder unemployed	43.7	44.8	49.0	49.1	49.8	48.5	48.2	45.9	47.8	49.4	50.2	50.8	50.2
Other member(s) employed	8.5	9.7	9.8	10.0	9.6	10.5	9.3	10.2	10.9	9.7	10.4	11.0	10.6
Other member(s) unemployed	56.3	55.2	51.0	50.9	50.2	51.5	51.8	54.1	52.2	50.6	49.8	49.2	49.8
FAMILIES MAINTAINED BY MEN[1]													
With Unemployed Member(s), Total	100.0	100.0	100.0	100.0	100.0	100.0	100.0	100.0	100.0	100.0	100.0	100.0	100.0
No member employed	42.0	40.3	41.3	39.2	42.5	42.1	41.7	39.3	42.7	47.4	53.3	53.6	53.3
Some member(s) employed	58.0	59.7	58.7	60.8	57.5	57.9	58.3	60.7	57.3	52.6	46.7	46.4	46.7
Householder unemployed	52.2	52.9	56.8	55.7	53.7	56.1	55.0	56.6	60.0	61.6	61.7	59.4	57.4
Other member(s) employed	20.4	21.7	24.2	25.9	21.3	22.8	22.8	26.3	25.6	23.5	23.5	23.8	22.5
Other member(s) unemployed	47.8	47.1	43.2	44.3	46.3	43.9	45.0	43.4	40.0	38.4	38.3	40.6	42.6

Note: Detail may not sum to total due to rounding.

[1]No spouse present.

Table 1-23. Employment Status of the Population, by Sex, Marital Status, and Presence and Age of Own Children Under 18 Years, Annual Averages, 2003–2012

(Thousands of people, percent.)

Characteristic	2003 Both sexes	2003 Men	2003 Women	2004 Both sexes	2004 Men	2004 Women	2005 Both sexes	2005 Men	2005 Women	2006 Both sexes	2006 Men	2006 Women	2007 Both sexes	2007 Men	2007 Women
With Own Children Under 18 Years, Total															
Civilian noninstitutional population	64 932	28 402	36 530	64 758	28 272	36 486	64 482	28 065	36 417	65 941	29 449	36 492	66 801	29 684	37 117
Civilian labor force	52 727	26 739	25 988	52 288	26 607	25 681	52 056	26 399	25 657	53 590	27 730	25 861	54 370	28 002	26 368
Participation rate	81.2	94.1	71.1	80.7	94.1	70.4	80.7	94.1	70.5	81.3	94.2	70.9	81.4	94.3	71.0
Employed	50 103	25 638	24 466	49 957	25 696	24 261	49 882	25 587	24 294	51 561	26 948	24 614	52 373	27 216	25 157
Employment-population ratio	77.2	90.3	67.0	77.1	90.9	66.5	77.4	91.2	66.7	78.2	91.5	67.4	78.4	91.7	67.8
Full-time workers[1]	42 880	24 762	18 118	42 758	24 794	17 964	42 852	24 713	18 139	44 634	26 033	18 601	45 336	26 282	19 053
Part-time workers[2]	7 223	876	6 347	7 200	902	6 298	7 029	875	6 155	6 927	914	6 013	7 037	933	6 104
Unemployed	2 624	1 101	1 523	2 331	911	1 420	2 174	811	1 363	2 029	782	1 247	1 998	786	1 211
Unemployment rate	5.0	4.1	5.9	4.5	3.4	5.5	4.2	3.1	5.3	3.8	2.8	4.8	3.7	2.8	4.6
Married, Spouse Present															
Civilian noninstitutional population	52 476	26 049	26 427	52 109	25 852	26 258	51 519	25 578	25 942	52 930	26 908	26 022	53 432	27 205	26 227
Civilian labor force	42 776	24 638	18 138	42 247	24 449	17 798	41 905	24 215	17 690	43 336	25 494	17 842	43 824	25 784	18 041
Participation rate	81.5	94.6	68.6	81.1	94.6	67.8	81.3	94.7	68.2	81.9	94.7	68.6	82.0	94.8	68.8
Employed	41 128	23 712	17 416	40 847	23 703	17 144	40 614	23 556	17 058	42 134	24 854	17 280	42 625	25 134	17 492
Employment-population ratio	78.4	91.0	65.9	78.4	91.7	65.3	78.8	92.1	65.8	79.6	92.4	66.4	79.8	92.4	66.7
Full-time workers[1]	35 315	22 954	12 360	35 141	22 935	12 206	35 086	22 808	12 278	36 649	24 074	12 575	37 120	24 332	12 788
Part-time workers[2]	5 813	757	5 056	5 706	768	4 938	5 528	748	4 780	5 485	780	4 705	5 505	802	4 704
Unemployed	1 648	926	722	1 400	747	653	1 291	659	632	1 202	640	562	1 199	650	549
Unemployment rate	3.9	3.8	4.0	3.3	3.1	3.7	3.1	2.7	3.6	2.8	2.5	3.1	2.7	2.5	3.0
Other Marital Status[3]															
Civilian noninstitutional population	12 455	2 354	10 102	12 649	2 420	10 229	12 963	2 487	10 475	13 010	2 541	10 470	13 369	2 479	10 890
Civilian labor force	9 950	2 100	7 850	10 042	2 158	7 883	10 151	2 184	7 967	10 255	2 236	8 019	10 546	2 219	8 328
Participation rate	79.9	89.2	77.7	79.4	89.2	77.1	78.3	87.8	76.1	78.8	88.0	76.6	78.9	89.5	76.5
Employed	8 975	1 926	7 050	9 110	1 993	7 117	9 268	2 032	7 236	9 427	2 094	7 333	9 747	2 082	7 665
Employment-population ratio	72.1	81.8	69.8	72.0	82.4	69.6	71.5	81.7	69.1	72.5	82.4	70.0	72.9	84.0	70.4
Full-time workers[1]	7 566	1 807	5 759	7 617	1 859	5 757	7 766	1 905	5 861	7 985	1 960	6 026	8 216	1 950	6 266
Part-time workers[2]	1 411	118	1 291	1 494	134	1 360	1 502	127	1 375	1 442	134	1 308	1 531	132	1 400
Unemployed	976	175	800	931	165	766	883	152	731	827	142	686	799	137	662
Unemployment rate	9.8	8.3	10.2	9.3	7.6	9.7	8.7	7.0	9.2	8.1	6.3	8.5	7.6	6.2	8.0
With Own Children 6 to 17 Years, None Younger															
Civilian noninstitutional population	35 943	15 653	20 290	35 874	15 597	20 277	35 937	15 590	20 348	36 530	16 212	20 318	36 983	16 384	20 599
Civilian labor force	30 362	14 572	15 790	30 182	14 516	15 666	30 068	14 496	15 572	30 675	15 091	15 585	31 179	15 269	15 910
Participation rate	84.5	93.1	77.8	84.1	93.1	77.3	83.7	93.0	76.5	84.0	93.1	76.7	84.3	93.2	77.2
Employed	29 040	14 008	15 032	29 013	14 056	14 957	28 953	14 066	14 887	29 643	14 690	14 952	30 176	14 866	15 310
Employment-population ratio	80.8	89.5	74.1	80.9	90.1	73.8	80.6	90.2	73.2	81.1	90.6	73.6	81.6	90.7	74.3
Full-time workers[1]	25 116	13 558	11 557	25 069	13 597	11 473	25 074	13 606	11 468	25 835	14 206	11 629	26 288	14 378	11 910
Part-time workers[2]	3 925	450	3 475	3 944	459	3 485	3 880	460	3 419	3 808	485	3 323	3 888	488	3 400
Unemployed	1 322	564	758	1 170	460	709	1 115	430	684	1 032	400	632	1 003	403	600
Unemployment rate	4.4	3.9	4.8	3.9	3.2	4.5	3.7	3.0	4.4	3.4	2.7	4.1	3.2	2.6	3.8
With Own Children Under 6 Years															
Civilian noninstitutional population	28 988	12 749	16 240	28 884	12 675	16 210	28 545	12 475	16 070	29 411	13 237	16 174	29 818	13 299	16 518
Civilian labor force	22 365	12 167	10 198	22 106	12 091	10 014	21 988	11 903	10 085	22 915	12 639	10 276	23 192	12 733	10 458
Participation rate	77.2	95.4	62.8	76.5	95.4	61.8	77.0	95.4	62.8	77.9	95.5	63.5	77.8	95.7	63.3
Employed	21 063	11 630	9 433	20 944	11 640	9 304	20 928	11 521	9 407	21 919	12 257	9 661	22 197	12 350	9 847
Employment-population ratio	72.7	91.2	58.1	72.5	91.8	57.4	73.3	92.4	58.5	74.5	92.6	59.7	74.4	92.9	59.6
Full-time workers[1]	17 764	11 203	6 561	17 689	11 197	6 491	17 778	11 107	6 671	18 800	11 828	6 972	19 048	11 904	7 143
Part-time workers[2]	3 299	426	2 872	3 256	443	2 813	3 150	414	2 736	3 119	430	2 689	3 149	446	2 704
Unemployed	1 302	538	765	1 162	451	710	1 060	381	678	997	382	615	995	383	611
Unemployment rate	5.8	4.4	7.5	5.3	3.7	7.1	4.8	3.2	6.7	4.3	3.0	6.0	4.3	3.0	5.8
With No Own Children Under 18 Years															
Civilian noninstitutional population	154 714	76 510	78 204	156900	77 739	79 160	159751	79 237	80 514	162874	81 156	81 718	165066	82 489	82 577
Civilian labor force	92 319	50 036	42 284	93 511	50 771	42 740	95 545	51 914	43 631	97 837	53 525	44 312	98 754	54 134	44 620
Participation rate	59.7	65.4	54.1	59.6	65.3	54.0	59.8	65.5	54.2	60.1	66.0	54.2	59.8	65.6	54.0
Employed	86 233	46 294	39 939	87 748	47 282	40 467	90 171	48 709	41 462	92 866	50 554	42 312	93 674	51 039	42 635
Employment-population ratio	55.7	60.5	51.1	55.9	60.8	51.1	56.4	61.5	51.5	57.0	62.3	51.8	56.7	61.9	51.6
Full-time workers[1]	69 073	39 245	29 827	70 244	40 134	30 110	72 515	41 496	31 019	75 054	43 274	31 780	75 755	43 752	32 003
Part-time workers[2]	17 160	7 049	10 111	17 505	7 148	10 357	17 657	7 213	10 444	17 812	7 280	10 532	17 919	7 286	10 632
Unemployed	6 087	3 741	2 345	5 763	3 489	2 274	5 374	3 205	2 169	4 971	2 971	2 000	5 080	3 095	1 984
Unemployment rate	6.6	7.5	5.5	6.2	6.9	5.3	5.6	6.2	5.0	5.1	5.6	4.5	5.1	5.7	4.4

Note: Own children include sons, daughters, stepchildren, and adopted children. Not included are nieces, nephews, grandchildren, and other related and unrelated children. Detail may not sum to total due to rounding.

[1] Usually work 35 hours or more a week at all jobs.
[2] Usually work less than 35 hours a week at all jobs.
[3] Includes never-married, divorced, separated, and widowed persons.

Table 1-23. Employment Status of the Population, by Sex, Marital Status, and Presence and Age of Own Children Under 18 Years, Annual Averages, 2003–2012—Continued

(Thousands of people, percent.)

Characteristic	2008 Both sexes	2008 Men	2008 Women	2009 Both sexes	2009 Men	2009 Women	2010 Both sexes	2010 Men	2010 Women	2011 Both sexes	2011 Men	2011 Women	2012 Both sexes	2012 Men	2012 Women
With Own Children Under 18 Years, Total															
Civilian noninstitutional population	65 655	29 142	36 513	64 854	28 778	36 076	64 488	28 463	36 025	63 885	28 143	35 743	63 796	27 889	35 907
Civilian labor force	53 506	27 422	26 085	52 748	26 985	25 763	52 159	26 661	25 499	51 521	26 302	25 219	51 342	26 028	25 314
Participation rate	81.5	94.1	71.4	81.3	93.8	71.4	80.9	93.7	70.8	80.6	93.5	70.6	80.5	93.3	70.5
Employed	51 017	26 380	24 637	48 621	24 989	23 632	47 863	24 653	23 210	47 578	24 619	22 959	47 872	24 665	23 207
Employment-population ratio	77.7	90.5	67.5	75.0	86.8	65.5	74.2	86.6	64.4	74.5	87.5	64.2	75.0	88.4	64.6
Full-time workers[1]	43 967	25 338	18 629	41 003	23 583	17 419	7 581	1 477	6 104	7 303	1 374	5 930	7 200	1 317	5 883
Part-time workers[2]	7 050	1 042	6 008	7 618	1 406	6 212	74	87	64	74	88	64	75	88	65
Unemployed	2 490	1 041	1 448	4 128	1 996	2 132	4 296	2 008	2 289	3 943	1 683	2 260	3 470	1 362	2 108
Unemployment rate	4.7	3.8	5.6	7.8	7.4	8.3	8.2	7.5	9.0	7.7	6.4	9.0	6.8	5.2	8.3
Married, Spouse Present															
Civilian noninstitutional population	52 433	26 647	25 786	51 634	26 249	25 385	50 868	25 820	25 049	49 999	25 392	24 607	49 590	25 010	24 580
Civilian labor force	43 137	25 205	17 933	42 424	24 763	17 661	41 600	24 332	17 268	40 783	23 873	16 911	40 273	23 478	16 795
Participation rate	82.3	94.6	69.5	82.2	94.3	69.6	81.8	94.2	68.9	81.6	94.0	68.7	81.2	93.9	68.3
Employed	41 611	24 353	17 258	39 732	23 100	16 632	38 870	22 689	16 181	38 379	22 480	15 900	38 257	22 372	15 885
Employment-population ratio	79.4	91.4	66.9	76.9	88.0	65.5	76.4	87.9	64.6	76.8	88.5	64.6	77.1	89.4	64.6
Full-time workers[1]	36 128	23 444	12 685	33 846	21 871	11 975	5 728	1 245	4 482	5 440	1 158	4 282	5 299	1 097	4 202
Part-time workers[2]	5 482	909	4 573	5 886	1 229	4 657	76	88	65	77	88	65	77	89	65
Unemployed	1 527	852	675	2 692	1 663	1 029	2 730	1 643	1 087	2 404	1 393	1 011	2 017	1 106	910
Unemployment rate	3.5	3.4	3.8	6.3	6.7	5.8	6.6	6.8	6.3	5.9	5.8	6.0	5.0	4.7	5.4
Other Marital Status[3]															
Civilian noninstitutional population	13 222	2 495	10 727	13 221	2 529	10 691	13 620	2 643	10 977	13 886	2 751	11 135	14 206	2 879	11 327
Civilian labor force	10 369	2 217	8 152	10 325	2 223	8 102	10 559	2 329	8 230	10 737	2 429	8 308	11 068	2 549	8 519
Participation rate	78.4	88.9	76.0	78.1	87.9	75.8	77.5	88.1	75.0	77.3	88.3	74.6	77.9	88.6	75.2
Employed	9 406	2 027	7 379	8 889	1 889	7 000	8 994	1 964	7 029	9 198	2 139	7 059	9 615	2 294	7 322
Employment-population ratio	71.1	81.3	68.8	67.2	74.7	65.5	66.0	74.3	64.0	66.2	77.8	63.4	67.7	79.7	64.6
Full-time workers[1]	7 838	1 894	5 944	7 157	1 712	5 445	1 853	232	1 621	1 864	216	1 647	1 901	220	1 681
Part-time workers[2]	1 568	133	1 435	1 732	177	1 555	66	74	64	66	78	63	68	80	65
Unemployed	963	190	773	1 436	334	1 103	1 566	365	1 201	1 539	290	1 249	1 453	256	1 197
Unemployment rate	9.3	8.6	9.5	13.9	15.0	13.6	14.8	15.7	14.6	14.3	11.9	15.0	13.1	10.0	14.1
With Own Children 6 to 17 Years, None Younger															
Civilian noninstitutional population	36 581	16 256	20 325	35 885	15 982	19 903	35 402	15 639	19 763	35 027	15 431	19 596	35 353	15 539	19 814
Civilian labor force	30 846	15 128	15 718	30 200	14 821	15 379	29 625	14 515	15 110	29 193	14 289	14 904	29 234	14 347	14 887
Participation rate	84.3	93.1	77.3	84.2	92.7	77.3	83.7	92.8	76.5	77.6	87.0	70.2	77.6	87.6	69.7
Employed	29 590	14 588	15 003	28 059	13 775	14 284	27 421	13 482	13 939	27 178	13 422	13 756	27 421	13 620	13 801
Employment-population ratio	80.9	89.7	73.8	78.2	86.2	71.8	77.5	86.2	70.5	77.6	87.0	70.2	77.6	87.6	69.7
Full-time workers[1]	25 733	14 054	11 679	23 864	13 067	10 798	4 182	757	3 425	3 992	686	3 306	3 901	702	3 199
Part-time workers[2]	3 858	534	3 324	4 194	708	3 486	78	86	70	78	87	70	78	88	70
Unemployed	1 255	541	715	2 141	1 046	1 095	2 204	1 032	1 172	2 015	867	1 148	1 813	727	1 086
Unemployment rate	4.1	3.6	4.5	7.1	7.1	7.1	7.4	7.1	7.8	6.9	6.1	7.7	6.2	5.1	7.3
With Own Children Under 6 Years															
Civilian noninstitutional population	29 074	12 886	16 188	28 969	12 796	16 173	29 086	12 824	16 262	28 858	12 712	16 146	28 443	12 350	16 094
Civilian labor force	22 661	12 293	10 367	22 549	12 164	10 384	22 534	12 146	10 388	22 328	12 013	10 315	22 108	11 681	10 427
Participation rate	77.9	95.4	64.0	77.8	95.1	64.2	77.5	94.7	63.9	77.4	94.5	63.9	77.7	94.6	64.8
Employed	21 426	11 792	9 634	20 562	11 214	9 348	20 442	11 171	9 271	20 400	11 197	9 203	20 451	11 045	9 406
Employment-population ratio	73.7	91.5	59.5	71.0	87.6	57.8	70.3	87.1	57.0	70.7	88.1	57.0	71.9	89.4	58.4
Full-time workers[1]	18 234	11 284	6 950	17 138	10 517	6 622	3 399	720	2 679	3 311	687	2 624	3 299	615	2 684
Part-time workers[2]	3 193	508	2 684	3 424	697	2 726	70	87	57	71	88	57	72	89	58
Unemployed	1 234	501	733	1 987	950	1 036	2 092	975	1 117	1 928	816	1 112	1 657	635	1 021
Unemployment rate	5.4	4.1	7.1	8.8	7.8	10.0	9.3	8.0	10.8	8.6	6.8	10.8	7.5	5.4	9.8
With No Own Children Under 18 Years															
Civilian noninstitutional population	168 133	83 971	84 162	170 947	85 358	85 589	173 342	86 711	86 631	175732	88 175	87 558	179 488	89 455	90 033
Civilian labor force	100 780	55 098	45 682	101 394	55 138	46 256	101 729	55 324	46 405	102096	55 673	46 423	103 633	56 299	47 334
Participation rate	59.9	65.6	54.3	59.3	64.6	54.0	58.7	63.8	53.6	58.1	63.1	53.0	57.7	62.9	52.6
Employed	94 346	51 106	43 239	91 257	48 681	42 576	91 201	48 706	42 495	92 291	49 671	42 620	94 597	50 890	43 707
Employment-population ratio	56.1	60.9	51.4	53.4	57.0	49.7	52.6	56.2	49.1	52.5	56.3	48.7	52.7	56.9	48.5
Full-time workers[1]	76 064	43 515	32 549	71 631	40 368	31 263	19 769	8 381	11 387	20 010	8 584	11 426	20 460	8 761	11 699
Part-time workers[2]	18 282	7 592	10 690	19 626	8 313	11 313	53	56	49	52	56	49	53	57	48
Unemployed	6 435	3 992	2 443	10 137	6 457	3 680	10 528	6 618	3 910	9 805	6 002	3 803	9 036	5 409	3 627
Unemployment rate	6.4	7.2	5.3	10.0	11.7	8.0	10.3	12.0	8.4	9.6	10.8	8.2	8.7	9.6	7.7

Note: Own children include sons, daughters, stepchildren, and adopted children. Not included are nieces, nephews, grandchildren, and other related and unrelated children. Detail may not sum to total due to rounding.

[1] Usually work 35 hours or more a week at all jobs.
[2] Usually work less than 35 hours a week at all jobs.
[3] Includes never-married, divorced, separated, and widowed persons.

Table 1-24. Employment Status of Mothers with Own Children Under 3 Years of Age, by Age of Youngest Child and Marital Status, Annual Averages, 2003–2012

(Thousands of people, percent.)

Year and characteristic	Civilian noninsti- tutional population	Civilian labor force		Employed				Unemployed	
		Total	Percent of population	Total	Percent of population	Full-time workers[1]	Part-time workers[2]	Number	Percent of labor force
2003									
Total Mothers with Own Children Under 3 Years	9 450	5 563	58.9	5 115	54.1	3 430	1 685	446	8.0
2 years	2 987	1 896	63.5	1 752	58.7	1 205	547	143	7.5
1 year	3 353	1 997	59.6	1 842	54.9	1 223	619	154	7.7
Under 1 year	3 110	1 670	53.7	1 521	48.9	1 002	519	149	8.9
Married, Spouse Present with Own Children Under 3 Years	7 165	4 068	56.8	3 872	54.0	2 529	1 342	197	4.8
2 years	2 243	1 350	60.2	1 281	57.1	853	428	69	5.1
1 year	2 541	1 458	57.4	1 395	54.9	906	488	64	4.4
Under 1 year	2 381	1 260	52.9	1 196	50.2	770	426	64	5.1
Other Marital Status with Own Children Under 3 Years[3]	2 287	1 495	65.4	1 244	54.4	902	341	250	16.7
2 years	744	546	73.4	471	63.3	352	118	75	13.7
1 year	813	539	66.3	448	55.1	317	131	91	16.9
Under 1 year	730	410	56.2	325	44.5	233	92	84	20.5
2004									
Total Mothers with Own Children Under 3 Years	9 345	5 377	57.5	4 964	53.1	3 360	1 604	414	7.7
2 years	2 813	1 746	62.1	1 630	57.9	1 152	477	116	6.6
1 year	3 273	1 906	58.2	1 759	53.7	1 172	587	147	7.7
Under 1 year	3 259	1 725	52.9	1 575	48.3	1 035	540	151	8.7
Married, Spouse Present with Own Children Under 3 Years	7 071	3 910	55.3	3 740	52.9	2 513	1 227	170	4.4
2 years	2 111	1 246	59.0	1 200	56.8	839	361	46	3.7
1 year	2 519	1 401	55.6	1 337	53.1	877	459	65	4.6
Under 1 year	2 441	1 262	51.7	1 203	49.3	797	406	59	4.7
Other Marital Status with Own Children Under 3 Years[3]	2 274	1 467	64.5	1 224	53.8	847	377	243	16.6
2 years	702	499	71.1	430	61.2	314	116	70	13.9
1 year	754	505	66.9	422	56.0	295	127	82	16.3
Under 1 year	818	463	56.6	372	45.4	238	134	91	19.7
2005									
Total Mothers with Own Children Under 3 Years	9 365	5 470	58.4	5 077	54.2	3 501	1 576	393	7.2
2 years	2 845	1 773	62.3	1 654	58.1	1 162	492	119	6.7
1 year	3 287	1 958	59.6	1 823	55.5	1 247	576	135	6.9
Under 1 year	3 233	1 740	53.8	1 600	49.5	1 092	508	140	8.0
Married, Spouse Present with Own Children Under 3 Years	6 951	3 939	56.7	3 776	54.3	2 588	1 188	164	4.2
2 years	2 118	1 268	59.9	1 214	57.3	840	374	55	4.3
1 year	2 435	1 389	57.0	1 337	54.9	901	436	52	3.7
Under 1 year	2 398	1 282	53.5	1 225	51.1	847	378	58	4.5
Other Marital Status with Own Children Under 3 Years[3]	2 414	1 531	63.4	1 301	53.9	913	388	230	15.0
2 years	726	504	69.5	440	60.6	322	118	64	12.7
1 year	852	569	66.8	486	57.0	346	139	83	14.6
Under 1 year	836	457	54.7	375	44.9	245	130	82	18.0
2006									
Total Mothers with Own Children Under 3 Years	9 431	5 675	60.2	5 315	56.4	3 751	1 564	360	6.3
2 years	2 864	1 847	64.5	1 746	61.0	1 280	466	101	5.5
1 year	3 318	2 006	60.5	1 883	56.7	1 305	577	123	6.1
Under 1 year	3 248	1 822	56.1	1 686	51.9	1 166	520	136	7.4
Married, Spouse Present with Own Children Under 3 Years	6 998	4 076	58.2	3 933	56.2	2 756	1 177	143	3.5
2 years	2 114	1 305	61.7	1 265	59.8	910	354	40	3.1
1 year	2 494	1 456	58.4	1 404	56.3	962	442	52	3.6
Under 1 year	2 390	1 315	55.0	1 264	52.9	883	381	51	3.9
Other Marital Status with Own Children Under 3 Years[3]	2 433	1 600	65.7	1 382	56.8	996	386	217	13.6
2 years	750	543	72.3	481	64.2	369	112	61	11.3
1 year	824	550	66.7	479	58.1	344	135	71	13.0
Under 1 year	859	507	59.0	422	49.2	283	139	85	16.7
2007									
Total Mothers with Own Children Under 3 Years	9 659	5 721	59.2	5 354	55.4	3 783	1 571	367	6.4
2 years	2 812	1 808	64.3	1 694	60.2	1 225	469	114	6.3
1 year	3 501	2 068	59.1	1 938	55.4	1 350	589	130	6.3
Under 1 year	3 346	1 845	55.1	1 721	51.4	1 208	513	123	6.7
Married, Spouse Present with Own Children Under 3 Years	7 018	4 027	57.4	3 888	55.4	2 730	1 157	140	3.5
2 years	2 076	1 281	61.7	1 230	59.2	881	349	51	4.0
1 year	2 536	1 433	56.5	1 388	54.7	954	434	46	3.2
Under 1 year	2 406	1 313	54.6	1 270	52.8	896	374	43	3.3
Other Marital Status with Own Children Under 3 Years[3]	2 641	1 694	64.1	1 466	55.5	1 052	414	227	13.4
2 years	736	528	71.6	464	63.1	344	120	63	12.0
1 year	965	635	65.8	551	57.1	396	155	84	13.2
Under 1 year	940	531	56.5	451	48.0	312	139	80	15.1

Note: Own children include sons, daughters, stepchildren, and adopted children. Not included are nieces, nephews, grandchildren, and other related and unrelated children. Detail may not sum to total due to rounding. Updated population controls are introduced annually with the release of January data.

[1]Usually work 35 hours or more a week at all jobs.
[2]Usually work less than 35 hours a week at all jobs.
[3]Includes never-married, divorced, separated, and widowed persons.

Table 1-24. Employment Status of Mothers with Own Children Under 3 Years of Age, by Age of Youngest Child and Marital Status, Annual Averages, 2003–2012—*Continued*

(Thousands of people, percent.)

Year and characteristic	Civilian noninsti-tutional population	Civilian labor force						Unemployed	
		Total	Percent of population	Employed				Number	Percent of labor force
				Total	Percent of population	Full-time workers[1]	Part-time workers[2]		
2008									
Total Mothers with Own Children Under 3 Years	9 595	5 792	60.4	5 354	55.8	3 782	1 573	438	7.6
2 years	2 934	1 852	63.1	1 734	59.1	1 264	470	118	6.4
1 year	3 342	2 069	61.9	1 905	57.0	1 337	568	164	7.9
Under 1 year	3 319	1 871	56.4	1 715	51.7	1 180	535	156	8.4
Married, Spouse Present with Own Children Under 3 Years	6 868	4 035	58.7	3 848	56.0	2 717	1 132	186	4.6
2 years	2 088	1 255	60.1	1 206	57.8	871	335	49	3.9
1 year	2 414	1 450	60.1	1 380	57.2	970	410	70	4.8
Under 1 year	2 366	1 330	56.2	1 263	53.4	875	388	67	5.0
Other Marital Status with Own Children Under 3 Years[3]	2 727	1 758	64.4	1 506	55.2	1 065	441	252	14.3
2 years	847	597	70.5	528	62.4	393	135	69	11.5
1 year	928	619	66.7	525	56.6	367	159	94	15.1
Under 1 year	953	542	56.8	452	47.5	305	147	89	16.5
2009									
Total Mothers with Own Children Under 3 Years	9 476	5 787	61.1	5 191	54.8	3 626	1 565	595	10.3
2 years	2 848	1 855	65.1	1 693	59.4	1 195	498	162	8.7
1 year	3 398	2 104	61.9	1 880	55.3	1 314	566	224	10.6
Under 1 year	3 231	1 828	56.6	1 619	50.1	1 117	502	209	11.4
Married, Spouse Present with Own Children Under 3 Years	6 784	4 047	59.7	3 780	55.7	2 657	1 123	267	6.6
2 years	2 053	1 288	62.7	1 208	58.8	858	350	80	6.2
1 year	2 425	1 465	60.4	1 369	56.4	963	406	96	6.6
Under 1 year	2 306	1 293	56.1	1 204	52.2	836	368	90	7.0
Other Marital Status with Own Children Under 3 Years[3]	2 693	1 740	64.6	1 411	52.4	969	442	328	18.9
2 years	795	567	71.3	485	61.0	337	148	82	14.4
1 year	973	639	65.6	511	52.5	351	160	127	20.0
Under 1 year	925	534	57.8	415	44.9	281	134	119	22.3
2010									
Total Mothers with Own Children Under 3 Years	9 503	5 770	60.7	5 114	53.8	3 570	1 543	656	11.4
2 years	2 968	1 908	64.3	1 708	57.5	1 200	509	199	10.5
1 year	3 351	2 062	61.5	1 815	54.2	1 243	572	246	12.0
Under 1 year	3 184	1 800	56.5	1 590	49.9	1 128	462	210	11.7
Married, Spouse Present with Own Children Under 3 Years	6 642	3 941	59.3	3 670	55.3	2 596	1 074	271	6.9
2 years	2 055	1 275	62.1	1 195	58.2	841	354	80	6.3
1 year	2 344	1 403	59.8	1 301	55.5	896	405	101	7.2
Under 1 year	3 184	1 800	56.5	1 590	49.9	1 128	462	210	11.7
Other Marital Status with Own Children Under 3 Years[3]	2 862	1 828	63.9	1 444	50.5	974	470	385	21.0
2 years	914	633	69.2	514	56.2	359	155	119	18.8
1 year	1 007	659	65.5	514	51.0	346	168	145	22.0
Under 1 year	941	537	57.0	416	44.2	269	147	121	22.5
2011									
Total Mothers with Own Children Under 3 Years	9 259	5 613	60.6	4 977	53.8	3 486	1 492	635	11.3
2 years	2 893	1 848	63.9	1 645	56.9	1 169	476	202	11.0
1 year	3 353	2 083	62.1	1 844	55.0	1 296	548	239	11.5
Under 1 year	3 013	1 682	55.8	1 488	49.4	1 021	467	194	11.5
Married, Spouse Present with Own Children Under 3 Years	6 488	3 854	59.4	3 603	55.5	2 594	1 009	251	6.5
2 years	1 999	1 220	61.0	1 138	56.9	822	316	82	6.7
1 year	2 381	1 434	60.2	1 342	56.4	967	375	92	6.4
Under 1 year	2 109	1 200	56.9	1 123	53.3	805	318	77	6.4
Other Marital Status with Own Children Under 3 Years[3]	2 771	1 759	63.5	1 375	49.6	892	483	384	21.8
2 years	894	628	70.3	508	56.8	347	161	120	19.2
1 year	973	649	66.8	502	51.6	329	173	147	22.6
Under 1 year	905	482	53.2	365	40.3	216	149	117	24.2
2012									
Total Mothers with Own Children Under 3 Years	9 134	5 612	61.4	5 047	55.3	3 552	1 495	564	10.1
2 years	2 829	1 832	64.7	1 656	58.6	1 177	479	175	9.6
1 year	3 256	2 044	62.8	1 845	56.7	1 272	572	199	9.7
Under 1 year	3 049	1 737	57.0	1 546	50.7	1 102	444	190	11.0
Married, Spouse Present with Own Children Under 3 Years	6 334	3 808	60.1	3 600	56.8	2 595	1 005	208	5.5
2 years	1 940	1 190	61.8	1 134	58.5	816	318	64	5.4
1 year	2 288	1 409	61.6	1 332	58.2	928	405	77	5.5
Under 1 year	2 106	1 200	57.0	1 134	53.8	852	282	66	5.5
Other Marital Status with Own Children Under 3 Years[3]	2 800	1 804	64.4	1 447	51.7	957	490	357	19.8
2 years	889	633	71.2	522	58.8	361	161	111	17.5
1 year	968	634	65.5	512	52.9	345	167	122	19.2
Under 1 year	943	537	56.9	412	43.7	251	162	124	23.2

Note: Own children include sons, daughters, stepchildren, and adopted children. Not included are nieces, nephews, grandchildren, and other related and unrelated children. Detail may not sum to total due to rounding. Updated population controls are introduced annually with the release of January data.

[1] Usually work 35 hours or more a week at all jobs.
[2] Usually work less than 35 hours a week at all jobs.
[3] Includes never-married, divorced, separated, and widowed persons.

UNEMPLOYMENT

Figure 1-3. Unemployment Rate by Race and Sex, 1972–2012

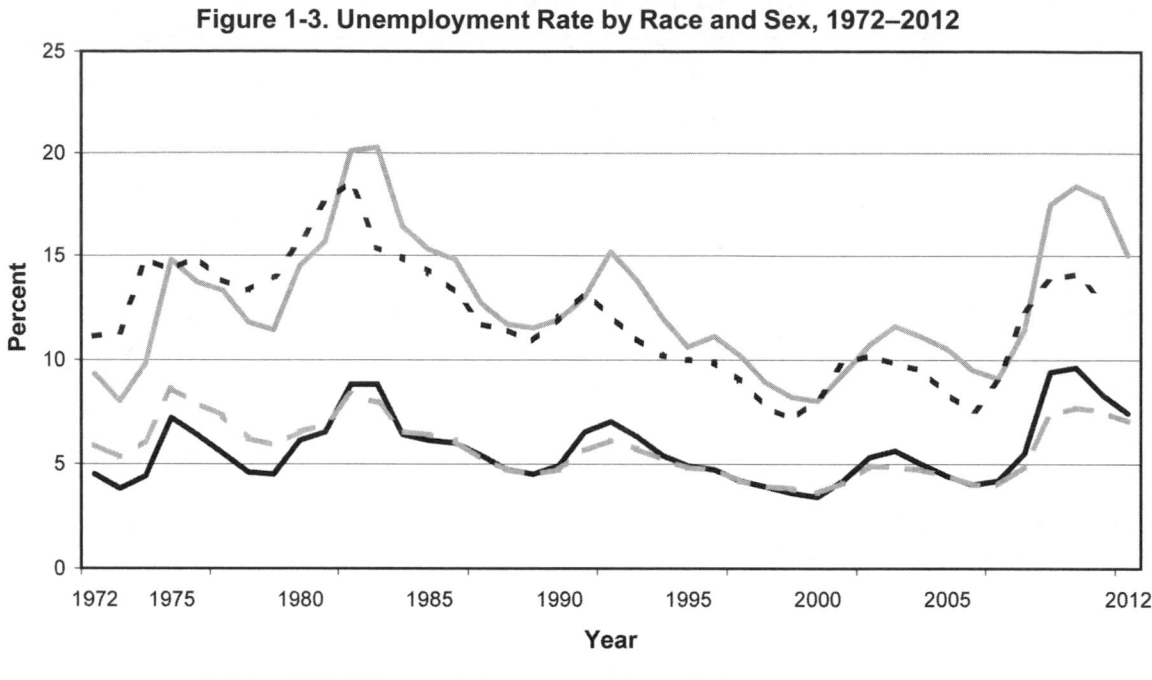

The unemployment rate declined from 8.9 percent in 2011 to 8.1 percent in 2012. Although the unemployment rate continued to be higher for men (8.2 percent) than for women (7.9 percent), the gap was closing. In 2011, men had an unemployment rate of 9.4 percent compared with an unemployment rate of 8.5 percent for women. Black men had the highest unemployment rate at 15.0 percent, followed by Black women with an unemployment rate of 12.8 percent. From 2010 to 2011, the unemployment rate decreased by 2.0 percent for Blacks and 0.7 percent for Whites. (See Table 1-27.)

OTHER HIGHLIGHTS

- While the unemployment rate decreased for every age group in 2012, the disparity in unemployment rates among age groups continued to be substantial as younger workers experienced much higher levels of unemployment. In 2012, the unemployment rate for those age 16 to 19 years was 24.0 percent, while it was only 5.9 percent for those age 55 to 64 years and 6.2 percent for those age 65 years and over. (See Table 1-27.)

- Among the major industries, construction had the highest unemployment rate at 13.9 percent, followed by agriculture and private wage salary workers (12.4 percent) and leisure and hospitality workers (10.4 percent). Government had the lowest unemployment rate at 4.3 percent. (See Table 1-29.)

- The median duration of unemployment declined to 19.3 weeks after remaining steady at 21.4 weeks in 2010 and 2011. (See Table 1-30.)

- In 2012, unemployment rates ranged from a low of 3.1 percent in North Dakota to a high of 11.1 percent in Nevada. (See Table 1-5.)

Table 1-25. Unemployment Rate, by Selected Characteristics, 1948–2012

(Unemployment as a percent of civilian labor force.)

Year	All civilian workers	Both sexes, 16 to 19 years	Men, 20 years and over	Women, 20 years and over	White[1]	Black[1]	Asian[1]	Hispanic[2]	Men Single, never married	Men Married, spouse present	Men Widowed, divorced, or separated	Women Single, never married	Women Married, spouse present	Women Widowed, divorced, or separated
1948	3.8	9.2	3.2	3.6	...	...	...	...	...	...	...	...	...	...
1949	5.9	13.4	5.4	5.3	...	...	...	...	...	...	...	...	...	...
1950	5.3	12.2	4.7	5.1	...	...	...	...	...	...	...	...	...	...
1951	3.3	8.2	2.5	4.0	...	...	...	...	...	...	...	...	...	...
1952	3.0	8.5	2.4	3.2	...	...	...	...	...	...	...	...	...	...
1953	2.9	7.6	2.5	2.9	...	...	...	...	...	...	...	...	...	...
1954	5.5	12.6	4.9	5.5	5.0	...	...	...	...	...	...	...	...	...
1955	4.4	11.0	3.8	4.4	3.9	...	...	...	8.6	2.6	7.1	5.0	3.7	5.0
1956	4.1	11.1	3.4	4.2	3.6	...	...	...	7.7	2.3	6.2	5.3	3.6	5.0
1957	4.3	11.6	3.6	4.1	3.8	...	...	...	9.2	2.8	6.8	5.6	4.3	4.7
1958	6.8	15.9	6.2	6.1	6.1	...	...	...	13.3	5.1	11.2	7.4	6.5	6.7
1959	5.5	14.6	4.7	5.2	4.8	...	...	...	11.6	3.6	8.6	7.1	5.2	6.2
1960	5.5	14.7	4.7	5.1	5.0	...	...	...	11.7	3.7	8.4	7.5	5.2	5.9
1961	6.7	16.8	5.7	6.3	6.0	...	...	...	13.1	4.6	10.3	8.7	6.4	7.4
1962	5.5	14.7	4.6	5.4	4.9	...	...	...	11.2	3.6	9.9	7.9	5.4	6.4
1963	5.7	17.2	4.5	5.4	5.0	...	...	...	12.4	3.4	9.6	8.9	5.4	6.7
1964	5.2	16.2	3.9	5.2	4.6	...	...	...	11.5	2.8	8.9	8.7	5.1	6.4
1965	4.5	14.8	3.2	4.5	4.1	...	...	...	10.1	2.4	7.2	8.2	4.5	5.4
1966	3.8	12.8	2.5	3.8	3.4	...	...	...	8.6	1.9	5.5	7.9	3.7	4.7
1967	3.8	12.9	2.3	4.2	3.4	...	...	...	8.3	1.8	4.9	7.5	4.5	4.6
1968	3.6	12.7	2.2	3.8	3.2	...	...	...	8.0	1.6	4.2	7.6	3.9	4.2
1969	3.5	12.2	2.1	3.7	3.1	...	...	...	8.0	1.5	4.0	7.3	3.9	4.0
1970	4.9	15.3	3.5	4.8	4.5	...	...	...	11.2	2.6	6.4	9.0	4.9	5.2
1971	5.9	16.9	4.4	5.7	5.4	...	...	...	13.2	3.2	7.4	10.5	5.7	6.3
1972	5.6	16.2	4.0	5.4	5.1	10.4	...	...	12.4	2.8	7.0	10.1	5.4	6.1
1973	4.9	14.5	3.3	4.9	4.3	9.4	...	7.5	10.4	2.3	5.4	9.4	4.7	5.8
1974	5.6	16.0	3.8	5.5	5.0	10.5	...	8.1	11.8	2.7	6.2	10.5	5.3	6.3
1975	8.5	19.9	6.8	8.0	7.8	14.8	...	12.2	16.1	5.1	11.0	13.0	7.9	8.9
1976	7.7	19.0	5.9	7.4	7.0	14.0	...	11.5	14.9	4.2	9.8	12.1	7.1	8.7
1977	7.1	17.8	5.2	7.0	6.2	14.0	...	10.1	13.5	3.6	8.2	12.1	6.5	7.9
1978	6.1	16.4	4.3	6.0	5.2	12.8	...	9.1	11.7	2.8	6.6	10.9	5.5	6.9
1979	5.8	16.1	4.2	5.7	5.1	12.3	...	8.3	11.1	2.8	6.5	10.4	5.1	6.7
1980	7.1	17.8	5.9	6.4	6.3	14.3	...	10.1	13.6	4.2	8.6	10.9	5.8	7.2
1981	7.6	19.6	6.3	6.8	6.7	15.6	...	10.4	14.6	4.3	9.1	11.9	6.0	8.1
1982	9.7	23.2	8.8	8.3	8.6	18.9	...	13.8	17.7	6.5	12.4	13.6	7.4	9.5
1983	9.6	22.4	8.9	8.1	8.4	19.5	...	13.7	17.3	6.5	13.0	13.1	7.0	9.9
1984	7.5	18.9	6.6	6.8	6.5	15.9	...	10.7	13.5	4.6	9.4	11.1	5.7	8.4
1985	7.2	18.6	6.2	6.6	6.2	15.1	...	10.5	12.7	4.3	9.2	10.7	5.6	8.3
1986	7.0	18.3	6.1	6.2	6.0	14.5	...	10.6	12.2	4.4	8.8	10.7	5.2	7.7
1987	6.2	16.9	5.4	5.4	5.3	13.0	...	8.8	11.1	3.9	7.6	9.5	4.3	7.0
1988	5.5	15.3	4.8	4.9	4.7	11.7	...	8.2	9.9	3.3	7.0	8.6	3.9	6.3
1989	5.3	15.0	4.5	4.7	4.5	11.4	...	8.0	9.6	3.0	6.3	8.4	3.7	5.9
1990	5.6	15.5	5.0	4.9	4.8	11.4	...	8.2	10.1	3.4	6.9	8.7	3.8	6.0
1991	6.8	18.7	6.4	5.7	6.1	12.5	...	10.0	12.4	4.4	9.0	10.1	4.5	6.9
1992	7.5	20.1	7.1	6.3	6.6	14.2	...	11.6	13.2	5.1	9.8	10.8	5.0	7.6
1993	6.9	19.0	6.4	5.9	6.1	13.0	...	10.8	12.4	4.4	9.0	10.3	4.6	7.3
1994	6.1	17.6	5.4	5.4	5.3	11.5	...	9.9	11.0	3.7	7.4	9.7	4.1	6.6
1995	5.6	17.3	4.8	4.9	4.9	10.4	...	9.3	10.1	3.3	6.9	9.1	3.9	5.9
1996	5.4	16.7	4.6	4.8	4.7	10.5	...	8.9	10.0	3.0	6.5	9.1	3.6	5.7
1997	4.9	16.0	4.2	4.4	4.2	10.0	...	7.7	9.2	2.7	5.8	8.8	3.1	5.2
1998	4.5	14.6	3.7	4.1	3.9	8.9	...	7.2	8.5	2.4	4.8	7.8	2.9	4.9
1999	4.2	13.9	3.5	3.8	3.7	8.0	...	6.4	7.8	2.2	4.6	7.4	2.7	4.5
2000	4.0	13.1	3.3	3.6	3.5	7.6	3.6	5.7	7.6	2.0	4.3	6.8	2.7	4.2
2001	4.7	14.7	4.2	4.1	4.2	8.6	4.5	6.6	8.9	2.7	5.1	7.7	3.1	4.7
2002	5.8	16.5	5.3	5.1	5.1	10.2	5.9	7.5	10.3	3.6	6.8	8.9	3.7	6.1
2003	6.0	17.5	5.6	5.1	5.2	10.8	6.0	7.7	11.0	3.8	7.3	9.1	3.7	6.1
2004	5.5	17.0	5.0	4.9	4.8	10.4	4.4	7.0	10.5	3.1	6.3	8.7	3.5	5.9
2005	5.1	16.6	4.4	4.6	4.4	10.0	4.0	6.0	9.5	2.8	5.6	8.3	3.3	5.4
2006	4.6	15.4	4.0	4.1	4.0	8.9	3.0	5.2	8.6	2.4	5.2	7.7	2.9	4.9
2007	4.6	15.7	4.1	4.0	4.1	8.3	3.2	5.6	8.8	2.5	5.3	7.2	2.8	5.0
2008	5.8	18.7	5.4	4.9	5.2	10.1	4.0	7.6	11.0	3.4	7.1	8.5	3.6	5.9
2009	9.3	24.3	9.6	7.5	8.5	14.8	7.3	12.1	16.3	6.6	12.8	12.0	5.5	9.2
2010	9.6	25.9	9.8	8.0	8.7	16.0	7.5	12.5	16.5	6.8	12.8	12.8	5.9	9.6
2011	8.9	24.4	8.7	7.9	7.9	15.8	7.0	11.5	15.1	5.8	11.1	12.5	5.6	9.7
2012	8.1	24.0	7.5	7.3	7.2	13.8	5.9	10.3	13.7	4.9	9.4	11.8	5.3	8.7

Note: See notes and definitions for information on historical comparability.

[1]Beginning in 2003, persons who selected this race group only; persons who selected more than one race group are not included. Prior to 2003, persons who reported more than one race group were included in the group they identified as their main race.
[2]May be of any race.
... = Not available.

Table 1-26. Unemployed Persons, by Age, Sex, Race, and Hispanic Origin, 1948–2012

(Thousands of people.)

Race, Hispanic origin, sex, and year	16 years and over	16 to 19 years			20 years and over						
		Total	16 to 17 years	18 to 19 years	Total	20 to 24 years	25 to 34 years	35 to 44 years	45 to 54 years	55 to 64 years	65 years and over
ALL RACES											
Both Sexes											
1948	2 276	409	180	228	1 869	455	457	347	290	226	93
1949	3 637	576	238	337	3 060	680	776	603	471	384	146
1950	3 288	513	226	287	2 776	561	702	530	478	368	137
1951	2 055	336	168	168	1 718	273	435	354	318	238	103
1952	1 883	345	180	165	1 539	268	389	325	274	195	86
1953	1 834	307	150	157	1 529	256	379	325	280	218	70
1954	3 532	501	221	247	3 032	504	793	680	548	374	132
1955	2 852	450	211	239	2 403	396	577	521	436	355	120
1956	2 750	478	231	247	2 274	395	554	476	429	311	109
1957	2 859	497	230	266	2 362	430	573	499	448	300	111
1958	4 602	678	299	379	3 923	701	993	871	731	472	154
1959	3 740	654	301	354	3 085	543	726	673	603	405	135
1960	3 852	712	325	387	3 140	583	752	671	614	396	122
1961	4 714	828	363	465	3 886	723	890	850	751	516	159
1962	3 911	721	312	409	3 191	636	712	688	605	411	141
1963	4 070	884	420	462	3 187	658	732	674	589	410	126
1964	3 786	872	436	437	2 913	660	607	605	543	378	117
1965	3 366	874	411	463	2 491	557	529	546	436	322	103
1966	2 875	837	395	441	2 041	446	441	426	369	265	92
1967	2 975	839	400	438	2 140	511	480	422	383	256	86
1968	2 817	838	414	426	1 978	543	443	371	314	219	88
1969	2 832	853	436	416	1 978	560	453	358	320	216	72
1970	4 093	1 106	537	569	2 987	866	718	515	476	309	104
1971	5 016	1 262	596	665	3 755	1 130	933	630	573	381	109
1972	4 882	1 308	633	676	3 573	1 132	878	576	510	368	111
1973	4 365	1 235	634	600	3 130	1 008	866	451	430	290	88
1974	5 156	1 422	699	722	3 733	1 212	1 044	559	498	321	99
1975	7 929	1 767	799	968	6 161	1 865	1 776	951	893	520	155
1976	7 406	1 719	796	924	5 687	1 714	1 710	849	758	510	147
1977	6 991	1 663	781	881	5 330	1 629	1 650	785	666	450	147
1978	6 202	1 583	796	787	4 620	1 483	1 422	694	552	345	123
1979	6 137	1 555	739	816	4 583	1 442	1 446	705	540	346	104
1980	7 637	1 669	778	890	5 969	1 835	2 024	940	676	399	94
1981	8 273	1 763	781	981	6 510	1 976	2 211	1 065	715	444	98
1982	10 678	1 977	831	1 145	8 701	2 392	3 037	1 552	966	647	107
1983	10 717	1 829	753	1 076	8 888	2 330	3 078	1 650	1 039	677	114
1984	8 539	1 499	646	854	7 039	1 838	2 374	1 335	828	566	97
1985	8 312	1 468	662	806	6 844	1 738	2 341	1 340	813	518	93
1986	8 237	1 454	665	789	6 783	1 651	2 390	1 371	790	489	91
1987	7 425	1 347	648	700	6 077	1 453	2 129	1 281	723	412	78
1988	6 701	1 226	573	653	5 475	1 261	1 929	1 166	657	375	87
1989	6 528	1 194	537	657	5 333	1 218	1 851	1 159	637	379	91
1990	7 047	1 212	527	685	5 835	1 299	1 995	1 328	723	386	105
1991	8 628	1 359	587	772	7 269	1 573	2 447	1 719	946	473	113
1992	9 613	1 427	641	787	8 186	1 649	2 702	1 976	1 138	589	132
1993	8 940	1 365	606	759	7 555	1 514	2 395	1 896	1 121	541	108
1994	7 996	1 320	624	696	6 676	1 373	2 067	1 627	971	485	153
1995	7 404	1 346	652	695	6 058	1 244	1 841	1 549	844	425	153
1996	7 236	1 306	617	689	5 929	1 239	1 757	1 505	883	406	139
1997	6 739	1 271	589	683	5 467	1 152	1 571	1 418	830	369	127
1998	6 210	1 205	573	632	5 005	1 081	1 419	1 258	782	343	122
1999	5 880	1 162	544	618	4 718	1 042	1 278	1 154	753	367	124
2000	5 692	1 081	502	579	4 611	1 022	1 207	1 133	762	355	132
2001	6 801	1 162	531	632	5 638	1 209	1 498	1 355	989	458	129
2002	8 378	1 253	540	714	7 124	1 430	1 890	1 691	1 315	635	163
2003	8 774	1 251	545	706	7 523	1 495	1 960	1 815	1 356	713	183
2004	8 149	1 208	554	653	6 942	1 431	1 784	1 578	1 288	682	179
2005	7 591	1 186	541	645	6 405	1 335	1 661	1 400	1 195	630	184
2006	7 001	1 119	509	610	5 882	1 234	1 521	1 279	1 094	595	159
2007	7 078	1 101	485	616	5 976	1 241	1 544	1 225	1 135	642	190
2008	8 924	1 285	563	722	7 639	1 545	1 949	1 604	1 473	803	264
2009	14 265	1 552	576	976	12 712	2 207	3 284	2 722	2 592	1 487	421
2010	14 825	1 528	582	945	13 297	2 329	3 386	2 703	2 769	1 660	449
2011	13 747	1 400	519	881	12 348	2 234	3 187	2 389	2 493	1 579	465
2012	12 506	1 397	533	863	11 109	2 054	2 764	2 158	2 181	1 470	482

Table 1-26. Unemployed Persons, by Age, Sex, Race, and Hispanic Origin, 1948–2012—*Continued*

(Thousands of people.)

Race, Hispanic origin, sex, and year	16 years and over	16 to 19 years			20 years and over						
		Total	16 to 17 years	18 to 19 years	Total	20 to 24 years	25 to 34 years	35 to 44 years	45 to 54 years	55 to 64 years	65 years and over
ALL RACES											
Men											
1948	1 559	256	113	142	1 305	324	289	233	201	177	81
1949	2 572	353	145	207	2 219	485	539	414	347	310	125
1950	2 239	318	139	179	1 922	377	467	348	327	286	117
1951	1 221	191	102	89	1 029	155	241	192	193	162	87
1952	1 185	205	116	89	980	155	233	192	182	145	73
1953	1 202	184	94	90	1 019	152	236	208	196	167	60
1954	2 344	310	142	168	2 035	327	517	431	372	275	112
1955	1 854	274	134	140	1 580	248	353	328	285	265	102
1956	1 711	269	134	135	1 442	240	348	278	270	216	90
1957	1 841	300	140	159	1 541	283	349	304	302	220	83
1958	3 098	416	185	231	2 681	478	685	552	492	349	124
1959	2 420	398	191	207	2 022	343	484	407	390	287	112
1960	2 486	426	200	225	2 060	369	492	415	392	294	96
1961	2 997	479	221	258	2 518	458	585	507	473	375	122
1962	2 423	408	188	220	2 016	381	445	404	382	300	103
1963	2 472	501	248	252	1 971	396	445	386	358	290	97
1964	2 205	487	257	230	1 718	384	345	324	319	263	85
1965	1 914	479	247	232	1 435	311	292	283	253	221	75
1966	1 551	432	220	212	1 120	221	239	219	196	179	65
1967	1 508	448	241	207	1 060	235	219	185	199	163	60
1968	1 419	426	234	193	993	258	205	171	165	132	61
1969	1 403	440	244	196	963	270	205	155	157	127	48
1970	2 238	599	306	294	1 638	479	391	253	247	198	71
1971	2 789	693	346	347	2 097	640	513	320	313	239	71
1972	2 659	711	357	355	1 948	628	466	284	272	227	73
1973	2 275	653	352	300	1 624	528	439	211	219	171	57
1974	2 714	757	394	362	1 957	649	546	266	250	183	63
1975	4 442	966	445	521	3 476	1 081	986	507	499	302	103
1976	4 036	939	443	496	3 098	951	914	431	411	296	94
1977	3 667	874	421	453	2 794	877	869	373	326	252	97
1978	3 142	813	426	388	2 328	768	691	314	277	198	81
1979	3 120	811	393	418	2 308	744	699	329	272	196	67
1980	4 267	913	429	485	3 353	1 076	1 137	482	357	243	58
1981	4 577	962	431	531	3 615	1 144	1 213	552	390	261	55
1982	6 179	1 090	469	621	5 089	1 407	1 791	879	550	393	69
1983	6 260	1 003	408	595	5 257	1 369	1 822	947	613	433	73
1984	4 744	812	348	464	3 932	1 023	1 322	728	450	356	53
1985	4 521	806	363	443	3 715	944	1 244	706	459	307	55
1986	4 530	779	355	424	3 751	899	1 291	763	440	301	58
1987	4 101	732	353	379	3 369	779	1 169	689	426	258	49
1988	3 655	667	311	356	2 987	676	1 040	617	366	240	49
1989	3 525	658	303	355	2 867	660	953	619	351	234	49
1990	3 906	667	283	384	3 239	715	1 092	711	413	249	59
1991	4 946	751	317	433	4 195	911	1 375	990	550	305	64
1992	5 523	806	357	449	4 717	951	1 529	1 118	675	378	67
1993	5 055	768	342	426	4 287	865	1 338	1 049	636	336	64
1994	4 367	740	342	398	3 627	768	1 113	855	522	281	88
1995	3 983	744	352	391	3 239	673	961	815	464	233	94
1996	3 880	733	347	387	3 146	675	903	786	484	223	76
1997	3 577	694	321	373	2 882	636	772	732	457	217	69
1998	3 266	686	330	355	2 580	583	699	609	420	201	69
1999	3 066	633	295	338	2 433	562	624	571	403	203	70
2000	2 975	599	281	317	2 376	547	602	557	398	189	83
2001	3 690	650	300	350	3 040	688	756	714	536	272	74
2002	4 597	700	301	399	3 896	792	1 023	897	725	373	87
2003	4 906	697	291	407	4 209	841	1 097	988	764	412	107
2004	4 456	664	292	372	3 791	811	980	839	684	373	104
2005	4 059	667	300	367	3 392	775	844	715	624	331	102
2006	3 753	622	271	352	3 131	705	810	642	569	318	88
2007	3 882	623	263	360	3 259	721	856	634	591	349	108
2008	5 033	736	312	425	4 297	920	1 119	875	804	425	153
2009	8 453	898	317	581	7 555	1 329	1 988	1 600	1 558	840	241
2010	8 626	863	315	548	7 763	1 398	1 993	1 534	1 614	962	262
2011	7 684	786	267	520	6 898	1 275	1 795	1 316	1 370	882	261
2012	6 771	787	291	497	5 984	1 163	1 476	1 124	1 142	811	268

Table 1-26. Unemployed Persons, by Age, Sex, Race, and Hispanic Origin, 1948–2012—*Continued*

(Thousands of people.)

Race, Hispanic origin, sex, and year	16 years and over	16 to 19 years			20 years and over						
		Total	16 to 17 years	18 to 19 years	Total	20 to 24 years	25 to 34 years	35 to 44 years	45 to 54 years	55 to 64 years	65 years and over
ALL RACES											
Women											
1948	717	153	67	86	564	131	168	114	89	49	12
1949	1 065	223	93	130	841	195	237	189	124	74	21
1950	1 049	195	87	108	854	184	235	182	151	82	20
1951	834	145	66	79	689	118	194	162	125	76	16
1952	698	140	64	76	559	113	156	133	92	50	13
1953	632	123	56	67	510	104	143	117	84	51	10
1954	1 188	191	79	79	997	177	276	249	176	99	20
1955	998	176	77	99	823	148	224	193	151	90	18
1956	1 039	209	97	112	832	155	206	198	159	95	19
1957	1 018	197	90	107	821	147	224	195	146	80	28
1958	1 504	262	114	148	1 242	223	308	319	239	123	30
1959	1 320	256	110	147	1 063	200	242	266	213	118	23
1960	1 366	286	125	162	1 080	214	260	256	222	102	26
1961	1 717	349	142	207	1 368	265	305	343	278	141	37
1962	1 488	313	124	189	1 175	255	267	284	223	111	38
1963	1 598	383	172	210	1 216	262	287	288	231	120	29
1964	1 581	385	179	207	1 195	276	262	281	224	115	32
1965	1 452	395	164	231	1 056	246	237	263	183	101	28
1966	1 324	405	175	229	921	225	202	207	173	86	27
1967	1 468	391	159	231	1 078	277	261	237	184	93	26
1968	1 397	412	180	233	985	285	238	200	149	87	27
1969	1 429	413	192	220	1 015	290	248	203	163	89	24
1970	1 855	506	231	275	1 349	387	327	262	229	111	33
1971	2 227	568	250	318	1 658	489	420	310	260	142	38
1972	2 222	598	276	322	1 625	503	413	293	237	141	38
1973	2 089	583	282	301	1 507	480	427	240	212	119	31
1974	2 441	665	305	360	1 777	564	497	294	248	137	36
1975	3 486	802	355	447	2 684	783	791	444	395	219	52
1976	3 369	780	352	429	2 588	763	795	417	346	214	53
1977	3 324	789	361	428	2 535	752	782	412	340	198	50
1978	3 061	769	370	399	2 292	714	731	381	275	148	43
1979	3 018	743	346	396	2 276	697	748	375	268	150	38
1980	3 370	755	349	407	2 615	760	886	459	318	155	36
1981	3 696	800	350	450	2 895	833	998	513	325	184	43
1982	4 499	886	362	524	3 613	985	1 246	673	416	254	38
1983	4 457	825	344	481	3 632	961	1 255	703	427	244	41
1984	3 794	687	298	390	3 107	815	1 052	607	378	211	45
1985	3 791	661	298	363	3 129	794	1 098	634	355	211	39
1986	3 707	675	310	365	3 032	752	1 099	609	350	189	33
1987	3 324	616	295	321	2 709	674	960	592	298	155	30
1988	3 046	558	262	297	2 487	585	889	550	291	136	38
1989	3 003	536	234	302	2 467	558	897	540	286	144	41
1990	3 140	544	243	301	2 596	584	902	617	310	137	46
1991	3 683	608	270	338	3 074	662	1 071	728	396	168	49
1992	4 090	621	283	338	3 469	698	1 173	858	463	210	66
1993	3 885	597	264	333	3 288	648	1 058	847	485	205	45
1994	3 629	580	282	298	3 049	605	954	772	449	204	66
1995	3 421	602	299	303	2 819	571	880	735	381	193	60
1996	3 356	573	270	303	2 783	564	854	720	399	183	63
1997	3 162	577	268	310	2 585	516	800	686	373	152	58
1998	2 944	519	242	277	2 424	498	720	650	362	141	53
1999	2 814	529	249	280	2 285	480	654	584	350	163	54
2000	2 717	483	221	262	2 235	475	604	577	364	165	50
2001	3 111	512	230	282	2 599	521	742	641	453	187	55
2002	3 781	553	238	315	3 228	638	866	795	591	263	76
2003	3 868	554	255	299	3 314	654	863	827	592	302	76
2004	3 694	543	262	281	3 150	619	804	739	605	309	75
2005	3 531	519	240	278	3 013	560	817	685	571	299	82
2006	3 247	496	238	258	2 751	530	711	637	524	277	71
2007	3 196	478	222	256	2 718	520	688	591	544	293	81
2008	3 891	549	251	297	3 342	625	830	730	669	377	111
2009	5 811	654	259	395	5 157	878	1 296	1 121	1 034	647	180
2010	6 199	665	268	397	5 534	931	1 392	1 169	1 156	698	187
2011	6 063	613	252	362	5 450	960	1 392	1 073	1 123	697	204
2012	5 734	609	242	367	5 125	891	1 288	1 034	1 039	659	214

Table 1-26. Unemployed Persons, by Age, Sex, Race, and Hispanic Origin, 1948–2012—*Continued*

(Thousands of people.)

Race, Hispanic origin, sex, and year	16 years and over	16 to 19 years			20 years and over						
		Total	16 to 17 years	18 to 19 years	Total	20 to 24 years	25 to 34 years	35 to 44 years	45 to 54 years	55 to 64 years	65 years and over
WHITE											
Both Sexes											
1954	2 859	423	191	232	2 436	394	610	540	447	329	115
1955	2 252	373	181	191	1 879	304	412	402	358	300	105
1956	2 159	382	191	191	1 777	297	406	363	355	258	98
1957	2 289	401	195	204	1 888	331	425	401	373	262	98
1958	3 680	541	245	297	3 139	541	756	686	614	405	136
1959	2 946	525	255	270	2 421	406	526	525	496	348	120
1960	3 065	575	273	302	2 490	456	573	520	502	330	109
1961	3 743	669	295	374	3 074	566	668	652	611	438	139
1962	3 052	580	262	318	2 472	488	515	522	485	345	117
1963	3 208	708	350	358	2 500	501	540	518	485	349	107
1964	2 999	708	365	342	2 291	508	441	472	447	323	100
1965	2 691	705	329	374	1 986	437	399	427	358	276	91
1966	2 255	651	315	336	1 604	338	323	336	298	227	80
1967	2 338	635	311	325	1 703	393	360	336	321	221	75
1968	2 226	644	326	318	1 582	422	330	297	269	187	80
1969	2 260	660	351	309	1 601	432	354	294	269	185	66
1970	3 339	871	438	432	2 468	679	570	433	415	275	95
1971	4 085	1 011	491	521	3 074	887	732	517	500	338	100
1972	3 906	1 021	515	506	2 885	887	679	459	439	324	95
1973	3 442	955	513	443	2 486	758	664	358	371	257	77
1974	4 097	1 104	561	544	2 993	925	821	448	427	283	88
1975	6 421	1 413	657	755	5 007	1 474	1 413	774	753	460	136
1976	5 914	1 364	649	715	4 550	1 326	1 329	682	637	448	128
1977	5 441	1 284	636	648	4 157	1 195	1 255	621	569	388	129
1978	4 698	1 189	631	558	3 509	1 059	1 059	543	453	290	104
1979	4 664	1 193	589	603	3 472	1 038	1 068	545	443	290	87
1980	5 884	1 291	625	666	4 593	1 364	1 528	740	550	335	74
1981	6 343	1 374	629	745	4 968	1 449	1 658	827	578	379	77
1982	8 241	1 534	683	851	6 707	1 770	2 283	1 223	796	549	86
1983	8 128	1 387	609	778	6 741	1 678	2 282	1 294	837	563	88
1984	6 372	1 116	510	605	5 256	1 282	1 723	1 036	660	475	81
1985	6 191	1 074	507	567	5 117	1 235	1 695	1 039	642	432	75
1986	6 140	1 070	509	561	5 070	1 149	1 751	1 056	629	407	78
1987	5 501	995	495	500	4 506	1 017	1 527	984	576	333	68
1988	4 944	910	437	473	4 033	874	1 371	890	520	309	69
1989	4 770	863	407	456	3 908	856	1 297	871	503	311	70
1990	5 186	903	401	502	4 283	899	1 401	983	582	330	88
1991	6 560	1 029	461	568	5 532	1 132	1 805	1 330	759	410	96
1992	7 169	1 037	484	553	6 132	1 156	1 967	1 483	915	495	116
1993	6 655	992	468	523	5 663	1 057	1 754	1 411	907	442	92
1994	5 892	960	471	489	4 933	952	1 479	1 184	779	407	132
1995	5 459	952	476	476	4 507	866	1 311	1 161	676	362	131
1996	5 300	939	456	484	4 361	854	1 223	1 117	709	336	122
1997	4 836	912	438	475	3 924	765	1 068	1 035	648	302	106
1998	4 484	876	424	451	3 608	731	978	901	620	276	101
1999	4 273	844	414	430	3 429	720	865	843	595	303	104
2000	4 121	795	386	409	3 326	682	835	817	591	294	107
2001	4 969	845	402	443	4 124	829	1 062	985	761	378	109
2002	6 137	925	407	518	5 212	977	1 340	1 237	1 004	518	137
2003	6 311	909	414	495	5 401	1 012	1 354	1 287	1 025	569	155
2004	5 847	890	414	476	4 957	959	1 211	1 130	953	557	148
2005	5 350	845	391	454	4 505	878	1 106	1 006	884	488	144
2006	5 002	794	375	419	4 208	832	1 029	920	813	480	135
2007	5 143	805	361	444	4 338	851	1 052	902	848	520	164
2008	6 509	947	422	524	5 562	1 087	1 336	1 196	1 094	634	216
2009	10 648	1 157	440	717	9 491	1 556	2 320	2 026	2 012	1 221	355
2010	10 916	1 128	445	683	9 788	1 614	2 358	1 969	2 130	1 344	373
2011	9 889	1 024	391	633	8 865	1 546	2 135	1 678	1 859	1 251	395
2012	8 915	1 004	397	607	7 911	1 353	1 881	1 514	1 614	1 144	405

Table 1-26. Unemployed Persons, by Age, Sex, Race, and Hispanic Origin, 1948–2012—*Continued*

(Thousands of people.)

Race, Hispanic origin, sex, and year	16 years and over	16 to 19 years			20 years and over						
		Total	16 to 17 years	18 to 19 years	Total	20 to 24 years	25 to 34 years	35 to 44 years	45 to 54 years	55 to 64 years	65 years and over
WHITE											
Men											
1954	1 913	266	125	142	1 647	260	408	341	299	241	98
1955	1 478	232	114	117	1 246	196	260	246	233	223	89
1956	1 366	221	112	108	1 145	186	265	212	225	177	81
1957	1 477	243	118	124	1 234	222	257	239	250	193	73
1958	2 489	333	149	184	2 156	382	525	436	404	299	110
1959	1 903	318	162	156	1 585	256	350	316	320	245	98
1960	1 988	341	167	174	1 647	295	376	330	317	243	86
1961	2 398	384	176	208	2 014	370	442	395	382	318	107
1962	1 915	334	158	176	1 581	300	332	311	308	246	84
1963	1 976	407	211	196	1 569	309	342	297	294	246	80
1964	1 779	400	217	183	1 379	310	262	255	266	216	70
1965	1 556	387	200	186	1 169	254	226	228	206	190	67
1966	1 241	340	178	162	901	172	185	173	160	154	57
1967	1 208	342	186	156	866	185	171	153	167	140	52
1968	1 142	328	185	143	814	206	162	140	142	111	55
1969	1 137	343	198	145	794	214	165	130	134	108	43
1970	1 857	485	255	230	1 372	388	316	212	216	177	64
1971	2 309	562	288	275	1 747	513	418	268	272	211	66
1972	2 173	564	288	276	1 610	506	375	231	237	199	60
1973	1 836	513	284	229	1 323	411	353	166	188	153	51
1974	2 169	584	311	274	1 585	505	434	218	213	161	53
1975	3 627	785	369	416	2 841	871	796	412	411	265	86
1976	3 258	754	368	385	2 504	750	730	346	341	259	78
1977	2 883	672	342	330	2 211	660	682	297	276	213	82
1978	2 411	615	338	277	1 797	558	525	250	227	169	68
1979	2 405	633	319	313	1 773	553	526	253	220	165	56
1980	3 345	716	347	369	2 629	827	884	378	291	206	44
1981	3 580	755	349	406	2 825	869	943	433	317	221	42
1982	4 846	854	387	467	3 991	1 066	1 385	696	460	331	53
1983	4 859	761	328	433	4 098	1 019	1 410	755	497	362	54
1984	3 600	608	280	328	2 992	722	991	572	363	302	42
1985	3 426	592	282	310	2 834	694	931	553	356	257	43
1986	3 433	576	276	299	2 857	645	978	586	349	248	51
1987	3 132	548	272	276	2 584	568	879	536	350	209	43
1988	2 766	499	239	260	2 268	480	777	477	293	200	40
1989	2 636	487	230	257	2 149	476	694	470	280	191	38
1990	2 935	504	214	290	2 431	510	796	530	330	214	51
1991	3 859	575	249	327	3 284	677	1 064	780	438	269	55
1992	4 209	590	270	319	3 620	686	1 155	858	543	318	58
1993	3 828	565	261	305	3 263	619	1 015	793	512	270	53
1994	3 275	540	259	280	2 735	555	827	626	417	236	74
1995	2 999	535	260	275	2 465	483	711	621	371	200	79
1996	2 896	532	260	273	2 363	478	655	592	383	188	67
1997	2 641	502	234	268	2 140	439	553	549	358	182	58
1998	2 431	510	254	257	1 920	405	512	441	342	164	58
1999	2 274	461	223	237	1 813	398	441	419	322	172	61
2000	2 177	446	217	229	1 731	368	428	403	302	162	68
2001	2 754	479	232	247	2 275	494	547	529	413	229	64
2002	3 459	516	228	288	2 943	562	772	672	554	305	77
2003	3 643	518	221	298	3 125	589	798	723	591	333	91
2004	3 282	497	224	274	2 785	560	694	620	516	307	88
2005	2 931	480	220	260	2 450	522	586	536	463	263	81
2006	2 730	449	202	247	2 281	483	567	482	417	259	73
2007	2 869	461	195	266	2 408	501	604	478	447	285	93
2008	3 727	548	231	317	3 179	668	784	662	604	337	124
2009	6 421	675	241	434	5 746	969	1 439	1 208	1 233	695	202
2010	6 476	648	246	402	5 828	995	1 452	1 131	1 249	785	216
2011	5 631	585	208	377	5 046	909	1 237	951	1 030	697	223
2012	4 931	584	222	362	4 347	792	1 044	794	856	637	224

Table 1-26. Unemployed Persons, by Age, Sex, Race, and Hispanic Origin, 1948–2012—*Continued*

(Thousands of people.)

Race, Hispanic origin, sex, and year	16 years and over	16 to 19 years			20 years and over						
		Total	16 to 17 years	18 to 19 years	Total	20 to 24 years	25 to 34 years	35 to 44 years	45 to 54 years	55 to 64 years	65 years and over
WHITE											
Women											
1954	946	157	66	90	789	134	202	199	148	88	17
1955	774	141	67	74	633	108	152	156	125	77	16
1956	793	161	79	83	632	111	141	151	130	81	17
1957	812	158	77	80	654	109	168	162	123	69	25
1958	1 191	208	96	113	983	159	231	250	210	106	26
1959	1 043	207	93	114	836	150	176	209	176	103	22
1960	1 077	234	106	128	843	161	197	190	185	87	23
1961	1 345	285	119	166	1 060	196	226	257	229	120	32
1962	1 137	246	104	142	891	188	183	211	177	99	33
1963	1 232	301	139	162	931	192	198	221	191	103	27
1964	1 220	308	148	159	912	198	179	217	181	107	30
1965	1 135	318	129	188	817	183	173	199	152	86	24
1966	1 014	311	137	174	703	166	138	163	138	73	23
1967	1 130	293	125	169	837	209	189	183	154	81	23
1968	1 084	316	141	175	768	216	168	157	127	76	25
1969	1 123	317	153	164	806	218	189	164	135	77	23
1970	1 482	386	183	202	1 096	291	254	221	199	98	31
1971	1 777	449	203	246	1 328	376	314	249	228	126	34
1972	1 733	457	227	230	1 275	381	304	227	202	125	35
1973	1 606	442	228	214	1 164	347	311	192	183	104	26
1974	1 927	519	250	270	1 408	420	387	230	214	122	35
1975	2 794	628	288	340	2 166	602	617	362	342	195	49
1976	2 656	611	280	330	2 045	577	598	336	296	188	49
1977	2 558	612	294	318	1 946	536	573	323	293	175	47
1978	2 287	574	292	281	1 713	500	533	294	226	122	37
1979	2 260	560	270	290	1 699	485	542	293	223	125	32
1980	2 540	576	278	298	1 964	537	645	362	259	129	31
1981	2 762	620	281	339	2 143	580	715	394	261	158	36
1982	3 395	680	296	384	2 715	704	898	527	337	217	33
1983	3 270	626	282	345	2 643	659	872	539	340	201	33
1984	2 772	508	231	277	2 264	559	731	464	297	173	39
1985	2 765	482	225	257	2 283	541	763	486	286	175	32
1986	2 708	495	233	262	2 213	504	773	470	281	159	27
1987	2 369	447	223	224	1 922	449	648	448	227	124	25
1988	2 177	412	198	214	1 766	393	594	413	227	110	30
1989	2 135	376	177	199	1 758	380	603	401	223	120	32
1990	2 251	399	187	212	1 852	389	605	453	251	116	37
1991	2 701	453	212	241	2 248	455	741	550	320	141	41
1992	2 959	447	214	233	2 512	469	811	625	372	177	58
1993	2 827	426	208	219	2 400	438	739	618	395	172	39
1994	2 617	420	211	208	2 197	397	652	558	361	170	58
1995	2 460	418	216	201	2 042	384	600	540	306	162	52
1996	2 404	407	196	211	1 998	376	568	525	326	148	55
1997	2 195	411	204	207	1 784	326	515	486	290	119	49
1998	2 053	365	171	195	1 688	327	467	460	279	112	43
1999	1 999	383	190	193	1 616	322	423	423	273	131	43
2000	1 944	349	168	180	1 595	314	407	414	289	133	39
2001	2 215	366	170	196	1 849	335	515	456	348	150	45
2002	2 678	409	179	230	2 269	415	567	565	449	213	60
2003	2 668	391	194	197	2 276	423	555	564	434	235	64
2004	2 565	393	191	202	2 172	399	516	510	437	250	60
2005	2 419	365	172	193	2 054	356	520	469	421	225	63
2006	2 271	345	173	172	1 927	349	462	437	395	222	62
2007	2 274	344	166	178	1 930	350	448	425	401	235	71
2008	2 782	399	191	207	2 384	419	552	534	489	298	92
2009	4 227	482	199	283	3 745	587	881	818	780	526	153
2010	4 440	480	199	281	3 960	619	906	839	881	559	157
2011	4 257	439	184	255	3 818	637	899	728	829	554	171
2012	3 985	420	176	245	3 564	561	837	720	758	508	181

Table 1-26. Unemployed Persons, by Age, Sex, Race, and Hispanic Origin, 1948–2012—*Continued*

(Thousands of people.)

Race, Hispanic origin, sex, and year	16 years and over	16 to 19 years			20 years and over						
		Total	16 to 17 years	18 to 19 years	Total	20 to 24 years	25 to 34 years	35 to 44 years	45 to 54 years	55 to 64 years	65 years and over
BLACK											
Both Sexes											
1974	965	297	127	170	666	261	201	95	65	33	10
1975	1 369	330	130	200	1 040	362	321	157	126	54	17
1976	1 334	330	134	195	1 005	350	338	145	101	54	16
1977	1 393	354	135	218	1 040	397	355	140	81	51	16
1978	1 330	360	150	210	972	379	320	127	82	47	17
1979	1 319	333	137	197	986	369	335	137	82	48	15
1980	1 553	343	134	210	1 209	426	433	171	109	53	18
1981	1 731	357	138	219	1 374	483	493	207	119	55	17
1982	2 142	396	130	266	1 747	565	662	278	141	84	17
1983	2 272	392	125	267	1 879	591	700	299	174	95	21
1984	1 914	353	122	230	1 561	504	577	253	138	75	15
1985	1 864	357	135	221	1 507	455	562	254	143	74	18
1986	1 840	347	138	209	1 493	453	564	269	127	69	10
1987	1 684	312	134	178	1 373	397	533	247	124	62	10
1988	1 547	288	121	167	1 259	349	502	230	111	51	15
1989	1 544	300	116	184	1 245	322	494	246	109	53	20
1990	1 565	268	112	156	1 297	349	505	278	106	44	14
1991	1 723	280	105	175	1 443	378	539	318	151	44	13
1992	2 011	324	127	197	1 687	421	610	402	178	64	13
1993	1 844	313	112	201	1 530	387	532	376	153	72	11
1994	1 666	300	127	173	1 366	351	468	346	130	55	16
1995	1 538	325	143	182	1 213	311	423	303	116	42	18
1996	1 592	310	133	177	1 282	327	454	313	127	48	13
1997	1 560	302	123	179	1 258	327	426	307	136	45	16
1998	1 426	281	124	156	1 146	301	366	294	125	45	16
1999	1 309	268	109	159	1 041	273	339	249	121	46	14
2000	1 241	230	96	134	1 011	281	289	254	131	38	20
2001	1 416	260	102	158	1 155	307	340	283	159	52	15
2002	1 693	260	103	156	1 433	365	407	349	215	76	21
2003	1 787	255	93	162	1 532	375	442	385	217	93	20
2004	1 729	241	103	138	1 487	353	441	341	245	86	21
2005	1 700	267	115	152	1 433	358	423	310	222	92	28
2006	1 549	253	102	151	1 296	318	388	276	214	81	19
2007	1 445	235	98	138	1 210	300	367	237	208	79	19
2008	1 788	246	98	148	1 542	355	458	301	275	117	36
2009	2 606	288	99	189	2 319	488	717	489	415	168	42
2010	2 852	291	97	194	2 562	539	776	534	461	204	47
2011	2 831	267	88	179	2 564	531	801	529	444	212	47
2012	2 544	272	94	179	2 272	510	640	457	397	209	59
BLACK											
Men											
1974	494	159	75	82	336	129	103	41	35	19	8
1975	741	170	71	100	571	195	169	83	78	33	13
1976	698	170	69	103	528	185	166	73	60	32	13
1977	698	187	73	114	512	197	170	63	40	31	12
1978	641	180	80	101	462	185	148	53	40	24	11
1979	636	164	68	97	473	174	152	66	44	27	10
1980	815	179	72	108	636	222	222	88	60	32	12
1981	891	188	73	115	703	248	245	102	65	32	10
1982	1 167	213	72	141	954	304	355	154	74	54	12
1983	1 213	211	70	142	1 002	313	358	162	96	59	14
1984	1 003	188	62	126	815	272	289	132	67	45	9
1985	951	193	69	124	757	224	268	127	85	43	11
1986	946	180	68	112	765	225	273	148	70	44	5
1987	826	160	70	90	666	186	253	122	61	39	6
1988	771	154	64	90	617	177	233	111	58	30	8
1989	773	153	65	88	619	162	226	129	59	33	10
1990	806	142	62	80	664	177	247	146	62	27	6
1991	890	145	54	91	745	201	252	172	87	25	7
1992	1 067	180	71	109	886	221	301	208	107	42	6
1993	971	170	66	104	801	201	260	201	87	46	7
1994	848	167	69	97	682	173	218	180	72	29	10
1995	762	168	73	95	593	153	195	150	63	21	11
1996	808	169	73	96	639	163	210	158	75	26	7
1997	747	162	70	92	585	165	178	141	72	22	7
1998	671	147	61	86	524	151	148	133	60	24	8
1999	626	145	60	85	480	135	143	114	60	22	7
2000	620	121	52	70	499	145	134	121	72	17	9
2001	709	136	51	85	573	150	159	142	84	31	7
2002	835	140	54	85	695	181	180	165	120	40	9
2003	891	132	49	83	760	192	212	189	109	47	10
2004	860	128	52	75	733	188	211	160	120	46	8
2005	844	145	63	82	699	192	189	143	116	45	14
2006	774	134	53	81	640	167	189	118	112	43	11
2007	752	130	55	75	622	166	186	114	106	41	10
2008	949	138	54	84	811	190	242	154	143	61	21
2009	1 448	161	55	106	1 286	264	406	270	230	91	24
2010	1 550	154	47	107	1 396	294	408	286	268	116	24
2011	1 502	142	39	102	1 360	278	426	277	233	125	21
2012	1 292	140	47	93	1 152	269	308	241	191	110	32

Table 1-26. Unemployed Persons, by Age, Sex, Race, and Hispanic Origin, 1948–2012—*Continued*

(Thousands of people.)

Race, Hispanic origin, sex, and year	16 years and over	16 to 19 years			20 years and over						
		Total	16 to 17 years	18 to 19 years	Total	20 to 24 years	25 to 34 years	35 to 44 years	45 to 54 years	55 to 64 years	65 years and over
BLACK											
Women											
1974	470	139	51	87	331	132	98	55	30	14	2
1975	629	160	60	100	469	167	153	75	48	22	4
1976	637	160	66	93	477	165	172	73	41	23	3
1977	695	167	63	104	528	200	185	77	41	21	4
1978	690	179	70	110	510	194	173	74	41	23	6
1979	683	169	69	100	513	195	183	71	38	21	5
1980	738	164	62	102	574	204	211	83	49	21	6
1981	840	169	65	104	671	235	248	105	54	23	7
1982	975	182	58	124	793	261	307	123	67	29	5
1983	1 059	181	56	125	878	278	342	137	77	36	7
1984	911	165	60	104	747	231	288	121	71	30	5
1985	913	164	66	98	750	231	295	127	58	31	7
1986	894	167	70	97	728	228	291	121	57	25	5
1987	858	152	64	88	706	211	280	125	63	23	4
1988	776	134	57	78	642	172	269	118	53	22	7
1989	772	147	51	96	625	160	267	118	50	21	9
1990	758	126	49	76	633	172	258	132	44	17	8
1991	833	135	51	84	698	177	288	145	64	19	6
1992	944	144	56	88	800	200	308	194	71	22	6
1993	872	143	46	97	729	186	272	175	66	26	5
1994	818	133	57	76	685	178	249	166	59	26	6
1995	777	157	. . .	87	620	158	228	153	53	20	7
1996	784	141	60	80	643	164	244	155	52	21	7
1997	813	140	53	87	673	163	248	166	64	24	9
1998	756	134	63	71	622	150	218	160	65	21	8
1999	684	123	49	74	561	138	196	135	61	25	7
2000	621	109	44	65	512	136	154	132	59	22	10
2001	706	124	52	72	582	157	181	141	75	21	8
2002	858	120	49	71	738	183	228	185	95	35	12
2003	895	123	44	79	772	183	230	195	109	46	10
2004	868	114	51	63	755	166	230	180	126	40	13
2005	856	123	52	70	734	166	233	168	106	47	14
2006	775	120	50	70	656	150	199	158	102	38	8
2007	693	106	43	63	588	135	181	123	103	38	9
2008	839	108	44	64	732	166	216	147	132	56	15
2009	1 159	127	44	82	1 032	223	311	219	185	77	17
2010	1 302	137	50	87	1 165	245	369	248	193	88	22
2011	1 329	125	49	76	1 204	253	376	252	211	86	25
2012	1 252	133	47	85	1 119	241	333	216	205	98	26
HISPANIC											
Both Sexes											
1975	508	123	. . .	. . .	. . .	. . .	. . .	. . .	. . .	. . .	. . .
1976	485	106	51	55	385	116	113	72	53	26	6
1977	456	113	50	60	344	98	114	56	48	24	5
1978	452	110	63	47	342	98	116	65	41	16	5
1979	434	106	54	51	329	100	102	65	37	20	4
1980	620	145	66	79	474	138	168	90	49	24	5
1981	678	144	60	84	533	171	178	92	57	31	5
1982	929	175	73	102	754	221	267	140	75	45	6
1983	961	167	64	104	793	214	270	156	93	54	5
1984	800	149	60	88	651	164	235	124	71	51	5
1985	811	141	55	85	670	171	256	123	73	41	7
1986	857	141	57	84	716	183	258	143	85	38	9
1987	751	136	57	79	615	152	222	128	75	33	5
1988	732	148	63	84	585	145	209	120	69	36	6
1989	750	132	59	73	618	158	218	124	76	36	6
1990	876	161	68	94	714	167	263	156	85	36	7
1991	1 092	179	79	99	913	214	332	206	110	44	8
1992	1 311	219	94	124	1 093	240	390	267	126	59	10
1993	1 248	201	86	115	1 047	237	354	261	132	54	10
1994	1 187	198	90	108	989	220	348	227	132	51	12
1995	1 140	205	96	109	934	209	325	224	106	54	16
1996	1 132	199	85	114	933	217	296	246	101	59	14
1997	1 069	197	87	110	872	206	269	229	99	56	13
1998	1 026	214	89	125	812	194	260	203	96	48	11
1999	945	196	79	117	750	171	233	190	104	42	10
2000	954	194	83	112	759	190	247	189	79	42	12
2001	1 138	208	84	123	931	212	315	228	111	56	9
2002	1 353	221	81	140	1 132	265	373	271	146	62	15
2003	1 441	192	79	113	1 249	273	419	294	183	69	10
2004	1 342	203	86	117	1 139	255	371	261	161	74	18
2005	1 191	191	78	113	1 000	227	324	231	142	61	15
2006	1 081	170	74	97	911	194	294	231	128	49	14
2007	1 220	197	78	119	1 023	213	322	238	161	70	19
2008	1 678	251	105	146	1 427	307	437	328	242	81	32
2009	2 706	321	109	212	2 385	429	731	584	416	186	38
2010	2 043	322	99	223	2 520	479	736	598	459	199	49
2011	2 629	300	96	203	2 329	473	669	524	424	195	45
2012	2 514	324	111	213	2 190	444	618	502	381	201	44

. . . = Not available.

Table 1-26. Unemployed Persons, by Age, Sex, Race, and Hispanic Origin, 1948–2012—*Continued*

(Thousands of people.)

Race, Hispanic origin, sex, and year	16 years and over	16 to 19 years			20 years and over						
		Total	16 to 17 years	18 to 19 years	Total	20 to 24 years	25 to 34 years	35 to 44 years	45 to 54 years	55 to 64 years	65 years and over
HISPANIC											
Men											
1975	296	...	...	...	225	...	...	...	...	...	...
1976	278	60	30	31	217	69	63	38	29	16	...
1977	253	60	27	33	195	57	65	28	22	15	...
1978	234	59	35	24	175	51	59	30	20	10	...
1979	223	55	29	27	168	52	50	33	19	11	...
1980	370	86	39	47	284	85	96	51	31	16	...
1981	408	87	40	47	321	105	113	49	31	19	...
1982	565	104	45	59	461	138	169	80	40	29	...
1983	591	100	38	62	491	134	168	92	57	36	...
1984	480	87	36	51	393	103	142	69	41	33	...
1985	483	82	34	49	401	108	156	69	40	23	...
1986	520	82	33	50	438	115	159	86	46	26	...
1987	451	77	32	45	374	88	137	77	46	22	...
1988	437	86	36	50	351	83	128	70	42	24	...
1989	423	81	36	45	342	88	113	69	43	25	...
1990	524	100	40	60	425	99	154	91	53	25	...
1991	685	110	47	62	575	139	210	126	62	33	...
1992	807	132	56	75	675	156	239	156	75	42	...
1993	747	118	50	68	629	144	217	148	79	33	...
1994	680	121	54	67	558	128	203	113	75	30	9
1995	651	121	59	63	530	123	185	120	57	33	13
1996	607	112	49	63	495	117	165	124	49	31	9
1997	582	110	47	63	471	125	137	113	54	35	8
1998	552	117	54	62	436	115	142	97	49	29	5
1999	480	106	42	63	374	96	109	83	54	24	7
2000	494	106	46	60	388	105	118	93	42	23	8
2001	611	117	52	65	495	129	152	116	55	36	6
2002	764	127	42	86	636	151	213	144	82	38	8
2003	809	116	42	74	693	157	239	153	98	41	5
2004	755	120	48	72	635	158	207	133	82	41	13
2005	647	112	42	70	536	134	168	119	74	31	9
2006	601	104	43	61	497	110	169	114	66	29	8
2007	695	119	44	74	576	121	189	126	92	35	13
2008	1 007	147	63	84	860	188	275	192	136	50	19
2009	1 670	196	66	131	1 474	255	470	364	246	117	21
2010	1 711	191	54	137	1 519	294	470	346	269	112	28
2011	1 527	182	53	129	1 345	277	395	297	231	116	28
2012	1 383	189	66	123	1 195	254	339	251	208	119	24
HISPANIC											
Women											
1975	212	...	...	...	160	...	...	...	...	...	...
1976	207	45	22	24	166	47	52	33	22	10	...
1977	204	50	23	27	153	40	49	28	25	11	...
1978	219	51	28	23	168	46	58	36	20	8	...
1979	211	50	26	24	160	48	52	32	18	10	...
1980	249	59	28	31	190	53	72	39	18	8	...
1981	269	57	20	37	212	65	65	43	25	13	...
1982	364	71	28	43	293	83	98	60	35	16	...
1983	369	68	26	42	302	80	102	65	36	18	...
1984	320	62	25	37	258	61	93	55	30	17	...
1985	327	58	22	37	269	63	100	54	32	18	...
1986	337	59	25	35	278	68	99	57	39	12	...
1987	300	59	25	34	241	64	85	51	29	11	...
1988	296	62	27	34	234	63	81	50	27	12	...
1989	327	51	23	28	276	70	105	55	33	11	...
1990	351	62	28	34	289	68	109	65	32	11	...
1991	407	69	32	37	339	74	122	80	48	12	...
1992	504	87	38	49	418	84	151	111	51	17	...
1993	501	83	36	47	418	93	136	113	53	21	...
1994	508	77	36	40	431	92	145	115	57	21	2
1995	488	84	38	46	404	86	140	104	50	21	3
1996	525	88	36	52	438	100	131	122	52	27	5
1997	488	87	40	46	401	81	132	117	46	21	4
1998	473	98	35	63	376	80	118	106	48	19	5
1999	466	90	36	54	376	75	124	107	50	17	3
2000	460	88	37	51	371	86	129	96	38	19	4
2001	527	91	33	58	436	83	163	112	56	20	3
2002	590	94	39	54	496	113	160	127	65	24	7
2003	631	76	37	39	555	116	180	141	86	28	5
2004	587	83	38	45	504	97	164	128	78	32	5
2005	544	80	36	43	464	93	156	112	68	30	6
2006	480	67	31	36	414	84	125	116	62	20	6
2007	525	79	34	45	446	92	134	111	69	35	6
2008	672	104	42	62	567	119	162	136	105	32	13
2009	1 036	125	44	81	911	174	260	220	170	70	17
2010	1 132	131	45	86	1 001	186	267	252	190	87	20
2011	1 102	118	44	74	984	196	274	227	192	78	17
2012	1 130	135	45	90	995	190	278	251	173	83	20

. . . = Not available.

Table 1-27. Unemployment Rates of Civilian Workers, by Age, Sex, Race, and Hispanic Origin, 1948–2012

(Percent of labor force.)

Race, Hispanic origin, sex, and year	16 years and over	16 to 19 years			20 years and over						
		Total	16 to 17 years	18 to 19 years	Total	20 to 24 years	25 to 34 years	35 to 44 years	45 to 54 years	55 to 64 years	65 years and over
ALL RACES											
Both Sexes											
1948	3.8	9.2	10.1	8.6	2.9	6.2	3.2	2.6	2.7	3.1	3.2
1949	5.9	13.4	14.0	13.0	4.8	9.3	5.4	4.4	4.2	5.2	4.9
1950	5.3	12.2	13.6	11.2	4.4	7.7	4.8	3.8	4.2	4.8	4.5
1951	3.3	8.2	9.6	7.1	2.8	4.1	3.0	2.5	2.7	3.1	3.4
1952	3.0	8.5	10.0	7.3	2.4	4.6	2.6	2.3	2.3	2.4	2.9
1953	2.9	7.6	8.7	6.8	2.4	4.7	2.5	2.2	2.3	2.7	2.2
1954	5.5	12.6	13.5	10.7	4.7	9.2	5.3	4.5	4.4	4.5	4.1
1955	4.4	11.0	12.3	10.0	3.6	7.0	3.8	3.4	3.4	4.2	3.6
1956	4.1	11.1	12.3	10.2	3.3	6.6	3.7	3.0	3.2	3.5	3.2
1957	4.3	11.6	12.5	10.9	3.4	7.1	3.9	3.1	3.3	3.4	3.4
1958	6.8	15.9	16.4	15.5	5.6	11.2	6.8	5.4	5.2	5.2	4.8
1959	5.5	14.6	15.3	14.0	4.4	8.5	5.0	4.2	4.2	4.4	4.3
1960	5.5	14.7	15.5	14.1	4.4	8.7	5.2	4.1	4.1	4.2	3.8
1961	6.7	16.8	18.3	15.8	5.4	10.4	6.2	5.2	5.0	5.4	5.1
1962	5.5	14.7	16.3	13.6	4.4	9.0	5.1	4.1	4.0	4.2	4.5
1963	5.7	17.2	19.3	15.6	4.3	8.8	5.2	4.0	3.8	4.1	4.1
1964	5.2	16.2	17.8	14.9	3.8	8.3	4.3	3.6	3.5	3.7	3.8
1965	4.5	14.8	16.5	13.5	3.2	6.7	3.7	3.2	2.8	3.1	3.3
1966	3.8	12.8	14.8	11.3	2.6	5.3	3.1	2.5	2.3	2.5	3.0
1967	3.8	12.9	14.6	11.6	2.6	5.7	3.2	2.5	2.4	2.4	2.8
1968	3.6	12.7	14.7	11.2	2.3	5.8	2.8	2.2	1.9	2.0	2.8
1969	3.5	12.2	14.5	10.5	2.2	5.7	2.8	2.2	1.9	1.9	2.2
1970	4.9	15.3	17.1	13.8	3.3	8.2	4.2	3.1	2.8	2.7	3.2
1971	5.9	16.9	18.7	15.5	4.0	10.0	5.3	3.9	3.4	3.3	3.5
1972	5.6	16.2	18.5	14.6	3.6	9.3	4.6	3.5	3.0	3.2	3.6
1973	4.9	14.5	17.3	12.4	3.1	7.8	4.2	2.7	2.5	2.6	3.0
1974	5.6	16.0	18.3	14.3	3.6	9.1	4.8	3.3	2.9	2.8	3.4
1975	8.5	19.9	21.4	18.9	6.0	13.6	7.8	5.6	5.2	4.6	5.2
1976	7.7	19.0	21.1	17.5	5.5	12.0	7.1	4.9	4.5	4.5	5.1
1977	7.1	17.8	19.9	16.2	4.9	11.0	6.5	4.4	3.9	3.9	5.0
1978	6.1	16.4	19.3	14.2	4.1	9.6	5.3	3.7	3.3	2.9	4.0
1979	5.8	16.1	18.1	14.7	3.9	9.1	5.2	3.6	3.2	2.9	3.4
1980	7.1	17.8	20.0	16.2	5.1	11.5	6.9	4.6	4.0	3.3	3.1
1981	7.6	19.6	21.4	18.4	5.4	12.3	7.3	5.0	4.2	3.7	3.2
1982	9.7	23.2	24.9	22.1	7.4	14.9	9.7	6.9	5.7	5.4	3.5
1983	9.6	22.4	24.5	21.1	7.5	14.5	9.7	7.0	6.2	5.6	3.7
1984	7.5	18.9	21.2	17.4	5.8	11.5	7.3	5.4	4.9	4.7	3.3
1985	7.2	18.6	21.0	17.0	5.6	11.1	7.0	5.1	4.7	4.3	3.2
1986	7.0	18.3	20.2	17.0	5.4	10.7	6.9	5.0	4.5	4.1	3.0
1987	6.2	16.9	19.1	15.2	4.8	9.7	6.0	4.5	4.0	3.5	2.5
1988	5.5	15.3	17.4	13.8	4.3	8.7	5.4	4.0	3.4	3.2	2.7
1989	5.3	15.0	17.2	13.6	4.0	8.6	5.2	3.8	3.2	3.2	2.6
1990	5.6	15.5	17.9	14.1	4.4	8.8	5.6	4.1	3.6	3.3	3.0
1991	6.8	18.7	21.0	17.2	5.4	10.8	6.9	5.2	4.5	4.1	3.3
1992	7.5	20.1	23.1	18.2	6.1	11.4	7.6	5.8	5.1	5.1	3.8
1993	6.9	19.0	21.4	17.5	5.6	10.5	6.9	5.5	4.8	4.7	3.2
1994	6.1	17.6	19.9	16.0	4.8	9.7	6.0	4.6	4.0	4.1	4.0
1995	5.6	17.3	20.2	15.3	4.3	9.1	5.4	4.3	3.3	3.6	4.0
1996	5.4	16.7	18.9	15.2	4.2	9.3	5.2	4.1	3.3	3.3	3.6
1997	4.9	16.0	18.2	14.5	3.8	8.5	4.7	3.8	3.0	2.9	3.3
1998	4.5	14.6	17.2	12.8	3.4	7.9	4.3	3.4	2.8	2.6	3.2
1999	4.2	13.9	16.3	12.4	3.1	7.5	4.0	3.0	2.6	2.7	3.1
2000	4.0	13.1	15.4	11.6	3.0	7.2	3.7	3.0	2.5	2.5	3.1
2001	4.7	14.7	17.2	13.1	3.7	8.3	4.6	3.6	3.1	3.0	2.9
2002	5.8	16.5	18.8	15.1	4.6	9.7	5.9	4.6	4.0	3.9	3.6
2003	6.0	17.5	19.1	16.4	4.8	10.0	6.1	4.9	4.1	4.1	3.8
2004	5.5	17.0	20.2	15.0	4.4	9.4	5.5	4.4	3.8	3.8	3.6
2005	5.1	16.6	19.1	14.9	4.0	8.8	5.1	3.9	3.5	3.3	3.5
2006	4.6	15.4	17.2	14.1	3.6	8.2	4.7	3.6	3.1	3.0	2.9
2007	4.6	15.7	17.5	14.5	3.6	8.2	4.7	3.4	3.2	3.1	3.3
2008	5.8	18.7	22.1	16.8	4.6	10.2	5.8	4.6	4.1	3.7	4.2
2009	9.3	24.3	25.9	23.4	7.9	14.7	9.9	7.9	7.2	6.6	6.4
2010	9.6	25.9	29.1	24.2	8.2	15.5	10.1	8.1	7.7	7.1	6.7
2011	8.9	24.4	27.7	22.9	7.6	14.6	9.5	7.3	7.1	6.6	6.5
2012	8.1	24.0	27.3	22.3	6.8	13.3	8.3	6.6	6.2	5.9	6.2

Table 1-27. Unemployment Rates of Civilian Workers, by Age, Sex, Race, and Hispanic Origin, 1948–2012—*Continued*

(Percent of labor force.)

Race, Hispanic origin, sex, and year	16 years and over	16 to 19 years			20 years and over						
		Total	16 to 17 years	18 to 19 years	Total	20 to 24 years	25 to 34 years	35 to 44 years	45 to 54 years	55 to 64 years	65 years and over
ALL RACES											
Men											
1948	3.6	9.8	10.2	9.5	3.2	6.9	2.8	2.4	2.5	3.1	3.4
1949	5.9	14.3	13.7	14.6	5.4	10.4	5.2	4.3	4.3	5.4	5.1
1950	5.1	12.7	13.3	12.3	4.7	8.1	4.4	3.6	4.0	4.9	4.8
1951	2.8	8.1	9.4	7.0	2.5	3.9	2.3	2.0	2.4	2.8	3.5
1952	2.8	8.9	10.5	7.4	2.4	4.6	2.2	1.9	2.2	2.4	3.0
1953	2.8	7.9	8.8	7.2	2.5	5.0	2.2	2.0	2.3	2.8	2.4
1954	5.3	13.5	13.9	13.2	4.9	10.7	4.8	4.1	4.3	4.5	4.4
1955	4.2	11.6	12.5	10.8	3.8	7.7	3.3	3.1	3.2	4.3	4.0
1956	3.8	11.1	11.7	10.5	3.4	6.9	3.3	2.6	3.0	3.5	3.5
1957	4.1	12.4	12.4	12.3	3.6	7.8	3.3	2.8	3.3	3.5	3.4
1958	6.8	17.1	16.3	17.8	6.2	12.7	6.5	5.1	5.3	5.5	5.2
1959	5.2	15.3	15.8	14.9	4.7	8.7	4.7	3.7	4.1	4.5	4.8
1960	5.4	15.3	15.5	15.0	4.7	8.9	4.8	3.8	4.1	4.6	4.2
1961	6.4	17.1	18.3	16.3	5.7	10.8	5.7	4.6	4.9	5.7	5.5
1962	5.2	14.7	16.0	13.8	4.6	8.9	4.5	3.6	3.9	4.6	4.6
1963	5.2	17.2	18.8	15.9	4.5	8.8	4.5	3.5	3.6	4.3	4.5
1964	4.6	15.8	17.1	14.6	3.9	8.1	3.5	2.9	3.2	3.9	4.0
1965	4.0	14.1	16.1	12.4	3.2	6.4	2.9	2.5	2.5	3.3	3.5
1966	3.2	11.7	13.7	10.2	2.5	4.6	2.4	2.0	1.9	2.6	3.1
1967	3.1	12.3	14.5	10.5	2.3	4.7	2.1	1.7	2.0	2.3	2.8
1968	2.9	11.6	13.9	9.7	2.2	5.1	1.9	1.6	1.6	1.9	2.8
1969	2.8	11.4	13.8	9.3	2.1	5.1	1.9	1.5	1.5	1.8	2.2
1970	4.4	15.0	16.9	13.4	3.5	8.4	3.5	2.4	2.4	2.8	3.3
1971	5.3	16.6	18.7	15.0	4.4	10.3	4.4	3.1	3.0	3.3	3.4
1972	5.0	15.9	18.3	14.1	4.0	9.3	3.8	2.7	2.6	3.2	3.6
1973	4.2	13.9	17.0	11.4	3.3	7.3	3.4	2.0	2.1	2.4	3.0
1974	4.9	15.6	18.4	13.3	3.8	8.8	4.0	2.6	2.4	2.6	3.3
1975	7.9	20.1	21.6	19.0	6.8	14.3	6.9	4.9	4.8	4.3	5.4
1976	7.1	19.2	21.4	17.6	5.9	12.1	6.2	4.1	4.0	4.2	5.1
1977	6.3	17.3	19.5	15.6	5.2	10.8	5.7	3.5	3.2	3.6	5.2
1978	5.3	15.8	19.1	13.3	4.3	9.2	4.4	2.8	2.7	2.8	4.2
1979	5.1	15.9	17.9	14.3	4.2	8.7	4.3	2.9	2.7	2.7	3.4
1980	6.9	18.3	20.4	16.7	5.9	12.5	6.7	4.1	3.6	3.4	3.1
1981	7.4	20.1	22.0	18.8	6.3	13.2	6.9	4.5	4.0	3.6	2.9
1982	9.9	24.4	26.4	23.1	8.8	16.4	10.1	6.9	5.6	5.5	3.7
1983	9.9	23.3	25.2	22.2	8.9	15.9	10.1	7.1	6.3	6.1	3.9
1984	7.4	19.6	21.9	18.3	6.6	11.9	7.2	5.2	4.6	5.0	3.0
1985	7.0	19.5	21.9	17.9	6.2	11.4	6.6	4.9	4.6	4.3	3.1
1986	6.9	19.0	20.8	17.7	6.1	11.0	6.7	5.1	4.4	4.3	3.2
1987	6.2	17.8	20.2	16.0	5.4	9.9	5.9	4.4	4.2	3.7	2.6
1988	5.5	16.0	18.2	14.6	4.8	8.9	5.3	3.8	3.5	3.5	2.5
1989	5.2	15.9	18.6	14.2	4.5	8.8	4.8	3.7	3.2	3.5	2.4
1990	5.7	16.3	18.4	15.0	5.0	9.1	5.5	4.1	3.7	3.8	3.0
1991	7.2	19.8	21.8	18.5	6.4	11.6	7.0	5.5	4.8	4.6	3.3
1992	7.9	21.5	24.6	19.5	7.1	12.2	7.8	6.1	5.6	5.8	3.3
1993	7.2	20.4	22.9	18.8	6.4	11.3	7.0	5.6	5.1	5.2	3.2
1994	6.2	19.0	21.0	17.6	5.4	10.2	5.9	4.5	4.0	4.4	4.0
1995	5.6	18.4	21.1	16.5	4.8	9.2	5.1	4.2	3.5	3.6	4.3
1996	5.4	18.1	20.8	16.3	4.6	9.5	4.9	4.0	3.5	3.3	3.4
1997	4.9	16.9	19.1	15.4	4.2	8.9	4.3	3.6	3.1	3.1	3.0
1998	4.4	16.2	19.1	14.1	3.7	8.1	3.9	3.0	2.8	2.8	3.1
1999	4.1	14.7	17.0	13.1	3.5	7.7	3.6	2.8	2.6	2.7	3.0
2000	3.9	14.0	16.8	12.2	3.3	7.3	3.4	2.8	2.4	2.4	3.3
2001	4.8	16.0	19.1	14.0	4.2	9.0	4.3	3.6	3.2	3.3	3.0
2002	5.9	18.1	21.1	16.4	5.3	10.2	5.8	4.5	4.2	4.3	3.4
2003	6.3	19.3	20.7	18.4	5.6	10.6	6.2	5.0	4.4	4.5	4.0
2004	5.6	18.4	22.0	16.3	5.0	10.1	5.5	4.3	3.9	3.9	3.7
2005	5.1	18.6	22.0	16.5	4.4	9.6	4.7	3.7	3.5	3.3	3.4
2006	4.6	16.9	18.6	15.7	4.0	8.7	4.5	3.3	3.1	3.0	2.8
2007	4.7	17.6	19.4	16.5	4.1	8.9	4.7	3.3	3.1	3.2	3.4
2008	6.1	21.2	25.2	19.0	5.4	11.4	6.1	4.6	4.2	3.8	4.5
2009	10.3	27.8	28.7	27.4	9.6	17.0	10.9	8.6	8.2	7.2	6.7
2010	10.5	28.8	31.8	27.4	9.8	17.8	10.9	8.5	8.6	8.0	7.1
2011	9.4	27.2	29.1	26.3	8.7	15.7	9.7	7.4	7.4	7.1	6.5
2012	8.2	26.8	30.6	25.0	7.5	14.3	8.2	6.4	6.2	6.3	6.2

Table 1-27. Unemployment Rates of Civilian Workers, by Age, Sex, Race, and Hispanic Origin, 1948–2012—*Continued*

(Percent of labor force.)

Race, Hispanic origin, sex, and year	16 years and over	16 to 19 years			20 years and over						
		Total	16 to 17 years	18 to 19 years	Total	20 to 24 years	25 to 34 years	35 to 44 years	45 to 54 years	55 to 64 years	65 years and over
ALL RACES											
Women											
1948	4.1	8.3	10.0	7.4	3.6	4.8	4.3	3.0	3.0	3.1	2.3
1949	6.0	12.3	14.4	11.2	5.3	7.3	5.9	4.7	4.0	4.4	3.8
1950	5.7	11.4	14.2	9.8	5.1	6.9	5.7	4.4	4.5	4.5	3.4
1951	4.4	8.3	10.0	7.2	4.0	4.4	4.5	3.8	3.5	4.0	2.9
1952	3.6	8.0	9.1	7.3	3.2	4.5	3.6	3.0	2.5	2.5	2.2
1953	3.3	7.2	8.5	6.4	2.9	4.3	3.4	2.5	2.3	2.5	1.4
1954	6.0	11.4	12.7	7.7	5.5	7.3	6.6	5.3	4.6	4.6	3.0
1955	4.9	10.2	12.0	9.1	4.4	6.1	5.3	4.0	3.6	3.8	2.3
1956	4.8	11.2	13.2	9.9	4.2	6.3	4.8	3.9	3.6	3.6	2.3
1957	4.7	10.6	12.6	9.4	4.1	6.0	5.3	3.8	3.2	3.0	3.4
1958	6.8	14.3	16.6	12.9	6.1	8.9	7.3	6.2	4.9	4.5	3.7
1959	5.9	13.5	14.4	13.0	5.2	8.1	5.9	5.1	4.2	4.1	2.8
1960	5.9	13.9	15.5	12.9	5.1	8.3	6.3	4.8	4.2	3.4	2.9
1961	7.2	16.3	18.3	15.1	6.3	9.8	7.4	6.4	5.1	4.5	4.0
1962	6.2	14.6	16.7	13.5	5.4	9.1	6.5	5.2	4.1	3.5	4.2
1963	6.5	17.2	20.2	15.2	5.4	8.9	6.9	5.1	4.2	3.6	3.2
1964	6.2	16.6	18.8	15.2	5.2	8.6	6.3	5.0	3.9	3.3	3.3
1965	5.5	15.7	17.2	14.8	4.5	7.3	5.5	4.6	3.2	2.8	2.9
1966	4.8	14.1	16.6	12.6	3.8	6.3	4.5	3.6	2.9	2.3	2.8
1967	5.2	13.5	14.8	12.8	4.2	7.0	5.4	4.1	3.1	2.4	2.7
1968	4.8	14.0	15.9	12.9	3.8	6.7	4.7	3.4	2.4	2.2	2.7
1969	4.7	13.3	15.5	11.8	3.7	6.3	4.6	3.4	2.6	2.2	2.3
1970	5.9	15.6	17.4	14.4	4.8	7.9	5.7	4.4	3.5	2.7	3.1
1971	6.9	17.2	18.7	16.2	5.7	9.6	7.0	5.2	4.0	3.3	3.6
1972	6.6	16.7	18.8	15.2	5.4	9.4	6.2	4.9	3.6	3.3	3.5
1973	6.0	15.3	17.7	13.5	4.9	8.5	5.8	3.9	3.2	2.8	2.9
1974	6.7	16.6	18.2	15.4	5.5	9.5	6.2	4.6	3.7	3.2	3.6
1975	9.3	19.7	21.2	18.7	8.0	12.7	9.1	6.8	5.9	5.1	5.0
1976	8.6	18.7	20.8	17.4	7.4	11.9	8.4	6.1	5.2	4.9	5.0
1977	8.2	18.3	20.5	16.9	7.0	11.2	7.7	5.7	5.1	4.4	4.7
1978	7.2	17.1	19.5	15.3	6.0	10.1	6.7	5.0	4.0	3.2	3.8
1979	6.8	16.4	18.3	15.0	5.7	9.6	6.5	4.6	3.9	3.2	3.3
1980	7.4	17.2	19.6	15.6	6.4	10.4	7.2	5.3	4.5	3.3	3.1
1981	7.9	19.0	20.7	17.9	6.8	11.2	7.7	5.7	4.6	3.8	3.6
1982	9.4	21.9	23.2	21.0	8.3	13.2	9.3	7.0	5.9	5.2	3.2
1983	9.2	21.3	23.7	19.9	8.1	12.9	9.1	6.9	6.0	5.0	3.4
1984	7.6	18.0	20.4	16.6	6.8	10.9	7.4	5.6	5.2	4.3	3.8
1985	7.4	17.6	20.0	16.0	6.6	10.7	7.4	5.5	4.8	4.3	3.3
1986	7.1	17.6	19.6	16.3	6.2	10.3	7.2	5.0	4.5	3.8	2.8
1987	6.2	15.9	18.0	14.3	5.4	9.4	6.2	4.6	3.7	3.1	2.4
1988	5.6	14.4	16.6	12.9	4.9	8.5	5.6	4.1	3.4	2.7	2.9
1989	5.4	14.0	15.7	13.0	4.7	8.3	5.6	3.9	3.2	2.8	2.9
1990	5.5	14.7	17.4	13.1	4.9	8.5	5.6	4.2	3.4	2.8	3.1
1991	6.4	17.5	20.2	15.9	5.7	9.8	6.8	4.8	4.2	3.4	3.3
1992	7.0	18.6	21.5	16.6	6.3	10.3	7.4	5.5	4.6	4.2	4.5
1993	6.6	17.5	19.8	16.1	5.9	9.7	6.8	5.3	4.5	4.0	3.1
1994	6.0	16.2	18.7	14.3	5.4	9.2	6.2	4.7	4.0	3.9	4.0
1995	5.6	16.1	19.2	14.0	4.9	9.0	5.7	4.4	3.2	3.6	3.7
1996	5.4	15.2	16.9	14.0	4.8	9.0	5.5	4.2	3.2	3.4	4.0
1997	5.0	15.0	17.2	13.6	4.4	8.1	5.2	4.0	2.9	2.7	3.6
1998	4.6	12.9	15.1	11.5	4.1	7.8	4.8	3.8	2.7	2.4	3.3
1999	4.3	13.2	15.5	11.6	3.8	7.2	4.4	3.3	2.5	2.6	3.2
2000	4.1	12.1	13.9	10.8	3.6	7.1	4.1	3.3	2.5	2.5	2.7
2001	4.7	13.4	15.2	12.2	4.1	7.5	5.1	3.7	3.0	2.7	2.9
2002	5.6	14.9	16.6	13.8	5.1	9.1	5.9	4.6	3.8	3.5	3.9
2003	5.7	15.6	17.5	14.2	5.1	9.3	5.9	4.9	3.7	3.7	3.6
2004	5.4	15.5	18.5	13.5	4.9	8.7	5.6	4.4	3.7	3.6	3.4
2005	5.1	14.5	16.5	13.1	4.6	7.9	5.6	4.1	3.5	3.3	3.5
2006	4.6	13.8	15.9	12.4	4.1	7.6	4.9	3.9	3.1	2.9	3.0
2007	4.5	13.8	15.7	12.5	4.0	7.3	4.6	3.6	3.2	3.0	3.1
2008	5.4	16.2	19.1	14.3	4.9	8.8	5.5	4.5	3.9	3.7	3.9
2009	8.1	20.7	23.1	19.4	7.5	12.3	8.6	7.1	6.0	6.0	6.1
2010	8.6	22.8	26.5	20.9	8.0	13.0	9.1	7.7	6.8	6.2	6.2
2011	8.5	21.7	26.3	19.3	7.9	13.4	9.1	7.2	6.7	6.1	6.5
2012	7.9	21.1	24.2	19.5	7.3	12.1	8.4	6.8	6.2	5.6	6.3

Table 1-27. Unemployment Rates of Civilian Workers, by Age, Sex, Race, and Hispanic Origin, 1948–2012—*Continued*

(Percent of labor force.)

Race, Hispanic origin, sex, and year	16 years and over	16 to 19 years			20 years and over						
		Total	16 to 17 years	18 to 19 years	Total	20 to 24 years	25 to 34 years	35 to 44 years	45 to 54 years	55 to 64 years	65 years and over
WHITE											
Both Sexes											
1954	5.0	12.1	13.2	5.0	4.6	8.3	4.6	4.0	4.0	4.3	3.9
1955	3.9	10.4	12.0	3.9	3.4	6.2	3.1	2.9	3.1	3.8	3.4
1956	3.6	10.1	11.5	3.6	3.2	5.7	3.1	2.6	2.9	3.2	3.1
1957	3.8	10.6	11.9	3.8	3.4	6.3	3.3	2.8	3.0	3.2	3.2
1958	6.1	14.4	15.2	6.1	5.6	9.9	5.9	4.8	4.8	4.9	4.6
1959	4.8	13.1	14.4	4.8	4.3	7.3	4.2	3.7	3.8	4.1	4.1
1960	5.0	13.5	14.6	5.0	4.3	7.9	4.5	3.6	3.8	3.9	3.7
1961	6.0	15.3	16.7	6.0	5.3	9.4	5.3	4.5	4.5	5.0	4.8
1962	4.9	13.3	15.3	4.9	4.2	7.9	4.2	3.6	3.6	3.9	4.0
1963	5.0	15.5	17.9	5.0	4.2	7.7	4.4	3.5	3.5	3.8	3.8
1964	4.6	14.8	16.5	4.6	3.8	7.3	3.6	3.2	3.2	3.5	3.5
1965	4.1	13.4	14.8	4.1	3.3	6.1	3.2	2.9	2.5	2.9	3.2
1966	3.4	11.2	13.3	3.4	2.6	4.6	2.6	2.3	2.1	2.4	2.9
1967	3.4	11.0	12.8	3.4	2.7	5.0	2.7	2.3	2.2	2.3	2.7
1968	3.2	11.0	12.9	3.2	2.5	5.2	2.4	2.0	1.8	1.9	2.8
1969	3.1	10.7	13.0	3.1	2.4	5.0	2.5	2.0	1.8	1.8	2.2
1970	4.5	13.5	15.5	4.5	3.7	7.3	3.8	3.0	2.7	2.7	3.2
1971	5.4	15.1	17.0	5.4	4.5	9.0	4.7	3.6	3.3	3.3	3.5
1972	5.1	14.2	16.6	5.1	4.1	8.4	4.1	3.2	2.9	3.1	3.4
1973	4.3	12.6	15.4	4.3	3.5	6.8	3.7	2.5	2.4	2.5	2.9
1974	5.0	14.0	16.3	5.0	4.1	8.0	4.4	3.1	2.8	2.8	3.3
1975	7.8	17.9	19.5	7.8	6.7	12.3	7.1	5.2	4.9	4.5	5.1
1976	7.0	16.9	19.0	7.0	5.9	10.7	6.3	4.5	4.2	4.3	4.9
1977	6.2	15.4	17.9	6.2	5.3	9.3	5.7	4.0	3.8	3.7	4.9
1978	5.2	13.9	17.0	5.2	4.3	8.0	4.6	3.3	3.0	2.7	3.8
1979	5.1	14.0	16.1	5.1	4.2	7.6	4.4	3.2	3.0	2.7	3.1
1980	6.3	15.5	17.9	6.3	5.4	9.9	6.1	4.2	3.7	3.1	2.7
1981	6.7	17.3	19.2	6.7	5.7	10.4	6.3	4.5	3.9	3.5	2.8
1982	8.6	20.4	22.8	8.6	7.6	12.8	8.5	6.3	5.4	5.1	3.1
1983	8.4	19.3	22.0	8.4	7.5	12.1	8.4	6.3	5.7	5.2	3.2
1984	6.5	16.0	18.8	6.5	5.7	9.3	6.2	4.8	4.4	4.4	3.0
1985	6.2	15.7	18.3	6.2	5.5	9.2	5.9	4.6	4.3	4.0	2.9
1986	6.0	15.6	17.6	6.0	5.3	8.7	5.9	4.5	4.1	3.8	2.9
1987	5.3	14.4	16.7	5.3	4.7	8.0	5.1	4.0	3.7	3.2	2.4
1988	4.7	13.1	15.3	4.7	4.1	7.1	4.5	3.5	3.1	3.0	2.4
1989	4.5	12.7	15.2	4.5	3.9	7.2	4.3	3.3	2.9	3.0	2.3
1990	4.8	13.5	15.8	4.8	4.3	7.3	4.6	3.6	3.3	3.2	2.8
1991	6.1	16.5	19.0	6.1	5.5	9.2	6.1	4.7	4.2	4.0	3.1
1992	6.6	17.2	20.3	6.6	6.0	9.5	6.7	5.2	4.8	4.9	3.7
1993	6.1	16.2	19.0	6.1	5.5	8.8	6.0	4.9	4.5	4.3	3.0
1994	5.3	15.1	17.6	5.3	4.7	8.1	5.2	4.0	3.7	3.9	3.8
1995	4.9	14.5	17.3	4.9	4.3	7.7	4.6	3.9	3.1	3.5	3.8
1996	4.7	14.2	16.4	4.7	4.1	7.8	4.4	3.6	3.1	3.2	3.5
1997	4.2	13.6	15.8	4.2	3.6	6.9	3.9	3.3	2.7	2.7	3.0
1998	3.9	12.6	14.8	3.9	3.3	6.5	3.7	2.9	2.6	2.4	2.9
1999	3.7	12.0	14.5	3.7	3.1	6.3	3.3	2.7	2.4	2.5	2.9
2000	3.5	11.4	13.9	3.5	3.0	5.9	3.2	2.6	2.2	2.4	2.8
2001	4.2	12.7	15.3	4.2	3.7	7.0	4.1	3.2	2.8	2.9	2.8
2002	5.1	14.5	16.7	5.1	4.6	8.1	5.2	4.1	3.7	3.7	3.5
2003	5.2	15.2	17.2	5.2	4.7	8.4	5.3	4.3	3.7	3.8	3.7
2004	4.8	15.0	17.9	4.8	4.3	7.9	4.7	3.9	3.4	3.6	3.3
2005	4.4	14.2	16.4	4.4	3.9	7.2	4.3	3.5	3.1	3.0	3.1
2006	4.0	13.2	15.1	4.0	3.6	6.9	4.0	3.2	2.8	2.8	2.8
2007	4.1	13.9	15.5	4.1	3.6	7.0	4.0	3.2	2.9	2.9	3.2
2008	5.2	16.8	19.9	5.2	4.6	9.0	5.1	4.3	3.7	3.4	4.0
2009	8.5	21.8	23.4	8.5	7.9	13.0	8.8	7.4	6.7	6.4	6.2
2010	8.7	23.2	26.3	8.7	8.1	13.5	8.9	7.4	7.2	6.8	6.4
2011	7.9	21.7	24.7	7.9	7.4	12.8	8.1	6.5	6.4	6.2	6.4
2012	7.2	21.5	24.8	7.2	6.6	11.4	7.3	5.9	5.7	5.5	6.0

Table 1-27. Unemployment Rates of Civilian Workers, by Age, Sex, Race, and Hispanic Origin, 1948–2012—*Continued*

(Percent of labor force.)

Race, Hispanic origin, sex, and year	16 years and over	16 to 19 years			20 years and over						
		Total	16 to 17 years	18 to 19 years	Total	20 to 24 years	25 to 34 years	35 to 44 years	45 to 54 years	55 to 64 years	65 years and over
WHITE											
Men											
1954	4.8	13.4	14.0	13.0	4.4	9.8	4.2	3.6	3.8	4.3	4.2
1955	3.7	11.3	12.2	10.4	3.3	7.0	2.7	2.6	2.9	3.9	3.8
1956	3.4	10.5	11.2	9.7	3.0	6.1	2.8	2.2	2.8	3.1	3.4
1957	3.6	11.5	11.9	11.1	3.2	7.0	2.7	2.5	3.0	3.4	3.2
1958	6.1	15.7	14.9	16.5	5.5	11.7	5.6	4.4	4.8	5.2	5.0
1959	4.6	14.0	15.0	13.0	4.1	7.5	3.8	3.2	3.7	4.2	4.5
1960	4.8	14.0	14.6	13.5	4.2	8.3	4.1	3.3	3.6	4.1	4.0
1961	5.7	15.7	16.5	15.2	5.1	10.1	4.9	4.0	4.4	5.3	5.2
1962	4.6	13.7	15.2	12.7	4.0	8.1	3.8	3.1	3.5	4.1	4.0
1963	4.7	15.9	17.8	14.2	3.9	7.8	3.9	2.9	3.3	4.0	4.1
1964	4.1	14.7	16.1	13.3	3.4	7.4	3.0	2.5	2.9	3.5	3.6
1965	3.6	12.9	14.7	11.3	2.9	5.9	2.6	2.3	2.3	3.1	3.4
1966	2.8	10.5	12.5	8.9	2.2	4.1	2.1	1.7	1.7	2.5	3.0
1967	2.7	10.7	12.7	9.0	2.1	4.2	1.9	1.6	1.8	2.2	2.7
1968	2.6	10.1	12.3	8.3	2.0	4.6	1.7	1.4	1.5	1.7	2.8
1969	2.5	10.0	12.5	7.9	1.9	4.6	1.7	1.4	1.4	1.7	2.2
1970	4.0	13.7	15.7	12.0	3.2	7.8	3.1	2.3	2.3	2.7	3.2
1971	4.9	15.1	17.1	13.5	4.0	9.4	4.0	2.9	2.9	3.2	3.4
1972	4.5	14.2	16.4	12.4	3.6	8.5	3.4	2.5	2.5	3.0	3.3
1973	3.8	12.3	15.2	10.0	3.0	6.6	3.0	1.8	2.0	2.4	2.9
1974	4.4	13.5	16.2	11.5	3.5	7.8	3.6	2.4	2.2	2.5	3.0
1975	7.2	18.3	19.7	17.2	6.2	13.1	6.3	4.5	4.4	4.1	5.0
1976	6.4	17.3	19.7	15.5	5.4	10.9	5.6	3.7	3.7	4.0	4.7
1977	5.5	15.0	17.6	13.0	4.7	9.3	5.0	3.1	3.0	3.3	4.9
1978	4.6	13.5	16.9	10.8	3.7	7.7	3.8	2.5	2.5	2.6	3.9
1979	4.5	13.9	16.1	12.2	3.6	7.5	3.7	2.5	2.5	2.5	3.2
1980	6.1	16.2	18.5	14.5	5.3	11.1	5.9	3.6	3.3	3.1	2.5
1981	6.5	17.9	19.9	16.4	5.6	11.6	6.1	4.0	3.6	3.4	2.4
1982	8.8	21.7	24.2	20.0	7.8	14.3	8.9	6.2	5.3	5.1	3.2
1983	8.8	20.2	22.6	18.7	7.9	13.8	9.0	6.4	5.7	5.6	3.2
1984	6.4	16.8	19.7	15.0	5.7	9.8	6.2	4.6	4.2	4.7	2.6
1985	6.1	16.5	19.2	14.7	5.4	9.7	5.7	4.3	4.1	4.0	2.7
1986	6.0	16.3	18.4	14.7	5.3	9.2	5.8	4.4	4.0	4.0	3.0
1987	5.4	15.5	17.9	13.7	4.8	8.4	5.2	3.9	3.9	3.4	2.5
1988	4.7	13.9	16.1	12.4	4.1	7.4	4.6	3.4	3.2	3.3	2.2
1989	4.5	13.7	16.4	12.0	3.9	7.5	4.1	3.2	2.9	3.1	2.1
1990	4.9	14.3	16.1	13.2	4.3	7.6	4.7	3.5	3.4	3.6	2.8
1991	6.5	17.6	19.7	16.3	5.8	10.2	6.4	5.0	4.4	4.6	3.1
1992	7.0	18.5	21.5	16.5	6.4	10.5	7.0	5.5	5.1	5.5	3.2
1993	6.3	17.7	20.2	16.0	5.7	9.6	6.2	5.0	4.7	4.7	2.9
1994	5.4	16.3	18.5	14.7	4.8	8.8	5.2	3.9	3.7	4.1	3.7
1995	4.9	15.6	18.2	13.8	4.3	7.9	4.5	3.8	3.2	3.4	4.0
1996	4.7	15.5	18.3	13.5	4.1	8.1	4.2	3.5	3.1	3.2	3.2
1997	4.2	14.3	16.3	12.9	3.6	7.3	3.7	3.2	2.8	3.0	2.7
1998	3.9	14.1	17.1	12.1	3.2	6.7	3.5	2.6	2.6	2.6	2.9
1999	3.6	12.6	15.1	10.8	3.0	6.5	3.1	2.4	2.4	2.6	2.9
2000	3.4	12.3	15.3	10.4	2.8	5.9	2.9	2.4	2.2	2.4	3.0
2001	4.2	13.9	17.4	11.7	3.7	7.8	3.8	3.1	2.9	3.2	2.8
2002	5.3	15.9	18.8	14.2	4.7	8.7	5.3	4.1	3.8	4.0	3.4
2003	5.6	17.1	18.5	16.1	5.0	9.1	5.5	4.4	4.0	4.2	3.8
2004	5.0	16.3	19.8	14.2	4.4	8.5	4.8	3.8	3.5	3.7	3.5
2005	4.4	16.1	18.9	14.3	3.8	7.9	4.1	3.3	3.0	3.0	3.1
2006	4.0	14.6	16.5	13.4	3.5	7.3	3.9	3.0	2.7	2.8	2.7
2007	4.2	15.7	17.0	14.8	3.7	7.6	4.1	3.0	2.8	3.0	3.3
2008	5.5	19.1	22.2	17.3	4.9	10.2	5.3	4.3	3.8	3.4	4.1
2009	9.4	25.2	25.9	24.8	8.8	15.3	9.8	8.0	7.7	6.8	6.3
2010	9.6	26.3	29.2	24.8	8.9	15.7	9.9	7.7	7.9	7.5	6.6
2011	8.3	24.5	26.6	23.5	7.7	13.9	8.4	6.6	6.7	6.6	6.4
2012	7.4	24.5	28.3	22.7	6.7	12.5	7.3	5.7	5.7	5.8	5.8

Table 1-27. Unemployment Rates of Civilian Workers, by Age, Sex, Race, and Hispanic Origin, 1948–2012—*Continued*

(Percent of labor force.)

Race, Hispanic origin, sex, and year	16 years and over	16 to 19 years			20 years and over						
		Total	16 to 17 years	18 to 19 years	Total	20 to 24 years	25 to 34 years	35 to 44 years	45 to 54 years	55 to 64 years	65 years and over
WHITE											
Women											
1954	5.5	10.4	12.0	9.4	5.1	6.4	5.7	4.9	4.4	4.5	2.8
1955	4.3	9.1	11.6	7.7	3.9	5.1	4.3	3.8	3.4	3.6	2.2
1956	4.2	9.7	12.1	8.3	3.7	5.1	4.0	3.5	3.3	3.5	2.3
1957	4.3	9.5	11.9	7.8	3.8	5.1	4.7	3.7	3.0	2.9	3.4
1958	6.2	12.7	15.6	11.0	5.6	7.3	6.6	5.6	4.9	4.3	3.5
1959	5.3	12.0	13.3	11.1	4.7	7.0	5.2	4.7	3.9	4.0	2.9
1960	5.3	12.7	14.5	11.5	4.6	7.2	5.7	4.2	4.0	3.3	2.8
1961	6.5	14.8	17.0	13.6	5.7	8.4	6.6	5.6	4.8	4.3	3.8
1962	5.5	12.8	15.6	11.3	4.7	7.7	5.4	4.5	3.7	3.5	4.0
1963	5.8	15.1	18.1	13.2	4.8	7.4	5.8	4.6	3.9	3.5	3.3
1964	5.5	14.9	17.1	13.2	4.6	7.1	5.2	4.5	3.6	3.5	3.4
1965	5.0	14.0	15.0	13.4	4.0	6.3	4.9	4.1	3.0	2.7	2.7
1966	4.3	12.1	14.5	10.7	3.3	5.3	3.7	3.3	2.7	2.2	2.7
1967	4.6	11.5	12.9	10.6	3.8	6.0	4.7	3.7	2.9	2.3	2.6
1968	4.3	12.1	13.9	11.0	3.4	5.9	3.9	3.1	2.3	2.1	2.8
1969	4.2	11.5	13.7	10.0	3.4	5.5	4.2	3.2	2.4	2.1	2.4
1970	5.4	13.4	15.3	11.9	4.4	6.9	5.3	4.3	3.4	2.6	3.3
1971	6.3	15.1	16.7	14.1	5.3	8.5	6.3	4.9	3.9	3.3	3.6
1972	5.9	14.2	17.0	12.3	4.9	8.2	5.5	4.4	3.5	3.3	3.7
1973	5.3	13.0	15.8	10.9	4.3	7.1	5.1	3.7	3.2	2.7	2.8
1974	6.1	14.5	16.4	13.0	5.1	8.2	5.8	4.3	3.6	3.2	3.9
1975	8.6	17.4	19.2	16.1	7.5	11.2	8.4	6.5	5.8	5.0	5.3
1976	7.9	16.4	18.2	15.1	6.8	10.4	7.6	5.8	5.0	4.8	5.3
1977	7.3	15.9	18.2	14.2	6.2	9.3	6.7	5.3	5.0	4.4	4.9
1978	6.2	14.4	17.1	12.4	5.2	8.3	5.8	4.5	3.8	3.0	3.7
1979	5.9	14.0	15.9	12.5	5.0	7.8	5.6	4.2	3.7	3.0	3.1
1980	6.5	14.8	17.3	13.1	5.6	8.5	6.3	4.9	4.3	3.1	3.0
1981	6.9	16.6	18.4	15.3	5.9	9.1	6.6	5.1	4.2	3.7	3.4
1982	8.3	19.0	21.2	17.6	7.3	10.9	8.0	6.4	5.5	5.0	3.1
1983	7.9	18.3	21.4	16.4	6.9	10.3	7.6	6.2	5.5	4.7	3.1
1984	6.5	15.2	17.8	13.6	5.8	8.8	6.1	5.0	4.8	4.0	3.7
1985	6.4	14.8	17.2	13.1	5.7	8.5	6.2	4.9	4.5	4.1	3.1
1986	6.1	14.9	16.7	13.6	5.4	8.1	6.1	4.5	4.3	3.7	2.6
1987	5.2	13.4	15.5	11.7	4.6	7.4	5.0	4.1	3.3	2.9	2.4
1988	4.7	12.3	14.4	10.8	4.1	6.7	4.5	3.7	3.1	2.5	2.6
1989	4.5	11.5	13.8	10.1	4.0	6.8	4.5	3.4	2.9	2.7	2.5
1990	4.7	12.6	15.5	10.9	4.1	6.8	4.6	3.7	3.2	2.7	2.8
1991	5.6	15.2	18.2	13.3	5.0	8.1	5.7	4.3	4.0	3.3	3.1
1992	6.1	15.8	18.9	13.7	5.5	8.3	6.2	4.9	4.3	4.0	4.5
1993	5.7	14.7	17.8	12.6	5.2	7.9	5.8	4.7	4.3	3.9	3.0
1994	5.2	13.8	16.6	11.8	4.6	7.4	5.1	4.2	3.7	3.7	3.9
1995	4.8	13.4	16.4	11.2	4.3	7.4	4.7	3.9	3.0	3.5	3.5
1996	4.7	12.9	14.4	11.7	4.1	7.4	4.6	3.8	3.1	3.1	3.8
1997	4.2	12.8	15.2	11.1	3.7	6.4	4.2	3.4	2.6	2.4	3.4
1998	3.9	10.9	12.4	9.8	3.4	6.3	3.9	3.3	2.5	2.2	3.0
1999	3.8	11.3	13.9	9.6	3.3	6.1	3.6	3.0	2.3	2.5	2.9
2000	3.6	10.4	12.5	9.0	3.1	5.8	3.5	2.9	2.3	2.4	2.4
2001	4.1	11.4	13.1	10.2	3.6	6.1	4.5	3.3	2.7	2.5	2.7
2002	4.9	13.1	14.6	12.1	4.4	7.4	5.0	4.1	3.5	3.3	3.5
2003	4.8	13.3	15.9	11.5	4.4	7.6	4.9	4.2	3.3	3.4	3.5
2004	4.7	13.6	16.1	11.9	4.2	7.1	4.6	3.9	3.3	3.5	3.1
2005	4.4	12.3	14.0	11.1	3.9	6.4	4.7	3.6	3.1	3.0	3.2
2006	4.0	11.7	13.8	10.2	3.6	6.3	4.1	3.4	2.9	2.8	3.0
2007	4.0	12.1	14.1	10.6	3.6	6.2	3.9	3.4	2.9	2.8	3.1
2008	4.9	14.4	17.6	12.3	4.4	7.5	4.8	4.3	3.5	3.5	3.8
2009	7.3	18.4	20.9	17.0	6.8	10.4	7.6	6.7	5.6	5.8	6.0
2010	7.7	20.0	23.4	18.1	7.2	11.0	7.7	7.1	6.4	6.0	6.0
2011	7.5	18.9	22.9	16.7	7.0	11.4	7.7	6.3	6.1	5.8	6.4
2012	7.0	18.4	21.4	16.7	6.5	10.1	7.2	6.3	5.7	5.2	6.3

Table 1-27. Unemployment Rates of Civilian Workers, by Age, Sex, Race, and Hispanic Origin, 1948–2012—*Continued*

(Percent of labor force.)

Race, Hispanic origin, sex, and year	16 years and over	16 to 19 years			20 years and over						
		Total	16 to 17 years	18 to 19 years	Total	20 to 24 years	25 to 34 years	35 to 44 years	45 to 54 years	55 to 64 years	65 years and over
BLACK											
Both Sexes											
1974	10.5	35.0	40.0	31.8	8.0	17.5	8.5	5.4	4.3	3.6	3.9
1975	14.8	39.5	41.6	38.1	12.3	24.5	13.0	8.9	8.3	5.9	6.6
1976	14.0	39.3	44.2	36.7	11.5	22.7	12.8	8.0	6.7	5.9	5.9
1977	14.0	41.1	44.5	39.2	11.5	24.2	12.7	7.4	5.3	5.5	5.9
1978	12.8	38.7	43.9	35.7	10.2	21.8	10.8	6.4	5.2	4.8	5.8
1979	12.3	36.5	40.2	34.4	10.1	20.6	10.8	6.7	5.2	4.9	5.3
1980	14.3	38.5	41.1	37.1	12.1	23.6	13.3	8.2	6.8	5.4	6.9
1981	15.6	41.4	44.8	39.5	13.4	26.4	14.7	9.5	7.4	5.5	7.0
1982	18.9	48.0	48.6	47.8	16.6	30.6	19.0	12.1	8.7	8.3	7.1
1983	19.5	48.5	50.5	47.6	17.3	31.6	19.0	12.4	10.7	9.2	9.2
1984	15.9	42.7	45.7	41.2	13.9	26.1	15.2	9.9	8.2	7.4	6.5
1985	15.1	40.2	43.6	38.3	13.1	24.5	14.5	9.5	8.2	7.0	7.0
1986	14.5	39.3	43.0	37.2	12.7	24.1	14.0	9.6	7.1	6.6	4.5
1987	13.0	34.7	39.7	31.6	11.3	21.8	12.8	8.4	6.8	5.6	3.9
1988	11.7	32.4	35.1	30.7	10.2	19.6	11.9	7.5	5.9	4.8	5.5
1989	11.4	32.4	32.9	32.2	9.9	18.0	11.5	7.6	5.6	5.2	6.9
1990	11.4	30.9	36.5	27.8	10.1	19.9	11.7	7.8	5.3	4.6	5.3
1991	12.5	36.1	39.5	34.4	11.1	21.6	12.7	8.5	7.4	4.4	5.2
1992	14.2	39.7	44.7	37.1	12.6	23.8	14.2	10.5	8.3	6.2	4.9
1993	13.0	38.8	39.7	38.4	11.4	21.9	12.6	9.5	6.9	7.1	4.7
1994	11.5	35.2	36.1	34.6	10.0	19.5	11.1	8.5	5.6	5.4	6.2
1995	10.4	35.7	39.1	33.4	8.7	17.7	9.9	7.3	4.8	4.0	6.7
1996	10.5	33.6	36.3	31.7	9.0	18.8	10.5	7.3	5.0	4.4	5.3
1997	10.0	32.4	35.0	30.8	8.6	18.3	9.9	7.0	5.0	4.2	6.1
1998	8.9	27.6	33.6	24.2	7.7	16.8	8.4	6.5	4.4	3.9	5.6
1999	8.0	27.9	31.0	26.2	6.8	14.6	7.6	5.3	4.0	3.9	5.0
2000	7.6	24.5	26.9	22.9	6.5	15.0	6.7	5.6	4.1	3.0	6.1
2001	8.6	29.0	30.8	27.9	7.4	16.3	8.1	6.3	4.8	3.9	4.3
2002	10.2	29.8	34.9	27.2	9.1	19.1	9.9	7.8	6.3	5.4	5.9
2003	10.8	33.0	32.2	33.5	9.7	19.8	10.9	8.6	6.2	6.3	5.4
2004	10.4	31.7	37.8	28.3	9.4	18.4	10.8	7.8	6.9	5.6	5.5
2005	10.0	33.3	41.2	29.0	8.8	18.3	10.2	7.1	6.0	5.6	6.9
2006	8.9	29.1	32.2	27.3	7.9	16.2	9.3	6.3	5.7	4.6	4.7
2007	8.3	29.4	32.6	27.4	7.2	15.2	8.6	5.4	5.4	4.3	4.5
2008	10.1	31.2	36.3	28.5	9.1	17.9	10.6	7.0	7.0	6.1	7.5
2009	14.8	39.5	43.1	37.8	13.7	24.9	16.7	11.7	10.4	8.4	8.5
2010	16.0	43.0	47.8	40.9	14.9	26.0	17.6	13.0	11.5	9.7	9.2
2011	15.8	41.3	47.1	38.9	14.9	25.2	18.1	13.1	11.2	9.8	8.4
2012	13.8	38.3	44.0	35.9	12.8	23.1	14.8	11.1	9.8	8.8	9.8
BLACK											
Men											
1974	9.8	33.1	39.9	28.3	7.4	16.2	8.1	4.3	4.2	3.6	5.3
1975	14.8	38.1	41.9	35.9	12.5	24.7	12.7	8.7	9.3	6.3	8.7
1976	13.7	37.5	40.8	36.0	11.4	22.6	12.0	7.5	7.3	6.3	8.7
1977	13.3	39.2	41.0	38.2	10.7	23.0	11.8	6.2	4.9	6.0	7.8
1978	11.8	36.7	43.0	32.9	9.3	21.0	9.8	5.1	4.9	4.4	6.6
1979	11.4	34.2	37.9	32.2	9.3	18.7	9.6	6.3	5.2	5.1	6.4
1980	14.5	37.5	39.7	36.2	12.4	23.7	13.4	8.2	7.2	6.2	8.7
1981	15.7	40.7	43.2	39.2	13.5	26.4	14.4	9.3	7.8	6.1	7.5
1982	20.1	48.9	52.7	47.1	17.8	31.5	20.1	13.4	9.0	10.3	9.3
1983	20.3	48.8	52.2	47.3	18.1	31.4	19.4	13.5	11.4	11.0	11.8
1984	16.4	42.7	44.0	42.2	14.3	26.6	15.0	10.4	7.9	8.9	7.9
1985	15.3	41.0	42.9	40.0	13.2	23.5	13.8	9.6	9.7	7.9	8.9
1986	14.8	39.3	41.4	38.2	12.9	23.5	13.5	10.9	7.8	8.0	4.3
1987	12.7	34.4	39.0	31.6	11.1	20.3	12.2	8.7	6.7	6.6	4.3
1988	11.7	32.7	34.4	31.7	10.1	19.4	11.0	7.6	6.2	5.2	5.6
1989	11.5	31.9	34.4	30.3	10.0	17.9	10.5	8.4	6.2	6.2	7.4
1990	11.9	31.9	38.8	28.0	10.4	20.1	11.5	8.4	6.3	5.4	4.6
1991	13.0	36.3	39.0	34.8	11.5	22.4	11.9	9.5	8.6	5.0	6.1
1992	15.2	42.0	47.5	39.1	13.5	24.6	14.2	11.2	10.3	8.1	4.9
1993	13.8	40.1	42.7	38.6	12.1	23.0	12.3	10.5	8.1	9.0	5.8
1994	12.0	37.6	39.3	36.5	10.3	19.4	10.6	9.1	6.5	6.0	8.2
1995	10.6	37.1	39.7	35.4	8.8	17.6	9.3	7.6	5.5	4.4	7.6
1996	11.1	36.9	39.9	34.9	9.4	19.2	10.1	7.8	6.3	5.2	5.0
1997	10.2	36.5	39.5	34.4	8.5	19.8	8.7	6.7	5.6	4.2	5.5
1998	8.9	30.1	33.9	27.9	7.4	18.0	7.3	6.2	4.4	4.5	5.2
1999	8.2	30.9	33.5	29.4	6.7	16.2	6.9	5.2	4.3	3.9	5.0
2000	8.0	26.2	28.5	24.7	6.9	16.6	6.7	5.8	4.8	2.7	6.3
2001	9.3	30.4	30.5	30.4	8.0	17.6	8.3	6.9	5.5	4.8	4.0
2002	10.7	31.3	36.6	28.7	9.5	20.0	9.4	8.0	7.4	6.1	5.0
2003	11.6	36.0	35.6	36.3	10.3	20.9	11.3	9.2	6.7	6.8	5.6
2004	11.1	35.6	40.8	32.7	9.9	20.3	10.9	8.0	7.2	6.4	4.2
2005	10.5	36.3	45.1	31.5	9.2	20.5	9.7	7.0	6.7	5.9	7.1
2006	9.5	32.7	34.8	31.5	8.3	17.2	9.5	5.9	6.3	5.5	5.8
2007	9.1	33.8	40.1	30.2	7.9	16.9	9.1	5.6	5.8	5.2	5.0
2008	11.4	35.9	43.9	32.0	10.2	19.3	11.8	7.7	7.7	7.1	9.5
2009	17.5	46.0	49.3	44.5	16.3	27.7	19.9	14.0	12.4	10.1	10.6
2010	18.4	45.4	49.4	43.9	17.3	29.8	19.3	14.9	14.4	12.2	10.4
2011	17.8	43.1	44.5	42.5	16.7	27.4	19.7	14.9	12.5	12.7	8.2
2012	15.0	41.3	47.2	38.9	14.0	25.6	15.2	12.6	10.2	10.1	11.5

Table 1-27. Unemployment Rates of Civilian Workers, by Age, Sex, Race, and Hispanic Origin, 1948–2012—*Continued*

(Percent of labor force.)

Race, Hispanic origin, sex, and year	16 years and over	16 to 19 years			20 years and over						
		Total	16 to 17 years	18 to 19 years	Total	20 to 24 years	25 to 34 years	35 to 44 years	45 to 54 years	55 to 64 years	65 years and over
BLACK											
Women											
1974	11.3	37.4	40.2	36.0	8.8	19.0	9.0	6.6	4.4	3.6	1.9
1975	14.8	41.0	41.2	40.6	12.2	24.3	13.4	9.0	7.0	5.3	3.6
1976	14.3	41.6	48.4	37.6	11.7	22.8	13.6	8.5	5.9	5.4	2.4
1977	14.9	43.4	49.5	40.4	12.3	25.5	13.6	8.7	5.8	4.8	3.4
1978	13.8	40.8	45.0	38.7	11.2	22.7	11.9	7.8	5.6	5.2	4.7
1979	13.3	39.1	42.7	36.9	10.9	22.6	12.1	7.2	5.2	4.7	3.9
1980	14.0	39.8	42.9	38.2	11.9	23.5	13.2	8.2	6.4	4.5	4.9
1981	15.6	42.2	46.5	39.8	13.4	26.4	14.9	9.8	6.9	4.7	6.0
1982	17.6	47.1	44.2	48.6	15.4	29.6	17.8	10.7	8.5	6.1	4.5
1983	18.6	48.2	48.6	48.0	16.5	31.8	18.6	11.4	9.9	7.3	6.3
1984	15.4	42.6	47.5	40.2	13.5	25.6	15.4	9.4	8.6	5.9	4.9
1985	14.9	39.2	44.3	36.4	13.1	25.6	15.1	9.3	6.8	6.0	5.2
1986	14.2	39.2	44.6	36.1	12.4	24.7	14.6	8.5	6.4	5.0	4.9
1987	13.2	34.9	40.5	31.7	11.6	23.3	13.5	8.1	6.9	4.5	3.4
1988	11.7	32.0	35.9	29.6	10.4	19.8	12.7	7.4	5.6	4.3	5.4
1989	11.4	33.0	31.1	34.0	9.8	18.1	12.5	7.0	5.0	4.2	6.4
1990	10.9	29.9	34.1	27.6	9.7	19.6	11.9	7.2	4.3	3.6	5.9
1991	12.0	36.0	40.1	33.9	10.6	20.7	13.4	7.6	6.2	3.8	4.4
1992	13.2	37.2	41.7	34.8	11.8	23.1	14.1	9.8	6.4	4.2	5.0
1993	12.1	37.4	36.1	38.1	10.7	20.9	12.9	8.6	5.8	5.1	3.6
1994	11.0	32.6	32.9	32.5	9.8	19.6	11.7	8.0	4.9	4.9	4.4
1995	10.2	34.3	38.5	31.5	8.6	17.8	10.5	7.0	4.2	3.6	. . .
1996	10.0	30.3	32.8	28.6	8.7	18.4	11.0	6.9	3.8	3.8	5.6
1997	9.9	28.7	30.3	27.8	8.8	17.1	10.9	7.2	4.4	4.1	6.6
1998	9.0	25.3	33.2	20.9	7.9	15.7	9.5	6.7	4.3	3.4	6.1
1999	7.8	25.1	28.5	23.3	6.8	13.4	8.3	5.5	3.8	3.9	5.0
2000	7.1	22.8	25.3	21.3	6.2	13.6	6.8	5.5	3.4	3.3	6.0
2001	8.1	27.5	31.2	25.4	7.0	15.3	8.0	5.8	4.3	3.1	4.6
2002	9.8	28.3	33.2	25.6	8.8	18.3	10.2	7.7	5.3	4.7	6.9
2003	10.2	30.3	29.1	31.1	9.2	18.8	10.5	8.1	5.8	5.9	5.3
2004	9.8	28.2	35.2	24.3	8.9	16.6	10.7	7.6	6.5	4.8	6.8
2005	9.5	30.3	37.3	26.6	8.5	16.3	10.6	7.2	5.4	5.3	6.6
2006	8.4	25.9	29.9	23.6	7.5	15.2	9.0	6.7	5.1	3.9	3.7
2007	7.5	25.3	26.4	24.7	6.7	13.6	8.1	5.3	5.0	3.7	4.0
2008	8.9	26.8	29.9	25.0	8.1	16.6	9.5	6.4	6.3	5.3	5.8
2009	12.4	33.4	37.2	31.7	11.5	22.2	13.8	9.7	8.7	7.1	6.6
2010	13.8	40.5	46.4	37.7	12.8	22.6	16.0	11.4	9.1	7.6	8.2
2011	14.1	39.4	49.5	34.8	13.2	23.1	16.5	11.6	10.0	7.4	8.5
2012	12.8	35.6	41.3	33.1	11.9	20.8	14.4	9.8	9.4	7.7	8.2
HISPANIC											
Both Sexes											
1975	12.2	27.7	30.0	26.5	10.3	16.7	9.9	8.6	8.1	7.7	9.9
1976	11.5	23.8	29.2	19.2	10.1	15.9	9.1	8.2	8.4	8.8	12.6
1977	10.1	22.9	27.0	19.6	8.5	12.0	8.6	6.1	7.3	8.2	9.2
1978	9.1	20.7	28.3	15.1	7.7	10.9	8.0	6.5	5.8	5.0	7.5
1979	8.3	19.2	26.0	14.9	7.0	10.4	6.7	6.2	5.2	6.0	5.7
1980	10.1	22.5	27.6	19.5	8.6	12.1	9.1	7.7	5.7	5.9	6.0
1981	10.4	23.9	28.0	21.7	9.1	13.9	8.8	7.4	6.4	7.3	5.4
1982	13.8	29.9	38.1	25.9	12.3	17.7	12.3	10.7	8.4	10.1	6.5
1983	13.7	28.4	33.8	25.8	12.3	16.7	11.9	11.3	10.0	10.9	5.8
1984	10.7	24.1	28.9	21.6	9.5	12.4	9.7	8.2	7.5	9.7	6.1
1985	10.5	24.3	27.8	22.5	9.4	12.6	9.9	7.7	7.4	7.8	8.1
1986	10.6	24.7	28.1	22.9	9.5	12.9	9.6	8.4	7.8	7.3	10.1
1987	8.8	22.3	27.7	19.5	7.8	10.6	7.7	6.7	6.9	6.0	6.5
1988	8.2	22.0	27.1	19.3	7.0	9.8	7.1	6.0	6.0	5.8	5.6
1989	8.0	19.4	26.4	16.0	7.2	10.7	7.0	5.9	6.3	5.8	5.3
1990	8.2	19.5	24.5	16.9	7.2	9.1	7.3	6.6	6.4	5.6	6.0
1991	10.0	22.9	31.9	18.7	9.0	11.6	9.2	8.1	8.0	6.5	7.0
1992	11.6	27.5	35.7	23.4	10.4	13.2	10.4	9.8	8.8	8.6	8.1
1993	10.8	26.1	35.1	21.8	9.7	13.1	9.3	9.1	8.6	8.0	6.6
1994	9.9	24.5	31.7	20.6	8.9	11.8	9.0	7.7	8.1	7.3	7.9
1995	9.3	24.1	33.1	19.5	8.2	11.5	8.2	7.2	6.4	7.5	10.6
1996	8.9	23.6	30.0	20.3	7.8	11.8	7.3	7.3	6.0	7.3	8.2
1997	7.7	21.6	27.7	18.4	6.8	10.3	6.3	6.4	5.1	6.5	6.8
1998	7.2	21.3	28.0	18.1	6.1	9.4	5.9	5.5	4.6	5.3	6.4
1999	6.4	18.6	23.7	16.3	5.5	8.3	5.4	4.8	4.8	4.5	5.0
2000	5.7	16.6	22.5	13.9	4.9	7.5	4.8	4.5	3.3	4.5	5.7
2001	6.6	17.7	24.0	15.0	5.8	8.1	5.9	5.2	4.3	5.6	4.5
2002	7.5	20.1	24.2	18.2	6.7	9.9	6.6	6.0	5.5	5.7	6.8
2003	7.7	20.0	24.6	17.7	7.0	10.2	7.0	6.0	6.3	5.7	3.9
2004	7.0	20.4	29.0	16.8	6.2	9.3	6.3	5.3	5.2	5.8	6.0
2005	6.0	18.4	23.6	16.0	5.3	8.6	5.3	4.5	4.4	4.4	4.9
2006	5.2	15.9	20.4	13.6	4.6	7.2	4.7	4.3	3.7	3.3	3.9
2007	5.6	18.1	22.5	16.0	5.0	7.8	4.9	4.3	4.3	4.5	4.9
2008	7.6	22.4	29.8	19.0	6.8	11.5	6.7	5.8	6.3	4.8	7.8
2009	12.1	30.2	36.3	27.8	11.2	16.2	11.4	10.2	10.1	10.0	8.0
2010	12.5	32.2	37.6	30.2	11.6	17.4	11.3	10.3	10.8	10.3	9.5
2011	11.5	31.1	38.3	28.5	10.6	15.7	10.4	9.2	9.9	9.7	8.8
2012	10.3	28.6	35.2	26.1	9.4	13.8	9.2	8.3	8.3	9.2	8.7

. . . = Not available.

Table 1-27. Unemployment Rates of Civilian Workers, by Age, Sex, Race, and Hispanic Origin, 1948–2012—*Continued*

(Percent of labor force.)

Race, Hispanic origin, sex, and year	16 years and over	16 to 19 years			20 years and over						
		Total	16 to 17 years	18 to 19 years	Total	20 to 24 years	25 to 34 years	35 to 44 years	45 to 54 years	55 to 64 years	65 years and over
HISPANIC											
Men											
1975	11.4	27.6	29.3	26.5	9.6	16.3	9.6	7.9	7.0	6.8	. . .
1976	10.8	23.3	28.7	19.7	9.4	16.0	8.1	7.0	7.4	8.7	. . .
1977	9.0	20.9	25.9	18.2	7.7	11.7	7.9	4.9	5.4	7.4	. . .
1978	7.7	19.7	27.5	13.9	6.4	9.4	6.6	4.8	4.8	4.4	. . .
1979	7.0	17.5	23.5	13.8	5.8	9.2	5.3	5.1	4.4	5.0	. . .
1980	9.7	21.9	26.2	19.3	8.3	12.2	8.3	7.1	6.0	5.9	. . .
1981	10.2	24.3	30.9	20.3	8.8	14.1	8.9	6.5	5.9	6.7	. . .
1982	13.6	31.3	40.2	26.8	12.1	18.2	12.4	9.9	7.5	10.0	. . .
1983	13.6	28.7	34.7	25.9	12.2	17.0	11.6	10.8	10.3	11.7	. . .
1984	10.5	25.2	31.5	22.2	9.3	12.5	9.2	7.6	7.2	10.2	. . .
1985	10.2	24.7	29.1	22.4	9.1	12.9	9.6	7.2	6.8	7.0	. . .
1986	10.5	24.5	28.5	22.4	9.5	13.0	9.5	8.5	7.0	8.0	. . .
1987	8.7	22.2	28.2	19.3	7.8	10.2	7.6	6.9	7.1	6.7	. . .
1988	8.1	22.7	29.5	19.5	7.0	9.2	7.0	5.9	6.1	6.7	. . .
1989	7.6	20.2	27.6	16.8	6.6	9.7	5.9	5.7	6.0	6.6	. . .
1990	8.0	19.5	24.0	17.4	7.0	8.4	6.9	6.5	6.8	6.5	. . .
1991	10.3	23.5	33.6	19.2	9.3	11.6	9.3	8.5	7.9	8.1	. . .
1992	11.7	28.2	36.6	24.0	10.5	13.7	10.1	9.8	8.9	10.2	. . .
1993	10.6	25.9	34.5	21.9	9.5	12.6	9.0	8.8	8.8	8.5	. . .
1994	9.4	26.3	33.3	22.5	8.3	10.8	8.4	6.6	8.1	7.4	10.5
1995	8.8	25.3	34.8	20.2	7.7	10.6	7.5	6.7	5.9	7.9	12.9
1996	7.9	22.5	31.5	18.4	6.9	10.3	6.6	6.3	5.1	6.7	8.3
1997	7.0	20.8	26.5	17.9	6.1	9.8	5.1	5.4	4.8	6.8	7.2
1998	6.4	20.6	29.0	16.4	5.4	8.9	5.2	4.5	4.2	5.3	5.0
1999	5.6	17.8	23.4	15.3	4.7	7.8	4.1	3.8	4.5	4.6	5.0
2000	5.0	15.7	22.3	12.8	4.2	6.6	3.7	3.8	3.1	4.1	6.2
2001	5.9	17.1	25.8	13.4	5.2	8.1	4.6	4.5	3.8	6.3	4.8
2002	7.2	20.2	22.9	19.1	6.4	9.3	6.1	5.4	5.5	6.2	6.3
2003	7.2	21.9	25.9	20.1	6.4	9.6	6.3	5.3	6.0	6.0	3.6
2004	6.5	21.2	30.7	17.6	5.8	9.4	5.5	4.5	4.7	5.7	6.9
2005	5.4	19.3	23.4	17.5	4.7	8.2	4.3	3.9	4.0	4.0	4.8
2006	4.8	17.3	22.6	14.8	4.2	6.7	4.2	3.6	3.4	3.5	3.7
2007	5.3	19.7	23.4	18.0	4.6	7.4	4.5	3.8	4.4	3.9	5.5
2008	7.6	23.4	30.9	19.9	6.8	11.8	6.6	5.6	6.2	5.1	7.8
2009	12.5	33.8	41.1	31.1	11.6	16.6	11.6	10.5	10.5	11.2	7.8
2010	12.7	34.6	41.0	32.6	11.7	18.2	11.6	9.8	11.2	10.6	9.4
2011	11.2	33.3	40.7	31.0	10.3	15.3	9.9	8.7	9.8	10.4	9.5
2012	9.9	30.5	40.6	26.9	8.9	13.8	8.4	7.2	8.2	9.8	8.6
HISPANIC											
Women											
1975	13.5	27.9	31.0	26.4	11.5	17.2	10.5	9.9	10.0	9.3	. . .
1976	12.7	22.2	30.3	18.7	11.4	15.8	10.8	10.0	9.8	9.0	. . .
1977	11.9	24.4	28.5	21.9	10.1	12.1	9.8	8.2	10.6	11.0	. . .
1978	11.3	21.8	29.9	16.6	9.8	13.0	10.3	9.2	7.4	7.2	. . .
1979	10.3	21.2	30.0	15.8	8.9	12.1	8.9	7.7	7.1	7.9	. . .
1980	10.7	23.4	29.7	19.8	9.2	12.0	10.6	8.6	5.3	5.8	. . .
1981	10.8	23.4	23.5	23.4	9.5	13.5	8.7	8.9	7.2	8.4	. . .
1982	14.1	28.2	35.1	25.0	12.5	16.8	12.2	11.9	9.9	10.4	. . .
1983	13.8	28.0	32.5	25.7	12.4	16.2	12.5	12.2	9.7	9.6	. . .
1984	11.1	22.8	26.1	21.0	9.9	12.2	10.3	9.1	7.9	8.8	. . .
1985	11.0	23.8	26.2	22.6	9.9	12.1	10.6	8.5	8.1	9.2	. . .
1986	10.8	25.1	27.6	23.6	9.6	12.9	9.8	8.2	8.9	6.2	. . .
1987	8.9	22.4	27.1	19.9	7.7	11.4	7.8	6.5	6.7	5.0	. . .
1988	8.3	21.0	24.5	18.9	7.1	10.7	7.2	6.2	5.9	4.6	. . .
1989	8.8	18.2	24.7	14.9	8.0	12.2	8.6	6.3	6.7	4.5	. . .
1990	8.4	19.4	25.4	16.2	7.5	10.4	8.0	6.7	6.0	4.3	. . .
1991	9.6	21.9	29.6	17.9	8.6	11.7	9.1	7.6	8.1	4.1	. . .
1992	11.4	26.4	34.5	22.4	10.2	12.4	11.0	9.7	8.5	6.2	. . .
1993	11.0	26.3	36.0	21.7	9.9	14.0	9.9	9.5	8.3	7.2	. . .
1994	10.7	22.2	29.7	18.1	9.8	13.5	10.1	9.2	8.0	7.1	3.6
1995	10.0	22.6	30.7	18.7	8.9	13.0	9.5	7.9	7.0	6.8	6.4
1996	10.2	25.1	28.2	23.3	9.2	14.1	8.5	8.7	7.2	8.1	8.0
1997	8.9	22.7	29.2	19.1	7.9	11.0	8.2	7.7	5.5	6.1	6.0
1998	8.2	22.1	26.4	20.2	7.1	10.1	7.2	6.9	5.1	5.4	8.8
1999	7.6	19.8	24.0	17.7	6.6	9.1	7.3	6.3	5.1	4.3	4.8
2000	6.8	18.0	22.7	15.6	5.9	9.0	6.4	5.4	3.6	5.0	4.8
2001	7.5	18.5	21.6	17.1	6.6	8.2	7.8	6.2	4.8	4.8	4.0
2002	8.0	19.9	25.8	17.0	7.2	10.8	7.4	6.7	5.5	5.0	7.5
2003	8.4	17.7	23.2	14.4	7.8	11.3	8.2	7.1	6.8	5.3	4.4
2004	7.6	19.3	27.0	15.5	7.0	9.1	7.6	6.4	5.8	5.8	4.6
2005	6.9	17.2	23.8	14.0	6.3	9.2	7.1	5.5	4.8	5.0	5.1
2006	5.9	14.1	18.1	11.9	5.3	8.1	5.5	5.5	4.2	3.1	4.2
2007	6.1	16.1	21.3	13.6	5.5	8.5	5.6	5.1	4.3	5.2	4.0
2008	7.7	21.1	28.1	18.0	6.9	11.1	6.8	6.0	6.4	4.4	7.7
2009	11.5	25.8	30.8	23.8	10.6	15.7	10.9	9.7	9.6	8.5	8.3
2010	12.3	29.1	34.2	27.0	11.4	16.2	10.9	11.1	10.4	9.9	9.6
2011	11.8	28.1	35.7	25.0	11.1	16.3	11.4	9.9	10.1	8.8	8.0
2012	10.9	26.4	29.4	25.1	10.1	13.9	10.4	9.7	8.5	8.5	8.8

. . . = Not available.

Table 1-28. Unemployed Persons and Unemployment Rates, by Selected Occupation, 2000–2012

(Thousands of people, percent of civilian labor force.)

Occupation	2000	2001	2002	2003	2004	2005	2006	2007	2008	2009	2010	2011	2012
Total Unemployed Persons, 16 Years and Over[1]	5 692	6 801	8 378	8 774	8 149	7 591	7 001	7 078	8 924	14 265	14 825	13 747	12 506
Management, professional, and related	827	1 102	1 482	1 556	1 346	1 172	1 065	1 090	1 463	2 531	2 566	2 458	2 318
Management, business, and financial operations	320	455	622	627	544	464	427	429	619	1 105	1 117	1 067	935
Professional and related	507	647	859	929	801	708	638	662	844	1 427	1 449	1 392	1 383
Services	1 132	1 311	1 544	1 681	1 617	1 587	1 485	1 521	1 769	2 605	2 819	2 727	2 540
Sales and office	1 446	1 652	2 110	2 070	1 937	1 820	1 667	1 638	2 006	3 143	3 315	3 135	2 775
Sales and related	673	779	998	995	912	874	812	835	980	1 501	1 596	1 481	1 318
Office and administrative support	773	873	1 112	1 076	1 025	946	856	804	1 026	1 642	1 719	1 653	1 457
Natural resources, construction, and maintenance ...	758	943	1 155	1 244	1 140	1 069	1 007	1 052	1 421	2 464	2 504	2 000	1 668
Farming, fishing, and forestry	133	163	142	136	132	103	101	89	112	179	193	181	167
Construction and extraction	507	626	788	814	786	751	699	781	1 067	1 825	1 809	1 414	1 181
Installation, maintenance, and repair	119	154	225	295	222	214	207	182	243	459	503	406	320
Production, transportation, and material moving	1 081	1 318	1 530	1 555	1 393	1 245	1 127	1 128	1 474	2 453	2 365	2 099	1 845
Production	575	759	848	807	714	677	544	564	746	1 322	1 206	1 025	865
Transportation and material moving	505	559	682	748	679	568	583	564	727	1 131	1 159	1 073	980
Total Unemployment Rate, 16 Years and Over[1] ...	4.0	4.7	5.8	6.0	5.5	5.1	4.6	4.6	5.8	9.3	9.6	8.9	8.1
Management, professional, and related	1.8	2.3	3.0	3.1	2.7	2.3	2.1	2.1	2.7	4.6	4.7	4.5	4.1
Management, business, and financial operations	1.6	2.2	3.0	3.1	2.6	2.2	2.0	1.9	2.7	4.9	5.1	4.7	4.0
Professional and related	1.9	2.3	3.0	3.2	2.8	2.4	2.1	2.1	2.7	4.4	4.5	4.3	4.2
Services	5.2	5.8	6.6	7.1	6.6	6.4	5.9	5.9	6.7	9.6	10.3	9.9	9.1
Sales and office	3.8	4.4	5.6	5.5	5.2	4.8	4.4	4.3	5.3	8.5	9.0	8.7	7.7
Sales and related	4.1	4.7	5.9	5.9	5.4	5.0	4.7	4.8	5.7	8.8	9.4	8.8	7.9
Office and administrative support	3.6	4.2	5.4	5.2	5.0	4.6	4.2	4.0	5.1	8.3	8.7	8.5	7.6
Natural resources, construction, and maintenance ...	5.3	6.4	7.8	8.1	7.3	6.5	6.0	6.3	8.8	15.6	16.1	13.3	11.5
Farming, fishing, and forestry	10.2	13.4	12.0	11.4	11.8	9.6	9.5	8.5	10.2	16.2	16.3	15.3	14.4
Construction and extraction	6.2	7.3	9.1	9.1	8.4	7.6	6.8	7.6	11.0	19.7	20.1	16.6	14.4
Installation, maintenance, and repair	2.4	3.2	4.6	5.5	4.2	3.9	3.7	3.4	4.5	8.5	9.3	7.7	6.2
Production, transportation, and material moving	5.1	6.4	7.6	7.9	7.2	6.5	5.8	5.8	7.6	13.3	12.8	11.3	9.8
Production	4.8	6.6	7.8	7.7	7.0	6.7	5.5	5.7	7.7	14.7	13.1	11.2	9.3
Transportation and material moving	5.6	6.2	7.4	8.2	7.4	6.2	6.2	6.0	7.6	12.0	12.4	11.4	10.3

[1]Includes persons with no work experience and persons whose last job was in the armed forces.

Table 1-29. Unemployed Persons and Unemployment Rates, by Class of Worker and Industry, 2000–2012

(Thousands of people, percent.)

Class of worker and industry	2000	2001	2002	2003	2004	2005	2006	2007	2008	2009	2010	2011	2012
Total Unemployed Persons, 16 Years and Over	5 692	6 801	8 378	8 774	8 149	7 591	7 001	7 078	8 924	14 265	14 825	13 747	12 506
Nonagricultural private wage and salary workers	4 483	5 540	6 926	7 131	6 484	5 989	5 523	5 559	7 118	11 654	11 808	10 655	9 531
Mining, quarrying, and oil and gas extraction	21	23	33	37	21	20	22	25	25	90	73	52	59
Construction	513	609	800	810	769	712	671	757	1 030	1 770	1 801	1 383	1 129
Manufacturing	691	992	1 205	1 166	966	812	699	706	945	1 890	1 622	1 373	1 122
Durable goods	400	630	789	762	590	485	410	436	597	1 279	1 074	887	693
Nondurable goods	290	362	416	404	375	326	289	270	348	611	548	485	430
Wholesale trade and retail trade	837	945	1 202	1 237	1 197	1 137	1 039	975	1 205	1 844	1 963	1 834	1 663
Transportation and utilities	193	236	274	283	236	232	229	233	312	525	492	484	410
Information	124	190	253	246	189	163	126	120	167	294	303	222	218
Financial activities	208	252	320	319	332	272	264	289	380	598	626	582	466
Professional and business services	573	768	1 009	1 042	861	792	746	740	921	1 522	1 561	1 430	1 358
Education and health services	383	463	570	640	617	627	568	575	698	1 100	1 243	1 217	1 232
Leisure and hospitality	720	833	961	1 006	972	921	865	896	1 102	1 543	1 592	1 527	1 403
Other services	219	229	301	347	324	301	293	241	332	477	533	551	470
Agriculture and related private wage and salary workers	134	153	139	140	129	104	95	78	123	200	211	190	188
Government workers	422	430	512	568	548	534	473	505	534	799	969	1 013	923
Self-employed and unpaid family workers	219	218	265	294	303	298	293	309	383	577	617	605	547
Total Unemployment Rate, 16 Years and Over[1]	4.0	4.7	5.8	6.0	5.5	5.1	4.6	4.6	5.8	9.3	9.6	8.9	8.1
Nonagricultural private wage and salary workers	4.1	5.0	6.2	6.3	5.7	5.2	4.7	4.7	5.9	9.8	9.9	9.0	7.9
Mining	4.4	4.2	6.3	6.7	3.9	3.1	3.2	3.4	3.1	11.6	9.4	6.1	6.0
Construction	6.2	7.1	9.2	9.3	8.4	7.4	6.7	7.4	10.6	19.0	20.6	16.4	13.9
Manufacturing	3.5	5.2	6.7	6.6	5.7	4.9	4.2	4.3	5.8	12.1	10.6	9.0	7.3
Durable goods	3.2	5.2	6.9	6.9	5.5	4.6	3.9	4.2	5.6	12.9	11.2	9.2	7.2
Nondurable goods	4.0	5.2	6.2	6.1	5.9	5.3	4.8	4.5	6.0	10.6	9.6	8.5	7.5
Wholesale trade and retail trade	4.3	4.9	6.1	6.0	5.8	5.4	4.9	4.7	5.9	9.0	9.5	8.9	8.1
Transportation and utilities	3.4	4.3	4.9	5.3	4.4	4.1	4.0	3.9	5.1	8.9	8.4	8.2	6.9
Information	3.2	4.9	6.9	6.8	5.7	5.0	3.7	3.6	5.0	9.2	9.7	7.3	7.6
Financial activities	2.4	2.9	3.5	3.5	3.6	2.9	2.7	3.0	3.9	6.4	6.9	6.4	5.1
Professional and business services	4.8	6.1	7.9	8.2	6.8	6.2	5.6	5.3	6.5	10.8	10.8	9.7	8.9
Education and health services	2.5	2.8	3.4	3.6	3.4	3.4	3.0	3.0	3.5	5.3	5.8	5.6	5.5
Leisure and hospitality	6.6	7.5	8.4	8.7	8.3	7.8	7.3	7.4	8.6	11.7	12.2	11.6	10.4
Other services	3.9	4.0	5.1	5.7	5.3	4.8	4.7	3.9	5.3	7.5	8.5	8.8	7.2
Agriculture and related private wage and salary workers	9.0	11.2	10.1	10.2	9.9	8.3	7.2	6.3	9.2	14.3	13.9	12.5	12.4
Government workers	2.1	2.2	2.5	2.8	2.7	2.6	2.3	2.3	2.4	3.6	4.4	4.7	4.3
Self-employed and unpaid family workers	2.1	2.1	2.6	2.7	2.8	2.7	2.7	2.8	3.6	5.5	5.9	6.0	5.4

Note: See notes and definitions for information on historical comparability.

[1] Includes persons with no work experience and persons whose last job was in the armed forces.

Table 1-30. Unemployed Persons, by Duration of Unemployment, 1948–2012

(Thousands of people, number of weeks.)

Year	Total unemployed	Duration of unemployment										Average duration, in weeks	Median duration, in weeks
		Less than 5 weeks		5 to 14 weeks		15 weeks and over		15 to 26 weeks		27 weeks and over			
		Number	Percent	Number	Percent	Number	Percent	Number	Percent	Number	Percent		
1948	2 276	1 300	57.1	669	29.4	309	13.6	193	8.5	116	5.1	8.6	...
1949	3 637	1 756	48.3	1 194	32.8	684	18.8	428	11.8	256	7.0	10.0	...
1950	3 288	1 450	44.1	1 055	32.1	782	23.8	425	12.9	357	10.9	12.1	...
1951	2 055	1 177	57.3	574	27.9	303	14.7	166	8.1	137	6.7	9.7	...
1952	1 883	1 135	60.3	516	27.4	232	12.3	148	7.9	84	4.5	8.4	...
1953	1 834	1 142	62.3	482	26.3	210	11.5	132	7.2	78	4.3	8.0	...
1954	3 532	1 605	45.4	1 116	31.6	812	23.0	495	14.0	317	9.0	11.8	...
1955	2 852	1 335	46.8	815	28.6	702	24.6	366	12.8	336	11.8	13.0	...
1956	2 750	1 412	51.3	805	29.3	533	19.4	301	10.9	232	8.4	11.3	...
1957	2 859	1 408	49.2	891	31.2	560	19.6	321	11.2	239	8.4	10.5	...
1958	4 602	1 753	38.1	1 396	30.3	1 452	31.6	785	17.1	667	14.5	13.9	...
1959	3 740	1 585	42.4	1 114	29.8	1 040	27.8	469	12.5	571	15.3	14.4	...
1960	3 852	1 719	44.6	1 176	30.5	957	24.8	503	13.1	454	11.8	12.8	...
1961	4 714	1 806	38.3	1 376	29.2	1 532	32.5	728	15.4	804	17.1	15.6	...
1962	3 911	1 663	42.5	1 134	29.0	1 119	28.6	534	13.7	585	15.0	14.7	...
1963	4 070	1 751	43.0	1 231	30.2	1 088	26.7	535	13.1	553	13.6	14.0	...
1964	3 786	1 697	44.8	1 117	29.5	973	25.7	491	13.0	482	12.7	13.3	...
1965	3 366	1 628	48.4	983	29.2	755	22.4	404	12.0	351	10.4	11.8	...
1966	2 875	1 573	54.7	779	27.1	526	18.3	287	10.0	239	8.3	10.4	...
1967	2 975	1 634	54.9	893	30.0	448	15.1	271	9.1	177	5.9	8.7	2.3
1968	2 817	1 594	56.6	810	28.8	412	14.6	256	9.1	156	5.5	8.4	4.5
1969	2 832	1 629	57.5	827	29.2	375	13.2	242	8.5	133	4.7	7.8	4.4
1970	4 093	2 139	52.3	1 290	31.5	663	16.2	428	10.4	235	5.8	8.6	4.9
1971	5 016	2 245	44.8	1 585	31.6	1 187	23.7	668	13.3	519	10.4	11.3	6.3
1972	4 882	2 242	45.9	1 472	30.2	1 167	23.9	601	12.3	566	11.6	12.0	6.2
1973	4 365	2 224	51.0	1 314	30.1	826	18.9	483	11.1	343	7.9	10.0	5.2
1974	5 156	2 604	50.5	1 597	31.0	955	18.5	574	11.1	381	7.4	9.8	5.2
1975	7 929	2 940	37.1	2 484	31.3	2 505	31.6	1 303	16.4	1 203	15.2	14.2	8.4
1976	7 406	2 844	38.4	2 196	29.6	2 366	32.0	1 018	13.8	1 348	18.2	15.8	8.2
1977	6 991	2 919	41.8	2 132	30.5	1 942	27.8	913	13.1	1 028	14.7	14.3	7.0
1978	6 202	2 865	46.2	1 923	31.0	1 414	22.8	766	12.3	648	10.5	11.9	5.9
1979	6 137	2 950	48.1	1 946	31.7	1 241	20.2	706	11.5	535	8.7	10.8	5.4
1980	7 637	3 295	43.2	2 470	32.3	1 871	24.5	1 052	13.8	820	10.7	11.9	6.5
1981	8 273	3 449	41.7	2 539	30.7	2 285	27.6	1 122	13.6	1 162	14.0	13.7	6.9
1982	10 678	3 883	36.4	3 311	31.0	3 485	32.6	1 708	16.0	1 776	16.6	15.6	8.7
1983	10 717	3 570	33.3	2 937	27.4	4 210	39.3	1 652	15.4	2 559	23.9	20.0	10.1
1984	8 539	3 350	39.2	2 451	28.7	2 737	32.1	1 104	12.9	1 634	19.1	18.2	7.9
1985	8 312	3 498	42.1	2 509	30.2	2 305	27.7	1 025	12.3	1 280	15.4	15.6	6.8
1986	8 237	3 448	41.9	2 557	31.0	2 232	27.1	1 045	12.7	1 187	14.4	15.0	6.9
1987	7 425	3 246	43.7	2 196	29.6	1 983	26.7	943	12.7	1 040	14.0	14.5	6.5
1988	6 701	3 084	46.0	2 007	30.0	1 610	24.0	801	12.0	809	12.1	13.5	5.9
1989	6 528	3 174	48.6	1 978	30.3	1 375	21.1	730	11.2	646	9.9	11.9	4.8
1990	7 047	3 265	46.3	2 257	32.0	1 525	21.6	822	11.7	703	10.0	12.0	5.3
1991	8 628	3 480	40.3	2 791	32.4	2 357	27.3	1 246	14.4	1 111	12.9	13.7	6.8
1992	9 613	3 376	35.1	2 830	29.4	3 408	35.4	1 453	15.1	1 954	20.3	17.7	8.7
1993	8 940	3 262	36.5	2 584	28.9	3 094	34.6	1 297	14.5	1 798	20.1	18.0	8.3
1994	7 996	2 728	34.1	2 408	30.1	2 860	35.8	1 237	15.5	1 623	20.3	18.8	9.2
1995	7 404	2 700	36.5	2 342	31.6	2 363	31.9	1 085	14.6	1 278	17.3	16.6	8.3
1996	7 236	2 633	36.4	2 287	31.6	2 316	32.0	1 053	14.6	1 262	17.4	16.7	8.3
1997	6 739	2 538	37.7	2 138	31.7	2 062	30.6	995	14.8	1 067	15.8	15.8	8.0
1998	6 210	2 622	42.2	1 950	31.4	1 637	26.4	763	12.3	875	14.1	14.5	6.7
1999	5 880	2 568	43.7	1 832	31.2	1 480	25.2	755	12.8	725	12.3	13.4	6.4
2000	5 692	2 558	44.9	1 815	31.9	1 318	23.2	669	11.8	649	11.4	12.6	5.9
2001	6 801	2 853	42.0	2 196	32.3	1 752	25.8	951	14.0	801	11.8	13.1	6.8
2002	8 378	2 893	34.5	2 580	30.8	2 904	34.7	1 369	16.3	1 535	18.3	16.6	9.1
2003	8 774	2 785	31.7	2 612	29.8	3 378	38.5	1 442	16.4	1 936	22.1	19.2	10.1
2004	8 149	2 696	33.1	2 382	29.2	3 072	37.7	1 293	15.9	1 779	21.8	19.6	9.8
2005	7 591	2 667	35.1	2 304	30.4	2 619	34.5	1 130	14.9	1 490	19.6	18.4	8.9
2006	7 001	2 614	37.3	2 121	30.3	2 266	32.4	1 031	14.7	1 235	17.6	16.8	8.3
2007	7 078	2 542	35.9	2 232	31.5	2 303	32.5	1 061	15.0	1 243	17.6	16.8	8.5
2008	8 924	2 932	32.8	2 804	31.4	3 188	35.7	1 427	16.0	1 761	19.7	17.9	9.4
2009	14 265	3 165	22.2	3 828	26.8	7 272	51.0	2 775	19.5	4 496	31.5	24.4	15.1
2010	14 825	2 771	18.7	3 267	22.0	8 786	59.3	2 371	16.0	6 415	43.3	33.0	21.4
2011	13 747	2 677	19.5	2 993	21.8	8 077	58.8	2 061	15.0	6 016	43.8	39.3	21.4
2012	12 506	2 644	21.1	2 866	22.9	6 996	55.9	1 859	14.9	5 136	41.1	39.4	19.3

. . . = Not available.

Table 1-31. Long-Term Unemployment, by Industry and Selected Occupation, 2000–2012

(Thousands of people.)

Length of unemployment, industry, and occupation	2000	2001	2002	2003	2004	2005	2006	2007	2008	2009	2010	2011	2012
UNEMPLOYED 15 WEEKS AND OVER													
Total	1 318	1 752	2 904	3 378	3 072	2 619	2 266	2 303	3 188	7 272	8 786	8 077	6 996
Wage and Salary Workers, by Industry													
Agriculture and related	32	44	39	44	38	29	30	28	42	96	100	99	92
Mining [1]	7	7	11	17	8	8	5	6	7	44	46	31	25
Construction	107	130	236	262	248	216	177	215	339	907	1 083	822	643
Manufacturing	184	303	528	575	467	326	257	259	385	1 059	1 122	922	702
Durable goods	99	183	348	389	293	199	140	162	246	702	773	611	443
Nondurable goods	86	120	180	186	174	127	116	97	139	357	350	311	259
Wholesale and retail trade	186	241	423	472	455	415	337	334	440	962	1 215	1 118	971
Transportation and utilities	57	71	124	132	114	91	87	95	142	290	343	343	262
Information	33	52	119	128	87	76	55	49	66	170	204	146	142
Financial activities	58	75	131	144	139	91	103	100	168	357	446	411	312
Professional and business services	143	217	377	440	345	299	266	247	346	810	985	878	793
Education and health services	124	149	232	300	304	271	263	253	320	691	898	910	907
Leisure and hospitality	146	196	279	328	321	277	259	274	356	755	898	830	740
Other services	54	58	95	132	126	117	97	80	132	245	310	336	261
Public administration	41	36	51	59	72	62	34	51	55	107	164	185	144
Experienced Workers, by Occupation													
Management, professional, and related	213	313	603	692	571	436	373	368	569	1 331	1 600	1 482	1 362
Services	246	323	447	564	565	511	464	482	595	1 243	1 557	1 500	1 356
Sales and office	331	419	759	810	750	641	561	560	741	1 675	2 048	1 949	1 622
Natural resources, construction, and maintenance	161	212	346	424	386	341	294	299	463	1 224	1 445	1 150	914
Production, transportation, and material moving	273	360	575	654	561	461	380	384	570	1 302	1 498	1 290	1 041
UNEMPLOYED 27 WEEKS AND OVER													
Total	649	801	1 535	1 936	1 779	1 490	1 235	1 243	1 761	4 496	6 415	6 016	5 136
Wage and Salary Workers, by Industry													
Agriculture and related	13	16	18	21	18	16	13	14	17	51	57	58	55
Mining [1]	4	3	5	10	6	4	3	3	4	23	37	22	17
Construction	44	60	111	132	133	108	92	107	168	530	773	617	464
Manufacturing	100	132	291	366	302	195	140	152	230	657	888	725	533
Durable goods	50	75	191	255	196	124	75	93	150	428	619	486	341
Nondurable goods	50	57	100	111	106	71	64	58	80	229	269	239	192
Wholesale and retail trade	80	114	226	261	261	230	183	171	237	607	904	833	731
Transportation and utilities	27	33	67	74	63	50	42	58	77	180	263	265	198
Information	18	21	62	80	58	41	30	29	38	115	159	116	107
Financial activities	32	34	131	88	79	56	56	50	97	232	332	315	245
Professional and business services	67	90	377	262	193	172	144	130	184	510	722	641	580
Education and health services	63	71	232	167	168	156	144	132	182	432	644	671	668
Leisure and hospitality	69	90	279	166	169	148	135	142	196	445	624	596	519
Other services	26	31	95	71	76	74	51	43	73	161	223	249	192
Public administration	23	18	51	33	44	38	21	29	29	66	121	140	112
Experienced Workers, by Occupation													
Management, professional, and related	101	135	340	429	356	269	206	207	569	840	6 415	1 121	1 022
Services	128	156	225	295	307	284	249	251	595	750	1 094	1 086	971
Sales and office	151	185	397	459	419	354	299	285	741	1 067	1 513	1 486	1 211
Natural resources, construction, and maintenance	74	96	164	229	221	186	158	157	463	724	1 042	855	676
Production, transportation, and material moving	140	162	313	388	336	261	206	219	570	814	1 142	973	773

Note: Beginning with data for January 2011, the Current Population Survey (CPS) uses the 2010 Census Occupational Classification system derived from the 2010 Standard Occupational Classification (SOC) system. The 2010 classification system replaces an earlier version that was based on the 2000 SOC. As a result of the classification change, CPS occupational data beginning with January 2011 data are not strictly comparable with earlier years.

[1] For 2009 through 2012, mining includes quarrying, and oil and gas extraction.

Table 1-32. Unemployed Persons and Unemployment Rates, by Reason for Unemployment, Sex, and Age, 1975–2012

(Thousands of people, percent.)

Sex, age, and year	Number of unemployed					Unemployed as a percent of the total civilian labor force			
	Total	Job losers and persons who completed temporary jobs	Job leavers	Entrants		Job losers and persons who completed temporary jobs	Job leavers	Entrants	
				Reentrants	New entrants			Reentrants	New entrants
Both Sexes, 16 Years and Over									
1975	7 929	4 386	827	1 892	823	4.7	0.9	2.0	0.9
1976	7 406	3 679	903	1 928	895	3.8	0.9	2.0	0.9
1977	6 991	3 166	909	1 963	953	3.2	0.9	2.0	1.0
1978	6 202	2 585	874	1 857	885	2.5	0.9	1.8	0.9
1979	6 137	2 635	880	1 806	817	2.5	0.8	1.7	0.8
1980	7 637	3 947	891	1 927	872	3.7	0.8	1.8	0.8
1981	8 273	4 267	923	2 102	981	3.9	0.8	1.9	0.9
1982	10 678	6 268	840	2 384	1 185	5.7	0.8	2.2	1.1
1983	10 717	6 258	830	2 412	1 216	5.6	0.7	2.2	1.1
1984	8 539	4 421	823	2 184	1 110	3.9	0.7	1.9	1.0
1985	8 312	4 139	877	2 256	1 039	3.6	0.8	2.0	0.9
1986	8 237	4 033	1 015	2 160	1 029	3.4	0.9	1.8	0.9
1987	7 425	3 566	965	1 974	920	3.0	0.8	1.6	0.8
1988	6 701	3 092	983	1 809	816	2.5	0.8	1.5	0.7
1989	6 528	2 983	1 024	1 843	677	2.4	0.8	1.5	0.5
1990	7 047	3 387	1 041	1 930	688	2.7	0.8	1.5	0.5
1991	8 628	4 694	1 004	2 139	792	3.7	0.8	1.7	0.6
1992	9 613	5 389	1 002	2 285	937	4.2	0.8	1.8	0.7
1993	8 940	4 848	976	2 198	919	3.8	0.8	1.7	0.7
1994	7 996	3 815	791	2 786	604	2.9	0.6	2.1	0.5
1995	7 404	3 476	824	2 525	579	2.6	0.6	1.9	0.4
1996	7 236	3 370	774	2 512	580	2.5	0.6	1.9	0.4
1997	6 739	3 037	795	2 338	569	2.2	0.6	1.7	0.4
1998	6 210	2 822	734	2 132	520	2.1	0.5	1.5	0.4
1999	5 880	2 622	783	2 005	469	1.9	0.6	1.4	0.3
2000	5 692	2 517	780	1 961	434	1.8	0.5	1.4	0.3
2001	6 801	3 476	835	2 031	459	2.4	0.6	1.4	0.3
2002	8 378	4 607	866	2 368	536	3.2	0.6	1.6	0.4
2003	8 774	4 838	818	2 477	641	3.3	0.6	1.7	0.4
2004	8 149	4 197	858	2 408	686	2.8	0.6	1.6	0.5
2005	7 591	3 667	872	2 386	666	2.5	0.6	1.6	0.4
2006	7 001	3 321	827	2 237	616	2.2	0.5	1.5	0.4
2007	7 078	3 515	793	2 142	627	2.3	0.5	1.4	0.4
2008	8 924	4 789	896	2 472	766	3.1	0.6	1.6	0.5
2009	14 265	9 160	882	3 187	1 035	5.9	0.6	2.1	0.7
2010	14 825	9 250	889	3 466	1 220	6.0	0.6	2.3	0.8
2011	13 747	8 106	956	3 401	1 284	5.3	0.6	2.2	0.8
2012	12 506	6 877	967	3 345	1 316	4.4	0.6	2.2	0.8
Both Sexes, 16 to 19 Years									
1975	1 767	450	155	529	634	5.1	1.7	6.0	7.1
1976	1 719	387	153	496	683	4.3	1.7	5.5	7.5
1977	1 663	318	156	477	711	3.4	1.7	5.1	7.6
1978	1 583	300	167	455	660	3.1	1.7	4.7	6.8
1979	1 555	319	184	452	599	3.3	1.9	4.7	6.2
1980	1 669	388	156	481	643	4.1	1.7	5.1	6.9
1981	1 763	385	162	487	728	4.3	1.8	5.4	8.1
1982	1 977	460	134	509	874	5.4	1.6	6.0	10.2
1983	1 829	370	110	482	867	4.6	1.3	5.9	10.6
1984	1 499	271	114	370	745	3.4	1.4	4.7	9.4
1985	1 468	275	113	390	689	3.5	1.4	4.9	8.7
1986	1 454	240	145	374	695	3.0	1.8	4.7	8.8
1987	1 347	210	146	375	617	2.7	1.8	4.7	7.7
1988	1 226	207	159	310	550	2.6	2.0	3.9	6.8
1989	1 194	198	200	345	452	2.5	2.5	4.3	5.7
1990	1 212	233	181	338	460	3.0	2.3	4.3	5.9
1991	1 359	289	180	365	524	4.0	2.5	5.0	7.2
1992	1 427	259	149	377	643	3.6	2.1	5.3	9.1
1993	1 365	233	151	353	628	3.3	2.1	4.9	8.8
1994	1 320	185	84	634	416	2.5	1.1	8.5	5.6
1995	1 346	214	102	615	415	2.8	1.3	7.9	5.3
1996	1 306	182	91	625	409	2.3	1.2	8.0	5.2
1997	1 271	174	104	606	388	2.2	1.3	7.6	4.9
1998	1 205	181	86	577	361	2.2	1.0	7.0	4.4
1999	1 162	173	114	547	328	2.1	1.4	6.6	3.9
2000	1 081	157	109	516	299	1.9	1.3	6.2	3.6
2001	1 162	185	98	568	311	2.3	1.2	7.2	3.9
2002	1 253	197	91	597	368	2.6	1.2	7.9	4.9
2003	1 251	188	85	554	424	2.6	1.2	7.7	5.9
2004	1 208	165	76	510	456	2.3	1.1	7.2	6.4
2005	1 186	155	76	489	466	2.2	1.1	6.8	6.5
2006	1 119	145	78	461	435	2.0	1.1	6.3	6.0
2007	1 101	176	71	435	419	2.5	1.0	6.2	6.0
2008	1 285	203	80	490	511	3.0	1.2	7.1	7.5
2009	1 552	271	56	548	677	4.2	0.9	8.6	10.6
2010	1 528	220	42	487	778	3.7	0.7	8.2	13.2
2011	1 400	181	52	429	739	3.2	0.9	7.5	12.9
2012	1 397	176	43	419	758	3.0	0.7	7.2	13.0

Note: See notes and definitions for information on historical comparability.

Table 1-32. Unemployed Persons and Unemployment Rates, by Reason for Unemployment, Sex, and Age, 1975–2012—*Continued*

(Thousands of people, percent.)

Sex, age, and year	Number of unemployed					Unemployed as a percent of the total civilian labor force			
	Total	Job losers and persons who completed temporary jobs	Job leavers	Entrants		Job losers and persons who completed temporary jobs	Job leavers	Entrants	
				Reentrants	New entrants			Reentrants	New entrants
Both Sexes, 16 Years and Over									
1975	7 929	4 386	827	1 892	823	4.7	0.9	2.0	0.9
1976	7 406	3 679	903	1 928	895	3.8	0.9	2.0	0.9
1977	6 991	3 166	909	1 963	953	3.2	0.9	2.0	1.0
1978	6 202	2 585	874	1 857	885	2.5	0.9	1.8	0.9
1979	6 137	2 635	880	1 806	817	2.5	0.8	1.7	0.8
1980	7 637	3 947	891	1 927	872	3.7	0.8	1.8	0.8
1981	8 273	4 267	923	2 102	981	3.9	0.8	1.9	0.9
1982	10 678	6 268	840	2 384	1 185	5.7	0.8	2.2	1.1
1983	10 717	6 258	830	2 412	1 216	5.6	0.7	2.2	1.1
1984	8 539	4 421	823	2 184	1 110	3.9	0.7	1.9	1.0
1985	8 312	4 139	877	2 256	1 039	3.6	0.8	2.0	0.9
1986	8 237	4 033	1 015	2 160	1 029	3.4	0.9	1.8	0.9
1987	7 425	3 566	965	1 974	920	3.0	0.8	1.6	0.8
1988	6 701	3 092	983	1 809	816	2.5	0.8	1.5	0.7
1989	6 528	2 983	1 024	1 843	677	2.4	0.8	1.5	0.5
1990	7 047	3 387	1 041	1 930	688	2.7	0.8	1.5	0.5
1991	8 628	4 694	1 004	2 139	792	3.7	0.8	1.7	0.6
1992	9 613	5 389	1 002	2 285	937	4.2	0.8	1.8	0.7
1993	8 940	4 848	976	2 198	919	3.8	0.8	1.7	0.7
1994	7 996	3 815	791	2 786	604	2.9	0.6	2.1	0.5
1995	7 404	3 476	824	2 525	579	2.6	0.6	1.9	0.4
1996	7 236	3 370	774	2 512	580	2.5	0.6	1.9	0.4
1997	6 739	3 037	795	2 338	569	2.2	0.6	1.7	0.4
1998	6 210	2 822	734	2 132	520	2.1	0.5	1.5	0.4
1999	5 880	2 622	783	2 005	469	1.9	0.6	1.4	0.3
2000	5 692	2 517	780	1 961	434	1.8	0.5	1.4	0.3
2001	6 801	3 476	835	2 031	459	2.4	0.6	1.4	0.3
2002	8 378	4 607	866	2 368	536	3.2	0.6	1.6	0.4
2003	8 774	4 838	818	2 477	641	3.3	0.6	1.7	0.4
2004	8 149	4 197	858	2 408	686	2.8	0.6	1.6	0.5
2005	7 591	3 667	872	2 386	666	2.5	0.6	1.6	0.4
2006	7 001	3 321	827	2 237	616	2.2	0.5	1.5	0.4
2007	7 078	3 515	793	2 142	627	2.3	0.5	1.4	0.4
2008	8 924	4 789	896	2 472	766	3.1	0.6	1.6	0.5
2009	14 265	9 160	882	3 187	1 035	5.9	0.6	2.1	0.7
2010	14 825	9 250	889	3 466	1 220	6.0	0.6	2.3	0.8
2011	13 747	8 106	956	3 401	1 284	5.3	0.6	2.2	0.8
2012	12 506	6 877	967	3 345	1 316	4.4	0.6	2.2	0.8
Both Sexes, 16 to 19 Years									
1975	1 767	450	155	529	634	5.1	1.7	6.0	7.1
1976	1 719	387	153	496	683	4.3	1.7	5.5	7.5
1977	1 663	318	156	477	711	3.4	1.7	5.1	7.6
1978	1 583	300	167	455	660	3.1	1.7	4.7	6.8
1979	1 555	319	184	452	599	3.3	1.9	4.7	6.2
1980	1 669	388	156	481	643	4.1	1.7	5.1	6.9
1981	1 763	385	162	487	728	4.3	1.8	5.4	8.1
1982	1 977	460	134	509	874	5.4	1.6	6.0	10.2
1983	1 829	370	110	482	867	4.6	1.3	5.9	10.6
1984	1 499	271	114	370	745	3.4	1.4	4.7	9.4
1985	1 468	275	113	390	689	3.5	1.4	4.9	8.7
1986	1 454	240	145	374	695	3.0	1.8	4.7	8.8
1987	1 347	210	146	375	617	2.7	1.8	4.7	7.7
1988	1 226	207	159	310	550	2.6	2.0	3.9	6.8
1989	1 194	198	200	345	452	2.5	2.5	4.3	5.7
1990	1 212	233	181	338	460	3.0	2.3	4.3	5.9
1991	1 359	289	180	365	524	4.0	2.5	5.0	7.2
1992	1 427	259	149	377	643	3.6	2.1	5.3	9.1
1993	1 365	233	151	353	628	3.3	2.1	4.9	8.8
1994	1 320	185	84	634	416	2.5	1.1	8.5	5.6
1995	1 346	214	102	615	415	2.8	1.3	7.9	5.3
1996	1 306	182	91	625	409	2.3	1.2	8.0	5.2
1997	1 271	174	104	606	388	2.2	1.3	7.6	4.9
1998	1 205	181	86	577	361	2.2	1.0	7.0	4.4
1999	1 162	173	114	547	328	2.1	1.4	6.6	3.9
2000	1 081	157	109	516	299	1.9	1.3	6.2	3.6
2001	1 162	185	98	568	311	2.3	1.2	7.2	3.9
2002	1 253	197	91	597	368	2.6	1.2	7.9	4.9
2003	1 251	188	85	554	424	2.6	1.2	7.7	5.9
2004	1 208	165	76	510	456	2.3	1.1	7.2	6.4
2005	1 186	155	76	489	466	2.2	1.1	6.8	6.5
2006	1 119	145	78	461	435	2.0	1.1	6.3	6.0
2007	1 101	176	71	435	419	2.5	1.0	6.2	6.0
2008	1 285	203	80	490	511	3.0	1.2	7.1	7.5
2009	1 552	271	56	548	677	4.2	0.9	8.6	10.6
2010	1 528	220	42	487	778	3.7	0.7	8.2	13.2
2011	1 400	181	52	429	739	3.2	0.9	7.5	12.9
2012	1 397	176	43	419	758	3.0	0.7	7.2	13.0

Note: See notes and definitions for information on historical comparability.

Table 1-33. Percent of the Population with Work Experience During the Year, by Age and Sex, 1987–2012

(Percent.)

Sex and year	Total	16 to 17 years	18 to 19 years	20 to 24 years	25 to 34 years	35 to 44 years	45 to 54 years	55 to 59 years	60 to 64 years	65 to 69 years	70 years and over
Both Sexes											
1987	69.7	51.8	76.6	85.5	85.7	86.1	81.6	69.4	51.3	26.2	10.2
1988	70.2	50.6	75.5	85.7	86.0	86.8	82.2	70.5	52.2	27.9	10.3
1989	70.5	51.9	75.4	84.9	86.6	86.9	82.8	70.4	52.5	28.4	10.0
1990	70.2	48.6	74.2	84.1	86.2	87.0	82.8	70.9	53.4	28.3	10.2
1991	69.5	43.4	70.8	83.4	85.9	86.6	83.0	70.3	52.9	27.2	9.8
1992	69.1	43.8	69.9	82.7	85.2	85.9	82.8	70.8	53.5	25.5	9.8
1993	69.2	42.1	70.4	82.0	85.0	85.3	82.8	71.6	51.6	27.5	10.7
1994	69.6	44.1	71.5	82.5	85.5	85.6	83.8	72.2	52.8	27.5	10.0
1995	69.6	44.4	71.2	82.0	85.6	85.9	83.4	72.2	53.3	28.0	10.2
1996	69.9	43.3	70.5	83.1	86.1	85.7	84.3	73.3	54.3	27.8	10.4
1997	70.1	43.6	70.5	83.0	87.1	85.9	84.4	73.8	53.8	28.5	10.0
1998	70.1	42.1	69.9	82.9	86.7	86.3	84.2	73.7	54.5	29.2	10.6
1999	70.7	43.7	71.2	82.7	87.3	86.9	85.0	72.3	55.8	30.5	11.6
2000	70.5	42.2	69.6	82.6	87.1	87.0	84.6	72.9	55.1	30.8	11.4
2001	69.4	37.7	66.7	80.8	86.1	85.8	83.7	73.5	56.7	30.6	10.5
2002	68.5	34.5	62.8	78.5	84.4	85.0	83.7	74.7	56.8	33.1	10.4
2003	67.8	32.0	61.7	77.5	83.7	84.0	82.9	73.9	56.5	33.2	11.4
2004	67.7	32.6	59.8	76.9	83.3	84.2	82.6	73.9	57.0	32.7	12.2
2005	67.8	31.1	60.1	77.3	83.7	84.1	82.8	74.4	58.2	32.0	12.1
2006	67.9	30.9	58.3	76.9	84.4	84.3	82.8	74.5	58.2	33.6	12.6
2007	67.8	28.5	57.3	76.6	84.2	84.4	82.4	75.6	59.7	35.2	13.0
2008	67.1	24.6	55.3	76.0	84.1	83.9	81.8	74.6	60.3	34.9	13.5
2009	65.0	21.9	48.7	71.0	81.6	82.0	80.5	73.8	59.3	35.3	12.8
2010	63.8	17.8	43.9	69.1	80.2	81.3	79.2	73.8	58.4	37.1	13.0
2011	63.4	17.0	44.8	69.8	79.7	81.3	79.0	72.0	59.5	36.5	13.3
2012	63.9	19.9	47.1	70.1	80.6	81.3	79.4	74.5	59.2	37.5	14.0
Men											
1987	78.9	52.4	77.4	90.4	94.3	94.1	91.9	83.3	63.2	34.2	15.4
1988	79.1	51.8	78.9	90.7	94.3	94.6	91.6	82.1	63.1	35.6	15.6
1989	79.4	53.2	77.7	89.9	94.7	94.7	91.9	82.0	64.2	35.4	15.1
1990	78.9	50.3	76.7	88.7	94.4	94.7	91.3	82.0	65.8	35.8	14.0
1991	77.9	45.4	72.2	87.9	93.5	93.6	91.3	81.5	63.6	35.0	14.4
1992	77.4	46.6	73.7	87.1	93.3	92.8	89.9	80.9	63.2	32.4	14.3
1993	76.8	43.9	71.4	86.6	92.5	92.0	89.3	79.8	59.1	34.3	15.3
1994	77.2	44.4	74.7	87.2	92.9	92.0	90.0	81.3	61.4	33.9	14.8
1995	77.0	43.7	73.6	86.4	92.6	92.2	89.7	81.5	62.1	34.5	14.9
1996	77.2	44.1	71.8	86.7	93.4	92.1	90.4	81.8	62.5	33.6	15.2
1997	77.1	43.4	70.3	86.6	94.1	92.3	90.7	81.4	62.9	33.8	13.9
1998	76.9	40.4	71.6	86.4	93.5	92.7	90.1	81.7	63.5	35.5	14.7
1999	77.3	44.7	72.3	85.5	93.9	93.2	89.9	79.2	65.1	37.4	16.5
2000	77.1	42.1	70.2	85.1	93.4	93.6	89.8	80.6	64.4	38.4	16.0
2001	76.3	37.4	67.7	84.8	93.2	92.2	89.1	80.4	64.3	37.8	14.5
2002	75.2	34.7	62.8	82.1	91.6	91.8	88.9	80.7	64.3	39.3	14.6
2003	74.3	32.8	61.7	80.2	90.8	90.9	87.7	80.9	63.1	37.3	15.8
2004	74.2	32.1	58.9	80.2	91.0	91.1	87.9	80.1	64.5	37.1	16.7
2005	74.6	31.1	60.7	80.8	91.3	91.6	88.2	80.1	64.3	37.6	17.0
2006	74.5	30.9	57.9	80.1	91.9	91.8	88.0	80.6	64.1	38.3	17.3
2007	74.3	28.5	59.0	80.5	90.5	91.5	88.2	80.3	66.2	39.3	17.9
2008	73.2	24.4	55.1	78.7	90.7	91.1	86.4	79.3	66.0	40.3	17.9
2009	70.8	22.2	48.0	73.3	87.7	89.1	85.0	78.3	64.8	39.8	17.2
2010	69.4	16.9	43.2	71.3	86.0	88.0	84.1	78.9	62.8	43.4	17.5
2011	69.0	16.1	43.2	71.6	86.2	88.1	84.3	76.7	64.0	42.6	18.2
2012	69.7	19.1	45.9	72.2	86.9	88.9	84.8	79.9	64.2	43.2	18.5
Women											
1987	61.3	51.1	75.8	81.0	77.3	78.5	71.9	56.7	41.0	19.6	6.8
1988	62.1	49.3	72.2	81.0	78.1	79.4	73.5	60.0	42.5	21.4	6.8
1989	62.3	50.6	73.1	80.2	78.6	79.3	74.2	59.9	42.4	22.5	6.7
1990	62.2	46.8	71.7	79.6	78.0	79.6	74.9	60.4	42.5	22.1	7.7
1991	61.8	41.4	69.4	79.0	78.3	79.9	75.3	59.9	43.6	20.6	6.7
1992	61.5	40.9	66.1	78.4	77.2	79.1	76.1	61.5	44.4	20.0	6.7
1993	62.1	40.3	69.4	77.5	77.6	78.7	76.5	63.9	44.7	22.1	7.7
1994	62.5	43.7	68.4	77.8	78.1	79.4	78.0	63.9	45.0	22.2	6.8
1995	62.8	45.2	68.7	77.7	78.8	79.8	77.6	63.2	45.6	22.4	7.1
1996	63.2	42.5	69.2	79.5	78.9	79.5	78.4	65.4	46.9	23.0	7.1
1997	63.6	43.9	70.7	79.5	80.1	79.6	78.4	66.7	45.6	24.0	7.3
1998	63.7	44.1	68.2	79.4	80.1	80.0	78.6	66.3	46.2	23.8	7.8
1999	64.5	42.6	70.1	79.9	80.9	80.7	80.3	66.2	47.3	24.4	8.2
2000	64.3	42.3	69.0	80.2	80.9	80.5	79.5	65.7	47.0	23.9	8.2
2001	63.1	38.1	65.7	76.9	79.2	79.5	78.6	67.1	49.8	24.2	7.9
2002	62.3	34.3	62.8	74.9	77.2	78.4	78.7	69.1	50.0	27.8	7.4
2003	61.7	31.2	61.6	74.6	76.6	77.2	78.4	67.3	50.7	29.6	8.3
2004	61.5	33.1	60.7	73.7	75.6	77.4	77.5	68.2	50.3	28.7	9.0
2005	61.4	31.2	59.6	73.7	76.1	76.8	77.6	68.9	52.7	27.1	8.7
2006	61.6	30.9	58.7	73.7	76.9	76.9	77.9	68.8	53.0	29.5	9.3
2007	61.6	28.5	55.6	72.6	77.8	77.4	76.9	71.2	53.7	31.5	9.5
2008	61.3	24.8	55.4	73.2	77.3	76.7	77.3	70.1	55.0	30.1	10.3
2009	59.6	21.6	49.5	68.6	75.4	75.0	76.1	69.5	54.4	31.1	9.7
2010	58.5	18.7	44.5	66.9	74.3	74.7	74.7	69.1	54.2	31.6	9.6
2011	58.1	18.0	46.5	68.0	73.4	74.7	73.8	67.7	55.4	31.0	9.6
2012	58.4	20.7	48.3	68.1	74.3	73.8	74.3	69.4	54.8	32.2	10.6

Note: See notes and definitions for information on historical comparability.

Table 1-34. Persons with Work Experience During the Year, by Industry and Class of Worker of Job Held the Longest, 2002–2012

(Thousands of people.)

Industry and class of worker	2002	2003	2004	2005	2006	2007	2008	2009	2010	2011	2012
TOTAL	151 546	151 553	153 024	155 127	157 352	158 468	158 317	154 772	153 141	154 330	157 050
Agriculture	2 490	2 521	2 492	2 344	2 332	2 407	2 382	2 581	2 383	2 470	2 176
Wage and salary workers	1 583	1 605	1 549	1 501	1 495	1 525	1 522	1 733	1 578	1 679	1 504
Self-employed workers	875	894	918	829	812	846	824	813	788	750	649
Unpaid family workers	33	22	25	14	25	36	37	35	17	42	22
Nonagricultural Industries	149 055	149 032	150 532	152 783	155 021	156 061	155 934	152 191	150 759	151 859	154 874
Wage and salary workers	139 909	139 747	140 885	143 002	145 152	146 485	146 521	142 946	141 686	142 962	145 787
Mining	594	576	630	696	758	746	840	778	771	890	1 146
Construction	9 488	9 423	10 076	10 423	10 989	10 547	10 234	9 443	8 633	8 607	8 445
Manufacturing	17 660	17 349	17 196	17 243	17 112	16 641	16 332	14 956	14 865	15 139	15 139
Durable goods	11 013	10 622	10 814	10 930	10 995	10 687	10 477	9 342	9 288	9 586	9 585
Nondurable goods	6 647	6 727	6 382	6 313	6 116	5 954	5 855	5 613	5 577	5 552	5 554
Wholesale and retail trade	21 615	21 650	22 091	22 479	21 822	21 837	21 838	21 210	20 854	20 685	20 485
Wholesale trade	4 402	4 691	4 470	4 517	4 395	4 017	4 016	3 849	3 921	3 601	3 606
Retail trade	17 213	16 959	17 621	17 962	17 427	17 820	17 822	17 361	16 933	17 084	16 879
Transportation and utilities	7 039	6 934	7 040	7 248	7 413	8 023	7 675	7 309	6 993	7 173	7 573
Transportation and warehousing	5 745	5 736	5 827	6 095	6 197	6 750	6 365	6 025	5 701	5 944	6 336
Utilities	1 294	1 198	1 213	1 153	1 216	1 273	1 310	1 284	1 292	1 229	1 237
Information	3 989	3 755	3 359	3 495	3 710	3 687	3 455	3 375	3 380	3 137	3 144
Financial activities	9 591	9 822	9 956	9 748	10 101	10 013	9 671	9 409	9 239	9 443	9 889
Finance and insurance	6 986	7 135	7 192	7 011	7 190	7 347	6 994	6 792	6 726	6 909	7 293
Real estate and rental and leasing	2 605	2 687	2 764	2 737	2 912	2 666	2 677	2 617	2 512	2 534	2 595
Professional and business services	13 883	13 485	13 277	13 537	14 412	14 659	14 868	14 633	15 094	15 339	15 924
Professional, scientific, and technical services	7 989	7 855	7 793	7 768	8 294	8 676	8 742	8 475	8 841	9 054	9 370
Management, administration, and waste management services	5 894	5 629	5 484	5 769	6 118	5 982	6 127	6 159	6 253	6 285	6 553
Education and health services	29 343	29 571	29 814	30 552	31 314	31 921	32 828	33 465	33 596	33 424	34 156
Education services	12 765	13 026	13 169	13 282	13 659	13 989	14 396	14 457	14 157	13 917	14 256
Health care and social assistance services	16 578	16 544	16 645	17 270	17 655	17 932	18 432	19 008	19 439	19 507	19 900
Leisure and hospitality	13 260	13 110	13 345	13 405	13 455	13 959	14 242	13 917	13 718	14 293	15 103
Arts, entertainment, and recreation	2 852	2 789	2 888	2 877	2 797	3 124	3 047	3 284	2 993	3 116	3 332
Accommodation and food services	10 408	10 321	10 457	10 528	10 658	10 835	11 195	10 633	10 725	11 177	11 771
Other services and private household	6 416	6 529	6 473	6 490	6 341	6 603	6 590	6 233	6 111	6 717	6 643
Private households	873	897	907	866	912	888	912	757	816	773	833
Public administration	6 290	6 734	6 897	6 917	7 076	7 095	7 121	7 332	7 597	7 270	7 333
Self-employed workers	9 023	9 169	9 520	9 658	9 733	9 451	9 332	9 121	8 962	8 778	8 955
Unpaid family workers	124	116	128	123	135	126	82	124	111	120	132

Note: See notes and definitions for information on historical comparability.

Table 1-35. Number of Persons with Work Experience During the Year, by Extent of Employment and Sex, 1987–2012

(Thousands of people.)

Sex and year	Total	Full-time workers				Part-time workers			
		Total	50 to 52 weeks	27 to 49 weeks	1 to 26 weeks	Total	50 to 52 weeks	27 to 49 weeks	1 to 26 weeks
Both Sexes									
1987	128 315	100 288	77 015	13 361	9 912	28 027	10 973	6 594	10 460
1988	130 451	102 131	79 627	12 875	9 629	28 320	11 384	6 624	10 312
1989	132 817	104 876	81 117	14 271	9 488	27 941	11 275	6 987	9 679
1990	133 535	105 323	80 932	14 758	9 633	28 212	11 507	7 012	9 693
1991	133 410	104 472	80 385	14 491	9 596	28 938	11 946	7 003	9 989
1992	133 912	104 813	81 523	13 587	9 703	29 099	12 326	6 841	9 932
1993	136 354	106 299	83 384	13 054	9 861	30 055	12 818	6 777	10 460
1994	138 468	108 141	85 764	13 051	9 326	30 327	12 936	6 956	10 435
1995	139 724	110 063	88 173	12 970	8 920	29 661	12 725	6 831	10 105
1996	142 201	112 313	90 252	12 997	9 064	29 888	13 382	6 643	9 863
1997	143 968	113 879	92 631	12 508	8 740	30 089	13 810	6 565	9 714
1998	145 566	116 412	95 772	12 156	8 484	29 155	13 538	6 480	9 137
1999	148 295	119 096	97 941	12 294	8 861	29 199	13 680	6 317	9 202
2000	149 361	120 591	100 349	12 071	8 171	28 770	13 865	6 161	8 744
2001	151 042	121 921	100 357	13 172	8 392	29 121	14 038	6 139	8 944
2002	151 546	121 726	100 659	12 544	8 523	29 819	14 635	6 184	9 000
2003	151 553	121 158	100 700	11 972	8 486	30 395	15 333	6 027	9 035
2004	153 024	122 404	102 427	11 862	8 115	30 621	15 552	6 077	8 992
2005	155 127	124 683	104 876	11 816	7 991	30 444	15 374	6 161	8 909
2006	157 352	127 340	107 734	11 736	7 870	30 012	15 131	6 223	8 657
2007	158 468	128 332	108 617	11 901	7 814	30 136	15 477	6 194	8 466
2008	158 317	125 937	104 023	13 421	8 493	32 380	16 562	6 630	9 188
2009	154 772	121 355	99 306	12 350	9 698	33 418	17 417	6 674	9 327
2010	153 141	119 940	99 250	11 705	8 985	33 201	17 122	6 582	9 497
2011	154 330	121 400	101 700	11 040	8 661	32 929	17 261	6 288	9 380
2012	157 050	123 229	103 078	11 708	8 442	33 821	17 494	6 681	9 646
Men									
1987	69 144	59 736	47 040	7 503	5 193	9 408	3 260	2 191	3 957
1988	70 021	60 504	48 299	7 329	4 876	9 517	3 468	2 199	3 850
1989	71 640	62 108	49 693	7 642	4 773	9 532	3 619	2 254	3 659
1990	71 953	62 319	49 175	8 188	4 956	9 634	3 650	2 322	3 662
1991	71 700	61 636	47 895	8 324	5 417	10 064	3 820	2 342	3 902
1992	72 007	61 722	48 300	7 965	5 457	10 285	3 864	2 354	4 067
1993	72 872	62 513	49 832	7 317	5 364	10 359	4 005	2 144	4 210
1994	73 958	63 634	51 582	7 094	4 958	10 324	3 948	2 358	4 018
1995	74 381	64 145	52 671	6 973	4 501	10 236	4 034	2 257	3 945
1996	75 760	65 356	53 795	6 891	4 670	10 404	4 321	2 136	3 947
1997	76 408	66 089	54 918	6 638	4 533	10 319	4 246	2 274	3 799
1998	76 918	67 250	56 953	6 208	4 089	9 669	4 197	2 090	3 382
1999	78 145	68 347	57 520	6 401	4 426	9 797	4 297	2 062	3 438
2000	78 804	68 925	58 756	6 094	4 075	9 879	4 485	1 957	3 437
2001	79 971	70 074	58 715	7 087	4 272	9 897	4 306	1 989	3 602
2002	80 282	70 132	58 765	6 804	4 563	10 151	4 519	2 042	3 590
2003	80 317	69 766	58 778	6 479	4 509	10 551	5 042	1 872	3 637
2004	81 261	70 780	60 096	6 428	4 256	10 482	4 987	1 992	3 503
2005	82 735	72 056	61 510	6 299	4 247	10 679	5 153	2 074	3 452
2006	83 767	73 578	63 058	6 373	4 147	10 189	4 747	2 046	3 396
2007	84 292	73 734	62 994	6 583	4 157	10 558	4 933	2 165	3 460
2008	83 889	72 204	59 869	7 645	4 690	11 685	5 425	2 457	3 803
2009	81 835	69 178	56 058	7 339	5 780	12 658	5 911	2 526	4 221
2010	81 076	68 402	56 416	6 760	5 225	12 674	5 883	2 523	4 267
2011	81 272	69 029	58 004	6 183	4 842	12 243	5 797	2 408	4 037
2012	82 910	70 181	59 022	6 547	4 611	12 729	6 199	2 481	4 049
Women									
1987	59 171	40 552	29 975	5 858	4 719	18 619	7 713	4 403	6 503
1988	60 430	41 627	31 328	5 546	4 753	18 803	7 916	4 425	6 462
1989	61 178	42 768	31 424	6 629	4 715	18 410	7 656	4 733	6 021
1990	61 582	43 004	31 757	6 570	4 677	18 578	7 857	4 690	6 031
1991	61 712	42 837	32 491	6 167	4 179	18 875	8 126	4 662	6 087
1992	61 904	43 090	33 223	5 621	4 246	18 814	8 462	4 487	5 865
1993	63 481	43 785	33 552	5 736	4 497	19 696	8 813	4 633	6 250
1994	64 511	44 508	34 182	5 957	4 369	20 003	8 988	4 598	6 417
1995	65 342	45 917	35 502	5 997	4 418	19 425	8 691	4 574	6 160
1996	66 439	46 955	36 457	6 105	4 393	19 484	9 061	4 507	5 916
1997	67 559	47 790	37 713	5 870	4 207	19 769	9 564	4 291	5 914
1998	68 648	49 162	38 819	5 948	4 395	19 486	9 341	4 390	5 755
1999	70 150	50 748	40 421	5 892	4 435	19 402	9 383	4 255	5 764
2000	70 556	51 665	41 593	5 977	4 095	18 891	9 380	4 204	5 307
2001	71 071	51 848	41 642	6 085	4 120	19 223	9 731	4 150	5 342
2002	71 263	51 593	41 893	5 741	3 959	19 671	10 117	4 143	5 411
2003	71 236	51 391	41 921	5 493	3 977	19 844	10 291	4 155	5 398
2004	71 763	51 624	42 331	5 434	3 859	20 139	10 565	4 085	5 489
2005	72 392	52 627	43 366	5 517	3 744	19 765	10 222	4 087	5 456
2006	73 585	53 762	44 676	5 364	3 723	19 823	10 384	4 178	5 261
2007	74 176	54 598	45 622	5 318	3 657	19 579	10 543	4 029	5 006
2008	74 428	53 733	44 154	5 776	3 803	20 695	11 137	4 172	5 385
2009	72 937	52 177	43 248	5 012	3 918	20 760	11 506	4 147	5 107
2010	72 066	51 538	42 834	4 944	3 760	20 528	11 239	4 058	5 230
2011	73 058	52 371	43 696	4 857	3 818	20 687	11 464	3 880	5 343
2012	74 140	53 048	44 055	5 161	3 831	21 092	11 295	4 200	5 597

Note: See notes and definitions for information on historical comparability.

Table 1-36. Percent Distribution of the Population with Work Experience During the Year, by Extent of Employment and Sex, 1987–2012

(Percent of total people with work experience.)

Sex and year	Total	Full-time workers				Part-time workers			
		Total	50 to 52 weeks	27 to 49 weeks	1 to 26 weeks	Total	50 to 52 weeks	27 to 49 weeks	1 to 26 weeks
Both Sexes									
1987	100.0	78.1	60.0	10.4	7.7	21.9	8.6	5.1	8.2
1988	100.0	78.3	61.0	9.9	7.4	21.7	8.7	5.1	7.9
1989	100.0	78.9	61.1	10.7	7.1	21.1	8.5	5.3	7.3
1990	100.0	78.9	60.6	11.1	7.2	21.2	8.6	5.3	7.3
1991	100.0	78.4	60.3	10.9	7.2	21.7	9.0	5.2	7.5
1992	100.0	78.2	60.9	10.1	7.2	21.7	9.2	5.1	7.4
1993	100.0	78.0	61.2	9.6	7.2	22.1	9.4	5.0	7.7
1994	100.0	78.0	61.9	9.4	6.7	21.8	9.3	5.0	7.5
1995	100.0	78.8	63.1	9.3	6.4	21.2	9.1	4.9	7.2
1996	100.0	79.0	63.5	9.1	6.4	21.0	9.4	4.7	6.9
1997	100.0	79.1	64.3	8.7	6.1	20.9	9.6	4.6	6.7
1998	100.0	80.0	65.8	8.4	5.8	20.1	9.3	4.5	6.3
1999	100.0	80.3	66.0	8.3	6.0	19.7	9.2	4.3	6.2
2000	100.0	80.8	67.2	8.1	5.5	19.3	9.3	4.1	5.9
2001	100.0	80.7	66.4	8.7	5.6	19.3	9.3	4.1	5.9
2002	100.0	80.3	66.4	8.3	5.6	19.7	9.7	4.1	5.9
2003	100.0	79.9	66.4	7.9	5.6	20.1	10.1	4.0	6.0
2004	100.0	80.0	66.9	7.8	5.3	20.1	10.2	4.0	5.9
2005	100.0	80.4	67.6	7.6	5.2	19.6	9.9	4.0	5.7
2006	100.0	80.9	68.5	7.5	5.0	19.1	9.6	4.0	5.5
2007	100.0	81.0	68.5	7.5	4.9	19.0	9.8	3.9	5.3
2008	100.0	79.5	65.7	8.5	5.4	20.5	10.5	4.2	5.8
2009	100.0	78.4	64.2	8.0	6.3	21.6	11.3	4.3	6.0
2010	100.0	78.3	64.8	7.6	5.9	21.7	11.2	4.3	6.2
2011	100.0	78.7	65.9	7.2	5.6	21.3	11.2	4.1	6.1
2012	100.0	78.5	65.6	7.5	5.4	21.5	11.1	4.3	6.1
Men									
1987	100.0	86.4	68.0	10.9	7.5	13.6	4.7	3.2	5.7
1988	100.0	86.5	69.0	10.5	7.0	13.6	5.0	3.1	5.5
1989	100.0	86.8	69.4	10.7	6.7	13.3	5.1	3.1	5.1
1990	100.0	86.6	68.3	11.4	6.9	13.4	5.1	3.2	5.1
1991	100.0	86.0	66.8	11.6	7.6	14.0	5.3	3.3	5.4
1992	100.0	85.8	67.1	11.1	7.6	14.3	5.4	3.3	5.6
1993	100.0	85.8	68.4	10.0	7.4	14.2	5.5	2.9	5.8
1994	100.0	86.0	69.7	9.6	6.7	13.9	5.3	3.2	5.4
1995	100.0	86.3	70.8	9.4	6.1	13.7	5.4	3.0	5.3
1996	100.0	86.3	71.0	9.1	6.2	13.7	5.7	2.8	5.2
1997	100.0	86.5	71.9	8.7	5.9	13.6	5.6	3.0	5.0
1998	100.0	87.4	74.0	8.1	5.3	12.6	5.5	2.7	4.4
1999	100.0	87.5	73.6	8.2	5.7	12.5	5.5	2.6	4.4
2000	100.0	87.5	74.6	7.7	5.2	12.6	5.7	2.5	4.4
2001	100.0	87.6	73.4	8.9	5.3	12.4	5.4	2.5	4.5
2002	100.0	87.4	73.2	8.5	5.7	12.6	5.6	2.5	4.5
2003	100.0	86.9	73.2	8.1	5.6	13.1	6.3	2.3	4.5
2004	100.0	87.1	74.0	7.9	5.2	12.9	6.1	2.5	4.3
2005	100.0	87.0	74.3	7.6	5.1	12.9	6.2	2.5	4.2
2006	100.0	87.8	75.3	7.6	5.0	12.2	5.7	2.4	4.1
2007	100.0	87.5	74.7	7.8	4.9	12.5	5.9	2.6	4.1
2008	100.0	86.1	71.4	9.1	5.6	13.9	6.5	2.9	4.5
2009	100.0	84.5	68.5	9.0	7.1	15.5	7.2	3.1	5.2
2010	100.0	84.4	69.6	8.3	6.4	15.6	7.3	3.1	5.3
2011	100.0	84.9	71.4	7.6	6.0	15.1	7.1	3.0	5.0
2012	100.0	84.6	71.2	7.9	5.6	15.4	7.5	3.0	4.9
Women									
1987	100.0	68.6	50.7	9.9	8.0	31.4	13.0	7.4	11.0
1988	100.0	68.9	51.8	9.2	7.9	31.1	13.1	7.3	10.7
1989	100.0	69.9	51.4	10.8	7.7	30.0	12.5	7.7	9.8
1990	100.0	69.9	51.6	10.7	7.6	30.2	12.8	7.6	9.8
1991	100.0	69.4	52.6	10.0	6.8	30.7	13.2	7.6	9.9
1992	100.0	69.7	53.7	9.1	6.9	30.4	13.7	7.2	9.5
1993	100.0	69.0	52.9	9.0	7.1	31.0	13.9	7.3	9.8
1994	100.0	69.0	53.0	9.2	6.8	30.9	13.9	7.1	9.9
1995	100.0	70.3	54.3	9.2	6.8	29.7	13.3	7.0	9.4
1996	100.0	70.7	54.9	9.2	6.6	29.3	13.6	6.8	8.9
1997	100.0	70.7	55.8	8.7	6.2	29.4	14.2	6.4	8.8
1998	100.0	71.6	56.5	8.7	6.4	28.4	13.6	6.4	8.4
1999	100.0	72.3	57.6	8.4	6.3	27.7	13.4	6.1	8.2
2000	100.0	73.2	58.9	8.5	5.8	26.8	13.3	6.0	7.5
2001	100.0	73.0	58.6	8.6	5.8	27.0	13.7	5.8	7.5
2002	100.0	72.5	50.8	8.1	5.6	27.6	14.2	5.8	7.6
2003	100.0	72.1	58.8	7.7	5.6	27.8	14.4	5.8	7.6
2004	100.0	72.0	59.0	7.6	5.4	28.0	14.7	5.7	7.6
2005	100.0	72.7	59.9	7.6	5.2	27.2	14.1	5.6	7.5
2006	100.0	73.1	60.7	7.3	5.1	26.9	14.1	5.7	7.1
2007	100.0	73.6	61.5	7.2	4.9	26.4	14.2	5.4	6.7
2008	100.0	72.2	59.3	7.8	5.1	27.8	15.0	5.6	7.2
2009	100.0	71.5	59.3	6.9	5.4	28.5	15.8	5.7	7.0
2010	100.0	71.5	59.4	6.9	5.2	28.5	15.6	5.6	7.3
2011	100.0	71.7	59.8	6.6	5.2	28.3	15.7	5.3	7.3
2012	100.0	71.6	59.4	7.0	5.2	28.4	15.2	5.7	7.5

Note: See notes and definitions for information on historical comparability.

Table 1-37. Extent of Unemployment During the Year, by Sex, 1987–2012

(Thousands of people, percent.)

Sex and extent of unemployment	1987	1988	1989	1990	1991	1992	1993	1994	1995	1996	1997	1998
BOTH SEXES												
Total Who Worked or Looked for Work	130 353	132 185	134 394	135 408	135 826	136 654	139 786	141 325	142 413	144 528	146 096	147 295
Percent with unemployment	14.1	12.9	12.9	14.6	15.7	15.7	14.7	13.4	12.7	11.6	10.7	9.5
Total with Unemployment	18 399	17 096	17 273	19 809	21 276	21 455	20 527	18 966	18 067	16 789	15 637	14 044
Did not work but looked for work	2 037	1 735	1 577	1 874	2 415	2 742	3 432	2 857	2 690	2 329	2 129	1 729
Worked during the year	16 362	15 362	15 697	17 936	18 861	18 714	17 094	16 109	15 377	14 460	13 508	12 316
Year-round workers with 1 or 2 weeks of unemployment	792	830	833	1 056	966	871	688	746	715	589	611	630
Part-year workers with unemployment	15 570	14 532	14 864	16 880	17 895	17 843	16 406	15 363	14 662	13 871	12 897	11 686
1 to 4 weeks	3 363	3 256	3 489	3 645	3 224	2 944	2 626	2 788	2 812	2 550	2 582	2 323
5 to 10 weeks	3 191	3 148	3 359	3 669	3 655	3 496	2 898	2 983	2 725	2 671	2 601	2 495
11 to 14 weeks	2 258	2 128	2 235	2 501	2 587	2 574	2 300	2 265	2 147	2 020	1 822	1 701
15 to 26 weeks	3 904	3 479	3 600	4 316	4 927	4 877	4 549	4 158	4 013	3 662	3 378	3 019
27 weeks or more	2 854	2 521	2 181	2 749	3 502	3 952	4 033	3 169	2 965	2 968	2 514	2 148
With 2 or more spells of unemployment	5 149	5 136	5 073	5 811	5 864	5 734	5 338	4 783	4 468	4 237	4 044	3 628
2 spells	2 442	2 460	2 460	2 855	2 738	2 698	2 572	2 207	1 963	1 982	1 853	1 650
3 or more spells	2 707	2 676	2 613	2 956	3 126	3 036	2 766	2 576	2 505	2 255	2 191	1 978
MEN												
Total Who Worked or Looked for Work	69 995	70 738	72 362	72 844	72 909	73 387	74 516	75 244	75 698	76 786	77 385	77 704
Percent with unemployment	15.0	13.7	13.5	15.5	17.3	17.5	15.7	14.1	13.2	11.9	11.1	9.4
Total with Unemployment	10 504	9 696	9 792	11 307	12 642	12 844	11 723	10 582	9 996	9 157	8 604	7 284
Did not work but looked for work	852	717	723	891	1 210	1 379	1 641	1 286	1 317	1 026	978	787
Worked during the year	9 653	8 978	9 071	10 415	11 432	11 466	10 082	9 296	8 679	8 130	7 626	6 497
Year-round workers with 1 or 2 weeks of unemployment	536	585	568	711	612	567	449	527	462	395	382	386
Part-year workers with unemployment	9 117	8 393	8 503	9 704	10 820	10 899	9 633	8 769	8 217	7 735	7 244	6 111
1 to 4 weeks	1 561	1 633	1 742	1 819	1 591	1 563	1 343	1 365	1 398	1 272	1 275	1 085
5 to 10 weeks	1 824	1 808	1 890	2 041	2 111	2 039	1 647	1 666	1 434	1 478	1 474	1 363
11 to 14 weeks	1 415	1 279	1 365	1 462	1 659	1 615	1 354	1 370	1 253	1 258	1 068	980
15 to 26 weeks	2 514	2 124	2 188	2 645	3 206	3 165	2 862	2 449	2 439	2 076	1 949	1 585
27 weeks or more	1 803	1 549	1 318	1 737	2 253	2 517	2 427	1 919	1 693	1 651	1 478	1 098
With 2 or more spells of unemployment	3 300	3 366	3 178	3 689	3 886	3 889	3 451	2 940	2 793	2 554	2 437	2 014
2 spells	1 488	1 560	1 517	1 676	1 742	1 781	1 580	1 266	1 110	1 109	1 078	880
3 or more spells	1 812	1 806	1 661	2 013	2 144	2 108	1 871	1 674	1 683	1 445	1 359	1 134
WOMEN												
Total Who Worked or Looked for Work	60 357	61 447	62 032	62 564	62 917	63 267	65 270	66 081	66 716	67 742	68 710	69 591
Percent with unemployment	13.1	12.0	12.1	13.6	13.7	13.6	13.5	12.7	12.1	11.3	10.2	9.7
Total with Unemployment	7 895	7 400	7 481	8 502	8 634	8 611	8 804	8 383	8 070	7 632	7 033	6 760
Did not work but looked for work	1 185	1 017	854	982	1 205	1 363	1 791	1 570	1 373	1 303	1 151	942
Worked during the year	6 710	6 382	6 628	7 520	7 427	7 247	7 014	6 813	6 696	6 330	5 882	5 816
Year-round workers with 1 or 2 weeks of unemployment	255	244	265	344	354	304	239	219	253	194	229	243
Part-year workers with unemployment	6 455	6 138	6 363	7 176	7 073	6 943	6 775	6 594	6 443	6 136	5 653	5 573
1 to 4 weeks	1 802	1 623	1 747	1 827	1 633	1 380	1 284	1 422	1 413	1 279	1 307	1 237
5 to 10 weeks	1 368	1 340	1 469	1 627	1 544	1 457	1 252	1 317	1 291	1 192	1 127	1 131
11 to 14 weeks	844	849	870	1 038	927	959	946	896	893	762	754	721
15 to 26 weeks	1 391	1 354	1 413	1 671	1 720	1 712	1 687	1 708	1 574	1 586	1 429	1 434
27 weeks or more	1 050	972	864	1 013	1 249	1 435	1 606	1 251	1 272	1 317	1 036	1 050
With 2 or more spells of unemployment	1 849	1 769	1 895	2 122	1 979	1 844	1 887	1 843	1 675	1 682	1 607	1 614
2 spells	954	899	943	1 179	997	916	992	941	853	872	775	770
3 or more spells	895	870	952	943	982	928	895	902	822	810	832	844

Table 1-37. Extent of Unemployment During the Year, by Sex, 1987–2012—*Continued*

(Thousands of people, percent.)

Sex and extent of unemployment	1999	2000	2001	2002	2003	2004	2005	2006	2007	2008	2009	2010	2011	2012
BOTH SEXES														
Total Who Worked or Looked for Work	149 798	150 786	153 056	154 205	154 315	155 576	157 549	159 259	160 565	161 506	160 624	159 706	160 545	162 574
Percent with unemployment	8.7	8.1	10.4	10.9	10.7	9.7	9.2	9.1	9.4	13.1	16.3	15.8	14.8	13.8
Total with Unemployment	13 068	12 269	15 843	16 824	16 462	15 074	14 558	14 447	15 130	21 231	26 151	25 262	23 752	22 460
Did not work but looked for work	1 503	1 425	2 014	2 660	2 762	2 551	2 422	1 907	2 097	3 189	5 851	6 564	6 216	5 525
Worked during the year	11 566	10 845	13 829	14 164	13 699	12 522	12 136	12 540	13 033	18 042	20 300	18 698	17 537	16 936
Year-round workers with 1 or 2 weeks of unemployment	562	573	602	584	534	465	431	450	500	763	693	591	417	465
Part-year workers with unemployment	11 004	10 272	13 227	13 580	13 165	12 057	11 705	12 090	12 533	17 279	19 607	18 107	17 119	16 470
1 to 4 weeks	2 361	2 233	2 368	2 002	1 839	1 985	1 941	2 601	2 593	2 794	2 528	2 267	2 211	2 252
5 to 10 weeks	2 218	2 014	2 557	2 373	2 264	2 100	2 170	2 107	2 090	2 944	2 562	2 397	2 276	2 351
11 to 14 weeks	1 594	1 505	2 038	1 970	1 749	1 773	1 698	1 615	1 888	2 438	2 414	2 302	2 064	2 176
15 to 26 weeks	2 803	2 641	3 683	3 848	3 778	3 448	3 349	3 176	3 373	4 859	5 698	5 116	4 949	4 715
27 weeks or more	2 028	1 879	2 582	3 387	3 535	2 751	2 547	2 592	2 589	4 244	6 405	6 025	5 619	4 976
With 2 or more spells of unemployment	3 225	3 079	3 421	3 226	3 093	2 896	3 095	3 076	3 108	3 991	4 152	3 875	3 527	3 763
2 spells	1 449	1 397	1 643	1 556	1 585	1 344	1 477	1 564	1 427	1 987	1 918	1 789	1 745	1 730
3 or more spells	1 776	1 682	1 779	1 670	1 508	1 552	1 618	1 513	1 681	2 004	2 234	2 086	1 782	2 033
MEN														
Total Who Worked or Looked for Work	78 905	79 546	80 975	81 651	81 804	82 478	83 951	84 736	85 368	85 563	85 161	84 738	84 486	85 778
Percent with unemployment	9.0	8.6	11.0	11.8	11.4	10.0	9.7	9.6	10.2	14.4	18.6	17.6	15.7	14.4
Total with Unemployment	7 091	6 806	8 928	9 621	9 339	8 256	8 116	8 115	8 698	12 331	15 877	14 900	13 273	12 388
Did not work but looked for work	760	742	1 004	1 369	1 487	1 217	1 216	969	1 076	1 674	3 325	3 662	3 214	2 868
Worked during the year	6 332	6 064	7 924	8 252	7 854	7 039	6 899	7 146	7 622	10 656	12 552	11 238	10 059	9 520
Year-round workers with 1 or 2 weeks of unemployment	373	379	421	365	359	289	296	295	365	484	458	379	271	310
Part-year workers with unemployment	5 959	5 685	7 502	7 887	7 495	6 750	6 603	6 850	7 257	10 172	12 093	10 859	9 788	9 210
1 to 4 weeks	1 166	1 070	1 247	1 075	958	1 028	1 052	1 283	1 367	1 523	1 466	1 186	1 170	1 189
5 to 10 weeks	1 168	1 135	1 446	1 342	1 314	1 170	1 209	1 267	1 214	1 701	1 594	1 423	1 240	1 364
11 to 14 weeks	937	880	1 207	1 186	1 039	1 021	1 024	961	1 163	1 467	1 558	1 441	1 277	1 243
15 to 26 weeks	1 655	1 595	2 191	2 282	2 178	2 065	1 923	1 868	2 058	3 035	3 564	3 233	2 941	2 719
27 weeks or more	1 033	1 005	1 412	2 002	2 006	1 466	1 395	1 472	1 455	2 445	3 911	3 577	3 159	2 696
With 2 or more spells of unemployment	1 845	1 809	2 100	1 920	1 882	1 828	1 975	1 936	1 992	2 623	2 865	2 623	2 450	2 328
2 spells	787	804	1 002	914	946	808	940	945	847	1 234	1 299	1 133	1 121	1 003
3 or more spells	1 058	1 005	1 099	1 006	936	1 020	1 035	991	1 145	1 389	1 566	1 491	1 329	1 325
WOMEN														
Total Who Worked or Looked for Work	70 893	71 240	72 081	72 554	72 511	73 097	73 598	74 523	75 197	75 943	75 463	74 968	76 060	76 797
Percent with unemployment	8.4	7.7	9.6	9.9	9.8	9.3	8.8	8.5	8.6	11.7	13.6	13.8	13.8	13.1
Total with Unemployment	5 976	5 463	6 915	7 203	7 123	6 818	6 442	6 332	6 432	8 900	10 274	10 362	10 479	10 073
Did not work but looked for work	743	683	1 010	1 291	1 275	1 334	1 206	938	1 021	1 514	2 526	2 903	3 002	2 657
Worked during the year	5 234	4 779	5 905	5 913	5 848	5 484	5 236	5 394	5 411	7 385	7 748	7 459	7 478	7 416
Year-round workers with 1 or 2 weeks of unemployment	189	193	180	220	176	177	136	154	135	279	235	211	147	155
Part-year workers with unemployment	5 045	4 586	5 725	5 693	5 672	5 307	5 100	5 240	5 276	7 106	7 513	7 248	7 331	7 261
1 to 4 weeks	1 194	1 164	1 121	927	882	957	888	1 317	1 226	1 270	1 061	1 081	1 041	1 064
5 to 10 weeks	1 050	878	1 111	1 031	950	929	961	840	876	1 243	968	974	1 036	987
11 to 14 weeks	657	625	831	784	710	752	674	655	725	971	857	861	787	933
15 to 26 weeks	1 148	1 045	1 492	1 566	1 600	1 384	1 426	1 307	1 316	1 823	2 134	1 883	2 008	1 997
27 weeks or more	996	874	1 170	1 385	1 530	1 285	1 151	1 120	1 134	1 800	2 494	2 448	2 459	2 280
With 2 or more spells of unemployment	1 379	1 270	1 321	1 306	1 211	1 069	1 120	1 140	1 116	1 368	1 287	1 252	1 077	1 435
2 spells	662	593	641	642	639	537	537	619	580	753	619	657	624	727
3 or more spells	717	677	680	664	572	532	583	521	536	616	668	595	453	707

Table 1-38. Percent Distribution of Persons with Unemployment During the Year, by Sex and Extent of Unemployment, 1987–2012

(Percent.)

Sex and extent of unemployment	1987	1988	1989	1990	1991	1992	1993	1994	1995	1996	1997	1998	1999
BOTH SEXES													
Total with Unemployment Who Worked During the Year	100.0	100.0	100.0	100.0	100.0	100.0	100.0	100.0	100.0	100.0	100.0	100.0	100.0
Year-round workers with 1 or 2 weeks of unemployment	4.8	5.4	5.3	5.9	5.1	4.7	4.0	4.6	4.6	4.1	4.5	5.1	4.9
Part-year workers with unemployment	95.2	94.5	94.6	94.1	94.8	95.4	96.1	95.4	95.4	96.0	95.5	95.0	95.1
1 to 4 weeks	20.6	21.2	22.2	20.3	17.1	15.7	15.4	17.3	18.3	17.6	19.1	18.9	20.4
5 to 10 weeks	19.5	20.5	21.4	20.5	19.4	18.7	17.0	18.5	17.7	18.5	19.3	20.3	19.2
11 to 14 weeks	13.8	13.8	14.2	13.9	13.7	13.8	13.5	14.1	14.0	14.0	13.5	13.8	13.8
15 to 26 weeks	23.9	22.6	22.9	24.1	26.1	26.1	26.6	25.8	26.1	25.3	25.0	24.5	24.2
27 weeks or more	17.4	16.4	13.9	15.3	18.5	21.1	23.6	19.7	19.3	20.6	18.6	17.5	17.5
With 2 or more spells of unemployment	31.4	33.4	32.3	32.4	31.1	30.6	31.2	29.7	29.1	29.3	29.9	29.5	27.9
2 spells	14.9	16.0	15.7	15.9	14.5	14.4	15.0	13.7	12.8	13.7	13.7	13.4	12.5
3 or more spells	16.5	17.4	16.6	16.5	16.6	16.2	16.2	16.0	16.3	15.6	16.2	16.1	15.4
MEN													
Total with Unemployment Who Worked During the Year	100.0	100.0	100.0	100.0	100.0	100.0	100.0	100.0	100.0	100.0	100.0	100.0	100.0
Year-round workers with 1 or 2 weeks of unemployment	5.6	6.5	6.3	6.8	5.4	4.9	4.4	5.7	5.3	4.9	5.0	5.9	5.9
Part-year workers with unemployment	94.5	93.4	93.7	93.2	94.6	95.0	95.5	94.3	94.7	95.1	95.1	94.1	94.0
1 to 4 weeks	16.2	18.2	19.2	17.5	13.9	13.6	13.3	14.7	16.1	15.6	16.7	16.7	18.4
5 to 10 weeks	18.9	20.1	20.8	19.6	18.5	17.8	16.3	17.9	16.5	18.2	19.3	21.0	18.4
11 to 14 weeks	14.7	14.2	15.1	14.0	14.5	14.1	13.4	14.7	14.4	15.5	14.0	15.1	14.8
15 to 26 weeks	26.0	23.7	24.1	25.4	28.0	27.6	28.4	26.4	28.1	25.5	25.6	24.4	26.1
27 weeks or more	18.7	17.2	14.5	16.7	19.7	21.9	24.1	20.6	19.5	20.3	19.4	16.9	16.3
With 2 or more spells of unemployment	34.2	37.5	35.0	35.4	34.0	33.9	34.3	31.6	32.2	31.4	31.9	31.0	29.1
2 spells	15.4	17.4	16.7	16.1	15.2	15.5	15.7	13.6	12.8	13.6	14.1	13.5	12.4
3 or more spells	18.8	20.1	18.3	19.3	18.8	18.4	18.6	18.0	19.4	17.8	17.8	17.5	16.7
WOMEN													
Total With Unemployment Who Worked During the Year	100.0	100.0	100.0	100.0	100.0	100.0	100.0	100.0	100.0	100.0	100.0	100.0	100.0
Year-round workers with 1 or 2 weeks of unemployment	3.8	3.8	4.0	4.6	4.8	4.2	3.4	3.2	3.8	3.1	3.9	4.2	3.6
Part-year workers with unemployment	96.3	96.1	96.0	95.3	95.3	95.7	96.6	96.7	96.2	96.9	96.1	95.8	96.4
1 to 4 weeks	26.9	25.4	26.4	24.3	22.0	19.0	18.3	20.9	21.1	20.2	22.2	21.3	22.8
5 to 10 weeks	20.4	21.0	22.2	21.6	20.8	20.1	17.8	19.3	19.3	18.8	19.2	19.4	20.1
11 to 14 weeks	12.6	13.3	13.1	13.8	12.5	13.2	13.5	13.1	13.3	12.0	12.8	12.4	12.6
15 to 26 weeks	20.7	21.2	21.3	22.2	23.2	23.6	24.1	25.1	23.5	25.1	24.3	24.7	21.9
27 weeks or more	15.7	15.2	13.0	13.4	16.8	19.8	22.9	18.3	19.0	20.8	17.6	18.0	19.0
With 2 or more spells of unemployment	27.5	27.7	28.6	28.2	26.6	25.4	26.9	27.0	25.0	26.6	27.3	27.7	26.3
2 spells	14.2	14.1	14.2	15.7	13.4	12.6	14.1	13.8	12.7	13.8	13.2	13.2	12.6
3 or more spells	13.3	13.6	14.4	12.5	13.2	12.8	12.8	13.2	12.3	12.8	14.1	14.5	13.7

Table 1-38. Percent Distribution of Persons with Unemployment During the Year, by Sex and Extent of Unemployment, 1987–2012—*Continued*

(Percent.)

Sex and extent of unemployment	2000	2001	2002	2003	2004	2005	2006	2007	2008	2009	2010	2011	2012
BOTH SEXES													
Total with Unemployment Who Worked During the Year	100.0	100.0	100.0	100.0	100.0	100.0	100.0	100.0	100.0	100.0	100.0	100.0	100.0
Year-round workers with 1 or 2 weeks of unemployment	5.3	4.4	4.1	3.9	3.7	3.6	3.6	3.8	4.2	3.4	3.2	2.4	2.7
Part-year workers with unemployment	94.8	95.6	95.9	96.1	96.3	96.4	96.4	96.1	95.8	96.5	96.8	97.6	97.3
1 to 4 weeks	20.6	17.1	14.1	13.4	15.9	16.0	20.7	19.9	15.5	12.5	12.1	12.6	13.3
5 to 10 weeks	18.6	18.5	16.8	16.5	16.8	17.9	16.8	16.0	16.3	12.6	12.8	13.0	13.9
11 to 14 weeks	13.9	14.7	13.9	12.8	14.2	14.0	12.9	14.5	13.5	11.9	12.3	11.8	12.8
15 to 26 weeks	24.4	26.6	27.2	27.6	27.5	27.6	25.3	25.9	26.9	28.1	27.4	28.2	27.8
27 weeks or more	17.3	18.7	23.9	25.8	22.0	20.9	20.7	19.8	23.5	31.5	32.2	32.0	29.4
With 2 or more spells of unemployment	28.4	24.8	22.8	22.6	23.1	25.5	24.5	23.8	22.1	20.5	20.7	20.1	22.2
2 spells	12.9	11.9	11.0	11.6	10.7	12.2	12.5	10.9	11.0	9.4	9.6	10.0	10.2
3 or more spells	15.5	12.9	11.8	11.0	12.4	13.3	12.1	12.9	11.1	11.0	11.2	10.2	12.0
MEN													
Total with Unemployment Who Worked During the Year	100.0	100.0	100.0	100.0	100.0	100.0	100.0	100.0	100.0	100.0	100.0	100.0	100.0
Year-round workers with 1 or 2 weeks of unemployment	6.3	5.3	4.4	4.6	4.1	4.3	4.1	4.8	4.5	3.7	3.4	2.7	3.3
Part-year workers with unemployment	93.6	94.7	95.6	95.4	95.9	95.7	95.9	95.2	95.5	96.4	96.6	97.3	96.7
1 to 4 weeks	17.6	15.7	13.0	12.2	14.6	15.3	18.0	17.9	14.3	11.7	10.5	11.6	12.5
5 to 10 weeks	18.7	18.2	16.3	16.7	16.6	17.5	17.7	15.9	16.0	12.7	12.7	12.3	14.3
11 to 14 weeks	14.5	15.2	14.4	13.2	14.5	14.8	13.4	15.3	13.8	12.4	12.8	12.7	13.1
15 to 26 weeks	26.3	27.6	27.7	27.7	29.3	27.9	26.1	27.0	28.5	28.4	28.8	29.2	28.6
27 weeks or more	16.5	17.8	24.3	25.5	20.8	20.2	20.6	19.1	22.9	31.2	31.8	31.4	28.3
With 2 or more spells of unemployment	29.9	26.5	23.3	24.0	26.0	28.6	27.1	26.1	24.6	22.8	23.3	24.4	24.5
2 spells	13.3	12.6	11.1	12.1	11.5	13.6	13.2	11.1	11.6	10.3	10.1	11.1	10.5
3 or more spells	16.6	13.9	12.2	11.9	14.5	15.0	13.9	15.0	13.0	12.5	13.3	13.2	13.9
WOMEN													
Total With Unemployment Who Worked During the Year	100.0	100.0	100.0	100.0	100.0	100.0	100.0	100.0	100.0	100.0	100.0	100.0	100.0
Year-round workers with 1 or 2 weeks of unemployment	4.0	3.1	3.7	3.0	3.2	2.6	2.9	2.5	3.8	3.0	2.8	2.0	2.1
Part-year workers with unemployment	96.0	96.9	96.3	97.0	96.8	97.4	97.1	97.4	96.2	96.9	97.2	98.0	97.9
1 to 4 weeks	24.3	19.0	15.7	15.1	17.4	17.0	24.4	22.6	17.2	13.7	14.5	13.9	14.3
5 to 10 weeks	18.4	18.8	17.4	16.2	16.9	18.4	15.6	16.2	16.8	12.5	13.1	13.9	13.3
11 to 14 weeks	13.1	14.1	13.3	12.1	13.7	12.9	12.1	13.4	13.1	11.1	11.5	10.5	12.6
15 to 26 weeks	21.9	25.3	26.5	27.4	25.2	27.2	24.2	24.3	24.7	27.5	25.2	26.8	26.9
27 weeks or more	18.3	19.8	23.4	26.2	23.5	22.0	20.8	20.9	24.4	32.1	32.8	32.9	30.8
With 2 or more spells of unemployment	26.6	22.4	22.1	20.7	19.5	21.4	21.1	20.6	18.5	16.6	16.8	14.4	19.3
2 spells	12.4	10.9	10.9	10.9	9.8	10.3	11.5	10.7	10.2	8.0	8.8	8.3	9.8
3 or more spells	14.2	11.5	11.2	9.8	9.7	11.1	9.7	9.9	8.3	8.6	8.0	6.1	9.5

Table 1-39. Number and Median Annual Earnings of Year-Round, Full-Time Wage and Salary Workers, by Age, Sex, and Race, 1987–2012

(Thousands of people, dollars.)

Sex, age, and race	1987	1988	1989	1990	1991	1992	1993	1994	1995	1996	1997	1998	1999
NUMBER													
Both Sexes, 16 Years and Over	71 069	73 598	74 898	74 728	74 449	75 517	77 427	79 875	83 407	85 611	86 905	89 748	91 722
16 to 24 years	7 563	7 400	7 471	6 978	6 571	6 224	6 685	6 684	6 892	6 809	7 063	7 618	7 631
25 to 44 years	42 211	44 036	45 082	45 086	44 811	45 022	45 951	47 150	48 695	49 225	49 513	50 264	50 532
25 to 34 years	22 884	23 727	23 721	23 201	22 541	22 469	22 637	23 193	23 310	23 071	23 186	23 048	22 952
35 to 44 years	19 327	20 309	21 361	21 885	22 270	22 553	23 314	23 957	25 385	26 154	26 327	27 216	27 580
45 to 54 years	12 764	13 506	13 848	14 070	14 718	15 652	16 424	17 366	18 436	19 714	20 109	21 274	22 375
55 to 64 years	7 406	7 529	7 321	7 458	7 219	7 590	7 208	7 500	8 122	8 455	8 901	9 273	9 594
65 years and over	1 125	1 127	1 177	1 137	1 130	1 029	1 159	1 174	1 263	1 408	1 318	1 318	1 590
Men, 16 Years and Over	42 490	43 785	45 107	44 574	43 523	43 894	45 494	47 255	49 334	50 407	50 772	52 509	53 132
16 to 24 years	4 145	4 165	4 223	3 982	3 596	3 457	3 853	3 918	4 094	3 942	4 021	4 479	4 347
25 to 44 years	25 293	26 246	27 321	27 069	26 353	26 335	27 161	28 000	28 940	29 282	29 453	29 763	29 738
25 to 34 years	13 659	14 163	14 439	13 941	13 303	13 146	13 400	13 749	13 844	13 817	13 735	13 612	13 471
35 to 44 years	11 634	12 083	12 882	13 128	13 050	13 189	13 761	14 251	15 096	15 465	15 718	16 151	16 267
45 to 54 years	7 726	8 086	8 276	8 168	8 479	8 908	9 522	10 120	10 589	11 372	11 388	12 030	12 546
55 to 64 years	4 654	4 616	4 562	4 650	4 403	4 588	4 238	4 460	4 884	4 908	5 133	5 438	5 498
65 years and over	672	672	725	705	694	606	719	757	827	903	775	801	1 003
Women, 16 Years and Over	28 579	29 812	29 791	30 155	30 925	31 622	31 933	32 619	34 073	35 203	36 133	37 239	38 591
16 to 24 years	3 418	3 235	3 249	2 995	2 976	2 767	2 832	2 767	2 798	2 867	3 041	3 140	3 285
25 to 44 years	16 918	17 790	17 760	18 017	18 458	18 688	18 790	19 150	19 755	19 942	20 060	20 503	20 794
25 to 34 years	9 225	9 564	9 282	9 260	9 238	9 323	9 237	9 444	9 467	9 254	9 451	9 437	9 481
35 to 44 years	7 693	8 226	8 478	8 757	9 220	9 365	9 553	9 706	10 288	10 688	10 609	11 066	11 313
45 to 54 years	5 037	5 420	5 572	5 902	6 239	6 744	6 902	7 246	7 847	8 343	8 721	9 244	9 829
55 to 64 years	2 752	2 913	2 758	2 808	2 816	3 002	2 970	3 040	3 238	3 547	3 767	3 836	4 096
65 years and over	453	455	451	433	436	423	439	417	436	505	543	517	586
White, 16 Years and Over	61 546	63 357	64 246	64 128	63 926	64 706	65 656	67 370	70 430	72 068	72 650	75 046	76 203
Men	37 461	38 449	39 430	38 915	38 018	38 267	39 347	40 589	42 608	43 554	43 429	44 901	45 211
Women	24 085	24 908	24 815	25 213	25 908	26 439	26 309	26 782	27 822	28 514	29 221	30 145	30 992
Black, 16 Years and Over	7 440	7 907	8 140	8 027	7 941	7 995	8 478	9 074	9 446	9 706	10 248	10 532	11 145
Men	3 838	3 976	4 219	4 162	4 001	4 011	4 259	4 598	4 686	4 682	5 026	5 202	5 411
Women	3 602	3 931	3 920	3 865	3 940	3 984	4 219	4 476	4 759	5 024	5 222	5 329	5 734
MEDIAN ANNUAL EARNINGS													
Both Sexes, 16 Years and Over	21 000	22 000	23 000	24 000	25 000	25 871	26 000	26 620	27 000	28 000	30 000	30 000	31 000
16 to 24 years	13 000	13 500	14 000	14 400	14 100	15 000	15 000	15 000	15 500	15 600	16 000	18 000	18 000
25 to 34 years	20 000	21 000	22 000	22 000	23 000	24 000	24 000	24 480	25 000	25 300	27 000	28 500	30 000
35 to 44 years	25 000	26 000	27 000	27 970	28 000	29 483	30 000	30 000	30 000	31 000	32 000	33 000	34 992
45 to 54 years	25 000	26 000	27 000	28 000	29 000	30 000	30 500	32 343	32 000	33 000	35 000	35 000	36 000
55 to 64 years	23 000	24 000	26 000	26 000	27 000	27 430	28 000	30 000	30 000	30 000	32 000	34 000	35 000
65 years and over	18 000	19 500	23 000	23 841	22 000	24 000	24 000	24 377	29 600	26 496	28 200	26 000	30 000
Men, 16 Years and Over	25 900	26 570	27 300	28 000	29 120	30 000	30 000	30 000	31 000	32 000	34 000	35 000	36 000
16 to 24 years	14 000	14 200	15 000	15 000	15 000	15 000	15 000	15 000	16 000	17 000	17 000	18 720	19 000
25 to 34 years	23 000	24 000	24 000	25 000	25 000	26 000	25 000	26 000	27 000	28 000	29 852	30 000	32 000
35 to 44 years	30 000	31 000	32 000	32 000	33 000	34 000	35 000	35 000	35 000	36 000	37 000	38 000	40 000
45 to 54 years	31 200	32 000	34 000	35 000	36 000	37 000	38 000	40 000	40 000	40 000	41 000	42 000	44 616
55 to 64 years	29 181	30 000	32 000	31 875	33 000	33 000	34 000	36 000	36 000	36 000	36 000	39 000	40 853
65 years and over	24 000	25 000	30 000	29 000	28 000	30 000	28 000	30 000	36 000	33 000	36 400	35 000	36 000
Women, 16 Years and Over	17 000	18 000	18 574	20 000	20 000	21 500	22 000	22 150	23 000	24 000	25 000	25 000	26 000
16 to 24 years	12 000	13 000	13 167	13 392	13 800	14 000	14 872	14 560	15 000	15 000	15 000	17 000	17 000
25 to 34 years	17 000	18 000	19 000	19 500	20 000	21 000	21 000	22 000	22 000	23 000	24 000	25 000	26 000
35 to 44 years	19 000	20 000	20 200	22 000	22 510	23 397	24 000	25 000	25 000	25 000	26 000	27 200	28 000
45 to 54 years	18 148	19 000	20 000	21 000	22 000	24 000	24 000	25 000	25 000	26 000	27 040	28 132	30 000
55 to 64 years	17 000	17 000	18 000	19 000	20 000	22 000	21 500	22 000	22 500	24 000	24 800	25 775	27 000
65 years and over	16 000	15 600	17 566	18 586	17 000	18 500	20 000	19 000	23 290	20 800	24 000	22 000	20 800
White, 16 Years and Over	22 000	23 000	24 000	25 000	25 000	26 200	27 000	28 000	28 000	29 000	30 000	31 000	32 000
Men	26 500	27 489	28 500	29 000	30 000	31 000	30 700	32 000	32 000	33 000	35 000	36 000	37 200
Women	17 000	18 000	19 000	20 000	20 500	22 000	22 000	23 000	23 000	24 000	25 000	26 000	27 000
Black, 16 Years and Over	17 000	18 000	19 000	19 350	20 000	21 000	20 800	21 000	22 000	23 784	24 000	25 000	25 760
Men	18 850	20 000	20 000	20 800	22 000	22 312	23 000	23 500	24 500	26 000	26 000	27 000	30 000
Women	15 500	16 200	17 115	18 000	18 500	20 000	19 843	20 000	20 000	21 000	22 000	23 000	24 000

Table 1-39. Number and Median Annual Earnings of Year-Round, Full-Time Wage and Salary Workers, by Age, Sex, and Race, 1987–2012—*Continued*

(Thousands of people, dollars.)

Sex, age, and race	2000	2001	2002	2003	2004	2005	2006	2007	2008	2009	2010	2011	2012
NUMBER													
Both Sexes, 16 Years and Over	94 359	94 531	94 526	94 731	96 098	98 632	101 353	102 441	98 493	94 012	94 110	96 562	97 879
16 to 24 years	8 384	7 989	7 903	7 631	7 702	7 956	8 113	8 064	7 242	6 302	6 073	6 411	6 424
25 to 44 years	51 159	49 939	49 120	48 343	48 421	49 149	50 056	49 725	47 364	44 579	44 441	45 166	45 812
25 to 34 years	23 044	22 744	22 657	22 512	22 405	22 808	23 613	23 646	22 786	21 572	21 894	21 989	22 690
35 to 44 years	28 115	27 195	26 463	25 831	26 016	26 341	26 443	26 080	24 578	23 007	22 546	23 177	23 122
45 to 54 years	23 307	23 855	23 999	24 507	25 074	25 661	26 338	26 566	25 722	24 877	24 388	24 782	24 593
55 to 64 years	9 870	10 948	11 584	12 207	12 812	13 605	14 340	15 248	15 286	15 274	16 073	16 622	17 255
65 years and over	1 639	1 800	1 921	2 042	2 090	2 262	2 507	2 837	2 879	2 980	3 135	3 582	3 795
Men, 16 Years and Over	54 477	54 630	54 420	54 575	55 610	57 020	58 533	58 673	55 973	52 362	52 793	54 542	55 489
16 to 24 years	4 602	4 605	4 570	4 421	4 493	4 663	4 812	4 719	4 112	3 494	3 462	3 649	3 730
25 to 44 years	30 080	29 271	28 855	28 499	28 763	29 151	29 589	29 004	27 546	25 324	25 449	25 959	26 476
25 to 34 years	13 497	13 386	13 400	13 288	13 430	13 629	13 933	13 706	13 208	12 085	12 475	12 616	13 043
35 to 44 years	16 583	15 885	15 455	15 211	15 333	15 522	15 655	15 298	14 337	13 239	12 974	13 343	13 433
45 to 54 years	13 045	13 363	13 330	13 616	13 975	14 382	14 758	14 810	14 199	13 521	13 373	13 723	13 690
55 to 64 years	5 693	6 253	6 502	6 872	7 165	7 489	7 905	8 449	8 397	8 289	8 727	9 066	9 315
65 years and over	1 057	1 138	1 163	1 165	1 213	1 334	1 469	1 692	1 720	1 733	1 782	2 146	2 278
Women, 16 Years and Over	39 887	39 901	40 106	40 156	40 488	41 613	42 820	43 768	42 520	41 650	41 318	42 020	42 390
16 to 24 years	3 782	3 384	3 333	3 210	3 209	3 293	3 301	3 345	3 130	2 808	2 611	2 762	2 694
25 to 44 years	21 081	20 668	20 264	19 844	19 656	19 997	20 467	20 721	19 819	19 255	18 992	19 207	19 336
25 to 34 years	9 548	9 358	9 257	9 224	8 974	9 179	9 679	9 940	9 578	9 487	9 420	9 373	9 647
35 to 44 years	11 533	11 310	11 007	10 620	10 682	10 818	10 788	10 782	10 240	9 768	9 572	9 834	9 689
45 to 54 years	10 263	10 493	10 669	10 891	11 099	11 279	11 580	11 757	11 524	11 356	11 016	11 059	10 903
55 to 64 years	4 178	4 695	5 082	5 335	5 647	6 116	6 434	6 799	6 889	6 984	7 346	7 556	7 940
65 years and over	583	662	758	877	877	927	1 038	1 146	1 158	1 247	1 354	1 436	1 518
White, 16 Years and Over	77 790	78 306	77 632	77 545	78 236	80 546	82 411	83 139	79 980	76 470	76 557	77 669	78 266
Men	46 105	46 373	45 823	45 816	46 317	47 790	48 897	48 825	46 608	43 622	44 018	45 037	45 460
Women	31 685	31 933	31 809	31 729	31 919	32 756	33 513	34 314	33 372	32 848	32 540	32 632	32 806
Black, 16 Years and Over	11 899	11 001	10 966	10 979	11 301	11 417	11 988	11 987	11 424	10 716	10 676	11 009	11 193
Men	5 636	5 281	5 150	5 196	5 470	5 402	5 679	5 689	5 377	4 952	4 957	5 111	5 323
Women	6 264	5 720	5 816	5 783	5 832	6 015	6 309	6 299	6 046	5 764	5 719	5 898	5 870
MEDIAN ANNUAL EARNINGS													
Both Sexes, 16 Years and Over	32 000	34 000	35 000	35 000	35 672	36 400	38 000	40 000	40 000	41 000	42 000	42 000	44 000
16 to 24 years	19 000	20 000	20 000	20 000	20 000	20 000	21 000	22 421	24 000	23 532	23 000	22 650	23 000
25 to 34 years	30 000	31 000	31 800	32 000	33 000	33 000	35 000	35 000	36 500	38 000	37 815	38 000	39 000
35 to 44 years	35 000	36 000	37 000	39 000	40 000	40 000	41 000	43 000	45 000	45 000	45 000	45 000	48 000
45 to 54 years	38 000	39 500	40 000	40 000	40 000	42 000	44 000	45 000	45 000	46 000	48 000	48 000	50 000
55 to 64 years	35 000	36 400	39 145	40 000	40 000	41 000	43 000	45 000	46 000	48 000	49 000	50 000	50 000
65 years and over	32 000	32 000	33 000	32 000	35 000	35 000	35 001	40 000	42 000	42 000	45 000	44 200	48 000
Men, 16 Years and Over	37 600	38 500	40 000	40 000	40 000	40 051	42 000	45 000	46 000	48 000	48 000	48 000	50 000
16 to 24 years	20 000	20 000	20 000	20 800	20 800	20 800	22 000	23 000	25 000	25 000	24 000	24 000	24 480
25 to 34 years	33 500	34 000	34 740	35 000	35 000	35 000	36 000	38 000	40 000	40 000	40 000	40 000	40 000
35 to 44 years	40 000	42 000	43 000	43 900	45 000	45 000	48 000	50 000	50 000	50 000	50 000	51 000	52 000
45 to 54 years	45 000	45 000	47 000	48 000	48 000	50 000	50 000	50 000	52 000	53 004	55 000	55 000	57 000
55 to 64 years	44 000	45 000	47 000	50 000	50 000	50 000	50 000	50 000	52 000	54 000	55 000	57 000	55 000
65 years and over	35 999	35 000	37 861	42 000	40 000	41 000	44 000	44 000	50 000	49 000	50 002	50 000	53 700
Women, 16 Years and Over	27 500	29 000	30 000	30 000	30 001	32 000	33 000	35 000	35 000	36 000	37 000	37 000	38 000
16 to 24 years	18 000	19 000	19 000	20 000	20 000	20 000	20 000	22 000	22 000	22 000	20 816	22 000	22 000
25 to 34 years	27 000	28 080	29 500	30 000	30 000	30 000	31 000	33 000	34 000	35 000	35 000	35 000	35 002
35 to 44 years	29 000	30 000	30 100	32 000	33 000	35 000	35 000	36 000	38 000	38 000	40 000	40 000	40 000
45 to 54 years	30 000	32 000	32 000	33 466	34 771	35 000	36 000	37 163	38 000	40 000	40 000	40 000	40 000
55 to 64 years	28 000	30 000	31 410	32 000	33 000	33 000	35 000	37 100	39 000	40 000	40 000	40 000	41 000
65 years and over	24 000	25 000	28 000	26 000	27 000	28 768	27 878	31 000	34 193	36 000	40 000	37 000	38 000
White, 16 Years and Over	34 000	35 000	35 000	36 000	37 000	38 000	40 000	40 000	41 600	42 000	43 502	44 000	45 000
Men	39 000	40 000	40 000	40 000	42 000	42 000	44 707	45 000	48 000	49 000	50 000	50 000	50 000
Women	28 000	30 000	30 000	31 000	31 800	32 000	34 000	35 000	35 500	36 002	38 000	38 000	39 520
Black, 16 Years and Over	26 000	28 500	29 000	30 000	30 000	30 000	31 000	33 000	34 000	35 000	35 000	35 000	35 000
Men	30 000	30 000	30 000	32 000	30 000	33 000	34 000	35 000	37 500	38 000	36 000	39 000	38 000
Women	25 000	26 000	26 000	27 000	28 000	29 141	30 000	30 000	30 002	32 000	32 000	34 000	34 000

Table 1-40. Number and Median Annual Earnings of Year-Round, Full-Time Wage and Salary Workers, by Sex and Occupation of Job Held the Longest, 2002–2012

(Thousands of people, dollars.)

Sex and occupation	2002	2003	2004	2005	2006	2007	2008	2009	2010	2011	2012
Both Sexes, Number of Workers											
Management, business, and financial operations	15 707	15 552	15 575	16 299	16 806	17 115	17 259	16 491	16 889	17 396	17 799
Management	11 350	11 102	11 125	11 685	11 866	12 191	12 256	11 733	11 804	12 140	12 548
Business and financial operations	4 357	4 450	4 451	4 613	4 941	4 924	5 003	4 758	5 085	5 256	5 251
Professional and related	19 149	19 607	19 592	20 093	21 268	21 939	21 748	21 831	21 966	22 165	22 751
Computer and mathematical	2 644	2 598	2 680	2 779	2 888	3 180	3 089	3 100	2 993	3 171	3 524
Architecture and engineering	2 257	2 273	2 349	2 361	2 491	2 467	2 360	2 133	2 409	2 451	2 398
Life, physical, and social sciences	1 094	1 010	999	1 096	1 142	1 026	1 044	1 054	993	991	1 050
Community and social services	1 694	1 698	1 632	1 728	1 835	1 791	1 754	1 827	1 905	1 784	1 846
Legal	1 006	1 149	1 087	1 093	1 168	1 159	1 228	1 230	1 255	1 226	1 350
Education, training, and library	4 606	4 918	4 742	4 894	5 195	5 482	5 478	5 500	5 510	5 390	5 285
Arts, design, entertainment, sports, and media	1 453	1 374	1 416	1 362	1 633	1 554	1 415	1 404	1 380	1 449	1 445
Health care practitioner and technical	4 395	4 586	4 688	4 780	4 916	5 278	5 380	5 583	5 521	5 703	5 852
Services	12 011	11 990	12 457	13 117	13 236	13 553	13 034	12 944	12 855	13 676	13 456
Health care support	1 767	1 703	1 781	2 027	2 081	2 027	2 019	2 135	2 008	2 236	2 037
Protective services	2 042	2 385	2 406	2 429	2 506	2 511	2 472	2 593	2 589	2 571	2 535
Food preparation and serving related	3 592	3 223	3 383	3 586	3 646	3 769	3 504	3 307	3 408	3 797	3 631
Building and grounds cleaning and maintenance	2 843	2 942	3 116	3 285	3 120	3 198	3 027	2 870	2 942	3 098	3 056
Personal care and services	1 767	1 735	1 771	1 790	1 883	2 048	2 012	2 038	1 908	1 974	2 196
Sales and office	23 791	23 766	23 619	24 010	24 467	24 472	23 058	22 320	21 859	21 949	22 121
Sales and related	9 929	9 804	9 951	10 251	10 497	10 301	9 763	9 275	9 187	9 191	9 312
Office and administrative support	13 862	13 962	13 668	13 758	13 970	14 171	13 294	13 045	12 671	12 758	12 810
Natural resources, construction, and maintenance	9 823	9 709	10 574	10 864	11 295	10 745	10 002	8 599	8 298	8 584	8 897
Farming, fishing, and forestry	573	562	629	556	585	607	581	555	532	562	539
Construction and extraction	5 256	5 070	5 711	6 145	6 484	5 885	5 158	4 172	4 029	4 283	4 329
Installation, maintenance, and repair	3 994	4 077	4 234	4 163	4 226	4 252	4 264	3 872	3 737	3 739	4 029
Production, transportation, and material moving	13 386	13 391	13 648	13 586	13 704	13 907	12 649	11 062	11 518	12 041	12 166
Production	7 736	7 670	7 787	7 623	7 762	7 589	6 652	5 834	6 226	6 574	6 410
Transportation and material moving	5 650	5 721	5 861	5 963	5 942	6 318	5 997	5 228	5 292	5 467	5 756
Armed forces	658	717	632	664	576	709	744	765	727	749	689
Both Sexes, Median Annual Earnings											
Management, business, and financial operations	50 000	52 000	55 000	57 000	60 000	60 000	60 800	60 000	64 000	65 000	65 000
Management	55 000	58 000	60 000	60 000	62 500	65 000	65 000	65 000	68 000	70 000	70 000
Business and financial operations	44 000	45 000	45 000	49 000	50 000	50 000	52 000	55 000	56 000	57 000	57 000
Professional and related	46 000	46 000	48 000	50 000	50 000	51 000	54 000	55 000	55 000	56 000	58 705
Computer and mathematical	60 000	60 000	62 000	62 400	68 000	70 000	70 000	72 000	70 000	73 000	75 000
Architecture and engineering	59 400	62 000	60 000	65 000	69 000	70 000	70 000	70 000	75 000	75 000	75 000
Life, physical, and social sciences	50 000	50 000	50 000	53 500	57 000	60 000	57 532	60 000	60 000	61 599	67 000
Community and social services	34 000	34 349	36 000	36 000	36 780	39 000	40 000	40 000	40 000	40 000	41 000
Legal	61 860	75 000	70 000	72 000	70 000	70 000	75 000	80 000	75 000	85 000	80 000
Education, training, and library	38 000	39 000	40 000	40 000	40 282	44 984	45 000	46 000	45 000	46 200	47 000
Arts, design, entertainment, sports, and media	43 500	40 000	40 000	42 000	45 000	44 297	47 000	49 000	48 000	50 000	50 000
Health care practitioner and technical	46 000	48 000	50 000	50 000	52 000	52 800	55 000	55 000	57 638	58 000	60 000
Services	22 000	22 000	22 000	23 000	24 000	25 000	25 000	26 000	26 000	26 000	27 000
Health care support	22 100	22 000	22 000	22 000	23 000	24 500	26 000	26 000	26 270	26 000	26 000
Protective services	38 000	42 000	42 000	42 000	45 000	45 000	45 000	46 000	48 000	50 000	50 000
Food preparation and serving related	18 000	18 000	18 000	19 656	19 000	20 000	20 800	20 000	20 800	21 000	21 840
Building and grounds cleaning and maintenance	20 000	20 000	20 000	21 000	23 000	23 000	24 000	24 024	25 000	24 002	25 000
Personal care and services	21 840	20 678	22 537	23 000	23 000	25 000	25 000	25 000	25 000	25 000	25 000
Sales and office	30 000	30 000	30 000	31 200	32 002	34 000	35 000	35 000	35 000	35 002	36 000
Sales and related	35 000	35 000	35 000	35 000	37 000	38 000	38 500	38 000	40 000	40 000	40 000
Office and administrative support	28 000	29 000	30 000	30 000	30 000	32 000	32 500	34 000	34 000	35 000	35 000
Natural resources, construction, and maintenance	33 000	34 000	35 000	35 000	35 000	36 000	40 000	40 000	40 000	40 000	40 000
Farming, fishing, and forestry	20 000	20 000	20 000	21 000	20 000	24 000	24 000	24 000	23 000	24 000	24 000
Construction and extraction	31 200	32 000	33 000	32 000	35 000	35 000	39 000	40 000	40 000	39 500	38 000
Installation, maintenance, and repair	36 000	38 000	38 300	40 000	40 000	40 000	42 000	44 192	43 981	44 018	44 000
Production, transportation, and material moving	28 704	30 000	30 000	30 200	30 000	33 000	34 000	34 000	34 000	35 000	36 000
Production	28 000	30 000	30 000	30 000	30 000	33 000	34 000	32 006	34 000	35 000	36 000
Transportation and material moving	29 000	30 000	30 000	30 800	30 000	33 800	34 000	35 000	33 000	35 000	36 000
Armed forces	36 000	36 000	40 000	39 000	40 000	42 000	45 000	47 000	47 000	45 000	45 000

Table 1-40. Number and Median Annual Earnings of Year-Round, Full-Time Wage and Salary Workers, by Sex and Occupation of Job Held the Longest, 2002–2012—*Continued*

(Thousands of people, dollars.)

Sex and occupation	2002	2003	2004	2005	2006	2007	2008	2009	2010	2011	2012
Men, Number of Workers											
Management, business, and financial operations	9 178	8 961	8 849	9 496	9 519	9 784	9 836	9 418	9 569	9 886	9 917
Management	7 145	6 991	6 911	7 477	7 361	7 619	7 714	7 300	7 249	7 497	7 666
Business and financial operations	2 033	1 970	1 938	2 019	2 157	2 165	2 122	2 117	2 320	2 389	2 252
Professional and related	9 299	9 535	9 497	9 561	10 387	10 274	10 074	10 036	10 126	10 228	10 731
Computer and mathematical	1 953	1 913	1 972	2 060	2 159	2 378	2 348	2 227	2 244	2 329	2 564
Architecture and engineering	1 984	2 004	2 049	2 041	2 174	2 172	2 068	1 859	2 110	2 144	2 073
Life, physical, and social sciences	667	668	626	668	748	611	581	575	562	605	615
Community and social services	726	730	705	713	756	744	675	707	701	679	742
Legal	490	610	537	490	546	515	595	645	605	616	686
Education, training, and library	1 407	1 476	1 386	1 421	1 587	1 651	1 535	1 650	1 601	1 522	1 504
Arts, design, entertainment, sports, and media	847	811	848	789	953	790	782	829	839	860	824
Health care practitioner and technical	1 225	1 323	1 374	1 378	1 464	1 413	1 490	1 544	1 464	1 473	1 724
Services	5 988	6 204	6 314	6 658	6 715	6 871	6 389	6 379	6 426	6 923	7 040
Health care support	181	178	208	240	252	261	204	247	242	268	269
Protective services	1 689	1 967	1 906	1 919	1 998	2 000	1 930	2 026	2 070	2 108	2 041
Food preparation and serving related	1 836	1 638	1 716	1 873	1 991	1 985	1 816	1 744	1 743	2 050	2 068
Building and grounds cleaning and maintenance	1 788	1 914	2 002	2 153	1 939	2 048	1 911	1 832	1 862	1 974	2 055
Personal care and services	494	508	482	473	535	576	527	530	508	523	606
Sales and office	9 453	9 398	9 380	9 464	9 747	9 694	9 128	8 680	8 872	8 971	8 874
Sales and related	5 933	5 891	5 892	5 896	6 125	6 019	5 690	5 231	5 363	5 425	5 436
Office and administrative support	3 520	3 507	3 488	3 568	3 622	3 675	3 438	3 449	3 509	3 545	3 439
Natural resources, construction, and maintenance	9 434	9 348	10 178	10 503	10 904	10 343	9 627	8 225	7 936	8 274	8 550
Farming, fishing, and forestry	463	470	536	469	482	516	489	425	430	474	445
Construction and extraction	5 156	4 972	5 576	6 026	6 344	5 753	5 056	4 068	3 909	4 192	4 245
Installation, maintenance, and repair	3 815	3 905	4 065	4 008	4 078	4 074	4 081	3 732	3 597	3 608	3 860
Production, transportation, and material moving	10 472	10 492	10 812	10 747	10 733	11 047	10 226	8 921	9 214	9 583	9 754
Production	5 517	5 513	5 637	5 503	5 525	5 461	4 983	4 370	4 612	4 813	4 814
Transportation and material moving	4 955	4 979	5 176	5 244	5 208	5 585	5 242	4 552	4 602	4 770	4 940
Armed forces	600	636	580	591	528	660	696	703	649	677	622
Men, Median Annual Earnings											
Management, business, and financial operations	60 000	60 200	65 000	69 000	68 000	70 000	72 000	72 000	75 000	75 000	75 000
Management	65 000	65 000	70 000	70 000	70 000	75 000	75 000	75 000	78 000	80 000	75 056
Business and financial operations	52 000	51 000	55 000	60 000	60 000	60 000	65 000	65 000	67 000	65 000	67 500
Professional and related	55 000	58 000	58 000	60 000	61 000	62 000	67 000	65 000	67 000	70 000	70 000
Computer and mathematical	60 000	65 000	65 000	65 000	70 000	70 000	74 000	75 000	75 000	79 000	80 000
Architecture and engineering	60 000	64 558	61 785	66 921	70 000	72 000	74 000	72 000	77 000	75 000	79 002
Life, physical, and social sciences	52 000	50 801	55 000	62 000	61 000	65 000	65 000	65 000	64 000	65 000	72 000
Community and social services	35 000	35 000	38 000	40 000	39 000	40 000	44 085	45 000	42 002	42 000	42 000
Legal	100 000	100 000	101 000	108 000	100 000	104 146	130 000	120 000	120 000	120 000	100 000
Education, training, and library	45 600	48 000	47 000	50 000	50 000	50 000	54 000	52 000	53 000	55 000	55 000
Arts, design, entertainment, sports, and media	46 000	45 000	45 000	50 000	50 000	50 000	52 000	50 000	50 000	55 000	55 000
Health care practitioner and technical	72 000	65 500	70 000	70 000	72 000	75 000	75 000	74 000	75 000	75 000	75 000
Services	25 000	26 000	25 000	26 000	29 000	29 000	30 000	30 000	30 002	30 000	30 000
Health care support	24 000	22 537	20 400	22 880	25 000	25 000	28 000	30 000	34 000	29 904	30 000
Protective services	40 000	44 000	44 000	45 000	46 886	49 000	49 000	49 500	50 000	50 000	54 000
Food preparation and serving related	20 000	18 720	18 720	20 000	20 000	21 000	21 500	21 000	23 000	23 400	24 000
Building and grounds cleaning and maintenance	24 500	22 156	24 000	24 000	25 000	25 000	27 012	26 000	28 600	27 000	28 000
Personal care and services	30 000	28 559	26 000	30 000	30 000	30 000	30 500	30 000	30 000	32 000	32 000
Sales and office	38 000	39 000	40 000	40 000	40 000	42 000	40 000	42 002	42 000	43 000	45 000
Sales and related	41 600	41 000	44 000	42 000	45 000	45 000	48 000	48 002	48 000	50 000	49 000
Office and administrative support	32 000	32 000	34 000	34 000	35 000	36 000	35 000	37 400	37 000	37 000	40 000
Natural resources, construction, and maintenance	33 592	34 283	35 000	35 000	35 674	36 000	40 000	40 000	40 000	40 000	40 000
Farming, fishing, and forestry	22 000	22 000	22 000	22 500	20 000	24 000	24 000	25 000	23 400	25 000	25 000
Construction and extraction	31 304	32 000	33 000	32 000	35 000	35 000	40 000	40 000	40 000	40 000	39 000
Installation, maintenance, and repair	36 000	38 000	38 870	40 000	40 000	40 000	42 685	45 000	44 000	45 000	44 000
Production, transportation, and material moving	30 000	32 000	33 000	34 000	33 358	35 000	35 360	35 198	36 000	38 500	40 000
Production	30 360	32 000	34 000	35 000	35 000	36 000	36 000	36 000	36 944	40 000	40 000
Transportation and material moving	30 000	30 000	32 000	32 760	32 000	35 000	35 000	35 000	35 000	37 440	38 638
Armed forces	36 000	36 000	40 000	40 000	40 000	42 000	45 000	47 000	47 000	45 000	45 000

Table 1-40. Number and Median Annual Earnings of Year-Round, Full-Time Wage and Salary Workers, by Sex and Occupation of Job Held the Longest, 2002–2012—*Continued*

(Thousands of people, dollars.)

Sex and occupation	2002	2003	2004	2005	2006	2007	2008	2009	2010	2011	2012
Women, Number of Workers											
Management, business, and financial operations	6 529	6 591	6 726	6 803	7 287	7 332	7 423	7 073	7 320	7 511	7 881
Management	4 205	4 111	4 214	4 209	4 504	4 573	4 542	4 432	4 555	4 643	4 882
Business and financial operations	2 324	2 479	2 512	2 594	2 783	2 759	2 881	2 641	2 765	2 867	2 999
Professional and related	9 851	10 071	10 095	10 532	10 881	11 664	11 675	11 795	11 840	11 937	12 020
Computer and mathematical	691	685	708	718	729	802	741	873	748	842	960
Architecture and engineering	273	269	300	320	317	295	293	274	299	307	325
Life, physical, and social sciences	428	342	373	428	394	415	462	479	431	386	435
Community and social services	968	968	927	1 015	1 079	1 047	1 079	1 119	1 204	1 105	1 104
Legal	516	539	550	603	622	645	633	585	650	610	664
Education, training, and library	3 199	3 441	3 356	3 473	3 608	3 831	3 944	3 850	3 909	3 868	3 781
Arts, design, entertainment, sports, and media	606	563	568	573	681	764	633	575	541	589	622
Health care practitioner and technical	3 170	3 263	3 314	3 403	3 452	3 865	3 890	4 039	4 057	4 230	4 129
Services	6 026	5 786	6 144	6 459	6 522	6 682	6 645	6 565	6 429	6 753	6 416
Health care support	1 586	1 525	1 573	1 787	1 829	1 766	1 815	1 888	1 766	1 969	1 768
Protective services	354	419	500	510	509	511	541	567	519	463	494
Food preparation and serving related	1 757	1 585	1 668	1 713	1 655	1 784	1 688	1 563	1 665	1 747	1 562
Building and grounds cleaning and maintenance	1 055	1 029	1 115	1 132	1 181	1 150	1 116	1 038	1 079	1 125	1 001
Personal care and services	1 274	1 228	1 289	1 317	1 349	1 471	1 485	1 508	1 400	1 451	1 590
Sales and office	14 338	14 368	14 239	14 546	14 720	14 778	13 930	13 640	12 986	12 979	13 247
Sales and related	3 996	3 913	4 060	4 355	4 372	4 282	4 073	4 044	3 824	3 766	3 876
Office and administrative support	10 342	10 455	10 180	10 191	10 348	10 496	9 856	9 596	9 162	9 213	9 371
Natural resources, construction, and maintenance	391	361	396	360	391	402	376	374	361	310	347
Farming, fishing, and forestry	111	92	93	87	104	92	91	130	102	87	94
Construction and extraction	100	97	135	119	140	132	101	104	120	91	85
Installation, maintenance, and repair	180	172	169	155	148	178	183	140	140	131	169
Production, transportation, and material moving	2 914	2 899	2 835	2 839	2 971	2 861	2 423	2 141	2 304	2 458	2 412
Production	2 219	2 157	2 150	2 120	2 237	2 128	1 668	1 464	1 614	1 761	1 596
Transportation and material moving	695	742	685	719	734	733	755	676	690	697	816
Armed forces	58	81	52	73	48	49	49	62	78	72	67
Women, Median Annual Earnings											
Management, business, and financial operations	41 000	43 000	43 000	46 000	50 000	50 000	50 000	50 000	52 779	52 000	54 000
Management	44 000	47 000	46 000	50 000	52 000	52 000	55 000	52 999	55 000	55 000	58 000
Business and financial operations	38 500	40 000	40 000	41 000	46 000	45 000	48 000	48 000	50 000	50 000	50 000
Professional and related	40 000	40 000	40 000	42 000	43 000	45 000	46 000	48 002	49 000	50 000	50 000
Computer and mathematical	51 627	52 000	57 000	57 000	60 000	60 000	62 000	65 000	65 000	65 000	66 002
Architecture and engineering	50 000	48 000	47 500	55 000	52 000	55 000	50 000	61 000	60 000	62 400	65 000
Life, physical, and social sciences	44 000	45 000	45 995	50 000	48 000	48 000	49 000	54 651	56 000	55 000	61 008
Community and social services	33 000	33 000	35 000	35 000	36 000	37 000	37 700	39 000	39 000	40 000	40 000
Legal	45 000	45 000	46 000	47 500	50 000	47 500	52 001	60 000	57 257	51 875	55 000
Education, training, and library	35 000	35 000	37 000	38 000	38 632	41 000	42 000	43 000	42 000	45 000	44 000
Arts, design, entertainment, sports, and media	40 000	35 000	36 000	35 000	38 000	40 000	40 000	45 000	42 000	43 000	45 000
Health care practitioner and technical	41 000	43 000	45 000	46 000	48 000	50 000	50 000	52 000	53 000	53 000	55 000
Services	20 000	20 000	20 000	20 000	20 500	22 000	23 516	24 000	23 000	23 000	24 000
Health care support	22 000	22 000	22 000	21 000	23 000	24 500	26 000	25 000	25 000	26 000	26 000
Protective services	30 900	32 000	32 000	34 344	37 896	35 000	35 000	38 000	38 500	42 000	42 000
Food preparation and serving related	16 160	17 000	16 000	18 000	18 000	19 000	20 000	19 000	19 000	20 000	20 000
Building and grounds cleaning and maintenance	16 441	16 000	16 866	18 000	19 000	19 500	20 000	20 000	20 000	20 020	20 000
Personal care and services	20 000	20 000	21 000	20 800	20 000	24 000	24 000	24 700	23 000	23 000	25 000
Sales and office	26 989	28 000	28 000	29 000	30 000	30 000	30 600	31 400	32 000	33 000	33 000
Sales and related	25 000	26 000	26 000	26 000	26 000	28 000	29 000	30 000	30 000	30 000	30 000
Office and administrative support	27 000	28 000	28 000	29 800	30 000	30 002	32 000	32 100	33 000	34 000	35 000
Natural resources, construction, and maintenance	26 000	28 000	30 000	30 200	27 000	37 025	30 000	30 000	30 000	30 000	32 000
Farming, fishing, and forestry	17 000	16 000	15 700	18 000	18 808	24 117	24 685	21 000	20 000	20 000	20 498
Construction and extraction	26 000	29 500	40 000	31 200	24 980	40 000	34 500	31 000	33 670	28 323	30 645
Installation, maintenance, and repair	34 000	37 000	33 000	36 000	40 000	42 000	33 913	38 139	41 888	35 000	43 889
Production, transportation, and material moving	22 000	22 100	23 000	23 000	23 000	25 000	25 000	25 000	25 000	25 000	27 560
Production	21 632	22 000	23 000	23 400	23 000	25 000	25 000	25 000	25 000	25 000	27 000
Transportation and material moving	22 000	22 710	23 000	21 000	24 000	27 000	24 000	25 000	25 000	26 000	28 000
Armed forces	40 000	32 000	35 100	32 652	32 000	41 000	32 000	43 600	50 000	52 000	48 000

Table 1-41. Distribution of Employed Wage and Salary Workers by Tenure with Current Employer, Age, Sex, Race, and Hispanic Origin, January 2012

(Thousands of people, percent.)

Characteristic	Number employed/ (in thousands)	Percent distribution by tenure with current employer								
		Total	12 months or less	13 to 23 months	2 years	3 to 4 years	5 to 9 years	10 to 14 years	15 to 19 years	20 years or more
Both Sexes										
16 years and over	125 516	100.0	21.1	6.3	4.9	16.6	21.8	12.5	6.1	10.6
16 to 19 years	3 925	100.0	72.9	11.9	6.9	7.8	0.4	-	-	-
20 years and over	121 591	100.0	19.5	6.1	4.8	16.9	22.4	12.9	6.3	11.0
20 to 24 years	12 712	100.0	48.9	12.8	10.6	20.4	7.1	0.2	-	-
25 to 34 years	28 381	100.0	25.5	8.4	6.9	24.5	27.2	6.8	0.7	-
35 to 44 years	27 477	100.0	16.1	5.4	4.3	16.8	27.0	17.8	8.8	3.8
45 to 54 years	28 535	100.0	12.5	4.5	2.9	13.0	22.0	16.8	9.5	18.7
55 to 64 years	19 339	100.0	9.4	2.8	2.3	10.8	20.2	16.4	9.8	28.3
65 years and over	5 148	100.0	7.8	2.0	2.1	11.8	20.7	16.6	9.2	29.7
Men										
16 years and over	64 552	100.0	21.0	6.3	5.0	16.2	21.3	12.2	6.4	11.5
16 to 19 years	1 839	100.0	71.2	13.3	7.8	7.4	0.4	-	-	-
20 years and over	62 713	100.0	19.6	6.1	4.9	16.5	21.9	12.6	6.5	11.9
20 to 24 years	6 559	100.0	48.8	12.5	10.4	20.6	7.4	0.2	-	-
25 to 34 years	15 104	100.0	24.7	8.5	7.3	23.8	27.8	7.0	0.9	-
35 to 44 years	14 570	100.0	16.3	5.4	4.0	16.1	26.8	17.3	9.8	4.4
45 to 54 years	14 361	100.0	12.6	4.5	2.8	12.5	19.6	16.6	10.0	21.4
55 to 64 years	9 470	100.0	10.0	2.5	2.7	10.1	18.8	15.6	9.2	31.2
65 years and over	2 648	100.0	7.8	1.3	1.9	11.8	21.7	16.9	8.9	29.7
Women										
16 years and over	60 964	100.0	21.3	6.3	4.8	17.1	22.2	12.7	5.9	9.7
16 to 19 years	2 085	100.0	74.4	10.7	6.2	8.2	0.5	-	-	-
20 years and over	58 879	100.0	19.4	6.2	4.7	17.4	23.0	13.2	6.1	10.1
20 to 24 years	6 153	100.0	49.0	13.1	10.7	20.3	6.7	0.2	-	-
25 to 34 years	13 276	100.0	26.5	8.4	6.4	25.3	26.5	6.5	0.5	-
35 to 44 years	12 907	100.0	15.9	5.4	4.6	17.5	27.4	18.4	7.7	3.1
45 to 54 years	14 174	100.0	12.4	4.5	3.1	13.6	24.4	17.0	9.0	16.0
55 to 64 years	9 868	100.0	8.8	3.2	1.9	11.6	21.4	17.2	10.5	25.5
65 years and over	2 499	100.0	7.7	2.8	2.4	11.9	19.7	16.3	9.6	29.7
White										
16 years and over	100 679	100.0	20.7	6.4	4.8	16.1	21.7	12.6	6.6	11.3
Men	52 641	100.0	20.5	6.5	4.7	15.7	21.1	12.4	6.8	12.3
Women	48 039	100.0	20.9	6.3	4.8	16.4	22.2	12.9	6.3	10.2
Black										
16 years and over	14 204	100.0	22.2	5.6	5.2	18.5	22.1	12.4	4.5	9.5
Men	6 526	100.0	22.9	5.1	5.5	18.9	21.9	10.8	4.8	10.0
Women	7 678	100.0	21.6	6.0	5.0	18.2	22.2	13.8	4.2	9.1
Asian										
16 years and over	6 933	100.0	21.1	6.6	5.3	20.5	23.8	11.3	4.8	6.6
Men	3 502	100.0	21.2	5.8	6.6	19.0	23.8	12.8	4.3	6.5
Women	3 432	100.0	21.0	7.3	4.0	22.1	23.9	9.8	5.2	6.7
Hispanic[1]										
16 years and over	19 763	100.0	23.6	5.9	6.6	20.1	23.7	10.9	4.2	5.1
Men	11 262	100.0	24.5	6.0	6.8	20.8	22.4	10.0	4.3	5.2
Women	8 501	100.0	22.3	5.6	6.4	19.2	25.4	12.0	4.2	4.9

[1]May be of any race.
- = Data represents or rounds to zero.

Table 1-42. Median Years of Tenure with Current Employer for Employed Wage and Salary Workers, 25 Years and Over, by Educational Attainment, Sex, and Age, January 2012

(Percent.)

Year, sex, and age	Total employed	25 to 34 years	35 to 44 years	45 to 54 years	55 to 64 years	65 years and over
Both Sexes	5.4	3.2	5.3	7.8	10.3	10.3
Less than a high school diploma	4.8	3.2	4.6	5.3	8.0	9.8
High school graduates, no college	5.8	3.3	5.0	8.5	10.3	10.2
Some college, no degree	5.2	3.1	5.1	7.4	10.3	10.2
Associate degree	5.7	3.2	5.6	7.7	10.4	10.4
College graduates	5.5	3.1	5.7	8.2	10.5	11.0
Bachelor's degree	5.2	3.1	5.7	7.8	10.4	11.6
Master's degree	6.3	3.4	6.0	8.6	10.4	10.2
Doctoral or professional degree	5.6	2.3	5.0	9.6	11.9	14.8
Men	5.5	3.2	5.4	8.5	10.7	10.2
Less than a high school diploma	4.7	3.4	4.8	5.4	8.2	10.5
High school graduates, no college	5.7	3.3	5.1	9.6	10.6	9.7
Some college, no degree	5.3	3.1	5.2	8.6	10.2	9.8
Associate degree	6.2	3.4	6.3	8.4	11.2	10.0
College graduates	5.7	3.1	5.7	8.6	11.3	11.3
Bachelor's degree	5.5	3.2	5.9	8.3	11.3	10.4
Master's degree	6.4	3.3	5.8	8.9	10.5	9.9
Doctoral or professional degree	5.9	2.3	4.8	9.7	13.4	15.3
Women	5.4	3.1	5.2	7.3	10.0	10.5
Less than a high school diploma	4.8	2.9	4.2	5.2	7.8	7.8
High school graduates, no college	6.0	3.3	5.0	7.8	10.0	11.4
Some college, no degree	5.2	3.2	5.0	6.5	10.3	10.8
Associate degree	5.3	3.1	5.1	7.2	9.8	11.3
College graduates	5.3	3.1	5.7	7.9	10.2	10.7
Bachelor's degree	5.0	3.0	5.6	7.4	10.1	12.3
Master's degree	6.3	3.4	6.2	8.4	10.4	10.3
Doctoral or professional degree	5.2	2.4	5.4	9.4	10.3	10.0

Table 1-43. Median Years of Tenure with Current Employer for Employed Wage and Salary Workers, by Age and Sex, Selected Years, February 1996–January 2012

(Number of years.)

Sex and age	February 1996	February 1998	February 2000	January 2002	January 2004	January 2006	January 2008	January 2010	January 2012
Both Sexes									
16 years and over	3.8	3.6	3.5	3.7	4.0	4.0	4.1	4.4	4.6
16 to 17 years	0.7	0.6	0.6	0.7	0.7	0.6	0.7	0.7	0.7
18 to 19 years	0.7	0.7	0.7	0.8	0.8	0.7	0.8	1.0	0.8
20 to 24 years	1.2	1.1	1.1	1.2	1.3	1.3	1.3	1.5	1.3
25 years and over	5.0	4.7	4.7	4.7	4.9	4.9	5.1	5.2	5.4
25 to 34 years	2.8	2.7	2.6	2.7	2.9	2.9	2.7	3.1	3.2
35 to 44 years	5.3	5.0	4.8	4.6	4.9	4.9	4.9	5.1	5.3
45 to 54 years	8.3	8.1	8.2	7.6	7.7	7.3	7.6	7.8	7.8
55 to 64 years	10.2	10.1	10.0	9.9	9.6	9.3	9.9	10.0	10.3
65 years and over	8.4	7.8	9.4	8.6	9.0	8.8	10.2	9.9	10.3
Men									
16 years and over	4.0	3.8	3.8	3.9	4.1	4.1	4.2	4.6	4.7
16 to 17 years	0.6	0.6	0.6	0.8	0.7	0.7	0.7	0.7	0.6
18 to 19 years	0.7	0.7	0.7	0.8	0.8	0.7	0.8	1.0	0.8
20 to 24 years	1.2	1.2	1.2	1.4	1.3	1.4	1.4	1.6	1.4
25 years and over	5.3	4.9	4.9	4.9	5.1	5.0	5.2	5.3	5.5
25 to 34 years	3.0	2.8	2.7	2.8	3.0	2.9	2.8	3.2	3.2
35 to 44 years	6.1	5.5	5.3	5.0	5.2	5.1	5.2	5.3	5.4
45 to 54 years	10.1	9.4	9.5	9.1	9.6	8.1	8.2	8.5	8.5
55 to 64 years	10.5	11.2	10.2	10.2	9.8	9.5	10.1	10.4	10.7
65 years and over	8.3	7.1	9.0	8.1	8.2	8.3	10.4	9.7	10.2
Women									
16 years and over	3.5	3.4	3.3	3.4	3.8	3.9	3.9	4.2	4.6
16 to 17 years	0.7	0.6	0.6	0.7	0.6	0.6	0.6	0.7	0.7
18 to 19 years	0.7	0.7	0.7	0.8	0.8	0.7	0.8	1.0	0.8
20 to 24 years	1.2	1.1	1.0	1.1	1.3	1.2	1.3	1.5	1.3
25 years and over	4.7	4.4	4.4	4.4	4.7	4.8	4.9	5.1	5.4
25 to 34 years	2.7	2.5	2.5	2.5	2.8	2.8	2.6	3.0	3.1
35 to 44 years	4.8	4.5	4.3	4.2	4.5	4.6	4.7	4.9	5.2
45 to 54 years	7.0	7.2	7.3	6.5	6.4	6.7	7.0	7.1	7.3
55 to 64 years	10.0	9.6	9.9	9.6	9.2	9.2	9.8	9.7	10.0
65 years and over	8.4	8.7	9.7	9.4	9.6	9.5	9.9	10.1	10.5

Table 1-44. Median Years of Tenure with Current Employer for Employed Wage and Salary Workers, by Industry, Selected Years, February 2000–January 2012

(Number of years.)

Industry	February 2000	January 2002	January 2004	January 2006	January 2008	January 2010	January 2012
TOTAL, 16 YEARS AND OVER	3.5	3.7	4.0	4.0	4.1	4.4	4.6
Private Sector	3.2	3.3	3.5	3.6	3.6	4.0	4.2
Agriculture and related industries	3.7	4.2	3.7	3.8	4.3	4.8	4.1
Nonagricultural industries	3.2	3.3	3.5	3.6	3.6	4.0	4.2
Mining	4.8	4.5	5.2	3.8	4.1	4.8	3.5
Construction	2.7	3.0	3.0	3.0	3.5	4.2	4.3
Manufacturing	4.9	5.4	5.8	5.5	5.9	6.1	6.0
Durable goods manufacturing	4.8	5.5	6.0	5.6	6.1	6.6	6.1
Nonmetallic mineral product	5.5	5.3	4.8	5.0	4.8	7.7	7.0
Primary metals and fabricated metal product	5.0	6.3	6.4	6.2	5.2	7.2	5.6
Machinery manufacturing	5.3	6.8	6.4	6.6	6.0	8.3	5.4
Computers and electronic product	3.9	4.7	5.2	5.9	6.7	5.9	7.7
Electrical equipment and appliances	5.0	5.5	9.8	6.2	6.2	5.0	5.9
Transportation equipment	6.4	7.0	7.7	7.2	7.8	8.3	7.1
Wood product	3.7	4.3	5.0	4.7	6.2	4.7	5.3
Furniture and fixtures	4.4	4.7	4.7	4.2	5.2	5.0	6.5
Miscellaneous manufacturing	3.7	4.5	4.6	3.9	4.7	5.4	4.8
Nondurable goods manufacturing	5.0	5.3	5.5	5.4	5.4	5.5	5.8
Food manufacturing	4.6	5.0	4.9	5.2	4.3	4.7	4.9
Beverage and tobacco product	5.5	4.6	8.0	5.4	6.9	8.1	6.4
Textiles, apparel, and leather	4.7	5.0	5.0	4.4	4.6	4.7	4.3
Paper and printing	5.1	6.2	6.9	6.3	5.5	6.8	9.7
Petroleum and coal product	9.5	9.8	11.4	5.0	4.3	5.1	6.4
Chemicals	6.0	5.7	5.3	6.1	7.6	7.3	6.1
Plastics and rubber product	4.6	5.3	5.7	5.0	5.3	7.4	6.1
Wholesale and retail trade	2.7	2.8	3.1	3.1	3.2	3.6	3.7
Wholesale trade	3.9	3.9	4.3	4.6	5.0	5.2	5.5
Retail trade	2.5	2.6	2.8	2.8	2.9	3.3	3.3
Transportation and utilities	4.7	4.9	5.3	4.9	5.1	5.3	5.6
Transportation and warehousing	4.0	4.3	4.7	4.3	4.6	5.0	5.3
Utilities	11.5	13.4	13.3	10.4	10.1	9.1	9.5
Information[1]	3.4	3.3	4.3	4.8	4.7	5.0	5.4
Publishing, except Internet	4.2	4.8	4.7	5.3	4.7	5.6	6.6
Motion picture and sound recording industries	1.6	2.3	2.2	1.9	1.9	3.8	2.6
Broadcasting, except Internet	3.6	3.1	4.0	4.6	3.4	4.3	4.9
Telecommunications	4.3	3.4	4.6	5.3	6.9	6.6	7.4
Financial activities	3.5	3.6	3.9	4.0	4.5	4.6	4.9
Finance and insurance	3.6	3.9	4.1	4.1	4.7	4.8	5.0
Finance	3.3	3.6	4.0	3.9	4.4	4.5	4.7
Insurance	4.4	4.5	4.4	4.7	5.2	5.5	5.7
Real estate and rental and leasing	3.1	3.0	3.3	3.4	3.7	3.9	4.5
Real estate	3.1	3.2	3.5	3.5	3.9	4.1	4.5
Rental and leasing services	3.0	2.2	2.9	3.1	3.0	3.3	4.2
Professional and business services	2.4	2.7	3.2	3.2	3.1	3.4	3.8
Professional and technical services	2.6	3.1	3.6	3.8	3.3	4.0	4.4
Management, administrative, and waste services[1]	2.0	2.1	2.6	2.5	2.5	2.9	3.1
Administrative and support services	1.8	1.9	2.4	2.4	2.4	2.8	3.0
Waste management and remediation services	3.6	4.3	3.4	4.1	4.1	2.9	4.4
Education and health services	3.4	3.5	3.6	4.0	4.1	4.1	4.4
Education services	3.2	3.6	3.8	4.0	4.3	4.4	4.3
Health care and social assistance	3.5	3.5	3.6	4.1	4.1	4.1	4.4
Hospitals	5.1	4.9	4.7	5.2	5.4	5.3	6.0
Health services, except hospitals	3.2	3.1	3.3	3.6	3.6	3.6	3.8
Social assistance	2.4	2.5	2.8	3.1	3.0	3.1	3.1
Leisure and hospitality	1.7	1.8	2.0	1.9	2.1	2.5	2.4
Arts, entertainment, and recreation	2.6	2.3	2.8	3.1	2.8	3.3	3.1
Accommodation and food services	1.5	1.6	1.9	1.6	1.9	2.3	2.3
Accommodation	2.8	2.7	3.1	2.5	3.1	3.3	3.8
Food services and drinking places	1.4	1.4	1.6	1.4	1.6	2.2	2.1
Other services	3.1	3.3	3.3	3.2	3.3	4.0	3.8
Other services, except private households	3.2	3.3	3.5	3.3	3.4	4.1	3.8
Repair and maintenance	3.0	3.0	3.2	2.9	3.0	4.0	3.7
Personal and laundry services	2.7	2.8	3.4	2.8	3.2	3.5	3.5
Membership associations and organizations	4.0	4.1	3.9	4.2	4.4	4.5	4.3
Other services, private households	3.0	2.7	2.3	2.8	2.8	3.4	3.3
Public Sector	7.1	6.7	6.9	6.9	7.2	7.2	7.8
Federal government	11.5	11.3	10.4	9.9	9.9	7.9	9.5
State government	5.5	5.4	6.4	6.3	6.5	6.4	6.4
Local government	6.7	6.2	6.4	6.6	7.1	7.5	8.1

Note: Data beginning in 2000 reflect the introduction of Census 2000 population controls. Data for 2004 forward reflect updated population controls introduced annually with the release of January data. Beginning with data for January 2009, industries reflect the introduction of the 2007 census industry classification system into the Current Population Survey (CPS). This industry classification system is derived from the 2007 North American Industry Classification System.

[1]Includes other industries not shown separately.

Table 1-45. Employment Status of the Population, by Sex and Marital Status, March 1990–March 2013

(Thousands of people, percent.)

Marital status and year	Men						Women					
		Labor force						Labor force				
		Total		Employed	Unemployed			Total		Employed	Unemployed	
	Population	Number	Percent of population		Number	Percent of labor force	Population	Number	Percent of population		Number	Percent of labor force
Single												
1990	25 757	18 829	73.1	16 893	1 936	10.3	21 088	14 003	66.4	12 856	1 147	8.2
1991	26 220	19 014	72.5	16 418	2 596	13.7	21 688	14 125	65.1	12 887	1 238	8.8
1992	26 529	19 229	72.5	16 401	2 828	14.7	21 738	14 072	64.7	12 793	1 279	9.1
1993	26 951	19 625	72.8	16 858	2 767	14.1	21 848	14 091	64.5	12 711	1 380	9.8
1994	28 350	20 365	71.8	17 826	2 539	12.5	22 885	14 903	65.1	13 419	1 484	10.0
1995	28 318	20 449	72.2	18 286	2 163	10.6	22 853	14 974	65.5	13 673	1 301	8.7
1996	28 695	20 561	71.7	18 097	2 464	12.0	23 632	15 417	65.2	14 084	1 333	8.6
1997	29 294	20 942	71.5	18 683	2 259	10.8	24 215	16 178	66.8	14 747	1 431	8.8
1998	29 558	21 255	71.9	19 124	2 131	10.0	24 808	16 885	68.1	15 626	1 259	7.5
1999	29 883	21 329	71.4	19 465	1 864	8.7	25 674	17 486	68.1	16 185	1 301	7.4
2000	30 232	21 641	71.6	19 823	1 818	8.4	25 863	17 749	68.6	16 446	1 303	7.3
2001	30 968	22 232	71.8	20 239	1 993	9.0	26 180	17 900	68.4	16 631	1 269	7.1
2002	32 220	22 761	70.6	20 066	2 695	11.8	26 942	18 079	67.1	16 499	1 580	8.7
2003	32 852	22 821	69.5	20 194	2 627	11.5	27 527	17 901	65.0	16 219	1 682	9.4
2004	33 786	23 212	68.7	20 434	2 778	12.0	28 033	18 089	64.5	16 506	1 583	8.8
2005	34 069	23 335	68.5	20 831	2 504	10.7	28 508	18 554	65.1	16 902	1 652	8.9
2006	34 906	24 369	69.8	21 961	2 408	9.9	29 357	18 989	64.7	17 444	1 545	8.1
2007	35 359	24 506	69.3	22 224	2 281	9.3	29 695	19 218	64.7	17 935	1 284	6.7
2008	36 522	25 229	69.1	22 695	2 534	10.0	30 772	19 889	64.6	18 369	1 520	7.6
2009	36 907	24 930	67.5	20 645	4 284	17.2	31 038	19 785	63.7	17 714	2 071	10.5
2010	38 110	25 663	67.3	21 038	4 626	18.0	32 085	19 973	62.3	17 517	2 457	12.3
2011	38 766	25 646	66.2	21 389	4 256	16.6	33 041	20 581	62.3	18 117	2 463	12.0
2012	38 933	25 615	65.8	21 838	3 778	14.7	34 241	21 417	62.5	18 895	2 523	11.8
2013	39 482	25 881	65.6	22 306	3 575	13.8	34 889	21 739	62.3	19 319	2 419	11.1
Married, Spouse Present												
1990	52 464	41 020	78.2	39 562	1 458	3.6	53 207	30 967	58.2	29 870	1 097	3.5
1991	52 460	40 883	77.9	38 843	2 040	5.0	53 176	31 103	58.5	29 668	1 435	4.6
1992	52 780	40 930	77.5	38 650	2 280	5.6	53 464	31 686	59.3	30 130	1 556	4.9
1993	53 488	41 255	77.1	39 069	2 186	5.3	54 146	32 158	59.4	30 757	1 401	4.4
1994	53 436	40 993	76.7	39 085	1 908	4.7	54 198	32 863	60.6	31 397	1 466	4.5
1995	54 166	41 806	77.2	40 262	1 544	3.7	54 902	33 563	61.1	32 267	1 296	3.9
1996	53 996	41 837	77.5	40 356	1 481	3.5	54 640	33 382	61.1	32 258	1 124	3.4
1997	53 981	41 967	77.7	40 628	1 339	3.2	54 611	33 907	62.1	32 836	1 071	3.2
1998	54 685	42 288	77.3	41 039	1 249	3.0	55 241	34 136	61.8	33 028	1 108	3.2
1999	55 256	42 557	77.0	41 476	1 081	2.5	55 801	34 349	61.6	33 403	946	2.8
2000	55 897	43 254	77.4	42 261	993	2.3	56 432	34 959	61.9	33 998	961	2.7
2001	56 152	43 463	77.4	42 245	1 218	2.8	56 740	35 234	62.1	34 273	961	2.7
2002	57 325	44 271	77.2	42 508	1 763	4.0	57 883	35 624	61.5	34 295	1 329	3.7
2003	57 940	44 700	77.1	42 797	1 903	4.3	58 545	36 185	61.8	34 806	1 379	3.8
2004	58 395	44 860	76.8	43 247	1 613	3.6	59 008	35 918	60.9	34 582	1 336	3.7
2005	58 854	45 263	76.9	43 763	1 500	3.3	59 449	35 809	60.2	34 738	1 071	3.0
2006	58 850	45 082	76.6	43 877	1 205	2.7	59 476	36 192	60.9	35 185	1 007	2.8
2007	60 126	46 129	76.7	44 813	1 317	2.9	60 656	37 335	61.6	36 370	965	2.6
2008	59 455	45 451	76.4	43 958	1 493	3.3	60 108	37 074	61.7	35 919	1 155	3.1
2009	60 132	45 741	76.1	42 667	3 074	6.7	60 818	37 536	61.7	35 540	1 996	5.3
2010	59 694	45 110	75.6	41 762	3 348	7.4	60 339	37 201	61.7	34 964	2 237	6.0
2011	59 477	44 553	74.9	41 667	2 886	6.5	60 095	36 383	60.5	34 340	2 043	5.6
2012	60 346	44 915	74.4	42 387	2 528	5.6	61 011	36 363	59.6	34 423	1 940	5.3
2013	60 630	44 904	74.1	42 760	2 145	4.8	61 269	36 292	59.2	34 601	1 691	4.7
Widowed, Divorced, or Separated												
1990	11 152	7 513	67.4	6 959	554	7.4	23 857	11 168	46.8	10 530	638	5.7
1991	11 588	7 804	67.3	6 985	819	10.5	24 105	11 145	46.2	10 386	759	6.8
1992	11 927	8 049	67.5	7 140	909	11.3	24 582	11 486	46.7	10 610	876	7.6
1993	11 861	7 956	67.1	7 055	901	11.3	24 661	11 308	45.9	10 528	780	6.9
1994	12 239	8 156	66.6	7 382	774	9.5	25 098	11 879	47.3	10 995	884	7.4
1995	12 410	8 315	67.0	7 632	683	8.2	25 373	12 001	47.3	11 308	693	5.8
1996	13 176	8 697	66.0	7 976	721	8.3	25 786	12 430	48.2	11 742	688	5.5
1997	14 113	9 420	66.7	8 715	705	7.5	26 301	12 814	48.7	12 071	743	5.8
1998	14 166	9 482	66.9	8 954	528	5.6	26 092	12 880	49.4	12 235	645	5.0
1999	14 225	9 449	66.4	8 971	478	5.1	26 199	12 951	49.4	12 307	644	5.0
2000	14 289	9 623	67.3	9 152	471	4.9	26 354	13 228	50.2	12 657	571	4.3
2001	14 392	9 421	65.5	8 927	494	5.2	26 747	13 454	50.3	12 887	567	4.2
2002	14 617	9 650	66.0	8 931	719	7.5	27 802	13 716	49.3	12 855	861	6.3
2003	15 180	9 855	64.9	9 020	835	8.5	28 240	14 154	50.1	13 240	914	6.5
2004	15 059	9 789	65.0	9 059	730	7.5	28 228	14 194	50.3	13 324	870	6.1
2005	15 779	10 256	65.0	9 569	687	6.7	28 576	14 233	49.8	13 472	761	5.3
2006	16 405	10 815	65.9	10 141	674	6.2	28 981	14 220	49.1	13 539	681	4.8
2007	16 247	10 799	66.5	10 150	650	6.0	28 950	14 320	49.5	13 620	700	4.9
2008	16 718	10 896	65.2	10 083	812	7.5	29 419	14 553	49.5	13 765	787	5.4
2009	16 719	10 687	63.9	9 224	1 463	13.7	29 471	14 449	49.0	13 169	1 281	8.9
2010	17 016	10 863	63.8	9 188	1 675	15.4	29 915	14 707	49.2	13 285	1 422	9.7
2011	17 744	11 095	62.5	9 676	1 420	12.8	29 876	14 610	48.9	13 221	1 389	9.5
2012	17 704	11 076	62.6	9 884	1 192	10.8	30 367	14 825	48.8	13 543	1 283	8.7
2013	18 090	11 045	61.1	9 968	1 077	10.8	30 633	14 688	47.9	13 494	1 193	8.1

Note: See notes and definitions for information on historical comparability.

Table 1-45. Employment Status of the Population, by Sex and Marital Status, March 1990–March 2013—*Continued*

(Thousands of people, percent.)

Marital status and year	Men						Women					
	Population	Labor force					Population	Labor force				
		Total		Employed	Unemployed			Total		Employed	Unemployed	
		Number	Percent of population		Number	Percent of labor force		Number	Percent of population		Number	Percent of labor force
Widowed												
1990	2 331	519	22.3	490	29	5.6	11 477	2 243	19.5	2 149	94	4.2
1991	2 385	486	20.4	448	38	7.8	11 288	2 150	19.0	2 044	106	4.9
1992	2 529	566	22.4	501	65	11.5	11 325	2 131	18.8	2 029	102	4.8
1993	2 468	596	24.1	535	61	10.2	11 214	1 961	17.5	1 856	105	5.4
1994	2 220	474	21.4	440	34	7.2	11 073	1 945	17.6	1 825	120	6.2
1995	2 282	496	21.7	469	27	5.4	11 080	1 941	17.5	1 844	97	5.0
1996	2 476	487	19.7	466	21	4.3	11 070	1 916	17.3	1 820	96	5.0
1997	2 686	559	20.8	529	30	5.4	11 058	2 018	18.2	1 926	92	4.6
1998	2 567	563	21.9	551	12	2.1	11 027	2 157	19.6	2 071	86	4.0
1999	2 540	562	22.1	532	30	5.3	10 943	2 039	18.6	1 942	97	4.8
2000	2 601	583	22.4	547	36	6.2	11 061	2 011	18.2	1 911	100	5.0
2001	2 638	568	21.5	546	22	3.9	11 182	2 137	19.1	2 045	92	4.3
2002	2 635	629	23.9	581	48	7.6	11 411	2 001	17.5	1 887	114	5.7
2003	2 694	628	23.3	588	40	6.4	11 295	2 087	18.5	1 991	96	4.6
2004	2 651	581	21.9	558	23	4.0	11 159	2 157	19.3	2 048	109	5.1
2005	2 729	618	22.6	590	28	4.5	11 125	2 111	19.0	2 005	106	5.0
2006	2 626	610	23.2	563	47	7.7	11 305	2 164	19.1	2 094	70	3.2
2007	2 697	631	23.4	588	43	6.8	11 220	2 058	18.3	1 971	87	4.2
2008	2 911	656	22.5	611	44	6.8	11 399	2 218	19.5	2 101	117	5.3
2009	2 813	632	22.5	543	90	14.2	11 446	2 174	19.0	2 032	143	6.6
2010	2 969	776	26.1	684	92	11.8	11 379	2 214	19.5	2 036	178	8.0
2011	2 931	698	23.8	648	50	7.1	11 310	2 291	20.3	2 118	173	7.6
2012	2 864	639	22.3	595	43	6.8	11 197	2 179	19.5	2 044	135	6.2
2013	3 122	686	22.0	631	55	8.1	11 234	2 132	19.0	1 987	145	6.8
Divorced												
1990	6 256	5 004	80.0	4 639	365	7.3	8 845	6 678	75.5	6 333	345	5.2
1991	6 586	5 262	79.9	4 722	540	10.3	9 152	6 779	74.1	6 365	414	6.1
1992	6 743	5 418	80.3	4 823	595	11.0	9 569	7 076	73.9	6 578	498	7.0
1993	6 770	5 330	78.7	4 736	594	11.1	9 879	7 183	72.7	6 736	447	6.2
1994	7 222	5 548	76.8	5 028	520	9.4	10 113	7 473	73.9	6 962	511	6.8
1995	7 343	5 739	78.2	5 266	473	8.2	10 262	7 559	73.7	7 206	353	4.7
1996	7 734	5 954	77.0	5 468	486	8.2	10 508	7 829	74.5	7 468	361	4.6
1997	8 191	6 298	76.9	5 851	447	7.1	11 102	8 092	72.9	7 666	426	5.3
1998	8 307	6 378	76.8	6 045	333	5.2	11 065	8 038	72.6	7 687	351	4.4
1999	8 529	6 481	76.0	6 151	330	5.1	11 130	8 171	73.4	7 841	330	4.0
2000	8 532	6 583	77.2	6 279	304	4.6	11 061	8 505	76.9	8 217	288	3.4
2001	8 580	6 403	74.6	6 074	329	5.1	11 719	8 662	73.9	8 335	327	3.8
2002	8 643	6 519	75.4	6 053	466	7.1	12 227	8 902	72.8	8 416	486	5.5
2003	8 938	6 621	74.1	6 052	569	8.6	12 653	9 191	72.6	8 673	518	5.6
2004	8 942	6 622	74.1	6 104	518	7.8	12 817	9 246	72.1	8 706	540	5.8
2005	9 196	6 754	73.4	6 281	473	7.0	12 950	9 253	71.5	8 836	417	4.5
2006	9 646	7 065	73.2	6 631	434	6.1	13 107	9 188	70.1	8 799	389	4.2
2007	9 608	7 110	74.0	6 679	431	6.1	13 214	9 334	70.6	8 896	439	4.7
2008	9 767	7 106	72.8	6 607	499	7.0	13 551	9 387	69.3	8 938	449	4.8
2009	9 938	7 052	71.0	6 064	988	14.0	13 301	9 176	69.0	8 402	774	8.4
2010	9 944	7 018	70.6	5 888	1 131	16.1	13 758	9 394	68.3	8 510	885	9.4
2011	10 635	7 394	69.5	6 430	965	13.0	13 757	9 230	67.1	8 407	823	8.9
2012	10 662	7 394	69.3	6 572	822	11.1	14 210	9 416	66.3	8 620	797	8.5
2013	10 923	7 420	67.9	6 718	702	9.5	14 428	9 416	65.3	8 704	713	7.6
Separated												
1990	2 565	1 990	77.6	1 830	160	8.0	3 535	2 247	63.6	2 048	199	8.9
1991	2 616	2 057	78.6	1 816	241	11.7	3 665	2 216	60.5	1 977	239	10.8
1992	2 655	2 065	77.8	1 816	249	12.1	3 688	2 279	61.8	2 003	276	12.1
1993	2 623	2 030	77.4	1 784	246	12.1	3 568	2 165	60.7	1 937	228	10.5
1994	2 797	2 134	76.3	1 914	220	10.3	3 911	2 461	62.9	2 208	253	10.3
1995	2 784	2 081	74.7	1 898	183	8.8	4 031	2 501	62.0	2 258	243	9.7
1996	2 966	2 255	76.0	2 041	214	9.5	4 209	2 684	63.8	2 453	231	8.6
1997	3 236	2 563	79.2	2 335	228	8.9	4 141	2 705	65.3	2 480	225	8.3
1998	3 293	2 542	77.2	2 358	184	7.2	4 000	2 683	67.1	2 476	207	7.7
1999	3 156	2 405	76.2	2 287	118	4.9	4 126	2 740	66.4	2 523	217	7.9
2000	3 157	2 456	77.8	2 326	130	5.3	4 012	2 711	67.6	2 528	183	6.8
2001	3 174	2 450	77.2	2 307	143	5.8	3 846	2 654	69.0	2 507	147	5.5
2002	3 339	2 502	74.9	2 297	205	8.2	4 164	2 812	67.5	2 551	261	9.3
2003	3 548	2 606	73.4	2 380	226	8.7	4 293	2 877	67.0	2 576	301	10.5
2004	3 466	2 586	74.6	2 397	189	7.3	4 251	2 791	65.7	2 569	222	8.0
2005	3 855	2 884	74.8	2 698	186	6.4	4 501	2 870	63.8	2 632	238	8.3
2006	4 132	3 141	76.0	2 947	194	6.2	4 569	2 869	62.8	2 647	222	7.7
2007	3 943	3 058	77.6	2 883	176	5.7	4 516	2 927	64.8	2 753	174	6.0
2008	4 040	3 134	77.6	2 865	269	8.6	4 469	2 947	65.9	2 726	221	7.5
2009	3 968	3 002	75.7	2 617	386	12.8	4 725	3 099	65.6	2 734	364	11.8
2010	4 103	3 069	74.8	2 616	452	14.7	4 778	3 099	64.8	2 739	359	11.6
2011	4 178	3 004	71.9	2 598	406	13.5	4 809	3 089	64.2	2 696	393	12.7
2012	4 177	3 044	72.9	2 717	327	10.7	4 960	3 230	65.1	2 879	351	10.9
2013	4 045	2 939	72.7	2 619	320	10.9	4 970	3 139	63.2	2 803	336	10.7

Note: See notes and definitions for information on historical comparability.

Table 1-46. Employment Status of All Women and Single Women, by Presence and Age of Children, March 1990–March 2013

(Thousands of women, percent.)

Presence and age of children and year	All women							Single women						
	Civilian labor force	Civilian labor force as percent of population	Employed			Unemployed		Civilian labor force	Civilian labor force as percent of population	Employed			Unemployed	
			Number	Percent full time	Percent part time	Number	Percent of labor force			Number	Percent full time	Percent part time	Number	Percent of labor force
Women with No Children Under 18 Years														
1990	33 942	52.3	32 391	74.4	25.6	1 551	4.6	12 478	68.1	11 611	65.9	34.1	866	6.9
1991	34 047	52.0	32 167	74.0	26.0	1 880	5.5	12 472	67.0	11 529	66.2	33.8	943	7.6
1992	34 487	52.3	32 481	74.3	25.7	2 006	5.8	12 355	66.9	11 374	66.6	33.4	982	7.9
1993	34 495	52.1	32 476	74.6	25.4	2 020	5.9	12 223	66.4	11 201	66.1	33.9	1 022	8.4
1994	35 454	53.1	33 343	72.7	27.3	2 110	6.0	12 737	66.8	11 674	64.5	35.5	1 063	8.3
1995	35 843	52.9	34 054	72.9	27.1	1 789	5.0	12 870	67.1	11 919	64.5	35.5	951	7.4
1996	36 509	53.0	34 698	73.3	26.7	1 811	5.0	13 172	66.1	12 255	64.6	35.4	918	7.0
1997	37 295	53.6	35 572	73.7	26.3	1 723	4.6	13 405	66.5	12 442	64.0	36.0	964	7.2
1998	38 253	54.1	36 680	74.1	25.9	1 573	4.1	13 888	67.2	13 082	64.8	35.2	806	5.8
1999	39 316	54.3	37 589	74.6	25.4	1 727	4.4	14 435	67.1	13 491	65.6	34.4	944	6.5
2000	40 142	54.8	38 408	75.4	24.6	1 733	4.3	14 677	67.6	13 713	66.6	33.4	964	6.6
2001	40 836	54.9	39 219	75.7	24.3	1 617	4.0	14 877	67.4	13 993	67.3	32.7	884	5.9
2002	41 278	54.0	39 038	75.1	24.9	2 241	5.4	14 855	65.6	13 682	65.9	34.1	1 173	7.9
2003	42 039	54.1	39 667	74.8	25.2	2 372	5.6	14 678	63.5	13 430	65.1	34.9	1 249	8.5
2004	42 289	53.8	40 000	74.6	25.4	2 289	5.4	14 828	63.0	13 670	65.5	34.5	1 157	7.8
2005	42 039	54.1	39 667	74.8	25.2	2 372	5.6	14 678	63.5	13 430	65.1	34.9	1 249	8.5
2006	43 392	53.6	41 440	75.3	24.7	1 952	4.5	15 673	63.4	14 547	66.5	33.5	1 125	7.2
2007	44 039	53.9	42 279	75.3	24.7	1 760	4.0	15 704	63.4	14 801	66.4	33.6	903	5.7
2008	45 585	54.3	43 417	75.7	24.3	2 168	4.8	16 378	63.4	15 261	67.4	32.6	1 116	6.8
2009	45 649	53.8	42 343	73.3	26.7	3 306	7.2	16 112	62.1	14 607	64.9	35.1	1 506	9.3
2010	46 098	53.5	42 256	73.5	26.5	3 842	8.3	16 331	60.7	14 533	65.6	34.4	1 798	11.0
2011	46 198	53.0	42 569	73.3	26.7	3 629	7.9	16 758	60.8	15 016	65.2	34.8	1 743	10.4
2012	47 222	52.6	43 494	74.0	26.0	3 728	7.9	17 310	60.7	15 473	66.3	33.7	1 837	10.6
2013	47 607	52.3	44 294	73.6	26.4	3 313	7.0	17 650	60.5	15 915	65.5	34.5	1 735	9.8
Women with Children Under 18 Years														
1990	22 196	66.7	20 865	73.0	27.0	1 331	6.0	1 525	55.2	1 244	79.1	20.9	280	18.4
1991	22 327	66.6	20 774	73.0	27.0	1 552	7.0	1 654	53.6	1 358	76.4	23.6	296	17.9
1992	22 756	67.2	21 052	73.8	26.2	1 704	7.5	1 716	52.5	1 420	75.9	24.1	297	17.3
1993	23 063	66.9	21 521	73.9	26.1	1 541	6.7	1 869	54.4	1 510	74.8	25.2	359	19.2
1994	24 191	68.4	22 467	70.8	29.2	1 724	7.1	2 166	56.9	1 745	73.9	26.1	421	19.4
1995	24 695	69.7	23 195	71.7	28.3	1 500	6.1	2 104	57.5	1 754	73.6	26.4	350	16.6
1996	24 720	70.2	23 386	72.6	27.4	1 334	5.4	2 245	60.5	1 829	73.5	26.5	416	18.5
1997	25 604	72.1	24 082	74.1	25.9	1 522	5.9	2 772	68.1	2 305	76.6	23.4	467	16.8
1998	25 647	72.3	24 209	74.0	26.0	1 438	5.6	2 997	72.5	2 544	75.6	24.4	453	15.1
1999	25 469	72.1	24 305	74.1	25.9	1 165	4.6	3 051	73.4	2 694	75.8	24.2	357	11.7
2000	25 795	72.9	24 693	74.6	25.4	1 102	4.3	3 073	73.9	2 734	79.7	20.3	339	11.0
2001	25 751	73.1	24 572	75.6	24.4	1 179	4.6	3 022	73.8	2 638	81.8	18.2	385	12.7
2002	26 140	72.2	24 612	74.8	25.2	1 529	5.8	3 224	75.3	2 818	79.1	20.9	406	12.6
2003	26 202	71.7	24 598	74.3	25.7	1 603	6.1	3 222	73.1	2 789	79.5	20.5	433	13.4
2004	25 913	70.7	24 413	74.2	25.8	1 501	5.8	3 262	72.6	2 836	76.8	23.2	426	13.1
2005	26 202	71.7	24 598	74.3	25.7	1 603	6.1	3 222	73.1	2 789	79.5	20.5	433	13.4
2006	26 009	70.6	24 728	75.6	24.4	1 281	4.9	3 317	71.5	2 896	77.8	22.2	420	12.7
2007	26 834	71.3	25 646	75.2	24.8	1 188	4.4	3 514	71.4	3 133	76.4	23.6	381	10.8
2008	25 930	71.2	24 637	75.7	24.3	1 294	5.0	3 511	71.0	3 108	78.0	22.0	403	11.5
2009	26 122	71.6	24 079	74.6	25.4	2 043	7.8	3 673	72.0	3 108	75.8	24.2	566	18.2
2010	25 783	71.3	23 510	73.7	26.3	2 273	8.8	3 642	70.1	2 984	71.9	28.1	659	18.1
2011	25 376	70.9	23 109	74.2	25.8	2 266	8.9	3 822	70.0	3 102	71.9	28.1	721	18.9
2012	25 384	70.9	23 366	75.4	24.6	2 018	7.9	4 108	71.5	3 422	73.2	26.8	686	16.7
2013	25 112	70.3	23 121	74.8	25.2	1 991	7.9	4 088	71.3	3 404	71.9	28.1	684	16.7
Women with Children Under 6 Years														
1990	9 397	58.2	8 732	69.6	30.4	664	7.1	929	48.7	736	75.0	25.0	194	20.9
1991	9 636	58.4	8 758	69.5	30.5	878	9.1	1 050	48.8	819	72.2	27.8	231	22.0
1992	9 573	58.0	8 662	70.2	29.8	911	9.5	1 029	45.8	829	73.2	26.8	200	19.4
1993	9 621	57.9	8 764	70.1	29.9	857	8.9	1 125	47.4	869	70.0	30.0	257	22.8
1994	10 328	60.3	9 394	67.1	32.9	935	9.1	1 379	52.2	1 062	70.0	30.0	317	23.0
1995	10 395	62.3	9 587	67.5	32.5	809	7.8	1 328	53.0	1 069	68.6	31.4	259	19.5
1996	10 293	62.3	9 592	68.4	31.6	701	6.8	1 378	55.1	1 099	67.3	32.7	279	20.2
1997	10 610	65.0	9 800	70.5	29.5	810	7.6	1 755	65.1	1 424	71.6	28.4	330	18.8
1998	10 619	65.2	9 839	69.8	30.2	780	7.3	1 755	67.3	1 448	71.7	28.3	307	17.5
1999	10 322	64.4	9 674	69.0	31.0	648	6.3	1 811	68.1	1 565	71.0	29.0	246	13.6
2000	10 316	65.3	9 763	70.5	29.5	553	5.4	1 835	70.5	1 603	75.3	24.7	232	12.6
2001	10 200	64.9	9 618	71.2	28.8	582	5.7	1 783	69.7	1 542	79.1	20.9	242	13.6
2002	10 193	64.1	9 441	70.4	29.6	752	7.4	1 819	71.0	1 568	74.5	25.5	251	13.8
2003	10 209	62.9	9 433	70.0	30.0	776	7.6	1 893	70.2	1 614	75.2	24.8	279	14.7
2004	10 131	62.2	9 407	69.4	30.6	724	7.1	1 885	68.4	1 605	70.1	29.9	279	14.8
2005	10 209	62.9	9 433	70.0	30.0	776	7.6	1 893	70.2	1 614	75.2	24.8	279	14.7
2006	10 430	63.0	9 779	72.0	28.0	651	6.2	1 934	68.6	1 659	72.8	27.2	276	14.3
2007	10 894	63.5	10 305	71.9	28.1	589	5.4	2 066	67.4	1 827	72.7	27.3	239	11.6
2008	10 452	63.6	9 794	72.1	27.9	657	6.3	1 982	66.0	1 705	72.2	27.8	277	14.0
2009	10 497	63.6	9 517	71.8	28.2	980	9.3	2 137	67.8	1 754	70.3	29.7	383	17.9
2010	10 536	64.2	9 452	70.9	29.1	1 085	10.3	2 076	65.6	1 643	67.0	33.0	433	20.9
2011	10 403	64.2	9 268	71.3	28.7	1 135	10.9	2 177	65.8	1 678	65.5	34.5	499	22.9
2012	10 462	64.7	9 458	72.6	27.4	1 004	9.6	2 408	68.1	1 958	69.0	31.0	450	18.7
2013	10 171	64.7	9 212	72.8	27.2	958	9.4	2 305	68.2	1 864	66.7	33.3	441	19.1

Note: See notes and definitions for information on historical comparability.

Table 1-47. Employment Status of Ever-Married Women and Married Women, Spouse Present, by Presence and Age of Children, March 1990–March 2013

(Thousands of women, percent.)

Presence and age of children and year	Ever-married women[1]							Married women, spouse present						
	Civilian labor force	Civilian labor force as percent of population	Employed			Unemployed		Civilian labor force	Civilian labor force as percent of population	Employed			Unemployed	
			Number	Percent full time	Percent part time	Number	Percent of labor force			Number	Percent full time	Percent part time	Number	Percent of labor force
Women with No Children Under 18 Years														
1990	21 464	46.1	20 779	79.1	20.9	685	3.2	14 467	51.1	14 068	77.3	22.7	399	2.8
1991	21 575	46.1	20 637	78.4	21.6	937	4.3	14 529	51.2	13 976	77.6	22.4	552	3.8
1992	22 132	46.6	21 108	78.5	21.5	1 024	4.6	14 851	51.9	14 247	77.8	22.2	604	4.1
1993	22 273	46.6	21 275	79.0	21.0	998	4.5	15 211	52.4	14 630	77.6	22.4	581	3.8
1994	22 716	47.6	21 669	77.1	22.9	1 047	4.6	15 234	53.2	14 641	75.6	24.4	593	3.9
1995	22 973	47.3	22 134	77.4	22.6	839	3.7	15 594	53.2	15 072	76.3	23.7	522	3.3
1996	23 337	47.7	22 444	78.1	21.9	893	3.8	15 628	53.4	15 123	76.8	23.2	506	3.2
1997	23 890	48.3	23 130	78.9	21.1	760	3.2	15 750	54.2	15 315	77.7	22.3	435	2.8
1998	24 366	48.7	23 598	79.3	20.7	767	3.1	16 007	54.1	15 581	78.3	21.7	426	2.7
1999	24 881	48.9	24 098	79.7	20.3	783	3.1	16 484	54.4	16 061	78.2	21.8	423	2.6
2000	25 465	49.4	24 695	80.3	19.7	769	3.0	16 786	54.7	16 357	79.1	20.9	429	2.6
2001	25 959	49.6	25 226	80.4	19.6	733	2.8	16 909	54.8	16 528	78.7	21.3	381	2.3
2002	26 423	49.1	25 356	80.0	20.0	1 068	4.0	17 353	54.8	16 780	78.4	21.6	573	3.3
2003	27 361	50.1	26 238	79.7	20.3	1 123	4.1	17 901	55.7	17 273	78.6	21.4	628	3.5
2004	27 461	49.8	26 329	79.3	20.7	1 131	4.1	17 965	55.0	17 367	78.6	21.4	598	3.3
2005	27 361	50.1	26 238	79.7	20.3	1 123	4.1	17 901	55.7	17 273	78.6	21.4	628	3.5
2006	27 719	49.3	26 893	80.1	19.9	827	3.0	18 124	54.8	17 691	79.3	20.7	434	2.4
2007	28 335	49.8	27 477	80.1	19.9	858	3.0	18 766	55.4	18 326	79.6	20.4	441	2.3
2008	29 207	50.3	28 156	80.2	19.8	1 052	3.6	19 188	55.9	18 650	79.8	20.2	539	2.8
2009	29 536	50.2	27 737	77.8	22.2	1 800	6.1	19 541	55.8	18 521	77.3	22.7	1 019	5.2
2010	29 767	50.2	27 723	77.7	22.3	2 044	6.9	19 579	55.8	18 454	77.3	22.7	1 125	5.7
2011	29 440	49.4	27 553	77.7	22.3	1 886	6.4	19 316	54.6	18 285	77.4	22.6	1 031	5.3
2012	29 912	48.8	28 021	78.2	21.8	1 891	6.3	19 617	53.6	18 536	77.8	22.2	1 081	5.5
2013	29 956	48.4	28 379	78.1	21.9	1 578	5.3	19 507	53.3	18 706	77.5	22.5	801	4.1
Women with Children Under 18 Years														
1990	20 671	67.8	19 621	72.6	27.4	1 051	5.1	16 500	66.3	15 803	69.8	30.2	698	4.2
1991	20 673	67.9	19 416	72.8	27.2	1 257	6.1	16 575	66.8	15 692	70.1	29.9	883	5.3
1992	21 040	68.8	19 633	73.6	26.4	1 407	6.7	16 835	67.8	15 884	71.3	28.7	952	5.7
1993	21 194	68.3	20 011	73.9	26.1	1 183	5.6	16 947	67.5	16 127	71.4	28.6	820	4.8
1994	22 025	69.8	20 722	70.5	29.5	1 303	5.9	17 628	69.0	16 755	68.0	32.0	873	5.0
1995	22 591	71.1	21 441	71.5	28.5	1 150	5.1	17 969	70.2	17 195	68.8	31.2	774	4.3
1996	22 475	71.4	21 556	72.5	27.5	919	4.1	17 754	70.0	17 136	69.6	30.4	618	3.5
1997	22 831	72.6	21 777	73.9	26.1	1 054	4.6	18 157	71.1	17 521	71.6	28.4	636	3.5
1998	22 650	72.3	21 665	73.8	26.2	985	4.3	18 129	70.6	17 447	71.5	28.5	682	3.8
1999	22 419	71.9	21 611	73.9	26.1	808	3.6	17 865	70.1	17 342	71.5	28.5	523	2.9
2000	22 722	72.7	21 960	74.0	26.0	763	3.4	18 174	70.6	17 641	71.7	28.3	533	2.9
2001	22 729	73.0	21 934	74.9	25.1	795	3.5	18 325	70.8	17 745	72.6	27.4	580	3.2
2002	22 917	71.8	21 794	74.3	25.7	1 122	4.9	18 271	69.6	17 515	71.7	28.3	756	4.1
2003	22 979	71.5	21 809	73.7	26.3	1 170	5.1	18 284	69.2	17 533	71.0	29.0	751	4.1
2004	22 651	70.5	21 576	73.8	26.2	1 075	4.7	17 953	68.2	17 215	71.3	28.7	738	4.1
2005	22 979	71.5	21 809	73.7	26.3	1 170	5.1	18 284	69.2	17 533	71.0	29.0	751	4.1
2006	22 692	70.5	21 831	75.3	24.7	861	3.8	18 067	68.4	17 494	73.0	27.0	574	3.2
2007	23 320	71.3	22 513	75.0	25.0	807	3.5	18 569	69.3	18 045	72.6	27.4	524	2.8
2008	22 419	71.2	21 529	75.4	24.6	890	4.0	17 886	69.4	17 269	73.6	26.4	616	3.4
2009	22 449	71.5	20 972	74.5	25.5	1 477	6.6	17 995	69.8	17 018	73.1	26.9	977	5.4
2010	22 141	71.5	20 526	74.0	26.0	1 615	7.3	17 622	69.7	16 510	72.6	27.4	1 112	6.3
2011	21 553	71.1	20 008	74.6	25.4	1 546	7.2	17 067	69.1	16 055	73.1	26.9	1 012	5.9
2012	21 276	70.7	19 944	75.8	24.2	1 332	6.3	16 746	68.5	15 887	74.1	25.9	859	5.1
2013	21 024	70.1	19 717	75.3	24.7	1 306	6.2	16 786	68.1	15 896	74.1	25.9	890	5.3
Women with Children Under 6 Years														
1990	8 467	59.5	7 996	69.1	30.9	471	5.6	7 247	58.9	6 901	67.4	32.6	346	4.8
1991	8 585	59.9	7 938	69.2	30.8	647	7.5	7 434	59.9	6 933	67.5	32.5	501	6.7
1992	8 544	60.0	7 832	69.9	30.1	711	8.3	7 333	59.9	6 819	68.5	31.5	514	7.0
1993	8 496	59.6	7 895	70.2	29.8	600	7.1	7 289	59.6	6 840	68.8	31.2	450	6.2
1994	8 949	61.8	8 332	66.7	33.3	617	6.9	7 723	61.7	7 291	65.4	34.6	432	5.6
1995	9 067	63.9	8 517	67.4	32.6	550	6.1	7 759	63.5	7 349	66.1	33.9	409	5.3
1996	8 915	63.6	8 493	68.6	31.4	422	4.7	7 590	62.7	7 297	66.5	33.5	293	3.9
1997	8 856	64.9	8 376	70.3	29.7	480	5.4	7 582	63.6	7 252	69.1	30.9	330	4.4
1998	8 864	64.8	8 391	69.5	30.5	473	5.3	7 655	63.7	7 309	68.1	31.9	346	4.5
1999	8 511	63.7	8 109	68.6	31.4	402	4.7	7 246	61.8	6 979	67.1	32.9	267	3.7
2000	8 481	64.3	8 159	69.5	30.5	321	3.8	7 341	62.8	7 087	68.1	31.9	254	3.5
2001	8 417	64.0	8 077	69.7	30.3	340	4.0	7 319	62.5	7 062	68.5	31.5	257	3.5
2002	8 373	62.8	7 873	69.6	30.4	501	6.0	7 166	60.8	6 804	67.7	32.3	363	5.1
2003	8 315	61.4	7 818	68.9	31.1	497	6.0	7 175	59.8	6 826	67.1	32.9	349	4.9
2004	8 246	61.0	7 801	69.3	30.7	445	5.4	7 107	59.3	6 774	68.1	31.9	332	4.7
2005	8 315	61.4	7 818	68.9	31.1	497	6.0	7 175	59.8	6 826	67.1	32.9	349	4.9
2006	8 496	61.9	8 121	71.8	28.2	375	4.4	7 366	60.3	7 092	70.6	29.4	274	3.7
2007	8 829	62.7	8 479	71.7	28.3	350	4.0	7 664	61.5	7 407	70.8	29.2	257	3.4
2008	8 470	63.0	8 089	72.1	27.9	381	4.5	7 285	61.6	6 999	70.9	29.1	285	3.9
2009	8 360	62.6	7 763	72.1	27.9	597	7.1	7 231	61.6	6 805	71.4	28.6	426	5.9
2010	8 460	63.8	7 809	71.7	28.3	651	7.7	7 227	62.5	6 741	71.5	28.5	486	6.7
2011	8 226	63.7	7 590	72.5	27.5	636	7.7	7 061	62.3	6 608	71.9	28.1	453	6.4
2012	8 054	63.7	7 501	73.5	26.5	554	6.9	6 878	62.3	6 491	72.7	27.3	387	5.6
2013	7 866	63.7	7 349	74.3	25.7	517	6.6	6 737	62.0	6 384	74.1	25.9	352	5.2

[1] Ever-married women are women who are, or have ever been, married.

Table 1-48. Employment Status of Women Who Maintain Families, by Marital Status and Presence and Age of Children, March 1995–March 2013

(Thousands of women, percent.)

Marital status, age of children, and year	Civilian noninstitutional population	Civilian labor force					Not in the labor force
		Number	Percent of the population	Employed	Unemployed		
					Number	Percent of the labor force	
Total, Women Who Maintain Families							
1995	12 762	8 192	64.2	7 527	665	8.1	4 570
1996	12 993	8 460	65.1	7 832	628	7.4	4 532
1997	13 258	8 998	67.9	8 192	806	9.0	4 260
1998	13 102	8 976	68.5	8 309	667	7.4	4 127
1999	13 191	9 213	69.8	8 596	617	6.7	3 978
2000	13 145	9 226	70.2	8 592	634	6.9	3 918
2001	12 930	9 034	69.9	8 453	581	6.4	3 897
2002	13 489	9 523	70.6	8 755	768	8.1	3 966
2003	14 000	9 759	69.7	8 898	861	8.8	4 241
2004	14 165	9 869	69.7	9 054	815	8.3	4 297
2005	14 391	9 941	69.1	9 140	801	8.1	4 450
2006	14 485	9 966	68.8	9 227	739	7.4	4 520
2007	14 833	10 172	68.6	9 510	661	6.5	4 662
2008	14 820	10 166	68.6	9 447	719	7.1	4 654
2009	14 813	10 140	68.5	9 034	1 106	10.9	4 673
2010	15 214	10 206	67.1	9 027	1 179	11.6	5 008
2011	15 461	10 462	67.7	9 141	1 321	12.6	5 000
2012	16 122	11 009	68.3	9 807	1 202	10.9	5 113
2013	15 914	10 793	67.8	9 589	1 204	11.2	5 121
Women with No Children Under 18 Years							
1995	4 610	2 471	53.6	2 394	77	3.1	2 139
1996	4 847	2 552	52.7	2 462	90	3.5	2 295
1997	4 909	2 663	54.2	2 571	92	3.5	2 246
1998	4 952	2 649	53.5	2 578	71	2.7	2 303
1999	4 942	2 667	54.0	2 556	111	4.2	2 275
2000	5 097	2 707	53.1	2 546	161	5.9	2 390
2001	5 185	2 772	53.5	2 668	104	3.8	2 413
2002	5 119	2 764	54.0	2 628	136	4.9	2 355
2003	5 457	2 934	53.8	2 728	206	7.0	2 522
2004	5 551	3 052	55.0	2 855	197	6.5	2 499
2005	5 692	3 095	54.4	2 961	134	4.3	2 597
2006	5 693	3 088	54.2	2 945	143	4.6	2 604
2007	5 823	3 124	53.7	2 990	134	4.3	2 699
2008	6 022	3 352	55.7	3 167	185	5.5	2 670
2009	6 068	3 332	54.9	3 075	258	7.7	2 735
2010	6 414	3 417	53.3	3 131	286	8.4	2 997
2011	6 403	3 455	54.0	3 131	324	9.4	2 948
2012	6 773	3 779	55.8	3 464	316	8.4	2 994
2013	6 822	3 790	55.5	3 466	324	8.5	3 032
Women with Children Under 18 Years							
1995	8 152	5 720	70.2	5 132	588	10.3	2 431
1996	8 146	5 908	72.5	5 370	538	9.1	2 237
1997	8 348	6 335	75.9	5 621	714	11.3	2 014
1998	8 151	6 327	77.6	5 731	596	9.4	1 823
1999	8 248	6 546	79.4	6 040	506	7.7	1 702
2000	8 048	6 520	81.0	6 046	474	7.3	1 528
2001	7 746	6 261	80.8	5 785	476	7.6	1 484
2002	8 370	6 759	80.8	6 127	632	9.4	1 611
2003	8 543	6 825	79.9	6 170	655	9.6	1 718
2004	8 614	6 817	79.1	6 199	618	9.1	1 798
2005	8 699	6 846	78.7	6 179	667	9.7	1 853
2006	8 793	6 878	78.2	6 282	596	8.7	1 915
2007	9 010	7 047	78.2	6 520	527	7.5	1 963
2008	8 798	6 814	77.4	6 280	535	7.8	1 984
2009	8 745	6 807	77.8	5 959	848	12.5	1 938
2010	8 800	6 789	77.1	5 896	893	13.2	2 011
2011	9 059	7 007	77.4	6 009	998	14.2	2 052
2012	9 349	7 230	77.3	6 343	887	12.3	2 119
2013	9 092	7 003	77.0	6 123	880	12.6	2 089
Single Women with No Children Under 18 Years							
1995	779	534	68.5	508	26	4.9	245
1996	895	588	65.7	572	16	2.7	308
1997	860	585	68.0	563	22	3.8	275
1998	893	637	71.3	613	24	3.8	256
1999	969	674	69.6	638	36	5.3	295
2000	1 004	720	71.7	642	78	10.8	284
2001	1 096	787	71.8	756	31	3.9	309
2002	1 154	796	69.0	747	49	6.2	358
2003	1 254	814	64.9	713	101	12.4	440
2004	1 381	977	70.7	887	90	9.2	404
2005	1 388	926	66.7	855	71	7.7	463
2006	1 370	933	68.1	861	72	7.7	437
2007	1 413	986	69.8	930	57	5.7	427
2008	1 515	1 057	69.8	989	68	6.5	458
2009	1 531	1 069	69.8	967	102	9.6	462

Note: See notes and definitions for information on historical comparability.

Table 1-48. Employment Status of Women Who Maintain Families, by Marital Status and Presence and Age of Children, March 1995–March 2013—*Continued*

(Thousands of women, percent.)

Marital status, age of children, and year	Civilian noninstitutional population	Civilian labor force					Not in the labor force
		Number	Percent of the population	Employed	Unemployed		
					Number	Percent of the labor force	
Single Women with No Children Under 18 Years—*Continued*							
2010	1 718	1 166	67.9	1 041	125	10.7	552
2011	1 729	1 178	68.2	1 047	132	11.2	551
2012	1 836	1 241	67.6	1 099	143	11.5	595
2013	1 933	1 322	68.4	1 178	144	10.9	611
Single Women with Children Under 18 Years							
1995	2 613	1 510	57.8	1 261	249	16.5	1 102
1996	2 639	1 633	61.9	1 346	287	17.6	1 006
1997	3 012	2 087	69.3	1 749	338	16.2	925
1998	3 083	2 280	74.0	1 960	320	14.0	803
1999	3 163	2 415	76.4	2 146	269	11.1	748
2000	3 167	2 413	76.2	2 151	262	10.9	754
2001	3 097	2 351	75.9	2 055	296	12.6	745
2002	3 315	2 566	77.4	2 241	325	12.7	749
2003	3 421	2 584	75.5	2 272	312	12.1	837
2004	3 414	2 568	75.2	2 233	335	13.0	846
2005	3 591	2 708	75.4	2 325	383	14.1	882
2006	3 671	2 710	73.8	2 370	340	12.5	961
2007	3 748	2 782	74.2	2 491	291	10.4	966
2008	3 721	2 743	73.7	2 448	295	10.8	978
2009	3 872	2 877	74.3	2 448	429	14.9	995
2010	3 948	2 868	72.6	2 379	488	17.0	1 081
2011	4 193	3 072	73.3	2 522	550	17.9	1 120
2012	4 442	3 263	73.5	2 746	517	15.8	1 179
2013	4 403	3 220	73.1	2 698	522	16.2	1 183
Widowed, Divorced, or Separated Women with No Children Under 18 Years							
1995	3 831	1 938	50.6	1 887	51	2.6	1 894
1996	3 952	1 964	49.7	1 890	74	3.8	1 988
1997	4 049	2 077	51.3	2 008	69	3.3	1 971
1998	4 058	2 011	49.6	1 965	46	2.3	2 047
1999	3 974	1 993	50.2	1 918	75	3.8	1 980
2000	4 093	1 987	48.5	1 904	83	4.2	2 106
2001	4 088	1 985	48.6	1 912	73	3.7	2 104
2002	3 964	1 968	49.6	1 882	86	4.4	1 997
2003	4 203	2 121	50.5	2 016	105	5.0	2 082
2004	4 170	2 075	49.8	1 968	107	5.2	2 095
2005	4 304	2 170	50.4	2 106	64	2.9	2 135
2006	4 323	2 156	49.9	2 084	72	3.3	2 168
2007	4 410	2 138	48.5	2 061	77	3.6	2 272
2008	4 507	2 295	50.9	2 178	117	5.1	2 213
2009	4 536	2 263	49.9	2 108	155	6.9	2 273
2010	4 696	2 251	47.9	2 090	161	7.1	2 445
2011	4 674	2 276	48.7	2 084	192	8.4	2 397
2012	4 937	2 538	51.4	2 365	173	6.8	2 399
2013	4 889	2 468	50.5	2 288	180	7.3	2 421
Widowed, Divorced, or Separated Women with Children Under 18 Years							
1995	5 539	4 210	76.0	3 871	339	8.1	1 329
1996	5 507	4 275	77.6	4 024	251	5.9	1 231
1997	5 337	4 248	79.6	3 872	376	8.9	1 089
1998	5 068	4 047	79.9	3 771	276	6.8	1 020
1999	5 086	4 131	81.2	3 894	237	5.7	955
2000	4 881	4 107	84.1	3 895	212	5.2	774
2001	4 649	3 910	84.1	3 730	180	4.6	739
2002	5 056	4 193	82.9	3 886	307	7.3	862
2003	5 122	4 241	82.8	3 898	343	8.1	881
2004	5 201	4 249	81.7	3 966	283	6.7	952
2005	5 108	4 137	81.0	3 854	283	6.8	971
2006	5 121	4 167	81.4	3 912	255	6.1	955
2007	5 262	4 266	81.1	4 029	237	5.5	997
2008	5 077	4 071	80.2	3 832	239	5.9	1 006
2009	4 873	3 930	80.7	3 511	420	10.7	943
2010	4 852	3 922	80.8	3 517	405	10.3	931
2011	4 866	3 935	80.9	3 487	448	11.4	931
2012	4 907	3 966	80.8	3 597	370	9.3	940
2013	4 689	3 783	80.7	3 425	358	9.5	906

Note: See notes and definitions for information on historical comparability.

Table 1-49. Number and Age of Children in Families, by Type of Family and Labor Force Status of Mother, March 1990–March 2013

(Thousands of children.)

Age of children and year	Total children	Mother in labor force	Mother not in labor force	Married-couple families			Families maintained by women			Families maintained by men
				Total	Mother in labor force	Mother not in labor force	Total	Mother in labor force	Mother not in labor force	
Children Under 18 Years										
1990	59 596	36 712	21 110	45 898	29 077	16 820	11 925	7 635	4 290	1 774
1991	60 330	36 968	21 526	45 912	29 056	16 856	12 582	7 912	4 670	1 836
1992	61 262	38 081	21 176	45 966	29 882	16 084	13 291	8 199	5 093	2 005
1993	62 020	38 542	21 444	46 499	30 054	16 445	13 487	8 488	4 999	2 034
1994	63 407	40 186	21 188	47 247	31 279	15 968	14 127	8 907	5 220	2 033
1995	63 989	41 365	20 421	47 675	32 190	15 486	14 111	9 176	4 935	2 202
1996	64 506	41 573	20 449	47 484	31 764	15 720	14 538	9 809	4 729	2 484
1997	64 710	42 747	19 223	47 529	32 263	15 265	14 441	10 483	3 958	2 740
1998	65 043	43 156	19 069	47 909	32 533	15 376	14 317	10 623	3 694	2 818
1999	65 191	43 419	19 074	47 945	32 193	15 752	14 547	11 226	3 322	2 699
2000	65 601	44 188	18 674	48 902	33 149	15 753	13 960	11 039	2 921	2 739
2001	65 777	44 051	18 864	49 352	33 436	15 916	13 563	10 615	2 948	2 862
2002	65 978	43 821	19 243	48 836	32 673	16 163	14 228	11 149	3 079	2 914
2003	66 521	43 769	19 782	49 004	32 411	16 593	14 547	11 359	3 189	2 970
2004	66 386	43 144	20 229	48 656	31 892	16 764	14 717	11 252	3 465	3 014
2005	66 526	43 239	20 179	48 688	31 886	16 802	14 729	11 352	3 377	3 108
2006	66 883	43 278	20 440	48 853	31 946	16 908	14 865	11 332	3 532	3 165
2007	67 228	44 116	20 073	48 927	32 496	16 431	15 263	11 620	3 643	3 038
2008	67 153	43 798	19 966	48 303	32 110	16 193	15 461	11 688	3 773	3 388
2009	66 913	43 509	20 074	48 384	32 065	16 315	15 204	11 444	3 759	3 326
2010	66 811	43 335	19 913	47 730	31 686	16 044	15 518	11 649	3 869	3 563
2011	66 804	42 882	20 260	47 051	30 902	16 149	16 091	11 980	4 111	3 662
2012	66 472	42 643	19 885	45 989	30 228	15 761	16 539	12 414	4 125	3 944
2013	66 661	42 454	20 012	46 254	30 294	15 960	16 211	12 159	4 052	4 195
Children 6 to 17 Years Years										
1990	39 095	25 805	12 079	29 726	20 067	9 659	8 157	5 737	2 420	1 211
1991	39 470	25 806	12 392	29 598	19 907	9 691	8 599	5 899	2 701	1 272
1992	40 064	26 666	12 067	29 673	20 586	9 087	9 060	6 079	2 980	1 331
1993	40 622	27 046	12 291	30 233	20 796	9 437	9 104	6 249	2 854	1 285
1994	41 795	28 179	12 287	30 895	21 663	9 233	9 570	6 516	3 054	1 329
1995	42 423	28 931	12 000	31 298	22 239	9 059	9 633	6 692	2 941	1 492
1996	42 964	29 381	11 897	31 231	22 092	9 139	10 047	7 289	2 758	1 685
1997	43 488	30 308	11 400	31 509	22 602	8 906	10 199	7 705	2 493	1 781
1998	43 771	30 579	11 367	31 707	22 706	9 001	10 238	7 873	2 365	1 826
1999	44 110	30 885	11 370	31 975	22 706	9 269	10 281	8 179	2 101	1 855
2000	44 562	31 531	11 198	32 732	23 393	9 339	9 997	8 138	1 859	1 833
2001	44 458	31 411	11 153	32 957	23 599	9 358	9 608	7 813	1 795	1 894
2002	44 865	31 437	11 510	32 799	23 296	9 504	10 148	8 142	2 006	1 918
2003	45 273	31 559	11 635	32 782	23 160	9 622	10 412	8 399	2 013	2 080
2004	45 066	31 040	11 968	32 506	22 736	9 769	10 502	8 304	2 199	2 058
2005	45 027	30 930	11 995	32 412	22 565	9 847	10 514	8 366	2 148	2 102
2006	45 039	30 591	12 250	32 311	22 315	9 996	10 530	8 276	2 254	2 198
2007	45 155	31 252	11 855	32 417	22 788	9 629	10 690	8 464	2 226	2 048
2008	44 909	30 853	11 874	31 990	22 413	9 577	10 737	8 440	2 297	2 182
2009	44 595	30 600	11 811	31 966	22 425	9 537	10 449	8 175	2 274	2 180
2010	44 456	30 209	11 922	31 468	21 957	9 510	10 663	8 251	2 412	2 325
2011	44 471	29 904	12 244	31 072	21 365	9 707	11 076	8 539	2 537	2 323
2012	45 049	30 143	12 315	30 923	21 163	9 760	11 535	8 980	2 556	2 591
2013	45 492	30 091	12 694	31 411	21 352	10 058	11 375	8 738	2 636	2 707
Children Under 6 Years										
1990	20 502	10 907	9 031	16 171	9 010	7 161	3 767	1 897	1 870	563
1991	20 860	11 162	9 134	16 313	9 148	7 165	3 983	2 013	1 969	563
1992	21 198	11 415	9 109	16 293	9 296	6 997	4 232	2 119	2 112	674
1993	21 398	11 496	9 153	16 266	9 258	7 008	4 383	2 239	2 145	749
1994	21 612	12 007	8 901	16 352	9 617	6 735	4 556	2 391	2 166	704
1995	21 566	12 435	8 421	16 377	9 951	6 427	4 478	2 484	1 995	710
1996	21 542	12 192	8 552	16 253	9 672	6 581	4 491	2 520	1 971	799
1997	21 222	12 439	7 823	16 020	9 661	6 359	4 243	2 778	1 464	959
1998	21 272	12 577	7 703	16 201	9 827	6 375	4 079	2 751	1 328	992
1999	21 081	12 533	7 704	15 971	9 487	6 484	4 267	3 046	1 220	844
2000	21 039	12 657	7 476	16 170	9 757	6 413	3 963	2 901	1 062	906
2001	21 318	12 640	7 711	16 395	9 837	6 558	3 956	2 802	1 153	968
2002	21 113	12 384	7 733	16 037	9 377	6 660	4 080	3 007	1 073	996
2003	21 248	12 210	8 147	16 222	9 251	6 971	4 136	2 960	1 176	890
2004	21 321	12 104	8 261	16 151	9 156	6 995	4 214	2 948	1 266	956
2005	21 498	12 308	8 184	16 276	9 321	6 955	4 216	2 987	1 229	1 006
2006	21 844	12 687	8 190	16 542	9 631	6 911	4 335	3 057	1 278	968
2007	22 073	12 864	8 218	16 509	9 708	6 802	4 572	3 156	1 416	991
2008	22 244	12 946	8 092	16 313	9 697	6 616	4 724	3 248	1 476	1 207
2009	22 318	12 909	8 263	16 418	9 640	6 778	4 755	3 270	1 485	1 146
2010	22 355	13 127	7 991	16 262	9 729	6 533	4 855	3 398	1 457	1 237
2011	22 333	12 978	8 015	15 979	9 537	6 442	5 015	3 441	1 573	1 340
2012	21 423	12 500	7 570	15 066	9 065	6 001	5 004	3 435	1 569	1 353
2013	21 169	12 363	7 317	14 844	8 942	5 902	4 837	3 421	1 416	1 489

Note: See notes and definitions for information on historical comparability.

Table 1-50. Number of Families and Median Family Income, by Type of Family and Earner Status of Members, 1990–2012

(Thousands of families, dollars.)

Number and type of families and median family income	1990	1991	1992	1993	1994	1995	1996	1997	1998	1999	2000
NUMBER OF FAMILIES											
Married-Couple Families, Total	52 241	52 549	53 254	53 248	53 929	53 621	53 654	54 362	54 829	55 352	55 650
No earners	6 765	7 101	7 250	7 281	7 225	7 276	7 145	7 286	7 257	7 160	7 297
One earner	11 630	11 553	12 053	11 806	11 715	11 708	11 493	11 700	12 246	12 290	12 450
Husband	9 110	8 907	9 182	8 715	8 673	8 792	8 611	8 770	9 173	9 062	9 319
Wife	1 816	1 987	2 145	2 405	2 364	2 251	2 207	2 298	2 411	2 585	2 545
Other family member	703	659	726	686	678	666	674	632	662	643	586
Two earners	25 896	26 037	26 344	26 742	27 263	27 180	27 260	27 712	27 593	28 010	28 329
Husband and wife	23 697	23 880	24 255	24 543	25 123	25 274	25 274	25 731	25 696	26 134	26 447
Husband and other family member	1 711	1 633	1 447	1 582	1 565	1 393	1 483	1 406	1 306	1 325	1 277
Husband not an earner	487	524	642	617	574	513	502	575	590	552	605
Three earners or more	7 950	7 858	7 606	7 419	7 727	7 456	7 756	7 664	7 733	7 892	7 575
Husband and wife	7 029	7 052	6 882	6 723	6 987	6 770	7 126	7 023	7 102	7 220	6 917
Husband, not wife	756	595	550	535	543	531	479	478	456	528	537
Husband not an earner	165	211	175	162	196	155	150	163	176	144	120
Families Maintained by Women, Total	11 771	12 214	12 504	12 982	12 771	13 007	13 277	13 115	13 206	13 164	12 950
No earners	2 623	2 925	2 968	3 100	2 848	2 664	2 574	2 332	2 143	1 883	1 786
One earner	5 672	5 926	6 184	6 407	6 506	6 815	7 027	7 091	7 351	7 441	7 462
Householder	4 585	4 812	5 042	5 278	5 415	5 590	5 817	5 841	6 167	6 127	6 132
Other family member	1 087	1 114	1 142	1 129	1 091	1 225	1 211	1 251	1 183	1 314	1 331
Two earners or more	3 476	3 363	3 352	3 476	3 417	3 527	3 675	3 692	3 712	3 840	3 702
Householder and other family member(s)	3 146	3 058	2 998	3 139	3 126	3 225	3 431	3 398	3 399	3 508	3 376
Householder not an earner	330	305	354	337	291	302	245	294	313	332	325
Families Maintained by Men, Total	2 948	3 079	3 094	2 992	3 287	3 557	3 924	3 982	4 041	4 086	4 316
No earners	296	310	345	329	383	357	359	344	381	376	380
One earner	1 396	1 541	1 544	1 593	1 705	1 800	1 972	2 104	2 027	2 044	2 223
Householder	1 133	1 289	1 305	1 352	1 428	1 548	1 667	1 791	1 725	1 721	1 879
Other family member	263	253	239	241	277	253	305	313	302	323	344
Two earners or more	1 257	1 228	1 204	1 070	1 198	1 400	1 593	1 534	1 634	1 666	1 713
Householder and other family member(s)	1 180	1 157	1 117	1 002	1 128	1 302	1 469	1 427	1 532	1 522	1 585
Householder not an earner	76	71	88	67	71	98	124	107	102	143	128
MEDIAN FAMILY INCOME											
Married-Couple Families, Total	39 802	40 746	42 000	43 000	44 893	47 000	49 614	51 475	54 043	56 792	59 200
No earners	19 221	20 415	20 023	19 983	20 604	21 888	22 622	23 782	24 525	25 262	25 356
One earner	31 020	31 671	32 500	32 084	33 393	35 100	36 468	39 140	40 519	41 261	44 424
Husband	32 422	33 208	34 714	34 401	35 000	36 052	38 150	40 300	42 000	44 200	47 010
Wife	25 228	26 500	27 343	27 502	28 661	32 098	30 301	34 050	35 625	35 546	36 458
Other family member	33 262	33 042	33 622	30 254	32 578	37 784	39 644	40 317	42 414	41 120	45 492
Two earners	44 000	45 359	47 737	49 650	51 190	53 500	56 000	58 020	61 300	64 007	67 500
Husband and wife	44 031	45 516	48 050	49 980	51 500	53 626	56 392	58 564	61 900	64 950	68 132
Husband and other family member	42 602	45 000	45 694	48 862	48 517	52 530	49 610	53 854	57 680	53 541	56 503
Husband not an earner	39 494	40 495	40 124	38 800	42 800	47 121	46 990	47 979	50 955	52 466	53 430
Three earners or more	59 336	61 120	61 640	63 535	66 172	68 996	70 400	75 593	78 973	81 940	83 990
Husband and wife	55 846	61 448	62 674	64 099	66 674	69 371	71 148	76 105	79 907	83 000	84 634
Husband, not wife	59 675	60 592	57 015	60 712	63 633	60 360	61 824	68 890	71 001	69 561	79 050
Husband not an earner	49 107	44 874	47 551	54 805	54 655	61 196	55 495	62 684	63 205	69 275	68 050
Families Maintained by Women, Total	16 351	16 054	16 431	16 800	17 600	19 306	19 416	20 470	21 875	23 100	25 000
No earners	5 880	6 060	5 964	6 492	6 805	7 440	7 092	7 476	7 737	8 010	8 988
One earner	15 987	16 284	16 468	16 745	17 226	18 824	18 500	19 000	20 000	20 092	22 306
Householder	15 001	15 542	15 905	15 700	16 603	17 890	18 000	18 000	18 800	19 000	21 400
Other family member	20 173	20 220	19 709	20 800	21 300	23 166	21 000	22 870	25 981	26 800	27 524
Two earners or more	30 500	31 508	32 705	33 300	33 820	35 000	36 400	39 275	40 000	41 144	43 035
Householder and other family member(s)	30 367	31 550	33 280	33 165	33 357	34 674	36 400	39 000	39 713	40 855	43 000
Householder not an earner	32 800	29 477	30 460	35 394	37 531	39 444	38 249	47 471	43 725	48 004	45 600
Families Maintained by Men, Total	28 493	28 000	27 400	25 856	27 486	30 000	31 500	32 984	35 000	37 000	37 040
No earners	11 386	11 196	9 416	10 900	11 293	12 240	12 030	14 252	15 468	13 752	14 946
One earner	25 000	23 715	23 020	22 300	24 011	25 337	26 100	26 897	29 125	31 038	30 160
Householder	24 150	23 309	23 000	22 079	24 000	25 069	25 874	27 000	29 125	30 483	30 816
Other family member	27 620	25 720	24 359	26 916	26 253	27 291	28 584	25 486	28 241	34 756	29 118
Two earners or more	40 000	37 700	39 000	38 000	41 439	43 100	44 275	49 900	51 288	51 040	55 010
Householder and other family member(s)	40 256	37 550	39 300	38 363	41 534	43 000	43 065	50 000	50 954	50 960	55 400
Householder not an earner	34 064	40 000	36 445	33 700	37 386	55 133	47 001	44 786	68 257	57 407	51 945

Note: See notes and definitions for information on historical comparability.

Table 1-50. Number of Families and Median Family Income, by Type of Family and Earner Status of Members, 1990–2012—*Continued*

(Thousands of families, dollars.)

Number and type of families and median family income	2001	2002	2003	2004	2005	2006	2007	2008	2009	2010	2011	2012
NUMBER OF FAMILIES												
Married-Couple Families, Total	56 798	57 362	57 767	58 180	58 225	59 050	58 490	59 181	58 521	58 135	59 071	59 327
No earners	7 662	7 803	8 043	7 998	8 017	8 091	7 914	8 083	8 467	8 626	9 152	9 101
One earner	12 852	13 503	14 061	14 385	14 301	14 562	14 272	14 625	15 046	15 421	15 981	15 841
Husband	9 573	10 121	10 478	10 853	10 611	10 706	10 396	10 567	10 570	10 895	11 308	11 276
Wife	2 689	2 821	3 027	2 993	3 097	3 264	3 267	3 437	3 854	3 935	4 016	3 894
Other family member	590	560	557	539	593	591	608	620	621	591	658	671
Two earners	28 779	28 891	28 693	28 806	28 802	29 216	29 256	29 466	28 371	27 821	27 661	27 902
Husband and wife	26 829	26 966	26 860	26 758	26 833	27 241	27 264	27 531	26 298	25 801	25 581	25 718
Husband and other family member	1 424	1 391	1 322	1 462	1 376	1 358	1 393	1 308	1 363	1 317	1 370	1 447
Husband not an earner	526	534	511	586	594	616	599	627	710	703	710	738
Three earners or more	7 504	7 165	6 970	6 991	7 104	7 181	7 048	7 008	6 638	6 267	6 277	6 482
Husband and wife	6 859	6 565	6 349	6 459	6 535	6 620	6 452	6 393	6 024	5 609	5 621	5 865
Husband, not wife	530	455	467	381	445	397	452	432	425	466	462	435
Husband not an earner	115	145	154	152	124	165	144	182	189	192	193	182
Families Maintained by Women, Total	13 517	14 033	14 196	14 404	14 505	14 852	14 846	14 842	15 236	15 491	16 154	15 949
No earners	2 076	2 228	2 451	2 610	2 616	2 627	2 502	2 678	3 076	3 297	3 373	3 300
One earner	7 693	8 153	8 012	8 074	8 052	8 303	8 418	8 381	8 475	8 638	8 790	8 621
Householder	6 436	6 832	6 725	6 788	6 724	6 904	7 020	6 978	6 941	7 158	7 303	7 170
Other family member	1 257	1 321	1 286	1 285	1 329	1 398	1 398	1 404	1 533	1 480	1 487	1 451
Two earners or more	3 748	3 652	3 733	3 720	3 836	3 923	3 925	3 783	3 685	3 555	3 991	4 028
Householder and other family member(s)	3 442	3 290	3 364	3 399	3 468	3 547	3 572	3 467	3 281	3 149	3 552	3 623
Householder not an earner	306	362	369	321	368	376	353	316	405	406	439	405
Families Maintained by Men, Total	4 499	4 747	4 778	4 953	5 193	5 119	5 181	5 301	5 630	5 649	5 975	6 308
No earners	461	466	530	492	537	555	532	611	539	775	838	883
One earner	2 319	2 434	2 466	2 573	2 661	2 584	2 703	2 636	2 801	2 911	3 106	3 242
Householder	1 911	2 026	2 053	2 152	2 196	2 155	2 297	2 199	2 261	2 389	2 535	2 698
Other family member	408	408	413	421	464	429	406	437	539	521	571	544
Two earners or more	1 719	1 847	1 782	1 888	1 995	1 979	1 947	2 054	2 030	1 963	2 031	2 183
Householder and other family member(s)	1 629	1 709	1 625	1 736	1 848	1 828	1 812	1 889	1 822	1 751	1 811	1 951
Householder not an earner	90	138	157	152	147	152	134	165	208	212	220	232
MEDIAN FAMILY INCOME												
Married-Couple Families, Total	60 100	61 000	62 388	63 627	65 586	69 300	72 802	72 805	71 464	72 224	73 678	75 002
No earners	25 900	25 954	26 312	26 798	28 376	30 000	30 134	31 164	32 093	32 350	33 756	33 584
One earner	44 400	45 000	46 546	47 749	50 000	50 400	52 686	53 865	53 087	55 000	56 609	58 415
Husband	47 500	48 004	48 948	50 000	52 000	53 360	55 350	56 000	55 333	56 533	59 842	60 002
Wife	36 140	39 072	41 180	41 000	43 505	45 000	47 000	47 015	47 550	50 150	52 007	52 517
Other family member	44 270	40 927	45 936	46 324	50 263	49 352	48 922	55 114	55 166	57 264	56 914	53 195
Two earners	69 543	71 282	73 309	75 100	76 960	81 500	85 012	85 500	86 361	88 500	90 001	91 651
Husband and wife	70 000	72 150	74 500	76 000	77 539	82 762	86 000	86 842	87 939	90 000	90 976	93 125
Husband and other family member	65 240	62 848	60 100	66 120	67 350	68 828	71 573	68 755	73 720	74 973	77 888	76 408
Husband not an earner	58 725	54 840	58 000	63 050	65 622	63 657	68 032	66 445	70 017	72 317	72 644	73 906
Three earners or more	86 090	88 632	93 000	94 212	98 000	103 803	106 747	105 618	107 000	107 542	111 000	114 201
Husband and wife	87 000	89 962	94 353	95 524	99 800	104 045	107 630	106 493	108 703	108 714	112 943	115 800
Husband, not wife	76 230	82 180	77 316	87 000	79 417	91 965	101 771	99 731	85 574	93 000	96 756	90 956
Husband not an earner	80 661	68 400	91 771	73 137	84 638	97 510	92 428	93 961	95 251	100 105	97 491	96 968
Families Maintained by Women, Total	25 064	26 000	26 000	26 400	27 000	28 218	30 000	29 698	29 025	28 774	29 848	30 000
No earners	8 160	8 808	8 344	8 400	8 228	8 657	8 873	9 404	10 037	9 600	9 600	10 299
One earner	23 008	24 597	24 752	25 040	25 308	26 393	27 795	28 060	29 000	29 009	28 912	29 558
Householder	22 001	23 760	23 832	24 801	24 505	25 381	26 644	27 000	27 928	27 924	27 488	28 077
Other family member	28 476	29 524	28 857	29 700	31 700	31 462	31 950	34 814	34 421	33 957	35 161	35 000
Two earners or more	45 244	46 580	47 576	48 549	50 000	52 400	55 749	54 369	54 500	55 047	56 000	58 694
Householder and other family member(s)	44 842	46 000	46 701	47 974	48 989	51 479	55 010	54 306	54 448	54 000	55 500	57 561
Householder not an earner	51 000	51 248	57 267	56 799	64 805	61 699	64 094	54 978	56 203	61 781	60 015	71 367
Families Maintained by Men, Total	36 000	37 440	37 914	40 000	40 293	41 130	44 001	43 050	41 000	42 500	43 000	42 000
No earners	12 840	15 200	15 408	14 167	13 950	15 462	12 921	15 557	15 653	16 176	17 945	18 006
One earner	30 800	30 139	32 097	35 000	35 001	35 100	37 716	36 806	35 116	37 707	38 000	35 500
Householder	30 500	30 014	31 355	35 000	35 075	35 011	37 720	37 569	35 117	37 990	38 069	36 000
Other family member	31 052	32 000	35 525	35 438	35 000	37 840	37 522	34 404	35 086	37 041	36 983	34 892
Two earners or more	55 024	55 000	57 840	57 600	60 024	61 000	63 600	64 077	64 747	66 000	67 301	65 017
Householder and other family member(s)	54 850	55 220	57 400	57 058	60 000	61 000	64 000	63 416	64 743	65 200	66 708	65 024
Householder not an earner	61 824	49 852	64 658	65 400	70 879	62 000	60 498	69 794	65 618	71 962	73 242	64 799

Note: See notes and definitions for information on historical comparability.

Table 1-51. Employment Status of the Foreign-Born and Native-Born Populations, by Selected Characteristics, 2011–2012

(Thousands of people, percent.)

Year and characteristic	Civilian noninstitutional population	Civilian labor force				
		Total	Participation rate	Employed	Unemployed	
					Number	Rate
2011						
TOTAL						
Both sexes, 16 years and over	239 618	153 617	64.1	139 869	13 747	8.9
Men	116 317	81 975	70.5	74 290	7 684	9.4
Women	123 300	71 642	58.1	65 579	6 063	8.5
FOREIGN BORN						
Both sexes, 16 years and over	36 420	24 391	67.0	22 183	2 208	9.1
Men	18 090	14 379	79.5	13 120	1 260	8.8
Women	18 331	10 012	54.6	9 063	949	9.5
Age						
16 to 24 years	3 631	1 971	54.3	1 695	276	14.0
25 to 34 years	7 562	5 758	76.1	5 255	503	8.7
35 to 44 years	8 492	6 843	80.6	6 301	542	7.9
45 to 54 years	7 089	5 799	81.8	5 274	525	9.1
55 to 64 years	4 737	3 161	66.7	2 870	290	9.2
65 years and over	4 909	860	17.5	788	72	8.3
Race and Hispanic Origin						
White, non-Hispanic	7 617	4 583	60.2	4 237	346	7.6
Black, non-Hispanic	3 002	2 137	71.2	1 870	267	12.5
Asian, non-Hispanic	8 306	5 449	65.6	5 086	363	6.7
Hispanic[1]	17 132	11 963	69.8	10 751	1 212	10.1
Educational Attainment						
Total, 25 years and over	32 790	22 420	68.4	20 488	1 932	8.6
Less than a high school diploma	9 532	5 721	60.0	5 086	634	11.1
High school graduate, no college[2]	8 488	5 674	66.8	5 145	529	9.3
Some college or associate's degree	5 389	3 927	72.9	3 584	343	8.7
Bachelor's degree or higher[3]	9 381	7 098	75.7	6 673	425	6.0
NATIVE BORN						
Both sexes, 16 years and over	203 197	129 226	63.6	117 686	11 539	8.9
Men	98 228	67 595	68.8	61 170	6 425	9.5
Women	104 970	61 630	58.7	56 516	5 115	8.3
Age						
16 to 24 years	34 567	19 026	55.0	15 668	3 358	17.7
25 to 34 years	33 801	27 967	82.7	25 282	2 685	9.6
35 to 44 years	31 006	25 817	83.3	23 970	1 847	7.2
45 to 54 years	36 753	29 560	80.4	27 593	1 967	6.7
55 to 64 years	32 250	20 604	63.9	19 315	1 289	6.3
65 years and over	34 819	6 252	18.0	5 858	393	6.3
Race and Hispanic Origin						
White, non-Hispanic	153 541	90 751	64.3	91 609	7 142	7.2
Black, non-Hispanic	24 911	14 973	60.1	12 526	2 447	16.3
Asian, non-Hispanic	2 917	1 793	61.5	1 647	147	8.2
Hispanic[1]	17 306	10 934	63.2	9 518	1 417	13.0
Educational Attainment						
Total, 25 years and over	168 630	110 200	65.4	102 019	8 181	7.4
Less than a high school diploma	15 590	5 878	37.7	4 881	998	17.0
High school graduates, no college[2]	53 444	31 670	59.3	28 679	2 992	9.4
Some college or associate's degree	47 700	32 904	69.0	30 310	2 594	7.9
Bachelor's degree or higher[3]	51 896	39 747	76.6	38 149	1 598	4.0

Note: Updated population controls are introduced annually with the release of January data.

[1] May be of any race.
[2] Includes persons with a high school diploma or equivalent.
[3] Includes persons with bachelor's, master's, professional, and doctoral degrees.

Table 1-51. Employment Status of the Foreign-Born and Native-Born Populations, by Selected Characteristics, 2011–2012—*Continued*

(Thousands of people, percent.)

Year and characteristic	Civilian noninstitutional population	Civilian labor force				
		Total	Participation rate	Employed	Unemployed	
					Number	Rate
2012						
TOTAL						
Both sexes, 16 years and over	243 284	154 975	63.7	142 469	12 506	8.1
Men	117 343	82 327	70.2	75 555	6 771	8.2
Women	125 941	72 648	57.7	66 914	5 734	7.9
FOREIGN BORN						
Both sexes, 16 years and over	37 727	25 026	66.3	23 006	2 021	8.1
Men	18 365	14 424	78.5	13 342	1 082	7.5
Women	19 362	10 602	54.8	9 663	939	8.9
Age						
16 to 24 years	3 724	1 905	51.2	1 632	273	14.3
25 to 34 years	7 674	5 840	76.1	5 373	468	8.0
35 to 44 years	8 710	6 997	80.3	6 518	479	6.8
45 to 54 years	7 509	6 071	80.9	5 622	449	7.4
55 to 64 years	5 021	3 332	66.4	3 051	282	8.5
65 years and over	5 089	880	17.3	810	70	8.0
Race and Hispanic Origin						
White, non-Hispanic	7 595	4 564	60.1	4 242	322	7.1
Black, non-Hispanic	3 068	2 166	70.6	1 925	241	11.1
Asian, non-Hispanic	9 146	5 919	64.7	5 582	337	5.7
Hispanic[1]	17 507	12 087	69.0	10 988	1 099	9.1
Educational Attainment						
Total, 25 years and over	34 002	23 121	68.0	21 374	1 747	7.6
Less than a high school diploma	9 497	5 688	59.9	5 126	562	9.9
High school graduates, no college[2]	8 713	5 783	66.4	5 314	469	8.1
Some college or associate degree	5 670	4 028	71.0	3 713	315	7.8
Bachelor's degree and higher[3]	10 122	7 621	75.3	7 221	401	5.3
NATIVE BORN						
Both sexes, 16 years and over	205 558	129 948	63.2	119 464	10 485	8.1
Men	98 979	67 903	68.6	62 213	5 690	8.4
Women	106 579	62 046	58.2	57 251	4 795	7.7
Age						
16 to 24 years	35 059	19 379	55.3	16 202	3 177	16.4
25 to 34 years	33 301	27 625	83.0	25 328	2 297	8.3
35 to 44 years	30 932	25 737	83.2	24 058	1 679	6.5
45 to 54 years	36 188	28 983	80.1	27 252	1 731	6.0
55 to 64 years	33 297	21 377	64.2	20 189	1 189	5.6
65 years and over	36 780	6 847	18.6	6 435	412	6.0
Race and Hispanic Origin						
White, non-Hispanic	152 742	97 328	63.7	90 949	6 379	6.6
Black, non-Hispanic	25 137	15 089	60.0	12 925	2 164	14.3
Asian, non-Hispanic	3 277	2 014	61.5	1 880	134	6.7
Hispanic[1]	19 252	12 304	63.9	10 890	1 414	11.5
Educational Attainment						
Total, 25 years and over	170 499	110 569	64.9	103 261	7 308	6.6
Less than a high school diploma	15 384	5 640	36.7	4 797	843	14.9
High school graduates, no college[2]	53 099	30 988	58.4	28 404	2 584	8.3
Some college or associate degree	48 624	33 332	68.5	30 992	2 339	7.0
Bachelor's degree or higher[3]	53 392	40 609	76.1	39 067	1 542	3.8

Note: Updated population controls are introduced annually with the release of January data.

[1] May be of any race.
[2] Includes persons with a high school diploma or equivalent.
[3] Includes persons with bachelor's, master's, professional, and doctoral degrees.

Table 1-52. Employment Status of the Foreign-Born and Native-Born Populations Age 16 Years and Over, by Sex and Presence and Age of Youngest Child, Annual Averages, 2011–2012

(Thousands of people, percent.)

Characteristic	2011			2012		
	Both sexes	Men	Women	Both sexes	Men	Women
FOREIGN BORN						
With Own Children Under 18 Years						
Civilian noninstitutional population	14 472	6 965	7 508	14 796	6 896	7 901
Civilian labor force	11 024	6 533	4 490	11 229	6 466	4 763
Participation rate	76.2	93.8	59.8	75.9	93.8	60.3
Employed	10 062	6 032	4 030	10 378	6 063	4 315
Employment-population ratio	69.5	86.6	53.7	70.1	87.9	54.6
Unemployed	961	501	460	851	403	448
Unemployment rate	8.7	7.7	10.2	7.6	6.2	9.4
With Own Children 6 to 17 Years, None Younger						
Civilian noninstitutional population	7 484	3 474	4 010	7 896	3 576	4 319
Civilian labor force	5 941	3 215	2 725	6 223	3 326	2 897
Participation rate	79.4	92.6	68.0	78.8	93.0	67.1
Employed	5 437	2 969	2 468	5 753	3 115	2 638
Employment-population ratio	72.6	85.5	61.5	72.9	87.1	61.1
Unemployed	504	247	257	469	211	259
Unemployment rate	8.5	7.7	9.4	7.5	6.3	8.9
With Own Children Under 6 Years						
Civilian noninstitutional population	6 989	3 491	3 497	6 901	3 319	3 581
Civilian labor force	5 083	3 318	1 765	5 006	3 140	1 865
Participation rate	72.7	95.0	50.5	72.5	94.6	52.1
Employed	4 625	3 063	1 562	4 625	2 948	1 677
Employment-population ratio	66.2	87.7	44.7	67.0	88.8	46.8
Unemployed	457	255	203	381	192	189
Unemployment rate	9.0	7.7	11.5	7.6	6.1	10.1
With Own Children Under 3 Years						
Civilian noninstitutional population	3 961	2 019	1 942	3 828	1 864	1 964
Civilian labor force	2 802	1 925	877	2 697	1 772	925
Participation rate	70.8	95.4	45.2	70.5	95.1	47.1
Employed	2 547	1 784	762	2 497	1 671	827
Employment-population ratio	64.3	88.4	39.3	65.2	89.6	42.1
Unemployed	256	141	115	200	101	98
Unemployment rate	9.1	7.3	13.1	7.4	5.7	10.6
With No Own Children Under 18 Years						
Civilian noninstitutional population	21 948	11 125	10 823	22 930	11 469	11 461
Civilian labor force	13 368	7 846	5 521	13 797	7 958	5 840
Participation rate	60.9	70.5	51.0	60.2	69.4	51.0
Employed	12 121	7 088	5 033	12 628	7 279	5 348
Employment-population ratio	55.2	63.7	46.5	55.1	63.5	46.7
Unemployed	1 247	758	489	1 170	679	491
Unemployment rate	9.3	9.7	8.9	8.5	8.5	8.4

Note: Updated population controls are introduced annually with the release of January data.

Table 1-52. Employment Status of the Foreign-Born and Native-Born Populations Age 16 Years and Over, by Sex and Presence and Age of Youngest Child, Annual Averages, 2011–2012—*Continued*

(Thousands of people, percent.)

Characteristic	2011			2012		
	Both sexes	Men	Women	Both sexes	Men	Women
NATIVE BORN						
With Own Children Under 18 Years						
Civilian noninstitutional population	51 190	22 218	28 972	50 823	22 048	28 776
Civilian labor force	41 879	20 675	21 204	41 525	20 488	21 037
Participation rate	81.8	93.1	73.2	81.7	92.9	73.1
Employed	38 703	19 357	19 346	38 723	19 397	19 326
Employment-population ratio	75.6	87.1	66.8	76.2	88.0	67.2
Unemployed	3 176	1 318	1 858	2 802	1 091	1 711
Unemployment rate	7.6	6.4	8.8	6.7	5.3	8.1
With Own Children 6 to 17 Years, None Younger						
Civilian noninstitutional population	27 961	12 194	15 767	27 890	12 200	15 690
Civilian labor force	23 584	11 271	12 314	23 350	11 219	12 131
Participation rate	84.3	92.4	78.1	83.7	92.0	77.3
Employed	22 037	10 627	11 410	21 969	10 676	11 293
Employment-population ratio	78.8	87.1	72.4	78.8	87.5	72.0
Unemployed	1 548	644	903	1 382	544	838
Unemployment rate	6.6	5.7	7.3	5.9	4.8	6.9
With Own Children Under 6 Years						
Civilian noninstitutional population	23 229	10 024	13 205	22 933	9 847	13 086
Civilian labor force	18 295	9 404	8 891	18 175	9 268	8 907
Participation rate	78.8	93.8	67.3	79.3	94.1	68.1
Employed	16 666	8 730	7 936	16 754	8 721	8 034
Employment-population ratio	71.7	87.1	60.1	73.1	88.6	61.4
Unemployed	1 629	674	955	1 421	548	873
Unemployment rate	8.9	7.2	10.7	7.8	5.9	9.8
With Own Children Under 3 Years						
Civilian noninstitutional population	13 655	5 932	7 723	13 293	5 718	7 575
Civilian labor force	10 536	5 567	4 969	10 314	5 400	4 914
Participation rate	77.2	93.8	64.3	77.6	94.4	64.9
Employed	9 577	5 160	4 418	9 494	5 075	4 419
Employment-population ratio	70.1	87.0	57.2	71.4	88.8	58.3
Unemployed	958	407	551	821	325	496
Unemployment rate	9.1	7.3	11.1	8.0	6.0	10.1
With No Own Children Under 18 Years						
Civilian noninstitutional population	152 007	76 010	75 998	154 734	76 931	77 803
Civilian labor force	87 346	46 920	40 426	88 423	47 415	41 008
Participation rate	57.5	61.7	53.2	57.1	61.6	52.7
Employed	78 983	41 814	37 170	80 741	42 817	37 924
Employment-population ratio	52.0	55.0	48.9	52.2	55.7	48.7
Unemployed	8 363	5 107	3 256	7 683	4 599	3 084
Unemployment rate	9.6	10.9	8.1	8.7	9.7	7.5

Note: Updated population controls are introduced annually with the release of January data.

Table 1-53. Employment Status of the Foreign-Born and Native-Born Populations Age 25 Years and Over, by Educational Attainment, Race, and Hispanic Origin, Annual Averages, 2011–2012

(Thousands of people, percent.)

Characteristic	2011				2012			
	Less than a high school diploma	High school graduate, no college[1]	Some college or associate's degree	Bachelor's degree or higher[2]	Less than a high school diploma	High school graduate, no college[1]	Some college or associate's degree	Bachelor's degree or higher[2]
FOREIGN BORN								
White, Non-Hispanic								
Civilian noninstitutional population	815	1 884	1 407	2 935	789	1 778	1 434	3 019
Civilian labor force	274	978	899	2 144	256	932	879	2 200
Participation rate	33.6	51.9	63.9	73.0	32.4	52.4	61.3	72.9
Employed	243	897	832	2 019	233	864	818	2 078
Employment-population ratio	29.9	47.6	59.1	68.8	29.6	48.6	57.0	68.8
Unemployed	30	81	67	125	23	68	61	122
Unemployment rate	11.1	8.3	7.4	5.8	8.9	7.3	6.9	5.5
Black, Non-Hispanic								
Civilian noninstitutional population	391	810	709	752	368	812	693	813
Civilian labor force	204	594	578	614	182	591	544	680
Participation rate	52.1	73.3	81.5	81.6	49.5	72.7	78.5	83.7
Employed	163	516	512	556	153	520	488	631
Employment-population ratio	41.7	63.7	72.2	74.0	41.6	64.0	70.4	77.7
Unemployed	41	78	66	57	29	71	56	49
Unemployment rate	19.9	13.2	11.4	9.3	16.0	12.0	10.3	7.2
Asian, Non-Hispanic								
Civilian noninstitutional population	955	1 628	1 149	3 892	978	1 658	1 306	4 364
Civilian labor force	404	1 014	807	2 936	438	1 011	894	3 251
Participation rate	42.3	62.3	70.3	75.4	44.8	61.0	68.5	74.5
Employed	366	935	749	2 785	407	949	837	3 104
Employment-population ratio	38.3	57.4	65.2	71.6	41.6	57.2	64.1	71.1
Unemployed	39	79	58	150	31	62	57	147
Unemployment rate	9.6	7.8	7.2	5.1	7.1	6.2	6.4	4.5
Hispanic[3]								
Civilian noninstitutional population	7 331	4 072	2 052	1 687	7 319	4 360	2 147	1 798
Civilian labor force	4 815	3 032	1 586	1 309	4 789	3 175	1 642	1 386
Participation rate	65.7	74.4	77.3	77.6	65.4	72.8	76.5	77.1
Employed	4 294	2 746	1 437	1 221	4 312	2 911	1 507	1 308
Employment-population ratio	58.6	67.4	70.0	72.4	58.9	66.8	70.2	72.8
Unemployed	521	286	149	88	476	263	134	78
Unemployment rate	10.8	9.4	9.4	6.7	9.9	8.3	8.2	5.6
NATIVE BORN								
White, Non-Hispanic								
Civilian noninstitutional population	9 841	41 003	36 755	44 100	9 533	40 294	36 922	44 806
Civilian labor force	3 609	23 710	24 997	33 543	3 372	22 863	24 868	33 777
Participation rate	36.7	57.8	68.0	76.1	35.4	56.7	67.4	75.4
Employed	3 103	21 813	23 315	32 316	2 946	21 234	23 363	32 596
Employment-population ratio	31.5	53.2	63.4	73.3	30.9	52.7	63.3	72.7
Unemployed	506	1 897	1 682	1 226	426	1 629	1 505	1 182
Unemployment rate	14.0	8.0	6.7	3.7	12.6	7.1	6.1	3.5
Black, Non-Hispanic								
Civilian noninstitutional population	2 924	7 075	5 924	3 866	2 799	7 000	6 097	4 068
Civilian labor force	1 015	4 297	4 188	3 013	910	4 204	4 275	3 157
Participation rate	34.7	60.7	70.7	77.9	32.5	60.1	70.1	77.6
Employed	745	3 613	3 635	2 810	703	3 626	3 793	2 966
Employment-population ratio	25.5	51.1	61.4	72.7	25.1	51.8	62.2	72.9
Unemployed	270	684	553	203	207	578	482	191
Unemployment rate	26.6	15.9	13.2	6.7	22.7	13.7	11.3	6.1
Asian, Non-Hispanic								
Civilian noninstitutional population	119	397	451	1 090	135	397	474	1 237
Civilian labor force	46	221	317	862	52	222	350	979
Participation rate	39.0	55.8	70.3	79.1	38.6	56.0	73.8	79.1
Employed	41	207	292	814	49	210	323	944
Employment-population ratio	34.9	52.1	64.8	74.7	36.6	52.8	68.2	76.3
Unemployed	5	15	25	48	3	13	27	34
Unemployment rate	10.4	6.7	7.8	5.6	5.0	5.7	7.6	3.5
Hispanic[3]								
Civilian noninstitutional population	2 281	3 927	3 414	2 074	2 461	4 273	3 831	2 413
Civilian labor force	1 043	2 781	2 628	1 722	1 131	2 993	2 942	1 998
Participation rate	45.7	70.8	77.0	83.0	46.0	70.0	76.8	82.8
Employed	862	2 470	2 393	1 636	957	2 702	2 708	1 902
Employment-population ratio	37.8	62.9	70.1	78.9	38.9	63.2	70.7	78.8
Unemployed	181	311	235	86	174	291	234	96
Unemployment rate	17.4	11.2	8.9	5.0	15.4	9.7	8.0	4.8

Note: Updated population controls are introduced annually with the release of January data.

[1]Includes persons with a high school diploma or equivalent.
[2]Includes persons with bachelor's, master's, professional, and doctoral degrees.
[3]May be of any race.

Table 1-54. Employed Foreign-Born and Native-Born Persons Age 16 Years and Over, by Occupation and Sex, 2011–2012 Annual Averages

(Thousands of people, percent.)

Occupation	2011					
	Foreign born			Native born		
	Both sexes	Male	Female	Both sexes	Male	Female
TOTAL EMPLOYED	22 183	13 120	9 063	117 686	61 170	56 516
Percent Employed	100.0	100.0	100.0	100.0	100.0	100.0
Management, professional, and related	28.6	26.5	31.6	39.3	36.1	42.7
Management, business, and financial operations	11.0	11.2	10.7	16.3	17.7	14.8
Management	7.6	8.5	6.3	11.5	13.6	9.3
Business and financial operations	3.4	2.6	4.5	4.7	4.1	5.5
Professional and related	17.6	15.4	20.9	23.0	18.4	27.9
Computer and mathematical	3.5	4.5	2.0	2.4	3.4	1.3
Architecture and engineering	2.0	2.8	0.7	2.0	3.3	0.6
Life, physical, and social sciences	1.0	0.9	1.2	0.9	0.9	0.9
Community and social services	0.9	0.7	1.2	1.8	1.2	2.5
Legal	0.4	0.2	0.7	1.4	1.4	1.4
Education, training, and library	3.7	2.1	5.9	6.6	3.3	10.3
Arts, design, entertainment, sports, and media	1.4	1.4	1.3	2.1	2.1	2.1
Health care practitioner and technical	4.8	2.6	7.9	5.7	2.7	8.9
Services	24.6	19.3	32.2	16.4	13.7	19.4
Health care support	2.6	0.7	5.4	2.4	0.5	4.3
Protective services	0.9	1.3	0.4	2.5	3.9	1.1
Food preparation and serving related	7.9	7.8	7.9	5.1	4.1	6.2
Building and grounds cleaning and maintenance	8.8	8.0	10.0	3.0	3.8	2.2
Personal care and services	4.3	1.5	8.4	3.4	1.4	5.6
Sales and office	17.5	12.6	24.5	24.8	17.6	32.6
Sales and related	8.7	7.4	10.7	11.4	11.1	11.7
Office and administrative support	8.7	5.2	13.8	13.4	6.6	20.8
Natural resources, construction, and maintenance	13.5	21.8	1.5	8.5	15.7	0.7
Farming, fishing, and forestry	1.9	2.4	1.0	0.5	0.8	0.2
Construction and extraction	8.5	14.1	0.3	4.5	8.3	0.2
Installation, maintenance, and repair	3.2	5.2	0.2	3.6	6.6	0.3
Production, transportation, and material moving	15.8	19.8	10.1	11.0	16.9	4.7
Production	8.7	9.3	7.7	5.3	7.5	2.9
Transportation and material moving	7.2	10.5	2.4	5.7	9.3	1.8

Occupation	2012					
	Foreign born			Native born		
	Both sexes	Male	Female	Both sexes	Male	Female
TOTAL EMPLOYED	23 006	13 342	9 663	119 464	62 213	57 251
Percent Employed	100.0	100.0	100.0	100.0	100.0	100.0
Management, professional, and related	30.0	28.0	32.8	39.5	36.1	43.1
Management, business, and financial operations	11.6	11.7	11.6	16.7	18.0	15.3
Management	8.1	9.0	6.9	11.9	13.9	9.6
Business and financial operations	3.5	2.7	4.6	4.9	4.1	5.7
Professional and related	18.4	16.3	21.2	22.7	18.1	27.7
Computer and mathematical	3.8	5.0	2.1	2.5	3.5	1.4
Architecture and engineering	2.2	3.3	0.8	2.0	3.2	0.5
Life, physical, and social sciences	1.0	1.0	1.1	0.9	1.0	0.9
Community and social services	0.8	0.6	1.1	1.7	1.2	2.3
Legal	0.5	0.3	0.7	1.4	1.4	1.4
Education, training, and library	3.7	2.2	5.8	6.4	3.2	10.0
Arts, design, entertainment, sports, and media	1.4	1.2	1.6	2.1	2.1	2.1
Health care practitioner and technical	5.0	2.7	8.1	5.7	2.6	9.1
Services	25.2	19.5	33.2	16.5	13.7	19.4
Health care support	2.7	0.6	5.6	2.4	0.6	4.4
Protective services	1.0	1.4	0.4	2.4	3.6	1.1
Food preparation and serving related	8.0	7.7	8.3	5.2	4.2	6.2
Building and grounds cleaning and maintenance	8.6	7.8	9.8	3.0	3.8	2.1
Personal care and services	4.9	2.0	9.0	3.4	1.5	5.6
Sales and office	16.5	12.1	22.6	24.6	17.7	32.0
Sales and related	8.4	7.5	9.7	11.3	11.1	11.5
Office and administrative support	8.1	4.6	12.9	13.3	6.6	20.5
Natural resources, construction, and maintenance	12.7	21.0	1.4	8.3	15.2	0.7
Farming, fishing, and forestry	1.8	2.3	1.1	0.5	0.7	0.2
Construction and extraction	8.0	13.5	0.2	4.3	8.1	0.3
Installation, maintenance, and repair	3.0	5.1	0.1	3.5	6.4	0.3
Production, transportation, and material moving	15.5	19.4	10.1	11.2	17.2	4.8
Production	8.4	9.1	7.3	5.5	7.9	2.9
Transportation and material moving	7.1	10.2	2.8	5.8	9.4	1.9

Note: Updated population controls are introduced annually with the release of January data.

Table 1-55. Median Usual Weekly Earnings of Full-Time Wage and Salary Workers for the Foreign-Born and Native-Born Populations, by Selected Characteristics, Annual Averages, 2011–2012 Annual Averages

(Thousands of people, dollars, percent.)

Year and characteristic	Foreign born		Native born		Earnings of foreign born as a percent of earnings of native born[1]
	Number	Median weekly earnings	Number	Median weekly earnings	
2011					
Both Sexes, 16 Years and Over	16 441	609	84 015	780	78.0
Men	10 177	624	45 794	879	71.0
Women	6 264	585	38 222	701	83.5
Age					
16 to 24 years	1 081	405	7 643	448	90.3
25 to 34 years	4 120	569	20 177	718	79.3
35 to 44 years	4 812	671	18 970	875	76.7
45 to 54 years	3 962	680	21 172	899	75.6
55 to 64 years	2 039	662	13 602	910	72.8
65 years and over	429	621	2 452	760	81.8
Race and Hispanic Origin					
White, non-Hispanic	2 876	883	64 359	837	105.5
Black, non-Hispanic	1 467	614	9 638	617	99.5
Asian, non-Hispanic	3 876	868	1 226	878	98.8
Hispanic[2]	8 044	489	7 103	636	77.0
Educational Attainment					
Total, 25 years and over	15 361	628	76 373	831	75.6
Less than a high school diploma	3 822	417	3 197	497	83.9
High school graduate, no college[3]	3 828	530	21 328	661	80.2
Some college	2 580	665	22 625	746	89.2
Bachelor's degree or higher[4]	5 131	1 148	29 222	1 151	99.8
2012					
Both Sexes, 16 Years and Over	17 089	625	85 659	797	78.4
Men	10 385	665	46 901	898	74.1
Women	6 704	589	38 758	710	82.9
Age					
16 to 24 years	994	403	8 036	452	89.2
25 to 34 years	4 275	591	20 310	729	81.1
35 to 44 years	4 972	692	19 112	897	77.1
45 to 54 years	4 267	683	21 079	913	74.8
55 to 64 years	2 142	667	14 376	929	71.8
65 years and over	439	628	2 747	778	80.7
Race and Hispanic Origin					
White, non-Hispanic	2 906	898	64 284	857	104.8
Black, non-Hispanic	1 459	640	10 002	623	102.8
Asian, non-Hispanic	4 213	922	1 385	937	98.4
Hispanic[2]	8 316	501	7 986	641	78.1
Educational Attainment					
Total, 25 years and over	16 095	652	77 623	851	76.7
Less than a high school diploma	3 879	428	3 131	510	84.0
High school graduates, no college[3]	3 899	550	21 339	675	81.5
Some college	2 702	673	23 124	758	88.8
Bachelor's degree and higher[4]	5 615	1 164	30 029	1 165	100.0

Note: Updated population controls are introduced annually with the release of January data.

[1]These figures are computed using unrounded medians and may differ slightly from percentages computed using the rounded medians displayed in this table.
[2]May be of any race.
[3]Includes persons with a high school diploma or equivalent.
[4]Includes persons with bachelor's, master's, professional, and doctoral degrees.

Table 1-56. Percent Distribution of the Civilian Labor Force Age 25 to 64 Years, by Educational Attainment, Sex, and Race, March 1990–March 2013

(Thousands of people, percent.)

Sex, race, and year	Civilian labor force	Percent distribution				
		Total	Less than a high school diploma	4 years of high school only	1 to 3 years of college	4 or more years of college
Both Sexes						
1990	99 175	100.0	13.4	39.5	20.7	26.4
1991	100 480	100.0	13.0	39.4	21.1	26.5
1992	102 387	100.0	12.2	36.2	25.2	26.4
1993	103 504	100.0	11.5	35.2	26.3	27.0
1994	104 868	100.0	11.0	34.0	27.7	27.3
1995	106 519	100.0	10.8	33.1	27.8	28.3
1996	108 037	100.0	10.9	32.9	27.7	28.5
1997	110 514	100.0	10.9	33.0	27.4	28.6
1998	111 857	100.0	10.7	32.8	27.4	29.1
1999	112 542	100.0	10.3	32.3	27.4	30.0
2000	114 052	100.0	9.8	31.8	27.9	30.4
2001	115 073	100.0	9.8	31.4	28.1	30.7
2002	117 738	100.0	10.1	30.6	27.7	31.6
2003	119 261	100.0	10.1	30.1	27.8	31.9
2004	119 392	100.0	9.7	30.1	27.8	32.4
2005	120 461	100.0	9.8	30.1	27.8	32.3
2006	122 541	100.0	9.8	29.6	28.0	32.6
2007	124 581	100.0	9.8	29.3	27.3	33.6
2008	125 493	100.0	9.0	28.8	27.9	34.4
2009	125 655	100.0	9.0	28.7	27.9	34.3
2010	126 363	100.0	8.8	29.1	27.5	34.5
2011	125 385	100.0	8.5	28.2	28.0	35.4
2012	125 726	100.0	8.6	27.5	27.9	36.0
2013	125 744	100.0	8.2	27.0	28.1	36.7
Men						
1990	54 476	100.0	15.1	37.2	19.7	28.0
1991	55 165	100.0	14.7	37.5	20.2	27.6
1992	55 917	100.0	13.9	34.7	23.8	27.5
1993	56 544	100.0	13.2	33.9	24.7	28.1
1994	56 633	100.0	12.7	32.9	25.8	28.6
1995	57 454	100.0	12.2	32.3	25.7	29.7
1996	58 121	100.0	12.7	32.2	26.0	29.1
1997	59 268	100.0	12.8	32.2	25.8	29.2
1998	59 905	100.0	12.3	32.3	25.8	29.6
1999	60 030	100.0	11.7	32.0	25.8	30.5
2000	60 510	100.0	11.1	31.8	26.1	30.9
2001	61 091	100.0	11.0	31.6	26.3	31.1
2002	62 794	100.0	11.8	30.6	25.9	31.7
2003	63 466	100.0	12.0	30.1	25.8	32.1
2004	63 699	100.0	11.5	30.5	25.8	32.2
2005	64 562	100.0	11.6	31.4	25.4	31.6
2006	65 708	100.0	11.8	30.7	25.7	31.8
2007	66 742	100.0	11.7	30.6	25.1	32.7
2008	66 957	100.0	11.0	30.3	25.8	33.0
2009	66 843	100.0	10.8	30.4	26.0	32.8
2010	67 261	100.0	10.6	31.2	25.3	32.9
2011	66 801	100.0	10.2	30.4	25.5	33.9
2012	66 539	100.0	10.1	29.7	25.9	34.3
2013	66 594	100.0	9.9	29.1	26.2	34.8
Women						
1990	44 699	100.0	11.3	42.4	21.9	24.5
1991	45 315	100.0	10.9	41.6	22.2	25.2
1992	46 469	100.0	10.2	37.9	26.9	25.0
1993	46 961	100.0	9.3	36.7	28.2	25.8
1994	48 235	100.0	9.1	35.3	29.8	25.8
1995	49 065	100.0	9.1	34.1	30.2	26.6
1996	49 916	100.0	8.8	33.7	29.7	27.8
1997	51 246	100.0	8.7	34.0	29.3	28.0
1998	51 953	100.0	8.8	33.3	29.3	28.6
1999	52 512	100.0	8.7	32.7	29.2	29.5
2000	53 541	100.0	8.4	31.8	30.0	29.8
2001	53 982	100.0	8.5	31.1	30.1	30.2
2002	54 944	100.0	8.2	30.6	29.7	31.5
2003	55 795	100.0	8.0	30.1	30.1	31.8
2004	55 693	100.0	7.7	29.6	30.2	32.5
2005	55 899	100.0	7.8	28.6	30.5	33.1
2006	56 833	100.0	7.6	28.2	30.6	33.6
2007	57 839	100.0	7.5	27.9	29.9	34.6
2008	58 536	100.0	6.7	27.0	30.4	35.9
2009	58 811	100.0	7.0	26.9	30.2	35.9
2010	59 102	100.0	6.8	26.8	30.1	36.3
2011	58 584	100.0	6.5	25.7	30.7	37.1
2012	59 187	100.0	6.8	25.1	30.2	37.9
2013	59 150	100.0	6.3	24.6	30.2	38.9

Table 1-56. Percent Distribution of the Civilian Labor Force Age 25 to 64 Years, by Educational Attainment, Sex, and Race, March 1990–March 2013—*Continued*

(Thousands of people, percent.)

Sex, race, and year	Civilian labor force	Percent distribution				
		Total	Less than a high school diploma	4 years of high school only	1 to 3 years of college	4 or more years of college
White[1]						
1990	85 238	100.0	12.6	39.6	20.6	27.1
1991	86 344	100.0	12.2	39.3	21.1	27.4
1992	87 656	100.0	11.3	36.1	25.5	27.1
1993	88 457	100.0	10.7	35.0	26.4	27.9
1994	89 009	100.0	10.5	33.7	27.7	28.1
1995	90 192	100.0	10.0	32.8	27.8	29.3
1996	91 506	100.0	10.4	32.8	27.5	29.3
1997	93 179	100.0	10.4	32.8	27.3	29.5
1998	93 527	100.0	10.2	32.7	27.4	29.8
1999	94 216	100.0	9.8	32.2	27.2	30.8
2000	95 073	100.0	9.5	31.8	27.7	31.0
2001	95 562	100.0	9.5	31.0	28.0	31.4
2002	97 699	100.0	9.8	30.6	27.6	32.0
2003	98 241	100.0	9.9	30.0	27.7	32.4
2004	98 030	100.0	9.5	29.8	27.8	32.9
2005	98 581	100.0	9.7	29.8	27.8	32.7
2006	100 205	100.0	9.7	29.3	28.1	32.9
2007	101 548	100.0	9.7	29.1	27.3	33.9
2008	102 077	100.0	8.9	28.7	27.8	34.6
2009	102 261	100.0	9.1	28.6	27.7	34.6
2010	102 634	100.0	8.8	29.0	27.4	34.8
2011	101 707	100.0	8.4	27.8	27.9	35.8
2012	100 382	100.0	8.6	27.4	27.7	36.4
2013	99 964	100.0	8.2	27.0	27.9	36.9
Black[1]						
1990	10 537	100.0	19.9	42.5	22.1	15.5
1991	10 650	100.0	19.5	42.9	22.1	15.4
1992	10 936	100.0	19.2	40.3	24.9	15.6
1993	11 051	100.0	16.8	39.5	27.6	16.1
1994	11 368	100.0	14.5	39.3	29.2	17.0
1995	11 695	100.0	14.1	38.6	29.6	17.7
1996	11 891	100.0	14.2	37.2	31.2	17.4
1997	12 253	100.0	14.3	37.8	31.3	16.6
1998	12 893	100.0	14.3	37.3	30.1	18.2
1999	12 945	100.0	13.0	37.2	30.4	19.5
2000	13 383	100.0	11.8	36.1	31.5	20.7
2001	13 617	100.0	12.0	37.1	31.1	19.8
2002	13 319	100.0	12.4	34.5	32.0	21.0
2003	13 315	100.0	11.3	35.6	31.5	21.6
2004	13 372	100.0	11.0	36.6	30.5	21.9
2005	13 635	100.0	11.2	37.3	29.9	21.6
2006	13 855	100.0	10.9	35.6	30.4	23.0
2007	14 186	100.0	10.1	35.4	31.4	23.1
2008	14 356	100.0	9.5	34.3	32.1	24.1
2009	14 325	100.0	8.5	35.1	33.0	23.5
2010	14 483	100.0	8.9	34.5	32.4	24.2
2011	14 377	100.0	8.5	33.8	33.1	24.6
2012	14 721	100.0	8.5	32.0	33.4	26.0
2013	14 869	100.0	8.5	31.4	33.4	26.7

[1]Beginning in 2003, persons who selected this race group only; persons who selected more than one race group are not included. Prior to 2003, persons who reported more than one race group were included in the group they identified as their main race.

Table 1-57. Labor Force Participation Rates of Persons Age 25 to 64 Years, by Educational Attainment, Sex, and Race, March 1990–March 2013

(Civilian labor force as a percent of the civilian noninstitutional population.)

Sex, race, and year	Participation rates				
	Total	Less than a high school diploma	4 years of high school only	1 to 3 years of college	4 or more years of college
Both Sexes					
1990	78.6	60.7	78.2	83.3	88.4
1991	78.6	60.7	78.1	83.2	88.4
1992	79.0	60.3	78.3	83.5	88.4
1993	78.9	59.6	77.7	82.9	88.3
1994	78.9	58.3	77.8	83.2	88.2
1995	79.3	59.8	77.3	83.2	88.7
1996	79.4	60.2	77.9	83.7	87.8
1997	80.1	61.7	78.5	83.7	88.5
1998	80.2	63.0	78.4	83.5	88.0
1999	80.0	62.7	78.1	83.0	87.6
2000	80.3	62.7	78.4	83.2	87.8
2001	80.2	63.5	78.4	83.0	87.0
2002	79.7	63.5	77.7	82.1	86.7
2003	79.4	64.1	76.9	81.9	86.2
2004	78.8	63.2	76.1	81.2	85.9
2005	78.5	62.9	75.7	81.1	85.7
2006	78.7	63.2	75.9	81.0	85.9
2007	79.0	63.7	76.3	81.1	85.9
2008	79.0	62.5	76.0	80.9	86.1
2009	78.6	62.3	75.7	80.3	85.9
2010	78.7	62.7	76.2	79.7	85.7
2011	77.6	61.0	74.3	78.6	85.3
2012	77.4	61.7	73.2	78.5	85.5
2013	77.2	60.9	73.0	78.1	85.1
Men					
1990	88.8	75.1	89.9	91.5	94.5
1991	88.6	75.1	89.3	92.0	94.2
1992	88.6	75.1	89.0	91.8	93.7
1993	88.1	74.9	88.1	90.6	93.7
1994	87.0	71.5	86.8	90.3	93.2
1995	87.4	72.0	86.9	90.1	93.8
1996	87.5	74.3	86.9	90.0	92.9
1997	87.7	75.2	86.4	90.6	93.5
1998	87.8	75.3	86.7	90.0	93.4
1999	87.5	74.4	86.6	89.4	93.0
2000	87.5	74.9	86.2	88.9	93.3
2001	87.4	75.4	85.8	89.1	92.9
2002	87.0	75.5	85.3	88.8	92.4
2003	86.4	76.1	84.3	87.5	92.2
2004	85.9	75.2	83.8	87.0	91.9
2005	86.0	75.7	83.7	87.5	91.7
2006	86.0	76.3	83.4	87.8	91.7
2007	86.2	75.7	83.9	87.2	92.4
2008	85.8	74.8	83.6	86.5	91.9
2009	85.1	73.7	82.3	86.0	91.9
2010	85.3	74.5	83.2	85.3	91.5
2011	84.0	73.3	81.8	83.2	91.1
2012	84.1	72.9	80.7	84.3	91.4
2013	84.0	72.7	80.5	83.8	91.4
Women					
1990	68.9	46.2	68.7	75.9	81.1
1991	69.1	46.2	68.6	75.2	81.8
1992	70.0	45.6	69.1	76.2	82.2
1993	70.0	44.2	68.8	76.1	82.2
1994	71.1	44.7	70.0	77.0	82.5
1995	71.5	47.2	68.9	77.3	82.8
1996	71.8	45.7	69.8	78.1	82.3
1997	72.8	47.1	71.4	77.6	83.2
1998	73.0	49.8	70.9	77.8	82.3
1999	72.8	50.5	70.4	77.4	81.9
2000	73.5	50.4	71.2	78.3	82.0
2001	73.4	51.7	71.3	77.7	80.9
2002	72.7	50.4	70.4	76.4	81.0
2003	72.6	50.5	69.8	77.1	80.1
2004	72.0	49.7	68.6	76.2	80.0
2005	71.4	48.7	67.4	75.8	79.8
2006	71.7	48.3	68.2	75.3	80.4
2007	72.1	49.6	68.4	76.0	79.7
2008	72.5	47.9	68.2	76.1	80.9
2009	72.4	49.0	68.7	75.4	80.5
2010	72.3	48.9	68.6	75.0	80.4
2011	71.3	46.8	66.1	74.7	80.0
2012	71.1	49.2	65.2	73.5	80.3
2013	70.8	47.3	65.1	73.3	79.6

Table 1-57. Labor Force Participation Rates of Persons Age 25 to 64 Years, by Educational Attainment, Sex, and Race, March 1990–March 2013—*Continued*

(Civilian labor force as a percent of the civilian noninstitutional population.)

Sex, race, and year	Participation rates				
	Total	Less than a high school diploma	4 years of high school only	1 to 3 years of college	4 or more years of college
White[1]					
1990	79.2	62.5	78.4	83.3	88.3
1991	79.4	62.5	78.3	83.1	88.6
1992	79.8	61.5	78.7	83.8	88.7
1993	79.7	61.1	78.2	83.1	88.8
1994	79.8	60.3	78.3	83.5	88.5
1995	80.1	61.6	77.9	83.4	88.8
1996	80.4	62.5	78.6	83.9	88.2
1997	81.0	63.8	79.2	83.9	89.0
1998	80.6	63.8	78.6	83.5	88.3
1999	80.6	64.2	78.5	83.3	87.9
2000	80.8	64.2	78.7	83.1	87.9
2001	80.7	64.5	78.7	83.1	87.2
2002	80.3	65.0	78.2	82.4	87.0
2003	80.1	65.7	77.5	82.3	86.5
2004	79.5	64.6	76.7	81.6	86.2
2005	79.2	63.8	76.4	81.5	86.1
2006	79.5	65.1	76.5	81.4	86.2
2007	79.6	65.1	77.2	81.4	86.1
2008	79.6	63.8	76.8	81.2	86.3
2009	79.4	64.7	76.4	80.7	86.2
2010	79.5	64.5	77.1	80.4	86.0
2011	78.5	62.9	75.3	79.3	85.5
2012	78.3	63.8	74.2	78.8	86.0
2013	78.0	63.0	73.9	78.5	85.6
Black[1]					
1990	74.6	54.5	78.2	84.2	92.0
1991	73.9	53.9	77.1	84.1	90.2
1992	74.4	55.4	76.9	83.4	89.1
1993	73.8	53.4	74.7	83.0	89.6
1994	73.5	49.4	75.2	82.4	89.5
1995	74.2	51.0	74.5	82.8	90.9
1996	73.7	50.1	74.3	83.0	87.9
1997	74.9	52.9	75.0	83.8	89.0
1998	77.7	59.3	77.0	85.0	88.8
1999	76.5	55.1	76.5	82.9	88.6
2000	77.9	55.5	77.0	84.2	90.3
2001	78.1	58.7	76.8	83.0	90.5
2002	76.4	56.6	75.0	81.7	88.9
2003	75.8	55.4	73.9	81.2	88.2
2004	75.0	55.2	73.4	79.0	87.9
2005	75.2	58.2	72.6	79.5	87.2
2006	75.0	54.0	73.3	79.6	87.7
2007	75.6	55.3	72.5	80.7	88.0
2008	75.6	54.3	72.8	80.0	87.5
2009	74.4	50.0	72.6	78.7	86.2
2010	74.2	52.2	71.7	77.5	87.0
2011	72.4	49.0	69.6	76.3	85.5
2012	72.9	50.8	68.6	77.2	85.7
2013	73.0	50.2	69.2	77.7	84.2

[1]Beginning in 2003, persons who selected this race group only; persons who selected more than one race group are not included. Prior to 2003, persons who reported more than one race group were included in the group they identified as their main race.

Table 1-58. Unemployment Rates of Persons Age 25 to 64 Years, by Educational Attainment and Sex, March 1990–March 2013

(Unemployment as a percent of the civilian labor force.)

Sex, race, and year	Unemployment rates				
	Total	Less than a high school diploma	4 years of high school only	1 to 3 years of college	4 or more years of college
Both Sexes					
1990	4.5	9.6	4.9	3.7	1.9
1991	6.1	12.3	6.7	5.0	2.9
1992	6.7	13.5	7.7	5.9	2.9
1993	6.4	13.0	7.3	5.5	3.2
1994	5.8	12.6	6.7	5.0	2.9
1995	4.8	10.0	5.2	4.5	2.5
1996	4.8	10.9	5.5	4.1	2.2
1997	4.4	10.4	5.1	3.8	2.0
1998	4.0	8.5	4.8	3.6	1.8
1999	3.5	7.7	4.0	3.1	1.9
2000	3.3	7.9	3.8	3.0	1.5
2001	3.5	8.1	4.2	2.9	2.0
2002	5.0	10.2	6.1	4.5	2.8
2003	5.3	9.9	6.4	5.2	3.0
2004	5.1	10.5	5.9	4.9	2.9
2005	4.4	9.0	5.5	4.1	2.3
2006	4.1	8.3	4.7	3.9	2.3
2007	3.9	8.5	4.7	3.7	1.8
2008	4.4	10.1	5.8	4.2	2.1
2009	8.1	15.8	10.4	8.0	4.3
2010	9.1	16.8	12.1	8.8	4.7
2011	8.3	16.2	10.9	8.1	4.4
2012	7.4	14.3	9.2	7.9	4.1
2013	6.6	12.7	8.7	6.5	3.8
Men					
1990	4.8	9.6	5.3	3.9	2.1
1991	6.8	13.4	7.7	5.2	3.2
1992	7.5	14.8	8.8	6.4	3.2
1993	7.3	14.1	8.7	6.3	3.4
1994	6.2	12.8	7.2	5.3	2.9
1995	5.1	10.9	5.7	4.4	2.6
1996	5.3	11.0	6.4	4.5	2.3
1997	4.7	9.9	5.6	4.0	2.1
1998	4.1	8.0	5.1	3.7	1.7
1999	3.5	7.0	4.1	3.2	1.9
2000	3.3	7.1	3.9	3.1	1.6
2001	3.7	7.5	4.6	3.2	1.9
2002	5.5	9.9	6.7	4.9	3.0
2003	5.8	9.5	6.9	6.0	3.2
2004	5.4	9.4	6.6	5.4	3.0
2005	4.7	7.9	6.0	4.3	2.5
2006	4.3	7.6	5.0	4.2	2.4
2007	4.3	8.4	5.5	3.9	1.9
2008	4.9	10.9	6.3	4.2	2.0
2009	9.5	16.5	12.4	9.3	4.7
2010	10.5	17.8	13.8	10.2	5.1
2011	9.2	16.7	12.2	8.7	4.6
2012	8.0	13.6	10.1	8.2	4.3
2013	6.9	11.9	9.2	6.5	3.7
Women					
1990	4.2	9.5	4.6	3.5	1.7
1991	5.2	10.7	5.5	4.8	2.5
1992	5.7	11.4	6.5	5.3	2.5
1993	5.2	11.2	5.8	4.6	2.9
1994	5.4	12.4	6.2	4.7	2.9
1995	4.4	8.6	4.6	4.5	2.4
1996	4.1	10.7	4.4	3.8	2.1
1997	4.1	11.3	4.5	3.6	2.0
1998	3.9	9.3	4.4	3.5	1.9
1999	3.5	8.8	3.9	3.0	1.9
2000	3.2	9.1	3.6	2.9	1.4
2001	3.3	8.9	3.8	2.6	2.0
2002	4.6	10.6	5.4	4.1	2.6
2003	4.8	10.6	5.9	4.4	2.8
2004	4.7	12.2	5.2	4.3	2.9
2005	4.2	10.9	4.8	4.0	2.2
2006	3.8	9.4	4.4	3.7	2.1
2007	3.4	8.5	3.8	3.6	1.8
2008	4.0	8.5	5.1	4.2	2.1
2009	6.6	14.5	7.9	6.7	4.0
2010	7.5	15.0	9.8	7.5	4.3
2011	7.2	15.2	9.1	7.5	4.3
2012	6.8	15.4	8.1	7.7	3.8
2013	6.3	14.1	8.1	6.4	3.8

Table 1-58. Unemployment Rates of Persons Age 25 to 64 Years, by Educational Attainment and Sex, March 1990–March 2013—*Continued*

(Unemployment as a percent of the civilian labor force.)

Sex, race, and year	Unemployment rates				
	Total	Less than a high school diploma	4 years of high school only	1 to 3 years of college	4 or more years of college
White[1]					
1990	4.0	8.3	4.4	3.3	1.8
1991	5.6	11.6	6.2	4.6	2.7
1992	6.0	12.9	6.8	5.3	2.7
1993	5.8	12.4	6.5	5.0	3.1
1994	5.2	11.7	5.8	4.5	2.6
1995	4.3	9.2	4.6	4.2	2.3
1996	4.2	10.2	4.6	3.7	2.1
1997	3.9	9.4	4.6	3.4	1.8
1998	3.5	7.5	4.2	3.2	1.7
1999	3.1	7.0	3.4	2.8	1.7
2000	3.0	7.5	3.3	2.7	1.4
2001	3.1	7.2	3.6	2.7	1.8
2002	4.6	9.1	5.5	4.1	2.6
2003	4.7	9.0	5.7	4.5	2.7
2004	4.6	9.6	5.4	4.4	2.8
2005	3.9	7.7	4.9	3.6	2.2
2006	3.5	7.1	4.0	3.5	2.1
2007	3.5	7.8	4.2	3.3	1.7
2008	4.0	9.2	5.1	3.7	1.9
2009	7.6	15.2	9.9	7.4	4.0
2010	8.4	16.3	11.3	8.1	4.3
2011	7.5	15.1	9.9	7.2	4.0
2012	6.7	13.5	8.3	6.9	3.7
2013	5.9	11.2	7.7	5.7	3.5
Black[1]					
1990	8.6	15.9	8.6	6.5	1.9
1991	10.1	15.9	10.3	8.0	5.2
1992	12.4	17.2	14.1	10.7	4.8
1993	10.9	17.3	12.4	8.7	4.1
1994	10.6	17.4	12.2	8.3	4.9
1995	7.7	13.7	8.4	6.3	4.1
1996	8.9	15.3	10.8	6.9	3.3
1997	8.1	16.6	8.2	6.1	4.4
1998	7.3	13.4	8.4	6.4	2.1
1999	6.3	12.0	6.7	5.2	3.3
2000	5.4	10.4	6.3	4.3	2.5
2001	6.5	14.0	7.7	4.3	3.3
2002	8.1	15.4	9.7	6.0	4.1
2003	9.0	14.7	9.9	8.9	4.7
2004	8.4	15.8	9.3	7.9	3.7
2005	8.3	17.9	8.6	7.5	3.6
2006	7.8	16.4	9.0	6.5	3.6
2007	6.5	14.0	7.7	5.7	2.5
2008	7.6	16.7	9.3	6.5	3.3
2009	12.1	22.0	14.0	11.2	7.2
2010	14.1	22.4	17.5	12.9	7.9
2011	13.9	25.0	16.6	12.7	7.7
2012	12.3	21.4	14.2	12.7	6.3
2013	11.4	22.8	14.2	10.0	6.1

[1]Beginning in 2003, persons who selected this race group only; persons who selected more than one race group are not included. Prior to 2003, persons who reported more than one race group were included in the group they identified as their main race.

Table 1-59. Workers Age 25 to 64 Years, by Educational Attainment, Occupation of Longest Job Held, and Sex, 2011–2012

(Thousands of people with work experience during the year.)

Year, sex, and occupation	Total	Less than a high school diploma	4 years of high school only	1 to 3 years of college	4 or more years of college
2011					
Both Sexes	125 188	10 391	34 165	35 113	45 520
Management, business, and financial operations	20 501	383	3 206	4 821	12 091
Management	14 294	342	2 531	3 513	7 909
Business and financial operations	6 207	41	675	1 308	4 182
Professional and related	28 610	164	2 078	6 071	20 297
Computer and mathematical	3 494	17	251	780	2 446
Architecture and engineering	2 648	. . .	227	602	1 819
Life, physical, and social sciences	1 164	1	53	114	995
Community and social services	2 174	30	192	380	1 572
Legal	1 494	6	78	231	1 178
Education, training, and library	7 858	24	532	1 028	6 274
Arts, design, entertainment, sports, and media	2 422	42	287	558	1 535
Health care practitioner and technical	7 357	44	458	2 377	4 478
Services	20 364	3 443	7 596	6 377	2 948
Health care support	3 059	251	1 034	1 414	361
Protective services	2 859	73	766	1 197	822
Food preparation and serving related	5 386	1 126	2 170	1 438	651
Building and grounds cleaning and maintenance	4 964	1 562	2 118	936	348
Personal care and services	4 096	431	1 507	1 391	767
Sales and office	27 659	1 245	8 576	10 276	7 563
Sales and related	11 914	690	3 500	3 744	3 980
Office and administrative support	15 745	555	5 076	6 531	3 584
Natural resources, construction, and maintenance	12 067	2 402	5 327	3 349	989
Farming, fishing, and forestry	883	435	293	96	59
Construction and extraction	6 959	1 542	3 222	1 674	522
Installation, maintenance, and repair	4 224	425	1 812	1 579	408
Production, transportation, and material moving	15 331	2 753	7 250	3 925	1 403
Production	7 816	1 393	3 716	1 965	741
Transportation and material moving	7 516	1 359	3 534	1 960	662
Armed forces	656	2	133	294	228
Men	65 963	6 473	19 405	17 214	22 870
Management, business, and financial operations	11 405	255	1 764	2 537	6 849
Management	8 684	231	1 549	2 103	4 801
Business and financial operations	2 722	25	215	434	2 048
Professional and related	11 812	60	731	2 127	8 894
Computer and mathematical	2 562	10	160	573	1 818
Architecture and engineering	2 289	. . .	190	550	1 549
Life, physical, and social sciences	648	1	42	79	526
Community and social services	750	14	55	113	569
Legal	723	. . .	7	19	696
Education, training, and library	1 930	2	50	158	1 720
Arts, design, entertainment, sports, and media	1 254	23	155	301	775
Health care practitioner and technical	1 655	9	71	334	1 241
Services	8 756	1 496	3 223	2 625	1 412
Health care support	321	15	101	144	62
Protective services	2 279	40	602	994	644
Food preparation and serving related	2 470	598	963	617	292
Building and grounds cleaning and maintenance	2 870	795	1 262	601	211
Personal care and services	816	48	296	269	203
Sales and office	10 220	433	2 855	3 362	3 570
Sales and related	6 326	222	1 669	1 934	2 501
Office and administrative support	3 895	211	1 186	1 428	1 069
Natural resources, construction, and maintenance	11 541	2 252	5 159	3 235	895
Farming, fishing, and forestry	679	321	243	71	44
Construction and extraction	6 803	1 517	3 166	1 642	478
Installation, maintenance, and repair	4 059	414	1 750	1 522	373
Production, transportation, and material moving	11 642	1 974	5 543	3 065	1 060
Production	5 439	843	2 622	1 474	501
Transportation and material moving	6 204	1 131	2 922	1 591	560
Armed forces	586	2	131	262	191
Women	59 226	3 917	14 760	17 899	22 650
Management, business, and financial operations	9 096	128	1 442	2 283	5 243
Management	5 610	111	982	1 410	3 108
Business and financial operations	3 486	17	460	874	2 135
Professional and related	16 798	103	1 347	3 944	11 403
Computer and mathematical	933	7	91	207	628
Architecture and engineering	359	. . .	36	52	270
Life, physical, and social sciences	516	. . .	11	36	469
Community and social services	1 424	15	137	268	1 003
Legal	771	6	71	212	482
Education, training, and library	5 927	21	482	870	4 554
Arts, design, entertainment, sports, and media	1 168	19	132	256	760
Health care practitioner and technical	5 701	34	387	2 043	3 237
Services	11 608	1 946	4 373	3 752	1 536
Health care support	2 738	235	933	1 271	299
Protective services	580	33	165	203	179
Food preparation and serving related	2 916	528	1 208	821	359
Building and grounds cleaning and maintenance	2 094	767	856	334	136
Personal care and services	3 280	383	1 211	1 122	564
Sales and office	17 439	811	5 721	6 914	3 993
Sales and related	5 588	468	1 831	1 810	1 479
Office and administrative support	11 851	343	3 889	5 104	2 514
Natural resources, construction, and maintenance	526	150	168	114	95
Farming, fishing, and forestry	204	114	50	25	15
Construction and extraction	157	26	56	31	44
Installation, maintenance, and repair	165	10	62	57	35
Production, transportation, and material moving	3 689	779	1 707	861	343
Production	2 377	551	1 094	492	240
Transportation and material moving	1 312	228	613	369	103
Armed forces	71	. . .	2	32	37

. . . = Not available.

Table 1-59. Workers Age 25 to 64 Years, by Educational Attainment, Occupation of Longest Job Held, and Sex, 2011–2012—*Continued*

(Thousands of people with work experience during the year.)

Year, sex, and occupation	Total	Less than a high school diploma	4 years of high school only	1 to 3 years of college	4 or more years of college
2012					
Both Sexes	126 567	10 030	33 757	36 028	46 752
Management, business, and financial operations	20 959	364	3 225	5 051	12 319
Management	14 792	323	2 570	3 760	8 139
Business and financial operations	6 167	41	656	1 291	4 180
Professional and related	29 157	168	1 951	6 320	20 718
Computer and mathematical	3 860	16	252	897	2 696
Architecture and engineering	2 460	6	214	545	1 695
Life, physical, and social sciences	1 206	5	64	123	1 015
Community and social services	2 181	21	163	422	1 576
Legal	1 594	6	77	247	1 265
Education, training, and library	8 025	45	513	1 043	6 424
Arts, design, entertainment, sports, and media	2 425	26	250	571	1 578
Health care practitioner and technical	7 404	44	419	2 471	4 471
Services	20 671	3 365	7 580	6 619	3 106
Health care support	2 928	216	982	1 356	373
Protective services	2 795	78	736	1 126	855
Food preparation and serving related	5 340	1 083	2 173	1 472	612
Building and grounds cleaning and maintenance	5 102	1 523	2 147	1 047	385
Personal care and services	4 506	465	1 542	1 618	881
Sales and office	27 726	1 196	8 552	10 048	7 931
Sales and related	11 820	606	3 410	3 679	4 125
Office and administrative support	15 907	590	5 141	6 369	3 806
Natural resources, construction, and maintenance	12 278	2 337	5 292	3 572	1 077
Farming, fishing, and forestry	771	363	242	100	65
Construction and extraction	6 991	1 596	3 147	1 718	530
Installation, maintenance, and repair	4 516	378	1 902	1 754	482
Production, transportation, and material moving	15 141	2 598	7 030	4 129	1 384
Production	7 581	1 314	3 450	2 112	704
Transportation and material moving	7 560	1 284	3 580	2 017	679
Armed forces	636	2	127	289	218
Men	66 889	6 378	19 222	17 918	23 371
Management, business, and financial operations	11 564	236	1 839	2 646	6 843
Management	8 998	216	1 625	2 224	4 934
Business and financial operations	2 566	21	214	422	1 909
Professional and related	12 214	51	742	2 321	9 100
Computer and mathematical	2 792	12	152	683	1 946
Architecture and engineering	2 086	6	185	487	1 408
Life, physical, and social sciences	670	2	46	83	539
Community and social services	748	11	64	139	533
Legal	771	. . .	10	30	731
Education, training, and library	1 964	3	41	144	1 776
Arts, design, entertainment, sports, and media	1 257	10	152	315	781
Health care practitioner and technical	1 928	7	93	440	1 387
Services	8 969	1 577	3 095	2 712	1 584
Health care support	329	15	88	156	69
Protective services	2 221	57	581	910	674
Food preparation and serving related	2 500	602	902	659	337
Building and grounds cleaning and maintenance	2 997	804	1 248	698	248
Personal care and services	921	99	276	289	256
Sales and office	10 209	435	2 750	3 338	3 686
Sales and related	6 285	217	1 636	1 849	2 584
Office and administrative support	3 924	219	1 114	1 489	1 102
Natural resources, construction, and maintenance	11 721	2 202	5 138	3 409	971
Farming, fishing, and forestry	570	259	197	63	52
Construction and extraction	6 841	1 577	3 092	1 669	502
Installation, maintenance, and repair	4 309	367	1 849	1 676	417
Production, transportation, and material moving	11 647	1 873	5 532	3 236	1 006
Production	5 423	842	2 509	1 598	473
Transportation and material moving	6 225	1 031	3 023	1 637	533
Armed forces	565	2	126	256	181
Women	59 679	3 652	14 534	18 111	23 381
Management, business, and financial operations	9 395	128	1 387	2 405	5 476
Management	5 793	107	945	1 537	3 205
Business and financial operations	3 601	20	442	868	2 271
Professional and related	16 942	117	1 209	3 999	11 618
Computer and mathematical	1 069	4	100	215	750
Architecture and engineering	374	. . .	29	58	287
Life, physical, and social sciences	537	3	18	40	476
Community and social services	1 434	10	98	283	1 043
Legal	822	6	67	216	533
Education, training, and library	6 062	42	472	899	4 648
Arts, design, entertainment, sports, and media	1 168	16	98	256	797
Health care practitioner and technical	5 477	37	325	2 031	3 084
Services	11 702	1 788	4 485	3 907	1 522
Health care support	2 598	201	894	1 200	304
Protective services	574	21	155	216	182
Food preparation and serving related	2 840	480	1 271	814	275
Building and grounds cleaning and maintenance	2 105	719	899	349	137
Personal care and services	3 585	365	1 266	1 379	675
Sales and office	17 517	761	5 802	6 710	4 245
Sales and related	5 535	389	1 775	1 830	1 541
Office and administrative support	11 983	372	4 027	4 880	2 704
Natural resources, construction, and maintenance	558	135	153	163	106
Farming, fishing, and forestry	200	104	46	37	13
Construction and extraction	150	20	54	49	27
Installation, maintenance, and repair	207	11	53	77	65
Production, transportation, and material moving	3 494	725	1 498	893	377
Production	2 158	472	941	514	232
Transportation and material moving	1 335	253	557	379	146
Armed forces	71	. . .	1	34	37

. . . = Not available.

**Table 1-60. Percent Distribution of Workers Age 25 to 64 Years,
by Educational Attainment, Occupation of Longest Job Held, and Sex, 2011–2012**

(Percent of total workers in occupation.)

Year, sex, and occupation	Total	Less than a high school diploma	4 years of high school only	1 to 3 years of college	4 or more years of college
2011					
Both Sexes	100.0	8.3	27.3	28.0	36.4
Management, business, and financial operations	100.0	1.9	15.6	23.5	59.0
Management	100.0	2.4	17.7	24.6	55.3
Business and financial operations	100.0	0.7	10.9	21.1	67.4
Professional and related	100.0	0.6	7.3	21.2	70.9
Computer and mathematical	100.0	0.5	7.2	22.3	70.0
Architecture and engineering	100.0	. . .	8.6	22.7	68.7
Life, physical, and social sciences	100.0	0.1	4.6	9.8	85.5
Community and social services	100.0	1.4	8.8	17.5	72.3
Legal	100.0	0.4	5.2	15.5	78.9
Education, training, and library	100.0	0.3	6.8	13.1	79.8
Arts, design, entertainment, sports, and media	100.0	1.7	11.9	23.0	63.4
Health care practitioner and technical	100.0	0.6	6.2	32.3	60.9
Services	100.0	16.9	37.3	31.3	14.5
Health care support	100.0	8.2	33.8	46.2	11.8
Protective services	100.0	2.6	26.8	41.9	28.8
Food preparation and serving related	100.0	20.9	40.3	26.7	12.1
Building and grounds cleaning and maintenance	100.0	31.5	42.7	18.9	7.0
Personal care and services	100.0	10.5	36.8	34.0	18.7
Sales and office	100.0	4.5	31.0	37.2	27.3
Sales and related	100.0	5.8	29.4	31.4	33.4
Office and administrative support	100.0	3.5	32.2	41.5	22.8
Natural resources, construction, and maintenance	100.0	19.9	44.1	27.8	8.2
Farming, fishing, and forestry	100.0	49.2	33.2	10.9	6.7
Construction and extraction	100.0	22.2	46.3	24.0	7.5
Installation, maintenance, and repair	100.0	10.1	42.9	37.4	9.7
Production, transportation, and material moving	100.0	18.0	47.3	25.6	9.2
Production	100.0	17.8	47.5	25.1	9.5
Transportation and material moving	100.0	18.1	47.0	26.1	8.8
Armed forces	100.0	0.3	20.2	44.8	34.7
Men	100.0	9.8	29.4	26.1	34.7
Management, business, and financial operations	100.0	2.2	15.5	22.2	60.0
Management	100.0	2.7	17.8	24.2	55.3
Business and financial operations	100.0	0.9	7.9	16.0	75.2
Professional and related	100.0	0.5	6.2	18.0	75.3
Computer and mathematical	100.0	0.4	6.2	22.4	71.0
Architecture and engineering	100.0	. . .	8.3	24.0	67.7
Life, physical, and social sciences	100.0	0.2	6.5	12.1	81.1
Community and social services	100.0	1.9	7.3	15.0	75.8
Legal	100.0	. . .	1.0	2.7	96.3
Education, training, and library	100.0	0.1	2.6	8.2	89.1
Arts, design, entertainment, sports, and media	100.0	1.8	12.3	24.0	61.8
Health care practitioner and technical	100.0	0.6	4.3	20.2	75.0
Services	100.0	17.1	36.8	30.0	16.1
Health care support	100.0	4.8	31.3	44.7	19.2
Protective services	100.0	1.8	26.4	43.6	28.2
Food preparation and serving related	100.0	24.2	39.0	25.0	11.8
Building and grounds cleaning and maintenance	100.0	27.7	44.0	21.0	7.4
Personal care and services	100.0	5.9	36.2	33.0	24.9
Sales and office	100.0	4.2	27.9	32.9	34.9
Sales and related	100.0	3.5	26.4	30.6	39.5
Office and administrative support	100.0	5.4	30.5	36.7	27.5
Natural resources, construction, and maintenance	100.0	19.5	44.7	28.0	7.8
Farming, fishing, and forestry	100.0	47.3	35.8	10.5	6.5
Construction and extraction	100.0	22.3	46.5	24.1	7.0
Installation, maintenance, and repair	100.0	10.2	43.1	37.5	9.2
Production, transportation, and material moving	100.0	17.0	47.6	26.3	9.1
Production	100.0	15.5	48.2	27.1	9.2
Transportation and material moving	100.0	18.2	47.1	25.6	9.0
Armed forces	100.0	0.4	22.4	44.7	32.6
Women	100.0	6.6	24.9	30.2	38.2
Management, business, and financial operations	100.0	1.4	15.9	25.1	57.6
Management	100.0	2.0	17.5	25.1	55.4
Business and financial operations	100.0	0.5	13.2	25.1	61.2
Professional and related	100.0	0.6	8.0	23.5	67.9
Computer and mathematical	100.0	0.8	9.7	22.2	67.4
Architecture and engineering	100.0	. . .	10.2	14.6	75.3
Life, physical, and social sciences	100.0	. . .	2.1	7.0	90.9
Community and social services	100.0	1.1	9.7	18.8	70.5
Legal	100.0	0.8	9.2	27.5	62.5
Education, training, and library	100.0	0.4	8.1	14.7	76.8
Arts, design, entertainment, sports, and media	100.0	1.6	11.3	21.9	65.1
Health care practitioner and technical	100.0	0.6	6.8	35.8	56.8
Services	100.0	16.8	37.7	32.3	13.2
Health care support	100.0	8.6	34.1	46.4	10.9
Protective services	100.0	5.7	28.4	35.1	30.8
Food preparation and serving related	100.0	18.1	41.4	28.2	12.3
Building and grounds cleaning and maintenance	100.0	36.6	40.9	16.0	6.5
Personal care and services	100.0	11.7	36.9	34.2	17.2
Sales and office	100.0	4.7	32.8	39.6	22.9
Sales and related	100.0	8.4	32.8	32.4	26.5
Office and administrative support	100.0	2.9	32.8	43.1	21.2
Natural resources, construction, and maintenance	100.0	28.5	32.0	21.6	18.0
Farming, fishing, and forestry	100.0	55.8	24.4	12.3	7.6
Construction and extraction	100.0	16.4	35.8	19.9	27.9
Installation, maintenance, and repair	100.0	6.2	37.6	34.7	21.4
Production, transportation, and material moving	100.0	21.1	46.3	23.3	9.3
Production	100.0	23.2	46.0	20.7	10.1
Transportation and material moving	100.0	17.4	46.7	28.1	7.8
Armed forces	100.0	. . .	2.4	45.4	52.2

. . . = Not available.

Table 1-60. Percent Distribution of Workers Age 25 to 64 Years, by Educational Attainment, Occupation of Longest Job Held, and Sex, 2011–2012—*Continued*

(Percent of total workers in occupation.)

Year, sex, and occupation	Total	Less than a high school diploma	4 years of high school only	1 to 3 years of college	4 or more years of college
2012					
Both Sexes	100.0	7.9	26.7	28.5	36.9
Management, business, and financial operations	100.0	1.7	15.4	24.1	58.8
Management	100.0	2.2	17.4	25.4	55.0
Business and financial operations	100.0	0.7	10.6	20.9	67.8
Professional and related	100.0	0.6	6.7	21.7	71.1
Computer and mathematical	100.0	0.4	6.5	23.2	69.8
Architecture and engineering	100.0	0.2	8.7	22.2	68.9
Life, physical, and social sciences	100.0	0.4	5.3	10.2	84.1
Community and social services	100.0	1.0	7.5	19.4	72.2
Legal	100.0	0.3	4.8	15.5	79.4
Education, training, and library	100.0	0.6	6.4	13.0	80.0
Arts, design, entertainment, sports, and media	100.0	1.1	10.3	23.6	65.1
Health care practitioner and technical	100.0	0.6	5.7	33.4	60.4
Services	100.0	16.3	36.7	32.0	15.0
Health care support	100.0	7.4	33.5	46.3	12.7
Protective services	100.0	2.8	26.3	40.3	30.6
Food preparation and serving related	100.0	20.3	40.7	27.6	11.5
Building and grounds cleaning and maintenance	100.0	29.9	42.1	20.5	7.5
Personal care and services	100.0	10.3	34.2	35.9	19.6
Sales and office	100.0	4.3	30.8	36.2	28.6
Sales and related	100.0	5.1	28.9	31.1	34.9
Office and administrative support	100.0	3.7	32.3	40.0	23.9
Natural resources, construction, and maintenance	100.0	19.0	43.1	29.1	8.8
Farming, fishing, and forestry	100.0	47.1	31.4	13.0	8.4
Construction and extraction	100.0	22.8	45.0	24.6	7.6
Installation, maintenance, and repair	100.0	8.4	42.1	38.8	10.7
Production, transportation, and material moving	100.0	17.2	46.4	27.3	9.1
Production	100.0	17.3	45.5	27.9	9.3
Transportation and material moving	100.0	17.0	47.4	26.7	9.0
Armed forces	100.0	0.2	20.0	45.5	34.2
Men	100.0	9.5	28.7	26.8	34.9
Management, business, and financial operations	100.0	2.0	15.9	22.9	59.2
Management	100.0	2.4	18.1	24.7	54.8
Business and financial operations	100.0	0.8	8.3	16.5	74.4
Professional and related	100.0	0.4	6.1	19.0	74.5
Computer and mathematical	100.0	0.4	5.4	24.4	69.7
Architecture and engineering	100.0	0.3	8.9	23.3	67.5
Life, physical, and social sciences	100.0	0.3	6.8	12.4	80.5
Community and social services	100.0	1.5	8.6	18.6	71.2
Legal	100.0	. . .	1.2	4.0	94.8
Education, training, and library	100.0	0.2	2.1	7.3	90.4
Arts, design, entertainment, sports, and media	100.0	0.8	12.1	25.1	62.1
Health care practitioner and technical	100.0	0.4	4.8	22.8	71.9
Services	100.0	17.6	34.5	30.2	17.7
Health care support	100.0	4.6	26.8	47.5	21.1
Protective services	100.0	2.6	26.1	41.0	30.3
Food preparation and serving related	100.0	24.1	36.1	26.3	13.5
Building and grounds cleaning and maintenance	100.0	26.8	41.6	23.3	8.3
Personal care and services	100.0	10.8	30.0	31.4	27.8
Sales and office	100.0	4.3	26.9	32.7	36.1
Sales and related	100.0	3.4	26.0	29.4	41.1
Office and administrative support	100.0	5.6	28.4	37.9	28.1
Natural resources, construction, and maintenance	100.0	18.8	43.8	29.1	8.3
Farming, fishing, and forestry	100.0	45.5	34.5	11.0	9.1
Construction and extraction	100.0	23.0	45.2	24.4	7.3
Installation, maintenance, and repair	100.0	8.5	42.9	38.9	9.7
Production, transportation, and material moving	100.0	16.1	47.5	27.8	8.6
Production	100.0	15.5	46.3	29.5	8.7
Transportation and material moving	100.0	16.6	48.6	26.3	8.6
Armed forces	100.0	0.3	22.4	45.3	32.0
Women	100.0	6.1	24.4	30.3	39.2
Management, business, and financial operations	100.0	1.4	14.8	25.6	58.3
Management	100.0	1.9	16.3	26.5	55.3
Business and financial operations	100.0	0.6	12.3	24.1	63.1
Professional and related	100.0	0.7	7.1	23.6	68.6
Computer and mathematical	100.0	0.4	9.4	20.1	70.2
Architecture and engineering	100.0	. . .	7.8	15.6	76.6
Life, physical, and social sciences	100.0	0.5	3.4	7.5	88.6
Community and social services	100.0	0.7	6.9	19.7	72.7
Legal	100.0	0.7	8.2	26.3	64.9
Education, training, and library	100.0	0.7	7.8	14.8	76.7
Arts, design, entertainment, sports, and media	100.0	1.4	8.4	21.9	68.3
Health care practitioner and technical	100.0	0.7	5.9	37.1	56.3
Services	100.0	15.3	38.3	33.4	13.0
Health care support	100.0	7.7	34.4	46.2	11.7
Protective services	100.0	3.7	27.0	37.7	31.6
Food preparation and serving related	100.0	16.9	44.8	28.6	9.7
Building and grounds cleaning and maintenance	100.0	34.2	42.7	16.6	6.5
Personal care and services	100.0	10.2	35.3	37.1	17.4
Sales and office	100.0	4.3	33.1	38.3	24.2
Sales and related	100.0	7.0	32.1	33.1	27.8
Office and administrative support	100.0	3.1	33.6	40.7	22.6
Natural resources, construction, and maintenance	100.0	24.2	27.5	29.3	19.0
Farming, fishing, and forestry	100.0	51.8	22.8	18.7	6.7
Construction and extraction	100.0	13.2	36.2	32.3	18.3
Installation, maintenance, and repair	100.0	5.5	25.8	37.3	31.5
Production, transportation, and material moving	100.0	20.7	42.9	25.6	10.8
Production	100.0	21.9	43.6	23.8	10.7
Transportation and material moving	100.0	18.9	41.7	28.4	10.9
Armed forces	100.0	. . .	1.0	47.4	51.6

. . . = Not available.

Table 1-61. Median Annual Earnings of Year-Round, Full-Time Wage and Salary Workers Age 25 to 64 Years, by Educational Attainment and Sex, 2001–2012

(Thousands of workers, dollars.)

Year and sex	Total	Less than a high school diploma	4 years of high school only	1 to 3 years of college	4 or more years of college
2001					
Both Sexes					
Number of workers	84 743	7 623	25 522	23 719	27 879
Median annual earnings	35 000	20 800	29 000	35 000	50 000
Men					
Number of workers	48 887	5 049	14 655	12 968	16 215
Median annual earnings	40 000	24 000	33 800	40 000	60 000
Women					
Number of workers	35 856	2 574	10 867	10 751	11 664
Median annual earnings	30 000	17 000	24 000	30 000	42 000
2002					
Both Sexes					
Number of workers	84 702	7 578	25 078	23 604	28 443
Median annual earnings	36 000	21 000	30 000	35 100	52 000
Men					
Number of workers	48 687	5 102	14 306	12 677	16 602
Median annual earnings	41 000	23 400	34 000	41 500	61 000
Women					
Number of workers	36 015	2 476	10 772	10 927	11 841
Median annual earnings	30 000	18 000	25 000	30 000	43 500
2003					
Both Sexes					
Number of workers	85 058	7 245	25 352	23 702	28 759
Median annual earnings	37 752	21 000	30 000	36 000	53 000
Men					
Number of workers	48 988	4 879	14 657	12 766	16 686
Median annual earnings	42 000	24 000	35 000	42 000	62 000
Women					
Number of workers	36 070	2 366	10 695	10 936	12 073
Median annual earnings	32 000	18 000	25 111	31 000	45 000
2004					
Both Sexes					
Number of workers	86 306	7 648	25 786	23 897	28 976
Median annual earnings	38 000	21 840	30 000	37 000	55 000
Men					
Number of workers	49 904	5 178	15 263	12 822	16 642
Median annual earnings	42 900	24 000	35 000	43 000	65 000
Women					
Number of workers	36 402	2 470	10 523	11 074	12 334
Median annual earnings	32 000	18 000	25 280	31 200	45 000
2005					
Both Sexes					
Number of workers	88 415	7 758	26 023	24 623	30 012
Median annual earnings	39 768	22 880	31 000	38 000	55 000
Men					
Number of workers	51 022	5 376	15 451	13 199	16 996
Median annual earnings	44 000	25 000	35 360	45 000	65 000
Women					
Number of workers	37 393	2 381	10 571	11 424	13 016
Median annual earnings	33 644	18 200	26 000	32 000	46 700
2006					
Both Sexes					
Number of workers	90 733	7 951	26 233	24 737	31 812
Median annual earnings	40 000	23 000	32 000	39 482	57 588
Men					
Number of workers	52 252	5 485	15 525	13 204	18 038
Median annual earnings	45 000	25 000	36 665	45 000	68 000
Women					
Number of workers	38 481	2 466	10 708	11 533	13 774
Median annual earnings	35 000	19 000	26 800	33 000	49 000

Table 1-61. Median Annual Earnings of Year-Round, Full-Time Wage and Salary Workers Age 25 to 64 Years, by Educational Attainment and Sex, 2001–2012—*Continued*

(Thousands of workers, dollars.)

Year and sex	Total	Less than a high school diploma	4 years of high school only	1 to 3 years of college	4 or more years of college
2007					
Both Sexes					
Number of workers	91 540	7 123	25 925	25 574	32 918
Median annual earnings	41 000	24 000	33 000	40 000	60 000
Men					
Number of workers	52 262	4 902	15 390	13 655	18 316
Median annual earnings	47 000	25 000	38 000	45 188	70 000
Women					
Number of workers	39 277	2 221	10 535	11 919	14 603
Median annual earnings	35 000	19 200	27 120	35 000	50 000
2008					
Both Sexes					
Number of workers	88 373	6 600	24 531	24 887	32 355
Median annual earnings	42 000	24 000	34 000	40 000	60 000
Men					
Number of workers	50 141	4 503	14 480	13 283	17 876
Median annual earnings	49 564	27 000	39 040	47 000	72 000
Women					
Number of workers	38 231	2 097	10 051	11 604	14 479
Median annual earnings	36 000	19 567	28 000	35 000	50 000
2009					
Both Sexes					
Number of workers	84 730	5 847	23 277	23 515	32 091
Median annual earnings	43 000	24 000	34 320	40 000	60 000
Men					
Number of workers	47 135	3 809	13 620	12 283	17 424
Median annual earnings	50 000	26 000	40 000	49 000	71 000
Women					
Number of workers	37 595	2 037	9 657	11 233	14 667
Median annual earnings	38 000	20 000	29 000	35 000	52 000
2010					
Both Sexes					
Number of workers	84 902	5 548	22 768	23 725	32 861
Median annual earnings	44 217	24 000	35 000	40 000	60 000
Men					
Number of workers	47 549	3 653	13 526	12 405	17 965
Median annual earnings	50 000	26 500	40 000	48 000	72 000
Women					
Number of workers	37 353	1 895	9 241	11 321	14 896
Median annual earnings	38 000	20 000	30 000	35 000	51 000
2011					
Both Sexes					
Number of workers	86 570	5 858	22 921	23 947	33 843
Median annual earnings	45 000	25 000	35 000	41 000	62 000
Men					
Number of workers	48 748	3 971	13 750	12 705	18 322
Median annual earnings	50 000	27 819	40 000	50 000	75 000
Women					
Number of workers	37 822	1 887	9 171	11 243	15 521
Median annual earnings	39 000	20 000	30 000	35 000	52 000
2012					
Both Sexes					
Number of workers	87 660	5 671	22 628	24 217	35 144
Median annual earnings	45 000	24 750	35 000	41 500	63 000
Men					
Number of workers	49 481	3 874	13 629	13 051	18 927
Median annual earnings	50 000	26 000	40 000	49 000	75 000
Women					
Number of workers	38 179	1 797	8 999	11 165	16 217
Median annual earnings	40 000	20 000	30 000	35 395	54 000

Table 1-62. Employment Status of the Civilian Noninstitutional Population by Disability Status and Selected Characteristics, 2012 Annual Averages

(Thousands of people, percent.)

Characteristic	Civilian noninstitutional population	Civilian labor force							Not in labor force
		Total	Participation rate	Employed		Unemployed			
				Total	Percent	Total	Rate		
TOTAL									
Total, 16 Years and Over	243 284	154 975	63.7	142 469	58.6	12 506	8.1		88 310
Men	117 343	82 327	70.2	75 555	64.4	6 771	8.2		35 017
Women	125 941	72 648	57.7	66 914	53.1	5 734	7.9		53 293
PERSONS WITH A DISABILITY	28 251	5 816	20.6	5 037	17.8	779	13.4		22 435
Sex									
Men	12 929	3 190	24.7	2 770	21.4	420	13.2		9 739
Women	15 322	2 626	17.1	2 267	14.8	359	13.7		12 696
Age									
16 to 64 years	15 339	4 854	31.6	4 146	27.0	708	14.6		10 484
16 to 19 years	626	139	22.3	85	13.6	54	38.7		486
20 to 24 years	777	309	39.8	223	28.8	86	27.7		468
25 to 34 years	1 652	699	42.3	574	34.7	126	18.0		953
35 to 44 years	2 183	810	37.1	682	31.2	128	15.8		1 373
45 to 54 years	4 182	1 309	31.3	1 144	27.3	165	12.6		2 873
55 to 64 years	5 919	1 588	26.8	1 438	24.3	150	9.4		4 332
65 years and over	12 912	961	7.4	890	6.9	71	7.4		11 951
Race and Hispanic Origin									
White	22 854	4 820	21.1	4 228	18.5	592	12.3		18 035
Black or African American	3 732	635	17.0	503	13.5	132	20.8		3 097
Asian	709	125	17.7	111	15.6	15	11.8		583
Hispanic[1]	2 813	563	20.0	456	16.2	107	19.0		2 250
Educational Attainment									
Total, 25 years and over	26 848	5 367	20.0	4 728	17.6	640	11.9		21 481
Less than a high school diploma	6 109	599	9.8	500	8.2	99	16.5		5 509
High school graduates, no college[2]	9 851	1 726	17.5	1 518	15.4	208	12.1		8 126
Some college or associate degree	6 649	1 726	26.0	1 507	22.7	219	12.7		4 922
Bachelor's degree and higher[3]	4 239	1 316	31.0	1 203	28.4	113	8.6		2 923

[1]May be of any race.
[2]Includes persons with a high school diploma or equivalent.
[3]Includes persons with bachelor's, master's, professional, and doctoral degrees.

Table 1-63. Employed Full- and Part-Time Workers by Disability Status and Age, 2012 Annual Averages

(Thousands of people.)

Disability status and age	Employed			At work part-time for economic reasons[1]
	Total	Usually work full-time	Usually work part-time	
TOTAL				
Total, 16 Years and Over	142 469	114 809	27 661	8 122
16 to 64 years	135 224	110 589	24 635	7 850
65 years and over	7 245	4 220	3 025	272
Persons With a Disability				
16 years and over	5 037	3 366	1 670	362
16 to 64 years	4 146	2 933	1 213	325
65 years and over	890	433	457	37
Persons Without a Disability				
16 years and over	137 433	111 442	25 990	7 760
16 to 64 years	131 078	107 656	23 422	7 525
65 years and over	6 355	3 787	2 568	235

Note: Full time refers to persons who usually work 35 hours or more per week; part time refers to persons who usually work less than 35 hours per week.

[1]Refers to persons who, whether they usually work full or part time, worked 1 to 34 hours during the reference week for an economic reason such as slack work or unfavorable business conditions, inability to find full-time work, or seasonal declines in demand.

Table 1-64. Employed Persons by Disability Status, Occupation, and Sex, 2012 Annual Averages

(Number in thousands, percent.)

Occupation	Persons with a disability			Persons with no disability		
	Total	Men	Women	Total	Men	Women
TOTAL EMPLOYED	5 037	2 770	2 267	137 433	72 785	64 647
Occupation as a Percent of Total Employed						
Total	100.0	100.0	100.0	100.0	100.0	100.0
Management, professional, and related	32.2	30.9	33.8	38.1	34.8	41.9
Management, business, and financial operations	14.3	16.2	11.9	16.0	16.9	14.9
Management	10.8	13.2	7.8	11.3	13.0	9.3
Business and financial operations	3.5	3.0	4.1	4.7	3.9	5.6
Professional and related	17.9	14.7	21.8	22.2	17.9	27.0
Computer and mathematical	2.0	2.4	1.4	2.7	3.8	1.5
Architecture and engineering	1.6	2.8	0.2	2.0	3.3	0.6
Life, physical, and social science	0.8	0.8	0.7	0.9	1.0	0.9
Community and social services	1.9	1.6	2.3	1.6	1.1	2.2
Legal	1.1	1.1	1.2	1.3	1.2	1.4
Education, training, and library	5.0	2.5	8.1	6.0	3.0	9.4
Arts, design, entertainment, sports, and media	1.9	1.8	2.1	2.0	1.9	2.0
Healthcare practitioner and technical	3.6	1.8	5.9	5.7	2.7	9.0
Service	20.0	15.5	25.5	17.8	14.7	21.3
Healthcare support	2.4	0.5	4.8	2.5	0.6	4.6
Protective service	2.2	3.1	1.2	2.2	3.2	1.0
Food preparation and serving related	5.2	3.7	6.9	5.6	4.9	6.5
Building and grounds cleaning and maintenance	6.1	6.9	5.2	3.8	4.5	3.2
Personal care and service	4.1	1.4	7.3	3.7	1.6	6.1
Sales and office	23.5	16.0	32.7	23.3	16.8	30.6
Sales and related	10.4	9.5	11.5	10.9	10.5	11.3
Office and administrative support	13.1	6.5	21.1	12.4	6.3	19.3
Natural resources, construction, and maintenance	8.8	15.4	0.7	9.0	16.3	0.8
Farming, fishing, and forestry	0.6	1.0	0.2	0.7	1.0	0.3
Construction and extraction	4.6	8.2	0.2	4.9	9.1	0.3
Installation, maintenance, and repair	3.5	6.2	0.2	3.4	6.2	0.2
Production, transportation, and material moving	15.5	22.1	7.4	11.8	17.4	5.5
Production	7.7	10.5	4.3	5.9	8.0	3.5
Transportation and material moving	7.8	11.6	3.1	5.9	9.4	2.0

Table 1-65. Persons Not in the Labor Force by Disability Status, Age, and Sex, 2012 Annual Averages

(Thousands of people, percent distribution.)

Category	Total, 16 years and over	16 to 64 years			Total, 65 years and over
		Total	Men	Women	
Persons With a Disability					
Total not in the labor force	22 435	10 484	4 959	5 525	11 951
Persons who currently want a job	718	521	255	266	197
Marginally attached to the labor force[1]	229	189	101	88	40
Discouraged workers[2]	67	53	31	22	15
Other persons marginally attached to the labor force[3]	162	136	71	66	26
Persons Without a Disability					
Total not in the labor force	65 875	43 683	15 980	27 703	22 191
Persons who currently want a job	5 840	5 260	2 404	2 856	580
Marginally attached to the labor force[1]	2 287	2 124	1 083	1 041	163
Discouraged workers[2]	842	762	457	305	80
Other persons marginally attached to the labor force[3]	1 445	1 362	626	736	84

[1]Data refer to persons who want a job, have searched for work during the prior 12 months, and were available to take a job during the reference week, but had not looked for work in the past 4 weeks.
[2]Includes those who did not actively look for work in the prior 4 weeks for reasons such as thinks no work available, could not find work, lacks schooling or training, employer thinks too young or old, and other types of discrimination.
[3]Includes those who did not actively look for work in the prior 4 weeks for such reasons as school or family responsibilities, ill health, and transportation problems, as well as a number for whom reason for nonparticipation was not determined.

Table 1-66. Employment Status of Persons 18 Years and Over by Veteran Status, Period of Service, Sex, Race, and Hispanic or Latino Ethnicity, 2012 Annual Averages

(Thousands of people, percent.)

Characteristic	Civilian noninstitutional population	Civilian labor force		Employed		Unemployed		Not in labor force
		Total	Percent of population	Total	Percent of population	Total	Percent of labor force	
TOTAL								
Total, 18 Years and Over	234 393	153 022	65.3	141 050	60.2	11 972	7.8	81 371
Veterans	21 183	11 006	52.0	10 233	48.3	773	7.0	10 177
Gulf War era, total	5 615	4 618	82.3	4 263	75.9	355	7.7	997
Gulf War era II	2 566	2 071	80.7	1 866	72.7	205	9.9	496
Gulf War era I	3 049	2 548	83.6	2 398	78.6	150	5.9	501
WW II, Korean War, and Vietnam era	9 872	3 165	32.1	2 964	30.0	201	6.4	6 707
Other service periods	5 696	3 222	56.6	3 006	52.8	217	6.7	2 473
Nonveterans	213 211	142 017	66.6	130 817	61.4	11 200	7.9	71 194
MEN								
Total, 18 Years and Over	112 793	81 377	72.1	74 896	66.4	6 481	8.0	31 417
Veterans	19 368	9 884	51.0	9 204	47.5	680	6.9	9 484
Gulf War era, total	4 703	3 958	84.2	3 669	78.0	289	7.3	745
Gulf War era II	2 136	1 774	83.1	1 606	75.2	168	9.5	362
Gulf War era I	2 567	2 184	85.1	2 063	80.4	121	5.6	383
WW II, Korean War, and Vietnam era	9 554	3 063	32.1	2 866	30.0	197	6.4	6 491
Other service periods	5 112	2 863	56.0	2 669	52.2	194	6.8	2 248
Nonveterans	93 425	71 493	76.5	65 692	70.3	5 801	8.1	21 933
WOMEN								
Total, 18 Years and Over	121 600	71 645	58.9	66 154	54.4	5 492	7.7	49 955
Veterans	1 815	1 122	61.8	1 029	56.7	93	8.3	693
Gulf War era, total	912	660	72.4	594	65.1	66	10.0	252
Gulf War era II	431	297	68.9	259	60.2	37	12.5	134
Gulf War era I	482	364	75.5	335	69.5	29	8.0	118
WW II, Korean War, and Vietnam era	318	102	32.1	98	30.7	4	4.1	216
Other service periods	584	359	61.5	337	57.7	22	6.2	225
Nonveterans	119 785	70 524	58.9	65 125	54.4	5 399	7.7	49 261
WHITE								
Total, 18 Years and Over	186 587	122 080	65.4	113 562	60.9	8 518	7.0	64 507
Veterans	17 923	9 051	50.5	8 467	47.2	584	6.4	8 872
Gulf War era, total	4 298	3 566	83.0	3 313	77.1	253	7.1	733
Gulf War era II	1 971	1 596	81.0	1 447	73.4	149	9.4	375
Gulf War era I	2 327	1 970	84.6	1 866	80.2	103	5.3	357
WW II, Korean War, and Vietnam era	8 852	2 838	32.1	2 666	30.1	172	6.1	6 014
Other service periods	4 772	2 647	55.5	2 488	52.1	159	6.0	2 125
Nonveterans	168 664	113 029	67.0	105 094	62.3	7 934	7.0	55 635
BLACK								
Total, 18 Years and Over	28 562	18 219	63.8	15 768	55.2	2 451	13.5	10 342
Veterans	2 358	1 405	59.6	1 263	53.6	142	10.1	954
Gulf War era, total	918	729	79.4	657	71.6	72	9.8	189
Gulf War era II	389	314	80.7	273	70.2	41	13.0	75
Gulf War era I	528	415	78.5	384	72.7	31	7.4	113
WW II, Korean War, and Vietnam era	720	229	31.8	206	28.6	23	10.1	491
Other service periods	720	447	62.0	400	55.5	47	10.5	274
Nonveterans	26 203	16 815	64.2	14 505	55.4	2 309	13.7	9 389
ASIAN								
Total, 18 Years and Over	12 345	8 097	65.6	7 624	61.8	473	5.8	4 248
Veterans	293	170	58.0	160	54.7	10	5.8	123
Gulf War era, total	131	105	79.6	97	73.5	8	7.7	27
Gulf War era II	78	60	76.3	56	71.2	4	6.7	18
Gulf War era I	53	45	84.4	41	76.8	4	9.0	8
WW II, Korean War, and Vietnam era	115	33	28.6	32	27.6	1	. . .	82
Other service periods	47	33	69.6	32	68.2	1	. . .	14
Nonveterans	12 052	7 927	65.8	7 464	61.9	463	5.8	4 125
HISPANIC[1]								
Total, 18 Years and Over	34 792	23 999	69.0	21 602	62.1	2 396	10.0	10 793
Veterans	1 298	822	63.4	755	58.2	67	8.2	475
Gulf War era, total	582	480	82.4	434	74.6	46	9.5	102
Gulf War era II	308	246	79.9	217	70.5	29	11.7	62
Gulf War era I	274	234	85.3	217	79.2	17	7.2	40
WW II, Korean War, and Vietnam era	412	139	33.8	132	32.0	8	5.4	273
Other service periods	303	203	67.0	189	62.2	14	7.1	100
Nonveterans	33 494	23 176	69.2	20 848	62.2	2 329	10.0	10 318

Note: Veterans are men and women who served in the U.S. Armed Forces during World War II, the Korean War, the Vietnam era, the Gulf War era, and all other service periods. Nonveterans are men and women who never served in the U.S. Armed Forces. Other service periods include the periods between World War II and the Korean War, between the Korean War and the Vietnam era, and between the Vietnam era and the Gulf War era. Estimates for the above race groups (White, Black, and Asian) do not sum to totals because data are not presented for all races.

[1]May be of any race.
. . . = Not available.

Table 1-67. Employment Status of Persons 18 Years and Over by Veteran Status, Age, Period of Service, and Sex, 2012 Annual Averages

(Thousands of people, percent.)

Veteran status, age, period of service, and sex	Civilian noninstitutional population	Civilian labor force							Not in labor force
		Total	Percent of population	Employed		Unemployed			
				Total	Percent of population	Total	Percent of labor force		

Veteran status, age, period of service, and sex	Civilian noninstitutional population	Total	Percent of population	Total	Percent of population	Total	Percent of labor force	Not in labor force
TOTAL VETERANS								
Total, 18 years and over	21 183	11 006	52.0	10 233	48.3	773	7.0	10 177
18 to 24 years	301	225	74.7	179	59.5	46	20.4	76
25 to 34 years	1 585	1 298	81.8	1 169	73.8	128	9.9	288
35 to 44 years	2 267	2 008	88.6	1 892	83.5	116	5.8	259
45 to 54 years	3 516	2 900	82.5	2 705	76.9	195	6.7	616
55 to 64 years	4 565	2 728	59.8	2 553	55.9	175	6.4	1 837
65 years and over	8 948	1 847	20.6	1 734	19.4	113	6.1	7 101
Gulf War Era, Total								
Total, 18 years and over	5 615	4 618	82.3	4 263	75.9	355	7.7	997
18 to 24 years	301	225	74.7	179	59.5	46	20.4	76
25 to 34 years	1 585	1 298	81.8	1 169	73.8	128	9.9	288
35 to 44 years	1 916	1 699	88.7	1 603	83.7	96	5.6	217
45 to 54 years	1 159	981	84.6	923	79.6	59	6.0	178
55 to 64 years	517	369	71.4	348	67.3	21	5.8	148
65 years and over	136	46	34.0	41	30.2	5	11.1	90
Gulf War Era II								
Total, 18 years and over	2 566	2 071	80.7	1 866	72.7	205	9.9	496
18 to 24 years	301	225	74.7	179	59.5	46	20.4	76
25 to 34 years	1 234	997	80.8	891	72.2	106	10.6	237
35 to 44 years	467	397	85.0	377	80.7	20	5.0	70
45 to 54 years	387	334	86.4	309	79.8	26	7.7	52
55 to 64 years	150	107	71.0	101	66.9	6	5.8	44
65 years and over	26	10	. . .	9	. . .	1	. . .	16
Gulf War Era I								
Total, 25 years and over	3 049	2 548	83.6	2 398	78.6	150	5.9	501
25 to 34 years	351	301	85.6	279	79.3	22	7.4	50
35 to 44 years	1 449	1 302	89.8	1 226	84.6	76	5.8	147
45 to 54 years	772	647	83.8	614	79.5	33	5.1	126
55 to 64 years	367	263	71.6	247	67.4	15	5.8	104
65 years and over	110	36	32.8	32	29.0	4	11.6	74
World War II, Korean War, Vietnam War								
Total, 55 years and over	9 872	3 165	32.1	2 964	30.0	201	6.4	6 707
55 to 64 years	3 220	1 777	55.2	1 662	51.6	115	6.5	1 443
65 years and over	6 652	1 388	20.9	1 302	19.6	86	6.2	5 264
Other Service Periods								
Total, 35 years and over	5 696	3 222	56.6	3 006	52.8	217	6.7	2 473
35 to 44 years	351	309	88.1	289	82.3	20	6.6	42
45 to 54 years	2 357	1 919	81.4	1 783	75.6	136	7.1	438
55 to 64 years	828	582	70.3	543	65.7	38	6.6	246
65 years and over	2 160	413	19.1	391	18.1	22	5.3	1 747
TOTAL NONVETERANS								
Total, 18 years and over	213 211	142 017	66.6	130 817	61.4	11 200	7.9	71 194
18 to 24 years	29 591	19 107	64.6	16 236	54.9	2 871	15.0	10 484
25 to 34 years	39 389	32 167	81.7	29 531	75.0	2 636	8.2	7 222
35 to 44 years	37 375	30 726	82.2	28 684	76.7	2 042	6.6	6 649
45 to 54 years	40 183	32 156	80.0	30 168	75.1	1 988	6.2	8 027
55 to 64 years	33 755	21 984	65.1	20 686	61.3	1 298	5.9	11 771
65 years and over	32 917	5 876	17.8	5 511	16.7	365	6.2	27 041

Note: Veterans are men and women who served in the U.S. Armed Forces during World War II, the Korean War, the Vietnam era, the Gulf War era, and all other service periods. Nonveterans are men and women who never served in the U.S. Armed Forces. Other service periods include the periods between World War II and the Korean War, between the Korean War and the Vietnam era, and between the Vietnam era and the Gulf War era.

. . . = Not available.

Table 1-67. Employment Status of Persons 18 Years and Over by Veteran Status, Age, Period of Service, and Sex, 2012 Annual Averages—*Continued*

(Thousands of people, percent.)

Veteran status, age, period of service, and sex	Civilian noninstitutional population	Civilian labor force						Not in labor force
		Total	Percent of population	Employed		Unemployed		
				Total	Percent of population	Total	Percent of labor force	
VETERANS, MEN								
Total, 18 years and over	19 368	9 884	51.0	9 204	47.5	680	6.9	9 484
18 to 24 years	250	193	77.3	154	61.9	39	20.0	57
25 to 34 years	1 321	1 116	84.5	1 009	76.4	107	9.6	204
35 to 44 years	1 896	1 715	90.5	1 616	85.2	99	5.8	181
45 to 54 years	3 016	2 534	84.0	2 373	78.7	161	6.3	481
55 to 64 years	4 224	2 519	59.6	2 357	55.8	163	6.5	1 704
65 years and over	8 662	1 806	20.9	1 695	19.6	111	6.2	6 856
Gulf War Era, Total								
Total, 18 years and over	4 703	3 958	84.2	3 669	78.0	289	7.3	745
18 to 24 years	250	193	77.3	154	61.9	39	20.0	57
25 to 34 years	1 321	1 116	84.5	1 009	76.4	107	9.6	204
35 to 44 years	1 595	1 446	90.7	1 366	85.7	80	5.5	149
45 to 54 years	978	843	86.3	802	82.0	42	5.0	134
55 to 64 years	436	318	72.9	300	68.9	18	5.5	118
65 years and over	124	41	33.5	37	30.3	4	9.5	82
Gulf War Era II								
Total, 18 years and over	2 136	1 774	83.1	1 606	75.2	168	9.5	362
18 to 24 years	250	193	77.3	154	61.9	39	20.0	57
25 to 34 years	1 034	868	83.9	778	75.2	90	10.4	166
35 to 44 years	381	334	87.6	317	83.2	17	5.0	47
45 to 54 years	323	283	87.6	267	82.7	16	5.6	40
55 to 64 years	124	88	71.0	83	66.6	6	6.2	36
65 years and over	24	9	. . .	8	. . .	1	. . .	16
Gulf War Era I								
Total, 25 years and over	2 567	2 184	85.1	2 063	80.4	121	5.6	383
25 to 34 years	286	248	86.7	231	80.7	17	7.0	38
35 to 44 years	1 214	1 112	91.6	1 049	86.4	63	5.7	102
45 to 54 years	655	561	85.6	535	81.6	26	4.6	94
55 to 64 years	312	230	73.7	218	69.8	12	5.2	82
65 years and over	99	33	32.9	30	29.9	3	. . .	67
World War II, Korean War, and Vietnam War								
Total, 55 years and over	9 554	3 063	32.1	2 866	30.0	197	6.4	6 491
55 to 64 years	3 076	1 695	55.1	1 584	51.5	111	6.6	1 380
65 years and over	6 478	1 367	21.1	1 282	19.8	86	6.3	5 111
Other Service Periods								
Total, 35 years and over	5 112	2 863	56.0	2 669	52.2	194	6.8	2 248
35 to 44 years	301	269	89.4	250	82.9	20	7.3	32
45 to 54 years	2 038	1 691	83.0	1 572	77.1	119	7.0	347
55 to 64 years	712	506	71.0	472	66.3	34	6.7	206
65 years and over	2 060	397	19.3	376	18.2	22	5.5	1 663
NONVETERANS, MEN								
Total, 18 years and over	93 425	71 493	76.5	65 692	70.3	5 801	8.1	21 933
18 to 24 years	14 746	9 907	67.2	8 287	56.2	1 620	16.4	4 839
25 to 34 years	18 884	16 966	89.8	15 598	82.6	1 369	8.1	1 918
35 to 44 years	17 519	15 892	90.7	14 867	84.9	1 025	6.4	1 627
45 to 54 years	18 325	15 830	86.4	14 847	81.0	982	6.2	2 495
55 to 64 years	14 195	10 363	73.0	9 711	68.4	652	6.3	3 832
65 years and over	9 756	2 534	26.0	2 382	24.4	152	6.0	7 222

Note: Veterans are men and women who served in the U.S. Armed Forces during World War II, the Korean War, the Vietnam era, the Gulf War era, and all other service periods. Nonveterans are men and women who never served in the U.S. Armed Forces. Other service periods include the periods between World War II and the Korean War, between the Korean War and the Vietnam era, and between the Vietnam era and the Gulf War era.

. . . = Not available.

Table 1-67. Employment Status of Persons 18 Years and Over by Veteran Status, Age, Period of Service, and Sex, 2012 Annual Averages—*Continued*

(Thousands of people, percent.)

Veteran status, age, period of service, and sex	Civilian noninstitutional population	Civilian labor force						Not in labor force
		Total	Percent of population	Employed		Unemployed		
				Total	Percent of population	Total	Percent of labor force	
VETERANS, WOMEN								
Total, 18 years and over	1 815	1 122	61.8	1 029	56.7	93	8.3	693
18 to 24 years	52	32	62.2	25	48.1	7	...	20
25 to 34 years	265	181	68.5	160	60.5	21	11.6	83
35 to 44 years	371	293	79.0	276	74.4	17	5.8	78
45 to 54 years	501	366	73.1	332	66.3	34	9.2	135
55 to 64 years	341	209	61.2	196	57.5	12	6.0	133
65 years and over	286	41	14.3	39	13.8	1	3.2	245
Gulf Era, Total								
Total, 18 years and over	912	660	72.4	594	65.1	66	10.0	252
18 to 24 years	52	32	62.2	25	48.1	7	...	20
25 to 34 years	265	181	68.5	160	60.5	21	11.6	83
35 to 44 years	321	253	78.8	237	73.7	16	6.4	68
45 to 54 years	182	138	75.9	121	66.7	17	12.1	44
55 to 64 years	81	51	63.5	48	58.7	4	7.6	30
65 years and over	12	5	...	4	...	1	...	7
Gulf Era II								
Total, 18 years and over	431	297	68.9	259	60.2	37	12.5	134
18 to 24 years	52	32	62.2	25	48.1	7	...	20
25 to 34 years	200	129	64.4	113	56.4	16	12.5	71
35 to 44 years	87	64	73.4	60	69.6	3	5.2	23
45 to 54 years	64	52	80.6	42	65.3	10	19.0	12
55 to 64 years	26	19	...	18	...	1	...	8
65 years and over	2	2	...	2	...	0	...	0
Gulf Era I								
Total, 25 Years and over	482	364	75.5	335	69.5	29	8.0	118
25 to 34 years	65	52	80.8	48	73.3	5	9.3	12
35 to 44 years	235	189	80.7	177	75.3	13	6.8	45
45 to 54 years	117	86	73.4	79	67.5	7	8.0	31
55 to 64 years	55	33	60.0	30	54.1	3	...	22
65 years and over	10	3	...	2	...	1	...	7
World War II, Korean War, and Vietnam Era								
Total, 55 years and over	318	102	32.1	98	30.7	4	4.1	216
55 to 64 years	145	81	56.3	77	53.5	4	5.0	63
65 years and over	174	21	11.8	20	11.8	0	...	153
Other Service Periods								
Total, 35 years and over	584	359	61.5	337	57.7	22	6.2	225
35 to 44 years	50	40	80.3	39	78.8	1	1.8	10
45 to 54 years	319	228	71.4	211	66.1	17	7.5	91
55 to 64 years	115	76	65.6	71	61.8	4	5.9	40
65 years and over	100	16	15.5	16	15.5	0	...	84
NONVETERANS, WOMEN								
Total, 18 years and over	119 785	70 524	58.9	65 125	54.4	5 399	7.7	49 261
18 to 24 years	14 845	9 200	62.0	7 949	53.5	1 251	13.6	5 645
25 to 34 years	20 505	15 201	74.1	13 934	68.0	1 267	8.3	5 304
35 to 44 years	19 855	14 834	74.7	13 817	69.6	1 017	6.9	5 022
45 to 54 years	21 858	16 327	74.7	15 321	70.1	1 006	6.2	5 532
55 to 64 years	19 560	11 621	59.4	10 975	56.1	646	5.6	7 939
65 years and over	23 161	3 341	14.4	3 129	13.5	212	6.4	19 820

Note: Veterans are men and women who served in the U.S. Armed Forces during World War II, the Korean War, the Vietnam era, the Gulf War era, and all other service periods. Nonveterans are men and women who never served in the U.S. Armed Forces. Other service periods include the periods between World War II and the Korean War, between the Korean War and the Vietnam era, and between the Vietnam era and the Gulf War era.

. . . – Not available.

Table 1-68. Employment Status of Gulf War Veterans by Reserve or National Guard Service, August 2012, Not Seasonally Adjusted

(Thousands of people, percent.)

Reserve or National Guard status	Civilian noninstitutional population	Civilian labor force							Not in labor force
		Total	Percent of population	Employed		Unemployed			
				Total	Percent of population	Total	Percent of labor force		
GULF WAR ERA									
Total	5 654	4 634	82.0	4 258	75.3	376	8.1		1 020
Current or past member of Reserve or National Guard	1 615	1 370	84.8	1 269	78.6	101	7.3		245
Never a member of Reserve or National Guard	3 026	2 481	82.0	2 257	74.6	224	9.0		545
Reserve or National Guard membership not reported	1 013	783	77.3	732	72.2	51	6.5		230
GULF WAR ERA II									
Total	2 571	2 081	81.0	1 854	72.1	227	10.9		490
Current or past member of Reserve or National Guard	763	655	85.8	608	79.6	47	7.2		109
Never a member of Reserve or National Guard	1 377	1 083	78.7	935	67.9	148	13.7		293
Reserve or National Guard membership not reported	431	343	79.6	311	72.3	32	9.2		88
GULF WAR ERA I									
Total	3 083	2 553	82.8	2 403	78.0	149	5.8		530
Current or past member of Reserve or National Guard	851	715	84.0	661	77.7	54	7.5		136
Never a member of Reserve or National Guard	1 649	1 398	84.8	1 322	80.1	76	5.4		251
Reserve or National Guard membership not reported	583	440	75.5	420	72.1	20	4.4		143

Note: Veterans are men and women who served in the U.S. Armed Forces during World War II, the Korean War, the Vietnam era, the Gulf War era, and all other service periods. The Gulf War era began in August 1990 and continues to the present day. It is divided into two periods of service: Gulf War era II (September 2001–present) and Gulf War era I (August 1990–August 2001).

Table 1-69. Employed Persons 18 Years and Over by Occupation, Sex, Veteran Status, and Period of Service, 2012 Annual Averages

(Number in thousands, percent distribution.)

Occupation	Total veterans	Gulf War era			WWII, Korean War, and Vietnam War	Other services periods	Non-veteran
		Total	Gulf War era II	Gulf War era I			
TOTAL							
Total, 18 Years and Over	10 233	4 263	1 866	2 398	2 964	3 006	130 817
Percent	100.0	100.0	100.0	100.0	100.0	100.0	100.0
Management, professional, and related occupations	37.8	36.8	36.0	37.5	41.3	35.6	38.3
Management, business, and financial operations occupations	18.1	16.2	15.3	16.9	21.8	17.1	15.9
Professional and related occupations	19.7	20.6	20.7	20.5	19.4	18.5	22.4
Service occupations	14.2	16.8	17.9	15.9	11.5	13.4	17.8
Sales and office occupations	17.0	17.4	17.3	17.5	17.6	15.8	23.7
Sales and related occupations	8.9	8.3	8.1	8.4	11.0	7.8	10.8
Office and administrative support occupations	8.1	9.1	9.1	9.1	6.7	8.1	12.8
Natural resources, construction, and maintenance occupations	13.9	13.6	13.6	13.6	12.3	15.7	8.7
Farming, fishing, and forestry occupations	0.4	0.2	0.2	0.3	0.4	0.5	0.7
Construction and extraction occupations	6.4	5.6	4.9	6.2	6.1	7.7	4.8
Installation, maintenance, and repair occupations	7.1	7.7	8.5	7.1	5.8	7.5	3.1
Production, transportation, and material moving occupations	17.2	15.4	15.2	15.5	17.3	19.5	11.6
Production occupations	7.2	7.1	7.5	6.8	6.6	8.0	5.9
Transportation and material moving occupations	9.9	8.3	7.7	8.7	10.7	11.5	5.7
MEN							
Total, 18 Years and Over	9 204	3 669	1 606	206	2 866	2 669	65 692
Percent	100.0	100.0	100.0	100.0	100.0	100.0	100.0
Management, professional, and related occupations	36.6	34.9	33.9	35.7	41.2	34.0	34.7
Management, business, and financial operations occupations	18.1	16.1	15.4	16.7	22.1	16.6	16.9
Professional and related occupations	18.5	18.8	18.5	19.0	19.1	17.3	17.8
Service occupations	14.0	16.9	18.1	15.9	11.4	12.9	14.6
Sales and office occupations	15.8	15.6	16.0	15.2	17.3	14.4	16.8
Sales and related occupations	9.1	8.5	8.3	8.6	11.0	8.0	10.6
Office and administrative support occupations	6.6	7.1	7.7	6.6	6.3	6.4	6.2
Natural resources, construction, and maintenance occupations	15.3	15.6	15.4	15.7	12.7	17.5	16.4
Farming, fishing, and forestry occupations	0.4	0.2	0.2	0.3	0.5	0.6	1.1
Construction and extraction occupations	7.0	6.5	5.5	7.2	6.3	8.6	9.4
Installation, maintenance, and repair occupations	7.8	8.9	9.7	8.3	6.0	8.3	6.0
Production, transportation, and material moving occupations	18.4	17.1	16.6	17.5	17.5	21.2	17.5
Production occupations	7.7	7.9	8.2	7.6	6.6	8.7	8.2
Transportation and material moving occupations	10.7	9.2	8.4	9.8	10.9	12.5	9.3
WOMEN							
Total, 18 Years and Over	1 029	594	259	335	98	337	65 125
Percent	100.0	100.0	100.0	100.0	100.0	100.0	100.0
Management, professional, and related occupations	48.3	48.8	49.5	48.4	44.0	48.7	41.9
Management, business, and financial operations occupations	17.9	16.9	15.0	18.3	14.9	20.6	14.9
Professional and related occupations	30.4	32.0	34.5	30.1	29.1	28.0	27.0
Service occupations	16.2	16.3	16.7	16.1	14.0	16.7	21.2
Sales and office occupations	28.1	28.7	25.3	31.3	28.3	26.9	30.6
Sales and related occupations	7.0	7.1	7.1	7.1	9.9	5.9	11.1
Office and administrative support occupations	21.1	21.6	18.2	24.2	18.4	21.0	19.5
Natural resources, construction, and maintenance occupations	1.3	1.3	2.3	0.5	1.2	1.5	0.8
Farming, fishing, and forestry occupations	0.2	0.3	0.3	0.3	0.0	0.0	0.3
Construction and extraction occupations	0.6	0.5	1.0	0.1	1.2	0.6	0.3
Installation, maintenance, and repair occupations	0.6	0.5	1.1	0.1	0.0	0.8	0.2
Production, transportation, and material moving occupations	6.0	4.8	6.2	3.7	12.6	6.2	5.5
Production occupations	3.2	2.4	3.1	1.8	7.8	3.2	3.5
Transportation and material moving occupations	2.8	2.4	3.1	1.9	4.7	3.0	2.0

Note: Veterans are men and women who served in the U.S. Armed Forces during World War II, the Korean War, the Vietnam era, the Gulf War era, and all other service periods. Nonveterans are men and women who never served in the U.S. Armed Forces. Other service periods include the periods between World War II and the Korean War, between the Korean War and the Vietnam era, and between the Vietnam era and the Gulf War era.

Table 1-70. Employed Persons 18 Years and Over by Industry, Class of Worker, Sex, Veteran Status, and Period of Service, 2012 Annual Averages

(Number in thousands, percent distribution.)

Industry and class of worker	Total veterans	Gulf War era			WWII, Korean War, and Vietnam War	Other services periods	Non-veteran
		Total	Gulf War era II	Gulf War era I			
TOTAL							
Total, 18 Years and Over	10 233	4 263	1 866	2 398	2 964	3 006	130 817
Percent	100.0	100.0	100.0	100.0	100.0	100.0	100.0
Agriculture and related industries	1.7	0.6	0.6	0.6	3.6	1.5	1.5
Wage and salary workers	0.8	0.4	0.4	0.3	1.3	0.8	1.0
Self-employed workers	1.0	0.2	0.2	0.3	2.3	0.7	0.5
Nonagricultural industries	98.3	99.4	99.4	99.4	96.4	98.5	98.5
Wage and salary workers	91.0	95.8	97.1	94.8	84.4	90.7	92.4
Private industries	70.2	71.1	72.2	70.2	68.4	70.7	78.4
Mining	0.9	1.0	1.1	1.0	0.8	0.9	0.6
Construction	5.4	5.0	4.5	5.5	5.1	6.2	4.9
Manufacturing	12.6	12.3	11.3	13.1	11.9	13.9	9.9
Wholesale trade	2.6	2.4	1.7	2.9	2.6	2.8	2.5
Retail trade	8.8	8.9	10.1	7.9	9.7	7.6	10.8
Transportation and utilities	7.1	6.7	6.2	7.1	6.3	8.2	3.7
Information	2.1	2.6	2.6	2.6	1.7	1.9	1.8
Financial activities	4.6	4.1	4.1	4.1	5.7	4.1	6.3
Professional and business services	10.5	11.7	12.8	10.9	10.1	9.3	9.8
Education and health services	8.4	8.6	8.8	8.4	7.9	8.8	15.3
Leisure and hospitality	4.1	5.1	6.0	4.3	3.2	3.7	8.4
Other services	3.0	2.7	3.1	2.4	3.4	3.1	4.4
Government	20.8	24.7	24.8	24.7	16.0	20.0	14.0
Federal	8.5	11.8	13.6	10.4	5.2	7.2	2.1
State	4.5	4.4	4.0	4.6	4.4	4.9	4.4
Local	7.8	8.6	7.2	9.6	6.5	7.9	7.4
Self-employed workers	7.2	3.6	2.3	4.5	12.0	7.7	6.1
MEN							
Total, 18 Years and Over	9 204	3 669	1 606	2 063	2 866	2 669	65 692
Percent	100.0	100.0	100.0	100.0	100.0	100.0	100.0
Agriculture and related industries	1.9	0.6	0.7	0.6	3.6	1.7	2.1
Wage and salary workers	0.8	0.4	0.5	0.3	1.2	0.9	1.4
Self-employed workers	1.0	0.2	0.2	0.2	2.4	0.8	0.7
Nonagricultural industries	98.1	99.4	99.3	99.4	96.4	98.3	97.9
Wage and salary workers	90.6	95.8	96.9	95.0	84.3	90.2	90.9
Private industries	70.6	71.6	72.1	71.2	68.7	71.4	80.3
Mining	1.0	1.1	1.1	1.1	0.9	1.0	1.1
Construction	5.9	5.7	5.0	6.3	5.2	6.8	8.8
Manufacturing	13.3	13.2	11.9	14.1	12.1	14.7	13.6
Wholesale trade	2.7	2.6	1.9	3.2	2.6	2.9	3.4
Retail trade	8.8	8.9	10.2	7.8	9.8	7.5	10.6
Transportation and utilities	7.6	7.5	6.9	8.0	6.5	9.0	5.5
Information	2.2	2.7	2.6	2.7	1.7	1.9	2.3
Financial activities	4.5	3.9	3.9	3.9	5.7	4.1	5.4
Professional and business services	10.8	12.2	12.9	11.5	10.2	9.5	11.0
Education and health services	6.7	6.2	6.6	5.9	7.3	7.0	6.7
Leisure and hospitality	4.0	4.9	5.9	4.1	3.2	3.6	8.0
Other services	3.1	2.8	3.2	2.4	3.4	3.3	3.9
Government	20.0	24.2	24.8	23.7	15.6	18.9	10.6
Federal	8.1	11.5	13.6	9.9	5.0	6.8	1.9
State	4.4	4.4	4.0	4.7	4.3	4.6	3.2
Local	7.5	8.3	7.2	9.1	6.4	7.5	5.5
Self-employed workers	7.5	3.6	2.5	4.5	12.0	8.0	6.9
WOMEN							
Total, 18 Years and Over	1 029	594	259	335	98	337	65 125
Percent	100.0	100.0	100.0	100.0	100.0	100.0	100.0
Agriculture and related industries	0.6	0.6	0.4	0.8	2.1	0.1	0.8
Wage and salary workers	0.3	0.2	0.3	0.1	1.6	0.0	0.5
Self-employed workers	0.3	0.4	0.1	0.7	0.5	0.1	0.3
Nonagricultural industries	99.4	99.4	99.6	99.2	97.9	99.9	99.2
Wage and salary workers	94.8	95.9	98.3	94.1	88.4	94.7	93.8
Private industries	66.4	67.9	73.1	63.8	60.0	65.8	76.5
Mining	0.2	0.3	0.7	0.0	0.1	0.1	0.2
Construction	1.3	1.0	1.4	0.6	2.3	1.6	1.0
Manufacturing	6.9	7.1	7.6	6.7	4.8	7.2	6.2
Wholesale trade	1.2	0.9	0.4	1.3	1.2	1.9	1.5
Retail trade	8.6	8.9	10.0	8.0	7.1	8.5	11.0
Transportation and utilities	1.9	2.0	2.1	1.9	1.0	2.1	1.8
Information	1.9	2.1	2.3	1.9	0.6	2.0	1.4
Financial activities	4.9	5.0	5.0	4.9	6.3	4.4	7.1
Professional and business services	8.3	9.1	12.0	6.8	5.4	7.7	8.7
Education and health services	23.5	23.3	22.5	24.0	24.5	23.6	23.9
Leisure and hospitality	5.3	6.0	6.7	5.4	3.6	4.7	8.9
Other services	2.4	2.4	2.6	2.3	3.1	2.1	4.8
Government	28.4	28.1	25.2	30.3	28.4	28.9	17.3
Federal	12.3	13.7	13.8	13.7	10.9	10.3	2.2
State	5.6	4.0	3.8	4.2	7.5	7.7	5.7
Local	10.5	10.3	7.6	12.5	10.0	10.9	9.4
Self-employed workers	4.5	3.4	1.3	5.1	9.5	5.0	5.3

Note: Veterans are men and women who served in the U.S. Armed Forces during World War II, the Korean War, the Vietnam era, the Gulf War era, and all other service periods. Nonveterans are men and women who never served in the U.S. Armed Forces. Other service periods include the periods between World War II and the Korean War, between the Korean War and the Vietnam era, and between the Vietnam era and the Gulf War era.

Table 1-71. Employed Persons 18 Years and Over by Veteran Status, Presence of Service-Connected Disability, Period of Service, and Class of Worker, August 2012, Not Seasonally Adjusted

(Numbers in thousands, percent distribution.)

Veteran status, presence of disability, and period of service	Total employed (number)	Total employed (percent)	Agriculture and related industries	Nonagricultural industries						Self-employed, unincorporated, and unpaid family workers
				Wage and salary workers						
				Total	Private sector	Government				
						Total	Federal	State and local		
Veterans, Total[1]	10 228	100.0	1.7	98.3	70.3	20.5	8.3	12.1		7.5
With service-connected disability	1 301	100.0	0.7	99.3	59.0	34.4	19.4	15.1		5.8
Without service-connected disability	7 123	100.0	1.8	98.2	71.8	19.2	6.6	12.6		7.3
Gulf War Era, Total[1]	4 258	100.0	0.9	99.1	71.5	24.1	12.4	11.7		3.4
With service-connected disability	827	100.0	0.1	99.9	58.5	38.6	24.5	14.1		2.8
Without service-connected disability	2 722	100.0	0.9	99.1	75.2	20.9	8.7	12.2		3.0
Gulf War Era II[1]	1 854	100.0	0.6	99.4	72.3	24.8	15.3	9.5		2.4
With service-connected disability	460	100.0	-	100.0	62.3	36.6	24.4	12.2		1.1
Without service-connected disability	1 086	100.0	0.9	99.1	75.5	21.4	11.4	10.0		2.2
Gulf War Era I[1]	2 403	100.0	1.2	98.8	71.0	23.6	10.1	13.5		4.3
With service-connected disability	367	100.0	0.3	99.7	53.7	41.1	24.7	16.4		5.0
Without service-connected disability	1 636	100.0	0.9	99.1	75.1	20.5	7.0	13.6		3.5
WW II, Korean War, and Vietnam Era[1]	2 939	100.0	3.3	96.7	69.8	14.7	4.0	10.8		12.1
With service-connected disability	257	100.0	3.1	96.9	61.9	20.8	4.6	16.1		14.2
Without service-connected disability	2 127	100.0	3.3	96.7	71.1	14.8	4.4	10.4		10.8
Other Service Periods[1]	3 031	100.0	1.3	98.7	68.9	20.9	6.9	14.0		8.8
With service-connected disability	216	100.0	0.1	99.9	57.8	34.6	17.1	17.5		7.5
Without service-connected disability	2 274	100.0	1.4	98.6	68.3	21.2	6.1	15.1		9.1
Nonveterans	130 730	100.0	1.6	98.4	78.7	13.6	2.1	11.5		6.2

Note: Veterans are men and women who served in the U.S. Armed Forces during World War II, the Korean War, the Vietnam era, the Gulf War era, and all other service periods. Nonveterans are men and women who never served in the U.S. Armed Forces. Other service periods include the periods between World War II and the Korean War, between the Korean War and the Vietnam era, and between the Vietnam era and the Gulf War era.

[1]Includes veterans who did not report presence of disability.
- = Quantity represents or rounds to zero.

Table 1-72. Volunteers by Selected Characteristics, September 2013

(Numbers in thousands, percent.)

Characteristic	Total, both sexes			Men			Women		
	Civilian noninstitutional population	Volunteers		Civilian noninstitutional population	Volunteers		Civilian noninstitutional population	Volunteers	
		Number	Percent of population		Number	Percent of population		Number	Percent of population
Age									
Total, 16 years and over	246 168	62 615	25.4	118 807	26 404	22.2	127 361	36 211	28.4
16 to 24 years	38 822	8 466	21.8	19 569	3 733	19.1	19 253	4 734	24.6
16 to 19 years	16 745	4 383	26.2	8 515	1 932	22.7	8 230	2 451	29.8
20 to 24 years	22 077	4 083	18.5	11 055	1 800	16.3	11 022	2 283	20.7
25 years and over	207 346	54 148	26.1	99 237	22 671	22.8	108 108	31 477	29.1
25 to 34 years	41 685	9 118	21.9	20 585	3 686	17.9	21 101	5 432	25.7
35 to 44 years	39 599	12 098	30.6	19 398	4 967	25.6	20 201	7 131	35.3
45 to 54 years	43 167	12 184	28.2	21 087	5 263	25.0	22 079	6 921	31.3
55 to 64 years	39 172	10 191	26.0	18 824	4 358	23.1	20 348	5 833	28.7
65 years and over	43 723	10 558	24.1	19 344	4 398	22.7	24 379	6 160	25.3
Race and Hispanic or Latino Ethnicity									
White	194 610	52 685	27.1	95 013	22 435	23.6	99 597	30 250	30.4
Black or African American	30 462	5 637	18.5	13 790	2 260	16.4	16 672	3 377	20.3
Asian	13 314	2 525	19.0	6 227	990	15.9	7 087	1 535	21.7
Hispanic or Latino ethnicity[1]	37 713	5 838	15.5	18 898	2 450	13.0	18 814	3 388	18.0
Educational Attainment[2]									
Less than a high school diploma	24 461	2 204	9.0	12 105	941	7.8	12 356	1 264	10.2
High school graduates, no college[3]	60 794	10 138	16.7	29 774	4 221	14.2	31 019	5 917	19.1
Some college or associate degree	56 233	15 562	27.7	25 595	5 987	23.4	30 639	9 575	31.3
Bachelor's degree and higher[4]	65 857	26 244	39.8	31 763	11 522	36.3	34 094	14 722	43.2
Marital Status									
Single, never married	74 351	14 851	20.0	39 108	6 417	16.4	35 243	8 434	23.9
Married, spouse present	122 725	37 719	30.7	61 794	16 907	27.4	60 931	20 812	34.2
Other marital status[5]	49 092	10 045	20.5	17 904	3 080	17.2	31 187	6 965	22.3
Presence of Own Children Under 18 Years[6]									
Without own children under 18	180 102	40 847	22.7	89 507	17 646	19.7	90 594	23 201	25.6
With own children under 18	66 066	21 767	32.9	29 299	8 758	29.9	36 767	13 009	35.4
Employment Status									
Civilian labor force	157 196	43 162	27.5	83 338	20 008	24.0	73 859	23 154	31.3
Employed	145 740	40 401	27.7	77 067	18 775	24.4	68 673	21 626	31.5
Full time[7]	117 704	31 524	26.8	66 905	16 172	24.2	50 799	15 351	30.2
Part time[8]	28 036	8 877	31.7	10 162	2 603	25.6	17 874	6 275	35.1
Unemployed	11 456	2 761	24.1	6 271	1 233	19.7	5 186	1 528	29.5
Not in the labor force	88 972	19 452	21.9	35 469	6 396	18.0	53 502	13 057	24.4

Note: Data on volunteers relate to persons who performed unpaid volunteer activities for an organization at any point from September 1, 2012, through the survey period in September 2013.

[1]May be of any race.
[2]Data refer to persons 25 years and over.
[3]Includes persons with a high school diploma or equivalent.
[4]Includes persons with bachelor's, professional, and doctoral degrees.
[5]Includes divorced, separated, and widowed persons.
[6]Own children include sons, daughters, stepchildren, and adopted children. Not included are nieces, nephews, grandchildren, and other related and unrelated children.
[7]Usually work 35 hours or more a week at all jobs.
[8]Usually work less than 35 hours a week at all jobs.

Table 1-73. Volunteers by Annual Hours of Volunteer Activities and Selected Characteristics, September 2013

(Numbers in thousands, percent.)

Characteristic	Total volunteers	Percent distribution of total annual hours spent volunteering at all organizations							Median annual hours[1]
		Total	1 to 14 hour	15 to 49 hours	50 to 99 hours	100 to 499 hours	500 hours and over	Not reporting annual hours	
Sex									
Total, both sexes	62 615	100.0	21.3	25.2	15.1	27.3	5.8	5.3	50
Men	26 404	100.0	20.5	25.2	14.6	28.2	6.1	5.4	52
Women	36 211	100.0	21.9	25.1	15.5	26.7	5.6	5.2	50
Age									
Total, 16 years and over	62 615	100.0	21.3	25.2	15.1	27.3	5.8	5.3	50
16 to 24 years	8 466	100.0	23.0	27.6	15.7	22.6	4.1	7.0	40
16 to 19 years	4 383	100.0	22.6	30.5	16.2	21.0	3.6	6.2	40
20 to 24 years	4 083	100.0	23.4	24.6	15.1	24.3	4.7	7.9	42
25 years and over	54 148	100.0	21.0	24.8	15.0	28.1	6.1	5.0	52
25 to 34 years	9 118	100.0	27.6	26.9	13.4	21.6	5.0	5.5	36
35 to 44 years	12 098	100.0	23.6	26.6	15.7	25.5	3.6	4.9	45
45 to 54 years	12 184	100.0	20.8	25.9	15.5	28.3	5.0	4.6	52
55 to 64 years	10 191	100.0	19.7	23.8	15.3	29.2	7.2	4.6	52
65 years and over	10 558	100.0	14.1	20.4	14.8	35.2	9.8	5.7	86
Race and Hispanic or Latino Ethnicity									
White	52 685	100.0	21.1	25.5	15.3	27.5	5.5	5.1	50
Black or African American	5 637	100.0	21.2	22.2	14.4	27.2	8.1	6.9	52
Asian	2 525	100.0	26.2	23.5	14.9	23.4	5.2	6.8	42
Hispanic or Latino ethnicity[2]	5 838	100.0	22.7	23.4	15.2	26.1	6.9	5.7	52
Educational Attainment[3]									
Less than a high school diploma	2 204	100.0	23.6	21.8	13.2	25.2	8.8	7.4	50
High school graduates, no college[4]	10 138	100.0	21.6	22.8	13.9	28.4	6.7	6.6	52
Some college or associate degree	15 562	100.0	22.3	24.0	14.6	28.4	6.1	4.6	51
Bachelor's degree and higher[5]	26 244	100.0	19.8	26.2	15.9	28.0	5.6	4.5	52
Marital Status									
Single, never married	14 851	100.0	24.1	27.2	14.4	23.3	4.5	6.5	40
Married, spouse present	37 719	100.0	20.2	24.5	15.8	28.9	5.9	4.7	52
Other marital status[6]	10 045	100.0	21.2	24.5	13.7	27.5	7.4	5.7	52
Presence of Own Children Under 18 Years[7]									
Men:									
No own children under 18 years old	17 646	100.0	20.4	25.1	13.8	27.6	7.2	5.9	52
With own children under 18 years old	8 758	100.0	20.6	25.4	16.3	29.3	4.0	4.4	52
Women:									
No own children under 18 years old	23 201	100.0	20.2	23.8	15.3	28.2	6.6	5.9	52
With own children under 18 years old	13 009	100.0	25.0	27.6	15.9	24.0	3.6	4.0	40
Employment Status									
Civilian labor force	43 162	100.0	22.8	26.7	15.2	25.5	4.7	5.1	48
Employed	40 401	100.0	22.9	26.8	15.4	25.3	4.5	5.1	47
Full time[8]	31 524	100.0	23.7	26.8	15.4	24.9	4.1	5.0	44
Part time[9]	8 877	100.0	20.0	26.7	15.5	26.7	5.9	5.3	50
Unemployed	2 761	100.0	21.5	25.3	12.9	27.6	7.8	5.0	52
Not in the labor force	19 452	100.0	17.9	21.8	14.9	31.4	8.2	5.8	65

Note: Data on volunteers relate to persons who performed unpaid volunteer activities for an organization at any point from September 1, 2012, through the survey period in September 2013.

[1]For those reporting annual hours.
[2]May be of any race.
[3]Data refer to persons 25 years and over.
[4]Includes persons with a high school diploma or equivalent.
[5]Includes persons with bachelor's, professional, and doctoral degrees.
[6]Includes divorced, separated, and widowed persons.
[7]Own children include sons, daughters, stepchildren, and adopted children. Not included are nieces, nephews, grandchildren, and other related and unrelated children.
[8]Usually work 35 hours or more a week at all jobs.
[9]Usually work less than 35 hours a week at all jobs.

Table 1-74. Volunteers by Type of Main Organization for Which Volunteer Activities Were Performed and Selected Characteristics, September 2013

(Numbers in thousands, percent.)

Characteristic	Total volunteers	Percent distribution of volunteers by type of organization[1]										Not determined
		Total	Civic, political, professional, or international	Educational or youth service	Environmental or animal care	Hospital or other health	Public safety	Religious	Social or community service	Sport, hobby, cultural, or arts	Other	
Sex												
Total, both sexes	62 615	100.0	5.1	25.6	2.7	7.3	1.1	33.0	14.7	4.0	3.9	2.5
Men	26 404	100.0	6.4	24.2	2.5	5.8	2.0	32.0	15.3	4.8	4.4	2.5
Women	36 211	100.0	4.2	26.7	2.8	8.4	0.5	33.8	14.3	3.4	3.6	2.4
Age												
Total, 16 years and over	62 615	100.0	5.1	25.6	2.7	7.3	1.1	33.0	14.7	4.0	3.9	2.5
16 to 24 years	8 466	100.0	4.2	30.1	3.3	8.2	1.7	26.8	14.5	4.0	3.9	3.4
16 to 19 years	4 383	100.0	3.1	35.9	3.6	6.1	0.7	29.1	12.5	3.9	2.4	2.6
20 to 24 years	4 083	100.0	5.4	23.8	2.9	10.5	2.7	24.3	16.6	4.1	5.5	4.2
25 years and over	54 148	100.0	5.3	24.9	2.6	7.1	1.0	34.0	14.7	4.0	4.0	2.3
25 to 34 years	9 118	100.0	4.1	29.1	3.1	7.6	1.1	30.5	13.6	4.0	4.1	2.8
35 to 44 years	12 098	100.0	3.8	40.6	2.0	6.0	1.3	26.4	11.3	3.7	2.6	2.2
45 to 54 years	12 184	100.0	5.2	29.0	3.0	6.1	0.7	32.3	14.1	3.6	3.9	2.0
55 to 64 years	10 191	100.0	6.4	14.5	2.6	8.0	1.1	39.2	16.5	4.7	4.6	2.4
65 years and over	10 558	100.0	6.9	8.8	2.2	8.3	1.0	42.9	18.5	4.2	4.8	2.4
Race and Hispanic or Latino Ethnicity												
White	52 685	100.0	5.3	25.3	3.0	7.3	1.2	32.2	15.0	4.2	4.2	2.4
Black or African American	5 637	100.0	4.5	25.8	0.5	5.0	0.6	44.6	12.2	1.7	2.3	2.8
Asian	2 525	100.0	3.8	30.9	1.5	11.2	0.4	30.1	12.0	3.7	3.3	3.2
Hispanic or Latino ethnicity[2]	5 838	100.0	2.8	31.4	1.2	5.0	0.8	38.8	11.2	3.2	3.2	2.4
Educational Attainment[3]												
Less than a high school diploma	2 204	100.0	3.1	23.8	1.1	5.7	1.3	47.5	10.6	2.0	2.7	2.1
High school graduates, no college[4]	10 138	100.0	4.8	20.3	2.2	6.1	1.5	41.4	14.7	3.3	3.3	2.4
Some college or associate degree	15 562	100.0	5.0	24.2	2.6	7.3	1.3	34.8	15.3	3.3	4.1	2.1
Bachelor's degree and higher[5]	26 244	100.0	5.8	27.3	2.9	7.5	0.7	29.6	14.7	4.9	4.2	2.5
Marital Status												
Single, never married	14 851	100.0	5.0	27.3	3.7	8.5	1.1	26.4	15.7	4.6	4.6	3.1
Married, spouse present	37 719	100.0	5.0	26.9	2.2	6.2	1.1	36.0	13.3	3.7	3.4	2.1
Other marital status[6]	10 045	100.0	5.6	18.6	3.1	9.4	1.1	31.7	18.4	4.1	5.1	3.0
Presence of Own Children Under 18 Years[7]												
Men:												
No own children under 18 years old	17 646	100.0	7.4	17.3	3.1	6.5	2.1	32.9	17.9	4.9	5.3	2.7
With own children under 18 years old	8 758	100.0	4.4	38.3	1.2	4.4	1.9	30.3	10.0	4.8	2.6	2.2
Women:												
No own children under 18 years old	23 201	100.0	5.1	16.6	3.4	9.8	0.6	36.7	17.0	3.8	4.2	2.9
With own children under 18 years old	13 009	100.0	2.7	44.5	1.9	5.8	0.3	28.6	9.5	2.6	2.4	1.7
Employment Status												
Civilian labor force	43 162	100.0	5.4	28.0	2.8	7.3	1.2	30.6	14.1	4.2	3.8	2.6
Employed	40 401	100.0	5.4	28.0	2.9	7.4	1.2	30.7	14.0	4.2	3.8	2.6
Full time[8]	31 524	100.0	5.6	28.0	2.7	7.8	1.4	30.2	13.8	4.3	3.6	2.6
Part time[9]	8 877	100.0	4.5	28.1	3.4	6.3	0.5	32.3	14.6	3.9	4.1	2.4
Unemployed	2 761	100.0	5.7	27.6	2.7	5.8	2.2	29.3	16.0	3.9	4.4	2.4
Not in the labor force	19 452	100.0	4.5	20.5	2.3	7.1	0.9	38.5	16.0	3.6	4.3	2.3

Note: Data on volunteers relate to persons who performed unpaid volunteer activities for an organization at any point from September 1, 2012, through the survey period in September 2013.

[1]Main organization is defined as the organization for which the volunteer worked the most hours during the year.
[2]May be of any race.
[3]Data refer to persons 25 years and over.
[4]Includes persons with a high school diploma or equivalent.
[5]Includes persons with bachelor's, professional, and doctoral degrees.
[6]Includes divorced, separated, and widowed persons.
[7]Own children include sons, daughters, stepchildren, and adopted children. Not included are nieces, nephews, grandchildren, and other related and unrelated children.
[8]Usually work 35 hours or more a week at all jobs.
[9]Usually work less than 35 hours a week at all jobs.

Table 1-75. Main Volunteer Activity for Main Organization for Which Activities Were Performed and Selected Characteristics, September 2013

(Numbers in thousands, percent.)

Characteristic	Total volunteers	Percent distribution of main volunteer activity for main organization[1]					
		Coach, referee, or supervise sports teams	Tutor or teach	Mentor youth	Be an usher, greeter, or minister	Collect, prepare, distribute, or serve food	Collect, make, or distribute clothing, crafts, or goods other than food
Sex							
Total, both sexes	62 615	5.7	9.8	6.7	4.4	10.9	3.7
Men	26 404	9.9	7.5	6.8	5.3	8.8	2.2
Women	36 211	2.6	11.4	6.6	3.8	12.5	4.7
Age							
Total, 16 years and over	62 615	5.7	9.8	6.7	4.4	10.9	3.7
16 to 24 years	8 466	5.6	9.9	9.2	2.5	8.6	3.2
16 to 19 years	4 383	5.2	11.1	9.2	2.5	9.1	3.1
20 to 24 years	4 083	6.0	8.7	9.1	2.6	8.1	3.3
25 years and over	54 148	5.7	9.8	6.3	4.7	11.3	3.7
25 to 34 years	9 118	7.7	11.2	9.0	3.3	8.9	3.1
35 to 44 years	12 098	10.0	11.8	8.4	3.4	9.4	2.9
45 to 54 years	12 184	6.3	10.2	7.0	4.3	10.8	3.6
55 to 64 years	10 191	2.8	8.2	4.5	6.1	12.4	3.6
65 years and over	10 558	1.1	7.1	2.4	6.5	15.0	5.5
Race and Hispanic or Latino Ethnicity							
White	52 685	5.7	9.9	6.4	4.1	10.7	3.6
Black or African American	5 637	6.1	9.0	10.1	7.5	12.5	4.3
Asian	2 525	3.3	11.5	6.1	5.7	13.2	3.2
Hispanic or Latino ethnicity[2]	5 838	6.3	12.7	5.6	5.9	9.9	3.2
Educational Attainment[3]							
Less than a high school diploma	2 204	5.9	8.8	3.7	8.5	15.4	4.7
High school graduates, no college[4]	10 138	6.0	7.7	4.0	5.9	15.6	5.1
Some college or associate degree	15 562	5.2	8.4	6.2	5.1	12.4	4.0
Bachelor's degree and higher[5]	26 244	5.9	11.4	7.5	3.7	8.6	3.0
Marital Status							
Single, never married	14 851	5.3	8.9	8.6	3.3	9.6	3.5
Married, spouse present	37 719	6.3	10.7	6.7	4.9	10.7	3.3
Other marital status[6]	10 045	3.7	7.5	3.8	4.2	13.7	5.4
Presence of Own Children Under 18 Years[7]							
Men:							
No own children under 18 years old	17 646	5.5	6.7	6.1	5.8	9.7	2.4
With own children under 18 years old ...	8 758	18.8	9.1	8.3	4.2	7.1	1.7
Women:							
No own children under 18 years old	23 201	1.8	9.4	5.3	4.4	12.9	5.1
With own children under 18 years old ...	13 009	4.2	15.0	8.9	2.6	11.6	4.0
Employment Status							
Civilian labor force	43 162	7.2	9.8	7.4	4.0	10.1	3.0
Employed	40 401	7.4	9.8	7.4	4.1	9.9	3.0
Full time[8]	31 524	8.4	9.4	7.3	4.1	9.5	2.8
Part time[9]	8 877	3.6	11.2	7.6	4.1	11.2	3.7
Unemployed	2 761	5.2	9.1	7.9	2.7	12.4	3.5
Not in the labor force	19 452	2.3	9.8	5.0	5.3	12.8	5.1

Note: Data on volunteers relate to persons who performed unpaid volunteer activities for an organization at any point from September 1, 2012, through the survey period in September 2013.

[1]Main organization is defined as the organization for which the volunteer worked the most hours during the year.
[2]May be of any race.
[3]Data refer to persons 25 years and over.
[4]Includes persons with a high school diploma or equivalent.
[5]Includes persons with bachelor's, professional, and doctoral degrees.
[6]Includes divorced, separated, and widowed persons.
[7]Own children include sons, daughters, stepchildren, and adopted children. Not included are nieces, nephews, grandchildren, and other related and unrelated children.
[8]Usually work 35 hours or more a week at all jobs.
[9]Usually work less than 35 hours a week at all jobs.

Table 1-75. Main Volunteer Activity for Main Organization for Which Activities Were Performed and Selected Characteristics, September 2013—*Continued*

(Numbers in thousands, percent.)

Characteristic	Percent distribution of main volunteer activity for main organization[1]						
	Fundraise or sell items to raise money	Provide counseling, medical care, fire/EMS, or protective services	Provide general office services	Provide professional or management assistance, including serving on a board or committee	Engage in music, performance, or other artistic activities	Other	Equal time among all
Sex							
Total, both sexes	10.0	2.9	4.4	6.9	3.8	14.9	7.8
Men	8.0	3.3	3.0	8.4	3.8	14.4	7.3
Women	11.5	2.6	5.5	5.8	3.8	15.2	8.1
Age							
Total, 16 years and over	10.0	2.9	4.4	6.9	3.8	14.9	7.8
16 to 24 years	10.6	3.2	3.9	1.3	5.5	17.8	7.9
16 to 19 years	9.2	1.5	3.3	1.0	6.9	17.9	8.0
20 to 24 years	12.1	5.0	4.6	1.5	4.0	17.7	7.7
25 years and over	9.9	2.9	4.5	7.0	3.5	14.4	7.8
25 to 34 years	10.7	3.0	3.7	4.7	3.5	16.0	6.4
35 to 44 years	11.4	3.0	3.6	6.1	2.5	13.3	7.4
45 to 54 years	10.2	2.5	4.0	8.2	3.2	13.1	8.4
55 to 64 years	9.7	3.3	4.4	9.5	4.6	14.4	8.3
65 years and over	7.5	2.5	7.0	10.2	4.0	15.9	8.2
Race and Hispanic or Latino Ethnicity							
White	10.5	2.9	4.5	7.4	3.6	14.9	7.6
Black or African American	6.2	3.0	4.1	3.7	4.7	13.0	9.5
Asian	8.2	3.2	4.2	4.5	4.2	17.2	7.1
Hispanic or Latino ethnicity[2]	7.9	2.4	4.1	2.8	4.8	17.0	7.9
Educational Attainment[3]							
Less than a high school diploma	8.2	2.1	2.4	1.5	3.0	15.8	8.8
High school graduates, no college[4]	9.2	2.3	4.3	3.5	4.0	15.2	7.2
Some college or associate degree	10.4	2.7	5.3	5.4	3.4	14.9	8.2
Bachelor's degree and higher[5]	10.1	3.2	4.3	11.4	3.4	13.7	7.6
Marital Status							
Single, never married	10.1	3.2	4.1	3.6	4.7	17.8	7.6
Married, spouse present	10.0	2.6	4.3	8.5	3.4	13.3	7.9
Other marital status[6]	10.2	3.7	5.6	5.9	3.9	16.4	7.9
Presence of Own Children Under 18 Years[7]							
Men:							
No own children under 18 years old	8.3	3.3	3.2	8.8	4.2	15.8	7.8
With own children under 18 years old ...	7.5	3.3	2.4	7.5	3.1	11.6	6.4
Women:							
No own children under 18 years old	10.5	2.9	5.9	6.3	4.3	16.4	8.3
With own children under 18 years old ...	13.3	2.1	4.9	5.0	2.9	13.1	7.8
Employment Status							
Civilian labor force	10.7	3.1	3.6	7.4	3.7	14.2	7.5
Employed	11.0	3.1	3.6	7.6	3.6	13.9	7.5
Full time[8]	11.3	3.4	3.4	8.2	3.6	13.2	7.3
Part time[9]	9.8	2.2	4.2	5.8	3.8	16.3	8.1
Unemployed	7.1	2.7	4.4	4.0	4.7	18.6	8.0
Not in the labor force	8.4	2.5	6.3	5.8	4.1	16.3	8.4

Note: Data on volunteers relate to persons who performed unpaid volunteer activities for an organization at any point from September 1, 2012, through the survey period in September 2013.

[1]Main organization is defined as the organization for which the volunteer worked the most hours during the year.
[2]May be of any race.
[3]Data refer to persons 25 years and over.
[4]Includes persons with a high school diploma or equivalent.
[5]Includes persons with bachelor's, professional, and doctoral degrees.
[6]Includes divorced, separated, and widowed persons.
[7]Own children include sons, daughters, stepchildren, and adopted children. Not included are nieces, nephews, grandchildren, and other related and unrelated children.
[8]Usually work 35 hours or more a week at all jobs.
[9]Usually work less than 35 hours a week at all jobs.

CHAPTER 2: EMPLOYMENT, HOURS, AND EARNINGS

EMPLOYMENT AND HOURS

HIGHLIGHTS

The employment, hours, and earnings data in this section are presented by industry and state and are derived from the Current Employment Statistics (CES) survey, which covers approximately 554,000 individual worksites and 144,000 business and government agencies. The employment numbers differ from those presented in from the household survey in Chapter 1 because of dissimilarities in methodology, concepts, definitions, and coverage. As the CES survey data are obtained from payroll records, they are consistent for industry classifications.

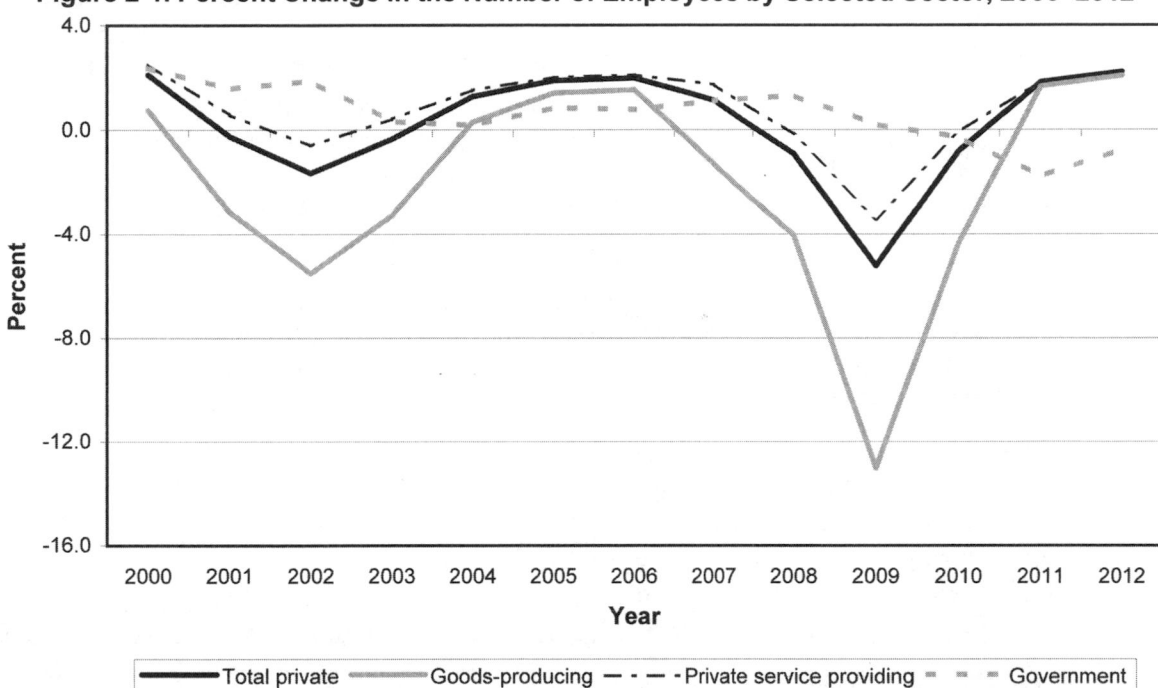

Figure 2-1. Percent Change in the Number of Employees by Selected Sector, 2000–2012

In 2012, total private employment increased for the second consecutive year after declining each year from 2008 to 2010. While employment increased in the goods-producing and private service-providing sectors from 2011 to 2012, it declined 0.8 percent in government in 2012. (See Table 2-1.)

OTHER HIGHLIGHTS

- Within the goods-producing industries, employment in construction increased slightly in 2012 after declining the previous five years. Employment in mining and logging increased 8.0 percent in 2012, while manufacturing employment increased 1.6 percent. (See Table 2-1.)

- From 2000 to 2012, the number of women employees on nonfarm payrolls has increased 4.3 percent. (See Table 2-2.)

- Average weekly hours of all employees on private nonfarm payrolls increased slightly in 2012 to 34.5 hours. Employees in mining and logging worked the longest week (43.9 hours), followed by workers in utilities (41.8 hours) and manufacturing (40.7). Workers in leisure and hospitality worked the shortest (26.1 hours). (See Table 2-6.)

NOTES AND DEFINITIONS

EMPLOYMENT, HOURS, AND EARNINGS

COLLECTION AND COVERAGE

The Bureau of Labor Statistics (BLS) conducts the Current Employment Statistics (CES), or establishment, survey. This survey collects monthly data on employment, hours, and earnings from a sample of nonfarm establishments (including government).

The CES sample includes about 144,000 businesses and government agencies and covers approximately 554,000 individual worksites. The reference period for the CES survey is the pay period which includes the 12th of the month.

The BLS publishes:

- Over 9,000 not seasonally adjusted special derivative series such as average weekly earnings, indexes, and constant dollar series for all employees and production and nonsupervisory employees.

- About 4,900 seasonally adjusted employment, hours, and earnings series for all employees, production and nonsupervisory employees, and women employees.

- Approximately 2,700 series for all employees and production and nonsupervisory employees covering average hourly earnings, average weekly hours. Also, in manufacturing, average weekly overtime hours are published monthly on a not seasonally adjusted basis and cover nearly 700 industries.

- About 2,200 not seasonally adjusted employment series for all employees, production and nonsupervisory employees, and women employees. The series for all employees include over 900 industries at various levels of aggregation.

INDUSTRY CLASSIFICATION

The CES survey completed a conversion from its original quota sample design to a probability-based sample survey design, and switched from the Standard Industrial Classification (SIC) system to the North American Industry Classification System (NAICS) in 2003. The industry-coding update included reconstruction of historical estimates in order to preserve time series for data users. The foundation of industrial classification with NAICS has changed how establishments are classified into industries and how businesses, as they exist today, are recognized. With the release of January 2008 data on February 1, 2008, the CES

National Nonfarm Payroll series was updated to the 2007 North American Industry Classification System (NAICS) from the 2002 NAICS basis. In February 2012, the CES National Nonfarm Payroll series was updated again from the 2007 version to the 2012 version of NAICS with the release of January data.

INDUSTRY EMPLOYMENT

Employment data refer to persons on establishment payrolls who received pay for any part of the pay period containing the 12th day of the month. The data exclude proprietors, the self-employed, unpaid volunteer or family workers, farm workers, and domestic workers. Salaried officers of corporations are included. Government employment covers only civilian employees; military personnel are excluded. Employees of the Central Intelligence Agency, the National Security Agency, the National Imagery and Mapping Agency, and the Defense Intelligence Agency are also excluded.

Persons on establishment payrolls who were on paid sick leave (for cases in which pay is received directly from the firm), paid holiday, or vacation leave, or who work during part of the pay period despite being unemployed or on strike during the rest of the period were counted as employed. Not counted as employed were persons on layoff, on leave without pay, on strike for the entire period, or who had been hired but had not yet reported during to their new jobs.

Beginning with the June 2003 publication of May 2003 data, the CES national federal government employment series has been estimated from a sample of federal establishments and benchmarked annually to counts from unemployment insurance tax records. It reflects employee counts as of the pay period containing the 12th day of the month, which is consistent with other CES industry series. Previously, the national series was an end-of-month count produced by the Office of Personnel Management.

The exclusion of farm employment, self-employment, and domestic service employment accounts from the payroll survey accounts for the differences in employment figures between the household and payroll surveys. The payroll survey also excludes workers on leave without pay. (These workers are counted as employed in the household survey.) Persons who worked in more than one establishment during the reporting period are counted each time their names appear on payrolls; these persons are only counted once in the household survey.

CONCEPTS AND DEFINITIONS

Production and related workers. This category includes working supervisors and all nonsupervisory workers (including group leaders and trainees) engaged in fabricating, processing, assembling, inspecting, receiving, storing, handling, packing, warehousing, shipping, trucking, hauling, maintenance, repair, janitorial, guard services, product development, auxiliary production for plant's own use (such as a power plant), recordkeeping, and other services closely associated with production operations.

Construction workers. This group includes the following employees in the construction division: working supervisors, qualified craft workers, mechanics, apprentices, helpers, and laborers engaged in new work, alterations, demolition, repair, maintenance, and the like, whether working at the site of construction or at jobs in shops or yards at tasks (such as precutting and pre-assembling) ordinarily performed by members of the construction trades.

Nonsupervisory workers. This category consists of employees such as office and clerical workers, repairers, salespersons, operators, drivers, physicians, lawyers, accountants, nurses, social workers, research aides, teachers, drafters, photographers, beauticians, musicians, restaurant workers, custodial workers, attendants, line installers and repairers, laborers, janitors, guards, and other employees at similar occupational levels whose services are closely associated with those of the employees listed. It excludes persons in executive, managerial, and supervisory positions.

Payroll. This refers to payments made to full- and part-time production, construction, or nonsupervisory workers who received pay for any part of the pay period containing the 12th day of the month. The payroll is reported before deductions of any kind, such as those for old age and unemployment insurance, group insurance, withholding tax, bonds, or union dues. Also included is pay for overtime, holidays, and vacation, as well as for sick leave paid directly by the firm. Bonuses (unless earned and paid regularly each pay period), other pay not earned in the pay period reported (such as retroactive pay), tips, and the value of free rent, fuel, meals, or other payment-in-kind are excluded. Employee benefits (such as health and other types of insurance and contributions to retirement, as paid by the employer) are also excluded.

Total hours. During the pay period, total hours include all hours worked (including overtime hours), hours paid for standby or reporting time, and equivalent hours for which employees received pay directly from the employer for sick leave, holidays, vacations, and other leave. Overtime and other premium pay hours are not converted to straight-time equivalent hours. The concept of total hours differs from those of scheduled hours and hours worked. The average weekly hours derived from paid total hours reflect the effects of such factors as unpaid absenteeism, labor turnover, part-time work, and work stoppages, as well as fluctuations in work schedules.

Average weekly hours. The workweek information relates to the average hours for which pay was received and is different from standard or scheduled hours. Such factors as unpaid absenteeism, labor turnover, part-time work, and work stoppages cause average weekly hours to be lower than scheduled hours of work for an establishment. Group averages further reflect changes in the workweeks of component industries.

Overtime hours. These are hours worked by production or related workers for which overtime premiums were paid because the hours were in excess of the number of hours of either the straight-time workday or the total workweek. Weekend and holiday hours are included only if overtime premiums were paid. Hours for which only shift differential, hazard, incentive, or other similar types of premiums were paid are excluded.

Average overtime hours. Overtime hours represent the portion of average weekly hours that exceeded regular hours and for which overtime premiums were paid. If an employee worked during a paid holiday at regular rates, receiving as total compensation his or her holiday pay plus straight-time pay for hours worked that day, no overtime hours would be reported.

Since overtime hours are premium hours by definition, weekly hours and overtime hours do not necessarily move in the same direction from month to month. Factors such as work stoppages, absenteeism, and labor turnover may not have the same influence on overtime hours as on average hours. Diverse trends at the industry group level may also be caused by a marked change in hours for a component industry in which little or no overtime was worked in both the previous and current months.

Industry hours and earnings. Average hours and earnings data are derived from reports of payrolls and hours for production and related workers in manufacturing and natural resources and mining, construction workers in construction, and nonsupervisory employees in private service-providing industries.

Average hourly earnings. Average hourly earnings are on a "gross" basis. They reflect not only changes in basic hourly and incentive wage rates but also such variable factors as premium pay for overtime and late-shift work and changes in output of workers paid on an incentive plan. They also reflect shifts in the number of employees between relatively high-paid and low-paid work and changes in workers' earnings in individual establishments. Averages for groups and divisions further reflect changes in average hourly earnings for individual industries.

Averages of hourly earnings differ from wage rates. Earnings are the actual return to the worker for a stated period; rates are the amount stipulated for a given unit of work or time. The earnings series do not measure the level of total labor costs on the part of the employer because the following items are excluded: irregular bonuses, retroactive items, payroll taxes paid by employers, and earnings for those employees not covered under the definitions of production workers, construction workers, or nonsupervisory employees.

Average hourly earnings, excluding overtime-premium pay, are computed by dividing the total production worker payroll for the industry group by the sum of total production worker hours and one-half of total overtime hours. No adjustments are made for other premium payment provisions, such as holiday pay, late-shift premiums, and overtime rates other than time and one-half.

Average weekly earnings. These estimates are derived by multiplying average weekly hours estimates by average hourly earnings estimates. Therefore, weekly earnings are affected not only by changes in average hourly earnings but also by changes in the length of the workweek. Monthly variations in factors, such as the proportion of part-time workers, work stoppages, labor turnover during the survey period, and absenteeism for which employees are not paid may cause the average workweek to fluctuate.

Long-term trends of average weekly earnings can be affected by structural changes in the makeup of the workforce. For example, persistent long-term increases in the proportion of part-time workers in retail trade and many of the services industries have reduced average workweeks in these industries and have affected the average weekly earnings series.

These earnings are in constant dollars and are calculated from the earnings averages for the current month using a deflator derived from the Consumer Price Index for Urban Wage Earnings and Clerical Workers (CPI-W). The reference year for these series is 1982.

Seasonally adjustment removes the change in employment that is due to normal seasonal hiring or layoffs, thus leaving an over-the-month change that reflects only employment changes due to trend and irregular movements. Seasonally adjusted estimates of employment and other series are generated using the X-12 ARIMA program developed by the United States Census Bureau.

DATA REVISIONS

CES revises published estimates to improve its data series by incorporating additional information that was not available at the time of the initial publication of the estimates. Each year, the CES incorporates a benchmark revision that re-anchors estimates to nearly complete employment counts available from Quarterly Census of Employment and Wages (QCEW) data, County Business Pattern data, and other state collected data. The benchmark helps to control for sampling error in the estimates. See more about the QCEW later in this chapter.

It can be nearly 2 years before not seasonally adjusted CES estimates are considered final. The first preliminary CES estimates of employment, hours, and earnings are published each month approximately 3 weeks after the reference period. Estimates are then revised twice before being held constant until the annual benchmark release. Second preliminary estimates for a given month are published the month following the initial release, and final sample-based estimates are published 2 months after the initial release. The annual benchmark revisions affect nearly 2 years of data, so most months are subject to revisions during 2 separate benchmark periods.

SOURCES OF ADDITIONAL INFORMATION

For further information on sampling, estimation methods, and data revisions for national data visit the Employment, Hours, and Earnings homepage on the BLS Web site at http://www.bls.gov/ces. For more information on state and area data, please visit the BLS Web site at http://www.bls.gov/sae.

Table 2-1. Employees on Nonfarm Payrolls, by Super Sector and Selected Component Groups, NAICS Basis, 2000–2012

(Thousands of people.)

Industry	2000	2001	2002	2003	2004	2005	2006	2007	2008	2009	2010	2011	2012
TOTAL	131 881	131 919	130 450	130 100	131 509	133 747	136 125	137 645	136 852	130 876	129 917	131 497	133 739
Total Private	111 091	110 800	108 937	108 517	109 888	111 943	114 151	115 427	114 342	108 321	107 427	109 411	111 822
Goods-Producing	24 649	23 873	22 557	21 816	21 882	22 190	22 530	22 233	21 335	18 558	17 751	18 047	18 410
Mining and Logging	599	606	583	572	591	628	684	724	767	694	705	788	851
Mining	520	533	512	503	523	562	620	664	710	643	655	739	800
Logging	79	74	70	69	68	65	64	60	57	50	50	49	50
Construction	6 787	6 826	6 716	6 735	6 976	7 336	7 691	7 630	7 162	6 016	5 518	5 533	5 641
Construction of buildings	1 633	1 589	1 575	1 576	1 630	1 712	1 805	1 774	1 642	1 357	1 230	1 222	1 236
Heavy and civil engineering	937	953	931	903	907	951	985	1 005	965	851	825	837	871
Specialty trade contractors	4 217	4 284	4 210	4 256	4 439	4 673	4 901	4 850	4 556	3 808	3 463	3 474	3 534
Manufacturing	17 263	16 441	15 259	14 509	14 315	14 227	14 155	13 879	13 406	11 847	11 528	11 726	11 919
Durable goods	10 877	10 336	9 485	8 964	8 925	8 956	8 981	8 808	8 463	7 284	7 064	7 273	7 462
Wood product	615	576	557	540	552	561	561	517	458	360	342	337	338
Nonmetallic mineral product	554	545	516	494	506	505	510	501	465	394	371	367	364
Primary metals	622	571	509	477	467	466	464	456	442	362	362	388	402
Fabricated metal product	1 753	1 676	1 549	1 479	1 497	1 522	1 553	1 563	1 528	1 312	1 282	1 347	1 411
Machinery	1 457	1 371	1 232	1 152	1 145	1 166	1 183	1 187	1 188	1 029	996	1 056	1 098
Computer and electronic product	1 820	1 749	1 507	1 355	1 323	1 316	1 308	1 273	1 244	1 137	1 095	1 104	1 094
Electrical equipment and appliances	591	557	497	460	445	434	433	429	424	374	360	366	370
Transportation equipment	2 057	1 939	1 830	1 775	1 767	1 772	1 769	1 712	1 608	1 348	1 333	1 382	1 456
Furniture and related product	680	643	605	574	574	566	558	529	478	384	357	353	350
Miscellaneous manufacturing	728	710	683	658	651	647	644	642	629	584	567	574	580
Nondurable goods	6 386	6 105	5 774	5 546	5 390	5 271	5 174	5 071	4 943	4 564	4 464	4 453	4 456
Food manufacturing	1 553	1 551	1 526	1 518	1 494	1 478	1 479	1 484	1 481	1 456	1 451	1 459	1 469
Beverage	175	177	174	169	166	167	171	176	177	169	167	171	178
Textile mills	378	333	291	261	237	218	195	170	151	124	119	120	118
Textile product mills	230	217	204	188	183	176	167	158	147	126	119	118	117
Apparel	484	415	350	304	278	251	232	215	199	168	157	152	148
Paper and paper product	605	578	547	516	496	484	471	458	445	407	395	387	379
Printing and related support activities	807	768	707	680	663	646	634	622	594	522	488	472	462
Petroleum and coal product	123	121	118	114	112	112	113	115	117	115	114	112	113
Chemicals	980	959	928	906	887	872	866	861	847	804	787	784	784
Plastics and rubber product	951	896	847	814	805	802	786	757	729	625	625	635	645
Private Service-Providing	86 442	86 927	86 380	86 701	88 006	89 753	91 621	93 194	93 008	89 764	89 676	91 363	93 411
Trade, Transportation, and Utilities	26 225	25 983	25 497	25 287	25 533	25 959	26 276	26 630	26 293	24 906	24 636	25 065	25 516
Wholesale Trade	5 933	5 773	5 652	5 608	5 663	5 764	5 905	6 015	5 943	5 587	5 452	5 543	5 673
Durable goods	3 251	3 130	3 008	2 941	2 951	2 999	3 075	3 122	3 052	2 810	2 714	2 765	2 830
Nondurable goods	2 065	2 031	2 015	2 005	2 010	2 022	2 041	2 062	2 048	1 966	1 928	1 939	1 972
Electronic markets, agents, and brokers	618	611	629	662	702	743	789	832	843	811	811	839	871
Retail Trade	15 280	15 239	15 025	14 917	15 058	15 280	15 353	15 520	15 283	14 522	14 440	14 668	14 875
Motor vehicle and parts dealers	1 847	1 855	1 879	1 883	1 902	1 919	1 910	1 908	1 831	1 638	1 629	1 691	1 732
Furniture and home furnishing stores	544	541	539	547	563	576	587	575	531	449	438	439	442
Electronic and appliance stores	647	633	595	574	572	585	581	583	570	516	522	527	512
Building material and garden supply stores	1 142	1 152	1 177	1 185	1 227	1 276	1 324	1 309	1 248	1 156	1 132	1 146	1 170
Food and beverage stores	2 993	2 951	2 882	2 838	2 822	2 818	2 821	2 844	2 862	2 830	2 808	2 823	2 859
Health and personal care stores	928	952	939	938	941	954	961	993	1 003	986	981	981	1 003
Gasoline stations	936	925	896	882	876	871	864	862	842	826	819	831	841
Clothing and clothing accessories stores	1 322	1 321	1 313	1 305	1 364	1 415	1 451	1 500	1 468	1 364	1 353	1 361	1 408
Sporting goods, hobby, and music stores	603	601	592	585	586	598	606	623	622	589	579	578	579
General merchandise stores	2 820	2 842	2 812	2 822	2 863	2 934	2 935	3 021	3 026	2 966	2 998	3 085	3 088
Miscellaneous store retailers	1 007	993	960	931	914	900	881	865	843	782	762	772	798
Nonstore retailers	492	474	444	427	429	435	433	438	438	421	421	434	443
Transportation and Warehousing	4 410	4 372	4 224	4 185	4 249	4 361	4 470	4 541	4 508	4 236	4 191	4 302	4 415
Air transportation	614	615	564	528	515	501	487	492	491	463	458	457	458
Rail transportation	232	227	218	218	226	228	228	234	231	218	216	228	230
Water transportation	56	54	53	55	56	61	63	66	67	63	62	61	63
Truck transportation	1 406	1 387	1 339	1 326	1 352	1 398	1 436	1 439	1 389	1 268	1 250	1 301	1 351
Transit and ground passenger transportation	372	375	381	382	385	389	399	412	423	422	430	440	448
Pipeline transportation	46	45	42	40	38	38	39	40	42	43	42	43	44
Scenic and sightseeing transportation	28	29	26	27	27	29	28	29	28	28	27	28	27
Support activities for transportation	537	539	525	520	535	552	571	584	592	549	543	562	578
Couriers and messengers	605	587	561	562	557	571	582	581	573	546	528	529	533
Warehousing and storage	514	514	517	528	558	595	638	665	672	637	633	653	682
Utilities	601	599	596	577	564	554	549	553	559	560	553	553	554
Information	3 630	3 629	3 395	3 188	3 118	3 061	3 038	3 032	2 984	2 804	2 707	2 674	2 678
Publishing industries, except Internet	1 035	1 021	964	925	909	904	902	901	880	796	759	749	738
Motion picture and sound recording industry	383	377	388	376	385	378	376	381	371	358	370	362	372
Broadcasting, except Internet	344	345	334	324	325	328	328	325	319	301	290	283	285
Internet publishing and broadcasting and web search portals	111	100	76	67	66	67	69	73	81	83	92	110	121
Telecommunications	1 397	1 424	1 281	1 167	1 115	1 071	1 048	1 031	1 019	966	903	874	858
Other information services	157	147	124	116	117	118	121	126	134	135	142	160	174

Table 2-1. Employees on Nonfarm Payrolls, by Super Sector and Selected Component Groups, NAICS Basis, 2000–2012—*Continued*

(Thousands of people.)

Industry	2000	2001	2002	2003	2004	2005	2006	2007	2008	2009	2010	2011	2012
Financial Activities	7 783	7 900	7 956	8 078	8 105	8 197	8 367	8 348	8 206	7 838	7 695	7 697	7 786
Finance and insurance	5 773	5 862	5 922	6 021	6 019	6 063	6 194	6 179	6 076	5 844	5 761	5 769	5 834
Monetary authorities, central bank	23	23	23	23	22	21	21	22	22	21	20	18	17
Credit intermediation	2 548	2 598	2 686	2 792	2 817	2 869	2 925	2 866	2 733	2 590	2 550	2 554	2 579
Securities, commodity contracts, and investments	805	831	789	758	766	786	818	849	864	811	801	811	814
Insurance carriers and related activities	2 317	2 326	2 342	2 367	2 333	2 303	2 342	2 354	2 367	2 333	2 304	2 300	2 337
Funds, trusts, and other financial vehicles	81	84	82	80	82	84	88	89	91	88	87	86	87
Real estate and rental and leasing	2 011	2 038	2 033	2 058	2 086	2 134	2 173	2 169	2 130	1 994	1 934	1 927	1 952
Real estate	1 316	1 343	1 357	1 387	1 419	1 461	1 499	1 500	1 485	1 420	1 396	1 401	1 417
Rental and leasing services	667	666	649	643	641	646	646	640	617	547	514	502	511
Lessors of nonfinancial intangible assets	28	29	28	27	26	27	28	28	28	27	25	24	24
Professional and Business Services	16 666	16 476	15 976	15 987	16 394	16 954	17 566	17 942	17 735	16 579	16 728	17 332	17 930
Professional and technical services	6 702	6 871	6 649	6 603	6 747	7 025	7 357	7 660	7 799	7 509	7 441	7 666	7 893
Management of companies and enterprises	1 796	1 779	1 705	1 687	1 724	1 759	1 811	1 866	1 905	1 867	1 872	1 934	2 008
Administrative and waste services	8 168	7 826	7 622	7 697	7 923	8 170	8 398	8 416	8 032	7 203	7 414	7 732	8 029
Administrative and support services	7 855	7 509	7 304	7 375	7 594	7 833	8 050	8 061	7 675	6 852	7 057	7 367	7 657
Waste management and remediation services	313	317	318	322	329	338	348	355	357	352	357	365	373
Education and Health Services	15 109	15 645	16 199	16 588	16 953	17 372	17 826	18 322	18 838	19 193	19 531	19 883	20 319
Education services	2 390	2 511	2 643	2 695	2 763	2 836	2 901	2 941	3 040	3 090	3 155	3 250	3 347
Health care and social assistance	12 718	13 134	13 556	13 893	14 190	14 536	14 925	15 380	15 798	16 103	16 375	16 634	16 972
Ambulatory health care services	4 320	4 462	4 633	4 786	4 952	5 114	5 286	5 474	5 647	5 793	5 975	6 136	6 318
Hospitals	3 954	4 051	4 160	4 245	4 285	4 345	4 423	4 515	4 627	4 667	4 679	4 722	4 791
Nursing and residential health facilities	2 583	2 676	2 743	2 786	2 818	2 855	2 893	2 958	3 016	3 082	3 124	3 168	3 194
Social assistance	1 860	1 946	2 020	2 075	2 135	2 222	2 324	2 433	2 508	2 560	2 599	2 608	2 669
Leisure and Hospitality	11 862	12 036	11 986	12 173	12 493	12 816	13 110	13 427	13 436	13 077	13 049	13 353	13 746
Arts, entertainment, and recreation	1 788	1 824	1 783	1 813	1 850	1 892	1 929	1 969	1 970	1 916	1 913	1 919	1 965
Performing arts and spectator sports	382	382	364	372	368	376	399	405	406	397	406	394	404
Museums, historical sites	110	115	114	115	118	121	124	130	132	129	128	133	136
Amusements, gambling, and recreation	1 296	1 327	1 305	1 327	1 364	1 395	1 406	1 434	1 433	1 389	1 379	1 392	1 426
Accommodation and food services	10 074	10 211	10 203	10 360	10 643	10 923	11 181	11 457	11 466	11 162	11 135	11 434	11 780
Accommodation	1 884	1 852	1 779	1 775	1 790	1 819	1 832	1 867	1 869	1 763	1 760	1 801	1 817
Food services and drinking places	8 189	8 359	8 425	8 584	8 854	9 104	9 349	9 590	9 598	9 399	9 376	9 633	9 963
Other Services	5 168	5 258	5 372	5 401	5 409	5 395	5 438	5 494	5 515	5 367	5 331	5 360	5 437
Repair and maintenance	1 242	1 257	1 247	1 234	1 229	1 236	1 249	1 253	1 227	1 150	1 139	1 169	1 191
Personal and laundry services	1 243	1 255	1 257	1 264	1 273	1 277	1 288	1 310	1 323	1 281	1 265	1 289	1 313
Membership associations and organizations	2 683	2 746	2 868	2 904	2 908	2 882	2 901	2 931	2 966	2 936	2 926	2 903	2 933
Government	20 790	21 118	21 513	21 583	21 621	21 804	21 974	22 218	22 509	22 555	22 490	22 086	21 917
Federal	2 865	2 764	2 766	2 761	2 730	2 732	2 732	2 734	2 762	2 832	2 977	2 859	2 814
Federal, excluding U.S. Postal Service	1 985	1 891	1 924	1 952	1 948	1 957	1 963	1 965	2 014	2 129	2 318	2 228	2 203
State	4 786	4 905	5 029	5 002	4 982	5 032	5 075	5 122	5 177	5 169	5 137	5 078	5 052
State, excluding education	2 756	2 792	2 786	2 748	2 744	2 772	2 782	2 804	2 823	2 809	2 764	2 704	2 667
Local	13 139	13 449	13 718	13 820	13 909	14 041	14 167	14 362	14 571	14 554	14 376	14 150	14 051
Local, excluding education	5 845	5 970	6 063	6 110	6 144	6 185	6 254	6 376	6 487	6 475	6 363	6 278	6 272

Table 2-2. Women Employees on Nonfarm Payrolls, by Super Sector and Selected Component Groups, NAICS Basis, 2000–2012

(Thousands of people.)

Industry	2000	2001	2002	2003	2004	2005	2006	2007	2008	2009	2010	2011	2012
TOTAL NONFARM	63 282	63 741	63 427	63 299	63 783	64 744	65 549	66 834	67 121	65 250	64 719	65 084	66 020
Total Private	51 511	51 726	51 100	50 963	51 448	52 355	53 331	54 256	54 213	52 350	51 890	52 472	53 526
Goods-Producing	6 297	5 961	5 486	5 192	5 117	5 104	5 083	5 041	4 866	4 289	4 088	4 057	4 091
Mining and logging	92	90	85	80	80	79	82	93	101	98	98	105	113
Construction	846	832	827	822	841	890	944	947	916	801	723	711	724
Manufacturing	5 359	5 039	4 574	4 290	4 197	4 135	4 057	4 001	3 848	3 390	3 268	3 241	3 254
Private Service-Providing	45 214	45 765	45 613	45 771	46 331	47 252	48 248	49 215	49 347	48 061	47 801	48 416	49 435
Trade, transportation, and utilities	10 859	10 768	10 466	10 321	10 364	10 535	10 627	10 849	10 782	10 233	10 007	10 091	10 285
Wholesale trade	1 827	1 770	1 718	1 700	1 714	1 738	1 796	1 831	1 820	1 705	1 640	1 667	1 704
Retail trade	7 680	7 635	7 449	7 339	7 387	7 524	7 587	7 758	7 713	7 361	7 226	7 280	7 417
Transportation and warehousing	1 202	1 212	1 149	1 134	1 117	1 130	1 098	1 110	1 098	1 024	1 002	1 009	1 027
Utilities	151	151	150	147	146	143	146	150	151	143	139	135	138
Information	1 697	1 684	1 554	1 428	1 366	1 333	1 306	1 285	1 260	1 170	1 104	1 084	1 076
Financial activities	4 697	4 784	4 822	4 892	4 876	4 923	5 055	4 988	4 851	4 648	4 530	4 490	4 520
Professional and business services	7 680	7 591	7 314	7 248	7 360	7 574	7 779	8 007	7 946	7 472	7 454	7 686	7 930
Education and health services	11 586	12 037	12 474	12 786	13 073	13 408	13 764	14 178	14 574	14 851	15 067	15 277	15 588
Leisure and hospitality	6 082	6 224	6 215	6 319	6 516	6 708	6 903	7 054	7 056	6 861	6 819	6 964	7 178
Other services	2 614	2 677	2 769	2 779	2 776	2 772	2 814	2 854	2 880	2 824	2 820	2 823	2 857
Government	11 771	12 015	12 327	12 337	12 335	12 389	12 218	12 578	12 908	12 900	12 829	12 611	12 494
Federal	1 231	1 148	1 155	1 173	1 168	1 177	1 194	1 202	1 224	1 259	1 326	1 269	1 247
State	2 464	2 534	2 621	2 599	2 562	2 575	2 630	2 651	2 684	2 628	2 639	2 643	2 646
Local	8 076	8 333	8 551	8 565	8 606	8 637	8 395	8 725	9 000	9 014	8 864	8 700	8 601

Table 2-3. Production Workers on Private Nonfarm Payrolls, by Super Sector, NAICS Basis, 2000–2012

(Thousands of people.)

Industry	2000	2001	2002	2003	2004	2005	2006	2007	2008	2009	2010	2011	2012
TOTAL PRIVATE	90 418	90 061	88 484	87 744	89 000	91 171	93 483	94 941	94 322	89 231	88 548	90 221	92 393
Goods-Producing	18 169	17 466	16 400	15 732	15 821	16 145	16 559	16 405	15 724	13 399	12 774	13 005	13 280
Mining and logging	446	457	436	420	440	473	519	547	574	510	525	594	643
Construction	5 295	5 332	5 196	5 123	5 309	5 611	5 903	5 883	5 521	4 567	4 172	4 184	4 243
Manufacturing	12 428	11 677	10 768	10 189	10 072	10 060	10 137	9 975	9 629	8 322	8 077	8 228	8 394
Private Service-Providing	72 249	72 595	72 084	72 012	73 179	75 027	76 924	78 537	78 598	75 832	75 774	77 217	79 112
Trade, transportation, and utilities	21 965	21 709	21 337	21 078	21 319	21 830	22 166	22 546	22 337	21 116	20 874	21 234	21 654
Wholesale trade	4 686	4 555	4 474	4 396	4 444	4 584	4 724	4 851	4 822	4 506	4 378	4 443	4 567
Retail trade	13 040	12 952	12 774	12 655	12 788	13 030	13 110	13 317	13 134	12 472	12 425	12 647	12 825
Transportation and warehousing	3 753	3 718	3 611	3 563	3 637	3 774	3 889	3 935	3 931	3 688	3 627	3 703	3 820
Utilities	485	483	478	464	450	443	443	444	450	451	444	441	442
Information	2 502	2 531	2 398	2 347	2 371	2 386	2 399	2 403	2 388	2 240	2 170	2 148	2 165
Financial activities	5 819	5 888	5 964	6 052	6 052	6 127	6 312	6 365	6 320	6 066	5 942	5 900	5 988
Professional and business services	13 790	13 588	13 049	12 911	13 287	13 854	14 446	14 784	14 585	13 520	13 699	14 251	14 805
Education and health services	13 362	13 846	14 311	14 532	14 771	15 129	15 539	15 999	16 488	16 841	17 125	17 421	17 819
Leisure and hospitality	10 516	10 662	10 576	10 666	10 955	11 263	11 568	11 861	11 873	11 560	11 507	11 772	12 134
Other services	4 296	4 373	4 449	4 426	4 425	4 438	4 494	4 578	4 606	4 488	4 458	4 491	4 547

Table 2-4. Production Workers on Manufacturing Payrolls, by Industry, NAICS Basis, 2000–2012

(Thousands of people.)

Industry	2000	2001	2002	2003	2004	2005	2006	2007	2008	2009	2010	2011	2012
Total Manufacturing	12 428	11 677	10 768	10 189	10 072	10 060	10 137	9 975	9 629	8 322	8 077	8 228	8 394
Durable Goods	7 659	7 164	6 530	6 152	6 140	6 220	6 355	6 250	5 975	4 990	4 829	4 986	5 146
Wood products	507	470	450	434	445	454	451	407	358	278	269	269	271
Nometallic mineral products	440	427	399	375	388	387	391	384	363	303	284	278	272
Primary metals	490	447	396	370	364	363	363	358	348	273	275	301	317
Fabricated metal products	1 326	1 254	1 147	1 093	1 109	1 129	1 162	1 171	1 143	961	935	994	1 051
Machinery	961	891	787	732	730	749	770	774	772	641	616	662	700
Computer and electronic products	949	876	744	673	656	700	756	744	730	654	629	630	631
Electrical equipment and appliances	433	402	352	320	307	300	303	305	305	266	251	248	247
Transportation equipment	1 498	1 399	1 310	1 269	1 265	1 277	1 304	1 275	1 177	948	937	972	1 021
Furniture and related products	544	509	475	445	444	436	433	409	364	284	263	260	258
Miscellaneous manufacturing	510	490	469	442	432	424	423	425	416	382	370	373	379
Nondurable Goods	4 769	4 513	4 238	4 037	3 932	3 841	3 782	3 725	3 653	3 332	3 248	3 241	3 248
Food manufacturing	1 228	1 221	1 202	1 193	1 178	1 170	1 172	1 184	1 184	1 161	1 152	1 158	1 169
Textile mills	315	276	242	217	194	174	158	137	122	99	96	98	96
Textile products mills	183	174	162	148	147	143	135	123	115	98	92	89	85
Apparel	404	341	286	242	219	193	182	173	163	132	120	112	109
Paper and paper products	468	446	421	393	374	365	357	351	344	313	302	295	287
Printing and related support	576	544	493	471	460	447	447	443	425	369	342	327	316
Petroleum and coal products	83	81	78	74	77	75	72	73	77	70	70	70	73
Chemicals	588	562	532	525	520	510	508	504	513	479	474	480	491
Plastics and rubber products	753	704	662	633	626	620	608	592	572	477	472	482	487

Table 2-5. Total Employees on Manufacturing Payrolls, by Industry, NAICS Basis, 2000–2012

(Thousands of people.)

Industry	2000	2001	2002	2003	2004	2005	2006	2007	2008	2009	2010	2011	2012
Total Manufacturing	17 263	16 441	15 259	14 509	14 315	14 227	14 155	13 879	13 406	11 847	11 528	11 726	11 919
Durable Goods	10 877	10 336	9 485	8 964	8 925	8 956	8 981	8 808	8 463	7 284	7 064	7 273	7 462
Wood products	615	576	557	540	552	561	561	517	458	360	342	337	338
Nometallic mineral products	554	545	516	494	506	505	510	501	465	394	371	367	364
Primary metals	622	571	509	477	467	466	464	456	442	362	362	388	402
Fabricated metal products	1 753	1 676	1 549	1 479	1 497	1 522	1 553	1 563	1 528	1 312	1 282	1 347	1 411
Machinery	1 457	1 371	1 232	1 152	1 145	1 166	1 183	1 187	1 188	1 029	996	1 056	1 098
Computer and electronic products	1 820	1 749	1 507	1 355	1 323	1 316	1 308	1 273	1 244	1 137	1 095	1 104	1 094
Electrical equipment and appliances	591	557	497	460	445	434	433	429	424	374	360	366	370
Transportation equipment	2 057	1 939	1 830	1 775	1 767	1 772	1 769	1 712	1 608	1 348	1 333	1 382	1 456
Furniture and related products	680	643	605	574	574	566	558	529	478	384	357	353	350
Miscellaneous manufacturing	728	710	683	658	651	647	644	642	629	584	567	574	580
Nondurable Goods	6 386	6 105	5 774	5 546	5 390	5 271	5 174	5 071	4 943	4 564	4 464	4 453	4 456
Food manufacturing	1 550	1 551	1 526	1 518	1 494	1 478	1 479	1 484	1 481	1 456	1 451	1 459	1 469
Beverage	175	177	174	169	166	167	171	176	177	169	167	171	178
Tobacco and tobacco products	32	32	34	31	29	25	24	22	22	19	17	16	14
Textile mills	378	333	291	261	237	218	195	170	151	124	119	120	118
Textile products mills	230	217	204	188	183	176	167	158	147	126	119	118	117
Apparel	484	415	350	304	278	251	232	215	199	168	157	152	148
Leather and allied products	69	58	50	45	42	40	37	34	33	29	28	29	29
Paper and paper products	605	578	547	516	496	484	471	458	445	407	395	387	379
Printing and related support	807	768	707	680	663	646	634	622	594	522	488	472	462
Petroleum and coal products	123	121	118	114	112	112	113	115	117	115	114	112	113
Chemicals	980	959	928	906	887	872	866	861	847	804	787	784	784
Plastics and rubber products	951	896	847	814	805	802	786	757	729	625	625	635	645

Table 2-6. Average Weekly Hours of All Employees on Private Nonfarm Payrolls by NAICS Super Sector, 2007–2012

(Hours per week, seasonally adjusted.)

Year and month	Total private	Mining and logging	Construction	Manufacturing	Trade, transportation, and utilities				Information	Financial activities	Professional and business services	Education and health services	Leisure and hospitality	Other services
					Total	Wholesale trade	Retail trade	Utilities						
2007	34.6	44.0	38.0	40.0	34.5	38.1	31.7	41.8	36.1	36.6	35.4	33.5	26.1	32.9
2008	34.5	43.7	37.8	39.8	34.4	38.4	31.4	42.0	36.5	36.5	35.2	33.7	25.9	32.9
2009	33.9	42.1	37.1	39.0	34.1	37.9	31.3	40.9	36.5	36.6	35.0	33.0	25.6	31.6
2010	34.1	43.4	37.8	40.2	34.2	38.1	31.3	41.1	36.5	36.9	35.4	32.8	25.7	31.6
2011	34.4	44.5	38.3	40.5	34.6	38.6	31.6	41.8	36.6	37.3	35.7	32.8	25.9	31.7
2012	34.5	43.9	38.8	40.7	34.6	38.7	31.6	41.8	36.6	37.4	36.0	32.9	26.1	31.6
2008														
January	34.6	43.7	38.3	40.0	34.6	38.3	31.7	42.3	36.5	36.5	35.2	33.6	26.0	32.6
February	34.6	43.8	38.3	40.1	34.6	38.4	31.7	42.2	36.5	36.6	35.2	33.7	25.9	32.9
March	34.7	44.8	38.2	40.3	34.6	38.5	31.7	42.7	36.5	36.6	35.4	34.0	25.9	33.1
April	34.6	42.9	38.1	39.9	34.5	38.4	31.5	42.0	36.6	36.6	35.2	33.8	26.0	33.0
May	34.6	43.5	38.0	40.0	34.5	38.4	31.5	42.2	36.5	36.7	35.3	33.8	26.0	32.9
June	34.6	44.0	38.0	40.1	34.5	38.5	31.5	42.4	36.6	36.6	35.2	33.8	25.9	32.8
July	34.5	43.3	37.8	39.8	34.5	38.6	31.4	41.8	36.6	36.5	35.3	33.8	25.8	32.9
August	34.5	43.7	37.9	39.9	34.5	38.7	31.4	41.6	36.6	36.7	35.3	33.7	25.9	33.0
September	34.4	42.8	37.5	39.6	34.4	38.5	31.4	41.8	36.7	36.5	35.2	33.7	25.8	32.9
October	34.4	44.3	38.3	39.6	34.4	38.4	31.3	41.6	36.7	36.6	35.3	33.6	25.9	32.8
November	34.3	44.0	37.2	39.4	34.3	38.3	31.3	41.7	36.6	36.6	35.2	33.6	25.7	32.9
December	34.1	43.3	37.4	39.1	34.0	38.3	30.7	41.5	36.7	36.6	35.1	33.5	25.6	32.9
2009														
January	34.2	43.0	37.2	38.8	34.3	38.4	31.3	41.6	36.5	36.7	35.1	33.6	25.6	32.6
February	34.0	42.9	37.3	39.0	34.2	38.2	31.2	41.9	36.5	36.6	35.0	33.2	25.5	32.1
March	33.9	42.5	37.2	38.6	34.2	38.0	31.2	41.1	36.4	36.6	35.0	33.1	25.5	31.5
April	33.8	41.9	37.1	38.7	34.1	37.9	31.2	40.9	36.3	36.6	35.0	33.0	25.5	31.3
May	33.8	41.5	37.2	38.5	34.2	37.9	31.3	40.5	36.5	36.6	35.1	32.9	25.5	31.5
June	33.8	41.9	37.2	38.7	34.0	37.8	31.2	40.4	36.4	36.4	35.0	32.8	25.5	31.4
July	33.8	42.0	37.4	38.9	34.0	37.7	31.2	40.8	36.5	36.6	35.0	32.9	25.5	31.4
August	33.8	42.2	37.3	39.2	34.0	37.7	31.1	40.8	36.3	36.5	35.0	32.9	25.5	31.5
September	33.9	42.2	37.0	39.1	34.2	37.6	31.5	40.4	36.4	36.6	35.0	32.9	25.6	31.4
October	33.8	42.0	37.2	39.2	34.1	37.7	31.3	40.6	36.4	36.7	34.9	32.7	25.5	31.4
November	33.9	42.5	37.4	39.6	34.1	37.8	31.3	40.9	36.6	36.6	35.2	32.7	25.6	31.5
December	33.9	42.4	37.2	39.7	34.0	37.7	31.1	40.6	36.5	36.7	35.2	32.8	25.6	31.6
2010														
January	34.0	43.0	37.4	39.9	34.0	37.8	31.2	40.5	36.6	36.8	35.4	33.0	25.6	31.6
February	33.9	43.0	36.4	39.6	34.0	37.8	31.3	40.6	36.4	36.8	35.1	32.8	25.7	31.6
March	34.0	43.3	37.3	40.0	34.0	37.9	31.2	40.5	36.5	36.9	35.4	32.8	25.7	31.6
April	34.1	43.6	38.0	40.2	34.2	38.1	31.3	40.9	36.5	36.9	35.3	32.8	25.8	31.7
May	34.2	43.9	37.7	40.5	34.2	38.1	31.3	41.3	36.6	37.0	35.4	32.8	25.8	31.7
June	34.1	43.3	37.7	40.2	34.2	38.1	31.3	41.1	36.6	37.2	35.2	32.8	25.7	31.6
July	34.2	43.8	37.6	40.2	34.4	38.2	31.5	41.2	36.6	37.0	35.5	32.8	25.8	31.7
August	34.2	43.9	37.9	40.3	34.4	38.2	31.5	41.3	36.7	37.0	35.4	32.8	25.8	31.8
September	34.3	43.4	38.2	40.4	34.4	38.4	31.4	41.3	36.6	37.1	35.6	32.8	25.8	31.9
October	34.3	43.7	38.1	40.4	34.5	38.4	31.5	41.7	36.8	37.1	35.7	32.8	25.9	31.8
November	34.2	42.9	38.1	40.4	34.4	38.3	31.4	41.4	36.6	37.1	35.5	32.8	25.9	31.7
December	34.3	44.0	37.9	40.4	34.6	38.4	31.6	42.0	36.5	37.1	35.7	32.7	25.8	31.7
2011														
January	34.2	44.5	37.6	40.3	34.4	38.5	31.4	41.8	36.5	37.1	35.6	32.7	25.8	31.7
February	34.3	44.1	37.7	40.4	34.5	38.5	31.4	41.4	36.6	37.1	35.7	32.7	25.9	31.7
March	34.3	44.4	37.9	40.5	34.6	38.6	31.5	42.1	36.6	37.0	35.7	32.8	25.8	31.8
April	34.4	44.5	38.1	40.4	34.7	38.6	31.7	42.0	36.6	37.2	35.7	32.9	26.0	31.8
May	34.4	44.8	38.5	40.5	34.5	38.6	31.5	41.9	36.7	37.2	35.7	33.0	25.8	31.8
June	34.3	44.6	38.3	40.4	34.6	38.7	31.5	41.7	36.6	37.3	35.7	32.8	25.8	31.8
July	34.4	44.2	38.4	40.3	34.6	38.7	31.6	41.4	36.7	37.4	35.8	33.0	25.9	31.8
August	34.3	44.1	38.2	40.4	34.5	38.6	31.5	41.4	36.5	37.2	35.7	32.7	25.9	31.6
September	34.4	44.6	38.3	40.4	34.7	38.8	31.7	42.4	36.7	37.5	35.8	32.8	25.9	31.7
October	34.4	45.4	38.2	40.6	34.6	38.8	31.7	42.3	36.7	37.4	35.8	32.8	26.1	31.7
November	34.4	43.9	38.2	40.5	34.6	38.8	31.7	41.7	36.8	37.4	35.8	32.8	26.1	31.7
December	34.5	44.6	38.5	40.6	34.7	38.8	31.8	41.1	36.7	37.3	35.9	32.8	26.1	31.7
2012														
January	34.5	45.4	38.6	40.9	34.7	38.8	31.8	41.3	36.7	37.3	35.8	32.8	26.2	31.7
February	34.6	44.6	38.8	40.9	34.7	38.8	31.9	41.3	36.8	37.3	35.9	32.9	26.1	31.7
March	34.5	44.0	38.6	40.7	34.7	38.7	31.9	41.4	36.6	37.2	35.9	32.9	26.1	31.8
April	34.5	43.9	38.8	40.8	34.6	38.7	31.7	41.8	36.6	37.2	36.0	32.9	26.1	31.7
May	34.4	43.6	38.5	40.6	34.6	38.7	31.6	41.6	36.6	37.1	35.9	32.9	26.0	31.6
June	34.4	44.0	38.5	40.6	34.6	38.7	31.6	41.6	36.6	37.1	35.9	32.9	26.1	31.6
July	34.4	44.1	38.5	40.7	34.5	38.6	31.5	42.0	36.5	37.1	36.0	32.9	26.0	31.7
August	34.4	43.5	38.6	40.5	34.5	38.6	31.5	41.8	36.5	37.2	36.0	32.8	26.0	31.5
September	34.5	43.5	38.9	40.6	34.5	38.6	31.5	41.8	36.5	37.3	36.1	32.9	26.0	31.5
October	34.3	43.4	38.7	40.5	34.4	38.5	31.4	41.6	36.2	37.1	35.8	32.8	26.0	31.5
November	34.4	43.2	39.0	40.7	34.6	38.5	31.6	42.6	36.4	37.2	35.9	32.8	26.0	31.5
December	34.5	43.5	39.3	40.8	34.5	38.6	31.4	42.2	36.5	37.2	36.0	32.8	26.1	31.5

Table 2-7. Average Weekly Hours of Production Workers on Private Nonfarm Payrolls, by Super Sector, NAICS Basis, 2000–2012

(Hours.)

Industry	2000	2001	2002	2003	2004	2005	2006	2007	2008	2009	2010	2011	2012
TOTAL PRIVATE	34.3	34.0	33.9	33.7	33.7	33.8	33.9	33.9	33.6	33.1	33.4	33.6	33.7
Goods-Producing	40.7	39.9	39.9	39.8	40.0	40.1	40.5	40.6	40.2	39.2	40.4	40.9	41.2
Mining and logging	44.4	44.6	43.2	43.6	44.5	45.6	45.6	45.9	45.1	43.2	44.6	46.7	46.6
Construction	39.2	38.7	38.4	38.4	38.3	38.6	39.0	39.0	38.5	37.6	38.4	39.0	39.3
Manufacturing	41.3	40.3	40.5	40.4	40.8	40.7	41.1	41.2	40.8	39.8	41.1	41.4	41.7
Trade, transportation, and utilities	33.8	33.5	33.6	33.6	33.5	33.4	33.4	33.3	33.2	32.9	33.3	33.7	33.8
Wholesale trade	38.8	38.4	38.0	37.9	37.8	37.7	38.0	38.2	38.2	37.6	37.9	38.5	38.7
Retail trade	30.7	30.7	30.9	30.9	30.7	30.6	30.5	30.2	30.0	29.9	30.2	30.5	30.5
Transportation and warehousing	37.4	36.7	36.8	36.8	37.2	37.0	36.9	37.0	36.4	36.0	37.1	37.8	38.0
Utilities	42.0	41.4	40.9	41.1	40.9	41.1	41.4	42.4	42.7	42.0	42.0	42.1	41.1
Information	36.8	36.9	36.5	36.2	36.3	36.5	36.6	36.5	36.7	36.6	36.3	36.2	36.0
Financial activities	35.9	35.8	35.6	35.5	35.6	36.0	35.8	35.9	35.9	36.1	36.2	36.4	36.8
Professional and business services	34.5	34.2	34.2	34.1	34.2	34.2	34.6	34.8	34.8	34.7	35.1	35.2	35.3
Education and health services	32.2	32.3	32.4	32.3	32.4	32.6	32.5	32.6	32.5	32.2	32.1	32.3	32.4
Leisure and hospitality	26.1	25.8	25.8	25.6	25.7	25.7	25.7	25.5	25.2	24.8	24.8	24.8	25.0
Other services	32.5	32.3	32.1	31.4	31.0	30.9	30.9	30.9	30.8	30.5	30.7	30.8	30.7

Table 2-8. Employees on Total Nonfarm Payrolls, by State and Selected Territory, 1970–2012

(Thousands of people.)

State	1970	1971	1972	1973	1974	1975	1976	1977	1978	1979	1980	1981	1982	1983	1984
UNITED STATES	71 006	71 335	73 798	76 912	78 389	77 069	79 502	82 593	86 826	89 932	90 528	91 289	89 677	90 280	94 530
Alabama	1 010	1 022	1 072	1 136	1 170	1 155	1 207	1 269	1 337	1 362	1 356	1 348	1 313	1 329	1 388
Alaska	93	98	104	110	128	162	172	163	164	167	169	186	200	214	226
Arizona	547	581	646	714	746	729	759	809	895	980	1 014	1 041	1 030	1 078	1 182
Arkansas	536	551	582	615	641	624	660	696	733	750	742	740	720	741	780
California	6 946	6 917	7 210	7 622	7 834	7 847	8 154	8 600	9 200	9 665	9 849	9 985	9 810	9 918	10 390
Colorado	750	787	869	936	960	964	1 003	1 058	1 150	1 218	1 251	1 295	1 317	1 327	1 402
Connecticut	1 198	1 164	1 190	1 239	1 264	1 223	1 240	1 282	1 346	1 398	1 427	1 438	1 429	1 444	1 517
Delaware	217	225	232	239	233	230	237	239	248	257	259	259	259	266	280
District of Columbia	567	567	572	574	580	577	576	579	596	613	606	611	598	597	614
Florida	2 152	2 276	2 513	2 779	2 864	2 746	2 784	2 933	3 181	3 381	3 576	3 736	3 762	3 905	4 204
Georgia	1 558	1 603	1 695	1 803	1 828	1 756	1 839	1 927	2 050	2 128	2 159	2 199	2 202	2 280	2 449
Hawaii	294	302	313	328	336	343	349	359	377	394	404	405	399	406	413
Idaho	208	217	237	252	267	273	291	307	331	338	330	328	312	318	331
Illinois	208	217	237	252	267	273	291	307	331	338	330	328	312	318	331
Indiana	1 849	1 841	1 922	2 028	2 031	1 942	2 024	2 114	2 206	2 236	2 130	2 115	2 028	2 030	2 122
Iowa	877	883	912	961	999	999	1 037	1 079	1 119	1 132	1 110	1 089	1 042	1 040	1 075
Kansas	679	678	718	763	790	801	835	871	913	947	945	950	921	922	961
Kentucky	910	932	988	1 039	1 066	1 058	1 103	1 148	1 210	1 245	1 210	1 196	1 161	1 152	1 214
Louisiana	1 034	1 056	1 129	1 176	1 221	1 250	1 314	1 365	1 464	1 517	1 579	1 631	1 607	1 565	1 602
Maine	332	332	344	355	362	357	375	388	406	416	418	419	416	425	446
Maryland	1 349	1 372	1 415	1 472	1 494	1 479	1 498	1 546	1 626	1 691	1 712	1 716	1 676	1 724	1 814
Massachusetts	2 244	2 211	2 252	2 333	2 354	2 273	2 324	2 416	2 526	2 604	2 654	2 672	2 642	2 697	2 856
Michigan	2 999	2 995	3 119	3 284	3 278	3 137	3 283	3 442	3 609	3 637	3 443	3 364	3 193	3 223	3 381
Minnesota	1 315	1 310	1 357	1 436	1 481	1 474	1 521	1 597	1 689	1 767	1 770	1 761	1 707	1 718	1 820
Mississippi	584	602	649	693	711	692	728	766	814	838	829	819	791	793	821
Missouri	1 668	1 661	1 700	1 771	1 789	1 741	1 798	1 862	1 953	2 011	1 970	1 957	1 923	1 937	2 033
Montana	199	205	215	224	234	238	251	265	280	284	280	282	274	276	281
Nebraska	484	491	517	541	562	558	572	594	610	631	628	623	610	611	635
Nevada	203	211	224	245	256	263	280	308	350	384	400	411	401	403	426
New Hampshire	259	260	279	298	300	293	313	337	360	379	385	395	394	410	442
New Jersey	2 606	2 608	2 673	2 760	2 783	2 700	2 754	2 837	2 962	3 027	3 060	3 099	3 093	3 165	3 329
New Mexico	293	306	328	346	360	370	390	415	444	461	465	476	474	480	503
New York	7 157	7 011	7 039	7 132	7 077	6 830	6 790	6 858	7 045	7 179	7 207	7 287	7 255	7 313	7 570
North Carolina	1 783	1 814	1 912	2 018	2 048	1 980	2 083	2 171	2 278	2 373	2 380	2 392	2 347	2 419	2 565
North Dakota	164	167	176	184	194	204	215	221	234	244	245	249	250	251	253
Ohio	3 881	3 840	3 938	4 113	4 169	4 016	4 095	4 230	4 395	4 485	4 367	4 318	4 124	4 093	4 260
Oklahoma	763	774	812	852	887	900	931	972	1 036	1 088	1 138	1 201	1 217	1 171	1 180
Oregon	711	729	775	816	838	837	879	937	1 009	1 056	1 045	1 019	961	967	1 007
Pennsylvania	4 352	4 291	4 400	4 507	4 515	4 436	4 513	4 565	4 716	4 806	4 753	4 729	4 580	4 524	4 655
Rhode Island	344	343	358	366	367	349	367	382	396	400	398	401	391	396	416
South Carolina	842	863	920	984	1 016	983	1 038	1 082	1 138	1 176	1 189	1 197	1 162	1 189	1 263
South Dakota	175	179	190	199	207	209	219	227	237	241	238	236	230	235	247
Tennessee	1 328	1 357	1 450	1 531	1 558	1 506	1 575	1 648	1 737	1 777	1 747	1 755	1 703	1 719	1 812
Texas	3 625	3 684	3 884	4 142	4 360	4 463	4 684	4 907	5 272	5 602	5 851	6 180	6 263	6 194	6 492
Utah	357	369	393	415	434	440	463	489	525	548	551	558	561	567	601
Vermont	148	148	154	161	163	162	168	178	191	198	200	204	203	206	215
Virginia	1 519	1 567	1 656	1 753	1 805	1 779	1 848	1 930	2 034	2 115	2 157	2 161	2 146	2 207	2 333
Washington	1 079	1 064	1 100	1 152	1 199	1 226	1 283	1 367	1 485	1 581	1 608	1 612	1 569	1 586	1 660
West Virginia	517	520	541	562	572	575	596	612	633	659	646	629	608	582	597
Wisconsin	1 530	1 525	1 581	1 661	1 703	1 677	1 726	1 799	1 887	1 960	1 938	1 923	1 867	1 867	1 949
Wyoming	108	111	117	126	137	146	157	171	187	201	210	224	218	203	204
Puerto Rico	. . .	. . .	. . .	. . .	. . .	. . .	. . .	. . .	. . .	. . .	693	680	642	646	684
Virgin Islands	. . .	. . .	. . .	. . .	. . .	33	31	32	34	36	37	38	37	36	37

. . . = Not available.

Table 2-8. Employees on Total Nonfarm Payrolls, by State and Selected Territory, 1970–2012—*Continued*

(Thousands of people.)

State	1985	1986	1987	1988	1989	1990	1991	1992	1993	1994	1995	1996	1997
UNITED STATES	97 511	99 474	102 088	105 345	108 014	109 487	108 377	108 745	110 876	114 333	117 336	119 757	122 853
Alabama	1 427	1 463	1 508	1 559	1 601	1 636	1 642	1 674	1 717	1 758	1 804	1 829	1 866
Alaska	231	221	210	214	227	237	242	246	252	258	261	263	268
Arizona	1 279	1 338	1 386	1 419	1 454	1 483	1 491	1 517	1 584	1 692	1 793	1 892	1 985
Arkansas	797	814	837	865	893	924	937	963	994	1 034	1 070	1 087	1 105
California	10 770	11 086	11 473	11 912	12 238	12 500	12 359	12 154	12 046	12 160	12 422	12 744	13 130
Colorado	1 419	1 408	1 413	1 436	1 482	1 521	1 545	1 597	1 671	1 756	1 835	1 901	1 980
Connecticut	1 558	1 598	1 638	1 667	1 666	1 620	1 557	1 526	1 531	1 544	1 562	1 582	1 608
Delaware	293	303	321	334	344	348	342	341	349	356	366	376	388
District of Columbia	629	640	656	674	681	686	677	674	670	659	643	623	618
Florida	4 410	4 599	4 848	5 067	5 261	5 364	5 275	5 339	5 552	5 780	5 976	6 164	6 400
Georgia	2 570	2 672	2 782	2 876	2 941	3 027	2 976	3 029	3 144	3 300	3 436	3 560	3 646
Hawaii	426	439	460	478	506	528	539	543	539	536	533	531	532
Idaho	336	328	333	349	366	385	398	414	433	459	475	489	506
Illinois	336	328	333	349	366	385	398	414	433	459	475	489	506
Indiana	2 169	2 222	2 305	2 396	2 479	2 522	2 507	2 554	2 627	2 713	2 786	2 814	2 858
Iowa	1 074	1 074	1 109	1 156	1 200	1 226	1 238	1 253	1 278	1 320	1 358	1 383	1 407
Kansas	968	985	1 005	1 035	1 064	1 092	1 097	1 116	1 135	1 167	1 200	1 228	1 270
Kentucky	1 250	1 274	1 328	1 382	1 433	1 471	1 475	1 509	1 548	1 597	1 643	1 672	1 711
Louisiana	1 591	1 518	1 484	1 512	1 538	1 588	1 611	1 625	1 656	1 720	1 770	1 808	1 848
Maine	458	477	501	527	542	535	514	512	519	532	538	542	554
Maryland	1 888	1 952	2 028	2 102	2 155	2 173	2 102	2 084	2 104	2 148	2 184	2 213	2 269
Massachusetts	2 931	2 992	3 071	3 138	3 118	2 988	2 824	2 798	2 843	2 907	2 980	3 039	3 114
Michigan	3 562	3 657	3 736	3 819	3 922	3 946	3 884	3 919	3 999	4 141	4 268	4 352	4 439
Minnesota	1 866	1 892	1 962	2 028	2 087	2 136	2 146	2 194	2 252	2 320	2 388	2 442	2 500
Mississippi	839	848	864	896	919	938	939	962	1 004	1 057	1 076	1 090	1 108
Missouri	2 095	2 143	2 198	2 259	2 315	2 345	2 309	2 334	2 394	2 470	2 521	2 568	2 639
Montana	279	275	274	283	291	297	304	317	326	340	352	362	367
Nebraska	650	652	667	688	708	731	740	752	769	798	819	837	856
Nevada	446	468	500	538	581	621	629	639	672	738	786	843	891
New Hampshire	466	490	513	529	529	508	482	487	502	523	540	554	570
New Jersey	3 414	3 488	3 576	3 651	3 690	3 635	3 499	3 458	3 493	3 553	3 601	3 639	3 724
New Mexico	520	526	529	548	562	580	585	602	626	657	682	695	708
New York	7 751	7 908	8 059	8 187	8 247	8 214	7 888	7 732	7 762	7 833	7 894	7 941	8 070
North Carolina	2 651	2 744	2 863	2 987	3 074	3 127	3 081	3 145	3 247	3 354	3 454	3 538	3 654
North Dakota	252	250	252	257	260	266	271	277	285	295	302	309	314
Ohio	4 373	4 472	4 583	4 701	4 818	4 882	4 819	4 848	4 918	5 076	5 221	5 296	5 392
Oklahoma	1 165	1 124	1 108	1 132	1 164	1 210	1 225	1 236	1 261	1 294	1 330	1 368	1 407
Oregon	1 030	1 058	1 100	1 153	1 206	1 256	1 254	1 276	1 318	1 372	1 428	1 485	1 537
Pennsylvania	4 730	4 791	4 915	5 042	5 138	5 173	5 086	5 078	5 126	5 195	5 256	5 309	5 409
Rhode Island	429	443	452	459	462	454	424	424	430	434	439	441	450
South Carolina	1 296	1 338	1 392	1 449	1 500	1 542	1 512	1 527	1 570	1 607	1 646	1 678	1 723
South Dakota	249	252	257	266	276	288	296	308	318	331	342	347	353
Tennessee	1 868	1 930	2 012	2 092	2 167	2 196	2 186	2 248	2 331	2 426	2 503	2 537	2 588
Texas	6 663	6 564	6 517	6 678	6 840	7 099	7 177	7 273	7 486	7 756	8 027	8 260	8 611
Utah	624	634	640	660	691	724	745	769	810	860	908	954	994
Vermont	225	234	246	256	262	258	249	251	257	264	270	275	279
Virginia	2 455	2 558	2 680	2 772	2 862	2 894	2 829	2 848	2 919	3 004	3 070	3 136	3 232
Washington	1 710	1 770	1 852	1 941	2 047	2 146	2 180	2 225	2 260	2 307	2 350	2 419	2 517
West Virginia	597	598	599	610	615	630	629	640	652	674	688	698	708
Wisconsin	1 983	2 024	2 090	2 168	2 236	2 292	2 302	2 358	2 413	2 491	2 559	2 601	2 656
Wyoming	207	196	183	189	193	198	203	206	210	217	219	221	225
Puerto Rico	692	728	764	818	837	846	838	858	872	898	930	973	989
Virgin Islands	37	38	40	42	42	43	44	45	49	44	42	41	42

Table 2-8. Employees on Total Nonfarm Payrolls, by State and Selected Territory, 1970–2012—*Continued*

(Thousands of people.)

State	1998	1999	2000	2001	2002	2003	2004	2005	2006	2007	2008	2009	2010	2011	2012
UNITED STATES	126 033	129 098	131 881	131 919	130 450	130 100	131 509	133 747	136 125	137 645	136 852	130 876	129 917	131 497	133 739
Alabama	1 898	1 920	1 931	1 909	1 883	1 876	1 902	1 945	1 980	2 006	1 992	1 886	1 871	1 870	1 883
Alaska	274	278	283	288	294	298	303	309	314	317	321	320	324	330	334
Arizona	2 075	2 163	2 243	2 266	2 268	2 299	2 385	2 513	2 639	2 679	2 623	2 433	2 386	2 411	2 460
Arkansas	1 122	1 142	1 159	1 154	1 146	1 145	1 158	1 178	1 199	1 204	1 202	1 165	1 163	1 170	1 177
California	13 597	13 992	14 489	14 602	14 458	14 394	14 533	14 802	15 061	15 174	14 983	14 085	13 937	14 099	14 394
Colorado	2 058	2 133	2 214	2 227	2 184	2 153	2 180	2 226	2 279	2 331	2 350	2 246	2 222	2 258	2 310
Connecticut	1 643	1 669	1 693	1 681	1 665	1 644	1 650	1 662	1 681	1 698	1 699	1 627	1 608	1 625	1 639
Delaware	400	413	420	420	415	416	425	433	438	439	437	417	414	417	418
District of Columbia	614	627	650	654	664	666	674	682	688	694	704	702	712	726	732
Florida	6 617	6 807	7 061	7 151	7 160	7 242	7 490	7 791	7 994	8 010	7 727	7 245	7 186	7 266	7 400
Georgia	3 772	3 885	3 979	3 971	3 897	3 870	3 923	4 025	4 112	4 167	4 123	3 901	3 861	3 901	3 953
Hawaii	531	535	551	555	557	568	583	602	617	625	619	592	587	594	605
Idaho	521	539	560	568	568	572	588	611	638	655	649	610	604	611	622
Illinois	521	539	560	568	568	572	588	611	638	655	649	610	610	611	622
Indiana	2 917	2 970	3 000	2 933	2 901	2 895	2 929	2 955	2 974	2 986	2 957	2 787	2 796	2 841	2 902
Iowa	1 443	1 469	1 478	1 466	1 447	1 440	1 457	1 480	1 504	1 519	1 524	1 479	1 469	1 486	1 508
Kansas	1 314	1 328	1 346	1 349	1 336	1 313	1 325	1 333	1 354	1 380	1 391	1 343	1 329	1 340	1 358
Kentucky	1 753	1 796	1 827	1 805	1 789	1 783	1 799	1 824	1 847	1 867	1 852	1 769	1 770	1 796	1 824
Louisiana	1 887	1 894	1 918	1 915	1 896	1 906	1 918	1 892	1 853	1 916	1 938	1 901	1 885	1 902	1 926
Maine	569	586	604	608	606	607	612	612	615	618	617	596	593	595	598
Maryland	2 326	2 392	2 455	2 472	2 480	2 486	2 517	2 555	2 588	2 607	2 599	2 522	2 517	2 543	2 574
Massachusetts	3 184	3 243	3 329	3 339	3 259	3 198	3 195	3 212	3 246	3 280	3 290	3 191	3 191	3 228	3 274
Michigan	4 514	4 585	4 676	4 564	4 487	4 416	4 399	4 390	4 326	4 268	4 162	3 870	3 863	3 952	4 024
Minnesota	2 564	2 622	2 685	2 690	2 664	2 660	2 681	2 723	2 758	2 771	2 763	2 655	2 641	2 689	2 728
Mississippi	1 135	1 155	1 155	1 131	1 125	1 116	1 126	1 132	1 143	1 154	1 149	1 098	1 092	1 093	1 103
Missouri	2 684	2 727	2 749	2 730	2 699	2 680	2 694	2 735	2 774	2 795	2 789	2 684	2 650	2 656	2 669
Montana	376	384	391	391	396	400	411	420	434	444	445	429	428	431	440
Nebraska	878	894	910	917	908	910	918	930	942	957	965	945	940	947	960
Nevada	926	983	1 027	1 051	1 052	1 088	1 153	1 223	1 280	1 292	1 264	1 148	1 117	1 125	1 143
New Hampshire	589	606	622	627	618	618	627	636	643	648	649	628	624	627	633
New Jersey	3 801	3 901	3 994	3 997	3 984	3 977	3 998	4 038	4 070	4 077	4 048	3 894	3 848	3 848	3 896
New Mexico	720	730	745	757	766	776	790	809	832	844	847	812	803	803	804
New York	8 239	8 459	8 638	8 595	8 462	8 410	8 465	8 537	8 618	8 734	8 793	8 556	8 567	8 689	8 800
North Carolina	3 759	3 849	3 915	3 893	3 835	3 787	3 834	3 912	4 037	4 141	4 131	3 904	3 870	3 917	3 988
North Dakota	320	324	328	330	330	333	338	345	352	358	367	367	376	397	430
Ohio	5 482	5 564	5 625	5 543	5 445	5 398	5 408	5 427	5 435	5 426	5 360	5 069	5 029	5 093	5 171
Oklahoma	1 454	1 475	1 502	1 520	1 499	1 471	1 487	1 525	1 566	1 595	1 618	1 568	1 556	1 578	1 608
Oregon	1 562	1 586	1 618	1 606	1 585	1 574	1 607	1 654	1 704	1 731	1 718	1 612	1 602	1 620	1 638
Pennsylvania	5 498	5 589	5 694	5 685	5 644	5 614	5 647	5 705	5 759	5 801	5 802	5 618	5 624	5 688	5 730
Rhode Island	458	466	477	478	479	484	488	491	493	493	482	460	459	462	465
South Carolina	1 786	1 833	1 862	1 825	1 806	1 810	1 835	1 869	1 909	1 948	1 929	1 816	1 812	1 832	1 858
South Dakota	360	370	378	379	378	378	384	390	399	406	411	404	403	408	414
Tennessee	2 642	2 689	2 733	2 688	2 664	2 663	2 706	2 743	2 783	2 797	2 775	2 620	2 615	2 661	2 714
Texas	8 940	9 157	9 429	9 511	9 412	9 367	9 494	9 737	10 063	10 391	10 604	10 304	10 341	10 576	10 880
Utah	1 023	1 048	1 075	1 081	1 073	1 074	1 104	1 148	1 204	1 253	1 252	1 189	1 182	1 208	1 249
Vermont	285	292	299	302	299	299	303	306	308	308	307	297	298	300	303
Virginia	3 320	3 412	3 516	3 519	3 496	3 499	3 585	3 664	3 729	3 766	3 768	3 646	3 642	3 687	3 727
Washington	2 598	2 651	2 714	2 700	2 657	2 660	2 704	2 780	2 862	2 936	2 962	2 825	2 789	2 825	2 871
West Virginia	719	726	736	735	733	727	737	746	756	758	762	746	747	756	765
Wisconsin	2 718	2 784	2 834	2 814	2 782	2 774	2 804	2 838	2 862	2 878	2 871	2 744	2 729	2 759	2 785
Wyoming	228	233	239	245	248	250	255	264	277	289	298	286	283	287	290
Puerto Rico	997	1 011	1 025	1 009	1 005	1 024	1 050	1 051	1 044	1 031	1 014	964	931	924	935
Virgin Islands	42	41	42	44	43	42	43	44	46	46	46	44	44	44	40

Table 2-9. Total Employees on Private Payrolls, by State and Selected Territory, 2000–2012

(Thousands of people.)

State	2000	2001	2002	2003	2004	2005	2006	2007	2008	2009	2010	2011	2012
UNITED STATES	111 091	110 800	108 937	108 517	109 888	111 943	114 151	115 427	114 342	108 321	107 427	109 411	111 822
Alabama	1 580	1 557	1 529	1 517	1 542	1 582	1 609	1 629	1 608	1 503	1 484	1 488	1 506
Alaska	209	210	214	217	222	228	233	236	239	236	239	245	250
Arizona	1 876	1 888	1 877	1 906	1 985	2 110	2 231	2 258	2 190	2 010	1 970	2 003	2 050
Arkansas	968	960	951	947	958	974	991	994	989	948	945	953	962
California	12 171	12 220	12 011	11 967	12 136	12 382	12 609	12 680	12 464	11 606	11 488	11 694	12 020
Colorado	1 877	1 883	1 829	1 797	1 821	1 863	1 912	1 957	1 966	1 855	1 828	1 865	1 916
Connecticut	1 451	1 437	1 416	1 399	1 407	1 418	1 435	1 449	1 447	1 378	1 364	1 385	1 400
Delaware	364	363	358	358	367	373	377	377	374	353	350	354	355
District of Columbia	426	428	433	435	443	449	455	463	469	461	465	479	489
Florida	6 059	6 128	6 121	6 188	6 424	6 710	6 895	6 887	6 600	6 131	6 074	6 173	6 322
Georgia	3 362	3 342	3 253	3 219	3 268	3 358	3 432	3 474	3 412	3 192	3 162	3 214	3 271
Hawaii	437	441	439	449	463	482	496	503	494	466	462	469	479
Idaho	451	458	456	459	474	496	522	538	530	490	485	494	505
Illinois	5 205	5 145	5 023	4 958	4 971	5 016	5 087	5 131	5 094	4 800	4 759	4 839	4 912
Indiana	2 595	2 523	2 484	2 473	2 503	2 529	2 548	2 555	2 516	2 349	2 359	2 414	2 474
Iowa	1 235	1 220	1 203	1 196	1 213	1 235	1 257	1 269	1 272	1 224	1 216	1 233	1 254
Kansas	1 101	1 101	1 085	1 063	1 074	1 082	1 099	1 122	1 131	1 082	1 066	1 080	1 099
Kentucky	1 519	1 493	1 474	1 471	1 489	1 511	1 529	1 543	1 529	1 445	1 440	1 461	1 487
Louisiana	1 544	1 542	1 521	1 526	1 535	1 518	1 505	1 560	1 573	1 532	1 518	1 545	1 576
Maine	504	506	503	503	507	507	510	514	513	493	489	493	496
Maryland	2 005	2 015	2 015	2 024	2 055	2 089	2 117	2 129	2 111	2 028	2 015	2 038	2 069
Massachusetts	2 894	2 899	2 823	2 773	2 774	2 787	2 817	2 848	2 853	2 743	2 751	2 794	2 836
Michigan	3 995	3 879	3 800	3 731	3 719	3 716	3 661	3 612	3 512	3 224	3 228	3 334	3 414
Minnesota	2 277	2 280	2 251	2 248	2 269	2 308	2 342	2 357	2 344	2 238	2 225	2 278	2 316
Mississippi	921	894	885	876	884	891	903	910	901	848	844	847	857
Missouri	2 323	2 302	2 268	2 248	2 265	2 306	2 340	2 355	2 343	2 232	2 203	2 217	2 232
Montana	307	307	311	315	324	334	346	357	357	339	336	341	351
Nebraska	756	760	749	751	758	769	779	795	801	776	771	778	792
Nevada	905	925	922	955	1 015	1 080	1 130	1 137	1 102	991	964	974	994
New Hampshire	538	541	530	528	537	545	551	554	554	531	528	535	542
New Jersey	3 406	3 394	3 370	3 355	3 364	3 397	3 422	3 429	3 399	3 242	3 208	3 229	3 275
New Mexico	562	572	575	581	592	607	635	649	649	613	604	607	610
New York	7 171	7 127	6 970	6 923	6 981	7 048	7 133	7 233	7 277	7 032	7 056	7 206	7 340
North Carolina	3 285	3 249	3 186	3 138	3 174	3 241	3 350	3 439	3 410	3 180	3 149	3 203	3 274
North Dakota	255	257	256	257	263	270	277	283	291	289	297	318	350
Ohio	4 840	4 749	4 645	4 595	4 607	4 627	4 635	4 629	4 563	4 281	4 249	4 329	4 414
Oklahoma	1 206	1 215	1 190	1 167	1 177	1 204	1 236	1 261	1 281	1 219	1 208	1 234	1 260
Oregon	1 339	1 324	1 300	1 295	1 324	1 369	1 417	1 442	1 420	1 313	1 302	1 325	1 347
Pennsylvania	4 966	4 954	4 902	4 866	4 900	4 957	5 011	5 053	5 050	4 858	4 863	4 947	5 008
Rhode Island	412	413	413	418	423	426	428	428	418	398	397	401	405
South Carolina	1 538	1 501	1 480	1 482	1 509	1 540	1 577	1 609	1 581	1 468	1 465	1 490	1 512
South Dakota	307	305	303	304	309	315	323	331	335	326	325	330	336
Tennessee	2 334	2 285	2 254	2 252	2 291	2 330	2 366	2 376	2 347	2 191	2 182	2 233	2 290
Texas	7 870	7 928	7 790	7 724	7 841	8 056	8 359	8 660	8 828	8 487	8 484	8 755	9 085
Utah	890	891	879	878	905	946	999	1 046	1 041	974	965	988	1 026
Vermont	249	252	249	247	251	253	254	255	253	243	243	246	249
Virginia	2 892	2 890	2 862	2 862	2 934	3 003	3 055	3 083	3 074	2 946	2 937	2 977	3 014
Washington	2 231	2 194	2 141	2 140	2 180	2 253	2 332	2 403	2 415	2 276	2 239	2 281	2 330
West Virginia	593	594	590	585	594	603	611	613	615	596	594	604	611
Wisconsin	2 428	2 400	2 367	2 361	2 392	2 423	2 446	2 462	2 449	2 323	2 309	2 344	2 374
Wyoming	179	184	185	187	191	199	212	222	229	215	210	214	216
Puerto Rico	739	726	710	723	742	747	744	734	714	675	664	665	676
Virgin Islands	29	32	30	29	31	32	33	33	33	31	31	31	29

Table 2-10. Employees on Manufacturing Payrolls, by State and Selected Territory, NAICS Basis, 2000–2012

(Thousands of people.)

State	2000	2001	2002	2003	2004	2005	2006	2007	2008	2009	2010	2011	2012
UNITED STATES	17 263	16 441	15 259	14 509	14 315	14 227	14 155	13 879	13 406	11 847	11 528	11 726	11 919
Alabama	351	326	307	294	292	299	303	296	284	247	236	237	243
Alaska	12	12	11	12	12	13	13	13	13	13	13	14	14
Arizona	210	202	184	175	177	182	186	182	173	154	149	151	155
Arkansas	240	227	214	206	204	202	200	191	184	164	160	159	156
California	1 856	1 781	1 634	1 545	1 523	1 505	1 490	1 464	1 425	1 282	1 242	1 248	1 253
Colorado	189	180	164	154	152	150	149	147	144	130	126	129	132
Connecticut	236	227	211	200	197	195	194	191	187	171	166	166	165
Delaware	42	39	37	36	35	33	34	33	32	28	26	26	26
District of Columbia	4	3	3	3	2	2	2	2	2	1	1	1	1
Florida	477	455	428	410	411	416	416	399	371	324	309	313	317
Georgia	538	505	471	452	448	450	448	431	409	358	345	351	355
Hawaii	16	16	15	15	15	15	15	15	15	14	13	13	13
Idaho	70	69	66	62	62	64	66	66	63	55	53	55	57
Illinois	871	815	754	714	697	688	683	675	657	577	561	574	583
Indiana	665	615	588	573	572	571	565	550	521	442	447	464	482
Iowa	252	240	227	220	223	229	231	230	227	203	201	206	210
Kansas	201	195	184	175	177	180	183	186	187	167	160	161	163
Kentucky	310	292	275	265	264	262	261	256	245	213	209	213	223
Louisiana	177	172	161	156	153	152	153	157	153	142	138	140	142
Maine	80	75	68	64	63	61	60	59	59	52	51	51	51
Maryland	172	166	155	145	141	139	135	132	128	119	114	113	109
Massachusetts	403	389	349	324	313	305	300	295	286	259	253	253	252
Michigan	897	821	761	718	698	678	648	617	572	463	474	510	537
Minnesota	397	379	356	343	343	347	346	342	336	300	293	301	305
Mississippi	223	201	188	179	180	178	176	170	160	141	136	135	137
Missouri	365	345	325	315	311	309	307	300	289	254	243	246	248
Montana	23	21	20	19	19	20	20	21	20	17	17	17	18
Nebraska	114	111	106	102	101	101	102	101	101	93	92	93	95
Nevada	43	44	43	44	46	48	50	50	48	40	38	38	39
New Hampshire	103	97	85	80	80	80	78	78	76	68	66	67	66
New Jersey	422	401	368	350	338	330	324	311	299	266	257	252	246
New Mexico	42	41	38	37	36	36	38	37	35	30	29	30	30
New York	749	707	651	612	596	579	566	552	532	476	457	459	458
North Carolina	758	704	644	599	577	565	553	539	516	448	432	434	440
North Dakota	24	24	24	24	25	26	26	26	26	24	23	24	25
Ohio	1 021	953	885	843	822	812	796	771	739	629	621	639	656
Oklahoma	177	170	152	143	142	145	149	151	150	129	123	130	135
Oregon	225	216	202	195	200	204	207	204	195	167	164	168	172
Pennsylvania	864	822	760	712	691	679	670	659	644	574	560	565	567
Rhode Island	71	68	62	59	57	55	53	51	48	42	40	40	40
South Carolina	336	313	289	275	267	260	252	249	241	213	207	215	220
South Dakota	44	41	38	38	39	40	42	42	43	38	37	39	41
Tennessee	497	454	429	413	412	409	399	380	361	309	299	304	314
Texas	1 067	1 026	948	899	890	897	924	934	925	839	812	836	863
Utah	126	122	114	112	115	118	123	128	126	113	111	114	117
Vermont	46	46	41	38	37	37	36	36	35	31	31	31	32
Virginia	364	341	320	305	299	296	288	278	265	239	231	231	232
Washington	332	316	285	267	264	273	286	293	291	266	258	269	280
West Virginia	76	72	69	65	63	62	61	59	57	51	49	50	49
Wisconsin	594	560	528	504	503	505	506	501	493	436	431	445	455
Wyoming	10	10	10	9	9	10	10	10	10	9	9	9	9
Puerto Rico	143	132	121	118	118	115	110	107	101	92	87	84	82
Virgin Islands	2	2	2	2	2	2	2	2	2	2	2	2	1

Table 2-11. Employees on Government Payrolls, by State and Selected Territory, NAICS Basis, 2000–2012

(Thousands of people.)

State	2000	2001	2002	2003	2004	2005	2006	2007	2008	2009	2010	2011	2012
UNITED STATES	20 790	21 118	21 513	21 583	21 621	21 804	21 974	22 218	22 509	22 555	22 490	22 086	21 917
Alabama	352	352	355	358	359	363	370	377	384	384	387	382	376
Alaska	74	78	80	81	81	81	81	81	82	84	85	85	84
Arizona	367	378	390	394	399	403	408	421	432	423	416	408	411
Arkansas	191	194	195	198	200	204	208	211	214	217	218	217	216
California	2 318	2 382	2 447	2 426	2 398	2 420	2 452	2 495	2 519	2 480	2 448	2 405	2 375
Colorado	337	344	355	356	358	363	367	375	384	390	394	393	395
Connecticut	242	244	249	246	243	244	246	249	252	248	244	240	239
Delaware	57	57	57	57	58	60	61	62	63	63	64	64	64
District of Columbia	224	226	232	231	231	234	233	231	235	240	247	247	242
Florida	1 002	1 024	1 039	1 053	1 066	1 081	1 099	1 123	1 127	1 115	1 112	1 093	1 079
Georgia	617	630	644	651	655	667	680	693	711	709	699	687	682
Hawaii	115	114	118	119	120	120	121	122	125	126	125	125	126
Idaho	109	110	112	113	114	115	116	117	119	120	119	117	117
Illinois	840	850	861	853	845	846	846	849	856	858	854	838	832
Indiana	405	410	417	423	426	426	426	431	440	438	437	427	428
Iowa	243	245	244	245	245	245	247	250	253	255	253	253	254
Kansas	245	248	251	250	251	251	254	258	260	261	262	260	259
Kentucky	308	312	315	312	310	314	318	323	323	324	331	334	337
Louisiana	374	374	375	379	382	374	348	356	364	369	366	357	350
Maine	100	102	103	104	105	105	104	104	104	104	104	102	101
Maryland	450	457	465	462	462	466	471	478	488	494	502	505	505
Massachusetts	435	440	436	426	422	425	429	433	437	438	439	435	437
Michigan	681	685	687	685	680	674	665	656	650	647	636	617	610
Minnesota	408	409	414	412	412	415	416	415	419	417	416	411	412
Mississippi	234	238	240	241	242	241	239	244	248	250	249	246	246
Missouri	426	429	431	432	429	429	434	440	446	452	448	439	437
Montana	84	84	85	86	87	86	88	87	88	90	92	90	90
Nebraska	154	157	159	160	160	161	162	162	164	168	170	168	168
Nevada	122	127	130	134	138	143	149	156	161	157	154	150	149
New Hampshire	84	86	88	90	90	91	92	93	95	96	96	92	91
New Jersey	589	603	614	622	633	642	647	648	649	652	640	619	620
New Mexico	183	186	191	195	198	201	198	195	198	199	200	196	194
New York	1 467	1 467	1 492	1 487	1 484	1 489	1 485	1 501	1 516	1 524	1 511	1 482	1 460
North Carolina	630	644	649	649	660	671	687	703	721	724	721	713	714
North Dakota	72	73	74	75	75	75	76	76	76	78	80	79	80
Ohio	785	794	800	803	802	800	800	797	796	788	780	765	757
Oklahoma	296	305	309	304	310	321	330	334	337	348	348	344	347
Oregon	279	282	286	280	282	285	286	290	298	300	300	295	292
Pennsylvania	728	731	742	748	747	748	748	748	752	760	761	740	722
Rhode Island	64	65	66	66	66	65	65	64	64	62	62	61	60
South Carolina	324	324	327	328	326	329	332	339	348	348	347	342	347
South Dakota	71	73	74	75	75	75	75	76	76	78	79	78	78
Tennessee	399	403	410	411	415	413	417	421	428	428	433	428	424
Texas	1 559	1 583	1 623	1 643	1 652	1 681	1 703	1 731	1 776	1 818	1 857	1 821	1 795
Utah	185	190	195	197	199	202	204	207	212	215	218	220	224
Vermont	49	50	51	52	52	53	54	54	54	55	55	54	54
Virginia	625	629	635	638	651	662	675	683	694	700	705	710	712
Washington	483	505	516	521	524	527	530	534	546	550	550	544	541
West Virginia	143	141	143	142	143	144	145	145	147	150	153	152	154
Wisconsin	406	414	415	413	412	415	415	416	422	421	420	415	411
Wyoming	61	62	63	64	64	65	65	67	69	72	73	73	74
Puerto Rico	286	282	295	301	307	304	300	297	299	289	268	259	259
Virgin Islands	13	12	13	13	12	12	12	13	13	13	13	12	12

EARNINGS

Figure 2-2. Average Hourly Earnings of All Employees on Nonfarm Payrolls by Industry, 2012

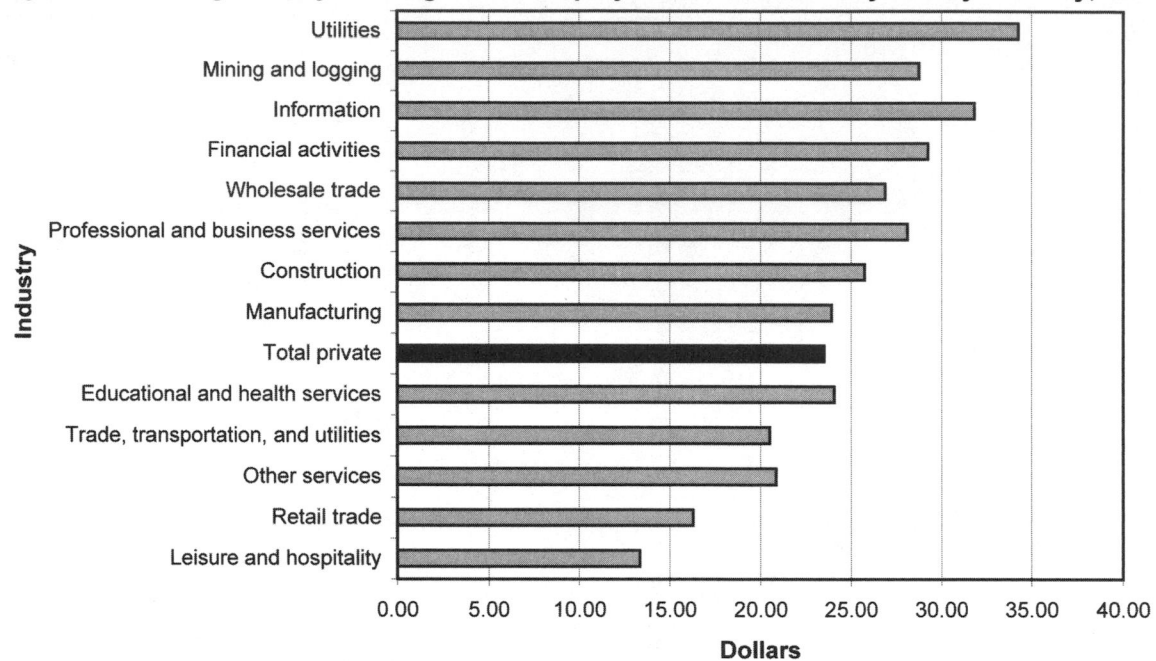

Workers in utilities had the highest average hourly earnings at $34.24, followed by those in information ($31.81), financial activities ($29.27), and mining and logging ($28.75). The average hourly earnings for all private employees was $23.53 in 2012. Earnings increased the most in the financial activity sector (4.9 percent) and the least in the information sector (0.7 percent). (See Table 2-12.)

OTHER HIGHLIGHTS

- Average hourly earnings for all employees also varied significantly by state in 2012. Earnings were highest in the District of Columbia ($36.84), followed by Connecticut ($28.14) and Massachusetts ($28.13). Arkansas had the lowest average hourly earnings ($18.57), followed by Mississippi ($18.83) and South Dakota ($19.42). (See Table 2-13.)

- In 2012, average weekly earnings increased 2.4 percent for all employees on nonfarm payrolls. However, when adjusted for inflation, average weekly earnings only increased 0.4 percent. Average weekly earnings of all employees on nonfarm payrolls ranged from $348.96 in leisure and hospitality to $1,432.53 in utilities. (See Table 2-15.)

- From 2011 to 2012, average weekly earnings declined by at least 0.1 percent in the following states: Utah (-3.0 percent), Delaware (-1.7 percent), South Carolina (-1.5 percent), Vermont (-1.0 percent), Florida (-0.7 percent), Maryland (-0.6 percent), New Mexico (-0.5 percent), California (-0.2 percent), and Connecticut (0.1 percent). (See Table 2-17.)

Table 2-12. Average Hourly Earnings of All Employees on Total Private Payrolls, by NAICS Super Sector, 2007–2012

(Dollars, seasonally adjusted.)

Year and month	Total private	Mining and logging	Construction	Manufacturing	Trade, transportation, and utilities				Information	Financial activities	Professional and business services	Education and health services	Leisure and hospitality	Other services
					Total	Whole-sale trade	Retail trade	Utilities						
2007	20.97	24.91	23.02	21.50	18.58	23.96	15.13	30.27	28.09	25.64	24.68	21.35	12.39	17.62
2008	21.62	26.20	23.96	22.16	18.93	24.37	15.21	32.22	28.66	26.18	25.82	22.12	12.77	18.17
2009	22.22	27.29	24.83	23.04	19.32	25.41	15.39	32.84	29.40	26.53	27.03	22.41	12.97	19.54
2010	22.60	27.39	25.19	23.31	19.65	26.13	15.56	32.55	30.53	27.21	27.24	22.96	13.08	20.16
2011	23.06	28.10	25.41	23.69	20.04	26.38	15.86	33.62	31.59	27.90	27.76	23.62	13.23	20.50
2012	23.53	28.75	25.75	23.93	20.50	26.89	16.29	34.24	31.81	29.27	28.11	24.23	13.37	20.85
2008														
January	21.27	25.43	23.43	21.70	18.71	24.09	15.11	31.47	28.42	26.02	25.15	21.79	12.62	17.90
February	21.34	24.85	23.52	21.80	18.78	24.15	15.16	32.20	28.34	26.07	25.21	21.92	12.67	17.90
March	21.44	26.46	23.58	21.98	18.79	24.21	15.14	31.73	28.59	26.12	25.34	22.02	12.74	18.00
April	21.44	24.97	23.64	21.88	18.83	24.21	15.20	30.98	28.65	26.12	25.48	21.98	12.74	18.00
May	21.53	25.48	23.80	22.00	18.92	24.28	15.24	32.25	28.48	26.16	25.63	22.02	12.75	18.10
June	21.61	25.87	23.90	22.18	18.97	24.40	15.22	32.67	28.67	26.19	25.73	22.07	12.78	18.20
July	21.65	26.28	23.98	22.10	18.98	24.43	15.21	31.94	28.83	26.26	25.83	22.11	12.79	18.20
August	21.76	26.69	24.20	22.22	19.08	24.63	15.29	32.58	28.87	26.29	26.03	22.21	12.82	18.30
September	21.78	26.63	24.21	22.26	19.03	24.43	15.27	32.62	28.85	26.42	26.10	22.27	12.83	18.30
October	21.83	26.58	24.24	22.45	19.01	24.43	15.24	32.59	28.76	26.31	26.30	22.30	12.82	18.40
November	21.94	27.57	24.41	22.60	19.07	24.61	15.26	32.74	28.78	26.27	26.54	22.43	12.82	18.40
December	22.01	27.31	24.58	22.63	19.15	24.71	15.28	32.83	28.89	26.31	26.66	22.45	12.84	18.50
2009														
January	22.02	27.45	24.55	22.79	19.15	24.85	15.31	32.87	28.84	26.30	26.71	22.43	12.87	18.64
February	22.08	27.51	24.57	22.91	19.20	24.92	15.32	33.33	28.82	26.30	26.84	22.42	12.88	18.83
March	22.11	27.69	24.75	23.01	19.23	25.01	15.34	33.06	28.83	26.27	26.95	22.20	12.88	19.50
April	22.14	27.58	24.79	23.03	19.23	25.17	15.31	32.90	28.92	26.27	27.05	22.27	12.90	19.51
May	22.14	27.54	24.78	23.01	19.27	25.29	15.37	32.83	29.19	26.38	27.00	22.27	12.86	19.57
June	22.17	27.43	24.86	23.03	19.24	25.31	15.34	32.75	29.36	26.47	27.04	22.36	12.91	19.54
July	22.22	27.29	24.85	23.10	19.28	25.35	15.38	32.74	29.67	26.52	27.07	22.39	12.97	19.61
August	22.27	27.37	24.90	23.13	19.44	25.73	15.50	32.84	29.63	26.60	27.04	22.41	13.00	19.66
September	22.29	27.15	24.86	23.14	19.41	25.69	15.50	32.57	29.62	26.70	27.18	22.40	13.04	19.82
October	22.35	27.30	24.99	23.13	19.42	25.74	15.42	32.84	29.82	26.79	27.11	22.57	13.10	19.89
November	22.39	27.06	25.04	23.19	19.47	25.82	15.45	32.80	29.93	26.91	27.07	22.59	13.16	19.97
December	22.41	26.97	25.01	23.14	19.51	25.91	15.46	32.75	29.88	26.93	27.12	22.57	13.15	20.03
2010														
January	22.46	27.09	25.11	23.17	19.60	26.17	15.50	32.62	29.90	27.00	27.15	22.59	13.13	20.06
February	22.47	27.14	25.22	23.22	19.58	26.17	15.49	32.42	30.16	27.00	27.22	22.62	13.11	20.11
March	22.50	27.12	25.16	23.18	19.62	26.15	15.55	32.32	30.18	27.06	27.18	22.71	13.09	20.13
April	22.54	27.23	25.10	23.20	19.65	26.13	15.62	32.26	30.18	27.19	27.18	22.86	13.07	20.11
May	22.57	27.44	25.16	23.31	19.62	26.13	15.51	32.27	30.30	27.24	27.24	22.91	13.08	20.12
June	22.56	27.41	25.13	23.23	19.61	26.09	15.53	32.34	30.41	27.17	27.26	22.93	13.06	20.14
July	22.62	27.57	25.19	23.36	19.63	26.12	15.55	32.56	30.48	27.38	27.27	23.01	13.08	20.09
August	22.66	27.57	25.18	23.44	19.61	26.03	15.52	32.67	30.68	27.33	27.37	23.09	13.10	20.08
September	22.70	27.78	25.19	23.44	19.72	26.19	15.59	32.63	30.97	27.35	27.38	23.10	13.10	20.15
October	22.76	27.64	25.30	23.46	19.77	26.23	15.65	32.75	31.15	27.40	27.42	23.19	13.10	20.25
November	22.76	27.75	25.32	23.41	19.75	26.20	15.63	32.48	31.26	27.41	27.39	23.23	13.10	20.38
December	22.80	27.56	25.36	23.49	19.79	26.23	15.66	33.01	31.08	27.57	27.33	23.34	13.10	20.32
2011														
January	22.89	27.96	25.48	23.64	19.86	26.30	15.72	33.21	31.47	27.54	27.51	23.35	13.17	20.42
February	22.89	28.04	25.41	23.50	19.89	26.28	15.75	33.32	31.54	27.61	27.54	23.34	13.18	20.40
March	22.91	28.11	25.32	23.55	19.89	26.19	15.74	33.45	31.82	27.65	27.54	23.41	13.18	20.34
April	22.96	28.29	25.37	23.60	19.96	26.30	15.80	33.88	31.76	27.71	27.62	23.46	13.21	20.38
May	23.03	28.25	25.35	23.68	19.99	26.30	15.84	33.69	31.58	27.73	27.66	23.61	13.25	20.44
June	23.04	27.74	25.36	23.68	20.03	26.38	15.82	33.89	31.50	27.81	27.75	23.58	13.23	20.46
July	23.13	27.68	25.37	23.74	20.10	26.44	15.95	33.51	31.48	27.89	27.94	23.74	13.21	20.53
August	23.10	28.00	25.47	23.71	20.08	26.42	15.86	33.63	31.59	27.95	27.84	23.68	13.21	20.53
September	23.14	28.07	25.48	23.76	20.04	26.37	15.81	33.85	31.39	28.09	27.85	23.76	13.27	20.55
October	23.22	28.23	25.47	23.88	20.17	26.52	15.95	33.82	31.70	28.25	27.93	23.82	13.30	20.59
November	23.22	28.30	25.46	23.75	20.20	26.53	16.01	33.77	31.63	28.35	27.95	23.82	13.32	20.61
December	23.26	28.39	25.50	23.84	20.22	26.52	16.03	33.63	31.72	28.36	27.92	23.88	13.33	20.63
2012														
January	23.28	28.07	25.51	23.87	20.21	26.50	16.03	33.65	31.63	28.60	27.87	24.05	13.32	20.63
February	23.33	28.52	25.56	23.85	20.23	26.53	16.08	33.51	31.64	28.74	27.91	24.12	13.32	20.65
March	23.40	28.70	25.64	23.88	20.30	26.67	16.11	33.76	31.66	28.88	28.03	24.17	13.35	20.70
April	23.42	28.68	25.67	23.91	20.36	26.69	16.17	33.70	31.75	28.90	27.97	24.15	13.35	20.75
May	23.43	28.62	25.71	23.80	20.40	26.73	16.20	33.85	31.73	29.10	28.03	24.10	13.33	20.76
June	23.50	28.70	25.74	23.92	20.50	26.82	16.33	33.99	31.78	29.12	28.05	24.21	13.38	20.78
July	23.54	28.73	25.78	23.94	20.53	26.84	16.33	34.59	31.82	29.22	28.09	24.22	13.40	20.83
August	23.53	28.65	25.77	23.91	20.54	26.88	16.35	34.24	31.49	29.33	28.04	24.26	13.39	20.90
September	23.60	28.88	25.84	23.97	20.57	26.93	16.39	34.50	31.77	29.44	28.14	24.31	13.40	20.98
October	23.58	28.64	25.84	23.92	20.58	27.00	16.41	34.21	31.70	29.51	28.10	24.29	13.39	20.98
November	23.67	28.93	25.93	24.03	20.63	27.20	16.37	35.14	31.85	29.66	28.22	24.40	13.39	21.01
December	23.75	29.14	25.97	24.07	20.73	27.36	16.48	34.89	32.18	29.80	28.29	24.47	13.38	21.10

Table 2-13. Average Hourly Earnings of All Employees on Total Private Payrolls, by State, NAICS Basis, 2007–2012

(Dollars.)

State	2007	2008	2009	2010	2011	2012
UNITED STATES	20.97	21.62	22.22	22.60	23.06	23.53
Alabama	19.37	19.56	19.68	19.86	20.14	20.21
Alaska	24.70	25.01	24.80	23.90	24.51	25.58
Arizona	19.84	20.69	22.03	22.16	22.56	22.60
Arkansas	16.27	17.21	17.97	18.08	18.36	18.57
California	24.68	24.70	25.47	26.38	26.91	26.85
Colorado	23.13	23.80	23.78	23.79	23.95	24.61
Connecticut	26.59	27.71	27.81	28.08	28.24	28.14
Delaware	21.98	22.73	22.30	22.72	22.32	22.01
District of Columbia	33.54	32.37	31.37	34.18	35.44	36.84
Florida	20.57	21.00	21.61	21.44	21.46	21.62
Georgia	20.44	20.77	21.08	21.57	21.83	21.75
Hawaii	20.68	20.80	21.11	21.65	22.16	22.72
Idaho	16.51	17.53	19.26	21.03	20.79	21.03
Illinois	22.94	22.67	23.05	23.15	23.58	24.31
Indiana	19.94	20.30	20.56	20.57	20.65	21.38
Iowa	18.01	18.35	20.01	20.38	20.22	20.87
Kansas	19.64	20.13	20.18	20.08	20.51	21.03
Kentucky	17.73	18.07	18.82	19.40	19.80	20.06
Louisiana	18.73	19.22	19.46	19.55	20.63	21.36
Maine	18.74	18.96	19.16	19.45	19.96	20.96
Maryland	24.04	24.56	25.42	26.17	25.80	25.95
Massachusetts	26.07	26.38	26.84	27.13	27.62	28.13
Michigan	21.55	21.61	21.89	22.26	22.34	22.44
Minnesota	23.13	23.23	23.41	23.85	24.54	24.95
Mississippi	16.46	16.89	17.87	18.05	18.13	18.83
Missouri	19.79	20.57	20.94	21.19	20.79	21.48
Montana	17.80	18.44	19.86	20.19	20.67	20.70
Nebraska	19.92	19.79	20.19	20.89	20.84	20.95
Nevada	19.64	19.75	19.56	19.13	19.36	19.83
New Hampshire	22.06	22.66	22.70	22.98	23.00	23.71
New Jersey	24.84	25.32	25.92	25.96	25.64	26.45
New Mexico	18.57	18.73	18.92	19.57	19.70	19.82
New York	25.26	25.48	25.70	26.06	26.48	27.18
North Carolina	19.26	19.92	20.61	20.63	20.91	21.71
North Dakota	18.34	18.76	19.21	20.19	21.45	22.77
Ohio	20.22	20.11	19.95	20.22	21.07	22.02
Oklahoma	17.33	17.42	18.06	19.18	20.35	20.90
Oregon	20.61	20.93	21.33	21.56	21.75	22.23
Pennsylvania	20.07	20.43	20.75	21.21	21.85	22.62
Rhode Island	22.17	22.50	22.52	22.67	23.73	25.00
South Carolina	18.76	18.80	19.17	19.89	20.58	20.09
South Dakota	16.47	16.53	17.94	18.55	19.05	19.42
Tennessee	19.01	19.40	19.52	19.94	20.20	20.12
Texas	21.07	21.30	21.39	21.36	21.97	22.21
Utah	21.41	21.10	22.48	24.31	23.11	22.28
Vermont	20.42	21.35	22.41	23.01	23.03	22.79
Virginia	22.46	22.31	22.58	23.54	24.66	24.98
Washington	24.19	25.23	26.32	26.95	27.26	27.34
West Virginia	17.04	17.71	18.09	18.65	18.94	19.56
Wisconsin	20.45	20.67	21.13	21.35	21.85	22.38
Wyoming	20.04	20.83	21.06	21.45	22.18	22.56

. . . = Not available.

Table 2-14. Average Hourly Earnings of Production Workers on Private Nonfarm Payrolls, by Super Sector, NAICS Basis, 2000–2012

(Dollars.)

Industry	2000	2001	2002	2003	2004	2005	2006	2007	2008	2009	2010	2011	2012
TOTAL PRIVATE	14.02	14.55	14.97	15.38	15.70	16.13	16.76	17.44	18.08	18.63	19.07	19.46	19.77
Goods-Producing	15.27	15.78	16.33	16.80	17.19	17.60	18.02	18.67	19.33	19.90	20.28	20.67	20.95
Mining and logging	16.55	17.00	17.19	17.56	18.07	18.72	19.90	20.97	22.50	23.29	23.82	24.50	25.79
Construction	17.48	18.00	18.52	18.95	19.23	19.46	20.02	20.95	21.87	22.66	23.22	23.65	23.98
Manufacturing	14.32	14.76	15.29	15.74	16.14	16.56	16.81	17.26	17.75	18.24	18.61	18.93	19.08
Private Service-Providing	13.63	14.19	14.59	15.00	15.30	15.74	16.42	17.11	17.77	18.36	18.81	19.21	19.52
Trade, transportation, and utilities	13.31	13.70	14.02	14.34	14.58	14.92	15.39	15.78	16.16	16.48	16.82	17.15	17.42
Wholesale trade	16.28	16.77	16.98	17.36	17.65	18.16	18.91	19.59	20.13	20.84	21.54	21.97	22.24
Retail trade	10.87	11.29	11.67	11.90	12.08	12.36	12.57	12.75	12.87	13.01	13.25	13.51	13.81
Transportation and warehousing	15.05	15.33	15.76	16.25	16.52	16.70	17.27	17.72	18.41	18.81	19.16	19.49	19.54
Utilities	22.75	23.58	23.96	24.77	25.61	26.68	27.40	27.88	28.83	29.48	30.04	30.82	31.61
Information	19.07	19.80	20.20	21.01	21.40	22.06	23.23	23.96	24.78	25.45	25.87	26.62	27.01
Financial activities	15.04	15.65	16.25	17.21	17.58	17.98	18.83	19.67	20.32	20.90	21.55	21.93	22.83
Professional and business services	15.52	16.33	16.80	17.21	17.48	18.08	19.13	20.15	21.18	22.35	22.78	23.12	23.28
Education and health services	13.95	14.64	15.21	15.64	16.15	16.71	17.38	18.11	18.87	19.49	20.12	20.77	21.09
Leisure and hospitality	8.32	8.57	8.81	9.00	9.15	9.38	9.75	10.41	10.84	11.12	11.31	11.45	11.62
Other services	12.73	13.27	13.72	13.84	13.98	14.34	14.77	15.42	16.09	16.59	17.06	17.32	17.59

Table 2-15. Average Weekly Earnings of All Employees on Nonfarm Payrolls, by Industry, in Current and 1982–1984 Dollars, NAICS Basis, 2007–2012

(Dollars.)

Industry	2007	2008	2009	2010	2011	2012
TOTAL PRIVATE						
Current dollars	725.25	745.00	753.54	770.82	792.71	811.99
1982–1984 dollars	349.78	346.02	351.24	353.50	352.41	353.66
Goods-Producing						
Current dollars	873.48	899.62	916.07	952.07	976.37	994.75
1982–1984 dollars	421.27	417.84	427.00	436.62	434.06	433.26
Mining and logging						
Current dollars	1 094.81	1 144.63	1 150.12	1 189.32	1 250.91	1 263.46
1982–1984 dollars	528.02	531.64	536.09	545.42	556.11	550.30
Construction						
Current dollars	875.06	905.68	922.54	952.78	973.85	997.82
1982–1904 dollars	422.04	420.65	430.01	436.94	432.94	434.60
Manufacturing						
Current dollars	861.19	882.19	898.44	937.34	958.84	974.29
1982–1984 dollars	415.35	409.74	418.78	429.86	426.27	424.35
Private Service-Providing						
Current dollars	690.09	709.79	719.27	734.98	756.14	775.34
1982–1984 dollars	332.83	329.67	335.27	337.06	336.15	337.70
Trade, transportation, and utilities						
Current dollars	641.51	651.96	659.78	672.58	692.51	708.84
1982–1984 dollars	309.40	302.81	307.54	308.44	307.87	308.74
Wholesale trade						
Current dollars	913.03	936.17	963.44	994.71	1 019.05	1 041.35
1982–1984 dollars	440.35	434.82	449.08	456.17	453.03	453.56
Retail trade						
Current dollars	479.81	478.00	481.18	487.66	500.75	515.22
1982–1984 dollars	231.41	222.01	224.29	223.64	222.62	224.40
Transportation and warehousing						
Current dollars	758.22	780.55	780.53	803.81	834.65	844.18
1982–1984 dollars	365.69	362.54	363.82	368.63	371.06	367.68
Utilities						
Current dollars	1 264.16	1 352.81	1 343.66	1 338.50	1 404.36	1 432.53
1982–1984 dollars	609.70	628.33	626.31	613.83	624.33	623.94
Information						
Current dollars	1 014.35	1 047.50	1 073.27	1 114.65	1 156.56	1 165.28
1982–1984 dollars	489.22	486.52	500.27	511.18	514.17	507.54
Financial activities						
Current dollars	937.69	956.24	971.73	1 004.14	1 039.66	1 093.60
1982–1984 dollars	452.24	444.14	452.94	460.50	462.20	476.32
Professional and business services						
Current dollars	874.68	909.23	947.10	963.57	991.87	1 012.88
1982–1984 dollars	421.85	422.30	441.46	441.89	440.95	441.16
Education and health services						
Current dollars	715.66	745.03	739.27	752.26	774.76	797.13
1982–1984 dollars	345.16	346.04	344.59	344.98	344.43	347.19
Leisure and hospitality						
Current dollars	323.54	330.32	331.64	336.83	342.67	348.96
1982–1984 dollars	156.04	153.42	154.58	154.47	152.34	151.99
Other services						
Current dollars	578.84	597.13	618.18	637.65	649.87	659.48
1982–1984 dollars	279.17	277.34	288.15	292.42	288.91	287.24

Table 2-16. Average Weekly Earnings of Production Workers on Nonfarm Payrolls, by Industry, in Current and 1982–1984 Dollars, NAICS Basis, 2000–2012

(Dollars.)

Industry	2000	2001	2002	2003	2004	2005	2006	2007	2008	2009	2010	2011	2012
TOTAL PRIVATE													
Current dollars	481.36	494.05	507.03	518.41	529.23	544.44	567.89	590.24	608.11	617.50	637.18	654.73	666.99
1982–1984 dollars	285.00	284.76	288.25	288.33	286.85	285.05	288.12	291.09	288.13	294.57	297.79	295.49	294.83
Goods-Producing													
Current dollars	621.86	629.91	651.61	669.13	688.32	705.31	730.16	757.50	776.63	779.68	818.96	844.89	862.09
1982–1984 dollars	368.18	363.06	370.44	372.15	373.07	369.27	370.45	373.58	367.98	371.93	382.75	381.31	381.07
Mining and logging													
Current dollars	734.88	757.96	741.97	765.94	804.01	853.87	907.95	962.63	1 014.69	1 006.67	1 063.11	1 144.64	1 201.92
1982–1984 dollars	435.10	436.86	421.81	426.00	435.78	447.05	460.65	474.75	480.77	480.21	496.86	516.59	531.28
Construction													
Current dollars	685.78	695.86	711.82	727.00	735.55	750.37	781.59	816.23	842.61	851.76	891.83	921.84	942.75
1982–1984 dollars	406.03	401.07	404.67	404.34	398.67	392.86	396.54	402.55	399.24	406.32	416.81	416.04	416.72
Manufacturing													
Current dollars	591.01	595.19	618.62	636.03	658.52	673.30	690.88	711.53	724.46	726.12	765.18	784.29	794.81
1982–1984 dollars	349.92	343.05	351.69	353.74	356.92	352.51	350.52	350.91	343.26	346.38	357.62	353.96	351.33
Private Service-Providing													
Current dollars	446.01	461.32	474.31	485.26	494.71	509.69	532.92	555.00	574.63	588.54	606.19	622.28	634.60
1982–1984 dollars	264.07	265.89	269.65	269.89	268.14	266.85	270.38	273.71	272.27	280.75	283.31	280.84	280.51
Trade, transportation, and utilities													
Current dollars	449.96	459.53	471.27	481.14	488.51	498.46	514.37	525.91	536.11	541.88	559.63	577.71	588.70
1982–1984 dollars	266.41	264.86	267.92	267.60	264.78	260.97	260.97	259.37	254.02	258.49	261.55	260.73	260.22
Wholesale trade													
Current dollars	631.24	643.45	644.38	657.29	666.79	685.00	718.50	748.94	769.62	784.49	816.50	845.44	860.74
1982–1984 dollars	373.74	370.86	366.33	365.57	361.40	358.64	364.54	369.36	364.66	374.23	381.60	381.56	380.47
Retail trade													
Current dollars	333.41	346.16	360.84	367.18	371.13	377.58	383.12	385.00	386.21	388.57	400.07	412.09	421.85
1982–1984 dollars	197.40	199.52	205.14	204.22	201.15	197.69	194.38	189.87	182.99	185.36	186.98	185.98	186.47
Transportation and warehousing													
Current dollars	562.56	562.57	579.91	598.41	614.89	618.55	636.80	654.95	670.22	677.56	710.85	737.00	742.23
1982–1984 dollars	333.07	324.25	329.68	332.82	333.27	323.85	323.08	323.01	317.56	323.22	332.22	332.62	328.09
Utilities													
Current dollars	955.09	977.25	979.26	1 017.44	1 048.01	1 095.91	1 135.57	1 182.65	1 230.65	1 239.34	1 262.89	1 296.92	1 298.19
1982–1984 dollars	565.48	563.26	556.71	565.87	568.03	573.77	576.14	583.26	583.10	591.20	590.23	585.32	573.84
Information													
Current dollars	700.92	731.18	737.94	760.84	776.72	805.11	850.64	874.45	908.78	931.08	939.85	964.85	971.22
1982–1984 dollars	414.99	421.43	419.52	423.16	420.99	421.52	431.58	431.26	430.59	444.15	439.25	435.45	429.31
Financial activities													
Current dollars	540.39	560.46	578.94	611.65	625.50	646.48	673.48	706.33	729.61	755.08	780.19	798.71	840.57
1982–1984 dollars	319.95	323.03	329.13	340.18	339.02	338.47	341.69	348.35	345.70	360.20	364.63	360.47	371.56
Professional and business services													
Current dollars	535.07	557.84	574.60	587.02	597.54	618.71	662.27	700.82	737.90	775.81	798.54	813.37	822.19
1982–1984 dollars	316.80	321.52	326.66	326.48	323.87	323.93	336.01	345.63	349.63	370.09	373.21	367.09	363.43
Education and health services													
Current dollars	449.29	473.39	492.74	505.69	523.78	544.59	564.94	590.09	613.73	628.45	646.65	670.24	682.74
1982–1984 dollars	266.01	272.85	280.13	281.25	283.89	285.13	286.63	291.02	290.79	299.79	302.22	302.49	301.79
Leisure and hospitality													
Current dollars	217.20	220.73	227.31	230.49	234.86	241.36	250.34	265.54	273.39	275.95	280.87	283.82	290.43
1982–1984 dollars	128.60	127.22	129.23	128.19	127.30	126.37	127.01	130.96	129.54	131.64	131.27	128.09	128.38
Other services													
Current dollars	413.30	428.64	439.87	434.41	433.04	443.40	456.50	477.06	495.57	506.26	523.70	532.63	539.31
1982–1984 dollars	244.70	247.05	250.07	241.61	234.71	232.15	231.61	235.27	234.81	241.50	244.76	240.38	238.39

Table 2-17. Average Weekly Earnings of All Employees on Total Private Payrolls, by State, NAICS Basis, 2007–2012

(Dollars.)

State	2007	2008	2009	2010	2011	2012
UNITED STATES	725.25	745.00	753.54	770.82	792.71	811.99
Alabama	708.94	704.16	684.86	697.09	710.94	727.56
Alaska	876.85	882.85	868.00	843.67	877.46	905.53
Arizona	698.37	720.01	766.64	780.03	789.60	791.00
Arkansas	571.08	605.79	621.76	630.99	642.60	648.09
California	851.46	844.74	860.89	896.92	925.70	923.64
Colorado	807.24	828.24	815.65	816.00	826.28	861.35
Connecticut	912.04	942.14	917.73	935.06	957.34	956.76
Delaware	753.91	768.27	729.21	736.13	738.79	726.33
District of Columbia	1 217.50	1 158.85	1 135.59	1 203.14	1 258.12	1 318.87
Florida	728.18	739.20	756.35	761.12	746.81	741.57
Georgia	727.66	733.18	729.37	748.48	757.50	761.25
Hawaii	674.17	678.08	686.08	710.12	740.14	770.21
Idaho	566.29	594.27	647.14	704.51	704.78	706.61
Illinois	789.14	777.58	792.92	796.36	815.87	843.56
Indiana	707.87	710.50	711.38	722.01	722.75	741.89
Iowa	615.94	620.23	666.33	694.96	687.48	715.84
Kansas	681.51	700.52	690.16	684.73	707.60	733.95
Kentucky	654.24	654.13	666.23	684.82	693.00	696.08
Louisiana	670.53	701.53	702.51	713.58	748.87	773.23
Maine	640.91	650.33	638.03	657.41	678.64	714.74
Maryland	836.59	852.23	876.99	892.40	887.52	882.30
Massachusetts	873.35	886.37	901.82	911.57	914.22	928.29
Michigan	752.10	739.06	728.94	750.16	764.03	767.45
Minnesota	779.48	775.88	763.17	787.05	817.18	838.32
Mississippi	587.62	601.28	632.60	648.00	652.68	670.35
Missouri	680.78	709.67	709.87	718.34	721.41	743.21
Montana	633.68	595.61	619.63	658.19	680.04	687.24
Nebraska	667.32	666.92	680.40	712.35	710.64	714.40
Nevada	732.57	730.75	700.25	659.99	665.98	674.22
New Hampshire	734.60	743.25	742.29	760.64	763.60	784.80
New Jersey	844.56	850.75	870.91	877.45	869.20	888.72
New Mexico	642.52	663.04	664.09	684.95	691.47	687.75
New York	861.37	868.87	866.09	883.43	902.97	924.12
North Carolina	670.25	683.26	696.62	703.48	717.21	749.00
North Dakota	605.22	607.82	614.72	658.19	731.45	799.23
Ohio	687.48	681.73	658.35	677.37	710.06	750.88
Oklahoma	606.55	618.41	633.91	682.81	720.39	739.86
Oregon	704.86	707.43	708.16	724.42	735.15	751.37
Pennsylvania	678.37	688.49	684.75	706.29	731.98	750.98
Rhode Island	742.70	767.25	763.43	768.51	783.09	827.50
South Carolina	675.36	669.28	665.20	692.17	716.18	705.16
South Dakota	543.51	543.84	597.40	626.99	645.80	673.87
Tennessee	671.05	682.88	687.10	703.88	711.04	712.25
Texas	769.06	771.06	752.93	766.82	808.50	808.44
Utah	747.21	730.06	804.78	863.01	808.85	784.26
Vermont	696.32	734.44	764.18	786.94	776.11	768.02
Virginia	790.59	780.85	781.27	833.32	872.96	874.30
Washington	853.91	872.96	905.41	921.69	943.20	945.96
West Virginia	599.81	623.39	622.30	650.89	653.43	672.86
Wisconsin	672.81	682.11	680.39	700.28	723.24	747.49
Wyoming	725.45	764.46	747.63	770.06	800.70	821.18

NOTES AND DEFINITIONS

QUARTERLY CENSUS OF EMPLOYMENT AND WAGES

The Quarterly Census of Employment and Wages (QCEW), often referred to as the ES-202 program, is a cooperative endeavor of the Bureau of Labor Statistics (BLS) and the State Employment Security Agencies (SESAs). Using quarterly data submitted by the agencies, BLS summarizes the employment and wage data for workers covered by state unemployment insurance laws and civilian workers covered by the Unemployment Compensation for Federal Employees (UCFE) program.

Since the introduction of 2001 data, the QCEW data have been coded according to the North American Classification System, either NAICS 2002, which was used for the data up through 2006; NAICS 2007, which was used for data from 2007 through 2010; or NAICS 2012, which was introduced with the release of first quarter data in 2011. As a result of the revision, approximately 8 percent of establishments, 11 percent of employment, and 6 percent of total wages were reclassified into different industries within private industry.

NAICS is the statistical classification standard underlying all establishment-based federal economic statistics classified by industry. Before 2001, QCEW data were coded according to the Standard Industrial Classification (SIC) system. Due to the differences in the classification systems, data coded according to NAICS are often not directly comparable to SIC coded data.

The QCEW data series is the most complete universe of employment and wage information by industry, county, and state. It includes 98 percent of all wage and salary civilian employment. These data serve as the basic source of benchmark information for employment by industry in the Current Employment Statistics (CES) survey, which is described in the first section of notes in this chapter. Therefore, the entire employment series is not presented here. The wage series is presented because the CES only provides earnings only for production and nonsupervisory employees. The QCEW is more comprehensive. BLS aggregates the data by industry and ownership; these aggregations are available at the national, state, county, and metropolitan statistical area (MSA) levels.

COLLECTION AND COVERAGE

Employment data under the QCEW program represent the number of covered workers who worked during, or received pay for, the pay period including the 12th of the month. Excluded are members of the armed forces, the self-employed, proprietors, domestic workers, unpaid family workers, and railroad workers covered by the railroad unemployment insurance system. Wages represent total compensation paid during the calendar quarter, regardless of when services were performed. Included in wages are pay for vacation and other paid leave, bonuses, stock options, tips, the cash value of meals and lodging, and, in some states, contributions to deferred compensation plans (such as 401(k) plans). The QCEW program does provide partial information on agricultural industries and employees in private households.

Data from the QCEW program serve as an important input to many BLS programs. The QCEW data are used as the benchmark source for employment by the Current Employment Statistics program and the Occupational employment statistics program. The UI administrative records collected under the QCEW program serve as a sampling frame for BLS establishment surveys.

In addition, data from the QCEW program serve as an input to other federal and state programs. The Bureau of Economic Analysis (BEA) of the Department of Commerce uses QCEW data as the base for developing the wage and salary component of personal income. The Employment and Training Administration (ETA) of the Department of Labor and the SESAs use QCEW data to administer the employment security program. The QCEW data accurately reflect the extent of coverage of the state UI laws and are used to measure UI revenues; national, state and local area employment; and total and UI taxable wage trends.

SOURCES OF ADDITIONAL INFORMATION

Additional information is available on the BLS Web site at http://www.bls.gov/cew.

Table 2-18. Employment and Average Annual Pay for Covered Workers,[1] by Industry, NAICS Basis, 2007–2012

(Number, dollars.)

Industry	2007		2008		2009	
	Employment	Average annual pay	Employment	Average annual pay	Employment	Average annual pay
Total Private	114 012 221	44 362	113 188 643	45 371	106 947 104	45 155
Natural resources and mining	1 826 609	45 733	1 882 426	49 170	1 783 558	47 425
Agriculture, forestry, fishing, and hunting	1 166 333	25 191	1 169 029	25 986	1 142 192	26 031
Construction	7 562 732	46 784	7 124 886	49 013	5 948 837	49 322
Manufacturing	13 833 022	53 489	13 382 697	54 400	11 810 371	54 873
Wholesale trade	5 987 206	60 719	5 954 915	61 843	5 561 787	61 595
Retail trade	15 509 017	26 124	15 307 933	26 179	14 544 111	26 162
Transportation and warehousing	4 292 445	42 615	4 271 969	42 962	3 985 037	42 823
Utilities	549 539	82 275	557 983	84 153	560 713	84 877
Information	3 029 789	69 140	2 989 161	70 787	2 807 721	71 191
Financial activities	8 145 981	73 980	7 968 376	74 133	7 589 821	70 045
Professional and business services	17 859 796	55 139	17 705 280	57 476	16 488 835	58 344
Education and health services	17 433 162	40 528	17 954 103	41 984	18 321 635	43 042
Leisure and hospitality	13 327 559	18 495	13 395 477	18 946	13 001 028	18 899
Other services	4 438 439	27 970	4 484 907	28 773	4 369 780	28 814
Total Government	21 353 885	44 968	21 617 017	46 568	21 660 738	47 552
Federal	2 726 300	64 871	2 762 055	66 293	2 826 713	67 756
State	4 611 395	45 903	4 642 650	47 980	4 639 715	48 742
Local	14 016 190	40 790	14 212 311	42 274	14 194 311	43 140

Industry	2010		2011		2012	
	Employment	Average annual pay	Employment	Average annual pay	Employment	Average annual pay
Total Private	106 201 232	46 455	108 184 795	47 815	110 645 869	49 200
Natural resources and mining	1 798 592	49 820	1 890 359	53 691	1 988 119	55 944
Agriculture, forestry, fishing, and hunting	1 146 962	26 636	1 160 311	27 543	1 189 986	28 619
Construction	5 489 499	49 597	5 473 045	50 693	5 586 553	52 298
Manufacturing	11 487 496	57 526	11 701 497	59 210	11 904 945	60 496
Wholesale trade	5 466 463	63 629	5 545 802	66 142	5 656 717	68 226
Retail trade	14 481 324	26 652	14 666 625	27 118	14 864 946	27 731
Transportation and warehousing	3 943 659	44 197	4 055 639	45 336	4 158 046	46 612
Utilities	551 287	86 791	549 921	90 609	549 681	93 722
Information	2 703 886	74 395	2 674 852	78 331	2 677 224	81 955
Financial activities	7 401 812	73 977	7 416 409	77 366	7 506 950	80 110
Professional and business services	16 712 011	60 145	17 298 233	61 902	17 887 637	64 487
Education and health services	18 656 160	43 604	19 035 334	44 383	19 405 016	45 285
Leisure and hospitality	13 006 814	19 387	13 294 603	19 772	13 739 315	20 218
Other services	4 349 563	29 370	4 408 735	29 916	4 548 785	30 090
Total Government	21 619 210	48 202	21 226 299	49 205	21 050 509	49 757
Federal	2 980 813	69 198	2 863 132	73 001	2 820 722	73 340
State	4 606 001	48 960	4 553 697	50 252	4 523 704	51 366
Local	14 032 396	43 493	13 809 471	43 926	13 706 083	44 373

[1]Includes workers covered by unemployment insurance (UI) and Unemployment Compensation for Federal Employees (UCFE) programs.

Table 2-19. Employment and Average Annual Pay for Covered Workers,[1] by State and Selected Territory, 2007–2012

(Number, dollars.)

State	2007		2008		2009	
	Employment	Average annual pay	Employment	Average annual pay	Employment	Average annual pay
UNITED STATES	135 366 106	44 458	134 805 659	45 563	128 607 842	45 559
Alabama	1 952 091	37 492	1 936 489	38 734	1 829 487	39 422
Alaska	310 810	43 972	315 285	45 805	313 802	47 103
Arizona	2 647 691	41 551	2 583 215	42 518	2 396 362	42 832
Arkansas	1 173 852	34 118	1 172 208	34 919	1 134 488	35 692
California	15 640 575	50 538	15 494 915	51 487	14 629 953	51 566
Colorado	2 292 630	45 396	2 310 865	46 614	2 201 427	46 861
Connecticut	1 686 043	58 029	1 687 902	58 395	1 615 356	57 771
Delaware	423 412	47 308	423 083	47 569	402 343	47 770
District of Columbia	678 119	73 450	685 069	76 518	681 875	77 483
Florida	7 945 162	39 746	7 666 374	40 568	7 182 815	40 970
Georgia	4 077 184	42 178	4 031 467	42 585	3 796 429	42 902
Hawaii	625 862	39 466	619 703	40 675	592 171	41 328
Idaho	660 683	33 544	653 108	33 897	613 814	34 124
Illinois	5 869 157	47 685	5 841 692	48 719	5 551 930	48 358
Indiana	2 905 725	37 528	2 872 442	38 403	2 705 331	38 270
Iowa	1 485 627	35 738	1 490 575	36 964	1 445 627	37 158
Kansas	1 356 966	37 044	1 366 878	38 178	1 317 029	38 154
Kentucky	1 801 907	36 480	1 791 017	37 434	1 710 677	37 996
Louisiana	1 868 986	38 229	1 890 007	40 381	1 849 303	40 579
Maine	602 321	35 129	602 074	36 317	581 796	36 617
Maryland	2 547 351	48 241	2 537 752	49 535	2 461 109	50 579
Massachusetts	3 234 357	55 244	3 245 983	56 746	3 135 497	56 267
Michigan	4 179 122	55 244	4 070 914	56 746	3 775 435	56 267
Minnesota	2 687 482	44 375	2 679 527	45 826	2 569 651	45 319
Mississippi	1 135 336	32 291	1 131 096	33 508	1 081 138	33 847
Missouri	2 719 380	38 603	2 715 183	40 361	2 607 595	40 022
Montana	436 656	32 224	437 591	33 305	421 566	33 762
Nebraska	916 580	35 238	922 929	36 243	901 470	36 644
Nevada	1 284 502	42 149	1 252 987	42 984	1 138 036	42 743
New Hampshire	630 204	43 863	628 763	44 912	605 004	44 932
New Jersey	3 961 341	53 853	3 934 789	55 280	3 771 296	55 168
New Mexico	821 484	36 379	825 736	37 910	791 509	38 529
New York	8 554 012	59 439	8 608 351	60 288	8 343 862	57 739
North Carolina	4 062 955	38 909	4 043 486	39 740	3 823 299	39 844
North Dakota	341 705	33 086	350 440	35 075	349 560	35 970
Ohio	5 306 812	39 917	5 235 972	40 784	4 943 970	40 900
Oklahoma	1 534 802	35 491	1 550 489	37 284	1 497 855	37 238
Oregon	1 727 886	39 569	1 713 764	40 500	1 607 915	40 757
Pennsylvania	5 652 547	43 239	5 658 771	44 381	5 468 176	44 829
Rhode Island	480 132	41 646	469 701	43 029	448 842	43 439
South Carolina	1 891 255	35 393	1 876 081	36 252	1 765 739	36 759
South Dakota	1 891 255	31 655	1 876 081	32 822	1 765 739	33 352
Tennessee	2 745 099	39 082	2 721 990	39 996	2 565 288	40 242
Texas	10 231 906	44 695	10 452 907	45 939	10 149 694	45 692
Utah	1 219 207	37 054	1 221 052	37 980	1 157 704	38 614
Vermont	303 448	36 956	302 627	38 328	292 406	38 778
Virginia	3 672 958	45 995	3 665 654	47 241	3 545 623	48 239
Washington	2 925 908	45 021	2 950 773	46 569	2 836 283	47 470
West Virginia	706 172	34 106	709 657	35 987	691 998	36 897
Wisconsin	2 780 924	38 050	2 772 889	39 119	2 644 190	39 131
Wyoming	277 721	39 254	286 333	41 487	274 758	40 709
Puerto Rico	1 016 362	24 741	1 001 120	25 554	954 555	26 359
Virgin Islands	45 922	36 521	45 796	37 005	43 799	37 299

[1]Includes workers covered by the unemployment insurance (UI) and Unemployment Compensation for Federal Employees (UCFE) programs.

Table 2-19. Employment and Average Annual Pay for Covered Workers,[1] by State and Selected Territory, 2007–2012—*Continued*

(Number, dollars.)

State	2010		2011		2012	
	Employment	Average annual pay	Employment	Average annual pay	Employment	Average annual pay
UNITED STATES	127 820 442	46 751	129 411 095	48 043	131 696 378	49 289
Alabama	1 813 155	40 289	1 813 497	41 186	1 828 248	41 990
Alaska	316 691	48 230	322 084	49 383	327 378	50 614
Arizona	2 356 789	43 299	2 378 248	44 581	2 431 788	45 593
Arkansas	1 134 071	36 254	1 139 682	37 280	1 146 811	38 226
California	14 414 461	53 285	14 567 128	55 013	14 959 808	56 784
Colorado	2 176 986	47 868	2 213 059	49 082	2 266 503	50 563
Connecticut	1 595 713	59 465	1 612 292	61 145	1 627 748	62 085
Delaware	399 078	48 669	402 959	50 499	405 646	51 734
District of Columbia	693 274	80 200	707 359	81 529	714 930	82 783
Florida	7 109 630	41 581	7 195 232	42 313	7 341 002	43 211
Georgia	3 753 934	43 899	3 792 209	45 090	3 841 767	46 267
Hawaii	586 772	41 709	593 668	42 473	605 240	43 385
Idaho	605 571	34 900	607 504	35 626	614 463	36 152
Illinois	5 502 322	49 497	5 566 648	50 840	5 636 918	52 194
Indiana	2 709 831	39 256	2 755 826	40 248	2 812 347	41 240
Iowa	1 436 340	38 146	1 452 769	39 204	1 475 884	40 343
Kansas	1 297 779	38 936	1 303 799	39 989	1 320 285	41 118
Kentucky	1 712 178	38 720	1 734 503	39 646	1 761 043	40 451
Louisiana	1 832 357	41 461	1 848 399	42 375	1 871 037	43 300
Maine	577 790	37 338	579 838	38 020	583 196	38 606
Maryland	2 453 197	51 739	2 478 505	53 008	2 511 669	54 035
Massachusetts	3 149 169	57 770	3 189 753	59 671	3 242 273	60 898
Michigan	3 770 225	57 770	3 854 837	59 671	3 935 694	60 898
Minnesota	2 558 310	46 787	2 602 988	47 858	2 644 408	49 349
Mississippi	1 074 617	34 343	1 076 488	34 976	1 085 748	35 875
Missouri	2 573 703	40 679	2 585 009	41 461	2 607 420	42 695
Montana	419 231	34 595	422 726	35 791	430 315	37 096
Nebraska	896 936	37 324	901 584	38 269	920 295	39 268
Nevada	1 108 238	42 512	1 115 062	43 102	1 132 140	43 667
New Hampshire	600 697	45 957	605 853	47 281	612 419	48 272
New Jersey	3 735 703	56 382	3 734 660	57 546	3 768 935	58 644
New Mexico	781 694	39 264	781 226	40 032	785 455	40 698
New York	8 340 732	60 291	8 444 791	61 792	8 563 125	62 669
North Carolina	3 788 581	41 119	3 838 300	42 121	3 907 085	43 110
North Dakota	358 635	38 128	379 432	41 778	411 709	45 909
Ohio	4 908 571	41 788	4 968 724	42 972	5 048 166	44 244
Oklahoma	1 485 400	38 237	1 507 558	40 108	1 540 292	41 633
Oregon	1 598 173	41 675	1 616 634	43 090	1 642 434	44 258
Pennsylvania	5 472 171	45 733	5 535 283	47 035	5 558 414	48 397
Rhode Island	447 408	44 645	448 570	45 705	450 711	46 716
South Carolina	1 758 204	37 553	1 780 690	38 427	1 810 150	39 286
South Dakota	1 758 204	34 331	1 780 690	35 413	1 810 150	36 534
Tennessee	2 558 438	41 572	2 602 604	42 454	2 653 392	43 961
Texas	10 182 150	46 952	10 422 295	48 735	10 727 642	50 579
Utah	1 150 737	39 389	1 176 530	40 279	1 215 983	41 301
Vermont	293 058	39 434	295 512	40 293	299 519	40 967
Virginia	3 536 676	49 651	3 578 848	50 657	3 619 176	51 646
Washington	2 808 698	48 516	2 844 622	50 256	2 894 703	51 962
West Virginia	692 448	37 675	701 905	39 092	710 590	39 727
Wisconsin	2 633 572	39 966	2 664 920	41 003	2 695 404	41 966
Wyoming	271 151	41 963	274 743	43 394	278 595	44 580
Puerto Rico	930 319	26 617	923 451	26 678	937 634	26 948
Virgin Islands	44 267	38 936	43 799	38 597	40 533	38 862

[1]Includes workers covered by the unemployment insurance (UI) and Unemployment Compensation for Federal Employees (UCFE) programs.

BUSINESS EMPLOYMENT DYNAMICS

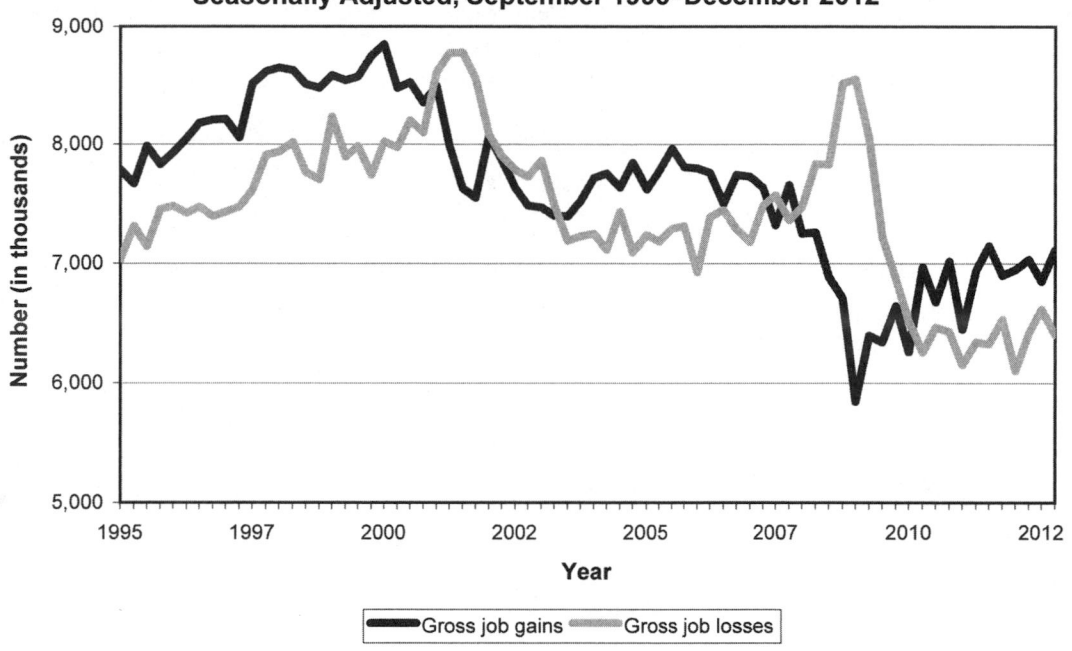

Figure 2-3. Private Sector Gross Job Gains and Gross Job Losses, Seasonally Adjusted, September 1995–December 2012

The change in the number of jobs is the net result of the gross increase in the number of jobs from expanding and opening establishments and the gross decrease in jobs from contracting and closing establishments. The net gain of 709,000 jobs in the fourth quarter of 2012 resulted from 7.110 million gross job gains and 6.401 million gross job losses. There was a net gain of jobs in eleven consecutive quarters from June 2010 to December 2012. In contrast, there was a net loss in nine consecutive quarters from the first quarter of 2008 through the first quarter of 2010. (See Table 2-20.)

OTHER HIGHLIGHTS

- Of the 6.401 million jobs that were lost in the fourth quarter of 2012, 81.2 percent resulted from contracting establishments while 18.8 percent were the result of establishments closing. (See Table 2-20.)

- The service-providing industries experienced a net job gain of 665,000 in the fourth quarter of 2012. Within the service-providing industry, professional and business services experienced the greatest net job gain at 174,000. (See Table 2-22.)

- In construction, gross job gains exceeded gross job losses by 63,000 in the fourth quarter of 2012—more than in any other goods-producing sector. (See Table 2-22.)

- Job gains exceeded job losses in all states except for Alaska (-1,020), Maine (-2,248) and West Virginia (-602) in the fourth quarter of 2012. (See Table 2-23.)

NOTES AND DEFINITIONS

BUSINESS EMPLOYMENT DYNAMICS (BED)

The Business Employment Dynamics (BED) data are a set of statistics generated from the federal-state cooperative program known as the Quarterly Census of Employment and Wages (QCEW), or the ES-202 program. These quarterly data series consist of gross job gains and gross job losses statistics from 1992 forward.

The Bureau of Labor Statistics (BLS) compiles the BED data from existing quarterly state unemployment insurance (UI) records. Most employers in the United States are required to file quarterly reports on the employment and wages of workers covered by UI laws and to pay quarterly UI taxes. The quarterly UI reports are sent by the State Workforce Agencies (SWAs) to BLS. These reports form the basis of the BLS establishment universe-sampling frame.

In the BED program, the quarterly UI records are linked across quarters to provide a longitudinal history for each establishment. The linkage process allows the tracking of net employment changes at the establishment level, which in turn allows estimations of jobs gained at opening and expanding establishments and of jobs lost at closing and contracting establishments. BLS publishes three different establishment-based employment measures for every given quarter. Each of these measures—the Current Employment Statistics (CES) survey, the QCEW program, and the BED data—makes use of the quarterly UI employment reports. However, each measure has somewhat different types of universal coverage, estimation procedures, and publication products. (See the notes and corresponding tables for CES and QCEW in earlier sections of this chapter.)

CONCEPTS AND DEFINITIONS

The BED data measure the net change in employment at the establishment level. These changes can come about in four different ways. A net increase in employment can come from either opening establishments or expanding establishments. A net decrease in employment can come from either closing establishments or contracting establishments.

Gross job gains include the sum of all jobs added at either opening or expanding establishments.

Gross job losses include the sum of all jobs lost in either closing or contracting establishments. The net change in employment is the difference between gross job gains and gross job losses.

Openings consist of establishments with positive third-month employment for the first time in the current quarter, with no links to the prior quarter, or with positive third-month employment in the current quarter, following zero employment in the previous quarter.

Expansions include establishments with positive employment in the third month in both the previous and current quarters, with a net increase in employment over this period.

Closings consist of establishments with positive third-month employment in the previous quarter, with no employment or zero employment reported in the current quarter.

Contractions include establishments with positive employment in the third month in both the previous and current quarters, with a net decrease in employment over this period.

SOURCES OF ADDITIONAL INFORMATION

For additional information, see BLS news release 13-1524, "Business Employment Dynamics: Fourth Quarter 2012." These resources can be found on the BLS Web site at http://www.bls.gov.

Table 2-20. Private Sector Gross Job Gains and Job Losses, Seasonally Adjusted, March 1997–December 2012

(Thousands of jobs.)

Year and month	Net change[1]	Gross job gains			Gross job losses		
		Total	Expanding establishments	Opening establishments	Total	Contracting establishments	Closing establishments
1997							
March	784	8 214	6 407	1 807	7 430	5 886	1 544
June	584	8 055	6 330	1 725	7 471	5 931	1 540
September	901	8 515	6 718	1 797	7 614	5 927	1 687
December	708	8 617	6 697	1 920	7 909	6 024	1 885
1998							
March	711	8 648	6 599	2 049	7 937	6 077	1 860
June	610	8 629	6 552	2 077	8 019	6 224	1 795
September	742	8 508	6 607	1 901	7 766	6 093	1 673
December	768	8 475	6 737	1 738	7 707	6 025	1 682
1999							
March	353	8 585	6 626	1 959	8 232	6 395	1 837
June	644	8 539	6 661	1 878	7 895	6 210	1 685
September	588	8 571	6 734	1 837	7 983	6 250	1 733
December	1 005	8 749	6 956	1 793	7 744	6 076	1 668
2000							
March	827	8 849	6 960	1 889	8 022	6 342	1 680
June	503	8 479	6 794	1 685	7 976	6 373	1 603
September	324	8 525	6 756	1 769	8 201	6 479	1 722
December	251	8 351	6 673	1 678	8 100	6 444	1 656
2001							
March	-119	8 491	6 728	1 763	8 610	6 717	1 893
June	-780	7 991	6 302	1 689	8 771	7 036	1 735
September	-1 148	7 630	5 945	1 685	8 778	6 990	1 788
December	-1 009	7 547	5 912	1 635	8 556	6 870	1 686
2002							
March	-10	8 071	6 298	1 773	8 081	6 434	1 647
June	-30	7 868	6 145	1 723	7 898	6 274	1 624
September	-151	7 630	6 039	1 591	7 781	6 248	1 533
December	-241	7 483	5 938	1 545	7 724	6 185	1 539
2003							
March	-393	7 467	5 928	1 539	7 860	6 307	1 553
June	-90	7 398	5 929	1 469	7 488	6 030	1 458
September	204	7 392	5 923	1 469	7 188	5 828	1 360
December	297	7 521	6 005	1 516	7 224	5 800	1 424
2004							
March	470	7 715	6 204	1 511	7 245	5 795	1 450
June	644	7 754	6 235	1 519	7 110	5 639	1 471
September	206	7 633	6 060	1 573	7 427	5 888	1 539
December	757	7 844	6 243	1 601	7 087	5 663	1 424
2005							
March	384	7 620	6 131	1 489	7 236	5 801	1 435
June	593	7 774	6 231	1 543	7 181	5 776	1 405
September	677	7 965	6 387	1 578	7 288	5 844	1 444
December	494	7 807	6 252	1 555	7 313	5 948	1 365
2006							
March	874	7 797	6 354	1 443	6 923	5 636	1 287
June	371	7 758	6 246	1 512	7 387	6 015	1 372
September	52	7 499	6 061	1 438	7 447	6 097	1 350
December	455	7 740	6 223	1 517	7 285	5 941	1 344
2007							
March	549	7 727	6 297	1 430	7 178	5 881	1 297
June	149	7 632	6 222	1 410	7 483	6 079	1 404
September	-252	7 318	5 847	1 471	7 570	6 215	1 355
December	299	7 658	6 196	1 462	7 359	6 012	1 347
2008							
March	-225	7 246	5 834	1 412	7 471	6 102	1 369
June	-578	7 254	5 846	1 408	7 832	6 352	1 480
September	-944	6 886	5 523	1 363	7 830	6 448	1 382
December	-1 809	6 706	5 354	1 352	8 515	7 034	1 481
2009							
March	-2 710	5 844	4 655	1 189	8 554	7 132	1 422
June	-1 659	6 391	5 088	1 303	8 050	6 667	1 383
September	-880	6 340	5 125	1 215	7 220	5 863	1 357
December	-229	6 640	5 316	1 324	6 869	5 589	1 280
2010							
March	-262	6 256	5 086	1 170	6 518	5 313	1 205
June	715	6 966	5 684	1 282	6 251	5 086	1 165
September	210	6 675	5 423	1 252	6 465	5 240	1 225
December	591	7 015	5 642	1 373	6 424	5 202	1 222
2011							
March	296	6 448	5 278	1 170	6 152	5 015	1 137
June	602	6 940	5 642	1 298	6 338	5 108	1 230
September	819	7 144	5 785	1 359	6 325	5 181	1 144
December	368	6 896	5 549	1 347	6 528	5 250	1 278
2012							
March	847	6 946	5 702	1 244	6 099	4 995	1 104
June	613	7 027	5 738	1 289	6 414	5 259	1 155
September	233	6 847	5 552	1 295	6 614	5 436	1 178
December	709	7 110	5 769	1 341	6 401	5 199	1 202

[1]Net change is the difference between total gross job gains and total gross job losses.

Table 2-21. Private Sector Gross Job Gains and Job Losses, as a Percent of Employment,[1] Seasonally Adjusted, March 1997–December 2012

(Percent.)

Year and month	Net change[2]	Gross job gains			Gross job losses		
		Total	Expanding establishments	Opening establishments	Total	Contracting establishments	Closing establishments
1997							
March	0.9	8.2	6.4	1.8	7.3	5.8	1.5
June	0.6	7.9	6.2	1.7	7.3	5.8	1.5
September	1.0	8.4	6.6	1.8	7.4	5.8	1.6
December	0.8	8.4	6.5	1.9	7.6	5.8	1.8
1998							
March	0.7	8.4	6.4	2.0	7.7	5.9	1.8
June	0.6	8.3	6.3	2.0	7.7	6.0	1.7
September	0.7	8.1	6.3	1.8	7.4	5.8	1.6
December	0.7	8.0	6.4	1.6	7.3	5.7	1.6
1999							
March	0.3	8.0	6.2	1.8	7.7	6.0	1.7
June	0.6	8.0	6.2	1.8	7.4	5.8	1.6
September	0.6	8.0	6.3	1.7	7.4	5.8	1.6
December	1.0	8.1	6.4	1.7	7.1	5.6	1.5
2000							
March	0.8	8.1	6.4	1.7	7.3	5.8	1.5
June	0.4	7.7	6.2	1.5	7.3	5.8	1.5
September	0.2	7.7	6.1	1.6	7.5	5.9	1.6
December	0.2	7.5	6.0	1.5	7.3	5.8	1.5
2001							
March	-0.1	7.7	6.1	1.6	7.8	6.1	1.7
June	-0.8	7.2	5.7	1.5	8.0	6.4	1.6
September	-1.1	6.9	5.4	1.5	8.0	6.4	1.6
December	-1.0	7.0	5.5	1.5	8.0	6.4	1.6
2002							
March	0.0	7.5	5.9	1.6	7.5	6.0	1.5
June	0.0	7.3	5.7	1.6	7.3	5.8	1.5
September	-0.1	7.1	5.6	1.5	7.2	5.8	1.4
December	-0.3	6.9	5.5	1.4	7.2	5.8	1.4
2003							
March	-0.5	6.9	5.5	1.4	7.4	5.9	1.5
June	0.0	7.0	5.6	1.4	7.0	5.6	1.4
September	0.1	6.9	5.5	1.4	6.8	5.5	1.3
December	0.3	7.0	5.6	1.4	6.7	5.4	1.3
2004							
March	0.5	7.2	5.8	1.4	6.7	5.4	1.3
June	0.6	7.2	5.8	1.4	6.6	5.2	1.4
September	0.3	7.1	5.6	1.5	6.8	5.4	1.4
December	0.7	7.2	5.7	1.5	6.5	5.2	1.3
2005							
March	0.4	7.0	5.6	1.4	6.6	5.3	1.3
June	0.6	7.1	5.7	1.4	6.5	5.2	1.3
September	0.6	7.2	5.8	1.4	6.6	5.3	1.3
December	0.4	7.0	5.6	1.4	6.6	5.4	1.2
2006							
March	0.9	7.0	5.7	1.3	6.1	5.0	1.1
June	0.3	6.8	5.5	1.3	6.5	5.3	1.2
September	0.1	6.7	5.4	1.3	6.6	5.4	1.2
December	0.3	6.8	5.5	1.3	6.5	5.3	1.2
2007							
March	0.5	6.8	5.5	1.3	6.3	5.2	1.1
June	0.2	6.7	5.5	1.2	6.5	5.3	1.2
September	-0.3	6.4	5.1	1.3	6.7	5.5	1.2
December	0.2	6.7	5.4	1.3	6.5	5.3	1.2
2008							
March	-0.3	6.3	5.1	1.2	6.6	5.4	1.2
June	-0.6	6.3	5.1	1.2	6.9	5.6	1.3
September	-0.8	6.1	4.9	1.2	6.9	5.7	1.2
December	-1.6	6.0	4.8	1.2	7.6	6.3	1.3
2009							
March	-2.4	5.4	4.3	1.1	7.8	6.5	1.3
June	-1.6	5.9	4.7	1.2	7.5	6.2	1.3
September	-0.9	5.9	4.8	1.1	6.8	5.5	1.3
December	-0.2	6.3	5.0	1.3	6.5	5.3	1.2
2010							
March	-0.2	5.9	4.8	1.1	6.1	5.0	1.1
June	0.7	6.6	5.4	1.2	5.9	4.8	1.1
September	0.2	6.3	5.1	1.2	6.1	4.9	1.2
December	0.6	6.6	5.3	1.3	6.0	4.9	1.1
2011							
March	0.2	6.0	4.9	1.1	5.8	4.7	1.1
June	0.6	6.5	5.3	1.2	5.9	4.8	1.1
September	0.8	6.7	5.4	1.3	5.9	4.8	1.1
December	0.3	6.3	5.1	1.2	6.0	4.8	1.2
2012							
March	0.7	6.3	5.2	1.1	5.6	4.6	1.0
June	0.5	6.4	5.2	1.2	5.9	4.8	1.1
September	0.2	6.2	5.0	1.2	6.0	4.9	1.1
December	0.6	6.4	5.2	1.2	5.8	4.7	1.1

[1]The rates measure gross job gains and job losses as a percentage of the average of the previous and current employment.
[2]Net change is the difference between total gross job gains and total gross job losses.

Table 2-22. Three-Month Private Sector Job Gains and Losses, by Industry, Seasonally Adjusted, December 2011–December 2012

(Thousands of jobs.)

Industry	Gross job gains and job losses (3 months ended)					Gross job gains and losses as a percent of employment (3 months ended)				
	December 2011	March 2012	June 2012	September 2012	December 2012	December 2011	March 2012	June 2012	September 2012	December 2012
TOTAL PRIVATE[1]										
Gross job gains	6 854	6 946	7 027	6 847	7 110	6.3	6.3	6.4	6.2	6.4
Gross job losses	6 486	6 099	6 414	6 614	6 401	6.0	5.6	5.9	6.0	5.8
Net employment change	368	847	613	233	709	0.3	0.7	0.5	0.2	0.6
Goods-Producing										
Gross job gains	1 348	1 402	1 396	1 338	1 359	7.0	7.3	7.2	6.9	7.0
Gross job losses	1 352	1 254	1 302	1 301	1 315	7.0	6.5	6.7	6.7	6.7
Net employment change	-4	148	94	37	44	0.0	0.8	0.5	0.2	0.3
Natural Resources and Mining										
Gross job gains	293	293	300	277	279	15.1	14.8	15.1	14.0	14.0
Gross job losses	269	266	293	276	288	13.9	13.4	14.8	13.9	14.4
Net employment change	24	27	7	1	-9	1.2	1.4	0.3	0.1	-0.4
Construction										
Gross job gains	623	675	641	648	667	11.3	12.2	11.5	11.6	11.9
Gross job losses	656	622	639	614	604	11.8	11.2	11.4	11.0	10.7
Net employment change	-33	53	2	34	63	-0.5	1.0	0.1	0.6	1.2
Manufacturing										
Gross job gains	432	434	455	413	413	3.6	3.7	3.8	3.5	3.4
Gross job losses	427	366	370	411	423	3.7	3.0	3.1	3.5	3.5
Net employment change	5	68	85	2	-10	-0.1	0.7	0.7	0.0	-0.1
Service-Providing[1]										
Gross job gains	5 506	5 544	5 631	5 509	5 751	6.1	6.2	6.2	6.1	6.3
Gross job losses	5 134	4 845	5 112	5 313	5 086	5.8	5.4	5.6	5.9	5.6
Net employment change	372	699	519	196	665	0.3	0.8	0.6	0.2	0.7
Wholesale Trade										
Gross job gains	275	285	287	267	280	4.9	5.1	5.1	4.7	4.9
Gross job losses	251	244	252	262	257	4.5	4.3	4.4	4.7	4.5
Net employment change	24	41	35	5	23	0.4	0.8	0.7	0.0	0.4
Retail Trade										
Gross job gains	892	899	896	848	921	6.1	6.0	6.0	5.6	6.2
Gross job losses	813	845	819	875	829	5.6	5.7	5.5	5.8	5.6
Net employment change	79	54	77	-27	92	0.5	0.3	0.5	-0.2	0.6
Transportation and Warehousing										
Gross job gains	244	213	220	221	263	5.9	5.1	5.3	5.3	6.3
Gross job losses	202	215	201	208	211	4.9	5.1	4.8	5.0	5.0
Net employment change	42	-2	19	13	52	1.0	0.0	0.5	0.3	1.3
Utilities										
Gross job gains	12	12	11	12	14	2.2	2.2	2.0	2.2	2.6
Gross job losses	11	11	13	13	12	2.0	2.0	2.4	2.4	2.2
Net employment change	1	1	-2	-1	2	0.2	0.2	-0.4	-0.2	0.4
Information										
Gross job gains	127	114	123	129	141	4.8	4.2	4.6	4.8	5.2
Gross job losses	138	113	126	140	121	5.1	4.2	4.7	5.2	4.5
Net employment change	-11	1	-3	-11	20	-0.3	0.0	-0.1	-0.4	0.7
Financial Activities										
Gross job gains	369	341	360	354	376	5.0	4.6	4.8	4.7	5.0
Gross job losses	346	319	330	333	326	4.7	4.3	4.4	4.4	4.3
Net employment change	23	22	30	21	50	0.3	0.3	0.4	0.3	0.7
Professional and Business Services										
Gross job gains	1 387	1 280	1 362	1 325	1 403	8.2	7.3	7.6	7.4	7.8
Gross job losses	1 176	1 148	1 215	1 256	1 229	6.9	6.5	6.8	7.0	6.8
Net employment change	211	132	147	69	174	1.3	0.8	0.8	0.4	1.0
Education and Health Services										
Gross job gains	842	821	799	840	836	4.5	4.2	4.1	4.3	4.3
Gross job losses	704	697	768	746	717	3.8	3.6	3.9	3.9	3.6
Net employment change	138	124	31	94	119	0.7	0.6	0.2	0.4	0.7
Leisure and Hospitality										
Gross job gains	1 131	1 238	1 212	1 162	1 176	8.6	9.1	8.8	8.5	8.5
Gross job losses	1 100	975	1 102	1 169	1 091	8.4	7.2	8.0	8.5	7.8
Net employment change	31	263	110	-7	85	0.2	1.9	0.8	0.0	0.7
Other Services										
Gross job gains	272	279	290	275	269	7.3	7.4	7.6	7.2	7.0
Gross job losses	267	251	259	281	266	7.2	6.6	6.7	7.3	6.9
Net employment change	5	28	31	-6	3	0.1	0.8	0.9	-0.1	0.1

[1]Includes unclassified sector, not shown separately.

Table 2-23. Private Sector Job Gains and Losses, by State and Selected Territory, Seasonally Adjusted, December 2011–December 2012

(Number.)

State	Gross job gains (3 months ended)					Gross job losses (3 months ended)				
	December 2011	March 2012	June 2012	September 2012	December 2012	December 2011	March 2012	June 2012	September 2012	December 2012
UNITED STATES	6 854 000	6 946 000	7 027 000	6 847 000	7 110 000	6 486 000	6 099 000	6 414 000	6 614 000	6 401 000
Alabama	84 902	91 664	86 636	83 851	85 704	86 811	80 725	82 955	83 306	80 669
Alaska	22 945	26 693	27 530	22 445	24 240	26 148	22 241	23 495	25 672	25 260
Arizona	141 007	128 274	128 793	135 745	142 500	122 629	118 427	125 041	117 227	119 631
Arkansas	59 014	54 609	52 314	51 668	56 703	50 570	53 188	53 856	57 464	50 392
California	859 658	851 650	894 003	844 915	919 234	779 826	755 035	776 483	795 400	774 546
Colorado	128 595	125 624	136 640	131 864	134 421	122 675	114 020	118 410	123 134	117 054
Connecticut	72 755	76 984	75 561	72 837	75 395	70 840	67 975	68 910	75 227	71 198
Delaware	21 495	21 643	21 869	21 192	23 491	21 336	20 549	22 030	21 369	19 541
District of Columbia	25 702	28 382	27 380	27 410	31 906	24 711	21 358	25 248	28 636	25 818
Florida	435 381	415 877	431 131	457 853	455 616	412 001	362 860	395 664	423 743	399 755
Georgia	201 650	218 487	209 942	201 628	217 427	200 263	190 064	196 142	198 881	188 763
Hawaii	25 022	25 388	27 415	27 160	26 609	22 485	25 215	23 961	22 743	20 912
Idaho	37 046	38 298	40 455	41 233	40 125	37 708	38 801	37 818	35 434	36 684
Illinois	266 469	263 612	265 911	271 148	258 830	258 087	233 030	243 549	263 946	251 875
Indiana	141 985	151 917	141 219	138 626	143 227	133 390	121 368	132 146	133 678	130 952
Iowa	71 149	76 178	71 500	70 809	71 392	68 595	63 144	64 753	68 605	68 038
Kansas	65 001	70 479	64 309	60 448	67 871	61 692	56 328	61 195	64 860	58 658
Kentucky	87 176	90 342	88 382	83 055	93 554	81 718	80 583	80 246	85 735	80 606
Louisiana	99 191	116 182	103 796	101 975	107 395	96 098	100 163	105 425	102 711	91 414
Maine	33 038	34 973	38 534	32 673	34 238	34 945	34 820	33 537	35 673	36 486
Maryland	128 539	134 976	128 774	128 971	129 764	122 002	115 216	121 718	128 148	127 138
Massachusetts	144 205	154 949	164 755	149 438	151 216	150 404	137 152	137 124	155 111	148 085
Michigan	202 960	203 456	207 062	207 299	205 504	198 242	173 801	192 021	197 226	183 401
Minnesota	125 786	142 219	138 414	136 191	134 577	130 800	129 890	121 959	128 083	130 799
Mississippi	51 504	56 245	50 119	53 633	57 216	50 410	47 444	55 578	52 107	51 673
Missouri	135 130	129 293	133 660	127 233	138 250	122 259	117 792	134 163	128 691	122 509
Montana	28 859	27 526	28 856	27 400	29 068	26 620	26 029	26 533	25 705	27 260
Nebraska	43 312	44 158	43 558	42 551	44 816	39 971	38 129	39 222	41 491	39 881
Nevada	57 458	58 292	62 766	58 249	60 294	55 206	52 978	53 406	57 228	56 082
New Hampshire	35 786	34 728	37 456	34 114	34 580	33 721	32 426	33 920	36 227	34 128
New Jersey	209 431	203 715	209 311	197 518	203 835	195 955	190 411	189 291	202 355	198 718
New Mexico	37 164	41 135	40 507	38 580	44 250	40 290	35 763	41 590	39 230	37 406
New York	436 423	466 516	466 207	454 607	466 748	426 749	399 950	429 311	443 564	440 756
North Carolina	202 558	210 882	205 622	202 081	211 726	191 808	179 984	196 910	193 077	190 051
North Dakota	32 270	34 497	26 806	28 903	29 218	19 899	20 369	22 207	25 009	23 917
Ohio	252 833	260 540	253 914	241 581	263 759	238 467	224 267	229 793	250 160	238 558
Oklahoma	75 051	76 212	76 079	73 753	82 091	73 191	65 995	68 331	73 607	68 685
Oregon	92 624	94 240	94 439	97 220	95 654	92 328	87 988	89 229	86 297	91 054
Pennsylvania	276 936	290 187	264 855	264 397	265 032	245 749	246 817	266 763	266 195	252 649
Rhode Island	23 838	25 161	25 079	23 706	24 574	24 926	23 785	23 337	24 729	23 675
South Carolina	90 346	93 884	89 273	85 519	97 458	82 032	80 792	86 862	87 308	79 795
South Dakota	21 579	21 808	22 284	21 046	20 959	19 441	19 892	20 663	20 682	20 519
Tennessee	136 418	133 838	134 381	124 873	138 078	116 607	113 151	125 736	124 155	114 673
Texas	522 310	533 617	549 198	532 447	553 932	456 424	445 061	458 036	473 461	450 359
Utah	69 738	68 992	71 874	68 688	74 490	60 954	58 811	60 288	61 913	61 715
Vermont	20 184	17 953	18 231	17 200	18 800	16 318	17 360	17 602	17 307	17 530
Virginia	177 651	175 293	169 738	186 995	177 043	174 723	159 817	168 085	179 241	165 510
Washington	163 346	158 587	173 163	163 111	166 655	162 721	148 380	148 738	153 439	153 804
West Virginia	37 872	40 700	36 043	36 427	36 002	32 794	35 173	40 260	38 609	36 604
Wisconsin	125 731	136 346	133 444	125 268	131 552	130 742	118 700	120 808	127 601	122 830
Wyoming	19 756	18 401	17 401	18 081	20 277	17 401	18 588	19 123	18 364	17 704
Puerto Rico	45 676	41 120	46 152	42 434	46 915	37 845	40 496	38 353	43 922	40 722
Virgin Islands	1 845	1 688	1 843	1 512	1 981	1 920	2 070	4 106	2 173	1 599

Table 2-24. Private Sector Job Gains and Losses as a Percent of Total Employment, by State and Selected Territory, Seasonally Adjusted, December 2011–December 2012

(Percent.)

State	Gross job gains (3 months ended)					Gross job losses (3 months ended)				
	December 2011	March 2012	June 2012	September 2012	December 2012	December 2011	March 2012	June 2012	September 2012	December 2012
UNITED STATES	6.3	6.3	6.4	6.2	6.4	6.0	5.6	5.9	6.0	5.8
Alabama	5.9	6.3	5.9	5.7	5.8	6.0	5.6	5.6	5.7	5.5
Alaska	9.4	10.8	11.1	9.0	9.8	10.7	9.0	9.4	10.3	10.1
Arizona	7.0	6.3	6.3	6.7	6.9	6.0	5.9	6.1	5.7	5.8
Arkansas	6.2	5.7	5.5	5.5	6.0	5.3	5.6	5.7	6.1	5.3
California	7.1	7.0	7.2	6.8	7.4	6.5	6.2	6.3	6.4	6.2
Colorado	7.0	6.7	7.3	6.9	7.1	6.6	6.1	6.3	6.5	6.2
Connecticut	5.3	5.6	5.5	5.2	5.4	5.2	4.9	4.9	5.4	5.1
Delaware	6.3	6.3	6.4	6.2	6.8	6.2	6.0	6.4	6.2	5.7
District of Columbia	5.6	6.1	5.8	5.8	6.8	5.4	4.6	5.3	6.1	5.5
Florida	7.0	6.7	6.9	7.3	7.1	6.7	5.8	6.3	6.7	6.3
Georgia	6.4	6.9	6.6	6.4	6.8	6.4	6.0	6.1	6.2	5.9
Hawaii	5.2	5.3	5.7	5.6	5.4	4.7	5.3	5.0	4.7	4.3
Idaho	7.4	7.6	8.0	8.2	7.9	7.5	7.7	7.5	7.0	7.2
Illinois	5.6	5.4	5.5	5.5	5.3	5.4	4.8	5.0	5.4	5.2
Indiana	6.0	6.3	5.8	5.7	5.9	5.6	5.1	5.5	5.5	5.4
Iowa	5.8	6.2	5.8	5.7	5.7	5.7	5.2	5.2	5.6	5.5
Kansas	6.1	6.6	6.0	5.6	6.3	5.8	5.3	5.7	6.1	5.4
Kentucky	6.1	6.3	6.1	5.7	6.5	5.7	5.6	5.5	5.9	5.5
Louisiana	6.5	7.5	6.7	6.6	7.0	6.4	6.6	6.9	6.7	5.9
Maine	6.8	7.2	7.9	6.7	7.0	7.3	7.2	6.9	7.3	7.5
Maryland	6.4	6.7	6.3	6.3	6.4	6.1	5.7	6.0	6.3	6.3
Massachusetts	5.2	5.6	5.9	5.3	5.4	5.5	4.9	4.9	5.6	5.3
Michigan	6.1	6.1	6.1	6.2	6.0	6.0	5.2	5.7	5.9	5.4
Minnesota	5.6	6.3	6.1	6.0	5.9	5.8	5.8	5.4	5.6	5.7
Mississippi	6.1	6.6	5.9	6.4	6.8	6.1	5.7	6.5	6.2	6.1
Missouri	6.3	6.0	6.1	5.9	6.4	5.7	5.4	6.1	5.9	5.6
Montana	8.4	8.0	8.3	7.9	8.3	7.8	7.5	7.6	7.3	7.8
Nebraska	5.8	5.9	5.7	5.6	5.9	5.3	5.1	5.2	5.5	5.2
Nevada	6.0	5.9	6.4	5.9	6.0	5.7	5.4	5.4	5.7	5.7
New Hampshire	6.9	6.6	7.1	6.4	6.5	6.5	6.2	6.4	6.9	6.4
New Jersey	6.5	6.4	6.5	6.2	6.4	6.2	6.0	5.9	6.3	6.2
New Mexico	6.3	6.9	6.7	6.4	7.4	6.7	6.0	6.9	6.6	6.2
New York	6.1	6.5	6.5	6.3	6.4	6.0	5.6	6.0	6.2	6.1
North Carolina	6.4	6.6	6.4	6.3	6.5	6.0	5.6	6.1	6.0	5.9
North Dakota	10.0	10.3	7.9	8.3	8.3	6.2	6.1	6.5	7.2	6.8
Ohio	5.9	6.0	5.8	5.6	6.1	5.6	5.2	5.3	5.7	5.5
Oklahoma	6.3	6.3	6.3	6.1	6.7	6.1	5.5	5.6	6.0	5.6
Oregon	6.9	6.9	6.9	7.1	7.0	6.8	6.5	6.6	6.4	6.6
Pennsylvania	5.7	5.9	5.4	5.4	5.5	5.1	5.0	5.5	5.4	5.1
Rhode Island	6.1	6.4	6.4	6.0	6.3	6.4	6.1	5.9	6.3	6.0
South Carolina	6.2	6.4	6.1	5.8	6.6	5.6	5.5	5.9	5.9	5.4
South Dakota	6.6	6.6	6.7	6.4	6.3	6.0	6.1	6.3	6.2	6.2
Tennessee	6.2	6.0	6.0	5.6	6.1	5.3	5.1	5.6	5.5	5.1
Texas	6.0	6.1	6.2	5.9	6.1	5.3	5.0	5.2	5.2	5.0
Utah	7.2	6.9	7.2	6.9	7.3	6.2	5.9	6.1	6.1	6.1
Vermont	8.3	7.3	7.4	7.0	7.6	6.7	7.0	7.1	7.0	7.1
Virginia	6.1	6.1	5.8	6.4	6.0	6.1	5.5	5.8	6.1	5.6
Washington	7.2	6.8	7.4	7.0	7.1	7.1	6.5	6.4	6.6	6.5
West Virginia	6.7	7.1	6.3	6.4	6.4	5.8	6.2	7.1	6.8	6.5
Wisconsin	5.5	6.0	5.8	5.4	5.7	5.7	5.2	5.2	5.5	5.3
Wyoming	9.3	8.6	8.2	8.6	9.5	8.2	8.6	9.0	8.7	8.4
Puerto Rico	6.8	6.1	6.8	6.2	6.8	5.6	6.0	5.6	6.3	5.9
Virgin Islands	6.0	5.5	6.2	5.3	7.0	6.2	6.8	13.9	7.7	5.6

CHAPTER 3: OCCUPATIONAL EMPLOYMENT AND WAGES

OCCUPATIONAL EMPLOYMENT AND WAGES

HIGHLIGHTS

This chapter presents employment and wage statistics from the Bureau of Labor Statistics Occupational Employment Statistics (OES) program.

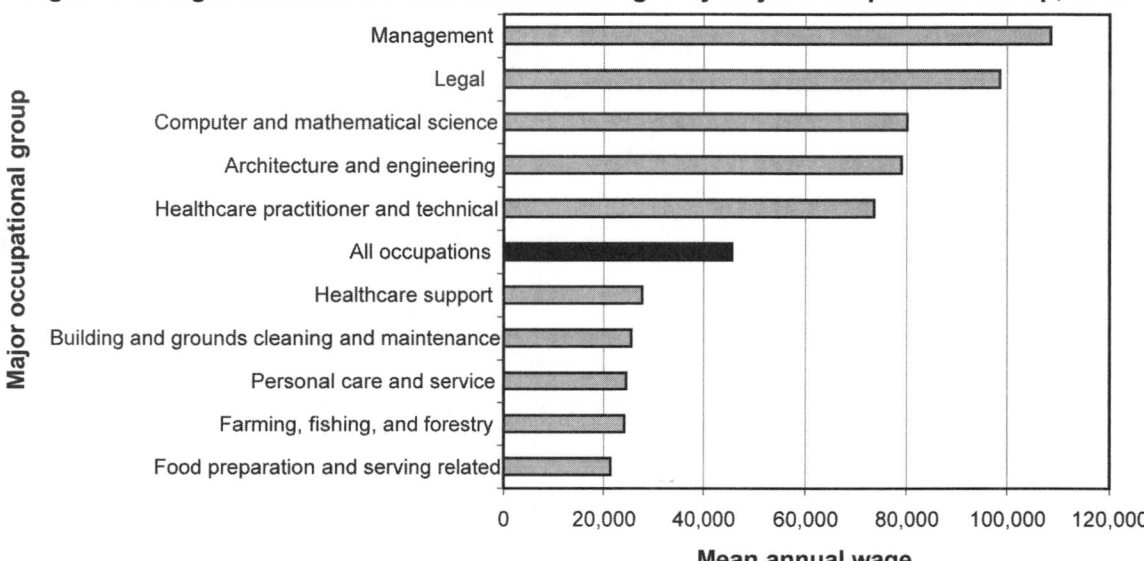

Figure 3-1. Highest and Lowest Mean Annual Wages by Major Occupational Group, 2012

Workers in management had the highest mean annual wage ($108,570), followed by those in legal occupations ($98,570), and computer and mathematical science occupations ($80,180) in 2012. Meanwhile, workers in food preparation and serving-related workers ($21,380) and personal care and services ($24,550) had the lowest mean annual wages. (See Table 3-1.)

OTHER HIGHLIGHTS

- Within management, chief executives had the highest salary at $176,840, while legislators had the lowest at $38,590. (See Table 3-3.)

- The mean annual wage increased for all the major occupational groups in 2012 except for the following: farming, fishing, and forestry occupations; food preparation and serving-related occupations; and personal care and service occupations. Wages grew the fastest in architecture and engineering at 2.4 percent. (See Table 3-1.)

- Nurse anesthetists ($154,390), computer network architects ($94,000), and nurse practitioners ($91,450) had the highest median annual wages among the 24 new occupations in the Standard Occupational Classification (SOC) system. (See Table 3-2.)

- In May 2012, the mean average wages of those in the education, training, or library professions ranged from $25,310 for teacher assistants to $115,550 for postsecondary law teachers. (See Table 3-3.)

NOTES AND DEFINITIONS

COLLECTION AND COVERAGE

The Occupational Employment Statistics (OES) survey is a federal-state cooperative program conducted by the Bureau of Labor Statistics (BLS) and the State Workforce Agencies (SWAs). The OES program collects data on wage and salary workers in nonfarm establishments in order to produce employment and wage estimates for approximately 800 occupations. Data from self-employed persons are not collected and are not included in the estimates.

Every six months, forms are mailed to two semiannual panels of around 200,000 taking three years to fully collect a sample of 1.2 million establishments. May 2012 estimates are based on responses from six semiannual panels collected over a 3-year period: May 2012, November 2011, May 2011, November 2010, May 2010, and November 2009.

SCOPE OF THE SURVEY

Prior to 1996, the OES program collected only occupational employment data for selected industries in each year of the three-year survey cycle, and produced only industry-specific estimates of occupational employment. The 1996 survey round was the first year that the OES program began collecting occupational employment and wage data in every State. In addition, the program's three-year survey cycle was modified to collect data from all covered industries each year. In 1997, the OES program began producing estimates of cross-industry as well as industry-specific occupational employment and wages.

In 1999, the OES survey began using the Standard Occupational Classification (SOC) system. The SOC system is the first occupational classification system for federal agencies required by the Office of Management and Budget (OMB). The May 2012 estimates are the first estimates based on the 2010 Standard Occupational Classification (SOC) system. In addition to 22 major occupational groups and 821 detailed occupations, employment and wage estimates for 94 minor groups and 458 broad occupations are available for the first time.

In 2002, the OES survey switched from the Standard Industrial Classification System (SIC) to the North American Industry Classification System (NAICS). In 2008, the OES survey switched to the 2007 NAICS from the 2002 NAICS. The most significant revisions were in the information sector, particularly within the telecommunications area. The May 2012 OES estimates are the first to be produced using the 2012 North American Industry Classification System

(NAICS). More information about NAICS can be found on the BLS Web site at http://www.bls.gov/bls/naics.htm.

CONCEPTS AND DEFINITIONS

Employment is the estimate of total wage and salary employment in an occupation across the industries in which it was reported. The OES survey defines employment as the number of workers who can be classified as full-time or part-time employees, including workers on paid vacations or other types of leave; workers on unpaid short-term absences; employees who are salaried officers, executives, or staff members of incorporated firms; employees temporarily assigned to other units; and employees for whom the reporting unit is their permanent duty station regardless of whether that unit prepares their paycheck.

Occupations are classified based on work performed and required skills. Employees are assigned to an occupation based on the work they perform and not on their education or training. Employees who perform the duties of two or more occupations are reported as being in either the occupation that requires the highest level of skill or the occupation in which the most time is spent (if there is no measurable difference in skill requirements).

Wages are money that is paid or received for work or services performed in a specified period. Base rate, cost-of-living allowances, guaranteed pay, hazardous-duty pay, incentive pay (including commissions and production bonuses), tips, and on-call pay are included.

Mean wage refers to an average wage; an occupational mean wage estimate is calculated by summing the wages of all the employees in a given occupation and then dividing the total wages by the number of employees.

An *establishment* is defined as an economic unit that processes goods or provides services, such as a factory, store, or mine.

An *industry* is a group of establishments that produce similar products or provide similar services.

ADDITIONAL INFORMATION

For additional data including area data, see BLS news release USDL 13-0543, "Occupational Employment and Wages, May 2012," and special reports on the BLS Web site at http://www.bls.gov/OES/.

Table 3-1. Employment and Wages, by Major Occupational Group, May 2009–May 2012

(Number, percent, dollars.)

Occupation	May 2009 Employment		Mean hourly wage	Mean annual wage[1]	May 2010 Employment		Mean hourly wage	Mean annual wage[1]
	Number	Percent			Number	Percent		
All Occupations	130 647 610	100.0	20.90	43 460	127 097 160	100.0	16.27	44 410
Management	6 116 380	4.7	49.47	102 900	6 022 860	4.7	43.96	105 440
Business and financial operations	6 063 670	4.6	31.68	65 900	6 090 910	4.8	29.17	67 690
Computer and mathematical sciences	3 303 690	2.5	36.68	76 290	3 283 950	2.6	35.44	77 230
Architecture and engineering	2 412 730	1.8	35.38	73 590	2 305 530	1.8	36.32	75 550
Life, physical, and social sciences	1 308 380	1.0	31.57	65 660	1 064 510	0.8	31.92	66 390
Community and social services	1 891 320	1.4	20.55	42 750	1 901 180	1.5	20.76	43 180
Legal	999 020	0.8	46.07	95 820	992 650	0.8	46.60	96 940
Education, training, and library	8 488 740	6.5	23.81	49 530	8 457 870	6.7	24.25	50 440
Arts, design, entertainment, sports, and media	1 745 670	1.3	24.87	51 720	1 716 640	1.4	25.14	52 290
Health care practitioner and technical	7 200 950	5.5	33.51	69 690	7 346 580	5.8	34.27	71 280
Health care support	3 886 690	3.0	12.84	26 710	3 962 930	3.1	12.94	26 920
Protective services	3 172 420	2.4	20.07	41 740	3 187 810	2.5	20.43	42 490
Food preparation and serving related	11 218 260	8.6	10.04	20 880	11 027 340	8.7	10.21	21 240
Building and grounds cleaning and maintenance	4 269 480	3.3	12.00	24 970	4 175 550	3.3	12.16	25 300
Personal care and services	3 461 910	2.6	11.87	24 680	3 425 220	2.7	11.82	24 590
Sales and related	13 715 050	10.5	17.32	36 020	13 437 980	10.6	17.69	36 790
Office and administrative support	22 336 450	17.1	15.86	32 990	21 503 800	16.9	16.09	33 470
Farming, fishing, and forestry	419 200	0.3	11.53	23 990	408 040	0.3	11.70	24 330
Construction and extraction	5 751 630	4.4	20.84	43 350	5 072 530	4.0	21.09	43 870
Installation, maintenance, and repair	5 114 150	3.9	20.30	42 210	4 928 960	3.9	20.58	42 810
Production	8 927 130	6.8	16.01	33 290	8 236 340	6.5	16.24	33 770
Transportation and material moving	8 844 700	6.8	15.47	32 180	8 547 980	6.7	15.70	32 660

Occupation	May 2011 Employment		Mean hourly wage	Mean annual wage[1]	May 2012 Employment		Mean hourly wage	Mean annual wage[1]
	Number	Percent			Number	Percent		
All Occupations	128 278 550	100.0	21.74	45 230	130 287 700	100.0	22.01	45 790
Management	6 183 820	4.8	51.64	107 410	6 390 430	4.9	52.20	108 570
Business and financial operations	6 178 070	4.8	33.05	68 740	6 419 370	4.9	33.44	69 550
Computer and mathematical sciences	3 406 720	2.7	37.85	78 730	3 578 220	2.7	38.55	80 180
Architecture and engineering	2 310 830	1.8	37.08	77 120	2 356 530	1.8	37.98	79 000
Life, physical, and social sciences	1 082 370	0.8	32.44	67 470	1 104 100	0.8	32.87	68 360
Community and social services	1 890 410	1.5	21.07	43 830	1 882 080	1.4	21.27	44 240
Legal	1 002 330	0.8	47.30	98 380	1 023 020	0.8	47.39	98 570
Education, training, and library	8 409 060	6.6	24.46	50 870	8 374 910	6.4	24.62	51 210
Arts, design, entertainment, sports, and media	1 725 670	1.3	25.89	53 850	1 750 130	1.3	26.20	54 490
Health care practitioner and technical	7 514 980	5.9	34.97	72 730	7 649 930	5.9	35.35	73 540
Health care support	3 954 070	3.1	13.16	27 370	3 915 460	3.0	13.36	27 780
Protective services	3 202 500	2.5	20.54	42 730	3 207 790	2.5	20.70	43 050
Food preparation and serving related	11 218 710	8.7	10.30	21 430	11 546 880	8.9	10.28	21 380
Building and grounds cleaning and maintenance	4 191 750	3.3	12.29	25 560	4 246 260	3.3	12.34	25 670
Personal care and services	3 619 250	2.8	11.84	24 620	3 810 750	2.9	11.80	24 550
Sales and related	13 646 450	10.6	18.04	37 520	13 835 090	10.6	18.26	37 990
Office and administrative support	21 384 330	16.7	16.40	34 120	21 355 350	16.4	16.54	34 410
Farming, fishing, and forestry	409 590	0.3	11.68	24 300	427 670	0.3	11.65	24 230
Construction and extraction	4 956 770	3.9	21.46	44 630	4 978 290	3.8	21.61	44 960
Installation, maintenance, and repair	4 988 980	3.9	20.86	43 390	5 069 590	3.9	21.09	43 870
Production	8 365 980	6.5	16.45	34 220	8 594 170	6.6	16.59	34 500
Transportation and material moving	8 635 940	6.7	15.96	33 200	8 771 690	6.7	16.15	33 590

[1]The annual wage has been calculated by multiplying the hourly mean wage by a "year-round, full-time" hours figure of 2,080 hours; for occupations with no published hourly mean wage, the annual wage has been directly calculated from the reported survey data.

Table 3-2. National Employment and Wages for Occupations Identified as New in the Standard Occupational Classification System, May 2012

(Number, dollars.)

Occupation	Employment	Mean wages		Median hourly wages
		Hourly	Annual[1]	
Fundraisers	48 530	26.55	55 220	24.37
Information security analysts	72 670	42.93	89 290	41.43
Web developers	102 940	31.78	66 100	30.05
Computer network architects	137 890	45.19	94 000	43.75
Computer network support specialists	167 980	30.27	62 960	28.41
Community health workers	38 020	18.02	37 490	16.64
Special education teachers, preschool	21 770	([2])	57 770	([2])
Special education teachers, all other	39 260	([2])	56 160	([2])
Exercise physiologists	5 820	22.89	47 610	21.53
Nurse anesthetists	34 180	74.22	154 390	71.23
Nurse midwives	5 710	43.78	91 070	43.08
Nurse practitioners	105 780	43.97	91 450	43.25
Magnetic resonance imaging technologists	29 560	31.45	65 410	31.42
Ophthalmic medical technicians	29 170	17.11	35 590	16.46
Hearing aid specialists	4 980	22.49	46 780	19.92
Genetic counselors	2 000	26.84	55 820	27.31
Orderlies	53 920	12.35	25 700	11.53
Phlebotomists	100 380	14.86	30 910	14.29
Transportation security screeners	47 200	17.85	37 130	17.71
Morticians, undertakers, and funeral directors	23 070	25.33	52 690	22.52
Financial clerks, all other	39 290	19.03	39 580	17.72
Solar photovoltaic installers	4 710	19.53	40 620	18.22
Wind turbine service technicians	3 200	23.23	48 320	22.10
Food processing workers, all other	37 570	11.96	24 880	11.12

[1]Annual wages have been calculated by multiplying the hourly mean wage by a "year-round, full-time" hours figure of 2,080 hours; for occupations with no published hourly mean wage, the annual wage has been directly calculated from the reported survey data.

[2]Wages for some occupations that do not generally entail year-round, full-time employment are reported as either hourly wages or annual salaries (depending on how employees are typically paid).

Table 3-3. Employment and Wages, by Occupation, May 2012

(Number of people, dollars.)

Occupation	May 2012			
	Employment	Median hourly wage	Mean hourly wage	Mean annual wage[1]
ALL OCCUPATIONS	130 287 700	16.71	22.01	45 790
Management Occupations				
Top executives	2 212 150	47.86	57.72	120 060
Chief executives	255 940	80.84	85.02	176 840
General and operations managers	1 899 460	45.88	55.22	114 850
Legislators	56 760	([2])	([2])	38 590
Advertising, marketing, promotions, public relations, and sales managers	598 110	51.90	58.24	121 150
Advertising and promotions managers	28 420	42.59	51.47	107 060
Marketing and sales managers	516 170	53.05	59.26	123 260
Marketing managers	171 430	57.44	62.44	129 870
Sales managers	344 730	50.60	57.68	119 980
Public relations and fundraising managers	53 520	45.89	52.05	108 260
Operations specialties managers	1 532 610	48.42	53.54	111 350
Administrative services managers	264 090	38.98	42.63	88 660
Computer and information systems managers	309 740	58.15	62.08	129 130
Financial managers	484 910	52.76	59.26	123 260
Industrial production managers	160 550	42.88	46.87	97 490
Purchasing managers	69 400	48.16	51.06	106 200
Transportation, storage, and distribution managers	98 600	39.34	42.75	88 920
Compensation and benefits managers	19 960	45.79	50.92	105 920
Human resources managers	98 020	47.94	52.69	109 590
Training and development managers	27 350	45.86	49.91	103 810
Other management occupations	2 047 560	39.39	43.46	90 400
Farmers, ranchers, and other agricultural managers	3 970	33.32	35.45	73 730
Construction managers	207 580	39.80	43.73	90 960
Education administrators	426 670	39.87	42.38	88 150
Education administrators, preschool and childcare center/program	48 410	21.13	24.55	51 060
Education administrators, elementary and secondary school	225 970	([2])	([2])	90 800
Education administrators, postsecondary	122 930	41.58	47.77	99 370
Education administrators, all other	29 360	36.95	39.37	81 890
Architectural and engineering managers	187 640	60.03	64.06	133 240
Food service managers	189 510	23.06	25.28	52 580
Funeral service managers	9 130	32.08	38.43	79 930
Gaming managers	4 490	31.36	34.32	71 390
Lodging managers	29 730	22.50	26.35	54 800
Medical and health services managers	293 490	42.59	47.34	98 460
Natural sciences managers	48 560	55.64	62.69	130 400
Postmasters and mail superintendents	23 790	30.31	29.85	62 080
Property, real estate, and community association managers	159 570	25.29	30.56	63 570
Social and community service managers	115 360	28.83	30.99	64 460
Emergency management directors	9 550	28.73	31.12	64 730
Managers, all other	338 520	48.51	50.79	105 650
Business and Financial Operations Occupations				
Business operations specialists	3 987 180	29.92	32.66	67 940
Agents and business managers of artists, performers, and athletes	11 770	30.47	42.61	88 620
Buyers and purchasing agents	399 990	27.35	29.29	60 920
Buyers and purchasing agents, farm products	10 370	26.79	28.74	59 770
Wholesale and retail buyers, except farm products	108 670	24.75	27.60	57 420
Purchasing agents, except wholesale, retail, and farm products	280 950	28.25	29.96	62 310
Claims adjusters, appraisers, examiners, and investigators	275 050	28.78	29.56	61 480
Claims adjusters, examiners, and investigators	263 280	28.83	29.58	61 530
Insurance appraisers, auto damage	11 770	28.18	28.96	60 230
Compliance officers	227 500	29.82	31.23	64 960
Cost estimators	195 230	28.30	30.33	63 080
Human resources workers	471 340	26.73	28.79	59 890
Human resources specialists	394 380	26.83	29.16	60 660
Farm labor contractors	1 030	14.74	18.55	38 590
Labor relations specialists	75 930	26.28	27.02	56 210
Logisticians	119 560	34.99	36.38	75 670
Management analysts	540 440	37.79	42.34	88 070
Meeting, convention, and event planners	70 480	22.02	23.96	49 830
Fundraisers	48 530	24.37	26.55	55 220
Compensation, benefits, and job analysis specialists	85 620	28.41	29.90	62 200
Training and development specialists	217 930	26.89	28.64	59 560
Market research analysts and marketing specialists	392 740	28.99	32.39	67 380
Business operations specialists, all other	931 010	31.31	33.90	70 520
Financial specialists	2 432 190	30.32	34.70	72 180
Accountants and auditors	1 129 340	30.55	34.15	71 040
Appraisers and assessors of real estate	59 530	23.82	26.53	55 180
Budget analysts	58 280	33.31	34.66	72 100
Credit analysts	61 240	29.36	33.42	69 500
Financial analysts and advisors	507 090	34.51	41.46	86 240
Financial analysts	239 810	37.00	42.98	89 410

[1]Annual wages have been calculated by multiplying the hourly mean wage by a "year-round, full-time" hours figure of 2,080 hours; for occupations with no published hourly mean wage, the annual wage has been directly calculated from the reported survey data.
[2]Wages for some occupations that do not generally entail year-round, full-time employment are reported as either hourly wages or annual salaries (depending on how employees are typically paid).

Table 3-3. Employment and Wages, by Occupation, May 2012—*Continued*

(Number of people, dollars.)

Occupation	May 2012			
	Employment	Median hourly wage	Mean hourly wage	Mean annual wage[1]
Business and Financial Operations Occupations—*Continued*				
Personal financial advisors	175 470	32.46	43.66	90 820
Insurance underwriters	91 810	30.22	33.27	69 200
Financial examiners	28 060	36.44	40.49	84 220
Credit counselors and loan officers	314 300	27.65	32.70	68 010
Credit counselors	27 640	18.95	21.00	43 670
Loan officers	286 670	28.76	33.82	70 350
Tax examiners, collectors and preparers, and revenue agents	126 700	21.14	23.62	49 120
Tax examiners and collectors, and revenue agents	65 560	24.25	26.95	56 050
Tax preparers	61 140	16.22	20.05	41 700
Financial specialists, all other	147 630	29.40	32.22	67 020
Computer and Mathematical Occupations				
Computer occupations	3 456 500	36.67	38.47	80 020
Computer and information research scientists	24 880	49.13	49.84	103 670
Computer and information analysts	554 710	38.68	40.64	84 520
Computer systems analysts	482 040	38.31	40.29	83 800
Information security analysts	72 670	41.43	42.93	89 290
Software developers and programmers	1 397 780	41.87	43.50	90 470
Computer programmers	316 790	35.71	37.63	78 260
Software developers, applications	586 340	43.30	44.85	93 280
Software developers, systems software	391 700	47.59	49.30	102 550
Web developers	102 940	30.05	31.78	66 100
Database and systems administrators and network architects	599 800	36.96	38.90	80 910
Database administrators	111 590	37.06	38.04	79 120
Network and computer systems administrators	350 320	34.88	36.69	76 320
Computer network architects	137 890	43.75	45.19	94 000
Computer support specialists	693 610	23.51	25.59	53 230
Computer user support specialists	525 630	22.32	24.10	50 130
Computer network support specialists	167 980	28.41	30.27	62 960
Computer occupations, all other	185 730	39.01	39.36	81 860
Mathematical science occupations	121 720	36.67	40.74	84 740
Actuaries	21 340	45.04	51.29	106 680
Mathematicians	3 250	48.73	48.69	101 280
Operations research analysts	69 180	34.66	38.38	79 830
Statisticians	25 570	36.33	38.25	79 570
Miscellaneous mathematical science occupations	2 370	27.12	30.63	63 720
Mathematical technicians	1 150	27.32	30.87	64 220
Mathematical science occupations, all other	1 220	26.98	30.41	63 250
Architecture and Engineering Occupations				
Architects, surveyors, and cartographers	150 150	31.91	34.16	71 040
Architects, except naval	98 470	34.47	37.01	76 990
Architects, except landscape and naval	82 720	35.14	37.83	78 690
Landscape architects	15 750	30.86	32.71	68 030
Surveyors, cartographers, and photogrammetrists	51 680	27.18	28.71	59 720
Cartographers and photogrammetrists	11 490	27.62	29.63	61 640
Surveyors	40 190	27.04	28.45	59 180
Engineers	1 530 090	41.44	43.73	90 960
Aerospace engineers	80 420	49.87	50.39	104 810
Agricultural engineers	2 470	35.58	37.20	77 370
Biomedical engineers	18 810	41.81	43.84	91 200
Chemical engineers	32 190	45.36	49.17	102 270
Civil engineers	258 100	38.14	40.45	84 140
Computer hardware engineers	79 580	48.52	49.99	103 980
Electrical and electronics engineers	295 520	43.09	44.89	93 380
Electrical engineers	160 560	42.27	44.14	91 810
Electronics engineers, except computer	134 960	44.14	45.79	95 250
Environmental engineers	50 850	38.89	40.93	85 140
Industrial engineers, including health and safety	243 620	37.83	39.36	81 870
Health and safety engineers, except mining safety engineers and inspectors	23 490	36.94	38.35	79 760
Industrial engineers	220 130	37.92	39.47	82 100
Marine engineers and naval architects	6 880	42.36	46.22	96 140
Materials engineers	22 740	40.94	42.06	87 490
Mechanical engineers	252 540	38.74	40.75	84 770
Mining and geological engineers, including mining safety engineers	7 640	40.54	43.87	91 250
Nuclear engineers	19 930	50.13	51.51	107 140
Petroleum engineers	36 410	62.64	70.90	147 470
Engineers, all other	122 410	44.24	44.87	93 330
Drafters, engineering technicians, and mapping technicians	676 280	24.87	25.82	53 700
Drafters	189 570	23.86	25.25	52 520
Architectural and civil drafters	83 410	23.01	24.30	50 550
Electrical and electronics drafters	28 160	26.78	28.12	58 490
Mechanical drafters	63 220	24.21	25.61	53 270
Drafters, all other	14 780	22.17	23.58	49 050
Engineering technicians, except drafters	439 710	25.92	26.63	55 390

[1]Annual wages have been calculated by multiplying the hourly mean wage by a "year-round, full-time" hours figure of 2,080 hours; for occupations with no published hourly mean wage, the annual wage has been directly calculated from the reported survey data.

Table 3-3. Employment and Wages, by Occupation, May 2012—*Continued*

(Number of people, dollars.)

Occupation	May 2012			
	Employment	Median hourly wage	Mean hourly wage	Mean annual wage[1]
Architecture and Engineering Occupations—*Continued*				
Aerospace engineering and operations technicians	9 750	29.58	29.80	61 980
Civil engineering technicians	70 790	22.87	23.66	49 220
Electrical and electronics engineering technicians	144 460	27.81	27.92	58 070
Electro-mechanical technicians	16 990	24.91	25.71	53 480
Environmental engineering technicians	18 590	21.80	23.74	49 380
Industrial engineering technicians	67 400	24.51	25.53	53 100
Mechanical engineering technicians	46 630	24.99	25.88	53 830
Engineering technicians, except drafters, all other	65 090	28.58	29.25	60 830
Surveying and mapping technicians	47 000	19.07	20.52	42 680
Life, Physical, and Social Science Occupations				
Life scientists	260 030	33.07	37.32	77 620
Agricultural and food scientists	28 220	28.18	30.99	64 470
Animal scientists	2 120	29.65	35.29	73 400
Food scientists and technologists	13 680	27.92	30.84	64 140
Soil and plant scientists	12 410	28.24	30.43	63 290
Biological scientists	94 680	33.58	36.84	76 630
Biochemists and biophysicists	26 410	39.17	43.01	89 470
Microbiologists	18 550	31.86	35.22	73 250
Zoologists and wildlife biologists	18 650	27.74	30.05	62 500
Biological scientists, all other	31 080	34.95	36.64	76 220
Conservation scientists and foresters	27 920	28.40	29.52	61 400
Conservation scientists	18 460	29.38	30.57	63 590
Foresters	9 470	26.90	27.47	57 140
Medical scientists	100 270	36.58	41.85	87 040
Epidemiologists	4 850	31.38	34.33	71 400
Medical scientists, except epidemiologists	95 420	37.01	42.23	87 830
Life scientists, all other	8 940	31.41	35.93	74 740
Physical scientists	274 610	35.99	40.08	83 360
Astronomers and physicists	19 960	51.14	54.28	112 900
Astronomers	2 150	46.37	49.30	102 550
Physicists	17 820	51.37	54.88	114 150
Atmospheric and space scientists	10 190	42.91	43.27	90 010
Chemists and materials scientists	92 920	35.13	37.49	77 970
Chemists	84 950	34.50	36.96	76 870
Materials scientists	7 970	42.78	43.15	89 740
Environmental scientists and geoscientists	126 300	33.53	38.48	80 040
Environmental scientists and specialists, including health	84 240	30.56	33.16	68 970
Geoscientists, except hydrologists and geographers	35 180	43.70	51.33	106 780
Hydrologists	6 880	36.31	37.94	78 920
Physical scientists, all other	25 230	44.06	45.06	93 720
Social scientists and related workers	235 390	33.31	35.51	73 870
Economists	15 760	44.16	47.83	99 480
Survey researchers	17 370	21.66	24.47	50 890
Psychologists	114 970	33.31	35.45	73 740
Clinical, counseling, and school psychologists	103 590	32.53	34.72	72 220
Industrial-organizational psychologists	1 030	40.18	47.50	98 800
Psychologists, all other	10 350	43.28	41.53	86 380
Sociologists	2 340	36.04	38.86	80 820
Urban and regional planners	37 620	31.36	32.67	67 950
Miscellaneous social scientists and related workers	47 330	35.93	37.71	78 440
Anthropologists and archeologists	6 060	27.61	28.95	60 230
Geographers	1 510	35.94	35.59	74 020
Historians	3 340	25.23	28.00	58 240
Political scientists	5 750	49.04	50.29	104 600
Social scientists and related workers, all other	30 660	36.80	38.25	79 560
Life, physical, and social science technicians	334 060	19.78	21.61	44 950
Agricultural and food science technicians	18 280	16.38	17.49	36 390
Biological technicians	72 740	19.11	20.48	42 600
Chemical technicians	61 300	20.64	22.18	46 130
Geological and petroleum technicians	15 360	25.34	28.79	59 880
Nuclear technicians	8 040	33.20	33.52	69 720
Social science research assistants	26 370	17.86	19.60	40 760
Miscellaneous life, physical, and social science technicians	131 970	19.81	21.39	44 480
Environmental science and protection technicians, including health	30 890	19.83	21.43	44 570
Forensic science technicians	12 440	25.41	26.79	55 730
Forest and conservation technicians	31 720	16.31	17.80	37 030
Life, physical, and social science technicians, all other	56 920	20.74	22.18	46 130
Community and Social Service Occupations				
Counselors, social workers, and other community and social service specialists	1 811 660	19.43	21.26	44 220
Counselors	598 250	21.18	22.84	47 510
Substance abuse and behavioral disorder counselors	80 130	18.52	19.67	40 920
Educational, guidance, school, and vocational counselors	237 480	25.77	27.00	56 170
Marriage and family therapists	34 270	22.44	23.69	49 270

[1]Annual wages have been calculated by multiplying the hourly mean wage by a "year-round, full-time" hours figure of 2,080 hours; for occupations with no published hourly mean wage, the annual wage has been directly calculated from the reported survey data.

Table 3-3. Employment and Wages, by Occupation, May 2012—*Continued*

(Number of people, dollars.)

Occupation	May 2012			
	Employment	Median hourly wage	Mean hourly wage	Mean annual wage[1]
Community and Social Service Occupations—*Continued*				
Mental health counselors	115 080	19.27	20.81	43 290
Rehabilitation counselors	104 070	16.29	17.95	37 330
Counselors, all other	27 220	21.06	22.15	46 060
Social workers	582 270	21.25	22.78	47 370
Child, family, and school social workers	273 920	19.97	21.78	45 300
Healthcare social workers	140 000	23.96	24.74	51 460
Mental health and substance abuse social workers	109 920	19.22	20.84	43 340
Social workers, all other	58 430	26.23	26.38	54 870
Miscellaneous community and social service specialists	631 150	16.41	18.37	38 200
Health educators	55 270	23.46	25.53	53 100
Probation officers and correctional treatment specialists	86 780	23.17	25.18	52 380
Social and human service assistants	351 400	13.87	14.85	30 880
Community health workers	38 020	16.64	18.02	37 490
Community and social service specialists, all other	99 680	19.74	20.99	43 660
Religious workers	70 410	19.40	21.41	44 540
Clergy	44 000	21.18	23.02	47 880
Directors, religious activities and education	18 310	17.92	20.50	42 640
Religious workers, all other	8 110	12.69	14.73	30 650
Legal				
Lawyers, judges, and related workers	641 020	53.24	60.99	126 860
Lawyers and judicial law clerks	593 120	53.91	62.21	129 410
Lawyers	581 920	54.58	62.93	130 880
Judicial law clerks	11 200	22.66	25.29	52 610
Judges, magistrates, and other judicial workers	47 900	45.84	45.83	95 340
Administrative law judges, adjudicators, and hearing officers	14 150	41.94	43.26	89 970
Arbitrators, mediators, and conciliators	6 520	29.46	37.12	77 200
Judges, magistrate judges, and magistrates	27 220	55.65	49.26	102 470
Legal support workers	382 000	22.53	24.57	51 100
Paralegals and legal assistants	267 030	22.59	24.15	50 220
Miscellaneous legal support workers	114 970	22.39	25.55	53 150
Court reporters	18 590	23.15	25.48	53 010
Title examiners, abstractors, and searchers	49 390	20.18	22.26	46 310
Legal support workers, all other	47 000	25.32	29.03	60 390
Education, Training, and Library Occupations				
Postsecondary teachers	1 496 810	(2)	(2)	73 770
Business teachers, postsecondary	82 460	(2)	(2)	85 730
Math and computer teachers, postsecondary	87 880	(2)	(2)	75 800
Computer science teachers, postsecondary	34 350	(2)	(2)	79 870
Mathematical science teachers, postsecondary	53 530	(2)	(2)	73 190
Engineering and architecture teachers, postsecondary	41 260	(2)	(2)	96 330
Architecture teachers, postsecondary	7 290	(2)	(2)	78 770
Engineering teachers, postsecondary	33 970	(2)	(2)	100 100
Life sciences teachers, postsecondary	63 020	(2)	(2)	86 350
Agricultural sciences teachers, postsecondary	10 500	(2)	(2)	83 990
Biological science teachers, postsecondary	50 040	(2)	(2)	87 060
Forestry and conservation science teachers, postsecondary	2 490	(2)	(2)	82 020
Physical sciences teachers, postsecondary	50 190	(2)	(2)	86 130
Atmospheric, earth, marine, and space sciences teachers, postsecondary	10 930	(2)	(2)	91 930
Chemistry teachers, postsecondary	20 430	(2)	(2)	81 460
Environmental science teachers, postsecondary	4 990	(2)	(2)	86 080
Physics teachers, postsecondary	13 840	(2)	(2)	88 470
Social sciences teachers, postsecondary	115 380	(2)	(2)	79 290
Anthropology and archeology teachers, postsecondary	5 690	(2)	(2)	82 860
Area, ethnic, and cultural studies teachers, postsecondary	9 710	(2)	(2)	77 690
Economics teachers, postsecondary	13 390	(2)	(2)	97 770
Geography teachers, postsecondary	4 460	(2)	(2)	71 890
Political science teachers, postsecondary	16 770	(2)	(2)	81 860
Psychology teachers, postsecondary	38 060	(2)	(2)	74 240
Sociology teachers, postsecondary	16 880	(2)	(2)	73 080
Social sciences teachers, postsecondary, all other	10 430	(2)	(2)	82 570
Health teachers, postsecondary	208 350	(2)	(2)	91 810
Health specialties teachers, postsecondary	152 130	(2)	(2)	100 370
Nursing instructors and teachers, postsecondary	56 220	(2)	(2)	68 640
Education and library science teachers, postsecondary	67 430	(2)	(2)	65 380
Education teachers, postsecondary	62 920	(2)	(2)	65 000
Library science teachers, postsecondary	4 510	(2)	(2)	70 770
Law, criminal justice, and social work teachers, postsecondary	39 090	(2)	(2)	85 300
Criminal justice and law enforcement teachers, postsecondary	14 020	(2)	(2)	62 770
Law teachers, postsecondary	15 260	(2)	(2)	115 550
Social work teachers, postsecondary	9 810	(2)	(2)	70 430
Arts, communications, and humanities teachers, postsecondary	271 550	(2)	(2)	70 450
Art, drama, and music teachers, postsecondary	92 570	(2)	(2)	73 340
Communications teachers, postsecondary	30 030	(2)	(2)	68 540
English language and literature teachers, postsecondary	72 680	(2)	(2)	67 980

[1]Annual wages have been calculated by multiplying the hourly mean wage by a "year-round, full-time" hours figure of 2,080 hours; for occupations with no published hourly mean wage, the annual wage has been directly calculated from the reported survey data.
[2]Wages for some occupations that do not generally entail year-round, full-time employment are reported as either hourly wages or annual salaries (depending on how employees are typically paid).

Table 3-3. Employment and Wages, by Occupation, May 2012—*Continued*

(Number of people, dollars.)

Occupation	May 2012			
	Employment	Median hourly wage	Mean hourly wage	Mean annual wage[1]
Education, Training, and Library Occupations—*Continued*				
Foreign language and literature teachers, postsecondary	29 810	([2])	([2])	66 730
History teachers, postsecondary	23 590	([2])	([2])	73 090
Philosophy and religion teachers, postsecondary	22 880	([2])	([2])	71 210
Miscellaneous postsecondary teachers	470 200	([2])	([2])	59 110
Graduate teaching assistants	120 160	([2])	([2])	33 030
Home economics teachers, postsecondary	4 700	([2])	([2])	68 260
Recreation and fitness studies teachers, postsecondary	19 410	([2])	([2])	64 490
Vocational education teachers, postsecondary	121 550	23.07	25.37	52 770
Postsecondary teachers, all other	204 380	([2])	([2])	77 500
Preschool, primary, secondary, and special education school teachers	4 033 290	([2])	([2])	54 550
Preschool and kindergarten teachers	497 720	15.89	18.17	37 800
Preschool teachers, except special education	340 350	13.04	14.79	30 750
Kindergarten teachers, except special education	157 370	([2])	([2])	53 030
Elementary and middle school teachers	1 999 790	([2])	([2])	56 180
Elementary school teachers, except special education	1 360 380	([2])	([2])	56 130
Middle school teachers, except special and career/technical education	620 900	([2])	([2])	56 280
Career/technical education teachers, middle school	18 510	([2])	([2])	56 270
Secondary school teachers	1 047 550	([2])	([2])	57 710
Secondary school teachers, except special and career/technical education	959 770	([2])	([2])	57 770
Career/technical education teachers, secondary school	87 780	([2])	([2])	57 140
Special education teachers	488 230	([2])	([2])	58 140
Special education teachers, preschool	21 770	([2])	([2])	57 770
Special education teachers, kindergarten and elementary school	197 740	([2])	([2])	56 700
Special education teachers, middle school	96 380	([2])	([2])	59 320
Special education teachers, secondary school	133 080	([2])	([2])	60 090
Special education teachers, all other	39 260	([2])	([2])	56 160
Other teachers and instructors	1 137 130	14.47	17.95	37 340
Adult basic and secondary education and literacy teachers and instructors	66 040	23.36	25.06	52 130
Self-enrichment education teachers	179 650	16.98	19.40	40 360
Miscellaneous teachers and instructors	891 450	13.72	17.13	35 630
Substitute teachers	619 700	12.47	14.22	29 590
Teachers and instructors, all other, except substitute teachers	271 740	([2])	([2])	49 430
Librarians, curators, and archivists	266 950	21.31	22.62	47 060
Archivists, curators, and museum technicians	26 440	21.35	23.64	49 180
Archivists	5 640	22.76	24.43	50 810
Curators	10 370	23.84	26.25	54 600
Museum technicians and conservators	10 430	18.38	20.63	42 920
Librarians	140 280	26.62	27.49	57 190
Library technicians	100 230	14.74	15.54	32 320
Other education, training, and library occupations	1 440 720	([2])	([2])	30 180
Audio-visual and multimedia collections specialists	8 690	20.84	22.03	45 820
Farm and home management advisors	11 060	22.48	23.43	48 730
Instructional coordinators	133 100	28.87	30.01	62 420
Teacher assistants	1 185 700	([2])	([2])	25 310
Education, training, and library workers, all other	102 180	17.60	19.85	41 280
Arts, Design, Entertainment, Sports, and Media Occupations				
Art and design workers	499 620	20.31	24.02	49 960
Artists and related workers	84 990	30.44	35.52	73 870
Art directors	31 570	38.88	45.32	94 260
Craft artists	4 810	14.23	16.94	35 240
Fine artists, including painters, sculptors, and illustrators	12 480	21.56	25.96	54 000
Multimedia artists and animators	29 270	29.50	33.44	69 560
Artists and related workers, all other	6 850	28.77	29.65	61 680
Designers	414 630	18.77	21.67	45 060
Commercial and industrial designers	29 030	28.66	30.02	62 430
Fashion designers	16 560	30.22	34.92	72 620
Floral designers	47 110	11.45	12.28	25 550
Graphic designers	191 440	21.22	23.43	48 730
Interior designers	40 750	22.89	25.47	52 970
Merchandise displayers and window trimmers	73 490	12.70	13.88	28 860
Set and exhibit designers	8 680	24.18	26.11	54 310
Designers, all other	7 560	21.79	24.56	51 080
Entertainers and performers, sports and related workers	489 840	18.52	27.35	56 890
Actors, producers, and directors	157 550	28.89	40.64	84 520
Actors	70 540	20.26	35.97	...
Producers and directors	87 010	34.31	44.42	92 390
Athletes, coaches, umpires, and related workers	229 830	([2])	([2])	38 520
Athletes and sports competitors	12 450	([2])	([2])	75 760
Coaches and scouts	201 800	([2])	([2])	36 680
Umpires, referees, and other sports officials	15 570	([2])	([2])	32 600
Dancers and choreographers	18 790	15.87	20.04	41 680

[1]Annual wages have been calculated by multiplying the hourly mean wage by a "year-round, full-time" hours figure of 2,080 hours; for occupations with no published hourly mean wage, the annual wage has been directly calculated from the reported survey data.
[2]Wages for some occupations that do not generally entail year-round, full-time employment are reported as either hourly wages or annual salaries (depending on how employees are typically paid).
. . . = Not available.

Table 3-3. Employment and Wages, by Occupation, May 2012—*Continued*

(Number of people, dollars.)

Occupation	May 2012			
	Employment	Median hourly wage	Mean hourly wage	Mean annual wage[1]
Arts, Design, Entertainment, Sports, and Media Occupations—*Continued*				
Dancers	11 390	14.16	19.02	([2])
Choreographers	7 400	18.33	21.60	44 930
Musicians, singers, and related workers	67 050	23.13	29.61	([2])
Music directors and composers	24 940	22.77	25.68	53 420
Musicians and singers	42 100	23.50	31.94	([2])
Entertainers and performers, sports and related workers, all other	16 630	15.58	22.64	([2])
Media and communication workers	551 020	24.49	28.45	59 180
Announcers	39 460	13.34	19.95	41 490
Radio and television announcers	31 340	13.47	20.13	41 860
Public address system and other announcers	8 120	12.61	19.27	40 070
News analysts, reporters and correspondents	50 740	17.83	23.32	48 510
Broadcast news analysts	5 170	26.63	37.68	78 380
Reporters and correspondents	45 570	17.25	21.69	45 120
Public relations specialists	201 280	26.04	29.80	61 980
Writers and editors	187 190	27.62	31.31	65 130
Editors	99 040	25.90	30.02	62 440
Technical writers	46 160	31.49	32.65	67 910
Writers and authors	41 990	26.89	32.90	68 420
Miscellaneous media and communication workers	72 350	21.81	25.55	53 150
Interpreters and translators	50 320	21.84	25.68	53 410
Media and communication workers, all other	22 030	21.71	25.27	52 550
Media and communication equipment workers	209 640	18.97	22.76	47 350
Broadcast and sound engineering technicians and radio operators	101 510	19.81	22.45	46 690
Audio and video equipment technicians	54 310	20.12	22.13	46 040
Broadcast technicians	31 640	18.21	21.18	44 050
Radio operators	1 280	20.23	20.79	43 240
Sound engineering technicians	14 280	22.27	26.60	55 340
Photographers	56 140	13.70	17.47	36 330
Television, video, and motion picture camera operators and editors	37 910	22.25	27.66	57 540
Camera operators, television, video, and motion picture	16 410	19.38	23.56	49 010
Film and video editors	21 500	24.66	30.80	64 060
Media and communication equipment workers, all other	14 090	33.08	32.97	68 570
Healthcare Practitioners and Technical Workers				
Health diagnosing and treating practitioners	4 680 350	35.29	44.18	91 890
Chiropractors	27 740	31.81	38.25	79 550
Dentists	109 570	71.79	80.25	166 910
Dentists, general	93 580	69.83	78.48	163 240
Oral and maxillofacial surgeons	4 990	([3])	104.06	216 440
Orthodontists	5 530	([3])	89.58	186 320
Prosthodontists	310	81.31	80.83	168 120
Dentists, all other specialists	5 150	74.51	79.22	164 780
Dietitians and nutritionists	58 240	26.56	27.00	56 170
Optometrists	29 180	47.03	52.80	109 810
Pharmacists	281 560	56.09	55.27	114 950
Physicians and surgeons	611 650	([3])	91.38	190 060
Anesthesiologists	29 930	([3])	111.94	232 830
Family and general practitioners	110 050	82.70	86.95	180 850
Internists, general	45 210	([3])	92.08	191 520
Obstetricians and gynecologists	20 880	([3])	104.21	216 760
Pediatricians, general	30 560	74.35	80.59	167 640
Psychiatrists	24 210	83.33	85.35	177 520
Surgeons	42 410	([3])	110.84	230 540
Physicians and surgeons, all other	308 410	([3])	88.86	184 820
Physician assistants	83 640	43.72	44.45	92 460
Podiatrists	9 090	55.98	63.69	132 470
Therapists	591 350	33.66	34.50	71 760
Occupational therapists	105 540	36.25	36.73	76 400
Physical therapists	191 460	38.39	38.99	81 110
Radiation therapists	18 230	37.29	38.66	80 410
Recreational therapists	19 180	20.33	21.29	44 280
Respiratory therapists	116 960	26.86	27.50	57 200
Speech-language pathologists	121 690	33.59	34.97	72 730
Exercise physiologists	5 820	21.53	22.89	47 610
Therapists, all other	12 480	25.58	27.29	56 760
Veterinarians	56 020	40.61	44.83	93 250
Registered nurses	2 633 980	31.48	32.66	67 930
Nurse anesthetists	34 180	71.23	74.22	154 390
Nurse midwives	5 710	43.08	43.78	91 070
Nurse practitioners	105 780	43.25	43.97	91 450
Audiologists	12 060	33.52	35.04	72 890
Health diagnosing and treating practitioners, all other	30 590	34.96	41.22	85 740
Health technologists and technicians	2 827 170	19.41	21.12	43 930
Clinical laboratory technologists and technicians	318 620	22.99	23.59	49 070

[1]Annual wages have been calculated by multiplying the hourly mean wage by a "year-round, full-time" hours figure of 2,080 hours; for occupations with no published hourly mean wage, the annual wage has been directly calculated from the reported survey data.
[2]Wages for some occupations that do not generally entail year-round, full-time employment are reported as either hourly wages or annual salaries (depending on how employees are typically paid).
[3]Median hourly wage is equal to or greater than $90.00 per hour.

Table 3-3. Employment and Wages, by Occupation, May 2012—*Continued*

(Number of people, dollars.)

Occupation	May 2012			
	Employment	Median hourly wage	Mean hourly wage	Mean annual wage[1]
Healthcare Practitioners and Technical Workers—*Continued*				
Medical and clinical laboratory technologists	160 700	27.69	28.19	58 640
Medical and clinical laboratory technicians	157 920	17.90	18.91	39 340
Dental hygienists	190 290	33.75	33.99	70 700
Diagnostic related technologists and technicians	353 060	27.81	28.45	59 170
Cardiovascular technologists and technicians	50 530	25.04	25.51	53 050
Diagnostic medical sonographers	57 700	31.66	31.90	66 360
Nuclear medicine technologists	20 480	33.74	34.06	70 840
Radiologic technologists	194 790	26.26	27.14	56 450
Magnetic resonance imaging technologists	29 560	31.42	31.45	65 410
Emergency medical technicians and paramedics	232 860	14.91	16.53	34 370
Health practitioner support technologists and technicians	668 870	15.06	15.98	33 240
Dietetic technicians	24 660	12.62	13.79	28 680
Pharmacy technicians	353 340	14.10	14.63	30 430
Psychiatric technicians	67 760	14.45	15.93	33 140
Respiratory therapy technicians	13 460	22.48	22.84	47 510
Surgical technologists	97 150	20.09	20.91	43 480
Veterinary technologists and technicians	83 350	14.56	15.13	31 470
Ophthalmic medical technicians	29 170	16.46	17.11	35 590
Licensed practical and licensed vocational nurses	718 800	19.97	20.39	42 400
Medical records and health information technicians	182 370	16.42	17.68	36 770
Opticians, dispensing	64 930	16.03	16.83	35 010
Miscellaneous health technologists and technicians	97 380	20.17	22.40	46 590
Orthotists and prosthetists	7 890	30.13	33.64	69 960
Hearing aid specialists	4 980	19.92	22.49	46 780
Health technologists and technicians, all other	84 510	19.57	21.35	44 400
Other healthcare practitioners and technical occupations	142 410	26.02	27.86	57 960
Occupational health and safety specialists and technicians	71 500	30.39	31.25	65 000
Occupational health and safety specialists	59 610	32.11	32.67	67 960
Occupational health and safety technicians	11 890	22.81	24.11	50 150
Miscellaneous health practitioners and technical workers	70 910	21.39	24.45	50 860
Athletic trainers	20 780	(^{2})	(^{2})	44 010
Genetic counselors	2 000	27.31	26.84	55 820
Healthcare practitioners and technical workers, all other	48 130	22.20	25.78	53 610
Healthcare Support				
Nursing, psychiatric, and home health aides	2 391 750	11.07	11.69	24 320
Home health aides	839 930	10.01	10.49	21 830
Psychiatric aides	77 880	11.82	12.83	26 680
Nursing assistants	1 420 020	11.74	12.32	25 620
Orderlies	53 920	11.53	12.35	25 700
Occupational therapy and physical therapist assistants and aides	155 970	20.25	20.63	42 920
Occupational therapy assistants and aides	37 460	23.53	23.15	48 160
Occupational therapy assistants	29 500	25.60	25.52	53 090
Occupational therapy aides	7 950	12.91	14.36	29 870
Physical therapist assistants and aides	118 510	18.96	19.84	41 260
Physical therapist assistants	69 810	25.08	25.15	52 320
Physical therapist aides	48 700	11.48	12.22	25 410
Other healthcare support occupations	1 367 740	14.72	15.43	32 100
Massage therapists	71 040	17.29	19.40	40 350
Miscellaneous healthcare support occupations	1 296 700	14.63	15.21	31 640
Dental assistants	300 160	16.59	16.86	35 080
Medical assistants	553 140	14.12	14.69	30 550
Medical equipment preparers	50 230	14.82	15.51	32 260
Medical transcriptionists	74 810	16.36	16.66	34 650
Pharmacy aides	42 600	10.51	11.28	23 460
Veterinary assistants and laboratory animal caretakers	71 500	11.12	11.90	24 740
Phlebotomists	100 380	14.29	14.86	30 910
Healthcare support workers, all other	103 890	15.77	16.29	33 880
Protective Service				
Supervisors of protective service workers	266 920	30.70	32.77	68 170
First-line supervisors of law enforcement workers	144 680	34.39	36.31	75 530
First-line supervisors of correctional officers	44 830	27.81	29.31	60 970
First-line supervisors of police and detectives	99 860	37.63	39.45	82 060
First-line supervisors of fire fighting and prevention workers	60 600	32.79	34.23	71 190
First-line supervisors of protective service workers, all other	61 640	22.03	23.05	47 940
Fire fighting and prevention workers	311 360	21.92	23.16	48 180
Firefighters	297 700	21.75	23.00	47 850
Fire inspectors	13 660	24.94	26.61	55 350
Fire inspectors and investigators	11 860	25.96	27.60	57 400
Forest fire inspectors and prevention specialists	1 800	17.20	20.13	41 860
Law enforcement workers	1 212 010	23.93	25.98	54 040
Bailiffs, correctional officers, and jailers	451 100	18.74	20.87	43 410
Bailiffs	16 240	17.71	19.15	39 840
Correctional officers and jailers	434 870	18.77	20.94	43 550

[1]Annual wages have been calculated by multiplying the hourly mean wage by a "year-round, full-time" hours figure of 2,080 hours; for occupations with no published hourly mean wage, the annual wage has been directly calculated from the reported survey data.
[2]Wages for some occupations that do not generally entail year-round, full-time employment are reported as either hourly wages or annual salaries (depending on how employees are typically paid).

Table 3-3. Employment and Wages, by Occupation, May 2012—*Continued*

(Number of people, dollars.)

Occupation	May 2012			
	Employment	Median hourly wage	Mean hourly wage	Mean annual wage[1]
Protective Service—*Continued*				
Detectives and criminal investigators	109 230	35.72	37.43	77 860
Fish and game wardens	6 320	23.11	23.75	49 400
Parking enforcement workers	9 210	17.16	17.70	36 810
Police officers	636 140	26.57	27.78	57 770
Police and sheriff's patrol officers	632 000	26.57	27.78	57 770
Transit and railroad police	4 140	26.54	27.83	57 880
Other protective service workers	1 417 510	11.65	13.36	27 790
Animal control workers	13 890	15.23	16.09	33 470
Private detectives and investigators	23 390	21.99	24.42	50 780
Security guards and gaming surveillance officers	1 055 580	11.55	13.12	27 290
Gaming surveillance officers and gaming investigators	9 150	14.23	15.40	32 040
Security guards	1 046 420	11.52	13.10	27 240
Miscellaneous protective service workers	324 650	11.53	13.24	27 530
Crossing guards	70 390	11.50	12.58	26 160
Lifeguards, ski patrol, and other recreational protective service workers	125 770	9.11	9.96	20 720
Transportation security screeners	47 200	17.71	17.85	37 130
Protective service workers, all other	81 290	14.65	16.19	33 680
Food Preparation and Serving Related				
Supervisors of food preparation and serving workers	914 970	14.48	16.05	33 390
Chefs and head cooks	97 370	20.42	22.39	46 570
First-line supervisors of food preparation and serving workers	817 600	14.07	15.30	31 820
Cooks and food preparation workers	2 870 010	9.66	10.52	21 890
Cooks	2 084 640	9.88	10.70	22 260
Cooks, fast food	504 740	8.85	9.03	18 780
Cooks, institution and cafeteria	395 280	10.99	11.70	24 340
Cooks, private household	540	11.29	13.38	27 840
Cooks, restaurant	1 000 710	10.59	11.20	23 300
Cooks, short order	162 320	9.48	10.21	21 240
Cooks, all other	21 050	11.18	12.17	25 310
Food preparation workers	785 370	9.28	10.05	20 910
Food and beverage serving workers	6 485 990	8.88	9.54	19 840
Bartenders	538 220	9.09	10.40	21 630
Fast food and counter workers	3 378 030	8.80	9.04	18 810
Combined food preparation and serving workers, including fast food	2 943 810	8.78	9.00	18 720
Counter attendants, cafeteria, food concession, and coffee shop	434 220	8.92	9.34	19 430
Waiters and waitresses	2 332 020	8.92	9.95	20 710
Food servers, nonrestaurant	237 740	9.44	10.58	22 010
Other food preparation and serving related workers	1 275 900	8.91	9.36	19 470
Dining room and cafeteria attendants and bartender helpers	395 750	8.89	9.47	19 690
Dishwashers	501 910	8.88	9.10	18 930
Hosts and hostesses, restaurant, lounge, and coffee shop	341 400	8.93	9.41	19 570
Food preparation and serving related workers, all other	36 850	9.76	11.25	23 390
Building and Grounds Cleaning and Maintenance				
Supervisors of building and grounds cleaning and maintenance workers	269 700	18.08	19.47	40 500
First-line supervisors of housekeeping and janitorial workers	170 690	16.98	18.19	37 830
First-line supervisors of landscaping, lawn service, and groundskeeping workers	99 010	20.27	21.68	45 100
Building cleaning and pest control workers	3 067 210	10.37	11.60	24 130
Building cleaning workers	3 005 830	10.31	11.52	23 970
Janitors and cleaners, except maids and housekeeping cleaners	2 097 380	10.73	11.95	24 850
Maids and housekeeping cleaners	894 920	9.41	10.49	21 820
Building cleaning workers, all other	13 530	13.25	14.13	29 390
Pest control workers	61 380	14.45	15.47	32 190
Grounds maintenance workers	909 350	11.53	12.72	26 460
Grounds maintenance workers	909 350	11.53	12.72	26 460
Landscaping and groundskeeping workers	830 640	11.33	12.44	25 870
Pesticide handlers, sprayers, and applicators, vegetation	23 650	14.55	15.38	32 000
Tree trimmers and pruners	39 750	15.54	16.27	33 850
Grounds maintenance workers, all other	15 300	12.86	14.72	30 620
Personal Care and Service				
Supervisors of personal care and service workers	174 450	17.61	19.10	39 740
First-line supervisors of gaming workers	32 490	21.81	22.12	46 010
Gaming supervisors	24 760	23.70	23.89	49 700
Slot supervisors	7 730	15.57	16.44	34 200
First-line supervisors of personal service workers	141 960	16.90	18.41	38 300
Animal care and service workers	161 310	9.60	11.02	22 920
Animal trainers	11 170	12.15	14.59	30 340
Nonfarm animal caretakers	150 140	9.46	10.75	22 370
Entertainment attendants and related workers	530 880	9.06	10.23	21 280
Gaming services workers	123 860	9.09	11.09	23 080
Gaming dealers	98 310	8.96	10.77	22 410
Gaming and sports book writers and runners	12 710	10.49	11.92	24 790
Gaming service workers, all other	12 850	11.29	12.74	26 500
Motion picture projectionists	8 030	9.53	10.38	21 600
Ushers, lobby attendants, and ticket takers	106 860	9.01	9.77	20 320

[1] Annual wages have been calculated by multiplying the hourly mean wage by a "year-round, full-time" hours figure of 2,080 hours; for occupations with no published hourly mean wage, the annual wage has been directly calculated from the reported survey data.

Table 3-3. Employment and Wages, by Occupation, May 2012—*Continued*

(Number of people, dollars.)

Occupation	May 2012			
	Employment	Median hourly wage	Mean hourly wage	Mean annual wage[1]
Personal Care and Service—*Continued*				
Miscellaneous entertainment attendants and related workers	292 130	9.06	10.03	20 870
Amusement and recreation attendants	256 400	9.00	9.63	20 020
Costume attendants	5 660	17.67	21.55	44 830
Locker room, coatroom, and dressing room attendants	19 190	9.21	10.28	21 390
Entertainment attendants and related workers, all other	10 890	12.09	13.17	27 400
Funeral service workers	60 000	14.24	17.70	36 820
Embalmers	5 040	20.31	21.00	43 680
Funeral attendants	31 890	10.87	11.66	24 250
Morticians, undertakers, and funeral directors	23 070	22.52	25.33	52 690
Personal appearance workers	478 160	10.67	12.68	26 370
Barbers, hairdressers, hairstylists and cosmetologists	368 500	10.95	12.89	26 820
Barbers	12 590	12.06	13.23	27 520
Hairdressers, hairstylists, and cosmetologists	355 910	10.91	12.88	26 790
Miscellaneous personal appearance workers	109 660	9.64	11.97	24 890
Makeup artists, theatrical and performance	1 950	30.99	32.49	67 580
Manicurists and pedicurists	62 330	9.24	10.31	21 440
Shampooers	13 570	8.80	8.94	18 600
Skincare specialists	31 810	13.77	15.25	31 720
Baggage porters, bellhops, and concierges	66 360	11.00	12.27	25 510
Baggage porters, bellhops, and concierges	66 360	11.00	12.27	25 510
Baggage porters and bellhops	40 480	9.64	11.10	23 090
Concierges	25 880	13.10	14.09	29 310
Tour and travel guides	35 480	11.74	13.19	27 440
Tour and travel guides	35 480	11.74	13.19	27 440
Tour guides and escorts	31 270	11.51	12.63	26 280
Travel guides	4 210	14.80	17.34	36 060
Other personal care and service workers	2 304 120	9.92	11.29	23 490
Childcare workers	624 520	9.38	10.25	21 310
Personal care aides	985 230	9.57	10.01	20 830
Recreation and fitness workers	543 800	11.71	14.60	30 370
Fitness trainers and aerobics instructors	234 070	15.25	17.74	36 900
Recreation workers	309 730	10.69	12.22	25 430
Residential advisors	83 760	11.79	12.72	26 470
Personal care and service workers, all other	66 810	9.90	11.26	23 420
Sales and Related				
Supervisors of sales workers	1 457 580	18.92	22.99	47 820
First-line supervisors of retail sales workers	1 214 170	17.70	19.67	40 910
First-line supervisors of non-retail sales workers	243 420	33.68	39.58	82 320
Retail sales workers	8 326 900	9.56	11.35	23 610
Cashiers	3 335 980	9.13	9.81	20 410
Gaming change persons and booth cashiers	21 970	11.87	12.38	25 740
Counter and rental clerks and parts salespersons	650 920	12.05	13.81	28 720
Counter and rental clerks	432 650	11.12	12.93	26 900
Parts salespersons	218 270	14.21	15.54	32 320
Retail salespersons	4 340 000	10.15	12.17	25 310
Sales representatives, services	1 549 470	24.56	32.97	68 580
Advertising sales agents	145 500	22.26	27.54	57 270
Insurance sales agents	336 740	23.15	30.48	63 400
Securities, commodities, and financial services sales agents	330 470	34.48	48.51	100 910
Travel agents	64 680	16.64	17.78	36 970
Sales representatives, services, all other	672 080	24.45	29.22	60 770
Sales representatives, wholesale and manufacturing	1 778 860	27.82	33.02	68 690
Sales representatives, wholesale and manufacturing	1 778 860	27.82	33.02	68 690
Sales representatives, wholesale and manufacturing, technical and scientific products	364 830	36.04	41.20	85 690
Sales representatives, wholesale and manufacturing, except technical and scientific products	1 414 030	26.07	30.91	64 300
Other sales and related workers	722 280	13.75	20.52	42 670
Models, demonstrators, and product promoters	77 500	11.40	13.49	28 060
Demonstrators and product promoters	73 170	11.47	13.55	28 180
Models	4 330	9.02	12.55	26 110
Real estate brokers and sales agents	199 830	20.19	27.50	57 210
Real estate brokers	37 270	28.05	38.57	80 220
Real estate sales agents	162 560	18.82	24.97	51 930
Sales engineers	65 410	44.15	47.74	99 290
Telemarketers	245 550	10.74	12.29	25 570
Miscellaneous sales and related workers	134 000	12.21	15.94	33 160
Door-to-door sales workers, news and street vendors, and related workers	6 650	10.32	12.68	26 380
Sales and related workers, all other	127 350	12.41	16.11	33 510
Office and Administrative Support				
Supervisors of office and administrative support workers	1 359 150	23.72	25.40	52 830
First-line supervisors of office and administrative support workers	1 359 150	23.72	25.40	52 830
Communications equipment operators	139 000	12.47	13.34	27 760
Switchboard operators, including answering service	125 490	12.20	12.91	26 860
Telephone operators	10 710	15.79	16.67	34 670
Communications equipment operators, all other	2 800	19.35	19.96	41 530
Financial clerks	3 324 780	15.71	16.55	34 420
Bill and account collectors	385 890	15.61	16.50	34 320
Billing and posting clerks	490 850	16.08	16.61	34 540
Bookkeeping, accounting, and auditing clerks	1 606 260	16.91	17.62	36 640

[1]Annual wages have been calculated by multiplying the hourly mean wage by a "year-round, full-time" hours figure of 2,080 hours; for occupations with no published hourly mean wage, the annual wage has been directly calculated from the reported survey data.

Table 3-3. Employment and Wages, by Occupation, May 2012—*Continued*

(Number of people, dollars.)

Occupation	May 2012			
	Employment	Median hourly wage	Mean hourly wage	Mean annual wage[1]
Office and Administrative Support—*Continued*				
Gaming cage workers	18 230	11.83	12.54	26 070
Payroll and timekeeping clerks	172 740	18.12	18.69	38 880
Procurement clerks	69 750	18.38	18.43	38 340
Tellers	541 770	11.99	12.40	25 790
Financial clerks, all other	39 290	17.72	19.03	39 580
Information and record clerks	5 240 790	14.28	15.35	31 940
Brokerage clerks	61 870	20.40	21.34	44 390
Correspondence clerks	10 150	17.38	17.75	36 920
Court, municipal, and license clerks	122 710	16.75	17.76	36 950
Credit authorizers, checkers, and clerks	51 650	16.16	17.15	35 680
Customer service representatives	2 299 750	14.70	15.92	33 110
Eligibility interviewers, government programs	130 340	19.49	19.74	41 060
File clerks	158 580	12.59	13.48	28 030
Hotel, motel, and resort desk clerks	229 000	9.78	10.56	21 960
Interviewers, except eligibility and loan	196 660	14.38	15.04	31 270
Library assistants, clerical	104 030	11.27	12.35	25 680
Loan interviewers and clerks	192 010	16.98	17.40	36 180
New accounts clerks	55 320	15.25	15.84	32 950
Order clerks	208 800	14.18	15.04	31 280
Human resources assistants, except payroll and timekeeping	139 200	18.03	18.43	38 340
Receptionists and information clerks	966 150	12.49	13.00	27 050
Reservation and transportation ticket agents and travel clerks	135 930	15.58	16.14	33 580
Information and record clerks, all other	178 650	17.91	18.15	37 750
Material recording, scheduling, dispatching, and distributing workers	3 830 120	13.65	15.54	32 310
Cargo and freight agents	78 750	19.10	20.34	42 310
Couriers and messengers	76 830	12.23	12.99	27 020
Dispatchers	280 530	17.26	18.41	38 300
Police, fire, and ambulance dispatchers	95 640	17.45	18.27	38 010
Dispatchers, except police, fire, and ambulance	184 890	17.16	18.49	38 450
Meter readers, utilities	39 530	17.28	18.52	38 510
Postal service workers	509 030	25.53	24.55	51 070
Postal service clerks	69 310	25.53	24.26	50 460
Postal service mail carriers	305 490	27.16	25.11	52 220
Postal service mail sorters, processors, and processing machine operators	134 230	25.52	23.44	48 750
Production, planning, and expediting clerks	278 490	21.03	21.85	45 450
Shipping, receiving, and traffic clerks	690 780	13.95	14.76	30 700
Stock clerks and order fillers	1 806 310	10.60	11.75	24 440
Weighers, measurers, checkers, and samplers, recordkeeping	69 870	13.42	14.30	29 750
Secretaries and administrative assistants	3 615 090	16.99	18.16	37 780
Executive secretaries and executive administrative assistants	803 040	22.84	24.14	50 220
Legal secretaries	216 730	20.27	21.34	44 380
Medical secretaries	509 640	15.07	15.71	32 670
Secretaries and administrative assistants, except legal, medical, and executive	2 085 680	15.58	16.13	33 560
Other office and administrative support workers	3 846 420	13.74	14.62	30 410
Computer operators	71 560	18.46	19.10	39 720
Data entry and information processing workers	303 840	14.47	15.11	31 430
Data entry keyers	207 280	13.47	14.05	29 220
Word processors and typists	96 560	16.96	17.40	36 190
Desktop publishers	15 960	17.81	18.77	39 040
Insurance claims and policy processing clerks	226 260	17.17	17.93	37 300
Mail clerks and mail machine operators, except postal service	102 410	12.93	13.53	28 140
Office clerks, general	2 808 100	13.21	14.07	29 270
Office machine operators, except computer	66 820	13.44	14.22	29 580
Proofreaders and copy markers	11 300	15.76	16.88	35 110
Statistical assistants	14 870	19.15	19.72	41 010
Office and administrative support workers, all other	225 310	14.94	15.90	33 070
Farming, Fishing, and Forestry Occupations				
Supervisors of farming, fishing, and forestry workers	19 340	20.99	22.31	46 410
Agricultural workers	365 760	9.14	10.54	21 920
Agricultural inspectors	13 570	20.27	20.41	42 460
Animal breeders	1 460	16.47	17.90	37 230
Graders and sorters, agricultural products	39 060	9.21	10.04	20 870
Miscellaneous agricultural workers	311 670	9.09	10.14	21 080
Agricultural equipment operators	22 820	12.43	13.17	27 390
Farmworkers and laborers, crop, nursery, and greenhouse	253 670	8.98	9.61	19 990
Farmworkers, farm, ranch, and aquacultural animals	29 570	10.61	11.56	24 040
Agricultural workers, all other	5 610	12.09	14.00	29 120
Fishing and hunting workers	610	16.35	17.98	37 410
Fishers and related fishing workers	570	16.07	17.74	36 900
Forest, conservation, and logging workers	41 960	15.57	16.30	33 910
Forest and conservation workers	7 910	11.70	13.75	28 600
Logging workers	34 050	16.17	16.90	35 140
Fallers	5 150	16.95	19.64	40 860
Logging equipment operators	23 240	16.05	16.41	34 130
Log graders and scalers	2 770	15.81	16.12	33 540
Logging workers, all other	2 890	16.47	16.66	34 650

[1]Annual wages have been calculated by multiplying the hourly mean wage by a "year-round, full-time" hours figure of 2,080 hours; for occupations with no published hourly mean wage, the annual wage has been directly calculated from the reported survey data.

Table 3-3. Employment and Wages, by Occupation, May 2012—*Continued*

(Number of people, dollars.)

Occupation	May 2012			
	Employment	Median hourly wage	Mean hourly wage	Mean annual wage[1]
Construction and Extraction Occupations				
Supervisors of construction and extraction workers	456 640	28.70	30.40	63 230
First-line supervisors of construction trades and extraction workers	456 640	28.70	30.40	63 230
Construction trades workers	3 671 980	18.74	21.09	43 860
Boilermakers	17 660	27.19	26.84	55 830
Brickmasons, blockmasons, and stonemasons	68 420	21.61	23.40	48 670
Brickmasons and blockmasons	57 090	22.33	24.22	50 370
Stonemasons	11 330	17.96	19.29	40 120
Carpenters	567 820	19.20	21.41	44 520
Carpet, floor, and tile installers and finishers	66 540	17.50	19.51	40 590
Carpet installers	25 350	17.66	19.68	40 930
Floor layers, except carpet, wood, and hard tiles	9 980	17.07	18.48	38 450
Floor sanders and finishers	4 150	15.98	17.13	35 640
Tile and marble setters	27 050	17.81	20.10	41 820
Cement masons, concrete finishers, and terrazzo workers	138 560	17.23	19.20	39 930
Cement masons and concrete finishers	135 200	17.19	19.17	39 870
Terrazzo workers and finishers	3 350	19.11	20.40	42 440
Construction laborers	814 470	14.42	16.58	34 490
Construction equipment operators	393 410	19.70	21.88	45 510
Paving, surfacing, and tamping equipment operators	54 460	17.23	19.31	40 170
Pile-driver operators	3 800	23.31	26.67	55 480
Operating engineers and other construction equipment operators	335 160	20.13	22.24	46 270
Drywall installers, ceiling tile installers, and tapers	91 180	18.23	20.99	43 660
Drywall and ceiling tile installers	75 810	17.89	20.38	42 380
Tapers	15 370	21.77	24.01	49 940
Electricians	519 850	23.96	25.50	53 030
Glaziers	42 350	18.08	20.24	42 090
Insulation workers	50 760	17.28	19.71	41 000
Insulation workers, floor, ceiling, and wall	22 540	15.56	17.49	36 390
Insulation workers, mechanical	28 220	18.83	21.48	44 680
Painters and paperhangers	187 790	16.91	18.55	38 590
Painters, construction and maintenance	184 330	16.92	18.55	38 590
Paperhangers	3 460	16.63	18.57	38 630
Pipelayers, plumbers, pipefitters, and steamfitters	383 970	22.82	24.75	51 480
Pipelayers	43 590	17.40	19.22	39 970
Plumbers, pipefitters, and steamfitters	340 370	23.62	25.46	52 950
Plasterers and stucco masons	21 040	17.85	20.13	41 860
Reinforcing iron and rebar workers	15 330	22.07	24.59	51 140
Roofers	97 650	16.97	18.63	38 760
Sheet metal workers	133 420	20.81	22.54	46 870
Structural iron and steel workers	57 070	22.18	24.40	50 740
Solar photovoltaic installers	4 710	18.22	19.53	40 620
Helpers, construction trades	210 460	12.77	13.57	28 230
Helpers, construction trades	210 460	12.77	13.57	28 230
Helpers–brickmasons, blockmasons, stonemasons, and tile and marble setters	24 310	13.57	14.95	31 100
Helpers–carpenters	35 870	12.29	13.09	27 230
Helpers–electricians	59 610	13.30	13.86	28 840
Helpers–painters, paperhangers, plasterers, and stucco masons	10 980	11.68	12.68	26 360
Helpers–pipelayers, plumbers, pipefitters, and steamfitters	46 510	12.82	13.65	28 380
Helpers–roofers	12 200	11.20	12.03	25 030
Helpers, construction trades, all other	20 980	12.31	13.18	27 420
Other construction and related workers	382 000	19.05	20.94	43 540
Construction and building inspectors	89 280	25.70	26.55	55 230
Elevator installers and repairers	19 700	36.85	35.64	74 140
Fence erectors	21 250	14.52	15.58	32 410
Hazardous materials removal workers	37 440	18.07	20.03	41 660
Highway maintenance workers	141 180	16.95	17.43	36 240
Rail-track laying and maintenance equipment operators	16 870	22.08	22.21	46 200
Septic tank servicers and sewer pipe cleaners	24 020	16.36	17.29	35 970
Miscellaneous construction and related workers	32 260	16.79	18.40	38 260
Segmental pavers	1 490	16.21	17.18	35 740
Construction and related workers, all other	30 770	16.82	18.45	38 380
Extraction workers	257 220	19.54	21.16	44 010
Derrick, rotary drill, and service unit operators, oil, gas, and mining	104 230	21.43	24.02	49 960
Derrick operators, oil and gas	21 950	22.55	23.43	48 740
Rotary drill operators, oil and gas	25 090	23.66	27.18	56 540
Service unit operators, oil, gas, and mining	57 180	20.18	22.86	47 540
Earth drillers, except oil and gas	17 680	19.61	21.08	43 840
Explosives workers, ordnance handling experts, and blasters	6 330	23.38	23.74	49 380
Mining machine operators	23 290	24.15	23.62	49 120
Continuous mining machine operators	13 640	24.98	24.49	50 940
Mine cutting and channeling machine operators	6 750	23.05	22.38	46 540
Mining machine operators, all other	2 900	22.51	22.40	46 590
Rock splitters, quarry	4 490	15.52	16.28	33 870
Roof bolters, mining	6 790	26.11	26.08	54 240
Roustabouts, oil and gas	59 320	16.41	17.21	35 800
Helpers–extraction workers	25 840	15.13	16.18	33 660
Extraction workers, all other	9 250	18.66	19.09	39 710

[1]Annual wages have been calculated by multiplying the hourly mean wage by a "year-round, full-time" hours figure of 2,080 hours; for occupations with no published hourly mean wage, the annual wage has been directly calculated from the reported survey data.

Table 3-3. Employment and Wages, by Occupation, May 2012—*Continued*

(Number of people, dollars.)

Occupation	May 2012			
	Employment	Median hourly wage	Mean hourly wage	Mean annual wage[1]
Installation, Maintenance, and Repair Occupations				
Supervisors of installation, maintenance, and repair workers	421 650	28.97	30.07	62 540
Electrical and electronic equipment mechanics, installers, and repairers	572 810	22.38	23.21	48 280
Computer, automated teller, and office machine repairers	113 480	17.60	18.53	38 550
Radio and telecommunications equipment installers and repairers	224 000	25.86	25.57	53 180
Radio, cellular, and tower equipment installers and repairers	15 780	21.11	22.24	46 260
Telecommunications equipment installers and repairers, except line installers	208 220	26.22	25.82	53 710
Miscellaneous electrical and electronic equipment mechanics, installers, and repairers	235 330	22.48	23.22	48 310
Avionics technicians	16 810	26.61	26.65	55 440
Electric motor, power tool, and related repairers	19 020	17.42	18.50	38 470
Electrical and electronics installers and repairers, transportation equipment	15 530	24.63	25.41	52 850
Electrical and electronics repairers, commercial and industrial equipment	66 440	25.31	25.45	52 940
Electrical and electronics repairers, powerhouse, substation, and relay	23 920	33.08	32.40	67 380
Electronic equipment installers and repairers, motor vehicles	12 590	15.07	16.16	33 600
Electronic home entertainment equipment installers and repairers	27 050	16.86	17.76	36 940
Security and fire alarm systems installers	53 960	19.73	20.77	43 210
Vehicle and mobile equipment mechanics, installers, and repairers	1 438 930	18.50	19.61	40 780
Aircraft mechanics and service technicians	119 160	26.55	26.78	55 690
Automotive technicians and repairers	747 210	17.72	18.97	39 460
Automotive body and related repairers	135 610	18.45	20.12	41 840
Automotive glass installers and repairers	14 780	15.70	16.14	33 580
Automotive service technicians and mechanics	596 830	17.60	18.78	39 060
Bus and truck mechanics and diesel engine specialists	230 030	20.35	20.99	43 660
Heavy vehicle and mobile equipment service technicians and mechanics	163 490	21.07	21.53	44 780
Farm equipment mechanics and service technicians	34 150	16.71	17.16	35 680
Mobile heavy equipment mechanics, except engines	110 200	22.14	22.66	47 140
Rail car repairers	19 140	23.32	22.80	47 430
Small engine mechanics	60 690	15.69	16.44	34 190
Motorboat mechanics and service technicians	18 380	17.08	17.86	37 140
Motorcycle mechanics	14 950	15.93	16.78	34 910
Outdoor power equipment and other small engine mechanics	27 350	14.67	15.30	31 820
Miscellaneous vehicle and mobile equipment mechanics, installers, and repairers	118 350	11.56	12.70	26 410
Bicycle repairers	10 490	11.61	12.14	25 250
Recreational vehicle service technicians	10 970	16.61	17.36	36 120
Tire repairers and changers	96 880	11.25	12.23	25 440
Other installation, maintenance, and repair occupations	2 636 210	18.63	20.00	41 600
Control and valve installers and repairers	56 060	21.90	23.17	48 180
Mechanical door repairers	15 750	17.36	18.55	38 590
Control and valve installers and repairers, except mechanical door	40 310	24.50	24.97	51 930
Heating, air conditioning, and refrigeration mechanics and installers	240 480	20.98	22.03	45 830
Home appliance repairers	34 510	16.91	17.92	37 270
Industrial machinery installation, repair, and maintenance workers	430 030	22.02	22.84	47 500
Industrial machinery mechanics	301 560	22.56	23.41	48 690
Maintenance workers, machinery	88 450	19.53	20.28	42 190
Millwrights	38 050	23.80	24.39	50 730
Refractory materials repairers, except brickmasons	1 970	19.89	20.13	41 870
Line installers and repairers	245 480	27.99	27.24	56 670
Electrical power-line installers and repairers	112 450	30.41	29.94	62 280
Telecommunications line installers and repairers	133 040	24.72	24.96	51 920
Precision instrument and equipment repairers	59 930	21.05	22.09	45 960
Camera and photographic equipment repairers	2 590	18.26	20.07	41 750
Medical equipment repairers	35 740	21.43	22.55	46 910
Musical instrument repairers and tuners	7 130	14.73	16.17	33 620
Watch repairers	2 670	18.10	19.03	39 570
Precision instrument and equipment repairers, all other	11 800	25.13	25.42	52 880
Maintenance and repair workers, general	1 230 270	16.93	17.88	37 190
Wind turbine service technicians	3 200	22.10	23.23	48 320
Miscellaneous installation, maintenance, and repair workers	336 260	14.95	16.68	34 690
Coin, vending, and amusement machine servicers and repairers	36 080	14.98	15.72	32 700
Commercial divers	3 480	22.54	26.32	54 750
Fabric menders, except garment	770	12.99	13.72	28 540
Locksmiths and safe repairers	16 190	18.06	18.83	39 160
Manufactured building and mobile home installers	3 310	13.50	14.50	30 160
Riggers	14 690	20.51	21.44	44 590
Signal and track switch repairers	8 600	26.66	26.63	55 390
Helpers–installation, maintenance, and repair workers	124 370	11.64	12.88	26 780
Installation, maintenance, and repair workers, all other	128 770	17.60	18.95	39 410
Production Occupations				
Supervisors of production workers	568 820	25.98	27.61	57 420
Assemblers and fabricators	1 718 700	13.74	14.89	30 970
Aircraft structure, surfaces, rigging, and systems assemblers	41 180	22.09	23.33	48 520
Electrical, electronics, and electromechanical assemblers	261 780	14.14	15.10	31 400
Coil winders, tapers, and finishers	14 300	14.83	15.39	32 000
Electrical and electronic equipment assemblers	197 500	13.85	14.89	30 970
Electromechanical equipment assemblers	49 990	15.12	15.84	32 950
Engine and other machine assemblers	40 750	17.36	18.14	37 730
Structural metal fabricators and fitters	78 340	17.19	17.91	37 260
Miscellaneous assemblers and fabricators	1 296 650	13.14	14.30	29 730

[1]Annual wages have been calculated by multiplying the hourly mean wage by a "year-round, full-time" hours figure of 2,080 hours; for occupations with no published hourly mean wage, the annual wage has been directly calculated from the reported survey data.

Table 3-3. Employment and Wages, by Occupation, May 2012—*Continued*

(Number of people, dollars.)

Occupation	May 2012			
	Employment	Median hourly wage	Mean hourly wage	Mean annual wage[1]
Production Occupations—*Continued*				
Fiberglass laminators and fabricators	17 580	13.86	14.40	29 960
Team assemblers	1 006 980	13.29	14.38	29 910
Timing device assemblers and adjusters	1 140	12.31	13.98	29 080
Assemblers and fabricators, all other	270 950	12.46	13.98	29 070
Food processing workers	720 970	11.72	12.68	26 380
Bakers	157 230	11.13	12.05	25 060
Butchers and other meat, poultry, and fish processing workers	372 060	11.74	12.61	26 230
Butchers and meat cutters	134 210	13.70	14.42	30 000
Meat, poultry, and fish cutters and trimmers	158 480	10.98	11.39	23 690
Slaughterers and meat packers	79 370	11.70	11.99	24 930
Miscellaneous food processing workers	191 690	12.39	13.34	27 750
Food and tobacco roasting, baking, and drying machine operators and tenders	20 350	13.67	14.22	29 580
Food batchmakers	100 520	12.77	13.63	28 340
Food cooking machine operators and tenders	33 250	12.67	13.51	28 090
Food processing workers, all other	37 570	11.12	11.96	24 880
Metal workers and plastic workers	1 837 280	17.01	17.88	37 190
Computer control programmers and operators	162 860	17.67	18.53	38 550
Computer-controlled machine tool operators, metal and plastic	138 870	17.10	17.70	36 810
Computer numerically controlled machine tool programmers, metal and plastic	23 990	22.08	23.39	48 640
Forming machine setters, operators, and tenders, metal and plastic	132 800	16.30	16.97	35 300
Extruding and drawing machine setters, operators, and tenders, metal and plastic	74 490	15.54	16.37	34 060
Forging machine setters, operators, and tenders, metal and plastic	22 270	16.37	16.74	34 830
Rolling machine setters, operators, and tenders, metal and plastic	36 040	17.98	18.35	38 160
Machine tool cutting setters, operators, and tenders, metal and plastic	333 520	15.13	15.86	32 980
Cutting, punching, and press machine setters, operators, and tenders, metal and plastic	182 570	14.27	14.95	31 090
Drilling and boring machine tool setters, operators, and tenders, metal and plastic	20 660	16.32	17.32	36 020
Grinding, lapping, polishing, and buffing machine tool setters, operators, and tenders, metal and plastic	69 510	15.20	15.90	33 070
Lathe and turning machine tool setters, operators, and tenders, metal and plastic	37 920	17.57	18.08	37 600
Milling and planing machine setters, operators, and tenders, metal and plastic	22 840	17.22	18.01	37 460
Machinists	388 370	18.99	19.65	40 860
Metal furnace operators, tenders, pourers, and casters	31 140	17.88	18.55	38 590
Metal-refining furnace operators and tenders	20 520	18.70	19.26	40 060
Pourers and casters, metal	10 620	16.37	17.19	35 750
Model makers and patternmakers, metal and plastic	9 830	21.32	21.86	45 470
Model makers, metal and plastic	5 700	22.04	22.58	46 970
Patternmakers, metal and plastic	4 130	20.40	20.86	43 400
Molders and molding machine setters, operators, and tenders, metal and plastic	136 950	13.84	14.67	30 510
Foundry mold and coremakers	12 510	14.68	15.19	31 600
Molding, coremaking, and casting machine setters, operators, and tenders, metal and plastic	124 440	13.77	14.62	30 400
Multiple machine tool setters, operators, and tenders, metal and plastic	85 110	16.33	16.85	35 060
Tool and die makers	76 430	22.60	23.31	48 490
Welding, soldering, and brazing workers	379 140	17.35	18.32	38 100
Welders, cutters, solderers, and brazers	329 710	17.45	18.46	38 410
Welding, soldering, and brazing machine setters, operators, and tenders	49 430	16.69	17.33	36 060
Miscellaneous metal workers and plastic workers	101 120	15.72	16.74	34 820
Heat treating equipment setters, operators, and tenders, metal and plastic	21 760	16.35	17.01	35 380
Layout workers, metal and plastic	12 380	20.22	20.35	42 330
Plating and coating machine setters, operators, and tenders, metal and plastic	34 420	14.29	15.30	31 830
Tool grinders, filers, and sharpeners	11 950	16.49	17.09	35 560
Metal workers and plastic workers, all other	20 620	14.93	16.48	34 280
Printing workers	267 390	16.40	17.14	35 640
Prepress technicians and workers	41 420	17.91	18.76	39 020
Printing press operators	173 010	16.68	17.35	36 090
Print binding and finishing workers	52 960	14.30	15.17	31 560
Textile, apparel, and furnishings workers	575 080	10.58	11.62	24 170
Laundry and dry-cleaning workers	198 750	9.58	10.35	21 540
Pressers, textile, garment, and related materials	52 850	9.46	9.97	20 730
Sewing machine operators	142 380	10.23	11.11	23 110
Shoe and leather workers	9 180	11.56	12.44	25 880
Shoe and leather workers and repairers	5 750	11.52	12.52	26 050
Shoe machine operators and tenders	3 420	11.69	12.31	25 600
Tailors, dressmakers, and sewers	30 360	12.20	13.69	28 480
Sewers, hand	5 500	10.97	12.21	25 390
Tailors, dressmakers, and custom sewers	24 870	12.64	14.02	29 170
Textile machine setters, operators, and tenders	75 520	12.27	12.54	26 080
Textile bleaching and dyeing machine operators and tenders	11 350	11.64	12.27	25 520
Textile cutting machine setters, operators, and tenders	15 620	11.56	12.24	25 460
Textile knitting and weaving machine setters, operators, and tenders	21 110	12.76	12.96	26 950
Textile winding, twisting, and drawing out machine setters, operators, and tenders	27 440	12.43	12.50	26 010
Miscellaneous textile, apparel, and furnishings workers	66 040	14.53	15.72	32 710
Extruding and forming machine setters, operators, and tenders, synthetic and glass fibers	17 620	15.59	15.75	32 750
Fabric and apparel patternmakers	6 500	18.58	21.53	44 790
Upholsterers	27 840	14.39	15.26	31 750
Textile, apparel, and furnishings workers, all other	14 080	12.47	13.93	28 970
Woodworkers	200 680	13.67	14.49	30 140

[1]Annual wages have been calculated by multiplying the hourly mean wage by a "year-round, full-time" hours figure of 2,080 hours; for occupations with no published hourly mean wage, the annual wage has been directly calculated from the reported survey data.

Table 3-3. Employment and Wages, by Occupation, May 2012—*Continued*

(Number of people, dollars.)

Occupation	May 2012			
	Employment	Median hourly wage	Mean hourly wage	Mean annual wage[1]
Production Occupations—*Continued*				
Cabinetmakers and bench carpenters	78 140	14.90	15.84	32 940
Furniture finishers	13 740	13.70	14.38	29 900
Model makers and patternmakers, wood	2 030	15.81	16.95	35 250
Model makers, wood	1 270	13.85	15.26	31 740
Patternmakers, wood	770	19.15	19.73	41 030
Woodworking machine setters, operators, and tenders	99 830	12.85	13.40	27 870
Sawing machine setters, operators, and tenders, wood	38 720	12.59	13.23	27 520
Woodworking machine setters, operators, and tenders, except sawing	61 110	13.00	13.51	28 100
Woodworkers, all other	6 940	13.15	14.49	30 150
Plant and system operators	308 150	25.88	26.29	54 690
Power plant operators, distributors, and dispatchers	60 070	32.80	32.71	68 050
Nuclear power reactor operators	7 140	36.05	36.55	76 020
Power distributors and dispatchers	11 590	34.47	35.44	73 710
Power plant operators	41 350	31.79	31.29	65 080
Stationary engineers and boiler operators	36 350	25.75	26.37	54 860
Water and wastewater treatment plant and system operators	108 440	20.56	21.46	44 630
Miscellaneous plant and system operators	103 280	27.88	27.61	57 430
Chemical plant and system operators	38 170	26.15	26.03	54 150
Gas plant operators	12 380	29.39	29.37	61 090
Petroleum pump system operators, refinery operators, and gaugers	41 020	29.73	29.20	60 730
Plant and system operators, all other	11 710	25.55	25.32	52 660
Other production occupations	2 397 100	14.10	15.43	32 100
Chemical processing machine setters, operators, and tenders	97 460	20.81	21.50	44 720
Chemical equipment operators and tenders	56 030	22.64	23.06	47 950
Separating, filtering, clarifying, precipitating, and still machine setters, operators, and tenders	41 430	18.55	19.39	40 340
Crushing, grinding, polishing, mixing, and blending workers	177 000	15.52	16.28	33 870
Crushing, grinding, and polishing machine setters, operators, and tenders	29 320	15.31	16.03	33 340
Grinding and polishing workers, hand	30 470	13.41	14.06	29 250
Mixing and blending machine setters, operators, and tenders	117 210	16.27	16.92	35 200
Cutting workers	70 300	14.43	15.01	31 230
Cutters and trimmers, hand	13 740	11.79	12.82	26 650
Cutting and slicing machine setters, operators, and tenders	56 560	15.11	15.55	32 340
Extruding, forming, pressing, and compacting machine setters, operators, and tenders	68 080	15.05	15.81	32 880
Furnace, kiln, oven, drier, and kettle operators and tenders	20 140	17.08	17.83	37 080
Inspectors, testers, sorters, samplers, and weighers	454 010	16.57	17.90	37 240
Jewelers and precious stone and metal workers	22 060	16.99	18.67	38 840
Medical, dental, and ophthalmic laboratory technicians	78 400	15.90	17.12	35 600
Dental laboratory technicians	36 790	17.35	18.91	39 320
Medical appliance technicians	12 230	17.35	18.37	38 200
Ophthalmic laboratory technicians	29 380	13.74	14.35	29 850
Packaging and filling machine operators and tenders	367 700	12.43	13.54	28 160
Painting workers	142 570	15.79	17.01	35 380
Coating, painting, and spraying machine setters, operators, and tenders	79 970	14.68	15.32	31 870
Painters, transportation equipment	46 290	19.04	20.96	43 600
Painting, coating, and decorating workers	16 310	13.36	14.07	29 270
Semiconductor processors	21 380	15.88	16.72	34 780
Photographic process workers and processing machine operators	45 760	11.11	12.57	26 140
Miscellaneous production workers	832 240	12.16	13.59	28 270
Adhesive bonding machine operators and tenders	16 800	14.34	15.28	31 780
Cleaning, washing, and metal pickling equipment operators and tenders	16 050	12.60	13.59	28 280
Cooling and freezing equipment operators and tenders	8 130	13.56	14.43	30 020
Etchers and engravers	8 610	13.65	14.53	30 230
Molders, shapers, and casters, except metal and plastic	31 010	14.08	14.79	30 770
Paper goods machine setters, operators, and tenders	95 690	16.68	17.14	35 660
Tire builders	17 360	19.81	18.91	39 340
Helpers–production workers	419 840	10.96	11.84	24 620
Production workers, all other	218 740	12.95	14.61	30 380
Transportation and Material Moving Occupations				
Supervisors of transportation and material moving workers	372 930	23.52	24.82	51 620
Aircraft cargo handling supervisors	6 720	23.04	24.44	50 830
First-line supervisors of helpers, laborers, and material movers, hand	168 910	21.72	22.69	47 180
First-line supervisors of transportation and material-moving machine and vehicle operators	197 300	25.60	26.65	55 430
Air transportation workers	216 470	(2	(2	83 340
Aircraft pilots and flight engineers	101 260	(2	(2	111 960
Airline pilots, copilots, and flight engineers	66 270	(2	(2	128 760
Commercial pilots	34 990	(2	(2	80 140
Air traffic controllers and airfield operations specialists	30 250	49.27	49.36	102 670
Air traffic controllers	23 260	58.91	56.94	118 430
Airfield operations specialists	6 990	23.12	24.17	50 270
Flight attendants	84 960	(2	(2	42 340
Motor vehicle operators	3 618 180	15.77	16.87	35 090
Ambulance drivers and attendants, except emergency medical technicians	18 540	11.27	11.97	24 900
Bus drivers	652 590	14.21	15.13	31 480
Bus drivers, transit and intercity	162 840	17.59	18.50	38 470
Bus drivers, school or special client	489 750	13.50	14.01	29 150
Driver/sales workers and truck drivers	2 719 630	16.61	17.65	36 710
Driver/sales workers	394 110	10.90	13.33	27 730
Heavy and tractor-trailer truck drivers	1 556 510	18.37	19.40	40 360

[1]Annual wages have been calculated by multiplying the hourly mean wage by a "year-round, full-time" hours figure of 2,080 hours; for occupations with no published hourly mean wage, the annual wage has been directly calculated from the reported survey data.
[2]Wages for some occupations that do not generally entail year-round, full-time employment are reported as either hourly wages or annual salaries (depending on how employees are typically paid).

Table 3-3. Employment and Wages, by Occupation, May 2012—*Continued*

(Number of people, dollars.)

Occupation	May 2012			
	Employment	Median hourly wage	Mean hourly wage	Mean annual wage[1]
Transportation and Material Moving Occupations—*Continued*				
Light truck or delivery services drivers	769 010	14.13	16.32	33 940
Taxi drivers and chauffeurs	167 360	10.97	12.09	25 140
Motor vehicle operators, all other	60 050	12.95	15.15	31 510
Rail transportation workers	122 720	25.44	26.10	54 280
Locomotive engineers and operators	43 810	24.45	25.61	53 260
Locomotive engineers	37 060	25.13	26.36	54 830
Locomotive firers	1 580	21.60	23.34	48 550
Rail yard engineers, dinkey operators, and hostlers	5 170	19.82	20.89	43 450
Railroad brake, signal, and switch operators	24 380	24.68	24.16	50 260
Railroad conductors and yardmasters	42 740	26.30	27.30	56 770
Subway and streetcar operators	8 750	30.16	27.99	58 220
Rail transportation workers, all other	3 040	26.48	26.41	54 930
Water transportation workers	76 160	23.55	28.14	58 530
Sailors and marine oilers	31 500	18.36	19.11	39 760
Ship and boat captains and operators	33 900	30.12	33.95	70 610
Captains, mates, and pilots of water vessels	30 860	31.80	35.46	73 760
Motorboat operators	3 040	16.92	18.54	38 560
Ship engineers	10 760	34.08	36.29	75 480
Other transportation workers	329 100	10.38	13.02	27 090
Bridge and lock tenders	3 460	22.09	20.82	43 300
Parking lot attendants	126 520	9.39	10.35	21 540
Automotive and watercraft service attendants	108 510	9.69	10.38	21 600
Traffic technicians	6 340	18.45	20.42	42 480
Transportation inspectors	24 310	30.62	31.96	66 470
Transportation attendants, except flight attendants	23 790	10.33	11.52	23 960
Transportation workers, all other	36 190	14.84	16.50	34 330
Material moving workers	4 036 120	11.65	13.15	27 350
Conveyor operators and tenders	39 540	14.24	15.08	31 360
Crane and tower operators	43 040	22.73	24.33	50 610
Dredge, excavating, and loading machine operators	49 660	18.73	20.32	42 260
Dredge operators	1 740	17.87	20.73	43 120
Excavating and loading machine and dragline operators	45 020	18.41	20.12	41 850
Loading machine operators, underground mining	2 900	23.28	23.11	48 060
Hoist and winch operators	3 050	19.21	22.94	47 710
Industrial truck and tractor operators	496 570	14.53	15.43	32 090
Laborers and material movers, hand	3 213 370	10.95	12.17	25 310
Cleaners of vehicles and equipment	302 960	9.54	10.87	22 620
Laborers and freight, stock, and material movers, hand	2 143 940	11.49	12.70	26 410
Machine feeders and offbearers	105 790	13.04	13.79	28 680
Packers and packagers, hand	660 670	9.57	10.80	22 470
Pumping station operators	30 570	22.23	22.85	47 520
Gas compressor and gas pumping station operators	4 350	24.59	24.92	51 840
Pump operators, except wellhead pumpers	11 870	21.45	22.88	47 590
Wellhead pumpers	14 350	21.97	22.18	46 140
Refuse and recyclable material collectors	117 670	15.83	16.94	35 230
Mine shuttle car operators	2 990	25.05	24.67	51 310
Tank car, truck, and ship loaders	12 390	21.20	22.31	46 400
Material moving workers, all other	27 260	17.94	19.73	41 040

[1]Annual wages have been calculated by multiplying the hourly mean wage by a "year-round, full-time" hours figure of 2,080 hours; for occupations with no published hourly mean wage, the annual wage has been directly calculated from the reported survey data.

CHAPTER 4: LABOR FORCE AND EMPLOYMENT PROJECTIONS BY INDUSTRY AND OCCUPATION

LABOR FORCE AND EMPLOYMENT PROJECTIONS BY INDUSTRY AND OCCUPATION

HIGHLIGHTS

Every two years, the Bureau of Labor Statistics (BLS) develops decade-long projections for industry output, employment, and occupations. This chapter presents the employment outlook for the 2012–2022 period. The projections are based on a set of explicit assumptions and an application of a model of economic relationships.

Figure 4-1. Percent Change and Projected Percent Change in the Civilian Labor Force, 1992–2022

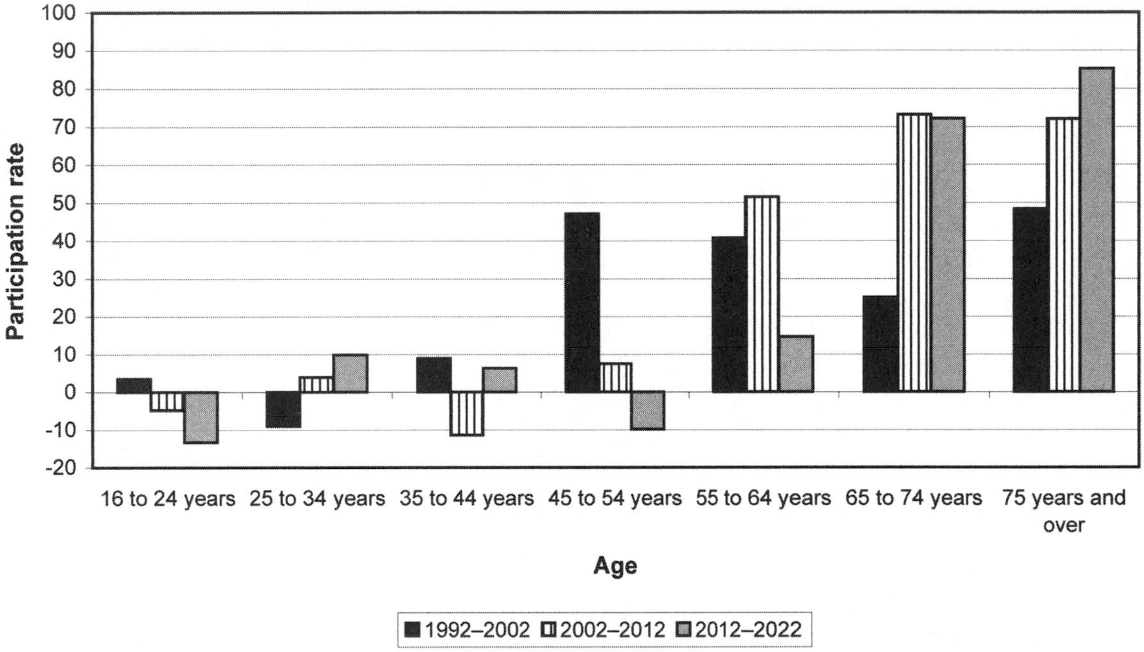

From 2012 to 2022, the civilian labor force is projected to grow by 5.5 percent, a much slower rate than the 7.0 percent increase from 2002 to 2012 or the 13.1 percent increase from 1992 to 2002. The aging of baby boomers has lead to a significant increase of older workers in the labor force. By 2022, persons 55 years of age and over are expected to make up 25.6 percent of the labor force. (See Table 4-1.)

OTHER HIGHLIGHTS

- While the number of persons 55 years and over in the labor force is expected to increase, the number of 16- to 24-year-olds in the labor force is expected to decline. In 1992, 16- to 24-year-olds made up 16.9 percent of the labor force. It is projected that by 2022, this age group will only make up 11.3 percent of the labor force. (See Table 4-1.)

- The slower growth in the labor force is expected to limit economic growth. From 2012 to 2022, gross domestic product is expected to only grow by 2.6 percent annually, which is slower than the growth seen in previous years. (See Table 4-1.)

- From 2012 to 2022, the number of Hispanics in the labor force is projected to increase by 27.8 percent, followed by the number of Asians at 23.8 percent and the number of Blacks at 10.0 percent. Meanwhile, the number of non-Hispanic Whites in the labor force is projected to decrease by 2.4 percent. (Hispanics may be of any race.) (See Table 4-1.)

NOTES AND DEFINITIONS

The Bureau of Labor Statistics (BLS) develops long-term projections of likely employment patterns in the U.S. economy. Since the early 1970s, projections have been prepared on a 2-year cycle. The last projections were released in December 2013. The projections cover the future size and composition of the labor force, aggregate economic growth, detailed estimates of industry production, and industry and occupational employment. The resulting data serve a variety of users who need information about expected patterns of economic growth and the effects these patterns are expected to have on employment. For example, information about future employment opportunities by occupation is used by counselors, educators, and others helping people choose a career and by officials who plan education and training programs.

The labor force projections are a function of two components—projections of the population and projections of labor force participation rates. Population projections are provided by the Census Bureau for detailed age, sex, race, and ethnicity groupings. BLS extrapolates participation rates for these same categories by applying well-specified smoothing and time series techniques to historical time series for the detailed participation rates.

CONCEPTS AND DEFINITIONS

Economic dependency ratio. This ratio is measured *by* measured by estimating the number of persons in the total population (including all Armed Forces personnel overseas and children) who are *not* in the labor force per hundred of those who are.

Employment. In the employment projections survey, employment is defined as a count of jobs, not a count of individual workers.

Employment change. The numerical change in employment measures the projected number of job gains or losses.

Employment change, percent. The percent change in employment measures the projected rate of change of employment in an occupation. A rapidly growing occupation usually indicates favorable prospects for employment. However, even modest employment growth in a large occupation can result in many more job openings due to growth than can rapid employment growth in a small occupation.

Job openings due to growth and replacement needs. Estimates of the projected number of net entrants into an occupation. For occupations that require training, the data may be used to assess the minimum number of workers who will need to be trained. The number of openings due to growth is the positive employment change from 2012 to 2022. If employment declines, then there are no job openings due to growth. The number of openings due to replacement needs is the net number of workers leaving an occupation who will need to be replaced.

ON-THE-JOB TRAINING TERMS

Apprenticeship. An apprenticeship is a formal relationship between a worker and sponsor that combines technical instruction and on-the-job training. The typical programs provides at least 2,000 hours of on-the-job training per year over a 3- to 5-year period and 144 hours of technical instruction.

Internship/residency. An internship or residency typically involves supervised training in a professional setting such as a classroom or hospital. Internships and/or residency programs are often required for certification or to obtain a license in fields such as architecture, counseling, medicine, and teaching.

Moderate-term on-the-job training. Skills needed for a worker to become fully qualified can be acquired during 1 to 12 months of combined on-the-job experience and informal training.

Short-term on-the-job training. Skills needed for a worker to become fully qualified can be acquired during a short demonstration of job duties or during 1 month or less of on-the-job experience or instruction. Examples include retail salespersons and waiters and waitresses.

Long-term on-the-job training. More than 12 months of on-the-job training or, alternatively, combined work experience and formal classroom instruction are needed for workers to develop the skills to become fully qualified. This category includes formal or informal apprenticeships that may last up to 5 years.

SOURCES OF ADDITIONAL INFORMATION

A complete presentation of the projections, including analysis of results and additional tables and a comprehensive description of the methodology, can be found in the December 2013 edition of the *Monthly Labor Review*, which is available on the BLS Web site at www.bls.gov/opub/mlr/mlrhome.htm. In addition, more information on employment projections can be found on the BLS Web site at http://www.bls.gov/emp/.

Table 4-1. Civilian Labor Force, by Age, Sex, Race, and Hispanic Origin, 1992, 2002, 2012, and Projected 2022

(Numbers in thousands, percent.)

Age, sex, race, and Hispanic origin	Labor force				Change			Percent change		
	1992	2002	2012	2022	1992–2002	2002–2012	2012–2022	1992–2002	2002–2012	2012–2022
Both Sexes, 16 Years and Over	128 105	144 863	154 975	163 450	16 758	10 112	8 475	13.1	7.0	5.5
16 to 24 years	21 617	22 366	21 285	18 462	749	-1 081	-2 823	3.5	-4.8	-13.3
16 to 19 years	7 096	7 586	5 823	4 473	490	-1 763	-1 350	6.9	-23.2	-23.2
20 to 24 years	14 521	14 780	15 462	13 989	259	682	-1 473	1.8	4.6	-9.5
25 to 54 years	91 429	101 720	101 253	103 195	10 291	-467	1 942	11.3	-0.5	1.9
25 to 34 years	35 369	32 196	33 465	36 786	-3 173	1 269	3 321	-9.0	3.9	9.9
35 to 44 years	33 899	36 927	32 734	34 810	3 028	-4 193	2 076	8.9	-11.4	6.3
45 to 54 years	22 160	32 597	35 054	31 600	10 437	2 457	-3 454	47.1	7.5	-9.9
55 years and over	15 060	20 777	32 437	41 793	5 717	11 660	9 356	38.0	56.1	28.8
55 to 64 years	11 587	16 308	24 710	28 317	4 721	8 402	3 607	40.7	51.5	14.6
65 to 74 years	2 932	3 665	6 344	10 915	733	2 679	4 571	25.0	73.1	72.1
75 years and over	542	804	1 383	2 561	262	579	1 178	48.3	72.0	85.2
Men, 16 Years and Over	69 964	77 500	82 327	86 913	7 536	4 827	4 586	10.8	6.2	5.6
16 to 24 years	11 521	11 639	11 050	9 582	118	-589	-1 468	1.0	-5.1	-13.3
16 to 19 years	3 751	3 870	2 940	2 316	119	-930	-624	3.2	-24.0	-21.2
20 to 24 years	7 770	7 769	8 110	7 266	-1	341	-844	0.0	4.4	-10.4
25 to 54 years	49 882	54 568	54 053	55 768	4 686	-515	1 715	9.4	-0.9	3.2
25 to 34 years	19 495	17 596	18 083	20 212	-1 899	487	2 129	-9.7	2.8	11.8
35 to 44 years	18 347	19 829	17 607	19 061	1 482	-2 222	1 454	8.1	-11.2	8.3
45 to 54 years	12 040	17 143	18 363	16 495	5 103	1 220	-1 868	42.4	7.1	-10.2
55 years and over	8 561	11 293	17 224	21 563	2 732	5 931	4 339	31.9	52.5	25.2
55 to 64 years	6 551	8 750	12 879	14 370	2 199	4 129	1 491	33.6	47.2	11.6
65 to 74 years	1 681	2 079	3 508	5 748	398	1 429	2 240	23.7	68.7	63.9
75 years and over	329	464	837	1 445	135	373	608	41.0	80.4	72.6
Women, 16 Years and Over	58 141	67 364	72 648	76 537	9 223	5 284	3 889	15.9	7.8	5.4
16 to 24 years	10 096	10 728	10 235	8 880	632	-493	-1 355	6.3	-4.6	-13.2
16 to 19 years	3 345	3 716	2 883	2 156	371	-833	-727	11.1	-22.4	-25.2
20 to 24 years	6 750	7 012	7 352	6 724	262	340	-628	3.9	4.8	-8.5
25 to 54 years	41 547	47 152	47 200	47 427	5 605	48	227	13.5	0.1	0.5
25 to 34 years	15 875	14 600	15 382	16 574	-1 275	782	1 192	-8.0	5.4	7.7
35 to 44 years	15 552	17 098	15 127	15 749	1 546	-1 971	622	9.9	-11.5	4.1
45 to 54 years	10 120	15 454	16 692	15 104	5 334	1 238	-1 588	52.7	8.0	-9.5
55 years and over	6 499	9 484	15 213	20 230	2 985	5 729	5 017	45.9	60.4	33.0
55 to 64 years	5 035	7 558	11 830	13 947	2 523	4 272	2 117	50.1	56.5	17.9
65 to 74 years	1 251	1 586	2 836	5 167	335	1 250	2 331	26.8	78.8	82.2
75 years and over	213	340	546	1 117	127	206	571	59.6	60.6	104.6
White, 16 Years and Over	108 837	120 150	123 684	126 923	11 313	3 534	3 239	10.4	2.9	2.6
Men	60 168	65 308	66 921	68 989	5 140	1 613	2 068	8.5	2.5	3.1
Women	48 669	54 842	56 763	57 934	6 173	1 921	1 171	12.7	3.5	2.1
Black, 16 Years and Over	14 162	16 565	18 400	20 247	2 403	1 835	1 847	17.0	11.1	10.0
Men	6 997	7 794	8 594	9 547	797	800	953	11.4	10.3	11.1
Women	7 166	8 772	9 805	10 700	1 606	1 033	895	22.4	11.8	9.1
Asian, 16 Years and Over	5 106	6 604	8 188	10 135	1 498	1 584	1 947	29.3	24.0	23.8
Men	2 799	3 567	4 334	5 341	768	767	1 007	27.4	21.5	23.2
Women	2 305	3 037	3 853	4 794	732	816	941	31.8	26.9	24.4
All Other Groups,[1] 16 Years and Over	. . .	1 544	4 703	6 145	. . .	. . .	1 442	. . .	. . .	30.7
Men	. . .	831	2 478	3 036	. . .	. . .	558	. . .	. . .	22.5
Women	. . .	713	2 227	3 109	. . .	. . .	882	. . .	. . .	39.6
Hispanic,[2] 16 Years and Over	11 338	17 943	24 391	31 179	6 605	6 448	6 788	58.3	35.9	27.8
Men	6 900	10 610	14 026	17 925	3 710	3 416	3 899	53.8	32.2	27.8
Women	4 439	7 334	10 365	13 254	2 895	3 031	2 889	65.2	41.3	27.9
Non-Hispanic, 16 Years and Over	116 767	126 920	130 584	132 271	10 153	3 664	1 687	8.7	2.9	1.3
Men	63 064	66 890	68 301	68 988	3 826	1 411	687	6.1	2.1	1.0
Women	53 702	60 030	62 283	63 283	6 328	2 253	1 000	11.8	3.8	1.6
White Non-Hispanic, 16 Years and Over	98 724	103 349	101 892	99 431	4 625	-1 457	-2 461	4.7	-1.4	-2.4
Men	53 984	55 340	54 325	53 282	1 356	-1 015	-1 043	2.5	-1.8	-1.9
Women	44 740	48 009	47 567	46 149	3 269	-442	-1 418	7.3	-0.9	-3.0

[1]The "All other groups" category includes respondents who reported the racial categories of "American Indian and Alaska Native" or "Native Hawaiian and Other Pacific Islander," as well as those who reported two or more races. This category was not defined prior to 2003.
[2]May be of any race.
. . . = Not available.

Table 4-1. Civilian Labor Force, by Age, Sex, Race, and Hispanic Origin, 1992, 2002, 2012, and Projected 2022—*Continued*

(Numbers in thousands, percent.)

Age, sex, race, and Hispanic origin	Percent distribution				Annual growth rate (percent)		
	1992	2002	2012	2022	1992–2002	2002–2012	2012–2022
Both Sexes, 16 Years and Over	100.0	100.0	100.0	100.0	1.2	0.7	0.5
16 to 24 years	16.9	15.4	13.7	11.3	0.3	-0.5	-1.4
16 to 19 years	5.5	5.2	3.8	2.7	0.7	-2.6	-2.6
20 to 24 years	11.3	10.2	10.0	8.6	0.2	0.5	-1.0
25 to 54 years	71.4	70.2	65.3	63.1	1.1	0.0	0.2
25 to 34 years	27.6	22.2	21.6	22.5	-0.9	0.4	1.0
35 to 44 years	26.5	25.5	21.1	21.3	0.9	-1.2	0.6
45 to 54 years	17.3	22.5	22.6	19.3	3.9	0.7	-1.0
55 years and over	11.8	14.3	20.9	25.6	3.3	4.6	2.6
55 to 64 years	9.0	11.3	15.9	17.3	3.5	4.2	1.4
65 to 74 years	2.3	2.5	4.1	6.7	2.3	5.6	5.6
75 years and over	0.4	0.6	0.9	1.6	4.0	5.6	6.4
Men, 16 Years and Over	54.6	53.5	53.1	53.2	1.0	0.6	0.5
16 to 24 years	9.0	8.0	7.1	5.9	0.1	-0.5	-1.4
16 to 19 years	2.9	2.7	1.9	1.4	0.3	-2.7	-2.4
20 to 24 years	6.1	5.4	5.2	4.4	0.0	0.4	-1.1
25 to 54 years	38.9	37.7	34.9	34.1	0.9	-0.1	0.3
25 to 34 years	15.2	12.1	11.7	12.4	-1.0	0.3	1.1
35 to 44 years	14.3	13.7	11.4	11.7	0.8	-1.2	0.8
45 to 54 years	9.4	11.8	11.8	10.1	3.6	0.7	-1.1
55 years and over	6.7	7.8	11.1	13.2	2.8	4.3	2.3
55 to 64 years	5.1	6.0	8.3	8.8	2.9	3.9	1.1
65 to 74 years	1.3	1.4	2.3	3.5	2.1	5.4	5.1
75 years and over	0.3	0.3	0.5	0.9	3.5	6.1	5.6
Women, 16 Years and Over	45.4	46.5	46.9	46.8	1.5	0.8	0.5
16 to 24 years	7.9	7.4	6.6	5.4	0.6	-0.5	-1.4
16 to 19 years	2.6	2.6	1.9	1.3	1.1	-2.5	-2.9
20 to 24 years	5.3	4.8	4.7	4.1	0.4	0.5	-0.9
25 to 54 years	32.4	32.5	30.5	29.0	1.3	0.0	0.0
25 to 34 years	12.4	10.1	9.9	10.1	-0.8	0.5	0.7
35 to 44 years	12.1	11.8	9.8	9.6	1.0	-1.2	0.4
45 to 54 years	7.9	10.7	10.8	9.2	4.3	0.8	-1.0
55 years and over	5.1	6.5	9.8	12.4	3.9	4.8	2.9
55 to 64 years	3.9	5.2	7.6	8.5	4.1	4.6	1.7
65 to 74 years	1.0	1.1	1.8	3.2	2.4	6.0	6.2
75 years and over	0.2	0.2	0.4	0.7	4.8	4.9	7.4
White, 16 Years and Over	85.0	82.9	79.8	77.7	1.0	0.3	0.3
Men	47.0	45.1	43.2	42.2	0.8	0.2	0.3
Women	38.0	37.9	36.6	35.4	1.2	0.3	0.2
Black, 16 Years and Over	11.1	11.4	11.9	12.4	1.6	1.1	1.0
Men	5.5	5.4	5.5	5.8	1.1	1.0	1.1
Women	5.6	6.1	6.3	6.5	2.0	1.1	0.9
Asian, 16 Years and Over	4.0	4.6	5.3	6.2	2.6	2.2	2.2
Men	2.2	2.5	2.8	3.3	2.5	2.0	2.1
Women	1.8	2.1	2.5	2.9	2.8	2.4	2.2
All Other Groups,[1] 16 Years and Over	...	...	3.0	3.8	...	...	2.7
Men	...	...	1.6	1.9	...	...	2.1
Women	...	...	1.4	1.9	...	...	3.4
Hispanic,[2] 16 Years and Over	8.9	12.4	15.7	19.1	4.7	3.1	2.5
Men	5.4	7.3	9.1	11.0	4.4	2.8	2.5
Women	3.5	5.1	6.7	8.1	5.1	3.5	2.5
Non-Hispanic, 16 Years and Over	91.1	87.6	84.3	80.9	0.8	0.3	0.1
Men	49.2	46.2	44.1	42.2	0.6	0.2	0.1
Women	41.9	41.4	40.2	38.7	1.1	0.4	0.2
White Non-Hispanic, 16 Years and Over	77.1	71.3	65.7	60.8	0.5	-0.1	-0.2
Men	42.1	38.2	35.1	32.6	0.2	-0.2	-0.2
Women	34.9	33.1	30.7	28.2	0.7	-0.1	-0.3

[1]The "All other groups" category includes respondents who reported the racial categories of "American Indian and Alaska Native" or "Native Hawaiian and Other Pacific Islander," as well as those who reported two or more races. This category was not defined prior to 2003.
[2]May be of any race.
. . . = Not available.

PROJECTED EMPLOYMENT

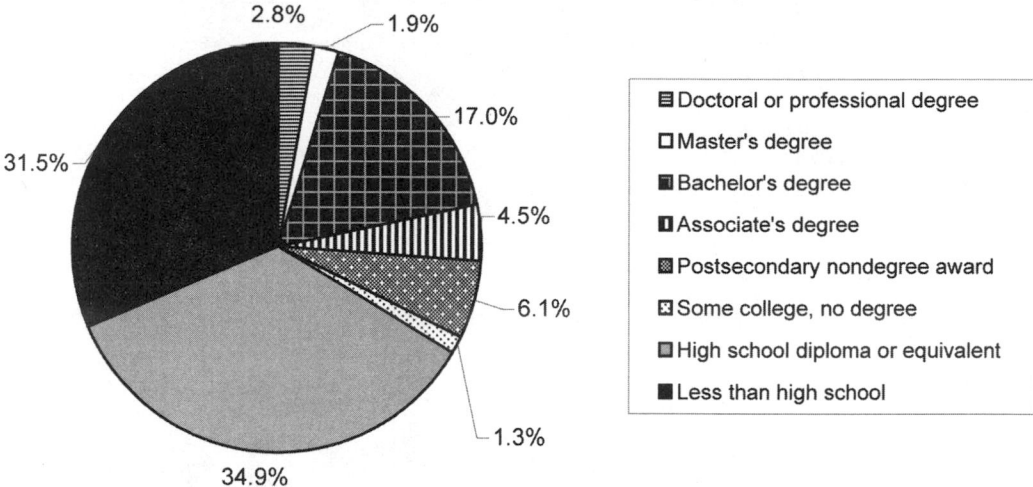

Figure 4-2. Percent Distribution of Projected Job Openings Due to Growth and Replacement Needs by Education Category, 2012–2022

Legend:
- Doctoral or professional degree
- Master's degree
- Bachelor's degree
- Associate's degree
- Postsecondary nondegree award
- Some college, no degree
- High school diploma or equivalent
- Less than high school

In 2022, only 1.9 percent of job openings will require a master's degree. However, the number of job openings that require a master's degree will grow by 18.4 percent—more than any other education category. Over 18 percent of jobs in 2022 will require a bachelor's degree, while 39.1 percent will require a high school diploma or equivalent. (See Table 4-9.)

OTHER HIGHLIGHTS

- Although employment is projected to remain very small at 2,500, the number of industrial organization psychologists is expected to grow faster than any other occupation. Among larger occupations, the number of personal care aides and homes health aides is expected to increase rapidly from 2012 to 2022, growing at rates of 48.8 percent and 48.5 percent, respectively. (See Table 4-2.)

- The occupations projected to add the largest number of jobs from 2012 to 2022 include personal health care aides (580,000), registered nurses (526,800), and retail sales persons (434,700). (See Table 4-3.)

- Meanwhile, the industries expected to experience the largest declines in employment from 2012 to 2022 include general federal non-defense government compensation (-180,300), postal service (-169,100), and newspaper, periodical, book, and directory publishers (-105,000). (See Table 4-5.)

- The median age of the labor force has gradually increased from 37.1 years in 1992 to 41.9 in 2012. In 2022, the median age is expected to increase even further to 42.6 years. (See Table 4-6.)

Table 4-2. Fastest-Growing Occupations, 2012 and Projected 2022

(Numbers in thousands, percent.)

Occupation	Employment		Change, 2012–2022		Mean annual wage, 2012
	2012	2022	Number	Percent	
TOTAL, ALL OCCUPATIONS	145 355.8	160 983.7	15 628.0	10.8	34 750
Industrial-organizational psychologists	1.6	2.5	0.9	53.4	83 580
Personal care aides	1 190.6	1 771.4	580.8	48.8	19 910
Home health aides	875.1	1 299.3	424.2	48.5	20 820
Insulation workers, mechanical	28.9	42.4	13.5	46.7	39 170
Interpreters and translators	63.6	92.9	29.3	46.1	45 430
Diagnostic medical sonographers	58.8	85.9	27.0	46.0	65 860
Helpers–brickmasons, blockmasons, stonemasons, and tile and marble setters	24.4	34.9	10.5	43.0	28 220
Occupational therapy assistants	30.3	43.2	12.9	42.6	53 240
Genetic counselors	2.1	3.0	0.9	41.2	56 800
Physical therapist assistants	71.4	100.7	29.3	41.0	52 160
Physical therapist aides	50.0	70.1	20.1	40.1	23 880
Skincare specialists	44.4	62.0	17.7	39.8	28 640
Physician assistants	86.7	120.0	33.3	38.4	90 930
Segmental pavers	1.8	2.4	0.7	38.1	33 720
Helpers–electricians	60.8	83.3	22.4	36.9	27 670
Information security analysts	75.1	102.5	27.4	36.5	86 170
Occupational therapy aides	8.4	11.4	3.0	36.2	26 850
Health specialties teachers, postsecondary	190.0	258.6	68.6	36.1	81 140
Medical secretaries	525.6	714.9	189.2	36.0	31 350
Physical therapists	204.2	277.7	73.5	36.0	79 860
Orthotists and prosthetists	8.5	11.5	3.0	35.5	62 670
Brickmasons and blockmasons	71.0	96.2	25.2	35.5	46 440
Nursing instructors and teachers, postsecondary	67.8	91.8	24.0	35.4	64 850
Nurse practitioners	110.2	147.3	37.1	33.7	89 960
Audiologists	13.0	17.3	4.3	33.6	69 720
Dental hygienists	192.8	256.9	64.2	33.3	70 210
Meeting, convention, and event planners	94.2	125.4	31.3	33.2	45 810
Therapists, all other	28.8	37.9	9.1	31.7	53 210
Market research analysts and marketing specialists	415.7	547.2	131.5	31.6	60 300
Substance abuse and behavioral disorder counselors	89.6	117.7	28.2	31.4	38 520

Table 4-3. Occupations with the Largest Job Growth, 2012–2022

(Numbers in thousands, percent.)

Occupation	Employment		Change, 2012–2022		Mean annual wage, 2012
	2012	2022	Number	Percent	
TOTAL, ALL OCCUPATIONS	145 355.8	160 983.7	15 628.0	10.8	34 750
Personal care aides	1 190.6	1 771.4	580.8	48.8	19 910
Registered nurses	2 711.5	3 238.4	526.8	19.4	65 470
Retail salespersons	4 447.0	4 881.7	434.7	9.8	21 110
Home health aides	875.1	1 299.3	424.2	48.5	20 820
Combined food preparation and serving workers, including fast food	2 969.3	3 391.2	421.9	14.2	18 260
Nursing assistants	1 479.8	1 792.0	312.2	21.1	24 420
Secretaries and administrative assistants, except legal, medical, and executive	2 324.4	2 632.3	307.8	13.2	32 410
Customer service representatives	2 362.8	2 661.4	298.7	12.6	30 580
Janitors and cleaners, except maids and housekeeping cleaners	2 324.0	2 604.0	280.0	12.1	22 320
Construction laborers	1 071.1	1 331.0	259.8	24.3	29 990
General and operations managers	1 972.7	2 216.8	244.1	12.4	95 440
Laborers and freight, stock, and material movers, hand	2 197.3	2 439.2	241.9	11.0	23 890
Carpenters	901.2	1 119.4	218.2	24.2	39 940
Bookkeeping, accounting, and auditing clerks	1 799.8	2 004.5	204.6	11.4	35 170
Heavy and tractor-trailer truck drivers	1 701.5	1 894.1	192.6	11.3	38 200
Medical secretaries	525.6	714.9	189.2	36.0	31 350
Childcare workers	1 312.7	1 496.8	184.1	14.0	19 510
Office clerks, general	2 983.5	3 167.6	184.1	6.2	27 470
Maids and housekeeping cleaners	1 434.6	1 618.0	183.4	12.8	19 570
Licensed practical and licensed vocational nurses	738.4	921.3	182.9	24.8	41 540
First-line supervisors of office and administrative support workers	1 418.1	1 589.6	171.5	12.1	49 330
Elementary school teachers, except special education	1 361.2	1 529.1	167.9	12.3	53 400
Accountants and auditors	1 275.4	1 442.2	166.7	13.1	63 550
Medical assistants	560.8	723.7	162.9	29.0	29 370
Cooks, restaurant	1 024.1	1 174.2	150.1	14.7	22 030
Software developers, applications	613.0	752.9	139.9	22.8	90 060
Landscaping and groundskeeping workers	1 124.9	1 264.0	139.2	12.4	23 570
Receptionists and information clerks	1 006.7	1 142.6	135.9	13.5	25 990
Management analysts	718.7	852.5	133.8	18.6	78 600
Sales representatives, wholesale and manufacturing, except technical and scientific products	1 480.7	1 612.8	132.0	8.9	54 230

Table 4-4. Economic Dependency Ratio, 1992, 2002, 2012, and Projected 2022

(Number.)

Group	1992	2002	2012	2022
TOTAL POPULATION	91.7	97.5	101.7	106.5
Under age 16	43.6	44.7	42.3	42.0
Ages 16 to 64	26.9	32.3	37.5	37.1
Ages 65 and older	21.2	21.5	22.9	28.2

Table 4-5. Industries with the Largest Wage and Salary Employment Growth and Declines, 2012–2022

(Number in thousands, percent.)

Industry	Sector	Employment		Change, 2012–2022	Annual rate of change, 2012–2022
		2012	2022		
Largest Growth					
Construction	Construction	5 640.9	7 263.0	1 622.1	2.6
Offices of health practitioners	Health care and social assistance	3 968.0	5 193.8	1 225.8	2.7
Retail trade	Retail trade	14 875.3	15 966.2	1 090.9	0.7
Food services and drinking places	Leisure and hospitality	9 963.3	10 851.5	888.2	0.9
Hospitals, private	Health care and social assistance	4 791.0	5 605.8	814.8	1.6
Employment services	Professional and business services	3 147.9	3 929.6	781.7	2.2
Nursing and residential care facilities	Health care and social assistance	3 193.5	3 954.2	760.7	2.2
Home health care services	Health care and social assistance	1 198.6	1 914.3	715.7	4.8
Individual and family services	Health care and social assistance	1 311.4	2 022.9	711.5	4.4
Computer systems design and related services	Professional and business services	1 620.3	2 229.0	608.7	3.2
Largest Declines					
General federal non-defense government compensation	Federal government	1 556.6	1 376.3	-180.3	-1.2
Postal Service	Federal government	611.2	442.1	-169.1	-3.2
Newspaper, periodical, book, and directory publishers	Information	451.8	346.8	-105.0	-2.6
Apparel manufacturing	Manufacturing	148.1	62.3	-85.8	-8.3
State government enterprises	State and local government	499.5	442.0	-57.5	-1.2
Other miscellaneous manufacturing	Manufacturing	268.4	211.1	-57.3	-2.4
Air transportation	Transportation and Warehousing	458.3	406.2	-52.1	-1.2
Textile mills and textile product mills	Manufacturing	234.6	183.1	-51.5	-2.4
Telecommunications	Information	858.0	807.0	-51.0	-0.6
Electric power generation, transmission and distribution	Utilities	396.8	350.6	-46.2	-1.2

Table 4-6. Median Age of the Labor Force by Sex, Race, and Ethnicity, 1992, 2002, 2012, and Projected 2022

(Number.)

	1992	2002	2012	2022
TOTAL	37.1	39.8	41.9	42.6
Sex				
Men	37.2	39.8	41.8	42.2
Women	37.0	40.0	42.1	43.1
Race				
White	37.3	40.2	42.6	43.3
Black	35.5	38.1	39.7	40.3
Asian	36.2	38.8	40.9	42.9
Ethnicity				
Hispanic origin[1]	32.5	34.0	36.9	38.9
White non-Hispanic	37.8	41.1	44.2	44.8

[1] May be of any race.

Table 4-7. Employment and Output, by Industry, 2002, 2012, and Projected 2022

(Number, percent, dollars.)

Industry	Employment							Output				
	Number of jobs (thousands)			Change		Average annual rate of change (percent)		Billions of chained (2005) dollars			Average annual rate of change (percent)	
	2002	2012	2022	2002–2012	2012–2022	2002–2012	2012–2022	2002	2012	2022	2002–2012	2012–2022
TOTAL	142 295	145 356	160 984	3 061	15 628	0.2	1.0	21 008	23 229	30 150	1.0	2.6
Nonagriculture Wage and Salary	131 028	134 428	149 751	3 399	15 324	0.3	1.1	20 732	22 920	29 769	1.0	2.6
Mining	512	800	922	288	121	4.6	1.4	383	474	599	2.1	2.4
Oil and gas extraction	122	187	221	65	34	4.4	1.7	263	320	411	2.0	2.5
Mining, except oil and gas	211	223	229	12	7	0.6	0.3	67	69	85	0.2	2.1
Coal mining	74	87	83	12	-3.4	1.5	-0.4	28	29	35	0.2	2.0
Metal ore mining	29	45	42	16	-4	4.6	-0.8	16	6	8	-9.1	2.5
Nonmetallic mineral mining and quarrying	107	91	104	-16	14	-1.7	1.4	24	35	43	4.1	2.0
Support activities for mining	180	391	472	211	81	8.1	1.9	56	97	119	5.5	2.1
Utilities	596	554	498	-42	-56	-0.7	-1.1	403	318	397	-2.4	2.3
Electric power generation, transmission and distribution	434	397	351	-37	-46	-0.9	-1.2	253	218	278	-1.5	2.5
Natural gas distribution	115	110	92	-5	-18	-0.4	-1.7	144	89	106	-4.7	1.8
Water, sewage and other systems	47.9	47.7	55.2	-0.2	7.5	0.0	1.5	8.8	5.9	7.4	-3.8	2.2
Construction	6 716	5 641	7 263	-1 075	1 622	-1.7	2.6	1 165	774	1 160	-4.0	4.1
Manufacturing	15 259	11 919	11 369	-3 340	-550	-2.4	-0.5	4 321	4 408	5 605	0.2	2.4
Food manufacturing	1 526	1 469	1 442	-57	-27	-0.4	-0.2	498	490	575	-0.2	1.6
Animal food manufacturing	51	53	48	2	-5	0.4	-1.0	28	20	25	-3.2	2.0
Grain and oilseed milling	62	60	57	-2	-3	-0.3	-0.5	55	44	51	-2.3	1.5
Sugar and confectionery product manufacturing	84	67	54	-18	-13	-2.3	-2.2	27	38	45	3.5	1.6
Fruit and vegetable preserving and specialty food manufacturing	183	170	150	-14	-19	-0.8	-1.2	56	58	67	0.3	1.5
Dairy product manufacturing	137	136	130	-1	-6	-0.1	-0.5	72	75	89	0.4	1.8
Animal slaughtering and processing	517	485	518	-32	33	-0.6	0.7	142	152	178	0.6	1.6
Seafood product preparation and packaging	44	39	36	-4	-4	-1.0	-1.0	9	9	10	-0.2	1.6
Bakeries and tortilla manufacturing	297	284	272	-12	-13	-0.4	-0.5	49	49	57	0.0	1.5
Other food manufacturing	151	174	177	23	3	1.5	0.2	60	48	57	-2.1	1.6
Beverage and tobacco product	207	192	188	-15	-4	-0.8	-0.2	123	179	197	3.8	1.0
Beverage manufacturing	174	178	176	4	-2	0.2	-0.1	75	85	92	1.3	0.8
Tobacco manufacturing	34	14	12	-19	-2	-8.1	-1.5	48	93	104	6.9	1.1
Textile mills and textile product mills	495	235	183	-261	-52	-7.2	-2.4	79	44	41	-5.6	-0.8
Apparel manufacturing	350	148	62	-202	-86	-8.2	-8.3	40	18	17	-7.6	-0.6
Leather and allied product manufacturing	50	29	18	-21	-11	-5.2	-4.5	6	3	2	-8.2	-1.0
Wood product manufacturing	555	338	388	-217	50	-4.8	1.4	100	71	97	-3.4	3.2
Sawmills and wood preservation	121	84	94	-37	9	-3.5	1.0	31	22	28	-3.6	2.8
Veneer, plywood, and engineered wood product manufacturing	116	64	84	-52	20	-5.8	2.7	24	20	27	-1.8	3.0
Other wood product manufacturing	318	190	212	-128	22	-5.0	1.1	45	30	42	-4.1	3.6
Paper manufacturing	547	379	345	-168	-34	-3.6	-0.9	162	139	159	-1.5	1.4
Pulp, paper, and paperboard mills	165	108	87	-56	-21	-4.1	-2.2	75	66	77	-1.2	1.4
Converted paper product manufacturing	382	271	258	-111	-13	-3.4	-0.5	87	72	82	-1.8	1.3
Printing and related support activities	707	462	434	-244	-28	-4.2	-0.6	102	82	92	-2.2	1.2
Petroleum and coal products manufacturing	118	113	103	-5	-10	-0.4	-0.9	429	422	544	-0.2	2.6
Chemical manufacturing	928	784	733	-144	-50	-1.7	-0.7	534	528	707	-0.1	3.0
Basic chemical manufacturing	170	143	126	-27	-17	-1.7	-1.2	134	120	150	-1.1	2.3
Resin, synthetic rubber, and artificial synthetic fibers and filaments manufacturing	115	92	83	-23	-9	-2.2	-1.0	86	88	111	0.2	2.4
Pesticide, fertilizer, and other agricultural chemical manufacturing	45	37	30	-8	-7	-1.9	-2.1	22	20	25	-1.0	2.2
Pharmaceutical and medicine manufacturing	291	271	284	-20	13	-0.7	0.5	157	140	198	-1.1	3.5
Paint, coating, and adhesive manufacturing	72	57	52	-15	-4	-2.3	-0.8	30	34	46	1.2	3.3
Soap, cleaning compound, and toilet preparation manufacturing	121	103	90	-17	-13	-1.5	-1.4	65	77	108	1.8	3.4
Other chemical product and preparation manufacturing	114	81	68	-33	-13	-3.3	-1.7	40	54	76	3.1	3.5
Plastics and rubber products manufacturing	847	645	594	-202	-51	-2.7	-0.8	192	159	195	-1.9	2.1
Plastics product manufacturing	663	516	477	-147	-39	-2.5	-0.8	157	128	153	-2.0	1.8
Rubber product manufacturing	184	129	117	-55	-12	-3.5	-1.0	35	31	41	-1.2	2.9
Nonmetallic mineral product manufacturing	516	364	408	-152	44	-3.4	1.1	103	81	113	-2.3	3.4
Clay product and refractory manufacturing	72	41	44	-31	4	-5.5	0.9	9	7	10	-1.6	2.8
Glass and glass product manufacturing	124	80	64	-44	-16	-4.3	-2.2	22	22	30	-0.2	3.2
Cement and concrete product manufacturing	230	162	219	-68	57	-3.5	3.1	50	38	54	-2.6	3.6
Lime, gypsum and other nonmetallic mineral product manufacturing	91	82	80	-9	-1	-1.1	-0.1	22	13	18	-4.8	3.3
Primary metal manufacturing	509	402	356	-108	-46	-2.3	-1.2	181	239	265	2.8	1.0
Iron and steel mills and ferroalloy manufacturing	107	94	79	-14	-15	-1.4	-1.7	68	73	80	0.6	1.0
Steel product manufacturing from purchased steel	63	60	57	-3	-3	-0.5	-0.5	23	23	30	0.2	2.5
Alumina and aluminum production and processing	80	60	51	-20	-9	-2.9	-1.6	32	62	61	6.9	-0.2
Nonferrous metal (except aluminum) production and processing	81	62	54	-20	-8	-2.7	-1.3	30	34	39	1.3	1.5
Foundries	178	127	115	-52	-12	-3.3	-1.0	29	47	54	4.9	1.3
Fabricated metal product manufacturing	1 548	1 411	1 493	-137	82	-0.9	0.6	268	258	333	-0.4	2.6
Forging and stamping	113	99	95	-14	-4	-1.3	-0.4	24	24	29	0.4	1.7
Cutlery and handtool manufacturing	64	40	35	-25	-4	-4.7	-1.1	11	16	17	3.8	0.5
Architectural and structural metals manufacturing	399	341	410	-58	69	-1.5	1.9	66	65	88	0.0	3.1
Boiler, tank, and shipping container manufacturing	96	96	99	1	2	0.1	0.2	26	20	22	-2.4	0.9
Hardware manufacturing	42	25	19	-17	-6	-5.1	-2.5	11	20	26	6.0	2.7
Spring and wire product manufacturing	70	42	31	-28	-10	-5.1	-2.8	10	13	19	2.9	3.7
Machine shops; turned product; and screw, nut, and bolt manufacturing	318	362	373	44	10	1.3	0.3	46	36	48	-2.6	3.2
Coating, engraving, heat treating, and allied activities	149	136	142	-13	6	-0.9	0.4	20	19	26	-0.4	2.8
Other fabricated metal product manufacturing	296	270	288	-26	18	-0.9	0.7	54	45	58	-1.8	2.5
Machinery manufacturing	1 232	1 098	1 017	-134	-81	-1.1	-0.8	249	302	401	1.9	2.9
Agriculture, construction, and mining machinery manufacturing	200	245	224	45	-22	2.1	-0.9	50	38	44	-2.8	1.7
Industrial machinery manufacturing	132	105	98	-26	-7	-2.2	-0.7	30	52	64	5.7	2.1
Commercial and service industry machinery manufacturing	130	88	82	-41	-7	-3.8	-0.8	21	37	51	5.7	3.3
Ventilation, heating, air-conditioning, and commercial refrigeration equipment manufacturing	168	128	124	-40	-4	-2.7	-0.3	34	45	60	3.0	2.8
Metalworking machinery manufacturing	216	177	154	-39	-23	-2.0	-1.4	25	35	46	3.3	2.9
Engine, turbine, and power transmission equipment manufacturing	101	102	99	2	-3	0.2	-0.3	38	38	54	0.1	3.6
Other general purpose machinery manufacturing	286	252	237	-34	-15	-1.2	-0.6	52	59	84	1.4	3.6

Table 4-7. Employment and Output, by Industry, 2002, 2012, and Projected 2022—*Continued*

(Number, percent, dollars.)

Industry	Number of jobs (thousands) 2002	2012	2022	Change 2002–2012	2012–2022	Avg annual rate of change (percent) 2002–2012	2012–2022	Billions of chained (2005) dollars 2002	2012	2022	Avg annual rate of change (percent) 2002–2012	2012–2022
Manufacturing—*Continued*												
Computer and electronic product manufacturing	1 507	1 094	952	-413	-142	-3.2	-1.4	310	448	684	3.7	4.3
Computer and peripheral equipment manufacturing	250	159	119	-91	-40	-4.4	-2.9	48	139	336	11.3	9.2
Communications equipment manufacturing	179	110	79	-70	-31	-4.8	-3.3	59	62	80	0.4	2.6
Audio and video equipment manufacturing	42	20	16	-22	-4	-7.2	-1.9	8	12	16	4.7	2.4
Semiconductor and other electronic component manufacturing	524	384	353	-140	-31	-3.1	-0.8	98	149	221	4.3	4.1
Navigational, measuring, electromedical, and control instruments manufacturing	457	400	367	-56	-33	-1.3	-0.9	95	83	111	-1.4	3.0
Manufacturing and reproducing magnetic and optical media	55	21	17	-34	-4	-9.2	-2.0	7	16	20	8.3	2.7
Electrical equipment, appliance, and component manufacturing	496	370	319	-126	-51	-2.9	-1.5	105	92	119	-1.3	2.6
Electric lighting equipment manufacturing	72	46	40	-26	-6	-4.4	-1.4	12	14	18	1.3	2.6
Household appliance manufacturing	98	55	49	-44	-6	-5.7	-1.1	21	26	36	2.2	3.2
Electrical equipment manufacturing	175	143	123	-32	-20	-2.0	-1.5	32	24	31	-2.9	2.7
Other electrical equipment and component manufacturing	152	127	107	-25	-20	-1.8	-1.7	39	28	36	-3.1	2.4
Transportation equipment manufacturing	1 830	1 456	1 457	-374	1	-2.3	0.0	645	664	871	0.3	2.8
Motor vehicle manufacturing	265	168	176	-97	8	-4.5	0.5	236	241	336	0.2	3.4
Motor vehicle body and trailer manufacturing	152	125	135	-27	10	-1.9	0.8	27	14	20	-6.0	3.3
Motor vehicle parts manufacturing	734	480	508	-254	28	-4.2	0.6	201	199	283	-0.1	3.6
Aerospace product and parts manufacturing	470	497	466	27	-31	0.6	-0.6	137	149	175	0.9	1.6
Railroad rolling stock manufacturing	22	24	21	1	-3	0.6	-1.2	9	10	10	0.8	0.6
Ship and boat building	147	129	117	-18	-13	-1.3	-1.0	24	29	33	2.3	1.1
Other transportation equipment manufacturing	39	32	34	-6	1	-1.8	0.4	13	21	29	4.6	3.5
Furniture and related product manufacturing	607	350	356	-257	6	-5.4	0.2	79	51	68	-4.2	2.9
Household and institutional furniture and kitchen cabinet manufacturing	402	216	222	-186	6	-6.0	0.3	46	32	41	-3.5	2.4
Office furniture (including fixtures) manufacturing	151	99	99	-52	0.3	-4.1	0.0	25	14	21	-5.6	4.0
Other furniture related product manufacturing	54	35	34	-19	-1	-4.3	-0.2	8	5	7	-4.8	2.8
Miscellaneous manufacturing	683	580	522	-104	-58	-1.6	-1.1	128	146	202	1.3	3.3
Medical equipment and supplies manufacturing	303	311	310	8	-1	0.3	0.0	63	62	92	0.0	4.0
Other miscellaneous manufacturing	380	268	211	-112	-57	-3.4	-2.4	66	83	109	2.4	2.8
Wholesale Trade	5 652	5 673	6 143	20	470	0.0	0.8	945	1 116	1 598	1.7	3.7
Retail Trade	15 025	14 875	15 966	-150	1 091	-0.1	0.7	1 070	1 271	1 748	1.7	3.2
Transportation and Warehousing	4 224	4 415	4 742	191	327	0.4	0.7	647	688	913	0.6	2.9
Air transportation	564	458	406	-105	-52	-2.0	-1.2	110	126	165	1.3	2.8
Rail transportation	218	230	221	12	-9	0.6	-0.4	52	63	80	1.8	2.5
Water transportation	53	63	75	10	12	1.8	1.8	32	32	40	0.2	2.3
Truck transportation	1 339	1 351	1 471	12	120	0.1	0.9	240	236	314	-0.2	2.9
Transit and ground passenger transportation	381	448	526	67	78	1.6	1.6	29	28	34	-0.5	1.8
Pipeline transportation	42	44	36	2	-8	0.5	-1.9	25	16	22	-4.2	3.0
Scenic and sightseeing transportation and support activities for transportation	550	606	721	55	116	1.0	1.8	53	59	79	1.1	2.9
Postal Service	842	611	442	-231	-169	-3.2	-3.2	69	57	54	-1.9	-0.6
Couriers and messengers	561	533	489	-28	-44	-0.5	-0.9	63	77	107	2.0	3.4
Warehousing and storage	517	682	796	165	114	2.8	1.6	42	52	73	2.2	3.4
Information	3 395	2 678	2 612	-717	-65	-2.3	-0.2	957	1 186	1 670	2.2	3.5
Publishing industries	964	738	706	-226	-32	-2.6	-0.4	260	303	437	1.6	3.7
Newspaper, periodical, book, and directory publishers	711	452	347	-259.1	-105	-4.4	-2.6	156	184	237	1.6	2.6
Software publishers	253	286	359	33	73	1.2	2.3	105	118	206	1.1	5.7
Motion picture, video, and sound recording industries	388	372	350	-16	-22	-0.4	-0.6	86	86	100	-0.1	1.5
Broadcasting (except Internet)	334	285	297	-49	11	-1.6	0.4	85	74	97	-1.3	2.7
Telecommunications	1 281	858	807	-423	-51	-3.9	-0.6	423	560	780	2.8	3.4
Data processing, hosting, related services, and other information services	428	424	453	-3	29	-0.1	0.7	105	166	263	4.7	4.7
Finance and Insurance	5 814	5 834	6 335	21	501	0.0	0.8	1 663	1 928	2 677	1.5	3.3
Monetary authorities, credit intermediation, and related activities	2 709	2 596	2 720	-113	124	-0.4	0.5	699	802	1 118	1.4	3.4
Securities, commodity contracts, and other financial investments and related activities	789	814	1 001	25	187	0.3	2.1	316	469	742	4.0	4.7
Insurance carriers and related activities	2 233	2 337	2 507	104	170	0.5	0.7	564	558	700	-0.1	2.3
Insurance carriers	1 413	1 425	1 447	12	22	0.1	0.2	429	412	512	-0.4	2.2
Agencies, brokerages, and other insurance related activities	820	912	1 060	92	147	1.1	1.5	136	146	189	0.7	2.6
Funds, trusts, and other financial vehicles	82	87	107	5	20	0.6	2.1	85	102	132	1.8	2.6
Real estate, rental, and leasing	2 033	1 952	2 202	-81	250	-0.4	1.2	1 086	1 240	1 656	1.3	2.9
Real estate	1 357	1 416	1 578	60	161	0.4	1.1	876	978	1 286	1.1	2.8
Rental and leasing services and lessors of intangible assets	677	536	624	-141	89	-2.3	1.5	211	262	371	2.2	3.5
Automotive equipment rental and leasing	195	173	188	-22	15	-1.2	0.8	38	53	74	3.4	3.5
Consumer goods rental and general rental centers	352	206	242	-146	36	-5.2	1.6	23	42	56	6.1	2.9
Commercial and industrial machinery and equipment rental and leasing	102	132	167	30	35	2.6	2.4	43	41	58	-0.5	3.5
Lessors of nonfinancial intangible assets (except copyrighted works)	28	24	27	-3	3	-1.3	1.1	106	126	183	1.7	3.8
Professional, Scientific, and Technical Services	6 649	7 892	9 716	1 243	1 824	1.7	2.1	1 136	1 416	1 944	2.2	3.2
Legal services	1 115	1 122	1 211	7	89	0.1	0.8	232	218	264	-0.6	1.9
Accounting, tax preparation, bookkeeping, and payroll services	837	913	1 019	75	106	0.9	1.1	117	128	162	0.9	2.4
Architectural, engineering, and related services	1 246	1 323	1 596	77	272	0.6	1.9	185	252	371	3.1	3.9
Specialized design services	124	116	139	-8	23	-0.6	1.8	23	29	40	2.5	3.2
Computer systems design and related services	1 153	1 620	2 229	468	609	3.5	3.2	159	307	492	6.8	4.8
Management, scientific, and technical consulting services	708	1 121	1 577	413	456	4.7	3.5	141	149	206	0.6	3.3
Scientific research and development services	538	638	724	100	86	1.7	1.3	117	133	157	1.3	1.7
Advertising and related services	441	430	460	-12	31	-0.3	0.7	85	132	182	4.5	3.3
Other professional, scientific, and technical services	487	610	761	122	152	2.3	2.2	79	81	107	0.2	2.8
Management of companies and enterprises	1 705	2 008	2 061	303	53	1.6	0.3	281	368	539	2.7	3.9
Administrative and support and waste management and remediation services	7 622	8 030	9 636	408	1 606	0.5	1.8	500	641	838	2.5	2.7
Administrative and support services	7 304	7 657	9 180	353	1 524	0.5	1.8	438	566	749	2.6	2.8
Office administrative services	289	426	571	138	145	4.0	3.0	41	38	52	-0.6	3.1
Facilities support services	103	126	164	23	39	2.0	2.7	15	16	18	0.3	1.4
Employment services	3 273	3 148	3 930	-125	782	-0.4	2.2	117	164	229	3.5	3.4
Business support services	757	828	983	71	156	0.9	1.7	56	63	76	1.3	1.9
Travel arrangement and reservation services	252	193	170	-59	-22	-2.6	-1.2	30	43	55	3.6	2.5
Investigation and security services	724	818	920	94	102	1.2	1.2	36	47	62	2.6	2.8
Services to buildings and dwellings	1 606	1 830	2 109	224	279	1.3	1.4	105	145	193	3.3	2.9
Other support services	300	288	332	-12	44	-0.4	1.4	38	50	66	2.8	2.7

Table 4-7. Employment and Output, by Industry, 2002, 2012, and Projected 2022—*Continued*

(Number, percent, dollars.)

Industry	Employment							Output				
	Number of jobs (thousands)			Change		Average annual rate of change (percent)		Billions of chained (2005) dollars			Average annual rate of change (percent)	
	2002	2012	2022	2002–2012	2012–2022	2002–2012	2012–2022	2002	2012	2022	2002–2012	2012–2022
Professional, Scientific, and Technical Services —*Continued*												
Waste management and remediation services	318	373	455	54	83	1.6	2.0	62	74	90	1.8	1.9
Education services	2 643	3 347	4 022	704	675	2.4	1.9	196	190	231	-0.3	2.0
Elementary and secondary schools	786	912	995	126	83	1.5	0.9	34	35	37	0.5	0.6
Junior colleges, colleges, universities, and professional schools	1 424	1 763	2 197	340	433	2.2	2.2	118	108	136	-0.8	2.3
Other educational services	434	672	830	238	159	4.5	2.1	44	46	58	0.4	2.2
Health care and social assistance	13 556	16 972	21 966	3 416	4 994	2.3	2.6	1 263	1 599	2 174	2.4	3.1
Ambulatory health care services	4 633	6 318	8 782	1 685	2 464	3.2	3.3	565	745	1 071	2.8	3.7
Offices of health practitioners	3 178	3 968	5 194	790	1 226	2.2	2.7	420	577	818	3.2	3.6
Outpatient, laboratory, and other ambulatory care services	775	1 151	1 674	376	522	4.0	3.8	112	126	188	1.2	4.0
Home health care services	680	1 199	1 914	519	716	5.8	4.8	33	42	65	2.4	4.5
Hospitals, private	4 160	4 791	5 606	631	815	1.4	1.6	446	536	683	1.8	2.5
Nursing and residential care facilities	2 743	3 194	3 954	450	761	1.5	2.2	143	185	249	2.6	3.0
Social assistance	2 020	2 669	3 624	650	955	2.8	3.1	109	133	173	2.0	2.6
Individual and family services	773	1 311	2 023	539	712	5.4	4.4	48	51	68	0.7	2.8
Community, and vocational rehabilitation services	503	502	549	-0.3	47	0.0	0.9	24	35	46	3.6	2.7
Child day care services	744	856	1 052	111	196	1.4	2.1	37	47	60	2.4	2.4
Arts, entertainment, and recreation	1 783	1 966	2 185	183	219	1.0	1.1	182	209	260	1.4	2.2
Performing arts, spectator sports, and related industries	364	404	438	41	34	1.1	0.8	88	109	139	2.2	2.4
Performing arts companies	121	108	109	-13	1	-1.1	0.1	14	18	22	2.5	1.8
Spectator sports	120	129	136	9	7	0.7	0.6	30	40	51	3.0	2.4
Promoters of events, and agents and managers	83	121	140	38	19	3.8	1.5	20	21	27	0.8	2.3
Independent artists, writers, and performers	40	47	52	7	6	1.5	1.2	24	30	40	2.3	2.9
Museums, historical sites, and similar institutions	114	136	157	22	21	1.8	1.5	12	20	25	5.1	2.2
Amusement, gambling, and recreation industries	1 305	1 426	1 590	120	164	0.9	1.1	82	80	96	-0.3	1.9
Accommodation and food services	10 203	11 780	12 850	1 577	1 070	1.4	0.9	592	702	874	1.7	2.2
Accommodation	1 779	1 817	1 999	38	182	0.2	1.0	159	211	269	2.9	2.5
Food services and drinking places	8 425	9 963	10 852	1 539	888	1.7	0.9	432	492	605	1.3	2.1
Other services	6 129	6 174	6 823	46	649	0.1	1.0	512	502	609	-0.2	1.9
Repair and maintenance	1 247	1 190	1 392	-56	202	-0.5	1.6	176	167	198	-0.5	1.7
Automotive repair and maintenance	900	830	997	-69	167	-0.8	1.8	108	101	127	-0.7	2.3
Electronic and precision equipment repair and maintenance	107	99	105	-8	5	-0.8	0.5	21	29	33	3.2	1.4
Commercial and industrial machinery and equipment (except automotive and electronic) repair and maintenance	157	193	222	36	29	2.1	1.4	26	21	22	-2.1	0.2
Personal and household goods repair and maintenance	83	68	69	-15	1	-2.0	0.2	21	18	18	-1.7	0.5
Personal and laundry services	1 257	1 313	1 455	56	142	0.4	1.0	133	119	148	-1.1	2.3
Personal care services	529	628	722	99	94	1.7	1.4	45	41	57	-0.9	3.2
Death care services	140	133	144	-7	11	-0.5	0.8	17	15	18	-1.4	2.0
Drycleaning and laundry services	368	298	313	-70	15	-2.1	0.5	25	26	32	0.3	2.1
Other personal services	221	254	276	33	22	1.4	0.8	45	36	42	-2.0	1.5
Religious, grantmaking, civic, professional, and similar organizations	2 868	2 933	3 227	66	294	0.2	1.0	189	202	244	0.7	1.9
Religious organizations	1 654	1 693	1 830	39	137	0.2	0.8	69	69	89	0.1	2.6
Grantmaking and giving services and social advocacy organizations	300	375	443	74	68	2.2	1.7	43	54	69	2.3	2.4
Civic, social, professional, and similar organizations	913	866	954	-48	88	-0.5	1.0	77	78	87	0.2	1.1
Private households	757	738	749	-19	11	-0.3	0.2	14	15	18	0.8	1.9
Federal Government	2 766	2 814	2 406	48	-408	0.2	-1.6	782	1 006	885	2.6	-1.3
Postal Service	842	611	442	-231	-169	-3.2	-3.2	69	57	54	-1.9	-0.6
Federal electric utilities	33	23	22	-10	-1	-3.5	-0.6	11	12	15	0.7	2.5
Federal enterprises except the Postal Service and electric utilities	54	73	61	19	-12	3.1	-1.7	7	8	10	1.1	2.7
Federal defense government compensation	499	550	505	52	-45	1.0	-0.9	204	239	200	1.6	-1.8
Federal defense government consumption of fixed capital	0	0	0	0	0	0.0	0.0	65	87	73	3.0	-1.8
Federal defense government except compensation and consumption of fixed capital	0	0	0	0	0	0.0	0.0	182	286	258	4.6	-1.0
Federal non-defense government compensation-except enterprises	1 338	1 557	1 376	218	-180	1.5	-1.2	127	146	126	1.4	-1.5
Federal non-defense government consumption of fixed capital	0	0	0	0	0	0.0	0.0	24	34	29	3.4	-1.5
Federal non-defense government except compensation and consumption of fixed capital	0	0	0	0	0	0.0	0.0	94	140	123	4.0	-1.3
Federal government except enterprises	1 837	2 107	1 881	270	-226	1.4	-1.1	695	931	807	3.0	-1.4
State and Local Government	18 747	19 103	20 032	356	929	0.2	0.5	1 698	1 772	2 012	0.4	1.3
Local government passenger transit	247	269	282	22	12	0.9	0.5	11	13	15	1.8	1.8
Local government enterprises except passenger transit	1 200	1 311	1 473	112	162	0.9	1.2	150	181	225	1.9	2.2
Local government hospitals-compensation	642	654	669	12	15.1	0.2	0.2	45	47	51	0.5	0.7
Local government educational services-compensation	7 654	7 779	8 234	125	454	0.2	0.6	373	365	393	-0.2	0.7
Local government excluding enterprises, educational services, and hospitals-compensation	3 975	4 038	4 190	63	153	0.2	0.4	203	212	228	0.4	0.7
State government enterprises	545	500	442	-45	-58	-0.9	-1.2	22	23	29	0.8	2.2
State government hospitals-compensation	349	347	343	-2	-4	-0.1	-0.1	35	33	36	-0.5	0.7
State government educational services-compensation	2 243	2 385	2 531	143	146	0.6	0.6	103	114	123	1.0	0.7
State government, other compensation	1 892	1 820	1 869	-72	49	-0.4	0.3	118	112	120	-0.6	0.7
State and local government capital services	0	0	0	0	0	0.0	0.0	104	132	142	2.4	0.7
General state and local government except compensation and capital services	0	0	0	0	0	0.0	0.0	535	540	650	0.1	1.9
Owner-Occupied Dwellings	0	0	0	0	0	0.0	0.0	977	1 157	1 472	1.7	2.4
Agriculture, Forestry, Fishing, and Hunting	2 245	2 113	1 889	-133	-224	-0.6	-1.1	276	307	376	1.1	2.1
Crop production	934	946	876	12	-70	0.1	-0.8	106	113	138	0.7	2.0
Animal production	1 021	894	750	-127	-144	-1.3	-1.7	128	158	194	2.2	2.1
Forestry	15	9	10	-6	1	-5.0	0.6	8	7	9	-0.3	2.2
Logging	98	68	58	-31	-9	-3.7	-1.4	15	14	17	-0.9	2.5
Fishing, hunting and trapping	53	39	38	-14	-1.2	-3.0	-0.3	7	6	7	-0.5	1.0
Support activities for agriculture and forestry	124	157	157	33	1	2.4	0.0	15	11	14	-3.1	2.4
Nonagriculture Self-Employed and Unpaid Family Worker	9 021	8 816	9 343	-206	528	-0.2	0.6	. . .	. . .	. . .	. . .	. . .

. . . = Not available.

Table 4-8. Employment by Occupation, 2012 and Projected 2022

(Numbers in thousands, percent.)

Occupation	Employment				Change, 2012–2022		Total job openings due to growth and net replacements, 2012–2022[1]
	Number		Percent distribution		Number	Percent	
	2012	2022	2012	2022			
TOTAL, ALL OCCUPATIONS	145 356	160 984	100.0	100.0	15 628	10.8	50 557
Management	8 862	9 498	6.1	5.9	637	7.2	2 587
Top executives	2 362	2 627	1.6	1.6	265	11.2	717
Chief executives	330	348	0.2	0.2	17	5.3	88
General and operations managers	1 973	2 217	1.4	1.4	244	12.4	613
Legislators	58	62	0.0	0.0	4	6.4	16
Advertising, marketing, promotions, public relations, and sales managers	637	700	0.4	0.4	63	9.9	203
Advertising and promotions managers	36	38	0.0	0.0	2	6.9	13
Marketing and sales managers	540	592	0.4	0.4	53	9.8	169
Marketing managers	180	203	0.1	0.1	23	12.7	62
Sales managers	359	389	0.2	0.2	30	8.3	107
Public relations and fundraising managers	62	70	0.0	0.0	8	12.9	21
Operations specialties managers	1 648	1 800	1.1	1.1	152	9.2	459
Administrative services managers	281	315	0.2	0.2	34	12.2	80
Computer and information systems managers	333	384	0.2	0.2	51	15.3	97
Financial managers	532	579	0.4	0.4	47	8.9	147
Industrial production managers	173	169	0.1	0.1	-4	-2.4	31
Purchasing managers	72	73	0.0	0.0	2	2.1	17
Transportation, storage, and distribution managers	105	110	0.1	0.1	5	4.9	29
Compensation and benefits managers	21	21	0.0	0.0	1	3.1	6
Human resources managers	103	116	0.1	0.1	14	13.2	41
Training and development managers	29	32	0.0	0.0	3	11.2	11
Other management occupations	4 215	4 371	2.9	2.7	156	3.7	1 207
Farmers, ranchers, and other agricultural managers	931	751	0.6	0.5	-180	-19.3	150
Construction managers	485	563	0.3	0.3	78	16.1	155
Education administrators	491	542	0.3	0.3	51	10.3	181
Education administrators, preschool and childcare center/program	64	75	0.0	0.0	11	17.0	28
Education administrators, elementary and secondary school	232	245	0.2	0.2	13	5.7	75
Education administrators, postsecondary	162	185	0.1	0.1	24	14.5	66
Education administrators, all other	34	37	0.0	0.0	3	9.0	12
Architectural and engineering managers	194	207	0.1	0.1	13	6.7	61
Food service managers	321	326	0.2	0.2	5	1.6	62
Funeral service managers	9	10	0.0	0.0	1	12.5	3
Gaming managers	5	5	0.0	0.0	0.4	7.5	1
Lodging managers	50	51	0.0	0.0	1	1.4	16
Medical and health services managers	316	389	0.2	0.2	73	23.2	150
Natural sciences managers	52	54	0.0	0.0	3	5.7	14
Postmasters and mail superintendents	23	17	0.0	0.0	-6	-24.2	5
Property, real estate, and community association managers	297	332	0.2	0.2	35	11.8	102
Social and community service managers	133	161	0.1	0.1	28	20.8	55
Emergency management directors	10	11	0.0	0.0	1	8.3	2
Managers, all other	898	951	0.6	0.6	53	5.9	249
Business and Financial Operations	7 168	8 066	4.9	5.0	898	12.5	2 352
Business operations specialists	4 432	5 009	3.0	3.1	577	13.0	1 344
Agents and business managers of artists, performers, and athletes	18	20	0.0	0.0	2	9.7	6
Buyers and purchasing agents	433	451	0.3	0.3	18	4.2	105
Buyers and purchasing agents, farm products	14	15	0.0	0.0	1	5.9	4
Wholesale and retail buyers, except farm products	125	134	0.1	0.1	9	7.1	40
Purchasing agents, except wholesale, retail, and farm products	294	302	0.2	0.2	8	2.9	62
Claims adjusters, appraisers, examiners, and investigators	311	322	0.2	0.2	11	3.5	83
Claims adjusters, examiners, and investigators	298	309	0.2	0.2	12	3.9	80
Insurance appraisers, auto damage	14	13	0.0	0.0	-1	-5.3	3
Compliance officers	240	251	0.2	0.2	11	4.6	55
Cost estimators	202	255	0.1	0.2	53	26.2	118
Human resources workers	496	528	0.3	0.3	32	6.6	124
Human resources specialists	418	451	0.3	0.3	33	7.9	110
Labor relations specialists	78	77	0.1	0.0	-1	-0.8	14
Logisticians	126	154	0.1	0.1	28	21.9	42
Management analysts	719	852	0.5	0.5	134	18.6	245
Meeting, convention, and event planners	94	125	0.1	0.1	31	33.2	44
Fundraisers	66	77	0.0	0.0	11	17.3	24
Compensation, benefits, and job analysis specialists	92	97	0.1	0.1	5	5.8	22
Training and development specialists	229	264	0.2	0.2	35	15.5	77
Market research analysts and marketing specialists	416	547	0.3	0.3	132	31.6	188
Business operations specialists, all other	992	1 065	0.7	0.7	73	7.4	209
Financial specialists	2 735	3 056	1.9	1.9	321	11.7	1 007
Accountants and auditors	1 275	1 442	0.9	0.9	167	13.1	544
Appraisers and assessors of real estate	84	88	0.1	0.1	5	5.6	12
Budget analysts	62	66	0.0	0.0	4	6.1	28
Credit analysts	62	68	0.0	0.0	6	10.4	22
Financial analysts and advisors	583	676	0.4	0.4	93	16.0	226
Financial analysts	253	292	0.2	0.2	39	15.5	101
Personal financial advisors	223	284	0.2	0.2	60	27.0	96
Insurance underwriters	106	100	0.1	0.1	-6	-6.1	29
Financial examiners	29	31	0.0	0.0	2	6.3	9
Credit counselors and loan officers	328	357	0.2	0.2	29	8.9	89
Credit counselors	31	37	0.0	0.0	6	20.7	12
Loan officers	297	320	0.2	0.2	23	7.7	77
Tax examiners, collectors and preparers, and revenue agents	157	163	0.1	0.1	6	3.8	50
Tax examiners and collectors, and revenue agents	70	67	0.0	0.0	-3	-3.9	24
Tax preparers	88	96	0.1	0.1	9	9.9	26
Financial specialists, all other	156	165	0.1	0.1	9	6.1	26

Note: Data may not sum to totals or 100 percent due to rounding.

[1]Total job openings represent the sum of employment increases and net replacements. If employment change is negative, job openings due to growth are zero and total job openings equal net replacements.

Table 4-8. Employment by Occupation, 2012 and Projected 2022—*Continued*

(Numbers in thousands, percent.)

Occupation	Employment				Change, 2012–2022		Total job openings due to growth and net replacements, 2012–2022[1]
	Number		Percent distribution		Number	Percent	
	2012	2022	2012	2022			
Computer and Mathematical	3 815	4 500	2.6	2.8	686	18.0	1 308
Computer occupations	3 682	4 334	2.5	2.7	651	17.7	1 240
Computer and information research scientists	27	31	0.0	0.0	4	15.3	8
Computer and information analysts	596	751	0.4	0.5	155	26.1	249
Computer systems analysts	521	648	0.4	0.4	128	24.5	210
Information security analysts	75	102	0.1	0.1	27	36.5	39
Software developers and programmers	1 503	1 783	1.0	1.1	280	18.6	522
Computer programmers	344	372	0.2	0.2	28	8.3	118
Software developers, applications	613	753	0.4	0.5	140	22.8	218
Software developers, systems software	405	488	0.3	0.3	83	20.4	135
Web developers	141	170	0.1	0.1	28	20.1	51
Database and systems administrators and network architects	629	710	0.4	0.4	82	13.0	184
Database administrators	119	137	0.1	0.1	18	15.1	40
Network and computer systems administrators	366	409	0.3	0.3	43	11.7	100
Computer network architects	143	164	0.1	0.1	21	14.6	44
Computer support specialists	722	845	0.5	0.5	123	17.0	236
Computer user support specialists	548	658	0.4	0.4	111	20.2	197
Computer network support specialists	175	187	0.1	0.1	12	6.9	40
Computer occupations, all other	206	214	0.1	0.1	8	3.8	40
Mathematical science occupations	132	167	0.1	0.1	34	26.1	68
Actuaries	24	31	0.0	0.0	6	26.1	13
Mathematicians	4	4	0.0	0.0	1	22.7	2
Operations research analysts	73	93	0.1	0.1	20	26.7	36
Statisticians	28	35	0.0	0.0	7	26.7	16
Miscellaneous mathematical science occupations	4	4	0.0	0.0	0.5	12.9	2
Mathematical technicians	2	2	0.0	0.0	0.2	12.6	1
Mathematical science occupations, all other	2	2	0.0	0.0	0.3	13.3	1
Architecture and Engineering	2 474	2 654	1.7	1.6	180	7.3	764
Architects, surveyors, and cartographers	182	210	0.1	0.1	28	15.5	70
Architects, except naval	128	149	0.1	0.1	21	16.8	52
Architects, except landscape and naval	107	126	0.1	0.1	19	17.3	44
Landscape architects	20	23	0.0	0.0	3	14.3	8
Surveyors, cartographers, and photogrammetrists	54	61	0.0	0.0	7	12.4	18
Cartographers and photogrammetrists	12	14	0.0	0.0	2	19.6	5
Surveyors	42	47	0.0	0.0	4	10.3	13
Engineers	1 590	1 726	1.1	1.1	136	8.6	544
Aerospace engineers	83	89	0.1	0.1	6	7.3	25
Agricultural engineers	3	3	0.0	0.0	0.1	4.8	1
Biomedical engineers	19	25	0.0	0.0	5	26.6	10
Chemical engineers	33	35	0.0	0.0	2	4.5	9
Civil engineers	273	327	0.2	0.2	54	19.7	120
Computer hardware engineers	83	89	0.1	0.1	6	7.4	24
Electrical and electronics engineers	306	319	0.2	0.2	13	4.1	79
Electrical engineers	166	174	0.1	0.1	8	4.7	44
Electronics engineers, except computer	140	145	0.1	0.1	5	3.4	35
Environmental engineers	53	61	0.0	0.0	8	15.3	21
Industrial engineers, including health and safety	247	260	0.2	0.2	13	5.1	85
Health and safety engineers, except mining safety engineers and inspectors	24	27	0.0	0.0	3	11.0	10
Industrial engineers	223	233	0.2	0.1	10	4.5	75
Marine engineers and naval architects	7	8	0.0	0.0	1	10.3	3
Materials engineers	23	23	0.0	0.0	0.2	0.9	8
Mechanical engineers	258	270	0.2	0.2	12	4.5	100
Mining and geological engineers, including mining safety engineers	8	9	0.0	0.0	1	12.0	3
Nuclear engineers	20	22	0.0	0.0	2	9.3	7
Petroleum engineers	38	48	0.0	0.0	10	25.5	20
Engineers, all other	133	138	0.1	0.1	5	3.8	30
Drafters, engineering technicians, and mapping technicians	703	718	0.5	0.4	15	2.1	150
Drafters	200	202	0.1	0.1	2	1.1	32
Architectural and civil drafters	88	88	0.1	0.1	1	0.8	12
Electrical and electronics drafters	30	32	0.0	0.0	3	9.6	7
Mechanical drafters	67	63	0.0	0.0	-3	-4.9	9
Drafters, all other	16	18	0.0	0.0	2	12.7	4
Engineering technicians, except drafters	449	454	0.3	0.3	5	1.2	100
Aerospace engineering and operations technicians	10	10	0.0	0.0	0	-0.4	2
Civil engineering technicians	73	74	0.1	0.0	0.4	0.6	16
Electrical and electronics engineering technicians	146	146	0.1	0.1	0	0.0	30
Electro-mechanical technicians	17	18	0.0	0.0	1	3.9	4
Environmental engineering technicians	19	22	0.0	0.0	4	18.4	7
Industrial engineering technicians	68	66	0.0	0.0	-2	-3.2	14
Mechanical engineering technicians	48	50	0.0	0.0	2	4.7	12
Engineering technicians, except drafters, all other	68	68	0.0	0.0	1	0.9	15
Surveying and mapping technicians	54	61	0.0	0.0	7	13.5	17
Life, Physical, and Social Science	1 249	1 375	0.9	0.9	126	10.1	488
Life scientists	294	322	0.2	0.2	27	9.2	105
Agricultural and food scientists	38	42	0.0	0.0	4	9.3	16
Animal scientists	3	3	0.0	0.0	0.2	8.8	1
Food scientists and technologists	19	22	0.0	0.0	2	10.8	8
Soil and plant scientists	16	18	0.0	0.0	1	7.5	7
Biological scientists	104	111	0.1	0.1	8	7.3	37
Biochemists and biophysicists	29	35	0.0	0.0	5	18.6	14
Microbiologists	20	22	0.0	0.0	1	7.0	7
Zoologists and wildlife biologists	20	21	0.0	0.0	1	4.9	7
Biological scientists, all other	34	34	0.0	0.0	-0.2	-0.6	10

Note: Data may not sum to totals or 100 percent due to rounding.

[1]Total job openings represent the sum of employment increases and net replacements. If employment change is negative, job openings due to growth are zero and total job openings equal net replacements.

Table 4-8. Employment by Occupation, 2012 and Projected 2022—*Continued*

(Numbers in thousands, percent.)

Occupation	Employment				Change, 2012–2022		Total job openings due to growth and net replacements, 2012–2022[1]
	Number		Percent distribution		Number	Percent	
	2012	2022	2012	2022			
Life, Physical, and Social Science—*Continued*							
Conservation scientists and foresters	34	35	0.0	0.0	1	2.5	11
Conservation scientists	22	22	0.0	0.0	0.1	0.5	7
Foresters	12	13	0.0	0.0	1	6.1	4
Medical scientists	108	122	0.1	0.1	14	13.1	37
Epidemiologists	5	6	0.0	0.0	0.5	10.2	2
Medical scientists, except epidemiologists	103	117	0.1	0.1	14	13.3	36
Life scientists, all other	10	11	0.0	0.0	1	10.2	3
Physical scientists	297	328	0.2	0.2	31	10.3	111
Astronomers and physicists	23	26	0.0	0.0	2	10.3	8
Astronomers	3	3	0.0	0.0	0.3	10.0	1
Physicists	21	23	0.0	0.0	2	10.4	7
Atmospheric and space scientists	11	12	0.0	0.0	1	10.0	4
Chemists and materials scientists	96	102	0.1	0.1	5	5.6	30
Chemists	88	93	0.1	0.1	5	5.6	28
Materials scientists	8	9	0.0	0.0	0.4	5.2	3
Environmental scientists and geoscientists	136	156	0.1	0.1	20	14.7	60
Environmental scientists and specialists, including health	90	103	0.1	0.1	13	14.6	40
Geoscientists, except hydrologists and geographers	38	44	0.0	0.0	6	15.8	17
Hydrologists	7	8	0.0	0.0	1	10.4	3
Physical scientists, all other	31	33	0.0	0.0	2	5.9	8
Social scientists and related workers	290	323	0.2	0.2	33	11.3	111
Economists	17	19	0.0	0.0	2	13.9	7
Survey researchers	18	21	0.0	0.0	3	17.6	6
Psychologists	160	179	0.1	0.1	19	11.7	62
Clinical, counseling, and school psychologists	145	162	0.1	0.1	16	11.3	56
Industrial-organizational psychologists	2	2	0.0	0.0	1	53.4	1
Psychologists, all other	13	15	0.0	0.0	1	10.7	5
Sociologists	3	3	0.0	0.0	0.4	15.0	1
Urban and regional planners	39	43	0.0	0.0	4	10.3	21
Miscellaneous social scientists and related workers	54	58	0.0	0.0	4	7.7	13
Anthropologists and archeologists	7	9	0.0	0.0	1	19.4	3
Geographers	2	2	0.0	0.0	0.5	29.0	1
Historians	4	4	0.0	0.0	0.2	6.0	1
Political scientists	7	8	0.0	0.0	1	21.3	2
Social scientists and related workers, all other	35	36	0.0	0.0	1	1.9	6
Life, physical, and social science technicians	367	402	0.3	0.2	35	9.5	162
Agricultural and food science technicians	26	27	0.0	0.0	1	2.9	10
Biological technicians	80	88	0.1	0.1	8	10.0	32
Chemical technicians	64	70	0.0	0.0	6	9.4	22
Geological and petroleum technicians	16	18	0.0	0.0	2	15.1	8
Nuclear technicians	8	9	0.0	0.0	1	14.9	4
Social science research assistants	30	34	0.0	0.0	4	15.0	16
Miscellaneous life, physical, and social science technicians	144	156	0.1	0.1	12	8.5	70
Environmental science and protection technicians, including health	33	39	0.0	0.0	6	18.8	19
Forensic science technicians	13	14	0.0	0.0	1	5.8	6
Forest and conservation technicians	34	33	0.0	0.0	-1	-3.5	13
Life, physical, and social science technicians, all other	64	70	0.0	0.0	6	10.1	32
Community and Social Service	2 375	2 783	1.6	1.7	409	17.2	963
Counselors, social workers, and other community and social service specialists	1 941	2 309	1.3	1.4	368	19.0	814
Counselors	666	802	0.5	0.5	137	20.6	278
Substance abuse and behavioral disorder counselors	90	118	0.1	0.1	28	31.4	47
Educational, guidance, school, and vocational counselors	262	294	0.2	0.2	31	11.9	87
Marriage and family therapists	38	49	0.0	0.0	12	30.6	20
Mental health counselors	128	165	0.1	0.1	37	28.5	64
Rehabilitation counselors	118	141	0.1	0.1	23	19.9	48
Counselors, all other	30	36	0.0	0.0	6	19.4	12
Social workers	607	722	0.4	0.4	114	18.8	243
Child, family, and school social workers	286	329	0.2	0.2	43	15.1	104
Healthcare social workers	146	186	0.1	0.1	39	26.8	70
Mental health and substance abuse social workers	114	140	0.1	0.1	26	22.8	50
Social workers, all other	61	67	0.0	0.0	6	9.5	19
Miscellaneous community and social service specialists	668	786	0.5	0.5	118	17.6	293
Health educators	59	70	0.0	0.0	11	19.0	27
Probation officers and correctional treatment specialists	90	89	0.1	0.1	-1	-1.0	24
Social and human service assistants	373	454	0.3	0.3	81	21.8	179
Community health workers	40	51	0.0	0.0	10	25.1	21
Community and social service specialists, all other	106	122	0.1	0.1	16	15.1	44
Religious workers	434	474	0.3	0.3	40	9.3	149
Clergy	240	263	0.2	0.2	24	9.8	73
Directors, religious activities and education	134	146	0.1	0.1	11	8.4	57
Religious workers, all other	60	65	0.0	0.0	5	8.9	19
Legal	1 247	1 380	0.9	0.9	133	10.7	334
Lawyers, judges, and related workers	824	900	0.6	0.6	77	9.3	209
Lawyers and judicial law clerks	772	847	0.5	0.5	75	9.8	199
Lawyers	760	835	0.5	0.5	75	9.8	196
Judicial law clerks	12	13	0.0	0.0	0.5	4.3	2
Judges, magistrates, and other judicial workers	52	53	0.0	0.0	1	2.5	10
Administrative law judges, adjudicators, and hearing officers	15	15	0.0	0.0	-0.3	-1.7	2
Arbitrators, mediators, and conciliators	8	9	0.0	0.0	1	10.4	2
Judges, magistrate judges, and magistrates	28	29	0.0	0.0	1	2.3	5

Note: Data may not sum to totals or 100 percent due to rounding.

[1]Total job openings represent the sum of employment increases and net replacements. If employment change is negative, job openings due to growth are zero and total job openings equal net replacements.

Table 4-8. Employment by Occupation, 2012 and Projected 2022—*Continued*

(Numbers in thousands, percent.)

Occupation	Employment				Change, 2012–2022		Total job openings due to growth and net replacements, 2012–2022[1]
	Number		Percent distribution		Number	Percent	
	2012	2022	2012	2022			
Legal—*Continued*							
Legal support workers	423	480	0.3	0.3	56	13.3	125
Paralegals and legal assistants	277	323	0.2	0.2	46	16.7	91
Miscellaneous legal support workers	146	156	0.1	0.1	10	6.9	34
Court reporters	21	23	0.0	0.0	2	9.6	6
Title examiners, abstractors, and searchers	68	74	0.0	0.0	6	9.2	17
Legal support workers, all other	57	59	0.0	0.0	2	3.1	11
Education, Training, and Library	9 116	10 132	6.3	6.3	1 016	11.1	2 897
Postsecondary teachers	1 831	2 134	1.3	1.3	304	16.6	579
Business teachers, postsecondary	103	118	0.1	0.1	15	14.7	31
Math and computer teachers, postsecondary	105	118	0.1	0.1	13	12.0	28
Computer science teachers, postsecondary	42	47	0.0	0.0	5	12.7	12
Mathematical science teachers, postsecondary	63	71	0.0	0.0	7	11.5	17
Engineering and architecture teachers, postsecondary	52	58	0.0	0.0	6	12.2	14
Architecture teachers, postsecondary	9	10	0.0	0.0	1	14.3	3
Engineering teachers, postsecondary	42	48	0.0	0.0	5	11.8	11
Life sciences teachers, postsecondary	77	91	0.1	0.1	13	17.2	25
Agricultural sciences teachers, postsecondary	13	14	0.0	0.0	1	8.0	3
Biological science teachers, postsecondary	61	73	0.0	0.0	12	19.5	21
Forestry and conservation science teachers, postsecondary	3	3	0.0	0.0	0.3	9.9	1
Physical sciences teachers, postsecondary	62	70	0.0	0.0	8	13.2	18
Atmospheric, earth, marine, and space sciences teachers, postsecondary	13	15	0.0	0.0	2	11.4	4
Chemistry teachers, postsecondary	25	29	0.0	0.0	4	13.7	7
Environmental science teachers, postsecondary	6	7	0.0	0.0	1	13.2	2
Physics teachers, postsecondary	17	20	0.0	0.0	2	13.8	5
Social sciences teachers, postsecondary	143	163	0.1	0.1	20	13.9	42
Anthropology and archeology teachers, postsecondary	7	8	0.0	0.0	1	12.5	2
Area, ethnic, and cultural studies teachers, postsecondary	12	14	0.0	0.0	2	15.8	4
Economics teachers, postsecondary	17	19	0.0	0.0	2	14.2	5
Geography teachers, postsecondary	6	6	0.0	0.0	1	10.6	1
Political science teachers, postsecondary	21	24	0.0	0.0	3	14.6	6
Psychology teachers, postsecondary	48	54	0.0	0.0	7	14.2	14
Sociology teachers, postsecondary	21	23	0.0	0.0	3	12.7	6
Social sciences teachers, postsecondary, all other	12	14	0.0	0.0	2	13.4	4
Health teachers, postsecondary	258	350	0.2	0.2	93	35.9	131
Health specialties teachers, postsecondary	190	259	0.1	0.2	69	36.1	97
Nursing instructors and teachers, postsecondary	68	92	0.0	0.1	24	35.4	34
Education and library science teachers, postsecondary	85	97	0.1	0.1	12	14.4	25
Education teachers, postsecondary	79	91	0.1	0.1	12	14.6	24
Library science teachers, postsecondary	6	6	0.0	0.0	1	10.8	1
Law, criminal justice, and social work teachers, postsecondary	49	56	0.0	0.0	7	14.9	15
Criminal justice and law enforcement teachers, postsecondary	16	18	0.0	0.0	2	13.1	5
Law teachers, postsecondary	20	24	0.0	0.0	4	17.6	6
Social work teachers, postsecondary	12	14	0.0	0.0	2	13.1	4
Arts, communications, and humanities teachers, postsecondary	333	382	0.2	0.2	49	14.7	99
Art, drama, and music teachers, postsecondary	114	133	0.1	0.1	18	16.0	36
Communications teachers, postsecondary	36	41	0.0	0.0	5	12.7	10
English language and literature teachers, postsecondary	87	97	0.1	0.1	11	12.2	24
Foreign language and literature teachers, postsecondary	36	41	0.0	0.0	6	15.3	11
History teachers, postsecondary	29	33	0.0	0.0	4	13.6	8
Philosophy and religion teachers, postsecondary	31	37	0.0	0.0	6	19.3	11
Miscellaneous postsecondary teachers	563	630	0.4	0.4	67	11.9	152
Graduate teaching assistants	150	166	0.1	0.1	16	10.3	38
Home economics teachers, postsecondary	6	6	0.0	0.0	0.5	9.6	1
Recreation and fitness studies teachers, postsecondary	23	26	0.0	0.0	3	12.2	6
Vocational education teachers, postsecondary	136	152	0.1	0.1	16	11.8	37
Postsecondary teachers, all other	248	280	0.2	0.2	32	13.0	70
Preschool, primary, secondary, and special education school teachers	4 115	4 545	2.8	2.8	429	10.4	1 401
Preschool and kindergarten teachers	597	694	0.4	0.4	97	16.2	264
Preschool teachers, except special education	438	515	0.3	0.3	76	17.4	199
Kindergarten teachers, except special education	158	179	0.1	0.1	21	13.0	65
Elementary and middle school teachers	1 994	2 239	1.4	1.4	245	12.3	684
Elementary school teachers, except special education	1 361	1 529	0.9	0.9	168	12.3	467
Middle school teachers, except special and career/technical education	614	690	0.4	0.4	76	12.4	211
Career/technical education teachers, middle school	18	19	0.0	0.0	1	5.2	5
Secondary school teachers	1 041	1 098	0.7	0.7	57	5.5	340
Secondary school teachers, except special and career/technical education	956	1 009	0.7	0.6	53	5.5	313
Career/technical education teachers, secondary school	85	90	0.1	0.1	4	5.0	28
Special education teachers	484	514	0.3	0.3	30	6.3	113
Special education teachers, preschool	22	26	0.0	0.0	4	16.2	7
Special education teachers, kindergarten and elementary school	195	207	0.1	0.1	12	6.2	45
Special education teachers, middle school	95	100	0.1	0.1	5	5.2	21
Special education teachers, secondary school	131	137	0.1	0.1	6	4.6	28
Special education teachers, all other	41	45	0.0	0.0	4	9.5	11
Other teachers and instructors	1 375	1 502	0.9	0.9	127	9.2	361
Adult basic and secondary education and literacy teachers and instructors	77	84	0.1	0.1	7	8.7	20
Self-enrichment education teachers	316	360	0.2	0.2	44	13.9	98
Teachers and instructors, all other	982	1 058	0.7	0.7	76	7.7	244
Librarians, curators, and archivists	284	307	0.2	0.2	23	8.2	120
Archivists, curators, and museum technicians	29	33	0.0	0.0	3	11.4	10
Archivists	6	8	0.0	0.0	1	16.6	2
Curators	11	13	0.0	0.0	1	12.5	4
Museum technicians and conservators	11	12	0.0	0.0	1	7.1	3
Librarians	148	159	0.1	0.1	11	7.4	44
Library technicians	106	115	0.1	0.1	9	8.4	66

Note: Data may not sum to totals or 100 percent due to rounding.

[1]Total job openings represent the sum of employment increases and net replacements. If employment change is negative, job openings due to growth are zero and total job openings equal net replacements.

Table 4-8. Employment by Occupation, 2012 and Projected 2022—*Continued*

(Numbers in thousands, percent.)

Occupation	Employment				Change, 2012–2022		Total job openings due to growth and net replacements, 2012–2022[1]
	Number		Percent distribution		Number	Percent	
	2012	2022	2012	2022			
Education, Training, and Library—*Continued*							
Other education, training, and library occupations	1 510	1 644	1.0	1.0	133	8.8	435
Audio-visual and multimedia collections specialists	10	10	0.0	0.0	-0.1	-0.8	1
Farm and home management advisors	14	15	0.0	0.0	1	9.7	2
Instructional coordinators	148	166	0.1	0.1	18	12.5	31
Teacher assistants	1 223	1 328	0.8	0.8	105	8.6	383
Education, training, and library workers, all other	116	124	0.1	0.1	8	7.1	18
Arts, Design, Entertainment, Sports, and Media	2 571	2 752	1.8	1.7	181	7.0	800
Art and design workers	754	793	0.5	0.5	40	5.3	240
Artists and related workers	195	203	0.1	0.1	8	4.0	54
Art directors	75	77	0.1	0.0	2	3.0	20
Craft artists	11	12	0.0	0.0	0.4	3.3	3
Fine artists, including painters, sculptors, and illustrators	29	30	0.0	0.0	1	3.8	8
Multimedia artists and animators	69	73	0.0	0.0	4	6.3	21
Artists and related workers, all other	11	11	0.0	0.0	-0.2	-1.5	3
Designers	558	590	0.4	0.4	32	5.7	185
Commercial and industrial designers	39	41	0.0	0.0	2	4.4	12
Fashion designers	22	22	0.0	0.0	-1	-3.0	6
Floral designers	62	57	0.0	0.0	-5	-8.0	16
Graphic designers	260	277	0.2	0.2	17	6.7	86
Interior designers	55	62	0.0	0.0	7	12.8	22
Merchandise displayers and window trimmers	99	109	0.1	0.1	10	10.1	36
Set and exhibit designers	11	12	0.0	0.0	1	6.3	4
Designers, all other	10	11	0.0	0.0	1	8.0	4
Entertainers and performers, sports and related workers	767	830	0.5	0.5	63	8.2	284
Actors, producers, and directors	183	189	0.1	0.1	6	3.4	67
Actors	80	83	0.1	0.1	3	4.1	29
Producers and directors	104	106	0.1	0.1	3	2.8	38
Athletes, coaches, umpires, and related workers	276	315	0.2	0.2	38	13.9	120
Athletes and sports competitors	15	16	0.0	0.0	1	6.7	5
Coaches and scouts	244	280	0.2	0.2	36	14.8	108
Umpires, referees, and other sports officials	18	19	0.0	0.0	1	7.7	6
Dancers and choreographers	26	29	0.0	0.0	3	13.2	11
Dancers	16	16	0.0	0.0	1	5.9	5
Choreographers	10	13	0.0	0.0	2	24.3	5
Musicians, singers, and related workers	245	257	0.2	0.2	12	5.0	78
Music directors and composers	78	81	0.1	0.1	4	4.5	24
Musicians and singers	167	176	0.1	0.1	9	5.2	54
Entertainers and performers, sports and related workers, all other	37	39	0.0	0.0	3	7.3	7
Media and communication workers	727	787	0.5	0.5	60	8.3	216
Announcers	52	53	0.0	0.0	1	1.5	12
Radio and television announcers	41	41	0.0	0.0	0	-0.1	9
Public address system and other announcers	11	12	0.0	0.0	1	7.6	3
News analysts, reporters and correspondents	58	50	0.0	0.0	-7	-12.6	20
Broadcast news analysts	6	6	0.0	0.0	-0.1	-2.3	2
Reporters and correspondents	52	45	0.0	0.0	-7	-13.8	18
Public relations specialists	229	256	0.2	0.2	27	12.0	59
Writers and editors	294	302	0.2	0.2	8	2.9	82
Editors	115	112	0.1	0.1	-3	-2.4	28
Technical writers	50	57	0.0	0.0	7	14.8	23
Writers and authors	129	133	0.1	0.1	4	3.0	32
Miscellaneous media and communication workers	94	125	0.1	0.1	31	32.7	44
Interpreters and translators	64	93	0.0	0.1	29	46.1	38
Media and communication workers, all other	31	32	0.0	0.0	2	4.9	6
Media and communication equipment workers	323	341	0.2	0.2	18	5.4	60
Broadcast and sound engineering technicians and radio operators	123	133	0.1	0.1	11	8.6	33
Audio and video equipment technicians	68	77	0.0	0.0	9	13.7	22
Broadcast technicians	37	38	0.0	0.0	1	3.2	8
Radio operators	1	1	0.0	0.0	0	1.2	0.3
Sound engineering technicians	17	17	0.0	0.0	0.1	0.7	3
Photographers	136	142	0.1	0.1	6	4.3	20
Television, video, and motion picture camera operators and editors	50	51	0.0	0.0	1	2.8	5
Camera operators, television, video, and motion picture	21	23	0.0	0.0	1	5.5	3
Film and video editors	28	28	0.0	0.0	0.2	0.6	2
Media and communication equipment workers, all other	15	15	0.0	0.0	-0.2	-1.5	2
Healthcare Practitioners and Technical Occupations	8 050	9 783	5.5	6.1	1 733	21.5	3 378
Health diagnosing and treating practitioners	5 005	6 020	3.4	3.7	1 015	20.3	2 042
Chiropractors	44	51	0.0	0.0	6	14.6	15
Dentists	147	170	0.1	0.1	23	15.9	59
Dentists, general	126	146	0.1	0.1	21	16.3	51
Oral and maxillofacial surgeons	7	8	0.0	0.0	1	16.1	3
Orthodontists	8	9	0.0	0.0	1	16.3	3
Prosthodontists	0.4	0.5	0.0	0.0	0.1	15.0	0.2
Dentists, all other specialists	6	7	0.0	0.0	0.4	6.3	2
Dietitians and nutritionists	67	82	0.0	0.1	14	21.1	22
Optometrists	33	41	0.0	0.0	8	24.4	18
Pharmacists	286	328	0.2	0.2	41	14.5	110

Note: Data may not sum to totals or 100 percent due to rounding.

[1] Total job openings represent the sum of employment increases and net replacements. If employment change is negative, job openings due to growth are zero and total job openings equal net replacements.

Table 4-8. Employment by Occupation, 2012 and Projected 2022—*Continued*

(Numbers in thousands, percent.)

Occupation	Employment				Change, 2012–2022		Total job openings due to growth and net replacements, 2012–2022[1]
	Number		Percent distribution		Number	Percent	
	2012	2022	2012	2022			
Healthcare Practitioners and Technical Occupations—*Continued*							
Physicians and surgeons	691	815	0.5	0.5	123	17.8	296
Anesthesiologists	34	42	0.0	0.0	8	24.4	17
Family and general practitioners	124	142	0.1	0.1	18	14.6	49
Internists, general	51	59	0.0	0.0	7	14.1	20
Obstetricians and gynecologists	24	27	0.0	0.0	3	14.4	9
Pediatricians, general	35	40	0.0	0.0	5	15.7	14
Psychiatrists	27	32	0.0	0.0	4	16.2	11
Surgeons	48	59	0.0	0.0	11	23.2	23
Physicians and surgeons, all other	349	414	0.2	0.3	65	18.7	153
Physician assistants	87	120	0.1	0.1	33	38.4	49
Podiatrists	11	13	0.0	0.0	2	22.5	5
Therapists	644	816	0.4	0.5	172	26.7	287
Occupational therapists	113	146	0.1	0.1	33	29.0	48
Physical therapists	204	278	0.1	0.2	74	36.0	124
Radiation therapists	19	24	0.0	0.0	4	23.5	8
Recreational therapists	20	22	0.0	0.0	3	13.4	7
Respiratory therapists	119	142	0.1	0.1	23	19.1	40
Speech-language pathologists	134	160	0.1	0.1	26	19.4	46
Exercise physiologists	6	6	0.0	0.0	1	9.2	1
Therapists, all other	29	38	0.0	0.0	9	31.7	12
Veterinarians	70	79	0.0	0.0	8	12.0	31
Registered nurses	2 712	3 238	1.9	2.0	527	19.4	1 053
Nurse anesthetists	35	44	0.0	0.0	9	24.9	16
Nurse midwives	6	8	0.0	0.0	2	28.6	3
Nurse practitioners	110	147	0.1	0.1	37	33.7	58
Audiologists	13	17	0.0	0.0	4	33.6	7
Health diagnosing and treating practitioners, all other	47	51	0.0	0.0	4	7.9	14
Health technologists and technicians	2 893	3 590	2.0	2.2	698	24.1	1 275
Clinical laboratory technologists and technicians	326	396	0.2	0.2	71	21.7	156
Medical and clinical laboratory technologists	164	187	0.1	0.1	23	13.8	66
Medical and clinical laboratory technicians	162	209	0.1	0.1	48	29.7	90
Dental hygienists	193	257	0.1	0.2	64	33.3	114
Diagnostic related technologists and technicians	361	456	0.2	0.3	96	26.5	146
Cardiovascular technologists and technicians	52	67	0.0	0.0	16	30.4	23
Diagnostic medical sonographers	59	86	0.0	0.1	27	46.0	35
Nuclear medicine technologists	21	25	0.0	0.0	4	20.2	7
Radiologic technologists	199	241	0.1	0.1	42	20.8	70
Magnetic resonance imaging technologists	30	37	0.0	0.0	7	23.6	11
Emergency medical technicians and paramedics	239	294	0.2	0.2	55	23.1	121
Health practitioner support technologists and technicians	678	821	0.5	0.5	144	21.2	210
Dietetic technicians	25	30	0.0	0.0	4	18.0	7
Pharmacy technicians	355	426	0.2	0.3	71	19.9	106
Psychiatric technicians	71	74	0.0	0.0	3	3.9	10
Respiratory therapy technicians	14	16	0.0	0.0	2	16.9	4
Surgical technologists	98	128	0.1	0.1	29	29.8	39
Veterinary technologists and technicians	85	110	0.1	0.1	25	29.5	33
Ophthalmic medical technicians	30	38	0.0	0.0	9	29.8	12
Licensed practical and licensed vocational nurses	738	921	0.5	0.6	183	24.8	363
Medical records and health information technicians	186	228	0.1	0.1	41	22.1	90
Opticians, dispensing	68	84	0.0	0.1	16	23.4	35
Miscellaneous health technologists and technicians	104	133	0.1	0.1	28	27.4	39
Orthotists and prosthetists	8	12	0.0	0.0	3	35.5	4
Hearing aid specialists	5	7	0.0	0.0	1	25.2	2
Health technologists and technicians, all other	90	115	0.1	0.1	24	26.7	33
Other healthcare practitioners and technical occupations	152	172	0.1	0.1	20	13.2	62
Occupational health and safety specialists and technicians	76	81	0.1	0.1	6	7.4	26
Occupational health and safety specialists	63	67	0.0	0.0	4	6.6	21
Occupational health and safety technicians	13	14	0.0	0.0	1	10.9	5
Miscellaneous health practitioners and technical workers	77	91	0.1	0.1	14	19.0	35
Athletic trainers	23	28	0.0	0.0	5	21.2	11
Genetic counselors	2	3	0.0	0.0	1	41.2	2
Healthcare practitioners and technical workers, all other	52	60	0.0	0.0	9	17.1	23
Healthcare Support	4 110	5 266	2.8	3.3	1 156	28.1	1 938
Nursing, psychiatric, and home health aides	2 492	3 242	1.7	2.0	750	30.1	1 224
Home health aides	875	1 299	0.6	0.8	424	48.5	591
Psychiatric aides	82	87	0.1	0.1	5	6.0	20
Nursing assistants	1 480	1 792	1.0	1.1	312	21.1	594
Orderlies	55	64	0.0	0.0	9	16.6	19
Occupational therapy and physical therapist assistants and aides	160	225	0.1	0.1	65	40.8	102
Occupational therapy assistants and aides	39	55	0.0	0.0	16	41.2	26
Occupational therapy assistants	30	43	0.0	0.0	13	42.6	20
Occupational therapy aides	8	11	0.0	0.0	3	36.2	5
Physical therapist assistants and aides	121	171	0.1	0.1	49	40.7	76
Physical therapist assistants	71	101	0.0	0.1	29	41.0	45
Physical therapist aides	50	70	0.0	0.0	20	40.1	31
Other healthcare support occupations	1 459	1 799	1.0	1.1	340	23.3	612
Massage therapists	133	163	0.1	0.1	30	22.6	44
Miscellaneous healthcare support occupations	1 326	1 636	0.9	1.0	310	23.4	568
Dental assistants	303	378	0.2	0.2	74	24.5	137
Medical assistants	561	724	0.4	0.4	163	29.0	270
Medical equipment preparers	52	62	0.0	0.0	10	20.3	20
Medical transcriptionists	84	90	0.1	0.1	6	7.6	22
Pharmacy aides	43	48	0.0	0.0	5	11.1	13
Veterinary assistants and laboratory animal caretakers	75	82	0.1	0.1	7	9.5	21
Phlebotomists	101	128	0.1	0.1	27	26.7	46
Healthcare support workers, all other	107	125	0.1	0.1	17	16.0	38

Note: Data may not sum to totals or 100 percent due to rounding.

[1]Total job openings represent the sum of employment increases and net replacements. If employment change is negative, job openings due to growth are zero and total job openings equal net replacements.

Table 4-8. Employment by Occupation, 2012 and Projected 2022—*Continued*

(Numbers in thousands, percent.)

Occupation	Employment				Change, 2012–2022		Total job openings due to growth and net replacements, 2012–2022[1]
	Number		Percent distribution		Number	Percent	
	2012	2022	2012	2022			
Protective Service	3 325	3 588	2.3	2.2	263	7.9	1 147
Supervisors of protective service workers	282	298	0.2	0.2	16	5.8	105
First-line supervisors of law enforcement workers	150	157	0.1	0.1	7	4.6	54
First-line supervisors of correctional officers	47	49	0.0	0.0	2	4.0	18
First-line supervisors of police and detectives	104	109	0.1	0.1	5	4.9	36
First-line supervisors of fire fighting and prevention workers	62	66	0.0	0.0	4	6.3	30
First-line supervisors of protective service workers, all other	69	75	0.0	0.0	6	8.0	21
Fire fighting and prevention workers	321	342	0.2	0.2	21	6.6	109
Firefighters	307	327	0.2	0.2	20	6.6	104
Fire inspectors	14	15	0.0	0.0	1	5.7	5
Fire inspectors and investigators	12	13	0.0	0.0	1	6.2	4
Forest fire inspectors and prevention specialists	2	2	0.0	0.0	0.1	2.8	1
Law enforcement workers	1 259	1 324	0.9	0.8	64	5.1	426
Bailiffs, correctional officers, and jailers	470	493	0.3	0.3	23	4.9	148
Bailiffs	17	18	0.0	0.0	1	5.3	5
Correctional officers and jailers	453	475	0.3	0.3	22	4.9	142
Detectives and criminal investigators	115	118	0.1	0.1	2	2.0	28
Fish and game wardens	7	7	0.0	0.0	0.1	1.2	2
Parking enforcement workers	10	10	0.0	0.0	0	-0.2	3
Police officers	658	697	0.5	0.4	39	5.9	245
Police and sheriff's patrol officers	654	693	0.4	0.4	39	5.9	244
Transit and railroad police	4	4	0.0	0.0	0.1	3.4	1
Other protective service workers	1 463	1 624	1.0	1.0	161	11.0	507
Animal control workers	15	16	0.0	0.0	1	7.7	4
Private detectives and investigators	30	33	0.0	0.0	3	11.2	12
Security guards and gaming surveillance officers	1 084	1 214	0.7	0.8	130	12.0	296
Gaming surveillance officers and gaming investigators	9	10	0.0	0.0	1	7.0	2
Security guards	1 074	1 204	0.7	0.7	130	12.1	294
Miscellaneous protective service workers	335	361	0.2	0.2	26	7.9	194
Crossing guards	71	74	0.0	0.0	3	4.3	14
Lifeguards, ski patrol, and other recreational protective service workers	130	143	0.1	0.1	13	10.2	102
Transportation security screeners	51	54	0.0	0.0	3	5.9	15
Protective service workers, all other	82	90	0.1	0.1	7	8.6	64
Food Preparation and Serving Related	11 780	12 882	8.1	8.0	1 102	9.4	5 514
Supervisors of food preparation and serving workers	964	1 079	0.7	0.7	115	12.0	374
Chefs and head cooks	115	122	0.1	0.1	6	5.2	25
First-line supervisors of food preparation and serving workers	848	958	0.6	0.6	109	12.9	349
Cooks and food preparation workers	2 956	3 190	2.0	2.0	234	7.9	892
Cooks	2 148	2 354	1.5	1.5	205	9.6	632
Cooks, fast food	517	514	0.4	0.3	-2	-0.5	102
Cooks, institution and cafeteria	409	463	0.3	0.3	54	13.2	135
Cooks, private household	7	7	0.0	0.0	-0.1	-0.8	1
Cooks, restaurant	1 024	1 174	0.7	0.7	150	14.7	352
Cooks, short order	166	167	0.1	0.1	0.5	0.3	33
Cooks, all other	26	29	0.0	0.0	3	12.7	8
Food preparation workers	808	837	0.6	0.5	29	3.6	260
Food and beverage serving workers	6 563	7 229	4.5	4.5	666	10.1	3 480
Bartenders	551	617	0.4	0.4	66	11.9	269
Fast food and counter workers	3 408	3 828	2.3	2.4	420	12.3	1 824
Combined food preparation and serving workers, including fast food	2 969	3 391	2.0	2.1	422	14.2	1 556
Counter attendants, cafeteria, food concession, and coffee shop	439	437	0.3	0.3	-2	-0.5	268
Waiters and waitresses	2 362	2 494	1.6	1.5	132	5.6	1 268
Food servers, nonrestaurant	241	290	0.2	0.2	49	20.1	119
Other food preparation and serving related workers	1 297	1 384	0.9	0.9	87	6.7	769
Dining room and cafeteria attendants and bartender helpers	403	435	0.3	0.3	32	8.0	209
Dishwashers	508	540	0.3	0.3	32	6.2	256
Hosts and hostesses, restaurant, lounge, and coffee shop	347	366	0.2	0.2	19	5.5	280
Food preparation and serving related workers, all other	38	42	0.0	0.0	4	9.8	24
Building and Grounds Cleaning and Maintenance	5 522	6 213	3.8	3.9	691	12.5	1 826
Supervisors of building and grounds cleaning and maintenance workers	457	515	0.3	0.3	58	12.8	142
First-line supervisors of housekeeping and janitorial workers	250	282	0.2	0.2	32	12.8	92
First-line supervisors of landscaping, lawn service, and groundskeeping workers	207	234	0.1	0.1	26	12.7	50
Building cleaning and pest control workers	3 838	4 317	2.6	2.7	478	12.5	1 220
Building cleaning workers	3 773	4 239	2.6	2.6	466	12.3	1 190
Janitors and cleaners, except maids and housekeeping cleaners	2 324	2 604	1.6	1.6	280	12.1	717
Maids and housekeeping cleaners	1 435	1 618	1.0	1.0	183	12.8	468
Building cleaning workers, all other	14	17	0.0	0.0	2	15.0	5
Pest control workers	65	78	0.0	0.0	13	19.7	31
Grounds maintenance workers	1 227	1 381	0.8	0.9	154	12.6	464
Landscaping and groundskeeping workers	1 125	1 264	0.8	0.8	139	12.4	423
Pesticide handlers, sprayers, and applicators, vegetation	30	33	0.0	0.0	3	11.2	11
Tree trimmers and pruners	53	63	0.0	0.0	10	18.5	23
Grounds maintenance workers, all other	19	21	0.0	0.0	2	10.0	7
Personal Care and Service	5 376	6 498	3.7	4.0	1 123	20.9	2 289
Supervisors of personal care and service workers	301	332	0.2	0.2	32	10.6	88
First-line supervisors of gaming workers	49	53	0.0	0.0	4	7.6	14
Gaming supervisors	38	42	0.0	0.0	3	8.2	11
Slot supervisors	11	11	0.0	0.0	1	5.8	3
First-line supervisors of personal service workers	252	280	0.2	0.2	28	11.1	74
Animal care and service workers	232	268	0.2	0.2	35	15.2	77
Animal trainers	42	48	0.0	0.0	6	14.8	24
Nonfarm animal caretakers	191	220	0.1	0.1	29	15.3	52

Note: Data may not sum to totals or 100 percent due to rounding.

[1]Total job openings represent the sum of employment increases and net replacements. If employment change is negative, job openings due to growth are zero and total job openings equal net replacements.

Table 4-8. Employment by Occupation, 2012 and Projected 2022—*Continued*

(Numbers in thousands, percent.)

Occupation	Employment				Change, 2012–2022		Total job openings due to growth and net replacements, 2012–2022[1]
	Number		Percent distribution		Number	Percent	
	2012	2022	2012	2022			
Personal Care and Service—*Continued*							
Entertainment attendants and related workers	549	596	0.4	0.4	47	8.6	284
Gaming services workers	128	142	0.1	0.1	14	10.8	36
Gaming dealers	100	112	0.1	0.1	11	11.4	29
Gaming and sports book writers and runners	15	16	0.0	0.0	1	7.8	4
Gaming service workers, all other	13	14	0.0	0.0	1	9.4	4
Motion picture projectionists	8	6	0.0	0.0	-2	-26.5	3
Ushers, lobby attendants, and ticket takers	109	111	0.1	0.1	2	1.7	59
Miscellaneous entertainment attendants and related workers	304	338	0.2	0.2	34	11.1	186
Amusement and recreation attendants	267	298	0.2	0.2	30	11.3	164
Costume attendants	6	6	0.0	0.0	0.4	6.6	3
Locker room, coatroom, and dressing room attendants	20	22	0.0	0.0	2	10.4	12
Entertainment attendants and related workers, all other	12	13	0.0	0.0	1	9.2	7
Funeral service workers	61	64	0.0	0.0	2	4.2	16
Embalmers	5	4	0.0	0.0	-1	-15.0	1
Funeral attendants	32	33	0.0	0.0	0.50	1.4	7
Morticians, undertakers, and funeral directors	24	26	0.0	0.0	3	12.1	8
Personal appearance workers	816	930	0.6	0.6	114	14.0	284
Barbers, hairdressers, hairstylists and cosmetologists	663	747	0.5	0.5	83	12.6	240
Barbers	52	58	0.0	0.0	6	11.1	19
Hairdressers, hairstylists, and cosmetologists	611	689	0.4	0.4	78	12.7	221
Miscellaneous personal appearance workers	153	184	0.1	0.1	31	20.3	44
Makeup artists, theatrical and performance	3	3	0.0	0.0	0.1	3.1	0.3
Manicurists and pedicurists	87	100	0.1	0.1	14	15.6	21
Shampooers	19	19	0.0	0.0	-0.3	-1.5	2
Skincare specialists	44	62	0.0	0.0	18	39.8	21
Baggage porters, bellhops, and concierges	67	78	0.0	0.0	11	16.5	28
Baggage porters and bellhops	41	46	0.0	0.0	5	12.1	15
Concierges	26	32	0.0	0.0	6	23.4	13
Tour and travel guides	47	51	0.0	0.0	4	7.7	26
Tour guides and escorts	41	45	0.0	0.0	3	8.3	23
Travel guides	6	6	0.0	0.0	0.2	3.6	3
Other personal care and service workers	3 302	4 179	2.3	2.6	877	26.5	1 486
Childcare workers	1 313	1 497	0.9	0.9	184	14.0	570
Personal care aides	1 191	1 771	0.8	1.1	581	48.8	666
Recreation and fitness workers	612	695	0.4	0.4	82	13.5	155
Fitness trainers and aerobics instructors	267	300	0.2	0.2	34	12.5	65
Recreation workers	345	394	0.2	0.2	49	14.2	90
Residential advisors	90	108	0.1	0.1	18	20.7	57
Personal care and service workers, all other	97	108	0.1	0.1	11	11.1	38
Sales and Related	15 105	16 200	10.4	10.1	1 096	7.3	5 627
Supervisors of sales workers	1 998	2 065	1.4	1.3	68	3.4	470
First-line supervisors of retail sales workers	1 603	1 674	1.1	1.0	71	4.4	420
First-line supervisors of non-retail sales workers	394	391	0.3	0.2	-3	-0.8	50
Retail sales workers	8 467	9 051	5.8	5.6	583	6.9	3 725
Cashiers	3 361	3 448	2.3	2.1	86	2.6	1 540
Cashiers	3 339	3 425	2.3	2.1	86	2.6	1 530
Gaming change persons and booth cashiers	22	22	0.0	0.0	0	0.1	10
Counter and rental clerks and parts salespersons	659	721	0.5	0.4	62	9.4	230
Counter and rental clerks	438	484	0.3	0.3	47	10.6	158
Parts salespersons	221	237	0.2	0.1	16	7.0	72
Retail salespersons	4 447	4 882	3.1	3.0	435	9.8	1 956
Sales representatives, services	1 728	1 914	1.2	1.2	186	10.8	633
Advertising sales agents	155	154	0.1	0.1	-1	-0.7	48
Insurance sales agents	443	489	0.3	0.3	46	10.4	150
Securities, commodities, and financial services sales agents	355	394	0.2	0.2	40	11.2	123
Travel agents	73	64	0.1	0.0	-9	-12.1	11
Sales representatives, services, all other	702	812	0.5	0.5	110	15.7	302
Sales representatives, wholesale and manufacturing	1 863	2 032	1.3	1.3	169	9.1	532
Sales representatives, wholesale and manufacturing, technical and scientific products	382	420	0.3	0.3	37	9.7	112
Sales representatives, wholesale and manufacturing, except technical and scientific products	1 481	1 613	1.0	1.0	132	8.9	421
Other sales and related workers	1 049	1 138	0.7	0.7	89	8.5	266
Models, demonstrators, and product promoters	83	96	0.1	0.1	13	16.1	37
Demonstrators and product promoters	78	91	0.1	0.1	13	16.1	35
Models	5	6	0.0	0.0	1	15.3	2
Real estate brokers and sales agents	422	469	0.3	0.3	47	11.0	86
Real estate brokers	80	88	0.1	0.1	9	10.8	16
Real estate sales agents	342	380	0.2	0.2	38	11.1	70
Sales engineers	66	72	0.0	0.0	6	8.9	17
Telemarketers	250	269	0.2	0.2	19	7.7	71
Miscellaneous sales and related workers	228	232	0.2	0.1	4	1.8	54
Door-to-door sales workers, news and street vendors, and related workers	93	78	0.1	0.0	-14	-15.3	9
Sales and related workers, all other	136	154	0.1	0.1	18	13.5	45
Office and Administrative Support	22 470	24 004	15.5	14.9	1 534	6.8	6 765
Supervisors of office and administrative support workers	1 418	1 590	1.0	1.0	172	12.1	508
First-line supervisors of office and administrative support workers	1 418	1 590	1.0	1.0	172	12.1	508
Communications equipment operators	145	126	0.1	0.1	-19	-12.9	28
Switchboard operators, including answering service	131	114	0.1	0.1	-17	-13.2	24
Telephone operators	11	10	0.0	0.0	-1	-13.1	3
Communications equipment operators, all other	3	3	0.0	0.0	0.1	4.6	1

Note: Data may not sum to totals or 100 percent due to rounding.

[1]Total job openings represent the sum of employment increases and net replacements. If employment change is negative, job openings due to growth are zero and total job openings equal net replacements.

Table 4-8. Employment by Occupation, 2012 and Projected 2022—*Continued*

(Numbers in thousands, percent.)

Occupation	Employment				Change, 2012–2022		Total job openings due to growth and net replacements, 2012–2022[1]
	Number		Percent distribution		Number	Percent	
	2012	2022	2012	2022			
Office and Administrative Support—*Continued*							
Financial clerks	3 567	3 959	2.5	2.5	391	11.0	1 098
Bill and account collectors	397	456	0.3	0.3	58	14.7	170
Billing and posting clerks	514	607	0.4	0.4	93	18.1	188
Bookkeeping, accounting, and auditing clerks	1 800	2 004	1.2	1.2	205	11.4	370
Gaming cage workers	18	20	0.0	0.0	1	7.3	5
Payroll and timekeeping clerks	180	202	0.1	0.1	22	12.5	62
Procurement clerks	72	74	0.0	0.0	1	2.0	28
Tellers	545	551	0.4	0.3	6	1.0	260
Financial clerks, all other	41	45	0.0	0.0	4	10.9	16
Information and record clerks	5 413	5 911	3.7	3.7	499	9.2	1 952
Brokerage clerks	62	64	0.0	0.0	2	3.8	18
Correspondence clerks	11	12	0.0	0.0	0.5	4.2	3
Court, municipal, and license clerks	130	144	0.1	0.1	14	10.6	34
Credit authorizers, checkers, and clerks	52	50	0.0	0.0	-2	-3.2	6
Customer service representatives	2 363	2 661	1.6	1.7	299	12.6	942
Eligibility interviewers, government programs	138	152	0.1	0.1	14	10.1	42
File clerks	164	159	0.1	0.1	-5	-3.3	38
Hotel, motel, and resort desk clerks	232	263	0.2	0.2	32	13.7	142
Interviewers, except eligibility and loan	204	226	0.1	0.1	21	10.4	60
Library assistants, clerical	110	127	0.1	0.1	16	14.7	64
Loan interviewers and clerks	196	213	0.1	0.1	17	8.7	30
New accounts clerks	56	53	0.0	0.0	-3	-4.9	14
Order clerks	213	207	0.1	0.1	-5	-2.5	56
Human resources assistants, except payroll and timekeeping	147	145	0.1	0.1	-2	-1.1	37
Receptionists and information clerks	1 007	1 143	0.7	0.7	136	13.5	407
Reservation and transportation ticket agents and travel clerks	139	120	0.1	0.1	-20	-14.0	18
Information and record clerks, all other	189	172	0.1	0.1	-17	-8.8	41
Material recording, scheduling, dispatching, and distributing workers	3 858	3 760	2.7	2.3	-99	-2.6	1 130
Cargo and freight agents	80	91	0.1	0.1	12	14.5	33
Couriers and messengers	98	87	0.1	0.1	-11	-11.1	13
Dispatchers	289	318	0.2	0.2	29	10.0	112
Police, fire, and ambulance dispatchers	98	106	0.1	0.1	8	7.7	36
Dispatchers, except police, fire, and ambulance	191	212	0.1	0.1	21	11.2	76
Meter readers, utilities	40	32	0.0	0.0	-8	-19.2	10
Postal service workers	492	353	0.3	0.2	-139	-28.3	122
Postal service clerks	67	46	0.0	0.0	-21	-31.8	10
Postal service mail carriers	295	216	0.2	0.1	-79	-26.8	103
Postal service mail sorters, processors, and processing machine operators	130	91	0.1	0.1	-39	-29.8	9
Production, planning, and expediting clerks	285	295	0.2	0.2	10	3.6	81
Shipping, receiving, and traffic clerks	696	702	0.5	0.4	7	1.0	190
Stock clerks and order fillers	1 807	1 801	1.2	1.1	-6	-0.3	546
Weighers, measurers, checkers, and samplers, recordkeeping	72	80	0.0	0.0	7	10.2	23
Secretaries and administrative assistants	3 947	4 427	2.7	2.7	480	12.1	972
Executive secretaries and executive administrative assistants	874	863	0.6	0.5	-10	-1.2	105
Legal secretaries	223	216	0.2	0.1	-7	-3.1	27
Medical secretaries	526	715	0.4	0.4	189	36.0	252
Secretaries and administrative assistants, except legal, medical, and executive	2 324	2 632	1.6	1.6	308	13.2	588
Other office and administrative support workers	4 122	4 232	2.8	2.6	110	2.7	1 077
Computer operators	75	62	0.1	0.0	-13	-17.0	7
Data entry and information processing workers	325	244	0.2	0.2	-80	-24.8	30
Data entry keyers	220	166	0.2	0.1	-54	-24.6	26
Word processors and typists	104	78	0.1	0.0	-26	-25.1	4
Desktop publishers	16	16	0.0	0.0	-1	-5.5	3
Insurance claims and policy processing clerks	254	275	0.2	0.2	21	8.1	88
Mail clerks and mail machine operators, except postal service	108	99	0.1	0.1	-10	-8.8	25
Office clerks, general	2 984	3 168	2.1	2.0	184	6.2	811
Office machine operators, except computer	69	62	0.0	0.0	-7	-10.2	16
Proofreaders and copy markers	13	13	0.0	0.0	-0.2	-1.4	2
Statistical assistants	17	19	0.0	0.0	2	9.2	6
Office and administrative support workers, all other	260	275	0.2	0.2	15	5.7	88
Farming, Fishing, and Forestry	947	915	0.7	0.6	-32	-3.4	271
Supervisors of farming, fishing, and forestry workers	46	45	0.0	0.0	-1	-2.5	10
First-line supervisors of farming, fishing, and forestry workers	46	45	0.0	0.0	-1	-2.5	10
Agricultural workers	816	789	0.6	0.5	-26	-3.2	246
Agricultural inspectors	17	17	0.0	0.0	-0.2	-1.0	5
Animal breeders	1	1	0.0	0.0	-0.3	-23.4	0.4
Graders and sorters, agricultural products	49	48	0.0	0.0	-1	-2.0	9
Miscellaneous agricultural workers	748	723	0.5	0.4	-25	-3.3	231
Agricultural equipment operators	59	61	0.0	0.0	2	3.9	20
Farmworkers and laborers, crop, nursery, and greenhouse	597	568	0.4	0.4	-29	-4.9	181
Farmworkers, farm, ranch, and aquacultural animals	78	80	0.1	0.0	2	2.2	25
Agricultural workers, all other	14	15	0.0	0.0	0.5	3.4	5
Fishing and hunting workers	31	30	0.0	0.0	-2	-4.9	6
Fishers and related fishing workers	31	30	0.0	0.0	-2	-5.0	6
Forest, conservation, and logging workers	54	51	0.0	0.0	-3	-6.2	10
Forest and conservation workers	10	11	0.0	0.0	0.5	4.5	2
Logging workers	44	40	0.0	0.0	-4	-8.7	7
Fallers	7	4	0.0	0.0	-3	-43.3	1
Logging equipment operators	30	31	0.0	0.0	1	2.0	5
Log graders and scalers	4	2	0.0	0.0	-1	-31.6	0.5
Logging workers, all other	4	3	0.0	0.0	-0.5	-12.1	1

Note: Data may not sum to totals or 100 percent due to rounding.

[1]Total job openings represent the sum of employment increases and net replacements. If employment change is negative, job openings due to growth are zero and total job openings equal net replacements.

Table 4-8. Employment by Occupation, 2012 and Projected 2022—*Continued*

(Numbers in thousands, percent.)

Occupation	Employment				Change, 2012–2022		Total job openings due to growth and net replacements, 2012–2022[1]
	Number		Percent distribution		Number	Percent	
	2012	2022	2012	2022			
Construction and Extraction	6 092	7 394	4.2	4.6	1 302	21.4	2 353
Supervisors of construction and extraction workers	546	674	0.4	0.4	128	23.5	187
First-line supervisors of construction trades and extraction workers	546	674	0.4	0.4	128	23.5	187
Construction trades workers	4 653	5 666	3.2	3.5	1 013	21.8	1 810
Boilermakers	18	19	0.0	0.0	1	3.7	9
Brickmasons, blockmasons, and stonemasons	85	114	0.1	0.1	29	34.5	38
Brickmasons and blockmasons	71	96	0.0	0.1	25	35.5	33
Stonemasons	14	18	0.0	0.0	4	29.2	6
Carpenters	901	1 119	0.6	0.7	218	24.2	329
Carpet, floor, and tile installers and finishers	96	108	0.1	0.1	12	12.3	29
Carpet installers	37	40	0.0	0.0	3	8.7	10
Floor layers, except carpet, wood, and hard tiles	14	16	0.0	0.0	2	13.0	4
Floor sanders and finishers	6	7	0.0	0.0	1	14.8	2
Tile and marble setters	39	45	0.0	0.0	6	15.0	13
Cement masons, concrete finishers, and terrazzo workers	144	186	0.1	0.1	42	28.9	58
Cement masons and concrete finishers	141	182	0.1	0.1	41	29.1	57
Terrazzo workers and finishers	4	4	0.0	0.0	1	19.8	1
Construction laborers	1 071	1 331	0.7	0.8	260	24.3	489
Construction equipment operators	410	488	0.3	0.3	78	19.1	165
Paving, surfacing, and tamping equipment operators	55	66	0.0	0.0	11	19.7	19
Pile-driver operators	4	5	0.0	0.0	1	27.5	2
Operating engineers and other construction equipment operators	351	418	0.2	0.3	66	18.9	144
Drywall installers, ceiling tile installers, and tapers	114	132	0.1	0.1	18	15.7	29
Drywall and ceiling tile installers	95	110	0.1	0.1	15	15.9	24
Tapers	19	22	0.0	0.0	3	14.8	5
Electricians	584	698	0.4	0.4	115	19.7	225
Glaziers	47	55	0.0	0.0	8	17.2	19
Insulation workers	52	72	0.0	0.0	20	37.6	26
Insulation workers, floor, ceiling, and wall	23	29	0.0	0.0	6	26.2	9
Insulation workers, mechanical	29	42	0.0	0.0	14	46.7	17
Painters and paperhangers	320	382	0.2	0.2	63	19.6	111
Painters, construction and maintenance	316	379	0.2	0.2	63	19.8	110
Paperhangers	4	3	0.0	0.0	0	-0.5	1
Pipelayers, plumbers, pipefitters, and steamfitters	435	528	0.3	0.3	92	21.2	147
Pipelayers	48	59	0.0	0.0	10	20.8	16
Plumbers, pipefitters, and steamfitters	387	469	0.3	0.3	82	21.3	130
Plasterers and stucco masons	23	26	0.0	0.0	3	15.0	4
Reinforcing iron and rebar workers	16	19	0.0	0.0	4	23.1	6
Roofers	133	148	0.1	0.1	15	11.4	43
Sheet metal workers	142	164	0.1	0.1	22	15.5	49
Structural iron and steel workers	58	71	0.0	0.0	13	21.8	32
Solar photovoltaic installers	5	6	0.0	0.0	1	24.5	2
Helpers, construction trades	213	279	0.1	0.2	65	30.6	99
Helpers–brickmasons, blockmasons, stonemasons, and tile and marble setters	24	35	0.0	0.0	10	43.0	14
Helpers–carpenters	36	47	0.0	0.0	11	29.6	16
Helpers–electricians	61	83	0.0	0.1	22	36.9	32
Helpers–painters, paperhangers, plasterers, and stucco masons	11	12	0.0	0.0	1	10.2	3
Helpers–pipelayers, plumbers, pipefitters, and steamfitters	47	61	0.0	0.0	13	27.9	21
Helpers–roofers	12	14	0.0	0.0	2	17.3	4
Helpers, construction trades, all other	21	27	0.0	0.0	5	24.3	9
Other construction and related workers	412	464	0.3	0.3	52	12.5	131
Construction and building inspectors	102	115	0.1	0.1	12	12.2	37
Elevator installers and repairers	20	24	0.0	0.0	5	24.6	8
Fence erectors	25	32	0.0	0.0	8	30.0	13
Hazardous materials removal workers	38	43	0.0	0.0	5	14.2	13
Highway maintenance workers	148	156	0.1	0.1	8	5.7	30
Rail-track laying and maintenance equipment operators	17	18	0.0	0.0	1	5.2	4
Septic tank servicers and sewer pipe cleaners	25	32	0.0	0.0	7	25.8	12
Miscellaneous construction and related workers	38	43	0.0	0.0	6	14.5	12
Segmental pavers	2	2	0.0	0.0	1	38.1	1
Construction and related workers, all other	36	41	0.0	0.0	5	13.4	11
Extraction workers	267	311	0.2	0.2	44	16.4	126
Derrick, rotary drill, and service unit operators, oil, gas, and mining	108	130	0.1	0.1	22	19.9	65
Derrick operators, oil and gas	23	27	0.0	0.0	4	18.8	14
Rotary drill operators, oil and gas	26	31	0.0	0.0	5	18.6	15
Service unit operators, oil, gas, and mining	59	72	0.0	0.0	12	20.9	36
Earth drillers, except oil and gas	20	23	0.0	0.0	4	19.2	9
Explosives workers, ordnance handling experts, and blasters	6	7	0.0	0.0	0.3	5.2	2
Mining machine operators	24	25	0.0	0.0	0.2	0.8	5
Continuous mining machine operators	14	14	0.0	0.0	-0.1	-0.6	3
Mine cutting and channeling machine operators	7	7	0.0	0.0	0.2	2.7	2
Mining machine operators, all other	3	3	0.0	0.0	0.1	2.7	1
Rock splitters, quarry	5	5	0.0	0.0	1	17.4	1
Roof bolters, mining	7	6	0.0	0.0	-0.3	-4.2	2
Roustabouts, oil and gas	61	73	0.0	0.0	12	19.2	28
Helpers–extraction workers	26	31	0.0	0.0	4	16.6	11
Extraction workers, all other	10	11	0.0	0.0	1	13.5	3

Note: Data may not sum to totals or 100 percent due to rounding.

[1]Total job openings represent the sum of employment increases and net replacements. If employment change is negative, job openings due to growth are zero and total job openings equal net replacements.

Table 4-8. Employment by Occupation, 2012 and Projected 2022—*Continued*

(Numbers in thousands, percent.)

Occupation	Employment				Change, 2012–2022		Total job openings due to growth and net replacements, 2012–2022[1]
	Number		Percent distribution		Number	Percent	
	2012	2022	2012	2022			
Installation, Maintenance, and Repair	5 515	6 046	3.8	3.8	531	9.6	1 814
Supervisors of installation, maintenance, and repair workers	436	470	0.3	0.3	34	7.8	152
First-line supervisors of mechanics, installers, and repairers	436	470	0.3	0.3	34	7.8	152
Electrical and electronic equipment mechanics, installers, and repairers	618	643	0.4	0.4	26	4.1	140
Computer, automated teller, and office machine repairers	133	138	0.1	0.1	5	3.8	33
Radio and telecommunications equipment installers and repairers	234	243	0.2	0.2	10	4.1	42
Radio, cellular, and tower equipment installers and repairs	16	18	0.0	0.0	1	6.6	3
Telecommunications equipment installers and repairers, except line installers	217	226	0.1	0.1	8	3.9	38
Miscellaneous electrical and electronic equipment mechanics, installers, and repairers	251	262	0.2	0.2	11	4.4	66
Avionics technicians	17	18	0.0	0.0	0.5	2.9	4
Electric motor, power tool, and related repairers	21	20	0.0	0.0	-1	-4.1	4
Electrical and electronics installers and repairers, transportation equipment	16	16	0.0	0.0	0.4	2.3	4
Electrical and electronics repairers, commercial and industrial equipment	69	71	0.0	0.0	2	3.4	16
Electrical and electronics repairers, powerhouse, substation, and relay	24	24	0.0	0.0	-0.1	-0.2	5
Electronic equipment installers and repairers, motor vehicles	15	14	0.0	0.0	-1	-5.9	1
Electronic home entertainment equipment installers and repairers	31	32	0.0	0.0	0.4	1.2	11
Security and fire alarm systems installers	58	67	0.0	0.0	9	15.9	21
Vehicle and mobile equipment mechanics, installers, and repairers	1 610	1 751	1.1	1.1	140	8.7	545
Aircraft mechanics and service technicians	122	125	0.1	0.1	3	2.4	36
Automotive technicians and repairers	873	957	0.6	0.6	83	9.5	295
Automotive body and related repairers	154	175	0.1	0.1	20	13.3	50
Automotive glass installers and repairers	18	20	0.0	0.0	2	13.6	7
Automotive service technicians and mechanics	701	762	0.5	0.5	60	8.6	238
Bus and truck mechanics and diesel engine specialists	251	272	0.2	0.2	22	8.6	75
Heavy vehicle and mobile equipment service technicians and mechanics	176	192	0.1	0.1	16	9.2	67
Farm equipment mechanics and service technicians	36	39	0.0	0.0	3	9.5	14
Mobile heavy equipment mechanics, except engines	119	132	0.1	0.1	12	10.3	47
Rail car repairers	21	22	0.0	0.0	0.5	2.5	7
Small engine mechanics	68	72	0.0	0.0	4	5.6	18
Motorboat mechanics and service technicians	21	22	0.0	0.0	1	5.5	6
Motorcycle mechanics	17	18	0.0	0.0	1	6.1	5
Outdoor power equipment and other small engine mechanics	30	32	0.0	0.0	2	5.5	8
Miscellaneous vehicle and mobile equipment mechanics, installers, and repairers	120	132	0.1	0.1	12	10.2	54
Bicycle repairers	11	13	0.0	0.0	3	25.1	6
Recreational vehicle service technicians	11	12	0.0	0.0	1	8.7	5
Tire repairers and changers	98	107	0.1	0.1	9	8.7	43
Other installation, maintenance, and repair occupations	2 850	3 182	2.0	2.0	332	11.6	976
Control and valve installers and repairers	57	60	0.0	0.0	4	6.3	23
Mechanical door repairers	16	20	0.0	0.0	4	23.8	9
Control and valve installers and repairers, except mechanical door	41	41	0.0	0.0	-0.2	-0.5	14
Heating, air conditioning, and refrigeration mechanics and installers	268	324	0.2	0.2	56	20.9	124
Home appliance repairers	44	44	0.0	0.0	0.3	0.7	14
Industrial machinery installation, repair, and maintenance workers	450	527	0.3	0.3	77	17.2	188
Industrial machinery mechanics	319	380	0.2	0.2	60	18.9	152
Maintenance workers, machinery	89	99	0.1	0.1	10	11.1	21
Millwrights	39	47	0.0	0.0	7	18.4	13
Refractory materials repairers, except brickmasons	2	2	0.0	0.0	0	0.4	1
Line installers and repairers	249	268	0.2	0.2	18	7.3	91
Electrical power-line installers and repairers	114	125	0.1	0.1	10	8.9	50
Telecommunications line installers and repairers	135	143	0.1	0.1	8	6.0	41
Precision instrument and equipment repairers	70	85	0.0	0.1	14	20.0	34
Camera and photographic equipment repairers	3	3	0.0	0.0	0.1	3.3	1
Medical equipment repairers	42	55	0.0	0.0	13	30.3	25
Musical instrument repairers and tuners	8	9	0.0	0.0	0.5	6.2	3
Watch repairers	3	3	0.0	0.0	0.1	1.9	1
Precision instrument and equipment repairers, all other	14	14	0.0	0.0	1	4.5	4
Maintenance and repair workers, general	1 325	1 450	0.9	0.9	125	9.4	380
Wind turbine service technicians	3	4	0.0	0.0	1	24.5	1
Miscellaneous installation, maintenance, and repair workers	384	420	0.3	0.3	36	9.3	123
Coin, vending, and amusement machine servicers and repairers	41	40	0.0	0.0	-1	-2.1	4
Commercial divers	4	5	0.0	0.0	1	29.4	2
Fabric menders, except garment	1	1	0.0	0.0	-0.1	-10.4	0.2
Locksmiths and safe repairers	22	24	0.0	0.0	2	7.4	9
Manufactured building and mobile home installers	5	4	0.0	0.0	-1	-15.1	1
Riggers	15	19	0.0	0.0	4	23.3	7
Signal and track switch repairers	9	9	0.0	0.0	-0.1	-1.2	2
Helpers—installation, maintenance, and repair workers	128	145	0.1	0.1	18	13.7	56
Installation, maintenance, and repair workers, all other	160	174	0.1	0.1	14	8.8	41
Production	8 942	9 018	6.2	5.6	76	0.8	2 151
Supervisors of production workers	595	584	0.4	0.4	-10	-1.8	84
First-line supervisors of production and operating workers	595	584	0.4	0.4	-10	-1.8	84
Assemblers and fabricators	1 755	1 819	1.2	1.1	64	3.7	372
Aircraft structure, surfaces, rigging, and systems assemblers	42	44	0.0	0.0	2	5.8	9
Electrical, electronics, and electromechanical assemblers	263	245	0.2	0.2	-19	-7.1	32
Coil winders, tapers, and finishers	14	13	0.0	0.0	-2	-10.5	2
Electrical and electronic equipment assemblers	198	185	0.1	0.1	-14	-6.8	24
Electromechanical equipment assemblers	50	47	0.0	0.0	-4	-7.1	6
Engine and other machine assemblers	42	41	0.0	0.0	-1	-1.4	7
Structural metal fabricators and fitters	80	86	0.1	0.1	6	7.7	38
Miscellaneous assemblers and fabricators	1 329	1 404	0.9	0.9	75	5.6	286
Fiberglass laminators and fabricators	18	17	0.0	0.0	-1	-4.1	3
Team assemblers	1 032	1 081	0.7	0.7	50	4.8	213
Timing device assemblers and adjusters	1	1	0.0	0.0	0	-2.6	0.2
Assemblers and fabricators, all other	278	304	0.2	0.2	26	9.4	70

Note: Data may not sum to totals or 100 percent due to rounding.

[1]Total job openings represent the sum of employment increases and net replacements. If employment change is negative, job openings due to growth are zero and total job openings equal net replacements.

Table 4-8. Employment by Occupation, 2012 and Projected 2022—*Continued*

(Numbers in thousands, percent.)

Occupation	Employment				Change, 2012–2022		Total job openings due to growth and net replacements, 2012–2022[1]
	Number		Percent distribution		Number	Percent	
	2012	2022	2012	2022			
Production—*Continued*							
Food processing workers	747	770	0.5	0.5	23	3.1	221
Bakers	168	177	0.1	0.1	9	5.6	50
Butchers and other meat, poultry, and fish processing workers	381	394	0.3	0.2	13	3.5	109
Butchers and meat cutters	137	143	0.1	0.1	6	4.8	40
Meat, poultry, and fish cutters and trimmers	163	172	0.1	0.1	9	5.3	49
Slaughterers and meat packers	81	79	0.1	0.0	-2	-2.4	20
Miscellaneous food processing workers	198	199	0.1	0.1	0.5	0.2	62
Food and tobacco roasting, baking, and drying machine operators and tenders	20	20	0.0	0.0	0.2	0.9	5
Food batchmakers	105	102	0.1	0.1	-3	-2.6	34
Food cooking machine operators and tenders	33	33	0.0	0.0	-0.2	-0.6	9
Food processing workers, all other	40	43	0.0	0.0	3	8.1	14
Metal workers and plastic workers	1 898	1 894	1.3	1.2	-4	-0.2	469
Computer control programmers and operators	165	192	0.1	0.1	27	16.5	73
Computer-controlled machine tool operators, metal and plastic	140	161	0.1	0.1	20	14.5	60
Computer numerically controlled machine tool programmers, metal and plastic	24	31	0.0	0.0	7	27.6	14
Forming machine setters, operators, and tenders, metal and plastic	134	116	0.1	0.1	-18	-13.7	26
Extruding and drawing machine setters, operators, and tenders, metal and plastic	75	63	0.1	0.0	-12	-15.9	14
Forging machine setters, operators, and tenders, metal and plastic	23	20	0.0	0.0	-3	-12.8	4
Rolling machine setters, operators, and tenders, metal and plastic	36	33	0.0	0.0	-4	-9.9	7
Machine tool cutting setters, operators, and tenders, metal and plastic	339	300	0.2	0.2	-38	-11.4	48
Cutting, punching, and press machine setters, operators, and tenders, metal and plastic	185	168	0.1	0.1	-16	-8.9	16
Drilling and boring machine tool setters, operators, and tenders, metal and plastic	21	16	0.0	0.0	-5	-22.5	4
Grinding, lapping, polishing, and buffing machine tool setters, operators, and tenders, metal and plastic	72	62	0.0	0.0	-9	-12.6	16
Lathe and turning machine tool setters, operators, and tenders, metal and plastic	39	33	0.0	0.0	-5	-14.0	7
Milling and planing machine setters, operators, and tenders, metal and plastic	23	20	0.0	0.0	-3	-12.6	4
Machinists	398	432	0.3	0.3	35	8.8	126
Metal furnace operators, tenders, pourers, and casters	32	27	0.0	0.0	-4	-13.6	4
Metal-refining furnace operators and tenders	21	18	0.0	0.0	-2	-10.9	3
Pourers and casters, metal	11	9	0.0	0.0	-2	-18.7	1
Model makers and patternmakers, metal and plastic	11	11	0.0	0.0	0.4	3.8	2
Model makers, metal and plastic	6	6	0.0	0.0	0.1	2.2	1
Patternmakers, metal and plastic	4	5	0.0	0.0	0.3	6.0	1
Molders and molding machine setters, operators, and tenders, metal and plastic	138	116	0.1	0.1	-21	-15.4	17
Foundry mold and coremakers	12	10	0.0	0.0	-2	-16.2	2
Molding, coremaking, and casting machine setters, operators, and tenders, metal and plastic	125	106	0.1	0.1	-19	-15.4	15
Multiple machine tool setters, operators, and tenders, metal and plastic	86	74	0.1	0.0	-11	-13.2	17
Tool and die makers	79	78	0.1	0.0	-1	-1.4	5
Welding, soldering, and brazing workers	411	442	0.3	0.3	31	7.6	132
Welders, cutters, solderers, and brazers	357	378	0.2	0.2	21	5.8	108
Welding, soldering, and brazing machine setters, operators, and tenders	54	64	0.0	0.0	11	19.8	24
Miscellaneous metal workers and plastic workers	108	106	0.1	0.1	-3	-2.8	20
Heat treating equipment setters, operators, and tenders, metal and plastic	22	22	0.0	0.0	-0.4	-1.9	4
Layout workers, metal and plastic	13	12	0.0	0.0	-0.4	-3.0	2
Plating and coating machine setters, operators, and tenders, metal and plastic	35	32	0.0	0.0	-3	-8.6	7
Tool grinders, filers, and sharpeners	13	13	0.0	0.0	0.1	0.4	2
Metal workers and plastic workers, all other	26	27	0.0	0.0	1	2.9	4
Printing workers	276	262	0.2	0.2	-14	-5.3	52
Prepress technicians and workers	43	37	0.0	0.0	-6	-12.9	11
Printing press operators	178	171	0.1	0.1	-7	-3.9	31
Print binding and finishing workers	55	53	0.0	0.0	-2	-3.7	10
Textile, apparel, and furnishings workers	658	611	0.5	0.4	-47	-7.1	135
Laundry and dry-cleaning workers	211	231	0.1	0.1	20	9.7	83
Pressers, textile, garment, and related materials	54	56	0.0	0.0	1	2.6	7
Sewing machine operators	161	120	0.1	0.1	-42	-25.8	8
Shoe and leather workers	12	10	0.0	0.0	-2	-20.1	2
Shoe and leather workers and repairers	9	7	0.0	0.0	-1	-14.0	1
Shoe machine operators and tenders	4	2	0.0	0.0	-1	-35.3	1
Tailors, dressmakers, and sewers	61	59	0.0	0.0	-2	-3.1	6
Sewers, hand	11	10	0.0	0.0	-1	-9.3	1
Tailors, dressmakers, and custom sewers	50	49	0.0	0.0	-1	-1.8	5
Textile machine setters, operators, and tenders	76	58	0.1	0.0	-18	-23.5	12
Textile bleaching and dyeing machine operators and tenders	11	9	0.0	0.0	-3	-24.0	2
Textile cutting machine setters, operators, and tenders	16	11	0.0	0.0	-4	-27.1	2
Textile knitting and weaving machine setters, operators, and tenders	22	16	0.0	0.0	-5	-24.5	4
Textile winding, twisting, and drawing out machine setters, operators, and tenders	28	22	0.0	0.0	-6	-20.5	4
Miscellaneous textile, apparel, and furnishings workers	82	77	0.1	0.0	-5	-5.9	16
Extruding and forming machine setters, operators, and tenders, synthetic and glass fibers	18	16	0.0	0.0	-2	-12.2	3
Fabric and apparel patternmakers	6	5	0.0	0.0	-2	-25.0	1
Upholsterers	41	41	0.0	0.0	0.3	0.7	11
Textile, apparel, and furnishings workers, all other	16	15	0.0	0.0	-1	-8.2	1
Woodworkers	222	239	0.2	0.1	17	7.5	46
Cabinetmakers and bench carpenters	86	90	0.1	0.1	4	4.1	10
Furniture finishers	15	15	0.0	0.0	0.5	3.3	3
Model makers and patternmakers, wood	2	2	0.0	0.0	0.1	3.5	0.4
Model makers, wood	1	1	0.0	0.0	0.1	5.5	0.3
Patternmakers, wood	1	1	0.0	0.0	0	0.2	0.1
Woodworking machine setters, operators, and tenders	102	113	0.1	0.1	12	11.5	26
Sawing machine setters, operators, and tenders, wood	40	46	0.0	0.0	5	13.5	17
Woodworking machine setters, operators, and tenders, except sawing	62	68	0.0	0.0	6	10.2	10
Woodworkers, all other	18	18	0.0	0.0	1	5.0	7

Note: Data may not sum to totals or 100 percent due to rounding.

[1]Total job openings represent the sum of employment increases and net replacements. If employment change is negative, job openings due to growth are zero and total job openings equal net replacements.

Table 4-8. Employment by Occupation, 2012 and Projected 2022—*Continued*

(Numbers in thousands, percent.)

Occupation	Employment				Change, 2012–2022		Total job openings due to growth and net replacements, 2012–2022[1]
	Number		Percent distribution		Number	Percent	
	2012	2022	2012	2022			
Production—*Continued*							
Plant and system operators	314	312	0.2	0.2	-2	-0.8	118
Power plant operators, distributors, and dispatchers	61	56	0.0	0.0	-5	-7.6	19
Nuclear power reactor operators	7	7	0.0	0.0	0	0.5	2
Power distributors and dispatchers	12	12	0.0	0.0	-0.1	-0.9	4
Power plant operators	42	37	0.0	0.0	-4	-10.8	13
Stationary engineers and boiler operators	38	39	0.0	0.0	1	3.1	13
Water and wastewater treatment plant and system operators	111	120	0.1	0.1	9	7.7	48
Miscellaneous plant and system operators	105	97	0.1	0.1	-8	-7.2	39
Chemical plant and system operators	38	34	0.0	0.0	-4	-11.5	14
Gas plant operators	12	11	0.0	0.0	-1	-8.8	5
Petroleum pump system operators, refinery operators, and gaugers	42	40	0.0	0.0	-2	-5.1	16
Plant and system operators, all other	12	12	0.0	0.0	0.1	0.7	4
Other production occupations	2 477	2 527	1.7	1.6	50	2.0	655
Chemical processing machine setters, operators, and tenders	98	92	0.1	0.1	-6	-6.0	34
Chemical equipment operators and tenders	56	52	0.0	0.0	-5	-8.3	20
Separating, filtering, clarifying, precipitating, and still machine setters, operators, and tenders	41	40	0.0	0.0	-1	-2.9	14
Crushing, grinding, polishing, mixing, and blending workers	182	177	0.1	0.1	-5	-2.7	51
Crushing, grinding, and polishing machine setters, operators, and tenders	30	30	0.0	0.0	-1	-2.3	8
Grinding and polishing workers, hand	32	31	0.0	0.0	-0.5	-1.7	9
Mixing and blending machine setters, operators, and tenders	120	116	0.1	0.1	-4	-3.1	34
Cutting workers	73	66	0.0	0.0	-7	-9.7	12
Cutters and trimmers, hand	14	12	0.0	0.0	-2	-15.3	2
Cutting and slicing machine setters, operators, and tenders	58	53	0.0	0.0	-5	-8.4	10
Extruding, forming, pressing, and compacting machine setters, operators, and tenders	71	68	0.0	0.0	-2	-3.2	19
Furnace, kiln, oven, drier, and kettle operators and tenders	20	20	0.0	0.0	-1	-4.3	5
Inspectors, testers, sorters, samplers, and weighers	464	490	0.3	0.3	26	5.5	128
Jewelers and precious stone and metal workers	33	30	0.0	0.0	-3	-9.8	7
Medical, dental, and ophthalmic laboratory technicians	83	88	0.1	0.1	6	6.7	34
Dental laboratory technicians	39	40	0.0	0.0	1	2.6	14
Medical appliance technicians	13	14	0.0	0.0	1	6.4	5
Ophthalmic laboratory technicians	31	35	0.0	0.0	4	12.1	14
Packaging and filling machine operators and tenders	369	371	0.3	0.2	2	0.6	89
Painting workers	150	155	0.1	0.1	6	3.7	33
Coating, painting, and spraying machine setters, operators, and tenders	84	84	0.1	0.1	0.4	0.5	16
Painters, transportation equipment	49	54	0.0	0.0	5	10.4	14
Painting, coating, and decorating workers	17	17	0.0	0.0	0	0.2	3
Semiconductor processors	21	16	0.0	0.0	-6	-27.1	5
Photographic process workers and processing machine operators	47	47	0.0	0.0	0.1	0.2	14
Miscellaneous production workers	867	908	0.6	0.6	41	4.7	224
Adhesive bonding machine operators and tenders	17	17	0.0	0.0	0.1	0.6	4
Cleaning, washing, and metal pickling equipment operators and tenders	16	16	0.0	0.0	-0.1	-0.6	4
Cooling and freezing equipment operators and tenders	8	8	0.0	0.0	0.1	1.0	2
Etchers and engravers	10	9	0.0	0.0	-0.4	-3.8	2
Molders, shapers, and casters, except metal and plastic	42	45	0.0	0.0	3	7.5	17
Paper goods machine setters, operators, and tenders	95	88	0.1	0.1	-8	-8.0	8
Tire builders	17	16	0.0	0.0	-2	-8.8	4
Helpers--production workers	420	450	0.3	0.3	30	7.1	102
Production workers, all other	242	259	0.2	0.2	18	7.3	81
Transportation and Material Moving	9 246	10 036	6.4	6.2	791	8.6	2 992
Supervisors of transportation and material moving workers	380	412	0.3	0.3	32	8.4	136
Aircraft cargo handling supervisors	7	7	0.0	0.0	0	0.7	2
First-line supervisors of helpers, laborers, and material movers, hand	172	186	0.1	0.1	15	8.5	62
First-line supervisors of transportation and material-moving machine and vehicle operators	201	218	0.1	0.1	17	8.6	73
Air transportation workers	221	215	0.2	0.1	-6	-2.6	62
Aircraft pilots and flight engineers	104	103	0.1	0.1	-1	-0.8	34
Airline pilots, copilots, and flight engineers	66	62	0.0	0.0	-4	-6.6	19
Commercial pilots	38	41	0.0	0.0	4	9.4	14
Air traffic controllers and airfield operations specialists	32	33	0.0	0.0	1	2.3	15
Air traffic controllers	25	25	0.0	0.0	0.4	1.4	11
Airfield operations specialists	7	8	0.0	0.0	0.4	5.1	4
Flight attendants	85	79	0.1	0.0	-6	-6.5	14
Motor vehicle operators	3 945	4 314	2.7	2.7	369	9.3	1 013
Ambulance drivers and attendants, except emergency medical technicians	19	25	0.0	0.0	6	31.1	9
Bus drivers	654	712	0.5	0.4	58	8.9	178
Bus drivers, transit and intercity	171	187	0.1	0.1	17	9.8	48
Bus drivers, school or special client	484	525	0.3	0.3	41	8.5	130
Driver/sales workers and truck drivers	2 975	3 236	2.0	2.0	261	8.8	737
Driver/sales workers	432	469	0.3	0.3	37	8.5	106
Heavy and tractor-trailer truck drivers	1 702	1 894	1.2	1.2	193	11.3	465
Light truck or delivery services drivers	842	874	0.6	0.5	32	3.8	167
Taxi drivers and chauffeurs	233	269	0.2	0.2	36	15.5	64
Motor vehicle operators, all other	64	72	0.0	0.0	7	11.5	25
Rail transportation workers	126	123	0.1	0.1	-3	-2.6	39
Locomotive engineers and operators	45	43	0.0	0.0	-2	-4.5	14
Locomotive engineers	38	36	0.0	0.0	-2	-3.9	11
Locomotive firers	2	1	0.0	0.0	-1	-42.0	0.5
Rail yard engineers, dinkey operators, and hostlers	5	5	0.0	0.0	0.1	2.4	2
Railroad brake, signal, and switch operators	25	24	0.0	0.0	-1	-2.6	8
Railroad conductors and yardmasters	44	42	0.0	0.0	-1	-2.9	13
Subway and streetcar operators	9	10	0.0	0.0	1	6.5	3
Rail transportation workers, all other	3	3	0.0	0.0	0.1	2.2	1

Note: Data may not sum to totals or 100 percent due to rounding.

[1]Total job openings represent the sum of employment increases and net replacements. If employment change is negative, job openings due to growth are zero and total job openings equal net replacements.

Table 4-8. Employment by Occupation, 2012 and Projected 2022—*Continued*

(Numbers in thousands, percent.)

Occupation	Employment				Change, 2012–2022		Total job openings due to growth and net replacements, 2012–2022[1]
	Number		Percent distribution		Number	Percent	
	2012	2022	2012	2022			
Transportation—*Continued*							
Water transportation workers	82	92	0.1	0.1	11	13.3	48
Sailors and marine oilers	32	37	0.0	0.0	5	15.5	19
Ship and boat captains and operators	39	44	0.0	0.0	5	13.1	23
Captains, mates, and pilots of water vessels	35	40	0.0	0.0	5	13.8	21
Motorboat operators	3	4	0.0	0.0	0.2	5.7	2
Ship engineers	11	12	0.0	0.0	1	7.8	6
Other transportation workers	335	372	0.2	0.2	37	11.1	161
Bridge and lock tenders	4	4	0.0	0.0	-0.1	-2.0	1
Parking lot attendants	128	138	0.1	0.1	9	7.3	71
Automotive and watercraft service attendants	110	129	0.1	0.1	20	18.1	51
Traffic technicians	7	7	0.0	0.0	1	11.7	3
Transportation inspectors	26	29	0.0	0.0	3	11.2	12
Transportation attendants, except flight attendants	23	26	0.0	0.0	3	11.0	6
Transportation workers, all other	37	39	0.0	0.0	2	5.1	16
Material moving workers	4 158	4 508	2.9	2.8	351	8.4	1 532
Conveyor operators and tenders	39	40	0.0	0.0	1	3.4	12
Crane and tower operators	44	51	0.0	0.0	7	16.8	22
Dredge, excavating, and loading machine operators	56	64	0.0	0.0	8	15.1	13
Dredge operators	2	2	0.0	0.0	0.3	13.3	0.4
Excavating and loading machine and dragline operators	51	59	0.0	0.0	8	16.2	12
Loading machine operators, underground mining	3	3	0.0	0.0	0	-0.6	0.3
Hoist and winch operators	3	3	0.0	0.0	0.1	2.7	1
Industrial truck and tractor operators	509	495	0.3	0.3	-14	-2.7	117
Laborers and material movers, hand	3 296	3 616	2.3	2.2	320	9.7	1 287
Cleaners of vehicles and equipment	325	361	0.2	0.2	36	11.1	126
Laborers and freight, stock, and material movers, hand	2 197	2 439	1.5	1.5	242	11.0	922
Machine feeders and offbearers	106	108	0.1	0.1	2	2.0	23
Packers and packagers, hand	667	707	0.5	0.4	40	6.0	215
Pumping station operators	34	38	0.0	0.0	4	10.7	16
Gas compressor and gas pumping station operators	5	5	0.0	0.0	-0.1	-3.1	2
Pump operators, except wellhead pumpers	13	15	0.0	0.0	1	10.8	6
Wellhead pumpers	16	19	0.0	0.0	2	14.8	8
Refuse and recyclable material collectors	133	155	0.1	0.1	22	16.2	49
Mine shuttle car operators	3	3	0.0	0.0	-0.1	-3.7	1
Tank car, truck, and ship loaders	12	13	0.0	0.0	0.3	2.7	4
Material moving workers, all other	29	30	0.0	0.0	2	5.3	9

Note: Data may not sum to totals or 100 percent due to rounding.

[1]Total job openings represent the sum of employment increases and net replacements. If employment change is negative, job openings due to growth are zero and total job openings equal net replacements.

Table 4-9. Employment and Total Job Openings by Education, Work Experience, and On-the Job Training Category, 2012 and Projected 2022

(Numbers in thousands, percent, dollars.)

Education, work experience, and on-the-job training	Employment				Change, 2012–2022		Total job openings due to growth and replacement needs, 2012–2022[1]		Median annual wage
	Number		Percent distribution		Number	Percent	Number	Percent distribution	
	2012	2022	2012	2022					
TOTAL, ALL OCCUPATIONS	145 355.8	160 983.7	100.0	100.0	15 628.0	10.8	50 557.3	100.0	34 750
Typical Education Needed for Entry									
Doctoral or professional degree	4 002.4	4 640.8	2.8	2.9	638.4	16.0	1 426.8	2.8	96 420
Master's degree	2 432.2	2 880.7	1.7	1.8	448.5	18.4	950.8	1.9	63 400
Bachelor's degree	26 033.0	29 176.7	17.9	18.1	3 143.6	12.1	8 618.7	17.0	67 140
Associate's degree	5 954.9	7 000.9	4.1	4.3	1 046.0	17.6	2 269.5	4.5	57 590
Postsecondary non-degree award	8 554.2	9 891.2	5.9	6.1	1 337.1	15.6	3 067.2	6.1	34 760
Some college, no degree	1 987.2	2 212.2	1.4	1.4	225.0	11.3	642.6	1.3	28 730
High school diploma or equivalent	58 264.4	62 895.2	40.1	39.1	4 630.8	7.9	17 667.4	34.9	35 170
Less than high school	38 127.6	42 286.0	26.2	26.3	4 158.4	10.9	15 914.3	31.5	20 110
Work Experience in a Related Occupation[2]									
More than 5 years	4 831.9	5 091.8	3.3	3.2	259.9	5.4	1 330.9	2.6	90 760
Less than 5 years	16 167.7	17 663.5	11.1	11.0	1 495.9	9.3	4 863.4	9.6	52 270
None	124 356.2	138 228.4	85.6	85.9	13 872.2	11.2	44 363.0	87.7	32 260
Typical On-the-Job Training									
Internship/residency	5 989.1	6 658.9	4.1	4.1	669.8	11.2	1 997.8	4.0	53 570
Apprenticeship	2 336.9	2 855.2	1.6	1.8	518.3	22.2	879.8	1.7	45 440
Long-term	6 876.5	7 448.7	4.7	4.6	572.2	8.3	2 163.7	4.3	41 810
Moderate-term	23 057.8	24 968.5	15.9	15.5	1 910.8	8.3	6 841.0	13.5	36 950
Short-term	58 928.4	64 673.7	40.5	40.2	5 745.3	9.7	22 273.7	44.1	22 960
None	48 167.2	54 378.8	33.1	33.8	6 211.6	12.9	16 401.3	32.4	56 970

[1]Total job openings represent the sum of employment increases and replacement needs. If employment change is negative, then job openings due to growth are zero and total job openings equals replacements.
[2]Indicates if work experience in a related occupation is commonly considered necessary by employers for entry, or is a commonly accepted substitute for formal types of training.

Table 4-10. Civilian Labor Force: Entrants and Leavers, 2002, 2012, and Projected 2022

(Numbers in thousands, percent.)

Characteristic	2002	2002–2012			2012	2012–2022			2022
		Entrants	Leavers	Stayers		Entrants	Leavers	Stayers	
NUMBER, 16 YEARS AND OVER									
Total	144 863	33 226	23 115	121 749	154 975	35 429	26 954	128 021	163 450
Men	77 500	17 742	12 915	64 585	82 327	19 723	15 137	67 190	86 913
Women	67 364	15 484	10 200	57 164	72 648	15 706	11 817	60 831	76 537
White	120 150	24 115	20 581	99 569	123 684	25 821	22 583	101 101	126 923
Men	65 308	13 292	11 679	53 629	66 921	14 789	12 722	54 199	68 989
Women	54 842	10 823	8 902	45 940	56 763	11 032	9 861	46 902	57 934
Black	16 565	4 541	2 708	13 858	18 400	5 033	3 185	15 184	20 247
Men	7 794	2 109	1 309	6 485	8 594	2 523	1 570	6 994	9 547
Women	8 772	2 432	1 399	7 373	9 805	2 510	1 615	8 190	10 700
Asian	6 604	2 394	811	5 793	8 188	3 025	1 078	7 109	10 135
Men	3 567	1 237	470	3 097	4 334	1 601	594	3 740	5 341
Women	3 037	1 157	341	2 696	3 853	1 424	484	3 369	4 794
All other groups[1]	1 544	...	...	...	4 703	...	...	...	6 145
Men	831	...	...	...	2 478	...	...	...	3 036
Women	713	...	...	...	2 227	...	...	...	3 109
Hispanic origin[2]	17 943	7 969	1 522	16 422	24 391	9 220	2 432	21 959	31 179
Men	10 610	4 292	876	9 734	14 026	5 371	1 472	12 554	17 925
Women	7 334	3 677	646	6 688	10 365	3 849	960	9 405	13 254
Other than Hispanic origin	126 920	25 257	21 593	105 327	130 584	26 209	24 522	106 062	132 271
Men	66 890	13 450	12 039	54 851	68 301	14 352	13 665	54 636	68 988
Women	60 030	11 807	9 554	50 476	62 283	11 857	10 857	51 426	63 283
White Non-Hispanic	103 349	17 863	19 320	84 029	101 892	17 858	20 319	81 573	99 431
Men	55 340	9 597	10 612	44 728	54 325	10 235	11 278	43 047	53 282
Women	48 009	8 266	8 708	39 301	47 567	7 623	9 041	38 526	46 149
SHARE, 16 YEARS AND OVER									
Total	100.0	100.0	100.0	100.0	100.0	100.0	100.0	100.0	100.0
Men	53.5	53.4	55.9	53.0	53.1	55.7	56.2	52.5	53.2
Women	46.5	46.6	44.1	47.0	46.9	44.3	43.8	47.5	46.8
White	82.9	72.6	89.0	81.8	79.8	72.9	83.8	79.0	77.7
Men	45.1	40.0	50.5	44.0	43.2	41.7	47.2	42.3	42.2
Women	37.9	32.6	38.5	37.7	36.6	31.1	36.6	36.6	35.4
Black	11.4	13.7	11.7	11.4	11.9	14.2	11.8	11.9	12.4
Men	5.4	6.3	5.7	5.3	5.5	7.1	5.8	5.5	5.8
Women	6.1	7.3	6.1	6.1	6.3	7.1	6.0	6.4	6.5
Asian	4.6	7.2	3.5	4.8	5.3	8.5	4.0	5.6	6.2
Men	2.5	3.7	2.0	2.5	2.8	4.5	2.2	2.9	3.3
Women	2.1	3.5	1.5	2.2	2.5	4.0	1.8	2.6	2.9
All other groups[1]	...	...	...	...	3.0	...	...	...	3.8
Men	...	...	...	...	1.6	...	...	...	1.9
Women	...	...	...	...	1.4	...	...	...	1.9
Hispanic origin[2]	12.4	24.0	6.6	13.5	15.7	26.0	9.0	17.2	19.1
Men	7.3	12.9	3.8	8.0	9.1	15.2	5.5	9.8	11.0
Women	5.1	11.1	2.8	5.5	6.7	10.9	3.6	7.3	8.1
Other than Hispanic	87.6	76.0	93.4	86.5	84.3	74.0	91.0	82.8	80.9
Men	46.2	40.5	52.1	45.1	44.1	40.5	50.7	42.7	42.2
Women	41.4	35.5	41.3	41.5	40.2	33.5	40.3	40.2	38.7
White Non-Hispanic	71.3	53.8	83.6	69.0	65.7	50.4	75.4	63.7	60.8
Men	38.2	28.9	45.9	36.7	35.1	28.9	41.8	33.6	32.6
Women	33.1	24.9	37.7	32.3	30.7	21.5	33.5	30.1	28.2

[1]The "All other groups" category includes those classified as of multiple racial origin and the race categories of American Indian and Alaska Native and Native Hawaiian and Other Pacific Islanders.
[2]May be of any race.
... = Not available.

CHAPTER 5: PRODUCTIVITY AND COSTS

HIGHLIGHTS

This chapter covers two kinds of productivity measures produced by the Bureau of Labor Statistics (BLS): output per hour (or labor productivity) and multifactor productivity. Multifactor productivity is designed to combine the joint influence of technological change, efficiency improvements, returns to scale, and other factors on economic growth.

Figure 5-1. Percent Change in Output Per Hour in Information Industries, 2010–2011

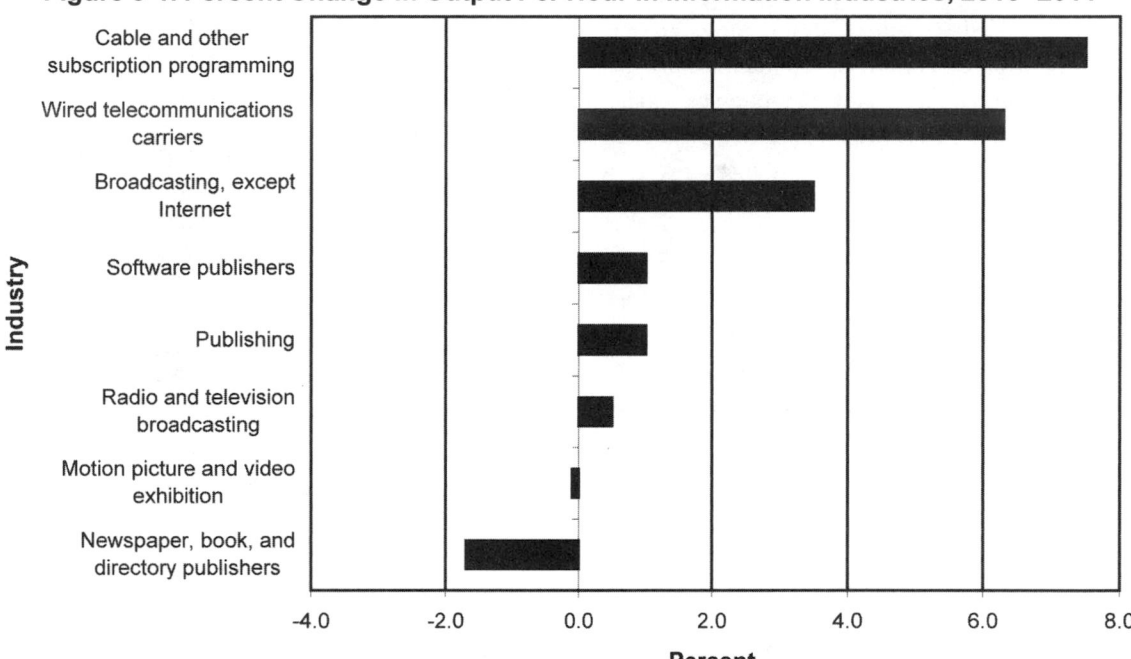

From 2010 to 2011, output per hour increased in seven out of nine information industries declining in newspaper, book, and directory publishing and motion picture and video exhibition. Wireless telecommunications carriers experienced the largest increase at 10.0 percent, followed by cable and other subscription programming at 7.5 percent. (See Table 5-2.)

OTHER HIGHLIGHTS

- Labor productivity grew 1.8 percent in manufacturing as output grew 4.2 percent and hours grew 2.3 percent. Employment and hours continued to increase in 2012 in the manufacturing, business, and nonfinancial sectors after showing sharp declines just a few years earlier. (See Table 5-1.)

- Output per hour increased in 63 percent of the 52 service-providing and mining industries in 2011, while unit labor costs declined in 35 percent of industries in 2011. (See Table 5-2.)

- Between 1987 and 2012, labor productivity increased 3.0 percent in wholesale trade and 2.8 percent in retail trade, but only 0.6 percent in food services and drinking places. (See Table 5-3.)

NOTES AND DEFINITIONS

PRODUCTIVITY AND COSTS

The Bureau of Labor Statistics (BLS) produces labor productivity and costs (LPC) measures for sectors of the U.S. economy. Productivity is a measure of economic efficiency that shows how effectively economic inputs are converted into output. The Major Sector Productivity program develops quarterly labor productivity measures for the major U.S. economic sectors including the business sector, the nonfarm business sector, nonfinancial corporations, and manufacturing, along with subsectors of durable and nondurable goods manufacturing. The Industry Productivity program develops annual labor productivity and unit labor cost measures for U.S. industries. In addition, the BLS produces multifactor productivity measures.

Quarterly labor productivity measures are available for business and nonfarm business sectors, nonfinancial corporations, and the manufacturing sector. Annual labor productivity measures are available for selected 2-, 3-, 4-, 5-, and 6-digit NAICS industries.

CONCEPTS AND DEFINITIONS

Business sector output is an annual-weighted index constructed after excluding from gross domestic product (GDP) the following outputs: general government, nonprofit institutions, paid employees of private households, and the rental value of owner-occupied dwellings. Corresponding exclusions also are made in labor inputs. The nonfarm business sector output also excludes the farm sector. Gross domestic product data are prepared by the Bureau of Economic Analysis of the U.S. Department of Commerce as part of the National Income and Product Accounts.

Hourly compensation costs are defined as the sum of wage and salary accruals and supplements to wages and salaries. Wage and salary accruals consist of the monetary remuneration of employees, including the compensation of corporate officers; commissions, tips, and bonuses; voluntary employee contributions to certain deferred compensation plans, such as 401(k) plans; employee gains from exercising nonqualified stock options; and receipts in kind that represent income. Supplements to wages and salaries consist of employer contributions for social insurance and employer payments (including payments in kind) to private pension and profit-sharing plans, group health and life insurance plans, and privately administered workers' compensation plans. For employees (wage and salary workers), hourly compensation is measured relative to hours at work and includes payments made by employers for time not at work, such as vacation,

holiday, and sick pay. Because compensation costs for the business and nonfarm business sectors would otherwise be severely understated, an estimate of the hourly compensation of proprietors of unincorporated businesses is made by assuming that their hourly compensation is equal to that of employees in the same sector.

Hours at work include paid time working, traveling between job sites, coffee breaks, and machine downtime. Hours at work, however, exclude hours for which employees are paid but not at work.

The *nonfarm business sector* is a subset of the domestic economy and excludes the economic activities of the following: general government, private households, nonprofit organizations serving individuals, and farms.

Nonfinancial corporations are a subset of the domestic economy and excludes the economic activities of the following: general government, private households, nonprofit organizations serving individuals, and those corporations classified as offices of bank holding companies, offices of other holding companies, or offices in the finance and insurance sector.

Nonlabor payments include profits, consumption of fixed capital, taxes on production and imports less subsidies, net interest and miscellaneous payments, business current transfer payments, rental income of persons, and the current surplus of government enterprises.

Output is measured as an annual-weighted index of the changes in the various products or services (in real terms) provided for sale outside the industry. Real industry output is usually derived by deflating nominal sales or values of production using BLS price indexes, but for some industries it is measured by physical quantities of output. Industry output measures are constructed primarily using data from the economic censuses and annual surveys of the U.S. Census Bureau, U.S. Department of Commerce, together with information on price changes primarily from BLS. Output measures for some mining and utilities industries are based on physical quantity data from the Energy Information Administration, U.S. Department of Energy, while output measures for some transportation industries are based on physical quantity data from the Bureau of Transportation Statistics, U.S. Department of Transportation. Other data sources for some industries include the U.S. Geological Survey, U.S. Department of the Interior; the U.S. Postal Service; the Federal Deposit Insurance Corporation; and the Postal Rate Commission.

Productivity measures describe the relationship between industry output and the labor time involved in its production. They show the changes from period to period in the amount of goods and services produced per hour. Although the labor productivity measures relate output to hours of employees or all persons in an industry, they do not measure the specific contribution of labor or any other factor of production. Rather, they reflect the joint effects of many influences, including changes in technology; capital investment; utilization of capacity, energy, and materials; the use of purchased services inputs, including contract employment services; the organization of production; managerial skill; and the characteristics and effort of the workforce.

Unit labor costs show the growth in compensation relative to that of real output. These costs are calculated by dividing total labor compensation by real output. Changes in unit labor costs can be approximated by subtracting the change in productivity from the change in hourly compensation.

MULTIFACTOR PRODUCTIVITY CONCEPTS AND DEFINITIONS

For the private business and private nonfarm business sectors, the growth rate of multifactor productivity is measured as the growth rate of output less the growth rate of combined inputs of labor and capital. Labor is measured by a weighted average of the number of hours worked classified by education, work experience, and gender. Capital services measure the flow of services from the stocks of equipment and software, structures, land, and inventories. For the manufacturing sector, multifactor productivity is the growth rate of output less the combined inputs of labor, capital, and intermediate purchases. Labor is measured by the number of hours worked. Capital services measure the flow of services from the stocks of equipment and software, structures, land, and inventories. Intermediate purchases are composed of materials, fuels, electricity, and purchased services.

Sectoral output is defined as gross output excluding intra-industry transactions. This measure defines output as deliveries to consumers outside the sector, in an effort to avoid the problem of double-counting that occurs when one establishment provides materials used by other establishments in the same industry.

Value-added output is defined as gross output (sales or receipts and other income, plus inventory change) minus intermediate inputs (goods and service inputs purchased from other domestic industries and foreign sources).

SOURCES OF ADDITIONAL INFORMATION

Productivity concepts and methodology are described in Chapters 10 and 11 of the *BLS Handbook of Methods*. More information on productivity can be found in BLS news releases on the BLS Web site at http://www.bls.gov/lpc/.

Table 5-1. Indexes of Productivity and Related Data, 1947–2012

(2009 = 100.)

Year	Business											
	Output per hour	Output	Hours	Hourly compensation	Real hourly compensation	Unit labor costs	Unit nonlabor payments	Implicit price deflator	Employment	Output per job	Compensation in current dollars	Nonlabor payments in current dollars
1947	21.5	12.3	57.2	3.8	33.7	17.9	12.9	15.8	48.4	25.4	2.2	1.6
1948	22.4	12.9	57.6	4.2	33.8	18.6	14.3	16.8	48.9	26.4	2.4	1.8
1949	22.9	12.8	55.7	4.2	34.7	18.4	14.1	16.6	47.8	26.7	2.4	1.8
1950	24.8	14.0	56.5	4.5	36.7	18.2	14.8	16.8	48.3	29.0	2.6	2.1
1951	25.6	14.9	58.3	5.0	37.3	19.4	16.3	18.1	49.6	30.1	2.9	2.4
1952	26.3	15.4	58.4	5.3	38.8	20.0	16.0	18.3	49.8	30.9	3.1	2.5
1953	27.3	16.2	59.2	5.6	41.0	20.5	15.6	18.5	50.5	32.0	3.3	2.5
1954	27.9	16.0	57.2	5.8	42.0	20.7	15.6	18.6	49.3	32.4	3.3	2.5
1955	29.1	17.3	59.3	5.9	43.2	20.3	16.6	18.8	50.7	34.0	3.5	2.9
1956	29.2	17.6	60.2	6.3	45.4	21.6	16.3	19.4	51.7	33.9	3.8	2.9
1957	30.1	17.9	59.4	6.7	46.8	22.3	16.8	20.0	51.6	34.6	4.0	3.0
1958	31.0	17.6	56.7	7.0	47.5	22.7	17.2	20.4	49.7	35.4	4.0	3.0
1959	32.1	19.0	59.1	7.3	49.1	22.8	17.6	20.6	51.2	37.0	4.3	3.3
1960	32.6	19.3	59.2	7.6	50.3	23.3	17.4	20.8	51.5	37.5	4.5	3.4
1961	33.8	19.7	58.3	7.9	51.7	23.4	17.7	21.0	50.9	38.7	4.6	3.5
1962	35.4	21.0	59.3	8.3	53.5	23.3	18.2	21.2	51.6	40.7	4.9	3.8
1963	36.8	22.0	59.7	8.5	54.6	23.2	18.7	21.3	51.9	42.3	5.1	4.1
1964	38.0	23.3	61.5	8.9	56.0	23.4	19.1	21.6	52.8	44.2	5.4	4.5
1965	39.4	25.0	63.5	9.2	57.1	23.4	19.9	21.9	54.4	46.0	5.8	5.0
1966	41.0	26.7	65.2	9.8	59.3	24.0	20.3	22.4	56.0	47.7	6.4	5.4
1967	41.9	27.3	65.0	10.4	60.8	24.7	20.7	23.0	56.7	48.1	6.7	5.6
1968	43.4	28.6	66.0	11.2	62.9	25.8	21.4	23.9	57.9	49.5	7.4	6.1
1969	43.6	29.5	67.7	12.0	63.8	27.4	21.7	25.0	59.7	49.5	8.1	6.4
1970	44.5	29.5	66.3	12.9	64.9	28.9	22.2	26.1	59.5	49.6	8.5	6.6
1971	46.3	30.6	66.2	13.6	65.9	29.5	24.1	27.2	59.6	51.4	9.0	7.4
1972	47.8	32.6	68.2	14.5	67.9	30.3	25.1	28.2	61.4	53.1	9.9	8.2
1973	49.2	34.9	70.8	15.6	68.9	31.8	26.6	29.6	64.0	54.5	11.1	9.3
1974	48.4	34.3	71.0	17.1	67.9	35.3	28.6	32.5	65.0	52.8	12.1	9.8
1975	50.1	34.0	67.9	18.9	68.9	37.8	32.7	35.7	63.0	53.9	12.9	11.1
1976	51.7	36.3	70.1	20.4	70.3	39.5	34.8	37.6	65.0	55.8	14.3	12.6
1977	52.7	38.4	72.8	22.1	71.3	41.9	36.8	39.8	67.8	56.6	16.1	14.1
1978	53.3	40.8	76.6	23.9	72.2	44.9	39.3	42.6	71.5	57.0	18.3	16.0
1979	53.3	42.2	79.1	26.3	72.3	49.3	41.9	46.2	74.3	56.8	20.8	17.7
1980	53.3	41.8	78.5	29.1	72.1	54.6	44.3	50.3	74.5	56.1	22.8	18.5
1981	54.5	43.0	79.0	31.8	72.0	58.4	50.0	54.9	75.2	57.2	25.1	21.5
1982	54.1	41.7	77.2	34.2	72.9	63.2	51.0	58.1	74.0	56.4	26.4	21.3
1983	56.0	44.0	78.6	35.7	73.1	63.7	55.0	60.1	74.7	59.0	28.1	24.2
1984	57.6	47.9	83.2	37.3	73.3	64.7	57.8	61.8	78.4	61.1	31.0	27.7
1985	58.9	50.1	85.1	39.2	74.5	66.5	59.4	63.6	80.4	62.3	33.3	29.8
1986	60.6	52.0	85.8	41.4	77.3	68.4	59.0	64.4	81.7	63.6	35.5	30.6
1987	60.9	53.8	88.3	43.0	77.6	70.6	59.0	65.7	83.9	64.1	38.0	31.7
1988	61.8	56.1	90.8	45.2	78.8	73.2	60.3	67.8	86.5	64.9	41.1	33.8
1989	62.5	58.2	93.1	46.6	77.9	74.5	64.3	70.3	88.4	65.9	43.4	37.5
1990	63.9	59.2	92.6	49.6	79.0	77.6	65.5	72.6	88.9	66.6	46.0	38.8
1991	65.1	58.9	90.4	52.1	79.9	80.0	67.2	74.6	87.6	67.2	47.1	39.6
1992	68.0	61.3	90.2	55.1	82.6	81.1	68.5	75.8	87.1	70.4	49.8	42.0
1993	68.1	63.1	92.7	56.0	81.8	82.2	71.2	77.6	88.9	70.9	51.9	44.9
1994	68.6	66.2	96.4	56.5	80.9	82.3	74.3	79.0	92.0	71.9	54.5	49.2
1995	68.9	68.2	99.1	57.6	80.5	83.6	75.8	80.4	94.6	72.2	57.1	51.7
1996	70.9	71.4	100.7	60.0	81.7	84.6	77.4	81.6	96.6	73.9	60.4	55.3
1997	72.3	75.2	104.0	62.2	82.9	86.0	78.3	82.8	99.3	75.8	64.7	58.9
1998	74.5	79.1	106.1	65.9	86.6	88.4	76.0	83.2	101.3	78.0	69.9	60.1
1999	77.3	83.6	108.2	68.8	88.5	89.0	76.4	83.7	103.0	81.2	74.4	63.9
2000	79.9	87.4	109.4	73.8	91.9	92.4	75.4	85.3	104.7	83.4	80.7	65.9
2001	82.1	87.9	107.1	77.2	93.5	94.0	76.7	86.8	104.0	84.6	82.7	67.5
2002	85.6	89.5	104.5	78.9	94.1	92.2	80.8	87.4	101.7	88.0	82.5	72.3
2003	88.9	92.3	103.9	81.9	95.5	92.1	83.8	88.6	101.5	91.0	85.1	77.3
2004	91.8	96.5	105.2	85.7	97.3	93.4	86.9	90.7	102.8	93.8	90.1	83.8
2005	93.7	100.2	106.9	88.8	97.6	94.8	91.7	93.5	104.7	95.7	94.9	91.8
2006	94.6	103.3	109.2	92.3	98.2	97.5	94.0	96.1	106.7	96.8	100.8	97.1
2007	96.0	105.5	109.9	96.4	99.7	100.4	95.3	98.2	107.6	98.1	105.9	100.5
2008	96.8	104.3	107.7	99.0	98.6	102.2	96.3	99.7	106.0	98.3	106.6	100.5
2009	100.0	100.0	100.0	100.0	100.0	100.0	100.0	100.0	100.0	100.0	100.0	100.0
2010	103.3	103.1	99.9	102.0	100.3	98.8	104.4	101.1	98.8	104.4	101.9	107.7
2011	103.6	105.6	101.9	104.4	99.6	100.8	106.8	103.3	100.3	105.3	106.4	112.8
2012	105.1	109.5	104.1	107.2	100.1	102.0	109.6	105.1	102.3	107.0	111.6	119.9

Table 5-1. Indexes of Productivity and Related Data, 1947–2012—*Continued*

(2009 = 100.)

Year	Nonfarm business											
	Output per hour	Output	Hours	Hourly compen-sation	Real hourly compen-sation	Unit labor costs	Unit nonlabor payments	Implicit price deflator	Employment	Output per job	Compen-sation in current dollars	Nonlabor payments in current dollars
1947	24.9	12.1	48.5	4.1	36.1	16.5	12.2	14.7	40.6	29.7	2.0	1.5
1948	25.5	12.6	49.3	4.5	36.3	17.5	13.2	15.7	41.4	30.3	2.2	1.7
1949	26.3	12.5	47.4	4.6	37.8	17.5	13.6	15.9	40.3	31.0	2.2	1.7
1950	28.0	13.7	48.9	4.9	39.5	17.4	14.2	16.0	41.2	33.3	2.4	1.9
1951	28.8	14.7	51.2	5.3	39.8	18.4	15.3	17.1	43.1	34.2	2.7	2.2
1952	29.3	15.2	51.8	5.6	41.2	19.0	15.2	17.4	43.6	34.8	2.9	2.3
1953	30.0	16.0	53.1	5.9	43.2	19.6	15.2	17.8	44.9	35.5	3.1	2.4
1954	30.6	15.7	51.3	6.1	44.3	19.9	15.2	17.9	43.7	35.9	3.1	2.4
1955	31.9	17.0	53.4	6.3	46.0	19.7	16.2	18.3	45.0	37.8	3.4	2.8
1956	31.8	17.4	54.7	6.7	48.1	21.1	15.9	18.9	46.3	37.5	3.7	2.8
1957	32.6	17.7	54.4	7.1	49.3	21.7	16.4	19.5	46.6	38.0	3.8	2.9
1958	33.3	17.4	52.1	7.4	49.8	22.1	16.6	19.8	44.9	38.6	3.8	2.9
1959	34.5	18.8	54.5	7.6	51.4	22.2	17.2	20.1	46.6	40.4	4.2	3.2
1960	34.9	19.1	54.8	8.0	52.7	22.8	16.8	20.3	47.1	40.7	4.4	3.2
1961	36.1	19.6	54.2	8.2	53.9	22.9	17.2	20.5	46.7	41.9	4.5	3.4
1962	37.7	20.9	55.4	8.6	55.5	22.7	17.8	20.7	47.6	43.9	4.7	3.7
1963	39.0	21.9	56.0	8.9	56.7	22.7	18.2	20.8	48.1	45.4	5.0	4.0
1964	40.1	23.3	58.1	9.1	57.7	22.8	18.8	21.1	49.3	47.3	5.3	4.4
1965	41.4	25.0	60.4	9.4	58.7	22.8	19.4	21.4	51.0	49.0	5.7	4.8
1966	42.9	26.8	62.4	10.0	60.4	23.3	19.9	21.9	53.0	50.5	6.2	5.3
1967	43.7	27.3	62.4	10.6	62.0	24.2	20.2	22.6	53.9	50.6	6.6	5.5
1968	45.2	28.7	63.5	11.4	64.0	25.2	21.0	23.4	55.2	52.1	7.2	6.0
1969	45.3	29.6	65.4	12.2	64.8	26.8	21.2	24.5	57.2	51.8	7.9	6.3
1970	46.0	29.6	64.3	13.0	65.6	28.3	21.7	25.6	57.2	51.7	8.4	6.4
1971	47.8	30.7	64.2	13.8	66.7	28.9	23.5	26.7	57.4	53.5	8.9	7.2
1972	49.4	32.7	66.3	14.7	68.8	29.7	24.3	27.5	59.1	55.4	9.7	8.0
1973	50.9	35.1	69.0	15.8	69.7	31.1	24.8	28.5	61.7	56.9	10.9	8.7
1974	50.1	34.6	69.1	17.3	68.7	34.6	27.0	31.4	62.7	55.1	12.0	9.3
1975	51.4	34.0	66.1	19.1	69.6	37.2	31.4	34.8	60.9	55.8	12.6	10.7
1976	53.2	36.4	68.5	20.6	70.9	38.7	33.8	36.7	63.0	57.8	14.1	12.3
1977	54.1	38.5	71.2	22.3	72.0	41.2	35.8	39.0	65.9	58.5	15.9	13.8
1978	54.8	41.1	74.9	24.2	73.1	44.2	37.9	41.6	69.5	59.0	18.1	15.6
1979	54.7	42.4	77.6	26.5	73.1	48.5	40.2	45.1	72.5	58.5	20.6	17.1
1980	54.7	42.0	76.9	29.4	72.8	53.8	43.2	49.4	72.7	57.8	22.6	18.2
1981	55.5	43.0	77.5	32.2	72.9	58.0	48.5	54.1	73.5	58.5	25.0	20.8
1982	55.0	41.6	75.8	34.6	73.7	62.9	49.9	57.5	72.4	57.6	26.2	20.8
1983	57.4	44.3	77.3	36.1	74.0	62.9	54.2	59.3	73.1	60.7	27.9	24.1
1984	58.6	48.1	82.0	37.7	74.1	64.3	56.4	61.0	77.0	62.4	30.9	27.1
1985	59.6	50.1	84.1	39.5	75.1	66.3	58.4	63.0	79.2	63.3	33.2	29.3
1986	61.4	52.0	84.8	41.8	78.0	68.1	58.1	63.9	80.6	64.5	35.4	30.2
1987	61.7	53.9	87.3	43.4	78.4	70.3	58.0	65.2	82.9	65.0	37.9	31.2
1988	62.7	56.3	89.8	45.6	79.5	72.7	59.4	67.2	85.5	65.9	41.0	33.4
1989	63.3	58.4	92.3	46.9	78.4	74.2	63.2	69.6	87.4	66.8	43.3	36.9
1990	64.5	59.3	91.9	49.9	79.3	77.3	64.5	71.9	88.1	67.4	45.8	38.2
1991	65.7	59.0	89.7	52.3	80.4	79.7	66.4	74.2	86.6	68.1	47.0	39.2
1992	68.5	61.3	89.5	55.5	83.1	81.0	67.6	75.4	86.2	71.2	49.7	41.5
1993	68.6	63.2	92.2	56.2	82.1	81.9	70.5	77.1	88.2	71.7	51.8	44.6
1994	69.3	66.2	95.5	56.9	81.4	82.1	73.6	78.6	91.1	72.7	54.3	48.7
1995	69.8	68.5	98.2	58.0	81.1	83.1	75.4	79.9	93.7	73.1	56.9	51.7
1996	71.6	71.6	99.9	60.4	82.2	84.3	76.5	81.0	95.9	74.6	60.3	54.7
1997	72.8	75.3	103.4	62.5	83.3	85.8	77.7	82.4	98.6	76.4	64.6	58.5
1998	75.0	79.3	105.7	66.1	86.9	88.1	75.7	82.9	100.8	78.6	69.8	60.0
1999	77.6	83.9	108.0	68.9	88.7	88.7	76.4	83.6	102.7	81.7	74.4	64.1
2000	80.2	87.5	109.1	74.0	92.1	92.2	75.4	85.2	104.5	83.8	80.7	66.0
2001	82.4	88.1	107.0	77.2	93.5	93.7	76.7	86.6	103.9	84.8	82.6	67.6
2002	85.9	89.7	104.4	79.0	94.2	91.9	81.0	87.4	101.5	88.3	82.4	72.6
2003	89.1	92.5	103.8	81.9	95.6	92.0	83.6	88.5	101.4	91.2	85.0	77.3
2004	91.9	96.6	105.2	85.7	97.3	93.3	86.2	90.3	102.8	94.0	90.1	83.3
2005	93.8	100.3	106.9	88.8	97.6	94.7	91.5	93.4	104.7	95.8	94.9	91.8
2006	94.6	103.5	109.3	92.3	98.2	97.5	93.9	96.0	106.7	96.9	100.9	97.2
2007	96.2	105.8	110.0	96.3	99.6	100.1	94.9	97.9	107.7	98.3	105.9	100.5
2008	96.9	104.5	107.8	98.9	98.5	102.0	95.8	99.4	106.1	98.5	106.6	100.1
2009	100.0	100.0	100.0	100.0	100.0	100.0	100.0	100.0	100.0	100.0	100.0	100.0
2010	103.3	103.2	99.9	102.1	100.4	98.8	104.0	101.0	98.8	104.4	102.0	107.3
2011	103.8	105.7	101.9	104.6	99.7	100.8	105.5	102.7	100.3	105.5	106.6	111.5
2012	105.3	109.7	104.1	107.4	100.3	102.0	108.3	104.6	102.3	107.2	111.8	118.7

Table 5-1. Indexes of Productivity and Related Data, 1947–2012—*Continued*

(2009 = 100.)

Year	Nonfinancial corporations												
	Output per hour	Output	Hours	Hourly compensation	Real hourly compensation	Unit labor costs	Unit nonlabor costs	Unit profits	Implicit price deflator	Employment	Output per job	Compensation in current dollars	Nonlabor payments in current dollars
1947	23.6	9.7	41.1	4.7	41.1	19.9	11.1	30.9	18.4	34.9	27.8	1.9	1.6
1948	25.1	10.4	41.5	5.2	41.9	20.5	11.6	36.9	19.6	35.4	29.4	2.1	1.9
1949	26.5	10.3	39.0	5.3	43.8	20.1	12.5	33.5	19.2	33.8	30.6	2.1	1.9
1950	28.5	11.7	41.0	5.6	45.7	19.8	12.0	37.9	19.3	35.1	33.3	2.3	2.2
1951	28.2	12.3	43.7	6.1	46.2	21.8	12.6	40.7	21.0	37.3	33.1	2.7	2.4
1952	28.9	12.8	44.3	6.5	48.0	22.5	13.1	36.7	21.2	37.8	33.8	2.9	2.5
1953	30.0	13.7	45.7	6.9	50.3	22.8	13.1	34.4	21.1	39.2	35.0	3.1	2.6
1954	31.3	13.6	43.4	7.1	51.7	22.7	13.4	33.5	21.0	37.6	36.2	3.1	2.5
1955	33.2	15.2	45.9	7.4	53.7	22.1	13.0	39.1	21.2	39.3	38.8	3.4	3.0
1956	33.4	15.8	47.1	7.8	56.3	23.4	13.9	36.6	21.9	40.6	38.8	3.7	3.1
1957	34.1	16.0	46.8	8.3	57.7	24.3	15.0	35.2	22.6	40.8	39.2	3.9	3.2
1958	34.9	15.4	44.1	8.6	58.3	24.7	16.4	31.9	23.0	38.6	39.8	3.8	3.1
1959	36.6	17.1	46.7	8.9	60.1	24.4	15.8	37.1	23.2	40.4	42.3	4.2	3.6
1960	37.2	17.7	47.5	9.3	61.4	25.0	16.2	34.2	23.3	41.3	42.8	4.4	3.7
1961	38.4	18.1	47.1	9.6	62.8	25.0	16.5	34.3	23.4	41.0	44.1	4.5	3.8
1962	40.1	19.6	48.9	10.0	64.6	24.8	16.3	36.8	23.5	42.4	46.3	4.9	4.2
1963	41.6	20.8	50.0	10.3	65.7	24.7	16.2	39.0	23.6	43.3	48.1	5.1	4.6
1964	42.3	22.3	52.7	10.5	66.1	24.8	16.2	40.3	23.8	44.9	49.7	5.5	5.0
1965	43.4	24.2	55.7	10.8	66.9	24.8	16.1	43.5	24.2	47.2	51.1	6.0	5.6
1966	44.2	26.0	58.7	11.4	68.7	25.7	16.2	43.5	24.7	49.9	52.0	6.7	6.0
1967	45.0	26.7	59.3	12.0	70.4	26.7	17.1	40.7	25.3	51.3	52.0	7.1	6.2
1968	46.7	28.4	60.9	12.9	72.4	27.6	18.3	40.8	26.2	53.1	53.5	7.8	6.9
1969	46.7	29.6	63.3	13.8	73.4	29.5	19.8	36.9	27.3	55.5	53.2	8.7	7.2
1970	47.0	29.3	62.3	14.7	74.1	31.3	22.3	30.3	28.5	55.6	52.7	9.2	7.2
1971	48.9	30.5	62.3	15.6	75.2	31.8	23.4	34.4	29.6	55.8	54.6	9.7	8.0
1972	49.9	32.8	65.7	16.4	76.7	32.8	23.4	37.5	30.5	58.6	55.9	10.8	8.9
1973	50.4	34.8	69.0	17.6	77.3	34.8	24.7	39.0	32.2	61.8	56.2	12.1	9.9
1974	49.4	34.2	69.3	19.2	76.1	38.8	28.4	35.6	35.3	63.0	54.3	13.3	10.4
1975	51.3	33.7	65.8	21.2	77.0	41.2	32.5	43.0	38.8	60.6	55.7	13.9	11.9
1976	53.0	36.5	68.8	22.7	78.2	42.9	32.2	50.8	40.5	63.3	57.7	15.7	13.5
1977	54.5	39.2	72.0	24.6	79.4	45.1	33.4	55.1	42.7	66.5	58.9	17.7	15.3
1978	55.2	41.7	75.7	26.8	80.9	48.6	34.8	58.6	45.5	70.3	59.4	20.3	17.1
1979	54.7	43.1	78.7	29.3	80.6	53.5	37.7	56.3	49.1	73.8	58.4	23.1	18.3
1980	54.6	42.7	78.2	32.2	79.9	59.1	44.2	50.8	53.8	74.1	57.6	25.2	19.6
1981	56.0	44.4	79.3	35.2	79.6	62.8	50.3	59.6	58.7	75.3	58.9	27.9	23.4
1982	56.3	43.4	77.2	37.5	80.0	66.7	55.8	55.6	62.2	73.6	59.0	28.9	24.2
1983	58.2	45.5	78.3	39.1	79.9	67.1	56.1	64.4	63.5	74.0	61.6	30.6	26.5
1984	59.5	49.6	83.3	40.8	80.1	68.5	55.8	75.5	65.4	78.3	63.3	34.0	30.2
1985	60.9	51.9	85.2	42.8	81.3	70.2	57.0	72.7	66.5	80.5	64.5	36.4	31.7
1986	62.3	53.3	85.5	45.2	84.3	72.5	60.0	60.2	67.5	81.7	65.2	38.6	32.0
1987	63.6	56.1	88.2	46.8	84.5	73.5	60.5	64.4	68.7	83.9	66.8	41.2	34.5
1988	65.5	59.5	90.9	49.1	85.5	75.0	61.7	68.9	70.4	86.7	68.6	44.6	37.8
1989	64.7	60.7	93.7	50.5	84.3	78.0	65.1	62.9	72.6	88.9	68.2	47.3	39.2
1990	65.4	61.5	94.1	53.0	84.3	81.0	68.1	59.3	74.9	90.5	68.0	49.8	40.5
1991	67.0	61.2	91.4	55.4	85.1	82.8	71.0	60.8	76.9	88.5	69.1	50.7	41.9
1992	68.8	63.1	91.8	58.3	87.4	84.9	69.7	63.0	78.0	88.6	71.2	53.5	42.9
1993	68.8	64.6	94.0	59.1	86.4	85.9	69.6	73.2	79.7	90.3	71.6	55.5	45.6
1994	70.0	68.6	98.0	59.9	85.7	85.5	70.0	87.4	81.1	93.6	73.3	58.7	51.1
1995	70.8	71.9	101.5	60.8	85.0	85.8	70.3	92.5	81.9	97.0	74.2	61.7	54.7
1996	73.7	76.1	103.3	63.1	86.0	85.7	69.4	99.2	82.2	99.4	76.6	65.3	58.7
1997	75.7	81.2	107.3	65.3	87.0	86.2	69.1	101.7	82.7	102.6	79.2	70.0	63.0
1998	78.3	85.8	109.6	69.0	90.7	88.2	69.3	90.5	82.7	105.1	81.7	75.7	64.2
1999	80.8	90.5	112.1	72.2	93.0	89.4	70.6	84.1	83.2	107.3	84.4	81.0	67.1
2000	84.1	95.5	113.5	77.5	96.5	92.2	73.2	70.0	84.2	109.4	87.3	88.0	69.1
2001	84.6	93.4	110.4	79.4	96.2	93.8	78.4	56.9	85.3	108.0	86.5	87.7	68.0
2002	88.0	94.2	107.1	80.9	96.5	91.9	78.9	69.2	85.7	104.9	89.8	86.6	72.0
2003	91.5	96.3	105.2	83.6	97.5	91.3	78.1	84.4	86.6	103.5	93.0	87.9	76.8
2004	94.7	100.6	106.3	86.6	98.3	91.5	77.5	102.7	88.5	104.4	96.4	92.0	84.6
2005	96.5	103.9	107.7	89.2	98.1	92.5	81.0	116.7	91.6	106.1	98.0	96.1	93.8
2006	98.3	107.9	109.8	92.0	97.9	93.6	83.1	131.0	94.4	107.7	100.2	101.0	103.1
2007	98.8	109.0	110.3	95.5	98.8	96.6	88.6	116.8	96.3	108.4	100.6	105.3	104.5
2008	99.2	107.6	108.5	98.3	97.9	99.0	94.3	105.4	98.3	106.9	100.7	106.6	104.6
2009	100.0	100.0	100.0	100.0	100.0	100.0	100.0	100.0	100.0	100.0	100.0	100.0	100.0
2010	105.4	105.6	100.2	101.8	100.1	96.6	96.7	129.0	100.0	99.0	106.7	101.9	110.9
2011	105.7	108.8	103.0	103.9	99.1	98.3	97.4	139.0	102.3	101.0	107.7	107.0	117.6
2012	107.1	112.9	105.4	106.8	99.8	99.7	97.5	144.2	103.7	103.4	109.2	112.5	123.7

. . . = Not available.

Table 5-1. Indexes of Productivity and Related Data, 1947–2012—*Continued*

(2009 = 100.)

Year	Manufacturing											
	Output per hour	Output	Hours	Hourly compen-sation	Real hourly compen-sation	Unit labor costs	Unit nonlabor payments	Implicit price deflator	Employment	Output per job	Compen-sation in current dollars	Nonlabor payments in current dollars
1947	...	...	...	...	...	...	...	...	...	...	...	...
1948	...	...	...	...	...	...	...	...	...	...	...	...
1949	...	...	...	...	...	...	...	...	...	...	...	...
1950	...	...	...	...	...	...	...	...	...	...	...	...
1951	...	...	...	...	...	...	...	...	...	...	...	...
1952	...	...	...	...	...	...	...	...	...	...	...	...
1953	...	...	...	...	...	...	...	...	...	...	...	...
1954	...	...	...	...	...	...	...	...	...	...	...	...
1955	...	...	...	...	...	...	...	...	...	...	...	...
1956	...	...	...	...	...	...	...	...	...	...	...	...
1957	...	...	...	...	...	...	...	...	...	...	...	...
1958	...	...	...	...	...	...	...	...	...	...	...	...
1959	...	...	...	...	...	...	...	...	...	...	...	...
1960	...	...	...	...	...	...	...	...	...	...	...	...
1961	...	...	...	...	...	...	...	...	...	...	...	...
1962	...	...	...	...	...	...	...	...	...	...	...	...
1963	...	...	...	...	...	...	...	...	...	...	...	...
1964	...	...	...	...	...	...	...	...	...	...	...	...
1965	...	...	...	...	...	...	...	...	...	...	...	...
1966	...	...	...	...	...	...	...	...	...	...	...	...
1967	...	...	...	...	...	...	...	...	...	...	...	...
1968	...	...	...	...	...	...	...	...	...	...	...	...
1969	...	...	...	...	...	...	...	...	...	...	...	...
1970	...	...	...	...	...	...	...	...	...	...	...	...
1971	...	...	...	...	...	...	...	...	...	...	...	...
1972	...	...	...	...	...	...	...	...	...	...	...	...
1973	...	...	...	...	...	...	...	...	...	...	...	...
1974	...	...	...	...	...	...	...	...	...	...	...	...
1975	...	...	...	...	...	...	...	...	...	...	...	...
1976	...	...	...	...	...	...	...	...	...	...	...	...
1977	...	...	...	...	...	...	...	...	...	...	...	...
1978	...	...	...	...	...	...	...	...	...	...	...	...
1979	...	...	...	...	...	...	...	...	...	...	...	...
1980	...	...	...	...	...	...	...	...	...	...	...	...
1981	...	...	...	...	...	...	...	...	...	...	...	...
1982	...	...	...	...	...	...	...	...	...	...	...	...
1983	...	...	...	...	...	...	...	...	...	...	...	...
1984	...	...	...	...	...	...	...	...	...	...	...	...
1985	...	...	...	...	...	...	...	...	...	...	...	...
1986	...	...	...	...	...	...	...	...	...	...	...	...
1987	49.1	73.1	148.8	44.4	80.3	90.5	66.4	73.0	147.3	49.6	66.1	48.5
1988	50.1	76.8	153.3	46.2	80.4	92.1	68.8	75.2	149.9	51.2	70.8	52.9
1989	50.6	78.1	154.3	47.7	79.7	94.3	72.5	78.5	150.8	51.8	73.6	56.6
1990	51.7	77.8	150.4	50.1	79.7	96.8	75.1	81.0	148.5	52.4	75.4	58.4
1991	53.1	76.5	144.1	52.8	81.2	99.6	74.7	81.5	143.3	53.4	76.2	57.1
1992	55.1	79.0	143.3	55.6	83.3	100.9	75.5	82.5	140.9	56.1	79.7	59.7
1993	56.5	82.1	145.3	56.3	82.3	99.7	76.6	82.9	141.1	58.2	81.8	62.9
1994	58.5	87.0	148.7	57.2	81.9	97.8	78.1	83.5	142.9	60.9	85.1	68.0
1995	61.2	91.5	149.7	58.3	81.5	95.3	80.8	84.8	144.9	63.2	87.2	74.0
1996	63.4	94.7	149.4	60.0	81.7	94.8	81.7	85.3	144.7	65.4	89.7	77.3
1997	66.8	101.6	152.0	62.1	82.8	93.0	81.0	84.3	146.0	69.6	94.5	82.3
1998	70.5	106.9	151.7	65.2	85.7	92.5	77.6	81.6	147.2	72.6	98.9	83.0
1999	73.9	111.3	150.6	68.2	87.7	92.2	77.8	81.8	144.9	76.8	102.7	86.7
2000	77.1	114.7	148.7	73.3	91.3	95.0	78.8	83.3	144.5	79.4	109.0	90.4
2001	78.6	109.2	139.0	75.5	91.5	96.1	77.6	82.7	137.8	79.2	105.0	84.7
2002	84.2	108.8	129.2	78.0	93.0	92.6	77.8	81.8	127.9	85.1	100.7	84.6
2003	89.5	109.9	122.9	82.2	95.8	91.8	80.1	83.3	121.9	90.2	100.9	88.1
2004	91.5	111.9	122.2	85.2	96.7	93.1	85.1	87.3	120.2	93.1	104.1	95.2
2005	95.9	115.9	120.8	88.4	97.1	92.1	93.0	92.8	119.6	96.9	106.8	107.8
2006	96.8	117.8	121.7	90.6	96.3	93.6	96.9	96.0	118.9	99.1	110.2	114.1
2007	100.5	120.3	119.7	94.1	97.4	93.6	102.4	100.0	116.8	103.0	112.6	123.1
2008	99.9	114.8	114.9	96.7	96.3	96.7	110.5	106.7	112.7	101.9	111.1	126.8
2009	100.0	100.0	100.0	100.0	100.0	100.0	100.0	100.0	100.0	100.0	100.0	100.0
2010	106.3	106.3	99.9	102.4	100.7	96.3	107.8	104.7	97.2	109.3	102.4	114.5
2011	107.3	109.5	102.1	103.8	98.9	96.7	120.3	113.9	98.5	111.2	105.9	131.8
2012	109.2	114.1	104.4	105.7	98.7	96.8	...	...	100.3	113.7	110.4	...

. . . = Not available.

Table 5-2. Average Annual Percent Change in Output Per Hour and Related Series, Selected Industries, 1987–2011 and 2010–2011

(Number, percent.)

Industry	NAICS code	2011 employment (thousands)	Average annual percent change, 1987–2011			Annual percent change, 2010–2011		
			Output per hour	Output	Hours	Output per hour	Output	Hours
Mining								
Mining	21	759	-0.4	0.1	0.5	-11.3	4.2	17.5
Oil and gas extraction	211	173	0.5	-0.2	-0.7	-11.0	4.7	17.6
Mining, except oil and gas	212	221	1.5	0.4	-1.1	-5.1	2.7	8.2
Coal mining	2121	88	1.6	-0.1	-1.7	-4.6	5.0	10.1
Metal ore mining	2122	42	1.5	1.9	0.4	-18.5	-2.0	20.2
Nonmetallic mineral mining and quarrying	2123	91	0.7	-0.3	-1.0	2.8	4.3	1.4
Support activities for mining	213	365	1.3	4.1	2.7	-3.0	19.9	23.6
Utilities								
Power generation and supply	2211	398	1.9	0.7	-1.2	-5.6	-4.5	1.1
Natural gas distribution	2212	108	2.7	1.2	-1.5	4.3	0.7	-3.4
Transportation and Warehousing								
Air transportation	481	425	3.1	2.7	-0.4	0.3	1.9	1.6
Line-haul railroads	482111	179	3.9	2.0	-1.8	-2.7	3.8	6.8
Truck transportation	484	1 496	0.6	1.7	1.1	1.1	5.1	4.0
General freight trucking	4841	1 079	1.4	2.3	0.9	2.3	5.3	2.9
General freight trucking, local	48411	282	3.0	3.6	0.6	2.4	7.7	5.2
General freight trucking, long-distance	48412	797	1.4	2.3	0.9	2.5	4.8	2.2
Used household and office goods moving	48421	87	-1.2	-1.1	0.1	-12.1	-3.5	9.8
Postal service	491	631	0.9	-0.3	-1.2	1.1	-2.7	-3.8
Couriers and messengers	492	561	-0.8	1.2	2.0	0.6	-0.5	-1.1
Warehousing and storage	493	659	2.9	5.8	2.8	3.3	8.1	4.6
General warehousing and storage	49311	553	5.2	8.0	2.7	6.0	10.1	3.9
Refrigerated warehousing and storage	49312	51	-0.2	3.1	3.3	-11.8	-1.8	11.3
Information								
Publishing	511	789	3.8	3.5	-0.3	1.0	2.4	1.4
Newspaper, book, and directory publishers	5111	517	0.0	-1.8	-1.8	-1.7	-2.5	-0.8
Software publishers	5112	272	13.0	19.7	6.0	1.0	6.4	5.3
Motion picture and video exhibition	51213	124	1.4	1.6	0.2	-0.1	-2.3	-2.2
Broadcasting, except Internet	515	291	2.1	2.6	0.5	3.5	2.9	-0.6
Radio and television broadcasting	5151	216	1.0	0.7	-0.4	0.5	0.8	0.3
Cable and other subscription programming	5152	76	3.9	7.5	3.5	7.5	4.8	-2.5
Wired telecommunications carriers	5171	590	4.3	3.3	-1.0	6.3	0.9	-5.2
Wireless telecommunications carriers	5172	170	10.4	20.7	9.3	10.0	10.5	0.5
Finance and Insurance								
Commercial banking	52211	1 315	3.6	3.6	-0.1	-2.8	-1.0	1.8
Real Estate and Rental and Leasing								
Passenger car rental	532111	101	2.6	2.7	0.1	15.2	12.9	-2.0
Truck, trailer and RV rental and leasing	53212	56	2.9	2.0	-0.9	5.9	4.1	-1.7
Video tape and disc rental	53223	41	6.4	1.7	-4.4	43.3	-16.0	-41.4
Professional and Technical Services								
Tax preparation services	541213	148	0.6	2.7	2.1	1.2	-0.4	-1.6
Architectural services	54131	177	1.2	2.0	0.8	5.3	3.9	-1.4
Engineering services	54133	922	0.9	2.7	1.7	-1.7	1.9	3.6
Advertising agencies	54181	195	2.2	2.5	0.3	-0.8	5.0	5.9
Photography studios, portrait	541921	69	0.8	1.8	1.0	11.7	1.4	-9.2
Administrative and Waste Services								
Employment placement agencies	561311	238	6.4	7.2	0.8	9.0	15.7	6.1
Travel arrangement and reservation services	5615	214	7.5	3.5	-3.6	-2.0	5.4	7.5
Travel agencies	56151	98	5.9	4.2	-1.6	3.5	6.5	2.9
Janitorial services	56172	1 262	2.0	3.7	1.6	2.5	4.0	1.5
Health Care and Social Assistance								
Medical and diagnostic laboratories	6215	244	2.9	6.2	3.2	-2.2	3.9	6.3
Medical laboratories	621511	168	2.5	5.7	3.1	-1.1	7.2	8.4
Diagnostic imaging centers	621512	76	3.3	6.9	3.5	-2.6	-1.4	1.3
Arts, Entertainment, and Recreation								
Amusement and theme parks	71311	144	-0.5	2.3	2.8	-0.9	4.6	5.5
Bowling centers	71395	69	0.2	-1.6	-1.8	-0.6	4.3	4.9
Accommodation and Food Services								
Accommodation and food services	72	11 699	0.8	2.1	1.2	0.8	3.6	2.7
Accommodation	721	1 825	1.7	2.3	0.6	4.9	3.6	-1.3
Traveler accommodation	7211	1 752	1.7	2.4	0.6	4.8	3.5	-1.2
Food services and drinking places	722	9 873	0.6	2.0	1.4	-0.1	3.6	3.6
Full-service restaurants	7221	4 648	0.6	2.1	1.4	1.3	5.0	3.7
Limited-service eating places	7222	4 166	0.6	2.1	1.6	-2.1	2.8	5.0
Special food services	7223	692	1.4	2.4	0.9	3.3	2.5	-0.8
Drinking places (alcoholic beverages)	7224	368	-0.3	-0.7	-0.4	2.1	-0.3	-2.4

Table 5-2. Average Annual Percent Change in Output Per Hour and Related Series, Selected Industries, 1987–2011 and 2010–2011—*Continued*

(Number, percent.)

Industry	NAICS code	2011 employment (thousands)	Average annual percent change, 1987–2011			Annual percent change, 2010–2011		
			Output per hour	Output	Hours	Output per hour	Output	Hours
Other Services								
Automotive repair and maintenance	8111	1 035	1.0	1.2	0.1	7.7	3.4	-4.0
Reupholstery and furniture repair	81142	20	-0.6	-3.2	-2.6	5.5	-0.3	-5.5
Personal care services	8121	1 104	2.2	3.3	1.0	6.6	3.2	-3.2
Hair, nail and skin care services	81211	923	2.2	3.0	0.8	5.4	2.1	-3.2
Funeral homes and funeral services	81221	104	-0.7	-0.5	0.2	-4.5	0.3	5.0
Drycleaning and laundry services	8123	320	1.6	0.5	-1.2	9.4	3.6	-5.3
Coin-operated laundries and drycleaners	81231	42	2.5	0.4	-2.0	15.7	-0.3	-13.8
Drycleaning and laundry services	81232	155	1.1	-1.1	-2.2	9.4	1.9	-6.9
Linen and uniform supply	81233	123	1.2	1.8	0.6	7.5	6.5	-0.9
Photofinishing	81292	14	2.8	-4.3	-6.9	16.6	10.4	-5.3
Manufacturing								
Food	311	1 493	1.0	1.2	0.2	-0.1	-0.4	-0.3
Animal food	3111	52	2.3	1.7	-0.5	-7.1	-3.3	4.1
Grain and oilseed milling	3112	59	1.7	1.0	-0.7	-8.1	-6.3	2.0
Sugar and confectionery products	3113	68	1.0	-0.1	-1.1	-7.0	-0.9	6.5
Fruit and vegetable preserving and specialty	3114	173	1.0	0.9	-0.1	2.5	-0.2	-2.6
Dairy products	3115	134	1.6	1.0	-0.6	-3.2	-0.5	2.7
Animal slaughtering and processing	3116	493	1.0	2.0	1.0	3.2	1.6	-1.6
Seafood product preparation and packaging	3117	39	0.8	-0.1	-0.8	-2.7	-2.3	0.5
Bakeries and tortilla manufacturing	3118	305	0.5	0.2	-0.3	0.7	-0.4	-1.1
Other food products	3119	171	0.7	2.0	1.3	2.4	2.3	0.0
Beverages and tobacco products	312	192	0.6	-0.3	-0.9	-5.7	1.2	7.4
Beverages	3121	176	1.7	1.4	-0.3	-4.1	3.7	8.2
Tobacco and tobacco products	3122	16	1.6	-3.3	-4.7	-3.7	-4.7	-1.0
Textile mills	313	129	3.4	-2.7	-5.8	-1.9	-2.1	-0.1
Fiber, yarn, and thread mills	3131	29	2.6	-2.7	-5.2	-10.4	-9.1	1.5
Fabric mills	3132	62	4.4	-2.6	-6.6	-1.2	-0.6	0.6
Textile and fabric finishing and coating mills	3133	38	1.8	-3.2	-4.9	2.9	0.1	-2.7
Textile product mills	314	125	1.0	-1.9	-2.9	6.6	1.2	-5.1
Textile furnishings mills	3141	57	0.6	-2.7	-3.2	12.1	3.8	-7.4
Other textile product mills	3149	68	2.1	-0.6	-2.6	0.8	-2.1	-2.9
Apparel	315	169	-1.0	-7.8	-6.9	1.0	-2.8	-3.7
Apparel knitting mills	3151	23	-0.3	-7.6	-7.3	-6.1	-15.7	-10.3
Cut and sew apparel	3152	134	-1.1	-7.9	-7.0	1.5	-0.4	-1.9
Accessories and other apparel	3159	12	-1.4	-6.8	-5.5	14.0	0.4	-11.9
Leather and allied products	316	30	2.0	-4.3	-6.2	-0.3	0.5	0.8
Leather and hide tanning and finishing	3161	4	1.8	-3.4	-5.1	13.7	6.3	-6.4
Footwear	3162	13	2.3	-5.6	-7.7	-5.4	-1.8	3.8
Other leather products	3169	14	0.5	-3.8	-4.2	-1.7	-1.3	0.4
Wood products	321	360	1.3	-0.9	-2.2	0.8	1.0	0.2
Sawmills and wood preservation	3211	90	2.1	-0.3	-2.4	-5.9	-0.5	5.8
Plywood and engineered wood products	3212	62	1.0	-1.2	-2.2	2.6	2.5	-0.1
Other wood products	3219	207	1.0	-1.0	-2.0	3.7	1.4	-2.2
Paper and paper products	322	388	1.9	-0.2	-2.0	2.7	0.1	-2.5
Pulp, paper, and paperboard mills	3221	109	2.9	-0.4	-3.2	1.1	0.4	-0.7
Converted paper products	3222	279	1.4	0.0	-1.4	3.3	0.0	-3.2
Printing and related support activities	323	496	1.4	-0.7	-2.1	4.7	-0.9	-5.3
Petroleum and coal products	324	113	2.7	1.2	-1.4	1.9	1.3	-0.5
Chemicals	325	791	1.5	0.7	-0.9	0.3	-0.2	-0.6
Basic chemicals	3251	142	2.4	0.3	-2.1	-0.9	-1.8	-0.9
Resin, rubber, and artificial fibers	3252	91	2.4	0.4	-1.9	-0.2	-1.2	-1.1
Agricultural chemicals	3253	37	2.1	0.3	-1.7	-6.9	-3.9	3.3
Pharmaceuticals and medicines	3254	271	0.2	2.1	1.9	2.7	2.0	-0.6
Paints, coatings, and adhesives	3255	57	1.3	-0.7	-1.9	7.8	1.6	-5.7
Soaps, cleaning compounds, and toiletries	3256	106	2.5	1.8	-0.7	-0.7	3.6	4.4
Other chemical products and preparations	3259	86	2.4	0.0	-2.3	0.3	-2.8	-3.1
Plastics and rubber products	326	637	1.9	1.2	-0.8	-0.9	1.8	2.7
Plastics products	3261	510	1.8	1.3	-0.4	-1.5	0.6	2.1
Rubber products	3262	127	2.4	0.4	-1.9	1.6	6.9	5.2
Nonmetallic mineral products	327	384	1.1	-0.3	-1.4	2.6	1.7	-1.0
Clay products and refractories	3271	51	0.8	-1.8	-2.6	4.3	0.4	-3.7
Glass and glass products	3272	85	2.4	0.1	-2.2	4.3	4.8	0.5
Cement and concrete products	3273	166	0.1	-0.5	-0.6	1.4	-0.5	-1.8
Lime and gypsum products	3274	14	1.2	-0.9	-2.1	7.1	4.4	-2.5
Other nonmetallic mineral products	3279	69	1.7	0.8	-0.9	0.3	2.1	1.8
Primary metals	331	391	2.3	0.2	-2.1	-2.0	7.5	9.7
Iron and steel mills and ferroalloy production	3311	93	4.3	1.8	-2.3	-0.1	9.5	9.7
Steel products from purchased steel	3312	57	-0.7	-1.1	-0.5	-7.6	6.9	15.7
Alumina and aluminum production	3313	57	2.7	0.0	-2.6	5.7	6.1	0.4
Other nonferrous metal production	3314	62	1.1	-1.2	-2.2	1.3	1.7	0.4
Foundries	3315	123	2.0	-0.2	-2.2	-6.0	10.1	17.1

Table 5-2. Average Annual Percent Change in Output Per Hour and Related Series, Selected Industries, 1987–2011 and 2010–2011—*Continued*

(Number, percent.)

Industry	NAICS code	2011 employment (thousands)	Average annual percent change, 1987–2011			Annual percent change, 2010–2011		
			Output per hour	Output	Hours	Output per hour	Output	Hours
Manufacturing—*Continued*								
Fabricated metal products	332	1 373	1.4	0.8	-0.6	1.9	7.9	5.9
Forging and stamping	3321	95	2.7	1.3	-1.4	1.5	10.2	8.5
Cutlery and hand tools	3322	41	2.2	-0.6	-2.7	3.3	-0.1	-3.2
Architectural and structural metals	3323	337	0.6	0.5	-0.1	-2.8	3.0	5.9
Boilers, tanks, and shipping containers	3324	90	0.7	0.0	-0.7	0.8	10.8	9.9
Hardware	3325	24	0.5	-3.5	-4.0	-1.5	-0.5	1.0
Spring and wire products	3326	42	. . .	. . .	. . .	5.6	3.3	-2.1
Machine shops and threaded products	3327	354	2.0	2.7	0.7	3.5	13.6	9.7
Coating, engraving, and heat treating metals	3328	132	2.8	2.7	-0.2	3.6	10.2	6.4
Other fabricated metal products	3329	259	1.4	0.3	-1.1	6.3	7.9	1.5
Machinery	333	1 069	2.5	1.5	-1.0	4.8	12.8	7.6
Agriculture, construction, and mining machinery	3331	228	2.8	3.2	0.4	6.9	17.5	9.9
Industrial machinery	3332	104	2.6	1.3	-1.3	6.4	13.1	6.3
Commercial and service industry machinery	3333	93	1.6	-0.5	-2.0	3.3	4.3	1.0
HVAC and commercial refrigeration equipment	3334	130	2.0	1.1	-1.0	-2.2	3.5	5.8
Metalworking machinery	3335	173	2.2	0.4	-1.8	7.8	18.2	9.6
Turbine and power transmission equipment	3336	98	1.9	1.5	-0.4	7.9	19.6	10.8
Computer and electronic products	334	1 111	10.7	8.0	-2.5	4.4	4.0	-0.4
Computer and peripheral equipment	3341	158	18.4	13.4	-4.3	-22.9	-28.5	-7.3
Communications equipment	3342	116	5.3	2.3	-2.8	5.3	5.7	0.4
Audio and video equipment	3343	20	2.3	-2.4	-4.6	19.7	16.5	-2.7
Semiconductors and electronic components	3344	387	16.1	14.2	-1.6	8.5	14.8	5.8
Electronic instruments	3345	406	4.1	1.8	-2.1	6.4	3.2	-3.0
Magnetic media manufacturing and reproduction	3346	25	1.3	-0.8	-2.1	-2.4	-9.0	-6.7
Electrical equipment and appliances	335	368	2.5	-0.1	-2.5	4.8	5.8	1.0
Electric lighting equipment	3351	46	2.2	-0.5	-2.6	10.0	6.2	-3.5
Household appliances	3352	57	3.4	-0.2	-3.5	-0.5	-2.1	-1.6
Electrical equipment	3353	140	2.2	-0.3	-2.4	5.1	6.0	0.8
Other electrical equipment and components	3359	126	2.2	0.0	-2.1	4.3	8.7	4.2
Transportation equipment	336	1 398	3.1	1.3	-1.7	1.2	5.6	4.4
Motor vehicles	3361	159	4.0	1.3	-2.6	7.4	11.6	3.9
Motor vehicle bodies and trailers	3362	117	1.0	0.5	-0.5	1.6	9.6	7.9
Motor vehicle parts	3363	455	3.3	1.9	-1.3	1.3	7.2	5.9
Aerospace products and parts	3364	488	1.8	-0.3	-2.1	-4.2	-1.4	2.9
Railroad rolling stock	3365	21	5.2	4.1	-1.0	5.2	17.0	11.1
Ship and boat building	3366	123	2.3	0.6	-1.7	-1.3	0.5	1.8
Other transportation equipment	3369	35	5.4	5.0	-0.4	-7.8	-6.4	1.5
Furniture and related products	337	376	1.5	-0.7	-2.2	-0.2	2.8	3.0
Household and institutional furniture	3371	238	1.3	-1.3	-2.5	-5.1	-2.5	2.7
Office furniture and fixtures	3372	101	1.2	-0.3	-1.6	4.1	10.8	6.4
Other furniture-related products	3379	37	2.4	1.2	-1.2	9.9	5.2	-4.3
Miscellaneous manufacturing	339	626	2.9	2.4	-0.5	-1.3	1.0	2.3
Medical equipment and supplies	3391	311	3.3	4.3	0.9	-2.4	-1.6	0.8
Other miscellaneous manufacturing	3399	314	2.3	0.7	-1.6	0.6	4.6	4.0

. . . = Not available.

Table 5-3. Average Annual Percent Change in Output Per Hour and Related Series, Wholesale Trade, Retail Trade, Food Services and Drinking Places, 1987–2012 and 2011–2012

(Number, percent.)

Industry	NAICS code	2012 employment (thousands)	Average annual percent change, 1987–2012			Annual percent change, 2011–2012		
			Output per hour	Output	Hours	Output per hour	Output	Hours
Wholesale Trade								
Wholesale trade	42	5 816	3.0	3.4	0.3	2.5	3.9	1.4
Durable goods	423	2 909	4.9	4.9	0.0	5.0	6.2	1.1
Motor vehicles and parts	4231	323	4.2	3.7	-0.4	18.0	17.7	-0.3
Furniture and furnishings	4232	99	1.9	1.1	-0.7	-0.1	1.4	1.5
Lumber and construction supplies	4233	187	1.8	1.6	-0.1	10.5	11.1	0.6
Commercial equipment	4234	631	13.6	13.9	0.2	4.2	3.6	-0.5
Metals and minerals	4235	123	-0.4	-0.4	0.0	9.9	11.2	1.2
Electric goods	4236	324	7.6	7.1	-0.5	-2.4	-0.3	2.1
Hardware and plumbing	4237	228	1.6	1.9	0.4	4.3	4.8	0.4
Machinery and supplies	4238	657	2.3	2.2	-0.1	1.4	4.6	3.1
Miscellaneous durable goods	4239	337	0.4	1.5	1.1	-9.8	-8.5	1.4
Nondurable goods	424	2 033	1.3	1.4	0.2	0.1	1.5	1.4
Paper and paper products	4241	123	1.4	0.6	-0.7	-4.3	0.5	5.0
Druggists' goods	4242	197	3.3	4.8	1.4	-8.6	-4.9	4.0
Apparel and piece goods	4243	147	2.5	2.1	-0.4	4.5	3.6	-0.9
Grocery and related products	4244	740	1.1	1.8	0.7	2.3	2.8	0.5
Farm product raw materials	4245	82	0.8	-1.1	-1.9	-0.3	-1.4	-1.1
Chemicals	4246	126	0.6	1.0	0.4	-1.5	3.7	5.3
Petroleum	4247	97	2.4	0.3	-2.0	4.7	3.8	-0.8
Alcoholic beverages	4248	173	-0.1	1.8	1.9	-0.8	1.2	2.0
Miscellaneous nondurable goods	4249	349	0.3	-0.1	-0.4	3.7	5.0	1.3
Electronic markets and agents and brokers	425	874	1.3	3.7	2.4	2.1	4.4	2.3
Retail Trade								
Retail trade	44-45	15 691	2.8	3.2	0.4	2.4	3.7	1.2
Motor vehicle and parts dealers	441	1 794	1.8	2.4	0.6	1.5	6.0	4.4
Automobile dealers	4411	1 132	1.9	2.5	0.6	1.0	6.9	5.9
Other motor vehicle dealers	4412	137	2.4	3.0	0.6	2.3	5.7	3.3
Auto parts, accessories, and tire stores	4413	525	1.3	1.9	0.6	-2.9	-1.3	1.6
Furniture and home furnishings stores	442	476	4.1	3.5	-0.5	8.8	8.7	-0.1
Furniture stores	4421	226	3.4	2.9	-0.4	8.4	5.5	-2.7
Home furnishings stores	4422	250	4.9	4.3	-0.6	9.1	12.4	3.1
Electronics and appliance stores	443	518	12.3	13.6	1.1	7.0	6.9	-0.1
Building material and garden supply stores	444	1 206	2.6	3.2	0.6	4.2	3.5	-0.6
Building material and supplies dealers	4441	1 054	2.3	3.2	0.8	4.0	3.3	-0.6
Lawn and garden equipment and supplies stores	4442	152	4.3	3.6	-0.6	5.4	4.7	-0.7
Food and beverage stores	445	2 959	0.3	0.2	-0.1	-1.7	0.9	2.6
Grocery stores	4451	2 548	0.2	0.2	0.0	-1.6	0.6	2.2
Specialty food stores	4452	248	0.3	-0.2	-0.5	2.4	7.0	4.5
Beer, wine and liquor stores	4453	163	2.0	0.9	-1.0	-4.4	3.0	7.7
Health and personal care stores	446	1 034	2.1	3.3	1.1	-0.2	-0.4	-0.2
Gasoline stations	447	854	1.7	1.0	-0.7	0.1	1.1	0.9
Clothing and clothing accessories stores	448	1 496	4.2	4.0	-0.2	-0.6	3.1	3.8
Clothing stores	4481	1 130	4.4	4.6	0.2	-3.4	2.6	6.2
Shoe stores	4482	193	3.6	2.3	-1.2	6.4	2.3	-3.8
Jewelry, luggage, and leather goods stores	4483	174	3.8	3.1	-0.7	7.4	6.9	-0.4
Sporting goods, hobby, book, and music stores	451	667	4.1	4.0	-0.1	7.3	6.3	-0.9
Sporting goods and musical instrument store	4511	540	4.7	5.2	0.4	7.0	8.5	1.4
Book, periodical, and music stores	4512	127	2.7	0.9	-1.7	8.5	-1.9	-9.6
General merchandise stores	452	3 096	3.1	4.8	1.6	6.0	3.1	-2.7
Department stores	4521	1 501	0.4	1.4	1.0	3.9	-2.0	-5.7
Other general merchandise stores	4529	1 595	5.9	8.4	2.4	5.1	5.3	0.2
Miscellaneous store retailers	453	966	3.7	3.6	-0.1	-0.8	6.7	7.5
Florists	4531	83	2.9	-0.1	-2.9	-5.2	9.8	15.9
Office supplies, stationery and gift stores	4532	325	5.8	4.9	-0.8	-0.3	4.7	4.9
Used merchandise stores	4533	215	4.1	5.9	1.7	-6.9	9.0	17.0
Other miscellaneous store retailers	4539	344	1.7	2.7	0.9	4.2	7.2	2.8
Nonstore retailers	454	625	8.5	8.7	0.2	5.5	8.0	2.3
Electronic shopping and mail-order houses	4541	333	10.7	14.6	3.6	3.1	9.9	6.6
Vending machine operators	4542	44	0.8	-2.4	-3.1	7.5	-0.5	-7.4
Direct selling establishments	4543	248	3.1	1.2	-1.8	3.8	1.7	-2.0
Food Services and Drinking Places								
Food services and drinking places	722	10 212	0.6	2.1	1.5	-0.1	4.6	4.7
Full-service restaurants	7221	4 788	0.6	2.2	1.6	1.0	5.8	4.7
Limited-service eating places	7222	4 328	0.5	2.2	1.7	-2.0	3.1	5.2
Special food services	7223	721	1.4	2.5	1.1	0.9	6.0	5.0
Drinking places, alcoholic beverages	7224	374	0.0	-0.5	-0.5	7.6	4.5	-2.9

Table 5-4. Indexes of Multifactor Productivity and Related Measures, 1990–2012

(2009 =100 for private business and 2005 = 100 for manufacturing.)

Sector	1990	1991	1992	1993	1994	1995	1996	1997	1998	1999	2000
PRIVATE BUSINESS											
Productivity											
Output per hour of all persons	63.2	64.4	67.3	67.4	68.0	68.3	70.4	71.7	73.9	76.7	79.3
Output per unit of capital services	117.8	113.8	116.0	115.7	117.1	115.9	116.0	116.0	115.0	114.3	112.3
Multifactor productivity	82.8	82.1	84.4	84.2	84.8	84.7	86.2	87.0	88.4	90.2	91.6
Real value-added output	58.6	58.3	60.8	62.6	65.6	67.7	70.9	74.7	78.6	83.1	86.9
Inputs											
Labor input	84.9	84.0	84.9	87.6	91.5	94.0	95.8	99.6	101.9	104.3	105.6
Capital services	49.7	51.2	52.4	54.1	56.0	58.4	61.1	64.4	68.3	72.8	77.4
Combined input quantity	70.7	71.0	72.0	74.3	77.4	79.9	82.2	85.8	88.9	92.2	94.8
Capital hours ratio	53.7	56.6	58.0	58.3	58.1	58.9	60.7	61.8	64.3	67.1	70.6
PRIVATE NONFARM BUSINESS											
Productivity											
Output per hour of all persons	63.8	65.0	67.8	68.0	68.7	69.2	71.1	72.2	74.4	77.0	79.6
Output per unit of capital services	120.8	116.5	118.3	118.2	119.3	118.2	117.9	117.6	116.6	115.6	113.2
Multifactor productivity	83.8	83.2	85.3	85.2	85.7	85.9	87.2	87.7	89.2	90.8	92.1
Real value-added output	58.7	58.4	60.8	62.7	65.6	68.0	71.1	74.8	78.8	83.4	87.0
Inputs											
Labor input	84.2	83.2	84.1	86.9	90.5	92.9	95.0	98.8	101.2	103.9	105.2
Capital services	48.6	50.1	51.4	53.1	55.0	57.5	60.3	63.6	67.6	72.1	76.9
Combined input quantity	70.0	70.2	71.3	73.6	76.6	79.1	81.5	85.3	88.4	91.8	94.5
Capital hours ratio	52.8	55.8	57.3	57.5	57.6	58.5	60.3	61.4	63.9	66.7	70.3
MANUFACTURING											
Productivity											
Output per hour	53.9	55.3	57.5	58.9	61.0	63.8	66.1	69.7	73.5	77.1	80.5
Output per unit of capital services	92.4	88.8	89.7	91.1	94.1	95.7	95.1	97.7	98.4	99.0	99.5
Sector output	67.2	66.0	68.2	70.9	75.1	79.0	81.7	87.7	92.3	96.1	99.0
Inputs											
Labor hours	124.5	119.3	118.7	120.3	123.1	123.9	123.6	125.8	125.5	124.7	123.1
Combined input quantity	87.0	85.8	89.2	90.4	93.3	96.5	99.5	104.0	108.1	111.2	110.6
Energy	88.1	87.9	87.0	89.9	93.1	95.8	93.3	91.4	94.9	117.0	127.6
Materials	66.9	66.6	72.4	72.9	76.1	80.2	87.4	94.4	102.3	108.7	106.6
Capital services	72.7	74.3	76.0	77.8	79.8	82.6	85.9	89.8	93.8	97.1	99.5
Purchased services	83.5	82.9	89.0	89.7	93.2	97.8	97.4	101.4	104.9	105.9	104.4

Sector	2001	2002	2003	2004	2005	2006	2007	2008	2009	2010	2011	2012
PRIVATE BUSINESS												
Productivity												
Output per hour of all persons	81.7	85.2	88.5	91.4	93.3	94.3	95.8	96.6	100.0	103.2	103.6	105.1
Output per unit of capital services	108.0	106.7	107.3	109.4	110.0	109.6	108.7	104.9	100.0	102.8	104.0	106.3
Multifactor productivity	92.1	94.0	96.5	99.2	100.6	101.0	101.3	100.1	100.0	102.6	103.2	104.7
Real value-added output	87.5	89.1	91.9	96.1	99.8	103.1	105.3	104.1	100.0	103.2	105.7	109.6
Inputs												
Labor input	103.7	101.8	101.4	102.5	104.5	107.0	108.4	106.9	100.0	100.6	102.9	105.7
Capital services	81.0	83.5	85.7	87.9	90.8	94.0	96.9	99.3	100.0	100.4	101.6	103.1
Combined input quantity	95.1	94.8	95.3	96.9	99.2	102.0	104.0	104.0	100.0	100.5	102.4	104.7
Capital hours ratio	75.6	79.9	82.5	83.6	84.9	86.0	88.1	92.1	100.0	100.5	99.6	98.8
PRIVATE NONFARM BUSINESS												
Productivity												
Output per hour of all persons	81.9	85.6	88.7	91.5	93.4	94.3	96.0	96.7	100.0	103.3	103.7	105.3
Output per unit of capital services	108.9	107.3	107.7	109.8	110.4	110.2	109.4	105.2	100.0	102.8	104.3	106.8
Multifactor productivity	92.5	94.4	96.7	99.5	100.9	101.2	101.6	100.3	100.0	102.7	103.4	105.0
Real value-added output	87.7	89.3	92.1	96.3	99.9	103.2	105.7	104.3	100.0	103.2	105.8	109.8
Inputs												
Labor input	103.5	101.4	101.1	102.4	104.3	107.0	108.5	106.9	100.0	100.6	102.9	105.7
Capital services	80.6	83.3	85.5	87.7	90.5	93.7	96.6	99.1	100.0	100.4	101.4	102.8
Combined input quantity	94.9	94.5	95.2	96.8	99.1	102.0	104.0	104.0	100.0	100.5	102.3	104.6
Capital hours ratio	75.2	79.8	82.4	83.4	84.6	85.6	87.7	91.9	100.0	100.5	99.4	98.6
MANUFACTURING												
Productivity												
Output per hour	81.9	87.9	93.4	95.5	100.0	100.9	104.8	104.2	104.3	110.9	111.8	. . .
Output per unit of capital services	93.8	93.3	94.5	96.9	100.0	100.9	101.6	94.7	82.4	88.0	90.6	. . .
Sector output	94.2	93.9	94.9	96.5	100.0	101.6	103.8	99.1	86.3	91.7	94.5	. . .
Inputs												
Labor hours	115.0	106.9	101.6	101.1	100.0	100.7	99.0	95.1	82.7	82.7	84.6	. . .
Combined input quantity	106.3	102.6	99.9	98.0	100.0	99.3	100.6	96.6	86.0	87.5	89.5	. . .
Energy	139.4	107.8	96.8	90.7	100.0	95.8	96.4	97.1	74.9	76.1	77.6	. . .
Materials	99.8	100.8	99.2	98.4	100.0	98.9	98.8	93.9	80.6	84.6	90.0	. . .
Capital services	100.5	100.7	100.4	99.6	100.0	100.7	102.1	104.6	104.8	104.2	104.3	. . .
Purchased services	102.6	99.3	98.5	92.4	100.0	97.3	105.7	95.6	85.4	86.5	83.8	. . .

. . . = Not available.

CHAPTER 6: COMPENSATION OF EMPLOYEES

HIGHLIGHTS

This chapter discusses the Employment Cost Index (ECI), which covers changes in wages and salaries and benefits; the Employer Costs for Employee Compensation (ECEC); and employee participation in various benefit plans.

Figure 6-1. Access to Retirement Benefits in Private Industry and State and Local Government by Occupation, March 2013

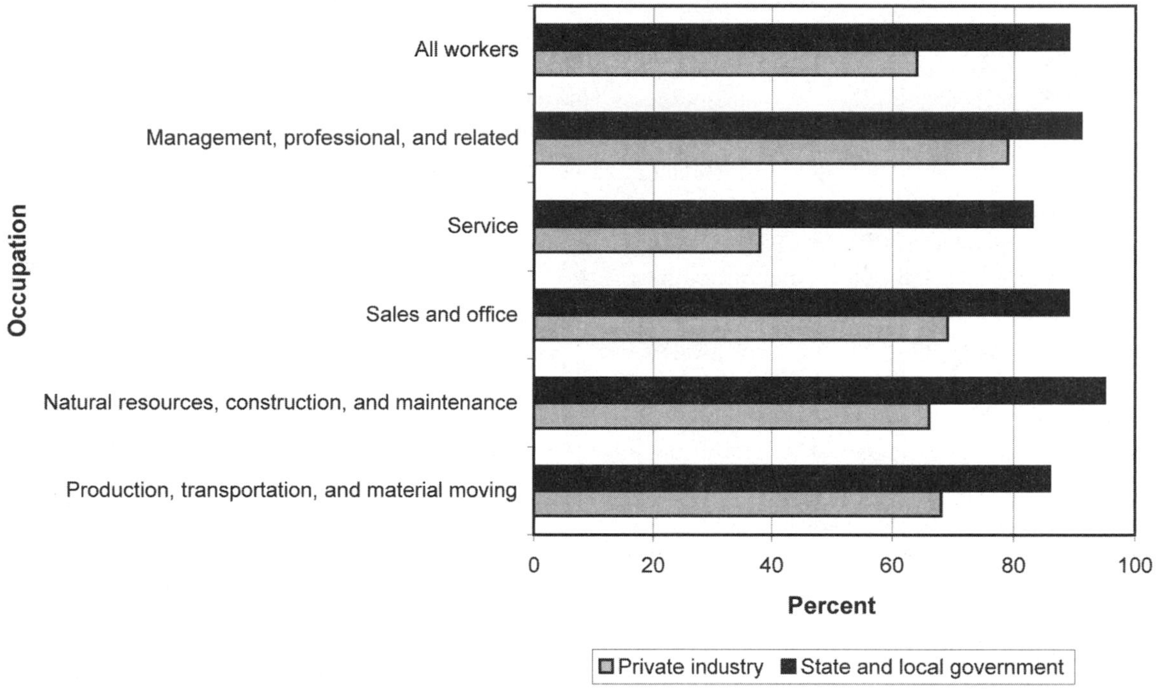

Among all occupations, state and local government workers were far more likely to have access to retirement benefits than those in the private sector. Eighty-nine percent of state and local government workers had access to retirement benefits compared with 64 percent of private industry workers. (See Table 6-9.)

OTHER HIGHLIGHTS

- Wages and salaries made up 70.3 percent of employee compensation for private industry workers in June 2013. Legally required benefits, such as Social Security, Medicare, and insurance, make up the next largest categories at 8.2 percent each, followed by paid leave at 6.9 percent. (See Table 6-5.)

- Total employer compensation costs per hour varied among the different Census divisions, ranging from $34.81 in the New England states (Connecticut, Maine, Massachusetts, New Hampshire, Rhode Island and Vermont) to $24.51 in the East South Central states (Alabama, Kentucky, Mississippi, and Tennessee). (See Table 6-6.)

- Union workers were far more likely to have access to retirement and medical benefits than those that were not in a union. In March 2013, 94 percent of union workers in private industry had access to retirement benefits compared with only 61 percent of nonunion workers. Similarly, 95 percent of union workers had access to medical care benefits compared with 67 percent of nonunion workers. (See Tables 6-9 and 6-10.)

NOTES AND DEFINITIONS

NATIONAL COMPENSATION SURVEY

The National Compensation Survey (NCS) is an establishment survey conducted by the Office of Compensation Levels and Trends (OCLT) at the Bureau of Labor Statistics (BLS). It provides data for the Employment Cost Index (ECI), the Employer Costs for Employee Compensation (ECEC), the occupational earnings series, and the employee benefits survey.

EMPLOYMENT COST INDEX

The ECI is a measure of the change in the cost of labor, independent of the influence of employment shifts among occupations and industry categories. The total compensation series includes changes in wages and salaries and in employer costs for employee benefits. The ECI calculates indexes of total compensation, wages and salaries, and benefits separately for all civilian workers in the United States (as defined by the NCS), for private industry workers, and for workers in state and local government. For all of these categories, the ECI calculates the same indexes by occupational group, worker attribute, industry group, and establishment characteristic. Seasonally adjusted series are calculated as well.

It was developed in the mid-1970s in response to the rapid acceleration of both wages and prices at that time. Monetary and fiscal policymakers needed a more accurate measure of the actual changes in employers' labor costs.

Data for the June 2013 reference period were collected from a probability sample of approximately 45,700 occupational observations selected from a sample of about 9,200 establishments in private industry and approximately 9,100 occupations from a sample of about 1,400 establishments in state and local governments. The state and local government sample, which is replaced less frequently than the private industry sample, was replaced in its entirety in September 2007. The private industry sample is rotated over approximately 5 years, which makes the sample more representative of the economy and reduces respondent burden. Data are collected for the pay period including the 12th day of the survey months of March, June, September, and December. The sample is replaced on a cross-area, cross-industry basis.

CONCEPTS AND DEFINITIONS

Compensation is a term used to encompass the entire range of wages and benefits, both current and deferred, that employees receive in return for their work. In the Employment Cost Index (ECI), compensation includes the employer's cost of wages and salaries, plus the employer's cost of providing employee benefits.

Lump-sum payments are payments made to employees in lieu of a general wage rate increase. The payment may be a fixed amount as set forth in a labor agreement or an amount determined by a formula—for example, 2.5 percent of an employee's earnings during the prior year. Lump-sum payments are not incorporated into an employee's base pay rate or salary, but are considered as nonproduction bonuses in the Employment Cost Index and Employer Costs for Employee Compensation series.

Wages and salaries are defined as the hourly straight-time wage rate or, for workers not paid on an hourly basis, straight-time earnings divided by the corresponding hours. Straight-time wage and salary rates are total earnings before payroll deductions, excluding premium pay for overtime and for work on weekends and holidays, shift differentials, and nonproduction bonuses such as lump-sum payments provided in lieu of wage increases. Production bonuses, incentive earnings, commission payments, and cost-of-living adjustments are included in straight-time wage and salary rates.

Benefits covered by the ECI are as follows: paid leave—vacations, holidays, sick leave, and personal leave; supplemental pay-premium pay for work in addition to the regular work schedule (such as overtime, weekends, and holidays), shift differentials, and nonproduction bonuses (such as referral bonuses and attendance bonuses); insurance benefits—life, health, short-term disability, and long-term disability; retirement and savings benefits—defined benefit and defined contribution plans; and legally required benefits—Social Security, Medicare, federal and state unemployment insurance, and workers' compensation.

SOURCES OF ADDITIONAL INFORMATION

Additional information on ECI methodology and more tables are available in Chapter 8 of the *BLS Handbook of Methods* and BLS new releases. The BLS publication *Compensation and Working Conditions* contains articles on all aspects of the NCS. All of these resources are on the BLS Web site at http://www.bls.gov/ncs/ect/.

Table 6-1. Employment Cost Index, Private Industry Workers, Total Compensation[1] and Wages and Salaries, by Selected Industry and Occupation, 2001–2013

(December 2005 = 100.)

Characteristic and year	Total compensation					Wages and salaries				
	Indexes				Percent change for 12 months (ended December)	Indexes				Percent change for 12 months (ended December)
	March	June	September	December		March	June	September	December	
WORKERS BY INDUSTRY										
Total Private										
2001	85.0	85.8	86.7	87.3	4.1	87.6	88.4	89.2	89.9	3.8
2002	88.2	89.2	89.7	90.0	3.1	90.7	91.6	92.0	92.2	2.6
2003	91.4	92.3	93.2	93.6	4.0	93.3	94.0	94.8	95.1	3.1
2004	94.9	95.9	96.7	97.2	3.8	95.7	96.5	97.3	97.6	2.6
2005	98.2	98.9	99.5	100.0	2.9	98.3	98.9	99.5	100.0	2.5
2006	100.8	101.7	102.5	103.2	3.2	100.7	101.7	102.5	103.2	3.2
2007	104.0	104.9	105.7	106.3	3.0	104.3	105.1	106.0	106.6	3.3
2008	107.3	108.0	108.7	108.9	2.4	107.6	108.4	109.1	109.4	2.6
2009	109.3	109.6	110.0	110.2	1.2	109.8	110.1	110.6	110.8	1.3
2010	111.1	111.7	112.2	112.5	2.1	111.4	111.9	112.4	112.8	1.8
2011	113.3	114.3	114.6	115.0	2.2	113.2	113.8	114.3	114.6	1.6
2012	115.7	116.4	116.8	117.1	1.8	115.3	115.9	116.4	116.6	1.7
2013	117.9	118.6	119.0	. . .	. . .	117.3	118.1	118.5	. . .	. . .
Goods-Producing[2]										
2001	83.9	84.7	85.3	86.0	3.6	87.9	88.8	89.3	90.0	3.6
2002	87.0	87.7	88.2	89.0	3.5	90.7	91.4	91.9	92.6	2.9
2003	90.5	91.5	92.1	92.6	4.0	93.3	94.1	94.6	94.9	2.5
2004	94.5	95.4	96.5	96.9	4.6	95.6	96.2	97.2	97.2	2.4
2005	98.0	99.0	99.8	100.0	3.2	97.9	98.7	99.5	100.0	2.9
2006	100.3	101.3	102.0	102.5	2.5	100.7	101.8	102.3	102.9	2.9
2007	102.9	103.9	104.4	105.0	2.4	103.9	104.7	105.4	106.0	3.0
2008	106.1	106.8	107.2	107.5	2.4	107.1	108.0	108.6	109.0	2.8
2009	107.9	108.2	108.4	108.6	1.0	109.2	109.5	109.8	110.0	0.9
2010	109.7	110.3	111.0	111.1	2.3	110.5	110.9	111.5	111.6	1.5
2011	112.0	113.2	113.4	113.8	2.4	112.2	112.7	113.2	113.5	1.7
2012	114.1	114.7	115.3	115.6	1.6	114.0	114.5	115.1	115.4	1.7
2013	116.4	117.0	117.5	. . .	. . .	116.1	116.8	117.4	. . .	. . .
Service-Providing[3]										
2001	85.4	86.2	87.1	87.8	4.4	87.4	88.3	89.2	89.8	3.8
2002	88.7	89.7	90.2	90.4	3.0	90.7	91.7	92.0	92.1	2.6
2003	91.7	92.5	93.6	94.0	4.0	93.3	93.9	94.9	95.2	3.4
2004	95.1	96.1	96.8	97.3	3.5	95.8	96.6	97.3	97.7	2.6
2005	98.3	98.9	99.5	100.0	2.8	98.4	99.0	99.5	100.0	2.4
2006	101.0	101.8	102.7	103.4	3.4	100.8	101.7	102.6	103.3	3.3
2007	104.3	105.2	106.1	106.7	3.2	104.4	105.3	106.1	106.8	3.4
2008	107.7	108.5	109.1	109.4	2.5	107.7	108.6	109.3	109.6	2.6
2009	109.8	110.1	110.5	110.8	1.3	110.0	110.3	110.8	111.1	1.4
2010	111.6	112.1	112.6	113.0	2.0	111.7	112.3	112.7	113.1	1.8
2011	113.8	114.6	115.0	115.3	2.0	113.5	114.1	114.6	114.9	1.6
2012	116.3	117.0	117.3	117.6	2.0	115.6	116.3	116.7	117.0	1.8
2013	118.4	119.1	119.6	. . .	. . .	117.7	118.4	118.9	. . .	. . .
WORKERS BY OCCUPATION										
Management, Professional, and Related[4]										
2001	85.0	86.0	86.8	87.4	4.5	87.0	88.0	88.9	89.5	4.1
2002	88.3	89.2	89.5	89.7	2.6	90.4	91.3	91.6	91.7	2.5
2003	91.6	92.3	93.3	93.8	4.6	93.3	94.0	94.8	95.3	3.9
2004	94.9	95.7	96.5	97.1	3.5	96.0	96.5	97.3	97.8	2.6
2005	98.5	99.1	99.6	100.0	3.0	98.6	99.2	99.6	100.0	2.2
2006	101.1	101.9	102.9	103.5	3.5	101.1	102.0	103.0	103.6	3.6
2007	104.6	105.5	106.4	106.8	3.2	104.9	105.8	106.7	107.2	3.5
2008	108.1	108.9	109.6	109.9	2.9	108.5	109.3	110.1	110.5	3.1
2009	110.4	110.5	110.6	110.7	0.7	111.1	111.1	111.3	111.5	0.9
2010	111.8	112.2	112.7	113.0	2.1	112.5	112.9	113.4	113.7	2.0
2011	114.1	114.8	115.1	115.4	2.1	114.4	114.9	115.3	115.5	1.6
2012	116.4	117.1	117.4	117.7	2.0	116.3	117.0	117.3	117.7	1.9
2013	118.5	119.4	119.9	. . .	. . .	118.4	119.4	119.8	. . .	. . .

[1]Includes wages, salaries, and employer costs for employee benefits.
[2]Includes mining, construction, and manufacturing.
[3]Includes the following industries: wholesale trade; retail trade; transportation and warehousing; utilities; information; finance and insurance; real estate and rental and leasing; professional, scientific, and technical services; management of companies and enterprises; administrative and support and waste management and remediation services; education services; health care and social assistance; arts, entertainment, and recreation; accommodation and food services; and other services, except public administration.
[4]Includes the following occupational groups: management, business, and financial; professional and related; sales and related; and office and administrative support.
. . . = Not available.

Table 6-1. Employment Cost Index, Private Industry Workers, Total Compensation[1] and Wages and Salaries, by Selected Industry and Occupation, 2001–2013—*Continued*

(December 2005 = 100.)

Characteristic and year	Total compensation					Wages and salaries				
	Indexes				Percent change for 12 months (ended December)	Indexes				Percent change for 12 months (ended December)
	March	June	September	December		March	June	September	December	
Management, Business, and Financial										
2001	86.1	87.1	87.8	88.5	4.4	87.3	88.3	89.1	89.8	4.1
2002	89.5	90.7	90.7	90.6	2.4	90.8	92.2	92.4	92.1	2.6
2003	93.3	93.9	94.9	95.4	5.3	94.8	95.5	96.4	96.7	5.0
2004	95.9	96.8	97.3	97.9	2.6	96.8	97.5	98.1	98.5	1.9
2005	99.1	99.6	99.7	100.0	2.1	99.2	99.7	99.5	100.0	1.5
2006	101.3	102.0	102.7	103.1	3.1	101.3	102.2	102.8	103.1	3.1
2007	104.3	105.1	106.0	106.3	3.1	104.7	105.5	106.3	106.6	3.4
2008	108.0	108.7	109.3	109.5	3.0	108.2	109.0	109.7	110.0	3.2
2009	109.6	109.7	109.7	109.9	0.4	110.3	110.3	110.4	110.8	0.7
2010	111.3	111.7	112.0	112.3	2.2	112.0	112.6	112.8	113.2	2.2
2011	113.6	114.5	114.8	115.0	2.4	113.9	114.4	114.9	115.0	1.6
2012	116.0	116.9	116.9	117.1	1.8	115.7	116.7	116.7	116.9	1.7
2013	118.0	119.3	119.6	...	...	117.9	119.3	119.4	...	...
Professional and Related										
2001	84.1	85.0	86.0	86.5	4.7	86.9	87.8	88.7	89.3	4.1
2002	87.3	87.9	88.5	89.1	3.0	90.1	90.5	91.0	91.4	2.4
2003	90.3	91.0	92.0	92.6	3.9	92.1	92.7	93.6	94.2	3.1
2004	94.1	94.8	95.8	96.5	4.2	95.3	95.7	96.7	97.2	3.2
2005	98.0	98.8	99.5	100.0	3.6	98.2	98.8	99.6	100.0	2.9
2006	101.0	101.8	103.1	103.9	3.9	100.9	101.8	103.1	104.0	4.0
2007	104.9	105.9	106.7	107.3	3.3	105.1	106.0	107.0	107.6	3.5
2007	102.4	103.6	104.2	105.2	2.8	102.8	104.0	104.4	105.5	2.8
2008	105.0	106.2	106.0	105.5	0.3	105.3	106.6	106.4	105.7	0.2
2009	104.3	104.5	105.3	105.8	0.3	104.3	104.7	105.7	106.2	0.5
2010	105.8	107.5	107.4	108.1	2.2	106.2	108.0	107.8	108.7	2.4
2011	107.8	109.8	110.3	110.7	2.4	107.8	109.8	110.4	110.9	2.0
2012	111.4	112.6	113.1	112.8	1.9	111.5	112.8	113.7	113.2	2.1
2013	113.6	114.5	115.1	...	...	113.6	114.6	115.2	...	...
Office and Administrative Support										
2001	84.2	84.9	85.9	86.6	4.6	87.0	87.7	88.8	89.4	4.2
2002	87.9	88.6	89.3	89.9	3.8	90.7	91.3	91.8	92.4	3.4
2003	91.0	92.0	92.8	93.3	3.8	93.1	93.9	94.4	94.7	2.5
2004	94.7	95.8	96.5	97.2	4.2	95.6	96.4	97.1	97.6	3.1
2005	98.1	98.9	99.5	100.0	2.9	98.2	99.0	99.4	100.0	2.5
2006	100.9	101.9	102.7	103.4	3.4	100.9	101.9	102.6	103.3	3.3
2007	104.5	105.4	106.0	106.7	3.2	104.5	105.4	106.0	106.7	3.3
2008	107.8	108.5	109.2	109.6	2.7	107.7	108.5	109.2	109.7	2.8
2009	110.5	110.9	111.3	111.6	1.8	110.6	111.1	111.4	111.8	1.9
2010	112.6	113.1	113.7	114.0	2.2	112.2	112.6	113.3	113.6	1.6
2011	115.1	115.8	116.2	116.5	2.2	114.4	114.8	115.4	115.7	1.8
2012	117.5	118.1	118.4	118.7	1.9	116.4	117.0	117.4	117.7	1.7
2013	119.7	120.4	120.7	...	...	118.6	119.3	119.7	...	...
Natural Resources, Construction, and Maintenance										
2001	84.3	85.0	86.4	86.6	4.0	87.6	88.4	89.9	90.0	3.8
2002	87.4	88.5	89.3	89.7	3.6	90.5	91.7	92.3	92.6	2.9
2003	90.8	92.0	92.8	93.3	4.0	93.2	94.1	94.8	95.2	2.8
2004	94.8	96.1	96.5	97.1	4.1	95.8	96.7	97.1	97.5	2.4
2005	97.9	98.9	99.5	100.0	3.0	97.8	98.7	99.4	100.0	2.6
2006	100.8	102.1	103.0	103.6	3.6	100.7	101.8	102.8	103.4	3.4
2007	104.0	105.0	105.9	106.7	3.0	104.2	105.1	106.2	107.1	3.6
2008	107.6	108.3	109.0	109.6	2.7	108.1	109.0	109.8	110.5	3.2
2009	109.9	110.3	110.8	111.2	1.5	110.6	111.0	111.6	112.0	1.4
2010	112.2	112.7	113.1	113.3	1.9	112.5	112.8	113.1	113.3	1.2
2011	113.8	114.9	115.5	115.8	2.2	113.7	114.4	115.2	115.4	1.9
2012	116.3	117.0	117.7	117.8	1.7	115.6	116.0	116.6	116.7	1.1
2013	118.6	119.1	119.9	...	...	117.2	117.6	118.5	...	...
Construction, Extraction, Farming, Fishing, and Forestry										
2001	84.2	85.1	86.2	86.4	3.8	87.8	88.9	89.8	90.0	3.6
2002	87.3	88.1	88.8	89.5	3.6	90.6	91.3	91.9	92.4	2.7
2003	90.3	91.6	92.5	93.1	4.0	92.7	93.7	94.6	94.9	2.7
2004	94.7	95.8	96.4	97.2	4.4	95.8	96.6	96.9	97.5	2.7
2005	97.7	98.7	99.5	100.0	2.9	97.8	98.5	99.3	100.0	2.6
2006	100.7	102.2	103.1	103.7	3.7	100.7	102.0	103.0	103.7	3.7
2007	104.4	105.7	106.5	107.4	3.6	104.7	105.8	106.7	107.8	4.0
2008	108.6	109.7	110.3	110.8	3.2	109.2	110.1	110.8	111.5	3.4
2009	110.9	111.5	112.0	112.4	1.4	111.4	111.7	112.3	112.7	1.1
2010	113.1	113.6	114.3	114.4	1.8	112.9	113.3	113.9	114.0	1.2
2011	114.8	115.5	116.0	116.5	1.8	114.5	114.9	115.4	115.7	1.5
2012	116.6	117.1	117.8	117.9	1.2	115.7	116.0	116.8	116.7	0.9
2013	118.6	118.9	119.9	...	...	117.1	117.3	118.2	...	...

[1]Includes wages, salaries, and employer costs for employee benefits.
. . . = Not available.

Table 6-1. Employment Cost Index, Private Industry Workers, Total Compensation[1] and Wages and Salaries, by Selected Industry and Occupation, 2001–2013—*Continued*

(December 2005 = 100.)

Characteristic and year	Total compensation					Wages and salaries				
	Indexes				Percent change for 12 months (ended December)	Indexes				Percent change for 12 months (ended December)
	March	June	September	December		March	June	September	December	
Installation, Maintenance, and Repair										
2001	84.4	84.9	86.8	86.8	4.1	87.4	87.9	90.1	90.1	4.3
2002	87.4	89.1	90.0	90.1	3.8	90.4	92.2	92.9	92.9	3.1
2003	91.4	92.5	93.1	93.6	3.9	93.8	94.6	95.1	95.5	2.8
2004	95.0	96.3	96.7	97.0	3.6	95.9	96.8	97.3	97.4	2.0
2005	98.1	99.3	99.6	100.0	3.1	97.8	99.1	99.5	100.0	2.7
2006	100.9	102.1	103.0	103.4	3.4	100.7	101.6	102.6	103.0	3.0
2007	103.5	104.1	105.2	105.8	2.3	103.7	104.2	105.6	106.1	3.0
2008	106.3	106.6	107.4	108.1	2.2	106.8	107.6	108.5	109.3	3.0
2009	108.6	108.9	109.4	109.8	1.6	109.7	110.2	110.7	111.2	1.7
2010	111.1	111.5	111.6	111.9	1.9	112.1	112.1	112.1	112.5	1.2
2011	112.6	114.2	114.9	115.0	2.8	112.7	113.9	115.0	115.0	2.2
2012	116.1	116.8	117.5	117.8	2.4	115.5	115.9	116.4	116.7	1.5
2013	118.6	119.3	119.9	. . .	. . .	117.5	118.0	119.0	. . .	. . .
Production, Transportation, and Material Moving										
2001	85.3	85.8	86.7	87.4	3.6	88.7	89.4	90.2	91.0	3.9
2002	88.4	89.1	89.7	90.3	3.3	91.9	92.4	92.8	93.3	2.5
2003	91.5	92.4	93.2	93.6	3.7	94.0	94.6	95.1	95.4	2.3
2004	95.5	96.5	97.4	97.8	4.5	96.0	96.7	97.6	97.8	2.5
2005	98.5	99.0	99.7	100.0	2.2	98.3	98.9	99.6	100.0	2.2
2006	100.4	101.1	101.7	102.3	2.3	100.6	101.2	101.8	102.4	2.4
2007	102.5	103.3	103.9	104.5	2.2	103.1	103.8	104.5	105.0	2.5
2008	105.5	106.0	106.6	106.9	2.3	106.0	106.8	107.5	107.8	2.7
2009	107.7	108.1	108.6	108.9	1.9	108.3	108.8	109.4	109.6	1.7
2010	109.9	110.5	111.3	111.5	2.4	109.8	110.3	111.1	111.3	1.6
2011	112.2	113.5	113.8	114.2	2.4	111.6	112.0	112.5	112.8	1.3
2012	114.5	115.1	115.7	116.0	1.6	113.7	114.0	114.7	115.1	2.0
2013	116.7	117.2	117.5	. . .	. . .	115.8	116.2	116.7	. . .	. . .
Production										
2001	84.9	85.2	86.0	86.7	3.2	88.4	89.1	89.7	90.5	3.7
2002	87.7	88.3	88.8	89.4	3.1	91.3	91.8	92.3	92.8	2.5
2003	91.0	91.7	92.5	93.0	4.0	93.6	94.1	94.8	95.1	2.5
2004	95.3	96.4	97.4	97.7	5.1	95.6	96.5	97.4	97.5	2.5
2005	98.6	99.1	99.6	100.0	2.4	98.3	98.9	99.5	100.0	2.6
2006	100.4	101.0	101.6	102.0	2.0	100.7	101.2	101.7	102.2	2.2
2007	102.1	102.8	103.2	104.0	2.0	103.1	103.6	104.2	104.6	2.3
2008	104.8	105.2	105.8	106.1	2.0	105.6	106.4	107.2	107.4	2.7
2009	107.1	107.6	108.0	108.2	2.0	108.1	108.5	109.0	109.3	1.8
2010	109.5	110.0	110.7	110.8	2.4	109.6	110.0	110.5	110.5	1.1
2011	111.7	113.2	113.4	113.8	2.7	111.1	111.5	112.0	112.3	1.6
2012	113.8	114.4	114.8	115.0	1.1	113.2	113.5	113.9	114.2	1.7
2013	115.7	116.1	116.3	. . .	. . .	115.0	115.5	116.0	. . .	. . .
Transportation and Material Moving										
2001	85.8	86.7	87.7	88.5	4.2	89.0	89.9	90.8	91.6	4.1
2002	89.5	90.2	90.9	91.4	3.3	92.6	93.1	93.6	94.0	2.6
2003	92.4	93.4	94.0	94.4	3.3	94.7	95.3	95.6	95.8	1.9
2004	95.7	96.7	97.5	97.9	3.7	96.4	97.1	97.9	98.2	2.5
2005	98.3	99.0	99.8	100.0	2.1	98.5	98.9	99.7	100.0	1.8
2006	100.4	101.2	102.0	102.6	2.6	100.4	101.2	102.0	102.6	2.6
2007	103.1	104.1	104.9	105.3	2.6	103.2	104.1	105.0	105.4	2.7
2008	106.4	107.2	107.7	107.9	2.5	106.5	107.4	108.0	108.3	2.8
2009	108.4	108.9	109.6	109.7	1.7	108.5	109.2	109.9	110.1	1.7
2010	110.4	111.2	112.2	112.5	2.6	110.2	110.8	111.8	112.2	1.9
2011	113.0	114.0	114.4	114.9	2.1	112.2	112.8	113.2	113.6	1.2
2012	115.5	116.0	117.0	117.6	2.3	114.4	114.8	115.7	116.3	2.4
2013	118.2	118.6	119.2	. . .	. . .	116.9	117.0	117.7	. . .	. . .
Service										
2001	87.1	87.7	88.2	89.4	3.8	89.7	90.2	90.6	91.7	3.4
2002	90.2	90.6	91.5	92.0	2.9	92.5	92.8	93.4	93.9	2.4
2003	93.0	93.4	94.4	95.0	3.3	94.5	94.8	95.6	96.1	2.3
2004	95.9	96.7	97.2	97.7	2.8	96.4	96.9	97.4	97.9	1.9
2005	98.5	99.0	99.5	100.0	2.4	98.6	99.0	99.6	100.0	2.1
2006	100.8	101.5	102.3	103.1	3.1	100.6	101.3	102.0	102.9	2.9
2007	104.5	105.2	106.4	107.0	3.8	104.6	105.3	106.5	107.1	4.1
2008	107.8	108.7	109.4	109.8	2.6	107.9	108.8	109.7	110.1	2.8
2009	110.7	110.9	111.7	111.8	1.8	111.0	111.2	112.1	112.3	2.0
2010	112.4	112.7	113.3	113.5	1.5	112.6	112.7	113.3	113.5	1.1
2011	114.5	114.7	115.0	115.4	1.7	114.2	114.2	114.6	115.1	1.4
2012	116.0	116.4	116.8	117.4	1.7	115.4	115.8	116.2	116.8	1.5
2013	117.9	118.3	118.4	. . .	. . .	117.2	117.6	117.6	. . .	. . .

[1]Includes wages, salaries, and employer costs for employee benefits.
. . . = Not available.

Table 6-2. Employment Cost Index, Private Industry Workers, Total Compensation[1] and Wages and Salaries, by Bargaining Status and Selected Industry, 2001–2013

(December 2005 = 100.)

Characteristic and year	Total compensation					Wages and salaries				
	Indexes				Percent change for 12 months (ended December)	Indexes				Percent change for 12 months (ended December)
	March	June	September	December		March	June	September	December	
WORKERS BY BARGAINING STATUS AND INDUSTRY										
Union Workers										
2001	82.0	82.9	83.7	84.8	4.2	86.5	87.4	88.3	89.6	4.3
2002	85.7	86.5	87.5	88.2	4.0	90.2	91.1	91.9	92.6	3.3
2003	89.5	90.7	91.6	92.3	4.6	93.0	93.8	94.4	94.9	2.5
2004	94.5	95.9	96.7	97.3	5.4	95.6	96.4	97.1	97.6	2.8
2005	97.9	98.8	99.6	100.0	2.8	97.9	98.7	99.5	100.0	2.5
2006	100.5	101.8	102.4	103.0	3.0	100.3	101.2	101.7	102.3	2.3
2007	102.7	103.9	104.4	105.1	2.0	102.8	103.7	104.4	104.7	2.3
2008	105.9	106.7	107.4	108.0	2.8	105.5	106.7	107.4	108.1	3.2
2009	109.1	109.8	110.5	111.1	2.9	108.8	109.6	110.2	110.9	2.6
2010	112.8	113.7	114.6	114.8	3.3	111.5	112.1	112.7	112.9	1.8
2011	115.6	117.1	117.4	117.9	2.7	113.6	114.0	114.6	114.9	1.8
2012	118.3	119.3	120.2	120.5	2.2	115.6	116.2	116.9	117.4	2.2
2013	121.5	122.1	122.5	...	...	118.4	119.0	119.6	...	...
Union Workers, Goods-Producing[2]										
2001	81.9	82.7	83.4	84.0	2.9	87.2	88.2	88.9	89.5	3.5
2002	84.8	85.5	86.4	87.1	3.7	90.0	90.9	91.7	92.4	3.2
2003	88.9	90.2	90.9	91.7	5.3	92.9	94.0	94.5	95.0	2.8
2004	94.6	95.9	96.7	97.2	6.0	95.4	96.3	96.9	97.1	2.2
2005	97.7	98.8	99.6	100.0	2.9	97.5	98.5	99.2	100.0	3.0
2006	99.9	101.2	101.8	102.2	2.2	100.5	101.6	101.9	102.3	2.3
2007	101.5	102.8	103.1	104.0	1.8	102.7	103.6	104.3	104.3	2.0
2008	104.6	105.6	106.2	106.9	2.8	105.2	106.4	107.1	107.7	3.3
2009	108.0	108.9	109.5	110.0	2.9	108.2	108.8	109.5	109.8	1.9
2010	111.9	112.6	113.8	113.9	3.5	110.2	110.7	111.1	111.2	1.3
2011	114.3	116.4	116.3	116.9	2.6	111.7	112.1	112.8	112.9	1.5
2012	115.8	116.6	117.7	118.0	0.9	113.5	113.8	114.4	115.0	1.9
2013	118.6	118.8	119.2	...	...	115.7	115.9	116.8	...	...
Union Workers, Manufacturing										
2001	81.1	81.4	82.0	83.0	2.7	87.3	88.1	88.8	89.7	3.7
2002	84.1	84.7	85.4	86.5	4.2	90.3	90.8	91.6	92.5	3.1
2003	88.6	89.5	90.1	91.0	5.2	93.3	94.2	94.5	95.0	2.7
2004	95.6	96.7	97.5	97.8	7.5	95.5	96.2	97.0	97.1	2.2
2005	98.3	99.1	99.7	100.0	2.2	97.6	98.3	99.0	100.0	3.0
2006	99.3	100.1	100.5	100.8	0.8	100.6	101.2	101.4	101.7	1.7
2007	99.2	100.0	100.0	101.0	0.2	102.0	102.5	102.9	102.6	0.9
2008	101.4	101.7	102.1	102.8	1.8	103.4	104.4	104.9	105.5	2.8
2009	104.4	104.8	105.3	105.8	2.9	106.0	106.4	107.0	107.3	1.7
2010	108.6	109.1	110.5	110.5	4.4	107.8	108.2	108.6	108.7	1.3
2011	110.9	113.8	113.2	113.8	3.0	109.4	109.8	110.6	110.7	1.8
2012	112.1	112.8	113.6	113.7	-0.1	111.5	111.8	112.1	112.5	1.6
2013	113.9	114.1	113.8	...	...	113.5	113.9	114.4	...	...
Union Workers, Service-Providing[3]										
2001	82.0	83.0	84.0	85.5	5.2	85.9	86.8	87.8	89.6	4.9
2002	86.4	87.3	88.4	89.1	4.2	90.3	91.2	92.0	92.7	3.5
2003	90.1	91.1	92.3	92.8	4.2	93.1	93.6	94.4	94.8	2.3
2004	94.4	95.8	96.6	97.3	4.8	95.7	96.5	97.3	98.0	3.4
2005	98.1	98.8	99.6	100.0	2.8	98.2	99.0	99.7	100.0	2.0
2006	101.0	102.2	102.9	103.6	3.6	100.1	100.9	101.6	102.2	2.2
2007	103.7	104.7	105.4	106.0	2.3	102.9	103.8	104.6	104.9	2.6
2008	107.0	107.5	108.3	108.8	2.6	105.8	106.9	107.7	108.3	3.2
2009	110.9	110.6	111.3	111.9	2.8	109.2	110.1	110.8	111.6	3.0
2010	113.4	114.5	115.2	115.5	3.2	112.4	113.1	113.8	114.2	2.3
2011	116.8	117.7	118.3	118.8	2.9	115.0	115.3	115.8	116.3	1.8
2012	120.4	121.5	122.2	122.6	3.2	117.0	117.9	118.7	119.1	2.4
2013	123.9	124.9	125.2	...	...	120.4	121.3	121.7	...	...

[1]Includes wages, salaries, and employer costs for employee benefits.
[2]Includes mining, construction, and manufacturing.
[3]Includes the following industries: wholesale trade; retail trade; transportation and warehousing; utilities; information; finance and insurance; real estate and rental and leasing; professional, scientific, and technical services; management of companies and enterprises; administrative and support and waste management and remediation services; education services; health care and social assistance; arts, entertainment, and recreation; accommodation and food services; and other services, except public administration.
. . . = Not available.

Table 6-2. Employment Cost Index, Private Industry Workers, Total Compensation[1] and Wages and Salaries, by Bargaining Status and Selected Industry, 2001–2013—Continued

(December 2005 = 100.)

Characteristic and year	Total compensation					Wages and salaries				
	Indexes				Percent change for 12 months (ended December)	Indexes				Percent change for 12 months (ended December)
	March	June	September	December		March	June	September	December	
Nonunion Workers										
2001	85.5	86.3	87.2	87.8	4.2	87.7	88.6	89.3	89.9	3.7
2002	88.7	89.6	90.0	90.3	2.8	90.8	91.7	92.0	92.2	2.6
2003	91.8	92.5	93.5	93.9	4.0	93.3	94.0	94.9	95.1	3.1
2004	95.0	95.9	96.7	97.2	3.5	95.8	96.5	97.3	97.6	2.6
2005	98.3	98.9	99.5	100.0	2.9	98.3	98.9	99.5	100.0	2.5
2006	100.9	101.7	102.6	103.2	3.2	100.8	101.8	102.7	103.3	3.3
2007	104.2	105.1	105.9	106.5	3.2	104.5	105.3	106.2	106.9	3.5
2008	107.5	108.3	108.9	109.1	2.4	107.9	108.7	109.4	109.6	2.5
2009	109.4	109.6	109.9	110.1	0.9	110.0	110.2	110.6	110.9	1.2
2010	110.9	111.4	111.8	112.1	1.8	111.4	111.9	112.4	112.7	1.6
2011	113.0	113.8	114.2	114.5	2.1	113.2	113.8	114.3	114.6	1.7
2012	115.3	116.0	116.3	116.6	1.8	115.2	115.9	116.3	116.5	1.7
2013	117.3	118.0	118.5	...	...	117.2	117.9	118.4	...	...
Nonunion, Goods-Producing[2]										
2001	84.7	85.5	86.0	86.7	3.8	88.1	89.0	89.5	90.1	3.6
2002	87.8	88.5	88.8	89.7	3.5	91.0	91.6	91.9	92.7	2.9
2003	91.1	91.9	92.6	92.9	3.6	93.4	94.1	94.6	94.9	2.4
2004	94.5	95.2	96.4	96.8	4.2	95.6	96.2	97.3	97.3	2.5
2005	98.1	99.0	99.9	100.0	3.3	98.0	98.7	99.6	100.0	2.8
2006	100.5	101.4	102.0	102.5	2.5	100.7	101.9	102.4	103.0	3.0
2007	103.3	104.2	104.8	105.4	2.8	104.2	105.0	105.8	106.4	3.3
2008	106.5	107.1	107.6	107.7	2.2	107.7	108.4	109.0	109.3	2.7
2009	107.9	108.0	108.0	108.2	0.5	109.5	109.7	109.9	110.1	0.7
2010	109.1	109.5	110.1	110.2	1.8	110.6	111.0	111.6	111.7	1.5
2011	111.3	112.2	112.5	112.9	2.5	112.3	112.9	113.3	113.7	1.8
2012	113.5	114.1	114.6	114.9	1.8	114.2	114.7	115.3	115.5	1.6
2013	115.7	116.4	116.9	...	...	116.2	117.0	117.5	...	...
Nonunion Workers, Manufacturing										
2001	84.5	85.3	85.8	86.3	3.6	88.5	89.4	89.8	90.3	3.4
2002	87.6	88.4	88.7	89.4	3.6	91.4	92.0	92.4	92.9	2.9
2003	91.2	91.9	92.6	92.8	3.8	93.9	94.5	94.9	95.2	2.5
2004	94.4	95.3	96.4	96.6	4.1	95.8	96.5	97.5	97.5	2.4
2005	98.2	99.1	99.8	100.0	3.5	98.4	99.0	99.8	100.0	2.6
2006	100.3	101.3	101.7	102.1	2.1	100.7	101.8	102.0	102.5	2.5
2007	102.8	103.7	104.1	104.6	2.4	103.6	104.2	104.9	105.5	2.9
2008	105.6	106.2	106.6	106.8	2.1	106.6	107.3	108.0	108.2	2.6
2009	107.1	107.3	107.3	107.5	0.7	108.6	108.9	109.1	109.3	1.0
2010	108.5	109.2	109.9	110.0	2.3	109.8	110.5	111.1	111.2	1.7
2011	111.6	112.5	112.8	113.0	2.7	112.1	112.6	113.0	113.3	1.9
2012	113.9	114.4	115.0	115.3	2.0	114.1	114.6	115.2	115.4	1.9
2013	116.3	117.0	117.5	...	...	116.2	117.1	117.5	...	...
Nonunion, Service-Providing[3]										
2001	85.7	86.5	87.5	88.0	4.1	87.6	88.5	89.3	89.9	3.8
2002	88.9	89.9	90.4	90.5	2.8	90.8	91.7	92.0	92.1	2.4
2003	91.9	92.7	93.7	94.1	4.0	93.3	94.0	94.9	95.2	3.4
2004	95.2	96.1	96.9	97.3	3.4	95.8	96.6	97.3	97.7	2.6
2005	98.3	98.9	99.4	100.0	2.8	98.4	99.0	99.5	100.0	2.4
2006	101.0	101.8	102.7	103.4	3.4	100.8	101.7	102.7	103.4	3.4
2007	104.4	105.3	106.2	106.8	3.3	104.6	105.4	106.3	107.0	3.5
2008	107.7	108.6	109.2	109.4	2.4	107.9	108.8	109.4	109.7	2.5
2009	109.8	110.0	110.4	110.6	1.1	110.1	110.3	110.8	111.0	1.2
2010	111.3	111.9	112.3	112.7	1.9	111.6	112.2	112.6	113.0	1.8
2011	113.5	114.3	114.7	115.0	2.0	113.4	114.0	114.5	114.8	1.6
2012	115.8	116.5	116.8	117.1	1.8	115.5	116.2	116.5	116.8	1.7
2013	117.8	118.5	119.0	...	...	117.4	118.2	118.6	...	...

[1]Includes wages, salaries, and employer costs for employee benefits.
[2]Includes mining, construction, and manufacturing.
[3]Includes the following industries: wholesale trade; retail trade; transportation and warehousing; utilities; information; finance and insurance; real estate and rental and leasing; professional, scientific, and technical services; management of companies and enterprises; administrative and support and waste management and remediation services; education services; health care and social assistance; arts, entertainment, and recreation; accommodation and food services; and other services, except public administration.
... = Not available.

Table 6-3. Employment Cost Index, Private Industry Workers, Total Compensation[1] and Wages and Salaries, by Region, and Metropolitan Area Status, 2001–2013

(December 2005 = 100.)

Geography type and year	Total compensation					Wages and salaries				
	Indexes				Percent change for 12 months (ended December)	Indexes				Percent change for 12 months (ended December)
	March	June	September	December		March	June	September	December	
CENSUS REGIONS AND DIVISIONS										
Northeast										
2001	84.3	85.3	86.2	86.7	3.8	86.8	87.8	88.6	89.2	3.8
2002	87.7	88.6	88.9	89.3	3.0	90.2	91.0	91.1	91.5	2.6
2003	90.6	91.4	92.4	92.9	4.0	92.4	93.2	94.1	94.5	3.3
2004	94.2	95.5	96.3	96.6	4.0	95.3	96.3	97.1	97.2	2.9
2005	97.6	98.5	99.2	100.0	3.5	97.8	98.6	99.2	100.0	2.9
2006	100.9	101.8	102.5	103.3	3.3	100.8	101.7	102.5	103.1	3.1
2007	104.0	105.1	106.2	106.8	3.4	104.0	105.0	106.1	106.6	3.4
2008	107.4	108.1	108.7	109.5	2.5	107.5	108.2	108.7	109.6	2.8
2009	109.8	110.2	110.7	111.0	1.4	109.9	110.3	110.8	111.1	1.4
2010	111.8	112.7	113.1	113.6	2.3	111.7	112.6	112.9	113.4	2.1
2011	114.4	115.3	115.7	116.1	2.2	113.7	114.6	114.9	115.3	1.7
2012	116.5	117.1	117.6	117.8	1.5	115.8	116.4	116.7	117.0	1.5
2013	118.7	119.4	119.7	...	...	117.6	118.4	118.7	...	...
New England										
2006	100.7	101.4	102.1	103.1	3.1	100.7	101.5	102.3	103.1	3.1
2007	103.6	104.8	105.4	106.1	2.9	103.6	104.8	105.7	106.3	3.1
2008	106.7	107.1	107.8	109.5	3.2	107.1	107.6	108.3	110.3	3.8
2009	109.9	110.2	111.2	111.5	1.8	110.5	110.6	111.7	112.1	1.6
2010	112.3	113.1	113.4	114.1	2.3	112.6	113.4	113.5	114.3	2.0
2011	114.8	116.0	116.2	116.3	1.9	114.5	115.9	116.0	116.0	1.5
2012	116.9	117.4	118.0	118.5	1.9	116.6	117.2	117.8	118.2	1.9
2013	118.9	120.0	120.5	...	...	118.6	119.8	120.5	...	...
Middle Atlantic										
2006	100.9	101.9	102.6	103.3	3.3	100.8	101.7	102.5	103.1	3.1
2007	104.2	105.3	106.5	107.1	3.7	104.2	105.1	106.4	106.7	3.5
2008	107.8	108.6	109.1	109.5	2.2	107.6	108.4	109.0	109.4	2.5
2009	109.8	110.2	110.6	110.8	1.2	109.7	110.1	110.4	110.7	1.2
2010	111.6	112.5	113.0	113.4	2.3	111.3	112.3	112.7	113.1	2.2
2011	114.3	115.1	115.5	116.0	2.3	113.4	114.0	114.5	115.0	1.7
2012	116.4	117.0	117.4	117.6	1.4	115.4	116.1	116.4	116.5	1.3
2013	118.6	119.2	119.5	...	...	117.3	117.9	118.0	...	...
South										
2001	86.4	87.2	88.1	88.7	4.2	88.9	89.7	90.5	91.0	3.6
2002	89.5	90.5	91.2	91.2	2.8	91.8	92.7	93.3	93.2	2.4
2003	92.0	92.7	93.6	93.9	3.0	93.5	94.1	94.9	95.0	1.9
2004	95.2	96.2	97.1	97.7	4.0	95.8	96.7	97.5	98.0	3.2
2005	98.9	99.3	99.7	100.0	2.4	98.9	99.3	99.7	100.0	2.0
2006	101.0	101.6	102.8	103.5	3.5	101.0	101.6	102.9	103.6	3.6
2007	104.3	105.3	106.1	106.7	3.1	104.6	105.6	106.5	107.0	3.3
2008	107.8	108.5	109.1	109.3	2.4	108.1	109.1	109.8	110.0	2.8
2009	109.8	110.1	110.6	110.7	1.3	110.4	110.7	111.3	111.5	1.4
2010	111.5	112.0	112.5	112.8	1.9	111.9	112.4	112.9	113.4	1.7
2011	113.4	114.3	114.7	115.0	2.0	113.7	114.4	115.0	115.2	1.6
2012	116.0	116.8	117.2	117.7	2.3	116.0	116.7	117.3	117.8	2.3
2013	118.6	119.3	119.7	...	...	118.7	119.3	119.7	...	...
South Atlantic										
2006	101.2	101.9	103.1	103.8	3.8	101.3	101.9	103.2	103.9	3.9
2007	104.9	106.0	106.8	107.3	3.4	105.0	106.1	106.9	107.5	3.5
2008	108.5	109.1	109.7	109.8	2.3	108.6	109.5	110.2	110.3	2.6
2009	110.3	110.7	111.3	111.5	1.5	110.8	111.3	111.9	112.2	1.7
2010	112.2	112.6	113.0	113.3	1.6	112.5	112.9	113.3	113.7	1.3
2011	113.8	114.6	115.1	115.4	1.9	114.0	114.6	115.4	115.6	1.7
2012	116.4	117.3	117.8	118.3	2.5	116.4	117.3	118.0	118.5	2.5
2013	119.1	119.8	120.2	...	...	119.2	120.0	120.2	...	...
East South Central										
2006	100.7	100.9	101.5	102.3	2.3	100.7	101.5	102.1	103.1	3.1
2007	103.3	103.8	104.8	105.4	3.0	104.2	104.5	105.6	106.3	3.1
2008	106.5	107.2	108.0	108.0	2.5	107.2	107.9	109.0	109.0	2.5
2009	108.5	108.7	109.2	109.3	1.2	109.2	109.5	110.1	110.2	1.1
2010	110.0	110.8	111.0	110.9	1.5	110.8	111.4	111.6	111.5	1.2
2011	112.1	112.7	113.0	113.2	2.1	112.6	112.9	113.4	113.5	1.8
2012	114.0	115.1	115.3	115.8	2.3	114.1	114.8	114.9	115.4	1.7
2013	116.8	116.9	117.5	...	...	116.3	116.4	116.8	...	...
West South Central										
2006	100.7	101.4	102.7	103.4	3.4	100.6	101.2	102.7	103.4	3.4
2007	103.7	104.8	105.6	106.1	2.6	104.1	105.3	106.1	106.6	3.1
2008	107.3	108.2	108.7	109.0	2.7	107.8	108.8	109.4	109.8	3.0
2009	109.4	109.5	109.9	109.9	0.8	110.1	110.2	110.8	110.9	1.0
2010	110.8	111.4	112.2	112.7	2.5	111.3	111.9	112.8	113.5	2.3
2011	113.2	114.4	114.7	115.0	2.0	113.7	114.5	115.0	115.2	1.5
2012	116.2	116.8	117.0	117.6	2.3	116.1	116.6	117.1	117.7	2.2
2013	118.5	119.3	119.8	...	...	118.7	119.5	120.0	...	...

[1] Includes wages, salaries, and employer costs for employee benefits.
. . . = Not available.

Table 6-3. Employment Cost Index, Private Industry Workers, Total Compensation[1] and Wages and Salaries, by Region, and Metropolitan Area Status, 2001–2013—*Continued*

(December 2005 = 100.)

Geography type and year	Total compensation					Wages and salaries				
	Indexes				Percent change for 12 months (ended December)	Indexes				Percent change for 12 months (ended December)
	March	June	September	December		March	June	September	December	
Midwest										
2001	84.8	85.4	86.1	86.7	3.5	86.8	87.6	88.3	88.9	3.3
2002	88.0	88.7	89.0	89.5	3.2	90.3	91.0	91.3	91.7	3.1
2003	92.1	92.8	93.6	94.0	5.0	94.2	94.7	95.2	95.5	4.1
2004	95.0	95.9	96.6	96.9	3.1	95.6	96.1	96.9	97.1	1.7
2005	97.8	98.4	99.5	100.0	3.2	97.8	98.2	99.4	100.0	3.0
2006	100.7	101.7	102.3	102.8	2.8	100.4	101.4	102.0	102.6	2.6
2007	103.3	104.2	104.6	105.3	2.4	103.6	104.4	105.0	105.6	2.9
2008	106.0	107.0	107.4	107.6	2.2	106.3	107.5	107.9	108.0	2.3
2009	107.9	108.1	108.4	108.6	0.9	108.4	108.6	108.9	109.2	1.1
2010	109.9	110.4	111.0	111.3	2.5	109.9	110.4	110.9	111.2	1.8
2011	112.2	113.3	113.6	113.9	2.3	111.8	112.2	112.7	112.9	1.5
2012	114.7	115.3	115.6	115.9	1.8	113.8	114.3	114.7	115.0	1.9
2013	116.4	117.0	117.4	...	...	115.5	116.0	116.6	...	...
East North Central										
2006	100.7	101.7	102.3	102.8	2.8	100.3	101.4	101.9	102.5	2.5
2007	103.2	104.1	104.4	105.0	2.1	103.6	104.4	104.7	105.3	2.7
2008	105.5	106.5	106.9	107.0	1.9	105.8	107.0	107.3	107.4	2.0
2009	107.0	107.3	107.5	107.8	0.7	107.5	107.7	108.0	108.3	0.8
2010	109.2	109.8	110.3	110.5	2.5	109.1	109.7	110.1	110.3	1.8
2011	111.6	112.7	113.1	113.2	2.4	110.9	111.3	111.8	111.9	1.5
2012	113.9	114.5	114.6	114.8	1.4	112.7	113.1	113.4	113.5	1.4
2013	115.4	116.0	116.4	...	...	114.1	114.7	115.3	...	...
West North Central										
2006	100.6	101.5	102.4	102.7	2.7	100.6	101.5	102.4	102.7	2.7
2007	103.5	104.3	105.3	105.9	3.1	103.8	104.5	105.6	106.3	3.5
2008	107.3	108.4	108.8	109.0	2.9	107.9	108.9	109.5	109.7	3.2
2009	109.9	110.2	110.6	110.7	1.6	110.7	110.8	111.2	111.4	1.5
2010	111.6	112.0	112.8	113.2	2.3	111.9	112.4	113.1	113.5	1.9
2011	113.9	114.8	115.0	115.6	2.1	114.0	114.5	114.9	115.4	1.7
2012	116.9	117.5	118.2	118.7	2.7	116.5	117.1	118.0	118.5	2.7
2013	119.1	119.4	119.9	...	...	119.0	119.2	119.8	...	...
West										
2001	84.1	85.0	85.9	86.9	5.2	87.4	88.3	89.2	90.2	4.8
2002	87.4	88.5	89.1	89.8	3.3	90.4	91.5	92.0	92.4	2.4
2003	90.9	92.0	93.2	93.8	4.5	93.0	93.9	95.1	95.5	3.4
2004	95.3	96.2	96.9	97.4	3.8	96.4	97.0	97.7	98.0	2.6
2005	98.4	99.3	99.7	100.0	2.7	98.4	99.3	99.6	100.0	2.0
2006	100.6	101.8	102.5	103.0	3.0	100.7	102.1	102.7	103.2	3.2
2007	104.2	104.9	105.7	106.5	3.4	104.8	105.4	106.2	107.0	3.7
2008	107.8	108.4	109.3	109.4	2.7	108.3	108.9	109.9	110.1	2.9
2009	109.9	110.0	110.3	110.6	1.1	110.5	110.8	111.2	111.6	1.4
2010	111.3	111.7	112.3	112.5	1.7	112.0	112.4	112.9	113.0	1.3
2011	113.5	114.3	114.6	115.1	2.3	113.6	114.1	114.5	114.9	1.7
2012	115.7	116.3	116.8	116.8	1.5	115.4	116.1	116.5	116.4	1.3
2013	117.6	118.5	119.2	...	...	117.1	118.1	118.8	...	...
Mountain										
2006	101.0	101.8	102.7	103.1	3.1	100.6	101.7	102.8	103.2	3.2
2007	105.2	105.2	106.6	107.5	4.3	105.3	105.5	106.7	107.8	4.5
2008	108.4	109.4	110.3	110.4	2.7	108.9	109.9	110.8	111.0	3.0
2009	110.5	110.6	110.9	111.0	0.5	111.1	111.4	111.9	111.9	0.8
2010	111.3	112.3	113.0	112.8	1.6	112.3	113.2	114.1	113.7	1.6
2011	113.4	113.9	114.8	115.3	2.2	113.7	114.1	115.0	115.2	1.3
2012	115.4	116.0	116.5	115.7	0.3	115.2	115.7	116.3	115.2	0.0
2013	116.6	118.1	118.7	...	...	116.0	117.8	118.3	...	...
Pacific										
2006	100.5	101.8	102.5	103.0	3.0	100.8	102.2	102.7	103.3	3.3
2007	103.9	104.8	105.4	106.1	3.0	104.6	105.3	106.0	106.8	3.4
2008	107.6	108.1	108.9	109.1	2.8	108.1	108.6	109.6	109.8	2.8
2009	109.7	109.9	110.1	110.5	1.3	110.3	110.6	110.9	111.5	1.5
2010	111.4	111.5	112.0	112.4	1.7	112.0	112.1	112.4	112.8	1.2
2011	113.6	114.5	114.6	115.1	2.4	113.6	114.1	114.4	114.9	1.9
2012	115.9	116.5	117.0	117.4	2.0	115.5	116.3	116.7	117.0	1.8
2013	118.1	118.7	119.5	...	...	117.6	118.3	119.1	...	...

[1]Includes wages, salaries, and employer costs for employee benefits.
. . . = Not available.

Table 6-4. Employment Cost Index, Benefits, by Industry and Occupation, 2001–2013

(December 2005 = 100.)

Characteristic and year	Indexes				Percent change for 12 months (ended December)
	March	June	September	December	
Civilian Workers[1]					
2001	78.0	78.8	79.9	80.8	1.1
2002	81.5	82.5	83.5	84.6	1.3
2003	86.3	87.5	88.9	90.0	1.2
2004	92.1	93.7	94.8	95.9	1.2
2005	97.5	98.4	99.4	100.2	0.8
2006	100.8	101.7	102.7	103.7	1.0
2007	104.0	105.2	106.0	107.0	0.9
2008	107.5	108.1	108.8	109.3	0.5
2009	109.6	109.9	110.4	110.9	0.5
2010	112.0	112.6	113.5	114.1	0.5
2011	115.4	116.8	117.0	117.8	0.7
2012	118.5	119.3	119.9	120.6	0.6
2013	121.3	121.8	122.6	. . .	. . .
Total Private					
2001	78.8	79.5	80.6	81.5	1.1
2002	82.3	83.3	84.1	85.0	1.1
2003	87.0	88.1	89.4	90.5	1.2
2004	92.9	94.4	95.4	96.5	1.2
2005	98.0	98.8	99.7	100.3	0.6
2006	100.8	101.6	102.5	103.4	0.9
2007	103.1	104.2	105.0	105.9	0.9
2008	106.4	106.9	107.5	107.9	0.4
2009	108.1	108.2	108.6	109.0	0.4
2010	110.3	110.9	111.7	112.2	0.4
2011	113.6	115.2	115.4	116.2	0.7
2012	116.7	117.4	117.9	118.6	0.6
2013	119.1	119.6	120.3	. . .	. . .
State and Local Government Workers					
2001	75.2	76.3	77.4	78.0	0.8
2002	78.8	79.9	81.4	82.9	1.8
2003	84.1	85.4	86.9	88.0	1.3
2004	89.5	91.1	92.5	93.9	1.5
2005	95.6	96.8	98.4	99.9	1.5
2006	100.8	102.0	103.5	105.1	1.5
2007	107.1	108.7	109.7	110.9	1.1
2008	111.4	112.4	113.3	114.1	0.7
2009	115.3	116.2	116.8	117.7	0.8
2010	118.2	119.1	120.2	121.1	0.7
2011	122.0	122.6	123.1	123.6	0.4
2012	124.8	125.9	127.0	127.9	0.7
2013	129.2	130.0	130.7	. . .	. . .
WORKERS BY OCCUPATION					
Management, Professional, and Related					
2002	82.7	83.7	84.2	85.2	1.2
2003	87.1	88.0	89.5	90.7	1.3
2004	91.9	93.4	94.5	95.9	1.5
2005	97.9	98.8	99.8	100.4	0.6
2006	101.0	101.7	102.8	103.8	1.0
2007	103.5	104.8	105.5	106.4	0.9
2008	107.1	107.8	108.5	109.0	0.5
2009	108.5	108.7	108.9	109.3	0.4
2010	109.9	110.3	111.0	111.7	0.6
2011	113.1	114.5	114.8	115.8	0.9
2012	116.4	117.1	117.7	118.5	0.7
2013	118.3	119.2	120.2	. . .	. . .
Sales and Office					
2002	81.8	83.2	84.2	85.1	1.1
2003	86.6	88.0	89.3	90.4	1.2
2004	92.5	94.2	95.2	96.1	0.9
2005	97.5	98.4	99.3	100.2	0.9
2006	100.7	101.5	102.1	103.0	0.9
2007	103.3	104.2	105.2	106.1	0.9
2008	106.5	106.9	107.6	108.0	0.4
2009	108.0	108.0	108.6	108.9	0.3
2010	110.1	110.9	111.7	112.1	0.4
2011	113.3	114.8	115.3	115.8	0.4
2012	116.6	117.4	117.4	117.9	0.4
2013	118.9	119.4	120.2	. . .	. . .
Natural Resources, Construction, and Maintenance					
2002	81.2	82.1	83.3	84.6	1.6
2003	86.0	87.6	88.7	90.3	1.8
2004	92.9	94.5	95.4	96.9	1.6
2005	98.0	98.9	99.7	100.4	0.7
2006	101.1	102.4	103.4	104.4	1.0
2007	103.5	104.5	105.2	106.3	1.0
2008	106.6	106.7	107.4	108.0	0.6
2009	108.2	108.6	109.1	109.8	0.6
2010	111.6	112.1	112.9	113.5	0.5
2011	114.1	115.6	116.1	117.2	0.9
2012	117.9	118.8	119.8	120.6	0.7
2013	121.6	121.8	122.5	. . .	. . .

[1]Includes workers in the private nonfarm economy, except those in private households, and workers in the public sector, except those in the federal government.
. . . = Not available.

Table 6-4. Employment Cost Index, Benefits, by Industry and Occupation, 2001–2013—*Continued*

(December 2005 = 100.)

Characteristic and year	Indexes				Percent change for 12 months (ended December)
	March	June	September	December	
Production, Transportation, and Material Moving					
2002	81.8	82.7	83.7	84.8	1.3
2003	86.7	88.1	89.4	90.4	1.1
2004	94.4	96.0	97.1	98.0	0.9
2005	98.7	99.2	99.9	100.1	0.2
2006	100.0	100.8	101.6	102.3	0.7
2007	101.1	102.3	102.7	103.9	1.2
2008	104.4	104.4	104.8	105.3	0.5
2009	106.4	106.6	107.1	107.6	0.5
2010	109.9	110.6	111.7	112.2	0.4
2011	113.5	116.3	116.3	117.2	0.8
2012	116.1	116.9	117.6	118.2	0.5
2013	118.7	118.9	119.1	. . .	. . .
Service					
2002	83.5	84.4	86.0	86.8	0.9
2003	88.5	89.4	90.8	92.0	1.3
2004	94.3	95.9	96.7	97.3	0.6
2005	98.0	98.8	99.5	100.3	0.8
2006	101.3	102.1	103.0	103.9	0.9
2007	104.0	105.0	106.0	107.0	0.9
2008	107.4	108.3	108.7	109.2	0.5
2009	109.5	109.8	110.4	110.9	0.5
2010	111.4	112.3	113.3	114.0	0.6
2011	115.1	115.9	116.0	116.9	0.8
2012	117.7	118.1	118.8	119.7	0.8
2013	119.6	120.2	120.8	. . .	. . .
WORKERS BY INDUSTRY					
Goods-producing industries[2]					
2001	76.5	77.0	77.8	78.7	1.1
2002	79.9	80.6	81.2	82.5	1.6
2003	85.2	86.5	87.5	88.4	1.0
2004	92.4	93.8	95.0	96.5	1.6
2005	98.3	99.5	100.3	100.2	-0.1
2006	99.4	100.3	101.3	102.0	0.7
2007	100.9	102.1	102.4	103.4	1.0
2008	104.0	104.3	104.6	105.0	0.4
2009	105.4	105.5	105.6	106.1	0.5
2010	108.3	108.8	109.9	110.4	0.5
2011	111.7	113.9	113.8	114.8	0.9
2012	114.1	114.7	115.6	116.4	0.7
2013	117.0	117.1	117.6	. . .	. . .
Manufacturing					
2001	75.4	75.8	76.4	77.4	1.2
2002	78.8	79.7	80.3	81.5	1.5
2003	84.7	85.7	86.8	87.5	0.8
2004	92.7	94.1	95.4	96.1	0.7
2005	98.2	99.4	100.1	100.1	0.0
2006	98.6	99.6	100.7	101.1	0.4
2007	99.4	100.8	100.9	101.9	1.0
2008	102.2	102.0	102.4	102.8	0.4
2009	103.4	103.4	103.4	103.9	0.5
2010	106.5	107.2	108.7	109.2	0.5
2011	111.0	113.7	113.4	114.3	0.8
2012	113.1	113.7	114.7	115.5	0.7
2013	115.7	115.8	116.3	. . .	. . .
Service-Providing[3]					
2001	79.7	80.5	81.7	82.6	1.1
2002	83.2	84.4	85.2	86.0	0.9
2003	87.7	88.8	90.2	91.4	1.3
2004	93.0	94.6	95.5	96.5	1.0
2005	97.9	98.6	99.4	100.3	0.9
2006	101.3	102.2	103.0	104.0	1.0
2007	104.0	105.1	106.0	106.9	0.8
2008	107.4	108.0	108.7	109.1	0.4
2009	109.2	109.3	109.9	110.2	0.3
2010	111.1	111.7	112.3	112.9	0.5
2011	114.3	115.7	116.0	116.8	0.7
2012	117.8	118.5	118.9	119.5	0.5
2013	119.9	120.6	121.4	. . .	. . .

[2]Includes mining, construction, and manufacturing.
[3]Includes the following industries: wholesale trade; retail trade; transportation and warehousing; utilities; information; finance and insurance; real estate and rental and leasing; professional, scientific, and technical services; management of companies and enterprises; administrative and support and waste management and remediation services; education services; health care and social assistance; arts, entertainment, and recreation; accommodation and food services; and other services, except public administration.
. . . = Not available.

NOTES AND DEFINITIONS

EMPLOYER COSTS FOR EMPLOYEE COMPENSATION (ECEC)

The ECEC series measures the average cost to employers for wages and salaries, and for benefits, per employee hour worked. The series provides quarterly data on employer costs per hour worked for total compensation, wages and salaries, total benefits, and the following benefits: paid leave—vacations, holidays, sick leave, and personal leave; supplemental pay—premium pay for work in addition to the regular work schedule (such as overtime, weekend, and holiday work) and for shift differentials, and nonproduction bonuses (such as yearend, referral, and attendance bonuses); insurance benefits—life, health, short-term disability, and long-term disability insurance; retirement and savings benefits—defined benefit and defined contribution plans; and legally required benefits—Social Security, Medicare, federal and state unemployment insurance, and workers' compensation. Cost data are presented both in dollar amounts and as percentages of total compensation. The ECEC uses current employment weights to reflect the composition of today's labor force.

Differences in the estimates for the state and local government and private industry sectors stem from factors such as variation in work activities and in occupational structures. Manufacturing and sales, for example, make up a large part of private industry work activities but are rare in state and local government. In contrast, professional and administrative support occupations (including teachers) account for two-thirds of the state and local government workforce but less than one-half of private industry.

The cost levels for June 2013 were collected from a probability sample of 45,700 occupations selected from a sample of about 9,200 establishments in private industry and approximately 9,100 occupations from a sample of about 1,400 establishments in state and local governments.

ECEC includes the civilian economy, which includes data from both private industry and state and local government. Excluded from private industry are the self-employed and farm and private household workers. Federal government workers are excluded from the public sector. The private industry series and the state and local government series provide data for the two sectors separately.

SOURCES OF ADDITIONAL INFORMATION

Additional information may be obtained from BLS news release 13-1835, "Employer Costs for Employee Compensation—June 2013," and Chapter 8 of the *BLS Handbook of Methods*.

Table 6-5. Employer Compensation Costs Per Hour Worked for Employee Compensation and Costs as a Percent of Total Compensation: Private Industry Workers, by Major Industry Group, June 2013

(Dollars, percent of total cost.)

Compensation component	All workers		Goods-producing[1]						Service-providing[2]			
			All goods-producing[1]		Construction		Manufacturing		All service-providing[2]		Trade, transportation, and utilities	
	Cost	Percent	Cost	Percent	Cost	Percent	Cost	Percent	Cost	Percent	Cost	Percent
TOTAL COMPENSATION	29.11	100.0	34.57	100.0	34.37	100.0	33.84	100.0	27.98	100.0	24.59	100.0
Wages and Salaries	20.47	70.3	23.12	66.9	23.86	69.4	22.29	65.9	19.92	71.2	17.33	70.5
Total Benefits	8.64	29.7	11.44	33.1	10.52	30.6	11.55	34.1	8.07	28.8	7.27	29.5
Paid leave	2.00	6.9	2.26	6.5	1.49	4.3	2.54	7.5	1.94	6.9	1.48	6.0
Vacation	1.04	3.6	1.19	3.5	0.76	2.2	1.35	4.0	1.00	3.6	0.78	3.2
Holiday	0.61	2.1	0.79	2.3	0.54	1.6	0.88	2.6	0.58	2.1	0.44	1.8
Sick	0.24	0.8	0.20	0.6	0.13	0.4	0.23	0.7	0.25	0.9	0.19	0.8
Personal	0.10	0.4	0.08	0.2	0.06	0.2	0.09	0.3	0.11	0.4	0.07	0.3
Supplemental pay	0.80	2.8	1.31	3.8	0.93	2.7	1.40	4.2	0.70	2.5	0.57	2.3
Overtime and premium pay[3]	0.25	0.8	0.55	1.6	0.59	1.7	0.52	1.5	0.18	0.7	0.25	1.0
Shift differentials	0.06	0.2	0.08	0.2	(4)	(5)	0.12	0.4	0.06	0.2	0.02	0.1
Nonproduction bonuses	0.49	1.7	0.67	2.0	0.33	1.0	0.77	2.3	0.46	1.6	0.29	1.2
Insurance	2.39	8.2	3.28	9.5	2.64	7.7	3.54	10.5	2.20	7.9	2.18	8.9
Life insurance	0.04	0.1	0.06	0.2	0.04	0.1	0.06	0.2	0.04	0.1	0.03	0.1
Health insurance	2.25	7.7	3.09	8.9	2.52	7.3	3.33	9.8	2.08	7.4	2.07	8.4
Short-term disability	0.05	0.2	0.08	0.2	0.06	0.2	0.09	0.3	0.05	0.2	0.04	0.1
Long-term disability	0.04	0.1	0.05	0.1	0.02	0.1	0.05	0.2	0.04	0.2	0.05	0.2
Retirement and savings	1.07	3.7	1.57	4.5	1.94	5.6	1.29	3.8	0.97	3.4	0.89	3.6
Defined benefit plans	0.47	1.6	0.82	2.4	1.23	3.6	0.57	1.7	0.40	1.4	0.45	1.8
Defined contribution plans	0.60	2.1	0.75	2.2	0.71	2.1	0.72	2.1	0.57	2.0	0.44	1.8
Legally required benefits	2.39	8.2	3.02	8.7	3.52	10.3	2.77	8.2	2.26	8.1	2.15	8.7
Social Security and Medicare	1.70	5.9	1.96	5.7	1.96	5.7	1.92	5.7	1.65	5.9	1.44	5.8
Social Security[6]	1.37	4.7	1.57	4.6	1.58	4.6	1.55	4.6	1.33	4.7	1.16	4.7
Medicare	0.34	1.2	0.38	1.1	0.38	1.1	0.38	1.1	0.33	1.2	0.28	1.1
Federal unemployment insurance	0.04	0.1	0.03	0.1	0.03	0.1	0.03	0.1	0.04	0.1	0.04	0.2
State unemployment insurance	0.23	0.8	0.31	0.9	0.39	1.1	0.28	0.8	0.22	0.8	0.20	0.8
Workers' compensation	0.41	1.4	0.72	2.1	1.15	3.3	0.53	1.6	0.35	1.3	0.47	1.9

Compensation component	Service-providing[2]											
	Information		Financial activities		Professional and business services		Education and health services		Leisure and hospitality		Other services	
	Cost	Percent	Cost	Percent	Cost	Percent	Cost	Percent	Cost	Percent	Cost	Percent
TOTAL COMPENSATION	47.15	100.0	40.75	100.0	34.92	100.0	30.79	100.0	12.68	100.0	25.19	100.0
Wages and Salaries	30.85	65.4	27.44	67.3	25.16	72.0	22.01	71.5	10.00	78.9	18.33	72.8
Total Benefits	16.30	34.6	13.31	32.7	9.76	28.0	8.77	28.5	2.67	21.1	6.86	27.2
Paid leave	4.20	8.9	3.39	8.3	2.59	7.4	2.36	7.7	0.40	3.2	1.50	6.0
Vacation	2.18	4.6	1.74	4.3	1.35	3.9	1.19	3.9	0.22	1.8	0.72	2.8
Holiday	1.07	2.3	1.00	2.5	0.81	2.3	0.67	2.2	0.12	1.0	0.50	2.0
Sick	0.50	1.1	0.48	1.2	0.30	0.9	0.34	1.1	0.04	0.3	0.21	0.8
Personal	0.44	0.9	0.18	0.4	0.13	0.4	0.15	0.5	0.02	0.1	0.08	0.3
Supplemental pay	1.46	3.1	2.10	5.2	0.85	2.4	0.57	1.8	0.15	1.2	0.31	1.2
Overtime and premium pay[3]	0.31	0.7	0.14	0.4	0.17	0.5	0.20	0.6	0.07	0.6	0.12	0.5
Shift differentials	0.05	0.1	0.02	(5)	0.02	0.1	0.20	0.7	(4)	(5)	(4)	(5)
Nonproduction bonuses	1.10	2.3	1.94	4.8	0.66	1.9	0.16	0.5	0.07	0.6	0.19	0.7
Insurance	4.58	9.7	3.42	8.4	2.44	7.0	2.51	8.1	0.61	4.8	1.84	7.3
Life insurance	0.06	0.1	0.05	0.1	0.05	0.1	0.03	0.1	(4)	(5)	0.03	0.1
Health insurance	4.25	9.0	3.20	7.9	2.27	6.5	2.39	7.8	0.59	4.6	1.76	7.0
Short-term disability	0.20	0.4	0.11	0.3	0.06	0.2	0.04	0.1	(4)	(5)	0.03	0.1
Long-term disability	0.07	0.1	0.06	0.2	0.06	0.2	0.05	0.1	(4)	(5)	0.02	0.1
Retirement and savings	2.86	6.1	1.67	4.1	1.19	3.4	0.96	3.1	0.14	1.1	0.99	3.9
Defined benefit plans	1.67	3.5	0.50	1.2	0.46	1.3	0.29	1.0	0.05	0.4	0.54	2.1
Defined contribution plans	1.19	2.5	1.17	2.9	0.73	2.1	0.67	2.2	0.09	0.7	0.45	1.8
Legally required benefits	3.21	6.8	2.72	6.7	2.70	7.7	2.38	7.7	1.37	10.8	2.22	8.8
Social Security and Medicare	2.64	5.6	2.25	5.5	2.06	5.9	1.83	6.0	0.87	6.8	1.52	6.0
Social Security[6]	2.11	4.5	1.78	4.4	1.64	4.7	1.47	4.8	0.70	5.5	1.22	4.9
Medicare	0.53	1.1	0.47	1.2	0.41	1.2	0.36	1.2	0.17	1.3	0.29	1.2
Federal unemployment insurance	0.04	0.1	0.04	0.1	0.04	0.1	0.03	0.1	0.04	0.4	0.03	0.1
State unemployment insurance	0.25	0.5	0.23	0.6	0.26	0.7	0.19	0.6	0.20	1.6	0.28	1.1
Workers' compensation	0.29	0.6	0.20	0.5	0.34	1.0	0.33	1.1	0.26	2.0	0.39	1.6

Note: Individual items may not sum to totals due to rounding.

[1]Includes mining, construction, and manufacturing. The agriculture, forestry, farming, and hunting sector is excluded.
[2]Includes utilities; wholesale trade; retail trade; transportation and warehousing; information; finance and insurance; real estate and rental and leasing; professional and technical services; management of companies and enterprises; administrative and waste services; education services; health care and social assistance; arts, entertainment, and recreation; accommodation and food services; and other services, except public administration.
[3]Includes premium pay for work in addition to the regular work schedule (such as overtime, weekends, and holidays).
[4]Cost per hour worked is $0.01 or less.
[5]Less than 0.05 percent.
[6]Comprises the Old Age, Survivors, and Disability Insurance (OASDI) program.

Table 6-6. Employer Compensation Costs Per Hour Worked for Employee Compensation and Costs as a Percent of Total Compensation: Private Industry Workers, by Census Region and Area, June 2013

(Dollars, percent of total costs.)

Compensation component	Census region and division[1]					
	Northeast		Northeast divisions			
			New England		Middle Atlantic	
	Cost	Percent	Cost	Percent	Cost	Percent
TOTAL COMPENSATION	33.50	100.0	34.81	100.0	33.02	100.0
Wages and Salaries	23.06	68.8	24.29	69.8	22.61	68.5
Total Benefits	10.44	31.2	10.52	30.2	10.41	31.5
Paid leave	2.50	7.5	2.54	7.3	2.48	7.5
Vacation	1.26	3.8	1.30	3.7	1.24	3.8
Holiday	0.75	2.2	0.79	2.3	0.73	2.2
Sick	0.33	1.0	0.31	0.9	0.34	1.0
Personal	0.16	0.5	0.14	0.4	0.17	0.5
Supplemental pay	1.03	3.1	0.94	2.7	1.06	3.2
Overtime and premium pay[2]	0.24	0.7	0.24	0.7	0.24	0.7
Shift differentials	0.07	0.2	0.09	0.2	0.07	0.2
Nonproduction bonuses	0.71	2.1	0.61	1.8	0.75	2.3
Insurance	2.90	8.6	2.85	8.2	2.91	8.8
Life insurance	0.05	0.1	0.05	0.1	0.05	0.2
Health insurance	2.71	8.1	2.67	7.7	2.73	8.3
Short-term disability	0.08	0.3	0.07	0.2	0.09	0.3
Long-term disability	0.05	0.2	0.05	0.2	0.05	0.2
Retirement and savings	1.29	3.8	1.40	4.0	1.25	3.8
Defined benefit plans	0.57	1.7	0.62	1.8	0.56	1.7
Defined contribution plans	0.71	2.1	0.78	2.2	0.69	2.1
Legally required benefits	2.74	8.2	2.80	8.0	2.71	8.2
Social Security and Medicare	1.91	5.7	2.01	5.8	1.88	5.7
Social Security	1.53	4.6	1.61	4.6	1.50	4.5
Medicare	0.39	1.1	0.40	1.1	0.38	1.2
Federal unemployment insurance	0.04	0.1	0.03	0.1	0.04	0.1
State unemployment insurance	0.33	1.0	0.33	0.9	0.33	1.0
Workers' compensation	0.45	1.4	0.43	1.2	0.46	1.4

Compensation component	Census region and division[1]							
	South		South divisions					
			South Atlantic		East South Central		West South Central	
	Cost	Percent	Cost	Percent	Cost	Percent	Cost	Percent
TOTAL COMPENSATION	26.51	100.0	26.79	100.0	24.51	100.0	26.85	100.0
Wages and Salaries	19.01	71.7	19.31	72.1	17.29	70.5	19.20	71.5
Total Benefits	7.50	28.3	7.48	27.9	7.22	29.5	7.65	28.5
Paid leave	1.75	6.6	1.81	6.8	1.59	6.5	1.71	6.4
Vacation	0.89	3.4	0.94	3.5	0.80	3.3	0.86	3.2
Holiday	0.55	2.1	0.56	2.1	0.52	2.1	0.55	2.1
Sick	0.21	0.8	0.22	0.8	0.18	0.8	0.21	0.8
Personal	0.09	0.4	0.10	0.4	0.08	0.3	0.09	0.3
Supplemental pay	0.75	2.8	0.65	2.4	0.73	3.0	0.92	3.4
Overtime and premium pay[2]	0.27	1.0	0.23	0.9	0.30	1.2	0.34	1.3
Shift differentials	0.06	0.2	0.06	0.2	0.06	0.2	0.05	0.2
Nonproduction bonuses	0.42	1.6	0.36	1.4	0.37	1.5	0.53	2.0
Insurance	2.01	7.6	2.00	7.5	2.05	8.4	2.02	7.5
Life insurance	0.04	0.1	0.03	0.1	0.04	0.2	0.04	0.1
Health insurance	1.90	7.2	1.88	7.0	1.93	7.9	1.91	7.1
Short-term disability	0.04	0.2	0.05	0.2	0.04	0.2	0.04	0.1
Long-term disability	0.04	0.1	0.04	0.1	0.04	0.2	0.04	0.1
Retirement and savings	0.87	3.3	0.87	3.3	0.82	3.4	0.87	3.2
Defined benefit plans	0.34	1.3	0.34	1.3	0.39	1.6	0.32	1.2
Defined contribution plans	0.52	2.0	0.53	2.0	0.43	1.8	0.54	2.0
Legally required benefits	2.12	8.0	2.14	8.0	2.02	8.2	2.13	7.9
Social Security and Medicare	1.59	6.0	1.61	6.0	1.48	6.0	1.61	6.0
Social Security	1.28	4.8	1.30	4.8	1.19	4.9	1.30	4.8
Medicare	0.31	1.2	0.32	1.2	0.28	1.2	0.32	1.2
Federal unemployment insurance	0.03	0.1	0.04	0.1	0.03	0.1	0.02	0.1
State unemployment insurance	0.16	0.6	0.17	0.6	0.15	0.6	0.16	0.6
Workers' compensation	0.33	1.3	0.33	1.2	0.36	1.5	0.33	1.2

Note: Individual items may not sum to totals due to rounding.

[1]The states that comprise the Census divisions are: New England—Connecticut, Maine, Massachusetts, New Hampshire, Rhode Island, and Vermont; Middle Atlantic—New Jersey, New York, and Pennsylvania; South Atlantic—Delaware, District of Columbia, Florida, Georgia, Maryland, North Carolina, South Carolina, Virginia, and West Virginia; East South Central—Alabama, Kentucky, Mississippi, and Tennessee; West South Central—Arkansas, Louisiana, Oklahoma, and Texas; East North Central—Illinois, Indiana, Michigan, Ohio, and Wisconsin; West North Central—Iowa, Kansas, Minnesota, Missouri, Nebraska, North Dakota, and South Dakota; Mountain—Arizona, Colorado, Idaho, Montana, Nevada, New Mexico, Utah, and Wyoming; and Pacific—Alaska, California, Hawaii, Oregon, and Washington.
[2]Comprises the Old-Age, Survivors, and Disability Insurance (OASDI) program.

Table 6-6. Employer Compensation Costs Per Hour Worked for Employee Compensation and Costs as a Percent of Total Compensation: Private Industry Workers, by Census Region and Area, June 2013—*Continued*

(Dollars, percent of total costs.)

Compensation component	Census region and division[1]					
	Midwest		Midwest divisions			
			East North Central		West North Central	
	Cost	Percent	Cost	Percent	Cost	Percent
TOTAL COMPENSATION	27.89	100.0	28.26	100.0	27.14	100.0
Wages and Salaries	19.39	69.5	19.46	68.9	19.24	70.9
Total Benefits	8.50	30.5	8.80	31.1	7.90	29.1
Paid leave	1.85	6.7	1.87	6.6	1.82	6.7
Vacation	0.99	3.6	1.01	3.6	0.97	3.6
Holiday	0.58	2.1	0.58	2.0	0.57	2.1
Sick	0.19	0.7	0.19	0.7	0.21	0.8
Personal	0.09	0.3	0.10	0.4	0.07	0.3
Supplemental pay	0.73	2.6	0.81	2.9	0.57	2.1
Overtime and premium pay[2]	0.24	0.9	0.26	0.9	0.20	0.7
Shift differentials	0.07	0.3	0.08	0.3	0.05	0.2
Nonproduction bonuses	0.42	1.5	0.47	1.7	0.33	1.2
Insurance	2.53	9.1	2.65	9.4	2.30	8.5
Life insurance	0.04	0.1	0.04	0.1	0.04	0.1
Health insurance	2.40	8.6	2.51	8.9	2.17	8.0
Short-term disability	0.06	0.2	0.06	0.2	0.05	0.2
Long-term disability	0.04	0.2	0.04	0.2	0.04	0.2
Retirement and savings	1.10	3.9	1.14	4.0	1.01	3.7
Defined benefit plans	0.52	1.9	0.59	2.1	0.37	1.4
Defined contribution plans	0.58	2.1	0.55	1.9	0.64	2.4
Legally required benefits	2.28	8.2	2.33	8.2	2.20	8.1
Social Security and Medicare	1.62	5.8	1.64	5.8	1.59	5.9
Social Security	1.31	4.7	1.32	4.7	1.28	4.7
Medicare	0.32	1.1	0.32	1.1	0.31	1.2
Federal unemployment insurance	0.04	0.1	0.04	0.1	0.03	0.1
State unemployment insurance	0.24	0.9	0.25	0.9	0.22	0.8
Workers' compensation	0.39	1.4	0.40	1.4	0.35	1.3

Compensation component	Census region and division[1]					
	West		West divisions			
			Mountain		Pacific	
	Cost	Percent	Cost	Percent	Cost	Percent
TOTAL COMPENSATION	30.58	100.0	27.78	100.0	31.82	100.0
Wages and Salaries	21.60	70.6	19.87	71.6	22.37	70.3
Total Benefits	8.98	29.4	7.90	28.4	9.45	29.7
Paid leave	2.09	6.8	1.92	6.9	2.17	6.8
Vacation	1.10	3.6	1.05	3.8	1.12	3.5
Holiday	0.63	2.0	0.53	1.9	0.67	2.1
Sick	0.28	0.9	0.24	0.9	0.30	0.9
Personal	0.09	0.3	0.10	0.4	0.08	0.2
Supplemental pay	0.76	2.5	0.69	2.5	0.79	2.5
Overtime and premium pay[2]	0.22	0.7	0.22	0.8	0.22	0.7
Shift differentials	0.05	0.2	0.04	0.1	0.05	0.2
Nonproduction bonuses	0.49	1.6	0.43	1.6	0.52	1.6
Insurance	2.35	7.7	2.02	7.3	2.50	7.9
Life insurance	0.03	0.1	0.03	0.1	0.04	0.1
Health insurance	2.24	7.3	1.92	6.9	2.39	7.5
Short-term disability	0.03	0.1	0.03	0.1	0.04	0.1
Long-term disability	0.04	0.1	0.05	0.2	0.04	0.1
Retirement and savings	1.16	3.8	1.03	3.7	1.22	3.8
Defined benefit plans	0.52	1.7	0.34	1.2	0.60	1.9
Defined contribution plans	0.64	2.1	0.69	2.5	0.62	2.0
Legally required benefits	2.61	8.5	2.24	8.1	2.78	8.7
Social Security and Medicare	1.78	5.8	1.62	5.8	1.85	5.8
Social Security	1.42	4.7	1.29	4.6	1.48	4.7
Medicare	0.35	1.2	0.33	1.2	0.37	1.2
Federal unemployment insurance	0.04	0.1	0.03	0.1	0.04	0.1
State unemployment insurance	0.25	0.8	0.19	0.7	0.28	0.9
Workers' compensation	0.54	1.8	0.40	1.4	0.61	1.9

Note: Individual items may not sum to totals due to rounding.

[1]The states that comprise the Census divisions are: New England—Connecticut, Maine, Massachusetts, New Hampshire, Rhode Island, and Vermont; Middle Atlantic—New Jersey, New York, and Pennsylvania; South Atlantic—Delaware, District of Columbia, Florida, Georgia, Maryland, North Carolina, South Carolina, Virginia, and West Virginia; East South Central—Alabama, Kentucky, Mississippi, and Tennessee; West South Central—Arkansas, Louisiana, Oklahoma, and Texas; East North Central—Illinois, Indiana, Michigan, Ohio, and Wisconsin; West North Central—Iowa, Kansas, Minnesota, Missouri, Nebraska, North Dakota, and South Dakota; Mountain—Arizona, Colorado, Idaho, Montana, Nevada, New Mexico, Utah, and Wyoming; and Pacific—Alaska, California, Hawaii, Oregon, and Washington.

[2]Comprises the Old-Age, Survivors, and Disability Insurance (OASDI) program.

Table 6-7. Employer Compensation Costs Per Hour Worked for Employee Compensation and Costs as a Percent of Total Compensation: State and Local Government, by Major Occupational and Injury Group, June 2013

(Dollars, percent of total compensation.)

Characteristic	Total compensation	Wages and salaries	Benefit costs					
			Total	Paid leave	Supplemental pay	Insurance	Retirement and savings	Legally required benefits
COSTS PER HOUR WORKED								
State and Local Government Workers	42.09	27.16	14.93	3.10	0.35	5.11	3.81	2.56
Occupational Group								
Management, professional, and related	51.22	34.43	16.80	3.44	0.25	5.67	4.49	2.94
Professional and related	50.25	34.00	16.25	3.10	0.25	5.63	4.46	2.82
Teachers[1]	57.56	40.26	17.30	2.78	0.14	6.11	5.17	3.10
Primary, secondary, and special education school teachers	58.07	40.23	17.84	2.52	0.16	6.78	5.41	2.97
Sales and office	29.02	17.47	11.55	2.53	0.20	4.56	2.41	1.86
Office and administrative support	29.24	17.55	11.69	2.56	0.20	4.63	2.44	1.86
Service	31.77	18.69	13.08	2.78	0.59	4.24	3.36	2.12
Industry Group								
Education and health services	44.14	29.60	14.54	2.75	0.22	5.31	3.76	2.50
Education services	44.90	30.32	14.58	2.59	0.16	5.41	3.94	2.49
Elementary and secondary schools	44.41	30.03	14.38	2.27	0.16	5.58	3.97	2.41
Junior colleges, colleges, and universities	47.16	31.83	15.33	3.85	0.14	4.64	3.91	2.80
Health care and social assistance	39.79	25.46	14.33	3.67	0.58	4.74	2.76	2.59
Hospitals	44.57	28.79	15.78	4.21	0.74	5.10	3.01	2.72
Public administration	40.38	24.21	16.16	3.79	0.57	5.00	4.12	2.68
PERCENT OF TOTAL COMPENSATION								
State and Local Government Workers	100.0	64.5	35.5	7.4	0.8	12.2	9.0	6.1
Occupational Group								
Management, professional, and related	100.0	67.2	32.8	6.7	0.5	11.1	8.8	5.7
Professional and related	100.0	67.7	32.3	6.2	0.5	11.2	8.9	5.6
Teachers[1]	100.0	69.9	30.1	4.8	0.2	10.6	9.0	5.4
Primary, secondary, and special education school teachers	100.0	69.3	30.7	4.3	0.3	11.7	9.3	5.1
Sales and office	100.0	60.2	39.8	8.7	0.7	15.7	8.3	6.4
Office and administrative support	100.0	60.0	40.0	8.8	0.7	15.8	8.3	6.4
Service	100.0	58.8	41.2	8.7	1.8	13.3	10.6	6.7
Industry Group								
Education and health services	100.0	67.1	32.9	6.2	0.5	12.0	8.5	5.7
Education services	100.0	67.5	32.5	5.8	0.3	12.0	8.8	5.5
Elementary and secondary schools	100.0	67.6	32.4	5.1	0.4	12.6	8.9	5.4
Junior colleges, colleges, and universities	100.0	67.5	32.5	8.2	0.3	9.8	8.3	5.9
Health care and social assistance	100.0	64.0	36.0	9.2	1.4	11.9	6.9	6.5
Hospitals	100.0	64.6	35.4	9.4	1.7	11.4	6.7	6.1
Public administration	100.0	60.0	40.0	9.4	1.4	12.4	10.2	6.6

Note: Individual items may not sum to totals due to rounding.

[1]Includes postsecondary teachers; primary, secondary, and special education teachers; and other teachers and instructors.

Table 6-8. Employer Compensation Costs Per Hour Worked for Employee Compensation and Costs as a Percent of Total Compensation: Private Industry Workers, by Establishment Employment Size, June 2013

(Dollars, percent.)

Compensation component	1–99 workers						100 workers or more					
	1–99 workers		1–49 workers		50–99 workers		100 workers or more		100–499 workers		500 workers or more	
	Cost	Percent	Cost	Percent	Cost	Percent	Cost	Percent	Cost	Percent	Cost	Percent
TOTAL COMPENSATION	23.91	100.0	23.09	100.0	26.64	100.0	35.22	100.0	29.76	100.0	43.15	100.0
Wages and Salaries	17.70	74.0	17.28	74.8	19.13	71.8	23.71	67.3	20.56	69.1	28.29	65.6
Total Benefits	6.21	26.0	5.81	25.2	7.51	28.2	11.50	32.7	9.19	30.9	14.86	34.4
Paid leave	1.37	5.7	1.27	5.5	1.73	6.5	2.73	7.8	2.12	7.1	3.62	8.4
Vacation	0.70	2.9	0.64	2.8	0.91	3.4	1.43	4.1	1.10	3.7	1.91	4.4
Holiday	0.45	1.9	0.42	1.8	0.53	2.0	0.81	2.3	0.65	2.2	1.04	2.4
Sick	0.16	0.7	0.15	0.6	0.19	0.7	0.35	1.0	0.25	0.8	0.48	1.1
Personal	0.07	0.3	0.06	0.3	0.10	0.4	0.15	0.4	0.12	0.4	0.18	0.4
Supplemental pay	0.47	2.0	0.43	1.9	0.61	2.3	1.19	3.4	0.78	2.6	1.78	4.1
Overtime and premium pay[1]	0.17	0.7	0.15	0.7	0.24	0.9	0.33	0.9	0.30	1.0	0.38	0.9
Shift differentials	(3)	(3)	(3)	(3)	0.03	0.1	0.12	0.3	0.06	0.2	0.20	0.5
Nonproduction bonuses	0.29	1.2	0.27	1.2	0.34	1.3	0.74	2.1	0.43	1.4	1.19	2.8
Insurance	1.62	6.8	1.49	6.5	2.03	7.6	3.29	9.3	2.71	9.1	4.12	9.6
Life insurance	0.03	0.1	0.02	0.1	0.03	0.1	0.05	0.2	0.05	0.2	0.06	0.1
Health insurance	1.54	6.4	1.42	6.2	1.93	7.3	3.09	8.8	2.55	8.6	3.86	8.9
Short-term disability	0.03	0.1	0.03	0.1	0.04	0.1	0.08	0.2	0.06	0.2	0.10	0.2
Long-term disability	0.02	0.1	0.02	0.1	0.03	0.1	0.07	0.2	0.04	0.1	0.10	0.2
Retirement and savings	0.60	2.5	0.52	2.2	0.86	3.2	1.62	4.6	1.18	4.0	2.26	5.2
Defined benefit plans	0.23	1.0	0.20	0.8	0.33	1.3	0.75	2.1	0.52	1.8	1.08	2.5
Defined contribution plans	0.37	1.5	0.32	1.4	0.53	2.0	0.87	2.5	0.66	2.2	1.18	2.7
Legally required benefits	2.14	9.0	2.10	9.1	2.28	8.6	2.68	7.6	2.40	8.1	3.07	7.1
Social Security and Medicare	1.46	6.1	1.43	6.2	1.58	5.9	1.99	5.7	1.72	5.8	2.39	5.5
Social Security[4]	1.17	4.9	1.15	5.0	1.26	4.7	1.59	4.5	1.38	4.6	1.91	4.4
Medicare	0.28	1.2	0.28	1.2	0.31	1.2	0.40	1.1	0.34	1.1	0.49	1.1
Federal unemployment insurance	0.04	0.2	0.04	0.2	0.04	0.1	0.03	0.1	0.03	0.1	0.03	0.1
State unemployment insurance	0.23	1.0	0.23	1.0	0.25	0.9	0.23	0.7	0.23	0.8	0.23	0.5
Workers' compensation	0.41	1.7	0.41	1.8	0.42	1.6	0.42	1.2	0.42	1.4	0.42	1.0

[1]Includes premium pay for work in addition to the regular work schedule (such as overtime, weekends, and holidays).
[2]Cost per hour worked is $0.01 or less.
[3]Less than .05 percent.
[4]Comprises the Old-Age, Survivors, and Disability Insurance (OASDI) program.

NOTES AND DEFINITIONS

EMPLOYEE BENEFITS SURVEY

The Employee Benefits Survey provides data on the incidence and provisions of selected employee benefit plans.

COLLECTION AND COVERAGE

The March 2013 National Compensation Survey (NCS) benefits survey represented nearly 125 million civilian workers; of this number, about 106 million were private industry workers and 19 million were state and local government workers. It included a sample of 11,893 establishments.

DEFINITIONS

Access to a benefit is determined on an occupational basis within an establishment. An employee is considered to have access to a benefit if it is available for his or her use.

Participation refers to the proportion of employees covered by a benefit. There will be cases whernemployees with access to a plan will not participate. For example, some employees may decline to participate in a health insurance plan if there is an employee cost involved.

A *private establishment* is an economic unit that produces goods or services, a central administrative office, or an auxiliary unit providing support services to a company. For private industries, the establishment is usually at a single physical location. For state and local governments, an establishment is defined as an agency or entity, such as a school district, college, university, hospital, nursing home, administrative body, court, police department, fire department, health or social service operation, highway maintenance operation, urban transit operation, or other governmental unit. It provides services under the authority of a specific state or local government organization within a defined geographic area or jurisdiction.

Take-up rates are the percentage of workers with access to a plan who participate in the plan. They are computed by using the number of workers participating in a plan divided by the number of workers with access to the plan, times 100 and rounded to the nearest one percent. Since the computation of take-up rates is based on the number of workers collected, rather than the rounded percentage estimates, the take-up rates in the tables may not equal the ratio of participation to access estimates.

An employee is considered to be a *union worker* when all the following conditions are met: 1) a labor organization is recognized as the bargaining agent for all workers in the occupation; 2) wage and salary rates are determined through collective bargaining or negotiations; 3) settlement terms, which must include earnings provisions and may include benefit provisions, are embodied in a signed, mutually binding collective bargaining agreement.

SOURCES OF ADDITIONAL INFORMATION

For more information, see Bureau of Labor Statistics (BLS) news release 13-1344, "Employee Benefits in the United States in the United States—March 2013," which is available on the BLS Web site at http://www.bls.gov/ncs/ebs/.

Table 6-9. Retirement Benefits:[1] Access, Participation, and Take-Up Rates,[2] March 2013

(Percent.)

Characteristic	Civilian[3]			Private industry			State and local government		
	Access	Participation	Take-up rate	Access	Participation	Take-up rate	Access	Participation	Take-up rate
ALL WORKERS	68	54	80	64	49	76	89	85	95
Worker Characteristics									
Management, professional, and related	83	73	88	79	68	85	91	87	95
Management, business, and financial	85	76	89	84	74	88	-	-	-
Professional and related	82	72	88	77	64	83	91	87	95
Teachers	86	81	94	-	-	-	91	86	95
Primary, secondary, and special education school teachers	95	91	96	-	-	-	99	95	97
Registered nurses	78	66	84	-	-	-	-	-	-
Service	45	30	67	38	21	56	83	79	95
Protective service	79	63	80	62	29	46	90	87	96
Sales and office	70	54	77	69	51	74	89	85	96
Sales and related	67	43	64	67	43	64	-	-	-
Office and administrative support	73	60	83	70	57	81	90	86	96
Natural resources, construction, and maintenance	69	56	82	66	53	79	95	92	96
Construction, extraction, farming, fishing, and forestry	65	53	81	61	47	77	-	-	-
Installation, maintenance, and repair	73	60	82	71	57	81	-	-	-
Production, transportation, and material moving	69	52	76	68	51	75	86	82	95
Production	73	57	78	72	56	78	-	-	-
Transportation and material moving	65	48	74	64	46	72	-	-	-
Full-time workers	78	65	83	74	59	80	99	94	95
Part-time workers	37	21	57	37	20	53	39	35	91
Union workers	95	89	93	94	86	92	97	93	95
Nonunion workers	63	48	76	61	45	73	83	78	95
Average Wage Within the Following Percentiles[4]									
Lowest 25 percent	40	22	54	38	18	48	73	69	95
Lowest 10 percent	28	11	38	28	10	35	58	55	94
Second 25 percent	70	54	77	65	47	72	93	88	95
Third 25 percent	80	68	85	75	62	82	95	90	95
Highest 25 percent	89	80	90	85	75	89	98	93	95
Highest 10 percent	90	82	91	87	78	90	98	92	94
Establishment Characteristics									
Goods-producing industries	75	61	81	75	61	81	-	-	-
Service-providing industries	67	53	79	62	46	74	89	85	95
Education and health services	76	65	86	67	52	78	90	85	94
Educational services	86	80	93	71	60	84	90	86	95
Elementary and secondary schools	90	86	95	-	-	-	92	88	96
Junior colleges, colleges, and universities	87	78	89	89	76	85	86	79	91
Health care and social assistance	68	54	79	66	51	77	89	82	92
Hospitals	90	77	86	-	-	-	95	85	89
Public administration	91	87	96	-	-	-	91	87	96
Number of Workers									
1 to 99 workers	50	36	72	49	35	71	77	74	96
1 to 49 workers	45	33	73	45	32	72	69	66	95
50 to 99 workers	65	46	71	63	43	68	89	86	97
100 workers or more	85	71	84	82	65	79	91	86	95
100 to 499 workers	80	61	76	79	58	73	87	84	96
500 workers or more	89	80	90	87	76	87	92	87	95
Geographic Areas[5]									
New England	68	55	81	65	50	77	86	82	96
Middle Atlantic	67	55	83	63	51	81	91	84	92
East North Central	70	56	81	68	53	78	84	82	97
West North Central	73	58	79	70	53	76	91	83	92
South Atlantic	67	52	77	63	46	73	90	84	93
East South Central	72	57	80	66	48	73	92	89	97
West South Central	68	52	77	65	46	71	89	86	97
Mountain	66	51	77	63	45	72	88	86	97
Pacific	65	53	82	60	46	77	91	88	98

[1]Includes defined benefit pension plans and defined contribution retirement plans. Workers are considered as having access or as participating if they have access to or participate in at least one of these plan types.
[2]The take-up rate is an estimate of the percentage of workers with access to a plan who participate in the plan, rounded for presentation.
[3]Includes workers in the private nonfarm economy except those in private households, and workers in the public sector, except the federal government.
[4]The percentile groupings are based on the average wage for each occupation surveyed, which may include workers both above and below the threshold.
[5]The states that comprise the Census divisions are: New England—Connecticut, Maine, Massachusetts, New Hampshire, Rhode Island, and Vermont; Middle Atlantic—New Jersey, New York, and Pennsylvania; South Atlantic—Delaware, District of Columbia, Florida, Georgia, Maryland, North Carolina, South Carolina, Virginia, and West Virginia; East South Central—Alabama, Kentucky, Mississippi, and Tennessee; West South Central—Arkansas, Louisiana, Oklahoma, and Texas; East North Central—Illinois, Indiana, Michigan, Ohio, and Wisconsin; West North Central—Iowa, Kansas, Minnesota, Missouri, Nebraska, North Dakota, and South Dakota; Mountain—Arizona, Colorado, Idaho, Montana, Nevada, New Mexico, Utah, and Wyoming; and Pacific—Alaska, California, Hawaii, Oregon, and Washington.
- = No workers in this area or data does not meet standards of reliability or precision.

Table 6-10. Medical Care Benefits: Access, Participation, and Take-Up Rates,[1] March 2013

(Percent.)

Characteristic	Civilian[2]			Private industry			State and local government		
	Access	Participation	Take-up rate	Access	Participation	Take-up rate	Access	Participation	Take-up rate
ALL WORKERS	72	54	75	70	51	73	87	73	84
Worker Characteristics									
Management, professional, and related	88	69	79	87	67	77	89	74	83
Management, business, and financial	94	73	78	94	73	77	-	-	-
Professional and related	85	68	79	84	65	77	89	74	83
Teachers	86	70	81	-	-	-	88	73	82
Primary, secondary, and special education school teachers	97	79	82	-	-	-	98	80	82
Registered nurses	81	60	74	-	-	-	-	-	-
Service	46	31	67	40	25	61	81	69	85
Protective service	70	58	83	45	32	71	88	77	87
Sales and office	73	53	74	71	52	72	87	73	84
Sales and related	62	43	69	62	43	69	-	-	-
Office and administrative support	79	59	75	77	57	74	87	73	84
Natural resources, construction, and maintenance	79	60	77	77	58	75	95	83	87
Construction, extraction, farming, fishing, and forestry	73	58	79	70	54	77	-	-	-
Installation, maintenance, and repair	84	63	75	83	61	74	-	-	-
Production, transportation, and material moving	76	58	76	76	57	75	82	68	83
Production	84	64	77	84	64	76	-	-	-
Transportation and material moving	69	52	75	69	51	74	-	-	-
Full-time workers	88	67	77	85	64	75	99	84	84
Part-time workers	24	13	56	24	13	54	24	17	73
Union workers	95	79	83	95	79	83	95	79	84
Nonunion workers	68	50	73	67	48	72	80	68	84
Average Wage Within the Following Percentiles[3]									
Lowest 25 percent	38	23	60	34	20	57	68	56	82
Lowest 10 percent	21	11	52	20	10	50	54	42	78
Second 25 percent	78	58	74	74	53	72	91	78	86
Third 25 percent	88	70	79	86	66	77	94	80	86
Highest 25 percent	94	75	80	93	72	78	97	80	83
Highest 10 percent	95	76	80	94	74	79	97	82	85
Establishment Characteristics									
Goods-producing industries	86	68	79	86	68	79	-	-	-
Service-providing industries	70	52	74	66	48	72	87	73	84
Education and health services	79	60	76	74	52	71	88	72	82
Educational services	85	68	80	77	57	74	88	72	82
Elementary and secondary schools	88	70	80	-	-	-	89	71	80
Junior colleges, colleges, and universities	86	71	82	90	68	76	84	72	86
Health care and social assistance	74	54	72	73	52	71	89	74	83
Hospitals	89	69	78	-	-	-	94	79	84
Public administration	88	78	88	-	-	-	88	78	88
Number of Workers									
1 to 99 workers	57	41	72	57	40	71	74	64	86
1 to 49 workers	53	38	72	53	38	71	64	55	86
50 to 99 workers	70	50	71	69	48	70	88	76	86
100 workers or more	86	66	77	85	63	75	89	74	84
100 to 499 workers	83	62	75	82	61	74	85	71	84
500 workers or more	89	70	79	88	67	76	90	76	84
Geographic Areas[4]									
New England	73	52	72	70	49	70	87	70	80
Middle Atlantic	72	56	77	70	52	75	86	77	90
East North Central	73	53	72	72	51	71	80	62	78
West North Central	70	51	73	67	48	72	85	69	81
South Atlantic	73	54	74	70	50	72	89	76	85
East South Central	76	60	78	72	53	74	92	84	92
West South Central	73	55	75	70	51	74	91	74	81
Mountain	69	51	74	67	48	72	87	72	83
Pacific	71	56	79	68	52	77	88	74	84

[1]The take-up rate is an estimate of the percentage of workers with access to a plan who participate in the plan, rounded for presentation.
[2]Includes workers in the private nonfarm economy except those in private households, and workers in the public sector, except the federal government.
[3]The percentile groupings are based on the average wage for each occupation surveyed, which may include workers both above and below the threshold.
[4]The states that comprise the Census divisions are: New England—Connecticut, Maine, Massachusetts, New Hampshire, Rhode Island, and Vermont; Middle Atlantic—New Jersey, New York, and Pennsylvania; South Atlantic—Delaware, District of Columbia, Florida, Georgia, Maryland, North Carolina, South Carolina, Virginia, and West Virginia; East South Central—Alabama, Kentucky, Mississippi, and Tennessee; West South Central—Arkansas, Louisiana, Oklahoma, and Texas; East North Central—Illinois, Indiana, Michigan, Ohio, and Wisconsin; West North Central—Iowa, Kansas, Minnesota, Missouri, Nebraska, North Dakota, and South Dakota; Mountain—Arizona, Colorado, Idaho, Montana, Nevada, New Mexico, Utah, and Wyoming; and Pacific—Alaska, California, Hawaii, Oregon, and Washington.
- = No workers in this area or data does not meet standards of reliability or precision.

Table 6-11. Medical Plans: Share of Premium Paid by Employer and Employee for Single Coverage, March 2013

(Percent.)

Characteristic	Civilian[1]		Private industry		State and local government	
	Employer share of premium	Employee share of premium	Employer share of premium	Employee share of premium	Employer share of premium	Employee share of premium
ALL WORKERS	81	19	79	21	87	13
Worker Characteristics						
Management, professional, and related	82	18	81	19	87	13
Management, business, and financial	81	19	79	21	-	-
Professional and related	83	17	81	19	87	13
Teachers	87	13	-	-	87	13
Primary, secondary, and special education school teachers	87	13	-	-	87	13
Registered nurses	80	20	-	-	-	-
Service	80	20	77	23	87	13
Protective service	85	15	75	25	87	13
Sales and office	78	22	77	23	88	12
Sales and related	72	28	72	28	-	-
Office and administrative support	81	19	79	21	88	12
Natural resources, construction, and maintenance	82	18	81	19	88	12
Construction, extraction, farming, fishing, and forestry	84	16	83	17	-	-
Installation, maintenance, and repair	80	20	79	21	-	-
Production, transportation, and material moving	80	20	79	21	87	13
Production	79	21	79	21	-	-
Transportation and material moving	80	20	80	20	-	-
Full-time workers	81	19	79	21	87	13
Part-time workers	74	26	72	28	81	19
Union workers	87	13	87	13	87	13
Nonunion workers	79	21	78	22	87	13
Average Wage Within the Following Percentiles[2]						
Lowest 25 percent	75	25	73	27	87	13
Lowest 10 percent	72	28	71	29	88	12
Second 25 percent	79	21	78	22	87	13
Third 25 percent	81	19	80	20	88	12
Highest 25 percent	83	17	81	19	87	13
Highest 10 percent	83	17	81	19	89	11
Establishment Characteristics						
Goods-producing industries	81	19	81	19	-	-
Service-providing industries	81	19	78	22	87	13
Education and health services	83	17	80	20	86	14
Educational services	85	15	81	19	86	14
Elementary and secondary schools	86	14	-	-	86	14
Junior colleges, colleges, and universities	85	15	79	21	88	12
Health care and social assistance	81	19	80	20	86	14
Hospitals	82	18	-	-	87	13
Public administration	88	12	-	-	88	12
Number of Workers						
1 to 99 workers	79	21	79	21	90	10
1 to 49 workers	80	20	79	21	91	9
50 to 99 workers	78	22	77	23	90	10
100 workers or more	81	19	79	21	87	13
100 to 499 workers	79	21	78	22	88	12
500 workers or more	83	17	81	19	86	14
Geographic Areas[3]						
New England	78	22	77	23	84	16
Middle Atlantic	83	17	81	19	89	11
East North Central	80	20	79	21	88	12
West North Central	81	19	78	22	91	9
South Atlantic	79	21	76	24	86	14
East South Central	80	20	77	23	87	13
West South Central	80	20	79	21	86	14
Mountain	82	18	81	19	88	12
Pacific	82	18	81	19	85	15

[1]Includes workers in the private nonfarm economy except those in private households, and workers in the public sector, except the federal government.
[2]The percentile groupings are based on the average wage for each occupation surveyed, which may include workers both above and below the threshold.
[3]The states that comprise the Census divisions are: New England—Connecticut, Maine, Massachusetts, New Hampshire, Rhode Island, and Vermont; Middle Atlantic—New Jersey, New York, and Pennsylvania; South Atlantic—Delaware, District of Columbia, Florida, Georgia, Maryland, North Carolina, South Carolina, Virginia, and West Virginia; East South Central—Alabama, Kentucky, Mississippi, and Tennessee; West South Central—Arkansas, Louisiana, Oklahoma, and Texas; East North Central—Illinois, Indiana, Michigan, Ohio, and Wisconsin; West North Central—Iowa, Kansas, Minnesota, Missouri, Nebraska, North Dakota, and South Dakota; Mountain—Arizona, Colorado, Idaho, Montana, Nevada, New Mexico, Utah, and Wyoming; and Pacific—Alaska, California, Hawaii, Oregon, and Washington.
- = No workers in this area or data does not meet standards of reliability or precision.

Table 6-12. Medical Plans: Share of Premiums Paid by Employer and Employee for Family Coverage, March 2013
(Percent.)

Characteristic	Civilian[1]		Private industry		State and local government	
	Employer share of premium	Employee share of premium	Employer share of premium	Employee share of premium	Employer share of premium	Employee share of premium
ALL WORKERS	69	31	68	32	70	30
Worker Characteristics						
Management, professional, and related	70	30	70	30	69	31
Management, business, and financial	70	30	70	30	-	-
Professional and related	70	30	70	30	68	32
Teachers	67	33	-	-	67	33
Primary, secondary, and special education school teachers	66	34	-	-	66	34
Registered nurses	71	29	-	-	-	-
Service	64	36	60	40	72	28
Protective service	74	26	60	40	78	22
Sales and office	67	33	66	34	72	28
Sales and related	62	38	62	38	-	-
Office and administrative support	69	31	68	32	72	28
Natural resources, construction, and maintenance	69	31	69	31	72	28
Construction, extraction, farming, fishing, and forestry	71	29	71	29	-	-
Installation, maintenance, and repair	67	33	67	33	-	-
Production, transportation, and material moving	72	28	72	28	71	29
Production	73	27	73	27	-	-
Transportation and material moving	71	29	72	28	-	-
Full-time workers	69	31	68	32	71	29
Part-time workers	64	36	63	37	69	31
Union workers	80	20	83	17	78	22
Nonunion workers	65	35	66	34	63	37
Average Wage Within the Following Percentiles[2]						
Lowest 25 percent	59	41	58	42	63	37
Lowest 10 percent	57	43	56	44	56	44
Second 25 percent	66	34	66	34	72	28
Third 25 percent	70	30	69	31	70	30
Highest 25 percent	73	27	73	27	74	26
Highest 10 percent	74	26	73	27	79	21
Establishment Characteristics						
Goods-producing industries	74	26	74	26	-	-
Service-providing industries	67	33	67	33	70	30
Education and health services	66	34	66	34	66	34
Educational services	66	34	65	35	66	34
Elementary and secondary schools	64	36	-	-	64	36
Junior colleges, colleges, and universities	71	29	69	31	72	28
Health care and social assistance	67	33	66	34	70	30
Hospitals	74	26	-	-	71	29
Public administration	77	23	-	-	77	23
Number of Workers						
1 to 99 workers	63	37	63	37	70	30
1 to 49 workers	63	37	63	37	72	28
50 to 99 workers	64	36	63	37	68	32
100 workers or more	72	28	72	28	70	30
100 to 499 workers	68	32	68	32	69	31
500 workers or more	74	26	77	23	71	29
Geographic Areas[3]						
New England	74	26	73	27	79	21
Middle Atlantic	75	25	73	27	87	13
East North Central	74	26	72	28	82	18
West North Central	67	33	66	34	69	31
South Atlantic	64	36	63	37	65	35
East South Central	61	39	64	36	55	45
West South Central	62	38	65	35	53	47
Mountain	68	32	69	31	64	36
Pacific	69	31	68	32	75	25

[1]Includes workers in the private nonfarm economy except those in private households, and workers in the public sector, except the federal government.
[2]The percentile groupings are based on the average wage for each occupation surveyed, which may include workers both above and below the threshold.
[3]The states that comprise the Census divisions are: New England—Connecticut, Maine, Massachusetts, New Hampshire, Rhode Island, and Vermont; Middle Atlantic—New Jersey, New York, and Pennsylvania; South Atlantic—Delaware, District of Columbia, Florida, Georgia, Maryland, North Carolina, South Carolina, Virginia, and West Virginia; East South Central—Alabama, Kentucky, Mississippi, and Tennessee; West South Central—Arkansas, Louisiana, Oklahoma, and Texas; East North Central—Illinois, Indiana, Michigan, Ohio, and Wisconsin; West North Central—Iowa, Kansas, Minnesota, Missouri, Nebraska, North Dakota, and South Dakota; Mountain—Arizona, Colorado, Idaho, Montana, Nevada, New Mexico, Utah, and Wyoming; and Pacific—Alaska, California, Hawaii, Oregon, and Washington.
- = No workers in this area or data does not meet standards of reliability or precision.

Table 6-13. Access to Paid Sick Leave, Vacation, and Holidays, March 2013

(Percent.)

Characteristic	Civilian[1]			Private industry			State and local government		
	Paid sick leave	Paid vacation	Paid holidays	Paid sick leave	Paid vacation	Paid holidays	Paid sick leave	Paid vacation	Paid holidays
ALL WORKERS	65	74	76	61	77	77	89	59	67
Worker Characteristics									
Management, professional, and related	85	75	79	83	88	89	90	43	55
Management, business, and financial	89	95	95	88	96	97	-	-	-
Professional and related	84	68	73	80	84	85	90	36	50
Teachers	85	17	34	-	-	-	88	12	30
Primary, secondary, and special education school teachers	95	12	29	-	-	-	95	8	26
Registered nurses	79	80	82	-	-	-	-	-	-
Service	47	58	57	40	55	53	85	76	78
Protective service	74	81	83	53	72	78	90	88	87
Sales and office	67	79	80	64	79	79	89	84	85
Sales and related	52	68	67	52	68	67	-	-	-
Office and administrative support	75	86	87	73	86	87	90	85	86
Natural resources, construction, and maintenance	57	82	85	53	81	84	95	95	96
Construction, extraction, farming, fishing, and forestry	44	71	77	38	68	75	-	-	-
Installation, maintenance, and repair	68	92	92	66	91	92	-	-	-
Production, transportation, and material moving	55	82	84	54	83	84	87	63	73
Production	55	91	92	55	91	92	-	-	-
Transportation and material moving	56	74	76	53	75	77	-	-	-
Full-time workers	78	87	88	74	91	90	98	67	74
Part-time workers	26	34	38	24	36	39	41	21	29
Union workers	84	75	81	71	91	92	97	57	69
Nonunion workers	62	74	75	60	75	76	82	62	66
Average Wage Within the Following Percentiles[2]									
Lowest 25 percent	34	51	51	30	49	49	75	56	63
Lowest 10 percent	21	39	37	20	39	36	62	41	49
Second 25 percent	69	83	84	63	83	84	93	84	87
Third 25 percent	79	89	90	74	90	90	93	66	74
Highest 25 percent	87	79	82	84	91	92	96	37	49
Highest 10 percent	90	78	81	87	92	92	98	36	46
Establishment Characteristics									
Goods-producing industries	57	89	91	57	89	91	-	-	-
Service-providing industries	67	72	73	62	74	74	89	59	67
Education and health services	80	65	71	74	78	80	89	42	55
Educational services	86	40	52	75	55	62	89	35	49
Elementary and secondary schools	90	27	41	-	-	-	90	26	41
Junior colleges, colleges, and universities	85	67	78	81	72	80	87	64	77
Health care and social assistance	75	82	84	74	82	83	89	87	89
Hospitals	87	90	91	-	-	-	93	93	94
Public administration	90	89	88	-	-	-	90	89	88
Number of Workers									
1 to 99 workers	52	69	68	51	69	68	79	66	69
1 to 49 workers	51	66	67	50	66	67	71	64	66
50 to 99 workers	59	76	74	56	76	74	90	69	74
100 workers or more	77	79	82	72	86	87	90	58	67
100 to 499 workers	69	81	82	66	84	85	87	60	64
500 workers or more	85	78	82	81	90	91	92	58	68
Geographic Areas[3]									
New England	69	72	73	65	75	77	89	48	53
Middle Atlantic	68	73	75	65	76	77	89	59	63
East North Central	60	74	76	56	78	78	85	53	65
West North Central	64	73	75	59	76	76	90	58	69
South Atlantic	66	77	79	61	79	80	92	66	77
East South Central	65	75	78	58	78	80	90	64	71
West South Central	67	76	76	63	80	80	86	54	56
Mountain	61	73	71	58	76	73	83	53	58
Pacific	67	72	73	63	73	73	91	66	73

[1]Includes workers in the private nonfarm economy except those in private households, and workers in the public sector, except the federal government.
[2]The percentile groupings are based on the average wage for each occupation surveyed, which may include workers both above and below the threshold.
[3]The states that comprise the Census divisions are: New England—Connecticut, Maine, Massachusetts, New Hampshire, Rhode Island, and Vermont; Middle Atlantic—New Jersey, New York, and Pennsylvania; South Atlantic—Delaware, District of Columbia, Florida, Georgia, Maryland, North Carolina, South Carolina, Virginia, and West Virginia; East South Central—Alabama, Kentucky, Mississippi, and Tennessee; West South Central—Arkansas, Louisiana, Oklahoma, and Texas; East North Central—Illinois, Indiana, Michigan, Ohio, and Wisconsin; West North Central—Iowa, Kansas, Minnesota, Missouri, Nebraska, North Dakota, and South Dakota; Mountain—Arizona, Colorado, Idaho, Montana, Nevada, New Mexico, Utah, and Wyoming; and Pacific—Alaska, California, Hawaii, Oregon, and Washington.
- = No workers in this area or data does not meet standards of reliability or precision.

Table 6-14. Quality of Life Benefits: Access for Civilian Workers,[1] March 2013

(Percent.)

Characteristic	Childcare[2]	Flexible workplace	Subsidized commuting	Wellness programs	Employee assistance programs
ALL WORKERS	10	6	6	38	52
Worker Characteristics					
Management, professional, and related	17	12	11	53	68
Management, business, and financial	19	18	15	56	69
Professional and related	16	9	9	52	68
Teachers	13	3	6	48	65
Primary, secondary, and special education school teachers	10	1	3	46	65
Registered nurses	23	5	9	68	77
Service	9	1	4	23	37
Protective service	10	3	10	42	62
Sales and office	8	5	7	40	54
Sales and related	4	3	3	39	53
Office and administrative support	11	6	9	40	55
Natural resources, construction, and maintenance	6	2	3	28	41
Construction, extraction, farming, fishing, and forestry	3	2	3	20	31
Installation, maintenance, and repair	9	2	3	35	49
Production, transportation, and material moving	5	2	3	30	46
Production	6	3	3	34	48
Transportation and material moving	3	2	3	26	44
Full-time workers	12	7	8	42	57
Part-time workers	6	1	3	25	36
Union workers	15	2	9	50	78
Nonunion workers	10	6	6	36	48
Average Wage Within the Following Percentiles[3]					
Lowest 25 percent	6	1	2	21	32
Lowest 10 percent	6	-	1	15	24
Second 25 percent	8	3	5	35	50
Third 25 percent	11	7	9	43	59
Highest 25 percent	17	12	12	56	72
Highest 10 percent	18	15	14	59	76
Establishment Characteristics					
Goods-producing industries	7	5	3	37	49
Service-providing industries	11	6	7	38	53
Education and health services	15	3	6	47	61
Educational services	13	4	8	49	67
Elementary and secondary schools	9	1	3	44	66
Junior colleges, colleges, and universities	26	-	18	67	78
Health care and social assistance	15	3	6	45	57
Hospitals	27	3	13	79	90
Public administration	17	6	17	54	77
Number of Workers					
1 to 99 workers	4	4	3	18	29
1 to 49 workers	4	4	3	16	25
50 to 99 workers	5	4	3	26	42
100 workers or more	16	7	9	56	74
100 to 499 workers	9	5	5	46	63
500 workers or more	22	9	14	65	84
Geographic Areas[4]					
New England	15	6	9	38	53
Middle Atlantic	12	5	8	37	53
East North Central	11	5	5	39	51
West North Central	10	5	5	37	49
South Atlantic	10	7	5	39	54
East South Central	10	7	4	40	50
West South Central	8	5	3	38	53
Mountain	11	3	9	34	53
Pacific	10	5	11	37	51

[1]Includes workers in the private nonfarm economy except those in private households, and workers in the public sector, except the federal government.
[2]A workplace program that provides for either the full or partial cost of caring for an employee's children in a nursery, day care center, or a baby sitter in facilities either on or off the employer's premises.
[3]The categories are based on the average wage for each occupation surveyed, which may include workers with earnings both above and below the threshold.
[4]The states that comprise the Census divisions are: New England—Connecticut, Maine, Massachusetts, New Hampshire, Rhode Island, and Vermont; Middle Atlantic—New Jersey, New York, and Pennsylvania; South Atlantic—Delaware, District of Columbia, Florida, Georgia, Maryland, North Carolina, South Carolina, Virginia, and West Virginia; East South Central—Alabama, Kentucky, Mississippi, and Tennessee; West South Central—Arkansas, Louisiana, Oklahoma, and Texas; East North Central—Illinois, Indiana, Michigan, Ohio, and Wisconsin; West North Central—Iowa, Kansas, Minnesota, Missouri, Nebraska, North Dakota, and South Dakota; Mountain—Arizona, Colorado, Idaho, Montana, Nevada, New Mexico, Utah, and Wyoming; and Pacific—Alaska, California, Hawaii, Oregon, and Washington.
- = No workers in this area or data does not meet standards of reliability or precision.

Table 6-15. Financial Benefits: Access for Civilian Workers,[1] March 2013

(Percent.)

Characteristic	Health savings account	Section 125 cafeteria benefits				Financial planning	Stock options			
		Flexible savings account	Dependent care reimbursement account	Healthcare reimbursement account	Pre-tax savings with no employer contributions		Total[2]	Performance	Signing	Other
ALL WORKERS	21	20	38	40	24	19	7	2	1	5
Worker Characteristics										
Management, professional, and related	29	31	57	61	34	27	9	3	2	6
Management, business, and financial	37	32	60	64	29	32	13	6	4	10
Professional and related	25	31	56	60	37	25	7	2	1	5
Teachers	20	33	49	57	52	19	-	-	-	-
Primary, secondary, and special education school teachers	20	34	48	58	53	18	-	-	-	-
Registered nurses	24	38	68	69	32	25	2	(³)	-	-
Service	9	11	23	24	18	11	2	-	-	2
Protective service	18	24	45	47	39	20	2	-	-	2
Sales and office	25	18	36	39	21	23	9	2	1	7
Sales and related	23	9	29	31	15	22	9	1	1	8
Office and administrative support	25	23	40	43	25	23	8	3	1	6
Natural resources, construction, and maintenance	17	16	27	31	20	15	5	2	-	3
Construction, extraction, farming, fishing, and forestry	11	12	17	20	17	9	2	-	-	2
Installation, maintenance, and repair	21	19	35	41	22	20	8	4	-	4
Production, transportation, and material moving	17	15	29	31	16	13	7	1	1	6
Production	18	18	32	35	16	15	6	2	1	5
Transportation and material moving	16	13	26	27	16	10	7	1	1	6
Full-time workers	24	24	44	48	27	22	7	2	1	6
Part-time workers	10	7	19	18	14	11	4	1	(³)	4
Union workers	18	24	49	54	42	26	5	3	1	3
Nonunion workers	21	19	36	38	20	18	7	2	1	6
Average Wage Within the Following Percentiles[4]										
Lowest 25 percent	9	7	18	18	14	10	4	(³)	-	3
Lowest 10 percent	4	3	11	9	10	5	4	-	-	3
Second 25 percent	22	19	34	38	22	18	6	2	1	5
Third 25 percent	24	24	44	47	27	22	7	2	1	6
Highest 25 percent	30	32	60	64	34	29	11	4	2	7
Highest 10 percent	33	33	65	69	36	31	12	5	3	9
Establishment Characteristics										
Goods-producing industries	19	18	33	36	16	17	7	3	1	5
Service-providing industries	21	20	39	41	25	20	7	2	1	5
Education and health services	20	28	47	52	37	18	1	-	(³)	1
Educational services	22	33	53	60	54	20	(³)	-	(³)	(³)
Elementary and secondary schools	20	34	49	57	53	18	-	-	-	-
Junior colleges, colleges, and universities	30	35	66	74	64	29	1	-	1	(³)
Health care and social assistance	19	24	44	47	25	17	2	-	-	1
Hospitals	22	41	73	75	33	29	2	(³)	-	2
Public administration	23	32	58	58	62	31	-	-	-	-
Number of Workers										
1 to 99 workers	13	10	19	22	13	9	4	1	1	3
1 to 49 workers	11	9	18	20	12	8	4	1	1	3
50 to 99 workers	17	15	24	29	19	14	6	1	1	5
100 workers or more	28	29	55	58	33	28	9	3	1	7
100 to 499 workers	27	21	43	45	24	25	8	2	1	6
500 workers or more	29	36	67	71	42	32	10	4	2	7
Geographic Areas[5]										
New England	16	16	43	43	25	18	7	2	1	6
Middle Atlantic	14	15	34	37	28	19	7	1	2	6
East North Central	23	18	35	39	24	21	7	2	1	5
West North Central	22	26	41	46	18	21	8	2	-	6
South Atlantic	23	23	38	40	23	20	6	2	1	5
East South Central	24	29	33	33	26	18	8	3	1	6
West South Central	20	22	41	44	23	21	6	1	1	5
Mountain	21	19	43	45	22	18	5	2	1	4
Pacific	22	17	37	40	23	18	7	3	2	4

[1]Includes workers in the private nonfarm economy except those in private households, and workers in the public sector, except the federal government.
[2]The sum of the individual components may be greater than the total because some employees may have access to more than one type of stock option.
[3]Less than 0.5.
[4]The categories are based on the average wage for each occupation surveyed, which may include workers with earnings both above and below the threshold.
[5]The states that comprise the Census divisions are: New England—Connecticut, Maine, Massachusetts, New Hampshire, Rhode Island, and Vermont; Middle Atlantic—New Jersey, New York, and Pennsylvania; South Atlantic—Delaware, District of Columbia, Florida, Georgia, Maryland, North Carolina, South Carolina, Virginia, and West Virginia; East South Central—Alabama, Kentucky, Mississippi, and Tennessee; West South Central—Arkansas, Louisiana, Oklahoma, and Texas; East North Central—Illinois, Indiana, Michigan, Ohio, and Wisconsin; West North Central—Iowa, Kansas, Minnesota, Missouri, Nebraska, North Dakota, and South Dakota; Mountain—Arizona, Colorado, Idaho, Montana, Nevada, New Mexico, Utah, and Wyoming; and Pacific—Alaska, California, Hawaii, Oregon, and Washington.
- = No workers in this area or data does not meet standards of reliability or precision.

Table 6-16. Nonproduction Bonuses: Access for Civilian Workers,[1] March 2013

(Percent.)

Characteristic	All nonproduc-tion bonuses[2]	Cash-profit sharing bonus	Employee recognition bonus	End-of-year-bonus	Holiday bonus	Payment in lieu of benefits bonus	Longevity bonus	Referral bonus	Other bonus[3]
ALL WORKERS	39	4	3	9	7	6	4	5	11
Worker Characteristics									
Management, professional, and related	45	6	5	10	5	9	2	7	15
Management, business, and financial	55	8	6	16	6	8	3	7	18
Professional and related	41	5	4	7	4	10	2	6	14
Teachers	26	-	2	-	1	13	2	(4)	10
Primary, secondary, and special education school teachers	29	-	2	-	-	14	2	-	11
Registered nurses	43	1	3	5	-	14	3	13	18
Service	26	1	2	5	6	3	3	3	7
Protective service	38	-	6	2	4	10	9	3	13
Sales and office	42	4	3	10	11	4	7	6	9
Sales and related	35	3	1	7	12	2	12	3	5
Office and administrative support	47	5	4	12	10	6	4	7	11
Natural resources, construction, and maintenance	38	5	3	10	10	3	2	4	11
Construction, extraction, farming, fishing, and forestry	33	3	1	12	10	2	2	1	8
Installation, maintenance, and repair	42	7	5	9	9	4	3	8	14
Production, transportation, and material moving	41	6	2	9	9	5	2	5	13
Production	47	9	2	12	10	5	3	5	16
Transportation and material moving	35	4	1	6	9	5	2	5	11
Full-time workers	45	5	4	10	8	7	4	6	14
Part-time workers	21	1	2	4	5	2	3	3	4
Union workers	36	5	4	3	2	14	3	3	15
Nonunion workers	39	4	3	10	8	4	4	6	11
Average Wage Within the Following Percentiles[5]									
Lowest 25 percent	26	1	1	6	7	2	4	4	6
Lowest 10 percent	20	(4)	1	5	6	1	1	3	3
Second 25 percent	39	4	3	9	11	5	5	4	9
Third 25 percent	45	5	4	10	8	8	4	6	14
Highest 25 percent	49	8	6	11	4	10	2	7	18
Highest 10 percent	51	8	6	13	4	10	2	6	17
Establishment Characteristics									
Goods-producing industries	49	10	2	14	10	5	2	5	16
Service-providing industries	37	3	3	8	7	6	4	5	11
Education and health services	32	1	3	5	4	9	2	5	10
Educational services	24	-	2	1	1	11	3	(4)	8
Elementary and secondary schools	25	-	1	1	1	13	3	-	10
Junior colleges, colleges, and universities	22	-	4	(4)	-	8	2	1	7
Health care and social assistance	38	1	3	9	6	8	2	8	11
Hospitals	45	2	3	4	1	17	3	13	17
Public administration	40	-	6	1	2	15	9	-	16
Number of Workers									
1 to 99 workers	35	3	2	11	10	3	1	3	8
1 to 49 workers	34	3	2	11	11	3	1	2	6
50 to 99 workers	38	4	3	10	6	4	2	5	12
100 workers or more	43	5	4	7	5	8	6	7	15
100 to 499 workers	42	4	3	7	8	5	8	8	12
500 workers or more	44	7	5	6	2	10	3	7	18
Geographic Areas[6]									
New England	34	2	-	9	2	8	2	5	10
Middle Atlantic	40	3	3	10	6	8	2	5	11
East North Central	42	6	3	10	6	8	5	5	14
West North Central	33	5	3	9	4	3	2	6	10
South Atlantic	42	4	4	7	11	4	4	6	13
East South Central	35	4	1	7	9	2	5	5	14
West South Central	46	5	2	12	12	3	5	7	13
Mountain	40	5	5	11	9	4	3	5	8
Pacific	32	4	4	7	5	7	2	3	8

[1]Includes workers in the private nonfarm economy except those in private households, and workers in the public sector, except the federal government.
[2]The sum of the individual components may be greater than the total because some employees may have access to more than one type of stock option.
[3]Includes all other bonuses provided to employees and not published separately.
[4]Less than 0.5.
[5]The categories are based on the average wage for each occupation surveyed, which may include workers with earnings both above and below the threshold.
[6]The states that comprise the Census divisions are: New England—Connecticut, Maine, Massachusetts, New Hampshire, Rhode Island, and Vermont; Middle Atlantic—New Jersey, New York, and Pennsylvania; South Atlantic—Delaware, District of Columbia, Florida, Georgia, Maryland, North Carolina, South Carolina, Virginia, and West Virginia; East South Central—Alabama, Kentucky, Mississippi, and Tennessee; West South Central—Arkansas, Louisiana, Oklahoma, and Texas; East North Central—Illinois, Indiana, Michigan, Ohio, and Wisconsin; West North Central—Iowa, Kansas, Minnesota, Missouri, Nebraska, North Dakota, and South Dakota; Mountain—Arizona, Colorado, Idaho, Montana, Nevada, New Mexico, Utah, and Wyoming; and Pacific—Alaska, California, Hawaii, Oregon, and Washington.

Table 6-17. Unmarried Domestic Partner Benefits: Access[1] for Civilian Workers,[2] March 2013

(Percent.)

Characteristic	Defined benefit retirement survivor benefits		Healthcare benefits	
	Same sex	Opposite sex	Same sex	Opposite sex
ALL WORKERS	15	14	32	26
Worker Characteristics				
Management, professional, and related	24	23	44	36
Management, business, and financial	22	22	52	44
Professional and related	25	24	40	32
Teachers	42	40	32	26
Primary, secondary, and special education school teachers	50	48	29	25
Registered nurses	19	19	33	24
Service	9	8	20	16
Protective service	27	26	27	19
Sales and office	13	13	32	28
Sales and related	5	5	25	22
Office and administrative support	17	17	36	31
Natural resources, construction, and maintenance	12	12	26	21
Construction, extraction, farming, fishing, and forestry	10	11	18	16
Installation, maintenance, and repair	14	13	33	25
Production, transportation, and material moving	10	9	27	23
Production	6	5	26	22
Transportation and material moving	13	13	28	24
Full-time workers	18	17	38	32
Part-time workers	6	6	12	10
Union workers	39	37	51	40
Nonunion workers	11	11	28	24
Average Wage Within the Following Percentiles[3]				
Lowest 25 percent	4	4	12	11
Lowest 10 percent	2	2	7	6
Second 25 percent	12	12	28	25
Third 25 percent	18	17	39	33
Highest 25 percent	27	26	52	42
Highest 10 percent	28	26	60	49
Establishment Characteristics				
Goods-producing industries	7	6	29	25
Service-providing industries	16	16	32	27
Education and health services	25	24	30	25
Educational services	43	42	34	28
Elementary and secondary schools	49	47	28	25
Junior colleges, colleges, and universities	36	35	49	38
Health care and social assistance	12	12	27	23
Hospitals	23	23	34	25
Public administration	48	47	38	31
Number of Workers				
1 to 99 workers	5	5	20	18
1 to 49 workers	4	4	17	15
50 to 99 workers	8	7	29	27
100 workers or more	24	23	43	34
100 to 499 workers	14	14	35	30
500 workers or more	34	32	50	38
Geographic Areas[4]				
New England	13	12	39	33
Middle Atlantic	18	17	37	29
East North Central	7	6	22	14
West North Central	11	10	27	24
South Atlantic	14	13	23	18
East South Central	19	19	17	13
West South Central	14	15	19	19
Mountain	14	14	39	32
Pacific	23	23	58	54

[1]The percentage of workers with access to the benefit reflects both the availability of the benefit and the employer's policy on providing the benefit to unmarried domestic partners.
[2]Includes workers in the private nonfarm economy except those in private households, and workers in the public sector, except the federal government.
[3]The categories are based on the average wage for each occupation surveyed, which may include workers with earnings both above and below the threshold.
[4]The states that comprise the Census divisions are: New England—Connecticut, Maine, Massachusetts, New Hampshire, Rhode Island, and Vermont; Middle Atlantic—New Jersey, New York, and Pennsylvania; South Atlantic—Delaware, District of Columbia, Florida, Georgia, Maryland, North Carolina, South Carolina, Virginia, and West Virginia; East South Central—Alabama, Kentucky, Mississippi, and Tennessee; West South Central—Arkansas, Louisiana, Oklahoma, and Texas; East North Central—Illinois, Indiana, Michigan, Ohio, and Wisconsin; West North Central—Iowa, Kansas, Minnesota, Missouri, Nebraska, North Dakota, and South Dakota; Mountain—Arizona, Colorado, Idaho, Montana, Nevada, New Mexico, Utah, and Wyoming; and Pacific—Alaska, California, Hawaii, Oregon, and Washington.

CHAPTER 7: RECENT TRENDS IN THE LABOR MARKET

HIGHLIGHTS

This chapter contains information on mass layoff events, initial claimants for unemployment insurance, movement of work, job openings, hires, and separations.

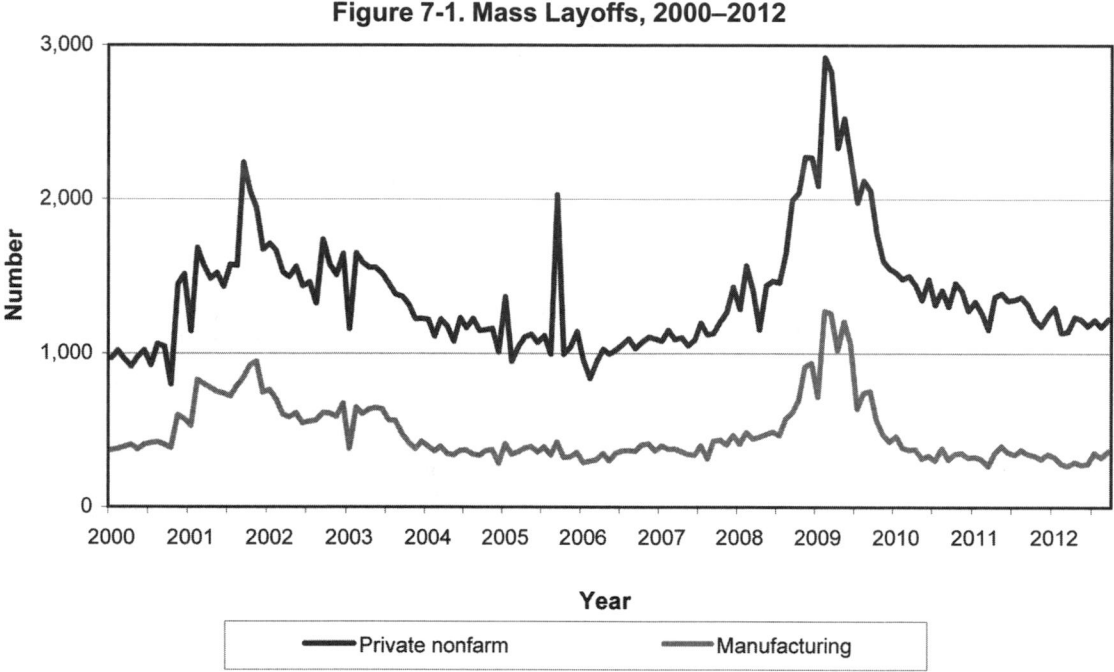

Figure 7-1. Mass Layoffs, 2000–2012

In May 2013, 1,301 mass layoff events occurred compared to a high 3,079 mass layoff events in February 2009 (seasonally adjusted). A mass layoff event is when there are 50 or more initial claims from an employer during the five-week period, regardless of duration. (See Table 7-1.)

OTHER HIGHLIGHTS

- Although the number of mass layoff events continued to decline in most sectors in 2012, they did increase in several industries, including wholesale trade, educational services, and transportation and warehousing. (See Table 7-3.)

- Manufacturing still accounted for the largest number of mass layoff events in 2012 at 3,886 even though the number of mass layoffs in manufacturing declined 11.6 percent from 2011 to 2012. (See Table 7-3.)

- According to data in October 2013, the number of job openings reached 3.92 million, representing the highest number of job openings since May 2008. The number of job openings were the highest in professional and business services (717,000), trade, transportation, and utilities (682,000), and education and health services (638,000). Meanwhile, they were the lowest in manufacturing (281,000) and construction (124,000). (See Table 7-7.)

NOTES AND DEFINITIONS

MASS LAYOFFS

COLLECTION AND COVERAGE

The Mass Layoff Statistics (MLS) program is a federal-state program that identifies, describes, and tracks the effects of major job cutbacks, using data from each state's unemployment insurance database. Employers that have at least 50 initial claims filed against them during a consecutive 5-week period are contacted by the state agency to determine whether these separations are of at least 31 days duration, and, if so, information is obtained on the total number of persons separated, the reasons for these separations, and recall expectations. Employers are identified according to industry classification and location, and unemployment insurance claimants are identified by such demographic factors as age, race, gender, ethnic group, and place of residence. The program yields information on an individual's entire spell of unemployment, to the point when regular unemployment insurance benefits are exhausted.

A given month contains an aggregation of the weekly unemployment insurance claims filings for the Sunday through Saturday weeks in that month. All weeks are included for the particular month, except if the first day of the month falls on Saturday. In this case, the week is included in the prior month's tabulations. This means that some months will contain 4 weeks and others 5 weeks; the number of weeks in a given month may be different from year to year, and the number of weeks in a year may vary.

The latest quarterly data in these tables are considered preliminary. After the initial publication of quarterly information, more data are collected as remaining employer interviews for the quarter are completed and additional initial claimant information associated with extended layoff events is received.

On March 1, 2013, President Obama ordered across-the-board spending cuts into effect. The Bureau of Labor Statistics (BLS) was required to cut its budget by more than $30 million. To achieve the saving, the Mass Layoffs Statistics program was one of the programs eliminated.

CONCEPTS AND DEFINITIONS

Employers in the MLS program include those covered by state unemployment insurance laws. Information on employers is obtained from the Quarterly Census of Employment and Wages (QCEW) program.

Extended layoff event is when there are fifty or more initial claims for unemployment insurance benefits from an employer during a 5-week period, with at least 50 workers separated for more than 30 days.

Initial claimant is a person who files any notice of unemployment to initiate a request either for a determination of entitlement to and eligibility for compensation, or for a subsequent period of unemployment within a benefit year or period of eligibility.

Layoff is the separation of persons from an employer as part of a mass layoff event. Such layoffs involve both persons subject to recall and those who are terminated by the establishment.

Mass layoff event is when there are fifty or more initial claims for unemployment insurance benefits from an employer during a five-week period, regardless of duration.

Movement-of-work action is relocation of work within the same company or to other companies, domestically or outside the United States. Because employers may cite more than one location to which work is moving, a layoff event may have more than one action associated with it.

Movement-of-work separations are the number of separations specifically associated with movement-of-work actions.

Outsourcing is the movement of work that was formerly conducted in-house by employees paid directly by a company to a different company under a contractual arrangement.

Seasonal adjustment is the process of estimating and removing the effect on time series data of regularly recurring seasonal events such as changes in the weather, holidays, and the beginning and ending of the school year. The use of seasonal adjustment makes it easier to observe fundamental changes in time series, particularly those associated with general economic expansions and contractions.

Separations are the total number of people laid off in an extended mass layoff event for more than 30 days, according to the employer.

Worksite closure is the complete closure of either multi-unit or single-unit employers or the partial closure of a multi-unit employer where entire worksites affected by layoffs are closed or planned to be closed.

SOURCES OF ADDITIONAL INFORMATION

For more extensive information and the latest edition of the Mass Layoffs news release, please see http://www.bls.gov/news.release/mmls.nr0.htm.

Table 7-1. Mass Layoff Events and Initial Claimants for Unemployment Insurance, 2000–May 2013, Seasonally Adjusted

(Number.)

Year and month	Total		Private nonfarm		Manufacturing	
	Events	Initial claimants	Events	Initial claimants	Events	Initial claimants
2000						
January	1 100	126 440	968	116 846	371	53 270
February	1 280	151 107	1 018	124 497	379	48 372
March	1 159	126 309	965	109 445	393	46 564
April	1 030	115 068	913	104 865	407	43 829
May	1 196	126 525	976	106 893	376	44 019
June	1 220	145 766	1 020	127 239	406	54 672
July	1 065	118 649	922	108 499	417	56 465
August	1 282	178 789	1 060	157 762	423	71 141
September	1 260	134 153	1 045	117 266	407	63 394
October	938	107 676	798	94 783	385	54 006
November	1 643	215 381	1 447	196 166	599	89 869
December	1 691	214 601	1 514	197 944	575	96 295
2001						
January	1 288	158 580	1 144	145 584	529	82 504
February	1 912	253 943	1 684	233 524	828	124 430
March	1 761	202 344	1 569	186 565	800	107 481
April	1 622	200 683	1 484	186 898	776	106 255
May	1 676	206 062	1 523	192 500	750	108 773
June	1 608	195 802	1 432	181 264	740	103 468
July	1 710	201 363	1 574	189 030	721	93 949
August	1 732	207 416	1 568	195 777	791	109 611
September	2 407	277 955	2 236	263 773	841	111 520
October	2 177	242 507	2 051	232 371	923	119 873
November	2 104	218 378	1 940	206 999	948	113 776
December	1 824	200 677	1 673	188 836	746	92 019
2002						
January	1 841	224 765	1 711	212 461	764	104 909
February	1 823	207 788	1 663	194 840	701	95 406
March	1 697	187 212	1 525	174 281	604	74 492
April	1 666	183 005	1 494	167 848	584	68 282
May	1 730	190 129	1 561	176 744	613	73 612
June	1 632	171 213	1 436	155 960	547	70 137
July	1 632	179 407	1 461	164 741	557	73 479
August	1 468	161 431	1 324	149 847	563	67 831
September	1 918	217 299	1 737	200 635	615	81 292
October	1 749	187 851	1 573	171 346	611	73 940
November	1 651	178 739	1 507	167 723	590	72 329
December	1 834	194 852	1 646	180 976	676	84 247
2003						
January	1 336	132 819	1 160	119 199	382	46 839
February	1 831	191 434	1 650	178 003	650	80 285
March	1 784	175 384	1 589	159 467	609	72 679
April	1 702	172 252	1 555	162 323	637	83 268
May	1 744	185 159	1 556	171 221	646	87 077
June	1 726	164 597	1 518	147 553	640	68 197
July	1 661	165 130	1 450	149 233	567	71 319
August	1 546	171 996	1 383	157 968	563	77 405
September	1 571	149 250	1 370	133 276	479	56 454
October	1 525	157 759	1 319	140 086	422	51 872
November	1 370	139 572	1 225	127 963	379	49 219
December	1 395	136 166	1 226	124 009	428	49 789
2004						
January	1 414	145 593	1 221	128 305	396	47 882
February	1 257	130 205	1 111	117 788	365	39 214
March	1 362	138 397	1 222	129 094	396	58 213
April	1 349	136 837	1 175	121 841	347	37 115
May	1 240	116 392	1 077	102 443	340	39 208
June	1 397	139 975	1 231	127 229	370	46 998
July	1 315	135 186	1 165	123 768	371	49 945
August	1 417	127 814	1 226	112 867	344	36 298
September	1 275	124 279	1 149	113 689	337	45 732
October	1 265	129 312	1 153	120 337	366	46 319
November	1 306	129 014	1 161	117 300	374	44 939
December	1 163	114 258	1 009	102 732	285	31 445
2005						
January	1 509	161 805	1 367	151 530	413	61 483
February	1 075	111 437	948	100 564	344	42 035
March	1 193	129 288	1 045	118 827	361	50 086
April	1 238	135 353	1 107	124 881	384	58 255
May	1 266	139 915	1 124	127 071	395	54 052
June	1 185	125 919	1 072	117 229	359	55 621
July	1 257	133 036	1 116	121 311	392	53 945
August	1 118	124 738	996	113 784	340	46 067
September	2 241	299 151	2 028	253 431	423	55 855
October	1 113	111 868	994	102 840	323	43 326
November	1 176	115 215	1 040	103 701	328	41 868
December	1 272	135 737	1 142	124 459	356	46 211
2006						
January	1 086	111 484	955	101 462	290	35 030
February	935	100 482	837	92 542	299	39 328
March	1 044	115 705	942	107 238	308	45 044
April	1 162	122 174	1 028	112 014	351	48 735
May	1 106	114 200	995	104 870	302	40 491
June	1 128	122 783	1 021	113 724	352	42 960
July	1 181	122 246	1 058	112 645	367	50 719
August	1 231	131 837	1 095	122 479	370	57 150
September	1 140	121 613	1 031	113 304	365	45 207
October	1 184	121 126	1 071	112 667	404	53 017
November	1 223	132 407	1 107	122 718	412	57 192
December	1 196	132 153	1 094	122 556	367	50 644

Table 7-1. Mass Layoff Events and Initial Claimants for Unemployment Insurance, 2000–May 2013, Seasonally Adjusted—*Continued*

(Number.)

Year and month	Total		Private nonfarm		Manufacturing	
	Events	Initial claimants	Events	Initial claimants	Events	Initial claimants
2007						
January	1 236	129 105	1 079	117 477	399	54 155
February	1 272	131 822	1 150	122 921	377	54 021
March	1 203	124 120	1 091	115 440	380	47 707
April	1 239	126 856	1 102	115 752	361	42 682
May	1 144	112 391	1 050	105 525	344	44 415
June	1 198	127 343	1 086	118 633	339	37 556
July	1 299	135 184	1 197	127 315	400	54 934
August	1 208	123 551	1 121	116 211	314	35 737
September	1 224	121 211	1 131	114 929	430	51 677
October	1 331	134 995	1 205	126 002	439	58 056
November	1 395	149 871	1 266	139 924	407	57 837
December	1 546	154 450	1 430	145 008	467	60 484
2008						
January	1 426	147 392	1 287	135 499	410	51 802
February	1 726	181 867	1 569	169 988	487	61 977
March	1 517	153 278	1 404	142 875	445	58 340
April	1 281	128 164	1 155	117 537	458	56 806
May	1 572	161 515	1 439	152 191	473	63 596
June	1 611	164 196	1 470	152 798	491	68 783
July	1 602	163 199	1 457	151 915	467	61 802
August	1 793	184 432	1 647	173 914	575	74 687
September	2 165	230 550	1 993	216 614	612	81 584
October	2 199	228 172	2 042	214 669	697	93 388
November	2 430	235 904	2 273	222 657	915	104 774
December	2 441	245 800	2 268	231 653	938	116 839
2009						
January	2 256	237 182	2 087	223 230	716	91 179
February	3 079	334 171	2 921	318 194	1 274	152 592
March	3 022	304 175	2 827	287 023	1 261	158 119
April	2 537	246 938	2 332	231 211	1 022	114 682
May	2 712	286 089	2 522	270 051	1 206	151 114
June	2 470	248 680	2 261	231 529	1 063	140 105
July	2 184	222 776	1 976	203 347	639	76 345
August	2 358	218 380	2 119	198 877	743	75 387
September	2 274	216 959	2 054	200 863	754	90 250
October	1 970	196 370	1 775	178 648	567	64 681
November	1 764	159 283	1 598	146 802	469	51 887
December	1 720	155 738	1 549	141 699	425	44 455
2010						
January	1 699	169 561	1 522	155 298	461	53 303
February	1 647	161 694	1 480	147 259	387	47 272
March	1 703	153 784	1 501	138 188	373	43 022
April	1 622	154 962	1 442	138 849	378	44 860
May	1 585	150 959	1 345	131 482	317	31 677
June	1 701	152 080	1 481	133 366	335	34 653
July	1 521	137 750	1 315	121 313	303	32 064
August	1 612	162 455	1 409	138 849	384	41 123
September	1 526	137 074	1 303	117 582	310	33 906
October	1 661	149 985	1 454	132 373	349	38 157
November	1 584	153 394	1 407	138 925	353	38 097
December	1 476	136 252	1 277	121 849	322	36 611
2011						
January	1 522	150 406	1 335	132 659	327	37 431
February	1 456	137 938	1 263	123 141	312	30 036
March	1 307	119 691	1 156	106 721	269	31 699
April	1 526	145 315	1 366	130 841	352	37 177
May	1 573	144 824	1 387	129 296	399	42 238
June	1 522	144 060	1 342	129 136	359	38 630
July	1 566	144 543	1 347	123 815	342	35 458
August	1 585	168 266	1 364	153 081	374	46 267
September	1 463	150 165	1 319	136 564	346	37 505
October	1 349	118 135	1 220	106 478	335	32 310
November	1 312	123 078	1 177	113 239	312	33 715
December	1 392	144 661	1 247	129 994	346	38 469
2012						
January	1 435	129 169	1 298	118 127	325	32 503
February	1 275	120 199	1 134	109 458	283	28 236
March	1 290	125 195	1 141	112 889	269	28 300
April	1 403	138 164	1 235	122 236	294	34 929
May	1 370	131 603	1 220	119 788	277	31 873
June	1 320	133 080	1 178	120 857	282	31 737
July	1 354	138 694	1 217	128 186	355	43 427
August	1 297	130 266	1 172	120 391	322	39 389
September	1 346	125 692	1 223	116 792	365	40 287
October	1 400	136 153	1 240	125 026	346	42 027
November	1 749	172 879	1 574	159 872	412	47 171
December	1 509	137 839	1 334	125 505	330	35 211
2013						
January	1 328	134 026	1 197	123 088	357	43 068
February	1 422	135 468	1 218	119 856	295	39 407
March	1 337	127 939	1 183	115 664	311	36 696
April	1 199	116 849	1 051	104 746	293	29 744
May	1 301	127 821	1 134	115 260	276	33 527

Table 7-2. Mass Layoff Events and Initial Claimants for Unemployment Insurance, 2000–May 2013, Not Seasonally Adjusted

(Number.)

Year and month	Total		Private nonfarm		Manufacturing	
	Events	Initial claimants	Events	Initial claimants	Events	Initial claimants
2000						
January	1 934	223 322	1 807	212 805	741	100 397
February	1 045	103 898	780	81 103	268	30 358
March	986	106 748	827	92 565	329	38 434
April	924	101 359	838	93 631	323	34 061
May	984	92 193	841	81 125	262	25 838
June	1 597	192 025	1 269	160 685	404	60 258
July	1 333	164 978	1 159	152 243	664	100 874
August	751	97 215	679	90 877	256	35 687
September	936	106 842	767	93 327	319	46 865
October	874	103 755	684	84 922	321	48 877
November	1 697	216 514	1 397	190 626	617	93 966
December	2 677	326 743	2 477	311 623	1 074	166 928
2001						
January	1 522	200 343	1 405	188 504	632	107 028
February	1 501	172 908	1 285	156 183	576	79 784
March	1 527	171 466	1 371	158 108	659	86 874
April	1 450	176 265	1 353	166 167	608	78 845
May	1 434	159 365	1 331	151 186	528	64 887
June	2 107	253 826	1 784	226 022	737	116 005
July	2 117	273 807	1 952	259 128	1 144	168 877
August	1 490	166 148	1 386	158 307	603	79 515
September	1 327	160 402	1 214	151 161	485	58 544
October	1 831	215 483	1 676	202 053	742	107 030
November	2 721	295 956	2 373	270 268	1 122	151 969
December	2 440	268 893	2 319	259 497	1 103	136 820
2002						
January	2 146	263 777	2 028	252 245	892	128 825
February	1 382	138 808	1 253	129 849	481	58 784
March	1 460	161 316	1 335	151 305	500	59 613
April	1 506	165 814	1 378	153 216	461	50 897
May	1 723	179 799	1 571	166 801	488	52 720
June	1 584	162 189	1 266	136 424	336	42 130
July	2 042	245 294	1 819	226 892	907	135 271
August	1 248	128 103	1 151	119 874	427	48 668
September	1 062	124 522	957	114 736	352	43 755
October	1 497	171 100	1 270	149 327	493	64 655
November	2 153	240 171	1 860	216 237	719	92 712
December	2 474	264 158	2 324	252 807	984	126 826
2003						
January	2 315	225 430	2 130	210 918	822	90 244
February	1 363	124 965	1 222	116 264	435	48 161
March	1 207	113 026	1 099	104 468	390	41 063
April	1 581	161 412	1 470	152 937	499	62 349
May	1 703	174 204	1 538	160 729	499	61 278
June	1 691	157 552	1 336	127 743	389	40 845
July	2 087	226 435	1 815	206 901	946	136 410
August	1 258	133 839	1 163	124 131	405	52 620
September	868	82 647	756	73 914	271	31 428
October	1 523	158 240	1 265	137 706	438	53 741
November	1 438	138 543	1 234	123 524	408	48 419
December	1 929	192 633	1 793	182 750	648	77 915
2004						
January	2 428	239 454	2 226	220 687	848	89 551
February	941	84 201	832	76 577	240	23 043
March	920	92 554	847	87 782	258	34 686
April	1 458	157 314	1 316	142 657	343	36 172
May	988	87 501	878	78 786	219	22 141
June	1 379	134 588	1 077	110 804	222	27 307
July	2 094	253 929	1 860	234 877	885	145 895
August	809	69 033	745	63 876	194	17 698
September	708	68 972	637	63 102	189	25 808
October	1 242	127 918	1 101	117 375	372	48 265
November	1 399	130 423	1 201	115 549	412	44 243
December	1 614	161 271	1 487	152 092	436	50 726
2005						
January	2 564	263 952	2 421	253 409	823	108 985
February	810	74 644	722	68 372	230	24 931
March	806	88 937	733	83 793	246	33 030
April	1 373	158 582	1 263	148 133	395	59 129
May	986	101 358	891	93 332	249	30 424
June	1 157	120 463	941	103 307	216	32 783
July	1 981	244 216	1 745	222 377	856	136 210
August	645	67 582	598	63 484	188	22 531
September	1 662	213 281	1 505	179 042	318	47 497
October	905	91 941	757	80 694	249	37 276
November	1 254	116 127	1 079	102 182	363	41 442
December	2 323	254 258	2 168	242 753	706	96 382
2006						
January	1 245	117 946	1 123	108 701	331	35 097
February	719	66 555	658	62 208	210	24 892
March	921	111 838	856	106 177	285	44 688
April	1 140	121 589	1 038	112 964	296	39 538
May	872	84 809	794	78 663	192	23 570
June	1 489	164 761	1 224	140 687	319	41 095
July	1 511	166 857	1 335	154 342	648	96 152
August	708	72 844	656	69 054	203	28 494
September	865	87 699	785	81 274	296	39 076
October	964	98 804	820	88 133	311	46 737
November	1 315	136 186	1 172	125 009	455	58 473
December	2 249	254 503	2 126	244 783	735	105 462

Table 7-2. Mass Layoff Events and Initial Claimants for Unemployment Insurance, 2000–May 2013, Not Seasonally Adjusted—*Continued*

(Number.)

Year and month	Total		Private nonfarm		Manufacturing	
	Events	Initial claimants	Events	Initial claimants	Events	Initial claimants
2007						
January	1 407	134 984	1 263	124 475	456	53 615
February	935	86 696	861	82 097	273	36 170
March	1 082	123 974	1 015	118 431	367	49 886
April	1 219	127 444	1 115	118 040	309	35 229
May	923	85 816	856	81 153	224	26 527
June	1 599	172 810	1 318	148 669	313	36 571
July	1 599	175 419	1 450	164 939	684	101 390
August	963	93 458	908	88 345	220	23 361
September	717	67 385	667	64 026	246	29 381
October	1 083	108 455	929	97 716	338	50 918
November	1 799	198 220	1 593	181 184	514	75 413
December	2 167	224 214	2 071	216 898	699	91 754
2008						
January	1 647	154 503	1 520	144 191	488	54 418
February	1 269	119 508	1 178	113 587	361	42 527
March	1 089	114 541	1 039	110 147	333	43 740
April	1 272	130 810	1 172	121 625	394	48 188
May	1 552	159 471	1 438	150 462	388	51 698
June	1 622	166 742	1 315	140 916	309	42 097
July	1 891	200 382	1 687	186 018	760	108 733
August	1 427	139 999	1 343	133 146	414	51 912
September	1 292	129 586	1 202	122 505	361	46 391
October	2 125	221 784	1 917	205 553	689	100 457
November	2 574	241 589	2 389	226 657	997	107 620
December	3 377	351 305	3 232	340 220	1 378	172 529
2009						
January	3 806	388 813	3 633	375 293	1 461	172 757
February	2 262	218 438	2 173	210 755	945	103 588
March	2 191	228 387	2 107	221 397	940	114 747
April	2 547	256 930	2 385	243 321	887	100 872
May	2 738	289 628	2 572	274 047	1 005	123 683
June	2 519	256 357	2 051	216 063	674	85 726
July	3 054	336 654	2 659	296 589	1 133	154 208
August	1 428	125 024	1 334	117 193	436	41 151
September	1 371	123 177	1 258	115 141	448	51 126
October	1 934	193 904	1 678	172 883	566	69 655
November	1 870	164 496	1 679	150 751	517	55 053
December	2 310	214 648	2 166	203 655	615	64 540
2010						
January	2 860	278 679	2 682	265 074	962	104 846
February	1 183	102 818	1 091	96 022	282	30 728
March	1 197	111 727	1 111	105 514	273	29 745
April	1 840	199 690	1 697	184 654	424	55 178
May	1 354	123 333	1 170	109 203	216	19 334
June	1 861	171 190	1 355	125 872	212	21 083
July	2 124	206 254	1 732	172 248	532	64 200
August	976	92 435	897	83 021	230	23 088
September	920	77 654	806	67 987	187	19 403
October	1 642	148 638	1 373	127 865	351	40 861
November	1 676	158 048	1 477	142 591	389	41 383
December	1 931	184 130	1 763	172 881	465	52 816
2011						
January	2 558	246 463	2 372	229 765	693	75 006
February	1 024	85 585	919	78 718	222	18 471
March	908	85 095	844	80 014	191	20 869
April	1 750	189 919	1 625	176 478	397	47 104
May	1 367	119 911	1 221	108 531	270	25 199
June	1 661	159 930	1 238	122 821	226	22 986
July	2 176	216 774	1 759	174 078	602	71 814
August	961	99 213	875	93 159	228	26 916
September	1 189	117 232	1 095	107 300	296	32 058
October	1 101	96 914	950	83 748	265	28 447
November	1 393	127 750	1 245	117 474	349	37 799
December	2 433	263 665	2 258	247 916	658	75 033
2012						
January	1 705	141 703	1 587	132 754	415	38 021
February	895	73 974	820	69 076	196	16 555
March	1 125	117 817	1 040	110 954	242	24 241
April	1 421	146 358	1 293	132 697	256	32 518
May	1 201	109 259	1 081	100 434	186	18 800
June	1 890	198 537	1 485	158 334	255	28 570
July	1 515	157 753	1 321	144 340	559	74 963
August	1 063	104 045	992	97 694	251	31 193
September	811	70 570	749	66 214	221	22 748
October	1 142	109 829	968	97 390	277	37 702
November	2 270	240 040	2 078	228 124	551	72 600
December	1 973	187 137	1 822	177 452	477	50 686
2013						
January	1 528	144 517	1 424	135 970	455	50 793
February	960	79 786	846	72 391	192	21 630
March	1 132	114 897	1 048	108 200	268	28 923
April	1 174	119 196	1 068	109 105	248	25 780
May	1 383	134 483	1 218	121 545	221	26 125

Table 7-3. Industry Distribution: Mass Layoff Events and Initial Claimants for Unemployment Insurance, 2000–May 2013

(Number, not seasonally adjusted.)

Industry	2000	2001	2002	2003	2004	2005	2006	2007	2008	2009	2010
						Mass layoff events					
ALL INDUSTRIES	15 738	21 467	20 277	18 963	15 980	16 466	13 998	15 493	21 137	28 030	19 564
Total, Private	15 028	20 763	19 376	17 846	15 018	15 534	13 238	14 714	20 130	26 437	17 887
Agriculture, forestry, fishing and hunting	1 503	1 314	1 164	1 025	811	711	651	668	698	742	733
Total, private nonfarm	13 525	19 449	18 212	16 821	14 207	14 823	12 587	14 046	19 432	25 695	17 154
Mining, quarrying, and oil and gas extraction	102	115	176	101	69	75	58	66	103	314	102
Utilities	37	33	44	40	25	25	20	20	28	39	30
Construction	1 638	1 688	1 939	2 013	1 821	1 975	1 546	1 952	2 393	2 833	2 262
Manufacturing	5 578	8 939	7 040	6 150	4 618	4 839	4 281	4 643	6 872	9 627	4 523
Food	826	879	826	850	797	751	648	595	678	771	745
Beverage and tobacco products	61	74	79	82	75	66	56	58	78	78	73
Textile mills	209	352	272	245	169	160	143	146	179	195	109
Textile product mills	83	91	113	111	93	86	66	63	69	76	59
Apparel	424	433	346	295	220	179	128	131	149	201	134
Leather and allied products	76	79	48	48	42	41	26	27	22	28	17
Wood products	381	359	383	350	226	273	341	418	557	553	309
Paper	148	212	167	156	82	98	86	78	146	241	93
Printing and related support activities	95	156	156	125	118	98	74	90	132	235	131
Petroleum and coal products	39	25	39	30	27	24	34	28	37	49	43
Chemicals	84	156	122	105	101	77	69	75	122	193	116
Plastics and rubber products	278	482	331	328	282	300	250	265	501	559	199
Nonmetallic mineral products	186	239	219	233	167	204	172	215	316	400	224
Primary metals	274	568	399	366	194	222	184	225	352	686	210
Fabricated metal products	327	675	482	397	322	311	288	293	574	949	292
Machinery	324	781	555	425	235	272	255	287	402	1 046	331
Computer and electronic products	231	1 050	817	481	230	217	173	190	285	626	198
Electrical equipment and appliance manufacturing	195	391	313	231	137	167	136	135	220	397	152
Transportation equipment	1 004	1 410	961	927	821	1 034	925	1 068	1 647	1 827	811
Furniture and related products	183	325	249	218	168	164	148	184	288	323	198
Miscellaneous manufacturing	150	202	163	147	112	95	79	72	118	194	79
Wholesale trade	236	334	336	318	222	251	184	220	363	653	328
Retail trade	906	1 249	1 351	1 327	1 165	1 196	991	1 048	1 457	1 965	1 574
Transportation and warehousing	717	908	947	965	853	1 011	934	982	1 267	1 491	1 160
Information	358	736	719	598	454	383	350	383	545	752	548
Finance and insurance	218	325	432	384	322	272	310	510	552	677	430
Real estate and rental and leasing	64	99	91	91	79	92	54	71	118	165	117
Professional and technical services	348	591	634	522	420	427	352	420	564	800	599
Management of companies and enterprises	40	47	40	35	38	27	28	42	61	104	60
Administrative and waste services	1 644	2 333	2 428	2 266	2 035	1 989	1 741	1 862	2 699	3 205	2 579
Educational services	34	51	69	82	60	70	63	67	100	149	161
Health care and social assistance	405	374	480	499	522	585	415	450	580	675	709
Arts, entertainment, and recreation	162	229	277	285	287	293	245	240	311	389	363
Accommodation and food services	729	1 032	916	886	980	1 083	844	905	1 238	1 606	1 386
Other services, except public administration	148	171	221	217	198	201	148	155	174	242	218
Unclassified	161	195	72	42	39	29	23	10	7	9	5
Government	710	704	901	1 117	962	932	760	779	1 007	1 593	1 677
Federal	172	143	125	134	142	154	119	134	118	166	204
State	152	165	171	205	177	196	130	136	184	305	292
Local	386	396	605	778	643	582	511	509	705	1 122	1 181

Table 7-3. Industry Distribution: Mass Layoff Events and Initial Claimants for Unemployment Insurance, 2000–May 2013—*Continued*

(Number, not seasonally adjusted.)

Industry	2011	2012	January 2013	February 2013	March 2013	April 2013	May 2013
			Mass layoff events				
ALL INDUSTRIES	18 521	17 080	1 528	960	1 132	1 174	1 383
Total, Private	17 046	15 966	1 466	928	1 097	1 125	1 255
Agriculture, forestry, fishing and hunting	645	730	42	82	49	57	37
Total, private nonfarm	16 401	15 236	1 424	846	1 048	1 068	1 218
Mining, quarrying, and oil and gas extraction	75	142	11	4	10	8	5
Utilities	30	30	4	...	(^{1})	(^{1})	(^{1})
Construction	1 994	1 806	188	103	126	97	135
Manufacturing	4 397	3 886	455	192	268	248	221
Food	810	750	58	41	57	75	57
Beverage and tobacco products	64	60	(^{1})	(^{1})	7	(^{1})	(^{1})
Textile mills	182	169	35	7	4	8	7
Textile product mills	61	62	5	6	(^{1})	4	4
Apparel	124	134	16	4	5	9	8
Leather and allied products	17	20	4	3	(^{1})	(^{1})	...
Wood products	279	175	26	11	14	8	6
Paper	95	69	5	3	6	3	6
Printing and related support activities	101	102	5	5	6	10	4
Petroleum and coal products	34	42	3	3	(^{1})	3	3
Chemicals	90	78	10	4	4	7	5
Plastics and rubber products	230	188	20	7	13	4	5
Nonmetallic mineral products	200	162	19	7	11	6	3
Primary metals	162	182	26	10	10	14	16
Fabricated metal products	246	243	29	14	23	15	12
Machinery	270	294	34	15	16	18	29
Computer and electronic products	184	192	15	12	12	17	11
Electrical equipment and appliance manufacturing	137	124	18	6	18	11	5
Transportation equipment	821	602	86	23	39	17	22
Furniture and related products	194	166	32	7	8	10	11
Miscellaneous manufacturing	96	72	7	3	9	6	5
Wholesale trade	262	282	28	12	12	19	26
Retail trade	1 448	1 393	136	128	84	96	103
Transportation and warehousing	1 180	1 194	87	34	90	116	45
Information	522	441	36	37	32	38	43
Finance and insurance	313	305	25	20	18	27	18
Real estate and rental and leasing	95	74	3	6	8	4	7
Professional and technical services	555	510	41	45	36	78	64
Management of companies and enterprises	49	58	7	(^{1})	5	5	4
Administrative and waste services	2 744	2 477	237	164	179	155	207
Educational services	167	182	10	8	4	11	12
Health care and social assistance	738	692	23	26	31	41	133
Arts, entertainment, and recreation	338	329	32	12	15	34	28
Accommodation and food services	1 294	1 221	86	45	117	80	130
Other services, except public administration	193	179	12	5	11	9	31
Unclassified	7	35	5	2	...	2	3
Government	1 475	1 114	62	32	35	49	128
Federal	149	91	9	7	3	9	8
State	331	238	19	13	12	13	36
Local	995	785	34	12	20	27	84

^{1}Data do not meet BLS or state agency disclosure standards.
. . . = Not available.

Table 7-3. Industry Distribution: Mass Layoff Events and Initial Claimants for Unemployment Insurance, 2000–May 2013—*Continued*

(Number, not seasonally adjusted.)

Industry	2000	2001	2002	2003	2004	2005	2006	2007	2008	2009	2010
	Initial claimants										
ALL INDUSTRIES	1 835 592	2 514 862	2 245 051	1 888 926	1 607 158	1 795 341	1 484 391	1 598 875	2 130 220	2 796 456	1 854 596
Total, Private	1 768 743	2 447 154	2 158 413	1 790 713	1 520 157	1 691 217	1 418 452	1 533 920	2 046 011	2 650 289	1 704 320
Agriculture, forestry, fishing and hunting	123 211	100 570	88 700	68 728	55 993	50 339	46 457	47 947	50 984	53 201	51 388
Total, private nonfarm	1 645 532	2 346 584	2 069 713	1 721 985	1 464 164	1 640 878	1 371 995	1 485 973	1 995 027	2 597 088	1 652 932
Mining, quarrying, and oil and gas extraction	9 271	14 887	16 672	9 852	5 985	6 483	5 582	5 327	9 273	27 872	8 192
Utilities	3 361	3 898	4 275	2 963	2 827	3 173	1 336	1 462	2 299	3 355	2 684
Construction	136 328	139 958	158 366	146 602	134 486	149 893	116 283	142 618	173 627	205 765	169 377
Manufacturing	782 543	1 236 178	904 856	744 473	565 535	670 620	583 274	610 215	870 310	1 137 106	502 665
Food	90 972	98 013	98 251	87 353	82 114	76 926	62 852	62 141	72 081	78 345	76 351
Beverage and tobacco products	5 955	6 242	6 564	6 775	6 594	4 714	4 404	4 679	6 466	7 205	5 952
Textile mills	33 064	57 009	43 511	37 734	19 669	22 213	19 070	19 527	21 620	23 439	13 872
Textile product mills	8 542	10 233	16 234	11 611	11 101	9 801	6 044	6 681	6 810	8 306	6 946
Apparel	40 474	50 423	41 320	29 887	24 729	21 889	14 170	11 508	13 970	18 545	11 663
Leather and allied products	8 204	7 867	3 903	5 170	4 733	4 960	2 757	3 077	2 862	2 280	2 187
Wood products	43 343	38 295	43 280	35 494	26 284	32 590	34 861	41 604	56 278	49 723	28 361
Paper	14 592	25 345	17 165	14 031	6 686	8 430	7 468	6 439	14 707	23 238	7 399
Printing and related support activities	9 030	13 799	15 019	9 976	10 534	8 005	6 131	7 414	12 000	22 793	11 396
Petroleum and coal products	3 609	2 518	3 611	2 292	2 343	2 262	2 874	2 333	3 114	3 689	3 405
Chemicals	8 960	15 659	11 161	10 811	8 707	7 713	6 164	6 665	10 227	15 692	9 880
Plastics and rubber products	35 828	59 024	38 596	35 054	28 409	30 714	26 098	24 611	49 196	58 926	17 354
Nonmetallic mineral products	19 272	25 246	21 712	22 031	15 389	18 956	15 980	19 204	27 834	32 179	18 013
Primary metals	38 835	81 601	48 671	40 641	23 193	27 469	21 866	27 016	37 765	76 288	20 467
Fabricated metal products	34 543	66 862	49 228	35 884	30 672	28 137	26 090	26 674	49 757	84 702	24 651
Machinery	57 793	121 724	87 710	60 370	28 407	33 713	40 069	45 831	53 673	164 176	44 916
Computer and electronic products	24 638	133 552	85 958	46 888	21 230	20 249	15 326	16 439	26 270	58 693	16 796
Electrical equipment and appliance manufacturing	39 205	60 387	48 413	36 496	24 443	30 804	24 503	23 274	37 732	48 250	20 199
Transportation equipment	228 380	303 139	176 505	178 282	163 026	253 681	221 257	228 213	323 622	304 693	133 554
Furniture and related products	23 252	39 362	33 640	24 551	16 315	18 168	17 366	19 510	33 617	39 554	22 467
Miscellaneous manufacturing	14 052	19 878	14 404	13 142	10 957	9 226	7 924	7 375	10 709	16 390	6 836
Wholesale trade	20 576	27 973	31 224	25 422	19 861	20 780	13 856	17 922	28 849	54 003	24 600
Retail trade	95 451	131 316	149 363	138 457	114 588	113 748	96 999	96 787	136 209	193 492	155 299
Transportation and warehousing	79 430	106 358	124 699	103 499	94 588	113 279	106 708	109 104	136 178	157 661	130 607
Information	80 618	103 122	100 982	80 715	72 820	72 100	64 365	64 404	70 066	96 127	75 518
Finance and insurance	17 532	27 881	36 099	27 870	24 954	20 884	22 213	40 917	42 152	55 876	33 122
Real estate and rental and leasing	4 564	7 611	7 324	6 412	6 329	7 615	4 082	5 139	8 754	11 567	7 861
Professional and technical services	57 135	77 862	82 223	52 700	49 547	49 719	40 739	49 223	57 144	72 962	56 713
Management of companies and enterprises	4 601	5 540	5 668	3 777	4 729	2 864	2 310	3 258	5 818	11 064	6 864
Administrative and waste services	191 073	258 542	257 530	206 765	184 369	187 156	153 655	168 460	246 670	294 709	221 024
Educational services	2 486	3 571	4 855	5 862	4 315	5 641	5 081	5 667	9 025	13 670	14 200
Health care and social assistance	36 759	32 255	40 364	38 108	40 118	51 371	33 972	38 848	44 139	52 058	55 205
Arts, entertainment, and recreation	14 399	20 542	23 517	21 387	21 191	27 564	16 531	16 874	21 550	29 853	28 366
Accommodation and food services	71 713	110 234	92 575	83 856	96 509	117 107	89 947	94 928	118 247	160 464	144 356
Other services, except public administration	13 287	15 742	20 049	18 617	18 226	18 753	13 478	13 936	14 310	18 889	15 849
Unclassified	24 405	23 114	9 072	4 648	3 187	2 128	1 584	884	407	595	430
Government	66 849	67 708	86 638	98 213	87 001	104 124	65 939	64 955	84 209	146 167	150 276
Federal	19 974	16 865	15 458	14 173	14 308	15 087	11 957	12 976	10 485	15 930	20 868
State	14 604	15 840	17 857	17 761	15 362	19 686	12 293	11 289	15 452	26 964	24 675
Local	32 271	35 003	53 323	66 279	57 331	69 351	41 689	40 690	58 272	103 273	104 733

Table 7-3. Industry Distribution: Mass Layoff Events and Initial Claimants for Unemployment Insurance, 2000–May 2013—*Continued*

(Number, not seasonally adjusted.)

Industry	2011	2012	January 2013	February 2013	March 2013	April 2013	May 2013
				Initial claimants			
ALL INDUSTRIES	1 808 451	1 666 931	144 517	79 786	114 897	119 196	134 483
Total, Private	1 667 632	1 566 198	139 018	77 091	111 521	114 638	123 833
Agriculture, forestry, fishing and hunting	47 630	50 735	3 048	4 700	3 321	5 533	2 288
Total, private nonfarm	1 620 002	1 515 463	135 970	72 391	108 200	109 105	121 545
Mining, quarrying, and oil and gas extraction	6 056	11 621	811	311	845	687	353
Utilities	2 658	9 702	(^{1})	(^{1})	(^{1})	. . .	243
Construction	152 071	139 537	13 212	8 221	9 526	7 185	11 463
Manufacturing	481 702	448 687	50 793	21 630	28 923	25 780	26 125
Food	85 240	83 747	6 530	3 879	5 218	8 477	6 040
Beverage and tobacco products	5 806	4 526	(^{1})	(^{1})	1 330	(^{1})	(^{1})
Textile mills	22 948	20 712	4 550	499	572	760	523
Textile product mills	6 158	5 890	403	470	(^{1})	499	371
Apparel	12 940	12 618	2 149	240	828	845	664
Leather and allied products	2 037	2 006	485	227	(^{1})	(^{1})	. . .
Wood products	26 674	15 213	2 517	1 075	1 079	721	530
Paper	8 035	5 915	314	220	322	213	554
Printing and related support activities	8 859	8 374	483	615	384	719	307
Petroleum and coal products	2 801	3 402	200	184	(^{1})	202	162
Chemicals	7 230	6 348	849	272	261	626	385
Plastics and rubber products	20 740	20 111	1 761	1 575	2 882	330	469
Nonmetallic mineral products	17 202	14 345	1 317	591	713	619	195
Primary metals	16 238	23 211	2 274	1 221	907	1 519	1 125
Fabricated metal products	22 218	21 041	2 522	947	1 873	1 596	804
Machinery	38 655	43 665	5 404	1 347	3 268	2 113	7 155
Computer and electronic products	14 286	14 807	1 287	684	1 002	1 184	729
Electrical equipment and appliance manufacturing	21 154	16 853	2 099	1 396	2 130	1 509	551
Transportation equipment	114 874	101 673	11 930	5 175	4 240	1 432	4 020
Furniture and related products	19 271	16 955	3 047	532	771	1 422	1 041
Miscellaneous manufacturing	8 336	7 275	488	388	729	640	329
Wholesale trade	21 212	23 641	2 334	854	1 098	1 364	1 674
Retail trade	143 652	131 122	13 622	10 111	8 204	9 833	9 008
Transportation and warehousing	134 588	138 775	6 419	3 833	12 753	12 688	5 188
Information	88 998	60 541	5 477	3 247	4 261	9 107	4 020
Finance and insurance	23 889	22 521	2 226	1 400	1 810	1 960	1 273
Real estate and rental and leasing	7 279	5 951	178	427	674	201	540
Professional and technical services	56 890	47 165	5 684	2 907	4 167	9 919	6 685
Management of companies and enterprises	3 897	5 849	976	(^{1})	471	434	407
Administrative and waste services	242 692	208 849	22 170	11 875	15 271	13 493	17 588
Educational services	14 663	15 968	609	442	302	939	980
Health care and social assistance	58 964	56 816	1 461	1 601	2 395	3 460	15 256
Arts, entertainment, and recreation	28 501	25 628	2 455	808	1 716	3 320	1 720
Accommodation and food services	136 133	146 554	6 391	4 046	14 725	7 939	15 553
Other services, except public administration	15 659	14 624	805	296	772	699	3 162
Unclassified	498	1 912	249	133	. . .	97	307
Government	140 819	100 733	5 499	2 695	3 376	4 558	10 650
Federal	14 690	7 636	933	561	317	1 074	782
State	34 500	22 729	1 435	1 178	1 559	1 257	2 902
Local	91 629	70 368	3 131	956	1 500	2 227	6 966

^{1}Data do not meet BLS or state agency disclosure standards.
. . . = Not available.

Table 7-4. Mass Layoff Events and Initial Claimants for Unemployment Insurance, by Region and State, 2000–May 2013

(Number.)

Region and state	2000	2001	2002	2003	2004	2005	2006	2007	2008	2009	2010
	Mass layoff events										
UNITED STATES[1]	15 738	21 467	20 277	18 963	15 980	16 466	13 998	15 493	21 137	28 030	19 564
Northeast	2 226	3 157	3 073	3 139	2 630	2 806	2 514	2 775	3 257	4 864	3 493
New England	427	691	615	493	359	426	352	358	427	745	504
Middle Atlantic	1 799	2 466	2 458	2 646	2 271	2 380	2 162	2 417	2 830	4 119	2 989
South	3 166	4 601	4 829	4 198	3 587	4 035	2 789	3 260	5 153	7 089	4 948
South Atlantic	1 538	2 249	2 275	2 068	1 802	1 585	1 475	1 727	2 561	3 782	2 753
East South Central	626	902	1 060	858	798	893	699	857	1 392	1 694	1 091
West South Central	1 002	1 450	1 494	1 272	987	1 557	615	676	1 200	1 613	1 104
Midwest	4 223	5 945	4 828	4 644	4 135	4 512	4 026	4 258	5 751	7 434	4 409
East North Central	3 309	4 682	3 679	3 622	3 292	3 585	3 183	3 381	4 551	5 734	3 286
West North Central	914	1 263	1 149	1 022	843	927	843	877	1 200	1 700	1 123
West	6 123	7 764	7 547	6 982	5 628	5 113	4 669	5 200	6 976	8 643	6 714
Mountain	596	836	726	638	512	537	443	558	831	1 291	947
Pacific	5 527	6 928	6 821	6 344	5 116	4 576	4 226	4 642	6 145	7 352	5 767
Alabama	119	169	428	332	274	244	138	276	444	493	365
Alaska	30	31	36	36	35	24	30	19	27	72	70
Arizona	107	161	170	146	110	109	72	99	146	255	192
Arkansas	85	95	76	60	54	52	40	69	116	117	71
California	5 008	6 145	6 045	5 651	4 547	4 104	3 702	4 130	5 403	6 377	5 110
Colorado	62	143	126	104	74	72	65	80	93	188	153
Connecticut	45	73	73	80	49	55	60	51	65	125	101
Delaware	13	33	19	23	13	9	9	17	38	57	47
District of Columbia	14	24	14	14	8	7	5	6	11	17	16
Florida	525	870	936	866	876	700	593	795	1 333	1 748	1 231
Georgia	164	215	310	403	323	323	317	350	476	618	429
Hawaii	38	77	74	55	37	33	48	46	88	106	56
Idaho	117	144	126	122	90	82	65	92	145	137	113
Illinois	647	870	824	775	663	647	600	641	871	1 309	804
Indiana	333	497	460	506	434	443	403	375	680	730	353
Iowa	230	319	251	249	169	212	188	192	303	423	243
Kansas	92	110	129	119	102	103	88	92	136	211	119
Kentucky	261	409	363	277	289	328	330	346	540	719	373
Louisiana	185	225	241	204	206	956	134	107	311	282	240
Maine	48	50	45	44	48	43	33	40	33	68	46
Maryland	68	73	85	94	80	55	120	128	85	141	128
Massachusetts	188	356	325	262	152	178	123	128	162	275	170
Michigan	969	1 359	612	604	866	1 032	922	949	1 156	1 305	634
Minnesota	198	304	279	260	213	237	205	199	245	377	221
Mississippi	102	121	82	81	61	155	71	80	167	135	147
Missouri	352	432	374	292	256	276	289	329	433	551	420
Montana	25	35	32	46	36	48	40	49	54	93	76
Nebraska	24	50	80	65	71	72	48	32	47	66	83
Nevada	214	246	178	148	121	138	117	135	251	369	240
New Hampshire	37	79	61	31	29	40	29	31	42	90	66
New Jersey	405	427	509	481	449	485	452	503	518	690	569
New Mexico	31	37	40	44	42	44	49	55	73	123	84
New York	244	441	765	932	836	806	717	733	897	1 367	1 121
North Carolina	172	288	245	246	167	166	129	93	196	325	315
North Dakota	10	30	24	22	22	14	18	22	26	47	30
Ohio	653	963	901	913	699	761	608	716	1 027	1 205	712
Oklahoma	61	122	122	121	86	58	55	69	79	150	71
Oregon	277	410	368	342	282	202	246	258	367	472	301
Pennsylvania	1 150	1 598	1 184	1 233	986	1 089	993	1 181	1 415	2 062	1 299
Rhode Island	71	82	72	41	51	65	52	54	64	90	71
South Carolina	288	452	364	170	159	142	140	177	284	493	272
South Dakota	8	18	12	15	10	13	7	11	10	25	7
Tennessee	144	203	187	168	174	166	160	155	241	347	206
Texas	671	1 008	1 055	887	641	491	386	431	694	1 064	722
Utah	39	66	50	24	33	37	30	43	61	113	77
Vermont	38	51	39	35	30	45	55	54	61	97	50
Virginia	271	275	263	229	156	170	143	142	116	330	290
Washington	174	265	298	260	215	213	200	189	260	325	230
West Virginia	23	19	39	23	20	13	19	19	22	53	25
Wisconsin	707	993	882	824	630	702	650	700	817	1 185	783
Wyoming	. . .	4	4	4	6	7	5	. . .	8	13	12

[1]Data for all states and the District of Columbia.
. . . = Not available.

Table 7-4. Mass Layoff Events and Initial Claimants for Unemployment Insurance, by Region and State, 2000–May 2013—*Continued*

(Number.)

Region and state	2011	2012	January 2013	February 2013	March 2013	April 2013	May 2013
				Mass layoff events			
UNITED STATES[1]	18 521	17 080	1 528	960	1 132	1 174	1 383
Northeast	3 508	3 601	272	159	229	272	182
New England	495	467	34	38	22	55	22
Middle Atlantic	3 013	3 134	238	121	207	217	160
South	5 025	4 538	515	237	290	310	428
South Atlantic	2 813	2 548	324	142	142	162	225
East South Central	1 113	960	129	39	67	56	96
West South Central	1 099	1 030	62	56	81	92	107
Midwest	4 216	3 618	339	146	230	203	292
East North Central	3 129	2 700	248	103	163	163	203
West North Central	1 087	918	91	43	67	40	89
West	5 772	5 323	402	418	383	389	481
Mountain	786	678	51	20	49	73	60
Pacific	4 986	4 645	351	398	334	316	421
Alabama	345	273	82	9	12	11	28
Alaska	54	57	(²)	4	7	4	8
Arizona	178	150	5	5	11	30	15
Arkansas	154	172	15	9	22	16	12
California	4 378	4 083	303	360	289	273	377
Colorado	114	104	11	(²)	4	12	9
Connecticut	88	92	11	15	...	7	6
Delaware	45	33	(²)	(²)	(²)	8	4
District of Columbia	22	17	3	(²)	...	...	3
Florida	1 091	852	56	55	58	54	78
Georgia	466	327	63	17	8	21	33
Hawaii	44	31	6	4	...	3	8
Idaho	110	82	9	3	8	4	(²)
Illinois	676	658	53	24	49	49	60
Indiana	327	277	22	12	16	10	27
Iowa	221	203	22	7	11	14	13
Kansas	112	116	7	8	11	3	11
Kentucky	390	349	24	15	29	21	18
Louisiana	214	174	9	6	5	14	16
Maine	63	60	10	(²)	7	6	(²)
Maryland	109	165	21	7	14	12	16
Massachusetts	170	157	7	10	7	20	5
Michigan	711	629	54	16	25	24	41
Minnesota	259	198	13	5	15	7	16
Mississippi	197	178	9	5	15	14	26
Missouri	375	296	41	15	19	14	37
Montana	63	48	7	...	(²)	5	6
Nebraska	87	71	7	6	8	(²)	7
Nevada	156	152	11	8	12	7	13
New Hampshire	47	46	...	(²)	3	5	(²)
New Jersey	585	671	36	24	41	46	21
New Mexico	83	74	...	(²)	5	5	10
New York	1 096	1 251	97	52	55	86	52
North Carolina	528	694	100	34	35	45	54
North Dakota	27	30	(²)	(²)	3	(²)	(²)
Ohio	668	583	62	25	36	45	44
Oklahoma	81	57	3	(²)	3	5	3
Oregon	281	242	23	13	13	14	19
Pennsylvania	1 332	1 212	105	45	111	85	87
Rhode Island	67	60	4	7	(²)	7	3
South Carolina	225	187	47	10	11	8	11
South Dakota	6	(²)	...	(²)	...	...	3
Tennessee	181	160	14	10	11	10	24
Texas	650	627	35	40	51	57	76
Utah	72	59	7	(²)	7	9	5
Vermont	60	52	(²)	4	4	10	5
Virginia	303	245	31	14	13	12	23
Washington	229	232	17	17	25	22	9
West Virginia	24	28	(²)	(²)	(²)	(²)	3
Wisconsin	747	553	57	26	37	35	31
Wyoming	10	9	(²)	...	(²)	(²)	...

[1]Data for all states and the District of Columbia.
[2]Data do not meet BLS or state agency disclosure standards.
. . . = Not available.

Table 7-4. Mass Layoff Events and Initial Claimants for Unemployment Insurance, by Region and State, 2000–May 2013—*Continued*

(Number.)

Region and state	2000	2001	2002	2003	2004	2005	2006	2007	2008	2009	2010
						Initial claimants					
UNITED STATES[1]	1 835 592	2 514 862	2 245 051	1 888 926	1 607 158	1 795 341	1 484 391	1 598 875	2 130 220	2 796 456	1 854 596
Northeast	235 083	340 246	338 965	306 462	270 788	280 628	254 684	273 079	316 191	465 208	350 507
New England	56 909	75 283	67 846	50 708	35 020	45 064	37 359	34 860	40 915	70 288	50 632
Middle Atlantic	178 174	264 963	271 119	255 754	235 768	235 564	217 325	238 219	275 276	394 920	299 875
South	360 330	546 222	545 907	435 387	355 561	485 505	312 892	356 812	533 687	691 460	469 957
South Atlantic	185 615	257 113	247 353	206 290	165 280	159 131	152 443	163 761	225 596	344 284	245 720
East South Central	69 619	107 661	127 477	98 450	91 565	131 138	95 861	115 114	180 702	183 287	113 934
West South Central	105 096	181 448	171 077	130 647	98 716	195 236	64 588	77 937	127 389	163 889	110 303
Midwest	583 290	841 597	614 121	552 140	485 255	571 950	508 798	509 431	676 591	892 202	466 753
East North Central	465 917	663 997	457 002	414 489	387 065	457 592	406 432	414 919	538 429	706 233	358 694
West North Central	117 373	177 600	157 119	137 651	98 190	114 358	102 366	94 512	138 162	185 969	108 059
West	656 889	786 797	746 058	594 937	495 554	457 258	408 017	459 553	603 751	747 586	567 379
Mountain	61 090	94 490	76 484	58 247	47 929	50 830	41 696	49 308	75 567	117 890	85 395
Pacific	595 799	692 307	669 574	536 690	447 625	406 428	366 321	410 245	528 184	629 696	481 984
Alabama	13 491	18 228	59 821	44 523	34 012	29 603	14 530	30 543	57 324	56 284	39 152
Alaska	2 706	2 814	2 846	2 973	2 930	2 326	2 770	1 798	2 888	7 056	6 796
Arizona	10 782	16 148	17 775	12 566	11 020	11 831	7 950	10 839	14 274	24 316	19 280
Arkansas	9 050	11 328	6 868	6 131	5 926	7 611	5 056	8 647	11 914	12 353	7 748
California	536 673	600 501	576 110	467 573	394 114	360 138	317 907	357 994	446 480	532 028	419 809
Colorado	5 967	14 127	12 601	9 422	6 856	6 759	5 905	6 567	8 200	16 424	13 915
Connecticut	4 393	6 122	7 360	7 054	4 203	4 972	6 595	4 975	5 505	10 559	8 835
Delaware	8 271	8 200	4 927	8 084	3 764	5 034	4 185	4 522	6 335	5 513	3 271
District of Columbia	1 572	2 301	1 688	1 160	807	565	346	418	1 195	1 504	1 352
Florida	39 407	70 889	71 635	61 863	63 087	51 535	42 593	55 696	94 656	131 190	88 776
Georgia	16 967	22 141	41 888	49 009	33 406	40 854	35 947	39 624	48 603	64 642	44 512
Hawaii	3 042	7 803	7 467	5 151	2 938	2 692	3 706	3 988	9 590	9 173	4 629
Idaho	13 121	17 144	15 579	13 690	8 148	7 233	5 665	8 245	13 591	12 405	9 267
Illinois	108 726	135 126	116 592	90 181	75 763	71 399	75 118	80 477	103 685	193 495	91 277
Indiana	50 892	71 521	67 134	70 393	58 853	62 574	56 395	47 923	80 027	84 555	42 895
Iowa	32 479	44 997	35 460	32 744	18 126	30 291	27 804	23 637	43 574	54 587	31 028
Kansas	13 145	21 657	18 186	16 102	10 782	9 740	9 785	10 654	17 243	27 741	13 212
Kentucky	33 975	60 327	42 094	34 709	37 809	55 078	61 246	59 399	89 953	87 321	46 854
Louisiana	14 799	28 373	22 113	17 329	16 519	120 600	12 915	13 042	31 664	26 098	20 739
Maine	7 407	4 713	4 377	3 828	4 293	3 445	2 622	3 035	2 536	5 922	4 058
Maryland	5 868	6 259	9 386	7 911	7 951	4 998	11 771	12 172	7 116	11 932	11 022
Massachusetts	27 907	36 693	33 705	25 352	13 960	18 114	11 188	10 785	14 911	25 608	15 749
Michigan	129 640	196 459	63 350	66 866	99 124	131 411	127 964	125 942	132 468	153 361	74 773
Minnesota	24 169	38 739	33 348	27 725	24 607	26 689	25 729	19 231	23 370	34 255	20 543
Mississippi	8 684	10 501	7 162	5 239	4 384	29 971	5 524	9 647	13 818	10 116	11 410
Missouri	43 765	60 026	57 373	50 379	35 034	37 005	29 324	33 557	43 451	54 046	32 586
Montana	3 489	4 048	3 570	4 379	3 600	4 567	3 726	3 873	4 731	8 260	6 094
Nebraska	2 102	6 363	8 371	6 761	6 764	8 332	5 907	3 440	5 204	7 371	7 061
Nevada	21 976	32 414	19 115	12 897	11 795	13 224	11 130	11 344	22 389	34 364	21 704
New Hampshire	4 615	10 903	8 080	3 030	2 726	4 666	2 996	3 053	3 873	8 548	7 214
New Jersey	45 173	52 530	63 369	49 815	51 252	48 732	51 128	52 738	51 623	68 149	61 398
New Mexico	2 243	3 045	2 894	3 129	3 071	3 469	4 226	4 619	6 253	9 680	6 509
New York	22 318	46 404	85 578	93 583	95 228	87 649	76 638	77 353	95 612	144 247	125 909
North Carolina	23 902	33 021	27 324	28 977	14 435	16 670	13 316	10 694	21 037	37 488	32 337
North Dakota	912	4 303	3 140	2 577	1 980	1 184	3 065	2 992	4 354	5 870	3 098
Ohio	94 419	139 218	103 577	102 864	86 850	113 165	80 291	83 429	131 813	147 712	71 382
Oklahoma	7 531	21 086	16 203	17 502	14 124	10 090	7 234	9 627	10 187	16 986	8 271
Oregon	32 159	55 449	44 944	35 508	28 401	22 231	24 386	29 391	42 780	52 900	31 404
Pennsylvania	110 683	166 029	122 172	112 356	89 288	99 183	89 559	108 128	128 041	182 524	112 568
Rhode Island	8 441	10 851	9 567	5 251	6 907	9 151	8 211	7 362	7 040	10 159	10 046
South Carolina	45 084	74 891	51 006	21 001	22 241	17 450	16 909	21 787	32 063	53 172	32 332
South Dakota	801	1 515	1 241	1 363	897	1 117	752	1 001	966	2 099	531
Tennessee	13 469	18 605	18 400	13 979	15 360	16 486	14 561	15 525	19 607	29 566	16 518
Texas	73 716	120 661	125 893	89 685	62 147	56 935	39 383	46 621	73 624	108 452	73 545
Utah	3 457	7 260	4 642	1 892	2 959	3 266	2 765	3 464	5 604	11 255	7 339
Vermont	4 146	6 001	4 757	6 193	2 931	4 716	5 747	5 650	7 050	9 492	4 730
Virginia	42 651	37 911	36 059	26 377	17 802	20 927	25 642	17 496	12 738	33 637	29 924
Washington	21 219	25 740	38 207	25 485	19 242	19 041	17 552	17 074	26 446	28 539	19 346
West Virginia	1 893	1 500	3 440	1 908	1 787	1 098	1 734	1 352	1 853	5 206	2 194
Wisconsin	82 240	121 673	106 349	84 185	66 475	79 043	66 664	77 148	90 436	127 110	78 367
Wyoming	. . .	304	308	272	480	481	329	. . .	525	1 186	1 287

[1]Data for all states and the District of Columbia.
. . . = Not available.

Table 7-4. Mass Layoff Events and Initial Claimants for Unemployment Insurance, by Region and State, 2000–May 2013—Continued

(Number.)

Region and state	2011	2012	January 2013	February 2013	March 2013	April 2013	May 2013
			Initial claimants				
UNITED STATES[1]	1 808 451	1 666 931	144 517	79 786	114 897	119 196	134 483
Northeast	367 033	385 979	21 049	15 631	23 264	28 395	16 595
New England	55 986	52 560	2 851	4 698	2 618	8 494	2 013
Middle Atlantic	311 047	333 419	18 198	10 933	20 646	19 901	14 582
South	487 823	452 035	52 634	19 264	32 616	29 555	45 661
South Atlantic	256 262	241 704	34 734	10 605	13 081	16 272	22 168
East South Central	119 348	100 887	11 540	4 056	7 405	5 356	12 308
West South Central	112 213	109 444	6 360	4 603	12 130	7 927	11 185
Midwest	444 743	388 102	31 994	15 411	26 698	19 909	33 002
East North Central	327 393	294 704	23 570	9 819	19 447	16 540	24 586
West North Central	117 350	93 398	8 424	5 592	7 251	3 369	8 416
West	508 852	440 815	38 840	29 480	32 319	41 337	39 225
Mountain	71 500	60 762	5 112	1 733	4 423	8 225	5 087
Pacific	437 352	380 053	33 728	27 747	27 896	33 112	34 138
Alabama	37 523	29 496	8 434	776	2 111	1 238	2 411
Alaska	5 631	5 845	([2])	361	634	545	657
Arizona	17 647	14 533	585	527	752	3 820	1 262
Arkansas	16 665	19 371	1 963	679	2 610	1 442	1 398
California	377 413	327 275	29 088	24 357	23 802	29 242	30 069
Colorado	11 036	9 896	1 787	([2])	298	1 379	930
Connecticut	7 679	9 098	771	1 656	. . .	742	441
Delaware	3 524	2 490	([2])	([2])	([2])	582	250
District of Columbia	2 022	1 512	259	([2])	. . .	. . .	177
Florida	79 766	62 173	3 784	3 090	4 547	4 148	4 914
Georgia	47 593	34 531	6 616	1 212	999	2 756	4 629
Hawaii	3 525	2 356	453	356	. . .	216	622
Idaho	9 158	6 913	670	201	881	711	([2])
Illinois	72 086	74 738	6 251	1 834	6 864	5 272	11 153
Indiana	39 956	34 656	2 138	2 115	1 982	807	2 285
Iowa	27 151	22 412	2 045	734	1 399	1 348	1 179
Kansas	16 111	13 067	622	2 956	878	169	1 603
Kentucky	47 950	40 596	1 738	2 267	3 237	2 209	2 193
Louisiana	18 042	14 468	545	492	260	942	2 154
Maine	5 383	5 896	899	([2])	515	780	([2])
Maryland	10 234	15 155	1 539	492	1 368	984	1 531
Massachusetts	21 084	17 392	587	840	516	3 021	338
Michigan	70 517	68 072	3 727	1 315	3 110	2 354	4 333
Minnesota	28 202	17 538	1 039	385	1 072	561	1 565
Mississippi	18 280	15 748	434	269	1 237	1 030	4 634
Missouri	32 823	28 432	4 037	840	2 674	1 101	2 723
Montana	5 407	4 220	543	. . .	([2])	437	422
Nebraska	9 381	7 925	557	448	816	([2])	903
Nevada	14 812	13 897	950	701	1 302	460	1 102
New Hampshire	5 488	5 577	. . .	([2])	792	902	([2])
New Jersey	66 811	85 979	2 933	2 020	4 031	4 217	2 033
New Mexico	6 063	5 437	. . .	([2])	458	445	836
New York	119 398	141 137	8 000	4 652	6 562	9 093	5 099
North Carolina	54 730	74 267	11 999	3 282	3 905	5 411	6 177
North Dakota	3 151	3 736	([2])	([2])	412	([2])	([2])
Ohio	71 334	63 076	6 460	2 211	3 942	4 459	3 547
Oklahoma	9 006	6 537	241	([2])	725	430	214
Oregon	29 795	23 197	2 880	1 203	1 204	1 080	2 057
Pennsylvania	124 838	106 303	7 265	4 261	10 053	6 591	7 450
Rhode Island	10 578	9 101	484	1 838	([2])	2 024	181
South Carolina	25 067	20 697	6 739	964	1 039	1 004	1 570
South Dakota	531	. . .	. . .	([2])	. . .	. . .	216
Tennessee	15 595	15 047	934	744	820	879	3 070
Texas	68 500	69 068	3 611	3 298	8 535	5 113	7 419
Utah	6 288	4 833	526	([2])	582	837	412
Vermont	5 774	5 496	. . .	244	739	1 025	672
Virginia	31 335	28 378	3 583	1 243	1 042	1 249	2 688
Washington	20 988	21 380	1 167	1 470	2 256	2 029	733
West Virginia	1 991	2 501	([2])	([2])	([2])	([2])	232
Wisconsin	73 500	54 162	4 994	2 344	3 549	3 648	3 268
Wyoming	1 089	1 033	. . .	. . .	([2])	([2])	. . .

[1] Data for all states and the District of Columbia.
[2] Data do not meet BLS or state agency disclosure standards.
. . . = Not available.

Table 7-5. Extended Mass Layoff Events by Reason for Layoff in Private Nonfarn Business, 2000–2013

(Number.)

Year and quarter	Business demand	Disaster/safety	Financial	Organizational	Production	Seasonal	Other miscellaneous
2000							
Quarter 1	315	45	104	147	21	325	97
Quarter 2	253	...	113	121	28	415	92
Quarter 3	292	...	89	118	26	174	91
Quarter 4	461	22	143	123	31	709	119
2001							
Quarter 1	635	19	212	230	44	232	138
Quarter 2	595	5	244	235	49	437	212
Quarter 3	717	10	242	238	32	191	153
Quarter 4	913	28	251	242	24	698	169
2002							
Quarter 1	687	14	177	310	25	240	109
Quarter 2	558	13	167	222	31	503	92
Quarter 3	483	3	164	214	26	167	85
Quarter 4	562	20	149	206	32	728	180
2003							
Quarter 1	564	15	148	218	31	283	196
Quarter 2	580	10	163	204	28	536	234
Quarter 3	460	3	96	175	25	182	207
Quarter 4	448	33	82	186	22	733	159
2004							
Quarter 1	416	17	116	206	20	359	205
Quarter 2	386	3	57	170	35	571	136
Quarter 3	322	15	63	160	21	191	114
Quarter 4	389	35	73	144	26	667	93
2005							
Quarter 1	378	31	64	175	22	373	99
Quarter 2	362	...	53	125	18	568	76
Quarter 3	315	346	48	133	31	183	80
Quarter 4	330	...	58	117	26	781	63
2006							
Quarter 1	361	38	60	147	22	248	87
Quarter 2	416	12	40	172	23	603	87
Quarter 3	446	4	57	135	21	177	89
Quarter 4	565	8	64	143	28	697	135
2007							
Quarter 1	437	20	99	127	24	261	142
Quarter 2	417	3	110	79	20	649	143
Quarter 3	421	3	122	99	15	218	140
Quarter 4	613	6	124	92	25	752	202
2008							
Quarter 1	600	8	122	114	29	246	221
Quarter 2	566	6	120	122	24	651	267
Quarter 3	642	32	192	122	30	216	347
Quarter 4	1 580	12	329	159	24	869	609
2009							
Quarter 1	2 160	6	428	201	17	340	827
Quarter 2	1 457	3	295	170	14	757	699
Quarter 3	941	4	172	113	15	286	503
Quarter 4	845	6	179	89	16	828	453
2010							
Quarter 1	738	7	165	117	15	418	410
Quarter 2	629	11	126	118	12	801	311
Quarter 3	487	...	110	83	17	372	300
Quarter 4	661	...	110	79	10	826	308
2011							
Quarter 1	564	7	120	94	24	391	290
Quarter 2	517	11	117	70	33	773	289
Quarter 3	629	9	102	76	17	303	257
Quarter 4	633	4	76	73	20	818	279
2012							
Quarter 1	519	4	115	75	16	325	240
Quarter 2	637	...	103	94	18	825	280
Quarter 3	485	...	83	75	21	216	241
Quarter 4	704	36	117	69	20	851	326
2013							
Quarter 1[1]	543	3	80	66	17	292	301

[1]Preliminary.
. . . = Not available.

Table 7-6. Extended Mass Layoffs by Age and Sex in Private Nonfarm Business, 2000–2013

(Number.)

Year and quarter	Men	Women	Sex unknown	Total persons by age				
				Under 30 years	30–44 years	45–54 years	55 years and over	Age unknown
2000								
Quarter 1	57.7	42.0	0.3	21.4	41.7	23.2	12.9	0.8
Quarter 2	45.3	54.5	0.3	19.2	39.7	23.4	14.8	2.8
Quarter 3	57.3	42.2	0.5	18.7	39.8	25.3	13.9	2.2
Quarter 4	64.4	34.9	0.7	20.9	40.7	24.2	12.5	1.7
2001								
Quarter 1	58.5	40.6	1.0	22.2	40.1	23.6	11.9	2.2
Quarter 2	49.9	48.9	1.3	18.2	40.0	25.3	14.9	1.5
Quarter 3	54.0	45.1	0.9	19.8	40.9	24.2	12.9	2.2
Quarter 4	64.0	35.7	0.3	20.0	40.6	24.3	13.0	2.0
2002								
Quarter 1	56.4	43.1	0.5	19.4	39.8	24.7	14.5	1.6
Quarter 2	49.7	50.0	0.3	18.8	39.4	24.6	16.1	1.2
Quarter 3	56.9	42.8	0.2	17.8	38.9	25.8	15.2	2.2
Quarter 4	64.4	35.4	0.2	18.8	39.4	25.0	14.4	2.4
2003								
Quarter 1	58.8	40.9	0.3	20.0	39.1	25.1	14.5	1.3
Quarter 2	49.3	49.8	0.9	17.3	37.5	25.9	17.4	1.9
Quarter 3	56.1	43.7	0.2	19.1	38.7	25.8	15.1	1.4
Quarter 4	65.0	34.8	0.3	19.7	38.0	26.3	15.1	1.0
2004								
Quarter 1	58.9	40.7	0.4	21.8	36.6	25.0	15.2	1.4
Quarter 2	46.1	53.6	0.3	16.7	36.0	26.2	19.3	1.8
Quarter 3	51.0	48.6	0.4	18.9	36.4	25.9	16.7	2.0
Quarter 4	65.7	33.9	0.3	18.8	37.4	26.3	16.1	1.3
2005								
Quarter 1	60.6	38.9	0.5	19.1	37.2	26.1	16.1	1.5
Quarter 2	44.4	55.1	0.6	14.6	35.0	27.6	20.9	1.9
Quarter 3	52.4	47.4	0.3	19.7	35.1	25.8	16.6	2.8
Quarter 4	67.6	32.0	0.3	18.0	36.0	26.7	16.6	2.7
2006								
Quarter 1	60.4	39.3	0.3	17.1	34.6	28.2	18.2	2.0
Quarter 2	45.3	54.2	0.5	15.5	33.1	27.0	22.3	2.1
Quarter 3	58.9	40.4	0.7	19.0	34.6	26.6	17.5	2.3
Quarter 4	69.6	30.1	0.3	18.3	36.4	27.9	16.7	0.7
2007								
Quarter 1	63.5	36.2	0.3	20.2	35.7	27.1	16.6	0.3
Quarter 2	45.1	54.2	0.8	16.2	33.4	26.9	23.1	0.5
Quarter 3	57.0	42.5	0.5	19.9	35.9	25.6	18.2	0.5
Quarter 4	70.0	29.6	0.4	19.5	36.0	27.4	16.7	0.4
2008								
Quarter 1	63.2	36.3	0.5	20.2	34.5	26.8	18.1	0.4
Quarter 2	49.7	49.7	0.5	17.9	33.8	26.0	21.5	0.8
Quarter 3	59.5	39.9	0.6	20.9	34.5	25.8	17.8	1.0
Quarter 4	68.3	30.8	0.9	20.2	35.5	26.9	16.7	0.8
2009								
Quarter 1	65.3	33.4	1.2	19.8	34.5	26.8	18.2	0.8
Quarter 2	57.8	41.5	0.7	18.4	33.9	26.7	20.5	0.5
Quarter 3	63.3	36.1	0.6	21.1	34.0	26.0	18.4	0.5
Quarter 4	69.0	30.6	0.5	20.4	34.4	26.5	18.2	0.4
2010								
Quarter 1	61.2	38.2	0.6	23.9	32.8	24.2	18.5	0.6
Quarter 2	49.6	50.3	0.1	20.2	31.8	24.7	22.7	0.6
Quarter 3	57.7	42.2	0.2	22.4	32.6	24.4	20.3	0.3
Quarter 4	69.2	30.7	0.1	21.2	34.1	25.7	18.5	0.5
2011								
Quarter 1	62.1	37.8	0.2	22.3	33.2	24.6	19.6	0.2
Quarter 2	48.0	51.8	0.2	19.1	32.0	24.7	23.9	0.2
Quarter 3	60.1	39.8	0.2	22.2	34.4	24.5	18.7	0.2
Quarter 4	67.5	32.4	0.2	21.9	34.2	25.3	18.5	0.1
2012								
Quarter 1	61.4	38.5	0.1	23.3	33.8	23.8	18.9	0.1
Quarter 2	49.4	50.5	0.1	20.0	32.6	24.3	23.0	0.1
Quarter 3	59.5	40.4	0.1	22.7	33.7	24.2	19.3	0.1
Quarter 4	68.4	31.5	0.1	21.0	33.7	25.7	19.6	0.1
2013								
Quarter 1[1]	62.9	36.9	0.2	22.0	34.0	24.1	19.8	0.1

[1]Preliminary.

NOTES AND DEFINITIONS

JOB OPENINGS AND LABOR TURNOVER SURVEY

Data from a sample of approximately 16,000 businesses for the Job Openings and Labor Turnover Survey (JOLTS) are collected and compiled monthly from a sample of business establishments by the Bureau of Labor Statistics (BLS). Each month, data are collected in a survey of business establishments for total employment, job openings, hires, quits, layoffs and discharges, and other separations. Data collection methods include computer-assisted telephone interviewing, touchtone data entry, fax, and mail.

CONCEPTS AND DEFINITIONS

The JOLTS program covers all private nonfarm establishments such as factories, offices, and stores, as well as federal, state, and local government entities in the 50 states and the District of Columbia.

Employment includes persons on the payroll who worked or received pay for the pay period that includes the 12th day of the reference month. Full-time, part-time, permanent, short-term, seasonal, salaried, and hourly employees are included, as are employees on paid vacations or other paid leave. Proprietors or partners of unincorporated businesses, unpaid family workers, or persons on leave without pay or on strike for the entire pay period, are not counted as employed. Employees of temporary help agencies, employee leasing companies, outside contractors, and consultants are counted by their employer of record, not by the establishment where they are working.

Job openings information is submitted by establishments for the last business day of the reference month. A job opening requires that: 1) a specific position exists and there is work available for that position, 2) work could start within 30 days regardless of whether a suitable candidate is found, and 3) the employer is actively recruiting from outside the establishment to fill the position. Included are full-time, part-time, permanent, short-term, and seasonal openings. Active recruiting means that the establishment is taking steps to fill a position by advertising in newspapers or on the Internet, posting help-wanted signs, accepting applications, or using other similar methods.

Jobs to be filled only by internal transfers, promotions, demotions, or recall from layoffs are excluded. Also excluded are jobs with start dates more than 30 days in the future, jobs for which employees have been hired but have not yet reported for work, and jobs to be filled by employees of temporary help agencies, employee leasing companies, outside contractors, or consultants. The job openings rate is computed by dividing the number of job openings by the sum of employment and job openings and multiplying that quotient by 100.

Hires are the total number of additions to the payroll occurring at any time during the reference month, including both new and rehired employees, full-time and part-time, permanent, short-term and seasonal employees, employees recalled to the location after a layoff lasting more than 7 days, on-call or intermittent employees who returned to work after having been formally separated, and transfers from other locations. The hires count does not include transfers or promotions within the reporting site, employees returning from strike, employees of temporary help agencies or employee leasing companies, outside contractors, or consultants. The hires rate is computed by dividing the number of hires by employment and multiplying that quotient by 100.

Separations are the total number of terminations of employment occurring at any time during the reference month, and are reported by type of separation—quits, layoffs and discharges, and other separations. Quits are voluntary separations by employees (except for retirements, which are reported as other separations). Layoffs and discharges are involuntary separations initiated by the employer and include layoffs with no intent to rehire, formal layoffs lasting or expected to last more than 7 days, discharges resulting from mergers, downsizing, or closings, firings or other discharges for cause, terminations of permanent or short-term employees, and terminations of seasonal employees. Other separations include retirements, transfers to other locations, deaths, and separations due to disability. Separations do not include transfers within the same location or employees on strike.

The separations rate is computed by dividing the number of separations by employment and multiplying that quotient by 100. The quits, layoffs and discharges, and other separations rates are computed similarly, dividing the number by employment and multiplying by 100.

The JOLTS annual level estimates for hires, quits, layoffs and discharges, other separations, and total separations are the sum of the 12 published monthly levels. The annual rate estimates are computed by dividing the annual level by the Current Employment Statistics (CES) annual average employment level, and multiplying that quotient by 100. This figure will be approximately equal to the sum of the 12 monthly rates.

Annual estimates are not calculated for job openings because job openings are a stock, or point-in-time, measurement for the last business day of each month. Only jobs still open on the last day of the month are counted. For the same reason job openings cannot be cumulated throughout each month, annual figures for job openings cannot be created by summing the monthly estimates. Hires and separations are flow measures and are cumulated over the month with a total reported for the month. Therefore, the annual figures can be created by summing the monthly estimates.

SOURCES OF ADDITIONAL INFORMATION

For more extensive information, see the Job Openings and Labor Turnover Survey (JOLTS) page on the BLS Web site at http://www.bls.gov/jlt/.

Table 7-7. Job Openings Levels and Rates, by Industry, 2002–October 2013

(Seasonally adjusted, levels in thousands, rates per 100.)

Year and month	Level											
	Total nonfarm[1]	Total private[1]	Construction	Manufacturing	Trade, transportation, and utilities[2]	Retail trade	Professional and business services	Education and health services	Leisure and hospitality[3]	Accommodation and food services	Government[4]	State and local government
2002												
January	3 572	3 204	103	248	571	382	586	751	385	334	369	330
February	3 370	2 935	111	248	490	312	494	749	397	355	434	392
March	3 560	3 137	130	225	596	358	545	728	450	345	422	374
April	3 373	2 986	91	238	545	325	530	698	409	352	387	345
May	3 482	3 067	108	245	551	327	629	641	426	362	415	369
June	3 251	2 880	127	240	525	333	531	708	320	275	371	345
July	3 403	2 987	95	249	522	352	591	668	410	371	416	373
August	3 415	2 998	117	240	513	317	600	688	415	361	417	373
September	3 290	2 891	127	229	511	328	564	703	380	343	399	353
October	3 560	3 165	126	228	589	397	692	652	401	356	395	351
November	3 513	3 091	112	226	499	303	667	705	415	367	422	370
December	3 056	2 696	96	215	430	235	566	629	370	336	360	320
2003												
January	3 618	3 211	115	212	516	315	894	608	407	373	408	356
February	3 378	3 003	94	196	526	332	787	585	357	304	375	328
March	3 056	2 710	89	189	489	311	634	570	354	322	346	304
April	3 107	2 762	143	192	440	307	496	615	424	335	345	317
May	3 108	2 799	97	195	498	322	605	623	392	355	309	269
June	3 196	2 810	107	194	504	324	601	591	421	356	385	321
July	3 106	2 783	127	184	506	300	676	520	365	315	323	263
August	3 182	2 881	105	209	542	339	765	543	345	303	301	251
September	3 051	2 756	54	200	536	350	657	539	373	330	295	252
October	3 140	2 814	79	202	575	377	573	579	407	359	327	285
November	3 286	2 992	104	251	581	376	648	577	391	353	294	254
December	3 255	2 949	108	220	567	319	622	533	504	447	306	260
2004												
January	3 322	3 003	126	231	521	321	586	620	429	363	319	269
February	3 415	3 085	118	215	547	382	679	586	437	377	331	284
March	3 394	3 046	124	252	612	381	547	592	430	384	348	299
April	3 524	3 170	131	268	607	388	691	596	412	371	354	291
May	3 620	3 271	135	299	627	409	666	603	425	360	349	318
June	3 423	3 089	114	268	633	396	710	514	445	399	334	282
July	3 807	3 463	113	272	687	429	754	589	450	406	344	303
August	3 623	3 299	131	277	643	434	685	594	460	417	324	284
September	3 754	3 403	113	263	695	471	706	601	468	408	352	301
October	3 836	3 445	144	284	623	415	732	645	469	410	391	343
November	3 383	3 013	149	246	547	314	607	602	393	341	370	323
December	3 808	3 415	148	271	633	389	705	637	463	390	393	331
2005												
January	3 638	3 313	140	284	602	406	646	587	540	480	325	285
February	3 757	3 401	154	276	679	421	686	607	502	435	356	316
March	3 916	3 572	148	273	706	472	739	683	516	450	344	299
April	4 057	3 695	143	278	710	480	796	642	551	481	362	324
May	3 877	3 519	142	271	706	428	790	661	477	419	358	307
June	4 064	3 698	142	278	691	424	883	640	497	417	366	323
July	4 155	3 760	147	313	682	426	851	692	506	418	395	350
August	4 102	3 733	149	299	685	431	871	649	505	438	369	324
September	4 275	3 860	161	340	707	418	831	668	493	452	415	364
October	4 221	3 854	171	270	753	448	842	657	500	439	367	321
November	4 437	4 067	232	387	817	535	849	650	545	477	371	323
December	4 278	3 854	161	346	711	465	831	651	566	498	424	367
2006												
January	4 296	3 916	140	317	696	455	875	698	554	490	380	331
February	4 282	3 887	141	360	685	407	847	729	586	538	395	340
March	4 472	4 037	183	380	725	415	746	723	554	495	434	389
April	4 438	4 014	186	363	739	426	713	722	553	484	424	373
May	4 487	4 066	182	317	791	450	868	683	562	502	421	376
June	4 333	3 903	187	345	701	417	754	703	492	437	430	381
July	4 076	3 585	208	313	679	362	618	630	566	502	491	432
August	4 498	4 049	202	337	750	435	749	773	547	488	449	397
September	4 563	4 075	185	342	866	464	692	778	546	449	489	446
October	4 434	4 023	164	349	791	427	714	777	585	497	411	366
November	4 705	4 273	160	352	791	449	803	781	708	623	432	394
December	4 583	4 167	128	363	872	519	701	773	633	566	416	382
2007												
January	4 602	4 148	251	357	845	463	782	720	581	483	454	408
February	4 483	4 045	267	356	759	467	710	660	578	504	438	388
March	4 707	4 267	211	384	859	437	811	719	580	502	440	390
April	4 498	4 046	178	351	825	402	790	758	541	457	452	394
May	4 479	4 037	166	357	704	373	795	773	591	528	442	390
June	4 690	4 257	157	354	798	458	805	801	596	530	433	392
July	4 404	3 946	158	359	786	416	699	718	606	547	459	416
August	4 491	4 041	159	323	807	404	766	765	611	543	450	403
September	4 536	4 088	124	313	769	388	776	840	642	575	448	401
October	4 275	3 851	143	294	707	360	749	738	611	542	424	378
November	4 396	3 945	132	338	753	387	750	731	683	583	452	399
December	4 256	3 827	127	303	730	386	783	738	585	539	430	373

[1] Includes natural resources and mining, information, financial activities, and other services, not shown separately.
[2] Includes wholesale trade and transportation, warehousing, and utilities, not shown separately.
[3] Includes arts, entertainment, and recreation, not shown separately.
[4] Includes federal government, not shown separately.

Table 7-7. Job Openings Levels and Rates, by Industry, 2002–October 2013—*Continued*

(Seasonally adjusted, levels in thousands, rates per 100.)

Year and month	Rate											
	Total[1]	Total private[1]	Construction	Manufacturing	Trade, transportation, and utilities[2]	Retail trade	Professional and business services	Education and health services	Leisure and hospitality[3]	Accommodation and food services	Government[4]	State and local government
2002												
January	2.7	2.8	1.5	1.6	2.2	2.5	3.5	4.5	3.1	3.2	1.7	1.7
February	2.5	2.6	1.6	1.6	1.9	2.0	3.0	4.5	3.2	3.4	2.0	2.1
March	2.7	2.8	1.9	1.4	2.3	2.3	3.3	4.3	3.6	3.3	1.9	2.0
April	2.5	2.7	1.3	1.5	2.1	2.1	3.2	4.2	3.3	3.3	1.8	1.8
May	2.6	2.7	1.6	1.6	2.1	2.1	3.8	3.8	3.4	3.4	1.9	1.9
June	2.4	2.6	1.9	1.5	2.0	2.2	3.2	4.2	2.6	2.6	1.7	1.8
July	2.5	2.7	1.4	1.6	2.0	2.3	3.6	3.9	3.3	3.5	1.9	1.9
August	2.6	2.7	1.7	1.6	2.0	2.1	3.6	4.1	3.4	3.4	1.9	1.9
September	2.5	2.6	1.9	1.5	2.0	2.1	3.4	4.1	3.1	3.2	1.8	1.8
October	2.7	2.8	1.9	1.5	2.3	2.6	4.2	3.8	3.2	3.3	1.8	1.8
November	2.6	2.8	1.6	1.5	1.9	2.0	4.0	4.1	3.3	3.4	1.9	1.9
December	2.3	2.4	1.4	1.4	1.7	1.5	3.4	3.7	3.0	3.2	1.6	1.7
2003												
January	2.7	2.9	1.7	1.4	2.0	2.1	5.3	3.6	3.2	3.5	1.9	1.9
February	2.5	2.7	1.4	1.3	2.0	2.2	4.7	3.4	2.9	2.9	1.7	1.7
March	2.3	2.4	1.3	1.3	1.9	2.0	3.8	3.3	2.8	3.0	1.6	1.6
April	2.3	2.5	2.1	1.3	1.7	2.0	3.0	3.6	3.4	3.2	1.6	1.7
May	2.3	2.5	1.4	1.3	1.9	2.1	3.7	3.6	3.1	3.3	1.4	1.4
June	2.4	2.5	1.6	1.3	2.0	2.1	3.6	3.4	3.4	3.3	1.8	1.7
July	2.3	2.5	1.9	1.3	2.0	2.0	4.1	3.0	2.9	3.0	1.5	1.4
August	2.4	2.6	1.5	1.4	2.1	2.2	4.6	3.2	2.8	2.8	1.4	1.3
September	2.3	2.5	0.8	1.4	2.1	2.3	3.9	3.1	3.0	3.1	1.4	1.3
October	2.4	2.5	1.1	1.4	2.2	2.5	3.4	3.4	3.2	3.3	1.5	1.5
November	2.5	2.7	1.5	1.7	2.2	2.5	3.9	3.3	3.1	3.3	1.3	1.3
December	2.4	2.6	1.6	1.5	2.2	2.1	3.7	3.1	3.9	4.1	1.4	1.4
2004												
January	2.5	2.7	1.8	1.6	2.0	2.1	3.5	3.6	3.4	3.3	1.5	1.4
February	2.6	2.8	1.7	1.5	2.1	2.5	4.0	3.4	3.4	3.5	1.5	1.5
March	2.5	2.7	1.8	1.7	2.4	2.5	3.3	3.4	3.3	3.5	1.6	1.6
April	2.6	2.8	1.9	1.8	2.3	2.5	4.1	3.4	3.2	3.4	1.6	1.5
May	2.7	2.9	1.9	2.0	2.4	2.6	3.9	3.4	3.3	3.3	1.6	1.7
June	2.5	2.7	1.6	1.8	2.4	2.6	4.2	2.9	3.4	3.6	1.5	1.5
July	2.8	3.1	1.6	1.9	2.6	2.8	4.4	3.4	3.5	3.7	1.6	1.6
August	2.7	2.9	1.8	1.9	2.5	2.8	4.0	3.4	3.6	3.8	1.5	1.5
September	2.8	3.0	1.6	1.8	2.6	3.0	4.1	3.4	3.6	3.7	1.6	1.6
October	2.8	3.0	2.0	1.9	2.4	2.7	4.2	3.6	3.6	3.7	1.8	1.8
November	2.5	2.7	2.1	1.7	2.1	2.0	3.5	3.4	3.0	3.1	1.7	1.7
December	2.8	3.0	2.0	1.9	2.4	2.5	4.1	3.6	3.5	3.5	1.8	1.7
2005												
January	2.7	2.9	1.9	2.0	2.3	2.6	3.7	3.3	4.1	4.2	1.5	1.5
February	2.8	3.0	2.1	1.9	2.6	2.7	3.9	3.4	3.8	3.9	1.6	1.6
March	2.9	3.1	2.0	1.9	2.7	3.0	4.2	3.8	3.9	4.0	1.6	1.5
April	3.0	3.2	1.9	1.9	2.7	3.1	4.5	3.6	4.1	4.2	1.6	1.7
May	2.8	3.1	1.9	1.9	2.7	2.7	4.5	3.7	3.6	3.7	1.6	1.6
June	3.0	3.2	1.9	1.9	2.6	2.7	5.0	3.6	3.7	3.7	1.7	1.7
July	3.0	3.2	2.0	2.2	2.6	2.7	4.8	3.8	3.8	3.7	1.8	1.8
August	3.0	3.2	2.0	2.1	2.6	2.7	4.9	3.6	3.8	3.8	1.7	1.7
September	3.1	3.3	2.1	2.3	2.6	2.7	4.6	3.7	3.7	4.0	1.9	1.9
October	3.0	3.3	2.2	1.9	2.8	2.8	4.7	3.6	3.7	3.9	1.7	1.7
November	3.2	3.5	3.0	2.7	3.0	3.4	4.7	3.6	4.1	4.2	1.7	1.7
December	3.1	3.3	2.1	2.4	2.6	2.9	4.6	3.6	4.2	4.3	1.9	1.9
2006												
January	3.1	3.3	1.8	2.2	2.6	2.9	4.8	3.8	4.1	4.2	1.7	1.7
February	3.1	3.3	1.8	2.5	2.5	2.6	4.6	4.0	4.3	4.6	1.8	1.7
March	3.2	3.4	2.3	2.6	2.7	2.6	4.1	3.9	4.1	4.3	1.9	2.0
April	3.2	3.4	2.3	2.5	2.7	2.7	3.9	3.9	4.1	4.2	1.9	1.9
May	3.2	3.4	2.3	2.2	2.9	2.9	4.7	3.7	4.1	4.3	1.9	1.9
June	3.1	3.3	2.4	2.4	2.6	2.6	4.1	3.8	3.6	3.8	1.9	1.9
July	2.9	3.0	2.6	2.2	2.5	2.3	3.4	3.4	4.1	4.3	2.2	2.2
August	3.2	3.4	2.6	2.3	2.8	2.8	4.1	4.2	4.0	4.2	2.0	2.0
September	3.2	3.4	2.3	2.4	3.2	2.9	3.8	4.2	4.0	3.9	2.2	2.3
October	3.1	3.4	2.1	2.4	2.9	2.7	3.9	4.1	4.2	4.2	1.8	1.9
November	3.3	3.6	2.0	2.4	2.9	2.8	4.3	4.2	5.1	5.2	1.9	2.0
December	3.2	3.5	1.6	2.5	3.2	3.3	3.8	4.1	4.5	4.8	1.8	1.9
2007												
January	3.2	3.5	3.1	2.5	3.1	2.9	4.2	3.8	4.2	4.1	2.0	2.1
February	3.2	3.4	3.4	2.5	2.8	2.9	3.8	3.5	4.1	4.2	1.9	2.0
March	3.3	3.6	2.7	2.7	3.1	2.7	4.3	3.8	4.2	4.2	1.9	2.0
April	3.2	3.4	2.3	2.5	3.0	2.5	4.2	4.0	3.9	3.9	2.0	2.0
May	3.2	3.4	2.1	2.5	2.6	2.3	4.2	4.1	4.2	4.4	2.0	2.0
June	3.3	3.6	2.0	2.5	2.9	2.9	4.3	4.2	4.3	4.4	1.9	2.0
July	3.1	3.3	2.0	2.5	2.9	2.6	3.7	3.8	4.3	4.6	2.0	2.1
August	3.2	3.4	2.0	2.3	2.9	2.5	4.1	4.0	4.4	4.5	2.0	2.0
September	3.2	3.4	1.6	2.2	2.8	2.4	4.1	4.4	4.6	4.8	2.0	2.0
October	3.0	3.2	1.9	2.1	2.6	2.3	4.0	3.8	4.3	4.5	1.9	1.9
November	3.1	3.3	1.7	2.4	2.7	2.4	4.0	3.8	4.8	4.8	2.0	2.0
December	3.0	3.2	1.7	2.2	2.7	2.4	4.2	3.8	4.1	4.5	1.9	1.9

[1]Includes natural resources and mining, information, financial activities, and other services, not shown separately.
[2]Includes wholesale trade and transportation, warehousing, and utilities, not shown separately.
[3]Includes arts, entertainment, and recreation, not shown separately.
[4]Includes federal government, not shown separately.

Table 7-7. Job Openings Levels and Rates, by Industry, 2002–October 2013—*Continued*

(Seasonally adjusted, levels in thousands, rates per 100.)

Year and month	Level											
	Total nonfarm[1]	Total private[1]	Construction	Manufacturing	Trade, transportation, and utilities[2]	Retail trade	Professional and business services	Education and health services	Leisure and hospitality[3]	Accommodation and food services	Government[4]	State and local government
2008												
January	4 224	3 810	125	293	672	344	753	720	604	543	414	375
February	4 026	3 614	126	272	649	343	772	747	560	488	412	371
March	4 003	3 587	98	252	603	380	788	775	564	500	417	369
April	3 906	3 519	88	275	602	360	775	729	524	462	388	360
May	3 947	3 518	156	282	630	388	674	721	542	478	428	374
June	3 777	3 344	110	249	545	312	746	734	479	430	434	381
July	3 784	3 346	109	247	615	370	657	741	433	375	438	372
August	3 643	3 241	86	252	557	348	675	705	420	360	402	333
September	3 233	2 821	129	216	527	322	610	581	378	341	411	349
October	3 384	2 997	71	238	614	431	613	631	399	339	387	325
November	3 155	2 787	68	164	562	382	583	620	289	256	368	334
December	3 011	2 719	87	159	488	337	551	612	320	283	292	265
2009												
January	2 853	2 419	32	120	529	417	502	621	244	214	434	315
February	2 807	2 439	67	137	418	306	535	568	291	263	368	302
March	2 550	2 188	50	114	389	254	448	512	280	253	362	251
April	2 292	1 942	21	97	330	201	421	497	304	279	350	281
May	2 415	2 143	37	93	468	328	401	526	257	235	272	229
June	2 377	2 054	58	97	421	273	370	512	257	240	323	264
July	2 179	1 906	42	93	301	190	425	523	240	225	273	216
August	2 282	1 986	61	124	430	254	345	534	206	187	296	269
September	2 477	2 187	67	126	383	267	441	532	306	280	290	226
October	2 409	2 018	63	130	332	215	425	512	227	211	392	261
November	2 390	2 051	67	144	325	211	422	522	232	207	339	244
December	2 451	2 134	68	172	335	207	439	541	215	198	318	258
2010												
January	2 751	2 315	56	145	365	243	431	585	261	242	436	237
February	2 577	2 224	68	165	397	277	401	523	241	220	353	230
March	2 614	2 202	79	155	479	343	388	505	232	204	411	250
April	3 142	2 521	78	175	435	277	516	525	277	249	621	248
May	2 849	2 482	76	184	422	264	579	502	293	251	367	236
June	2 645	2 322	76	197	419	254	483	469	293	244	323	225
July	2 922	2 612	94	225	423	270	518	515	323	281	311	231
August	2 905	2 601	57	180	427	250	596	473	353	318	304	235
September	2 784	2 459	72	184	411	233	552	510	318	284	324	235
October	3 033	2 703	73	206	457	263	595	590	308	273	329	264
November	3 051	2 746	86	222	434	258	718	532	259	230	305	222
December	2 930	2 549	47	194	457	275	599	533	291	250	381	296
2011												
January	2 868	2 548	64	220	489	280	467	519	302	265	320	256
February	3 017	2 709	49	220	477	250	607	540	383	335	307	254
March	3 104	2 785	68	225	507	274	591	571	358	315	319	266
April	3 025	2 689	88	225	528	316	556	541	310	275	335	289
May	2 937	2 635	91	207	495	291	556	559	301	270	301	252
June	3 180	2 837	61	206	539	351	620	591	351	301	343	295
July	3 286	2 978	75	233	577	341	674	597	341	274	307	251
August	3 172	2 842	101	235	505	332	589	620	385	344	330	287
September	3 465	3 060	77	242	579	348	706	572	410	353	406	351
October	3 308	2 965	71	229	602	325	593	604	403	344	343	275
November	3 118	2 819	78	231	582	316	505	596	415	358	299	247
December	3 384	3 031	69	261	594	345	628	595	421	384	353	298
2012												
January	3 415	3 066	77	255	573	321	674	636	431	360	350	296
February	3 526	3 114	74	259	569	349	668	659	417	368	412	342
March	3 848	3 453	96	324	641	410	786	680	433	381	396	326
April	3 523	3 163	67	254	552	321	668	674	452	375	360	283
May	3 774	3 361	70	302	608	364	746	701	441	389	414	346
June	3 792	3 420	77	310	584	337	751	717	451	408	372	301
July	3 499	3 118	70	271	566	314	625	657	461	409	380	331
August	3 632	3 222	79	257	613	371	709	651	420	363	409	331
September	3 603	3 216	83	242	648	389	609	712	378	329	387	317
October	3 646	3 295	100	265	618	392	661	667	438	389	350	289
November	3 789	3 421	96	271	731	475	649	691	481	428	368	301
December	3 612	3 235	95	242	704	436	575	670	453	394	377	313
2013												
January	3 611	3 194	104	253	645	390	690	579	453	401	417	340
February	3 899	3 478	116	274	644	396	709	672	488	437	421	357
March	3 875	3 473	108	271	669	424	692	687	500	436	402	344
April	3 800	3 400	99	243	715	455	731	662	468	410	401	330
May	3 907	3 479	102	237	784	514	632	660	477	419	428	367
June	3 869	3 459	120	210	712	473	685	665	483	434	411	356
July	3 808	3 402	99	234	655	413	664	670	493	446	406	357
August	3 844	3 459	109	268	694	418	658	732	514	438	385	339
September	3 883	3 508	112	256	726	459	629	675	550	492	375	324
October	3 925	3 552	124	281	682	419	717	638	559	483	373	334

[1]Includes natural resources and mining, information, financial activities, and other services, not shown separately.
[2]Includes wholesale trade and transportation, warehousing, and utilities, not shown separately.
[3]Includes arts, entertainment, and recreation, not shown separately.
[4]Includes federal government, not shown separately.

Table 7-7. Job Openings Levels and Rates, by Industry, 2002–October 2013—*Continued*

(Seasonally adjusted, levels in thousands, rates per 100.)

Year and month	Total[1]	Total private[1]	Construction	Manufacturing	Trade, transportation, and utilities[2]	Retail trade	Professional and business services	Education and health services	Leisure and hospitality[3]	Accommodation and food services	Government[4]	State and local government
2008												
January	3.0	3.2	1.6	2.1	2.5	2.2	4.0	3.7	4.3	4.5	1.8	1.9
February	2.8	3.0	1.7	1.9	2.4	2.2	4.1	3.9	4.0	4.1	1.8	1.9
March	2.8	3.0	1.3	1.8	2.2	2.4	4.2	4.0	4.0	4.2	1.8	1.8
April	2.8	3.0	1.2	2.0	2.2	2.3	4.1	3.7	3.7	3.9	1.7	1.8
May	2.8	3.0	2.1	2.0	2.3	2.5	3.6	3.7	3.9	4.0	1.9	1.9
June	2.7	2.8	1.5	1.8	2.0	2.0	4.0	3.8	3.4	3.6	1.9	1.9
July	2.7	2.8	1.5	1.8	2.3	2.4	3.6	3.8	3.1	3.2	1.9	1.8
August	2.6	2.8	1.2	1.8	2.1	2.2	3.7	3.6	3.0	3.0	1.7	1.7
September	2.3	2.4	1.8	1.6	2.0	2.1	3.3	3.0	2.7	2.9	1.8	1.7
October	2.4	2.6	1.0	1.8	2.3	2.8	3.4	3.2	2.9	2.9	1.7	1.6
November	2.3	2.4	1.0	1.2	2.1	2.5	3.2	3.2	2.1	2.2	1.6	1.7
December	2.2	2.4	1.3	1.2	1.9	2.2	3.1	3.1	2.4	2.4	1.3	1.3
2009												
January	2.1	2.1	0.5	0.9	2.0	2.7	2.9	3.2	1.8	1.9	1.9	1.6
February	2.1	2.2	1.0	1.1	1.6	2.0	3.1	2.9	2.2	2.3	1.6	1.5
March	1.9	2.0	0.8	0.9	1.5	1.7	2.6	2.6	2.1	2.2	1.6	1.3
April	1.7	1.8	0.3	0.8	1.3	1.4	2.5	2.5	2.3	2.4	1.5	1.4
May	1.8	1.9	0.6	0.8	1.8	2.2	2.4	2.7	1.9	2.1	1.2	1.1
June	1.8	1.9	1.0	0.8	1.7	1.8	2.2	2.6	1.9	2.1	1.4	1.3
July	1.6	1.7	0.7	0.8	1.2	1.3	2.5	2.7	1.8	2.0	1.2	1.1
August	1.7	1.8	1.0	1.1	1.7	1.7	2.1	2.7	1.6	1.6	1.3	1.3
September	1.9	2.0	1.1	1.1	1.5	1.8	2.6	2.7	2.3	2.5	1.3	1.1
October	1.8	1.8	1.1	1.1	1.3	1.5	2.5	2.6	1.7	1.9	1.7	1.3
November	1.8	1.9	1.2	1.2	1.3	1.4	2.5	2.6	1.8	1.8	1.5	1.2
December	1.9	2.0	1.2	1.5	1.3	1.4	2.6	2.7	1.6	1.8	1.4	1.3
2010												
January	2.1	2.1	1.0	1.3	1.5	1.7	2.5	2.9	2.0	2.1	1.9	1.2
February	2.0	2.0	1.2	1.4	1.6	1.9	2.4	2.6	1.8	2.0	1.5	1.2
March	2.0	2.0	1.4	1.3	1.9	2.3	2.3	2.5	1.8	1.8	1.8	1.3
April	2.4	2.3	1.4	1.5	1.7	1.9	3.0	2.6	2.1	2.2	2.7	1.3
May	2.1	2.3	1.4	1.6	1.7	1.8	3.4	2.5	2.2	2.2	1.6	1.2
June	2.0	2.1	1.4	1.7	1.7	1.7	2.8	2.3	2.2	2.1	1.4	1.1
July	2.2	2.4	1.7	1.9	1.7	1.8	3.0	2.6	2.4	2.5	1.4	1.2
August	2.2	2.4	1.0	1.5	1.7	1.7	3.4	2.4	2.6	2.8	1.3	1.2
September	2.1	2.2	1.3	1.6	1.6	1.6	3.2	2.5	2.4	2.5	1.4	1.2
October	2.3	2.4	1.3	1.8	1.8	1.8	3.4	2.9	2.3	2.4	1.5	1.3
November	2.3	2.5	1.5	1.9	1.7	1.8	4.1	2.6	1.9	2.0	1.3	1.1
December	2.2	2.3	0.9	1.6	1.8	1.9	3.4	2.6	2.2	2.2	1.7	1.5
2011												
January	2.2	2.3	1.2	1.9	1.9	1.9	2.7	2.6	2.2	2.3	1.4	1.3
February	2.3	2.4	0.9	1.9	1.9	1.7	3.4	2.7	2.8	2.9	1.4	1.3
March	2.3	2.5	1.2	1.9	2.0	1.8	3.3	2.8	2.6	2.7	1.4	1.4
April	2.3	2.4	1.6	1.9	2.1	2.1	3.1	2.7	2.3	2.4	1.5	1.5
May	2.2	2.4	1.6	1.7	1.9	2.0	3.1	2.7	2.2	2.3	1.3	1.3
June	2.4	2.5	1.1	1.7	2.1	2.3	3.5	2.9	2.6	2.6	1.5	1.5
July	2.4	2.6	1.3	1.9	2.2	2.3	3.7	2.9	2.5	2.3	1.4	1.3
August	2.4	2.5	1.8	2.0	2.0	2.2	3.3	3.0	2.8	2.9	1.5	1.5
September	2.6	2.7	1.4	2.0	2.2	2.3	3.9	2.8	3.0	3.0	1.8	1.8
October	2.4	2.6	1.3	1.9	2.3	2.2	3.3	2.9	2.9	2.9	1.5	1.4
November	2.3	2.5	1.4	1.9	2.3	2.1	2.8	2.9	3.0	3.0	1.3	1.3
December	2.5	2.7	1.2	2.2	2.3	2.3	3.4	2.9	3.0	3.2	1.6	1.5
2012												
January	2.5	2.7	1.4	2.1	2.2	2.1	3.7	3.1	3.1	3.0	1.6	1.5
February	2.6	2.7	1.3	2.1	2.2	2.3	3.6	3.2	3.0	3.1	1.8	1.8
March	2.8	3.0	1.7	2.6	2.5	2.7	4.2	3.3	3.1	3.2	1.8	1.7
April	2.6	2.8	1.2	2.1	2.1	2.1	3.6	3.2	3.2	3.1	1.6	1.5
May	2.7	2.9	1.2	2.5	2.3	2.4	4.0	3.3	3.1	3.2	1.9	1.8
June	2.8	3.0	1.4	2.5	2.2	2.2	4.0	3.4	3.2	3.4	1.7	1.5
July	2.5	2.7	1.2	2.2	2.2	2.1	3.4	3.1	3.2	3.4	1.7	1.7
August	2.6	2.8	1.4	2.1	2.3	2.4	3.8	3.1	3.0	3.0	1.8	1.7
September	2.6	2.8	1.4	2.0	2.5	2.5	3.3	3.4	2.7	2.7	1.7	1.6
October	2.6	2.8	1.7	2.2	2.4	2.6	3.5	3.2	3.1	3.2	1.6	1.5
November	2.7	2.9	1.7	2.2	2.8	3.1	3.5	3.3	3.4	3.5	1.7	1.6
December	2.6	2.8	1.6	2.0	2.7	2.8	3.1	3.2	3.2	3.2	1.7	1.6
2013												
January	2.6	2.7	1.8	2.1	2.4	2.5	3.7	2.7	3.2	3.2	1.9	1.8
February	2.8	3.0	2.0	2.2	2.4	2.6	3.7	3.2	3.4	3.5	1.9	1.8
March	2.8	3.0	1.8	2.2	2.5	2.7	3.6	3.2	3.4	3.5	1.8	1.8
April	2.7	2.9	1.7	2.0	2.7	2.9	3.8	3.1	3.2	3.3	1.8	1.7
May	2.8	3.0	1.7	1.9	2.9	3.3	3.3	3.1	3.3	3.3	1.9	1.9
June	2.8	2.9	2.0	1.7	2.7	3.0	3.6	3.1	3.3	3.5	1.8	1.8
July	2.7	2.9	1.7	1.9	2.5	2.6	3.5	3.1	3.4	3.5	1.8	1.8
August	2.7	2.9	1.8	2.2	2.6	2.7	3.4	3.4	3.5	3.5	1.7	1.7
September	2.8	3.0	1.9	2.1	2.7	2.9	3.3	3.2	3.7	3.9	1.7	1.7
October	2.8	3.0	2.1	2.3	2.5	2.7	3.7	3.0	3.8	3.8	1.7	1.7

[1]Includes natural resources and mining, information, financial activities, and other services, not shown separately.
[2]Includes wholesale trade and transportation, warehousing, and utilities, not shown separately.
[3]Includes arts, entertainment, and recreation, not shown separately.
[4]Includes federal government, not shown separately.

Table 7-8. Hires Levels¹ and Rates,² by Industry, 2002–October 2013

(Seasonally adjusted, levels in thousands, rates per 100.)

Year and month	Level³											
	Total⁴	Total private⁴	Construction	Manufacturing	Trade, transportation, and utilities⁵	Retail trade	Professional and business services	Education and health services	Leisure and hospitality⁶	Accommodation and food services	Government⁷	State and local government
2002												
January	4 858	4 549	426	351	984	694	916	512	804	687	309	271
February	4 903	4 580	426	388	1 001	670	942	474	848	731	324	280
March	4 637	4 320	406	354	915	621	941	455	769	633	318	277
April	4 984	4 651	420	407	1 037	716	945	486	828	700	332	284
May	4 997	4 646	409	406	1 021	720	1 006	466	811	688	350	300
June	4 840	4 517	417	394	1 016	707	869	496	793	670	323	285
July	5 047	4 720	448	401	1 043	739	936	483	874	708	327	290
August	4 845	4 510	412	370	984	676	915	453	834	699	335	287
September	4 862	4 581	429	386	1 027	710	937	457	817	682	281	228
October	4 811	4 480	426	355	969	687	983	453	788	681	331	281
November	4 893	4 530	415	376	999	716	974	440	814	674	362	313
December	4 965	4 661	430	369	1 006	716	1 031	474	826	676	305	267
2003												
January	5 000	4 671	457	389	958	677	963	496	869	710	329	285
February	4 676	4 393	351	357	960	704	935	447	798	679	284	245
March	4 402	4 115	411	334	918	635	730	431	773	640	287	248
April	4 583	4 299	432	316	892	638	911	435	798	663	285	260
May	4 589	4 326	444	318	908	650	834	469	836	675	263	231
June	4 725	4 424	449	338	953	670	903	471	807	688	301	260
July	4 616	4 285	429	340	930	633	908	437	729	618	331	296
August	4 637	4 395	476	343	971	682	885	450	801	674	242	207
September	4 744	4 487	460	334	988	671	875	501	798	686	257	223
October	4 896	4 571	411	345	1 080	761	897	492	829	702	325	284
November	4 666	4 388	451	363	956	673	834	472	826	694	279	240
December	4 980	4 671	445	360	1 053	728	876	452	926	797	310	268
2004												
January	4 819	4 527	438	365	1 092	751	858	470	821	691	292	255
February	4 712	4 401	439	361	1 032	719	722	470	861	706	310	268
March	5 157	4 815	512	393	1 098	740	908	476	877	744	342	306
April	5 131	4 827	444	419	1 111	773	995	466	857	725	304	253
May	4 943	4 655	435	391	1 042	714	886	459	886	742	288	264
June	4 991	4 697	460	375	1 046	698	935	438	865	727	294	261
July	4 891	4 586	414	383	1 072	756	900	459	835	696	305	271
August	5 094	4 795	430	409	1 106	747	932	488	868	735	299	269
September	5 057	4 733	444	388	1 072	726	920	462	897	729	324	293
October	5 155	4 824	494	376	1 119	781	897	502	887	748	331	295
November	5 199	4 855	437	370	1 130	807	993	490	859	753	344	304
December	5 190	4 866	452	358	1 135	802	992	501	853	733	324	278
2005												
January	5 193	4 857	451	352	1 105	756	966	483	908	769	336	297
February	5 224	4 908	494	363	1 121	768	1 029	486	855	731	316	281
March	5 210	4 899	442	364	1 135	811	989	524	890	757	311	273
April	5 308	4 988	512	370	1 144	799	993	517	878	740	320	285
May	5 320	5 002	497	384	1 154	784	1 028	509	849	728	318	279
June	5 303	5 005	476	349	1 138	794	1 070	500	945	777	298	260
July	5 310	4 961	432	370	1 137	809	1 051	497	922	784	349	317
August	5 443	5 133	512	373	1 142	808	1 089	502	910	774	310	272
September	5 455	5 153	521	397	1 127	780	1 083	535	942	778	302	258
October	5 026	4 720	498	396	1 076	742	847	486	885	765	306	271
November	5 232	4 894	497	380	1 108	712	901	501	916	796	338	297
December	5 143	4 814	479	361	1 127	742	897	498	917	792	328	285
2006												
January	5 194	4 889	490	375	1 114	777	953	485	933	827	305	261
February	5 377	5 033	471	367	1 166	817	954	497	983	870	344	293
March	5 363	4 988	475	415	1 127	790	937	480	962	834	375	319
April	5 096	4 740	457	361	1 117	784	848	501	868	748	355	294
May	5 532	5 179	470	392	1 174	812	1 168	570	877	734	353	291
June	5 357	4 999	409	409	1 192	842	1 014	491	905	764	358	301
July	5 419	5 049	462	383	1 159	791	973	546	938	787	370	305
August	5 222	4 851	410	371	1 166	775	936	518	893	765	371	306
September	5 237	4 840	405	348	1 113	766	977	536	868	766	397	323
October	5 187	4 871	396	341	1 113	771	966	525	924	789	316	282
November	5 540	5 190	472	362	1 144	796	1 100	522	1 024	881	350	302
December	5 261	4 938	450	365	1 092	767	963	523	979	842	323	282
2007												
January	5 279	4 916	418	378	1 146	806	981	522	929	785	363	302
February	5 183	4 810	323	393	1 106	771	989	510	937	799	373	304
March	5 354	4 981	442	372	1 148	787	981	530	910	771	373	295
April	5 180	4 802	380	361	1 083	726	906	516	973	827	378	303
May	5 314	4 936	398	381	1 101	778	973	558	932	803	378	299
June	5 237	4 873	429	387	1 073	715	858	539	940	806	364	298
July	5 121	4 778	407	372	1 046	714	941	502	912	792	342	256
August	5 145	4 756	400	374	1 045	738	932	529	917	790	389	305
September	5 156	4 790	388	370	1 099	787	948	521	889	750	366	286
October	5 201	4 881	400	376	1 107	760	971	536	921	785	321	291
November	5 150	4 807	385	399	1 090	780	975	540	894	753	342	296
December	4 971	4 613	367	353	1 033	750	905	487	908	772	358	311

¹Hires are the number of hires during the entire month.
²The hires rate is the number of hires during the entire month as a percent of total employment.
³Detail will not necessarily add to totals because of the independent seasonal adjustment of the various series.
⁴Includes natural resources and mining, information, financial activities, and other services, not shown separately.
⁵Includes wholesale trade and transportation, warehousing, and utilities, not shown separately.
⁶Includes arts, entertainment, and recreation, not shown separately.
⁷Includes federal government, not shown separately.
. . . = Not available.

Table 7-8. Hires Levels[1] and Rates,[2] by Industry, 2002–October 2013—*Continued*

(Seasonally adjusted, levels in thousands, rates per 100.)

Year and month	Rate											
	Total[4]	Total private[4]	Construction	Manufacturing	Trade, transportation, and utilities[5]	Retail trade	Professional and business services	Education and health services	Leisure and hospitality[6]	Accommodation and food services	Government[7]	State and local government
2002												
January	3.7	4.2	6.3	2.3	3.8	4.6	5.7	3.2	6.7	6.7	1.4	1.5
February	3.8	4.2	6.3	2.5	3.9	4.4	5.9	3.0	7.1	7.2	1.5	1.5
March	3.6	4.0	6.0	2.3	3.6	4.1	5.9	2.8	6.4	6.2	1.5	1.5
April	3.8	4.3	6.3	2.6	4.1	4.8	5.9	3.0	6.9	6.9	1.5	1.5
May	3.8	4.3	6.1	2.6	4.0	4.8	6.3	2.9	6.8	6.8	1.6	1.6
June	3.7	4.2	6.2	2.6	4.0	4.7	5.4	3.1	6.7	6.6	1.5	1.5
July	3.9	4.3	6.7	2.6	4.1	4.9	5.9	3.0	7.3	7.0	1.5	1.5
August	3.7	4.2	6.2	2.4	3.9	4.5	5.7	2.8	7.0	6.9	1.6	1.5
September	3.7	4.2	6.4	2.6	4.0	4.7	5.9	2.8	6.8	6.7	1.3	1.2
October	3.7	4.1	6.4	2.4	3.8	4.6	6.2	2.8	6.5	6.6	1.5	1.5
November	3.8	4.2	6.2	2.5	3.9	4.8	6.1	2.7	6.7	6.5	1.7	1.7
December	3.8	4.3	6.4	2.5	4.0	4.8	6.5	2.9	6.8	6.6	1.4	1.4
2003												
January	3.8	4.3	6.8	2.6	3.8	4.5	6.0	3.0	7.1	6.9	1.5	1.5
February	3.6	4.0	5.3	2.4	3.8	4.7	5.9	2.7	6.6	6.6	1.3	1.3
March	3.4	3.8	6.2	2.3	3.6	4.3	4.6	2.6	6.4	6.2	1.3	1.3
April	3.5	4.0	6.5	2.2	3.5	4.3	5.7	2.6	6.6	6.4	1.3	1.4
May	3.5	4.0	6.6	2.2	3.6	4.4	5.2	2.8	6.9	6.6	1.2	1.2
June	3.6	4.1	6.7	2.3	3.8	4.5	5.7	2.8	6.7	6.7	1.4	1.4
July	3.6	4.0	6.4	2.4	3.7	4.3	5.7	2.6	6.0	6.0	1.5	1.6
August	3.6	4.1	7.0	2.4	3.8	4.6	5.5	2.7	6.6	6.5	1.1	1.1
September	3.7	4.1	6.8	2.3	3.9	4.5	5.5	3.0	6.5	6.6	1.2	1.2
October	3.8	4.2	6.1	2.4	4.3	5.1	5.6	3.0	6.8	6.7	1.5	1.5
November	3.6	4.0	6.6	2.5	3.8	4.5	5.2	2.8	6.7	6.6	1.3	1.3
December	3.8	4.3	6.5	2.5	4.2	4.9	5.4	2.7	7.5	7.6	1.4	1.4
2004												
January	3.7	4.2	6.4	2.6	4.3	5.0	5.3	2.8	6.7	6.6	1.4	1.4
February	3.6	4.0	6.4	2.5	4.1	4.8	4.5	2.8	7.0	6.7	1.4	1.4
March	3.9	4.4	7.4	2.7	4.3	4.9	5.6	2.8	7.1	7.0	1.6	1.6
April	3.9	4.4	6.4	2.9	4.4	5.1	6.1	2.8	6.9	6.8	1.4	1.3
May	3.8	4.2	6.3	2.7	4.1	4.7	5.4	2.7	7.1	7.0	1.3	1.4
June	3.8	4.3	6.6	2.6	4.1	4.6	5.7	2.6	6.9	6.8	1.4	1.4
July	3.7	4.2	5.9	2.7	4.2	5.0	5.5	2.7	6.7	6.5	1.4	1.4
August	3.9	4.4	6.1	2.9	4.3	5.0	5.7	2.9	7.0	6.9	1.4	1.4
September	3.8	4.3	6.3	2.7	4.2	4.8	5.6	2.7	7.1	6.8	1.5	1.6
October	3.9	4.4	7.0	2.6	4.4	5.2	5.4	2.9	7.0	7.0	1.5	1.6
November	3.9	4.4	6.2	2.6	4.4	5.3	6.0	2.9	6.8	7.0	1.6	1.6
December	3.9	4.4	6.4	2.5	4.4	5.3	6.0	2.9	6.8	6.8	1.5	1.5
2005												
January	3.9	4.4	6.4	2.5	4.3	5.0	5.8	2.8	7.2	7.1	1.5	1.6
February	3.9	4.4	6.9	2.5	4.3	5.1	6.2	2.8	6.7	6.7	1.5	1.5
March	3.9	4.4	6.2	2.6	4.4	5.3	5.9	3.0	7.0	7.0	1.4	1.4
April	4.0	4.5	7.0	2.6	4.4	5.2	5.9	3.0	6.9	6.8	1.5	1.5
May	4.0	4.5	6.8	2.7	4.4	5.1	6.1	2.9	6.6	6.7	1.5	1.5
June	4.0	4.5	6.5	2.5	4.4	5.2	6.3	2.9	7.4	7.1	1.4	1.4
July	4.0	4.4	5.9	2.6	4.4	5.3	6.2	2.9	7.2	7.2	1.6	1.7
August	4.1	4.6	6.9	2.6	4.4	5.3	6.4	2.9	7.1	7.0	1.4	1.4
September	4.1	4.6	7.0	2.8	4.3	5.1	6.3	3.1	7.3	7.1	1.4	1.3
October	3.7	4.2	6.7	2.8	4.1	4.8	4.9	2.8	6.9	7.0	1.4	1.4
November	3.9	4.3	6.6	2.7	4.2	4.6	5.2	2.9	7.1	7.3	1.5	1.6
December	3.8	4.3	6.4	2.5	4.3	4.8	5.2	2.8	7.1	7.2	1.5	1.5
2006												
January	3.8	4.3	6.4	2.6	4.3	5.1	5.5	2.8	7.2	7.5	1.4	1.4
February	4.0	4.4	6.2	2.6	4.4	5.3	5.5	2.8	7.6	7.9	1.6	1.5
March	4.0	4.4	6.2	2.9	4.3	5.1	5.4	2.7	7.4	7.5	1.7	1.7
April	3.8	4.2	5.9	2.5	4.3	5.1	4.9	2.8	6.6	6.7	1.6	1.5
May	4.1	4.5	6.1	2.8	4.5	5.3	6.7	3.2	6.7	6.6	1.6	1.5
June	3.9	4.4	5.3	2.9	4.5	5.5	5.8	2.8	6.9	6.9	1.6	1.6
July	4.0	4.4	6.0	2.7	4.4	5.2	5.5	3.1	7.1	7.0	1.7	1.6
August	3.8	4.2	5.3	2.6	4.4	5.1	5.3	2.9	6.8	6.8	1.7	1.6
September	3.8	4.2	5.2	2.5	4.2	5.0	5.5	3.0	6.6	6.8	1.8	1.7
October	3.8	4.3	5.2	2.4	4.2	5.0	5.5	2.9	7.0	7.0	1.4	1.5
November	4.1	4.5	6.2	2.6	4.3	5.2	6.2	2.9	7.7	7.8	1.6	1.6
December	3.8	4.3	5.9	2.6	4.1	5.0	5.4	2.9	7.4	7.4	1.5	1.5
2007												
January	3.9	4.3	5.4	2.7	4.3	5.2	5.5	2.9	7.0	6.9	1.6	1.6
February	3.8	4.2	4.2	2.8	4.2	5.0	5.5	2.8	7.0	7.0	1.7	1.6
March	3.9	4.3	5.7	2.7	4.3	5.1	5.5	2.9	6.8	6.8	1.7	1.5
April	3.8	4.2	4.9	2.6	4.1	4.7	5.1	2.8	7.3	7.2	1.7	1.6
May	3.9	4.3	5.2	2.7	4.1	5.0	5.4	3.1	7.0	7.0	1.7	1.5
June	3.8	4.2	5.6	2.8	4.0	4.6	4.8	2.9	7.0	7.0	1.6	1.5
July	3.7	4.1	5.3	2.7	3.9	4.6	5.2	2.7	6.8	6.9	1.5	1.3
August	3.7	4.1	5.3	2.7	3.9	4.8	5.2	2.9	6.8	6.9	1.8	1.6
September	3.7	4.2	5.1	2.7	4.1	5.1	5.3	2.8	6.6	6.5	1.6	1.5
October	3.8	4.2	5.3	2.7	4.2	4.9	5.4	2.9	6.8	6.8	1.4	1.5
November	3.7	4.2	5.1	2.9	4.1	5.0	5.4	2.9	6.6	6.5	1.5	1.5
December	3.6	4.0	4.9	2.6	3.9	4.8	5.0	2.6	6.7	6.7	1.6	1.6

[1] Hires are the number of hires during the entire month.
[2] The hires rate is the number of hires during the entire month as a percent of total employment.
[4] Includes natural resources and mining, information, financial activities, and other services, not shown separately.
[5] Includes wholesale trade and transportation, warehousing, and utilities, not shown separately.
[6] Includes arts, entertainment, and recreation, not shown separately.
[7] Includes federal government, not shown separately.
. . . = Not available.

Table 7-8. Hires Levels[1] and Rates,[2] by Industry, 2002–October 2013—*Continued*

(Seasonally adjusted, levels in thousands, rates per 100.)

Year and month	Total[4]	Total private[4]	Construction	Manufacturing	Trade, transportation, and utilities[5]	Retail trade	Professional and business services	Education and health services	Leisure and hospitality[6]	Accommodation and food services	Government[7]	State and local government
2008												
January	4 927	4 601	369	331	1 036	711	890	561	875	730	326	292
February	4 895	4 577	371	317	1 046	732	808	556	942	788	318	276
March	4 811	4 483	381	310	992	696	870	554	842	716	328	295
April	4 897	4 589	384	335	1 016	687	894	570	861	740	308	278
May	4 678	4 367	360	321	920	643	817	548	885	753	312	288
June	4 739	4 438	398	310	1 003	689	893	515	809	701	301	277
July	4 505	4 215	365	264	972	672	805	526	796	688	290	266
August	4 609	4 320	408	279	985	684	804	524	821	668	289	268
September	4 378	4 105	351	285	917	635	794	487	789	691	273	251
October	4 509	4 212	381	313	941	643	791	528	781	661	297	273
November	3 960	3 693	347	248	761	538	756	488	685	598	267	240
December	4 182	3 912	334	267	868	605	812	497	703	594	269	247
2009												
January	4 202	3 864	350	195	861	548	736	541	699	580	338	294
February	4 008	3 748	342	247	779	533	710	524	680	582	259	236
March	3 784	3 538	300	234	820	541	648	469	629	556	245	222
April	3 887	3 519	299	198	859	626	693	465	621	541	368	223
May	3 792	3 539	325	176	823	554	669	471	681	593	252	231
June	3 626	3 363	265	189	704	488	592	492	641	547	263	234
July	3 840	3 609	313	239	729	492	695	508	650	519	230	197
August	3 789	3 511	270	241	767	532	654	512	660	540	279	255
September	3 878	3 639	313	266	822	524	691	499	634	525	240	220
October	3 792	3 479	303	243	710	487	697	502	617	515	313	270
November	3 960	3 687	302	279	772	499	800	482	670	556	273	240
December	3 829	3 587	321	243	794	514	679	482	621	527	242	221
2010												
January	3 882	3 595	309	265	744	534	751	453	655	555	287	232
February	3 822	3 542	291	257	787	536	746	455	587	509	279	236
March	4 186	3 838	386	252	895	652	759	504	645	538	348	257
April	4 098	3 765	352	271	805	554	772	479	674	553	332	228
May	4 378	3 645	313	246	770	530	769	459	647	541	733	235
June	4 026	3 739	286	251	818	555	807	490	660	525	287	232
July	4 090	3 833	336	273	851	576	782	517	678	549	257	215
August	3 911	3 663	350	256	763	541	761	462	648	540	248	210
September	3 946	3 698	313	250	826	556	746	494	673	561	248	217
October	4 073	3 787	361	272	804	566	768	483	651	556	287	256
November	4 100	3 811	342	283	817	561	803	506	634	540	289	260
December	4 125	3 844	362	263	785	508	886	474	636	537	281	252
2011												
January	3 939	3 672	282	262	832	573	819	451	620	529	266	235
February	4 052	3 821	354	258	869	570	838	455	636	539	231	199
March	4 203	3 951	361	265	836	579	891	453	730	602	253	224
April	4 036	3 766	351	255	814	574	830	471	669	557	270	245
May	4 107	3 868	359	262	821	561	873	461	659	544	239	208
June	4 142	3 872	374	255	836	574	776	491	718	597	270	248
July	4 077	3 859	322	253	832	588	820	473	721	605	218	192
August	4 187	3 926	335	254	805	541	893	488	705	586	261	236
September	4 304	4 026	375	241	827	572	892	478	746	601	278	252
October	4 159	3 904	318	237	824	546	871	472	716	586	254	226
November	4 264	3 978	319	230	854	581	852	478	775	618	285	254
December	4 174	3 876	313	258	793	503	842	490	733	612	298	267
2012												
January	4 192	3 915	327	249	862	579	791	498	762	615	277	260
February	4 489	4 181	348	258	829	565	985	539	775	624	309	276
March	4 435	4 133	323	259	862	577	896	514	813	654	301	271
April	4 252	3 962	262	252	862	575	859	485	766	623	290	256
May	4 526	4 231	321	261	882	589	968	541	748	621	296	265
June	4 357	4 081	347	283	855	573	921	486	729	616	275	245
July	4 171	3 893	362	237	843	561	823	486	723	612	278	260
August	4 405	4 083	301	232	903	591	897	495	767	640	322	289
September	4 217	3 934	337	227	833	560	857	493	712	612	283	251
October	4 287	4 031	318	234	911	617	864	489	752	627	255	225
November	4 420	4 134	386	234	900	597	912	471	697	589	286	256
December	4 195	3 915	280	236	890	600	798	506	759	629	280	246
2013												
January	4 298	4 015	326	219	868	586	878	507	747	643	283	249
February	4 451	4 138	353	231	936	651	845	499	762	646	313	266
March	4 227	3 931	320	201	821	562	831	520	776	653	295	264
April	4 395	4 100	283	222	868	598	912	544	809	686	295	262
May	4 490	4 206	317	239	889	620	890	541	802	678	284	258
June	4 318	4 036	309	225	842	586	928	470	793	660	282	253
July	4 497	4 219	307	222	906	635	1 001	530	753	639	277	253
August	4 559	4 261	298	248	936	659	979	556	749	643	298	273
September	4 632	4 338	299	251	923	634	999	534	813	678	294	268
October	4 509	4 205	307	235	950	669	873	531	831	681	304	277

[1]Hires are the number of hires during the entire month.
[2]The hires rate is the number of hires during the entire month as a percent of total employment.
[3]Detail will not necessarily add to totals because of the independent seasonal adjustment of the various series.
[4]Includes natural resources and mining, information, financial activities, and other services, not shown separately.
[5]Includes wholesale trade and transportation, warehousing, and utilities, not shown separately.
[6]Includes arts, entertainment, and recreation, not shown separately.
[7]Includes federal government, not shown separately.
. . . = Not available.

Table 7-8. Hires Levels[1] and Rates,[2] by Industry, 2002–October 2013—*Continued*

(Seasonally adjusted, levels in thousands, rates per 100.)

Year and month	Total[4]	Total private[4]	Construction	Manufacturing	Trade, transportation, and utilities[5]	Retail trade	Professional and business services	Education and health services	Leisure and hospitality[6]	Accommodation and food services	Government[7]	State and local government
2008												
January	3.6	4.0	4.9	2.4	3.9	4.6	4.9	3.0	6.5	6.3	1.5	1.5
February	3.5	4.0	5.0	2.3	3.9	4.7	4.5	3.0	7.0	6.8	1.4	1.4
March	3.5	3.9	5.1	2.3	3.7	4.5	4.8	3.0	6.2	6.2	1.5	1.5
April	3.6	4.0	5.2	2.5	3.8	4.5	5.0	3.0	6.4	6.4	1.4	1.4
May	3.4	3.8	4.9	2.4	3.5	4.2	4.6	2.9	6.6	6.5	1.4	1.5
June	3.5	3.9	5.5	2.3	3.8	4.5	5.0	2.7	6.0	6.1	1.3	1.4
July	3.3	3.7	5.1	2.0	3.7	4.4	4.5	2.8	5.9	6.0	1.3	1.3
August	3.4	3.8	5.7	2.1	3.8	4.5	4.5	2.8	6.1	5.8	1.3	1.4
September	3.2	3.6	5.0	2.2	3.5	4.2	4.5	2.6	5.9	6.0	1.2	1.3
October	3.3	3.7	5.5	2.4	3.6	4.3	4.5	2.8	5.8	5.8	1.3	1.4
November	2.9	3.3	5.1	1.9	3.0	3.6	4.4	2.6	5.1	5.3	1.2	1.2
December	3.1	3.5	5.0	2.1	3.4	4.1	4.7	2.6	5.3	5.2	1.2	1.2
2009												
January	3.1	3.5	5.3	1.6	3.4	3.7	4.3	2.8	5.3	5.1	1.5	1.5
February	3.0	3.4	5.3	2.0	3.1	3.6	4.2	2.7	5.2	5.2	1.1	1.2
March	2.9	3.2	4.8	1.9	3.3	3.7	3.9	2.5	4.8	5.0	1.1	1.1
April	3.0	3.2	4.9	1.6	3.4	4.3	4.2	2.4	4.8	4.9	1.6	1.1
May	2.9	3.3	5.3	1.5	3.3	3.8	4.0	2.5	5.2	5.3	1.1	1.2
June	2.8	3.1	4.4	1.6	2.8	3.4	3.6	2.6	4.9	4.9	1.2	1.2
July	2.9	3.4	5.3	2.0	2.9	3.4	4.2	2.6	5.0	4.6	1.0	1.0
August	2.9	3.3	4.6	2.1	3.1	3.7	4.0	2.7	5.1	4.8	1.2	1.3
September	3.0	3.4	5.4	2.3	3.3	3.6	4.2	2.6	4.9	4.7	1.1	1.1
October	2.9	3.2	5.3	2.1	2.9	3.4	4.2	2.6	4.7	4.6	1.4	1.4
November	3.1	3.4	5.3	2.4	3.1	3.5	4.9	2.5	5.2	5.0	1.2	1.2
December	3.0	3.4	5.7	2.1	3.2	3.6	4.1	2.5	4.8	4.8	1.1	1.1
2010												
January	3.0	3.4	5.5	2.3	3.0	3.7	4.5	2.3	5.1	5.0	1.3	1.2
February	3.0	3.3	5.3	2.2	3.2	3.7	4.5	2.3	4.5	4.6	1.2	1.2
March	3.2	3.6	7.0	2.2	3.6	4.5	4.6	2.6	5.0	4.9	1.5	1.3
April	3.2	3.5	6.3	2.4	3.3	3.8	4.6	2.5	5.2	5.0	1.5	1.2
May	3.4	3.4	5.7	2.1	3.1	3.7	4.6	2.4	5.0	4.9	3.2	1.2
June	3.1	3.5	5.2	2.2	3.3	3.8	4.8	2.5	5.1	4.7	1.3	1.2
July	3.1	3.6	6.1	2.4	3.5	4.0	4.7	2.6	5.2	4.9	1.1	1.1
August	3.0	3.4	6.3	2.2	3.1	3.7	4.5	2.4	5.0	4.8	1.1	1.1
September	3.0	3.4	5.7	2.2	3.3	3.8	4.4	2.5	5.1	5.0	1.1	1.1
October	3.1	3.5	6.6	2.4	3.2	3.9	4.6	2.5	5.0	5.0	1.3	1.3
November	3.1	3.5	6.2	2.4	3.3	3.9	4.7	2.6	4.8	4.8	1.3	1.3
December	3.2	3.6	6.6	2.3	3.2	3.5	5.2	2.4	4.8	4.8	1.3	1.3
2011												
January	3.0	3.4	5.2	2.3	3.4	3.9	4.8	2.3	4.7	4.7	1.2	1.2
February	3.1	3.5	6.5	2.2	3.5	3.9	4.9	2.3	4.8	4.8	1.0	1.0
March	3.2	3.6	6.6	2.3	3.4	4.0	5.2	2.3	5.5	5.3	1.1	1.2
April	3.1	3.5	6.4	2.2	3.3	3.9	4.8	2.4	5.0	4.9	1.2	1.3
May	3.1	3.5	6.5	2.2	3.3	3.8	5.0	2.3	5.0	4.8	1.1	1.1
June	3.2	3.5	6.8	2.2	3.3	3.9	4.5	2.5	5.4	5.2	1.2	1.3
July	3.1	3.5	5.8	2.2	3.3	4.0	4.7	2.4	5.4	5.3	1.0	1.0
August	3.2	3.6	6.0	2.2	3.2	3.7	5.1	2.4	5.3	5.1	1.2	1.2
September	3.3	3.7	6.7	2.0	3.3	3.9	5.1	2.4	5.6	5.2	1.3	1.3
October	3.1	3.5	5.7	2.0	3.3	3.7	5.0	2.4	5.3	5.1	1.2	1.2
November	3.2	3.6	5.7	2.0	3.4	3.9	4.9	2.4	5.7	5.3	1.3	1.3
December	3.1	3.5	5.6	2.2	3.1	3.4	4.8	2.4	5.4	5.3	1.4	1.4
2012												
January	3.2	3.5	5.8	2.1	3.4	3.9	4.5	2.5	5.6	5.3	1.2	1.4
February	3.4	3.8	6.2	2.2	3.3	3.8	5.5	2.7	5.7	5.3	1.0	1.4
March	3.3	3.7	5.7	2.2	3.4	3.9	5.0	2.5	5.9	5.6	1.1	1.4
April	3.2	3.6	4.7	2.1	3.4	3.9	4.8	2.4	5.6	5.3	1.2	1.3
May	3.4	3.8	5.7	2.2	3.5	4.0	5.4	2.7	5.5	5.3	1.1	1.4
June	3.3	3.7	6.2	2.4	3.4	3.9	5.1	2.4	5.3	5.2	1.2	1.3
July	3.1	3.5	6.4	2.0	3.3	3.8	4.6	2.4	5.3	5.2	1.0	1.4
August	3.3	3.6	5.3	1.9	3.5	4.0	5.0	2.4	5.6	5.4	1.2	1.5
September	3.1	3.5	6.0	1.9	3.3	3.8	4.8	2.4	5.2	5.2	1.3	1.3
October	3.2	3.6	5.6	2.0	3.6	4.1	4.8	2.4	5.4	5.3	1.2	1.2
November	3.3	3.7	6.8	2.0	3.5	4.0	5.0	2.3	5.0	5.0	1.3	1.3
December	3.1	3.5	4.9	2.0	3.5	4.0	4.4	2.5	5.5	5.3	1.4	1.3
2013												
January	3.2	3.6	5.7	1.8	3.4	3.9	4.8	2.5	5.4	5.4	1.3	1.3
February	3.3	3.7	6.1	1.9	3.6	4.3	4.6	2.4	5.5	5.4	1.4	1.4
March	3.1	3.5	5.5	1.7	3.2	3.7	4.5	2.5	5.5	5.4	1.4	1.4
April	3.2	3.6	4.9	1.9	3.4	4.0	5.0	2.6	5.8	5.7	1.4	1.4
May	3.3	3.7	5.5	2.0	3.4	4.1	4.8	2.6	5.7	5.6	1.3	1.4
June	3.2	3.5	5.3	1.9	3.2	3.9	5.0	2.3	5.6	5.4	1.3	1.3
July	3.3	3.7	5.3	1.9	3.5	4.2	5.4	2.6	5.3	5.3	1.3	1.3
August	3.3	3.7	5.1	2.1	3.6	4.3	5.3	2.7	5.3	5.3	1.4	1.4
September	3.4	3.8	5.1	2.1	3.5	4.2	5.4	2.6	5.7	5.6	1.3	1.4
October	3.3	3.7	5.3	2.0	3.6	4.4	4.7	2.6	5.8	5.6	1.4	1.4

[1] Hires are the number of hires during the entire month.
[2] The hires rate is the number of hires during the entire month as a percent of total employment.
[4] Includes natural resources and mining, information, financial activities, and other services, not shown separately.
[5] Includes wholesale trade and transportation, warehousing, and utilities, not shown separately.
[6] Includes arts, entertainment, and recreation, not shown separately.
[7] Includes federal government, not shown separately.
. . . = Not available.

Table 7-9. Separations Levels[1] and Rates,[2] by Industry, 2002–October 2013

(Seasonally adjusted, levels in thousands, rates per 100.)

Year and month	Level[3]											
	Total[4]	Total private[4]	Construction	Manufacturing	Trade, transportation, and utilities[5]	Retail trade	Professional and business services	Education and health services	Leisure and hospitality[6]	Accommodation and food services	Government[7]	State and local government
2002												
January	5 051	4 761	422	470	1 080	750	982	460	789	654	290	250
February	5 032	4 709	447	454	1 040	686	976	425	850	735	324	278
March	4 749	4 483	408	429	977	659	981	415	770	644	266	223
April	5 030	4 702	432	447	1 045	721	907	459	867	714	328	285
May	4 949	4 668	440	458	1 030	732	979	430	790	678	281	248
June	4 840	4 544	416	440	1 030	725	862	407	788	676	297	251
July	5 221	4 904	466	451	1 028	723	1 024	460	905	702	317	274
August	4 821	4 527	406	445	1 040	724	877	420	801	668	294	255
September	4 923	4 612	437	439	1 032	711	962	431	789	671	310	267
October	4 757	4 435	438	430	965	679	965	435	735	638	322	284
November	4 794	4 466	383	438	1 002	715	957	391	784	664	328	276
December	5 069	4 766	451	428	978	695	1 109	460	795	657	303	259
2003												
January	4 880	4 586	435	430	998	698	914	443	805	658	294	256
February	4 823	4 522	397	433	1 003	746	913	416	804	676	300	260
March	4 694	4 396	412	398	1 007	698	837	415	810	664	297	259
April	4 641	4 329	401	425	891	621	904	384	819	673	311	269
May	4 632	4 335	431	370	932	651	781	445	870	700	297	253
June	4 752	4 482	431	400	1 000	692	884	465	751	645	270	231
July	4 654	4 358	429	438	971	637	876	436	707	609	296	261
August	4 688	4 369	472	368	968	668	911	435	762	638	320	279
September	4 633	4 335	447	367	918	623	820	459	787	660	298	264
October	4 720	4 455	407	367	1 048	736	855	454	805	676	265	219
November	4 612	4 312	434	382	973	689	773	429	816	673	299	238
December	4 809	4 502	422	388	1 020	701	820	415	860	738	307	272
2004												
January	4 653	4 354	420	377	999	712	851	434	786	668	299	258
February	4 639	4 336	457	373	1 018	707	715	452	806	659	304	259
March	4 923	4 622	448	391	1 081	726	909	429	834	713	301	265
April	4 873	4 593	419	382	1 086	763	900	439	847	701	280	255
May	4 653	4 367	385	358	1 008	683	787	440	848	714	286	244
June	4 884	4 581	430	372	997	673	928	423	845	699	303	264
July	4 866	4 570	407	383	1 087	771	882	433	846	698	296	263
August	4 957	4 678	424	407	1 084	728	898	445	878	744	279	250
September	4 877	4 572	420	401	992	680	882	480	837	687	306	274
October	4 796	4 486	443	374	1 062	738	802	402	852	713	310	268
November	5 152	4 843	414	396	1 131	818	975	465	860	740	309	268
December	5 036	4 704	409	394	1 099	792	958	455	821	694	332	284
2005												
January	5 053	4 770	487	379	1 059	723	929	448	878	749	283	251
February	4 966	4 653	445	355	1 045	721	963	472	810	687	314	277
March	5 152	4 839	410	377	1 140	830	979	503	864	746	314	279
April	4 988	4 681	422	379	1 083	762	973	485	789	674	306	267
May	5 155	4 859	470	373	1 117	746	949	470	863	743	295	268
June	5 020	4 711	421	367	1 087	756	992	454	902	742	308	263
July	4 934	4 677	402	374	1 075	767	1 002	442	870	759	257	221
August	5 223	4 922	489	394	1 100	784	1 022	470	870	750	301	267
September	5 317	4 987	497	400	1 121	796	988	490	951	785	330	286
October	4 963	4 649	453	392	1 043	727	846	463	941	800	314	280
November	4 923	4 613	428	394	1 079	725	805	454	892	774	310	270
December	5 061	4 748	472	368	1 168	787	859	473	896	764	313	260
2006												
January	4 938	4 618	463	362	1 038	748	914	430	914	800	320	282
February	5 095	4 770	423	382	1 112	793	893	440	943	832	325	278
March	5 096	4 752	444	415	1 109	779	869	444	910	791	345	289
April	4 945	4 609	394	343	1 130	830	865	489	820	718	336	279
May	5 503	5 157	473	418	1 212	851	1 067	551	898	749	346	289
June	5 203	4 849	390	379	1 160	830	951	499	891	762	354	292
July	5 165	4 836	434	405	1 114	775	922	517	872	729	329	270
August	4 977	4 641	405	384	1 135	761	844	472	861	736	337	267
September	5 024	4 696	413	375	1 071	744	972	446	851	736	329	251
October	5 143	4 817	433	373	1 056	733	986	487	896	772	325	287
November	5 374	5 037	470	403	1 132	807	1 016	473	979	834	338	284
December	5 246	4 918	435	421	1 095	795	973	500	945	811	328	279
2007												
January	5 095	4 768	409	418	1 072	739	939	482	893	758	327	282
February	5 134	4 792	423	425	1 048	728	958	477	922	785	341	273
March	5 144	4 808	353	403	1 083	726	956	487	909	766	336	261
April	[2]5 150	4 805	391	387	1 090	749	933	476	937	790	345	273
May	5 153	4 790	413	395	1 094	769	891	512	913	793	363	288
June	5 063	4 716	403	388	1 063	731	833	488	936	806	346	268
July	[1]5 090	4 704	419	396	1 021	707	927	479	880	770	387	300
August	5 102	4 762	442	397	1 053	742	891	483	906	786	340	265
September	5 035	4 707	422	401	1 077	780	938	446	823	701	328	245
October	5 089	4 781	414	396	1 078	749	954	489	888	763	308	271
November	5 101	4 793	425	409	1 052	738	948	514	897	757	308	269
December	5 009	4 696	423	384	1 084	787	893	456	902	767	313	276

[1]Total separations are the number of separations during the entire month.
[2]The total separations rate is the number of total separations during the entire month as a percent of total employment.
[3]Detail will not necessarily add to totals because of the independent seasonal adjustment of the various series.
[4]Includes natural resources and mining, information, financial activities, and other services, not shown separately.
[5]Includes wholesale trade and transportation, warehousing, and utilities, not shown separately.
[6]Includes arts, entertainment, and recreation, not shown separately.
[7]Includes federal government, not shown separately.

Table 7-9. Separations Levels[1] and Rates,[2] by Industry, 2002–October 2013—*Continued*

(Seasonally adjusted, levels in thousands, rates per 100.)

Year and month	Rate											
	Total[4]	Total private[4]	Construc-tion	Manufac-turing	Trade, transpor-tation, and utilities[5]	Retail trade	Profes-sional and business services	Education and health services	Leisure and hospitality[6]	Accommo-dation and food services	Govern-ment[7]	State and local govern-ment
2002												
January	3.9	4.4	6.2	3.0	4.2	5.0	6.1	2.9	6.6	6.4	1.4	1.3
February	3.9	4.3	6.6	2.9	4.1	4.6	6.1	2.7	7.1	7.2	1.5	1.5
March	3.6	4.1	6.0	2.8	3.8	4.4	6.1	2.6	6.4	6.3	1.2	1.2
April	3.9	4.3	6.4	2.9	4.1	4.8	5.7	2.9	7.3	7.0	1.5	1.5
May	3.8	4.3	6.6	3.0	4.0	4.9	6.1	2.7	6.6	6.7	1.3	1.3
June	3.7	4.2	6.2	2.9	4.0	4.8	5.4	2.5	6.6	6.7	1.4	1.3
July	4.0	4.5	7.0	3.0	4.0	4.8	6.4	2.8	7.6	6.9	1.5	1.5
August	3.7	4.2	6.1	2.9	4.1	4.8	5.5	2.6	6.7	6.6	1.4	1.4
September	3.8	4.2	6.5	2.9	4.1	4.7	6.0	2.6	6.6	6.6	1.4	1.4
October	3.6	4.1	6.5	2.9	3.8	4.5	6.0	2.7	6.1	6.2	1.5	1.5
November	3.7	4.1	5.7	2.9	3.9	4.8	6.0	2.4	6.5	6.4	1.5	1.5
December	3.9	4.4	6.7	2.9	3.8	4.6	7.0	2.8	6.6	6.4	1.4	1.4
2003												
January	3.7	4.2	6.5	2.9	3.9	4.7	5.7	2.7	6.6	6.4	1.4	1.4
February	3.7	4.2	6.0	2.9	4.0	5.0	5.7	2.5	6.6	6.6	1.4	1.4
March	3.6	4.1	6.2	2.7	4.0	4.7	5.3	2.5	6.7	6.5	1.4	1.4
April	3.6	4.0	6.0	2.9	3.5	4.2	5.7	2.3	6.8	6.5	1.4	1.4
May	3.6	4.0	6.4	2.5	3.7	4.4	4.9	2.7	7.2	6.8	1.4	1.3
June	3.7	4.1	6.4	2.8	4.0	4.6	5.5	2.8	6.2	6.3	1.2	1.2
July	3.6	4.0	6.4	3.0	3.9	4.3	5.5	2.6	5.8	5.9	1.4	1.4
August	3.6	4.0	7.0	2.6	3.8	4.5	5.7	2.6	6.3	6.2	1.5	1.5
September	3.6	4.0	6.6	2.6	3.6	4.2	5.1	2.8	6.4	6.3	1.4	1.4
October	3.6	4.1	6.0	2.6	4.1	4.9	5.3	2.7	6.6	6.5	1.2	1.2
November	3.5	4.0	6.4	2.7	3.8	4.6	4.8	2.6	6.6	6.4	1.4	1.3
December	3.7	4.1	6.2	2.7	4.0	4.7	5.1	2.5	7.0	7.0	1.4	1.4
2004												
January	3.6	4.0	6.1	2.6	3.9	4.8	5.3	2.6	6.4	6.4	1.4	1.4
February	3.6	4.0	6.7	2.6	4.0	4.7	4.4	2.7	6.5	6.3	1.4	1.4
March	3.8	4.2	6.5	2.7	4.2	4.8	5.6	2.5	6.7	6.7	1.4	1.4
April	3.7	4.2	6.1	2.7	4.3	5.1	5.5	2.6	6.8	6.6	1.3	1.4
May	3.5	4.0	5.5	2.5	4.0	4.5	4.8	2.6	6.8	6.7	1.3	1.3
June	3.7	4.2	6.2	2.6	3.9	4.5	5.7	2.5	6.8	6.6	1.4	1.4
July	3.7	4.2	5.8	2.7	4.3	5.1	5.4	2.6	6.8	6.6	1.4	1.4
August	3.8	4.3	6.1	2.8	4.2	4.8	5.5	2.6	7.0	7.0	1.3	1.3
September	3.7	4.2	6.0	2.8	3.9	4.5	5.4	2.8	6.7	6.4	1.4	1.5
October	3.6	4.1	6.3	2.6	4.1	4.9	4.8	2.4	6.8	6.6	1.4	1.4
November	3.9	4.4	5.8	2.8	4.4	5.4	5.9	2.7	6.8	6.9	1.4	1.4
December	3.8	4.3	5.7	2.8	4.3	5.2	5.8	2.7	6.5	6.4	1.5	1.5
2005												
January	3.8	4.3	6.9	2.7	4.1	4.8	5.6	2.6	6.9	6.9	1.3	1.3
February	3.7	4.2	6.2	2.5	4.1	4.7	5.8	2.7	6.4	6.3	1.4	1.5
March	3.9	4.4	5.7	2.6	4.4	5.5	5.8	2.9	6.8	6.9	1.4	1.5
April	3.7	4.2	5.8	2.7	4.2	5.0	5.8	2.8	6.2	6.2	1.4	1.4
May	3.9	4.4	6.4	2.6	4.3	4.9	5.6	2.7	6.7	6.8	1.4	1.4
June	3.8	4.2	5.7	2.6	4.2	4.9	5.9	2.6	7.0	6.8	1.4	1.4
July	3.7	4.2	5.5	2.6	4.1	5.0	5.9	2.5	6.8	6.9	1.2	1.2
August	3.9	4.4	6.6	2.8	4.2	5.1	6.0	2.7	6.8	6.8	1.4	1.4
September	4.0	4.4	6.7	2.8	4.3	5.2	5.8	2.8	7.4	7.2	1.5	1.5
October	3.7	4.1	6.1	2.8	4.0	4.7	4.9	2.6	7.3	7.3	1.4	1.5
November	3.7	4.1	5.7	2.8	4.1	4.7	4.7	2.6	6.9	7.1	1.4	1.4
December	3.8	4.2	6.3	2.6	4.5	5.1	5.0	2.7	6.9	6.9	1.4	1.4
2006												
January	3.7	4.1	6.1	2.5	4.0	4.9	5.3	2.4	7.1	7.2	1.5	1.5
February	3.8	4.2	5.5	2.7	4.2	5.2	5.1	2.5	7.3	7.5	1.5	1.5
March	3.8	4.2	5.8	2.9	4.2	5.1	5.0	2.5	7.0	7.1	1.6	1.5
April	3.6	4.0	5.1	2.4	4.3	5.4	5.0	2.8	6.3	6.4	1.5	1.5
May	4.0	4.5	6.1	2.9	4.6	5.6	6.1	3.1	6.9	6.7	1.6	1.5
June	3.8	4.3	5.1	2.7	4.4	5.4	5.4	2.8	6.8	6.8	1.6	1.5
July	3.8	4.2	5.6	2.9	4.2	5.1	5.2	2.9	6.6	6.5	1.5	1.4
August	3.7	4.1	5.2	2.7	4.3	5.0	4.8	2.6	6.5	6.6	1.5	1.4
September	3.7	4.1	5.4	2.7	4.1	4.8	5.5	2.5	6.5	6.6	1.5	1.3
October	3.8	4.2	5.6	2.6	4.0	4.8	5.6	2.7	6.8	6.9	1.5	1.5
November	3.9	4.4	6.1	2.9	4.3	5.2	5.7	2.6	7.4	7.4	1.5	1.5
December	3.8	4.3	5.7	3.0	4.1	5.2	5.5	2.8	7.1	7.2	1.5	1.4
2007												
January	3.7	4.1	5.3	3.0	4.0	4.8	5.3	2.7	6.7	6.7	1.5	1.5
February	3.7	4.2	5.5	3.0	3.9	4.7	5.4	2.6	6.9	6.9	1.5	1.4
March	3.7	4.2	4.6	2.9	4.1	4.7	5.3	2.7	6.8	6.7	1.5	1.3
April	3.7	4.2	5.1	2.8	4.1	4.8	5.2	2.6	7.0	6.9	1.6	1.4
May	3.7	4.2	5.4	2.8	4.1	5.0	5.0	2.8	6.8	6.9	1.6	1.5
June	3.7	4.1	5.2	2.8	4.0	4.7	4.6	2.7	7.0	7.0	1.6	1.4
July	3.7	4.1	5.5	2.9	3.8	4.6	5.2	2.6	6.6	6.7	1.7	1.5
August	3.7	4.1	5.8	2.9	4.0	4.8	5.0	2.6	6.7	6.9	1.5	1.4
September	3.7	4.1	5.6	2.9	4.0	5.0	5.2	2.4	6.1	6.1	1.5	1.3
October	3.7	4.1	5.5	2.9	4.0	4.8	5.3	2.6	6.6	6.6	1.4	1.4
November	3.7	4.1	5.6	3.0	3.9	4.7	5.3	2.8	6.6	6.6	1.4	1.4
December	3.6	4.1	5.6	3.0	4.1	5.1	4.9	2.5	6.7	6.6	1.4	1.4

[1]Total separations are the number of separations during the entire month.
[2]The total separations rate is the number of total separations during the entire month as a percent of total employment.
[4]Includes natural resources and mining, information, financial activities, and other services, not shown separately.
[5]Includes wholesale trade and transportation, warehousing, and utilities, not shown separately.
[6]Includes arts, entertainment, and recreation, not shown separately.
[7]Includes federal government, not shown separately.

Table 7-9. Separations Levels[1] and Rates,[2] by Industry, 2002–October 2013—*Continued*

(Seasonally adjusted, levels in thousands, rates per 100.)

Year and month	Level[3]											
	Total[4]	Total private[4]	Construction	Manufacturing	Trade, transportation, and utilities[5]	Retail trade	Professional and business services	Education and health services	Leisure and hospitality[6]	Accommodation and food services	Government[7]	State and local government
2008												
January	4 990	4 698	402	373	1 053	727	920	508	894	752	293	253
February	5 032	4 749	404	369	1 065	741	874	510	963	811	283	250
March	4 821	4 528	401	357	989	687	890	508	853	722	292	267
April	5 167	4 867	460	398	1 119	785	944	535	856	732	299	272
May	4 820	4 541	412	352	1 012	696	822	501	905	769	279	257
June	4 927	4 649	454	374	1 071	738	933	467	827	715	277	254
July	4 694	4 440	414	331	1 020	713	882	481	809	695	255	235
August	4 866	4 569	437	328	1 082	741	864	485	854	699	297	275
September	4 772	4 485	416	368	1 033	702	866	464	814	698	287	268
October	4 934	4 637	452	403	1 050	714	912	505	803	691	297	271
November	4 693	4 429	478	366	988	675	907	451	740	651	264	241
December	4 826	4 554	454	420	1 033	695	928	473	734	623	272	245
2009												
January	4 945	4 653	480	496	999	628	876	487	734	617	291	269
February	4 700	4 422	437	430	880	568	881	501	733	632	278	262
March	4 617	4 356	443	422	987	623	774	466	696	608	261	242
April	4 706	4 443	459	390	1 053	739	862	481	690	587	262	240
May	4 198	3 878	376	363	900	577	713	400	640	567	320	237
June	4 165	3 851	364	348	788	516	714	461	674	556	314	240
July	4 228	3 932	421	303	822	541	733	484	678	534	296	272
August	4 055	3 786	348	282	813	546	700	486	706	586	268	243
September	4 067	3 776	372	301	904	578	688	478	606	539	291	271
October	3 956	3 694	357	280	802	546	699	461	649	529	263	233
November	3 921	3 651	326	287	803	504	721	443	675	559	270	231
December	3 986	3 697	384	255	810	537	666	458	664	555	289	252
2010												
January	3 884	3 612	378	280	741	484	692	432	653	542	272	257
February	3 876	3 585	352	268	760	505	711	434	602	532	291	258
March	3 994	3 694	346	253	848	616	750	440	633	521	300	264
April	3 895	3 607	353	244	798	568	704	472	629	525	288	246
May	3 871	3 559	348	214	760	519	730	419	628	529	312	247
June	4 204	3 664	300	237	819	564	746	462	646	513	540	265
July	4 204	3 762	355	252	812	558	782	495	685	531	442	257
August	3 968	3 536	328	262	763	544	714	438	633	522	433	283
September	3 953	3 573	331	240	783	535	737	488	615	514	380	273
October	3 827	3 566	346	264	751	529	719	420	659	536	261	222
November	3 926	3 615	329	258	806	562	687	464	629	528	311	282
December	4 049	3 754	414	251	751	507	827	464	605	507	294	272
2011												
January	3 854	3 588	309	234	782	528	777	422	634	524	267	239
February	3 854	3 585	315	230	808	534	770	437	590	506	268	243
March	3 971	3 706	339	247	790	556	788	432	689	566	265	239
April	3 744	3 459	353	232	715	514	785	413	611	507	284	254
May	4 001	3 701	338	251	796	555	826	432	657	533	300	272
June	3 959	3 686	365	233	781	531	794	448	662	556	273	239
July	3 963	3 650	309	233	778	544	794	433	688	577	314	283
August	4 073	3 787	336	240	798	550	840	459	702	584	286	253
September	4 075	3 799	338	233	802	563	829	418	729	587	277	246
October	3 961	3 683	311	227	791	530	826	433	652	535	278	246
November	4 081	3 765	320	234	779	526	798	460	716	567	316	278
December	3 994	3 677	295	237	770	517	789	467	696	575	316	284
2012												
January	3 906	3 622	304	211	808	558	700	476	711	580	284	258
February	4 202	3 914	341	237	811	562	906	471	715	570	288	255
March	4 180	3 885	313	220	836	566	849	462	763	622	294	264
April	4 122	3 813	277	238	827	557	806	459	730	578	309	276
May	4 447	4 123	349	248	849	594	964	480	749	618	324	292
June	4 292	3 988	336	266	853	569	895	487	702	600	304	272
July	3 978	3 686	354	222	795	540	766	448	693	587	293	262
August	4 341	4 051	298	248	895	604	895	470	748	635	289	259
September	4 052	3 806	336	239	821	559	846	438	678	573	246	213
October	4 079	3 751	288	220	828	551	784	456	726	613	328	291
November	4 179	3 885	359	229	774	512	849	465	694	584	294	255
December	4 062	3 772	263	231	840	595	813	468	729	604	290	251
2013												
January	4 173	3 872	315	215	854	580	845	486	715	614	302	259
February	4 180	3 884	322	225	863	583	770	482	730	627	296	251
March	4 123	3 819	316	203	820	557	780	482	738	631	304	260
April	4 287	3 987	300	224	857	604	858	518	779	659	300	256
May	4 381	4 081	306	249	883	613	848	544	734	626	300	261
June	4 228	3 913	310	224	789	549	891	480	740	633	315	281
July	4 273	3 992	292	238	838	568	934	490	731	612	281	247
August	4 405	4 138	297	246	917	650	947	516	720	619	267	235
September	4 477	4 203	279	246	872	619	959	515	814	671	274	241
October	4 249	3 911	280	214	875	597	805	485	776	651	338	297

[1]Total separations are the number of separations during the entire month.
[2]The total separations rate is the number of total separations during the entire month as a percent of total employment.
[3]Detail will not necessarily add to totals because of the independent seasonal adjustment of the various series.
[4]Includes natural resources and mining, information, financial activities, and other services, not shown separately.
[5]Includes wholesale trade and transportation, warehousing, and utilities, not shown separately.
[6]Includes arts, entertainment, and recreation, not shown separately.
[7]Includes federal government, not shown separately.

Table 7-9. Separations Levels[1] and Rates,[2] by Industry, 2002–October 2013—*Continued*

(Seasonally adjusted, levels in thousands, rates per 100.)

Year and month	Rate											
	Total[4]	Total private[4]	Construction	Manufacturing	Trade, transportation, and utilities[5]	Retail trade	Professional and business services	Education and health services	Leisure and hospitality[6]	Accommodation and food services	Government[7]	State and local government
2008												
January	3.6	4.1	5.4	2.7	3.9	4.7	5.1	2.7	6.6	6.5	1.3	1.3
February	3.6	4.1	5.4	2.7	4.0	4.8	4.9	2.7	7.1	7.0	1.3	1.3
March	3.5	3.9	5.4	2.6	3.7	4.4	5.0	2.7	6.3	6.3	1.3	1.4
April	3.8	4.2	6.3	2.9	4.2	5.1	5.3	2.9	6.3	6.4	1.3	1.4
May	3.5	3.9	5.7	2.6	3.8	4.5	4.6	2.7	6.7	6.7	1.2	1.3
June	3.6	4.0	6.3	2.8	4.1	4.8	5.2	2.5	6.1	6.2	1.2	1.3
July	3.4	3.9	5.8	2.5	3.9	4.7	5.0	2.5	6.0	6.0	1.1	1.2
August	3.6	4.0	6.1	2.5	4.1	4.9	4.9	2.6	6.4	6.1	1.3	1.4
September	3.5	3.9	5.9	2.8	4.0	4.6	4.9	2.4	6.1	6.1	1.3	1.4
October	3.6	4.1	6.5	3.1	4.0	4.7	5.2	2.7	6.0	6.1	1.3	1.4
November	3.5	3.9	7.0	2.8	3.8	4.5	5.2	2.4	5.6	5.7	1.2	1.2
December	3.6	4.1	6.8	3.3	4.0	4.7	5.4	2.5	5.5	5.5	1.2	1.2
2009												
January	3.7	4.2	7.3	4.0	3.9	4.3	5.1	2.6	5.6	5.5	1.3	1.4
February	3.5	4.0	6.8	3.5	3.5	3.9	5.2	2.6	5.6	5.6	1.2	1.3
March	3.5	4.0	7.0	3.5	3.9	4.3	4.6	2.4	5.3	5.4	1.2	1.2
April	3.6	4.1	7.5	3.2	4.2	5.1	5.2	2.5	5.3	5.3	1.2	1.2
May	3.2	3.6	6.2	3.1	3.6	4.0	4.3	2.1	4.9	5.1	1.4	1.2
June	3.2	3.6	6.1	3.0	3.2	3.6	4.3	2.4	5.2	5.0	1.4	1.2
July	3.2	3.7	7.1	2.6	3.3	3.7	4.5	2.5	5.2	4.8	1.3	1.4
August	3.1	3.5	6.0	2.4	3.3	3.8	4.3	2.5	5.4	5.3	1.2	1.2
September	3.1	3.5	6.4	2.6	3.7	4.0	4.2	2.5	4.6	4.8	1.3	1.4
October	3.1	3.4	6.2	2.4	3.3	3.8	4.3	2.4	5.0	4.8	1.2	1.2
November	3.0	3.4	5.7	2.5	3.3	3.5	4.4	2.3	5.2	5.0	1.2	1.2
December	3.1	3.5	6.8	2.2	3.3	3.7	4.0	2.4	5.1	5.0	1.3	1.3
2010												
January	3.0	3.4	6.8	2.4	3.0	3.4	4.2	2.2	5.0	4.9	1.2	1.3
February	3.0	3.4	6.4	2.3	3.1	3.5	4.3	2.2	4.7	4.8	1.3	1.3
March	3.1	3.5	6.2	2.2	3.5	4.3	4.5	2.3	4.9	4.7	1.3	1.3
April	3.0	3.4	6.4	2.1	3.2	3.9	4.2	2.4	4.8	4.7	1.3	1.3
May	3.0	3.3	6.3	1.9	3.1	3.6	4.4	2.2	4.8	4.8	1.4	1.3
June	3.2	3.4	5.4	2.1	3.3	3.9	4.5	2.4	5.0	4.6	2.4	1.4
July	3.2	3.5	6.4	2.2	3.3	3.9	4.7	2.5	5.2	4.8	2.0	1.3
August	3.1	3.3	5.9	2.3	3.1	3.8	4.3	2.2	4.8	4.7	1.9	1.5
September	3.0	3.3	6.0	2.1	3.2	3.7	4.4	2.5	4.7	4.6	1.7	1.4
October	2.9	3.3	6.3	2.3	3.0	3.6	4.3	2.1	5.0	4.8	1.2	1.1
November	3.0	3.3	6.0	2.2	3.3	3.9	4.1	2.4	4.8	4.7	1.4	1.5
December	3.1	3.5	7.6	2.2	3.0	3.5	4.9	2.4	4.6	4.5	1.3	1.4
2011												
January	3.0	3.3	5.7	2.0	3.2	3.6	4.6	2.1	4.8	4.7	1.2	1.2
February	2.9	3.3	5.8	2.0	3.2	3.7	4.5	2.2	4.5	4.5	1.2	1.3
March	3.0	3.4	6.2	2.1	3.2	3.8	4.6	2.2	5.2	5.0	1.2	1.2
April	2.9	3.2	6.4	2.0	2.9	3.5	4.6	2.1	4.6	4.5	1.3	1.3
May	3.0	3.4	6.1	2.1	3.2	3.8	4.8	2.2	4.9	4.7	1.4	1.4
June	3.0	3.4	6.6	2.0	3.1	3.6	4.6	2.3	5.0	4.9	1.2	1.2
July	3.0	3.3	5.6	2.0	3.1	3.7	4.6	2.2	5.1	5.0	1.4	1.5
August	3.1	3.5	6.1	2.0	3.2	3.7	4.8	2.3	5.2	5.1	1.3	1.3
September	3.1	3.5	6.1	2.0	3.2	3.8	4.7	2.1	5.4	5.1	1.3	1.3
October	3.0	3.3	5.6	1.9	3.1	3.6	4.7	2.2	4.8	4.6	1.3	1.3
November	3.1	3.4	5.7	2.0	3.1	3.6	4.6	2.3	5.3	4.9	1.4	1.5
December	3.0	3.3	5.3	2.0	3.0	3.5	4.5	2.3	5.1	5.0	1.4	1.5
2012												
January	2.9	3.3	5.4	1.8	3.2	3.8	4.0	2.4	5.2	5.0	1.3	1.4
February	3.2	3.5	6.0	2.0	3.2	3.8	5.1	2.3	5.2	4.9	1.3	1.3
March	3.1	3.5	5.6	1.8	3.3	3.8	4.8	2.3	5.6	5.3	1.3	1.4
April	3.1	3.4	4.9	2.0	3.3	3.8	4.5	2.3	5.3	4.9	1.4	1.4
May	3.3	3.7	6.2	2.1	3.3	4.0	5.4	2.4	5.5	5.3	1.5	1.5
June	3.2	3.6	6.0	2.2	3.4	3.8	5.0	2.4	5.1	5.1	1.4	1.4
July	3.0	3.3	6.3	1.9	3.1	3.6	4.3	2.2	5.0	5.0	1.3	1.4
August	3.2	3.6	5.3	2.1	3.5	4.1	5.0	2.3	5.4	5.4	1.3	1.4
September	3.0	3.4	6.0	2.0	3.2	3.8	4.7	2.1	4.9	4.8	1.1	1.1
October	3.0	3.3	5.1	1.8	3.2	3.7	4.3	2.2	5.2	5.2	1.5	1.5
November	3.1	3.5	6.3	1.9	3.0	3.4	4.7	2.3	5.0	4.9	1.3	1.3
December	3.0	3.3	4.6	1.9	3.3	4.0	4.5	2.3	5.2	5.1	1.3	1.3
2013												
January	3.1	3.4	5.5	1.8	3.3	3.9	4.7	2.4	5.1	5.1	1.4	1.4
February	3.1	3.4	5.6	1.9	3.3	3.9	4.2	2.3	5.2	5.2	1.4	1.3
March	3.0	3.4	5.4	1.7	3.2	3.7	4.2	2.3	5.3	5.2	1.4	1.4
April	3.2	3.5	5.2	1.9	3.3	4.0	4.7	2.5	5.5	5.5	1.4	1.3
May	3.2	3.6	5.3	2.1	3.4	4.1	4.6	2.6	5.2	5.2	1.4	1.4
June	3.1	3.4	5.3	1.9	3.0	3.6	4.8	2.3	5.2	5.2	1.4	1.5
July	3.1	3.5	5.0	2.0	3.2	3.7	5.0	2.4	5.2	5.0	1.3	1.3
August	3.2	3.6	5.1	2.1	3.5	4.3	5.1	2.5	5.1	5.1	1.2	1.2
September	3.3	3.7	4.8	2.1	3.3	4.1	5.1	2.5	5.7	5.5	1.3	1.3
October	3.1	3.4	4.8	1.8	3.3	3.9	4.3	2.3	5.4	5.3	1.5	1.5

[1]Total separations are the number of separations during the entire month.
[2]The total separations rate is the number of total separations during the entire month as a percent of total employment.
[4]Includes natural resources and mining, information, financial activities, and other services, not shown separately.
[5]Includes wholesale trade and transportation, warehousing, and utilities, not shown separately.
[6]Includes arts, entertainment, and recreation, not shown separately.
[7]Includes federal government, not shown separately.

Table 7-10. Quits Levels[1] and Rates,[2] by Industry, 2002–October 2013

(Seasonally adjusted, levels in thousands, rates per 100.)

Year and month	Level[3]											
	Total[4]	Total private[4]	Construction	Manufacturing	Trade, transportation, and utilities[5]	Retail trade	Professional and business services	Education and health services	Leisure and hospitality[6]	Accommodation and food services	Government[7]	State and local government
2002												
January	2 824	2 675	165	177	647	470	544	268	564	494	149	128
February	2 706	2 534	166	187	553	409	512	264	540	473	172	152
March	2 583	2 453	139	187	558	417	521	226	538	474	130	110
April	2 715	2 540	173	197	575	397	486	272	560	496	175	156
May	2 654	2 519	155	197	540	390	514	279	525	461	135	120
June	2 591	2 442	126	198	623	470	422	259	506	453	149	122
July	2 639	2 500	169	194	576	419	459	287	510	462	139	120
August	2 617	2 475	157	195	570	413	482	272	497	453	142	122
September	2 630	2 485	171	189	551	414	501	244	517	457	145	125
October	2 551	2 405	144	169	559	389	491	275	483	437	145	126
November	2 503	2 342	106	175	565	442	480	265	472	442	161	140
December	2 658	2 510	146	155	532	409	562	298	489	444	149	121
2003												
January	2 492	2 357	142	174	519	384	451	276	483	437	135	117
February	2 511	2 376	140	166	554	430	443	263	512	465	134	116
March	2 426	2 289	128	156	555	396	415	244	483	439	137	119
April	2 352	2 222	91	164	511	378	428	239	480	443	130	110
May	2 318	2 184	154	178	527	398	338	255	443	412	134	115
June	2 333	2 214	156	164	493	370	398	264	487	441	120	103
July	2 333	2 195	144	182	509	377	397	231	497	450	138	119
August	2 307	2 167	153	168	502	370	370	261	480	429	139	119
September	2 469	2 336	138	171	561	410	368	299	487	433	133	117
October	2 454	2 323	145	169	575	422	369	274	513	463	131	115
November	2 428	2 301	164	179	539	370	342	256	500	438	127	113
December	2 461	2 323	191	195	521	366	393	272	466	424	137	122
2004												
January	2 411	2 274	152	191	556	428	345	279	457	422	137	119
February	2 434	2 285	160	186	541	405	355	268	474	448	149	126
March	2 620	2 483	170	197	571	433	444	277	519	478	138	122
April	2 609	2 467	170	202	612	478	362	278	518	463	141	131
May	2 436	2 298	156	173	536	387	316	270	536	498	138	121
June	2 665	2 524	185	194	578	423	443	268	499	460	141	129
July	2 673	2 538	137	191	613	451	435	305	506	459	135	123
August	2 588	2 459	157	171	601	471	453	268	521	478	129	118
September	2 603	2 468	167	208	590	437	442	264	497	454	135	124
October	2 623	2 496	165	182	612	457	441	256	495	451	127	112
November	2 854	2 718	173	210	664	501	492	281	580	528	136	121
December	2 745	2 599	160	210	579	419	479	277	541	492	146	133
2005												
January	2 832	2 696	181	190	645	460	469	286	578	521	136	124
February	2 703	2 557	174	187	584	429	488	294	506	453	146	131
March	2 847	2 695	202	188	666	489	468	310	531	476	152	138
April	2 821	2 682	163	191	632	478	516	319	528	472	140	126
May	2 820	2 678	180	177	648	500	484	292	566	509	142	130
June	2 784	2 633	165	200	646	481	468	299	529	473	150	134
July	2 771	2 656	177	196	632	474	414	300	609	551	116	102
August	2 972	2 825	200	195	677	500	481	297	608	558	147	133
September	3 066	2 911	239	207	641	466	522	318	640	587	155	137
October	2 970	2 805	226	222	641	477	412	298	696	621	166	148
November	2 934	2 774	195	199	657	493	407	305	634	586	160	142
December	2 864	2 718	229	185	713	528	419	295	572	520	146	126
2006												
January	2 886	2 732	211	189	622	473	456	266	663	592	155	141
February	3 011	2 852	199	204	683	514	456	303	653	604	158	138
March	3 025	2 864	202	208	696	523	484	285	630	573	161	137
April	2 776	2 613	203	178	683	506	480	289	542	490	162	137
May	3 042	2 862	212	222	690	506	494	320	605	556	179	154
June	3 005	2 836	203	185	648	477	469	336	644	590	169	144
July	2 965	2 803	184	214	685	522	464	319	578	537	161	135
August	2 975	2 802	169	205	702	476	483	320	595	551	173	144
September	2 920	2 755	170	179	641	467	541	290	591	551	165	124
October	2 955	2 794	169	202	635	466	526	315	606	552	161	143
November	3 139	2 972	160	230	738	542	534	310	650	586	167	142
December	3 129	2 963	171	246	680	491	547	343	659	598	166	145
2007												
January	2 990	2 826	163	241	651	465	533	301	618	573	164	148
February	2 993	2 839	143	211	686	489	513	316	635	580	154	133
March	3 008	2 833	143	225	654	467	514	304	618	559	176	147
April	2 903	2 736	153	205	662	477	468	308	635	586	168	144
May	3 006	2 827	160	212	681	487	465	336	615	571	180	153
June	2 836	2 673	135	198	658	467	458	289	627	575	163	136
July	2 880	2 715	182	189	584	433	483	318	639	585	165	135
August	2 892	2 741	166	209	604	447	464	311	632	569	151	127
September	2 597	2 440	138	188	606	450	457	262	471	421	158	126
October	2 845	2 692	162	198	625	457	462	290	625	574	153	138
November	2 793	2 642	160	189	541	404	475	312	663	608	151	138
December	2 876	2 741	160	212	677	513	437	291	638	574	135	125

[1]Quits are the number of quits during the entire month.
[2]The quits rate is the number of quits during the entire month as a percent of total employment.
[3]Detail will not necessarily add to totals because of the independent seasonal adjustment of the various series.
[4]Includes natural resources and mining, information, financial activities, and other services, not shown separately.
[5]Includes wholesale trade and transportation, warehousing, and utilities, not shown separately.
[6]Includes arts, entertainment, and recreation, not shown separately.
[7]Includes federal government, not shown separately.

Table 7-10. Quits Levels[1] and Rates,[2] by Industry, 2002–October 2013—*Continued*

(Seasonally adjusted, levels in thousands, rates per 100.)

Year and month	Rate											
	Total[4]	Total private[4]	Construction	Manufacturing	Trade, transportation, and utilities[5]	Retail trade	Professional and business services	Education and health services	Leisure and hospitality[6]	Accommodation and food services	Government[7]	State and local government
2002												
January	2.2	2.4	2.4	1.1	2.5	3.1	3.4	1.7	4.7	4.8	0.7	0.7
February	2.1	2.3	2.5	1.2	2.2	2.7	3.2	1.6	4.5	4.7	0.8	0.8
March	2.0	2.3	2.1	1.2	2.2	2.8	3.3	1.4	4.5	4.7	0.6	0.6
April	2.1	2.3	2.6	1.3	2.3	2.6	3.0	1.7	4.7	4.9	0.8	0.8
May	2.0	2.3	2.3	1.3	2.1	2.6	3.2	1.7	4.4	4.5	0.6	0.6
June	2.0	2.2	1.9	1.3	2.4	3.1	2.6	1.6	4.3	4.5	0.7	0.7
July	2.0	2.3	2.5	1.3	2.3	2.8	2.9	1.8	4.3	4.5	0.6	0.6
August	2.0	2.3	2.3	1.3	2.2	2.8	3.0	1.7	4.2	4.4	0.7	0.6
September	2.0	2.3	2.5	1.2	2.2	2.8	3.1	1.5	4.3	4.5	0.7	0.7
October	2.0	2.2	2.2	1.1	2.2	2.6	3.1	1.7	4.0	4.2	0.7	0.7
November	1.9	2.2	1.6	1.2	2.2	3.0	3.0	1.6	3.9	4.3	0.7	0.7
December	2.0	2.3	2.2	1.0	2.1	2.7	3.5	1.8	4.0	4.3	0.7	0.6
2003												
January	1.9	2.2	2.1	1.2	2.0	2.6	2.8	1.7	4.0	4.2	0.6	0.6
February	1.9	2.2	2.1	1.1	2.2	2.9	2.8	1.6	4.2	4.5	0.6	0.6
March	1.9	2.1	1.9	1.1	2.2	2.7	2.6	1.5	4.0	4.3	0.6	0.6
April	1.8	2.1	1.4	1.1	2.0	2.5	2.7	1.4	4.0	4.3	0.6	0.6
May	1.8	2.0	2.3	1.2	2.1	2.7	2.1	1.5	3.7	4.0	0.6	0.6
June	1.8	2.0	2.3	1.1	2.0	2.5	2.5	1.6	4.0	4.3	0.6	0.5
July	1.8	2.0	2.1	1.3	2.0	2.5	2.5	1.4	4.1	4.4	0.6	0.6
August	1.8	2.0	2.3	1.2	2.0	2.5	2.3	1.6	3.9	4.1	0.6	0.6
September	1.9	2.2	2.0	1.2	2.2	2.7	2.3	1.8	4.0	4.2	0.6	0.6
October	1.9	2.1	2.1	1.2	2.3	2.8	2.3	1.6	4.2	4.4	0.6	0.6
November	1.9	2.1	2.4	1.2	2.1	2.5	2.1	1.5	4.1	4.2	0.6	0.6
December	1.9	2.1	2.8	1.4	2.1	2.4	2.4	1.6	3.8	4.0	0.6	0.7
2004												
January	1.8	2.1	2.2	1.3	2.2	2.9	2.1	1.7	3.7	4.0	0.6	0.6
February	1.9	2.1	2.3	1.3	2.1	2.7	2.2	1.6	3.8	4.3	0.7	0.7
March	2.0	2.3	2.5	1.4	2.2	2.9	2.7	1.6	4.2	4.5	0.6	0.6
April	2.0	2.3	2.5	1.4	2.4	3.2	2.2	1.6	4.2	4.4	0.7	0.7
May	1.9	2.1	2.2	1.2	2.1	2.6	1.9	1.6	4.3	4.7	0.6	0.6
June	2.0	2.3	2.7	1.4	2.3	2.8	2.7	1.6	4.0	4.3	0.7	0.7
July	2.0	2.3	2.0	1.3	2.4	3.0	2.6	1.8	4.0	4.3	0.6	0.7
August	2.0	2.2	2.2	1.2	2.4	3.1	2.8	1.6	4.2	4.5	0.6	0.6
September	2.0	2.2	2.4	1.5	2.3	2.9	2.7	1.6	4.0	4.2	0.6	0.7
October	2.0	2.3	2.3	1.3	2.4	3.0	2.7	1.5	3.9	4.2	0.6	0.6
November	2.2	2.5	2.4	1.5	2.6	3.3	3.0	1.6	4.6	4.9	0.6	0.6
December	2.1	2.3	2.3	1.5	2.3	2.8	2.9	1.6	4.3	4.6	0.7	0.7
2005												
January	2.1	2.4	2.5	1.3	2.5	3.0	2.8	1.7	4.6	4.8	0.6	0.7
February	2.0	2.3	2.4	1.3	2.3	2.8	2.9	1.7	4.0	4.2	0.7	0.7
March	2.1	2.4	2.8	1.3	2.6	3.2	2.8	1.8	4.2	4.4	0.7	0.7
April	2.1	2.4	2.2	1.3	2.4	3.1	3.1	1.8	4.1	4.3	0.6	0.7
May	2.1	2.4	2.5	1.2	2.5	3.3	2.9	1.7	4.4	4.7	0.7	0.7
June	2.1	2.4	2.3	1.4	2.5	3.1	2.8	1.7	4.1	4.3	0.7	0.7
July	2.1	2.4	2.4	1.4	2.4	3.1	2.4	1.7	4.7	5.0	0.5	0.5
August	2.2	2.5	2.7	1.4	2.6	3.3	2.8	1.7	4.7	5.1	0.7	0.7
September	2.3	2.6	3.2	1.5	2.5	3.0	3.1	1.8	5.0	5.4	0.7	0.7
October	2.2	2.5	3.0	1.6	2.5	3.1	2.4	1.7	5.4	5.7	0.8	0.8
November	2.2	2.5	2.6	1.4	2.5	3.2	2.4	1.7	4.9	5.3	0.7	0.7
December	2.1	2.4	3.0	1.3	2.7	3.4	2.4	1.7	4.4	4.7	0.7	0.7
2006												
January	2.1	2.4	2.8	1.3	2.4	3.1	2.6	1.5	5.1	5.4	0.7	0.7
February	2.2	2.5	2.6	1.4	2.6	3.3	2.6	1.7	5.0	5.4	0.7	0.7
March	2.2	2.5	2.6	1.5	2.7	3.4	2.8	1.6	4.8	5.2	0.7	0.7
April	2.0	2.3	2.6	1.3	2.6	3.3	2.8	1.6	4.1	4.4	0.7	0.7
May	2.2	2.5	2.7	1.6	2.6	3.3	2.8	1.8	4.6	5.0	0.8	0.8
June	2.2	2.5	2.6	1.3	2.5	3.1	2.7	1.9	4.9	5.3	0.8	0.7
July	2.2	2.5	2.4	1.5	2.6	3.4	2.6	1.8	4.4	4.8	0.7	0.7
August	2.2	2.4	2.2	1.4	2.7	3.1	2.7	1.8	4.5	4.9	0.8	0.7
September	2.1	2.4	2.2	1.3	2.4	3.0	3.1	1.6	4.5	4.9	0.7	0.6
October	2.2	2.4	2.2	1.4	2.4	3.0	3.0	1.8	4.6	4.9	0.7	0.7
November	2.3	2.6	2.1	1.6	2.8	3.5	3.0	1.7	4.9	5.2	0.8	0.7
December	2.3	2.6	2.2	1.8	2.6	3.2	3.1	1.9	5.0	5.3	0.8	0.7
2007												
January	2.2	2.5	2.1	1.7	2.5	3.0	3.0	1.7	4.6	5.0	0.7	0.8
February	2.2	2.5	1.9	1.5	2.6	3.2	2.9	1.7	4.8	5.1	0.7	0.7
March	2.2	2.5	1.9	1.6	2.5	3.0	2.9	1.7	4.6	4.9	0.8	0.8
April	2.1	2.4	2.0	1.5	2.5	3.1	2.6	1.7	4.7	5.1	0.8	0.7
May	2.2	2.4	2.1	1.5	2.6	3.1	2.6	1.8	4.6	5.0	0.8	0.8
June	2.1	2.3	1.8	1.4	2.5	3.0	2.6	1.6	4.7	5.0	0.7	0.7
July	2.1	2.4	2.4	1.4	2.2	2.8	2.7	1.7	4.8	5.1	0.7	0.7
August	2.1	2.4	2.2	1.5	2.3	2.9	2.6	1.7	4.7	5.0	0.7	0.7
September	1.9	2.1	1.8	1.4	2.3	2.9	2.5	1.4	3.5	3.7	0.7	0.6
October	2.1	2.3	2.1	1.4	2.3	2.9	2.6	1.6	4.6	5.0	0.7	0.7
November	2.0	2.3	2.1	1.4	2.0	2.6	2.6	1.7	4.9	5.3	0.7	0.7
December	2.1	2.4	2.1	1.5	2.5	3.3	2.4	1.6	4.7	5.0	0.6	0.6

[1]Quits are the number of quits during the entire month.
[2]The quits rate is the number of quits during the entire month as a percent of total employment.
[4]Includes natural resources and mining, information, financial activities, and other services, not shown separately.
[5]Includes wholesale trade and transportation, warehousing, and utilities, not shown separately.
[6]Includes arts, entertainment, and recreation, not shown separately.
[7]Includes federal government, not shown separately.

Table 7-10. Quits Levels[1] and Rates,[2] by Industry, 2002–October 2013—*Continued*

(Seasonally adjusted, levels in thousands, rates per 100.)

Year and month	Level[3]											
	Total[4]	Total private[4]	Construc-tion	Manufac-turing	Trade, transpor-tation, and utilities[5]	Retail trade	Profes-sional and business services	Education and health services	Leisure and hospitality[6]	Accommo-dation and food services	Govern-ment[7]	State and local govern-ment
2008												
January	2 860	2 720	144	197	658	481	444	316	612	545	140	128
February	2 839	2 697	164	193	615	433	484	303	603	554	141	130
March	2 610	2 480	111	187	572	410	403	315	593	550	130	121
April	2 904	2 754	169	180	626	451	532	335	593	545	151	141
May	2 666	2 531	134	157	595	415	466	268	625	575	135	128
June	2 645	2 512	143	159	575	414	474	283	572	530	133	126
July	2 472	2 345	148	142	539	393	443	293	551	498	127	120
August	2 447	2 298	160	141	557	413	355	280	517	476	149	140
September	2 447	2 316	110	149	556	413	406	277	534	487	131	124
October	2 414	2 291	109	140	542	379	441	286	523	485	123	116
November	2 106	1 994	89	123	492	361	364	250	458	429	113	108
December	2 086	1 960	84	101	508	363	364	236	445	419	126	118
2009												
January	1 986	1 880	82	109	451	339	356	241	429	402	106	100
February	1 906	1 806	86	102	374	281	286	263	424	390	100	97
March	1 830	1 729	84	85	434	319	277	234	393	363	101	98
April	1 765	1 666	68	82	368	266	300	229	393	355	99	95
May	1 739	1 640	79	86	371	272	297	235	376	338	99	89
June	1 742	1 647	78	88	374	285	274	255	382	337	95	89
July	1 702	1 592	69	87	386	283	262	237	368	330	110	106
August	1 673	1 573	63	80	385	290	254	241	385	347	100	89
September	1 601	1 509	72	93	369	262	255	257	296	284	92	86
October	1 669	1 572	56	76	374	276	274	257	351	320	98	94
November	1 772	1 672	84	72	401	271	272	250	390	350	100	91
December	1 717	1 606	83	71	375	284	268	258	361	330	111	99
2010												
January	1 694	1 591	95	82	340	243	273	238	399	343	103	99
February	1 765	1 651	75	102	400	305	287	232	376	344	114	103
March	1 793	1 681	80	86	388	289	302	235	367	336	112	100
April	1 890	1 789	67	93	449	345	305	286	374	337	101	93
May	1 773	1 676	59	84	410	309	294	237	376	342	96	84
June	1 891	1 764	65	96	406	306	357	259	346	318	127	101
July	1 839	1 722	73	95	423	325	330	241	368	339	117	96
August	1 817	1 702	86	105	390	285	335	231	372	337	115	98
September	1 893	1 777	83	97	426	328	340	247	370	331	116	104
October	1 882	1 777	74	98	405	317	368	248	390	337	104	96
November	1 823	1 718	53	99	432	330	301	254	370	329	105	96
December	1 960	1 852	93	101	400	297	366	244	393	351	107	100
2011												
January	1 813	1 700	62	100	374	267	361	231	375	338	113	104
February	1 906	1 797	67	93	447	306	381	233	363	324	109	102
March	1 943	1 840	72	109	434	330	371	250	394	350	104	96
April	1 864	1 759	102	105	408	314	356	237	380	340	105	96
May	1 956	1 836	85	107	467	352	356	248	372	333	120	112
June	1 863	1 762	77	105	431	328	335	236	399	358	101	92
July	1 956	1 816	70	104	407	305	383	233	393	351	140	131
August	2 036	1 914	70	96	436	329	389	265	439	393	123	113
September	2 020	1 912	79	99	452	333	391	243	421	374	108	98
October	1 928	1 815	74	108	450	328	357	236	371	330	113	101
November	2 009	1 881	102	118	419	297	371	240	389	352	128	118
December	1 995	1 859	67	110	452	335	363	253	398	348	136	126
2012												
January	1 964	1 840	64	95	446	326	369	260	393	351	124	114
February	2 106	1 986	79	104	476	353	385	297	424	370	119	107
March	2 152	2 021	76	104	467	336	392	272	471	422	131	119
April	2 080	1 940	75	114	455	332	383	258	433	390	141	129
May	2 151	2 019	79	113	446	324	427	263	457	404	132	120
June	2 148	2 016	82	111	481	339	389	264	452	403	132	123
July	2 093	1 964	82	106	468	341	369	270	430	385	129	118
August	2 139	2 013	74	111	468	327	376	275	432	391	126	117
September	1 976	1 870	77	107	446	328	372	242	396	364	106	97
October	2 079	1 929	93	96	461	318	360	255	437	394	150	137
November	2 140	2 010	90	106	465	344	394	280	442	400	130	119
December	2 126	1 999	68	116	452	328	413	273	451	413	127	115
2013												
January	2 260	2 128	134	98	491	362	375	299	472	426	132	121
February	2 286	2 159	106	102	501	354	385	289	491	437	127	116
March	2 099	1 967	91	94	446	318	372	281	445	397	131	120
April	2 185	2 040	98	109	470	340	410	283	454	412	146	134
May	2 233	2 098	103	112	453	321	418	283	464	422	135	124
June	2 205	2 063	106	99	461	329	455	286	436	390	142	131
July	2 342	2 208	100	114	459	347	541	285	454	406	134	122
August	2 364	2 240	102	106	527	406	490	288	453	407	124	113
September	2 327	2 217	96	123	533	403	453	297	474	431	111	100
October	2 385	2 255	85	108	565	402	426	285	527	483	131	117

[1]Quits are the number of quits during the entire month.
[2]The quits rate is the number of quits during the entire month as a percent of total employment.
[3]Detail will not necessarily add to totals because of the independent seasonal adjustment of the various series.
[4]Includes natural resources and mining, information, financial activities, and other services, not shown separately.
[5]Includes wholesale trade and transportation, warehousing, and utilities, not shown separately.
[6]Includes arts, entertainment, and recreation, not shown separately.
[7]Includes federal government, not shown separately.

Table 7-10. Quits Levels[1] and Rates,[2] by Industry, 2002–October 2013—*Continued*

(Seasonally adjusted, levels in thousands, rates per 100.)

Year and month	Rate											
	Total[4]	Total private[4]	Construction	Manufacturing	Trade, transportation, and utilities[5]	Retail trade	Professional and business services	Education and health services	Leisure and hospitality[6]	Accommodation and food services	Government[7]	State and local government
2008												
January	2.1	2.4	1.9	1.4	2.5	3.1	2.5	1.7	4.5	4.7	0.6	0.7
February	2.1	2.3	2.2	1.4	2.3	2.8	2.7	1.6	4.5	4.8	0.6	0.7
March	1.9	2.1	1.5	1.4	2.1	2.6	2.2	1.7	4.4	4.8	0.6	0.6
April	2.1	2.4	2.3	1.3	2.4	2.9	3.0	1.8	4.4	4.7	0.7	0.7
May	1.9	2.2	1.8	1.2	2.2	2.7	2.6	1.4	4.6	5.0	0.6	0.6
June	1.9	2.2	2.0	1.2	2.2	2.7	2.7	1.5	4.2	4.6	0.6	0.6
July	1.8	2.0	2.1	1.1	2.0	2.6	2.5	1.6	4.1	4.3	0.6	0.6
August	1.8	2.0	2.2	1.1	2.1	2.7	2.0	1.5	3.8	4.1	0.7	0.7
September	1.8	2.0	1.6	1.1	2.1	2.7	2.3	1.5	4.0	4.3	0.6	0.6
October	1.8	2.0	1.6	1.1	2.1	2.5	2.5	1.5	3.9	4.3	0.5	0.6
November	1.6	1.8	1.3	0.9	1.9	2.4	2.1	1.3	3.4	3.8	0.5	0.5
December	1.6	1.8	1.2	0.8	2.0	2.4	2.1	1.2	3.4	3.7	0.6	0.6
2009												
January	1.5	1.7	1.3	0.9	1.8	2.3	2.1	1.3	3.2	3.6	0.5	0.5
February	1.4	1.6	1.3	0.8	1.5	1.9	1.7	1.4	3.2	3.5	0.4	0.5
March	1.4	1.6	1.3	0.7	1.7	2.2	1.7	1.2	3.0	3.2	0.4	0.5
April	1.3	1.5	1.1	0.7	1.5	1.8	1.8	1.2	3.0	3.2	0.4	0.5
May	1.3	1.5	1.3	0.7	1.5	1.9	1.8	1.2	2.9	3.0	0.4	0.4
June	1.3	1.5	1.3	0.8	1.5	2.0	1.7	1.3	2.9	3.0	0.4	0.5
July	1.3	1.5	1.2	0.7	1.6	2.0	1.6	1.2	2.8	2.9	0.5	0.5
August	1.3	1.5	1.1	0.7	1.6	2.0	1.5	1.3	2.9	3.1	0.4	0.5
September	1.2	1.4	1.2	0.8	1.5	1.8	1.6	1.3	2.3	2.6	0.4	0.4
October	1.3	1.5	1.0	0.7	1.5	1.9	1.7	1.3	2.7	2.9	0.4	0.5
November	1.4	1.6	1.5	0.6	1.6	1.9	1.6	1.3	3.0	3.2	0.4	0.5
December	1.3	1.5	1.5	0.6	1.5	2.0	1.6	1.3	2.8	3.0	0.5	0.5
2010												
January	1.3	1.5	1.7	0.7	1.4	1.7	1.7	1.2	3.1	3.1	0.5	0.5
February	1.4	1.5	1.4	0.9	1.6	2.1	1.7	1.2	2.9	3.1	0.5	0.5
March	1.4	1.6	1.4	0.8	1.6	2.0	1.8	1.2	2.8	3.0	0.5	0.5
April	1.5	1.7	1.2	0.8	1.8	2.4	1.8	1.5	2.9	3.0	0.4	0.5
May	1.4	1.6	1.1	0.7	1.7	2.1	1.8	1.2	2.9	3.1	0.4	0.4
June	1.5	1.6	1.2	0.8	1.7	2.1	2.1	1.3	2.7	2.9	0.6	0.5
July	1.4	1.6	1.3	0.8	1.7	2.3	2.0	1.2	2.8	3.0	0.5	0.5
August	1.4	1.6	1.6	0.9	1.6	2.0	2.0	1.2	2.8	3.0	0.5	0.5
September	1.5	1.7	1.5	0.8	1.7	2.3	2.0	1.3	2.8	3.0	0.5	0.5
October	1.4	1.6	1.4	0.9	1.6	2.2	2.2	1.3	3.0	3.0	0.5	0.5
November	1.4	1.6	1.0	0.9	1.7	2.3	1.8	1.3	2.8	2.9	0.5	0.5
December	1.5	1.7	1.7	0.9	1.6	2.0	2.1	1.2	3.0	3.1	0.5	0.5
2011												
January	1.4	1.6	1.1	0.9	1.5	1.8	2.1	1.2	2.9	3.0	0.5	0.5
February	1.5	1.7	1.2	0.8	1.8	2.1	2.2	1.2	2.7	2.9	0.5	0.5
March	1.5	1.7	1.3	0.9	1.7	2.3	2.2	1.3	3.0	3.1	0.5	0.5
April	1.4	1.6	1.8	0.9	1.6	2.1	2.1	1.2	2.9	3.0	0.5	0.5
May	1.5	1.7	1.5	0.9	1.9	2.4	2.1	1.3	2.8	2.9	0.5	0.6
June	1.4	1.6	1.4	0.9	1.7	2.2	1.9	1.2	3.0	3.1	0.5	0.5
July	1.5	1.7	1.3	0.9	1.6	2.1	2.2	1.2	2.9	3.1	0.6	0.7
August	1.5	1.7	1.3	0.8	1.7	2.2	2.2	1.3	3.3	3.4	0.6	0.6
September	1.5	1.7	1.4	0.8	1.8	2.3	2.2	1.2	3.1	3.3	0.5	0.5
October	1.5	1.6	1.3	0.9	1.8	2.2	2.0	1.2	2.8	2.9	0.5	0.5
November	1.5	1.7	1.8	1.0	1.7	2.0	2.1	1.2	2.9	3.0	0.6	0.6
December	1.5	1.7	1.2	0.9	1.8	2.3	2.1	1.3	2.9	3.0	0.6	0.7
2012												
January	1.5	1.7	1.1	0.8	1.8	2.2	2.1	1.3	2.9	3.0	0.6	0.6
February	1.6	1.8	1.4	0.9	1.9	2.4	2.2	1.5	3.1	3.2	0.5	0.6
March	1.6	1.8	1.3	0.9	1.8	2.3	2.2	1.3	3.4	3.6	0.6	0.6
April	1.6	1.7	1.3	1.0	1.8	2.2	2.1	1.3	3.2	3.3	0.6	0.7
May	1.6	1.8	1.4	0.9	1.8	2.2	2.4	1.3	3.3	3.4	0.6	0.6
June	1.6	1.8	1.5	0.9	1.9	2.3	2.2	1.3	3.3	3.4	0.6	0.6
July	1.6	1.8	1.5	0.9	1.8	2.3	2.1	1.3	3.1	3.3	0.6	0.6
August	1.6	1.8	1.3	0.9	1.8	2.2	2.1	1.3	3.1	3.3	0.6	0.6
September	1.5	1.7	1.4	0.9	1.7	2.2	2.1	1.2	2.9	3.1	0.5	0.5
October	1.5	1.7	1.7	0.8	1.8	2.1	2.0	1.2	3.2	3.3	0.7	0.7
November	1.6	1.8	1.6	0.9	1.8	2.3	2.2	1.4	3.2	3.4	0.6	0.6
December	1.6	1.8	1.2	1.0	1.8	2.2	2.3	1.3	3.2	3.5	0.6	0.6
2013												
January	1.7	1.9	2.3	0.8	1.9	2.4	2.1	1.5	3.4	3.6	0.6	0.6
February	1.7	1.9	1.8	0.9	1.9	2.4	2.1	1.4	3.5	3.7	0.6	0.6
March	1.6	1.7	1.6	0.8	1.7	2.1	2.0	1.4	3.2	3.3	0.6	0.6
April	1.6	1.8	1.7	0.9	1.8	2.3	2.2	1.4	3.2	3.4	0.7	0.7
May	1.6	1.8	1.8	0.9	1.8	2.1	2.3	1.4	3.3	3.5	0.6	0.6
June	1.6	1.8	1.8	0.8	1.8	2.2	2.5	1.4	3.1	3.2	0.7	0.7
July	1.7	1.9	1.7	1.0	1.8	2.3	2.9	1.4	3.2	3.3	0.6	0.6
August	1.7	2.0	1.8	0.9	2.0	2.7	2.6	1.4	3.2	3.3	0.6	0.6
September	1.7	1.9	1.7	1.0	2.0	2.6	2.4	1.4	3.3	3.5	0.5	0.5
October	1.7	2.0	1.5	0.9	2.2	2.6	2.3	1.4	3.7	3.9	0.6	0.6

[1]Quits are the number of quits during the entire month.
[2]The quits rate is the number of quits during the entire month as a percent of total employment.
[4]Includes natural resources and mining, information, financial activities, and other services, not shown separately.
[5]Includes wholesale trade and transportation, warehousing, and utilities, not shown separately.
[6]Includes arts, entertainment, and recreation, not shown separately.
[7]Includes federal government, not shown separately.

Table 7-11. Layoffs and Discharges Levels and Rates, by Industry, 2002–October 2013

(Not seasonally adjusted, levels in thousands, rates per 100.)

Year and month	Level												
	Total	Total private	Mining and logging	Construc-tion	Manufac-turing	Durable goods	Non-durable goods	Trade, transpor-tation, and utilities	Whole-sale trade	Retail trade	Transpor-tation, ware-housing, and utilities	Infor-mation	Financial activities
2007	22 142	20 834	88	2 837	1 952	1 202	751	4 187	764	2 733	691	284	1 079
2008	24 181	23 030	120	3 430	2 252	1 446	807	4 720	894	3 029	794	362	1 031
2009	26 784	25 175	177	3 744	2 857	1 831	1 025	5 012	1 080	2 873	1 055	380	1 260
2010	21 773	19 727	98	3 113	1 652	953	699	3 712	741	2 309	661	295	783
2011	20 401	19 096	82	2 836	1 318	746	570	3 381	562	2 157	663	273	636
2012	20 546	19 336	134	2 745	1 263	793	469	3 493	621	2 200	674	262	607
2002													
January	2 495	2 429	10	335	318	201	117	605	70	451	84	81	137
February	1 624	1 577	7	253	196	108	88	403	70	263	71	24	55
March	1 432	1 390	10	202	189	132	56	282	59	163	59	36	44
April	1 798	1 740	11	200	231	147	84	329	55	219	55	52	57
May	1 622	1 525	7	212	192	116	76	374	80	257	37	30	75
June	1 725	1 577	5	228	196	118	78	269	49	160	60	40	87
July	2 138	2 003	14	251	211	126	86	334	89	200	44	38	73
August	1 930	1 780	8	234	202	142	61	313	50	206	57	37	81
September	2 017	1 845	6	233	199	127	72	368	65	228	74	25	67
October	2 091	2 012	7	327	244	153	91	353	48	256	49	38	56
November	1 881	1 808	6	296	201	120	82	339	82	201	56	53	68
December	2 169	2 106	10	326	257	140	117	485	75	321	88	29	63
2003													
January	2 602	2 531	14	377	273	167	106	640	84	495	61	69	121
February	1 611	1 558	9	226	187	114	73	358	39	282	37	37	39
March	1 488	1 441	8	223	186	112	75	287	47	197	43	38	65
April	1 819	1 750	7	250	235	144	91	277	59	175	43	20	42
May	1 592	1 491	5	205	139	81	59	291	65	172	54	26	51
June	1 925	1 777	7	206	195	124	71	362	51	227	84	35	48
July	2 023	1 895	8	235	219	125	95	371	87	192	91	28	103
August	2 159	1 968	10	318	154	106	48	349	64	219	65	26	50
September	1 929	1 759	4	285	149	92	57	253	52	154	47	19	73
October	2 147	2 071	6	291	169	99	70	424	80	273	71	31	59
November	1 813	1 722	7	288	165	117	48	344	39	257	49	31	45
December	2 186	2 101	17	273	173	101	72	602	61	417	123	33	58
2004													
January	2 462	2 388	10	331	203	122	81	621	75	458	88	42	77
February	1 559	1 511	8	261	138	79	59	412	69	292	52	30	35
March	1 538	1 484	5	222	149	93	55	309	57	180	72	42	56
April	1 844	1 793	6	200	167	83	84	336	92	194	50	27	47
May	1 521	1 428	6	168	132	66	66	349	60	209	80	32	36
June	1 728	1 561	4	187	134	91	43	280	55	164	62	43	57
July	1 843	1 707	6	216	164	105	59	370	67	237	66	23	47
August	2 139	1 982	8	256	200	138	61	328	76	175	77	20	104
September	2 065	1 868	5	214	150	97	54	311	50	191	70	40	70
October	2 059	1 960	7	302	190	112	78	364	67	220	77	31	81
November	1 864	1 777	9	268	161	106	55	365	63	236	67	20	69
December	2 180	2 074	8	296	158	97	60	626	44	454	128	23	74
2005													
January	2 476	2 405	10	419	207	137	71	566	75	412	78	37	117
February	1 573	1 521	6	238	119	78	41	374	49	262	62	15	70
March	1 595	1 545	5	165	145	81	63	301	38	213	50	23	59
April	1 751	1 690	7	214	166	112	54	326	69	196	61	19	88
May	1 637	1 531	4	216	140	93	47	364	79	181	104	30	57
June	1 811	1 652	5	187	130	80	50	329	46	203	81	18	28
July	1 873	1 749	6	188	133	84	49	355	62	226	66	23	62
August	2 016	1 841	7	257	154	106	48	311	46	209	57	17	53
September	2 050	1 886	8	231	151	89	62	379	34	266	78	19	76
October	1 843	1 759	7	232	151	94	57	352	72	209	71	19	85
November	1 621	1 548	4	237	150	73	77	347	77	185	85	25	60
December	1 939	1 843	8	285	147	81	66	524	78	283	164	21	61
2006													
January	2 167	2 081	5	334	172	84	88	570	57	427	86	17	87
February	1 420	1 369	6	181	116	63	52	328	60	235	33	18	61
March	1 353	1 288	8	178	157	86	71	255	38	158	59	16	72
April	1 672	1 608	10	143	142	65	77	298	52	217	29	35	80
May	1 672	1 561	3	177	143	87	57	329	56	216	57	12	50
June	1 687	1 479	2	127	142	76	66	349	47	241	62	15	52
July	1 798	1 645	4	199	143	89	55	334	98	181	54	20	73
August	1 741	1 595	6	211	144	87	57	312	47	206	60	19	80
September	1 840	1 666	9	194	162	101	61	313	53	195	65	16	67
October	1 970	1 876	5	257	154	95	59	338	67	206	65	30	73
November	1 864	1 787	6	322	147	96	51	304	51	203	51	21	66
December	1 973	1 887	7	293	157	91	66	463	45	337	81	26	84
2007													
January	2 197	2 111	10	317	189	118	72	546	55	388	103	53	99
February	1 449	1 399	5	224	154	98	57	266	34	193	39	26	73
March	1 446	1 395	4	154	138	90	48	260	50	153	58	19	100
April	1 776	1 715	6	207	144	88	56	296	61	173	62	18	92
May	1 524	1 406	6	181	129	77	52	299	54	203	42	22	72
June	1 727	1 560	4	205	141	88	53	261	47	171	42	18	63
July	1 855	1 642	6	186	178	108	70	345	88	200	57	32	105
August	1 990	1 808	9	260	159	96	63	333	70	217	46	27	98
September	2 173	2 034	8	262	172	108	64	341	67	232	43	15	109
October	2 053	1 971	9	264	198	123	75	382	82	239	61	19	103
November	1 940	1 880	11	277	192	119	73	413	69	261	83	16	72
December	2 012	1 913	10	300	158	89	68	445	87	303	55	19	93

Table 7-11. Layoffs and Discharges Levels and Rates, by Industry, 2002–October 2013—*Continued*

(Not seasonally adjusted, levels in thousands, rates per 100.)

Year and month	Finance and insurance	Real estate and rental and leasing	Professional and business services	Education and health services	Educational services	Health care and social assistance	Leisure and hospitality	Arts, entertainment, and recreation	Accommodation and food services	Other services	Government	Federal	State and local government
2007	592	488	4 679	1 711	369	1 341	3 078	864	2 213	936	1 308	219	1 090
2008	616	413	5 041	1 978	382	1 597	3 134	899	2 234	958	1 152	103	1 050
2009	690	569	5 016	2 182	452	1 728	3 316	832	2 483	1 230	1 610	224	1 383
2010	460	324	4 330	2 087	396	1 691	2 739	785	1 955	921	2 046	740	1 307
2011	349	291	4 587	1 813	366	1 447	3 090	929	2 159	1 079	1 309	134	1 176
2012	329	280	4 814	1 900	383	1 517	3 070	904	2 165	1 046	1 210	128	1 082
2002													
January	108	30	436	180	32	148	233	59	174	93	66	16	50
February	40	15	312	104	8	96	185	26	159	38	47	7	40
March	24	19	330	123	18	105	142	32	109	33	42	10	32
April	39	18	373	129	20	109	271	91	180	86	58	10	49
May	56	19	313	123	22	101	159	24	135	40	97	6	91
June	61	26	304	156	27	130	215	25	190	77	149	9	140
July	41	32	460	169	28	140	346	109	236	107	135	12	124
August	43	38	324	149	26	122	303	131	171	130	150	8	142
September	28	40	372	141	34	108	360	131	229	73	172	15	158
October	29	27	494	115	10	105	330	65	265	49	78	11	67
November	35	33	401	71	3	68	328	118	209	45	73	13	60
December	36	27	543	112	23	89	228	63	165	52	63	7	56
2003													
January	64	56	476	143	15	128	325	91	234	93	71	13	57
February	29	9	355	101	13	88	178	48	130	68	53	8	45
March	34	31	288	105	9	96	199	56	143	43	47	6	41
April	24	17	438	108	20	88	303	111	192	71	69	8	62
May	31	20	313	160	35	125	264	77	187	37	101	11	90
June	23	25	383	218	66	151	210	27	183	113	148	10	137
July	48	56	418	227	70	157	184	33	151	102	128	10	117
August	27	23	442	191	55	136	271	104	167	156	191	12	180
September	40	33	376	119	19	100	397	158	239	85	170	13	157
October	37	22	511	131	22	109	370	102	268	79	76	20	57
November	25	21	379	104	16	89	305	99	206	53	91	25	65
December	25	34	464	84	17	67	311	56	255	86	85	5	80
2004													
January	39	38	577	132	20	112	340	74	266	55	74	12	62
February	24	11	262	108	13	95	207	72	134	49	48	9	40
March	28	28	342	110	18	92	210	45	166	40	55	7	48
April	25	22	526	129	14	115	287	93	195	69	51	5	46
May	23	13	324	135	30	106	192	55	136	54	92	9	83
June	27	31	371	166	49	118	271	51	220	46	168	20	147
July	28	19	391	125	24	101	293	61	233	72	136	9	128
August	66	38	381	171	33	138	344	129	215	171	157	11	147
September	34	36	362	172	37	135	454	236	219	90	197	12	185
October	44	37	356	104	8	96	485	131	354	40	98	12	86
November	39	29	413	115	18	97	254	80	174	103	86	7	80
December	31	43	504	127	18	108	209	56	153	50	106	24	82
2005													
January	70	47	507	141	17	124	302	57	245	98	70	10	60
February	26	44	327	116	12	104	196	42	154	59	53	9	44
March	34	25	398	153	22	131	235	36	200	60	50	7	42
April	59	29	444	141	17	125	231	58	173	53	61	10	51
May	33	24	283	159	45	114	196	41	155	83	106	7	99
June	20	9	446	157	30	127	304	54	250	49	159	19	140
July	35	27	562	133	30	103	227	29	198	61	123	14	109
August	41	11	459	166	24	143	250	92	158	169	175	16	159
September	29	47	357	130	34	96	454	250	204	81	165	16	149
October	36	48	419	116	17	99	323	96	226	56	84	8	76
November	20	40	335	94	12	82	260	88	172	35	73	10	63
December	26	35	408	120	35	86	215	59	156	54	96	28	68
2006													
January	50	38	409	145	23	122	270	33	237	72	85	12	74
February	39	21	342	89	8	82	176	34	142	52	51	8	43
March	34	38	283	109	18	91	183	36	147	27	65	12	53
April	43	36	368	141	24	117	230	46	185	161	64	13	51
May	27	23	376	225	52	172	195	67	128	51	111	12	99
June	28	24	358	174	54	121	193	40	153	64	208	24	183
July	31	42	389	178	42	137	227	55	172	77	153	22	131
August	45	35	306	147	28	119	267	98	169	105	146	28	118
September	38	29	351	121	27	94	346	157	189	86	174	25	149
October	33	39	434	114	23	91	379	105	274	93	93	10	84
November	25	41	419	93	13	80	348	99	249	61	77	9	68
December	54	30	463	106	26	80	226	53	173	62	86	15	70
2007													
January	51	48	422	139	34	105	275	76	199	61	86	15	71
February	40	33	340	100	22	78	182	48	134	27	50	13	37
March	50	50	349	134	18	116	188	49	139	49	51	15	37
April	43	49	455	133	23	109	254	89	165	109	61	14	47
May	28	44	286	155	38	117	222	52	169	37	118	16	102
June	45	19	292	216	71	146	255	44	211	104	167	24	143
July	65	40	372	139	21	117	176	28	148	102	213	28	185
August	70	29	341	184	61	123	266	57	209	130	182	26	156
September	61	48	382	156	19	137	455	143	312	135	139	27	112
October	60	42	470	130	15	115	344	114	230	53	82	11	71
November	21	51	461	117	23	94	246	109	137	74	60	9	51
December	58	35	509	108	24	84	215	55	160	55	99	21	78

Table 7-11. Layoffs and Discharges Levels and Rates, by Industry, 2002–October 2013—*Continued*

(Not seasonally adjusted, levels in thousands, rates per 100.)

Year and month	Rate												
	Total	Total private	Mining and logging	Construction	Manufac-turing	Durable goods	Non-durable goods	Trade, transpor-tation, and utilities	Whole-sale trade	Retail trade	Transpor-tation, ware-housing, and utilities	Infor-mation	Financial activities
2007	16.1	18.1	12.2	37.2	14.1	13.6	14.8	15.7	12.7	17.6	13.6	9.4	13.0
2008	17.7	20.2	15.7	47.9	16.8	17.1	16.3	18.0	15.0	19.8	15.7	12.1	12.7
2009	20.5	23.3	25.5	62.2	24.1	25.1	22.5	20.1	19.3	19.8	22.0	13.6	16.2
2010	16.8	18.4	13.9	56.4	14.3	13.5	15.7	15.1	13.6	16.0	13.9	10.9	10.2
2011	15.5	17.5	10.4	51.3	11.2	10.3	12.8	13.5	10.1	14.7	13.7	10.2	8.3
2012	15.4	17.3	15.7	48.7	10.6	10.6	10.5	13.7	10.9	14.8	13.6	9.8	7.8
2002													
January	1.9	2.3	1.7	5.3	2.1	2.1	2.0	2.4	1.2	3.0	1.8	2.3	1.8
February	1.3	1.5	1.2	4.0	1.3	1.1	1.5	1.6	1.2	1.8	1.5	0.7	0.7
March	1.1	1.3	1.8	3.1	1.2	1.4	1.0	1.1	1.1	1.1	1.2	1.0	0.6
April	1.4	1.6	2.0	3.1	1.5	1.5	1.5	1.3	1.0	1.5	1.2	1.5	0.7
May	1.2	1.4	1.2	3.1	1.3	1.2	1.3	1.5	1.4	1.7	0.8	0.9	1.0
June	1.3	1.4	0.8	3.3	1.3	1.2	1.3	1.1	0.9	1.1	1.2	1.2	1.1
July	1.6	1.8	2.4	3.6	1.4	1.3	1.5	1.3	1.6	1.3	0.9	1.1	0.9
August	1.5	1.6	1.4	3.3	1.3	1.5	1.0	1.2	0.9	1.4	1.2	1.1	1.0
September	1.5	1.7	1.0	3.4	1.3	1.4	1.2	1.4	1.1	1.5	1.5	0.8	0.9
October	1.6	1.8	1.2	4.7	1.6	1.6	1.6	1.4	0.8	1.7	1.0	1.1	0.7
November	1.4	1.7	1.1	4.3	1.3	1.3	1.4	1.3	1.4	1.3	1.2	1.6	0.9
December	1.7	1.9	1.8	4.9	1.7	1.5	2.1	1.9	1.3	2.1	1.8	0.9	0.8
2003													
January	2.0	2.4	2.5	6.0	1.8	1.8	1.9	2.5	1.5	3.3	1.3	2.1	1.5
February	1.3	1.5	1.5	3.6	1.3	1.3	1.3	1.4	0.7	1.9	0.8	1.2	0.5
March	1.2	1.3	1.4	3.5	1.3	1.2	1.3	1.1	0.8	1.3	0.9	1.2	0.8
April	1.4	1.6	1.3	3.8	1.6	1.6	1.6	1.1	1.0	1.2	0.9	0.6	0.5
May	1.2	1.4	0.9	3.0	1.0	0.9	1.1	1.2	1.2	1.2	1.1	0.8	0.6
June	1.5	1.6	1.2	3.0	1.3	1.4	1.3	1.4	0.9	1.5	1.8	1.1	0.6
July	1.6	1.7	1.5	3.3	1.5	1.4	1.7	1.5	1.6	1.3	1.9	0.9	1.3
August	1.7	1.8	1.8	4.5	1.1	1.2	0.9	1.4	1.1	1.5	1.4	0.8	0.6
September	1.5	1.6	0.7	4.1	1.0	1.0	1.0	1.0	0.9	1.0	1.0	0.6	0.9
October	1.6	1.9	1.1	4.2	1.2	1.1	1.3	1.7	1.4	1.8	1.5	1.0	0.7
November	1.4	1.6	1.2	4.2	1.2	1.3	0.9	1.3	0.7	1.7	1.0	1.0	0.6
December	1.7	1.9	3.0	4.1	1.2	1.1	1.3	2.3	1.1	2.7	2.6	1.0	0.7
2004													
January	1.9	2.2	1.8	5.1	1.4	1.4	1.5	2.5	1.3	3.1	1.8	1.3	1.0
February	1.2	1.4	1.5	4.1	1.0	0.9	1.1	1.6	1.2	2.0	1.1	1.0	0.4
March	1.2	1.4	0.9	3.4	1.0	1.1	1.0	1.2	1.0	1.2	1.5	1.3	0.7
April	1.4	1.6	1.0	2.9	1.2	0.9	1.6	1.3	1.6	1.3	1.0	0.8	0.6
May	1.2	1.3	0.9	2.4	0.9	0.7	1.2	1.4	1.1	1.4	1.7	1.0	0.4
June	1.3	1.4	0.7	2.6	0.9	1.0	0.8	1.1	1.0	1.1	1.3	1.4	0.7
July	1.4	1.5	1.0	3.0	1.1	1.2	1.1	1.4	1.2	1.6	1.4	0.7	0.6
August	1.6	1.8	1.3	3.5	1.4	1.5	1.1	1.3	1.3	1.2	1.6	0.6	1.3
September	1.6	1.7	0.8	2.9	1.0	1.1	1.0	1.2	0.9	1.3	1.4	1.3	0.9
October	1.5	1.8	1.1	4.1	1.3	1.2	1.4	1.4	1.2	1.5	1.6	1.0	1.0
November	1.4	1.6	1.5	3.7	1.1	1.2	1.0	1.4	1.1	1.5	1.4	0.6	0.9
December	1.6	1.9	1.4	4.2	1.1	1.1	1.1	2.4	0.8	2.9	2.6	0.7	0.9
2005													
January	1.9	2.2	1.8	6.3	1.5	1.5	1.3	2.2	1.3	2.7	1.6	1.2	1.5
February	1.2	1.4	1.0	3.6	0.8	0.9	0.8	1.5	0.9	1.8	1.3	0.5	0.9
March	1.2	1.4	0.9	2.4	1.0	0.9	1.2	1.2	0.7	1.4	1.0	0.8	0.7
April	1.3	1.5	1.1	3.0	1.2	1.2	1.0	1.3	1.2	1.3	1.2	0.6	1.1
May	1.2	1.4	0.6	2.9	1.0	1.0	0.9	1.4	1.4	1.2	2.1	1.0	0.7
June	1.3	1.5	0.7	2.5	0.9	0.9	0.9	1.3	0.8	1.3	1.6	0.6	0.3
July	1.4	1.5	0.9	2.5	0.9	0.9	0.9	1.4	1.1	1.5	1.4	0.7	0.8
August	1.5	1.6	1.0	3.3	1.1	1.2	0.9	1.2	0.8	1.4	1.2	0.5	0.6
September	1.5	1.7	1.3	3.0	1.1	1.0	1.2	1.5	0.6	1.7	1.6	0.6	0.9
October	1.4	1.6	1.1	3.0	1.1	1.0	1.1	1.3	1.2	1.4	1.4	0.6	1.0
November	1.2	1.4	0.6	3.1	1.1	0.8	1.5	1.3	1.3	1.2	1.7	0.8	0.7
December	1.4	1.6	1.2	3.8	1.0	0.9	1.3	2.0	1.3	1.8	3.3	0.7	0.7
2006													
January	1.6	1.9	0.8	4.6	1.2	0.9	1.7	2.2	1.0	2.8	1.7	0.6	1.1
February	1.1	1.2	0.9	2.5	0.8	0.7	1.0	1.3	1.0	1.6	0.7	0.6	0.7
March	1.0	1.1	1.2	2.4	1.1	1.0	1.4	1.0	0.6	1.0	1.2	0.5	0.9
April	1.2	1.4	1.4	1.9	1.0	0.7	1.5	1.1	0.9	1.4	0.6	1.2	1.0
May	1.2	1.4	0.4	2.3	1.0	1.0	1.1	1.3	0.9	1.4	1.1	0.4	0.6
June	1.2	1.3	0.4	1.6	1.0	0.8	1.3	1.3	0.8	1.6	1.2	0.5	0.6
July	1.3	1.4	0.6	2.5	1.0	1.0	1.1	1.3	1.7	1.2	1.1	0.7	0.9
August	1.3	1.4	0.8	2.6	1.0	1.0	1.1	1.2	0.8	1.3	1.2	0.6	0.9
September	1.3	1.5	1.3	2.4	1.1	1.1	1.2	1.2	0.9	1.3	1.3	0.5	0.8
October	1.4	1.6	0.8	3.2	1.1	1.1	1.1	1.3	1.1	1.3	1.3	1.0	0.9
November	1.4	1.5	0.8	4.1	1.0	1.1	1.0	1.1	0.9	1.3	1.0	0.7	0.8
December	1.4	1.6	1.0	3.9	1.1	1.0	1.3	1.7	0.8	2.1	1.6	0.9	1.0
2007													
January	1.6	1.9	1.5	4.3	1.4	1.3	1.4	2.1	0.9	2.5	2.0	1.8	1.2
February	1.1	1.2	0.8	3.1	1.1	1.1	1.1	1.0	0.6	1.3	0.8	0.9	0.9
March	1.1	1.2	0.5	2.1	1.0	1.0	0.9	1.0	0.8	1.0	1.1	0.6	1.2
April	1.3	1.5	0.9	2.8	1.0	1.0	1.1	1.1	1.0	1.1	1.2	0.6	1.1
May	1.1	1.2	0.8	2.3	0.9	0.9	1.0	1.1	0.9	1.3	0.8	0.7	0.9
June	1.2	1.3	0.6	2.6	1.0	1.0	1.0	1.0	0.8	1.1	0.8	0.6	0.8
July	1.4	1.4	0.8	2.3	1.3	1.2	1.4	1.3	1.5	1.3	1.1	1.0	1.3
August	1.4	1.6	1.2	3.3	1.1	1.1	1.2	1.3	1.2	1.4	0.9	0.9	1.2
September	1.6	1.8	1.0	3.3	1.2	1.2	1.3	1.3	1.1	1.5	0.8	0.5	1.3
October	1.5	1.7	1.2	3.4	1.4	1.4	1.5	1.4	1.4	1.5	1.2	0.6	1.2
November	1.4	1.6	1.4	3.6	1.4	1.4	1.5	1.5	1.1	1.6	1.6	0.5	0.9
December	1.4	1.6	1.4	4.1	1.1	1.0	1.4	1.6	1.4	1.9	1.1	0.6	1.1

Table 7-11. Layoffs and Discharges Levels and Rates, by Industry, 2002–October 2013—*Continued*

(Not seasonally adjusted, levels in thousands, rates per 100.)

Year and month	Rate												
	Finance and insurance	Real estate and rental and leasing	Professional and business services	Education and health services	Educational services	Health care and social assistance	Leisure and hospitality	Arts, entertainment, and recreation	Accommodation and food services	Other services	Government	Federal	State and local government
2007	9.7	22.5	26.1	9.3	12.5	8.7	22.9	43.9	19.3	17.0	5.9	8.0	5.6
2008	10.2	19.4	28.4	10.5	12.6	10.1	23.3	45.6	19.5	17.4	5.1	3.7	5.3
2009	11.9	28.5	30.3	11.4	14.6	10.7	25.4	43.4	22.2	22.9	7.1	7.9	7.0
2010	8.0	16.8	25.9	10.7	12.6	10.3	21.0	41.0	17.6	17.3	9.1	24.9	6.7
2011	6.1	15.1	26.5	9.1	11.3	8.7	23.1	48.4	18.9	20.1	5.9	4.7	6.1
2012	5.6	14.3	26.9	9.4	11.4	8.9	22.3	46.0	18.4	19.2	5.5	4.5	5.7
2002													
January	1.9	1.5	2.8	1.1	1.3	1.1	2.0	3.7	1.8	1.8	0.3	0.6	0.3
February	0.7	0.8	2.0	0.6	0.3	0.7	1.6	1.6	1.6	0.7	0.2	0.3	0.2
March	0.4	1.0	2.1	0.8	0.6	0.8	1.2	1.9	1.1	0.6	0.2	0.4	0.2
April	0.7	0.9	2.3	0.8	0.7	0.8	2.3	5.3	1.8	1.6	0.3	0.3	0.3
May	1.0	0.9	2.0	0.8	0.8	0.7	1.3	1.3	1.3	0.7	0.4	0.2	0.5
June	1.1	1.3	1.9	1.0	1.1	1.0	1.7	1.2	1.8	1.4	0.7	0.3	0.7
July	0.7	1.5	2.9	1.1	1.2	1.0	2.8	5.4	2.3	2.0	0.7	0.4	0.7
August	0.7	1.9	2.0	0.9	1.1	0.9	2.4	6.5	1.6	2.4	0.7	0.3	0.8
September	0.5	1.9	2.3	0.9	1.3	0.8	3.0	7.1	2.2	1.4	0.8	0.5	0.8
October	0.5	1.3	3.1	0.7	0.3	0.8	2.7	3.7	2.6	0.9	0.4	0.4	0.4
November	0.6	1.6	2.5	0.4	0.1	0.5	2.8	7.1	2.1	0.8	0.3	0.5	0.3
December	0.6	1.3	3.4	0.7	0.8	0.6	1.9	3.8	1.6	1.0	0.3	0.2	0.3
2003													
January	1.1	2.8	3.1	0.9	0.6	0.9	2.8	5.6	2.4	1.7	0.3	0.5	0.3
February	0.5	0.5	2.3	0.6	0.4	0.6	1.5	2.9	1.3	1.3	0.2	0.3	0.2
March	0.6	1.5	1.8	0.6	0.3	0.7	1.7	3.3	1.4	0.8	0.2	0.2	0.2
April	0.4	0.9	2.8	0.6	0.7	0.6	2.5	6.3	1.9	1.3	0.3	0.3	0.3
May	0.5	1.0	2.0	1.0	1.3	0.9	2.1	4.1	1.8	0.7	0.5	0.4	0.5
June	0.4	1.2	2.4	1.3	2.7	1.1	1.7	1.3	1.7	2.1	0.7	0.4	0.7
July	0.8	2.6	2.6	1.4	2.9	1.1	1.4	1.6	1.4	1.9	0.6	0.4	0.7
August	0.5	1.1	2.7	1.2	2.3	1.0	2.1	5.0	1.6	2.9	0.9	0.4	1.0
September	0.7	1.6	2.3	0.7	0.7	0.7	3.2	8.4	2.3	1.6	0.8	0.5	0.8
October	0.6	1.0	3.1	0.8	0.8	0.8	3.0	5.8	2.6	1.5	0.3	0.7	0.3
November	0.4	1.0	2.3	0.6	0.5	0.6	2.5	5.9	2.0	1.0	0.4	0.9	0.3
December	0.4	1.6	2.9	0.5	0.6	0.5	2.6	3.3	2.5	1.6	0.4	0.2	0.4
2004													
January	0.7	1.9	3.7	0.8	0.7	0.8	2.9	4.5	2.6	1.0	0.3	0.4	0.3
February	0.4	0.6	1.7	0.6	0.5	0.7	1.7	4.4	1.3	0.9	0.2	0.3	0.2
March	0.5	1.4	2.1	0.6	0.6	0.7	1.7	2.6	1.6	0.7	0.2	0.2	0.2
April	0.4	1.1	3.2	0.8	0.5	0.8	2.3	5.1	1.8	1.3	0.2	0.2	0.2
May	0.4	0.6	2.0	0.8	1.1	0.7	1.5	2.9	1.3	1.0	0.4	0.3	0.4
June	0.5	1.4	2.2	1.0	1.9	0.8	2.1	2.5	2.0	0.8	0.8	0.7	0.8
July	0.5	0.9	2.4	0.8	1.0	0.7	2.2	2.8	2.1	1.3	0.7	0.3	0.7
August	1.1	1.8	2.3	1.0	1.4	1.0	2.6	6.1	2.0	3.1	0.8	0.4	0.8
September	0.6	1.7	2.2	1.0	1.4	0.9	3.6	12.2	2.0	1.7	0.9	0.4	1.0
October	0.7	1.8	2.1	0.6	0.3	0.7	3.9	7.2	3.3	0.7	0.4	0.4	0.4
November	0.7	1.4	2.5	0.7	0.6	0.7	2.1	4.7	1.6	1.9	0.4	0.2	0.4
December	0.5	2.1	3.0	0.7	0.6	0.8	1.7	3.3	1.4	0.9	0.5	0.9	0.4
2005													
January	1.2	2.3	3.1	0.8	0.6	0.9	2.5	3.5	2.4	1.8	0.3	0.4	0.3
February	0.4	2.1	2.0	0.7	0.4	0.7	1.6	2.5	1.5	1.1	0.2	0.3	0.2
March	0.6	1.2	2.4	0.9	0.8	0.9	1.9	2.1	1.9	1.1	0.2	0.3	0.2
April	1.0	1.4	2.6	0.8	0.6	0.9	1.8	3.1	1.6	1.0	0.3	0.4	0.3
May	0.5	1.1	1.7	0.9	1.6	0.8	1.5	2.1	1.4	1.5	0.5	0.3	0.5
June	0.3	0.4	2.6	0.9	1.2	0.9	2.3	2.5	2.2	0.9	0.7	0.7	0.7
July	0.6	1.3	3.3	0.8	1.2	0.7	1.7	1.3	1.7	1.1	0.6	0.5	0.6
August	0.7	0.5	2.7	1.0	0.9	1.0	1.9	4.2	1.4	3.1	0.8	0.6	0.9
September	0.5	2.2	2.1	0.7	1.2	0.7	3.5	12.6	1.8	1.5	0.8	0.6	0.8
October	0.6	2.2	2.4	0.7	0.6	0.7	2.5	5.2	2.1	1.0	0.4	0.3	0.4
November	0.3	1.9	1.9	0.5	0.4	0.6	2.1	5.0	1.6	0.7	0.3	0.4	0.3
December	0.4	1.6	2.4	0.7	1.2	0.6	1.7	3.4	1.4	1.0	0.4	1.0	0.3
2006													
January	0.8	1.8	2.4	0.8	0.8	0.8	2.2	2.0	2.2	1.3	0.4	0.4	0.4
February	0.6	1.0	2.0	0.5	0.3	0.6	1.4	2.0	1.3	1.0	0.2	0.3	0.2
March	0.5	1.8	1.6	0.6	0.6	0.6	1.4	2.0	1.3	0.5	0.3	0.4	0.3
April	0.7	1.7	2.1	0.8	0.8	0.8	1.8	2.4	1.7	3.0	0.3	0.5	0.3
May	0.4	1.1	2.1	1.3	1.8	1.2	1.5	3.3	1.1	0.9	0.5	0.4	0.5
June	0.5	1.1	2.0	1.0	2.0	0.8	1.4	1.8	1.3	1.2	1.0	0.9	1.0
July	0.5	1.9	2.2	1.0	1.6	0.9	1.6	2.5	1.5	1.4	0.7	0.8	0.7
August	0.7	1.6	1.7	0.8	1.1	0.8	1.9	4.4	1.5	1.9	0.7	1.0	0.7
September	0.6	1.3	2.0	0.7	0.9	0.6	2.6	7.8	1.7	1.6	0.8	0.9	0.8
October	0.5	1.8	2.4	0.6	0.7	0.6	2.9	5.5	2.4	1.7	0.4	0.4	0.4
November	0.4	1.9	2.3	0.5	0.4	0.5	2.7	5.5	2.2	1.1	0.3	0.3	0.3
December	0.9	1.4	2.6	0.6	0.8	0.5	1.7	2.9	1.5	1.1	0.4	0.6	0.4
2007													
January	0.8	2.2	2.4	0.8	1.2	0.7	2.2	4.4	1.8	1.1	0.4	0.6	0.4
February	0.6	1.5	1.9	0.5	0.7	0.5	1.4	2.7	1.2	0.5	0.2	0.5	0.2
March	0.8	2.3	2.0	0.7	0.6	0.8	1.5	2.7	1.2	0.9	0.2	0.5	0.2
April	0.7	2.3	2.5	0.7	0.0	0.7	1.9	4.7	1.5	2.0	0.3	0.5	0.2
May	0.4	2.0	1.6	0.8	1.3	0.8	1.6	2.6	1.5	0.7	0.5	0.6	0.5
June	0.7	0.8	1.6	1.2	2.6	0.9	1.8	2.0	1.8	1.9	0.8	0.9	0.7
July	1.1	1.8	2.1	0.8	0.8	0.8	1.3	1.3	1.3	1.8	1.0	1.0	1.0
August	1.1	1.3	1.9	1.0	2.3	0.8	1.9	2.6	1.8	2.3	0.9	0.9	0.9
September	1.0	2.2	2.1	0.8	0.7	0.9	3.3	7.0	2.7	2.5	0.6	1.0	0.6
October	1.0	1.9	2.6	0.7	0.5	0.7	2.6	5.9	2.0	1.0	0.4	0.4	0.4
November	0.3	2.4	2.5	0.6	0.7	0.6	1.9	5.9	1.2	1.3	0.3	0.3	0.3
December	1.0	1.6	2.8	0.6	0.8	0.5	1.6	3.0	1.4	1.0	0.4	0.8	0.4

Table 7-11. Layoffs and Discharges Levels and Rates, by Industry, 2002–October 2013—*Continued*

(Not seasonally adjusted, levels in thousands, rates per 100.)

Year and month	Level												
	Total	Total private	Mining and logging	Construction	Manufacturing	Durable goods	Non-durable goods	Trade, transportation, and utilities	Wholesale trade	Retail trade	Transportation, warehousing, and utilities	Information	Financial activities
2008													
January	2 337	2 251	11	350	182	124	59	553	96	375	82	36	124
February	1 505	1 468	11	199	135	77	58	331	57	231	42	18	59
March	1 492	1 436	7	229	121	77	44	256	53	155	47	28	73
April	1 765	1 713	8	245	189	119	70	316	80	186	50	21	94
May	1 617	1 511	5	211	145	89	56	297	62	190	44	16	66
June	1 856	1 701	6	219	169	104	65	368	75	245	48	32	74
July	1 982	1 852	12	229	164	116	48	388	54	253	81	20	112
August	2 244	2 076	6	250	166	118	48	392	69	248	75	18	108
September	2 051	1 920	6	296	187	115	73	355	68	211	76	34	80
October	2 313	2 232	11	348	253	157	96	429	81	277	71	53	80
November	2 237	2 177	18	417	227	143	84	398	74	251	73	40	74
December	2 782	2 693	19	437	314	207	106	637	125	407	105	46	87
2009													
January	3 308	3 191	16	544	443	316	126	738	185	442	111	62	195
February	2 022	1 969	16	299	276	187	89	394	85	236	72	32	115
March	2 003	1 945	23	296	285	211	74	372	88	195	89	33	108
April	2 428	2 356	17	345	280	205	75	481	102	308	70	39	103
May	1 916	1 729	14	239	223	147	76	376	115	201	60	26	96
June	2 001	1 750	11	212	200	132	68	317	72	174	71	29	98
July	2 333	2 142	15	313	191	106	85	361	79	198	84	31	122
August	2 226	2 013	9	266	186	94	92	319	82	175	62	19	111
September	2 241	2 050	11	300	180	102	78	407	63	238	106	16	74
October	2 107	2 016	15	313	212	122	90	336	62	211	63	23	113
November	1 903	1 827	12	267	212	108	104	334	64	192	77	28	45
December	2 296	2 187	18	350	169	101	68	577	83	303	190	42	80
2010													
January	2 357	2 255	12	375	216	163	53	547	84	382	81	49	109
February	1 424	1 374	8	222	135	77	58	249	63	144	42	22	50
March	1 480	1 411	7	209	127	72	55	312	53	229	31	21	55
April	1 585	1 509	9	249	127	64	62	240	57	146	37	18	60
May	1 568	1 398	8	231	99	61	38	231	59	130	42	26	70
June	1 913	1 490	5	173	108	53	55	309	51	196	63	21	44
July	2 103	1 792	6	249	132	69	63	315	81	181	52	21	75
August	1 948	1 636	7	223	141	76	65	247	48	164	35	24	54
September	1 795	1 565	7	235	127	72	55	260	72	145	42	17	49
October	1 755	1 661	7	251	166	97	69	276	53	161	62	21	93
November	1 781	1 685	9	303	148	79	70	294	57	192	45	23	59
December	2 064	1 951	13	393	126	70	56	432	63	239	129	32	65
2011													
January	2 147	2 071	10	332	140	74	66	560	54	402	105	31	106
February	1 275	1 231	4	209	105	57	48	247	46	170	31	18	48
March	1 338	1 288	3	211	106	64	42	233	43	155	35	33	39
April	1 442	1 374	9	223	102	51	51	196	32	134	30	16	31
May	1 534	1 404	6	201	112	60	52	209	62	122	25	20	35
June	1 685	1 530	6	212	93	56	37	246	59	145	42	18	53
July	1 772	1 599	5	215	103	61	41	276	46	176	55	25	46
August	1 853	1 679	7	238	128	73	55	250	33	167	50	20	51
September	1 873	1 703	8	255	111	64	47	247	45	159	43	20	61
October	1 792	1 699	5	233	102	59	43	247	43	140	64	23	63
November	1 780	1 713	8	238	107	63	44	273	46	180	47	21	56
December	1 910	1 805	11	269	109	64	44	397	53	207	136	28	47
2012													
January	2 022	1 948	14	314	112	62	50	495	75	342	79	32	55
February	1 388	1 338	11	211	94	56	39	230	36	160	35	25	35
March	1 345	1 294	12	191	82	48	34	235	55	145	35	24	43
April	1 616	1 554	11	178	99	59	40	235	48	143	44	21	50
May	1 736	1 591	12	218	100	57	43	257	47	170	40	21	47
June	1 728	1 574	9	188	122	79	43	258	39	158	61	17	43
July	1 577	1 450	7	252	95	59	35	230	44	136	51	20	49
August	1 989	1 814	12	193	117	79	38	324	54	212	57	31	63
September	1 856	1 722	10	266	110	78	32	262	63	143	55	18	36
October	1 764	1 672	10	199	124	81	43	288	58	180	50	17	71
November	1 739	1 676	10	302	111	72	39	224	52	124	49	16	71
December	1 786	1 703	16	233	97	63	33	455	50	287	118	20	44
2013													
January	1 905	1 836	19	235	118	77	41	494	52	332	110	18	74
February	1 219	1 168	12	182	92	61	31	241	41	158	42	20	49
March	1 329	1 267	9	189	83	58	25	233	30	162	41	11	44
April	1 614	1 556	14	178	89	58	30	251	29	175	47	22	43
May	1 593	1 477	9	159	101	67	34	303	45	204	54	24	49
June	1 567	1 405	6	150	90	53	37	218	33	146	39	35	39
July	1 595	1 478	14	179	89	50	40	290	75	156	59	25	57
August	1 816	1 682	9	163	129	79	51	277	35	171	71	31	67
September	1 916	1 780	11	168	104	64	39	225	48	129	48	33	96
October	1 511	1 422	16	183	98	63	35	211	44	125	42	23	80

Table 7-11. Layoffs and Discharges Levels and Rates, by Industry, 2002–October 2013—*Continued*

(Not seasonally adjusted, levels in thousands, rates per 100.)

Year and month	Level												
	Finance and insurance	Real estate and rental and leasing	Professional and business services	Education and health services	Educational services	Health care and social assistance	Leisure and hospitality	Arts, entertainment, and recreation	Accommodation and food services	Other services	Government	Federal	State and local government
2008													
January	78	45	505	171	25	146	249	63	186	69	86	17	69
February	36	23	304	128	15	113	229	58	171	54	37	7	30
March	52	20	364	130	12	118	173	57	115	56	57	6	51
April	64	30	445	133	35	98	207	67	140	55	53	9	44
May	32	34	261	207	40	167	205	61	144	98	106	5	101
June	53	21	378	210	56	154	195	38	156	51	154	9	145
July	67	45	395	210	48	162	198	29	170	124	129	6	123
August	70	38	421	205	51	154	377	144	233	131	168	8	160
September	43	37	375	149	22	127	358	122	236	79	131	7	125
October	37	43	434	138	26	113	384	116	268	101	81	9	72
November	32	42	531	110	22	88	303	77	226	58	60	5	56
December	52	35	628	187	30	157	256	67	189	82	90	15	74
2009													
January	112	83	569	190	22	168	299	73	225	136	117	10	106
February	68	47	451	146	18	128	182	36	146	57	53	5	48
March	61	47	401	141	13	128	204	37	167	83	58	6	52
April	64	39	576	185	31	154	248	62	186	83	72	11	61
May	71	25	313	150	51	99	207	25	182	83	187	62	125
June	57	41	339	216	62	154	228	40	188	100	252	61	190
July	73	49	424	300	95	205	232	51	181	153	192	8	183
August	47	64	360	251	71	179	346	102	244	146	213	9	204
September	30	44	351	173	31	141	373	109	264	164	191	8	183
October	45	68	362	145	24	121	404	135	269	91	91	11	80
November	23	21	412	133	12	120	328	100	228	58	76	18	58
December	39	41	458	152	22	131	265	62	203	76	108	15	93
2010													
January	43	66	444	160	20	139	247	45	203	97	102	6	96
February	28	22	327	138	11	127	128	18	109	96	51	8	43
March	33	22	338	122	13	110	171	55	116	48	69	13	57
April	38	23	419	139	17	122	195	65	130	54	75	18	58
May	43	27	318	161	39	122	190	46	144	65	170	38	131
June	27	17	296	234	73	162	232	58	174	68	424	239	184
July	38	37	410	291	69	222	215	59	156	77	310	153	158
August	39	15	307	222	62	160	262	93	170	150	312	130	182
September	41	8	303	201	39	162	304	121	183	61	230	89	141
October	58	35	305	114	12	101	341	102	239	89	94	26	68
November	30	29	354	138	18	120	280	80	200	76	96	11	85
December	42	23	509	167	23	144	174	43	131	40	113	9	104
2011													
January	48	58	430	135	21	114	244	59	185	83	76	11	65
February	27	21	293	112	19	92	126	22	103	71	45	5	40
March	28	11	318	102	15	88	197	52	145	46	50	6	44
April	13	18	433	107	16	91	173	59	114	83	69	9	59
May	25	10	370	151	37	114	225	62	163	75	130	7	124
June	27	27	375	242	66	176	212	36	176	72	155	10	145
July	27	19	372	210	64	146	223	34	190	123	173	9	165
August	28	24	378	205	36	169	283	92	190	118	175	23	151
September	40	22	352	136	31	105	390	184	206	122	169	20	150
October	24	40	393	125	18	107	383	121	262	126	94	14	80
November	31	25	404	148	21	127	373	152	220	86	67	11	56
December	31	16	469	140	22	118	261	56	205	74	106	9	97
2012													
January	28	27	343	176	39	138	315	74	242	89	75	9	66
February	19	16	413	98	10	87	158	45	113	62	50	6	44
March	20	23	350	114	11	103	193	63	130	50	51	6	45
April	34	17	452	150	21	129	229	104	124	129	62	7	55
May	29	18	439	188	50	138	221	55	165	89	145	6	139
June	20	23	401	267	75	192	193	29	164	77	154	9	145
July	25	24	335	204	59	145	199	30	170	60	126	6	120
August	36	27	459	186	36	150	332	91	240	97	175	18	157
September	22	14	402	136	20	116	362	142	220	120	134	21	113
October	34	37	364	131	21	110	355	108	247	112	92	16	76
November	43	28	438	109	14	95	291	93	197	105	63	12	51
December	19	26	418	141	27	114	222	70	153	56	83	12	71
2013													
January	35	38	464	144	19	126	216	43	173	53	69	10	59
February	36	12	276	130	16	114	130	21	108	36	51	15	35
March	26	18	328	115	16	99	192	40	152	63	62	14	48
April	26	17	476	142	21	122	250	80	170	92	59	18	41
May	29	20	372	174	33	141	197	46	151	89	116	11	105
June	18	21	377	198	57	140	204	31	174	87	162	10	152
July	36	20	342	190	63	126	209	35	174	82	117	9	109
August	40	27	416	235	64	171	269	64	204	87	135	12	122
September	51	46	415	153	41	111	461	207	254	115	136	12	124
October	42	30	315	118	18	100	316	134	182	62	89	19	70

Table 7-11. Layoffs and Discharges Levels and Rates, by Industry, 2002–October 2013—*Continued*

(Not seasonally adjusted, levels in thousands, rates per 100.)

Year and month	Rate												
	Total	Total private	Mining and logging	Construc-tion	Manufac-turing	Durable goods	Non-durable goods	Trade, transpor-tation, and utilities	Whole-sale trade	Retail trade	Transpor-tation, ware-housing, and utilities	Infor-mation	Financial activities
2008													
January	1.7	2.0	1.6	5.0	1.3	1.4	1.2	2.1	1.6	2.4	1.6	1.2	1.5
February	1.1	1.3	1.4	2.9	1.0	0.9	1.2	1.3	1.0	1.5	0.8	0.6	0.7
March	1.1	1.3	0.9	3.3	0.9	0.9	0.9	1.0	0.9	1.0	0.9	0.9	0.9
April	1.3	1.5	1.1	3.4	1.4	1.4	1.4	1.2	1.3	1.2	1.0	0.7	1.2
May	1.2	1.3	0.6	2.9	1.1	1.0	1.1	1.1	1.0	1.2	0.9	0.5	0.8
June	1.3	1.5	0.7	2.9	1.2	1.2	1.3	1.4	1.3	1.6	0.9	1.0	0.9
July	1.4	1.6	1.5	3.1	1.2	1.4	1.0	1.5	0.9	1.7	1.6	0.7	1.4
August	1.6	1.8	0.8	3.4	1.2	1.4	1.0	1.5	1.2	1.6	1.5	0.6	1.3
September	1.5	1.7	0.7	4.1	1.4	1.4	1.5	1.4	1.1	1.4	1.5	1.1	1.0
October	1.7	2.0	1.4	4.8	1.9	1.9	2.0	1.6	1.4	1.8	1.4	1.8	1.0
November	1.6	1.9	2.3	6.0	1.7	1.7	1.7	1.5	1.3	1.6	1.5	1.4	0.9
December	2.1	2.4	2.4	6.6	2.4	2.6	2.2	2.4	2.1	2.6	2.1	1.6	1.1
2009													
January	2.5	2.9	2.2	8.8	3.6	4.1	2.7	2.9	3.2	3.0	2.3	2.2	2.5
February	1.5	1.8	2.2	5.0	2.3	2.4	1.9	1.6	1.5	1.6	1.5	1.1	1.5
March	1.5	1.8	3.2	5.0	2.3	2.8	1.6	1.5	1.6	1.4	1.8	1.2	1.4
April	1.8	2.2	2.4	5.7	2.3	2.8	1.6	1.9	1.8	2.1	1.5	1.4	1.3
May	1.5	1.6	2.1	3.9	1.9	2.0	1.7	1.5	2.1	1.4	1.3	0.9	1.2
June	1.5	1.6	1.6	3.4	1.7	1.8	1.5	1.3	1.3	1.2	1.5	1.0	1.3
July	1.8	2.0	2.2	5.0	1.6	1.5	1.9	1.5	1.4	1.4	1.8	1.1	1.6
August	1.7	1.9	1.3	4.3	1.6	1.3	2.0	1.3	1.5	1.2	1.3	0.7	1.4
September	1.7	1.9	1.7	5.0	1.5	1.4	1.7	1.7	1.1	1.7	2.2	0.6	1.0
October	1.6	1.9	2.3	5.3	1.8	1.7	2.0	1.4	1.1	1.5	1.3	0.8	1.5
November	1.5	1.7	1.7	4.6	1.8	1.5	2.3	1.3	1.2	1.3	1.6	1.0	0.6
December	1.8	2.0	2.7	6.3	1.5	1.4	1.5	2.3	1.5	2.0	4.0	1.5	1.0
2010													
January	1.9	2.1	1.8	7.2	1.9	2.3	1.2	2.2	1.6	2.7	1.7	1.8	1.4
February	1.1	1.3	1.2	4.4	1.2	1.1	1.3	1.0	1.2	1.0	0.9	0.8	0.7
March	1.2	1.3	1.1	4.0	1.1	1.0	1.2	1.3	1.0	1.6	0.7	0.8	0.7
April	1.2	1.4	1.3	4.6	1.1	0.9	1.4	1.0	1.0	1.0	0.8	0.7	0.8
May	1.2	1.3	1.2	4.2	0.9	0.9	0.8	0.9	1.1	0.9	0.9	0.9	0.9
June	1.5	1.4	0.7	3.0	0.9	0.7	1.2	1.3	0.9	1.4	1.3	0.8	0.6
July	1.6	1.7	0.9	4.3	1.1	1.0	1.4	1.3	1.5	1.3	1.1	0.8	1.0
August	1.5	1.5	0.9	3.8	1.2	1.1	1.4	1.0	0.9	1.1	0.7	0.9	0.7
September	1.4	1.4	1.0	4.1	1.1	1.0	1.2	1.1	1.3	1.0	0.9	0.6	0.6
October	1.3	1.5	0.9	4.4	1.4	1.4	1.5	1.1	1.0	1.1	1.3	0.8	1.2
November	1.4	1.5	1.3	5.4	1.3	1.1	1.6	1.2	1.0	1.3	0.9	0.8	0.8
December	1.6	1.8	1.7	7.3	1.1	1.0	1.2	1.7	1.2	1.6	2.6	1.2	0.8
2011													
January	1.7	2.0	1.4	6.6	1.2	1.0	1.5	2.3	1.0	2.8	2.2	1.2	1.4
February	1.0	1.2	0.6	4.1	0.9	0.8	1.1	1.0	0.8	1.2	0.6	0.7	0.6
March	1.0	1.2	0.4	4.1	0.9	0.9	1.0	0.9	0.8	1.1	0.7	1.2	0.5
April	1.1	1.3	1.2	4.2	0.9	0.7	1.2	0.8	0.6	0.9	0.6	0.6	0.4
May	1.2	1.3	0.8	3.6	1.0	0.8	1.2	0.8	1.1	0.8	0.5	0.7	0.5
June	1.3	1.4	0.8	3.7	0.8	0.8	0.8	1.0	1.0	1.0	0.7	0.7	0.7
July	1.4	1.4	0.6	3.7	0.9	0.8	0.9	1.1	0.8	1.2	1.1	0.9	0.6
August	1.4	1.5	0.9	4.1	1.1	1.0	1.2	1.0	0.6	1.1	1.0	0.8	0.7
September	1.4	1.5	0.9	4.4	0.9	0.9	1.0	1.0	0.8	1.1	0.9	0.7	0.8
October	1.3	1.5	0.6	4.0	0.9	0.8	1.0	1.0	0.8	1.0	1.3	0.9	0.8
November	1.3	1.5	0.9	4.2	0.9	0.9	1.0	1.1	0.8	1.2	1.0	0.8	0.7
December	1.4	1.6	1.4	4.9	0.9	0.9	1.0	1.5	0.9	1.4	2.7	1.0	0.6
2012													
January	1.5	1.8	1.7	6.0	1.0	0.8	1.1	2.0	1.3	2.3	1.6	1.2	0.7
February	1.1	1.2	1.4	4.0	0.8	0.8	0.9	0.9	0.6	1.1	0.7	0.9	0.5
March	1.0	1.2	1.5	3.6	0.7	0.6	0.8	0.9	1.0	1.0	0.7	0.9	0.6
April	1.2	1.4	1.3	3.3	0.8	0.8	0.9	0.9	0.9	1.0	0.9	0.8	0.7
May	1.3	1.4	1.4	3.9	0.8	0.8	1.0	1.0	0.8	1.1	0.8	0.8	0.6
June	1.3	1.4	1.1	3.2	1.0	1.0	1.0	0.7	0.7	1.1	1.2	0.6	0.5
July	1.2	1.3	0.8	4.3	0.8	0.8	0.8	0.9	0.8	0.9	1.0	0.7	0.6
August	1.5	1.6	1.4	3.3	1.0	1.1	0.8	1.3	1.0	1.4	1.2	1.1	0.8
September	1.4	1.5	1.2	4.5	0.9	1.0	0.7	1.0	1.1	1.0	1.1	0.7	0.5
October	1.3	1.5	1.2	3.4	1.0	1.1	1.0	1.1	1.0	1.2	1.0	0.7	0.9
November	1.3	1.5	1.1	5.2	0.9	1.0	0.9	0.9	0.9	0.8	1.0	0.6	0.9
December	1.3	1.5	1.9	4.2	0.8	0.8	0.7	1.7	0.9	1.8	2.3	0.7	0.6
2013													
January	1.4	1.7	2.2	4.4	1.0	1.0	0.9	1.9	0.9	2.2	2.2	0.7	0.9
February	0.9	1.0	1.5	3.4	0.8	0.8	0.7	0.9	0.7	1.1	0.9	0.8	0.6
March	1.0	1.1	1.0	3.4	0.7	0.8	0.6	0.9	0.5	1.1	0.8	0.4	0.6
April	1.2	1.4	1.7	3.1	0.7	0.8	0.7	1.0	0.5	1.2	0.9	0.8	0.5
May	1.2	1.3	1.0	2.7	0.8	0.9	0.8	1.2	0.8	1.4	1.1	0.9	0.6
June	1.1	1.2	0.7	2.5	0.7	0.7	0.8	0.8	0.6	1.0	0.8	1.3	0.5
July	1.2	1.3	1.6	2.9	0.7	0.7	0.9	1.1	1.3	1.0	1.2	0.9	0.7
August	1.3	1.5	1.0	2.7	1.1	1.0	1.1	1.1	0.6	1.1	1.4	1.1	0.8
September	1.4	1.5	1.2	2.8	0.9	0.9	0.9	0.9	0.8	0.8	0.9	1.2	1.2
October	1.1	1.2	1.8	3.0	0.8	0.8	0.8	0.8	0.8	0.8	0.8	0.9	1.0

Table 7-11. Layoffs and Discharges Levels and Rates, by Industry, 2002–October 2013—*Continued*

(Not seasonally adjusted, levels in thousands, rates per 100.)

Year and month	Rate												
	Finance and insurance	Real estate and rental and leasing	Professional and business services	Education and health services	Educational services	Health care and social assistance	Leisure and hospitality	Arts, entertainment, and recreation	Accommodation and food services	Other services	Government	Federal	State and local government
2008													
January	1.3	2.1	2.9	0.9	0.9	0.9	1.9	3.6	1.7	1.3	0.4	0.6	0.4
February	0.6	1.1	1.7	0.7	0.5	0.7	1.8	3.2	1.5	1.0	0.2	0.3	0.1
March	0.9	1.0	2.1	0.7	0.4	0.8	1.3	3.1	1.0	1.0	0.2	0.2	0.3
April	1.1	1.4	2.5	0.7	1.1	0.6	1.5	3.4	1.2	1.0	0.2	0.3	0.2
May	0.5	1.6	1.5	1.1	1.3	1.1	1.5	3.0	1.2	1.8	0.5	0.2	0.5
June	0.9	1.0	2.1	1.1	2.0	1.0	1.4	1.7	1.3	0.9	0.7	0.3	0.7
July	1.1	2.0	2.2	1.1	1.7	1.0	1.4	1.3	1.4	2.2	0.6	0.2	0.7
August	1.2	1.8	2.4	1.1	1.8	1.0	2.7	6.5	2.0	2.4	0.8	0.3	0.9
September	0.7	1.8	2.1	0.8	0.7	0.8	2.6	6.1	2.0	1.4	0.6	0.2	0.6
October	0.6	2.0	2.4	0.7	0.8	0.7	2.9	6.0	2.4	1.8	0.4	0.3	0.4
November	0.5	2.0	3.0	0.6	0.7	0.6	2.3	4.3	2.0	1.1	0.3	0.2	0.3
December	0.9	1.7	3.6	1.0	0.9	1.0	2.0	3.7	1.7	1.5	0.4	0.6	0.4
2009													
January	1.9	4.1	3.4	1.0	0.7	1.1	2.4	4.2	2.1	2.5	0.5	0.4	0.5
February	1.2	2.4	2.7	0.8	0.6	0.8	1.4	2.1	1.3	1.1	0.2	0.2	0.2
March	1.0	2.4	2.4	0.7	0.4	0.8	1.6	2.1	1.5	1.5	0.3	0.2	0.3
April	1.1	1.9	3.5	1.0	0.9	1.0	1.9	3.3	1.7	1.5	0.3	0.4	0.3
May	1.2	1.3	1.9	0.8	1.6	0.6	1.6	1.3	1.6	1.5	0.8	2.2	0.6
June	1.0	2.0	2.0	1.1	2.1	1.0	1.7	1.9	1.6	1.8	1.1	2.2	1.0
July	1.3	2.4	2.6	1.6	3.4	1.3	1.7	2.3	1.6	2.8	0.9	0.3	1.0
August	0.8	3.2	2.2	1.3	2.6	1.1	2.5	4.7	2.1	2.7	1.0	0.3	1.1
September	0.5	2.2	2.1	0.9	1.0	0.9	2.8	5.4	2.3	3.1	0.9	0.3	0.9
October	0.8	3.4	2.2	0.7	0.7	0.7	3.1	7.3	2.4	1.7	0.4	0.4	0.4
November	0.4	1.1	2.5	0.7	0.4	0.7	2.6	5.7	2.1	1.1	0.3	0.6	0.3
December	0.7	2.1	2.8	0.8	0.7	0.8	2.1	3.6	1.9	1.4	0.5	0.5	0.5
2010													
January	0.7	3.5	2.7	0.8	0.7	0.9	2.0	2.7	1.9	1.8	0.5	0.2	0.5
February	0.5	1.2	2.0	0.7	0.3	0.8	1.0	1.1	1.0	1.8	0.2	0.3	0.2
March	0.6	1.2	2.1	0.6	0.4	0.7	1.4	3.2	1.1	0.9	0.3	0.4	0.3
April	0.7	1.2	2.5	0.7	0.5	0.7	1.5	3.5	1.2	1.0	0.3	0.6	0.3
May	0.8	1.4	1.9	0.8	1.2	0.7	1.4	2.3	1.3	1.2	0.7	1.1	0.7
June	0.5	0.9	1.8	1.2	2.5	1.0	1.7	2.7	1.5	1.3	1.9	7.5	0.9
July	0.7	1.9	2.4	1.5	2.4	1.4	1.6	2.6	1.4	1.4	1.5	5.0	0.9
August	0.7	0.8	1.8	1.2	2.2	1.0	1.9	4.2	1.5	2.8	1.5	4.4	1.0
September	0.7	0.4	1.8	1.0	1.3	1.0	2.3	6.0	1.6	1.1	1.0	3.1	0.7
October	1.0	1.8	1.8	0.6	0.4	0.6	2.6	5.5	2.1	1.7	0.4	0.9	0.3
November	0.5	1.5	2.1	0.7	0.5	0.7	2.2	4.5	1.8	1.4	0.4	0.4	0.4
December	0.7	1.2	3.0	0.8	0.7	0.9	1.4	2.4	1.2	0.8	0.5	0.3	0.5
2011													
January	0.8	3.1	2.6	0.7	0.7	0.7	2.0	3.6	1.7	1.6	0.3	0.4	0.3
February	0.5	1.1	1.7	0.6	0.6	0.6	1.0	1.3	0.9	1.3	0.2	0.2	0.2
March	0.5	0.6	1.9	0.5	0.4	0.5	1.5	3.0	1.3	0.9	0.2	0.2	0.2
April	0.2	1.0	2.5	0.5	0.5	0.5	1.3	3.2	1.0	1.6	0.3	0.3	0.3
May	0.4	0.5	2.1	0.8	1.1	0.7	1.7	3.1	1.4	1.4	0.6	0.2	0.6
June	0.5	1.4	2.1	1.2	2.2	1.1	1.5	1.6	1.5	1.3	0.7	0.4	0.8
July	0.5	1.0	2.1	1.1	2.2	0.9	1.6	1.5	1.6	2.3	0.8	0.3	0.9
August	0.5	1.2	2.2	1.0	1.2	1.0	2.0	4.2	1.6	2.2	0.8	0.8	0.8
September	0.7	1.1	2.0	0.7	1.0	0.6	2.9	9.2	1.8	2.3	0.8	0.7	0.8
October	0.4	2.0	2.2	0.6	0.5	0.6	2.9	6.4	2.3	2.3	0.4	0.5	0.4
November	0.5	1.3	2.3	0.7	0.6	0.8	2.8	8.5	1.9	1.6	0.3	0.4	0.3
December	0.5	0.8	2.7	0.7	0.6	0.7	2.0	3.2	1.8	1.4	0.5	0.3	0.5
2012													
January	0.5	1.4	2.0	0.9	1.2	0.8	2.4	4.3	2.2	1.7	0.3	0.3	0.3
February	0.3	0.8	2.4	0.5	0.3	0.5	1.2	2.6	1.0	1.2	0.2	0.2	0.2
March	0.3	1.2	2.0	0.6	0.3	0.6	1.4	3.5	1.1	0.9	0.2	0.2	0.2
April	0.6	0.9	2.5	0.7	0.6	0.8	1.7	5.5	1.1	2.4	0.3	0.2	0.3
May	0.5	0.9	2.5	0.9	1.5	0.8	1.6	2.7	1.4	1.6	0.7	0.2	0.7
June	0.3	1.2	2.2	1.3	2.4	1.1	1.3	1.3	1.4	1.4	0.7	0.3	0.8
July	0.4	1.2	1.9	1.0	1.9	0.9	1.4	1.3	1.4	1.1	0.6	0.2	0.7
August	0.6	1.3	2.5	0.9	1.2	0.9	2.3	4.1	2.0	1.8	0.8	0.7	0.9
September	0.4	0.7	2.2	0.7	0.6	0.7	2.6	7.0	1.8	2.2	0.6	0.7	0.6
October	0.6	1.9	2.0	0.6	0.6	0.6	2.6	5.6	2.1	2.1	0.4	0.6	0.4
November	0.7	1.4	2.4	0.5	0.4	0.6	2.1	5.1	1.7	1.9	0.3	0.4	0.3
December	0.3	1.3	2.3	0.7	0.8	0.7	1.6	3.8	1.3	1.0	0.4	0.4	0.4
2013													
January	0.6	2.0	2.6	0.7	0.6	0.7	1.6	2.5	1.5	1.0	0.3	0.4	0.3
February	0.6	0.6	1.5	0.6	0.4	0.7	1.0	1.2	0.9	0.7	0.2	0.6	0.2
March	0.5	0.9	1.8	0.6	0.5	0.6	1.4	2.2	1.3	1.2	0.3	0.5	0.2
April	0.4	0.8	2.6	0.7	0.6	0.7	1.8	4.1	1.4	1.7	0.3	0.6	0.2
May	0.5	1.0	2.0	0.8	1.0	0.8	1.4	2.2	1.2	1.6	0.5	0.4	0.5
June	0.3	1.0	2.0	1.0	1.8	0.8	1.4	1.3	1.4	1.6	0.7	0.4	0.8
July	0.6	1.0	1.8	0.9	2.1	0.7	1.4	1.5	1.4	1.5	0.6	0.3	0.6
August	0.7	1.3	2.2	1.1	2.1	1.0	1.8	2.8	1.6	1.6	0.6	0.4	0.7
September	0.9	2.3	2.2	0.7	1.2	0.6	3.2	10.0	2.1	2.1	0.6	0.5	0.7
October	0.7	1.9	1.7	0.6	0.5	0.6	2.2	6.7	1.5	1.1	0.4	0.7	0.4

CHAPTER 8: LABOR-MANAGEMENT RELATIONS

HIGHLIGHTS

This chapter contains information on historical trends in union membership, earnings, and work stoppages.

Figure 8-1. Numbers of Work Stoppages, 2012

While the number of work stoppages has declined dramatically since 1947, they have increased in recent years before remaining steady in 2012 at 19. In 2009, only five work stoppages involving 1,000 or more workers took place compared with 11 work stoppages in 2010 and 19 in 2011. From 2011 to 2012, the number of days idle increased slightly from 1,020 to 1,131 after increasing dramatically from 2010 to 2011. (See Table 8-1.)

OTHER HIGHLIGHTS

- Union membership was higher for men (12.0 percent) than for women (10.5 percent) in 2012. According to race, Black workers had the highest rate of union membership at 13.4 percent, followed by Whites at 11.1 percent, Hispanics at 9.8 percent, and Asians at 9.6 percent. Hispanics may be of any race. (See Table 8-2.)

- In 2012, the percentage of workers belonging to a union declined to 11.3 percent. Nearly 14.4 million workers were union members in 2011 compared with 17.7 million in 1983. (See Tables 8-2 and 8-5.)

- Workers in the public sector were far more likely to be in a union than those in the private sector (35.9 percent compared with 6.6 percent). In the private sector, workers in transportation and utilities had the highest unionization rate (20.6 percent), while those in agriculture and related industries (1.4 percent) had the lowest rate. (See Table 8-3.)

- In 2012, 19 states had higher union membership rates than average. From 2011 to 2012, union membership rates rose in 14 states and the District of Columbia, declined in 34 states, and remained unchanged in 2 states. (See Table 8-6.)

NOTES AND DEFINITIONS

WORK STOPPAGES

COLLECTION AND COVERAGE

Data on work stoppages measure the number and duration of major strikes or lockouts (involving 1,000 workers or more) during the year, the number of workers involved in these stoppages, and the amount of time lost due to these stoppages.

Information on work stoppages is obtained from reports issued by the Federal Mediation and Conciliation Service, state labor market information offices, Bureau of Labor Statistics (BLS) Strike Reports from the Office of Employment and Unemployment Statistics, and media sources such as the *Daily Labor Report* and the *Wall Street Journal.* One or both parties involved in the work stoppage (employer and/or union) is contacted to verify the duration of the stoppage and number of workers idled by the stoppage.

The International Labor Organization (ILO) publishes foreign work stoppages statistics. Data are available from the ILO at http://www.ilo.org/global/lang--en/index.htm.

CONCEPTS AND DEFINITIONS

Days of idleness is calculated by taking the number of workers involved in the strike or lockout and multiplying it by the number of days workers are off the job. The number of working days lost for every major work stoppage is based on a 5-day workweek (Monday through Friday), excluding federal holidays.

Major work stoppage includes both worker-initiated strikes and employer-initiated lockouts involving 1,000 workers or more. BLS does not distinguish between lockouts and strikes in its statistics.

Workers involved consists of workers directly involved in the stoppage. This category does not measure the indirect or secondary effect of stoppages on other establishments whose employees are idle from material shortages or lack of service.

SOURCES OF ADDITIONAL INFORMATION

Additional information is available in BLS news release USDL 13-0193, "Major Work Stoppages in 2012," on the BLS Web site at http://www.bls.gov/wsp/home.htm.

UNION MEMBERSHIP

COLLECTION AND COVERAGE

The estimates of union membership are obtained from the Current Population Survey (CPS), which provides basic information on the labor force, employment, and unemployment. The survey is conducted monthly for the Bureau of Labor Statistics by the U.S. Census Bureau from a scientifically selected national sample of about 60,000 households. The union membership and earnings data are tabulated from one-quarter of the CPS monthly sample and are limited to wage and salary workers. All self-employed workers are excluded. The data in these tables are annual averages.

The Census Bureau introduces adjustments to the population controls for the CPS as part of its annual update of population estimates. The effect of the revised population controls on the union affiliation data is unknown. However, the effect of the new controls on the monthly CPS estimates was to decrease the December 2011 employment level by 216,000. The updated controls had little or no effect on unemployment rates and other ratios.

CONCEPTS AND DEFINITIONS

Full-time workers are workers who usually work 35 hours or more per week at their sole or principal job.

Part-time workers are workers who usually work fewer than 35 hours per week at their sole or principal job.

Wage and salary workers are workers who receive wages, salaries, commissions, tips, payment in kind, or piece rates. The group includes employees in both the private and public sectors but, for the purposes of the union membership and earnings series, excludes all self-employed persons, regardless of whether their businesses are incorporated.

Hispanic or Latino ethnicity refers to persons who identified themselves in the enumeration process as being Spanish, Hispanic, or Latino. Persons whose ethnicity is identified as Hispanic or Latino may be of any race.

Union members are members of a labor union or an employee association similar to a union.

Represented by unions refers to union members, as well as to workers who have no union affiliation but whose jobs are covered by a union contract.

CHAPTER EIGHT: LABOR-MANAGEMENT RELATIONS

Median earnings is the amount which divides a given earnings distribution into two equal groups, one having earnings above the median and the other having earnings below the median. The estimating procedure places each reported or calculated weekly earnings value into $50-wide intervals centered around multiples of $50. The actual value is estimated through the linear interpolation of the interval in which the median lies.

Usual weekly earnings represent earnings before taxes and other deductions and include any overtime pay, commissions, or tips usually received (at the main job in the case of multiple jobholders). Prior to 1994, respondents were asked how much they usually earned per week. Since January 1994, respondents have been asked to identify the easiest way for them to report earnings (hourly, weekly, biweekly, twice monthly, monthly, annually, other) and how much they usually earn in the reported time period. Earnings reported on a basis other than weekly are converted to a weekly equivalent. The term "usual" is as perceived by the respondent. If the respondent asks for a definition of "usual," interviewers are instructed to define the term as more than half of the weeks worked during the past 4 or 5 months.

SOURCES OF ADDITIONAL INFORMATION

For additional information, see BLS news release USDL 13-0105, "Union Members–2012."

Table 8-1. Work Stoppages Involving 1,000 Workers or More, 1947–2012

(Number, percent.)

Year	Stoppages beginning during the year		Days idle during the year[1]	
	Number	Workers involved (thousands)[2]	Number (thousands)	Percent of estimated total working time[3]
1947	270	1 629	25 720	. . .
1948	245	1 435	26 127	0.22
1949	262	2 537	43 420	0.38
1950	424	1 698	30 390	0.26
1951	415	1 462	15 070	0.12
1952	470	2 746	48 820	0.38
1953	437	1 623	18 130	0.14
1954	265	1 075	16 630	0.13
1955	363	2 055	21 180	0.16
1956	287	1 370	26 840	0.20
1957	279	887	10 340	0.07
1958	332	1 587	17 900	0.13
1959	245	1 381	60 850	0.43
1960	222	896	13 260	0.09
1961	195	1 031	10 140	0.07
1962	211	793	11 760	0.08
1963	181	512	10 020	0.07
1964	246	1 183	16 220	0.11
1965	268	999	15 140	0.10
1966	321	1 300	16 000	0.10
1967	381	2 192	31 320	0.18
1968	392	1 855	35 367	0.20
1969	412	1 576	29 397	0.16
1970	381	2 468	52 761	0.29
1971	298	2 516	35 538	0.19
1972	250	975	16 764	0.09
1973	317	1 400	16 260	0.08
1974	424	1 796	31 809	0.16
1975	235	965	17 563	0.09
1976	231	1 519	23 962	0.12
1977	298	1 212	21 258	0.10
1978	219	1 006	23 774	0.11
1979	235	1 021	20 409	0.09
1980	187	795	20 844	0.09
1981	145	729	16 908	0.07
1982	96	656	9 061	0.04
1983	81	909	17 461	0.08
1984	62	376	8 499	0.04
1985	54	324	7 079	0.03
1986	69	533	11 861	0.05
1987	46	174	4 481	0.02
1988	40	118	4 381	0.02
1989	51	452	16 996	0.07
1990	44	185	5 926	0.02
1991	40	392	4 584	0.02
1992	35	364	3 989	0.01
1993	35	182	3 981	0.01
1994	45	322	5 021	0.02
1995	31	192	5 771	0.02
1996	37	273	4 889	0.02
1997	29	339	4 497	0.01
1998	34	387	5 116	0.02
1999	17	73	1 996	0.01
2000	39	394	20 419	0.06
2001	29	99	1 151	(4)
2002	19	46	660	(4)
2003	14	129	4 091	0.01
2004	17	171	3 344	0.01
2005	22	100	1 736	0.01
2006	20	70	2 688	0.01
2007	21	189	1 265	(4)
2008	15	72	1 954	0.01
2009	5	13	124	(4)
2010	11	45	302	(4)
2011	19	113	1 020	(4)
2012	19	148	1 131	(4)

[1]Days idle include all stoppages in effect during the reference period. For work stoppages that are still ongoing at the end of the calendar year, only those days of idleness during the calendar year are counted.
[2]Workers are counted more than once if involved in more than one stoppage during the reference period.
[3]Agricultural and government workers are included in the calculation of estimated working time; private household, forestry, and fishery workers are excluded.
[4]Less than 0.005 percent.
. . . = Not available.

Table 8-2. Union Affiliation of Employed Wage and Salary Workers, by Selected Characteristics, 2007–2012

(Numbers in thousands, percent.)

Characteristic	2007					2008					2009				
	Total employed	Member of union[1]		Represented by union[2]		Total employed	Member of union[1]		Represented by union[2]		Total employed	Member of union[1]		Represented by union[2]	
		Total	Percent of employed	Total	Percent of employed		Total	Percent of employed	Total	Percent of employed		Total	Percent of employed	Total	Percent of employed
SEX AND AGE															
Both Sexes, 16 Years and Over	129 767	15 670	12.1	17 243	13.3	129 377	16 098	12.4	17 761	13.7	124 490	15 327	12.3	16 904	13.6
16 to 24 years	19 395	939	4.8	1 068	5.5	18 705	930	5.0	1 062	5.7	17 173	813	4.7	941	5.5
25 years and over	110 372	14 731	13.3	16 176	14.7	110 672	15 168	13.7	16 699	15.1	107 317	14 514	13.5	15 962	14.9
25 to 34 years	29 409	3 050	10.4	3 358	11.4	29 276	3 120	10.7	3 443	11.8	28 067	2 942	10.5	3 262	11.6
35 to 44 years	30 296	3 972	13.1	4 362	14.4	29 708	3 993	13.4	4 365	14.7	28 066	3 669	13.1	4 035	14.4
45 to 54 years	29 731	4 664	15.7	5 087	17.1	29 787	4 767	16.0	5 228	17.6	29 054	4 551	15.7	4 994	17.2
55 to 64 years	16 752	2 691	16.1	2 967	17.7	17 430	2 887	16.6	3 209	18.4	17 599	2 926	16.6	3 186	18.1
65 years and over	4 183	355	8.5	402	9.6	4 471	401	9.0	454	10.2	4 530	425	9.4	485	10.7
Men, 16 Years and Over	67 468	8 767	13.0	9 494	14.1	66 846	8 938	13.4	9 724	14.5	63 539	8 441	13.3	9 176	14.4
16 to 24 years	9 959	551	5.5	627	6.3	9 537	555	5.8	617	6.5	8 555	493	5.8	560	6.5
25 years and over	57 509	8 217	14.3	8 867	15.4	57 309	8 383	14.6	9 107	15.9	54 984	7 947	14.5	8 616	15.7
25 to 34 years	15 994	1 736	10.9	1 884	11.8	15 780	1 750	11.1	1 909	12.1	14 952	1 633	10.9	1 786	11.9
35 to 44 years	16 070	2 318	14.4	2 501	15.6	15 653	2 307	14.7	2 491	15.9	14 679	2 077	14.1	2 250	15.3
45 to 54 years	15 040	2 578	17.1	2 745	18.3	14 988	2 608	17.4	2 812	18.8	14 421	2 492	17.3	2 693	18.7
55 to 64 years	8 286	1 403	16.9	1 532	18.5	8 657	1 525	17.6	1 682	19.4	8 647	1 536	17.8	1 654	19.1
65 years and over	2 119	181	8.5	205	9.7	2 230	193	8.7	213	9.6	2 285	211	9.2	233	10.2
Women, 16 Years and Over	62 299	6 903	11.1	7 749	12.4	62 532	7 160	11.4	8 036	12.9	60 951	6 887	11.3	7 727	12.7
16 to 24 years	9 436	388	4.1	441	4.7	9 168	374	4.1	445	4.8	8 619	320	3.7	381	4.4
25 years and over	52 863	6 514	12.3	7 308	13.8	53 364	6 785	12.7	7 592	14.2	52 333	6 567	12.5	7 346	14.0
25 to 34 years	13 416	1 313	9.8	1 474	11.0	13 496	1 370	10.1	1 534	11.4	13 116	1 309	10.0	1 476	11.3
35 to 44 years	14 226	1 653	11.6	1 861	13.1	14 055	1 685	12.0	1 874	13.3	13 387	1 593	11.9	1 785	13.3
45 to 54 years	14 691	2 086	14.2	2 341	15.9	14 799	2 159	14.6	2 416	16.3	14 633	2 060	14.1	2 302	15.7
55 to 64 years	8 466	1 288	15.2	1 435	17.0	8 773	1 363	15.5	1 527	17.4	8 952	1 390	15.5	1 532	17.1
65 years and over	2 065	174	8.4	197	9.5	2 241	208	9.3	241	10.7	2 245	215	9.6	252	11.2
RACE, HISPANIC ORIGIN, AND SEX															
White, 16 Years and Over[3]	105 515	12 487	11.8	13 715	13.0	105 052	12 863	12.2	14 222	13.5	101 581	12 330	12.1	13 595	13.4
Men	55 771	7 134	12.8	7 708	13.8	55 197	7 309	13.2	7 961	14.4	52 691	6 918	13.1	7 512	14.3
Women	49 743	5 352	10.8	6 007	12.1	49 855	5 555	11.1	6 261	12.6	48 889	5 412	11.1	6 083	12.4
Black, 16 Years and Over[3]	15 177	2 165	14.3	2 403	15.8	15 030	2 178	14.5	2 370	15.8	14 127	1 966	13.9	2 172	15.4
Men	6 945	1 097	15.8	1 205	17.3	6 809	1 081	15.9	1 159	17.0	6 257	964	15.4	1 046	16.7
Women	8 232	1 067	13.0	1 198	14.6	8 221	1 097	13.3	1 211	14.7	7 870	1 002	12.7	1 126	14.3
Asian, 16 Years and Over[3]	6 016	654	10.9	720	12.0	6 157	653	10.6	714	11.6	5 847	664	11.4	730	12.5
Men	3 168	324	10.2	348	11.0	3 216	310	9.6	339	10.6	3 075	332	10.8	370	12.0
Women	2 849	330	11.6	372	13.1	2 941	344	11.7	374	12.7	2 772	333	12.0	361	13.0
Hispanic, 16 Years and Over[4]	18 778	1 837	9.8	2 026	10.8	18 572	1 960	10.6	2 168	11.7	18 034	1 841	10.2	2 036	11.3
Men	11 163	1 108	9.9	1 208	10.8	10 998	1 204	11.0	1 317	12.0	10 518	1 108	10.5	1 199	11.4
Women	7 615	728	9.6	818	10.7	7 574	756	10.0	852	11.2	7 515	733	9.7	836	11.1
FULL- OR PART-TIME STATUS[5]															
Full-time workers	107 339	14 201	13.2	15 570	14.5	106 648	14 561	13.7	16 029	15.0	99 820	13 602	13.6	14 960	15.0
Part-time workers	22 172	1 437	6.5	1 635	7.4	22 497	1 505	6.7	1 697	7.5	24 431	1 698	7.0	1 913	7.8

[1]Data refer to members of a labor union or to an employee association similar to a union.
[2]Data refer to members of a labor union or to an employee association similar to a union, as well as to workers who report no union affiliation but whose jobs are covered by a union or an employee association contract.
[3]Beginning in 2003, persons who selected this race group only; persons who selected more than one race group are not included. Prior to 2003, persons who reported more than one race group were included in the group they identified as their main race. Additionally, estimates for the above race groups (White, Black, and Asian) do not sum to totals because data are not presented for all races.
[4]May be of any race.
[5]The distinction between full- and part-time workers is based on hours usually worked. Data will not sum to totals because full- or part-time status on the principal job is not identifiable for a small number of multiple job holders.

Table 8-2. Union Affiliation of Employed Wage and Salary Workers, by Selected Characteristics, 2007–2012—*Continued*

(Numbers in thousands, percent.)

Characteristic	2010					2011					2012				
	Total employed	Member of union[1]		Represented by union[2]		Total employed	Member of union[1]		Represented by union[2]		Total employed	Member of union[1]		Represented by union[2]	
		Total	Percent of employed	Total	Percent of employed		Total	Percent of employed	Total	Percent of employed		Total	Percent of employed	Total	Percent of employed
SEX AND AGE															
Both Sexes, 16 Years and Over	124 073	14 715	11.9	16 290	13.1	125 187	14 764	11.8	16 290	13.0	127 577	14 366	11.3	15 922	12.5
16 to 24 years	16 638	722	4.3	836	5.0	16 910	737	4.4	845	5.0	17 417	731	4.2	869	5.0
25 years and over	107 435	13 993	13.0	15 453	14.4	108 278	14 027	13.0	15 444	14.3	110 160	13 635	12.4	15 053	13.7
25 to 34 years	28 363	2 860	10.1	3 179	11.2	28 682	2 829	9.9	3 155	11.0	28 875	2 755	9.5	3 083	10.7
35 to 44 years	27 356	3 512	12.8	3 888	14.2	27 231	3 470	12.7	3 804	14.0	27 442	3 424	12.5	3 746	13.6
45 to 54 years	28 860	4 340	15.0	4 774	16.5	28 693	4 286	14.9	4 707	16.4	28 765	4 032	14.0	4 437	15.4
55 to 64 years	18 199	2 849	15.7	3 126	17.2	18 751	2 949	15.7	3 219	17.2	19 694	2 932	14.9	3 233	16.4
65 years and over	4 657	432	9.3	486	10.4	4 920	494	10.0	559	11.4	5 385	491	9.1	554	10.3
Men, 16 Years and Over	63 531	7 994	12.6	8 761	13.8	64 686	8 006	12.4	8 731	13.5	65 898	7 895	12.0	8 611	13.1
16 to 24 years	8 291	419	5.0	476	5.7	8 636	435	5.0	486	5.6	8 830	448	5.1	521	5.9
25 years and over	55 240	7 575	13.7	8 286	15.0	56 050	7 571	13.5	8 246	14.7	57 067	7 448	13.1	8 090	14.2
25 to 34 years	15 148	1 603	10.6	1 759	11.6	15 465	1 541	10.0	1 706	11.0	15 465	1 546	10.0	1 688	10.9
35 to 44 years	14 430	1 966	13.6	2 151	14.9	14 412	1 946	13.5	2 114	14.7	14 481	1 919	13.3	2 085	14.4
45 to 54 years	14 423	2 349	16.3	2 554	17.7	14 415	2 327	16.1	2 513	17.4	14 601	2 214	15.2	2 385	16.3
55 to 64 years	8 895	1 430	16.1	1 566	17.6	9 212	1 497	16.2	1 623	17.6	9 728	1 521	15.6	1 655	17.0
65 years and over	2 343	227	9.7	256	10.9	2 547	260	10.2	290	11.4	2 792	248	8.9	277	9.9
Women, 16 Years and Over	60 542	6 722	11.1	7 528	12.4	60 502	6 758	11.2	7 558	12.5	61 679	6 470	10.5	7 311	11.9
16 to 24 years	8 347	303	3.6	361	4.3	8 274	302	3.6	360	4.3	8 586	283	3.3	347	4.0
25 years and over	52 195	6 418	12.3	7 167	13.7	52 228	6 456	12.4	7 199	13.8	53 093	6 187	11.7	6 964	13.1
25 to 34 years	13 215	1 257	9.5	1 420	10.7	13 218	1 288	9.7	1 449	11.0	13 410	1 209	9.0	1 396	10.4
35 to 44 years	12 926	1 546	12.0	1 737	13.4	12 819	1 524	11.9	1 690	13.2	12 961	1 505	11.6	1 661	12.8
45 to 54 years	14 437	1 991	13.8	2 219	15.4	14 278	1 959	13.7	2 195	15.4	14 164	1 819	12.8	2 052	14.5
55 to 64 years	9 303	1 419	15.3	1 560	16.8	9 540	1 452	15.2	1 596	16.7	9 966	1 411	14.2	1 579	15.8
65 years and over	2 314	205	8.8	230	10.0	2 373	233	9.8	269	11.3	2 593	244	9.4	277	10.7
RACE, HISPANIC ORIGIN, AND SEX															
White, 16 Years and Over[3]	101 042	11 865	11.7	13 111	13.0	101 768	11 853	11.6	13 061	12.8	101 851	11 306	11.1	12 517	12.3
Men	52 565	6 588	12.5	7 208	13.7	53 418	6 568	12.3	7 156	13.4	53 542	6 359	11.9	6 933	12.9
Women	48 477	5 277	10.9	5 903	12.2	48 351	5 285	10.9	5 905	12.2	48 309	4 947	10.2	5 584	11.6
Black, 16 Years and Over[3]	14 195	1 896	13.4	2 115	14.9	14 249	1 927	13.5	2 140	15.0	14 975	2 009	13.4	2 220	14.8
Men	6 347	938	14.8	1 031	16.2	6 440	940	14.6	1 020	15.8	6 753	999	14.8	1 078	16.0
Women	7 848	958	12.2	1 085	13.8	7 808	987	12.6	1 119	14.3	8 222	1 009	12.3	1 142	13.9
Asian, 16 Years and Over[3]	5 900	645	10.9	713	12.1	6 153	623	10.1	690	11.2	6 953	668	9.6	758	10.9
Men	3 112	292	9.4	325	10.4	3 269	296	9.1	331	10.1	3 650	323	8.9	369	10.1
Women	2 787	353	12.6	388	13.9	2 884	327	11.4	359	12.4	3 303	345	10.4	388	11.8
Hispanic, 16 Years and Over[4]	18 263	1 820	10.0	2 021	11.1	18 733	1 826	9.7	2 015	10.8	20 144	1 982	9.8	2 197	10.9
Men	10 646	1 090	10.2	1 196	11.2	10 980	1 078	9.8	1 186	10.8	11 415	1 148	10.1	1 266	11.1
Women	7 616	730	9.6	825	10.8	7 754	748	9.6	829	10.7	8 730	834	9.6	931	10.7
FULL- OR PART-TIME STATUS[5]															
Full-time workers	99 531	13 125	13.2	14 498	14.6	100 457	13 177	13.1	14 487	14.4	102 749	12 847	12.5	14 173	13.8
Part-time workers	24 351	1 560	6.4	1 760	7.2	24 502	1 557	6.4	1 769	7.2	24 614	1 483	6.0	1 710	6.9

[1]Data refer to members of a labor union or to an employee association similar to a union.

[2]Data refer to members of a labor union or to an employee association similar to a union, as well as to workers who report no union affiliation but whose jobs are covered by a union or an employee association contract.

[3]Beginning in 2003, persons who selected this race group only; persons who selected more than one race group are not included. Prior to 2003, persons who reported more than one race group were included in the group they identified as their main race. Additionally, estimates for the above race groups (White, Black, and Asian) do not sum to totals because data are not presented for all races.

[4]May be of any race.

[5]The distinction between full- and part-time workers is based on hours usually worked. Data will not sum to totals because full- or part-time status on the principal job is not identifiable for a small number of multiple job holders.

Table 8-3. Union Affiliation of Wage and Salary Workers, by Occupation and Industry, 2011–2012

(Thousands of people, percent.)

Occupation and industry	2011					2012				
	Total employed	Member of union[1]		Represented by union[2]		Total employed	Member of union[1]		Represented by union[2]	
		Total	Percent of employed	Total	Percent of employed		Total	Percent of employed	Total	Percent of employed
OCCUPATION										
Management, professional, and related	45 520	5 896	13.0	6 693	14.7	46 897	5 751	12.3	6 514	13.9
Management, business, and financial operations	17 196	851	4.9	1 039	6.0	18 153	844	4.6	1 009	5.6
Management	11 593	538	4.6	668	5.8	12 259	500	4.1	610	5.0
Business and financial operations	5 603	313	5.6	371	6.6	5 894	344	5.8	399	6.8
Professional and related	28 324	5 045	17.8	5 654	20.0	28 743	4 907	17.1	5 505	19.2
Computer and mathematical	3 438	136	4.0	167	4.9	3 578	134	3.7	173	4.8
Architecture and engineering	2 615	191	7.3	227	8.7	2 701	206	7.6	240	8.9
Life, physical, and social science	1 174	139	11.8	164	13.9	1 219	132	10.8	150	12.3
Community and social service	2 268	374	16.5	418	18.4	2 239	361	16.1	406	18.1
Legal	1 378	69	5.0	93	6.7	1 428	70	4.9	87	6.1
Education, training, and library	8 343	3 067	36.8	3 381	40.5	8 325	2 944	35.4	3 267	39.2
Arts, design, entertainment, sports, and media	1 904	132	6.9	146	7.7	1 943	144	7.4	159	8.2
Health care practitioner and technical	7 204	938	13.0	1 058	14.7	7 309	916	12.5	1 023	14.0
Services	22 508	2 429	10.8	2 653	11.8	23 095	2 406	10.4	2 630	11.4
Health care support	3 178	268	8.4	297	9.3	3 340	277	8.3	321	9.6
Protective service	3 207	1 107	34.5	1 180	36.8	3 078	1 071	34.8	1 122	36.5
Food preparation and serving related	7 677	305	4.0	351	4.6	7 966	298	3.7	358	4.5
Building and grounds cleaning and maintenance	4 603	489	10.6	532	11.6	4 729	498	10.5	540	11.4
Personal care and service	3 843	260	6.8	294	7.6	3 983	263	6.6	289	7.3
Sales and office	30 580	2 114	6.9	2 362	7.7	30 685	2 070	6.7	2 357	7.7
Sales and related	13 189	401	3.0	455	3.4	13 366	389	2.9	465	3.5
Office and administrative support	17 390	1 714	9.9	1 908	11.0	17 319	1 681	9.7	1 892	10.9
Natural resources, construction, and maintenance	10 955	1 838	16.8	1 959	17.9	10 863	1 775	16.3	1 876	17.3
Farming, fishing, and forestry	940	32	3.4	38	4.0	949	32	3.4	38	4.1
Construction and extraction	5 575	1 064	19.1	1 120	20.1	5 567	1 054	18.9	1 108	19.9
Installation, maintenance, and repair	4 440	742	16.7	801	18.0	4 347	689	15.8	729	16.8
Production, transportation, and material moving	15 625	2 487	15.9	2 622	16.8	16 038	2 365	14.7	2 546	15.9
Production	7 739	1 104	14.3	1 159	15.0	8 116	1 002	12.3	1 084	13.4
Transportation and material moving	7 886	1 383	17.5	1 463	18.6	7 922	1 363	17.2	1 462	18.5
INDUSTRY										
Private sector	104 737	7 202	6.9	7 969	7.6	107 191	7 037	6.6	7 851	7.3
Agriculture and related industries	1 183	16	1.4	21	1.8	1 172	16	1.4	21	1.8
Nonagricultural industries	103 554	7 186	6.9	7 948	7.7	106 019	7 021	6.6	7 830	7.4
Mining	780	56	7.2	61	7.8	923	66	7.2	72	7.7
Construction	6 244	874	14.0	928	14.9	6 205	820	13.2	850	13.7
Manufacturing	13 599	1 424	10.5	1 521	11.2	13 941	1 338	9.6	1 468	10.5
Durable goods	8 530	871	10.2	924	10.8	8 787	830	9.4	906	10.3
Nondurable goods	5 070	553	10.9	596	11.8	5 154	507	9.8	563	10.9
Wholesale and retail trade	18 002	859	4.8	959	5.3	18 174	854	4.7	960	5.3
Wholesale trade	3 419	150	4.4	165	4.8	3 341	169	5.1	186	5.6
Retail trade	14 582	709	4.9	794	5.4	14 833	686	4.6	774	5.2
Transportation and utilities	5 239	1 108	21.1	1 159	22.1	5 359	1 105	20.6	1 174	21.9
Transportation and warehousing	4 355	887	20.4	932	21.4	4 520	898	19.9	948	21.0
Utilities	884	221	25.0	228	25.7	839	207	24.7	226	26.9
Information[3]	2 756	279	10.1	298	10.8	2 575	251	9.7	273	10.6
Publishing, except Internet	554	25	4.5	26	4.7	548	20	3.7	24	4.3
Motion pictures and sound recording	337	47	13.8	48	14.1	293	33	11.4	36	12.2
Broadcasting, except Internet	576	34	5.9	40	7.0	546	37	6.7	42	7.6
Telecommunications	1 064	166	15.6	175	16.4	956	149	15.6	160	16.8
Financial activities	8 086	132	1.6	165	2.0	8 196	156	1.9	203	2.5
Finance and insurance	6 111	64	1.1	86	1.4	6 195	73	1.2	102	1.7
Finance	3 932	37	1.0	53	1.3	4 054	45	1.1	62	1.5
Insurance	2 179	27	1.2	33	1.5	2 141	28	1.3	40	1.9
Real estate and rental and leasing	1 976	67	3.4	79	4.0	2 001	83	4.1	101	5.0
Professional and business services	12 171	250	2.1	322	2.6	12 726	310	2.4	388	3.0
Professional and technical services	7 244	90	1.2	131	1.8	7 630	93	1.2	140	1.8
Management, administrative, and waste services	4 927	160	3.3	191	3.9	5 096	217	4.3	248	4.9
Education and health services	19 855	1 715	8.6	1 982	10.0	20 394	1 658	8.1	1 891	9.3
Education services	4 020	523	13.0	621	15.5	4 190	520	12.4	592	14.1
Health care and social assistance	15 835	1 192	7.5	1 361	8.6	16 204	1 138	7.0	1 299	8.0
Leisure and hospitality	11 355	305	2.7	344	3.0	11 775	321	2.7	377	3.2
Arts, entertainment, and recreation	2 107	111	5.3	121	5.7	2 127	136	6.4	148	7.0
Accommodation and food services	9 247	194	2.1	224	2.4	9 648	185	1.9	229	2.4
Accommodation	1 350	96	7.1	105	7.8	1 354	89	6.5	101	7.5
Food services and drinking places	7 898	98	1.2	119	1.5	8 295	97	1.2	128	1.5
Other services[3]	5 467	184	3.4	209	3.8	5 750	143	2.5	174	3.0
Other services, except private households	4 723	167	3.5	189	4.0	5 028	133	2.6	163	3.2
Public sector	20 450	7 562	37.0	8 321	40.7	20 385	7 328	35.9	8 072	39.6
Federal government	3 568	1 004	28.1	1 185	33.2	3 552	956	26.9	1 114	31.4
State government	6 261	1 973	31.5	2 189	35.0	6 279	1 968	31.3	2 190	34.9
Local government	10 621	4 586	43.2	4 947	46.6	10 554	4 404	41.7	4 768	45.2

Note: Updated population controls are introduced annually with the release of January data. Data refer to the sole or principal job of full- and part-time workers. Excluded are all self-employed workers, regardless of whether or not their businesses are incorporated.

[1]Data refer to members of a labor union or an employee association similar to a union.
[2]Data refer to members of a labor union or an employee association similar to a union, as well as to workers who report no union affiliation but whose jobs are covered by a union or an employee association contract.
[3]Includes other industries, not shown separately.

Table 8-4. Median Weekly Earnings of Full-Time Wage and Salary Workers, by Union Affiliation, Occupation, and Industry, 2011–2012

(Dollars.)

Occupation and industry	2011				2012			
	Total	Member of union[1]	Represented by union[2]	Non-union	Total	Member of union[1]	Represented by union[2]	Non-union
OCCUPATION								
Management, professional, and related	1 082	1 090	1 082	1 082	1 108	1 108	1 092	1 111
Management, business, and financial operations	1 160	1 169	1 171	1 159	1 171	1 159	1 161	1 172
Management	1 237	1 287	1 300	1 232	1 248	1 261	1 274	1 247
Business and financial operations	1 038	999	999	1 042	1 058	1 060	1 024	1 060
Professional and related	1 029	1 074	1 064	1 017	1 053	1 098	1 077	1 046
Computer and mathematical	1 305	1 156	1 169	1 324	1 349	1 157	1 158	1 359
Architecture and engineering	1 315	1 304	1 325	1 314	1 337	1 368	1 350	1 335
Life, physical, and social science	1 108	1 229	1 218	1 085	1 134	1 209	1 177	1 127
Community and social service	813	993	1 000	771	838	1 007	1 003	783
Legal	1 277	1 222	1 376	1 273	1 328	1 174	1 173	1 342
Education, training, and library	919	1 038	1 020	814	915	1 050	1 028	814
Arts, design, entertainment, sports, and media	929	1 179	1 152	910	969	1 107	1 097	957
Health care practitioner and technical	995	1 132	1 125	975	1 028	1 151	1 142	1 010
Services	486	742	732	455	485	754	735	458
Health care support	487	519	518	484	482	527	522	477
Protective service	757	1 008	1 004	627	791	1 071	1 056	649
Food preparation and serving related	409	504	500	405	410	509	505	405
Building and grounds cleaning and maintenance	465	635	626	431	465	621	614	440
Personal care and service	453	534	527	444	468	524	515	462
Sales and office	638	775	771	624	655	789	776	642
Sales and related	670	660	669	670	689	689	668	691
Office and administrative support	623	803	791	608	643	808	796	624
Natural resources, construction, and maintenance	732	1 016	1 008	676	740	1 026	1 018	688
Farming, fishing, and forestry	430	(3)	(3)	426	435	(3)	(3)	430
Construction and extraction	717	1 017	1 010	647	740	1 040	1 026	682
Installation, maintenance, and repair	806	1 036	1 021	767	808	1 032	1 021	768
Production, transportation, and material moving	609	798	794	582	624	823	811	597
Production	605	781	778	583	627	816	807	605
Transportation and material moving	614	813	808	580	621	833	816	586
INDUSTRY								
Private sector	729	878	875	716	742	887	877	731
Agriculture and related industries	483	(3)	(3)	481	470	(3)	(3)	469
Nonagricultural industries	732	879	875	721	746	888	878	735
Mining	1 064	1 030	1 005	1 069	1 112	1 119	1 112	1 113
Construction	746	1 059	1 037	698	768	1 086	1 069	722
Manufacturing	787	836	835	780	797	872	863	786
Durable goods	818	889	887	809	827	891	884	819
Nondurable goods	737	771	771	729	737	827	817	722
Wholesale and retail trade	613	622	622	612	630	650	637	629
Wholesale trade	759	798	773	758	821	821	801	823
Retail trade	578	591	592	577	592	609	598	592
Transportation and utilities	805	987	985	762	828	998	989	789
Transportation and warehousing	763	941	939	726	778	948	934	746
Utilities	1 081	1 132	1 132	1 027	1 132	1 216	1 204	1 086
Information[4]	940	1 122	1 117	916	978	1 103	1 087	966
Publishing, except Internet	910	(3)	(3)	902	934	(3)	(3)	921
Motion pictures and sound recording	965	(3)	(3)	926	854	(3)	(3)	798
Broadcasting, except Internet	834	(3)	(3)	834	890	(3)	(3)	903
Telecommunications	987	1 113	1 109	950	1 064	1 162	1 163	1 039
Financial activities	866	824	822	866	889	795	779	893
Finance and insurance	907	819	826	908	941	852	831	944
Finance	910	(3)	820	911	952	(3)	762	955
Insurance	899	(3)	(3)	900	922	(3)	(3)	924
Real estate and rental and leasing	736	836	815	734	731	773	759	727
Professional and business services	880	872	883	880	910	826	843	912
Professional and technical services	1 149	1 193	1 211	1 149	1 165	1 183	1 133	1 165
Management, administrative, and waste services	569	706	693	562	582	699	708	577
Education and health services	736	870	878	722	748	879	876	736
Education services	858	938	942	833	864	918	922	844
Health care and social assistance	706	801	809	697	720	835	824	711
Leisure and hospitality	479	607	605	473	481	611	604	475
Arts, entertainment, and recreation	612	632	625	611	641	675	668	640
Accommodation and food services	447	594	594	441	445	596	588	438
Accommodation	515	598	596	508	542	613	609	527
Food services and drinking places	427	585	592	424	421	536	534	419
Other services[4]	626	917	901	619	622	807	763	618
Other services, except private households	654	960	919	643	649	828	774	645
Public sector	895	981	977	810	898	990	980	829
Federal government	1 063	1 038	1 043	1 092	1 072	1 035	1 045	1 113
State government	852	956	946	785	854	948	933	794
Local government	861	973	967	743	866	989	975	75

Note: Updated population controls are introduced annually with the release of January data. Data refer to the sole or principal job of full- and part-time workers. Excluded are all self-employed workers, regardless of whether or not their businesses are incorporated.

[1]Data refer to members of a labor union or an employee association similar to a union.
[2]Data refer to members of a labor union or an employee association similar to a union, as well as to workers who report no union affiliation but whose jobs are covered by a union or an employee association contract.
[3]Data not shown where base is less than 50,000.
[4]Includes other industries, not shown separately.

Table 8-5. Union or Employee Association Members Among Wage and Salary Employees, 1977–2012

(Numbers in thousands, percent.)

Year	Total wage and salary employment	Union or employee association member	Union or association members as a percent of total wage and salary employment
1977	81 334	19 335	23.8
1978	84 968	19 548	23.0
1979	87 117	20 986	24.1
1980	87 480	20 095	23.0
1981	...	...	...
1982	...	...	...
1983[1]	88 290	17 717	20.1
1984	92 194	17 340	18.8
1985	94 521	16 996	18.0
1986	96 903	16 975	17.5
1987	99 303	16 913	17.0
1988	101 407	17 002	16.8
1989	103 480	16 980	16.4
1990	103 905	16 740	16.1
1991	102 786	16 568	16.1
1992	103 688	16 390	15.8
1993	105 087	16 598	15.8
1994[2]	107 989	16 748	15.5
1995	110 038	16 360	14.9
1996	111 960	16 269	14.5
1997	114 533	16 110	14.1
1998	116 730	16 211	13.9
1999	118 963	16 477	13.9
2000	120 786	16 258	13.5
2001	122 482	16 387	13.4
2002	121 826	16 145	13.3
2003	122 358	15 776	12.9
2004	123 554	15 472	12.5
2005	125 889	15 685	12.5
2006	128 237	15 359	12.0
2007	129 767	15 670	12.1
2008	129 377	16 098	12.4
2009	124 490	15 327	12.3
2010	124 073	14 715	11.9
2011	125 187	14 764	11.8
2012	127 577	14 366	11.3

[1]Annual average data beginning in 1983 are not directly comparable with the data for 1977–1980.
[2]Data beginning in 1994 are not strictly comparable with data for 1993 and earlier years because of the introduction of a major redesign of the Current Population Survey questionnaire and collection methodology and the introduction of 1990 census–based population controls.
. . . = Not available.

Table 8-6. Union Affiliation of Employed Wage and Salary Workers, by State, 2011–2012

(Numbers in thousands, percent.)

State	2011					2012				
	Total employed	Member of union[1]		Represented by union[2]		Total employed	Member of union[1]		Represented by union[2]	
		Total	Percent of employed	Total	Percent of employed		Total	Percent of employed	Total	Percent of employed
UNITED STATES	125 187	14 764	11.8	16 290	13.0	127 577	14 366	11.3	15 922	12.5
Alabama	1 781	178	10.0	193	10.8	1 807	166	9.2	190	10.5
Alaska	306	68	22.1	73	23.7	298	67	22.4	71	23.9
Arizona	2 493	149	6.0	183	7.3	2 434	125	5.1	159	6.5
Arkansas	1 116	47	4.2	57	5.1	1 157	37	3.2	43	3.7
California	13 931	2 379	17.1	2 532	18.2	14 483	2 489	17.2	2 666	18.4
Colorado	2 186	179	8.2	203	9.3	2 165	169	7.8	190	8.8
Connecticut	1 542	259	16.8	272	17.7	1 541	216	14.0	232	15.1
Delaware	370	39	10.5	42	11.2	377	39	10.4	44	11.8
District of Columbia	281	23	8.3	28	9.9	309	27	8.6	32	10.3
Florida	7 283	460	6.3	557	7.6	7 602	440	5.8	555	7.3
Georgia	3 876	153	3.9	185	4.8	3 914	171	4.4	210	5.4
Hawaii	525	113	21.5	118	22.5	537	116	21.6	124	23.2
Idaho	594	31	5.1	36	6.1	613	29	4.8	36	5.8
Illinois	5 408	876	16.2	929	17.2	5 486	801	14.6	852	15.5
Indiana	2 681	302	11.3	333	12.4	2 702	246	9.1	269	10.0
Iowa	1 386	155	11.2	187	13.5	1 390	145	10.4	172	12.4
Kansas	1 268	97	7.6	128	10.1	1 248	85	6.8	105	8.4
Kentucky	1 678	150	8.9	173	10.3	1 742	174	10.0	198	11.4
Louisiana	1 717	77	4.5	91	5.3	1 733	107	6.2	130	7.5
Maine	554	63	11.3	74	13.4	559	64	11.5	78	13.9
Maryland	2 549	316	12.4	348	13.7	2 636	280	10.6	325	12.3
Massachusetts	2 882	422	14.6	445	15.4	2 896	417	14.4	470	16.2
Michigan	3 838	671	17.5	703	18.3	3 785	629	16.6	648	17.1
Minnesota	2 461	371	15.1	390	15.8	2 465	351	14.2	368	14.9
Mississippi	1 081	54	5.0	73	6.8	1 113	48	4.3	64	5.7
Missouri	2 531	275	10.9	316	12.5	2 507	224	8.9	253	10.1
Montana	377	49	13.0	55	14.6	392	54	13.9	65	16.5
Nebraska	828	65	7.9	83	10.0	864	52	6.0	70	8.1
Nevada	1 050	154	14.6	175	16.6	1 101	162	14.7	181	16.4
New Hampshire	617	68	11.1	77	12.5	621	65	10.5	74	12.0
New Jersey	3 816	615	16.1	641	16.8	3 796	611	16.1	636	16.8
New Mexico	726	49	6.8	65	9.0	780	50	6.5	68	8.7
New York	7 920	1 906	24.1	2 068	26.1	7 936	1 841	23.2	1 975	24.9
North Carolina	3 589	105	2.9	149	4.1	3 805	112	2.9	162	4.3
North Dakota	318	20	6.3	27	8.6	329	20	6.1	27	8.2
Ohio	4 813	647	13.4	706	14.7	4 800	604	12.6	665	13.9
Oklahoma	1 458	94	6.4	113	7.7	1 531	115	7.5	140	9.1
Oregon	1 574	270	17.1	286	18.1	1 526	240	15.7	250	16.4
Pennsylvania	5 348	779	14.6	846	15.8	5 452	734	13.5	787	14.4
Rhode Island	453	79	17.4	81	17.9	455	81	17.8	84	18.4
South Carolina	1 726	59	3.4	86	5.0	1 773	58	3.3	82	4.6
South Dakota	359	18	5.1	23	6.5	351	20	5.6	24	6.7
Tennessee	2 504	115	4.6	139	5.6	2 586	124	4.8	152	5.9
Texas	10 214	534	5.2	643	6.3	10 590	599	5.7	721	6.8
Utah	1 150	67	5.8	82	7.1	1 179	61	5.2	77	6.6
Vermont	290	35	12.0	39	13.5	288	31	10.7	38	13.1
Virginia	3 550	163	4.6	198	5.6	3 592	159	4.4	197	5.5
Washington	2 727	517	19.0	557	20.4	2 776	513	18.5	541	19.5
West Virginia	672	93	13.8	102	15.2	697	84	12.1	91	13.1
Wisconsin	2 538	339	13.3	358	14.1	2 605	293	11.2	312	12.0
Wyoming	250	18	7.2	21	8.4	252	17	6.7	20	8.1

Note: Updated population controls are introduced annually with the release of January data. Data refer to the sole or principal job of full- and part-time workers. Excluded are all self-employed workers, regardless of whether or not their businesses are incorporated.

[1] Data refer to members of a labor union or an employee association similar to a union.
[2] Data refer to members of a labor union or an employee association similar to a union, as well as to workers who report no union affiliation but whose jobs are covered by a union or an employee association contract.

CHAPTER 9: PRICES

PRICES

HIGHLIGHTS

This chapter examines the movement of prices, which is one of the most important indicators of the state of the economy. Several indexes are covered: the Producer Price Index (PPI), which gives information about prices received by producers; the Consumer Price Index (CPI), which gives information about prices paid by consumers; and the Import Price Index (MPI) and the Export Price Index (XPI), which give information about prices involved in various foreign trade, export, and import price indexes.

Figure 9-1. Percent Change in Producer Price Indexes by Selected Commodity Group, 2000–2012

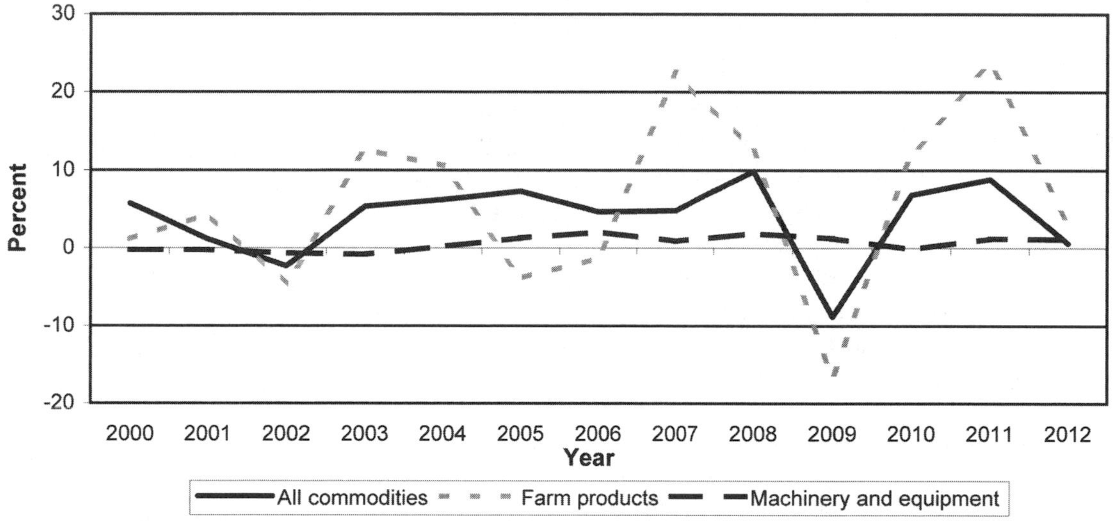

The PPI for all commodities increased slightly in 2012 after rising 8.8 percent in 2011 and 6.8 percent in 2010. Meanwhile, the PPI for farm products grew 3.1 percent after increasing 23.6 percent in 2011. (See Table 9-2.)

OTHER HIGHLIGHTS

- The PPI for crude materials for further processing declined 3.2 percent in 2012 after it rose quickly in 2010 and 2011. (See Table 9-1.)

- Among the industrial commodities listed in Table 9-2, the PPI for lumber and wood products grew the fastest at 3.5 percent, while the PPI for metals and metal products experienced the steepest decline at 2.7 percent. (See Table 9-2.)

- From 2000 through 2012, the producer price index increased 52.4 percent. Fuels and related products grew the fastest at 104.9 percent, followed by farm products at 93.5 percent. (See Table 9-2.)

NOTES AND DEFINITIONS

PRODUCER PRICE INDEX

COVERAGE

The Producer Price Index (PPI) measures average changes in prices received by domestic producers of goods and services. PPIs measure price change from the perspective of the seller. This contrasts with other measures, such as the Consumer Price Index (CPI). CPIs measure price change from the purchaser's perspective. Sellers' and purchasers' prices can differ due to government subsidies, sales and excise taxes, and distribution costs.

The PPI is the oldest continuous series of the federal government. When first published in 1902, it covered the years from 1890 through 1901 and was named the Wholesale Price Index (WPI). It was renamed the Producer Price Index in 1978. Many major commodity-based indexes are available from the early 1900s. Indexes for the major stage-of-processing categories are available from 1947 to present. Most manufacturing and mining industry indexes, however, are available only since the early 1980s; most indexes for services began being introduced in the mid-2000s.

Over 25,000 establishments provide approximately 100,000 price quotations per month today. Establishments report selling prices on the Tuesday that includes the 13th of each month, and they usually respond by mail or fax. Over 10,000 PPIs for individual products and groups of products are released each month.

PPIs are typically organized into one of three main structures: (1) industry classification, (2) commodity classification, and (3) commodity-based final demand-intermediate demand (FD-ID) system. The PPI publishes approximately 535 industry price indexes in combination with over 4,000 specific product line and product category sub-indexes, as well as roughly 500 indexes for groupings of industries. The commodity classification structure of the PPI organizes products and services by similarity or material composition, regardless of the industry classification of the producing establishment. Commodity-based FD-ID price indexes regroup commodity indexes for goods, services, and construction at the subproduct class (six-digit) level, according to the type of buyer and the amount of physical processing or assembling the products have undergone.

The PPI is widely used in many aspects of business and government. It is commonly used as an economic indicator, a deflator of other economic series, and a basis for contract escalation.

A PPI may go out of publication if there is not cooperation from a minimum number of establishments or if, in any given month, the index does not have actual prices from a minimum number of reporting units.

SOURCES OF ADDITIONAL INFORMATION

For more information on the underlying concepts and methodology of the Producer Price Index, see Chapter 14 in the *BLS Handbook of Methods*, which is available on the BLS Web site at http://www.bls.gov/opub/hom/.

Table 9-1. Producer Price Indexes, by Stage of Processing, 1947–2012

(1982 = 100.)

Year	Crude materials for further processing				Intermediate materials, supplies, and components						Finished goods		
	Total	Foodstuffs and feedstuffs	Nonfood materials, except fuel	Fuel	Total	Materials and components for construction	Components for manufacturing	Processed fuels and lubricants	Containers	Supplies	Total	Consumer goods	Capital equipment
1947	31.7	45.1	24.0	7.5	23.3	22.5	21.3	14.4	23.4	28.5	26.4	28.6	19.8
1948	34.7	48.8	26.7	8.9	25.2	24.9	23.0	16.4	24.4	29.8	28.5	30.8	21.6
1949	30.1	40.5	24.3	8.8	24.2	24.9	23.4	14.9	24.5	28.0	27.7	29.4	22.7
1950	32.7	43.4	27.8	8.8	25.3	26.2	24.3	15.2	25.2	29.0	28.2	29.9	23.2
1951	37.6	50.2	32.0	9.0	28.4	28.7	27.6	15.9	29.6	32.6	30.8	32.7	25.5
1952	34.5	47.3	27.8	9.0	27.5	28.5	27.6	15.7	28.0	32.6	30.6	32.3	25.9
1953	31.9	42.3	26.6	9.3	27.7	29.0	28.1	15.8	28.0	31.0	30.3	31.7	26.3
1954	31.6	42.3	26.1	8.9	27.9	29.1	28.3	15.8	28.5	31.7	30.4	31.7	26.7
1955	30.4	38.4	27.5	8.9	28.4	30.3	29.5	15.8	28.9	31.2	30.5	31.5	27.4
1956	30.6	37.6	28.6	9.5	29.6	31.8	32.2	16.3	31.0	32.0	31.3	32.0	29.5
1957	31.2	39.2	28.2	10.1	30.3	32.0	33.5	17.2	32.4	32.3	32.5	32.9	31.3
1958	31.9	41.6	27.1	10.2	30.4	32.0	33.8	16.2	33.2	33.1	33.2	33.6	32.1
1959	31.1	38.8	28.1	10.4	30.8	32.9	34.2	16.2	33.0	33.5	33.1	33.3	32.7
1960	30.4	38.4	26.9	10.5	30.8	32.7	34.0	16.6	33.4	33.3	33.4	33.6	32.8
1961	30.2	37.9	27.2	10.5	30.6	32.2	33.7	16.8	33.2	33.7	33.4	33.6	32.9
1962	30.5	38.6	27.1	10.4	30.6	32.1	33.4	16.7	33.6	34.5	33.5	33.7	33.0
1963	29.9	37.5	26.7	10.5	30.7	32.2	33.4	16.6	33.2	35.0	33.4	33.5	33.1
1964	29.6	36.6	27.2	10.5	30.8	32.5	33.7	16.2	32.9	34.7	33.5	33.6	33.4
1965	31.1	39.2	27.7	10.6	31.2	32.8	34.2	16.5	33.5	35.0	34.1	34.2	33.8
1966	33.1	42.7	28.3	10.9	32.0	33.6	35.4	16.8	34.5	36.5	35.2	35.4	34.6
1967	31.3	40.3	26.5	11.3	32.2	34.0	36.5	16.9	35.0	36.8	35.6	35.6	35.8
1968	31.8	40.9	27.1	11.5	33.0	35.7	37.3	16.5	35.9	37.1	36.6	36.5	37.0
1969	33.9	44.1	28.4	12.0	34.1	37.7	38.5	16.6	37.2	37.8	38.0	37.9	38.3
1970	35.2	45.2	29.1	13.8	35.4	38.3	40.6	17.7	39.0	39.7	39.3	39.1	40.1
1971	36.0	46.1	29.4	15.7	36.8	40.8	41.9	19.5	40.8	40.8	40.5	40.2	41.7
1972	39.9	51.5	32.3	16.8	38.2	43.0	42.9	20.1	42.7	42.5	41.8	41.5	42.8
1973	54.5	72.6	42.9	18.6	42.4	46.5	44.3	22.2	45.2	51.7	45.6	46.0	44.2
1974	61.4	76.4	54.5	24.8	52.5	55.0	51.1	33.6	53.3	56.8	52.6	53.1	50.5
1975	61.6	77.4	50.0	30.6	58.0	60.1	57.8	39.4	60.0	61.8	58.2	58.2	58.2
1976	63.4	76.8	54.9	34.5	60.9	64.1	60.8	42.3	63.1	65.8	60.8	60.4	62.1
1977	65.5	77.5	56.3	42.0	64.9	69.3	64.5	47.7	65.9	69.3	64.7	64.3	66.1
1978	73.4	87.3	61.9	48.2	69.5	76.5	69.2	49.9	71.0	72.9	69.8	69.4	71.3
1979	85.9	100.0	75.5	57.3	78.4	84.2	75.8	61.6	79.4	80.2	77.6	77.5	77.5
1980	95.3	104.6	91.8	69.4	90.3	91.3	84.6	85.0	89.1	89.9	88.0	88.6	85.8
1981	103.0	103.9	109.8	84.8	98.6	97.9	94.7	100.6	96.7	96.9	96.1	96.6	94.6
1982	100.0	100.0	100.0	100.0	100.0	100.0	100.0	100.0	100.0	100.0	100.0	100.0	100.0
1983	101.3	101.8	98.8	105.1	100.6	102.8	102.4	95.4	100.4	101.8	101.6	101.3	102.8
1984	103.5	104.7	101.0	105.1	103.1	105.6	105.0	95.7	105.9	104.1	103.7	103.3	105.2
1985	95.8	94.8	94.3	102.7	102.7	107.3	106.4	92.8	109.0	104.4	104.7	103.8	107.5
1986	87.7	93.2	76.0	92.2	99.1	108.1	107.5	72.7	110.3	105.6	103.2	101.4	109.7
1987	93.7	96.2	88.5	84.1	101.5	109.8	108.8	73.3	114.5	107.7	105.4	103.6	111.7
1988	96.0	106.1	85.9	82.1	107.1	116.1	112.3	71.2	120.1	113.7	108.0	106.2	114.3
1989	103.1	111.2	95.8	85.3	112.0	121.3	116.4	76.4	125.4	118.1	113.6	112.1	118.8
1990	108.9	113.1	107.3	84.8	114.5	122.9	119.0	85.9	127.7	119.4	119.2	118.2	122.9
1991	101.2	105.5	97.5	82.9	114.4	124.5	121.0	85.3	128.1	121.4	121.7	120.5	126.7
1992	100.4	105.1	94.2	84.0	114.7	126.5	122.0	84.5	127.7	122.7	123.2	121.7	129.1
1993	102.4	108.4	94.1	87.1	116.2	132.0	123.0	84.7	126.4	125.0	124.7	123.0	131.4
1994	101.8	106.5	97.0	82.4	118.5	136.6	124.3	83.1	129.7	127.0	125.5	123.3	134.1
1995	102.7	105.8	105.8	72.1	124.9	142.1	126.5	84.2	148.8	132.1	127.9	125.6	136.7
1996	113.8	121.5	105.7	92.6	125.7	143.6	126.9	90.0	141.1	135.9	131.3	129.5	138.3
1997	111.1	112.2	103.5	101.3	125.6	146.5	126.4	89.3	136.0	135.9	131.8	130.2	138.2
1998	96.8	103.9	84.5	86.7	123.0	146.8	125.9	81.1	140.8	134.8	130.7	128.9	137.6
1999	98.2	98.7	91.1	91.2	123.2	148.9	125.7	84.6	142.5	134.2	133.0	132.0	137.6
2000	120.6	100.2	118.0	136.9	129.2	150.7	126.2	102.0	151.6	136.9	138.0	138.2	138.8
2001	121.0	106.1	101.5	151.4	129.7	150.6	126.4	104.5	153.1	138.7	140.7	141.5	139.7
2002	108.1	99.5	101.0	117.3	127.8	151.3	126.1	96.3	152.1	138.9	138.9	139.4	139.1
2003	135.3	113.5	116.9	185.7	133.7	153.6	125.9	112.6	153.7	141.5	143.3	145.3	139.5
2004	159.0	127.0	149.2	211.4	142.6	166.4	127.4	124.3	159.3	146.7	148.5	151.7	141.4
2005	182.2	122.7	176.7	279.7	154.0	176.6	129.9	150.0	167.1	151.9	155.7	160.4	144.6
2006	184.8	119.3	210.0	241.5	164.0	188.4	134.5	162.8	175.0	157.0	160.4	166.0	146.9
2007	207.1	146.7	238.7	236.8	170.7	192.5	136.3	173.9	180.3	161.7	166.6	173.5	149.5
2008	251.8	163.4	308.5	298.3	188.3	205.4	140.3	206.2	191.8	173.8	177.1	186.3	153.8
2009	175.2	134.5	211.1	166.3	172.5	202.9	141.0	161.9	195.8	172.2	172.5	179.1	156.7
2010	212.2	152.4	280.8	188.0	183.4	205.7	142.2	185.2	201.2	175.0	179.8	189.1	157.3
2011	249.4	188.4	342.0	181.5	199.8	212.8	145.8	215.0	205.4	184.2	190.5	203.3	159.7
2012	241.3	196.3	332.4	143.9	200.7	218.4	147.7	213.2	206.9	188.9	194.2	207.3	162.8

Table 9-2. Producer Price Indexes, by Commodity Group, 1913–2012

(1982 = 100.)

Year	All commodities	Farm products	Processed foods and feeds	Industrial commodities													
				Total	Textile products and apparel	Hides, leather, and related products	Fuels and related products and power	Chemicals and related products	Rubber and plastics products	Lumber and wood products	Pulp, paper, and allied products	Metals and metal products	Machinery and equipment	Furniture and household durables	Non-metallic mineral products	Transportation equipment	Miscellaneous products
1913	12.0	18.0	...	11.9	...	...	...	...	...	...	...	...	...	...	...	...	...
1914	11.8	17.9	...	11.3	...	...	...	...	...	...	...	...	...	...	...	...	...
1915	12.0	18.0	...	11.6	...	...	...	...	...	...	...	...	...	...	...	...	...
1916	14.7	21.3	...	15.0	...	...	...	...	...	...	...	...	...	...	...	...	...
1917	20.2	32.6	...	19.5	...	...	...	...	...	...	...	...	...	...	...	...	...
1918	22.6	37.4	...	21.1	...	...	...	...	...	...	...	...	...	...	...	...	...
1919	23.9	39.8	...	22.0	...	...	...	...	...	...	...	...	...	...	...	...	...
1920	26.6	38.0	...	27.4	...	...	...	...	...	...	...	...	...	...	...	...	...
1921	16.8	22.3	...	17.8	...	...	...	...	...	...	...	...	...	...	...	...	...
1922	16.7	23.7	...	17.4	...	...	...	...	...	...	...	...	...	...	...	...	...
1923	17.3	24.9	...	17.8	...	...	...	...	...	...	...	...	...	...	...	...	...
1924	16.9	25.2	...	17.0	...	...	...	...	...	...	...	...	...	...	...	...	...
1925	17.8	27.7	...	17.5	...	...	...	...	...	...	...	...	...	...	...	...	...
1926	17.2	25.3	...	17.0	...	17.1	10.3	...	47.1	9.3	...	13.7	...	28.6	16.4	...	...
1927	16.5	25.1	...	16.0	...	18.4	9.1	...	35.7	8.8	...	12.9	...	27.9	15.7	...	...
1928	16.7	26.7	...	15.8	...	20.7	8.7	...	28.3	8.5	...	12.9	...	27.2	16.2	...	...
1929	16.4	26.4	...	15.6	...	18.6	8.6	...	24.6	8.8	...	13.3	...	27.0	16.0	...	...
1930	14.9	22.4	...	14.5	...	17.1	8.1	...	21.5	8.0	...	12.0	...	26.5	15.9	...	...
1931	12.6	16.4	...	12.8	...	14.7	7.0	...	18.3	6.5	...	10.8	...	24.4	14.9	...	...
1932	11.2	12.2	...	11.9	...	12.5	7.3	...	15.9	5.6	...	9.9	...	21.5	13.9	...	...
1933	11.4	13.0	...	12.1	...	13.8	6.9	16.2	16.7	6.7	...	10.2	...	21.6	14.7	...	...
1934	12.9	16.5	...	13.3	...	14.8	7.6	17.0	19.5	7.8	...	11.2	...	23.4	15.7	...	...
1935	13.8	19.8	...	13.3	...	15.3	7.6	17.7	19.6	7.5	...	11.2	...	23.2	15.7	...	...
1936	13.9	20.4	...	13.5	...	16.3	7.9	17.8	21.1	7.9	...	11.4	...	23.6	15.8	...	...
1937	14.9	21.8	...	14.5	...	17.9	8.0	18.6	24.9	9.3	...	13.1	...	26.1	16.1	...	...
1938	13.5	17.3	...	13.9	...	15.8	7.9	17.7	24.4	8.5	...	12.6	...	25.5	15.6	...	...
1939	13.3	16.5	...	13.9	...	16.3	7.5	17.6	25.4	8.7	...	12.5	14.8	25.4	15.3	...	...
1940	13.5	17.1	...	14.1	...	17.2	7.4	17.9	23.7	9.6	...	12.5	14.9	26.0	15.3	...	...
1941	15.1	20.8	...	15.1	...	18.4	7.9	19.5	25.5	11.5	...	12.8	15.1	27.6	15.7	...	...
1942	17.0	26.7	...	16.2	...	20.1	8.1	21.7	29.7	12.5	...	13.0	15.4	29.9	16.3	...	...
1943	17.8	30.9	...	16.5	...	20.1	8.3	21.9	30.5	13.2	...	12.9	15.2	29.7	16.4	...	...
1944	17.9	31.2	...	16.7	...	19.9	8.6	22.2	30.1	14.3	...	12.9	15.1	30.5	16.7	...	...
1945	18.2	32.4	...	17.0	...	20.1	8.7	22.3	29.2	14.5	...	13.1	15.1	30.5	17.4	...	...
1946	20.8	37.5	...	18.6	...	23.3	9.3	24.1	29.3	16.6	...	14.7	16.6	32.4	18.5	...	...
1947	25.6	45.1	33.0	22.7	50.6	31.7	11.1	32.1	29.2	25.8	25.1	18.2	19.3	37.2	20.7	...	26.6
1948	27.7	48.5	35.3	24.6	52.8	32.1	13.1	32.8	30.2	29.5	26.2	20.7	20.9	39.4	22.4	...	27.7
1949	26.3	41.9	32.1	24.1	48.3	30.4	12.4	30.0	29.2	27.3	25.1	20.9	21.9	40.1	23.0	...	28.2
1950	27.3	44.0	33.2	25.0	50.2	32.9	12.6	30.4	35.6	31.4	25.7	22.0	22.6	40.9	23.5	...	28.6
1951	30.4	51.2	36.9	27.6	56.0	37.7	13.0	34.8	43.7	34.1	30.5	24.5	25.3	44.4	25.0	...	30.3
1952	29.6	48.4	36.4	26.9	50.5	30.5	13.0	33.0	39.6	33.2	29.7	24.5	25.3	43.5	25.0	...	30.2
1953	29.2	43.8	34.8	27.2	49.3	31.0	13.4	33.4	36.9	33.1	29.6	25.3	25.9	44.4	26.0	...	31.0
1954	29.3	43.2	35.4	27.2	48.2	29.5	13.2	33.8	37.5	32.5	29.6	25.5	26.3	44.9	26.6	...	31.3
1955	29.3	40.5	33.8	27.8	48.2	29.4	13.2	33.7	42.4	34.1	30.4	27.2	27.2	45.1	27.3	...	31.3
1956	30.3	40.0	33.8	29.1	48.2	31.2	13.6	33.9	43.0	34.6	32.4	29.6	29.3	46.3	28.5	...	31.7
1957	31.2	41.1	34.8	29.9	48.3	31.2	14.3	34.6	42.8	32.8	33.0	30.2	31.4	47.5	29.6	...	32.6
1958	31.6	42.9	36.5	30.0	47.4	31.6	13.7	34.9	42.8	32.5	33.4	30.0	32.1	47.9	29.9	...	33.3
1959	31.7	40.2	35.6	30.5	48.1	35.9	13.7	34.8	42.6	34.7	33.7	30.6	32.8	48.0	30.3	...	33.4
1960	31.7	40.1	35.6	30.5	48.6	34.6	13.9	34.8	42.7	33.5	34.0	30.6	33.0	47.8	30.4	...	33.6
1961	31.6	39.7	36.2	30.4	47.8	34.9	14.0	34.5	41.1	32.0	33.0	30.5	33.0	47.5	30.5	...	33.7
1962	31.7	40.4	36.5	30.4	48.2	35.3	14.0	33.9	39.9	32.2	33.4	30.2	33.0	47.2	30.5	...	33.9
1963	31.6	39.6	36.8	30.3	48.2	34.3	13.9	33.5	40.1	32.8	33.1	30.3	33.1	46.9	30.3	...	34.2
1964	31.6	39.0	36.7	30.5	48.5	34.4	13.5	33.6	39.6	33.5	33.0	31.1	33.3	47.1	30.4	...	34.4

. . . = Not available.

Table 9-2. Producer Price Indexes, by Commodity Group, 1913–2012—*Continued*

(1982 = 100.)

Year	All com-modities	Farm products	Processed foods and feeds	Industrial commodities														
				Total	Textile products and apparel	Hides, leather, and related products	Fuels and related products and power	Chemi-cals and related products	Rubber and plastics products	Lumber and wood products	Pulp, paper, and allied products	Metals and metal products	Machin-ery and equip-ment	Furniture and house-hold durables	Non-metallic mineral products	Trans-porta-tion equip-ment	Miscel-laneous products
1965	32.3	40.7	38.0	30.9	48.8	35.9	13.8	33.9	39.7	33.7	33.3	32.0	33.7	46.8	30.4	. . .	34.7
1966	33.3	43.7	40.2	31.5	48.9	39.4	14.1	34.0	40.5	35.2	34.2	32.8	34.7	47.4	30.7	. . .	35.3
1967	33.4	41.3	39.8	32.0	48.9	38.1	14.4	34.2	41.4	35.1	34.6	33.2	35.9	48.3	31.2	. . .	36.2
1968	34.2	42.3	40.6	32.8	50.7	39.3	14.3	34.1	42.8	39.8	35.0	34.0	37.0	49.7	32.4	. . .	37.0
1969	35.6	45.0	42.7	33.9	51.8	41.5	14.6	34.2	43.6	44.0	36.0	36.0	38.2	50.7	33.6	40.4	38.1
1970	36.9	45.8	44.6	35.2	52.4	42.0	15.3	35.0	44.9	39.9	37.5	38.7	40.0	51.9	35.3	41.9	39.8
1971	38.1	46.6	45.5	36.5	53.3	43.4	16.6	35.6	45.2	44.7	38.1	39.4	41.4	53.1	38.2	44.2	40.8
1972	39.8	51.6	48.0	37.8	55.5	50.0	17.1	35.6	45.3	50.7	39.3	40.9	42.3	53.8	39.4	45.5	41.5
1973	45.0	72.7	58.9	40.3	60.5	54.5	19.4	37.6	46.6	62.2	42.3	44.0	43.7	55.7	40.7	46.1	43.3
1974	53.5	77.4	68.0	49.2	68.0	55.2	30.1	50.2	56.4	64.5	52.5	57.0	50.0	61.8	47.8	50.3	48.1
1975	58.4	77.0	72.6	54.9	67.4	56.5	35.4	62.0	62.2	62.1	59.0	61.5	57.9	67.5	54.4	56.7	53.4
1976	61.1	78.8	70.8	58.4	72.4	63.9	38.3	64.0	66.0	72.2	62.1	65.0	61.3	70.3	58.2	60.5	55.6
1977	64.9	79.4	74.0	62.5	75.3	68.3	43.6	65.9	69.4	83.0	64.6	69.3	65.2	73.2	62.6	64.6	59.4
1978	69.9	87.7	80.6	67.0	78.1	76.1	46.5	68.0	72.4	96.9	67.7	75.3	70.3	77.5	69.6	69.5	66.7
1979	78.7	99.6	88.5	75.7	82.5	96.1	58.9	76.0	80.5	105.5	75.9	86.0	76.7	82.8	77.6	75.3	75.5
1980	89.8	102.9	95.9	88.0	89.7	94.7	82.8	89.0	90.1	101.5	86.3	95.0	86.0	90.7	88.4	82.9	93.6
1981	98.0	105.2	98.9	97.4	97.6	99.3	100.2	98.4	96.4	102.8	94.8	99.6	94.4	95.9	96.7	94.3	96.1
1982	100.0	100.0	100.0	100.0	100.0	100.0	100.0	100.0	100.0	100.0	100.0	100.0	100.0	100.0	100.0	100.0	100.0
1983	101.3	102.4	101.8	101.1	100.3	103.2	95.9	100.3	100.8	107.9	103.3	101.8	102.7	103.4	101.6	102.8	104.8
1984	103.7	105.5	105.4	103.3	102.7	109.0	94.8	102.9	102.3	108.0	110.3	104.8	105.1	105.7	105.4	105.2	107.0
1985	103.2	95.1	103.5	103.7	102.9	108.9	91.4	103.7	101.9	106.6	113.3	104.4	107.2	107.1	108.6	107.9	109.4
1986	100.2	92.9	105.4	100.0	103.2	113.0	69.8	102.6	101.9	107.2	116.1	103.2	108.8	108.2	110.0	110.5	111.6
1987	102.8	95.5	107.9	102.6	105.1	120.4	70.2	106.4	103.0	112.8	121.8	107.1	110.4	109.9	110.0	112.5	114.9
1988	106.9	104.9	112.7	106.3	109.2	131.4	66.7	116.3	109.3	118.9	130.4	118.7	113.2	113.1	111.2	114.3	120.2
1989	112.2	110.9	117.8	111.6	112.3	136.3	72.9	123.0	112.6	126.7	137.8	124.1	117.4	116.9	112.6	117.7	126.5
1990	116.3	112.2	121.9	115.8	115.0	141.7	82.3	123.6	113.6	129.7	141.2	122.9	120.7	119.2	114.7	121.5	134.2
1991	116.5	105.7	121.9	116.5	116.3	138.9	81.2	125.6	115.1	132.1	142.9	120.2	123.0	121.2	117.2	126.4	140.8
1992	117.2	103.6	122.1	117.4	117.8	140.4	80.4	125.9	115.1	146.6	145.2	119.2	123.4	122.2	117.3	130.4	145.3
1993	118.9	107.1	124.0	119.0	118.0	143.7	80.0	128.2	116.0	174.0	147.3	119.2	124.0	123.7	120.0	133.7	145.4
1994	120.4	106.3	125.5	120.7	118.3	148.5	77.8	132.1	117.6	180.0	152.5	124.8	125.1	126.1	124.2	137.2	141.9
1995	124.7	107.4	127.0	125.5	120.8	153.7	78.0	142.5	124.3	178.1	172.2	134.5	126.6	128.2	129.0	139.7	145.4
1996	127.7	122.4	133.3	127.3	122.4	150.5	85.8	142.1	123.8	176.1	168.7	131.0	126.5	130.4	131.0	141.7	147.7
1997	127.6	112.9	134.0	127.7	122.6	154.2	86.1	143.6	123.2	183.8	167.9	131.8	125.9	130.8	133.2	141.6	150.9
1998	124.4	104.6	131.6	124.8	122.9	148.0	75.3	143.9	122.6	179.1	171.7	127.8	124.9	131.3	135.4	141.2	156.0
1999	125.5	98.4	131.1	126.5	121.1	146.0	80.5	144.2	122.5	183.6	174.1	124.6	124.3	131.7	138.9	141.8	166.6
2000	132.7	99.5	133.1	134.8	121.4	151.5	103.5	151.0	125.5	178.2	183.7	128.1	124.0	132.6	142.5	143.8	170.8
2001	134.2	103.8	137.3	135.7	121.3	158.4	105.3	151.8	127.2	174.4	184.8	125.4	123.7	133.2	144.3	145.2	181.3
2002	131.1	99.0	136.2	132.4	119.9	157.6	93.2	151.9	126.8	173.3	185.9	125.9	122.9	133.5	146.2	144.6	182.4
2003	138.1	111.5	143.4	139.1	119.8	162.3	112.9	161.8	130.1	177.4	190.0	129.2	121.9	133.9	148.2	145.7	179.6
2004	146.7	123.3	151.2	147.6	121.0	164.5	126.9	174.4	133.8	195.6	195.7	149.6	122.1	135.1	153.2	148.6	183.2
2005	157.4	118.5	153.1	160.2	122.8	165.4	156.4	192.0	143.8	196.5	202.6	160.8	123.7	139.4	164.2	151.0	195.1
2006	164.7	117.0	153.8	168.8	124.5	168.4	166.7	205.8	153.8	194.4	209.8	181.6	126.2	142.6	179.9	152.6	205.6
2007	172.6	143.4	165.1	175.1	125.8	173.6	177.6	214.8	155.0	192.4	216.9	193.5	127.3	144.7	186.2	155.0	210.3
2008	189.6	161.3	180.5	192.3	128.9	173.1	214.6	245.5	165.9	191.3	226.8	213.0	129.7	148.9	197.1	158.6	216.6
2009	172.9	134.6	176.2	174.8	129.5	157.0	158.7	229.4	165.2	182.8	225.6	186.8	131.3	153.1	202.4	162.2	217.5
2010	184.7	151.0	182.3	187.0	131.7	181.4	185.8	246.6	170.7	192.7	236.9	207.6	131.1	153.2	201.8	163.4	221.5
2011	201.0	186.7	197.5	202.0	141.7	199.9	215.9	275.1	182.7	194.7	245.1	225.9	132.7	156.4	205.0	166.1	229.2
2012	202.2	192.5	205.2	202.1	142.2	202.3	212.1	276.6	186.9	201.6	244.2	219.9	134.2	160.6	211.0	169.8	235.6

. . . = Not available.

CONSUMER PRICE INDEX

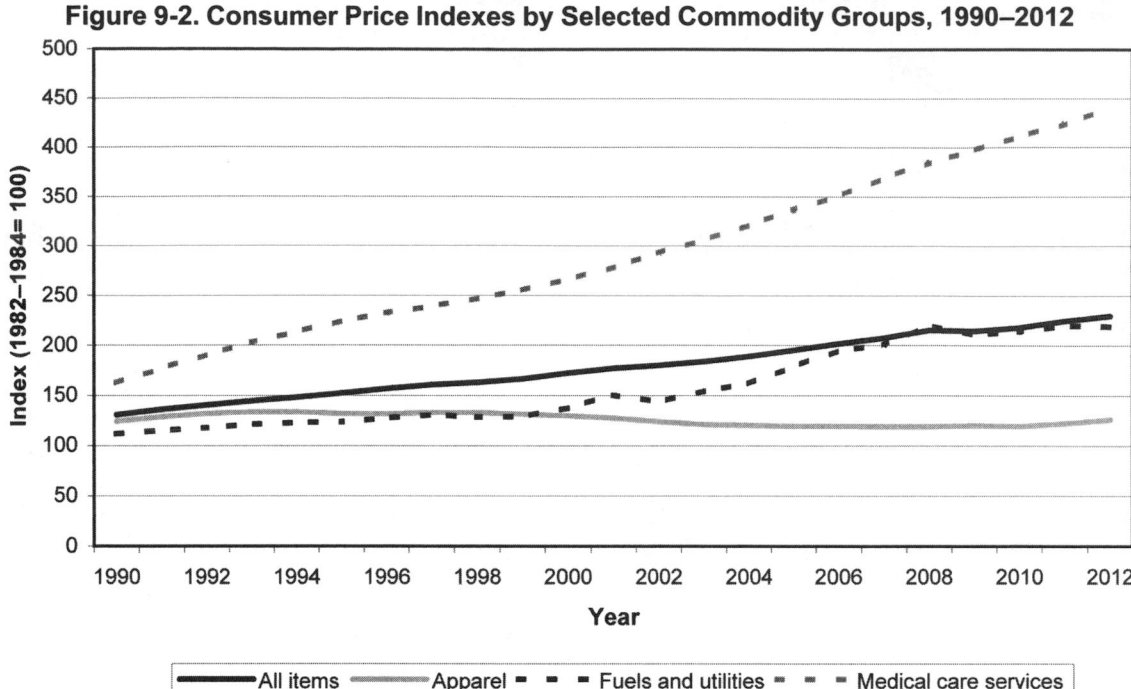

Figure 9-2. Consumer Price Indexes by Selected Commodity Groups, 1990–2012

The CPI for medical care has grown at a much faster rate than average. From 1990 to 2012, the CPI for all urban consumers grew 75.7 percent, while the CPI for medical care grew 154.9 percent. Within medical care, hospital and related services has grown the fastest at 277.6 percent from 1990 to 2012. (See Table 9-7.)

OTHER HIGHLIGHTS

- The CPI-U for most commodities and services increased from 2011 to 2012. In addition to medical care services, the CPI-U for energy commodities and gas increased by more than 3 percent. (See Table 9-4.)

- After declining for the first time since 1955 in 2009, the CPI-W continued to increase in 2012, rising 2.1 percent. (See Table 9-6.)

- The CPI-U in Pittsburgh, PA, increased 3.5 percent in 2012—faster than any other MSA listed in Table 9-9. The CPI-U grew the slowest in Chicago, IL-Gary, IN-Kenosha, WI at 1.5 percent from 2011 to 2012. (See Table 9-9.)

NOTES AND DEFINITIONS

CONSUMER PRICE INDEX

The Consumer Price Index (CPI) is a measure of the average change over time in the prices of consumer items—goods and services that people buy for day-to-day living. The CPI is a complex construct that combines economic theory with sampling and other statistical techniques and uses data from several surveys to produce a timely and precise measure of average price change for the consumption sector of the American economy.

The Bureau of Labor Statistics (BLS) publishes CPIs for the following population groups: (1) the CPI for Urban Wage Earners and Clerical Workers (CPI-W), which covers households of wage earners and clerical workers that make up approximately 32 percent of the total population, and (2) the CPI for All Urban Consumers (CPI-U) and the Chained CPI for All Urban Consumers (C-CPI-U), which cover approximately 87 percent of the total population and include, in addition to wage earners and clerical worker households, groups such as professional, managerial, and technical workers, the self-employed, short-term workers, the unemployed, and retirees and others not in the labor force. BLS began publishing the CPI-U in January 1978, but did not begin publishing the C-CPI-U until August 2002 with data beginning in January 2000. The CPI-W is much older than either the CPI-U or the C-CPI-U.

The CPIs are based on prices of food, clothing, shelter, fuels, transportation, doctors' and dentists' services, drugs, and other goods and services that people buy for day-to-day living. Prices are collected each month in 87 urban areas across the country from about 23,000 retail and service establishments. Data on rents are collected from about 50,000 landlords or tenants. All taxes directly associated with the purchase and use of items are included in the index.

Various indexes have been devised to measure different aspects of inflation. The CPI measures inflation as experienced by consumers in their day-to-day living expenses; the Producer Price Index (PPI), as described earlier in this chapter, measures inflation at earlier stages of the production process; the Employment Cost Index (ECI), as described in Chapter 6, measures it in the labor market; the BLS International Price Program measures it for imports and exports; and the Gross Domestic Product Deflator (GDP Deflator) measures inflation experienced by consumers themselves as well as governments and other institutions providing goods and services to consumers. Finally, there are specialized measures, such as measures of interest rates. The CPI is generally the best measure for adjusting payments to consumers when the intent is to allow consumers to purchase at today's prices, a market basket of goods and services equivalent to one that they could purchase in an earlier period.

The CPI does have some limitations, however. The CPI may not be applicable to all population groups. For example, the CPI-U is designed to measure inflation for the U.S. urban population and thus may not accurately reflect the experience of people living in rural areas. In addition, the CPI does not produce official estimates for the rate of inflation experienced by subgroups of the population, such as the elderly or the poor.

The Consumer Price Index Research Series Using Current Methods (CPI-U-RS), seen in Table 9-10, provides estimates for the period since 1977 of what the CPI would have been had the most current methods been in effect. Each time there are new methods introduced into the CPI, the CPI-U-RS is revised from 1978 forward.

The CPI-U-RS provides an annual inflation series that adjusts only for specified changes in BLS methodology. It does not incorporate all possible research results on past inflation.

SOURCES OF ADDITIONAL INFORMATION

An extensive description of the methodology is available in the updated version of Chapter 17 in the *BLS Handbook of Methods*. Additional detailed data can be found in the *Consumer Price Index Detailed Report* and in special reports. These resources can be found on the BLS Web site at http://www.bls.gov.

Table 9-3. Consumer Price Indexes, All Urban Consumers (CPI-U): U.S. City Average, Major Groups, 1957–2012

(1982–1984 = 100, unless otherwise specified.)

Year	All items	Food and beverages	Housing	Apparel	Transportation	Medical care	Recreation[1]	Education and communication[1]	Other goods and services
1957	28.1	...	...	44.5	27.7	19.7	...	...	...
1958	28.9	...	...	44.6	28.6	20.6	...	...	...
1959	29.1	...	...	45.0	29.8	21.5	...	...	...
1960	29.6	...	...	45.7	29.8	22.3	...	...	...
1961	29.9	...	...	46.1	30.1	22.9	...	...	...
1962	30.2	...	...	46.3	30.8	23.5	...	...	...
1963	30.6	...	...	46.9	30.9	24.1	...	...	...
1964	31.0	...	...	47.3	31.4	24.6	...	...	...
1965	31.5	...	...	47.8	31.9	25.2	...	...	...
1966	32.4	...	...	49.0	32.3	26.3	...	...	...
1967	33.4	35.0	30.8	51.0	33.3	28.2	...	...	35.1
1968	34.8	36.2	32.0	53.7	34.3	29.9	...	...	36.9
1969	36.7	38.1	34.0	56.8	35.7	31.9	...	...	38.7
1970	38.8	40.1	36.4	59.2	37.5	34.0	...	...	40.9
1971	40.5	41.4	38.0	61.1	39.5	36.1	...	...	42.9
1972	41.8	43.1	39.4	62.3	39.9	37.3	...	...	44.7
1973	44.4	48.8	41.2	64.6	41.2	38.8	...	...	46.4
1974	49.3	55.5	45.8	69.4	45.8	42.4	...	...	49.8
1975	53.8	60.2	50.7	72.5	50.1	47.5	...	...	53.9
1976	56.9	62.1	53.8	75.2	55.1	52.0	...	...	57.0
1977	60.6	65.8	57.4	78.6	59.0	57.0	...	...	60.4
1978	65.2	72.2	62.4	81.4	61.7	61.8	...	...	64.3
1979	72.6	79.9	70.1	84.9	70.5	67.5	...	...	68.9
1980	82.4	86.7	81.1	90.9	83.1	74.9	...	...	75.2
1981	90.9	93.5	90.4	95.3	93.2	82.9	...	...	82.6
1982	96.5	97.3	96.9	97.8	97.0	92.5	...	...	91.1
1983	99.6	99.5	99.5	100.2	99.3	100.6	...	...	101.1
1984	103.9	103.2	103.6	102.1	103.7	106.8	...	...	107.9
1985	107.6	105.6	107.7	105.0	106.4	113.5	...	...	114.5
1986	109.6	109.1	110.9	105.9	102.3	122.0	...	...	121.4
1987	113.6	113.5	114.2	110.6	105.4	130.1	...	...	128.5
1988	118.3	118.2	118.5	115.4	108.7	138.6	...	...	137.0
1989	124.0	124.9	123.0	118.6	114.1	149.3	...	...	147.7
1990	130.7	132.1	128.5	124.1	120.5	162.8	...	...	159.0
1991	136.2	136.8	133.6	128.7	123.8	177.0	...	...	171.6
1992	140.3	138.7	137.5	131.9	126.5	190.1	...	...	183.3
1993	144.5	141.6	141.2	133.7	130.4	201.4	90.7	85.5	192.9
1994	148.2	144.9	144.8	133.4	134.3	211.0	92.7	88.8	198.5
1995	152.4	148.9	148.5	132.0	139.1	220.5	94.5	92.2	206.9
1996	156.9	153.7	152.8	131.7	143.0	228.2	97.4	95.3	215.4
1997	160.5	157.7	156.8	132.9	144.3	234.6	99.6	98.4	224.8
1998	163.0	161.1	160.4	133.0	141.6	242.1	101.1	100.3	237.7
1999	166.6	164.6	163.9	131.3	144.4	250.6	102.0	101.2	258.3
2000	172.2	168.4	169.6	129.6	153.3	260.8	103.3	102.5	271.1
2001	177.1	173.6	176.4	127.3	154.3	272.8	104.9	105.2	282.6
2002	179.9	176.8	180.3	124.0	152.9	285.6	106.2	107.9	293.2
2003	184.0	180.5	184.8	120.9	157.6	297.1	107.5	109.8	298.7
2004	188.9	186.6	189.5	120.4	163.1	310.1	108.6	111.6	304.7
2005	195.3	191.2	195.7	119.5	173.9	323.2	109.4	113.7	313.4
2006	201.6	195.7	203.2	119.5	180.9	336.2	110.9	116.8	321.7
2007	207.3	203.3	209.6	119.0	184.7	351.1	111.4	119.6	333.3
2008	215.3	214.2	216.3	118.9	195.5	364.1	113.3	123.6	345.4
2009	214.5	218.2	217.1	120.1	179.3	375.6	114.3	127.4	368.6
2010	218.1	220.0	216.3	119.5	193.4	388.4	113.3	129.9	381.3
2011	224.9	227.9	219.1	122.1	212.4	400.3	113.4	131.5	387.2
2012	229.6	233.7	222.7	126.3	217.3	414.9	114.7	133.8	394.4

[1]December 1997 = 100.
. . . = Not available.

Table 9-4. Consumer Price Indexes, All Urban Consumers (CPI-U): U.S. City Average, Commodity, Service, and Special Groups, 1957–2012

(1982–1984 = 100, unless otherwise specified.)

Year	All items less food	All items less shelter	All items less medical care	All items less energy	All items less food and energy	Commodities	Commodities less food and beverages	Commodities less food and energy	Energy commodities	Nondurables	Nondurables less food	Nondurables less food and apparel
1957	28.0	29.7	28.7	28.9	28.9	32.6	. . .	37.4	21.6	30.9	32.9	28.5
1958	28.6	30.6	29.5	29.7	29.6	33.3	. . .	37.9	21.3	31.7	33.1	28.8
1959	29.2	30.8	29.8	29.9	30.2	33.3	. . .	38.4	21.5	31.5	33.5	29.2
1960	29.7	31.3	30.2	30.4	30.6	33.6	. . .	38.5	21.9	32.0	34.1	29.7
1961	30.0	31.7	30.5	30.7	31.0	33.8	. . .	38.6	21.9	32.2	34.3	29.8
1962	30.3	32.0	30.8	31.1	31.4	34.1	. . .	38.9	22.0	32.5	34.5	30.1
1963	30.7	32.4	31.1	31.5	31.8	34.4	. . .	39.2	22.1	32.9	34.8	30.4
1964	31.1	32.8	31.5	32.0	32.3	34.8	. . .	39.6	21.9	33.2	35.1	30.6
1965	31.6	33.3	32.0	32.5	32.7	35.2	. . .	39.8	22.6	33.8	35.6	31.2
1966	32.3	34.3	33.0	33.5	33.5	36.1	. . .	40.3	23.2	35.1	36.4	31.8
1967	33.4	35.2	33.7	34.4	34.7	36.8	38.3	41.3	23.9	35.7	37.6	32.6
1968	34.9	36.7	35.1	35.9	36.3	38.1	39.7	42.9	24.4	37.1	39.1	33.7
1969	36.8	38.4	37.0	38.0	38.4	39.9	41.4	44.7	25.2	38.9	40.9	34.9
1970	39.0	40.3	39.2	40.3	40.8	41.7	43.1	46.7	25.6	40.8	42.5	36.3
1971	40.8	42.0	40.8	42.0	42.7	43.2	44.7	48.5	26.1	42.1	44.0	37.6
1972	42.0	43.3	42.1	43.4	44.0	44.5	45.8	49.7	26.4	43.5	45.0	38.6
1973	43.7	46.2	44.8	46.1	45.6	47.8	47.3	51.1	29.1	47.5	46.9	40.3
1974	48.0	51.4	49.8	50.6	49.4	53.5	52.4	55.0	40.4	54.0	52.9	46.9
1975	52.5	56.0	54.3	55.1	53.9	58.2	57.3	60.1	43.4	58.3	57.0	51.5
1976	56.0	59.3	57.2	58.2	57.4	60.7	60.2	63.2	45.4	60.5	59.5	54.1
1977	59.6	63.1	60.8	61.9	61.0	64.2	63.6	66.5	48.7	64.0	62.5	57.2
1978	63.9	67.4	65.4	66.7	65.5	68.8	67.3	70.5	51.0	68.6	65.5	60.4
1979	71.2	74.2	72.9	73.4	71.9	76.6	75.2	76.4	68.7	77.2	74.6	71.2
1980	81.5	82.9	82.8	81.9	80.8	86.0	85.7	83.5	95.2	87.6	88.4	87.1
1981	90.4	91.0	91.4	90.1	89.2	93.2	93.1	90.0	107.6	95.2	96.7	96.8
1982	96.3	96.2	96.8	96.1	95.8	97.0	96.9	95.3	102.9	97.8	98.3	98.2
1983	99.7	99.8	99.6	99.6	99.6	99.8	100.0	100.2	99.0	99.7	100.0	100.0
1984	104.0	103.9	103.7	104.3	104.6	103.2	103.1	104.4	98.1	102.5	101.7	101.8
1985	108.0	107.0	107.2	108.4	109.1	105.4	105.2	107.1	98.2	104.8	104.1	104.1
1986	109.8	108.0	108.8	112.6	113.5	104.4	101.4	108.6	77.2	103.5	98.5	96.9
1987	113.6	111.6	112.6	117.2	118.2	107.7	104.0	111.8	80.2	107.5	101.8	100.3
1988	118.3	115.9	117.0	122.3	123.4	111.5	107.3	115.8	80.8	111.8	105.8	104.0
1989	123.7	121.6	122.4	128.1	129.0	116.7	111.6	119.6	87.9	118.2	111.7	111.3
1990	130.3	128.2	128.8	134.7	135.5	122.8	117.0	123.6	101.2	126.0	119.9	120.9
1991	136.1	133.5	133.8	140.9	142.1	126.6	120.4	128.8	99.1	130.3	124.5	125.7
1992	140.8	137.3	137.5	145.4	147.3	129.1	123.2	132.5	98.3	132.8	127.6	128.9
1993	145.1	141.4	141.2	150.0	152.2	131.5	125.3	135.2	97.3	135.1	129.3	130.7
1994	149.0	144.8	144.7	154.1	156.5	133.8	126.9	137.1	97.6	136.8	129.7	131.6
1995	153.1	148.6	148.6	158.7	161.2	136.4	128.9	139.3	98.8	139.3	130.9	134.1
1996	157.5	152.8	152.8	163.1	165.6	139.9	131.5	141.3	105.7	143.5	134.5	139.5
1997	161.1	155.9	156.3	167.1	169.5	141.8	132.2	142.3	105.7	146.4	136.3	141.8
1998	163.4	157.2	158.6	170.9	173.4	141.9	130.5	143.2	92.1	146.9	134.6	139.2
1999	167.0	160.2	162.0	174.4	177.0	144.4	132.5	144.1	100.0	151.2	139.4	147.5
2000	173.0	165.7	167.3	178.6	181.3	149.2	137.7	144.9	129.5	158.2	149.1	162.9
2001	177.8	169.7	171.9	183.5	186.1	150.7	137.2	145.3	125.2	160.6	149.1	164.1
2002	180.5	170.8	174.3	187.7	190.5	149.7	134.2	143.7	117.1	161.1	147.4	163.3
2003	184.7	174.6	178.1	190.6	193.2	151.2	134.5	140.9	136.7	165.3	151.9	172.1
2004	189.4	179.3	182.7	194.4	196.6	154.7	136.7	139.6	161.2	172.2	159.3	183.8
2005	196.0	186.1	188.7	198.7	200.9	160.2	142.5	140.3	197.4	180.2	170.1	201.2
2006	202.7	191.9	194.7	203.7	205.9	164.0	145.9	140.6	223.0	186.7	178.2	213.9
2007	208.1	196.6	200.1	208.9	210.7	167.5	147.5	140.1	241.0	193.5	184.0	223.4
2008	215.5	205.5	207.8	214.8	215.6	174.8	153.0	140.2	284.4	205.9	197.3	244.4
2009	214.0	203.3	206.6	218.4	219.2	169.7	144.4	142.0	205.3	198.5	181.5	218.7
2010	217.8	208.6	209.7	220.5	221.3	174.6	150.4	143.6	242.6	205.3	191.9	235.6
2011	224.5	217.0	216.3	224.8	225.0	183.9	159.9	145.5	306.4	219.0	209.6	262.1
2012	229.0	221.4	220.6	229.7	229.8	187.6	162.7	147.3	316.0	224.6	215.0	268.2

. . . = Not available.

Table 9-4. Consumer Price Indexes, All Urban Consumers (CPI-U): U.S. City Average, Commodity, Service, and Special Groups, 1957–2012—*Continued*

(1982–1984 = 100, unless otherwise specified.)

Year	Total services[1]	Rent of shelter[2]	Gasoline, all types	Transportation services	Medical care services	Other services	Services less medical care	Energy	Services less energy
1957	21.8	...	23.8	24.1	17.0	...	22.8	21.5	21.9
1958	22.6	...	23.5	25.6	17.9	...	23.6	21.5	22.7
1959	23.3	...	23.7	26.5	18.7	...	24.2	21.9	23.4
1960	24.1	...	24.4	27.2	19.5	...	25.0	22.4	24.2
1961	24.5	...	24.1	27.8	20.2	...	25.4	22.5	24.7
1962	25.0	...	24.3	28.3	20.9	...	25.9	22.6	25.2
1963	25.5	...	24.2	28.6	21.5	...	26.3	22.6	25.7
1964	26.0	...	24.1	29.2	22.0	...	26.8	22.5	26.2
1965	26.6	...	25.1	30.3	22.7	...	27.4	22.9	26.9
1966	27.6	...	25.6	31.6	23.9	...	28.3	23.3	28.0
1967	28.8	...	26.4	32.6	26.0	36.0	29.3	23.8	29.3
1968	30.3	...	26.8	33.9	27.9	38.1	30.8	24.2	30.9
1969	32.4	...	27.7	36.3	30.2	40.0	32.9	24.8	33.2
1970	35.0	...	27.9	40.2	32.3	42.2	35.6	25.5	36.0
1971	37.0	...	28.1	43.4	34.7	44.4	37.5	26.5	38.0
1972	38.4	...	28.4	44.4	35.9	45.6	38.9	27.2	39.4
1973	40.1	...	31.2	44.7	37.5	47.7	40.6	29.4	41.1
1974	43.8	...	42.2	46.3	41.4	51.3	44.3	38.1	44.8
1975	48.0	...	45.1	49.8	46.6	55.1	48.3	42.1	48.8
1976	52.0	...	47.0	56.9	51.3	58.4	52.2	45.1	52.7
1977	56.0	...	49.7	61.5	56.4	62.1	55.9	49.4	56.5
1978	60.8	...	51.8	64.4	61.2	66.4	60.7	52.5	61.3
1979	67.5	...	70.2	69.5	67.2	71.9	67.5	65.7	68.2
1980	77.9	...	97.5	79.2	74.8	78.7	78.2	86.0	78.5
1981	88.1	...	108.5	88.6	82.8	86.1	88.7	97.7	88.7
1982	96.0	...	102.8	96.1	92.6	93.5	96.4	99.2	96.3
1983	99.4	102.7	99.4	99.1	100.7	100.0	99.2	99.9	99.2
1984	104.6	107.7	97.8	104.8	106.7	106.5	104.4	100.9	104.5
1985	109.9	113.9	98.6	110.0	113.2	113.0	109.6	101.6	110.2
1986	115.4	120.2	77.0	116.3	121.9	119.4	114.6	88.2	116.5
1987	120.2	125.9	80.1	121.9	130.0	125.7	119.1	88.6	122.0
1988	125.7	132.0	80.8	128.0	138.3	132.6	124.3	89.3	127.9
1989	131.9	138.0	88.5	135.6	148.9	140.9	130.1	94.3	134.4
1990	139.2	145.5	101.0	144.2	162.7	150.2	136.8	102.1	142.3
1991	146.3	152.1	99.2	151.2	177.1	159.8	143.3	102.5	149.8
1992	152.0	157.3	99.0	155.7	190.5	168.5	148.4	103.0	155.9
1993	157.9	162.0	97.7	162.9	202.9	177.0	153.6	104.2	161.9
1994	163.1	167.0	98.2	168.6	213.4	185.4	158.4	104.6	167.6
1995	168.7	172.4	99.8	175.9	224.2	193.3	163.5	105.2	173.7
1996	174.1	178.0	105.9	180.5	232.4	201.4	168.7	110.1	179.4
1997	179.4	183.4	105.8	185.0	239.1	209.6	173.9	111.5	185.0
1998	184.2	189.6	91.6	187.9	246.8	216.9	178.4	102.9	190.6
1999	188.8	195.0	100.1	190.7	255.1	223.1	182.7	106.6	195.7
2000	195.3	201.3	128.6	196.1	266.0	229.9	188.9	124.6	202.1
2001	203.4	208.9	124.0	201.9	278.8	238.0	196.6	129.3	209.6
2002	209.8	216.7	116.0	209.1	292.9	246.4	202.5	121.7	217.5
2003	216.5	221.9	135.1	216.3	306.0	254.4	208.7	136.5	223.8
2004	222.8	227.9	159.7	220.6	321.3	261.3	214.5	151.4	230.2
2005	230.1	233.7	194.7	225.7	336.7	268.4	221.2	177.1	236.6
2006	238.9	241.9	219.9	230.8	350.6	277.5	229.6	196.9	244.7
2007	246.8	250.8	238.0	233.7	369.3	285.6	236.8	207.7	253.1
2008	255.5	257.2	277.5	244.1	384.9	295.8	245.0	236.7	261.0
2009	259.2	259.9	201.6	251.0	397.3	304.0	248.1	193.1	265.9
2010	261.3	258.8	238.6	259.8	411.2	309.6	249.6	211.4	268.3
2011	265.8	262.2	301.7	268.0	423.8	314.4	253.6	243.9	273.1
2012	271.4	267.8	311.5	272.9	440.3	322.3	258.5	246.1	279.7

[1]Includes tenants, household insurance, water, sewer, trash, and household operations services, not shown separately.
[2]December 1982 = 100.
. . . = Not available.

Table 9-5. Consumer Price Indexes, All Urban Consumers (CPI-U): U.S. City Average, Selected Groups and Purchasing Power of the Consumer Dollar, 1913–2012

(1982–1984 = 100, unless otherwise specified.)

Year	All items	Food	Rent of primary residence	Owners' equivalent of primary residence[1]	Apparel	Purchasing power of the consumer dollar
1913	9.9	10.0	21.0	...	14.9	1 007.7
1914	10.0	10.2	21.0	...	15.0	994.2
1915	10.1	10.0	21.1	...	15.3	984.3
1916	10.9	11.3	21.3	...	16.8	915.2
1917	12.8	14.5	21.2	...	20.2	779.3
1918	15.1	16.7	21.5	...	27.3	663.5
1919	17.3	18.6	23.3	...	36.2	577.9
1920	20.0	21.0	27.4	...	43.1	498.9
1921	17.9	15.9	31.5	...	33.2	558.5
1922	16.8	14.9	32.4	...	27.0	596.2
1923	17.1	15.4	33.2	...	27.1	585.7
1924	17.1	15.2	34.4	...	26.8	584.5
1925	17.5	16.5	34.6	...	26.3	570.1
1926	17.7	17.0	34.2	...	25.9	564.7
1927	17.4	16.4	33.7	...	25.3	575.5
1928	17.1	16.3	32.9	...	25.0	583.3
1929	17.1	16.5	32.1	...	24.7	583.3
1930	16.7	15.6	31.2	...	24.2	598.6
1931	15.2	12.9	29.6	...	22.0	656.3
1932	13.7	10.7	26.5	...	19.5	731.7
1933	13.0	10.4	22.9	...	18.8	771.2
1934	13.4	11.6	21.4	...	20.6	746.4
1935	13.7	12.4	21.4	...	20.8	728.1
1936	13.9	12.6	21.9	...	21.0	721.3
1937	14.4	13.1	22.9	...	22.0	696.1
1938	14.1	12.1	23.7	...	21.9	709.3
1939	13.9	11.8	23.7	...	21.6	719.5
1940	14.0	12.0	23.7	...	21.8	712.6
1941	14.7	13.1	24.2	...	22.8	678.8
1942	16.3	15.4	24.7	...	26.7	613.2
1943	17.3	17.1	24.7	...	27.8	577.9
1944	17.6	16.9	24.8	...	29.8	568.0
1945	18.0	17.3	24.8	...	31.4	555.2
1946	19.5	19.8	25.0	...	34.4	511.5
1947	22.3	24.1	25.8	...	39.9	447.4
1948	24.1	26.1	27.5	...	42.5	415.1
1949	23.8	25.0	28.7	...	40.8	419.3
1950	24.1	25.4	29.7	...	40.3	415.1
1951	26.0	28.2	30.9	...	43.9	384.6
1952	26.5	28.7	32.2	...	43.5	376.5
1953	26.7	28.3	33.9	...	43.1	373.5
1954	26.9	28.2	35.1	...	43.1	371.7
1955	26.8	27.8	35.6	...	42.9	373.2
1956	27.2	28.0	36.3	...	43.7	367.8
1957	28.1	28.9	37.0	...	44.5	354.9
1958	28.9	30.2	37.6	...	44.6	345.7
1959	29.1	29.7	38.2	...	45.0	342.7
1960	29.6	30.0	38.7	...	45.7	337.3
1961	29.9	30.4	39.2	...	46.1	334.0
1962	30.2	30.6	39.7	...	46.3	330.4
1963	30.6	31.1	40.1	...	46.9	326.5
1964	31.0	31.5	40.5	...	47.3	322.0
1965	31.5	32.2	40.9	...	47.8	316.6
1966	32.4	33.8	41.5	...	49.0	308.0
1967	33.4	34.1	42.2	...	51.0	299.3
1968	34.8	35.3	43.3	...	53.7	287.3
1969	36.7	37.1	44.7	...	56.8	272.6
1970	38.8	39.2	46.5	...	59.2	257.4
1971	40.5	40.4	48.7	...	61.1	246.6
1972	41.8	42.1	50.4	...	62.3	239.1
1973	44.4	48.2	52.5	...	64.6	225.1
1974	49.3	55.1	55.2	...	69.4	202.9
1975	53.8	59.8	58.0	...	72.5	185.9
1976	56.9	61.6	61.1	...	75.2	175.7
1977	60.6	65.5	64.8	...	78.6	164.9
1978	65.2	72.0	69.3	...	81.4	153.2
1979	72.6	79.9	74.3	...	84.9	138.0

[1]December 1982 = 100.
. . . = Not available.

Table 9-5. Consumer Price Indexes, All Urban Consumers (CPI-U): U.S. City Average, Selected Groups and Purchasing Power of the Consumer Dollar, 1913–2012—*Continued*

(1982–1984 = 100, unless otherwise specified.)

Year	All items	Food	Rent of primary residence	Owners' equivalent of primary residence[1]	Apparel	Purchasing power of the consumer dollar
1980	82.4	86.8	80.9	. . .	90.9	121.5
1981	90.9	93.6	87.9	. . .	95.3	109.8
1982	96.5	97.4	94.6	. . .	97.8	103.5
1983	99.6	99.4	100.1	102.5	100.2	100.3
1984	103.9	103.2	105.3	107.3	102.1	96.1
1985	107.6	105.6	111.8	113.2	105.0	92.8
1986	109.6	109.0	118.3	119.4	105.9	91.3
1987	113.6	113.5	123.1	124.8	110.6	88.0
1988	118.3	118.2	127.8	131.1	115.4	84.6
1989	124.0	125.1	132.8	137.4	118.6	80.7
1990	130.7	132.4	138.4	144.8	124.1	76.6
1991	136.2	136.3	143.3	150.4	128.7	73.4
1992	140.3	137.9	146.9	155.5	131.9	71.3
1993	144.5	140.9	150.3	160.5	133.7	69.2
1994	148.2	144.3	154.0	165.8	133.4	67.5
1995	152.4	148.4	157.8	171.3	132.0	65.6
1996	156.9	153.3	162.0	176.8	131.7	63.8
1997	160.5	157.3	166.7	181.9	132.9	62.3
1998	163.0	160.7	172.1	187.8	133.0	61.4
1999	166.6	164.1	177.5	192.9	131.3	60.0
2000	172.2	167.8	183.9	198.7	129.6	58.1
2001	177.1	173.1	192.1	206.3	127.3	56.5
2002	179.9	176.2	199.7	214.7	124.0	55.6
2003	184.0	180.0	205.5	219.9	120.9	54.4
2004	188.9	186.2	211.0	224.9	120.4	53.0
2005	195.3	190.7	217.3	230.2	119.5	51.2
2006	201.6	195.2	225.1	238.2	119.5	49.6
2007	207.3	202.9	234.7	246.2	119.0	48.2
2008	215.3	214.1	243.3	252.4	118.9	46.5
2009	214.5	218.0	248.8	256.6	120.1	46.6
2010	218.1	219.6	249.4	256.6	119.5	45.9
2011	224.9	227.8	253.6	259.6	122.1	44.5
2012	229.6	233.8	260.4	264.8	126.3	43.6

[1]December 1982 = 100.
. . . = Not available.

Table 9-6. Consumer Price Indexes, Urban Wage Earners and Clerical Workers (CPI-W): U.S. City Average, Major Groups, 1913–2012

(1982–1984 = 100, unless otherwise specified.)

Year	All items	Food and beverages	Housing	Apparel	Transportation	Medical care	Recreation[1]	Education and communication[1]	Other goods and services
1913	10.0	. . .	. . .	15.0	. . .	. . .	. . .	. . .	. . .
1914	10.1	. . .	. . .	15.1	. . .	. . .	. . .	. . .	. . .
1915	10.2	. . .	. . .	15.4	. . .	. . .	. . .	. . .	. . .
1916	11.0	. . .	. . .	16.9	. . .	. . .	. . .	. . .	. . .
1917	12.9	. . .	. . .	20.3	. . .	. . .	. . .	. . .	. . .
1918	15.1	. . .	. . .	27.5	. . .	. . .	. . .	. . .	. . .
1919	17.4	. . .	. . .	36.4	. . .	. . .	. . .	. . .	. . .
1920	20.1	. . .	. . .	43.3	. . .	. . .	. . .	. . .	. . .
1921	18.0	. . .	. . .	33.4	. . .	. . .	. . .	. . .	. . .
1922	16.9	. . .	. . .	27.2	. . .	. . .	. . .	. . .	. . .
1923	17.2	. . .	. . .	27.2	. . .	. . .	. . .	. . .	. . .
1924	17.2	. . .	. . .	26.9	. . .	. . .	. . .	. . .	. . .
1925	17.6	. . .	. . .	26.4	. . .	. . .	. . .	. . .	. . .
1926	17.8	. . .	. . .	26.0	. . .	. . .	. . .	. . .	. . .
1927	17.5	. . .	. . .	25.5	. . .	. . .	. . .	. . .	. . .
1928	17.2	. . .	. . .	25.1	. . .	. . .	. . .	. . .	. . .
1929	17.2	. . .	. . .	24.8	. . .	. . .	. . .	. . .	. . .
1930	16.8	. . .	. . .	24.3	. . .	. . .	. . .	. . .	. . .
1931	15.3	. . .	. . .	22.1	. . .	. . .	. . .	. . .	. . .
1932	13.7	. . .	. . .	19.6	. . .	. . .	. . .	. . .	. . .
1933	13.0	. . .	. . .	18.9	. . .	. . .	. . .	. . .	. . .
1934	13.5	. . .	. . .	20.7	. . .	. . .	. . .	. . .	. . .
1935	13.8	. . .	. . .	20.9	14.1	10.2	. . .	. . .	. . .
1936	13.9	. . .	. . .	21.1	14.2	10.3	. . .	. . .	. . .
1937	14.4	. . .	. . .	22.1	14.5	10.4	. . .	. . .	. . .
1938	14.2	. . .	. . .	22.0	14.6	10.4	. . .	. . .	. . .
1939	14.0	. . .	. . .	21.7	14.2	10.4	. . .	. . .	. . .
1940	14.1	. . .	. . .	21.9	14.1	10.4	. . .	. . .	. . .
1941	14.8	. . .	. . .	23.0	14.6	10.5	. . .	. . .	. . .
1942	16.4	. . .	. . .	26.8	15.9	10.8	. . .	. . .	. . .
1943	17.4	. . .	. . .	28.0	15.8	11.3	. . .	. . .	. . .
1944	17.7	. . .	. . .	30.0	15.8	11.6	. . .	. . .	. . .
1945	18.1	. . .	. . .	31.5	15.8	11.9	. . .	. . .	. . .
1946	19.6	. . .	. . .	34.6	16.6	12.6	. . .	. . .	. . .
1947	22.5	. . .	. . .	40.1	18.4	13.6	. . .	. . .	. . .
1948	24.2	. . .	. . .	42.7	20.4	14.5	. . .	. . .	. . .
1949	24.0	. . .	. . .	41.0	22.0	14.9	. . .	. . .	. . .
1950	24.2	. . .	. . .	40.5	22.6	15.2	. . .	. . .	. . .
1951	26.1	. . .	. . .	44.1	24.0	15.9	. . .	. . .	. . .
1952	26.7	. . .	. . .	43.7	25.6	16.8	. . .	. . .	. . .
1953	26.9	. . .	. . .	43.3	26.3	17.4	. . .	. . .	. . .
1954	27.0	. . .	. . .	43.3	25.9	17.9	. . .	. . .	. . .
1955	26.9	. . .	. . .	43.1	25.6	18.3	. . .	. . .	. . .
1956	27.3	. . .	. . .	44.0	26.1	19.0	. . .	. . .	. . .
1957	28.3	. . .	. . .	44.7	27.6	19.8	. . .	. . .	. . .
1958	29.1	. . .	. . .	44.8	28.4	20.7	. . .	. . .	. . .
1959	29.3	. . .	. . .	45.2	29.6	21.6	. . .	. . .	. . .
1960	29.8	. . .	. . .	45.9	29.6	22.4	. . .	. . .	. . .
1961	30.1	. . .	. . .	46.3	30.0	23.0	. . .	. . .	. . .
1962	30.4	. . .	. . .	46.6	30.6	23.6	. . .	. . .	. . .
1963	30.8	. . .	. . .	47.1	30.8	24.2	. . .	. . .	. . .
1964	31.2	. . .	. . .	47.5	31.2	24.7	. . .	. . .	. . .
1965	31.7	. . .	. . .	48.0	31.7	25.3	. . .	. . .	. . .
1966	32.6	. . .	. . .	49.2	32.2	26.4	. . .	. . .	. . .
1967	33.6	35.0	31.1	51.2	33.1	28.3	. . .	. . .	35.4
1968	35.0	36.2	32.3	54.0	34.1	30.0	. . .	. . .	37.2
1969	36.9	38.0	34.3	57.1	35.5	32.1	. . .	. . .	39.1
1970	39.0	40.1	36.7	59.5	37.3	34.1	. . .	. . .	41.3
1971	40.7	41.3	38.3	61.4	39.2	36.3	. . .	. . .	43.3
1972	42.1	43.1	39.8	62.7	39.7	37.5	. . .	. . .	45.1
1973	44.7	48.8	41.5	65.0	41.0	39.0	. . .	. . .	46.9
1974	49.6	55.5	46.2	69.8	45.5	42.6	. . .	. . .	50.2
1975	54.1	60.2	51.1	72.9	49.8	47.7	. . .	. . .	54.4
1976	57.2	62.0	54.2	75.6	54.7	52.3	. . .	. . .	57.6
1977	60.9	65.7	57.9	79.0	58.6	57.3	. . .	. . .	60.9
1978	65.6	72.1	62.9	81.7	61.5	62.1	. . .	. . .	64.8
1979	73.1	79.9	70.7	85.2	70.4	68.0	. . .	. . .	69.4

[1]December 1997 = 100.
. . . = Not available.

**Table 9-6. Consumer Price Indexes, Urban Wage Earners and Clerical Workers (CPI-W):
U.S. City Average, Major Groups, 1913–2012—*Continued***

(1982–1984 = 100, unless otherwise specified.)

Year	All items	Food and beverages	Housing	Apparel	Transportation	Medical care	Recreation[1]	Education and communication[1]	Other goods and services
1980	82.9	86.9	81.7	90.9	82.9	75.6	. . .	. . .	75.6
1981	91.4	93.6	91.1	95.6	93.0	83.5	. . .	. . .	82.5
1982	96.9	97.3	97.7	97.8	97.0	92.5	. . .	. . .	90.9
1983	99.8	99.5	100.0	100.2	99.2	100.5	. . .	. . .	101.3
1984	103.3	103.2	102.2	102.0	103.8	106.9	. . .	. . .	107.9
1985	106.9	105.5	106.6	105.0	106.4	113.6	. . .	. . .	114.2
1986	108.6	108.9	109.7	105.8	101.7	122.0	. . .	. . .	120.9
1987	112.5	113.3	112.8	110.4	105.1	130.2	. . .	. . .	127.8
1988	117.0	117.9	116.8	114.9	108.3	139.0	. . .	. . .	136.5
1989	122.6	124.6	121.2	117.9	113.9	149.6	. . .	. . .	147.4
1990	129.0	131.8	126.4	123.1	120.1	162.7	. . .	. . .	158.9
1991	134.3	136.5	131.2	127.4	123.1	176.5	. . .	. . .	171.7
1992	138.2	138.3	135.0	130.7	125.8	189.6	. . .	. . .	183.3
1993	142.1	141.2	138.5	132.4	129.4	200.9	91.2	86.0	192.2
1994	145.6	144.4	142.0	132.2	133.4	210.4	93.0	89.1	196.4
1995	149.8	148.3	145.4	130.9	138.8	219.8	94.7	92.3	204.2
1996	154.1	153.2	149.6	130.9	142.8	227.6	97.5	95.4	212.2
1997	157.6	157.2	153.4	132.1	143.6	234.0	99.7	98.5	221.6
1998	159.7	160.4	156.7	131.6	140.5	241.4	100.9	100.4	236.1
1999	163.2	163.8	160.0	130.1	143.4	249.7	101.3	101.5	261.9
2000	168.9	167.7	165.4	128.3	152.8	259.9	102.4	102.7	276.5
2001	173.5	173.0	172.1	126.1	153.6	271.8	103.6	105.3	289.5
2002	175.9	176.1	175.7	123.1	151.8	284.6	104.6	107.6	302.0
2003	179.8	179.9	180.4	120.0	156.3	296.3	105.5	109.0	307.0
2004	184.5	186.2	185.0	120.0	161.5	309.5	106.3	110.0	312.6
2005	191.0	190.5	191.2	119.1	173.0	322.8	106.8	111.4	322.2
2006	197.1	194.9	198.5	119.1	180.3	335.7	108.2	113.9	330.9
2007	202.8	202.5	204.8	118.5	184.3	350.9	108.6	116.3	344.0
2008	211.1	213.5	211.8	118.7	195.7	364.2	110.1	119.8	357.9
2009	209.6	217.5	213.1	119.8	176.7	376.1	111.0	123.0	391.6
2010	214.0	219.2	212.9	118.7	192.6	389.8	109.8	124.9	409.3
2011	221.6	227.3	215.8	121.3	213.3	402.2	109.9	125.5	416.9
2012	226.2	233.1	219.3	125.8	218.7	417.8	111.1	127.3	424.7

[1]December 1997 = 100.
. . . = Not available.

Table 9-7. Consumer Price Indexes, All Urban Consumers (CPI-U): U.S. City Average, by Expenditure Category, 1990–2012

(1982–1984 = 100, unless otherwise specified.)

Expenditure category	1990	1991	1992	1993	1994	1995	1996	1997	1998	1999	2000
ALL ITEMS	130.7	136.2	140.3	144.5	148.2	152.4	156.9	160.5	163.0	166.6	172.2
Food and Beverages	132.1	136.8	138.7	141.6	144.9	148.9	153.7	157.7	161.1	164.6	168.4
Food	132.4	136.3	137.9	140.9	144.3	148.4	153.3	157.3	160.7	164.1	167.8
Food at home	132.3	135.8	136.8	140.1	144.1	148.8	154.3	158.1	161.1	164.2	167.9
Cereals and bakery product	140.0	145.8	151.5	156.6	163.0	167.5	174.0	177.6	181.1	185.0	188.3
Meats, poultry, fish, and eggs	130.0	132.6	130.9	135.5	137.2	138.8	144.8	148.5	147.3	147.9	154.5
Dairy and related product	126.5	125.1	128.5	129.4	131.7	132.8	142.1	145.5	150.8	159.6	160.7
Fruits and vegetables	149.0	155.8	155.4	159.0	165.0	177.7	183.9	187.5	198.2	203.1	204.6
Nonalcoholic beverages and beverage materials	113.5	114.1	114.3	114.6	123.2	131.7	128.6	133.4	133.0	134.3	137.8
Other food at home	123.4	127.3	128.8	130.5	135.6	140.8	142.9	147.3	150.8	153.5	155.6
Sugar and sweets	124.7	129.3	133.1	133.4	135.2	137.5	143.7	147.8	150.2	152.3	154.0
Fats and oils	126.3	131.7	129.8	130.0	133.5	137.3	140.5	141.7	146.9	148.3	147.4
Other food	131.2	137.1	140.1	143.7	147.5	151.1	156.2	161.2	165.5	168.9	172.2
Other miscellaneous food[1]	...	...	...	...	...	...	...	...	102.6	104.9	107.5
Food away from home	133.4	137.9	140.7	143.2	145.7	149.0	152.7	157.0	161.1	165.1	169.0
Other food away from home[1]	...	...	...	...	...	...	...	...	101.6	105.2	109.0
Alcoholic beverages	129.3	142.8	147.3	149.6	151.5	153.9	158.5	162.8	165.7	169.7	174.7
Housing	128.5	133.6	137.5	141.2	144.8	148.5	152.8	156.8	160.4	163.9	169.6
Shelter	140.0	146.3	151.2	155.7	160.5	165.7	171.0	176.3	182.1	187.3	193.4
Rent of primary residence	138.4	143.3	146.9	150.3	154.0	157.8	162.0	166.7	172.1	177.5	183.9
Lodging away from home[1]	...	...	...	...	...	...	...	...	109.0	112.3	117.5
Owners' equivalent rent of primary residence[2]	144.8	150.4	155.5	160.5	165.8	171.3	176.8	181.9	187.8	192.9	198.7
Tenants' and household insurance[1]	...	...	...	...	...	...	...	...	99.8	101.3	103.7
Fuels and utilities	111.6	115.3	117.8	121.3	122.8	123.7	127.5	130.8	128.5	128.8	137.9
Household energy	104.5	106.7	108.1	111.2	111.7	111.5	115.2	117.9	113.7	113.5	122.8
Fuel oil and other fuels	99.3	94.6	90.7	90.3	88.8	88.1	99.2	99.8	90.0	91.4	129.7
Energy services	109.3	112.6	114.8	118.5	119.2	119.2	122.1	125.1	121.2	120.9	128.0
Water, sewer, and trash collection services[1]	...	...	...	...	...	...	...	...	101.6	104.0	106.5
Household furnishings and operations	113.3	116.0	118.0	119.3	121.0	123.0	124.7	125.4	126.6	126.7	128.2
Household operations[1]	...	...	...	...	...	...	...	...	101.5	104.5	110.5
Apparel	124.1	128.7	131.9	133.7	133.4	132.0	131.7	132.9	133.0	131.3	129.6
Men's and boys' apparel	120.4	124.2	126.5	127.5	126.4	126.2	127.7	130.1	131.8	131.1	129.7
Women's and girls' apparel	122.6	127.6	130.4	132.6	130.9	126.9	124.7	126.1	126.0	123.3	121.5
Infants' and toddlers' apparel	125.8	128.9	129.3	127.1	128.1	127.2	129.7	129.0	126.1	129.0	130.6
Footwear	117.4	120.9	125.0	125.9	126.0	125.4	126.6	127.6	128.0	125.7	123.8
Transportation	120.5	123.8	126.5	130.4	134.3	139.1	143.0	144.3	141.6	144.4	153.3
Private transportation	118.8	121.9	124.6	127.5	131.4	136.3	140.0	141.0	137.9	140.5	149.1
New and used motor vehicles[1]	...	...	...	91.8	95.5	99.4	101.0	100.5	100.1	100.1	100.8
New vehicles	121.4	126.0	129.2	132.7	137.6	141.0	143.7	144.3	143.4	142.9	142.8
Used cars and trucks	117.6	118.1	123.2	133.9	141.7	156.5	157.0	151.1	150.6	152.0	155.8
Motor fuel	101.2	99.4	99.0	98.0	98.5	100.0	106.3	106.2	92.2	100.7	129.3
Gasoline (all types)	101.0	99.2	99.0	97.7	98.2	99.8	105.9	105.8	91.6	100.1	128.6
Motor vehicle parts and equipment	100.9	102.2	103.1	101.6	101.4	102.1	102.2	101.9	101.1	100.5	101.5
Motor vehicle maintenance and repair	130.1	136.0	141.3	145.9	150.2	154.0	158.4	162.7	167.1	171.9	177.3
Public transportation	142.6	148.9	151.4	167.0	172.0	175.9	181.9	186.7	190.3	197.7	209.6
Medical Care	162.8	177.0	190.1	201.4	211.0	220.5	228.2	234.6	242.1	250.6	260.8
Medical care commodities	163.4	176.8	188.1	195.0	200.7	204.5	210.4	215.3	221.8	230.7	238.1
Medical care services	162.7	177.1	190.5	202.9	213.4	224.2	232.4	239.1	246.8	255.1	266.0
Professional services	156.1	165.7	175.8	184.7	192.5	201.0	208.3	215.4	222.2	229.2	237.7
Hospital and related services	178.0	196.1	214.0	231.9	245.6	257.8	269.5	278.4	287.5	299.5	317.3
Recreation[1]	...	...	...	90.7	92.7	94.5	97.4	99.6	101.1	102.0	103.3
Video and audio[1]	...	...	...	96.5	95.4	95.1	96.6	99.4	101.1	100.7	101.0
Education and Communication[1]	...	...	...	85.5	88.8	92.2	95.3	98.4	100.3	101.2	102.5
Education[1]	...	...	...	78.4	83.3	88.0	92.7	97.3	102.1	107.0	112.5
Educational books and supplies	171.3	180.3	190.3	197.6	205.5	214.4	226.9	238.4	250.8	261.7	279.9
Tuition, other school fees, and childcare	175.7	191.4	208.5	225.3	239.8	253.8	267.1	280.4	294.2	308.4	324.0
Communication[1]	...	...	...	96.7	97.6	98.8	99.6	100.3	98.7	96.0	93.6
Information and information processing[1]	...	...	...	97.7	98.6	98.7	99.5	100.4	98.5	95.5	92.8
Telephone services[1]	...	...	...	...	...	...	...	...	100.7	100.1	98.5
Information technology, hardware, and services[3]	93.5	88.6	83.7	78.8	72.0	63.8	57.2	50.1	39.9	30.5	25.9
Personal computers and peripheral equipment[1]	...	...	...	...	...	...	...	...	875.1	598.7	459.9
Other Goods and Services	159.0	171.6	183.3	192.9	198.5	206.9	215.4	224.8	237.7	258.3	271.1
Tobacco and smoking product	181.5	202.7	219.8	228.4	220.0	225.7	232.8	243.7	274.8	355.8	394.9
Personal care	128.2	132.8	136.5	139.0	141.5	143.1	144.3	144.2	148.3	151.8	153.7
Personal care product	128.2	132.8	136.5	139.0	141.5	143.1	144.3	144.2	148.3	151.8	153.7
Personal care services	132.8	137.0	140.0	144.0	147.9	151.5	156.6	162.4	166.0	171.4	178.1
Miscellaneous personal services	158.4	168.8	177.5	186.1	195.9	205.9	215.6	226.1	234.7	243.0	252.3

[1]December 1997 = 100.
[2]December 1982 = 100.
[3]December 1988 = 100.
. . . = Not available.

Table 9-7. Consumer Price Indexes, All Urban Consumers (CPI-U): U.S. City Average, by Expenditure Category, 1990–2012—*Continued*

(1982–1984 = 100, unless otherwise specified.)

Expenditure category	2001	2002	2003	2004	2005	2006	2007	2008	2009	2010	2011	2012
ALL ITEMS	177.1	179.9	184.0	188.9	195.3	201.6	207.3	215.3	214.5	218.1	224.9	229.6
Food and Beverages	173.6	176.8	180.5	186.6	191.2	195.7	203.3	214.2	218.2	220.0	227.9	233.7
Food	173.1	176.2	180.0	186.2	190.7	195.2	202.9	214.1	218.0	219.6	227.8	233.8
Food at home	173.4	175.6	179.4	186.2	189.8	193.1	201.2	214.1	215.1	215.8	226.2	231.8
Cereals and bakery product	193.8	198.0	202.8	206.0	209.0	212.8	222.1	244.9	252.6	250.4	260.3	267.7
Meats, poultry, fish, and eggs	161.3	162.1	169.3	181.7	184.7	186.6	195.6	204.7	203.8	207.7	223.2	231.0
Dairy and related product	167.1	168.1	167.9	180.2	182.4	181.4	194.8	210.4	197.0	199.2	212.7	217.3
Fruits and vegetables	212.2	220.9	225.9	232.7	241.4	252.9	262.6	278.9	272.9	273.5	284.7	282.8
Nonalcoholic beverages and beverage materials	139.2	139.2	139.8	140.4	144.4	147.4	153.4	160.0	163.0	161.6	166.8	168.6
Other food at home	159.6	160.8	162.6	164.9	167.0	169.6	173.3	184.2	191.2	191.1	197.4	204.8
Sugar and sweets	155.7	159.0	162.0	163.2	165.2	171.5	176.8	186.6	196.9	201.2	207.8	214.7
Fats and oils	155.7	155.4	157.4	167.8	167.7	168.0	172.9	196.8	201.2	200.6	219.2	232.6
Other food	176.0	177.1	178.8	179.7	182.5	185.0	188.2	198.1	205.5	204.6	209.3	216.6
Other miscellaneous food[1]	108.9	109.2	110.3	110.4	111.3	113.9	115.1	119.9	122.4	121.7	124.0	128.3
Food away from home	173.9	178.3	182.1	187.5	193.4	199.4	206.7	215.8	223.3	226.1	231.4	238.0
Other food away from home[1]	113.4	117.7	121.3	125.3	131.3	136.6	144.1	150.6	155.9	159.3	162.8	166.5
Alcoholic beverages	179.3	183.6	187.2	192.1	195.9	200.7	207.0	214.5	220.8	223.3	226.7	230.8
Housing	176.4	180.3	184.8	189.5	195.7	203.2	209.6	216.3	217.1	216.3	219.1	222.7
Shelter	200.6	208.1	213.1	218.8	224.4	232.1	240.6	246.7	249.4	248.4	251.6	257.1
Rent of primary residence	192.1	199.7	205.5	211.0	217.3	225.1	234.7	243.3	248.8	249.4	253.6	260.4
Lodging away from home[1]	118.6	118.3	119.3	125.9	130.3	136.0	142.8	143.7	134.2	133.7	137.4	140.5
Owners' equivalent rent of primary residence[2]	206.3	214.7	219.9	224.9	230.2	238.2	246.2	252.4	256.6	256.6	259.6	264.8
Tenants' and household insurance[1]	106.2	108.7	114.8	116.2	117.6	116.5	117.0	118.8	121.5	125.7	127.4	131.3
Fuels and utilities	150.2	143.6	154.5	161.9	179.0	194.7	200.6	220.0	210.7	214.2	220.4	219.0
Household energy	135.4	127.2	138.2	144.4	161.6	177.1	181.7	200.8	188.1	189.3	193.6	189.3
Fuel oil and other fuels	129.3	115.5	139.5	160.5	208.6	234.9	251.5	334.4	239.8	275.1	337.1	335.9
Energy services	142.4	134.4	145.0	150.6	166.5	182.1	186.3	202.2	193.6	192.9	194.4	189.7
Water, sewer, and trash collection services[1]	109.6	113.0	117.2	124.0	130.3	136.8	143.7	152.1	161.1	170.9	179.6	189.3
Household furnishings and operations	129.1	128.3	126.1	125.5	126.1	127.0	126.9	127.8	128.7	125.5	124.9	125.7
Household operations[1]	115.6	119.0	121.8	125.0	130.3	136.6	140.6	147.5	150.3	150.3	151.8	155.2
Apparel	127.3	124.0	120.9	120.4	119.5	119.5	119.0	118.9	120.1	119.5	122.1	126.3
Men's and boys' apparel	125.7	121.7	118.0	117.5	116.1	114.1	112.4	113.0	113.6	111.9	114.7	119.5
Women's and girls' apparel	119.3	115.8	113.1	113.0	110.8	110.7	110.3	107.5	108.1	107.1	109.2	113.0
Infants' and toddlers' apparel	129.2	126.4	122.1	118.5	116.7	116.5	113.9	113.8	114.5	114.2	113.6	119.7
Footwear	123.0	121.4	119.6	119.3	122.6	123.5	122.4	124.2	126.9	128.0	128.5	131.8
Transportation	154.3	152.9	157.6	163.1	173.9	180.9	184.7	195.5	179.3	193.4	212.4	217.3
Private transportation	150.0	148.8	153.6	159.4	170.2	177.0	180.8	191.0	174.8	188.7	207.6	212.8
New and used motor vehicles[1]	101.3	99.2	96.5	94.2	95.6	95.6	94.3	93.3	93.5	97.1	99.8	100.6
New vehicles	142.1	140.0	137.9	137.1	137.9	137.6	136.3	134.2	135.6	138.0	141.9	144.2
Used cars and trucks	158.7	152.0	142.9	133.3	139.4	140.0	135.7	134.0	127.0	143.1	149.0	150.3
Motor fuel	124.7	116.6	135.8	160.4	195.7	221.0	239.1	279.7	202.0	239.2	302.6	312.7
Gasoline (all types)	124.0	116.0	135.1	159.7	194.7	219.9	238.0	277.5	201.6	238.6	301.7	311.5
Motor vehicle parts and equipment	104.8	106.9	107.8	108.7	111.9	117.3	121.6	128.7	134.1	137.0	143.9	148.6
Motor vehicle maintenance and repair	183.5	190.2	195.6	200.2	206.9	215.6	223.0	233.9	243.3	248.0	253.1	257.6
Public transportation	210.6	207.4	209.3	209.1	217.3	226.6	230.0	250.5	236.3	251.4	269.4	271.4
Medical Care	272.8	285.6	297.1	310.1	323.2	336.2	351.1	364.1	375.6	388.4	400.3	414.9
Medical care commodities	247.6	256.4	262.8	269.3	276.0	285.9	290.0	296.0	305.1	314.7	324.1	333.6
Medical care services	278.8	292.9	306.0	321.3	336.7	350.6	369.3	384.9	397.3	411.2	423.8	440.3
Professional services	246.5	253.9	261.2	271.5	281.7	289.3	300.8	311.0	319.4	328.2	335.7	342.0
Hospital and related services	338.3	367.8	394.8	417.9	439.9	468.1	498.9	534.0	567.9	607.7	641.5	672.1
Recreation[1]	104.9	106.2	107.5	108.6	109.4	110.9	111.4	113.3	114.3	113.3	113.4	114.7
Video and audio[1]	101.5	102.8	103.6	104.2	104.2	104.6	102.9	102.6	101.3	99.1	98.4	99.4
Education and Communication[1]	105.2	107.9	109.8	111.6	113.7	116.8	119.6	123.6	127.4	129.9	131.5	133.8
Education[1]	118.5	126.0	134.4	143.7	152.7	162.1	171.4	181.3	190.9	199.3	207.8	216.3
Educational books and supplies	295.9	317.6	335.4	351.0	365.6	388.9	420.4	450.2	482.1	505.6	529.5	562.6
Tuition, other school fees, and childcare	341.1	362.1	386.7	414.3	440.9	468.1	494.1	522.1	549.0	573.2	597.2	621.0
Communication[1]	93.3	92.3	89.7	86.7	84.7	84.1	83.4	84.2	85.0	84.7	83.3	83.1
Information and information processing[1]	92.3	90.8	87.8	84.6	82.6	81.7	80.7	81.4	81.9	81.5	80.0	79.5
Telephone services[1]	99.3	99.7	98.3	95.8	94.9	95.8	98.2	100.5	102.4	102.4	101.2	101.7
Information technology, hardware, and services[3]	21.3	18.3	16.1	14.8	13.6	12.5	10.6	10.1	9.7	9.4	9.0	8.7
Personal computers and peripheral equipment[1]	330.1	248.4	196.9	171.2	143.2	120.9	108.4	94.9	82.3	76.4	68.9	62.3
Other Goods and Services	282.6	293.2	298.7	304.7	313.4	321.7	333.3	345.4	368.6	381.3	387.2	394.4
Tobacco and smoking product	425.2	461.5	469.0	478.0	502.8	519.9	554.2	588.7	730.3	807.3	834.8	853.5
Personal care	155.1	154.7	153.5	153.9	154.4	155.8	158.3	159.3	162.6	161.1	160.5	162.2
Personal care product	155.1	154.7	153.5	153.9	154.4	155.8	158.3	159.3	162.6	161.1	160.5	162.2
Personal care services	184.3	188.4	193.2	197.6	203.9	209.7	216.6	223.7	227.6	229.6	230.8	234.2
Miscellaneous personal services	263.1	274.4	283.5	293.9	303.0	313.6	325.0	338.9	344.5	354.1	362.9	372.7

[1]December 1997 = 100.
[2]December 1982 = 100.
[3]December 1988 = 100.

Table 9-8. Relative Importance of Components in the Consumer Price Index: U.S. City Average, Selected Groups, December 1997–December 2012

(Percent distribution.)

Index and year	All items	Food and beverages	Housing	Apparel	Transportation	Medical care	Recreation	Education and communication	Other goods and services
ALL URBAN CONSUMERS (CPI-U)									
December 1997	100.0	16.3	39.6	4.9	17.6	5.6	6.1	5.5	4.3
December 1998	100.0	16.4	39.8	4.8	17.0	5.7	6.1	5.5	4.6
December 1999	100.0	16.3	39.6	4.7	17.5	5.8	6.0	5.4	4.7
December 2000	100.0	16.2	40.0	4.4	17.6	5.8	5.9	5.3	4.8
December 2001[1]	100.0	16.4	40.5	4.2	16.6	6.0	5.9	5.4	4.9
December 2001[2]	100.0	15.7	40.9	4.4	17.1	5.8	6.0	5.8	4.3
December 2002	100.0	15.6	40.9	4.2	17.3	6.0	5.9	5.8	4.4
December 2003	100.0	15.4	42.1	4.0	16.9	6.1	5.9	5.9	3.8
December 2004	100.0	15.3	42.0	3.8	17.4	6.1	5.7	5.8	3.8
December 2005	100.0	15.1	42.2	3.7	17.7	6.2	5.6	5.8	3.7
December 2006	100.0	15.0	42.7	3.7	17.2	6.3	5.6	6.0	3.5
December 2007	100.0	14.9	42.4	3.7	17.7	6.2	5.6	6.1	3.3
December 2008	100.0	15.8	43.4	3.7	15.3	6.4	5.7	6.3	3.4
December 2009	100.0	14.8	42.0	3.7	16.7	6.5	6.4	6.4	3.5
December 2010	100.0	14.8	42.0	3.7	16.7	6.5	6.4	3.0	3.5
December 2011	100.0	15.3	41.0	3.6	16.9	7.1	6.0	6.8	3.4
December 2012	100.0	15.3	41.0	3.6	16.8	7.2	6.0	6.8	3.4
URBAN WAGE EARNERS AND WORKERS (CPI-W)									
December 1997	100.0	17.9	36.5	5.3	19.8	4.6	6.0	5.4	4.5
December 1998	100.0	18.0	36.7	5.2	19.2	4.7	5.9	5.4	5.0
December 1999	100.0	17.9	36.5	5.0	19.7	4.7	5.8	5.3	5.1
December 2000	100.0	17.8	36.8	4.8	19.9	4.7	5.7	5.2	5.2
December 2001[1]	100.0	18.0	37.3	4.6	18.8	4.9	5.7	5.3	5.4
December 2001[2]	100.0	17.2	38.1	4.8	19.4	4.6	5.6	5.6	4.5
December 2002	100.0	17.1	38.1	4.6	19.7	4.7	5.6	5.6	4.6
December 2003	100.0	17.2	39.1	4.4	19.1	5.0	5.7	5.6	3.9
December 2004	100.0	17.0	39.0	4.2	19.8	5.0	5.5	5.5	3.9
December 2005	100.0	16.8	39.2	4.0	20.1	5.1	5.4	5.4	3.9
December 2006	100.0	16.5	40.5	4.0	19.5	5.2	5.0	5.6	3.7
December 2007	100.0	15.9	40.0	4.0	20.1	5.2	5.3	6.0	3.5
December 2008	100.0	16.9	41.3	4.0	17.1	5.4	5.5	6.2	3.7
December 2009	100.0	16.4	39.8	3.8	18.6	5.3	6.0	6.2	3.9
December 2010	100.0	16.4	39.8	3.8	18.6	5.3	6.0	6.2	3.9
December 2011	100.0	15.9	39.8	3.6	19.0	5.7	5.6	6.8	3.5
December 2012	100.0	15.9	39.9	3.6	19.0	5.8	5.5	6.8	3.5

[1] 1993–1995 weights.
[2] 1999–2000 weights.

Table 9-9. Consumer Price Indexes, All Urban Consumers (CPI-U), All Items: Selected Metropolitan Statistical Areas, Selected Years, 1975–2012

(1982–1984 = 100, unless otherwise specified.)

Area	1975	1980	1985	1986	1987	1988	1989	1990	1991	1992	1993	1994	1995	1996	1997
NORTHEAST															
Boston-Brockton-Nashua, MA-NH-ME-CT	55.8	82.6	109.4	112.2	117.1	124.2	131.3	138.9	145.0	148.6	152.9	154.9	158.6	163.3	167.9
New York-Northern New Jersey-Long Island, NY-NJ-CT-PA	57.6	82.1	108.7	112.3	118.0	123.7	130.6	138.5	144.8	150.0	154.5	158.2	162.2	166.9	170.8
Philadelphia-Wilmington-Atlantic City, PA-NJ-DE-MD	56.8	83.6	108.8	111.5	116.8	122.4	128.3	135.8	142.2	146.6	150.2	154.6	158.7	162.8	166.5
Pittsburgh, PA	52.4	81.0	106.9	108.2	111.4	114.9	120.1	126.2	131.3	136.0	139.9	144.6	149.2	153.2	157.0
NORTH CENTRAL															
Chicago-Gary-Kenosha, IL-IN-WI	52.8	82.2	107.7	110.0	114.5	119.0	125.0	131.7	137.0	141.1	145.4	148.6	153.3	157.4	161.7
Cincinnati-Hamilton, OH-KY-IN	51.8	82.1	106.6	107.6	111.9	116.1	120.9	126.5	131.4	134.1	137.8	142.4	146.2	149.6	152.1
Cleveland-Akron, OH	50.2	78.9	107.8	109.4	112.7	116.7	122.7	129.0	134.2	136.8	140.3	144.4	147.9	152.0	156.1
Detroit-Ann Arbor-Flint, MI	53.9	85.3	106.8	108.3	111.7	116.1	122.3	128.6	133.1	135.9	139.6	144.0	148.6	152.5	156.3
Kansas City, MO-KS	53.2	83.6	107.7	108.7	113.1	117.4	121.6	126.0	131.2	134.3	138.1	141.3	145.3	151.6	155.8
Milwaukee-Racine, WI	50.8	81.4	107.0	107.4	111.5	115.9	120.8	126.2	132.2	137.1	142.1	147.0	151.0	154.7	157.7
Minneapolis-St. Paul, MN-WI	51.2	78.9	107.0	108.4	111.6	117.2	122.0	127.0	130.4	135.0	139.2	143.6	147.0	151.9	155.4
St. Louis, MO-IL	52.6	82.5	107.1	108.6	112.2	115.7	121.8	128.1	132.1	134.7	137.5	141.3	145.2	149.6	152.9
SOUTH															
Atlanta, GA	53.6	80.3	108.9	112.2	116.5	120.4	126.1	131.7	135.9	138.5	143.4	146.7	150.9	156.0	158.9
Dallas-Fort Worth, TX	50.4	81.5	108.2	109.9	112.9	116.1	119.5	125.1	130.8	133.9	137.3	141.2	144.9	148.8	151.4
Houston-Galveston-Brazoria, TX	51.4	82.7	104.9	103.9	106.5	109.5	114.1	120.6	125.1	129.1	133.4	137.9	139.8	142.7	145.4
Miami-Fort Lauderdale, FL	...	81.1	106.5	107.9	111.8	116.8	121.5	128.0	132.3	134.5	139.1	143.6	148.9	153.7	158.4
Tampa-St. Petersburg-Clearwater, FL[1]	...	...	...	...	100.0	103.7	107.2	111.7	116.4	119.2	124.0	126.5	129.7	131.6	134.0
Washington-Baltimore, DC-MD-VA-WV[2]	...	...	...	...	...	...	...	...	...	...	...	...	...	...	100.8
WEST															
Anchorage, AK	57.1	85.5	105.8	107.8	108.2	108.6	111.7	118.6	124.0	128.2	132.2	135.0	138.9	142.7	144.8
Denver-Boulder-Greeley, CO	48.4	78.4	107.1	107.9	110.8	113.7	115.8	120.9	125.6	130.3	135.8	141.8	147.9	153.1	158.1
Honolulu, HI	56.3	83.0	106.8	109.4	114.9	121.7	128.7	138.1	148.0	155.1	160.1	164.5	168.1	170.7	171.9
Los Angeles-Riverside-Orange County, CA	53.3	83.7	108.4	111.9	116.7	122.1	128.3	135.9	141.4	146.5	150.3	152.3	154.6	157.5	160.0
Phoenix-Mesa, AZ	...	...	...	...	...	...	...	...	...	...	...	...	...	...	...
Portland-Salem, OR-WA	53.5	87.2	106.7	108.2	110.9	114.7	120.4	127.4	133.9	139.8	144.7	148.9	153.2	158.6	164.0
San Diego, CA	47.6	79.4	110.4	113.5	117.5	123.4	130.6	138.4	143.4	147.4	150.6	154.5	156.8	160.9	163.7
San Francisco-Oakland-San Jose, CA	51.8	80.4	108.4	111.6	115.4	120.5	126.4	132.1	137.9	142.5	146.3	148.7	151.6	155.1	160.4
Seattle-Tacoma-Bremerton, WA	51.1	82.7	105.6	106.7	109.2	112.8	118.1	126.8	134.1	139.0	142.9	147.8	152.3	157.5	163.0

Area	1998	1999	2000	2001	2002	2003	2004	2005	2006	2007	2008	2009	2010	2011	2012
NORTHEAST															
Boston-Brockton-Nashua, MA-NH-ME-CT	171.7	176.0	183.6	191.5	196.5	203.9	209.5	216.4	223.1	227.4	235.4	233.8	237.4	243.9	247.7
New York-Northern New Jersey-Long Island, NY-NJ-CT-PA	173.6	177.0	182.5	187.1	191.9	197.8	204.8	212.7	220.7	226.9	235.8	236.8	240.9	247.7	252.6
Philadelphia-Wilmington-Atlantic City, PA-NJ-DE-MD	168.2	171.9	176.5	181.3	184.9	188.8	196.5	204.2	212.1	216.7	224.1	223.3	227.7	233.8	238.1
Pittsburgh, PA	159.2	162.5	168.0	172.5	174.0	177.5	183.0	189.8	195.7	201.5	211.3	212.1	215.4	225.1	232.9
NORTH CENTRAL															
Chicago-Gary-Kenosha, IL-IN-WI	165.0	168.4	173.8	178.3	181.2	184.5	188.6	194.3	198.3	204.8	212.5	210.0	212.9	218.7	222.0
Cincinnati-Hamilton, OH-KY-IN	155.1	159.2	164.8	167.9	170.0	173.4	176.5	181.6	188.6	193.9	201.5	200.6	204.7	211.1	216.3
Cleveland-Akron, OH	159.8	162.5	168.0	172.9	173.3	176.2	181.6	187.9	191.1	196.0	203.0	200.5	204.6	211.0	214.7
Detroit-Ann Arbor-Flint, MI	159.8	163.9	169.8	174.4	178.9	182.5	185.4	190.8	196.6	200.1	204.7	203.5	205.1	211.8	216.1
Kansas City, MO-KS	157.8	160.1	166.6	172.2	174.0	177.0	180.7	185.3	190.1	194.5	201.2	201.0	205.4	213.5	218.5
Milwaukee-Racine, WI	160.3	163.7	168.6	171.7	174.0	177.7	180.2	185.2	189.9	194.1	203.0	203.0	209.6	216.9	221.1
Minneapolis-St. Paul, MN-WI	158.3	163.3	170.1	176.5	179.6	182.7	187.9	193.1	196.2	201.2	209.0	207.9	211.7	219.3	224.5
St. Louis, MO-IL	154.5	157.6	163.1	167.3	169.1	173.4	180.3	186.2	189.5	193.2	198.7	198.5	203.2	209.8	214.8
SOUTH															
Atlanta, GA	161.2	164.8	170.6	176.2	178.2	180.8	183.2	188.9	193.8	200.0	206.5	201.0	203.5	209.1	212.8
Dallas-Fort Worth, TX	153.6	158.0	164.7	170.4	172.7	176.2	178.7	184.7	190.1	193.2	201.8	200.5	201.6	207.9	212.2
Houston-Galveston-Brazoria, TX	146.8	148.7	154.2	158.8	159.2	163.7	169.5	175.6	180.6	183.8	190.0	190.5	194.2	200.5	204.2
Miami-Fort Lauderdale, FL	160.5	162.4	167.8	173.0	175.5	180.6	185.6	194.3	203.9	212.4	222.1	221.4	223.1	230.9	235.2
Tampa-St. Petersburg-Clearwater, FL[1]	137.5	140.6	145.7	148.8	153.9	158.1	162.0	168.5	175.2	184.3	190.1	189.9	193.5	198.9	203.6
Washington-Baltimore, DC-MD-VA-WV[2]	102.1	104.2	107.6	110.4	113.0	116.2	119.5	124.3	128.8	133.5	139.5	139.8	142.2	147.0	150.2
WEST															
Anchorage, AK	146.9	148.4	150.9	155.2	158.2	162.5	166.7	171.8	177.3	181.2	189.5	191.7	195.1	201.4	205.9
Denver-Boulder-Greeley, CO	161.9	166.6	173.2	181.3	184.8	186.8	187.0	190.9	197.7	202.0	209.9	208.5	212.4	220.3	224.6
Honolulu, HI	171.5	173.3	176.3	178.4	180.3	184.5	190.6	197.8	209.4	219.5	228.9	230.0	234.9	243.6	249.5
Los Angeles-Riverside-Orange County, CA	162.3	166.1	171.6	177.3	182.2	187.0	193.2	201.8	210.4	217.3	225.0	223.2	225.9	231.9	236.6
Phoenix-Mesa, AZ	...	...	...	...	101.2	103.3	105.2	108.3	111.5	115.3	119.3	117.6	118.2	121.5	124.2
Portland-Salem, OR-WA	167.1	172.6	178.0	182.4	183.8	186.3	191.1	196.0	201.1	208.6	215.4	215.6	218.3	224.6	229.8
San Diego, CA	166.9	172.8	182.8	191.2	197.9	205.3	212.8	220.6	228.1	233.3	242.3	242.3	245.5	252.9	257.0
San Francisco-Oakland-San Jose, CA	165.5	172.5	180.2	189.9	193.0	196.4	198.8	202.7	209.2	216.0	222.8	224.4	227.5	233.4	239.7
Seattle-Tacoma-Bremerton, WA	167.7	172.8	179.2	185.7	189.3	192.3	194.7	200.2	207.6	215.7	224.7	226.0	226.7	232.8	238.7

[1]1987 = 100.
[2]November 1996 = 100.
. . . = Not available.

Table 9-10. Consumer Price Index Research Series, Using Current Methods (CPI-U-RS), by Month and Annual Average, 1977–2012

(December 1977 = 100.)

Year	January	February	March	April	May	June	July	August	September	October	November	December	Annual average
1977	100.0	. . .	. . .	. . .	. . .	. . .	. . .	. . .	. . .	. . .	. . .	. . .	. . .
1978	100.5	101.1	101.8	102.7	103.6	104.6	105.0	105.5	106.1	106.7	107.3	107.9	104.4
1979	108.7	109.7	110.7	111.8	113.0	114.1	115.2	116.0	117.1	117.9	118.5	119.5	114.4
1980	120.9	122.4	123.8	124.8	125.8	126.7	127.6	128.6	130.0	130.8	131.5	132.4	127.1
1981	133.6	135.3	136.4	137.1	137.9	138.7	139.7	140.7	141.8	142.4	142.9	143.4	139.2
1982	144.2	144.7	144.9	145.1	146.1	147.5	148.5	148.8	149.5	150.2	150.5	150.7	147.6
1983	151.1	151.2	151.3	152.4	153.2	153.8	154.4	154.8	155.6	156.0	156.2	156.4	153.9
1984	157.3	158.0	158.4	159.1	159.5	160.0	160.5	161.1	161.9	162.3	162.3	162.4	160.2
1985	162.6	163.3	164.0	164.7	165.3	165.8	166.1	166.4	167.0	167.4	167.9	168.3	165.7
1986	168.8	168.3	167.5	167.1	167.7	168.5	168.5	168.7	169.7	169.7	169.8	169.9	168.7
1987	170.9	171.6	172.3	173.2	173.7	174.3	174.6	175.6	176.4	176.8	176.9	176.8	174.4
1988	177.3	177.6	178.3	179.2	179.8	180.5	181.1	181.9	183.0	183.5	183.6	183.7	180.8
1989	184.6	185.2	186.2	187.5	188.4	188.8	189.3	189.5	190.2	190.9	191.2	191.5	188.6
1990	193.3	194.2	195.2	195.5	195.8	196.9	197.6	199.3	200.9	202.1	202.3	202.4	198.0
1991	203.3	203.5	203.6	203.9	204.4	204.9	205.0	205.6	206.4	206.6	207.1	207.2	205.1
1992	207.5	208.1	209.0	209.3	209.6	210.1	210.4	211.0	211.6	212.2	212.5	212.3	210.3
1993	212.9	213.7	214.3	214.9	215.3	215.5	215.6	216.1	216.4	217.1	217.3	217.1	215.5
1994	217.4	218.0	218.8	219.0	219.2	219.9	220.4	221.1	221.5	221.6	221.9	221.8	220.1
1995	222.6	223.3	224.0	224.7	225.1	225.6	225.7	226.1	226.5	227.1	226.9	226.8	225.4
1996	227.9	228.7	229.8	230.6	231.2	231.3	231.7	232.0	232.7	233.4	233.8	233.8	231.4
1997	234.5	235.2	235.6	235.9	235.8	236.2	236.3	236.7	237.5	237.9	237.8	237.4	236.4
1998	237.8	238.2	238.6	239.1	239.4	239.6	239.8	240.2	240.5	241.0	241.0	240.7	239.7
1999	241.4	241.7	242.4	244.1	244.1	244.2	244.9	245.6	246.7	247.2	247.3	247.3	244.7
2000	248.0	249.4	251.4	251.6	251.8	253.2	253.7	253.8	255.1	255.5	255.7	255.5	252.9
2001	257.1	258.2	258.8	259.8	260.9	261.4	260.6	260.7	261.8	260.9	260.4	259.4	260.0
2002	260.1	261.1	262.5	264.0	264.0	264.2	264.5	265.3	265.8	266.3	266.3	265.7	264.2
2003	266.8	268.9	270.5	269.9	269.5	269.8	270.1	271.1	271.9	271.7	270.9	270.6	270.1
2004	272.0	273.5	275.2	276.1	277.6	278.5	278.2	278.3	278.8	280.4	280.5	279.5	277.4
2005	280.0	281.6	283.8	285.7	285.5	285.6	286.9	288.3	291.9	292.5	290.2	288.9	286.7
2006	291.2	291.8	293.5	295.9	297.3	297.9	298.8	299.5	298.0	296.4	295.9	296.4	296.1
2007	297.2	298.8	301.6	303.5	305.4	306.0	305.9	305.3	306.2	306.8	308.6	308.4	304.5
2008	310.0	310.9	313.6	315.5	318.1	321.3	323.0	321.7	321.3	318.0	311.9	308.7	316.2
2009	310.1	311.6	312.4	313.1	314.0	316.7	316.2	316.9	317.1	317.5	317.7	317.1	315.0
2010	318.2	318.3	319.6	320.1	320.4	320.1	320.1	320.6	320.8	321.2	321.3	321.9	320.2
2011	323.4	325.0	328.2	330.3	331.8	331.5	331.8	332.7	333.2	332.5	332.2	331.4	330.3
2012	332.9	334.3	336.9	337.9	337.5	337.0	336.4	338.3	339.8	339.7	338.1	337.2	337.2

. . . = Not available.

NOTES AND DEFINITIONS

EXPORT AND IMPORT PRICE INDEXES

COLLECTION AND COVERAGE

The International Price Program (IPP) at the Bureau of Labor Statistics (BLS) produces Import/Export Price Indexes (MXP) which contain data on changes in the prices of goods and services traded between the United States and the rest of the world. Price indexes are available for nearly all merchandise categories. Military goods, works of art, used items, charity donations, railroad equipment, items leased for less than a year, rebuilt and repaired items, and selected exports are not included in the IPP program.

The (IPP) selects sample establishments based upon their relative trade value in imports and exports during the course of a year. After an establishment is selected for inclusion, a BLS field economist visits the establishment to enlist cooperation and to select the exact items that will be priced on a monthly basis. All information provided by the establishment is protected under BLS confidentiality rules.

The MXP are primarily used to deflate foreign trade statistics produced by the U.S. government. The MXP are also a valuable input into the processes of measuring inflation, formulating fiscal and monetary policy, forecasting future prices, conducting elasticity studies, measuring U.S. industrial competitiveness, analyzing exchange rates, negotiating trade contracts, and analyzing import prices by locality of origin. The IPP collects prices as close as possible to the first day of each reference month.

The formula used to calculate the MXP is a modified form of the Laspeyres index. A Laspeyres index uses fixed base period quantities to aggregate prices. This means that the quality of goods and services is fixed; new goods do not appear, and the prices of goods that disappear must be observable. Because these implications are not consistent with the actually workings of the economy, adjustments must be made to the index. All MXP data are not seasonally adjusted.

Items are classified by end use for the Bureau of Economic Analysis System, by industry according to the North American Industry Classification System (NAICS), and by product category according to the Harmonized System (HS). While classification by end use and product category are self-explanatory, a couple of notes are in order for classifying items by industry. In the NAICS tables, for both imports and exports, items are classified by output industry, not input industry. As an example, NAICS import index 326 (plastics and rubber products) includes outputs such as manufactured plastic rather than inputs such as petroleum. The NAICS classification structure also matches the classification system used by the PPI to produce the NAICS primary products indexes.

Although import and export transaction prices are used to calculate the MXP, the IPP does not publish price information. For this reason, the MXP cannot be used to measure differences in price levels among different products and services or among different localities of origin.

SOURCES OF ADDITIONAL INFORMATION

Concepts and methodology are described in Chapter 15 of the *BLS Handbook of Methods* and in monthly BLS press releases. These resources are available on the BLS Web site at http://www.bls.gov.

Table 9-11. U.S. Export Price Indexes for Selected Categories of Goods, by End Use, 2001–2012

(2000 = 100, unless otherwise indicated.)

Commodity	2001				2002				2003			
	March	June	September	December	March	June	September	December	March	June	September	December
ALL COMMODITIES	100.0	99.4	99.0	97.6	97.6	98.0	98.8	98.6	99.7	99.5	99.8	100.8
Foods, Feeds, and Beverages	101.0	100.4	102.6	100.7	99.7	101.5	109.8	108.7	108.2	111.3	115.3	122.4
Agricultural foods, feeds, and beverages excluding distilled beverages	101.2	101.2	103.6	101.6	100.0	101.7	110.7	109.5	108.1	111.2	116.3	123.8
Nonagricultural foods (fish, distilled beverages)	99.4	92.6	92.9	92.1	98.3	100.7	101.3	102.3	110.0	113.1	106.5	108.5
Industrial Supplies and Materials	98.9	97.2	95.2	91.4	91.9	94.6	95.9	96.0	100.6	100.1	100.2	102.5
Industrial supplies and materials, durable	98.6	97.6	95.9	93.8	94.4	96.0	96.4	96.6	99.2	99.7	100.4	103.3
Industrial supplies and materials, nondurable	99.0	96.9	94.8	90.0	90.4	93.9	95.8	95.8	101.7	100.6	100.4	102.2
Agricultural industrial supplies and materials	101.7	99.3	96.8	93.3	93.6	95.8	98.4	101.9	104.8	104.4	107.3	117.5
Fuels and lubricants	100.3	102.8	103.2	83.5	85.6	86.7	92.9	91.3	108.0	97.0	97.6	99.0
Nonagricultural supplies and materials excluding fuels and building materials	98.5	96.1	93.8	92.3	92.6	95.7	96.4	96.4	99.9	100.7	100.5	102.5
Selected building materials	97.5	97.0	95.5	94.2	94.2	94.2	96.2	96.2	96.4	96.3	98.4	99.5
Capital Goods	100.6	100.3	100.0	99.4	99.4	98.7	98.4	98.1	98.3	97.6	97.5	97.5
Electrical generating equipment	100.9	101.7	101.6	101.5	102.1	102.0	102.0	101.9	101.6	101.6	101.7	101.7
Nonelectrical machinery	99.7	99.1	98.6	97.7	97.5	96.6	96.0	95.4	95.6	94.5	94.3	94.1
Transportation equipment excluding motor vehicles[1]	...	...	...	100.0	100.9	100.8	101.7	102.5	103.5	104.0	105.1	105.7
Automotive Vehicles, Parts, and Engines	100.3	100.4	100.4	100.5	100.9	100.9	101.1	101.3	101.5	101.6	101.8	101.8
Consumer Goods, Excluding Automotives	99.6	99.4	99.7	99.9	99.1	99.1	99.3	99.3	99.4	99.6	99.4	99.9
Nondurables, manufactured	99.0	99.0	99.1	99.1	98.1	98.5	98.7	98.7	98.7	98.8	98.5	99.2
Durables, manufactured	100.2	100.0	100.4	100.5	99.7	99.4	99.6	99.6	99.7	100.1	100.1	100.3
Agricultural Commodities	101.3	100.9	102.5	100.2	98.9	100.7	108.6	108.2	107.5	110.0	114.7	122.7
Nonagricultural Commodities	99.9	99.3	98.6	97.4	97.5	97.8	98.0	97.8	99.1	98.7	98.6	99.1

Commodity	2004				2005				2006			
	March	June	September	December	March	June	September	December	March	June	September	December
ALL COMMODITIES	103.0	103.4	103.8	104.8	106.4	106.7	107.5	107.7	108.8	111.2	111.7	112.5
Foods, Feeds, and Beverages	130.5	129.1	118.7	116.9	120.9	125.2	122.8	121.9	121.7	125.6	128.8	138.7
Agricultural foods, feeds, and beverages excluding distilled beverages	132.4	131.1	119.3	116.6	120.7	125.6	122.6	121.7	121.5	125.7	129.1	140.5
Nonagricultural foods (fish, distilled beverages)	112.1	110.7	113.0	118.4	121.8	120.1	123.6	123.6	123.2	125.0	126.0	123.5
Industrial Supplies and Materials	108.1	109.9	114.0	118.0	122.3	122.3	127.4	127.9	131.3	138.8	139.5	139.4
Industrial supplies and materials, durable	110.3	111.8	116.0	120.2	122.6	122.7	123.4	129.1	135.7	146.2	146.9	150.1
Industrial supplies and materials, nondurable	107.0	108.9	112.9	116.9	122.2	122.1	129.8	127.4	129.0	134.9	135.7	133.9
Agricultural industrial supplies and materials	117.2	110.7	109.4	109.5	115.6	115.8	116.4	117.4	116.8	117.3	118.1	123.9
Fuels and lubricants	108.9	114.9	121.5	125.4	143.8	148.8	184.8	163.4	173.5	196.3	191.1	183.5
Nonagricultural supplies and materials excluding fuels and building materials	108.1	110.0	114.4	118.9	121.4	120.6	122.2	125.7	128.5	134.7	136.3	136.8
Selected building materials	102.3	103.4	104.0	104.4	105.3	106.2	105.7	106.5	108.5	109.8	110.0	111.5
Capital Goods	98.0	97.8	97.8	98.2	98.4	98.4	97.6	97.7	98.2	98.4	98.5	98.8
Electrical generating equipment	102.0	102.0	102.4	103.6	103.9	103.4	102.6	103.6	104.4	104.8	105.1	106.2
Nonelectrical machinery	94.5	94.1	93.9	93.9	93.9	93.7	92.7	92.5	92.7	92.7	92.6	92.6
Transportation equipment excluding motor vehicles[1]	106.6	107.2	108.3	109.5	111.1	111.8	112.6	113.8	116.0	117.1	117.7	119.1
Automotive Vehicles, Parts, and Engines	101.9	102.3	102.5	102.9	103.3	103.4	103.7	103.9	104.4	104.9	105.2	105.5
Consumer Goods, Excluding Automotives	100.2	100.4	101.0	101.2	101.6	101.5	101.9	101.9	102.3	103.5	104.0	104.0
Nondurables, manufactured	99.9	100.0	101.0	101.0	101.5	101.2	101.5	101.6	102.4	103.3	103.8	104.0
Durables, manufactured	100.1	100.7	100.9	101.1	101.5	101.5	101.8	101.5	101.3	102.4	103.1	102.8
Agricultural Commodities	129.7	127.4	117.6	115.4	119.9	123.9	121.5	121.0	120.7	124.1	127.1	137.3
Nonagricultural Commodities	100.9	101.5	102.8	104.1	105.4	105.4	106.5	106.8	108.0	110.3	110.6	110.7

[1]December 2001 = 100.
. . . = Not available.

Table 9-11. U.S. Export Price Indexes for Selected Categories of Goods, by End Use, 2001–2012—*Continued*

(2000 = 100, unless otherwise indicated.)

Commodity	2007				2008				2009			
	March	June	September	December	March	June	September	December	March	June	September	December
ALL COMMODITIES	108.8	111.2	111.7	112.5	123.8	126.1	124.9	115.8	115.5	117.8	117.9	119.7
Foods, Feeds, and Beverages	146.9	148.6	157.8	171.1	196.9	198.0	190.4	155.1	156.7	174.8	158.2	165.1
Agricultural foods, feeds, and beverages excluding distilled beverages	149.2	151.0	160.8	175.2	202.6	204.0	195.6	156.6	158.3	178.6	160.7	167.9
Nonagricultural foods (fish, distilled beverages)	128.0	128.5	133.0	136.1	148.3	146.1	145.5	143.5	144.4	141.5	137.3	140.9
Industrial Supplies and Materials	145.5	149.0	148.8	154.1	165.5	173.2	169.4	139.6	136.5	140.4	143.9	150.1
Industrial supplies and materials, durable	160.2	160.9	155.5	159.2	172.7	172.9	167.1	141.5	143.4	144.0	150.7	157.7
Industrial supplies and materials, nondurable	137.6	142.8	145.5	151.9	162.0	174.2	171.6	139.1	133.1	139.0	140.5	146.2
Agricultural industrial supplies and materials	127.3	128.7	140.0	144.7	159.3	158.0	157.4	126.1	122.9	131.0	142.2	152.5
Fuels and lubricants	188.8	201.1	200.9	222.8	249.5	297.2	267.2	166.8	146.9	175.2	171.9	189.6
Nonagricultural supplies and materials excluding fuels and building materials	143.5	146.1	145.0	148.5	158.2	161.6	160.8	138.8	138.2	138.5	142.7	147.3
Selected building materials	112.7	113.9	114.4	113.7	114.2	113.8	115.4	115.1	114.0	113.0	114.0	113.5
Capital Goods	99.2	99.6	99.9	100.6	101.2	102.0	101.8	101.5	102.3	103.1	103.5	103.3
Electrical generating equipment	106.0	106.5	106.7	107.5	108.6	108.9	109.5	109.0	106.8	107.2	107.4	109.3
Nonelectrical machinery	92.8	92.9	93.1	93.6	93.7	94.2	93.9	93.3	93.8	94.4	94.9	94.5
Transportation equipment excluding motor vehicles[1]	121.1	122.3	123.4	125.0	128.1	130.3	130.7	131.5	135.1	137.3	137.2	136.5
Automotive Vehicles, Parts, and Engines	105.9	106.1	106.3	106.7	107.1	107.4	107.9	108.0	108.2	108.0	108.0	108.2
Consumer Goods, Excluding Automotives	104.8	105.8	106.2	107.3	108.0	108.2	109.3	109.0	108.5	108.4	109.2	109.4
Nondurables, manufactured	105.0	106.7	107.0	108.2	109.3	110.1	109.0	107.2	107.1	108.5	109.4	110.0
Durables, manufactured	103.4	103.7	104.2	105.2	105.4	105.2	108.7	109.7	109.9	108.1	109.5	109.2
Agricultural Commodities	145.0	146.7	156.8	169.3	194.3	195.2	188.3	150.8	151.6	169.7	156.9	164.7
Nonagricultural Commodities	112.6	113.8	113.8	115.7	118.8	121.2	120.4	113.2	112.9	114.1	115.1	116.5

Commodity	2010				2011				2012			
	March	June	September	December	March	June	September	December	March	June	September	December
ALL COMMODITIES	121.2	122.2	123.7	127.5	132.7	134.5	135.3	132.1	134.1	131.7	134.5	133.6
Foods, Feeds, and Beverages	163.4	164.5	174.6	191.1	206.9	210.6	213.8	199.0	206.0	205.8	231.6	229.3
Agricultural foods, feeds, and beverages excluding distilled beverages	165.7	166.7	177.6	194.6	212.1	214.6	217.3	201.2	208.6	208.0	235.9	233.8
Nonagricultural foods (fish, distilled beverages)	145.9	147.2	149.4	161.1	157.9	174.6	184.6	183.8	186.2	190.1	193.0	187.9
Industrial Supplies and Materials	155.1	159.8	162.6	172.6	188.3	191.8	192.8	184.6	188.2	178.4	183.6	180.6
Industrial supplies and materials, durable	160.4	165.5	167.0	174.8	186.1	190.3	196.6	188.2	191.1	183.5	183.4	186.1
Industrial supplies and materials, nondurable	152.6	157.2	160.8	172.2	190.4	193.6	191.7	183.4	187.4	176.3	184.5	178.4
Agricultural industrial supplies and materials	155.7	162.5	173.2	223.0	258.9	234.8	212.5	200.7	201.4	189.2	201.2	196.3
Fuels and lubricants	197.0	208.0	213.1	233.9	276.4	284.0	284.6	270.6	280.4	248.3	272.9	253.8
Nonagricultural supplies and materials excluding fuels and building materials	152.2	155.8	158.0	164.4	173.8	178.5	181.2	173.8	176.3	171.0	171.6	172.4
Selected building materials	116.0	118.7	117.1	116.2	116.3	116.2	115.8	115.6	117.2	118.1	118.8	117.9
Capital Goods	103.8	103.5	103.5	103.9	104.0	104.6	104.6	104.6	105.9	105.8	105.6	105.7
Electrical generating equipment	109.8	109.3	108.7	109.8	111.1	113.6	114.1	112.8	113.1	114.3	113.9	114.3
Nonelectrical machinery	94.7	94.3	94.3	94.4	93.9	94.2	94.2	94.3	95.3	95.0	94.8	94.9
Transportation equipment excluding motor vehicles[1]	139.1	139.5	140.1	141.6	144.5	145.3	144.9	145.6	148.6	149.1	149.2	149.0
Automotive Vehicles, Parts, and Engines	108.6	108.5	108.7	109.1	109.7	110.3	111.4	111.9	112.5	112.9	112.9	112.9
Consumer Goods, Excluding Automotives	110.2	110.4	111.8	112.7	113.9	116.3	117.4	116.6	116.8	117.0	116.7	116.4
Nondurables, manufactured	111.9	111.5	112.9	114.0	113.4	114.1	114.7	113.9	114.9	114.9	115.3	115.6
Durables, manufactured	107.7	108.2	109.9	110.9	112.9	112.7	113.6	113.3	114.3	114.9	114.9	113.9
Agricultural Commodities	163.3	165.3	176.1	198.5	218.8	217.2	216.0	200.5	206.9	204.5	229.9	227.4
Nonagricultural Commodities	118.1	119.1	120.0	122.4	126.5	128.6	129.5	127.3	128.9	126.5	127.6	126.9

[1]December 2001 = 100.

Table 9-12. U.S. Import Price Indexes for Selected Categories of Goods, by End Use, 2001–2012

(2000 = 100, unless otherwise indicated.)

Commodity	2001				2002				2003			
	March	June	September	December	March	June	September	December	March	June	September	December
ALL COMMODITIES	98.3	97.6	95.9	91.4	92.8	94.1	95.5	95.2	99.1	96.2	96.2	97.5
Foods, Feeds, and Beverages	98.9	95.4	95.0	94.6	95.0	96.2	99.7	100.2	102.6	100.7	101.8	103.2
Agricultural foods, feeds, and beverages, excluding distilled beverages	101.0	97.0	97.8	98.3	99.5	101.3	105.4	106.0	109.6	107.1	108.3	110.9
Nonagricultural foods (fish and distilled beverages)	94.5	92.2	89.2	86.8	85.5	85.1	87.3	87.5	86.9	86.6	87.6	86.0
Industrial Supplies and Materials	96.0	95.5	91.0	77.6	84.9	89.8	95.2	94.6	109.7	98.2	98.9	103.6
Fuels and lubricants	91.1	90.9	86.1	61.6	76.4	85.8	96.2	94.7	125.2	100.3	99.4	107.2
Paper and paper base stocks	104.4	100.0	93.9	90.7	88.0	87.1	90.5	89.1	91.0	94.1	94.0	93.9
Materials associated with nondurable supplies and materials	102.8	100.3	97.9	96.2	95.9	97.1	99.4	100.1	104.2	103.0	102.5	104.4
Selected building materials	91.9	111.1	103.7	92.9	100.7	99.1	97.6	95.0	96.3	96.7	110.3	108.0
Unfinished metals related to durable goods	99.5	93.6	87.1	82.1	83.8	88.5	89.7	91.5	92.8	92.2	93.4	99.2
Finished metals related to durable goods	98.3	99.4	98.2	97.9	97.1	96.5	97.1	96.8	96.1	97.4	99.0	101.0
Nonmetals related to durable goods	101.6	100.6	100.4	99.0	97.2	96.7	96.9	97.1	97.9	98.2	97.5	98.2
Industrial Supplies and Materials, Durable	98.1	99.1	94.1	89.1	91.1	92.3	92.7	92.7	93.6	93.7	97.3	99.5
Industrial Supplies and Materials, Excluding Fuels[1]	...	...	...	...	101.0	102.1	103.4	103.6	105.8	105.7	107.9	110.1
Industrial Supplies and Materials, Excluding Petroleum	102.1	99.8	94.2	90.0	90.3	92.9	93.9	95.2	104.3	99.9	100.3	102.1
Industrial Supplies and Materials, Nondurable, Excluding Petroleum	106.4	100.7	94.2	90.9	89.3	93.4	95.2	98.1	117.1	107.2	103.8	105.0
Capital Goods	98.7	97.7	96.8	96.2	95.2	95.1	94.7	93.9	93.7	93.8	93.5	92.9
Electric generating equipment	102.1	101.8	101.4	100.6	95.5	95.1	95.7	94.9	95.5	96.6	95.8	96.8
Nonelectrical machinery	98.0	96.7	95.6	94.9	94.4	94.4	93.7	92.8	92.5	92.3	92.1	91.1
Transportation equipment, excluding motor vehicles[1]	...	...	...	100.0	100.5	100.4	101.0	101.0	101.6	102.0	102.2	102.8
Automotive Parts and Accessories	99.3	98.7	98.0	97.4	97.1	98.0	98.3	98.0	98.0	98.3	97.8	98.8
Consumer Goods, Excluding Automotive	99.8	99.3	99.1	98.7	98.2	98.1	98.1	98.0	97.9	98.1	97.9	98.1
Nondurables, manufactured	100.2	99.8	99.6	99.7	99.2	99.1	99.5	99.7	99.7	99.8	99.7	100.1
Nonmanufactured consumer goods	99.3	99.2	97.9	96.4	96.1	95.6	95.4	95.4	95.7	96.2	95.7	96.2
All Imports, Excluding Fuels	...	...	...	100.0	99.7	99.9	100.1	100.0	100.3	100.3	100.6	101.0
All Imports, Excluding Petroleum	100.0	98.9	97.3	96.2	95.8	96.2	96.4	96.5	98.1	97.3	97.3	97.7

Commodity	2004				2005				2006			
	March	June	September	December	March	June	September	December	March	June	September	December
ALL COMMODITIES	100.2	101.7	104.1	104.0	107.8	109.2	114.4	112.3	112.7	117.3	116.2	115.1
Foods, Feeds, and Beverages	105.9	106.9	108.7	111.5	115.9	114.1	114.2	117.5	117.0	118.0	120.9	122.6
Agricultural foods, feeds, and beverages, excluding distilled beverages	113.0	114.3	116.4	120.7	125.7	123.5	122.6	127.2	125.4	126.8	130.4	133.7
Nonagricultural foods (fish and distilled beverages)	90.1	90.3	91.4	91.0	94.0	93.1	95.6	95.9	98.3	98.5	99.8	97.9
Industrial Supplies and Materials	112.7	119.3	128.5	126.4	139.8	145.5	167.2	158.6	160.4	178.1	172.2	166.6
Fuels and lubricants	120.2	130.9	146.2	141.0	165.6	178.0	222.1	202.4	201.5	230.2	216.3	204.3
Paper and paper base stocks	95.6	99.0	101.1	101.3	103.8	103.8	104.3	106.1	107.7	111.3	113.1	112.8
Materials associated with nondurable supplies and materials	105.4	106.0	108.0	109.8	113.0	113.5	117.3	117.8	119.3	120.6	121.8	123.0
Selected building materials	118.4	120.5	125.6	115.6	122.7	118.1	117.6	116.9	118.0	117.2	115.8	110.6
Unfinished metals related to durable goods	114.9	124.4	133.1	138.5	140.4	139.9	138.2	145.8	161.1	193.2	194.4	195.9
Finished metals related to durable goods	104.8	108.1	112.4	114.7	115.9	116.6	117.3	117.6	119.2	125.3	128.4	128.9
Nonmetals related to durable goods	99.3	98.7	98.8	99.7	100.8	100.9	100.7	100.5	100.8	101.1	101.3	101.7
Industrial Supplies and Materials, Durable	108.5	112.8	117.8	118.0	120.8	119.7	119.1	121.4	127.2	139.1	139.8	139.2
Industrial Supplies and Materials, Excluding Fuels[1]	116.5	119.8	124.1	124.8	128.0	127.5	128.5	130.3	134.9	143.7	144.7	144.7
Industrial Supplies and Materials, Excluding Petroleum	107.9	112.5	114.4	118.8	119.9	120.2	126.8	132.2	128.1	133.9	135.1	138.3
Industrial Supplies and Materials, Nondurable, Excluding Petroleum	107.1	112.0	110.2	119.7	118.7	120.7	135.4	144.3	128.3	126.7	128.5	136.3
Capital Goods	93.1	92.2	92.0	92.2	92.3	92.3	91.5	91.0	91.1	91.2	91.3	91.5
Electric generating equipment	97.8	97.0	97.4	98.0	98.8	98.8	99.0	99.3	100.1	102.1	102.7	103.0
Nonelectrical machinery	91.2	90.1	89.8	89.9	89.8	89.8	88.7	88.1	88.0	87.8	87.8	87.9
Transportation equipment, excluding motor vehicles[1]	103.5	104.0	103.9	104.5	105.6	106.0	106.4	106.1	107.0	107.9	108.3	109.1
Automotive Parts and Accessories	99.6	100.1	100.2	101.5	101.8	102.0	102.1	101.8	101.6	102.7	103.2	103.0
Consumer Goods, Excluding Automotive	98.7	98.5	98.4	99.0	99.9	99.9	99.7	99.6	99.6	99.8	100.5	101.0
Nondurables, manufactured	101.3	100.9	100.8	101.4	102.8	102.8	103.1	102.7	102.8	102.6	103.0	103.4
Nonmanufactured consumer goods	96.4	96.8	97.9	98.2	100.3	101.8	100.6	101.2	98.2	98.6	100.5	101.8
All Imports, Excluding Fuels	102.4	102.7	103.4	104.0	105.0	104.9	104.8	105.1	105.7	107.2	107.8	108.1
All Imports, Excluding Petroleum	99.1	99.7	100.1	101.3	102.0	102.0	102.8	103.7	103.0	104.2	104.8	105.7

[1]December 2001 = 100.
... = Not available.

Table 9-12. U.S. Import Price Indexes for Selected Categories of Goods, by End Use, 2001–2012—*Continued*

(2000 = 100, unless otherwise indicated.)

Commodity	2007				2008				2009			
	March	June	September	December	March	June	September	December	March	June	September	December
ALL COMMODITIES	115.9	120.0	121.8	127.3	133.5	145.5	137.8	114.5	113.6	120.0	121.3	124.4
Foods, Feeds, and Beverages	124.6	127.8	131.8	134.4	141.8	147.7	147.9	142.3	137.0	139.8	140.6	143.7
Agricultural foods, feeds, and beverages, excluding distilled beverages	135.1	139.5	144.4	148.3	157.3	165.1	165.1	159.4	151.3	155.5	156.8	160.8
Nonagricultural foods (fish and distilled beverages)	101.3	101.5	103.5	103.0	106.8	108.4	109.1	103.8	104.8	104.4	104.1	104.9
Industrial Supplies and Materials	169.8	185.6	190.7	211.3	234.5	283.0	248.9	150.4	149.3	177.3	183.0	196.2
Fuels and lubricants	209.6	238.2	250.0	290.3	329.0	423.7	346.3	153.9	162.3	222.1	228.5	249.7
Paper and paper base stocks	111.5	110.8	111.2	109.2	114.1	117.3	119.9	113.2	106.6	101.8	99.1	103.1
Materials associated with nondurable supplies and materials	124.0	125.4	128.2	135.3	147.8	152.9	162.4	148.5	136.7	137.5	134.8	140.6
Selected building materials	111.4	113.1	116.9	116.0	114.1	119.2	122.7	118.1	116.2	116.0	118.9	120.9
Unfinished metals related to durable goods	202.9	219.7	209.1	217.2	241.5	273.2	255.4	185.7	171.6	178.3	204.0	221.5
Finished metals related to durable goods	125.4	133.7	134.8	135.0	145.8	158.7	159.9	140.8	132.7	133.2	137.1	140.4
Nonmetals related to durable goods	101.8	101.6	102.5	103.8	105.2	107.6	111.4	109.0	105.2	103.0	104.3	105.4
Industrial Supplies and Materials, Durable	141.0	148.4	146.3	149.1	158.9	173.5	169.7	141.8	134.7	136.0	145.7	152.5
Industrial Supplies and Materials, Excluding Fuels[1]	146.2	151.6	151.2	155.4	166.8	178.8	179.5	155.1	145.5	146.5	151.7	158.6
Industrial Supplies and Materials, Excluding Petroleum	139.3	144.6	141.0	147.5	159.4	173.7	167.4	146.0	133.1	132.1	134.4	145.2
Industrial Supplies and Materials, Nondurable, Excluding Petroleum	136.3	139.1	133.6	144.5	159.3	173.0	163.5	150.8	131.0	127.4	121.0	136.3
Capital Goods	91.1	91.3	91.9	92.2	92.2	93.2	93.3	92.7	91.8	91.9	91.9	91.9
Electric generating equipment	104.3	105.7	106.5	107.9	109.3	112.0	112.9	111.4	109.4	110.0	110.3	111.3
Nonelectrical machinery	87.2	87.2	87.7	87.7	87.5	88.2	88.2	87.5	86.6	86.5	86.5	86.4
Transportation equipment, excluding motor vehicles[1]	110.1	111.0	113.4	114.7	115.3	117.7	118.2	120.2	120.6	122.4	123.2	122.6
Automotive Parts and Accessories	103.5	103.3	103.6	104.8	106.2	106.7	107.4	108.8	108.9	108.5	109.2	110.0
Consumer Goods, Excluding Automotive	101.3	101.4	102.1	102.6	104.0	104.9	105.1	104.4	103.9	104.3	104.1	104.3
Nondurables, manufactured	104.1	104.3	105.0	105.5	107.5	107.9	108.2	108.2	108.4	108.1	107.8	107.9
Nonmanufactured consumer goods	102.2	102.6	103.4	103.8	104.3	106.6	106.6	103.6	101.2	101.4	101.2	102.1
All Imports, Excluding Fuels	108.4	109.5	110.1	111.4	113.9	116.5	116.8	112.7	110.7	111.2	111.9	113.0
All Imports, Excluding Petroleum	105.9	107.1	107.1	108.9	111.6	114.9	114.0	109.9	107.3	107.4	107.9	109.7

Commodity	2010				2011				2012			
	March	June	September	December	March	June	September	December	March	June	September	December
ALL COMMODITIES	126.3	125.2	125.7	131.0	139.3	142.2	141.7	142.2	144.2	138.7	140.8	139.4
Foods, Feeds, and Beverages	147.4	148.7	153.3	162.7	174.9	174.8	174.7	172.4	174.4	171.8	171.6	169.1
Agricultural foods, feeds, and beverages, excluding distilled beverages	165.8	166.1	171.1	182.6	198.9	197.0	196.5	194.0	196.3	193.4	194.4	190.7
Nonagricultural foods (fish and distilled beverages)	105.6	109.2	113.0	117.4	120.7	124.5	125.3	123.7	124.7	122.9	120.1	120.4
Industrial Supplies and Materials	205.0	199.5	200.1	222.6	256.3	266.1	262.5	263.6	272.0	245.5	255.8	249.3
Fuels and lubricants	262.4	245.8	247.1	285.2	343.7	359.0	348.2	356.3	371.0	317.7	343.1	328.2
Paper and paper base stocks	107.6	115.5	117.5	117.5	116.3	119.4	117.1	114.8	114.0	114.1	112.6	111.5
Materials associated with nondurable supplies and materials	144.6	146.2	147.7	157.0	165.8	173.0	175.9	175.1	177.7	183.3	176.0	175.6
Selected building materials	127.6	131.9	124.6	127.0	131.5	129.3	131.2	130.7	134.4	138.1	141.3	143.6
Unfinished metals related to durable goods	233.4	244.6	244.2	266.0	290.2	297.0	304.9	277.8	283.9	263.5	257.1	263.8
Finished metals related to durable goods	142.4	146.5	147.7	152.7	157.4	161.1	165.6	162.1	163.9	161.8	161.6	161.7
Nonmetals related to durable goods	107.1	107.2	107.7	108.7	112.1	114.3	116.3	115.2	115.4	115.0	114.2	114.4
Industrial Supplies and Materials, Durable	158.4	163.7	162.5	171.2	181.4	184.7	189.3	179.9	183.4	176.7	174.9	177.4
Industrial Supplies and Materials, Excluding Fuels[1]	164.3	168.9	168.9	178.0	187.8	192.8	196.6	190.0	192.9	191.1	187.1	188.4
Industrial Supplies and Materials, Excluding Petroleum	149.7	151.6	151.0	159.4	168.4	172.5	174.5	167.8	167.6	165.3	163.1	167.8
Industrial Supplies and Materials, Nondurable, Excluding Petroleum	139.4	137.5	137.5	145.5	153.1	158.2	157.4	153.5	149.5	151.7	149.1	155.9
Capital Goods	91.4	91.5	91.8	92.0	92.6	92.7	92.9	93.1	93.5	93.2	93.4	93.2
Electric generating equipment	111.0	111.4	112.7	113.7	115.6	117.1	118.4	118.4	118.9	118.8	119.5	119.7
Nonelectrical machinery	85.9	86.0	86.1	86.2	86.5	86.4	86.4	86.4	86.6	86.2	86.4	86.0
Transportation equipment, excluding motor vehicles[1]	121.5	121.3	121.6	121.9	124.8	126.1	126.4	130.0	133.1	133.8	133.8	134.8
Automotive Parts and Accessories	109.9	110.2	111.5	112.0	113.7	115.7	116.6	117.0	117.6	118.3	118.9	118.6
Consumer Goods, Excluding Automotive	104.5	104.4	104.2	104.2	104.7	105.8	106.6	107.7	107.6	107.6	107.3	107.6
Nondurables, manufactured	109.0	109.3	110.0	110.4	110.3	111.6	112.8	114.4	114.5	114.8	114.7	115.3
Nonmanufactured consumer goods	102.5	102.4	103.0	103.7	107.8	111.8	114.9	119.3	118.0	119.3	115.5	115.3
All Imports, Excluding Fuels	113.7	114.4	114.7	116.4	118.7	120.1	120.9	120.4	121.1	120.8	120.4	120.4
All Imports, Excluding Petroleum	110.3	110.7	111.0	112.6	115.0	116.4	117.0	116.4	116.7	116.3	116.0	116.5

[1] December 2001 = 100.

Table 9-13. U.S. Import Price Indexes for Selected Categories of Goods, by Locality of Origin, 1990–2012

(2000 = 100, unless otherwise indicated.)

Category and year	Relative importance (October 2013)[1]	Month			
		March	June	September	December
INDUSTRIALIZED COUNTRIES[2]					
Total Goods	100.0				
1990					89.8
1991		89.6	87.9	87.9	88.9
1992		89.2	89.6	90.9	90.1
1993		90.5	91.4	91.5	91.7
1994		92.3	93.4	94.8	96.1
1995		97.4	99.8	100.0	100.0
1996		99.7	98.8	99.3	99.4
1997		97.4	96.5	96.4	96.1
1998		94.6	94.0	93.3	93.8
1999		94.1	94.8	96.4	97.5
2000		99.5	100.1	100.9	101.4
2001		100.2	99.0	96.5	93.7
2002		94.3	95.7	96.9	96.7
2003		100.0	98.4	98.6	100.0
2004		103.4	104.7	106.3	107.5
2005		109.7	110.0	113.5	114.1
2006		113.5	117.4	117.0	116.4
2007		117.9	119.7	120.4	124.2
2008		130.9	139.6	135.1	119.1
2009		117.5	119.3	120.4	123.9
2010		125.7	124.0	124.5	128.1
2011		130.7	133.8	133.0	133.2
2012		132.9	130.2	131.3	131.1
Nonmanufactured Articles	12.0				
1990					68.6
1991		64.2	62.2	62.3	62.7
1992		62.0	63.8	64.6	63.7
1993		64.5	63.8	61.8	58.7
1994		58.2	64.3	64.3	64.1
1995		66.3	67.6	65.2	66.0
1996		71.6	72.3	76.0	84.3
1997		73.3	68.9	69.4	68.5
1998		59.3	56.8	57.2	55.7
1999		56.9	65.1	78.7	83.2
2000		92.7	102.2	107.5	118.2
2001		103.9	97.2	85.2	69.9
2002		82.9	93.8	102.4	102.7
2003		134.3	113.7	108.9	112.4
2004		122.9	133.1	138.7	147.1
2005		156.7	158.0	203.0	199.2
2006		170.9	190.0	183.7	184.9
2007		185.6	197.9	195.4	228.2
2008		275.6	346.8	279.0	154.5
2009		143.9	170.6	169.1	198.8
2010		209.7	188.0	188.2	218.3
2011		236.7	251.9	233.1	246.4
2012		229.7	202.7	224.1	215.4
Manufactured Articles	87.4				
1990					90.2
1991		91.6	90.1	90.1	91.3
1992		91.8	91.7	93.0	92.4
1993		92.8	93.8	94.1	94.6
1994		95.1	95.9	97.4	98.8
1995		100.0	102.6	102.9	102.9
1996		102.1	101.1	101.4	100.7
1997		99.5	98.9	98.8	98.6
1998		97.8	97.5	96.7	97.3
1999		97.6	97.7	98.1	98.9
2000		100.2	99.9	100.2	99.8
2001		99.9	99.2	97.6	96.0
2002		95.6	96.3	96.9	96.7
2003		97.8	97.7	98.2	99.4
2004		102.1	102.8	104.0	104.6
2005		106.3	106.6	106.7	107.7
2006		109.0	111.8	111.8	111.1
2007		112.5	113.5	114.5	116.3
2008		120.1	124.3	124.2	115.7
2009		114.9	114.9	116.1	117.9
2010		118.9	118.8	119.2	120.8
2011		122.0	124.1	124.9	123.9
2012		124.9	124.2	123.8	124.2

[1]Based on 2011 trade values.
[2]Includes Western Europe, Canada, Japan, Australia, New Zealand and South Africa.

Table 9-13. U.S. Import Price Indexes for Selected Categories of Goods, by Locality of Origin, 1990–2012—*Continued*

(2000 = 100, unless otherwise indicated.)

Category and year	Relative importance (October 2013)[1]	Month			
		March	June	September	December
OTHER COUNTRIES[3]					
Total Goods	100.0				
1990					107.2
1991		94.1	93.5	93.8	93.6
1992		92.2	94.7	95.0	94.4
1993		94.2	93.5	92.3	89.6
1994		90.1	94.2	95.0	95.7
1995		97.5	98.7	97.4	97.6
1996		99.8	99.0	101.3	102.7
1997		100.6	99.4	98.7	96.6
1998		92.4	90.7	89.5	86.8
1999		87.7	90.3	94.5	96.9
2000		99.8	100.4	102.5	99.5
2001		97.0	96.6	95.0	88.6
2002		90.9	92.2	94.3	93.4
2003		96.7	93.1	93.3	94.1
2004		96.3	97.9	101.5	99.7
2005		105.0	107.0	112.1	109.5
2006		110.8	115.5	114.0	111.8
2007		113.1	118.0	121.1	127.5
2008		133.3	147.3	139.0	111.2
2009		110.3	118.7	120.0	122.1
2010		124.2	123.1	123.7	129.0
2011		138.9	141.2	141.1	142.0
2012		145.0	138.7	140.7	138.8
Nonmanufactured Articles	22.8				
1990					88.2
1991		64.8	63.8	64.6	63.8
1992		61.0	65.5	66.0	63.7
1993		64.9	62.8	59.1	51.9
1994		52.0	63.8	64.8	65.5
1995		69.5	70.3	66.1	67.3
1996		73.7	72.1	80.9	84.5
1997		75.8	72.6	72.2	68.8
1998		57.1	54.9	54.5	46.8
1999		53.0	63.6	80.3	89.2
2000		99.9	102.4	109.2	97.4
2001		88.9	89.7	86.1	65.3
2002		81.3	88.2	99.6	96.4
2003		113.3	98.0	98.8	106.5
2004		118.1	123.2	141.5	130.3
2005		158.0	169.5	199.8	181.3
2006		191.7	215.4	204.6	191.1
2007		192.4	220.6	241.6	279.0
2008		314.6	402.3	336.0	160.2
2009		166.8	225.6	231.3	247.8
2010		260.8	248.9	254.0	288.8
2011		351.8	367.1	356.0	363.9
2012		390.1	337.0	356.0	343.2
Manufactured Articles	76.8				
1990					105.3
1991		105.2	105.1	104.9	105.2
1992		105.5	105.7	105.7	105.4
1993		104.6	104.5	104.2	103.7
1994		104.2	105.1	105.8	106.5
1995		107.3	108.8	108.6	108.4
1996		108.9	108.4	107.9	108.6
1997		108.4	107.8	107.0	105.3
1998		103.5	102.2	100.6	99.6
1999		98.8	98.9	99.0	99.3
2000		99.8	99.7	100.3	100.2
2001		99.6	98.8	97.9	96.0
2002		95.6	95.9	96.2	95.8
2003		96.5	95.1	95.1	94.5
2004		95.2	96.2	97.2	97.1
2005		98.4	98.7	99.3	99.6
2006		99.4	101.2	101.2	100.7
2007		102.0	103.6	104.1	106.0
2008		107.8	111.8	111.3	103.4
2009		101.7	103.5	104.3	104.5
2010		105.0	105.3	105.3	106.8
2011		110.0	110.6	111.8	111.8
2012		112.2	111.2	111.3	110.6

[1]Based on 2011 trade values.
[3]Includes Eastern Europe, Latin America, Organization of the Petroleum Exporting Countries (OPEC), and other countries in Asia, Africa and the Western Hemisphere.

Table 9-13. U.S. Import Price Indexes for Selected Categories of Goods, by Locality of Origin, 1990–2012—*Continued*

(2000 = 100, unless otherwise indicated.)

Category and year	Relative importance (October 2013)[1]	Month			
		March	June	September	December
CANADA					
Total Goods	100.0				
1990					90.2
1991		87.2	87.3	86.9	87.2
1992		86.5	87.4	87.5	86.3
1993		86.5	85.9	85.2	85.1
1994		85.5	87.2	88.1	90.2
1995		92.1	93.8	94.8	94.7
1996		94.3	93.5	93.8	95.1
1997		93.2	92.6	93.2	92.0
1998		90.1	89.7	89.3	88.7
1999		88.8	90.6	93.5	94.7
2000		97.2	99.8	102.4	105.6
2001		102.6	101.8	97.0	93.2
2002		96.1	97.8	99.6	99.2
2003		106.6	103.1	103.9	104.4
2004		110.0	112.3	114.4	116.6
2005		120.1	119.6	128.2	129.6
2006		125.4	130.6	129.7	129.2
2007		130.2	135.0	135.0	142.3
2008		152.0	171.2	160.1	129.8
2009		124.4	129.0	131.1	137.7
2010		143.7	139.3	139.9	148.1
2011		155.7	159.7	155.0	155.4
2012		153.6	147.4	150.7	149.4
Nonmanufactured Articles	30.2				
1990					66.8
1991		59.2	59.5	58.9	58.6
1992		58.1	60.7	61.2	60.0
1993		60.6	60.3	58.1	55.3
1994		54.7	61.1	60.1	60.3
1995		61.7	64.4	63.9	64.8
1996		70.3	70.7	74.4	84.3
1997		69.9	66.6	68.1	66.4
1998		58.4	56.6	56.5	56.3
1999		56.5	64.2	76.8	79.9
2000		89.3	103.6	107.6	124.4
2001		108.1	97.9	83.1	69.8
2002		83.8	96.8	104.1	104.9
2003		143.1	119.0	111.5	114.0
2004		126.1	138.0	138.9	150.5
2005		157.9	159.8	210.8	207.4
2006		171.3	189.2	183.1	187.1
2007		187.8	195.9	187.7	222.3
2008		273.7	345.1	273.0	150.8
2009		139.7	163.4	161.6	192.5
2010		204.6	181.3	182.0	211.4
2011		228.2	241.7	223.1	236.2
2012		216.9	192.0	210.3	204.6
Manufactured Articles	68.8				
1990					92.8
1991		93.2	93.1	93.0	93.6
1992		92.9	92.5	92.4	91.4
1993		91.6	90.8	90.4	90.9
1994		91.4	92.3	93.6	95.9
1995		98.0	99.4	100.7	100.5
1996		99.0	98.0	97.7	97.4
1997		98.0	98.0	98.3	97.3
1998		96.7	96.6	96.3	95.5
1999		95.5	96.1	96.9	97.7
2000		98.8	98.9	101.3	101.8
2001		101.6	102.8	99.9	98.1
2002		99.1	98.7	99.5	98.9
2003		100.9	101.1	103.2	103.3
2004		107.4	108.2	110.3	110.7
2005		113.7	112.9	113.1	115.6
2006		117.2	120.0	110.0	118.7
2007		119.5	123.7	125.3	127.6
2008		128.8	137.5	138.7	126.8
2009		122.7	123.0	125.8	127.3
2010		131.7	132.0	132.5	135.5
2011		140.5	141.9	141.1	137.8
2012		140.6	139.4	138.8	138.7

[1]Based on 2011 trade values.

Table 9-13. U.S. Import Price Indexes for Selected Categories of Goods, by Locality of Origin, 1990–2012—*Continued*

(2000 = 100, unless otherwise indicated.)

Category and year	Relative importance (October 2013)[1]	Month			
		March	June	September	December
EUROPEAN UNION					
Total Goods	100.0				
1990					93.8
1991		95.2	91.6	91.7	94.0
1992		94.2	94.9	97.7	93.1
1993		92.2	92.9	92.0	91.8
1994		91.9	93.1	94.9	96.2
1995		97.7	99.5	99.7	100.4
1996		101.3	101.0	101.7	101.9
1997		100.5	100.0	99.1	100.1
1998		98.9	98.8	98.7	99.4
1999		98.8	99.1	99.9	100.3
2000		100.8	100.1	100.0	98.9
2001		99.0	98.8	98.2	97.4
2002		97.4	99.2	101.0	100.9
2003		103.2	102.8	102.8	104.3
2004		107.4	108.5	110.0	111.6
2005		113.8	114.1	115.7	114.5
2006		117.7	120.4	120.5	119.6
2007		121.3	121.6	122.3	124.1
2008		129.7	133.9	131.5	124.3
2009		123.6	124.4	125.4	127.4
2010		128.3	127.7	128.4	129.1
2011		132.8	135.9	136.5	136.3
2012		136.3	135.0	134.3	133.8
Nonmanufactured Articles	1.0				
1990					74.8
1991		76.8	71.8	72.4	73.8
1992		73.0	73.9	74.9	74.1
1993		74.8	72.7	70.3	67.6
1994		67.6	73.5	71.9	72.0
1995		72.8	74.5	71.2	73.0
1996		78.8	80.6	85.7	91.7
1997		89.3	82.2	76.5	78.4
1998		65.6	58.7	58.8	53.4
1999		53.6	66.6	81.3	88.7
2000		100.4	102.9	107.9	106.2
2001		96.0	99.5	89.1	75.7
2002		86.6	88.7	99.6	104.1
2003		118.8	106.7	111.5	118.8
2004		128.4	135.1	157.9	163.1
2005		177.1	177.5	209.7	191.1
2006		211.4	231.9	219.9	198.7
2007		205.2	234.6	274.9	304.8
2008		323.4	400.2	332.3	230.8
2009		188.3	230.0	235.3	250.2
2010		252.4	250.4	251.9	274.1
2011		322.2	367.3	350.5	364.0
2012		403.4	340.5	377.5	370.0
Manufactured Articles	98.8				
1990					93.8
1991		94.8	92.1	92.0	94.4
1992		95.1	95.7	98.9	93.9
1993		93.0	93.8	93.0	92.8
1994		92.9	93.9	95.8	97.1
1995		98.6	100.4	100.9	101.5
1996		102.3	101.8	102.4	102.3
1997		101.0	100.8	100.1	101.0
1998		100.4	100.6	100.5	101.5
1999		100.9	100.6	100.8	100.8
2000		100.8	99.9	99.6	98.6
2001		99.2	98.8	98.7	98.4
2002		98.1	99.9	101.5	101.4
2003		103.3	103.2	103.2	104.5
2004		107.4	108.4	109.3	110.9
2005		112.8	113.0	113.8	112.9
2006		116.0	118.0	118.4	118.0
2007		119.5	119.2	119.7	121.1
2008		126.5	130.1	128.2	121.8
2009		121.5	122.1	123.0	124.9
2010		125.8	125.2	125.9	126.4
2011		129.6	132.3	133.0	132.7
2012		132.4	131.6	130.5	130.1

[1]Based on 2011 trade values.

Table 9-13. U.S. Import Price Indexes for Selected Categories of Goods, by Locality of Origin, 1990–2012—*Continued*

(2000 = 100, unless otherwise indicated.)

Category and year	Relative importance (October 2013)[1]	Month			
		March	June	September	December
LATIN AMERICA[4]					
Total Goods	100.0				
1997					89.0
1998		84.3	83.9	83.0	80.4
1999		81.7	85.3	90.7	94.2
2000		98.9	100.9	103.5	99.5
2001		99.5	98.9	97.2	90.6
2002		94.0	96.2	100.0	98.9
2003		104.8	99.6	99.8	102.6
2004		106.3	108.6	114.7	113.1
2005		122.1	126.3	133.8	131.0
2006		134.0	142.8	140.2	136.4
2007		138.1	146.3	152.3	161.5
2008		171.6	193.9	181.7	135.4
2009		132.1	146.7	148.5	154.0
2010		157.4	154.5	155.5	163.9
2011		179.7	181.4	179.8	181.5
2012		185.5	173.3	178.4	174.1
Nonmanufactured Articles	32.6				
1997					70.8
1998		60.8	59.7	59.4	51.9
1999		59.3	67.2	82.1	90.2
2000		100.2	103.5	107.8	93.6
2001		89.3	89.0	86.0	67.3
2002		83.5	90.7	103.0	99.3
2003		111.7	103.5	100.9	109.8
2004		121.1	125.9	144.6	130.1
2005		161.0	175.1	205.1	184.6
2006		195.5	217.2	205.7	197.1
2007		199.3	225.0	250.7	289.5
2008		320.9	409.2	348.3	181.5
2009		188.9	254.3	257.1	273.9
2010		286.4	269.3	270.8	314.4
2011		382.1	391.4	378.8	399.4
2012		418.8	354.0	383.5	360.6
Manufactured Articles	67.0				
1997					97.2
1998		94.8	95.0	93.8	93.5
1999		92.0	93.6	94.6	96.0
2000		98.3	99.6	101.6	102.3
2001		104.2	103.5	102.5	101.4
2002		101.5	102.4	104.2	103.8
2003		108.2	103.6	104.4	105.8
2004		107.5	109.1	112.0	113.9
2005		117.1	118.6	120.1	122.2
2006		123.2	128.9	128.4	125.8
2007		127.4	131.4	132.5	134.3
2008		139.3	146.0	145.4	127.7
2009		121.7	125.0	126.5	129.3
2010		130.3	130.5	129.5	131.9
2011		136.1	136.0	136.8	134.3
2012		135.1	133.6	133.8	133.1
CHINA[5]					
Total Goods	100.0				
2003					100.0
2004		99.5	99.7	99.6	99.0
2005		98.8	98.8	98.4	98.5
2006		97.9	97.4	97.4	97.3
2007		97.4	98.1	99.1	99.6
2008		101.1	102.8	103.7	102.4
2009		100.9	100.4	100.5	100.6
2010		100.1	100.4	100.5	101.4
2011		102.7	103.7	104.4	105.1
2012		105.4	104.9	104.7	104.5

[1]Based on 2011 trade values.
[4]Includes Mexico, Central America, South America, and the Caribbean.
[5]December 2003 = 100.

Table 9-13. U.S. Import Price Indexes for Selected Categories of Goods, by Locality of Origin, 1990–2012—*Continued*

(2000 = 100, unless otherwise indicated.)

Category and year	Relative importance (October 2013)[1]	Month			
		March	June	September	December
JAPAN					
Total Goods	100.0				
1990					93.7
1991		94.5	93.4	93.9	95.2
1992		95.8	95.5	96.4	97.7
1993		98.5	100.9	103.5	104.4
1994		105.2	105.8	107.0	108.0
1995		108.6	112.5	112.0	111.0
1996		110.1	108.4	107.8	106.5
1997		104.6	103.2	102.7	101.0
1998		99.8	98.2	96.8	98.0
1999		98.2	98.2	98.6	99.6
2000		99.6	100.0	99.9	99.9
2001		99.4	98.6	97.8	97.0
2002		95.6	95.4	95.0	94.6
2003		94.4	94.2	93.8	94.7
2004		95.2	95.1	95.3	95.9
2005		95.9	95.8	95.8	95.2
2006		94.6	94.7	94.4	94.1
2007		93.9	94.0	93.9	94.2
2008		94.6	95.1	94.9	96.0
2009		96.3	96.9	97.2	97.8
2010		98.1	98.6	99.0	99.8
2011		101.1	101.5	101.7	102.1
2012		102.4	102.6	102.9	102.8
ASIAN NEWLY INDUSTRIALIZED COUNTRIES[6]					
Total Goods	100.0				
1990					121.4
1991		120.4	120.3	120.4	121.0
1992		121.5	121.8	121.9	121.8
1993		121.5	121.2	121.2	120.8
1994		120.7	120.4	120.2	120.2
1995		120.9	121.3	121.5	120.8
1996		120.6	119.6	118.1	117.3
1997		116.6	115.3	113.8	111.3
1998		108.7	105.2	103.0	102.0
1999		101.3	100.8	100.7	100.8
2000		100.6	99.9	100.0	99.3
2001		97.3	96.4	95.2	93.8
2002		93.3	92.6	92.5	91.3
2003		91.2	91.5	91.7	90.9
2004		90.3	90.6	91.0	90.6
2005		90.9	90.0	89.7	88.5
2006		88.8	89.2	89.3	89.1
2007		88.7	88.5	88.8	88.9
2008		89.2	91.1	93.2	89.2
2009		85.4	85.7	86.1	86.5
2010		87.0	88.1	88.6	88.5
2011		91.0	92.4	91.8	90.6
2012		90.5	90.8	91.0	90.0

[1]Based on 2011 trade values.
[6]The Asian Newly Industrialized Countries are Hong Kong, Republic of Korea, Singapore, and Taiwan.

Table 9-14. U.S. International Price Indexes for Selected Transportation Services, 1990–2012

(2000 = 100.)

Category and year	March	June	September	December
AIR FREIGHT				
Import Air Freight				
1990	. . .	. . .	96.4	105.6
1991	104.5	100.4	99.8	101.8
1992	102.8	98.5	101.6	99.5
1993	97.5	104.2	104.5	103.8
1994	103.5	105.7	108.9	110.9
1995	115.8	118.7	112.9	115.1
1996	113.7	112.2	112.0	110.6
1997	104.1	104.5	102.5	100.1
1998	93.0	94.2	92.8	100.2
1999	101.5	98.7	100.6	102.8
2000	100.7	100.1	100.2	99.0
2001	98.9	96.0	95.9	95.6
2002	96.7	99.7	101.2	106.9
2003	110.2	111.5	116.8	114.9
2004	117.1	117.5	120.0	126.8
2005	128.6	128.4	129.7	128.9
2006	129.7	135.2	133.1	131.2
2007	130.7	132.3	134.2	141.8
2008	144.4	158.7	157.1	138.5
2009	132.9	132.8	134.8	163.9
2010	158.3	162.5	163.2	170.1
2011	172.8	184.3	185.5	177.1
2012	173.7	178.6	173.9	175.8
Export Air Freight				
1996	. . .	. . .	. . .	112.9
1997	111.1	110.4	109.0	105.4
1998	107.1	106.6	108.0	109.2
1999	102.1	102.5	100.8	99.1
2000	99.1	100.8	100.8	99.4
2001	99.7	98.4	98.6	97.9
2002	95.5	97.9	98.3	95.2
2003	96.3	95.2	95.1	95.4
2004	97.1	99.1	100.3	106.1
2005	106.4	110.1	110.9	112.0
2006	113.6	115.9	117.9	116.7
2007	117.0	117.0	119.8	127.1
2008	132.0	140.8	144.3	135.0
2009	124.1	117.4	121.6	122.9
2010	124.0	126.3	125.7	128.1
2011	139.2	147.4	146.4	144.2
2012	148.9	148.0	146.7	147.0
Inbound Air Freight				
1990	. . .	. . .	98.6	107.1
1991	105.3	103.4	103.3	105.8
1992	106.5	103.2	105.8	100.7
1993	98.7	104.9	105.1	104.6
1994	104.4	106.6	107.1	108.9
1995	113.6	116.5	111.0	111.7
1996	108.6	107.7	108.2	107.6
1997	101.3	101.8	100.3	97.9
1998	93.9	94.4	92.7	99.0
1999	99.6	97.6	99.5	102.8
2000	100.7	100.1	100.2	99.0
2001	97.9	95.1	94.9	95.1
2002	93.9	98.3	100.3	105.9
2003	108.8	109.4	112.5	112.9
2004	116.2	116.6	118.7	125.1
2005	126.3	125.6	127.5	124.6
2006	124.6	129.2	128.9	127.1
2007	126.6	127.3	129.6	138.1
2008	140.7	152.1	151.6	136.8
2009	127.5	125.1	127.4	147.3
2010	144.3	147.1	147.2	153.4
2011	157.0	164.4	164.2	160.7
2012	158.8	163.2	163.6	167.5

. . . = Not available.

Table 9-14. U.S. International Price Indexes for Selected Transportation Services, 1990–2012—*Continued*

(2000 = 100.)

Category and year	March	June	September	December
Outbound Air Freight				
1992	. . .	. . .	109.9	108.6
1993	106.9	106.1	105.0	105.9
1994	106.0	105.7	105.6	106.9
1995	108.2	108.1	108.6	107.8
1996	107.3	107.6	107.0	107.3
1997	108.0	107.3	107.7	105.7
1998	105.2	103.8	103.7	103.0
1999	100.3	100.4	100.3	99.2
2000	99.2	100.3	100.2	100.2
2001	100.1	98.0	97.6	97.8
2002	95.9	98.4	97.3	95.4
2003	97.2	95.4	95.5	94.9
2004	96.1	99.0	100.7	104.7
2005	103.8	107.2	112.4	112.0
2006	113.5	117.2	116.9	113.8
2007	112.3	114.3	117.0	124.3
2008	128.9	143.7	147.0	130.4
2009	119.7	112.1	111.9	114.6
2010	118.1	122.4	122.8	126.2
2011	136.4	142.1	143.9	144.6
2012	146.3	148.9	146.8	148.0
AIR PASSENGER FARES				
Import Air Passenger Fares				
1990	64.7	70.2	75.1	74.2
1991	77.7	79.2	80.5	77.1
1992	76.8	82.5	86.8	76.6
1993	76.5	82.4	83.0	76.0
1994	76.5	81.4	83.6	78.5
1995	80.2	88.1	86.4	82.6
1996	82.0	88.1	86.8	84.3
1997	84.7	95.5	94.0	88.0
1998	87.1	94.9	95.1	88.6
1999	87.5	98.9	99.5	89.7
2000	92.5	103.5	105.1	98.9
2001	101.1	112.8	116.4	105.7
2002	103.1	119.1	125.2	107.2
2003	108.6	122.3	125.9	107.0
2004	103.6	123.1	121.0	111.7
2005	110.0	128.1	124.0	116.3
2006	114.9	136.7	130.9	125.4
2007	122.9	144.6	140.2	135.3
2008	131.3	171.6	161.3	157.3
2009	134.9	147.3	137.9	152.3
2010	149.8	175.3	160.9	169.9
2011	161.2	184.0	174.6	179.5
2012	178.7	199.8	179.8	194.2
Export Air Passenger Fares				
1990	71.5	74.7	79.0	80.5
1991	82.7	84.3	85.2	83.0
1992	83.5	87.3	90.5	83.2
1993	84.5	89.7	91.0	86.0
1994	87.3	90.2	92.9	89.6
1995	92.4	99.4	96.4	91.6
1996	93.0	94.4	97.7	94.7
1997	85.3	97.7	95.0	87.4
1998	89.5	90.2	90.6	93.1
1999	95.5	96.8	100.6	98.6
2000	98.1	101.5	102.6	97.7
2001	99.6	100.4	102.5	98.4
2002	97.5	103.2	108.1	103.2
2003	108.4	117.0	118.0	118.4
2004	123.2	123.8	130.1	134.0
2005	136.3	136.2	139.5	128.3
2006	130.8	139.3	142.4	137.3
2007	140.2	147.3	154.6	155.7
2008	156.4	171.4	171.9	164.6
2009	141.7	138.2	141.3	156.1
2010	157.7	176.3	172.2	169.0
2011	172.8	186.6	192.7	191.1
2012	185.1	202.8	187.8	186.4

. . . = Not available.

CHAPTER 10: INTERNATIONAL LABOR COMPARISONS

HIGHLIGHTS

This chapter compares several summary statistics of labor force status, manufacturing productivity, and consumer prices for the United States with similar statistics for other countries. Different concepts and methodologies can make comparisons between countries difficult, but the Bureau of Labor Statistics (BLS) makes adjustments to reconcile as much of the data as possible.

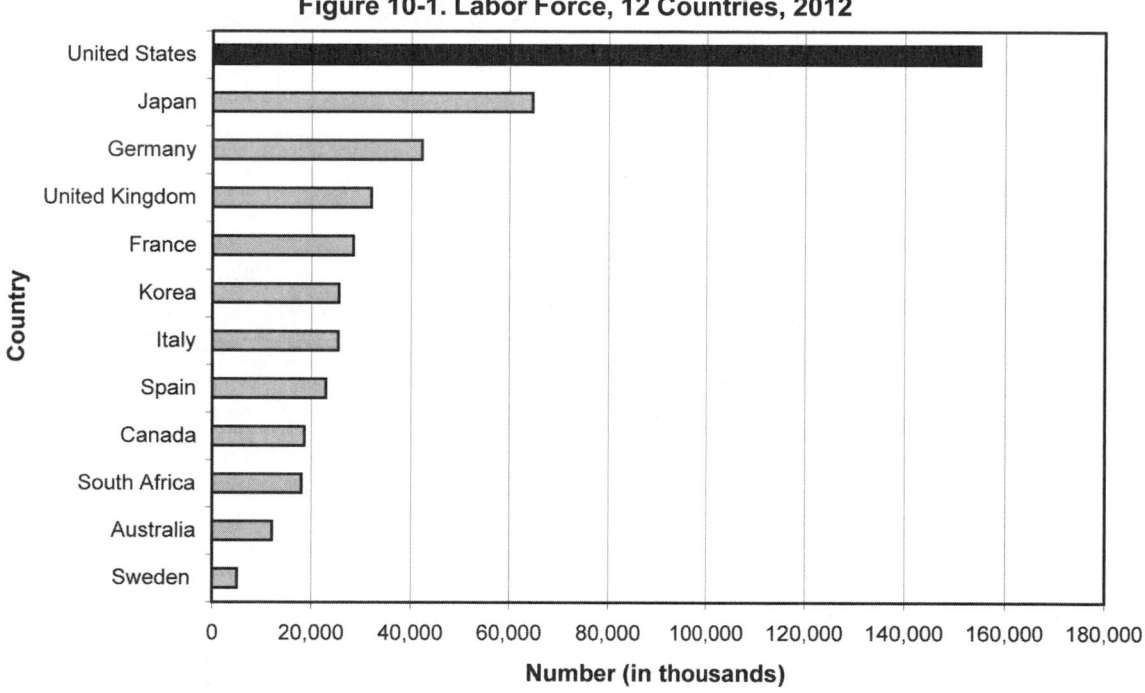

Figure 10-1. Labor Force, 12 Countries, 2012

In 2012, nearly 155 million people were in the labor force in the United States, nearly 65 million people were in the labor force in Japan, and 42 million people were in the labor force in Germany. Among the twelve countries being compared in Figure 10-1, Sweden had the smallest labor force at only 5.0 million; however, it had a higher labor force participation rate than the United States, Japan, or Germany. (See Table 10-1.)

OTHER HIGHLIGHTS

- Spain experienced the highest unemployment rate at 25.2 percent among all countries being compared in Table 10-1. Unemployment remained high in other parts of Western Europe as well. The unemployment rate in Italy climbed to 10.8 percent, while it increased to 10.0 percent in France. The unemployment rate in the United States dropped to 8.1 percent in 2012. (See Table 10-1.)

- The unemployment rates among youth varied from 7.5 percent in Japan to 53.7 percent in Spain. (See Table 10-3.)

- Although the Consumer Price Index (CPI-U) increased in most countries between 2011 and 2012, it declined in Switzerland by -0.7 percent and remained unchanged in Japan. (See Table 10-14.)

NOTES AND DEFINITIONS

COLLECTION AND COVERAGE

From its inception, the Bureau of Labor Statistics (BLS) has conducted a program of research and statistical analysis that compares labor conditions in the United States with those in selected foreign countries. The principal comparative measures of the International Labor Comparisons (ILC) program (formerly called the Foreign Labor Statistics program) cover the labor force, employment, and unemployment; trends in labor productivity and unit labor costs in manufacturing; hourly compensation costs for manufacturing production workers; and consumer prices. All of the measures are based upon statistical data and other source materials from (a) the statistical agencies of the foreign countries studied; (b) international and supranational bodies such as the United Nations, the International Labour Office (ILO), the Organisation for Economic Co-operation and Development (OECD), and the Statistical Office of the European Communities (EUROSTAT), which attempt to obtain comparable country data; and (c) private agencies such as banks, industry associations, and research institutions.

International statistical comparisons should be made with caution, as the statistical concepts and methods in each country are primarily fashioned to meet domestic (rather than international) needs. Whenever possible, BLS adjusts the data to improve comparability.

LABOR FORCE, EMPLOYMENT, AND UNEMPLOYMENT

To compare unemployment across countries, BLS publishes data for several countries that have been adjusted as closely as possible to U.S. concepts. BLS publishes additional annual labor force statistics on a civilian basis, including working-age population, labor force, employment by major economic sector (agriculture, industry, manufacturing, and services), unemployment, employment-population ratios by sex, unemployment rates by age and sex, and women's share of the labor force.

Foreign country data are adjusted as closely as possible to the U.S. definitions. Primary areas of adjustment address conceptual differences in upper age limits and definitions of employment and unemployment, provided that reliable data are available to make these adjustments. Adjustments are made where applicable to include employed and unemployed persons above upper age limits; some European countries do not include persons older than age 64 in their labor force measures, because a large portion of this population has retired. Adjustments are made to exclude active duty military from employment figures, although a small number of career

military may be included in some European countries. Adjustments are made to exclude unpaid family workers who worked fewer than 15 hours per week from employment figures; U.S. concepts do not include them in employment, but most foreign countries include all unpaid family workers regardless of the number of hours worked. Adjustments are made to include full-time students seeking work and available for work as unemployed when they are classified as not in the labor force.

Where possible, lower age limits are based on the age at which compulsory schooling ends in each country, rather than based on the U.S. standard of 16 years of age and over.

Some adjustments for comparability are not made because data are unavailable for adjustment purposes. For example, no adjustments to unemployment are usually made for deviations from U.S. concepts in the treatment of persons waiting to start a new job or passive job seekers. These conceptual differences have little impact on the measures. Furthermore, BLS studies have concluded that no adjustments should be made for persons on layoff who are counted as employed in some countries because of their strong job attachment, as evidenced by, for example, payment of salary or the existence of a recall date. In the United States, persons on layoff have weaker job attachment and are classified as unemployed. Finally, employment data by economic sector are not fully comparable with U.S. definitions for some countries because all data required to make adjustments at the sector level are not available. Therefore, the sum of employment by sector may not equal total adjusted employment.

HOURLY COMPENSATION COSTS

Measures of hourly compensation costs are prepared by BLS to assess international differences in manufacturing employer labor costs. For several reasons, comparisons based on the more readily available average earnings statistics published by many countries can be misleading. National definitions of average earnings differ considerably; average earnings do not include all items of labor compensation, and the omitted items of compensation frequently represent a large proportion of total compensation. For many years, data on hourly compensation costs covered production workers only; recently, the series has been extended to cover all employees as well.

Hourly compensation costs include (1) hourly direct pay and (2) employer social insurance expenditures and other labor taxes. Hourly direct pay includes all payments made directly to the worker, before payroll deductions of any kind, consisting of pay for time worked and other direct pay. Social insurance expenditures and other labor taxes include employer expenditures for legally required insurance programs, contractual and private benefit plans, and other labor taxes. Other labor taxes refer to taxes on payrolls or employment (or reductions to reflect subsidies), even if they do not finance programs that directly benefit workers, because such taxes are regarded as labor costs.

PRODUCTIVITY AND UNIT LABOR COSTS

Time series indexes of manufacturing labor productivity (output per hour) and unit labor costs are constructed from three basic aggregate measures: total real output, hours worked, and nominal compensation. Indexes for unit labor costs are prepared on a national currency basis and, using currency exchange rates, a U.S. dollar basis. With the additional collection of annual employment in manufacturing and the use of consumer price indexes, a total of 15 time series indexes are constructed.

The employment, hours, and compensation measures refer to employees (wage and salary workers) in Belgium and Taiwan and to all employed persons (employees plus the self-employed and unpaid family workers) in all other economies.

In general, the measures relate to total manufacturing as defined by the International Standard Industrial Classification (ISIC). However, the measures for France include parts of mining. Data for the United States are in accordance with the North American Industry Classification System (NAICS), except compensation data before 1987, which are based on SIC 1987. Canadian data are in accordance with NAICS starting in 1961.

The data for the most recent years are based on the United Nations System of National Accounts 1993 (SNA 93). For earlier years, data were compiled according to previously used systems.

To obtain historical time series, BLS sometimes links together data series that were compiled according to different accounting systems by national statistical offices.

REAL GROSS DOMESTIC PRODUCT PER CAPITA AND PER EMPLOYED PERSON

Measures of gross domestic product (GDP), population, and employment are obtained from national statistical sources. While these data are generally comparable to one another, some differences remain in the countries' statistical methodologies, which may affect comparability. The GDP measures used for all countries come from their national accounts sources. For all countries, the most recent series use the 1993 United Nations System of National Accounts (SNA 93). However, some earlier series have been prepared using 1968 United Nations System of National Accounts (SNA 68). The U.S. GDP series is based on the system of national income and product accounts (NIPAs) estimated by the Bureau of Economic Analysis (BEA).

SOURCES OF ADDITIONAL INFORMATION

An extensive description of the methodology can be found in Chapter 12 in the *BLS Handbook of Methods*. For more information on international comparisons, see the BLS reports titled "International Indexes of Consumer Prices" and "International Comparisons of Annual Labor Force Statistics, Adjusted to U.S. Concepts, 16 Countries, 1970–2012," on the BLS Web site at http://www.bls.gov/fls/.

Table 10-1. Employment Status of the Working-Age Population, Adjusted to U.S. Concepts, 12 Countries, 1975–2012

(Numbers in thousands, percent.)

Category and year	United States	Australia	Canada	France	Germany[1]	Italy	Japan	Korea	South Africa	Spain	Sweden	United Kingdom
Employed												
1975	85 846	5 866	9 284	20 869	25 536	19 395	51 532	11 691	...	...	4 056	24 770
1976	88 752	5 946	9 652	21 041	25 396	19 504	52 034	12 412	...	...	4 082	24 623
1977	92 017	6 000	9 825	21 235	25 428	19 668	52 720	12 812	...	12 466	4 093	24 650
1978	96 048	6 038	10 124	21 326	25 647	19 725	53 371	13 412	...	12 274	4 109	24 786
1979	98 824	6 111	10 561	21 392	26 074	19 932	54 040	13 602	...	12 106	4 174	25 043
1980	99 303	6 284	10 872	21 443	26 486	20 195	54 598	13 683	...	11 778	4 226	24 929
1981	100 397	6 416	11 192	21 345	26 453	20 279	55 057	14 023	...	11 475	4 219	24 268
1982	99 526	6 415	10 847	22 172	26 149	20 246	55 618	14 379	...	11 370	4 213	23 794
1983	100 834	6 300	10 936	22 134	25 765	20 320	56 545	14 505	...	11 312	4 218	23 619
1984	105 005	6 494	11 211	21 939	25 826	20 392	56 866	14 429	...	11 013	4 249	24 127
1985	107 150	6 697	11 557	21 966	26 018	20 492	57 255	14 970	...	10 902	4 293	24 434
1986	109 597	6 974	11 895	22 161	26 383	20 614	57 736	15 505	...	11 111	4 326	24 590
1987	112 440	7 129	12 221	22 161	26 584	20 591	58 315	16 354	...	11 646	4 340	25 084
1988	114 968	7 398	12 591	22 239	26 799	20 868	59 303	16 869	...	12 098	4 410	25 917
1989	117 342	7 720	12 876	22 556	27 201	20 773	60 493	17 560	...	12 539	4 480	26 600
1990	118 793	7 859	12 964	22 630	27 952	21 080	61 706	18 085	...	12 857	4 513	26 724
1991	117 718	7 676	12 754	22 535	36 871	21 364	62 920	18 649	...	12 963	4 447	26 018
1992	118 492	7 637	12 643	22 494	36 390	21 233	63 632	19 009	...	12 729	4 265	25 399
1993	120 259	7 680	12 705	22 323	35 989	21 091	63 826	19 234	...	12 208	4 027	25 173
1994	123 060	7 921	12 975	22 256	35 756	20 697	63 860	19 848	...	12 129	3 990	25 386
1995	124 900	8 236	13 210	22 535	35 780	20 555	63 897	20 414	...	12 424	4 053	25 684
1996	126 708	8 340	13 337	22 660	35 637	20 615	64 197	20 853	...	12 777	4 014	25 928
1997	129 558	8 429	13 639	22 592	35 508	20 643	64 897	21 214	...	13 253	3 974	26 407
1998	131 463	8 618	13 974	22 799	36 059	20 827	64 454	19 938	...	13 806	4 036	26 684
1999	133 488	8 762	14 326	23 101	36 042	21 045	63 924	20 291	...	14 584	4 116	27 049
2000	136 891	8 989	14 677	23 731	36 236	21 358	63 790	21 156	...	15 387	4 230	27 375
2001	136 933	9 088	14 860	24 063	36 350	21 720	63 460	21 572	...	16 023	4 303	27 618
2002	136 485	9 271	15 210	24 325	36 018	21 994	62 650	22 169	...	16 514	4 311	27 835
2003	137 736	9 485	15 576	24 369	35 615	22 020	62 511	22 139	...	17 179	4 301	28 096
2004	139 252	9 662	15 835	24 434	35 604	22 124	62 641	22 557	...	17 854	4 279	28 388
2005	141 730	9 998	16 032	24 596	36 123	22 290	62 908	22 856	...	18 823	4 334	28 681
2006	144 427	10 257	16 317	24 787	36 949	22 721	63 279	23 151	...	19 609	4 416	28 942
2007	146 047	10 576	16 704	25 212	37 763	22 953	63 659	23 433	...	20 208	4 530	29 148
2008	145 362	10 877	16 985	25 578	38 345	23 144	63 490	23 577	13 864	20 113	4 581	29 354
2009	139 877	10 954	16 732	25 345	38 279	22 760	62 561	23 506	13 453	18 735	4 487	28 878
2010	139 064	11 189	16 969	25 403	38 549	22 597	62 421	23 829	13 059	18 309	4 513	28 929
2011	139 869	11 389	17 238	25 489	39 549	22 712	62 332	24 244	13 263	17 972	4 615	29 078
2012	142 469	11 501	17 445	25 547	39 873	22 620	62 152	24 681	13 521	17 155	4 645	29 439
Unemployed												
1975	7 929	303	690	773	890	690	1 000	501	...	...	67	1 174
1976	7 406	298	716	870	890	790	1 080	499	...	...	66	1 414
1977	6 991	358	836	991	900	840	1 100	504	...	686	75	1 470
1978	6 202	405	898	1 038	870	850	1 240	437	...	915	94	1 453
1979	6 137	408	831	1 184	780	920	1 170	540	...	1 137	88	1 432
1980	7 637	409	854	1 276	770	920	1 140	748	...	1 500	86	1 833
1981	8 273	394	887	1 511	1 090	1 040	1 260	660	...	1 841	108	2 609
1982	10 678	495	1 298	1 653	1 560	1 160	1 360	654	...	2 094	137	2 875
1983	10 717	697	1 437	1 731	1 900	1 270	1 560	613	...	2 306	151	3 081
1984	8 539	641	1 377	2 028	1 970	1 280	1 610	568	...	2 671	136	3 241
1985	8 312	603	1 293	2 164	2 010	1 310	1 470	622	...	2 854	124	3 151
1986	8 237	613	1 205	2 199	1 860	1 680	1 630	611	...	2 809	117	3 160
1987	7 425	629	1 123	2 243	1 800	1 760	1 570	519	...	2 792	100	2 940
1988	6 701	576	999	2 167	1 810	1 790	1 440	435	...	2 704	86	2 445
1989	6 528	508	982	2 034	1 640	1 760	1 340	463	...	2 428	74	2 082
1990	7 047	585	1 083	1 976	1 460	1 590	1 280	454	...	2 297	84	2 053
1991	8 628	814	1 386	2 021	2 204	1 580	1 270	461	...	2 313	147	2 530
1992	9 613	925	1 507	2 258	2 615	1 680	1 350	490	...	2 602	261	2 822
1993	8 940	939	1 533	2 525	3 113	2 296	1 600	571	...	3 230	416	2 929
1994	7 996	856	1 372	2 690	3 318	2 493	1 720	504	...	3 455	426	2 676
1995	7 404	764	1 246	2 549	3 200	2 616	1 920	430	...	3 279	404	2 436
1996	7 236	779	1 282	2 710	3 505	2 619	2 040	435	...	3 192	441	2 296
1997	6 739	778	1 247	2 745	3 907	2 641	2 110	568	...	3 007	445	1 988
1998	6 210	721	1 160	2 652	3 693	2 681	2 540	1 490	...	2 727	368	1 788
1999	5 880	652	1 072	2 594	3 333	2 593	2 810	1 374	...	2 310	313	1 727
2000	5 692	602	955	2 239	3 065	2 408	2 920	979	...	2 095	260	1 587
2001	6 801	658	1 026	2 046	3 110	2 173	3 020	899	...	1 904	227	1 489
2002	8 378	630	1 146	2 107	3 396	2 058	3 216	752	...	2 155	234	1 529
2003	8 774	599	1 146	2 294	3 661	2 050	2 985	818	...	2 242	264	1 490
2004	8 149	551	1 091	2 411	4 107	1 960	2 726	860	...	2 214	300	1 426
2005	7 591	531	1 024	2 432	4 573	1 889	2 476	887	...	1 913	361	1 467
2006	7 001	516	949	2 432	4 257	1 673	2 346	827	...	1 837	332	1 674
2007	7 078	484	922	2 223	3 601	1 506	2 400	783	...	1 834	293	1 654
2008	8 924	483	951	2 064	3 136	1 692	2 410	769	4 104	2 591	296	1 783
2009	14 265	649	1 326	2 575	3 228	1 945	3 120	889	4 215	4 150	404	2 390
2010	14 825	617	1 294	2 640	2 946	2 102	3 100	920	4 332	4 632	420	2 476
2011	13 747	611	1 196	2 612	2 502	2 108	2 735	855	4 397	4 999	386	2 564
2012	12 506	635	1 171	2 824	2 317	2 744	2 490	820	4 541	5 769	398	2 547

[1]Unified Germany from 1991 onward; data for previous years relate to the former West Germany.
. . . = Not available.

Table 10-1. Employment Status of the Working-Age Population, Adjusted to U.S. Concepts, 12 Countries, 1975–2012—*Continued*

(Numbers in thousands, percent.)

Category and year	United States	Australia	Canada	France	Germany[1]	Italy	Japan	Korea	South Africa	Spain	Sweden	United Kingdom
Civilian Labor Force Participation Rate												
1975	61.2	63.2	61.1	55.7	55.0	47.7	62.4	58.3	...	...	65.9	63.1
1976	61.6	62.7	62.5	55.9	54.6	48.0	62.4	59.7	...	...	66.0	63.0
1977	62.3	62.7	62.8	56.2	54.4	48.2	62.5	59.4	...	51.9	66.0	62.8
1978	63.2	61.9	63.7	56.1	54.4	47.8	62.8	59.9	...	51.4	66.1	62.6
1979	63.7	61.6	64.5	56.1	54.5	48.0	62.7	59.5	...	50.9	66.6	62.7
1980	63.8	62.1	65.0	56.0	54.7	48.1	62.6	59.0	...	50.4	66.9	62.8
1981	63.9	61.9	65.7	55.8	54.7	48.3	62.6	58.5	...	49.8	66.8	62.7
1982	64.0	61.7	64.9	57.7	54.6	47.7	62.7	58.6	...	49.7	66.8	61.9
1983	64.0	61.4	65.2	57.3	54.3	47.5	63.1	57.7	...	49.6	66.7	61.6
1984	64.4	61.5	65.5	57.1	54.4	47.3	62.7	55.8	...	49.1	66.6	62.8
1985	64.8	61.7	66.0	57.0	54.7	47.2	62.2	56.6	...	48.7	66.9	62.9
1986	65.3	62.8	66.4	57.1	54.9	47.8	62.1	57.1	...	48.6	67.0	62.9
1987	65.6	63.0	66.8	56.7	55.0	47.6	61.8	58.3	...	49.8	66.5	63.2
1988	65.9	63.3	67.1	56.2	55.1	47.4	61.8	58.5	...	50.2	66.9	63.8
1989	66.5	64.2	67.5	56.2	55.2	47.3	62.1	59.6	...	50.1	67.3	64.3
1990	66.5	64.7	67.4	55.7	55.0	47.2	62.6	60.0	...	50.2	67.4	64.4
1991	66.2	64.2	66.8	55.3	58.8	47.8	63.1	60.6	...	50.2	67.0	63.7
1992	66.4	63.9	65.9	55.4	58.1	47.5	63.3	60.9	...	49.8	65.8	62.9
1993	66.3	63.6	65.5	55.3	57.8	49.4	63.2	60.9	...	49.7	64.5	62.6
1994	66.6	63.9	65.2	55.2	57.4	48.8	62.9	61.6	...	49.7	63.7	62.4
1995	66.6	64.6	64.9	55.2	57.1	48.6	62.8	61.9	...	49.6	64.0	62.4
1996	66.8	64.6	64.8	55.5	57.1	48.7	62.8	62.1	...	49.9	63.9	62.4
1997	67.1	64.3	65.1	55.1	57.3	48.7	63.0	62.5	...	50.2	63.3	62.5
1998	67.1	64.3	65.4	55.1	57.7	49.1	62.6	60.6	...	50.6	62.9	62.4
1999	67.1	64.0	65.8	55.2	56.9	49.3	62.0	60.6	...	51.2	62.7	62.8
2000	67.1	64.4	66.0	55.4	56.7	49.5	61.7	61.2	...	52.3	63.7	62.8
2001	66.8	64.4	66.1	55.2	56.7	49.7	61.2	61.4	...	52.8	63.7	62.7
2002	66.6	64.3	67.1	55.4	56.4	49.9	60.4	62.0	...	54.1	63.9	62.9
2003	66.2	64.6	67.7	55.5	56.0	49.6	59.9	61.5	...	55.3	63.9	62.9
2004	66.0	64.6	67.6	55.4	56.4	49.1	59.6	62.1	...	56.2	63.6	62.9
2005	66.0	65.4	67.3	55.3	57.5	48.7	59.5	62.0	...	57.1	64.8	63.1
2006	66.2	65.8	67.2	55.3	58.1	48.9	59.6	61.9	...	58.1	64.9	63.5
2007	66.0	66.2	67.5	55.4	58.3	48.6	59.8	61.8	...	58.7	65.3	63.4
2008	66.0	66.7	67.7	55.5	58.4	49.0	59.6	61.5	58.0	59.6	65.3	63.5
2009	65.4	66.7	67.2	55.8	58.5	48.4	59.3	60.8	56.1	59.7	64.8	63.4
2010	64.7	66.4	67.0	55.8	58.6	48.1	59.1	61.0	54.3	59.8	64.7	63.2
2011	64.1	66.5	66.8	55.6	59.2	48.1	58.7	61.1	54.3	59.8	65.1	63.2
2012	63.7	66.2	66.7	55.9	59.2	49.0	58.4	61.3	54.8	59.8	65.2	63.4
Unemployment Rate												
1975	8.5	4.9	6.9	3.6	3.4	3.4	1.9	4.1	...	...	1.6	4.5
1976	7.7	4.8	6.9	4.0	3.4	3.9	2.0	3.9	...	...	1.6	5.4
1977	7.1	5.6	7.8	4.5	3.4	4.1	2.0	3.8	...	5.2	1.8	5.6
1978	6.1	6.3	8.1	4.6	3.3	4.1	2.3	3.2	...	6.9	2.2	5.5
1979	5.8	6.3	7.3	5.2	2.9	4.4	2.1	3.8	...	8.6	2.1	5.4
1980	7.1	6.1	7.3	5.6	2.8	4.4	2.0	5.2	...	11.3	2.0	6.8
1981	7.6	5.8	7.3	6.6	4.0	4.9	2.2	4.5	...	13.8	2.5	9.7
1982	9.7	7.2	10.7	6.9	5.6	5.4	2.4	4.4	...	15.6	3.1	10.8
1983	9.6	10.0	11.6	7.3	6.9	5.9	2.7	4.1	...	16.9	3.5	11.5
1984	7.5	9.0	10.9	8.5	7.1	5.9	2.8	3.8	...	19.5	3.1	11.8
1985	7.2	8.3	10.1	9.0	7.2	6.0	2.5	4.0	...	20.7	2.8	11.4
1986	7.0	8.1	9.2	9.0	6.6	7.5	2.7	3.8	...	20.2	2.6	11.4
1987	6.2	8.1	8.4	9.2	6.3	7.9	2.6	3.1	...	19.3	2.3	10.5
1988	5.5	7.2	7.4	8.9	6.3	7.9	2.4	2.5	...	18.3	1.9	8.6
1989	5.3	6.2	7.1	8.3	5.7	7.8	2.2	2.6	...	16.2	1.6	7.3
1990	5.6	6.9	7.7	8.0	5.0	7.0	2.0	2.4	...	15.2	1.8	7.1
1991	6.8	9.6	9.8	8.2	5.6	6.9	2.0	2.4	...	15.1	3.2	8.9
1992	7.5	10.8	10.6	9.1	6.7	7.3	2.1	2.5	...	17.0	5.8	10.0
1993	6.9	10.9	10.8	10.2	8.0	9.8	2.4	2.9	...	20.9	9.4	10.4
1994	6.1	9.7	9.6	10.8	8.5	10.7	2.6	2.5	...	22.2	9.6	9.5
1995	5.6	8.5	8.6	10.2	8.2	11.3	2.9	2.1	...	20.9	9.1	8.7
1996	5.4	8.5	8.8	10.7	9.0	11.3	3.1	2.0	...	20.0	9.9	8.1
1997	4.9	8.5	8.4	10.8	9.9	11.3	3.1	2.6	...	18.5	10.1	7.0
1998	4.5	7.7	7.7	10.4	9.3	11.4	3.8	7.0	...	16.5	8.4	6.3
1999	4.2	6.9	7.0	10.1	8.5	11.0	4.2	6.3	...	13.7	7.1	6.0
2000	4.0	6.3	6.1	8.6	7.8	10.1	4.4	4.4	...	12.0	5.8	5.5
2001	4.7	6.8	6.5	7.8	7.9	9.1	4.5	4.0	...	10.6	5.0	5.1
2002	5.8	6.4	7.0	8.0	8.6	8.6	4.9	3.3	...	11.5	5.1	5.2
2003	6.0	5.9	6.9	8.6	9.3	8.5	4.6	3.6	...	11.5	5.8	5.0
2004	5.5	5.4	6.4	9.0	10.3	8.1	4.2	3.7	...	11.0	6.6	4.8
2005	5.1	5.0	6.0	9.0	11.2	7.8	3.8	3.7	...	9.2	7.7	4.9
2006	4.6	4.8	5.5	8.9	10.3	6.9	3.6	3.4	...	8.6	7.0	5.5
2007	4.6	4.4	5.2	8.1	8.7	6.2	3.6	3.2	...	8.3	6.1	5.4
2008	5.8	4.2	5.3	7.5	7.6	6.8	3.7	3.2	22.8	11.4	6.1	5.7
2009	9.3	5.6	7.3	9.2	7.8	7.9	4.8	3.6	23.9	18.1	8.3	7.6
2010	9.6	5.2	7.1	9.4	7.1	8.5	4.7	3.7	24.9	20.2	8.5	7.9
2011	8.9	5.1	6.5	9.3	5.9	8.5	4.2	3.4	24.9	21.8	7.7	8.1
2012	8.1	5.2	6.3	10.0	5.5	10.8	3.9	3.2	25.1	25.2	7.9	8.0

[1] Unified Germany from 1991 onward; data for previous years relate to the former West Germany.
... = Not available.

Table 10-2. Unemployment Rates by Sex and Country, Adjusted to U.S. Concepts, 12 Countries, 1975–2012

(Percent.)

Sex and year	United States	Australia	Canada	France	Germany¹	Italy	Japan	Korea	South Africa	Spain	Sweden	United Kingdom
Men												
1975	7.9	3.8	6.2	2.7	3.3	2.5	1.8	5.0	...	...	1.3	4.1
1976	7.1	3.9	6.3	2.8	3.0	2.7	2.2	5.0	...	...	1.3	5.2
1977	6.3	4.6	7.3	3.2	2.9	2.8	2.0	4.6	...	5.1	1.5	5.3
1978	5.3	5.4	7.5	3.4	2.7	2.8	2.2	3.7	...	6.5	2.1	5.1
1979	5.1	5.2	6.7	3.9	2.3	3.0	1.9	4.7	...	8.1	1.9	4.9
1980	6.9	5.1	6.9	3.9	2.3	2.9	1.7	6.2	...	10.6	1.7	6.7
1981	7.4	4.8	7.0	4.9	3.4	3.3	2.0	5.7	...	13.0	2.4	10.3
1982	9.9	6.4	11.1	5.4	5.0	3.8	2.1	5.5	...	14.4	3.0	11.6
1983	9.9	9.7	12.2	5.8	6.2	4.1	2.5	5.2	...	15.6	3.4	12.2
1984	7.4	8.7	11.1	7.0	6.2	4.2	2.5	4.8	...	18.2	3.0	12.0
1985	7.0	7.9	10.2	7.6	6.2	4.2	2.2	5.0	...	19.2	2.7	11.8
1986	6.9	7.7	9.3	7.6	5.6	5.2	2.4	4.9	...	18.3	2.6	11.8
1987	6.2	7.8	8.3	7.5	5.4	5.5	2.2	3.9	...	16.0	2.3	10.9
1988	5.5	6.8	7.2	7.1	5.3	5.5	2.0	3.0	...	14.1	1.9	8.8
1989	5.2	5.7	7.0	6.4	4.6	5.4	1.8	3.1	...	12.1	1.6	7.4
1990	5.7	6.7	7.9	6.3	4.2	4.8	1.7	2.9	...	11.1	1.9	7.4
1991	7.2	9.9	10.5	6.5	4.6	4.9	1.7	2.7	...	11.3	3.5	9.9
1992	7.9	11.4	11.6	7.4	5.5	5.3	1.8	2.8	...	13.2	6.8	11.8
1993	7.2	11.5	11.5	8.8	6.7	7.3	2.1	3.3	...	17.4	11.0	12.4
1994	6.2	10.0	10.2	9.5	7.3	8.3	2.3	2.8	...	18.1	11.0	11.3
1995	5.6	8.8	9.1	8.7	7.3	8.7	2.6	2.3	...	16.6	9.9	10.1
1996	5.4	8.8	9.2	9.4	8.4	8.7	2.8	2.4	...	15.9	10.4	9.5
1997	4.9	8.7	8.7	9.6	9.4	8.7	2.8	2.8	...	14.3	10.4	7.9
1998	4.4	8.0	8.0	9.1	8.9	8.8	3.5	7.8	...	12.1	8.7	7.0
1999	4.1	7.1	7.3	8.9	8.1	8.4	4.0	7.2	...	9.7	7.4	6.6
2000	3.9	6.5	6.3	7.3	7.6	7.8	4.1	5.0	...	8.4	6.2	6.0
2001	4.8	7.0	6.9	6.6	7.8	7.0	4.4	4.5	...	7.6	5.3	5.7
2002	5.9	6.5	7.6	7.2	8.8	6.6	4.7	3.7	...	8.3	5.6	5.8
2003	6.3	5.9	7.3	7.8	9.7	6.6	4.3	3.8	...	8.5	6.3	5.6
2004	5.6	5.3	6.8	8.2	10.6	6.5	3.9	3.9	...	8.2	6.9	5.2
2005	5.1	4.9	6.3	8.2	11.5	6.3	3.5	4.0	...	7.1	7.8	5.3
2006	4.6	4.7	5.8	8.2	10.4	5.5	3.3	3.8	...	6.4	6.9	5.8
2007	4.7	4.0	5.6	7.6	8.6	5.0	3.2	3.7	...	6.4	5.8	5.7
2008	6.1	4.0	5.8	7.0	7.5	5.6	3.2	3.6	19.8	10.1	5.8	6.2
2009	10.3	5.7	8.5	9.1	8.2	6.9	4.4	4.1	22.0	17.9	8.6	8.7
2010	10.5	5.1	7.8	9.1	7.6	7.7	4.5	4.0	22.8	19.9	8.6	8.7
2011	9.4	4.9	7.0	8.9	6.2	7.7	4.1	3.6	22.5	21.4	7.8	8.8
2012	8.2	5.2	6.7	9.9	5.7	10.0	3.6	3.4	22.9	24.9	8.2	8.4
Women												
1975	9.3	7.0	8.1	5.0	3.5	5.7	3.9	2.5	...	...	2.0	5.2
1976	8.6	6.4	7.9	5.8	3.9	6.7	3.9	2.0	...	...	2.0	5.9
1977	8.2	7.5	8.8	6.4	4.3	6.8	4.3	2.4	...	5.6	2.2	6.2
1978	7.2	7.9	9.1	6.5	4.2	6.9	4.3	2.2	...	8.0	2.4	6.2
1979	6.8	8.2	8.3	7.3	3.9	7.4	4.1	2.4	...	9.8	2.3	6.2
1980	7.4	7.9	7.9	8.1	3.6	7.4	3.3	3.5	...	13.0	2.3	7.1
1981	7.9	7.4	7.8	9.1	4.8	8.1	3.5	2.4	...	16.0	2.7	8.8
1982	9.4	8.5	10.1	9.1	6.5	8.7	3.5	2.5	...	18.4	3.4	9.5
1983	9.2	10.4	10.8	9.3	7.9	9.4	3.7	2.2	...	20.2	3.5	10.5
1984	7.6	9.5	10.7	10.4	8.5	9.3	3.3	2.2	...	22.6	3.2	11.6
1985	7.4	8.8	9.9	10.8	8.6	9.4	3.0	2.4	...	24.3	2.9	11.0
1986	7.1	8.7	9.1	10.8	8.1	11.8	3.2	2.1	...	24.4	2.7	10.9
1987	6.2	8.6	8.6	11.4	7.8	12.2	3.2	1.8	...	26.2	2.3	10.0
1988	5.6	7.9	7.6	11.2	7.8	12.3	2.9	1.7	...	26.4	1.9	8.3
1989	5.4	6.8	7.1	10.7	7.2	12.1	2.7	1.8	...	24.2	1.7	7.1
1990	5.5	7.2	7.5	10.2	6.1	10.8	2.5	1.8	...	22.9	1.8	6.8
1991	6.4	9.2	9.0	10.4	7.0	10.4	2.5	2.0	...	22.3	2.9	7.5
1992	7.0	10.0	9.4	11.2	8.4	10.8	2.5	2.1	...	23.8	4.6	7.7
1993	6.6	10.1	9.9	11.8	9.6	14.0	3.0	2.3	...	27.1	7.6	7.9
1994	6.0	9.4	8.8	12.4	10.1	14.7	3.1	2.0	...	29.0	8.2	7.4
1995	5.6	8.1	8.0	11.9	9.4	15.5	3.4	1.7	...	28.1	8.1	6.9
1996	5.4	8.2	8.2	12.2	9.6	15.3	3.5	1.6	...	26.7	9.3	6.4
1997	5.0	8.2	8.0	12.3	10.6	15.4	3.7	2.3	...	25.2	9.7	5.9
1998	4.6	7.4	7.2	11.9	9.8	15.5	4.2	5.7	...	23.5	8.0	5.4
1999	4.3	6.7	6.6	11.5	8.9	14.8	4.5	5.1	...	20.0	6.7	5.2
2000	4.1	6.1	5.8	10.1	8.1	13.6	4.8	3.6	...	17.5	5.4	4.9
2001	4.7	6.4	6.0	9.2	7.9	12.1	4.8	3.3	...	15.3	4.7	4.5
2002	5.6	6.2	6.4	8.9	8.3	11.4	5.2	2.8	...	16.4	4.7	4.5
2003	5.7	6.0	6.3	9.5	8.8	11.4	4.9	3.3	...	16.1	5.2	4.4
2004	5.4	5.5	6.0	9.9	10.0	10.6	4.6	3.4	...	15.1	6.1	4.3
2005	5.1	5.2	5.6	9.9	10.9	10.1	4.1	3.4	...	12.2	7.5	4.4
2006	4.6	4.9	5.2	9.7	10.2	8.8	4.0	2.9	...	11.6	7.1	5.0
2007	4.5	4.8	4.8	8.6	8.8	7.9	4.3	2.6	...	10.9	6.4	5.0
2008	5.4	4.6	4.8	7.9	7.7	8.5	4.3	2.6	26.4	13.1	6.3	5.1
2009	8.1	5.4	6.1	9.4	7.3	9.3	5.2	3.0	26.2	18.5	7.9	6.4
2010	8.6	5.4	6.2	9.7	6.5	9.7	5.0	3.3	27.5	20.6	8.4	6.9
2011	8.5	5.3	5.9	9.7	5.6	9.6	4.4	3.1	27.8	22.2	7.6	7.3
2012	7.9	5.3	5.8	10.0	5.2	11.9	4.2	3.0	27.8	25.5	7.6	7.4

¹Unified Germany from 1991 onward; data for previous years relate to the former West Germany.
. . . = Not available.

Table 10-3. Unemployment Rates Among Youth, Adjusted to U.S. Concepts, 12 Countries, 1970–2012

(Percent.)

Year	United States	Australia	Canada	France	Germany[1]	Italy	Japan	Korea	South Africa	Spain	Sweden	United Kingdom
1970	11.0	...	...	4.9	0.4	10.4	2.0	...	...	...	2.9	...
1971	12.7	...	...	5.5	0.6	10.3	2.1	...	...	...	5.1	...
1972	12.1	...	...	5.9	0.7	13.6	2.5	...	...	...	5.8	...
1973	10.5	...	...	5.8	0.8	13.2	2.3	...	...	...	5.3	...
1974	11.9	...	...	6.3	2.2	12.0	2.4	...	...	...	4.5	...
1975	16.1	...	...	7.9	4.7	13.2	3.1	...	...	...	3.8	...
1976	14.7	...	12.4	9.0	4.8	15.2	3.2	...	...	...	3.8	...
1977	13.6	...	13.8	10.6	5.0	14.9	3.6	...	...	12.4	4.5	...
1978	12.3	12.6	13.9	11.1	4.5	15.4	3.8	...	...	17.4	5.6	...
1979	11.8	13.0	12.6	12.7	3.6	16.0	3.7	...	...	21.3	5.1	...
1980	13.9	12.5	12.7	14.2	3.7	15.8	3.5	...	...	28.0	5.1	...
1981	14.9	11.4	12.6	16.8	5.7	17.3	4.0	...	...	34.0	6.4	...
1982	17.8	13.8	18.1	15.5	8.2	19.4	4.3	10.0	...	38.1	7.7	...
1983	17.2	18.3	19.1	16.5	9.6	20.9	4.6	9.2	...	41.2	8.1	...
1984	13.9	16.8	17.2	20.1	10.7	21.6	4.9	8.8	...	45.5	6.1	19.8
1985	13.6	15.2	15.6	20.2	10.0	22.2	4.7	10.0	...	47.0	5.9	18.0
1986	13.3	15.0	14.5	19.1	8.0	25.5	5.1	9.0	...	45.2	5.7	18.2
1987	12.2	14.9	13.0	18.2	7.4	25.8	5.0	7.6	...	42.1	5.3	15.4
1988	11.0	13.4	11.2	17.1	6.9	24.8	4.7	7.2	...	38.8	4.3	12.6
1989	10.9	11.2	10.5	15.4	5.5	23.9	4.4	6.8	...	33.2	4.0	10.1
1990	11.2	13.0	12.0	15.5	4.6	21.3	4.3	7.0	...	30.9	4.6	10.6
1991	13.4	17.5	15.4	16.1	5.6	21.2	4.2	7.3	...	29.5	8.0	14.3
1992	14.2	19.4	16.8	17.7	6.4	22.8	4.4	7.6	...	32.6	13.9	16.3
1993	13.4	18.7	16.7	20.7	7.8	27.3	5.1	9.0	...	41.1	23.5	18.0
1994	12.5	17.1	14.9	22.4	8.5	28.9	5.2	7.3	...	43.0	23.8	16.8
1995	12.1	15.4	13.9	20.5	8.4	30.1	5.9	6.3	...	40.4	20.2	15.7
1996	12.0	15.7	14.5	21.8	9.7	30.1	6.4	6.1	...	39.6	21.5	15.4
1997	11.3	16.1	15.5	22.2	10.6	29.9	6.4	7.6	...	36.5	21.1	14.1
1998	10.4	14.6	14.6	20.9	9.4	29.4	7.4	15.8	...	32.7	17.1	13.6
1999	9.9	13.3	13.4	20.6	8.8	28.2	8.7	14.1	...	26.8	14.6	12.9
2000	9.3	12.1	11.7	16.4	8.6	26.5	8.9	10.8	...	23.6	12.0	12.4
2001	10.6	13.5	11.9	15.7	8.5	23.4	9.1	10.2	...	21.4	12.0	12.0
2002	12.0	12.8	12.9	16.6	10.0	22.3	9.5	8.5	...	22.5	13.1	12.2
2003	12.4	12.0	12.8	18.7	10.8	24.0	9.6	10.1	...	23.0	14.0	12.5
2004	11.8	11.4	12.5	20.3	12.9	23.8	9.0	10.4	...	22.3	17.2	12.4
2005	11.3	10.6	11.4	20.9	15.5	24.2	8.1	10.2	...	20.0	22.4	13.1
2006	10.5	10.0	10.6	21.9	13.8	21.9	7.5	10.0	...	18.2	21.4	14.2
2007	10.5	9.4	10.0	19.4	11.9	20.6	7.6	8.8	...	18.5	18.9	14.4
2008	12.8	8.8	10.4	18.8	10.5	21.5	7.0	9.3	45.5	25.0	19.4	15.2
2009	17.6	11.5	13.9	23.5	11.2	25.7	9.0	9.8	48.1	38.5	24.9	19.2
2010	18.4	11.6	13.6	23.0	9.8	28.2	9.2	9.8	50.5	42.3	24.5	19.9
2011	17.3	11.4	12.8	22.2	8.7	29.4	8.1	9.6	49.8	47.1	22.5	21.2
2012	16.2	11.7	13.0	23.9	8.2	35.6	7.5	9.0	51.5	53.7	23.3	21.2

Note: Youth are defined as 16- to 24-year-olds in the United States, Canada, France, Sweden, and the United Kingdom; otherwise, they are defined as 15- to 24-year-olds.

[1]Unified Germany from 1991 onward; data for previous years relate to the former West Germany.
. . . = Not available.

Table 10-4. Employment-Population Ratios by Sex, Adjusted to U.S. Concepts, 12 Countries, 1975–2012
(Ratio.)

Sex and year	United States	Australia	Canada	France	Germany[1]	Italy	Japan	Korea	South Africa	Spain	Sweden	United Kingdom
Men												
1975	71.7	79.1	73.5	70.6	70.9	68.8	79.5	73.5	...	...	76.0	77.9
1976	72.0	78.3	74.2	70.2	70.3	68.5	79.2	73.6	...	...	75.5	76.7
1977	72.8	77.3	73.3	69.7	69.9	67.5	78.7	75.1	...	74.8	74.5	75.9
1978	73.8	75.5	73.4	69.0	69.7	66.8	78.2	75.0	...	72.7	73.5	75.3
1979	73.8	75.3	74.3	68.2	69.8	66.3	78.2	73.3	...	70.6	73.7	75.0
1980	72.0	75.1	74.0	67.5	69.6	66.0	77.9	71.7	...	67.7	73.6	73.3
1981	71.3	75.1	73.9	66.1	68.5	65.6	77.8	71.5	...	65.2	72.0	70.1
1982	69.0	73.4	69.3	67.2	67.0	64.4	77.4	70.9	...	63.5	71.3	68.0
1983	68.8	70.1	68.3	66.1	65.8	63.5	77.1	69.8	...	61.9	70.4	66.7
1984	70.7	70.5	68.9	64.4	65.7	62.9	76.4	68.7	...	59.1	70.2	67.3
1985	70.9	70.6	69.6	63.8	65.8	62.5	75.9	68.7	...	57.5	70.5	67.2
1986	71.0	70.8	70.4	63.3	66.3	61.8	75.4	68.6	...	57.7	70.6	66.6
1987	71.5	70.3	71.0	62.7	66.2	60.9	74.9	69.7	...	58.8	69.7	67.2
1988	72.0	70.9	71.6	62.2	65.9	60.4	75.0	70.7	...	59.6	70.3	69.0
1989	72.5	72.0	71.8	62.3	65.9	59.9	75.1	71.2	...	60.6	70.9	70.3
1990	72.0	71.3	70.6	61.5	65.6	60.0	75.4	71.8	...	61.0	70.6	70.0
1991	70.4	68.1	67.6	60.5	67.9	60.6	75.8	73.0	...	60.4	69.2	67.3
1992	69.8	66.5	65.7	59.8	66.3	59.8	76.1	73.6	...	57.9	65.7	64.8
1993	70.0	65.9	65.3	58.1	64.7	59.6	75.9	73.2	...	54.3	61.6	63.7
1994	70.4	67.0	65.9	57.4	63.8	58.1	75.4	74.2	...	53.2	60.9	64.2
1995	70.8	68.1	66.1	57.6	63.1	57.3	75.0	74.6	...	53.6	62.0	64.7
1996	70.9	67.9	65.8	57.5	62.1	57.1	74.9	74.4	...	54.0	61.5	64.8
1997	71.3	67.6	66.4	56.9	61.3	56.9	74.9	73.9	...	55.0	61.0	65.9
1998	71.6	67.9	66.8	56.7	61.9	56.9	73.9	69.2	...	56.7	62.1	66.2
1999	71.6	68.2	67.5	57.0	60.7	57.1	73.0	69.1	...	58.7	62.5	66.6
2000	71.9	68.4	68.2	58.0	60.6	57.4	72.5	70.7	...	60.2	64.2	66.9
2001	70.9	67.6	67.7	58.0	60.2	57.7	71.5	71.0	...	61.1	64.4	66.9
2002	69.7	67.8	67.9	57.8	58.9	58.1	70.4	72.2	...	61.2	64.3	66.7
2003	68.9	68.1	68.3	57.1	57.5	57.6	69.9	71.9	...	61.8	63.7	66.9
2004	69.2	68.8	68.5	56.5	57.3	56.9	69.6	72.0	...	62.3	63.0	66.9
2005	69.6	69.4	68.6	56.2	57.7	56.8	69.7	71.6	...	63.7	63.8	66.8
2006	70.1	69.8	68.4	56.1	58.6	57.3	69.9	71.3	...	64.5	64.5	66.7
2007	69.8	70.4	68.7	56.3	59.7	57.3	70.1	71.3	...	64.6	65.4	66.7
2008	68.5	70.7	68.8	56.7	60.5	56.9	69.7	70.9	52.7	62.2	65.5	66.4
2009	64.5	69.1	65.9	55.6	59.9	55.3	68.1	70.1	49.7	56.2	63.0	64.2
2010	63.7	69.5	66.2	55.4	60.2	54.4	67.7	70.1	47.7	54.3	63.3	63.8
2011	63.9	69.5	66.6	55.3	61.5	54.2	67.6	70.5	47.4	52.9	63.9	63.6
2012	64.4	68.9	66.6	55.1	61.7	53.2	67.3	70.8	47.5	50.1	63.5	64.0
Women												
1975	42.0	41.4	40.7	38.4	37.9	25.3	44.0	39.4	...	...	54.1	44.2
1976	43.2	41.5	42.6	38.9	37.8	25.8	44.1	42.3	...	...	54.7	44.0
1977	44.5	41.5	42.9	39.3	37.7	26.9	44.9	40.7	...	26.2	55.5	44.0
1978	46.4	41.0	44.0	39.6	37.9	26.8	45.5	42.3	...	25.4	56.1	44.4
1979	47.5	40.7	45.7	39.7	38.4	27.3	45.6	42.3	...	24.9	57.2	45.0
1980	47.7	41.9	46.9	39.6	38.8	27.9	45.6	41.3	...	23.8	58.0	45.1
1981	48.0	42.1	48.2	39.5	38.7	28.0	45.6	41.2	...	22.7	58.5	44.3
1982	47.7	41.5	47.0	41.6	38.1	27.6	45.9	42.3	...	22.4	58.4	43.5
1983	48.0	40.8	47.3	41.5	37.3	27.6	46.7	41.9	...	22.4	58.6	43.3
1984	49.5	41.8	48.2	41.4	37.3	27.6	46.4	39.8	...	21.7	59.1	44.4
1985	50.4	43.0	49.5	41.3	37.6	27.8	46.3	40.9	...	21.3	59.7	45.2
1986	51.4	45.0	50.7	41.7	38.1	28.1	46.2	42.2	...	21.5	60.1	45.8
1987	52.5	45.6	51.6	41.5	38.5	28.2	46.2	44.1	...	23.0	60.5	46.9
1988	53.4	46.8	53.0	41.4	39.0	28.3	46.6	44.2	...	24.0	61.2	48.4
1989	54.3	48.7	53.9	41.8	39.7	28.6	47.4	45.7	...	24.8	61.7	49.9
1990	54.3	49.4	54.1	42.0	40.5	29.2	48.0	46.2	...	25.7	61.8	50.3
1991	53.7	48.2	53.2	42.0	44.3	29.7	48.6	46.2	...	26.2	60.6	49.6
1992	53.8	47.8	52.4	41.9	43.4	29.7	48.7	46.1	...	26.1	58.4	49.1
1993	54.1	47.6	51.9	42.1	42.7	30.7	48.2	46.0	...	25.3	55.5	49.1
1994	55.3	48.6	52.4	41.9	42.3	30.3	48.0	46.9	...	25.2	54.3	49.3
1995	55.6	50.3	52.7	42.4	42.7	30.2	47.7	47.6	...	25.9	54.7	49.8
1996	56.0	50.4	52.6	42.5	42.8	30.5	47.6	48.1	...	26.8	53.9	50.4
1997	56.8	50.4	53.2	42.2	42.7	30.7	47.9	48.6	...	27.8	53.0	51.0
1998	57.1	51.0	54.3	42.6	43.5	31.2	47.4	44.4	...	28.7	53.3	51.4
1999	57.4	51.3	55.2	43.1	44.1	31.9	46.6	45.2	...	30.7	54.2	52.0
2000	57.5	52.5	56.0	44.0	44.4	32.7	46.4	47.0	...	32.8	56.1	52.5
2001	57.0	52.6	56.2	44.5	44.8	33.8	46.1	47.7	...	34.1	56.7	52.7
2002	56.3	52.9	57.1	44.9	44.7	34.3	45.4	48.4	...	35.2	57.1	53.0
2003	56.1	53.6	58.0	44.9	44.5	34.2	45.3	47.4	...	36.7	56.8	53.1
2004	56.0	53.7	58.2	44.9	44.3	34.2	45.5	48.3	...	38.3	56.1	53.4
2005	56.2	55.0	58.1	45.0	44.9	34.1	45.7	48.4	...	40.5	56.0	53.7
2006	56.6	55.7	58.6	45.1	46.0	34.7	46.0	48.8	...	42.2	56.4	53.8
2007	56.6	56.4	59.5	46.0	47.1	34.9	46.1	48.9	...	43.4	57.3	53.6
2008	56.2	57.2	59.6	46.5	47.8	35.3	45.9	48.7	37.4	43.7	57.3	53.8
2009	54.4	56.9	58.7	46.2	48.3	34.7	45.6	47.7	36.2	41.9	56.0	53.2
2010	53.6	56.6	58.5	46.0	48.9	34.5	45.7	47.8	34.3	41.4	55.2	52.9
2011	53.2	56.8	58.5	46.0	50.2	34.7	45.6	48.1	34.6	41.0	56.3	52.8
2012	53.1	56.7	58.5	46.0	50.4	35.0	45.7	48.4	34.9	39.7	56.7	52.9

[1]Unified Germany from 1991 onward; data for previous years relate to the former West Germany.
. . . = Not available.

Table 10-5. Women's Share of the Labor Force, Adjusted to U.S. Concepts, 12 Countries, 1970–2012

(Percent.)

Year	United States	Australia	Canada	France	Germany[1]	Italy	Japan	Korea	South Africa	Spain	Sweden	United Kingdom
1970	38.1	32.8	33.6	36.6	36.5	28.3	39.4	35.9	...	...	39.6	...
1971	38.2	33.2	34.4	37.0	36.8	28.3	39.1	36.1	...	...	40.3	37.3
1972	38.5	33.4	34.9	37.4	37.3	28.1	38.7	35.9	...	...	40.8	37.6
1973	38.9	34.1	35.6	37.7	37.7	28.8	38.7	36.9	...	...	41.1	38.1
1974	39.4	34.8	36.1	38.0	38.0	29.1	38.1	36.4	...	...	41.9	38.6
1975	40.0	35.5	36.9	38.2	38.5	29.4	37.9	35.9	...	...	42.7	38.8
1976	40.5	35.6	37.4	38.8	38.8	30.2	37.9	37.5	...	...	43.1	38.9
1977	41.0	36.1	37.9	39.4	39.0	31.4	38.7	36.5	...	28.1	43.8	39.2
1978	41.7	36.3	38.6	39.8	39.2	31.5	39.0	37.6	...	28.3	44.4	39.6
1979	42.1	36.4	39.2	40.2	39.3	32.2	39.1	37.8	...	28.5	44.8	40.0
1980	42.5	37.1	39.8	40.6	39.5	32.7	38.9	37.5	...	28.6	45.3	40.4
1981	43.0	37.2	40.5	41.0	39.7	33.0	38.9	37.3	...	28.4	46.1	40.5
1982	43.3	37.3	40.9	41.8	39.8	33.2	39.1	38.4	...	28.9	46.4	40.7
1983	43.5	37.5	41.4	42.1	39.8	33.5	39.6	38.5	...	29.7	46.7	41.1
1984	43.8	38.0	41.9	42.6	39.9	33.7	39.5	37.7	...	29.9	47.0	41.8
1985	44.2	38.6	42.4	42.8	40.1	34.0	39.5	38.3	...	30.1	47.2	42.1
1986	44.5	39.6	42.7	43.2	40.2	34.9	39.6	39.1	...	30.5	47.3	42.6
1987	44.8	40.0	43.1	43.5	40.3	35.3	39.8	39.9	...	32.7	47.7	42.9
1988	45.0	40.5	43.6	43.7	40.7	35.6	40.0	39.8	...	33.8	47.8	43.2
1989	45.2	41.1	43.9	43.9	41.0	36.0	40.3	40.4	...	34.1	47.8	43.5
1990	45.2	41.6	44.2	44.2	41.5	36.3	40.5	40.5	...	34.5	47.8	43.7
1991	45.3	41.8	44.6	44.5	42.8	36.3	40.6	40.2	...	34.9	47.7	43.8
1992	45.4	41.9	44.7	44.8	42.8	36.6	40.6	40.0	...	35.7	47.7	44.0
1993	45.5	42.1	44.9	45.3	42.8	37.9	40.5	40.0	...	36.2	47.7	44.3
1994	46.0	42.4	44.9	45.5	42.9	38.1	40.5	40.2	...	37.0	47.6	44.5
1995	46.1	42.9	45.1	45.8	43.1	38.4	40.5	40.3	...	37.6	47.6	44.7
1996	46.2	43.0	45.2	45.9	43.3	38.8	40.5	40.6	...	37.9	47.7	44.9
1997	46.2	43.1	45.3	45.8	43.4	39.0	40.7	41.0	...	38.3	47.5	45.1
1998	46.3	43.3	45.5	46.2	43.5	39.4	40.7	40.0	...	38.3	47.2	45.3
1999	46.5	43.5	45.7	46.3	44.0	39.8	40.6	40.5	...	38.7	47.4	45.4
2000	46.5	44.0	45.9	46.4	44.3	40.1	40.8	41.1	...	39.2	47.5	45.6
2001	46.5	44.3	46.0	46.6	44.4	40.5	40.9	41.4	...	39.3	47.7	45.6
2002	46.5	44.4	46.2	46.7	44.7	40.6	40.9	41.4	...	40.0	47.8	45.7
2003	46.6	44.8	46.5	47.0	45.0	40.7	41.1	41.0	...	40.6	47.8	45.7
2004	46.4	44.6	46.6	47.3	45.1	40.7	41.3	41.4	...	41.1	47.8	45.8
2005	46.4	45.0	46.5	47.4	45.2	40.5	41.4	41.5	...	41.4	47.5	45.9
2006	46.3	45.2	46.8	47.5	45.5	40.6	41.6	41.7	...	42.0	47.5	46.0
2007	46.4	45.3	47.0	47.8	45.7	40.6	41.6	41.7	...	42.4	47.6	45.8
2008	46.5	45.4	47.0	47.8	45.7	41.0	41.7	41.6	45.4	43.1	47.5	45.8
2009	46.7	45.5	47.2	48.0	45.9	41.1	42.0	41.3	45.2	44.0	47.4	46.0
2010	46.7	45.4	47.2	48.0	46.0	41.3	42.2	41.4	44.9	44.6	47.1	46.1
2011	46.6	45.6	47.2	48.1	46.2	41.6	42.1	41.5	45.4	45.2	47.3	46.2
2012	46.9	45.7	47.3	48.0	46.1	42.3	42.4	41.6	45.3	45.8	47.5	46.2

[1]Unified Germany from 1991 onward; data for previous years relate to the former West Germany.

Table 10-6. Percent of Employment in Agriculture, Adjusted to U.S. Concepts, 12 Countries, 1970–2012

(Percent.)

Year	United States	Australia	Canada	France	Germany[1]	Italy	Japan	Korea	South Africa	Spain	Sweden	United Kingdom[2]
1970	4.4	8.1	7.6	. . .	8.5	20.1	16.9	50.4	. . .	. . .	8.2	. . .
1971	4.3	7.7	7.5	16.0	8.0	20.1	15.5	48.2	. . .	. . .	7.8	3.1
1972	4.2	7.9	6.9	15.0	7.6	19.0	14.5	50.5	. . .	. . .	7.5	2.9
1973	4.1	7.4	6.5	14.1	7.2	18.2	13.1	49.8	. . .	. . .	7.1	2.9
1974	4.0	7.0	6.3	13.3	6.9	17.4	12.6	48.0	. . .	. . .	6.7	2.7
1975	4.0	6.9	6.1	12.9	6.7	16.7	12.4	45.7	. . .	. . .	6.5	2.7
1976	3.8	6.6	5.6	12.3	6.2	16.4	11.9	44.4	. . .	. . .	6.2	2.7
1977	3.6	6.7	5.4	11.8	5.9	15.8	11.6	41.7	. . .	20.4	6.1	2.7
1978	3.5	6.4	5.2	11.4	5.7	15.4	11.4	38.4	. . .	19.9	6.1	2.7
1979	3.4	6.5	5.1	11.1	5.3	14.9	10.8	35.8	. . .	19.2	5.8	2.6
1980	3.4	6.5	4.9	10.7	5.2	14.2	10.1	34.0	. . .	18.5	5.6	2.5
1981	3.4	6.5	4.8	10.4	5.0	13.3	9.7	34.2	. . .	17.9	5.6	2.6
1982	3.4	6.5	4.9	9.6	4.9	12.4	9.4	32.1	. . .	17.7	5.6	2.6
1983	3.4	6.6	5.0	9.3	4.8	12.3	8.9	29.7	. . .	17.9	5.5	2.6
1984	3.2	6.2	4.8	9.1	4.7	11.7	8.5	27.1	. . .	17.6	5.1	2.5
1985	3.0	6.1	4.7	8.7	4.5	11.0	8.4	24.9	. . .	17.6	4.9	2.2
1986	2.9	6.1	4.7	8.4	4.3	10.7	8.1	23.6	. . .	15.6	4.7	2.1
1987	2.9	5.8	4.5	8.0	4.1	10.4	8.0	21.9	. . .	14.5	4.5	2.2
1988	2.8	5.8	4.4	7.7	3.9	9.8	7.6	20.6	. . .	13.8	4.4	2.2
1989	2.7	5.5	4.2	7.3	3.7	9.3	7.3	19.6	. . .	12.5	4.3	2.1
1990	2.7	5.6	4.2	6.9	3.5	8.9	6.9	17.9	. . .	11.4	4.0	2.0
1991	2.8	5.5	4.3	6.6	4.1	8.5	6.4	14.6	. . .	10.2	3.8	2.2
1992	2.7	5.3	4.2	6.3	3.8	8.2	6.1	14.0	. . .	9.7	3.8	2.1
1993	2.6	5.3	4.3	6.0	3.5	6.4	5.7	13.5	. . .	9.6	4.0	1.9
1994	2.8	5.1	4.2	5.7	3.3	6.2	5.6	12.6	. . .	9.3	3.9	2.0
1995	2.8	4.9	4.0	5.5	3.1	5.9	5.5	11.8	. . .	8.8	3.5	2.0
1996	2.7	5.0	3.9	5.3	3.0	5.6	5.3	11.1	. . .	8.3	3.3	1.9
1997	2.6	5.1	3.8	5.2	2.9	5.4	5.1	10.8	. . .	8.1	3.1	1.6
1998	2.6	4.9	3.8	5.0	2.8	5.2	5.0	12.0	. . .	7.8	3.0	1.4
1999	2.5	4.9	3.5	4.9	2.8	4.9	4.9	11.3	. . .	7.1	3.1	1.2
2000	1.8	4.9	3.3	4.6	2.6	4.7	4.8	10.6	. . .	6.6	2.9	1.2
2001	1.7	4.8	2.8	4.5	2.6	4.6	4.7	10.0	. . .	6.5	2.6	1.1
2002	1.7	4.4	2.8	4.3	2.5	4.5	4.5	9.3	. . .	6.0	2.5	1.0
2003	1.7	3.9	2.7	4.2	2.5	4.4	4.4	8.8	. . .	5.7	2.5	1.0
2004	1.6	3.7	2.7	3.9	2.4	4.5	4.3	8.1	. . .	5.5	2.5	0.9
2005	1.6	3.6	2.7	3.7	2.4	4.2	4.2	7.9	. . .	5.2	2.3	1.0
2006	1.5	3.4	2.6	3.8	2.3	4.3	4.1	7.7	. . .	4.7	2.2	1.0
2007	1.4	3.3	2.5	3.5	2.3	4.0	4.1	7.4	. . .	4.5	2.2	1.0
2008	1.5	3.3	2.3	2.8	2.3	3.7	4.0	7.2	5.7	4.0	2.2	1.1
2009	1.5	3.3	2.3	3.0	1.7	3.7	4.0	7.0	5.1	4.1	2.2	1.1
2010	1.6	3.3	2.2	3.0	1.6	3.8	3.9	6.6	4.9	4.3	2.1	1.2
2011	1.6	2.9	2.1	3.0	1.6	3.7	3.8	6.4	4.6	4.2	2.0	1.2
2012	1.5	2.9	2.2	3.0	1.6	3.7	3.7	6.2	4.9	4.3	2.1	1.2

Note: Agriculture includes agriculture, forestry, hunting, and fishing.

[1]Unified Germany from 1991 onward; data for previous years relate to the former West Germany.
[2]Sectoral employment is only partially adjusted to U.S. concepts prior to 1984.
. . . = Not available.

Table 10-7. Percent of Employment in Industry, Adjusted to U.S. Concepts, 12 Countries, 1970–2012

(Percent.)

Year	United States	Australia	Canada	France	Germany[1]	Italy	Japan	Korea	South Africa	Spain	Sweden	United Kingdom[2]
1970	33.1	34.6	29.8	. . .	48.7	38.8	35.7	17.2	. . .	. . .	38.0	. . .
1971	31.7	34.4	29.4	39.4	47.7	39.0	35.9	17.7	. . .	. . .	37.1	41.8
1972	31.4	33.5	29.2	39.6	47.0	38.8	36.2	17.9	. . .	. . .	36.3	41.1
1973	32.0	33.4	29.5	39.6	46.8	38.4	37.0	19.6	. . .	. . .	36.3	40.8
1974	31.4	33.0	29.5	39.4	45.9	38.4	36.8	21.7	. . .	. . .	36.4	40.5
1975	29.5	31.5	28.1	38.9	44.5	38.3	35.6	23.5	. . .	. . .	35.8	38.9
1976	29.6	31.0	27.9	38.1	44.1	37.5	35.6	26.1	. . .	. . .	34.8	38.0
1977	29.7	30.4	27.5	37.8	43.8	37.6	35.1	27.2	. . .	37.3	33.7	37.9
1978	30.0	29.3	27.3	37.1	43.5	37.4	34.8	29.2	. . .	37.1	32.4	37.6
1979	30.2	29.0	27.5	36.6	43.3	37.0	34.7	29.7	. . .	36.6	31.9	37.2
1980	29.3	28.6	27.3	36.1	42.9	37.0	35.1	28.7	. . .	36.1	31.5	36.1
1981	28.9	28.3	26.9	35.5	42.2	36.5	35.1	27.5	. . .	35.2	30.6	34.2
1982	27.2	27.4	25.0	33.5	41.3	36.1	34.5	27.6	. . .	33.9	29.4	33.0
1983	25.7	25.9	24.2	32.8	40.6	35.1	34.4	28.9	. . .	33.3	29.1	31.9
1984	26.1	25.5	24.3	32.0	40.3	33.4	34.5	30.5	. . .	32.7	29.0	33.2
1985	25.8	24.8	24.3	31.0	40.1	32.6	34.6	30.5	. . .	31.5	29.1	32.8
1986	25.5	24.1	24.2	30.2	39.9	32.0	34.2	31.6	. . .	31.6	29.2	32.2
1987	25.0	23.9	24.1	29.8	39.5	31.5	33.5	33.8	. . .	32.1	28.7	31.2
1988	24.8	23.9	24.3	29.6	39.0	31.5	33.9	34.6	. . .	32.3	28.3	31.3
1989	24.7	24.2	24.3	29.4	38.9	31.5	34.1	34.8	. . .	32.5	28.4	31.1
1990	24.2	23.2	23.6	29.5	38.9	31.4	33.9	35.0	. . .	33.0	28.2	30.7
1991	23.4	22.0	22.0	29.2	39.8	31.4	34.2	36.5	. . .	32.7	27.2	31.0
1992	22.8	21.7	21.3	28.3	38.9	31.3	34.3	35.4	. . .	32.1	25.6	28.6
1993	22.3	21.9	20.7	27.2	37.8	32.5	34.0	33.7	. . .	30.3	24.5	28.1
1994	22.3	21.8	20.9	26.5	36.6	32.5	33.7	33.3	. . .	29.7	24.0	26.5
1995	22.4	21.4	21.2	26.1	35.3	32.1	33.1	33.1	. . .	29.5	25.0	26.2
1996	22.3	21.1	21.1	25.6	34.4	31.6	32.9	32.3	. . .	29.1	25.2	26.3
1997	22.4	20.9	21.5	25.4	33.9	31.4	32.8	31.1	. . .	29.5	25.0	24.3
1998	22.2	20.6	21.6	25.1	33.6	31.4	31.7	27.7	. . .	30.1	24.9	24.1
1999	21.7	20.2	21.7	24.9	33.2	31.1	31.3	27.2	. . .	30.4	24.2	23.3
2000	22.0	20.6	21.8	24.6	32.8	30.6	30.9	27.8	. . .	30.6	23.6	22.7
2001	21.3	19.8	21.7	24.6	32.3	30.4	30.1	27.2	. . .	30.9	23.1	22.2
2002	20.3	20.0	21.8	24.2	31.7	30.3	29.0	27.1	. . .	30.7	22.5	21.7
2003	20.0	19.9	21.6	23.8	31.0	30.3	28.5	27.3	. . .	30.3	22.0	20.9
2004	20.0	20.3	21.7	23.5	30.7	30.3	27.6	26.6	. . .	30.0	21.9	20.4
2005	19.8	20.1	21.4	23.2	29.2	30.4	27.1	26.1	. . .	29.3	21.1	20.2
2006	19.9	20.2	20.9	23.1	29.0	29.8	27.2	25.5	. . .	29.1	21.1	20.1
2007	19.8	20.2	20.4	22.8	29.2	29.9	27.0	25.1	. . .	28.9	20.8	20.2
2008	19.1	20.5	20.4	22.2	29.0	28.9	26.6	24.6	25.1	27.1	20.8	19.5
2009	17.6	19.9	19.1	21.4	27.5	28.3	25.6	23.7	23.6	23.7	19.2	18.2
2010	17.2	19.7	19.0	20.9	27.1	27.6	25.0	24.3	23.8	22.2	19.0	17.9
2011	17.3	19.5	19.1	20.9	26.9	27.3	24.9	24.2	23.6	20.8	19.0	17.7
2012	17.3	19.4	19.2	20.4	26.9	26.5	24.7	23.9	22.9	19.6	18.7	17.6

Note: Industry includes manufacturing, mining, and construction.

[1]Unified Germany from 1991 onward; data for previous years relate to the former West Germany.
[2]Sectoral employment is only partially adjusted to U.S. concepts prior to 1984.
. . . = Not available.

Table 10-8. Percent of Employment in Manufacturing, Adjusted to U.S. Concepts, 12 Countries, 1970–2012

(Percent.)

Year	United States	Australia	Canada	France	Germany[1]	Italy	Japan	Korea	South Africa	Spain	Sweden	United Kingdom[2]
1970	26.4	24.4	22.3	...	39.5	27.7	27.4	13.2	...	...	27.7	...
1971	24.7	24.1	21.8	28.5	37.4	28.0	27.4	13.4	...	...	27.4	33.6
1972	24.3	23.5	21.8	28.8	36.9	27.9	27.3	13.6	...	...	27.2	32.7
1973	24.8	23.3	22.0	28.9	36.7	27.9	27.8	15.8	...	...	27.6	32.1
1974	24.2	22.9	21.7	28.8	36.5	28.1	27.6	17.3	...	...	28.4	32.2
1975	22.7	21.3	20.2	28.5	35.7	28.0	26.1	18.6	...	...	28.1	30.8
1976	22.8	21.2	19.2	28.0	35.2	27.7	25.8	21.3	...	...	27.0	30.0
1977	22.7	20.9	18.8	27.7	35.1	27.6	25.3	21.6	...	26.3	26.0	30.2
1978	22.7	19.9	18.9	27.2	34.8	27.3	24.8	22.3	...	26.2	25.0	29.9
1979	22.7	19.6	19.2	26.7	34.5	26.9	24.6	22.8	...	26.1	24.7	29.3
1980	22.1	19.4	19.1	26.3	34.0	26.9	25.0	21.6	...	25.9	24.3	28.1
1981	21.7	19.2	18.5	25.8	33.4	26.3	25.1	20.4	...	25.4	23.4	26.3
1982	20.4	18.6	17.2	24.4	32.8	25.8	24.7	21.1	...	24.1	22.5	25.3
1983	18.4	17.8	16.8	24.1	32.2	25.0	24.8	22.5	...	23.7	22.4	24.1
1984	18.5	17.3	17.1	23.7	32.1	23.9	25.2	23.2	...	23.9	22.5	24.7
1985	18.1	16.1	17.0	23.0	32.3	23.2	25.3	23.4	...	23.1	22.6	24.6
1986	17.8	15.6	17.1	22.3	32.3	22.9	24.9	24.7	...	22.9	22.8	24.4
1987	17.3	15.4	16.7	21.8	32.0	22.5	24.4	27.0	...	23.0	22.0	23.0
1988	17.3	15.3	16.6	21.4	31.6	22.6	24.5	27.7	...	22.7	21.7	23.3
1989	17.2	15.1	16.5	21.2	31.6	22.8	24.5	27.8	...	22.5	21.7	22.5
1990	16.8	14.4	15.8	21.3	31.6	22.6	24.3	27.2	...	22.5	21.0	22.1
1991	16.3	13.8	14.8	21.1	30.7	22.1	24.6	27.6	...	21.8	19.9	22.6
1992	15.9	13.7	14.3	20.4	29.5	22.0	24.6	26.2	...	21.7	18.9	21.1
1993	15.4	13.5	14.0	19.7	28.1	24.0	23.9	24.5	...	20.5	18.3	20.9
1994	15.4	13.5	14.0	19.3	26.6	24.3	23.4	24.0	...	20.0	18.2	18.9
1995	15.5	13.0	14.4	19.0	25.2	24.1	22.7	23.6	...	19.4	19.0	18.8
1996	15.3	12.8	14.4	18.7	24.3	23.7	22.5	22.7	...	18.9	19.3	19.1
1997	15.2	12.9	14.8	18.6	24.0	23.5	22.2	21.4	...	19.1	19.2	16.6
1998	15.0	12.3	15.0	18.4	24.1	23.7	21.4	19.6	...	19.6	19.1	16.3
1999	14.3	11.8	15.3	18.2	23.8	23.4	21.0	19.8	...	19.2	18.5	15.6
2000	14.4	12.1	15.3	17.9	23.9	22.9	20.7	20.3	...	18.9	18.0	14.8
2001	13.5	11.6	15.0	17.8	23.7	22.4	20.2	19.8	...	18.8	17.5	14.2
2002	12.6	11.5	15.0	17.4	23.6	22.3	19.1	19.1	...	18.4	16.8	13.7
2003	12.3	11.0	14.6	17.0	23.3	22.1	18.8	19.0	...	17.7	16.2	12.6
2004	11.8	10.9	14.5	16.7	23.1	21.9	18.3	18.5	...	17.1	16.0	11.8
2005	11.5	10.4	13.8	16.4	22.2	21.6	18.1	18.1	...	16.5	15.0	11.5
2006	11.3	10.0	12.9	16.1	22.0	21.2	18.3	17.5	...	15.8	14.7	11.2
2007	11.2	9.9	12.1	15.7	22.2	21.2	18.3	17.1	...	15.3	14.3	11.1
2008	10.9	9.8	11.5	14.6	22.2	20.1	18.1	16.8	14.4	14.7	13.9	10.4
2009	10.2	9.3	10.6	13.9	20.5	19.5	17.3	16.3	13.4	13.4	12.5	9.7
2010	10.1	8.9	10.3	13.3	20.1	18.9	16.9	16.9	13.3	12.9	12.1	9.8
2011	10.2	8.5	10.2	13.4	20.0	19.0	16.8	16.9	13.3	12.8	12.1	9.8
2012	10.3	8.4	10.2	13.0	19.8	18.6	16.6	16.6	12.7	12.7	11.7	9.8

[1]Unified Germany from 1991 onward; data for previous years relate to the former West Germany.
[2]Sectoral employment is only partially adjusted to U.S. concepts prior to 1984.
. . . = Not available.

Table 10-9. Percent of Employment in Services Adjusted to U.S. Concepts, 12 Countries, 1970–2012

(Percent.)

Year	United States	Australia	Canada	France	Germany[1]	Italy	Japan	Korea	South Africa	Spain	Sweden	United Kingdom[2]
1970	62.5	57.3	62.6	. . .	42.8	41.1	47.4	32.4	. . .	. . .	53.9	. . .
1971	64.0	57.9	63.1	44.7	44.4	40.9	48.5	34.1	. . .	. . .	55.1	55.1
1972	64.3	58.6	63.9	45.4	45.4	42.2	49.4	31.7	. . .	. . .	56.2	56.1
1973	63.9	59.3	63.9	46.3	46.0	43.4	49.9	30.6	. . .	. . .	56.6	56.4
1974	64.6	60.1	64.2	47.3	47.2	44.2	50.6	30.3	. . .	. . .	56.9	56.9
1975	66.6	61.5	65.8	48.2	48.8	45.1	52.0	30.9	. . .	. . .	57.7	58.5
1976	66.6	62.4	66.5	49.5	49.6	46.1	52.5	29.5	. . .	. . .	59.0	59.4
1977	66.7	62.9	67.2	50.4	50.3	46.6	53.3	31.1	. . .	42.3	60.2	59.5
1978	66.5	64.3	67.5	51.5	50.8	47.2	53.8	32.4	. . .	43.0	61.5	59.8
1979	66.5	64.5	67.4	52.4	51.4	48.2	54.5	34.5	. . .	44.2	62.3	60.2
1980	67.3	64.9	67.8	53.2	51.9	48.8	54.8	37.3	. . .	45.4	62.9	61.4
1981	67.8	65.2	68.3	54.1	52.8	50.2	55.3	38.2	. . .	46.9	63.8	63.2
1982	69.4	66.1	70.1	56.9	53.7	51.6	56.0	40.3	. . .	48.4	64.9	64.4
1983	71.0	67.4	70.8	57.8	54.5	52.6	56.6	41.4	. . .	48.8	65.5	65.5
1984	70.8	68.2	70.9	58.9	55.1	54.8	56.9	42.4	. . .	49.7	65.9	64.3
1985	71.3	69.1	71.0	60.2	55.4	56.4	57.0	44.5	. . .	50.9	66.1	65.0
1986	71.6	69.8	71.1	61.4	55.8	57.3	57.6	44.8	. . .	52.8	66.1	65.7
1987	72.2	70.3	71.3	62.2	56.4	58.1	58.5	44.3	. . .	53.4	66.8	66.6
1988	72.4	70.3	71.4	62.8	57.0	58.8	58.5	44.8	. . .	53.9	67.3	66.5
1989	72.6	70.3	71.5	63.3	57.4	59.3	58.7	45.6	. . .	54.9	67.3	66.7
1990	73.1	71.2	72.3	63.6	57.6	59.6	59.2	47.1	. . .	55.6	67.9	67.3
1991	73.9	72.5	73.6	64.2	56.1	60.2	59.4	48.9	. . .	57.1	69.0	66.8
1992	74.5	73.0	74.4	65.4	57.3	60.6	59.5	50.6	. . .	58.2	70.6	69.3
1993	75.1	72.8	75.0	66.8	58.7	61.1	60.3	52.8	. . .	60.0	71.6	70.0
1994	74.9	73.1	74.9	67.7	60.0	61.3	60.8	54.2	. . .	61.0	72.1	71.5
1995	74.8	73.7	74.8	68.4	61.5	62.0	61.4	55.1	. . .	61.7	71.5	71.8
1996	75.0	73.9	75.0	69.1	62.6	62.8	61.8	56.6	. . .	62.5	71.6	71.8
1997	75.0	74.1	74.7	69.4	63.2	63.2	62.1	58.2	. . .	62.4	71.9	74.1
1998	75.2	74.5	74.7	69.8	63.6	63.4	63.3	60.3	. . .	62.2	72.2	74.5
1999	75.8	74.9	74.8	70.2	64.0	64.0	63.8	61.4	. . .	62.5	72.7	75.4
2000	76.2	74.4	74.9	70.8	64.5	64.7	64.3	61.6	. . .	62.8	73.5	76.1
2001	77.1	75.4	75.5	70.9	65.1	65.0	65.2	62.8	. . .	62.6	74.3	76.7
2002	78.0	75.6	75.4	71.4	65.8	65.3	66.5	63.6	. . .	63.3	75.0	77.3
2003	78.3	76.2	75.7	71.9	66.4	65.3	67.1	63.9	. . .	64.0	75.5	78.1
2004	78.4	76.0	75.7	72.6	66.9	65.2	68.0	65.3	. . .	64.5	75.6	78.7
2005	78.6	76.3	75.8	73.1	68.5	65.4	68.7	66.0	. . .	65.5	76.6	78.8
2006	78.5	76.3	76.4	73.1	68.7	65.9	68.8	66.8	. . .	66.1	76.7	78.9
2007	78.8	76.5	77.1	73.7	68.5	66.1	68.9	67.6	. . .	66.6	76.9	78.8
2008	79.5	76.2	77.3	75.0	68.7	67.4	69.4	68.3	69.2	68.9	77.1	79.5
2009	80.9	76.7	78.7	75.6	70.8	68.0	70.4	69.3	71.3	72.1	78.6	80.7
2010	81.2	77.0	78.9	76.1	71.3	68.5	71.1	69.1	71.3	73.6	78.9	80.9
2011	81.1	77.6	78.8	76.1	71.5	69.0	71.3	69.5	71.8	75.0	79.0	81.1
2012	81.2	77.7	78.6	76.6	71.6	69.8	71.7	69.9	72.3	76.1	79.2	81.3

[1]Unified Germany from 1991 onward; data for previous years relate to the former West Germany.
[2]Sectoral employment is only partially adjusted to U.S. concepts prior to 1984.
. . . = Not available.

Table 10-10. Inactivity Rates, Adjusted to U.S. Concepts, 12 Countries, 1970–2012

(Percent.)

Year	United States	Australia	Canada	France	Germany[1]	Italy	Japan	Korea	South Africa	Spain	Sweden	United Kingdom[2]
1970	39.6	37.9	42.2	43.8	43.1	51.0	35.5	42.4	. . .	. . .	36.0	. . .
1971	39.8	37.8	41.9	43.9	43.5	51.3	35.8	42.6	. . .	. . .	35.8	37.2
1972	39.6	37.7	41.4	44.1	43.8	52.3	36.2	42.3	. . .	. . .	35.8	37.1
1973	39.2	37.4	40.3	43.9	43.7	52.4	36.0	41.6	. . .	. . .	35.9	36.9
1974	38.7	37.0	39.5	43.8	44.3	52.3	36.9	41.1	. . .	. . .	35.1	36.9
1975	38.8	36.8	38.9	44.3	45.0	52.3	37.6	41.7	. . .	. . .	34.1	36.9
1976	38.4	37.3	37.5	44.1	45.4	52.0	37.6	40.3	. . .	. . .	34.0	37.0
1977	37.7	37.3	37.2	43.8	45.6	51.8	37.5	40.6	. . .	48.1	34.0	37.2
1978	36.8	38.1	36.3	43.9	45.6	52.2	37.2	40.1	. . .	48.6	33.9	37.4
1979	36.3	38.4	35.5	43.9	45.5	52.0	37.3	40.5	. . .	49.1	33.4	37.3
1980	36.2	37.9	35.0	44.0	45.3	51.9	37.4	41.0	. . .	49.6	33.1	37.2
1981	36.1	38.1	34.3	44.2	45.3	51.7	37.4	41.5	. . .	50.2	33.2	37.3
1982	36.0	38.3	35.1	42.3	45.4	52.3	37.3	41.4	. . .	50.3	33.2	38.1
1983	36.0	38.6	34.8	42.7	45.7	52.5	36.9	42.3	. . .	50.4	33.3	38.4
1984	35.6	38.5	34.5	42.9	45.6	52.7	37.3	44.2	. . .	50.9	33.4	37.2
1985	35.2	38.3	34.0	43.0	45.3	52.8	37.8	43.4	. . .	51.3	33.1	37.1
1986	34.7	37.2	33.6	42.9	45.1	52.2	37.9	42.9	. . .	51.4	33.0	37.1
1987	34.4	37.0	33.2	43.3	45.0	52.4	38.2	41.7	. . .	50.2	33.5	36.8
1988	34.1	36.7	32.9	43.8	44.9	52.6	38.2	41.5	. . .	49.8	33.1	36.2
1989	33.5	35.8	32.5	43.8	44.8	52.7	37.9	40.4	. . .	49.9	32.7	35.7
1990	33.5	35.3	32.6	44.3	45.0	52.8	37.4	40.0	. . .	49.8	32.6	35.6
1991	33.8	35.8	33.2	44.7	41.2	52.2	36.9	39.4	. . .	49.8	33.0	36.3
1992	33.6	36.1	34.1	44.6	41.9	52.5	36.7	39.1	. . .	50.2	34.2	37.1
1993	33.7	36.4	34.5	44.7	42.2	50.6	36.8	39.1	. . .	50.3	35.5	37.4
1994	33.4	36.1	34.8	44.8	42.6	51.2	37.1	38.4	. . .	50.3	36.3	37.6
1995	33.4	35.4	35.1	44.8	42.9	51.4	37.2	38.1	. . .	50.4	36.0	37.6
1996	33.2	35.4	35.2	44.5	42.9	51.3	37.2	37.9	. . .	50.1	36.1	37.6
1997	32.9	35.7	34.9	44.9	42.7	51.3	37.0	37.5	. . .	49.8	36.7	37.5
1998	32.9	35.7	34.6	44.9	42.3	50.9	37.4	39.4	. . .	49.4	37.1	37.6
1999	32.9	36.0	34.2	44.8	43.1	50.7	38.0	39.4	. . .	48.8	37.3	37.2
2000	32.9	35.6	34.0	44.6	43.3	50.5	38.3	38.8	. . .	47.7	36.3	37.2
2001	33.2	35.6	33.9	44.8	43.3	50.3	38.8	38.6	. . .	47.2	36.3	37.3
2002	33.4	35.7	32.9	44.6	43.6	50.1	39.6	38.0	. . .	45.9	36.1	37.1
2003	33.8	35.4	32.3	44.5	44.0	50.4	40.1	38.5	. . .	44.7	36.1	37.1
2004	34.0	35.4	32.4	44.6	43.6	50.9	40.4	37.9	. . .	43.8	36.4	37.1
2005	34.0	34.6	32.7	44.7	42.5	51.3	40.5	38.0	. . .	42.9	35.2	36.9
2006	33.8	34.2	32.8	44.7	41.9	51.1	40.4	38.1	. . .	41.9	35.1	36.5
2007	34.0	33.8	32.5	44.6	41.7	51.4	40.2	38.2	. . .	41.3	34.7	36.6
2008	34.0	33.3	32.3	44.5	41.6	51.0	40.4	38.5	42.0	40.4	34.7	36.5
2009	34.6	33.3	32.8	44.2	41.5	51.6	40.7	39.2	43.9	40.3	35.2	36.6
2010	35.3	33.6	33.0	44.2	41.4	51.9	40.9	39.0	45.7	40.2	35.3	36.8
2011	35.9	33.5	33.2	44.4	40.8	51.9	41.3	38.9	45.7	40.2	34.9	36.8
2012	36.3	33.8	33.3	44.1	40.8	51.0	41.6	38.7	45.2	40.2	34.8	36.6

[1]Unified Germany from 1991 onward; data for previous years relate to the former West Germany.
[2]Sectoral employment is only partially adjusted to U.S. concepts prior to 1984.
. . . = Not available.

Table 10-11. Inactivity Rates for Men, Adjusted to U.S. Concepts, 12 Countries, 1970–2012

(Percent.)

Year	United States	Australia	Canada	France	Germany[1]	Italy	Japan	Korea	South Africa	Spain	Sweden	United Kingdom[2]
1970	20.3	15.9	22.2	24.4	21.2	26.3	18.5	22.1	. . .	. . .	21.5	. . .
1971	20.9	16.2	22.7	25.3	22.5	26.6	18.1	22.8	. . .	. . .	22.0	16.9
1972	21.1	16.4	22.5	26.0	23.6	28.0	18.2	22.5	. . .	. . .	22.7	17.2
1973	21.2	16.9	21.8	26.3	24.2	28.8	18.2	23.2	. . .	. . .	23.2	17.7
1974	21.3	17.3	21.3	26.5	25.4	29.0	18.4	22.3	. . .	. . .	23.2	18.5
1975	22.1	17.8	21.6	27.4	26.7	29.4	19.0	22.6	. . .	. . .	23.0	18.7
1976	22.5	18.5	20.8	27.8	27.5	29.6	19.0	22.6	. . .	. . .	23.5	19.1
1977	22.3	19.0	21.0	28.0	28.1	30.5	19.7	21.3	. . .	21.2	24.4	19.8
1978	22.1	20.2	20.7	28.6	28.4	31.3	20.0	22.1	. . .	22.2	24.9	20.7
1979	22.2	20.5	20.4	29.1	28.5	31.7	20.3	23.1	. . .	23.2	24.9	21.2
1980	22.6	20.9	20.5	29.8	28.8	32.1	20.7	23.6	. . .	24.3	25.1	21.5
1981	23.0	21.2	20.6	30.5	29.1	32.2	20.7	24.2	. . .	25.0	26.2	21.9
1982	23.4	21.6	22.1	29.0	29.4	33.1	21.0	25.0	. . .	25.8	26.6	23.0
1983	23.6	22.4	22.3	29.8	29.9	33.8	20.9	26.3	. . .	26.7	27.1	23.9
1984	23.6	22.7	22.5	30.7	30.0	34.4	21.6	27.9	. . .	27.7	27.6	23.5
1985	23.7	23.3	22.5	31.0	29.9	34.7	22.4	27.7	. . .	28.8	27.5	23.9
1986	23.7	23.3	22.4	31.4	29.8	34.8	22.7	27.9	. . .	29.4	27.5	24.5
1987	23.8	23.8	22.6	32.2	30.1	35.5	23.4	27.5	. . .	30.0	28.7	24.5
1988	23.8	24.0	22.8	33.0	30.4	36.1	23.5	27.1	. . .	30.6	28.4	24.3
1989	23.6	23.6	22.8	33.4	30.9	36.6	23.6	26.6	. . .	31.1	27.9	24.1
1990	23.6	23.5	23.4	34.4	31.5	37.0	23.3	26.0	. . .	31.4	28.0	24.3
1991	24.2	24.4	24.5	35.3	28.9	36.3	22.9	25.0	. . .	31.9	28.3	25.3
1992	24.2	24.9	25.6	35.5	29.9	36.9	22.5	24.3	. . .	33.3	29.5	26.5
1993	24.6	25.5	26.3	36.2	30.7	35.7	22.4	24.3	. . .	34.2	30.8	27.3
1994	24.9	25.5	26.6	36.6	31.2	36.6	22.8	23.7	. . .	35.1	31.5	27.7
1995	25.0	25.3	27.2	36.9	31.9	37.2	23.0	23.6	. . .	35.7	31.2	28.0
1996	25.1	25.5	27.5	36.6	32.2	37.5	22.9	23.8	. . .	35.7	31.4	28.3
1997	25.0	26.0	27.3	37.0	32.4	37.7	22.9	23.9	. . .	35.8	31.9	28.5
1998	25.1	26.3	27.3	37.6	32.1	37.6	23.4	24.9	. . .	35.4	32.0	28.8
1999	25.3	26.6	27.1	37.5	33.9	37.7	23.9	25.6	. . .	35.0	32.5	28.6
2000	25.2	26.9	27.2	37.4	34.4	37.7	24.5	25.6	. . .	34.3	31.5	28.9
2001	25.6	27.3	27.3	37.9	34.7	38.0	25.2	25.7	. . .	33.9	32.0	29.1
2002	25.9	27.5	26.6	37.7	35.4	37.8	26.2	25.0	. . .	33.2	31.9	29.2
2003	26.5	27.6	26.3	38.1	36.3	38.4	27.0	25.3	. . .	32.5	32.0	29.2
2004	26.7	27.4	26.5	38.5	35.9	39.1	27.6	25.0	. . .	32.1	32.3	29.4
2005	26.7	27.0	26.8	38.7	34.8	39.4	27.7	25.4	. . .	31.5	30.8	29.5
2006	26.5	26.8	27.4	38.9	34.5	39.4	27.8	25.9	. . .	31.1	30.8	29.2
2007	26.8	26.7	27.2	39.1	34.6	39.7	27.6	26.0	. . .	31.0	30.5	29.3
2008	27.0	26.4	27.0	39.0	34.6	39.8	28.0	26.5	34.2	30.7	30.5	29.2
2009	28.0	26.7	28.0	38.9	34.7	40.6	28.7	26.9	36.3	31.6	31.1	29.8
2010	28.8	26.8	28.2	39.0	34.9	41.0	29.1	27.0	38.2	32.2	30.7	30.2
2011	29.5	26.9	28.3	39.3	34.4	41.3	29.5	26.9	38.8	32.8	30.7	30.3
2012	29.8	27.4	28.6	38.9	34.5	40.8	30.2	26.7	38.3	33.3	30.8	30.2

[1]Unified Germany from 1991 onward; data for previous years relate to the former West Germany.
[2]Sectoral employment is only partially adjusted to U.S. concepts prior to 1984.
. . . = Not available.

Table 10-12. Inactivity Rates for Women, Adjusted to U.S. Concepts, 12 Countries, 1970–2012

(Percent.)

Year	United States	Australia	Canada	France	Germany[1]	Italy	Japan	Korea	South Africa	Spain	Sweden	United Kingdom[2]
1970	56.7	59.6	61.7	61.0	61.6	73.6	50.8	60.7	...	...	50.0	...
1971	56.6	59.0	60.6	60.6	61.5	73.7	51.4	60.5	...	...	49.1	55.4
1972	56.1	58.8	59.8	60.2	61.0	74.4	52.2	60.4	...	...	48.5	55.1
1973	55.3	57.6	58.1	59.8	60.5	73.9	52.0	58.5	...	...	48.3	54.2
1974	54.3	56.5	57.0	59.4	60.6	73.5	53.5	58.5	...	...	46.7	53.6
1975	53.7	55.5	55.6	59.6	60.7	73.2	54.2	59.6	...	...	44.8	53.4
1976	52.7	55.7	53.8	58.7	60.7	72.4	54.1	56.8	...	...	44.1	53.3
1977	51.6	55.2	52.9	58.0	60.7	71.1	53.1	58.3	...	72.3	43.3	53.1
1978	50.0	55.5	51.5	57.6	60.4	71.2	52.5	56.7	...	72.3	42.5	52.6
1979	49.1	55.7	50.2	57.2	60.1	70.5	52.4	56.7	...	72.4	41.5	52.0
1980	48.5	54.5	49.0	56.9	59.7	69.9	52.8	57.2	...	72.6	40.7	51.4
1981	47.9	54.5	47.7	56.5	59.3	69.6	52.7	57.7	...	73.0	39.9	51.4
1982	47.4	54.6	47.7	54.2	59.3	69.7	52.4	56.6	...	72.6	39.5	51.9
1983	47.1	54.5	46.9	54.2	59.5	69.5	51.5	57.2	...	71.9	39.2	51.6
1984	46.4	53.9	46.1	53.8	59.3	69.5	52.0	59.3	...	72.0	38.9	49.8
1985	45.5	52.9	45.0	53.7	58.8	69.3	52.2	58.1	...	71.9	38.5	49.3
1986	44.7	50.7	44.3	53.2	58.6	68.1	52.2	56.9	...	71.5	38.3	48.6
1987	44.0	50.0	43.5	53.2	58.3	67.8	52.2	55.0	...	68.8	38.1	47.9
1988	43.4	49.2	42.6	53.4	57.7	67.7	52.0	55.0	...	67.4	37.6	47.2
1989	42.6	47.8	41.9	53.1	57.3	67.4	51.3	53.4	...	67.2	37.2	46.4
1990	42.5	46.8	41.5	53.2	56.9	67.2	50.7	53.0	...	66.7	37.0	46.1
1991	42.6	47.0	41.6	53.2	52.3	66.8	50.2	52.9	...	66.3	37.6	46.4
1992	42.2	46.9	42.2	52.8	52.6	66.7	50.0	52.9	...	65.7	38.7	46.8
1993	42.1	47.1	42.4	52.3	52.8	64.3	50.3	52.9	...	65.3	39.9	46.7
1994	41.2	46.4	42.6	52.1	52.9	64.5	50.5	52.2	...	64.5	40.8	46.7
1995	41.1	45.3	42.7	51.9	52.9	64.3	50.7	51.6	...	64.0	40.5	46.5
1996	40.7	45.0	42.7	51.6	52.6	63.9	50.6	51.1	...	63.5	40.6	46.2
1997	40.2	45.2	42.2	52.0	52.2	63.7	50.3	50.2	...	62.8	41.4	45.8
1998	40.2	45.0	41.5	51.6	51.8	63.1	50.6	52.9	...	62.5	42.0	45.6
1999	40.0	45.0	40.9	51.3	51.7	62.6	51.2	52.4	...	61.7	41.9	45.1
2000	40.1	44.2	40.5	51.1	51.6	62.1	51.3	51.2	...	60.3	40.8	44.8
2001	40.2	43.8	40.2	51.0	51.4	61.6	51.5	50.7	...	59.7	40.5	44.9
2002	40.4	43.7	39.1	50.7	51.3	61.3	52.1	50.2	...	57.9	40.1	44.5
2003	40.5	42.9	38.1	50.3	51.2	61.4	52.4	51.0	...	56.3	40.1	44.4
2004	40.8	43.1	38.1	50.2	50.8	61.7	52.4	50.1	...	55.0	40.2	44.2
2005	40.7	42.0	38.4	50.1	49.7	62.1	52.4	49.9	...	53.8	39.4	43.9
2006	40.6	41.4	38.2	50.0	48.8	61.9	52.1	49.7	...	52.3	39.2	43.4
2007	40.7	40.7	37.5	49.7	48.4	62.1	51.9	49.8	...	51.3	38.8	43.6
2008	40.5	40.0	37.4	49.5	48.2	61.4	52.0	50.0	49.2	49.7	38.8	43.3
2009	40.8	39.9	37.5	49.1	47.9	61.8	51.9	50.8	51.0	48.6	39.3	43.2
2010	41.4	40.2	37.6	49.0	47.6	61.8	51.9	50.6	52.6	47.9	39.7	43.2
2011	41.9	40.0	37.8	49.1	46.8	61.6	52.3	50.3	52.1	47.2	39.0	43.0
2012	42.3	40.1	37.9	48.8	46.8	60.3	52.3	50.1	51.7	46.8	38.7	42.8

[1]Unified Germany from 1991 onward; data for previous years relate to the former West Germany.
[2]Sectoral employment is only partially adjusted to U.S. concepts prior to 1984.
. . . = Not available.

Table 10-13. Consumer Price Indexes, 16 Countries, 1950–2012

(1982–1984 =100)

Year	United States	Australia	Austria	Bel-gium	Canada	Denmark	France	Ger-many[1]	Italy	Japan	Nether-lands	Norway	Spain	Sweden	Switzer-land	United Kingdom
1950	24.1	12.6	...	24.0	21.6	12.2	11.2	34.0	...	...	21.0	13.5	5.5	13.4	33.2	9.8
1951	26.0	15.0	...	26.3	23.8	13.6	13.1	36.6	...	...	23.1	15.7	6.0	15.7	34.8	10.7
1952	26.5	17.6	...	26.5	24.5	13.9	14.7	37.3	...	...	23.1	17.1	5.9	16.8	35.7	11.7
1953	26.7	18.4	...	26.4	24.2	13.8	14.5	36.7	10.3	...	23.1	17.5	6.0	16.9	35.4	12.1
1954	26.9	18.7	...	26.9	24.4	14.1	14.4	36.8	10.6	...	24.0	18.2	6.1	17.0	35.7	12.3
1955	26.8	19.0	...	26.7	24.4	15.0	14.6	37.3	10.9	...	24.5	18.4	6.3	17.5	36.0	12.8
1956	27.2	20.1	...	27.4	24.7	15.8	14.9	38.4	11.2	...	24.9	19.1	6.7	18.4	36.5	13.5
1957	28.1	20.7	...	28.2	25.6	16.0	15.3	39.1	11.4	...	26.5	19.7	7.4	19.2	37.2	14.0
1958	28.9	20.8	31.6	28.6	26.3	16.2	17.6	40.0	11.7	...	27.0	20.6	8.4	20.0	37.9	14.4
1959	29.1	21.2	32.0	29.0	26.4	16.5	18.7	40.3	11.7	...	27.2	21.2	9.0	20.2	37.7	14.5
1960	29.6	22.0	32.6	29.0	26.8	16.9	19.4	40.9	11.9	...	27.9	21.2	9.1	21.0	38.2	14.6
1961	29.9	22.5	33.8	29.3	27.1	17.6	20.0	42.0	12.2	...	28.4	21.7	9.2	21.5	38.9	15.1
1962	30.2	22.5	35.3	29.8	27.5	18.8	21.0	43.1	12.7	...	28.9	22.8	9.7	22.5	40.6	15.8
1963	30.6	22.6	36.2	30.4	27.8	19.7	22.0	44.4	13.7	...	30.0	23.3	10.6	23.2	42.0	16.1
1964	31.0	23.2	37.6	31.7	28.3	20.5	22.7	45.5	14.5	...	31.7	24.6	11.3	23.9	43.3	16.6
1965	31.5	24.0	39.5	32.9	29.0	21.8	23.3	46.9	15.2	...	33.3	25.7	12.8	25.2	44.8	17.4
1966	32.4	24.8	40.3	34.3	30.2	23.3	23.9	48.5	15.5	...	35.3	26.6	13.6	26.8	46.9	18.1
1967	33.4	25.7	41.9	35.3	31.3	25.0	24.6	49.4	16.1	...	36.4	27.7	14.5	27.9	48.8	18.6
1968	34.8	26.3	43.1	36.3	32.5	27.0	25.7	50.2	16.3	...	37.7	28.8	15.2	28.5	50.0	19.4
1969	36.7	27.2	44.4	37.6	34.0	27.9	27.3	51.1	16.7	...	40.5	29.5	15.5	29.2	51.2	20.5
1970	38.8	28.1	46.4	39.1	35.1	29.7	28.8	52.9	17.5	38.4	42.3	32.6	16.4	31.3	53.1	21.8
1971	40.5	29.9	48.5	40.8	36.1	31.5	30.3	55.7	18.4	41.0	45.5	34.8	17.7	33.6	56.6	23.8
1972	41.8	31.7	51.6	43.0	37.8	33.6	32.2	58.7	19.4	42.9	49.1	37.2	19.2	35.6	60.4	25.5
1973	44.4	34.5	55.5	46.0	40.8	36.7	34.6	62.8	21.6	48.0	53.0	40.1	21.4	38.0	65.6	27.8
1974	49.3	39.9	60.8	51.8	45.3	42.3	39.3	67.2	25.7	59.0	58.1	43.8	24.8	41.7	72.0	32.3
1975	53.8	45.9	65.9	58.5	50.1	46.4	43.9	71.2	30.0	66.0	64.0	48.9	29.0	45.8	76.9	40.1
1976	56.9	52.0	70.8	63.8	53.7	50.5	48.2	74.2	35.1	72.2	69.6	53.4	34.1	50.6	78.2	46.8
1977	60.6	58.4	74.7	68.4	58.1	56.2	52.7	77.0	41.0	78.0	74.3	58.4	42.4	56.3	79.2	54.2
1978	65.2	63.1	77.3	71.4	63.2	61.8	57.5	79.1	46.0	81.4	77.3	63.1	50.8	62.0	80.0	58.7
1979	72.6	68.9	80.2	74.6	69.1	67.7	63.6	82.3	52.8	84.4	80.6	66.0	58.8	66.4	82.9	66.6
1980	82.4	75.8	85.3	79.6	76.0	76.1	72.3	86.8	64.0	91.0	85.8	73.3	67.9	75.5	86.3	78.5
1981	90.9	83.0	91.0	85.6	85.5	85.0	82.0	92.2	75.4	95.3	91.6	83.2	77.8	84.6	91.9	87.9
1982	96.5	92.5	96.0	93.1	94.9	93.6	91.6	97.1	87.8	98.0	97.1	92.6	89.0	91.9	97.1	95.4
1983	99.6	101.8	99.2	100.3	100.4	100.1	100.5	100.2	100.7	99.8	99.8	100.5	99.9	100.0	99.9	99.8
1984	103.9	105.8	104.8	106.6	104.7	106.3	107.9	102.7	111.5	102.2	103.1	106.9	111.1	108.1	103.0	104.8
1985	107.6	112.9	108.2	111.8	108.9	111.3	114.2	104.8	121.8	104.2	105.4	112.9	120.9	116.1	106.5	111.1
1986	109.6	123.1	110.0	113.3	113.4	115.4	117.2	104.7	129.0	104.9	105.6	120.9	131.6	121.0	107.3	114.9
1987	113.6	133.6	111.6	115.0	118.4	120.1	120.9	104.9	135.1	104.9	105.1	131.5	138.5	126.0	108.9	119.7
1988	118.3	143.3	113.7	116.4	123.0	125.5	124.2	106.2	141.9	105.7	105.8	140.2	145.2	133.4	110.8	125.6
1989	124.0	154.1	116.6	120.0	129.3	131.5	128.6	109.2	150.8	108.1	107.0	146.6	155.0	142.0	114.3	135.4
1990	130.7	165.4	120.4	124.1	135.5	135.0	133.0	112.1	160.5	111.4	109.6	152.6	165.4	156.7	120.5	148.2
1991	136.2	170.6	124.4	128.1	143.1	138.2	137.3	116.3	170.6	115.0	113.8	157.9	175.2	171.5	127.6	156.9
1992	140.3	172.3	129.4	131.2	145.2	141.1	140.5	122.3	179.6	117.0	118.1	161.6	185.6	175.6	132.8	162.7
1993	144.5	175.4	134.1	134.8	147.9	142.9	143.5	127.6	187.8	118.5	120.5	165.2	194.1	183.8	137.1	165.3
1994	148.2	178.8	138.1	138.0	148.1	145.7	145.8	131.2	195.5	119.2	123.8	167.6	203.3	187.8	138.3	169.3
1995	152.4	187.1	141.2	140.1	151.4	148.8	148.4	133.4	205.8	119.1	126.0	171.8	212.8	192.4	140.8	175.2
1996	156.9	192.0	143.8	142.9	153.6	151.9	151.3	135.3	214.0	119.2	128.7	173.8	220.3	193.5	141.9	179.4
1997	160.5	192.4	145.7	145.3	156.2	155.2	153.2	137.9	218.3	121.5	131.5	178.4	224.7	194.7	142.7	185.1
1998	163.0	194.1	147.1	146.6	157.8	158.1	154.3	139.3	222.6	122.2	134.1	182.4	228.8	194.2	142.7	191.4
1999	166.6	197.0	147.9	148.3	160.5	162.0	155.0	140.0	226.3	121.8	137.0	186.6	234.1	195.1	143.8	194.3
2000	172.2	205.7	151.4	152.1	164.9	166.8	157.7	142.0	232.1	121.0	140.2	192.4	242.1	196.9	146.1	200.1
2001	177.1	214.8	155.4	155.8	169.0	170.7	160.3	144.8	238.5	120.1	146.1	198.2	250.8	201.6	147.5	203.6
2002	179.9	221.2	158.2	158.4	172.0	174.0	163.4	146.9	244.5	119.0	150.9	200.8	259.6	206.0	148.5	207.0
2003	184.0	227.2	160.3	160.9	177.6	178.5	166.8	148.5	251.0	118.7	154.0	205.7	267.5	209.9	149.4	213.0
2004	188.9	232.6	163.6	164.3	180.9	180.5	170.3	150.9	256.6	118.7	156.0	206.6	275.6	210.7	150.6	219.4
2005	195.3	238.8	167.4	168.8	184.9	183.8	173.4	153.2	261.5	118.3	158.6	209.9	284.9	211.7	152.5	225.6
2006	201.6	247.3	169.9	171.9	188.5	187.3	176.2	155.7	267.1	118.7	160.4	214.7	294.9	214.5	154.1	232.8
2007	207.3	253.1	173.6	175.0	192.7	190.5	178.9	159.2	272.0	118.7	163.0	216.3	303.1	219.3	155.2	242.7
2008	215.3	264.1	179.1	182.9	197.2	197.0	183.9	163.3	281.1	120.3	167.1	224.5	315.5	226.8	158.9	252.4
2009	214.5	268.8	180.0	182.8	197.7	199.6	184.1	163.9	283.3	118.7	169.0	229.2	314.6	225.7	158.1	251.1
2010	218.1	276.6	183.3	186.8	201.3	204.2	186.9	165.8	287.7	117.8	171.2	234.9	320.2	228.3	159.2	262.7
2011	224.9	285.8	189.3	193.4	207.2	209.8	190.8	169.6	295.7	117.5	175.2	237.8	330.5	235.1	159.7	276.3
2012	229.6	290.8	194.0	198.9	210.3	214.9	194.6	173.0	304.6	117.5	179.5	239.6	338.6	237.2	158.5	285.2

[1]Unified Germany from 1991 onward; data for previous years relate to the former West Germany.
... = Not available.

Table 10-14. Consumer Price Indexes, Annual Percent Change, 16 Countries, 1950–2012

(Percent.)

Year	United States	Austalia	Austria	Belgium	Canada	Den-mark	France	Ger-many[1]	Italy	Japan	Nether-lands	Norway	Spain	Sweden	Switzer-land	United Kingdom
1950–2012	3.7	5.2	...	3.5	3.7	4.7	4.7	2.7	...	...	3.5	4.7	6.9	4.7	2.6	5.6
1960–2012	4.0	5.1	3.5	3.8	4.0	5.0	4.5	2.8	6.4	...	3.6	4.8	7.2	4.8	2.8	5.9
1970–2012	4.3	5.7	3.5	3.9	4.4	4.8	4.7	2.9	7.0	2.7	3.5	4.9	7.5	4.9	2.6	6.3
1980–2012	3.3	4.3	2.6	2.9	3.2	3.3	3.1	2.2	5.0	0.8	2.3	3.8	5.1	3.6	1.9	4.1
1990–2012	2.6	2.6	2.2	2.2	2.0	2.1	1.7	2.0	3.0	0.2	2.3	2.1	3.3	1.9	1.3	3.0
2000–2012	2.4	2.9	2.1	2.3	2.0	2.1	1.8	1.7	2.3	-0.2	2.1	1.8	2.8	1.6	0.7	3.0
2010–2012	2.6	2.5	2.9	3.2	2.2	2.6	2.0	2.1	2.9	-0.2	2.4	1.0	2.8	1.9	-0.2	4.2
1950–1955	2.1	8.6	...	2.2	2.4	4.3	5.4	1.9	...	...	3.0	6.4	2.8	5.4	1.6	5.5
1955–1960	2.0	3.0	...	1.7	1.9	2.3	5.8	1.9	1.9	...	2.7	2.8	7.6	3.7	1.2	2.6
1960–1965	1.3	1.8	3.9	2.5	1.6	5.3	3.7	2.8	4.9	...	3.6	4.0	7.0	3.7	3.2	3.5
1965–1970	4.3	3.2	3.3	3.5	3.9	6.4	4.3	2.4	3.0	...	4.9	4.9	5.1	4.4	3.5	4.6
1970–1975	6.8	10.3	7.3	8.4	7.4	9.3	8.8	6.1	11.3	11.4	8.6	8.4	12.1	8.0	7.7	13.0
1975–1980	8.9	10.6	5.3	6.4	8.7	10.4	10.5	4.0	16.3	6.6	6.0	8.4	18.6	10.5	2.3	14.4
1980–1985	5.5	8.3	4.9	7.0	7.4	7.9	9.6	3.8	13.7	2.7	4.2	9.0	12.2	9.0	4.3	7.2
1985–1990	4.0	7.9	2.2	2.1	4.5	3.9	3.1	1.4	5.7	1.3	0.8	6.2	6.5	6.2	2.5	5.9
1990–1995	3.1	2.5	3.2	2.4	2.2	2.0	2.2	3.5	5.1	1.4	2.8	2.4	5.2	4.2	3.2	3.4
1995–2000	2.5	1.9	1.4	1.7	1.7	2.3	1.2	1.3	2.4	0.3	2.2	2.3	2.6	0.5	0.7	2.7
2000–2005	2.5	3.0	2.0	2.1	2.3	2.0	1.9	1.5	2.4	-0.5	2.5	1.8	3.3	1.5	0.9	2.4
2005–2010	2.2	3.0	1.8	2.0	1.7	2.1	1.5	1.6	1.9	-0.1	1.5	2.3	2.4	1.5	0.9	3.1
1950–1951	7.9	19.4	...	9.4	10.4	11.7	16.9	7.6	...	...	9.6	16.2	9.4	16.9	4.8	9.1
1951–1952	1.9	17.2	...	0.9	2.9	2.3	11.8	2.1	...	...	0.0	9.3	-2.0	7.2	2.6	9.2
1952–1953	0.8	4.5	...	-0.3	-1.4	-0.7	-1.2	-1.7	...	...	0.0	2.1	1.6	0.6	-0.7	3.1
1953–1954	0.7	1.6	...	1.8	0.7	1.8	-0.4	0.4	2.8	...	4.0	4.2	1.2	0.6	0.7	2.0
1954–1955	-0.4	1.5	...	-0.5	0.0	6.8	1.2	1.4	2.3	...	1.9	1.0	4.0	2.7	0.9	4.4
1955–1956	1.5	5.7	...	2.4	1.4	5.1	2.0	2.8	3.4	...	1.9	4.0	5.9	5.0	1.5	5.1
1956–1957	3.3	2.9	...	3.2	3.5	1.2	2.7	2.0	1.3	...	6.5	2.9	10.8	4.5	1.9	3.5
1957–1958	2.8	0.7	...	1.3	2.7	1.0	15.0	2.3	2.8	...	1.7	4.6	13.4	4.3	1.8	3.2
1958–1959	0.7	2.1	1.1	1.2	0.7	2.0	6.2	0.6	-0.4	...	0.8	2.7	7.3	0.8	-0.7	0.4
1959–1960	1.7	3.7	1.9	0.3	1.3	2.3	3.7	1.6	2.3	...	2.5	0.0	1.2	4.1	1.4	1.0
1960–1961	1.0	2.3	3.6	1.0	1.3	4.5	3.3	2.5	2.1	...	1.7	2.6	0.8	2.2	1.9	3.5
1961–1962	1.0	-0.3	4.4	1.4	1.3	6.5	4.7	2.8	4.7	...	1.9	5.0	5.7	4.8	4.3	4.3
1962–1963	1.3	0.6	2.7	2.1	1.3	5.2	4.8	3.0	7.5	...	3.8	2.4	8.7	3.0	3.4	1.9
1963–1964	1.3	2.9	3.8	4.2	1.9	3.7	3.4	2.4	5.9	...	5.5	5.5	7.0	3.1	3.1	3.3
1964–1965	1.6	3.4	5.0	4.1	2.4	6.4	2.5	3.2	4.6	...	5.2	4.4	13.2	5.2	3.4	4.7
1965–1966	2.9	3.3	2.2	4.2	4.2	6.9	2.7	3.3	2.3	...	5.8	3.5	6.2	6.6	4.7	3.9
1966–1967	3.1	3.5	4.0	2.9	3.4	7.4	2.6	1.9	3.7	...	3.1	4.1	6.4	4.0	4.0	2.6
1967–1968	4.2	2.5	2.8	2.8	3.9	8.0	4.6	1.6	1.4	...	3.7	3.9	5.0	2.0	2.4	4.7
1968–1969	5.5	3.3	3.0	3.7	4.8	3.5	6.5	1.8	2.7	...	7.4	2.5	2.2	2.7	2.5	5.4
1969–1970	5.7	3.4	4.4	3.9	3.0	6.5	5.2	3.6	4.9	...	4.4	10.5	5.7	6.9	3.6	6.4
1970–1971	4.4	6.1	4.7	4.3	3.0	5.9	5.5	5.2	4.8	6.7	7.5	6.7	8.2	7.4	6.6	9.4
1971–1972	3.2	6.0	6.3	5.4	4.8	6.7	6.2	5.4	5.7	4.6	7.8	6.8	8.3	6.0	6.7	7.1
1972–1973	6.2	9.1	7.5	7.0	7.8	9.3	7.3	7.1	10.8	11.8	8.0	7.8	11.4	6.7	8.7	9.1
1973–1974	11.0	15.4	9.5	12.7	11.0	15.3	13.7	6.9	19.1	23.1	9.6	9.1	15.7	9.9	9.8	16.0
1974–1975	9.1	15.2	8.4	12.8	10.7	9.6	11.8	6.0	17.0	11.8	10.2	11.7	17.0	9.8	6.7	24.2
1975–1976	5.8	13.3	7.3	9.2	7.2	9.0	9.6	4.2	16.8	9.5	8.8	9.3	17.6	10.4	1.7	16.5
1976–1977	6.5	12.3	5.5	7.1	8.0	11.1	9.4	3.7	17.0	8.0	6.7	9.2	24.5	11.3	1.3	15.8
1977–1978	7.6	8.0	3.6	4.5	8.9	10.0	9.1	2.7	12.1	4.4	4.1	8.1	19.8	10.1	1.1	8.3
1978–1979	11.3	9.1	3.7	4.5	9.3	9.6	10.8	4.1	14.8	3.6	4.2	4.6	15.7	7.2	3.6	13.4
1979–1980	13.5	10.1	6.4	6.6	10.0	12.3	13.6	5.4	21.2	7.8	6.5	11.0	15.6	13.6	4.0	18.0
1980–1981	10.3	9.5	6.8	7.6	12.5	11.7	13.4	6.3	17.8	4.8	6.7	13.4	14.5	12.1	6.5	11.9
1981–1982	6.2	11.4	5.4	8.7	10.9	10.1	11.8	5.2	16.5	2.8	6.0	11.4	14.4	8.6	5.7	8.6
1982–1983	3.2	10.0	3.4	7.7	5.8	6.9	9.6	3.2	14.7	1.8	2.8	8.5	12.2	8.9	2.9	4.6
1983–1984	4.3	4.0	5.6	6.4	4.3	6.3	7.4	2.5	10.8	2.4	3.3	6.4	11.3	8.0	3.0	5.0
1984–1985	3.6	6.7	3.2	4.9	4.0	4.7	5.8	2.0	9.2	2.0	2.2	5.6	8.8	7.4	3.4	6.1
1985–1986	1.9	9.1	1.7	1.3	4.1	3.7	2.7	-0.1	5.9	0.7	0.2	7.1	8.8	4.2	0.7	3.4
1986–1987	3.6	8.5	1.4	1.6	4.4	4.0	3.1	0.2	4.7	0.0	-0.5	8.7	5.2	4.2	1.5	4.2
1987–1988	4.1	7.2	1.9	1.2	3.9	4.5	2.7	1.2	5.0	0.8	0.7	6.7	4.8	5.8	1.8	4.9
1988–1989	4.8	7.5	2.6	3.1	5.1	4.8	3.6	2.8	6.3	2.2	1.1	4.6	6.8	6.4	3.2	7.8
1989–1990	5.4	7.3	3.3	3.4	4.8	2.6	3.4	2.6	6.5	3.1	2.5	4.1	6.7	10.4	5.4	9.5
1990–1991	4.2	3.2	3.3	3.2	5.6	2.4	3.2	3.7	6.3	3.3	3.9	3.5	5.9	9.4	5.8	5.9
1991–1992	3.0	1.0	4.0	2.4	1.4	2.1	2.4	5.1	5.3	1.7	3.7	2.3	5.9	2.4	4.1	3.7
1992–1993	3.0	1.8	3.6	2.8	1.9	1.2	2.1	4.4	4.6	1.3	2.1	2.3	4.6	4.7	3.2	1.6
1993–1994	2.6	2.0	2.9	2.4	0.1	2.0	1.6	2.8	4.1	0.6	2.8	1.4	4.7	2.2	0.8	2.4
1994–1995	2.8	4.6	2.2	1.5	2.2	2.1	1.8	1.8	5.3	-0.1	1.8	2.5	4.7	2.5	1.8	3.5
1995–1996	3.0	2.6	1.9	2.1	1.5	2.1	2.0	1.4	4.0	0.1	2.1	1.2	3.6	0.5	0.8	2.4
1996–1997	2.3	0.2	1.3	1.6	1.7	2.2	1.2	1.9	2.0	1.9	2.2	2.6	2.0	0.7	0.6	3.1
1997–1998	1.6	0.9	0.9	0.9	1.0	1.8	0.7	1.0	2.0	0.6	2.0	2.2	1.8	-0.3	0.0	3.4
1998–1999	2.2	1.5	0.6	1.1	1.8	2.5	0.5	0.6	1.7	-0.3	2.2	2.3	2.3	0.5	0.8	1.5
1999–2000	3.4	4.5	2.4	2.5	2.7	2.9	1.7	1.4	2.5	-0.7	2.3	3.1	3.4	0.9	1.6	3.0
2000–2001	2.8	4.4	2.7	2.5	2.5	2.4	1.7	1.9	2.7	-0.8	4.2	3.0	3.6	2.4	1.0	1.8
2001–2002	1.6	3.0	1.8	1.6	2.2	2.4	1.9	1.5	2.5	-0.9	3.3	1.3	3.5	2.2	0.6	1.7
2002–2003	2.3	2.7	1.3	1.6	2.8	2.1	2.1	1.0	2.7	-0.3	2.1	2.5	3.0	1.9	0.6	2.9
2003–2004	2.7	2.3	2.1	2.1	1.8	1.2	2.1	1.7	2.2	0.0	1.2	0.4	3.0	0.4	0.7	3.0
2004–2005	3.4	2.7	2.3	2.8	2.2	1.8	1.8	1.5	1.9	-0.3	1.7	1.6	3.4	0.5	1.3	2.8
2005–2006	3.2	3.6	1.5	1.8	2.0	1.9	1.6	1.6	2.1	0.3	1.2	2.3	3.5	1.4	1.0	3.2
2006–2007	2.8	2.3	2.2	1.8	2.2	1.7	1.5	2.3	1.8	0.0	1.6	0.8	2.8	2.2	0.7	4.3
2007–2008	3.8	4.4	3.2	4.5	2.3	3.4	2.8	2.6	3.3	1.4	2.5	3.8	4.1	3.4	2.4	4.0
2008–2009	-0.4	1.8	0.5	-0.1	0.3	1.3	0.1	0.4	0.8	-1.4	1.2	2.1	-0.3	-0.5	-0.5	-0.5
2009–2010	1.6	2.9	1.9	2.2	1.8	2.3	1.5	1.1	1.5	-0.7	1.3	2.5	1.8	1.2	0.7	4.6
2010–2011	3.2	3.3	3.3	3.5	2.9	2.8	2.1	2.3	2.8	-0.3	2.3	1.2	3.2	3.0	0.3	5.2
2011–2012	2.1	1.8	2.5	2.8	1.5	2.4	2.0	2.0	3.0	0.0	2.5	0.8	2.4	0.9	-0.7	3.2

[1]Unified Germany from 1991 onward; data for previous years relate to the former West Germany.
. . . = Not available.

Table 10-15. Harmonized Indexes of Consumer Prices (HICP), 16 Countries and Areas, 1996–2012

(2005 =100.)

Year	United States	Austria	Bel-gium	Den-mark	Euro Area	European Union[1]	France	Ger-many[1]	Italy	Japan	Nether-lands	Norway	Spain	Sweden	Switzer-land	United Kingdom
1996	...	87.2	85.3	84.3	84.6	84.9	86.6	88.6	81.8	101.8	80.4	84.3	77.9	87.5	...	88.1
1997	...	88.2	86.5	85.9	85.9	86.4	87.8	90.0	83.3	103.4	81.9	86.5	79.4	89.1	...	89.7
1998	84.1	89.0	87.3	87.0	86.9	87.5	88.3	90.5	85.0	104.1	83.4	88.2	80.8	90.0	...	91.1
1999	85.8	89.4	88.3	88.8	87.9	88.5	88.8	91.1	86.4	103.7	85.1	90.0	82.6	90.5	...	92.3
2000	88.7	91.2	90.7	91.2	89.7	90.2	90.5	92.4	88.6	102.8	87.1	92.8	85.5	91.7	...	93.1
2001	90.8	93.3	92.9	93.3	91.8	92.2	92.1	94.1	90.7	101.9	91.5	95.3	87.9	94.1	...	94.2
2002	91.6	94.8	94.3	95.6	93.9	94.1	93.9	95.4	93.1	100.7	95.1	96.1	91.0	95.9	...	95.4
2003	93.7	96.1	95.8	97.5	95.8	96.0	95.9	96.4	95.7	100.4	97.2	97.9	93.9	98.2	...	96.7
2004	96.3	97.9	97.5	98.3	97.9	97.9	98.1	98.1	97.8	100.4	98.5	98.5	96.7	99.2	...	98.0
2005	100.0	100.0	100.0	100.0	100.0	100.0	100.0	100.0	100.0	100.0	100.0	100.0	100.0	100.0	100.0	100.0
2006	103.2	101.7	102.3	101.8	102.2	102.2	101.9	101.8	102.2	100.3	101.7	102.5	103.6	101.5	101.0	102.3
2007	105.9	103.9	104.2	103.5	104.4	104.6	103.6	104.1	104.3	100.4	103.3	103.2	106.5	103.2	101.8	104.7
2008	110.6	107.3	108.9	107.3	107.8	108.4	106.8	107.0	108.0	102.0	105.5	106.7	110.9	106.7	104.2	108.5
2009	109.7	107.7	108.9	108.4	108.1	109.5	106.9	107.2	108.8	100.5	106.6	109.2	110.6	108.7	103.4	110.8
2010	112.4	109.5	111.4	110.8	109.8	111.8	108.8	108.4	110.6	99.7	107.6	111.8	112.9	110.8	104.1	114.5
2011	116.8	113.4	115.3	113.8	112.8	115.2	111.3	111.1	113.8	99.4	110.2	113.1	116.4	112.3	104.2	119.6
2012	119.4	116.3	118.3	116.5	115.7	118.3	113.8	113.5	117.5	99.4	113.3	113.6	119.2	113.4	103.4	123.0

[1]Data for Germany for years before 1991 pertain to the former West Germany.
. . . = Not available.

Table 10-16. Harmonized Indexes of Consumer Prices (HICP), 16 Countries and Areas, Annual Percent Change, 1996–2012

(Percent.)

Year	United States	Austria	Bel-gium	Den-mark	Euro Area	European Union[1]	France	Ger-many[1]	Italy	Japan	Nether-lands	Norway	Spain	Sweden	Switzer-land	United Kingdom
1996–2012	...	1.8	2.1	2.0	2.0	2.1	1.7	1.6	2.3	-0.1	2.2	1.9	2.7	1.6	...	2.1
2006–2012	2.5	2.3	2.4	2.3	2.1	2.5	1.8	1.8	2.4	-0.1	1.8	1.7	2.4	1.9	0.4	3.1
1996–2001	...	1.3	1.7	2.0	1.6	1.7	1.2	1.2	2.1	0.0	2.6	2.5	2.4	1.5	...	1.3
2001–2006	2.6	1.7	2.0	1.8	2.2	2.1	2.1	1.6	2.4	-0.3	2.1	1.5	3.3	1.5	...	1.7
2006–2011	2.5	2.2	2.4	2.3	2.0	2.4	1.8	1.8	2.2	-0.2	1.6	2.0	2.4	2.0	0.6	3.2
1996–1997	...	1.2	1.5	1.9	1.6	1.7	1.3	1.6	1.8	1.6	1.9	2.6	1.9	1.8	...	1.8
1997–1998	...	0.8	0.9	1.3	1.1	1.3	0.7	0.6	2.0	0.7	1.8	2.0	1.8	1.0	...	1.6
1998–1999	2.0	0.5	1.1	2.1	1.1	1.2	0.6	0.7	1.6	-0.4	2.0	2.0	2.2	0.6	...	1.3
1999–2000	3.4	2.0	2.7	2.7	2.1	1.9	1.8	1.4	2.5	-0.9	2.3	3.1	3.5	1.3	...	0.9
2000–2001	2.3	2.3	2.4	2.3	2.4	2.2	1.8	1.8	2.4	-0.9	5.1	2.7	2.8	2.7	...	1.2
2001–2002	0.9	1.7	1.6	2.5	2.2	2.1	1.9	1.4	2.6	-1.2	3.9	0.8	3.6	1.9	...	1.3
2002–2003	2.3	1.3	1.5	2.0	2.1	2.0	2.2	1.0	2.8	-0.3	2.2	1.9	3.1	2.3	...	1.4
2003–2004	2.8	2.0	1.9	0.8	2.1	2.0	2.3	1.8	2.2	0.0	1.4	0.6	3.1	1.0	...	1.3
2004–2005	3.9	2.1	2.5	1.7	2.2	2.2	1.9	1.9	2.2	-0.4	1.5	1.5	3.4	0.8	...	2.0
2005–2006	3.2	1.7	2.3	1.8	2.2	2.2	1.9	1.8	2.2	0.3	1.7	2.5	3.6	1.5	1.0	2.3
2006–2007	2.6	2.2	1.8	1.7	2.1	2.3	1.6	2.3	2.1	0.1	1.6	0.7	2.8	1.7	0.8	2.3
2007–2008	4.4	3.2	4.5	3.7	3.3	3.7	3.2	2.8	3.5	1.6	2.2	3.4	4.1	3.3	2.4	3.6
2008–2009	-0.9	0.4	0.0	1.0	0.3	1.0	0.1	0.2	0.7	-1.5	1.0	2.3	-0.2	1.9	-0.8	2.1
2009–2010	2.5	1.7	2.3	2.2	1.6	2.1	1.7	1.1	1.7	-0.8	0.9	2.4	2.0	1.9	0.7	3.3
2010–2011	3.9	3.6	3.5	2.7	2.7	3.1	2.3	2.5	2.9	-0.3	2.5	1.2	3.1	1.4	0.1	4.5
2011–2012	2.2	2.6	2.6	2.4	2.5	2.6	2.2	2.2	3.3	0.0	2.8	0.4	2.4	0.9	-0.8	2.8

[1]Data for Germany for years before 1991 pertain to the former West Germany.
. . . = Not available.

CHAPTER 11: CONSUMER EXPENDITURES

HIGHLIGHTS

The principal objective of the Consumer Expenditure (CE) Survey is to collect information about the buying habits of American households. The survey breaks down expenditures for different demographic categories, such as income, age, family size, and geographic location. These data are used in a variety of government, business, and academic research projects and provide important weights for the periodic revisions of the Consumer Price Index (CPI).

Figure 11-1. Consumer Expenditures, Annual Percent Change, 2010–2011 and 2011–2012

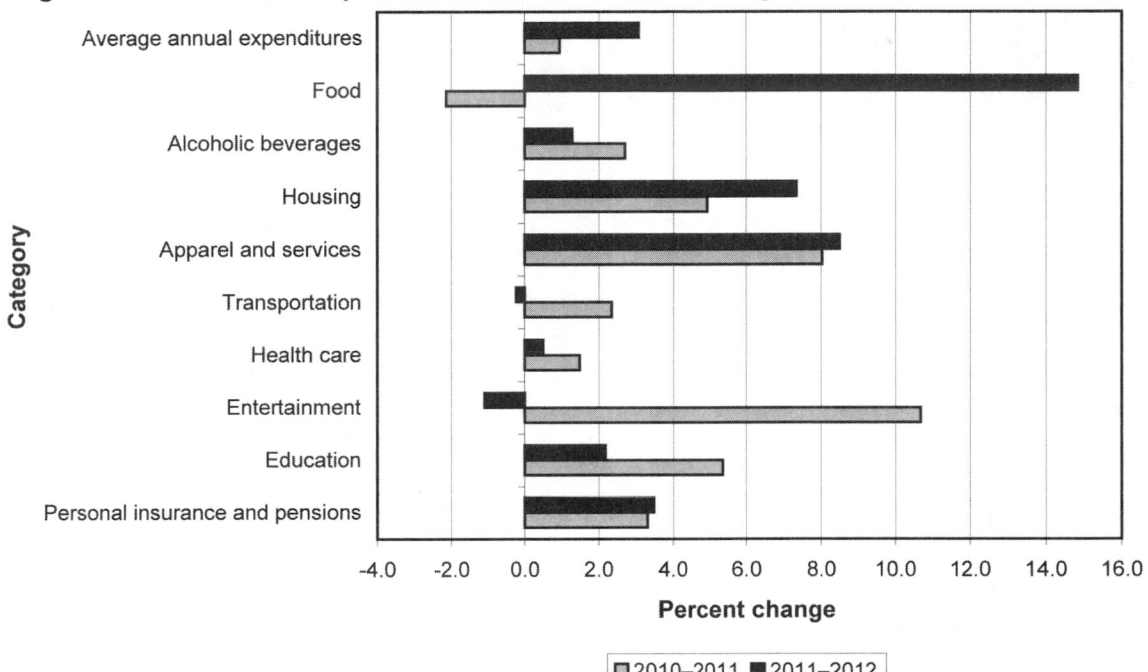

Average annual consumer expenditures increased 3.5 percent from 2011 to 2012. While average annual expenditures increased in most categories in 2012, they declined in reading (-5.2 percent), alcoholic beverages (-1.1), personal care products and services (-0.9), and apparel (-0.2). (See Table 11-1.)

OTHER HIGHLIGHTS

- Average annual expenditures increased 8.5 percent for transportation, 7.3 percent for health care, and 2.2 percent for food. (See Table 11-1.)

- Average annual consumer expenditures varied substantially by age group. Those aged 45 to 54 years had the highest average expenditures at $62,103, followed by those 35 to 44 years at $58,069. Older age groups typically spent more in health care, while those in younger age groups spent more on education. (See Table 11-10.)

- As educational attainment increased, so did average annual expenditures. Those with less than a high school diploma had average annual expenditures of $24,582, while those with a master's, professional, or doctoral degree had average annual expenditures of $82,606. (See Table 11-13.)

- Homeowners had far higher average annual expenditures than renters ($59,983 compared with $36,076). Meanwhile, those in urban areas had higher expenditures than those in rural areas ($52,227 compared with $42,699). (See Table 11-14.)

NOTES AND DEFINITIONS

PURPOSE, COLLECTION, AND COVERAGE

The buying habits of American consumers change over time because of changes in relative prices, real income, family size and composition, and other determinants of tastes and preferences. The introduction of new products into the marketplace and the emergence of new concepts in retailing also influence consumer buying habits. Data taken from the Consumer Expenditure Survey (CE), which is the only national survey that relates family expenditures to demographic characteristics, are of great importance to researchers. The survey data are also used to revise the Consumer Price Index market baskets and item samples.

Until the 1970s, the Bureau of Labor Statistics (BLS) conducted surveys of consumer expenditures approximately once every 10 years. The last such survey was conducted in 1972–1973. In late 1979, in a significant departure from previous methodology, BLS initiated a survey to be conducted on a continuous basis with rotating panels of respondents.

The current CE is similar to its 1972–1973 predecessor in that it consists of two separate components. Each component has its own questionnaire and sample: (1) the Interview Survey, in which an interviewer visits each consumer unit every three months for a twelve-month period; and (2) the Diary Survey, a recordkeeping survey completed by other consumer units for two consecutive one-week periods. The Census Bureau, under contract to BLS, collects the data for both components of the survey. Beginning in 1999, the sample was increased from 5,000 to 7,500 households.

In 2003, the survey modified the questions on race and Hispanic origin to comply with the new standards for maintaining, collecting, and presenting federal data on race and ethnicity for federal statistical agencies. Beginning with the data collected in 2003, the CE tables use data collected from the new race and ethnicity questions. A number of new classifications were made with publication of the 2003 data.

Beginning with the publication of the 2004 tables, the CE has been implementing multiple imputations of income data. Prior to 2004, the CE only published income data collected from complete income reporters. The introduction of multiply imputed income data affects the published CE tables in several ways, because income data are now published for all consumer units (instead of for complete reporters only). The most obvious result of this change is seen in the tables showing expenditures categorized by income before taxes, including income by quintile. Starting with the 2004 data, columns describing income, expenditures, and characteristics for "total complete reporting" and "incomplete reporting of

income" no longer appear in these tables, and the column titled "all consumer units" appears on all income tables. Due to the implementation of income imputation, data for 2004 are not strictly comparable to those of prior years, especially for the income tables. Averages for demographic characteristics and annual expenditures will change due to differences between the incomplete and complete income reporters in these categories. Furthermore, certain expenditures (such as personal insurance and pensions) are computed using income data. As a result of imputation, average annual values for these expenditures may be substantially different in the 2004 CE tables than in tables for previous years. The regular flow of data resulting from this design substantially enhances the usefulness of the survey through providing more timely information on consumption patterns within different kinds of consumer units.

The *Quarterly Interview Survey* is designed to collect data on the types of expenditures that respondents can be expected to recall after a period of three months or longer. These include relatively large expenditures (such as those for property, travel, automobiles, and major appliances) and expenditures that occur on a regular basis (such as those for rent, utilities, insurance premiums, and clothing). The interview also obtains "global estimates" for food and other selected items. The survey collects data for approximately 95 percent of total expenditures. Each sample household is interviewed once per quarter, for five consecutive quarters.

The *Diary Survey* is designed to collect data on expenditures for frequently purchased items that are more difficult to recall over longer periods of time. Respondents complete a diary of expenses for two consecutive 1-week periods. Expenditures for tobacco, drugs (including nonprescription drugs), and personal care supplies and services are also collected in the Diary Survey.

Participants in both surveys record dollar amounts for goods and services purchased during the reporting period, regardless of whether payment was made at the time of purchase. Excluded from both surveys are business-related expenditures and expenditures for which the family is reimbursed. Information is collected regarding demographic and family characteristics at the initial interview for each survey.

The tables in this chapter present integrated data from the Diary Survey and the Interview Survey and provide a complete accounting of consumer expenditures and income, which neither survey component is designed to do alone. Data for some expenditure items are only collected in one of the surveys. For example, the Diary Survey does not collect data for expenditures on overnight travel or information on reimbursements, while the Interview Survey records these purchases. Examples of expenditures for which reimbursements are netted out include those for medical care, auto repair, and construction, repairs, alterations, and maintenance of property.

For items unique to one survey or the other, the choice of which survey to use as the source of data is obvious. However, there is considerable overlap in coverage between the two surveys. Integrating the data thus presents the problem of determining the appropriate survey component. When data are available from both survey sources, the more reliable of the two (as determined by statistical methods) is selected. As a result, some items are selected from the Interview Survey and others are selected from the Diary Survey.

DATA INCLUDED IN THIS EDITION

Data for single characteristics are for calendar year 2012, and data for two cross-classified characteristics are for an average of calendar years 2011 and 2012. Income values from the survey are derived from "complete income reporters" only. Complete income reporters are defined as consumer units that provide values for at least one of the major sources of their income: wages and salaries, self-employment income, retirement income, dividends and interest, and welfare benefits. Some consumer units are defined as complete income reporters, even though they may not have provided a full accounting of all income from all sources.

Consumer units are classified by quintiles of income before taxes, age of reference person, size of consumer unit, region, composition of consumer unit, number of earners in consumer unit, housing tenure, race, type of area (urban or rural), and occupation.

CONCEPTS AND DEFINITIONS

A *consumer unit* comprises either (1) all members of a particular household related by blood, marriage, adoption, or other legal arrangements; (2) a person living alone, sharing a household with others, living as a roomer in a private home or lodging house or in permanent living quarters in a hotel or motel, but who is financially independent; or (3) two or more persons living together who pool their income to make joint expenditure decisions. Financial independence is determined by the three major expense categories: housing, food, and

other living expenses. To be considered financially independent, at least two of the three major expense categories have to be provided by the respondent. The terms "family," "household," and "consumer unit" are used interchangeably in descriptions of the CE.

An *earner* is a consumer unit member, 14 years of age or older, who reported having worked at least 1 week during the 12 months prior to the interview date.

The *education of reference person* refers to the number of years of formal education of the reference person, on the basis of the highest grade completed. If enrolled at time of the interview, the interviewer records the grade currently attended. Persons not reporting the extent of their education are classified under no school or not reported.

The *householder* or *reference person* is the first member of the consumer unit mentioned by the respondent as owner or renter of the premises at the time of the initial interview.

Housing tenure refers to the family's principal place of residence during the survey. "Owner" includes families living in their own homes, cooperatives or condominium apartments, or townhouses. "Renter" includes families paying rent, as well as families living rent-free in lieu of wages.

Quintiles of income before taxes refers to the ranking of complete income reporters in ascending order, according to the level of total before-tax income reported by the consumer unit. The ranking is then divided into five equal groups. Incomplete income reporters are not ranked and are shown separately.

Total expenditures include the transaction costs, including excise and sales taxes of goods and services acquired during the interview period. Estimates include expenditures for gifts and contributions and payments for pensions and personal insurance.

SOURCES OF ADDITIONAL INFORMATION

More extensive descriptions and tables can be found in an updated version of Chapter 16 in the *BLS Handbook of Methods* and in an anthology of articles relating to consumer expenditures. These resources can be found on the BLS Web site at http://www.bls.gov.

Table 11-1. Consumer Expenditures, Annual Average of All Consumer Units, 2000–2012

(Number, dollar, percent.)

Item	2000	2001	2002	2003	2004	2005	2006	2007	2008	2009	2010	2011	2012
NUMBER OF CONSUMER UNITS (THOUSANDS)	109 367	110 339	112 108	115 356	116 282	117 356	118 843	120 171	120 770	120 847	121 107	122 287	124 416
CONSUMER UNIT CHARACTERISTICS													
Income Before Taxes	44 649	47 507	49 430	51 128	54 453	58 712	60 533	63 091	63 563	62 857	62 481	63 685	65 596
Age of Reference Person	48.2	48.1	48.1	48.0	48.5	48.6	48.7	48.8	49.1	49.0	49.0	50.0	50.0
Average Number in Consumer Unit													
All persons	2.5	2.5	2.5	2.5	2.5	2.5	2.5	2.5	2.5	2.5	2.5	2.5	2.5
Children under 18 years	0.7	0.7	0.7	0.6	0.6	0.6	0.6	0.6	0.6	0.6	0.6	0.6	0.6
Persons 65 years and over	0.3	0.3	0.3	0.3	0.3	0.3	0.3	0.3	0.3	0.3	0.3	0.3	0.3
Earners	1.4	1.4	1.4	1.3	1.3	1.3	1.3	1.3	1.3	1.3	1.3	1.3	1.3
Vehicles	1.9	1.9	2.0	1.9	1.9	2.0	1.9	1.9	2.0	2.0	1.9	1.9	1.9
Percent Homeowner	66	66	66	67	68	67	67	67	66	66	66	65	64
With mortgage	39	40	41	41	42	43	43	43	42	41	41	40	39
Without mortgage	27	26	26	26	25	25	24	23	24	25	25	25	26
AVERAGE ANNUAL EXPENDITURES	38 045	39 518	40 677	40 817	43 395	46 409	48 398	49 638	50 486	49 067	48 109	49 705	51 442
Food	5 158	5 321	5 375	5 340	5 781	5 931	6 111	6 133	6 443	6 372	6 129	6 458	6 599
Food at home	3 021	3 086	3 099	3 129	3 347	3 297	3 417	3 465	3 744	3 753	3 624	3 838	3 921
Cereals and bakery products	453	452	450	442	461	445	446	460	507	506	502	531	538
Meats, poultry, fish, and eggs	453	452	798	825	880	764	797	777	846	841	784	832	852
Dairy products	325	332	328	328	371	378	368	387	430	406	380	407	419
Fruits and vegetables	521	522	552	535	561	552	592	600	657	656	679	715	731
Other food at home	927	952	970	999	1 075	1 158	1 212	1 241	1 305	1 343	1 278	1 353	1 380
Food away from home	2 137	2 235	2 276	2 211	2 434	2 634	2 694	2 668	2 698	2 619	2 505	2 620	2 678
Alcoholic Beverages	372	349	376	391	459	426	497	457	444	435	412	456	451
Housing	12 319	13 011	13 283	13 432	13 918	15 167	16 366	16 920	17 109	16 895	16 557	16 803	16 887
Shelter	7 114	7 602	7 829	7 887	7 998	8 805	9 673	10 023	10 183	10 075	9 812	9 825	9 891
Owned dwellings	4 602	4 979	5 165	5 263	5 324	5 958	6 516	6 730	6 760	6 543	6 277	6 148	6 056
Rented dwellings	2 034	2 134	2 160	2 179	2 201	2 345	2 590	2 602	2 724	2 860	2 900	3 029	3 186
Other lodging	478	489	505	445	473	502	567	691	698	672	635	648	649
Utilities, fuels, and public services	2 489	2 767	2 684	2 811	2 927	3 183	3 397	3 477	3 649	3 645	3 660	3 727	3 648
Household operations	684	676	706	707	753	801	948	984	998	1 011	1 007	1 122	1 159
Housekeeping supplies	482	509	545	529	594	611	640	639	654	659	612	615	610
Household furnishings and equipment	1 549	1 458	1 518	1 497	1 646	1 767	1 708	1 797	1 624	1 506	1 467	1 514	1 580
Apparel and Services	1 856	1 743	1 749	1 640	1 816	1 886	1 874	1 881	1 801	1 725	1 700	1 740	1 736
Transportation	7 417	7 633	7 759	7 781	7 801	8 344	8 508	8 758	8 604	7 658	7 677	8 293	8 998
Vehicle purchases (net outlay)	3 418	3 579	3 665	3 732	3 397	3 544	3 421	3 244	2 755	2 657	2 588	2 669	3 210
Gasoline and motor oil	1 291	1 279	1 235	1 333	1 598	2 013	2 227	2 384	2 715	1 986	2 132	2 655	2 756
Other vehicle expenses	2 281	2 375	2 471	2 331	2 365	2 339	2 355	2 592	2 621	2 536	2 464	2 454	2 490
Public and other transportation	427	400	389	385	441	448	505	538	513	479	493	516	542
Health Care	2 066	2 182	2 350	2 416	2 574	2 664	2 766	2 853	2 976	3 126	3 157	3 313	3 556
Health insurance	983	1 061	1 168	1 252	1 332	1 361	1 465	1 545	1 653	1 785	1 831	1 922	2 061
Medical services	568	573	590	591	648	677	670	709	727	736	722	768	839
Drugs	416	449	487	467	480	521	514	481	482	486	485	489	515
Medical supplies	99	100	105	107	114	105	117	118	114	119	119	134	142
Entertainment	1 863	1 953	2 079	2 060	2 218	2 388	2 376	2 698	2 835	2 693	2 504	2 572	2 605
Personal Care Products and Services	564	465	526	527	581	541	585	588	616	596	582	634	628
Reading	146	141	139	127	130	126	117	118	116	110	100	115	109
Education	632	648	752	783	905	940	888	945	1 046	1 068	1 074	1 051	1 207
Tobacco Products and Smoking Supplies	319	308	320	290	288	319	327	323	317	380	362	351	332
Miscellaneous	776	750	792	606	690	808	846	808	840	816	849	775	829
Cash Contributions	1 192	1 258	1 277	1 370	1 408	1 663	1 869	1 821	1 737	1 723	1 633	1 721	1 913
Personal Insurance and Pensions	3 365	3 737	3 899	4 055	4 823	5 204	5 270	5 336	5 605	5 471	5 373	5 424	5 591
Life and other personal insurance	399	410	406	397	390	381	322	309	317	309	318	317	353
Pensions and Social Security	2 966	3 326	3 493	3 658	4 433	4 823	4 948	5 027	5 288	5 162	5 054	5 106	5 238

Table 11-2. Shares of Annual Average Consumer Expenditures and Characteristics of All Consumer Units, 2000–2011[1]

(Number, dollar, percent.)

Item	2000	2001	2002	2003	2004	2005	2006	2007	2008	2009	2010	2011
NUMBER OF CONSUMER UNITS (THOUSANDS)	109 367	110 339	112 108	115 356	116 282	117 356	118 843	120 171	120 770	120 847	121 107	122 287
CONSUMER UNIT CHARACTERISTICS												
Income Before Taxes	44 649	47 507	49 430	51 128	54 453	58 712	60 533	63 091	63 563	62 857	62 481	63 685
Age of Reference Person	48.2	48.1	48.1	48.4	48.5	48.6	48.7	48.8	49.1	49.4	49.4	49.7
Average Number in Consumer Unit												
All persons	2.5	2.5	2.5	2.5	2.5	2.5	2.5	2.5	2.5	2.5	2.5	2.5
Children under 18 years	0.7	0.7	0.7	0.6	0.6	0.6	0.6	0.6	0.6	0.6	0.6	0.6
Persons 65 years and over	0.3	0.3	0.3	0.3	0.3	0.3	0.3	0.3	0.3	0.3	0.3	0.3
Earners	1.4	1.4	1.4	1.3	1.3	1.3	1.3	1.3	1.3	1.3	1.3	1.3
Vehicles	1.9	1.9	2.0	1.9	1.9	2.0	1.9	1.9	2.0	2.0	1.9	1.9
Percent Homeowner	66	66	66	67	68	67	67	67	66	66	66	65
With mortgage	39	40	41	41	42	43	43	43	42	41	41	40
Without mortgage	27	26	26	26	25	25	24	23	24	25	25	25
AVERAGE ANNUAL EXPENDITURES	38 045	39 518	40 677	40 817	43 395	46 409	48 398	49 638	50 486	49 067	48 109	49 705
Food	13.6	13.5	13.2	13.1	13.3	12.8	12.6	12.4	12.8	13.0	12.7	13.0
Food at home	7.9	7.8	7.6	7.7	7.7	7.1	7.1	7.0	7.4	7.6	7.5	7.7
Cereals and bakery products	1.2	1.1	1.1	1.1	1.1	1.0	0.9	0.9	1.0	1.0	1.0	1.1
Meats, poultry, fish, and eggs	2.1	2.1	2.0	2.0	2.0	1.6	1.6	1.6	1.7	1.7	1.6	1.7
Dairy products	0.9	0.8	0.8	0.8	0.9	0.8	0.8	0.8	0.9	0.8	0.8	0.8
Fruits and vegetables	1.4	1.3	1.4	1.3	1.3	1.2	1.2	1.2	1.3	1.3	1.4	1.4
Other food at home	2.4	2.4	2.4	2.4	2.5	2.5	2.5	2.5	2.6	2.7	2.7	2.7
Food away from home	5.6	5.7	5.6	5.4	5.6	5.7	5.6	5.4	5.3	5.3	5.2	5.3
Alcoholic Beverages	1.0	0.9	0.9	1.0	1.1	0.9	1.0	0.9	0.9	0.9	0.9	0.9
Housing	32.4	32.9	32.7	32.9	32.1	32.7	33.8	34.1	33.9	34.4	34.4	33.8
Shelter	18.7	19.2	19.2	19.3	18.4	19.0	20.0	20.2	20.2	20.5	20.4	19.8
Owned dwellings	12.1	12.6	12.7	12.9	12.3	12.8	13.5	13.6	13.4	13.3	13.0	12.4
Rented dwellings	5.3	5.4	5.3	5.3	5.1	5.1	5.4	5.2	5.4	5.8	6.0	6.1
Other lodging	1.3	1.2	1.2	1.1	1.1	1.1	1.2	1.4	1.4	1.4	1.3	1.3
Utilities, fuels, and public services	6.5	7.0	6.6	6.9	6.7	6.9	7.0	7.0	7.2	7.4	7.6	7.5
Household operations	1.8	1.7	1.7	1.7	1.7	1.7	2.0	2.0	2.0	2.1	2.1	2.3
Housekeeping supplies	1.3	1.3	1.3	1.3	1.4	1.3	1.3	1.3	1.3	1.3	1.3	1.2
Household furnishings and equipment	4.1	3.7	3.7	3.7	3.8	3.8	3.5	3.6	3.2	3.1	3.0	3.0
Apparel and Services	4.9	4.4	4.3	4.0	4.2	4.1	3.9	3.8	3.6	3.5	3.5	3.5
Transportation	19.5	19.3	19.1	19.1	18.0	18.0	17.6	17.6	17.0	15.6	16.0	16.7
Vehicle purchases (net outlay)	9.0	9.1	9.0	9.1	7.8	7.6	7.1	6.5	5.5	5.4	5.4	5.4
Gasoline and motor oil	3.4	3.2	3.0	3.3	3.7	4.3	4.6	4.8	5.4	4.0	4.4	5.3
Other vehicle expenses	6.0	6.0	6.1	5.7	5.5	5.0	4.9	5.2	5.2	5.2	5.1	4.9
Public and other transportation	1.1	1.0	1.0	0.9	1.0	1.0	1.0	1.1	1.0	1.0	1.0	1.0
Health Care	5.4	5.5	5.8	5.9	5.9	5.7	5.7	5.7	5.9	6.4	6.6	6.7
Health insurance	2.6	2.7	2.9	3.1	3.1	2.9	3.0	3.1	3.3	3.6	3.8	3.9
Medical services	1.5	1.4	1.5	1.4	1.5	1.5	1.4	1.4	1.4	1.5	1.5	1.5
Drugs	1.1	1.1	1.2	1.1	1.1	1.1	1.1	1.0	1.0	1.0	1.0	1.0
Medical supplies	0.3	0.3	0.3	0.3	0.3	0.2	0.2	0.2	0.2	0.2	0.2	0.3
Entertainment	4.9	4.9	5.1	5.0	5.1	5.1	4.9	5.4	5.6	5.5	5.2	5.2
Personal Care Products and Services	1.5	1.2	1.3	1.3	1.3	1.2	1.2	1.2	1.2	1.2	1.2	1.3
Reading	0.4	0.4	0.3	0.3	0.3	0.3	0.2	0.2	0.2	0.2	0.2	0.2
Education	1.7	1.6	1.8	1.9	2.1	2.0	1.8	1.9	2.1	2.2	2.2	2.1
Tobacco Products and Smoking Supplies	0.8	0.8	0.8	0.7	0.7	0.7	0.7	0.7	0.6	0.8	0.8	0.7
Miscellaneous	2.0	1.9	1.9	1.5	1.6	1.7	1.7	1.6	1.7	1.7	1.8	1.6
Cash Contributions	3.1	3.2	3.1	3.4	3.2	3.6	3.9	3.7	3.4	3.5	3.4	3.5
Personal Insurance and Pensions	8.8	9.5	9.6	9.9	11.1	11.2	10.9	10.8	11.1	11.2	11.2	10.9
Life and other personal insurance	1.0	1.0	1.0	1.0	0.9	0.8	0.7	0.6	0.6	0.6	0.7	0.6
Pensions and Social Security	7.8	8.4	8.6	9.0	10.2	10.4	10.2	10.1	10.5	10.5	10.5	10.3

[1]The separate expenditure shares table has been discontinued with the release of the 2012 data.

Table 11-3. Consumer Expenditures, Averages by Income Before Taxes, 2012

(Number, dollar, percent.)

Item	All consumer units	Less than $5,000	$5,000 to $9,999	$10,000 to $14,999	$15,000 to $19,999	$20,000 to $29,999	$30,000 to $39,999	$40,000 to $49,999	$50,000 to $69,999	$70,000 and over
NUMBER OF CONSUMER UNITS (THOUSANDS)	124 416	4 906	5 171	8 094	8 006	14 515	13 526	11 010	17 972	41 216
CONSUMER UNIT CHARACTERISTICS										
Income Before Taxes	65 596	-2 153	8 010	12 676	17 483	24 834	34 700	44 759	59 283	133 437
Income After Taxes	63 370	-2 070	8 203	12 811	17 786	25 066	34 745	44 276	58 199	127 102
Age of Reference Person	50.0	45.7	48.1	56.7	55.7	53.5	49.1	49.6	47.8	48.5
Average Number in Consumer Unit										
All persons	2.5	1.7	1.8	1.6	1.9	2.1	2.4	2.5	2.6	3.0
Children under 18 years	0.6	0.4	0.5	0.3	0.5	0.5	0.6	0.6	0.6	0.8
Persons 65 years and over	0.3	0.3	0.3	0.5	0.5	0.5	0.4	0.4	0.3	0.2
Earners	1.3	0.5	0.5	0.4	0.6	0.8	1.1	1.3	1.5	1.9
Vehicles	1.9	0.9	0.8	0.9	1.2	1.4	1.6	1.9	2.1	2.7
Percent Distribution										
Male	47	44	38	37	39	43	44	48	48	53
Female	53	56	62	63	61	57	56	52	52	47
Percent Homeowner	64	34	31	41	48	53	56	64	68	85
With mortgage	39	12	8	10	15	19	29	35	45	64
Without mortgage	26	21	24	31	33	34	27	29	23	21
AVERAGE ANNUAL EXPENDITURES	51 442	23 462	19 783	20 188	25 691	30 869	36 229	41 567	49 982	85 410
Food	6 599	3 747	3 035	3 211	3 959	4 271	4 962	5 698	6 518	10 205
Food at home	3 921	2 322	2 232	2 235	2 762	2 877	3 216	3 621	3 910	5 560
Cereals and bakery products	538	321	315	313	388	400	421	521	549	750
Meats, poultry, fish, and eggs	852	518	552	527	599	626	752	791	825	1 185
Dairy products	419	208	223	218	300	299	337	374	414	614
Fruits and vegetables	731	426	376	408	514	536	599	655	719	1 055
Other food at home	1 380	849	766	768	961	1 016	1 108	1 281	1 403	1 956
Food away from home	2 678	1 426	803	977	1 197	1 394	1 746	2 077	2 608	4 645
Alcoholic Beverages	451	149	148	117	193	219	335	352	420	804
Housing	16 887	9 116	8 240	8 178	10 116	11 728	13 224	14 645	16 278	25 809
Shelter	9 891	5 811	5 249	4 988	6 054	6 686	7 703	8 384	9 551	15 063
Owned dwellings	6 056	2 063	1 218	1 531	2 202	2 815	3 564	4 500	5 585	11 355
Rented dwellings	3 186	3 372	3 873	3 338	3 647	3 651	3 909	3 569	3 541	2 300
Other lodging	649	376	159	119	204	220	230	316	424	1 408
Utilities, fuels, and public services	3 648	1 898	1 947	2 161	2 609	2 894	3 225	3 557	3 823	4 917
Household operations	1 159	355	348	350	465	701	768	899	923	2 112
Housekeeping supplies	610	375	250	268	351	483	490	527	557	930
Household furnishings and equipment	1 580	677	445	411	636	964	1 038	1 278	1 425	2 787
Apparel and Services	1 736	928	763	593	947	1 064	1 163	1 398	1 559	2 932
Transportation	8 998	3 917	2 748	2 987	4 128	4 991	6 311	7 531	9 928	14 781
Vehicle purchases (net outlay)	3 210	1 582	774	697	1 100	1 425	1 751	2 197	3 855	5 711
Gasoline and motor oil	2 756	1 161	1 054	1 125	1 558	1 896	2 337	2 651	3 091	4 034
Other vehicle expenses	2 490	912	724	1 030	1 285	1 450	1 941	2 365	2 533	3 968
Public and other transportation	542	262	196	136	185	220	281	318	449	1 068
Health Care	3 556	1 363	1 318	1 731	2 196	2 844	2 906	3 244	3 689	5 212
Health insurance	2 061	753	754	1 052	1 273	1 664	1 696	1 926	2 235	2 951
Medical services	839	287	307	311	482	592	653	689	778	1 358
Drugs	515	278	218	313	342	503	461	526	527	667
Medical supplies	142	46	39	55	98	86	96	103	150	236
Entertainment	2 605	1 020	802	1 039	1 075	1 481	1 816	1 934	2 438	4 534
Personal Care Products and Services	628	240	233	249	290	412	423	479	606	1 058
Reading	109	40	44	43	50	65	77	87	103	185
Education	1 207	881	963	438	402	319	589	571	647	2 515
Tobacco Products and Smoking Supplies	332	280	339	288	298	336	384	364	374	306
Miscellaneous	829	462	346	305	410	766	557	666	727	1 316
Cash Contributions	1 913	1 101	463	550	796	1 104	1 130	1 193	1 819	3 450
Personal Insurance and Pensions	5 591	218	340	458	830	1 271	2 353	3 407	4 875	12 302
Life and other personal insurance	353	76	78	115	106	133	188	209	266	722
Pensions and Social Security	5 238	142	263	343	724	1 137	2 164	3 198	4 609	11 580

Table 11-4. Consumer Expenditures, Averages by Higher Income Before Taxes, 2012

(Number, dollar, percent.)

Item	All consumer units	Less than $70,000	$70,000 to $79,000	$80,000 to $99,999	$100,000 and over	$100,000 to $119,000	$120,000 to $149,999	$150,000 and over
NUMBER OF CONSUMER UNITS (THOUSANDS)	124 416	83 200	6 946	10 977	23 293	7 183	6 947	9 162
CONSUMER UNIT CHARACTERISTICS								
Income Before Taxes	65 596	31 989	74 689	88 974	171 910	108 977	132 318	251 270
Income After Taxes	63 370	31 798	72 762	86 313	162 529	105 714	127 434	233 684
Age of Reference Person	50.0	50.8	47.9	48.1	48.9	48.7	48.5	49.4
Average Number in Consumer Unit								
All persons	2.5	2.2	2.8	2.9	3.2	3.1	3.2	3.2
Children under 18 years	0.6	0.5	0.7	0.7	0.8	0.8	0.8	0.9
Persons 65 years and over	0.3	0.4	0.3	0.3	0.2	0.2	0.2	0.2
Earners	1.3	1.0	1.7	1.8	2.0	2.0	2.1	2.0
Vehicles	1.9	1.5	2.4	2.5	2.8	2.8	2.8	2.8
Percent Distribution								
Male	47	44	46	52	55	53	56	56
Female	53	56	54	48	45	47	44	44
Percent Homeowner	64	54	75	80	90	87	89	92
With mortgage	39	26	53	60	69	66	70	71
Without mortgage	26	28	23	20	21	21	20	22
AVERAGE ANNUAL EXPENDITURES	51 442	34 679	59 984	67 418	101 423	77 966	89 521	129 211
Food	6 599	4 842	8 250	8 612	11 527	9 599	11 287	13 375
Food at home	3 921	3 124	4 945	4 865	6 060	5 279	6 003	6 790
Cereals and bakery products	538	435	669	664	814	720	797	909
Meats, poultry, fish, and eggs	852	691	1 074	1 086	1 264	1 127	1 204	1 430
Dairy products	419	324	541	533	673	581	654	767
Fruits and vegetables	731	574	878	906	1 176	985	1 172	1 347
Other food at home	1 380	1 100	1 783	1 676	2 134	1 867	2 175	2 336
Food away from home	2 678	1 718	3 306	3 747	5 467	4 320	5 284	6 585
Alcoholic Beverages	451	279	583	659	937	737	899	1 140
Housing	16 887	12 476	18 456	21 039	30 243	23 410	27 330	37 877
Shelter	9 891	7 328	10 437	12 293	17 748	13 796	15 837	22 296
Owned dwellings	6 056	3 431	6 721	8 888	13 898	10 653	12 588	17 436
Rented dwellings	3 186	3 625	3 065	2 708	1 881	2 072	1 752	1 828
Other lodging	649	272	650	697	1 969	1 070	1 498	3 032
Utilities, fuels, and public services	3 648	3 020	4 149	4 432	5 374	4 795	5 158	5 992
Household operations	1 159	687	1 194	1 454	2 696	1 732	2 297	3 757
Housekeeping supplies	610	454	841	787	1 021	836	988	1 208
Household furnishings and equipment	1 580	986	1 835	2 073	3 404	2 252	3 050	4 624
Apparel and Services	1 736	1 152	2 209	2 394	3 399	2 509	3 184	4 315
Transportation	8 998	6 139	11 590	12 953	16 578	14 841	14 907	19 217
Vehicle purchases (net outlay)	3 210	1 972	4 267	5 283	6 343	6 126	5 146	7 421
Gasoline and motor oil	2 756	2 123	3 432	3 827	4 311	4 143	4 363	4 404
Other vehicle expenses	2 490	1 763	3 381	3 203	4 487	3 775	4 232	5 248
Public and other transportation	542	282	510	640	1 437	797	1 167	2 144
Health Care	3 556	2 737	4 167	4 535	5 843	5 277	5 448	6 593
Health insurance	2 061	1 620	2 476	2 702	3 210	2 911	3 109	3 521
Medical services	839	581	957	1 083	1 608	1 495	1 404	1 851
Drugs	515	440	540	574	748	665	710	847
Medical supplies	142	97	194	175	277	206	226	373
Entertainment	2 605	1 655	3 112	3 202	5 578	3 934	4 874	7 456
Personal Care Products and Services	628	417	898	822	1 213	1 049	1 110	1 422
Reading	109	72	141	148	216	162	204	267
Education	1 207	560	1 045	1 230	3 559	1 917	2 462	5 681
Tobacco Products and Smoking Supplies	332	344	384	357	259	311	250	225
Miscellaneous	829	588	794	946	1 648	1 313	1 392	2 108
Cash Contributions	1 913	1 151	1 878	2 381	4 422	2 683	3 196	6 716
Personal Insurance and Pensions	5 591	2 266	6 477	8 139	16 000	10 223	12 980	22 820
Life and other personal insurance	353	170	368	487	938	532	660	1 469
Pensions and Social Security	5 238	2 097	6 109	7 652	15 062	9 691	12 320	21 351

Table 11-5. Consumer Expenditures, Averages by Quintiles of Income Before Taxes, 2012

(Number, dollar, percent.)

Item	All consumer units	Lowest 20 percent	Second 20 percent	Third 20 percent	Fourth 20 percent	Highest 20 percent
NUMBER OF CONSUMER UNITS (THOUSANDS)	124 416	24 927	24 863	24 848	24 836	24 942
CONSUMER UNIT CHARACTERISTICS						
Income Before Taxes	65 596	9 988	27 585	47 265	75 952	167 010
Income After Taxes	63 370	10 171	27 743	46 777	73 970	158 024
Age of Reference Person	50.0	52.5	51.7	49.3	47.8	48.9
Average Number in Consumer Unit						
All persons	2.5	1.7	2.2	2.5	2.8	3.1
Children under 18 years	0.6	0.4	0.5	0.6	0.7	0.8
Persons 65 years and over	0.3	0.4	0.5	0.4	0.3	0.2
Earners	1.3	0.5	0.9	1.3	1.7	2.0
Vehicles	1.9	1.0	1.4	1.9	2.4	2.8
Percent Distribution						
Male	47	39	43	48	48	55
Female	53	61	57	52	52	45
Percent Homeowner	64	39	54	64	75	89
With mortgage	39	11	23	37	54	68
Without mortgage	26	28	31	27	21	21
AVERAGE ANNUAL EXPENDITURES	51 442	22 154	32 632	43 004	59 980	99 368
Food	6 599	3 502	4 524	5 798	7 831	11 334
Food at home	3 921	2 416	2 991	3 633	4 593	5 968
Cereals and bakery products	538	341	407	503	638	800
Meats, poultry, fish, and eggs	852	553	672	805	974	1 258
Dairy products	419	243	312	377	498	664
Fruits and vegetables	731	440	558	670	831	1 156
Other food at home	1 380	839	1 041	1 279	1 652	2 090
Food away from home	2 678	1 086	1 533	2 164	3 239	5 366
Alcoholic Beverages	451	152	260	363	559	922
Housing	16 887	8 836	12 258	14 755	18 863	29 705
Shelter	9 891	5 451	7 055	8 544	10 948	17 442
Owned dwellings	6 056	1 724	3 055	4 542	7 301	13 644
Rented dwellings	3 186	3 527	3 776	3 670	3 056	1 905
Other lodging	649	200	223	331	592	1 893
Utilities, fuels, and public services	3 648	2 177	2 980	3 561	4 192	5 330
Household operations	1 159	380	712	855	1 243	2 602
Housekeeping supplies	610	305	481	525	737	1 001
Household furnishings and equipment	1 580	522	1 031	1 271	1 743	3 330
Apparel and Services	1 736	759	1 132	1 313	2 121	3 352
Transportation	8 998	3 447	5 462	8 181	11 549	16 344
Vehicle purchases (net outlay)	3 210	993	1 603	2 781	4 479	6 193
Gasoline and motor oil	2 756	1 222	2 013	2 745	3 494	4 305
Other vehicle expenses	2 490	1 051	1 615	2 290	3 033	4 457
Public and other transportation	542	181	231	365	543	1 389
Health Care	3 556	1 677	2 787	3 363	4 169	5 785
Health insurance	2 061	994	1 621	1 969	2 541	3 179
Medical services	839	332	600	747	909	1 604
Drugs	515	287	476	531	546	733
Medical supplies	142	64	91	116	173	269
Entertainment	2 605	989	1 603	2 056	2 930	5 444
Personal Care Products and Services	628	255	407	509	775	1 194
Reading	109	44	69	87	135	212
Education	1 207	628	431	526	1 046	3 399
Tobacco Products and Smoking Supplies	332	301	342	386	356	273
Miscellaneous	829	376	635	736	779	1 617
Cash Contributions	1 913	698	1 109	1 310	2 189	4 252
Personal Insurance and Pensions	5 591	489	1 612	3 623	6 678	15 534
Life and other personal insurance	353	97	139	232	391	903
Pensions and Social Security	5 238	392	1 473	3 391	6 287	14 631

Table 11-6. Consumer Expenditures, Averages by Occupation of Reference Person, 2012

(Number, dollar, percent.)

Item	Self-employed workers	Wage and salary earners						Retired	All others, including those not reporting
		Total wage and salary earners	Managers and professional workers	Technical sales and clerical workers	Service workers	Construction workers and mechanics	Operators, fabricators, and laborers		
NUMBER OF CONSUMER UNITS (THOUSANDS)	6 058	76 929	31 412	19 690	13 335	4 097	8 396	22 812	18 617
CONSUMER UNIT CHARACTERISTICS									
Income Before Taxes	86 024	78 173	107 270	63 123	52 945	60 792	53 151	38 015	40 778
Income After Taxes	82 424	75 077	101 576	61 552	52 132	58 777	52 044	37 649	40 313
Age of Reference Person	49.6	43.9	45.1	43.2	42.6	42.6	43.9	74.0	46.0
Average Number in Consumer Unit									
All persons	2.6	2.6	2.6	2.5	2.7	2.8	2.7	1.7	2.8
Children under 18 years	0.6	0.7	0.7	0.6	0.8	0.8	0.8	0.1	0.9
Persons 65 years and over	0.2	0.1	0.1	0.1	0.1	0.1	0.1	1.2	0.2
Earners	1.8	1.7	1.7	1.7	1.7	1.8	1.7	0.2	0.6
Vehicles	2.1	2.0	2.2	1.9	1.8	2.4	2.0	1.6	1.5
Percent Distribution									
Male	60	51	49	38	46	93	75	42	32
Female	40	49	51	62	54	7	25	58	68
Percent Homeowner	71	63	73	58	49	64	57	80	49
With mortgage	45	46	56	41	34	45	37	20	28
Without mortgage	26	17	16	17	14	19	20	60	21
AVERAGE ANNUAL EXPENDITURES	61 645	57 431	73 079	49 627	44 275	50 035	41 511	38 699	39 195
Food	7 412	7 209	8 695	6 610	5 790	6 847	5 399	5 084	5 744
Food at home	4 447	4 079	4 631	3 799	3 572	4 179	3 413	3 292	3 885
Cereals and bakery products	558	560	633	523	512	589	438	451	548
Meats, poultry, fish, and eggs	995	877	934	820	809	1 025	832	698	895
Dairy products	471	439	512	413	366	419	342	341	418
Fruits and vegetables	896	757	884	678	673	749	616	646	680
Other food at home	1 525	1 446	1 668	1 365	1 213	1 398	1 184	1 156	1 344
Food away from home	2 966	3 129	4 064	2 811	2 218	2 668	1 986	1 792	1 859
Alcoholic Beverages	645	528	679	484	361	402	371	325	242
Housing	18 696	18 402	22 990	16 153	14 854	15 620	13 504	13 534	14 174
Shelter	11 084	10 936	13 747	9 599	8 980	8 484	7 857	7 352	8 292
Owned dwellings	7 350	6 735	9 380	5 358	4 431	5 321	4 417	4 913	4 228
Rented dwellings	2 808	3 494	3 170	3 792	4 223	2 885	3 144	1 835	3 695
Other lodging	926	707	1 197	449	327	278	296	605	370
Utilities, fuels, and public services	3 781	3 802	4 234	3 632	3 381	3 658	3 322	3 317	3 377
Household operations	1 194	1 287	1 914	963	809	763	715	1 012	800
Housekeeping supplies	708	616	744	539	491	563	526	630	536
Household furnishings and equipment	1 930	1 762	2 351	1 420	1 193	2 151	1 085	1 223	1 169
Apparel and Services	2 050	1 995	2 457	1 872	1 371	1 999	1 462	1 006	1 482
Transportation	9 540	10 470	12 010	9 660	9 221	10 524	8 593	6 082	6 340
Vehicle purchases (net outlay)	2 848	3 894	4 346	3 751	3 599	3 637	3 129	1 942	2 059
Gasoline and motor oil	3 076	3 166	3 416	2 937	2 793	3 838	3 035	1 731	2 210
Other vehicle expenses	3 051	2 789	3 264	2 550	2 449	2 741	2 158	1 977	1 727
Public and other transportation	565	621	983	422	381	308	270	431	344
Health Care	4 084	3 280	4 169	2 889	2 464	2 811	2 393	5 029	2 726
Health insurance	2 412	1 871	2 328	1 722	1 358	1 522	1 499	3 079	1 482
Medical services	993	829	1 106	636	709	778	465	958	680
Drugs	516	448	555	411	314	424	356	791	452
Medical supplies	163	131	179	121	82	87	73	200	112
Entertainment	3 796	2 871	3 852	2 408	1 992	2 689	1 749	1 960	1 935
Personal Care Products and Services	821	685	882	607	541	562	424	541	446
Reading	122	110	161	86	75	76	46	136	71
Education	1 304	1 478	2 284	1 017	970	669	739	214	1 277
Tobacco Products and Smoking Supplies	341	339	234	371	368	589	489	199	460
Miscellaneous	1 071	858	1 172	694	606	757	519	958	474
Cash Contributions	2 108	1 916	2 949	1 230	1 216	1 163	1 139	2 467	1 155
Personal Insurance and Pensions	9 656	7 291	10 545	5 546	4 446	5 326	4 683	1 166	2 667
Life and other personal insurance	627	370	536	271	218	209	304	316	235
Pensions and Social Security	9 029	6 920	10 009	5 275	4 228	5 118	4 379	849	2 432

Table 11-7. Consumer Expenditures, Averages by Number of Earners, 2012

(Number, dollar, percent.)

Item	All consumer units	Single consumer		Consumer units of two or more persons			
		No earner	One earner	No earner	One earner	Two earners	Three or more earners
NUMBER OF CONSUMER UNITS (THOUSANDS)	124 416	15 943	20 999	11 753	26 075	39 702	9 944
CONSUMER UNIT CHARACTERISTICS							
Income Before Taxes	65 596	19 704	45 033	33 243	63 836	94 352	110 647
Income After Taxes	63 370	19 590	42 400	33 164	61 604	91 013	107 809
Age of Reference Person	50.0	67.6	44.1	64.6	47.8	43.9	47.1
Average Number in Consumer Unit							
All persons	2.5	1.0	1.0	2.4	3.0	3.1	4.4
Children under 18 years	0.6	X	X	0.4	1.0	0.9	1.0
Persons 65 years and over	0.3	0.7	0.1	1.2	0.3	0.1	0.1
Earners	1.3	X	1.0	X	1.0	2.0	3.3
Vehicles	1.9	0.9	1.2	1.7	1.9	2.4	3.3
Percent Distribution							
Male	47	37	54	45	42	50	46
Female	53	63	46	55	58	50	54
Percent Homeowner	64	57	45	74	63	72	79
With mortgage	39	11	29	21	38	55	61
Without mortgage	26	46	16	53	25	17	18
AVERAGE ANNUAL EXPENDITURES	51 442	23 641	36 030	39 119	52 654	67 596	75 840
Food	6 599	2 953	3 890	5 757	7 142	8 512	10 372
Food at home	3 921	1 961	1 966	3 909	4 405	4 885	6 220
Cereals and bakery products	538	272	269	555	605	664	851
Meats, poultry, fish, and eggs	852	406	383	866	980	1 056	1 434
Dairy products	419	203	210	396	473	532	653
Fruits and vegetables	731	385	383	740	812	897	1 166
Other food at home	1 380	696	722	1 351	1 536	1 737	2 116
Food away from home	2 678	991	1 923	1 848	2 737	3 627	4 152
Alcoholic Beverages	451	125	500	312	408	607	537
Housing	16 887	9 845	12 807	13 522	17 845	21 047	21 641
Shelter	9 891	6 069	8 476	6 896	10 352	12 148	12 322
Owned dwellings	6 056	2 916	3 788	4 335	6 292	8 206	8 706
Rented dwellings	3 186	2 924	4 315	2 003	3 377	3 056	2 640
Other lodging	649	229	373	558	683	885	976
Utilities, fuels, and public services	3 648	2 247	2 324	3 561	3 973	4 313	5 288
Household operations	1 159	655	628	985	1 190	1 682	1 124
Housekeeping supplies	610	314	317	701	690	748	818
Household furnishings and equipment	1 580	559	1 061	1 381	1 640	2 157	2 091
Apparel and Services	1 736	548	1 094	1 192	1 961	2 330	2 718
Transportation	8 998	3 009	5 806	6 199	9 227	12 260	15 113
Vehicle purchases (net outlay)	3 210	702	1 889	2 078	3 318	4 566	5 668
Gasoline and motor oil	2 756	905	1 811	1 930	2 807	3 690	4 830
Other vehicle expenses	2 490	1 157	1 711	1 863	2 520	3 270	3 905
Public and other transportation	542	245	395	328	582	735	709
Health Care	3 556	2 829	1 968	4 984	3 787	3 881	4 499
Health insurance	2 061	1 568	1 042	3 130	2 215	2 246	2 593
Medical services	839	693	567	786	896	951	1 106
Drugs	515	457	284	871	543	519	586
Medical supplies	142	111	74	197	132	165	213
Entertainment	2 605	1 182	1 711	1 932	2 750	3 556	3 360
Personal Care Products and Services	628	304	435	501	660	811	907
Reading	109	78	86	126	108	123	136
Education	1 207	441	852	268	1 129	1 651	2 734
Tobacco Products and Smoking Supplies	332	224	272	325	363	357	455
Miscellaneous	829	515	745	988	843	915	930
Cash Contributions	1 913	1 400	1 547	2 424	1 736	2 202	2 206
Personal Insurance and Pensions	5 591	188	4 318	588	4 695	9 342	10 229
Life and other personal insurance	353	145	160	318	355	504	521
Pensions and Social Security	5 238	[1]42	4 158	[1]271	4 339	8 838	9 707

[1]Data are likely to have large sampling errors.
X = Not applicable.

Table 11-8. Consumer Expenditures, Averages by Size of Consumer Unit, 2012

(Number, dollar, percent.)

Item	All consumer units	One person	Two or more persons				
			Total	Two persons	Three persons	Four persons	Five or more persons
NUMBER OF CONSUMER UNITS (THOUSANDS)	124 416	36 942	87 474	39 676	18 980	16 852	11 966
CONSUMER UNIT CHARACTERISTICS							
Income Before Taxes	65 596	34 102	78 897	72 885	79 557	90 184	81 887
Income After Taxes	63 370	32 556	76 383	69 616	77 346	87 793	81 226
Age of Reference Person	50.0	54.3	48.2	54.3	45.6	41.7	41.5
Average Number in Consumer Unit							
All persons	2.5	1.0	3.1	2.0	3.0	4.0	5.7
Children under 18 years	0.6	X	0.9	0.1	0.7	1.6	2.8
Persons 65 years and over	0.3	0.3	0.3	0.6	0.2	0.1	0.1
Earners	1.3	0.6	1.6	1.2	1.7	1.9	2.1
Vehicles	1.9	1.0	2.3	2.1	2.3	2.4	2.4
Percent Distribution							
Male	47	47	47	49	44	47	42
Female	53	53	53	51	56	53	58
Percent Homeowner	64	50	70	73	67	70	66
With mortgage	39	21	46	38	50	57	50
Without mortgage	26	29	24	35	17	13	16
AVERAGE ANNUAL EXPENDITURES	51 442	30 716	60 097	55 068	60 943	67 622	64 963
Food	6 599	3 497	7 857	6 836	7 671	9 225	9 725
Food at home	3 921	1 964	4 712	3 932	4 612	5 563	6 351
Cereals and bakery products	538	270	646	512	628	781	943
Meats, poultry, fish, and eggs	852	392	1 038	862	1 029	1 189	1 447
Dairy products	419	207	505	414	488	616	685
Fruits and vegetables	731	384	871	742	844	1 043	1 116
Other food at home	1 380	711	1 651	1 400	1 624	1 934	2 160
Food away from home	2 678	1 533	3 145	2 904	3 058	3 662	3 374
Alcoholic Beverages	451	344	495	606	430	426	315
Housing	16 887	11 532	19 138	17 158	19 781	21 548	21 280
Shelter	9 891	7 437	10 926	9 786	11 468	12 240	12 001
Owned dwellings	6 056	3 412	7 172	6 268	7 297	8 608	7 951
Rented dwellings	3 186	3 715	2 963	2 619	3 360	2 906	3 553
Other lodging	649	311	791	898	811	726	497
Utilities, fuels, and public services	3 648	2 291	4 221	3 736	4 304	4 683	5 049
Household operations	1 159	640	1 378	1 052	1 569	1 943	1 360
Housekeeping supplies	610	316	729	688	703	773	845
Household furnishings and equipment	1 580	848	1 883	1 896	1 737	1 908	2 024
Apparel and Services	1 736	865	2 090	1 690	2 083	2 631	2 702
Transportation	8 998	4 599	10 848	10 055	10 803	12 001	11 914
Vehicle purchases (net outlay)	3 210	1 377	3 985	3 787	3 766	4 360	4 459
Gasoline and motor oil	2 756	1 420	3 320	2 808	3 432	3 833	4 115
Other vehicle expenses	2 490	1 472	2 911	2 804	3 016	3 073	2 865
Public and other transportation	542	330	632	655	588	735	476
Health Care	3 556	2 339	4 069	4 399	3 845	3 730	3 810
Health insurance	2 061	1 269	2 395	2 620	2 232	2 250	2 115
Medical services	839	622	930	923	945	864	1 024
Drugs	515	359	580	690	504	467	491
Medical supplies	142	90	164	166	165	149	181
Entertainment	2 605	1 485	3 071	2 829	2 939	3 667	3 249
Personal Care Products and Services	628	380	730	712	681	807	765
Reading	109	83	121	139	109	108	95
Education	1 207	675	1 432	917	1 954	2 124	1 339
Tobacco Products and Smoking Supplies	332	251	366	339	401	338	439
Miscellaneous	829	647	906	917	938	950	756
Cash Contributions	1 913	1 484	2 094	2 459	2 073	1 631	1 567
Personal Insurance and Pensions	5 591	2 535	6 881	6 015	7 235	8 433	7 008
Life and other personal insurance	353	154	437	468	416	435	366
Pensions and Social Security	5 238	2 382	6 445	5 546	6 818	7 998	6 642

X = Not applicable.

Table 11-9. Consumer Expenditures, Averages by Composition of Consumer Unit, 2012

(Number, dollar, percent.)

Item	Husband and wife consumer units							One parent, at least one child under 18 years	Single person and other consumer units
	Total	Husband and wife only	Husband and wife with children				Other husband and wife consumer units		
			Total	Oldest child under 6 years	Oldest child 6 to 17 years	Oldest child 18 years or over			
NUMBER OF CONSUMER UNITS (THOUSANDS)	60 428	25 936	29 252	5 676	14 797	8 778	5 241	6 524	57 463
CONSUMER UNIT CHARACTERISTICS									
Income Before Taxes	90 393	81 717	98 104	85 200	100 698	102 074	90 293	34 194	43 086
Income After Taxes	87 507	78 420	95 387	82 637	98 029	99 179	88 494	34 475	41 268
Age of Reference Person	50.1	58.4	42.8	32.7	40.9	52.7	49.9	38.0	51.3
Average Number in Consumer Unit									
All persons	3.2	2.0	3.9	3.5	4.2	3.9	4.9	2.9	1.7
Children under 18 years	0.9	X	1.6	1.5	2.2	0.6	1.4	1.7	0.2
Persons 65 years and over	0.4	0.7	0.1	(¹)	(¹)	0.2	0.6	(¹)	0.3
Earners	1.6	1.2	1.9	1.7	1.8	2.4	2.3	1.0	0.9
Vehicles	2.5	2.4	2.6	2.0	2.5	3.1	2.9	1.2	1.3
Percent Distribution									
Male	52	55	51	54	51	49	46	16	44
Female	48	45	49	46	49	51	54	84	56
Percent Homeowner	80	85	76	64	76	86	74	36	51
With mortgage	52	42	61	57	64	61	54	28	25
Without mortgage	27	43	15	7	12	25	20	8	26
AVERAGE ANNUAL EXPENDITURES	67 310	61 285	72 814	64 103	74 659	75 286	67 187	38 667	36 152
Food	8 615	7 463	9 611	7 331	10 458	9 626	9 431	5 895	4 528
Food at home	5 089	4 263	5 742	4 452	6 095	5 958	6 041	3 673	2 699
Cereals and bakery products	698	559	803	623	878	789	890	515	369
Meats, poultry, fish, and eggs	1 095	922	1 213	830	1 302	1 304	1 411	802	598
Dairy products	561	448	656	570	693	647	652	353	275
Fruits and vegetables	953	825	1 060	858	1 100	1 118	1 073	676	499
Other food at home	1 781	1 509	2 011	1 571	2 122	2 099	2 016	1 327	957
Food away from home	3 526	3 200	3 869	2 879	4 363	3 668	3 390	2 222	1 829
Alcoholic Beverages	553	670	475	503	502	411	351	175	377
Housing	20 771	18 258	22 980	23 621	23 432	21 803	20 803	14 593	13 061
Shelter	11 739	10 213	13 149	13 106	13 616	12 389	11 417	8 586	8 095
Owned dwellings	8 493	7 284	9 641	8 851	10 036	9 486	8 066	3 505	3 782
Rented dwellings	2 220	1 712	2 568	3 751	2 619	1 717	2 797	4 872	4 010
Other lodging	1 025	1 217	940	504	961	1 186	554	209	302
Utilities, fuels, and public services	4 487	3 997	4 752	3 867	4 797	5 250	5 430	3 298	2 806
Household operations	1 562	1 106	2 004	3 891	1 785	1 151	1 354	1 244	725
Housekeeping supplies	815	772	856	713	925	829	820	477	407
Household furnishings and equipment	2 169	2 170	2 220	2 044	2 309	2 183	1 782	989	1 027
Apparel and Services	2 235	1 760	2 685	2 450	2 870	2 523	2 250	2 113	1 154
Transportation	12 163	11 254	12 786	10 925	12 522	14 424	13 174	6 353	5 968
Vehicle purchases (net outlay)	4 594	4 355	4 732	4 357	4 523	5 328	5 003	2 104	1 881
Gasoline and motor oil	3 599	3 023	3 999	3 283	4 038	4 397	4 212	2 231	1 929
Other vehicle expenses	3 214	3 058	3 322	2 710	3 205	3 903	3 372	1 767	1 808
Public and other transportation	757	818	733	575	756	796	587	251	350
Health Care	4 828	5 407	4 310	3 381	4 167	5 150	4 854	1 704	2 430
Health insurance	2 860	3 251	2 518	2 119	2 439	2 909	2 840	924	1 349
Medical services	1 095	1 119	1 071	875	1 026	1 275	1 105	432	616
Drugs	682	845	526	270	513	712	749	278	365
Medical supplies	191	192	195	118	190	254	160	70	100
Entertainment	3 554	3 228	3 948	3 023	4 530	3 563	3 013	1 846	1 689
Personal Care Products and Services	804	781	835	678	908	812	769	518	454
Reading	145	172	126	96	125	148	117	50	79
Education	1 706	985	2 417	793	2 240	3 767	1 313	846	724
Tobacco Products and Smoking Supplies	314	282	317	236	299	401	457	248	360
Miscellaneous	954	987	950	936	956	948	814	946	683
Cash Contributions	2 550	3 117	2 078	1 705	1 955	2 528	2 375	720	1 378
Personal Insurance and Pensions	8 117	6 919	9 295	8 426	9 695	9 184	7 467	2 660	3 268
Life and other personal insurance	554	627	505	460	501	540	470	142	164
Pensions and Social Security	7 562	6 291	8 790	7 966	9 194	8 643	6 996	2 518	3 103

¹Value less than or equal to 0.05.
X = Not applicable.

Table 11-10. Consumer Expenditures, Averages by Age of Reference Person, 2012

(Number, dollar, percent.)

Item	All consumer units	Under 25 years	25 to 34 years	35 to 44 years	45 to 54 years	55 to 64 years	65 years and over	65 to 74 years	75 years and over
NUMBER OF CONSUMER UNITS (THOUSANDS)	124 416	8 159	20 112	21 598	24 624	22 770	27 154	14 993	12 161
CONSUMER UNIT CHARACTERISTICS									
Income Before Taxes	65 596	36 639	58 832	78 169	81 704	77 507	44 713	53 521	33 853
Income After Taxes	63 370	33 670	57 437	76 376	78 859	73 302	43 969	52 510	33 439
Age of Reference Person	50.0	21.7	29.6	39.4	49.6	59.1	74.8	68.9	82.1
Average Number in Consumer Unit									
All persons	2.5	2.0	2.8	3.4	2.7	2.1	1.7	1.8	1.5
Children under 18 years	0.6	0.4	1.1	1.4	0.6	0.2	0.1	0.1	(¹)
Persons 65 years and over	0.3	(¹)	(¹)	(¹)	0.1	0.1	1.4	1.4	1.3
Earners	1.3	1.3	1.5	1.6	1.7	1.3	0.5	0.6	0.2
Vehicles	1.9	1.2	1.7	2.0	2.3	2.2	1.6	1.9	1.3
Percent Distribution									
Male	47	50	47	46	47	49	43	48	38
Female	53	50	53	54	53	51	57	52	62
Percent Homeowner	64	15	40	62	72	79	80	80	79
With mortgage	39	10	35	52	53	43	22	30	11
Without mortgage	26	4	5	10	19	36	58	50	67
AVERAGE ANNUAL EXPENDITURES	51 442	31 411	49 544	58 069	62 103	55 636	40 410	45 968	33 530
Food	6 599	4 412	6 513	7 701	7 917	6 800	5 059	5 793	4 141
Food at home	3 921	2 529	3 680	4 490	4 707	4 012	3 273	3 719	2 716
Cereals and bakery products	538	355	512	632	633	527	459	490	421
Meats, poultry, fish, and eggs	852	573	755	999	1 047	887	686	804	539
Dairy products	419	251	394	497	498	433	342	385	289
Fruits and vegetables	731	456	683	808	872	733	659	723	580
Other food at home	1 380	894	1 335	1 555	1 657	1 432	1 127	1 318	887
Food away from home	2 678	1 883	2 833	3 210	3 210	2 788	1 785	2 074	1 426
Alcoholic Beverages	451	354	564	501	454	493	315	407	201
Housing	16 887	10 957	17 157	19 858	19 076	17 247	13 833	15 076	12 298
Shelter	9 891	7 285	10 458	11 849	11 244	9 728	7 605	8 372	6 659
Owned dwellings	6 056	1 307	4 552	7 676	7 625	6 991	5 101	5 970	4 030
Rented dwellings	3 186	5 748	5 603	3 691	2 712	1 788	1 828	1 557	2 162
Other lodging	649	230	304	483	907	949	676	845	467
Utilities, fuels, and public services	3 648	1 879	3 130	4 077	4 304	3 992	3 340	3 595	3 025
Household operations	1 159	538	1 338	1 559	1 080	1 029	1 076	1 004	1 164
Housekeeping supplies	610	303	538	618	668	736	597	670	507
Household furnishings and equipment	1 580	952	1 693	1 755	1 780	1 763	1 215	1 436	942
Apparel and Services	1 736	1 246	2 061	2 264	2 041	1 622	1 022	1 287	691
Transportation	8 998	6 410	9 724	9 991	10 644	9 519	6 538	8 214	4 468
Vehicle purchases (net outlay)	3 210	2 867	4 175	3 610	3 537	2 895	2 250	2 993	1 333
Gasoline and motor oil	2 756	1 931	2 822	3 342	3 421	2 887	1 775	2 222	1 224
Other vehicle expenses	2 490	1 322	2 238	2 532	3 046	3 046	2 041	2 414	1 579
Public and other transportation	542	291	489	506	640	691	472	585	332
Health Care	3 556	1 024	2 047	2 948	3 687	4 377	5 118	5 259	4 944
Health insurance	2 061	458	1 227	1 751	2 109	2 271	3 186	3 299	3 047
Medical services	839	406	525	720	892	1 210	935	974	887
Drugs	515	114	213	363	527	724	798	813	779
Medical supplies	142	47	82	114	159	172	200	174	231
Entertainment	2 605	1 257	2 382	3 232	3 051	2 911	2 020	2 413	1 532
Personal Care Products and Services	628	360	574	694	707	696	569	652	465
Reading	109	44	72	93	118	133	142	148	136
Education	1 207	1 886	1 021	1 050	2 426	1 118	236	245	223
Tobacco Products and Smoking Supplies	332	262	351	358	431	372	193	249	124
Miscellaneous	829	372	660	876	924	908	902	1 031	743
Cash Contributions	1 913	488	1 104	1 469	2 430	2 353	2 454	2 289	2 658
Personal Insurance and Pensions	5 591	2 339	5 313	7 033	8 196	7 088	2 009	2 904	906
Life and other personal insurance	353	50	144	325	446	517	397	484	290
Pensions and Social Security	5 238	2 289	5 169	6 709	7 749	6 571	1 612	2 420	616

¹Value less than or equal to 0.05.

Table 11-11. Consumer Expenditures, Averages by Race of Reference Person, 2012

(Number, dollar, percent.)

Item	All consumer units	White, Asian, and other races			Black
		Total	White and other races	Asian	
NUMBER OF CONSUMER UNITS (THOUSANDS)	124 416	108 778	103 386	5 393	15 637
CONSUMER UNIT CHARACTERISTICS					
Income Before Taxes	65 596	68 253	67 319	86 156	47 119
Income After Taxes	63 370	65 771	64 842	83 585	46 666
Age of Reference Person	50.0	50.4	50.7	44.1	47.7
Average Number in Consumer Unit					
All persons	2.5	2.5	2.5	2.8	2.5
Children under 18 years	0.6	0.6	0.6	0.7	0.8
Persons 65 years and over	0.3	0.4	0.4	0.3	0.2
Earners	1.3	1.3	1.3	1.4	1.1
Vehicles	1.9	2.0	2.0	1.6	1.3
Percent Distribution					
Male	47	48	48	55	38
Female	53	52	52	45	62
Percent Homeowner	64	67	68	54	43
With mortgage	39	40	40	40	28
Without mortgage	26	27	28	14	15
AVERAGE ANNUAL EXPENDITURES	51 442	53 290	52 870	61 399	38 627
Food	6 599	6 875	6 822	7 980	4 701
Food at home	3 921	4 059	4 044	4 367	2 973
Cereals and bakery products	538	557	556	584	404
Meats, poultry, fish, and eggs	852	855	846	1 034	836
Dairy products	419	443	446	372	254
Fruits and vegetables	731	760	747	1 037	530
Other food at home	1 380	1 443	1 448	1 339	949
Food away from home	2 678	2 816	2 777	3 613	1 728
Alcoholic Beverages	451	486	492	360	212
Housing	16 887	17 246	17 058	20 821	14 395
Shelter	9 891	10 099	9 904	13 841	8 441
Owned dwellings	6 056	6 402	6 299	8 380	3 645
Rented dwellings	3 186	2 994	2 902	4 770	4 521
Other lodging	649	702	703	691	275
Utilities, fuels, and public services	3 648	3 666	3 677	3 456	3 525
Household operations	1 159	1 209	1 195	1 469	810
Housekeeping supplies	610	632	638	497	459
Household furnishings and equipment	1 580	1 641	1 643	1 558	1 160
Apparel and Services	1 736	1 741	1 710	2 391	1 697
Transportation	8 998	9 322	9 280	10 117	6 751
Vehicle purchases (net outlay)	3 210	3 362	3 363	3 339	2 155
Gasoline and motor oil	2 756	2 817	2 825	2 659	2 329
Other vehicle expenses	2 490	2 571	2 566	2 658	1 927
Public and other transportation	542	571	525	1 461	340
Health Care	3 556	3 779	3 804	3 285	2 013
Health insurance	2 061	2 163	2 166	2 101	1 349
Medical services	839	915	926	704	307
Drugs	515	546	555	368	300
Medical supplies	142	155	157	112	57
Entertainment	2 605	2 761	2 784	2 303	1 526
Personal Care Products and Services	628	637	640	594	565
Reading	109	119	120	97	45
Education	1 207	1 289	1 184	3 295	641
Tobacco Products and Smoking Supplies	332	344	354	161	245
Miscellaneous	829	867	868	849	563
Cash Contributions	1 913	1 992	2 025	1 356	1 358
Personal Insurance and Pensions	5 591	5 832	5 730	7 789	3 914
Life and other personal insurance	353	357	357	361	321
Pensions and Social Security	5 238	5 475	5 373	7 428	3 593

Table 11-12. Consumer Expenditures, Averages by Hispanic Origin of Reference Person, 2012

(Number, dollar, percent.)

Item	All consumer units	Hispanic[1]	Not Hispanic		
			Total	White, Asian, and other races	Black
NUMBER OF CONSUMER UNITS (THOUSANDS)	124 416	15 597	108 819	93 385	15 434
CONSUMER UNIT CHARACTERISTICS					
Income Before Taxes	65 596	48 066	68 109	71 552	47 277
Income After Taxes	63 370	47 580	65 633	68 742	46 821
Age of Reference Person	50.0	42.8	51.1	51.6	47.7
Average Number in Consumer Unit					
All persons	2.5	3.3	2.4	2.3	2.5
Children under 18 years	0.6	1.1	0.5	0.5	0.8
Persons 65 years and over	0.3	0.2	0.4	0.4	0.2
Earners	1.3	1.6	1.2	1.3	1.1
Vehicles	1.9	1.6	1.9	2.0	1.3
Percent Distribution					
Male	47	45	47	48	38
Female	53	55	53	52	62
Percent Homeowner	64	46	67	71	43
With mortgage	39	30	40	42	28
Without mortgage	26	16	27	29	15
AVERAGE ANNUAL EXPENDITURES	51 442	42 268	52 757	55 097	38 634
Food	6 599	6 570	6 603	6 924	4 678
Food at home	3 921	4 116	3 893	4 050	2 954
Cereals and bakery products	538	534	538	561	402
Meats, poultry, fish, and eggs	852	1 037	826	825	835
Dairy products	419	427	418	446	251
Fruits and vegetables	731	820	718	750	528
Other food at home	1 380	1 298	1 392	1 468	938
Food away from home	2 678	2 454	2 710	2 875	1 724
Alcoholic Beverages	451	338	467	510	212
Housing	16 887	15 061	17 149	17 605	14 393
Shelter	9 891	9 215	9 987	10 244	8 432
Owned dwellings	6 056	4 185	6 324	6 763	3 664
Rented dwellings	3 186	4 843	2 949	2 694	4 491
Other lodging	649	187	715	787	278
Utilities, fuels, and public services	3 648	3 325	3 695	3 721	3 535
Household operations	1 159	728	1 221	1 288	815
Housekeeping supplies	610	568	616	642	462
Household furnishings and equipment	1 580	1 225	1 631	1 711	1 149
Apparel and Services	1 736	2 030	1 694	1 694	1 695
Transportation	8 998	8 306	9 097	9 485	6 755
Vehicle purchases (net outlay)	3 210	2 890	3 256	3 439	2 154
Gasoline and motor oil	2 756	2 727	2 760	2 831	2 328
Other vehicle expenses	2 490	2 294	2 518	2 615	1 934
Public and other transportation	542	395	563	600	339
Health Care	3 556	1 893	3 795	4 088	2 024
Health insurance	2 061	1 019	2 210	2 351	1 355
Medical services	839	528	883	978	310
Drugs	515	261	551	592	302
Medical supplies	142	85	151	166	57
Entertainment	2 605	1 588	2 751	2 953	1 531
Personal Care Products and Services	628	556	639	651	565
Reading	109	40	119	132	45
Education	1 207	488	1 310	1 423	631
Tobacco Products and Smoking Supplies	332	157	357	375	246
Miscellaneous	829	553	868	919	561
Cash Contributions	1 913	782	2 075	2 192	1 364
Personal Insurance and Pensions	5 591	3 905	5 833	6 146	3 934
Life and other personal insurance	353	112	387	398	324
Pensions and Social Security	5 238	3 793	5 446	5 749	3 610

[1]May be of any race.

Table 11-13. Consumer Expenditures, Averages by Education of Reference Person, 2012

(Number, dollar, percent.)

Item	All consumer units	Less than a college graduate					College graduate or more		
		Total	Less than a high school graduate	High school graduate	High school graduate with some college	Associate's degree	Total	Bachelor's degree	Master's, professional, or doctoral degree
NUMBER OF CONSUMER UNITS (THOUSANDS)	124 416	76 789	10 571	26 601	25 793	13 825	47 626	28 069	19 557
CONSUMER UNIT CHARACTERISTICS									
Income Before Taxes	65 596	44 603	25 159	39 357	48 224	62 809	99 444	85 802	119 023
Income After Taxes	63 370	43 846	25 199	38 825	47 519	60 913	94 849	82 083	113 172
Age of Reference Person	50.0	50.7	56.2	53.0	47.5	48.3	48.9	47.4	51.1
Average Number in Consumer Unit									
All persons	2.5	2.4	2.2	2.4	2.4	2.7	2.6	2.5	2.7
Children under 18 years	0.6	0.6	0.7	0.6	0.6	0.7	0.6	0.6	0.6
Persons 65 years and over	0.3	0.4	0.5	0.4	0.3	0.3	0.3	0.3	0.4
Earners	1.3	1.2	0.7	1.0	1.2	1.5	1.5	1.5	1.5
Vehicles	1.9	1.7	1.1	1.7	1.8	2.2	2.1	2.1	2.2
Percent Distribution									
Male	47	44	44	45	44	41	51	51	52
Female	53	56	56	55	56	59	49	49	48
Percent Homeowner	64	58	47	59	56	68	74	71	79
With mortgage	39	31	16	28	33	45	51	49	54
Without mortgage	26	27	32	32	23	22	23	22	25
AVERAGE ANNUAL EXPENDITURES	51 442	39 107	24 582	34 786	43 041	50 836	71 151	63 135	82 606
Food	6 599	5 409	3 913	4 944	5 749	6 658	8 435	7 928	9 143
Food at home	3 921	3 442	2 862	3 263	3 542	3 980	4 654	4 379	5 032
Cereals and bakery products	538	473	383	453	481	554	637	592	700
Meats, poultry, fish, and eggs	852	802	672	812	772	926	930	911	957
Dairy products	419	349	288	322	363	414	526	488	577
Fruits and vegetables	731	608	550	567	626	687	919	848	1 017
Other food at home	1 380	1 211	969	1 109	1 299	1 399	1 641	1 541	1 781
Food away from home	2 678	1 967	1 051	1 682	2 207	2 678	3 782	3 549	4 111
Alcoholic Beverages	451	292	108	236	350	416	696	650	759
Housing	16 887	13 197	9 388	12 143	14 241	16 146	22 815	20 230	26 512
Shelter	9 891	7 532	5 521	6 871	8 168	9 155	13 693	12 103	15 976
Owned dwellings	6 056	3 998	2 087	3 509	4 424	5 607	9 373	8 022	11 312
Rented dwellings	3 186	3 226	3 362	3 150	3 373	2 995	3 122	3 213	2 991
Other lodging	649	308	72	212	371	553	1 198	867	1 672
Utilities, fuels, and public services	3 648	3 318	2 541	3 280	3 333	3 957	4 181	3 935	4 534
Household operations	1 159	726	390	600	845	1 003	1 856	1 495	2 373
Housekeeping supplies	610	516	382	475	564	592	753	676	859
Household furnishings and equipment	1 580	1 106	554	918	1 331	1 439	2 331	2 021	2 770
Apparel and Services	1 736	1 329	1 042	1 083	1 540	1 588	2 366	2 226	2 565
Transportation	8 998	7 381	3 835	6 225	8 422	10 342	11 594	10 817	12 710
Vehicle purchases (net outlay)	3 210	2 621	932	1 880	3 290	4 090	4 161	3 827	4 641
Gasoline and motor oil	2 756	2 466	1 549	2 318	2 557	3 282	3 223	3 156	3 319
Other vehicle expenses	2 490	2 041	1 191	1 839	2 244	2 666	3 202	3 062	3 405
Public and other transportation	542	253	162	187	331	305	1 008	773	1 345
Health Care	3 556	2 885	2 004	2 823	2 949	3 560	4 635	4 196	5 263
Health insurance	2 061	1 698	1 173	1 747	1 638	2 116	2 646	2 417	2 973
Medical services	839	628	354	554	734	783	1 178	1 075	1 326
Drugs	515	455	426	416	474	516	609	540	706
Medical supplies	142	105	52	106	103	146	202	164	257
Entertainment	2 605	1 901	1 134	1 630	2 118	2 571	3 725	3 220	4 443
Personal Care Products and Services	628	468	292	388	530	627	881	769	1 039
Reading	109	69	29	53	81	107	175	135	232
Education	1 207	564	120	214	892	959	2 244	1 792	2 891
Tobacco Products and Smoking Supplies	332	426	331	497	421	372	179	219	123
Miscellaneous	829	654	307	691	728	703	1 110	926	1 373
Cash Contributions	1 913	1 106	599	1 012	1 214	1 473	3 213	2 411	4 364
Personal Insurance and Pensions	5 591	3 425	1 481	2 847	3 805	5 313	9 084	7 617	11 188
Life and other personal insurance	353	205	107	203	207	281	591	479	752
Pensions and Social Security	5 238	3 220	1 374	2 645	3 598	5 032	8 493	7 139	10 436

Table 11-14. Consumer Expenditures, Averages by Housing Tenure and Type of Area, 2012

(Number, dollar, percent.)

| Item | All consumer units | Housing tenure | | | | Type of area | | | |
| | | Homeowner | | | Renter | Urban | | | Rural |
		Total	Homeowner with mortgage	Homeowner without mortgage		Total	Central city	Other urban	
NUMBER OF CONSUMER UNITS (THOUSANDS)	124 416	79 945	47 946	31 999	44 471	114 117	36 929	77 188	10 299
CONSUMER UNIT CHARACTERISTICS									
Income Before Taxes	65 596	80 330	93 941	59 937	39 109	66 877	56 338	71 919	51 405
Income After Taxes	63 370	77 165	89 941	58 022	38 571	64 581	54 804	69 259	49 947
Age of Reference Person	50.0	54.5	48.5	63.6	42.0	49.7	47.3	50.8	54.1
Average Number in Consumer Unit									
All persons	2.5	2.6	2.9	2.1	2.3	2.5	2.3	2.6	2.4
Children under 18 years	0.6	0.6	0.8	0.3	0.7	0.6	0.6	0.6	0.6
Persons 65 years and over	0.3	0.4	0.2	0.8	0.2	0.3	0.3	0.4	0.4
Earners	1.3	1.4	1.7	0.9	1.1	1.3	1.2	1.3	1.2
Vehicles	1.9	2.3	2.4	2.1	1.2	1.8	1.4	2.1	2.5
Percent Distribution									
Male	47	47	49	45	45	47	46	47	46
Female	53	53	51	55	55	53	54	53	54
Percent Homeowner	64	100	100	100	X	63	47	70	82
With mortgage	39	60	100	X	X	39	29	43	37
Without mortgage	26	40	X	100	X	24	18	27	45
AVERAGE ANNUAL EXPENDITURES	51 442	59 983	68 228	47 255	36 076	52 227	45 115	55 577	42 699
Food	6 599	7 465	7 920	6 565	5 037	6 652	5 929	6 975	5 981
Food at home	3 921	4 357	4 579	3 899	3 134	3 929	3 496	4 119	3 827
Cereals and bakery products	538	599	631	531	428	540	474	569	515
Meats, poultry, fish, and eggs	852	937	994	819	700	850	773	884	883
Dairy products	419	473	499	419	322	420	365	444	409
Fruits and vegetables	731	809	845	733	591	739	675	766	642
Other food at home	1 380	1 539	1 610	1 396	1 094	1 381	1 210	1 456	1 378
Food away from home	2 678	3 108	3 341	2 666	1 903	2 723	2 433	2 856	2 154
Alcoholic Beverages	451	513	563	417	339	465	477	460	290
Housing	16 887	18 756	22 705	12 849	13 526	17 364	15 861	18 070	11 604
Shelter	9 891	10 307	13 590	5 387	9 142	10 289	9 882	10 484	5 470
Owned dwellings	6 056	9 349	12 591	4 492	135	6 237	4 562	7 038	4 048
Rented dwellings	3 186	57	50	67	8 812	3 389	4 828	2 701	935
Other lodging	649	901	949	828	195	663	492	745	487
Utilities, fuels, and public services	3 648	4 338	4 648	3 874	2 408	3 655	3 184	3 880	3 577
Household operations	1 159	1 439	1 638	1 139	655	1 201	1 013	1 291	693
Housekeeping supplies	610	725	734	705	403	610	480	667	612
Household furnishings and equipment	1 580	1 947	2 094	1 744	918	1 609	1 302	1 749	1 252
Apparel and Services	1 736	1 877	2 125	1 411	1 481	1 764	1 770	1 761	1 419
Transportation	8 998	10 658	12 110	8 468	6 013	9 011	6 949	9 991	8 862
Vehicle purchases (net outlay)	3 210	3 863	4 569	2 805	2 038	3 218	2 166	3 721	3 128
Gasoline and motor oil	2 756	3 188	3 584	2 593	1 979	2 717	2 099	3 012	3 189
Other vehicle expenses	2 490	2 962	3 286	2 463	1 638	2 505	2 086	2 699	2 323
Public and other transportation	542	645	671	607	357	571	598	559	222
Health Care	3 556	4 541	4 311	4 896	1 786	3 518	2 759	3 801	3 900
Health insurance	2 061	2 658	2 485	2 917	988	2 034	1 554	2 263	2 358
Medical services	839	1 059	1 093	1 007	443	834	694	900	894
Drugs	515	642	567	763	286	508	392	563	588
Medical supplies	142	183	167	210	70	143	119	154	140
Entertainment	2 605	3 196	3 536	2 657	1 541	2 635	2 119	2 874	2 278
Personal Care Products and Services	628	733	805	605	440	643	585	670	460
Reading	109	139	135	145	56	110	98	116	98
Education	1 207	1 383	1 756	818	891	1 270	1 087	1 358	507
Tobacco Products and Smoking Supplies	332	307	324	281	377	317	296	327	494
Miscellaneous	829	1 022	1 025	1 032	482	850	725	909	591
Cash Contributions	1 913	2 385	2 182	2 690	1 063	1 927	1 834	1 971	1 753
Personal Insurance and Pensions	5 591	7 007	8 733	4 421	3 045	5 700	4 627	6 213	4 381
Life and other personal insurance	353	478	539	386	127	361	257	410	264
Pensions and Social Security	5 238	6 529	8 194	4 035	2 917	5 339	4 370	5 803	4 117

X = Not applicable.

Table 11-15. Consumer Expenditures, Averages by Population Size of Area of Residence, 2012

(Number, dollar, percent.)

Item	All consumer units	Outside urban area	Urban consumer units						
			Total	Less than 100,000	100,000 to 249,999	250,000 to 999,999	1,000,000 to 2,499,999	2,500,000 to 4,999,999	5,000,000 and over
NUMBER OF CONSUMER UNITS (THOUSANDS)	124 416	24 900	99 516	19 236	9 857	21 495	15 646	17 191	16 092
CONSUMER UNIT CHARACTERISTICS									
Income Before Taxes	65 596	61 279	66 677	52 881	62 177	60 061	67 502	82 670	76 873
Income After Taxes	63 370	59 483	64 342	51 804	61 039	58 522	65 215	77 351	74 385
Age of Reference Person	50.0	53.8	49.1	48.8	49.0	48.8	49.3	48.9	49.8
Average Number in Consumer Unit									
All persons	2.5	2.5	2.5	2.4	2.5	2.4	2.5	2.5	2.6
Children under 18 years	0.6	0.6	0.6	0.6	0.7	0.6	0.6	0.6	0.6
Persons 65 years and over	0.3	0.4	0.3	0.3	0.3	0.3	0.3	0.3	0.3
Earners	1.3	1.3	1.3	1.2	1.3	1.3	1.3	1.4	1.3
Vehicles	1.9	2.5	1.7	1.8	1.9	1.8	1.8	1.7	1.4
Percent Distribution									
Male	47	47	47	44	44	46	49	50	45
Female	53	53	53	56	56	54	51	50	55
Percent Homeowner	64	82	60	60	62	61	62	59	54
With mortgage	39	42	38	34	40	38	42	41	33
Without mortgage	26	41	22	26	23	24	20	19	20
AVERAGE ANNUAL EXPENDITURES	51 442	49 191	52 005	43 672	48 647	50 196	52 898	60 684	56 327
Food	6 599	6 414	6 645	5 752	6 151	6 730	6 684	7 355	7 095
Food at home	3 921	3 991	3 903	3 458	3 894	4 009	3 816	4 292	3 976
Cereals and bakery products	538	535	539	464	545	560	539	584	549
Meats, poultry, fish, and eggs	852	874	847	767	822	812	836	925	924
Dairy products	419	426	417	377	408	453	413	427	421
Fruits and vegetables	731	673	746	615	752	745	685	878	813
Other food at home	1 380	1 484	1 354	1 235	1 367	1 439	1 344	1 478	1 268
Food away from home	2 678	2 423	2 742	2 293	2 257	2 720	2 867	3 063	3 119
Alcoholic Beverages	451	391	466	383	411	478	531	532	449
Housing	16 887	14 290	17 537	13 483	15 829	16 373	17 533	20 824	21 509
Shelter	9 891	7 337	10 529	7 338	8 969	9 455	10 529	12 959	14 140
Owned dwellings	6 056	5 618	6 165	4 420	5 518	5 793	6 303	7 485	7 602
Rented dwellings	3 186	1 147	3 696	2 426	2 951	3 091	3 500	4 546	5 765
Other lodging	649	572	668	492	500	570	727	929	773
Utilities, fuels, and public services	3 648	3 831	3 602	3 395	3 682	3 429	3 609	3 796	3 819
Household operations	1 159	850	1 236	869	1 199	1 144	1 202	1 536	1 531
Housekeeping supplies	610	674	594	562	573	640	586	610	580
Household furnishings and equipment	1 580	1 598	1 575	1 319	1 406	1 705	1 606	1 923	1 438
Apparel and Services	1 736	1 511	1 792	1 391	1 696	1 608	1 817	2 091	2 208
Transportation	8 998	9 775	8 804	8 571	9 217	8 423	9 417	9 676	7 816
Vehicle purchases (net outlay)	3 210	3 463	3 147	3 605	3 561	2 944	3 792	3 194	1 940
Gasoline and motor oil	2 756	3 364	2 604	2 508	2 641	2 604	2 641	2 885	2 359
Other vehicle expenses	2 490	2 641	2 452	2 158	2 592	2 352	2 395	2 731	2 614
Public and other transportation	542	307	601	300	423	523	589	865	903
Health Care	3 556	4 096	3 421	3 251	3 385	3 585	3 598	3 514	3 167
Health insurance	2 061	2 441	1 966	1 718	2 069	1 998	2 073	2 118	1 889
Medical services	839	918	819	860	716	839	913	808	724
Drugs	515	595	495	550	467	593	462	429	422
Medical supplies	142	142	142	123	132	155	150	159	132
Entertainment	2 605	2 846	2 545	2 306	2 327	2 618	2 639	2 818	2 504
Personal Care Products and Services	628	552	647	542	552	648	688	752	680
Reading	109	108	110	97	92	108	121	128	108
Education	1 207	781	1 314	800	994	1 229	1 229	1 593	2 023
Tobacco Products and Smoking Supplies ...	332	467	298	335	397	308	305	248	227
Miscellaneous	829	739	851	667	1 162	768	811	1 053	814
Cash Contributions	1 913	1 943	1 905	1 524	1 510	2 063	1 931	2 621	1 601
Personal Insurance and Pensions	5 591	5 278	5 669	4 572	4 922	5 257	5 595	7 481	6 125
Life and other personal insurance	353	353	352	257	350	358	277	532	342
Pensions and Social Security	5 238	4 925	5 317	4 315	4 573	4 898	5 318	6 950	5 783

Table 11-16. Consumer Expenditures, Averages by Region of Residence, 2012

(Number, dollar, percent.)

Item	All consumer units	Northeast	South	Midwest	West
		Region[1]			
NUMBER OF CONSUMER UNITS (THOUSANDS)	124 416	22 459	27 584	46 338	28 035
CONSUMER UNIT CHARACTERISTICS					
Income Before Taxes	65 596	72 036	65 217	60 219	69 700
Income After Taxes	63 370	69 289	62 652	58 488	67 404
Age of Reference Person	50.0	50.9	49.6	50.3	49.3
Average Number in Consumer Unit					
All persons	2.5	2.4	2.4	2.5	2.6
Children under 18 years	0.6	0.6	0.6	0.6	0.6
Persons 65 years and over	0.3	0.4	0.3	0.3	0.3
Earners	1.3	1.3	1.3	1.2	1.4
Vehicles	1.9	1.6	2.0	1.9	2.0
Percent Distribution					
Male	47	45	47	46	49
Female	53	55	53	54	51
Percent Homeowner	64	62	68	66	59
With mortgage	39	38	40	38	38
Without mortgage	26	24	27	28	21
AVERAGE ANNUAL EXPENDITURES	51 442	55 884	48 602	47 757	56 782
Food	6 599	6 962	6 393	6 156	7 246
Food at home	3 921	4 056	3 906	3 652	4 272
Cereals and bakery products	538	586	556	488	564
Meats, poultry, fish, and eggs	852	898	797	839	893
Dairy products	419	448	421	383	452
Fruits and vegetables	731	798	728	637	836
Other food at home	1 380	1 327	1 405	1 304	1 526
Food away from home	2 678	2 906	2 486	2 504	2 974
Alcoholic Beverages	451	535	437	375	524
Housing	16 887	19 745	15 012	15 280	19 103
Shelter	9 891	12 274	8 530	8 298	11 953
Owned dwellings	6 056	7 480	5 644	5 147	6 823
Rented dwellings	3 186	3 938	2 282	2 617	4 416
Other lodging	649	856	604	534	715
Utilities, fuels, and public services	3 648	3 979	3 455	3 704	3 481
Household operations	1 159	1 435	973	1 030	1 333
Housekeeping supplies	610	597	588	609	644
Household furnishings and equipment	1 580	1 460	1 466	1 640	1 691
Apparel and Services	1 736	1 833	1 564	1 662	1 950
Transportation	8 998	8 857	8 604	9 080	9 367
Vehicle purchases (net outlay)	3 210	2 906	3 216	3 413	3 115
Gasoline and motor oil	2 756	2 503	2 713	2 863	2 824
Other vehicle expenses	2 490	2 612	2 242	2 434	2 730
Public and other transportation	542	836	432	371	698
Health Care	3 556	3 572	3 844	3 234	3 795
Health insurance	2 061	2 162	2 295	1 861	2 079
Medical services	839	801	858	742	1 009
Drugs	515	452	550	508	541
Medical supplies	142	156	141	122	166
Entertainment	2 605	2 723	2 550	2 407	2 894
Personal Care Products and Services	628	635	572	628	680
Reading	109	134	107	82	137
Education	1 207	1 789	1 180	851	1 358
Tobacco Products and Smoking Supplies	332	354	341	364	250
Miscellaneous	829	938	808	665	1 033
Cash Contributions	1 913	1 798	1 851	1 699	2 417
Personal Insurance and Pensions	5 591	6 009	5 339	5 273	6 030
Life and other personal insurance	353	332	334	393	320
Pensions and Social Security	5 238	5 677	5 005	4 879	5 710

[1]The states that comprise the Census regions are: Northeast—Connecticut, Maine, Massachusetts, New Hampshire, New Jersey, New York, Pennsylvania, Rhode Island, and Vermont; South—Alabama, Arkansas, Delaware, District of Columbia, Florida, Georgia, Kentucky, Louisiana, Maryland, Mississippi, North Carolina, Oklahoma, South Carolina, Tennessee, Texas, Virginia, and West Virginia; Midwest—Illinois, Indiana, Iowa, Kansas, Michigan, Minnesota, Missouri, Nebraska, North Dakota, Ohio, South Dakota, and Wisconsin; and West—Alaska, Arizona, California, Colorado, Hawaii, Idaho, Montana, Nevada, New Mexico, Oregon, Utah, Washington, and Wyoming.

Table 11-17. Consumer Expenditures, Averages for Single Men by Income Before Taxes, 2011–2012

(Number, dollar, percent.)

Item	All single men	Complete reporting of income						
		Less than $5,000	$5,000 to $9,999	$10,000 to $14,999	$15,000 to $19,999	$20,000 to $29,999	$30,000 to $39,999	$40,000 and over
NUMBER OF CONSUMER UNITS (THOUSANDS)	17 055	1 470	1 407	2 036	1 670	2 710	2 131	5 632
CONSUMER UNIT CHARACTERISTICS								
Income Before Taxes	39 906	-3 356	7 938	12 575	17 355	24 683	34 394	85 156
Income After Taxes	37 899	-2 573	7 908	12 364	17 277	24 317	33 344	79 553
Age of Reference Person	48.9	41.1	44.6	51.8	56.2	51.2	47.3	48.2
Average Number in Consumer Unit								
All persons	1.0	1.0	1.0	1.0	1.0	1.0	1.0	1.0
Persons 65 years and over	0.2	0.1	0.2	0.3	0.4	0.3	0.2	0.1
Earners	0.7	0.5	0.4	0.4	0.4	0.6	0.8	0.9
Vehicles	1.2	0.7	0.7	0.9	1.2	1.2	1.3	1.5
Percent Homeowner	44	24	21	30	48	42	47	58
With mortgage	22	6	5	7	13	16	25	40
Without mortgage	22	17	16	23	35	26	22	19
AVERAGE ANNUAL EXPENDITURES	31 861	20 107	16 118	16 932	23 086	26 124	30 552	49 284
Food	3 832	2 811	2 504	2 558	2 755	3 128	3 828	5 172
Food at home	1 908	1 339	1 496	1 661	1 746	1 666	1 963	2 261
Cereals and bakery products	260	196	193	233	271	230	264	298
Meats, poultry, fish, and eggs	411	273	341	383	324	349	438	490
Dairy products	193	129	154	150	193	169	197	231
Fruits and vegetables	350	223	275	293	311	307	328	433
Other food at home	694	518	532	602	648	610	736	810
Food away from home	1 924	1 472	1 008	897	1 009	1 462	1 865	2 910
Alcoholic Beverages	508	277	386	256	248	301	572	774
Housing	11 198	6 942	6 181	6 712	8 316	10 109	11 351	16 426
Shelter	7 383	4 835	4 335	4 389	5 160	6 478	7 330	11 005
Owned dwellings	3 091	1 001	740	802	1 866	2 175	2 936	5 915
Rented dwellings	3 959	3 320	3 395	3 497	3 107	4 129	4 230	4 501
Other lodging	333	514	199	90	187	174	165	589
Utilities, fuels, and public services	2 187	1 273	1 235	1 587	2 048	2 172	2 304	2 885
Household operations	543	244	179	230	275	450	559	942
Housekeeping supplies	254	163	126	147	237	231	239	338
Household furnishings and equipment	832	427	307	360	596	779	919	1 256
Apparel and Services	817	521	463	293	713	442	944	1 244
Transportation	5 136	3 405	2 204	2 665	4 124	4 275	4 848	7 908
Vehicle purchases (net outlay)	1 592	1 314	567	559	1 361	1 155	1 368	2 656
Gasoline and motor oil	1 644	1 021	904	1 062	1 257	1 672	1 782	2 252
Other vehicle expenses	1 573	757	571	882	1 329	1 227	1 468	2 436
Public and other transportation	327	313	162	161	176	221	230	564
Health Care	1 794	694	654	1 057	1 938	1 967	1 840	2 482
Health insurance	999	318	360	620	1 010	1 097	1 099	1 385
Medical services	488	174	96	214	622	510	445	731
Drugs	240	183	176	179	230	286	257	262
Medical supplies	68	[1]18	[1]22	44	75	73	39	104
Entertainment	1 576	725	785	957	1 099	1 326	1 712	2 366
Personal Care Products and Services	205	121	126	123	111	161	183	318
Reading	73	37	44	36	50	64	74	115
Education	873	1 996	1 492	511	638	665	503	865
Tobacco Products and Smoking Supplies	344	276	373	378	314	421	376	302
Miscellaneous	631	697	209	342	354	669	496	940
Cash Contributions	1 769	1 448	407	597	1 717	1 154	1 150	3 161
Personal Insurance and Pensions	3 105	157	290	447	709	1 443	2 675	7 210
Life and other personal insurance	139	67	20	85	76	163	129	217
Pensions and Social Security	2 966	90	270	362	633	1 280	2 546	6 993

[1]Data are likely to have large sampling errors.
X = Not applicable.

Table 11-18. Consumer Expenditures, Averages for Single Women by Income Before Taxes, 2011–2012

(Number, dollar, percent.)

Item	All single women	Complete reporting of income						
		Less than $5,000	$5,000 to $9,999	$10,000 to $14,999	$15,000 to $19,999	$20,000 to $29,999	$30,000 to $39,999	$40,000 and over
NUMBER OF CONSUMER UNITS (THOUSANDS)	19 470	1 729	1 890	3 391	2 476	3 089	2 292	4 603
CONSUMER UNIT CHARACTERISTICS								
Income Before Taxes	29 424	2 322	8 090	12 678	17 356	24 368	34 431	68 092
Income After Taxes	28 438	2 450	8 117	12 625	17 298	24 124	33 817	64 404
Age of Reference Person	58.6	47.7	56.7	65.7	66.7	60.7	54.8	54.2
Average Number in Consumer Unit								
All persons	1.0	1.0	1.0	1.0	1.0	1.0	1.0	1.0
Persons 65 years and over	0.4	0.3	0.4	0.6	0.7	0.5	0.3	0.3
Earners	0.5	0.3	0.3	0.2	0.3	0.5	0.7	0.8
Vehicles	0.9	0.5	0.6	0.7	0.9	1.0	1.1	1.2
Percent Homeowner	55	30	35	49	57	60	60	71
With mortgage	22	8	8	10	11	20	31	46
Without mortgage	33	22	27	39	46	40	30	26
AVERAGE ANNUAL EXPENDITURES	29 617	17 919	16 084	17 762	22 756	28 096	33 574	50 577
Food	3 352	2 571	2 448	2 449	2 777	3 073	3 580	4 906
Food at home	2 104	1 687	1 733	1 795	1 923	1 921	2 174	2 756
Cereals and bakery products	291	231	283	263	273	274	283	353
Meats, poultry, fish, and eggs	382	377	361	341	345	332	407	465
Dairy products	230	162	173	196	214	204	270	300
Fruits and vegetables	427	308	332	362	378	397	436	577
Other food at home	774	610	584	632	712	713	777	1 061
Food away from home	1 248	884	715	655	854	1 152	1 406	2 149
Alcoholic Beverages	234	137	132	43	110	146	328	520
Housing	11 747	7 701	6 852	7 728	9 790	11 658	13 453	18 441
Shelter	7 243	4 832	4 301	4 658	5 766	6 801	8 391	11 781
Owned dwellings	3 717	1 443	1 200	1 763	2 518	3 319	4 329	7 652
Rented dwellings	3 249	3 143	2 978	2 786	3 123	3 288	3 709	3 555
Other lodging	277	247	123	109	124	195	352	574
Utilities, fuels, and public services	2 465	1 500	1 772	2 008	2 352	2 666	2 761	3 227
Household operations	774	507	233	339	759	1 093	845	1 175
Housekeeping supplies	394	261	220	264	366	386	472	559
Household furnishings and equipment	870	601	326	459	548	711	984	1 700
Apparel and Services	1 039	825	647	553	570	733	1 165	1 999
Transportation	3 916	2 024	1 617	2 004	2 952	4 052	4 905	6 815
Vehicle purchases (net outlay)	1 057	[1]681	[1]241	[1]306	822	1 013	1 390	2 076
Gasoline and motor oil	1 204	659	710	746	973	1 347	1 495	1 832
Other vehicle expenses	1 335	513	547	814	1 001	1 460	1 613	2 210
Public and other transportation	320	172	118	138	156	232	407	697
Health Care	2 604	1 216	1 433	2 061	2 734	2 787	2 731	3 734
Health insurance	1 472	703	742	1 214	1 736	1 669	1 650	1 886
Medical services	595	221	397	376	486	518	526	1 124
Drugs	419	207	230	362	401	492	440	554
Medical supplies	117	85	64	108	111	107	115	170
Entertainment	1 440	680	789	794	1 041	1 397	1 803	2 475
Personal Care Products and Services	534	233	281	265	358	444	704	999
Reading	98	38	43	55	79	90	111	182
Education	599	1 229	749	405	360	354	455	807
Tobacco Products and Smoking Supplies	174	176	169	195	130	174	224	158
Miscellaneous	597	352	338	360	494	606	775	923
Cash Contributions	1 199	505	356	554	843	1 239	1 263	2 412
Personal Insurance and Pensions	2 086	231	231	297	517	1 343	2 078	6 207
Life and other personal insurance	190	37	85	113	107	361	147	300
Pensions and Social Security	1 895	194	146	183	411	982	1 931	5 907

[1]Data are likely to have large sampling errors.

Table 11-19. Consumer Expenditures, Averages for Age Groups by Income Before Taxes: Reference Person Under 25 Years of Age, 2011–2012

(Number, dollar, percent.)

Item		Complete reporting of income						
	Total	Less than $5,000	$5,000 to $9,999	$10,000 to $14,999	$15,000 to $19,999	$20,000 to $29,999	$30,000 to $39,999	$40,000 and over
NUMBER OF CONSUMER UNITS (THOUSANDS)	7 951	1 361	1 028	834	755	1 111	905	1 957
CONSUMER UNIT CHARACTERISTICS								
Income Before Taxes	32 196	2 803	7 278	12 661	17 498	24 492	34 708	82 933
Income After Taxes	30 663	2 936	7 324	12 874	17 903	24 849	34 837	76 083
Age of Reference Person	21.7	20.7	21.0	21.6	21.6	22.1	22.2	22.3
Average Number in Consumer Unit								
All persons	2.1	1.3	1.5	1.5	2.0	2.1	2.6	2.8
Children under 18 years	0.4	0.2	0.2	0.3	0.5	0.5	0.7	0.5
Persons 65 years and over	([1])	([1])	([1])	([1])	([1])	([1])	([1])	([1])
Earners	1.3	0.7	0.8	0.9	1.1	1.3	1.6	2.0
Vehicles	1.1	0.4	0.6	0.7	1.0	1.1	1.4	1.9
Percent Distribution								
Male	48	44	50	48	43	45	51	53
Female	52	56	50	52	57	55	49	47
Percent Homeowner	15	2	2	3	9	10	19	38
With mortgage	10	1	1	1	3	7	13	30
Without mortgage	5	1	2	2	6	4	6	8
AVERAGE ANNUAL EXPENDITURES	30 675	15 786	17 906	19 614	24 915	29 366	35 536	51 336
Food	4 387	2 713	2 483	3 011	3 262	4 075	5 280	6 329
Food at home	2 460	1 143	1 206	1 724	1 933	2 156	3 151	3 681
Cereals and bakery products	346	138	166	245	301	324	410	516
Meats, poultry, fish, and eggs	551	212	215	388	409	430	736	882
Dairy products	248	119	146	158	177	240	310	364
Fruits and vegetables	441	207	207	259	342	417	587	659
Other food at home	874	468	472	673	704	745	1 109	1 260
Food away from home	1 926	1 569	1 277	1 287	1 328	1 919	2 129	2 648
Alcoholic Beverages	384	144	367	391	232	245	587	512
Housing	10 629	5 290	6 473	7 115	9 271	10 903	12 947	17 161
Shelter	7 016	3 891	4 829	4 991	6 246	7 142	7 967	10 985
Owned dwellings	1 292	[2]206	[2]145	[2]122	326	578	1 092	4 019
Rented dwellings	5 438	3 206	4 324	4 687	5 795	6 292	6 619	6 725
Other lodging	286	479	360	[2]183	[2]125	272	256	240
Utilities, fuels, and public services	1 898	718	835	1 215	1 655	1 986	2 539	3 317
Household operations	522	196	171	249	512	540	668	987
Housekeeping supplies	287	94	162	112	180	225	368	495
Household furnishings and equipment	906	390	476	549	678	1 010	1 404	1 377
Apparel and Services	1 340	1 120	947	613	952	1 030	1 659	2 055
Transportation	5 953	2 090	2 541	3 262	5 547	6 149	6 526	11 132
Vehicle purchases (net outlay)	2 478	[2]537	[2]890	[2]1071	[2]2883	2 744	2 387	4 996
Gasoline and motor oil	1 887	897	1 005	1 241	1 522	1 894	2 298	3 259
Other vehicle expenses	1 293	434	496	793	790	1 188	1 583	2 403
Public and other transportation	295	222	149	157	352	323	257	473
Health Care	935	381	322	349	681	1 135	1 191	1 754
Health insurance	457	143	179	[2]138	186	405	623	1 015
Medical services	332	113	55	108	399	634	376	506
Drugs	103	99	49	78	70	75	143	157
Medical supplies	43	[2]26	[2]38	[2]24	[2]27	21	49	76
Entertainment	1 297	593	699	768	902	1 306	1 612	2 198
Personal Care Products and Services	343	204	179	165	226	345	436	552
Reading	44	28	39	33	48	40	32	70
Education	2 065	2 781	2 995	2 501	1 988	1 391	1 518	1 551
Tobacco Products and Smoking Supplies	259	126	156	160	263	346	390	336
Miscellaneous	329	71	209	334	159	402	369	548
Cash Contributions	429	116	128	251	330	295	353	1 029
Personal Insurance and Pensions	2 281	130	369	661	1 052	1 703	2 638	6 109
Life and other personal insurance	58	2	[2]3	[2]9	[2]20	[2]18	[2]57	185
Pensions and Social Security	2 223	128	366	652	1 032	1 685	2 580	5 924

[1]Value less than or equal to 0.05.
[2]Data are likely to have large sampling errors.

Table 11-20. Consumer Expenditures, Averages for Age Groups by Income Before Taxes: Reference Person 25 to 34 Years of Age, 2011–2012

(Number, dollar, percent.)

Item	Total	Complete reporting of income								
		Less than $5,000	$5,000 to $9,999	$10,000 to $14,999	$15,000 to $19,999	$20,000 to $29,999	$30,000 to $39,999	$40,000 to $49,999	$50,000 to $69,999	$70,000 and over
NUMBER OF CONSUMER UNITS (THOUSANDS)	20 287	622	720	888	987	2 372	2 762	2 094	3 711	6 130
CONSUMER UNIT CHARACTERISTICS										
Income Before Taxes	58 503	411	8 268	12 730	17 719	24 995	34 567	44 615	59 102	111 622
Income After Taxes	57 141	940	8 773	13 491	18 790	25 534	35 168	44 543	57 937	106 973
Age of Reference Person	29.6	29.1	28.5	29.1	28.9	29.1	29.4	29.4	29.6	30.3
Average Number in Consumer Unit										
All persons	2.8	2.5	2.7	2.5	2.8	2.6	2.7	2.9	2.9	3.1
Children under 18 years	1.1	1.2	1.4	1.2	1.3	1.1	1.1	1.1	1.0	1.0
Persons 65 years and over	(1)	(1)	(1)	(1)	(1)	(1)	(1)	(1)	(1)	(1)
Earners	1.5	0.5	0.8	0.8	1.0	1.2	1.3	1.5	1.6	1.9
Vehicles	1.7	0.8	0.8	0.9	1.0	1.2	1.4	1.6	1.9	2.3
Percent Distribution										
Male	48	35	34	40	39	46	46	52	51	51
Female	52	65	66	60	61	54	54	48	49	49
Percent Homeowner	42	16	16	13	15	17	30	37	49	68
With mortgage	36	7	10	7	11	12	25	30	44	63
Without mortgage	5	9	6	5	5	4	5	7	5	4
AVERAGE ANNUAL EXPENDITURES	48 813	26 010	23 132	22 027	25 312	30 738	36 609	40 553	49 859	76 310
Food	6 360	3 882	4 199	3 715	3 983	4 445	5 394	5 473	6 274	9 092
Food at home	3 562	2 247	3 151	2 514	2 667	2 878	3 225	3 246	3 466	4 582
Cereals and bakery products	495	304	433	296	404	408	477	460	483	623
Meats, poultry, fish, and eggs	744	522	722	587	575	637	729	706	706	900
Dairy products	386	234	289	215	277	288	345	341	394	519
Fruits and vegetables	655	402	521	418	466	552	563	552	619	888
Other food at home	1 282	785	1 185	998	945	994	1 111	1 189	1 265	1 652
Food away from home	2 798	1 635	1 048	1 200	1 316	1 567	2 169	2 226	2 807	4 510
Alcoholic Beverages	538	489	134	160	235	283	443	400	517	898
Housing	17 090	9 529	9 451	9 641	10 698	12 177	13 624	14 832	17 117	25 024
Shelter	10 469	5 924	6 156	6 043	6 691	7 314	8 656	9 197	10 549	15 111
Owned dwellings	4 690	861	913	541	852	1 096	2 388	2 898	4 805	9 712
Rented dwellings	5 469	4 962	4 999	5 348	5 723	6 149	6 152	6 140	5 437	4 773
Other lodging	310	[2]100	[2]245	[2]154	[2]116	69	115	159	307	626
Utilities, fuels, and public services	3 214	2 379	1 962	2 303	2 605	2 446	2 783	3 210	3 426	4 039
Household operations	1 348	265	431	539	555	643	821	971	1 109	2 595
Housekeeping supplies	478	176	286	230	331	381	379	452	492	660
Household furnishings and equipment	1 580	786	616	526	515	1 393	985	1 003	1 542	2 619
Apparel and Services	1 938	1 788	1 030	791	1 534	1 524	1 691	1 421	1 852	2 798
Transportation	9 289	4 396	3 110	3 728	4 215	5 254	6 665	7 548	10 427	14 777
Vehicle purchases (net outlay)	3 685	[2]1 993	[2]610	[2]1 237	1 256	1 268	2 042	2 417	4 406	6 635
Gasoline and motor oil	2 774	1 075	1 321	1 489	1 943	2 094	2 396	2 699	3 007	3 754
Other vehicle expenses	2 321	1 122	872	797	839	1 701	1 912	2 040	2 550	3 449
Public and other transportation	509	206	307	205	178	191	314	393	464	940
Health Care	2 071	670	539	500	690	990	1 489	2 015	2 400	3 342
Health insurance	1 232	277	293	255	401	561	855	1 185	1 531	1 979
Medical services	536	152	122	136	163	258	397	574	554	887
Drugs	221	209	110	77	99	124	162	197	232	341
Medical supplies	82	[2]33	[2]13	[2]31	[2]26	47	75	60	82	135
Entertainment	2 403	883	939	1 019	798	1 435	1 593	1 928	2 456	4 018
Personal Care Products and Services	572	214	245	235	279	396	423	440	587	902
Reading	73	28	55	37	25	37	54	63	78	115
Education	1 035	2 671	1 927	646	763	1 144	784	732	1 012	1 052
Tobacco Products and Smoking Supplies	365	445	439	312	312	333	389	463	429	293
Miscellaneous	633	[2]339	354	137	190	271	496	545	509	1 145
Cash Contributions	1 117	516	292	445	453	623	753	862	1 048	1 963
Personal Insurance and Pensions	5 329	160	418	661	1 137	1 828	2 810	3 831	5 154	10 890
Life and other personal insurance	141	[2]30	[2]28	[2]28	42	42	73	91	127	293
Pensions and Social Security	5 188	130	390	633	1 095	1 786	2 737	3 740	5 027	10 597

1Value less than or equal to 0.05.
2Data are likely to have large sampling errors.

Table 11-21. Consumer Expenditures, Averages for Age Groups by Income Before Taxes: Reference Person 35 to 44 Years of Age, 2011–2012

(Number, dollar, percent.)

Item	Total	Complete reporting of income								
		Less than $5,000	$5,000 to $9,999	$10,000 to $14,999	$15,000 to $19,999	$20,000 to $29,999	$30,000 to $39,999	$40,000 to $49,999	$50,000 to $69,999	$70,000 and over
NUMBER OF CONSUMER UNITS (THOUSANDS)	21 648	424	609	674	943	1 987	2 330	2 018	3 434	9 228
CONSUMER UNIT CHARACTERISTICS										
Income Before Taxes	77 772	776	7 905	12 644	17 453	25 169	34 794	44 640	59 485	133 072
Income After Taxes	75 955	1 050	8 422	13 241	18 538	26 112	35 222	44 456	58 562	128 682
Age of Reference Person	39.5	40.2	39.3	39.4	39.6	39.7	39.0	39.4	39.5	39.6
Average Number in Consumer Unit										
All persons	3.3	2.3	2.7	2.4	2.9	3.0	3.1	3.4	3.4	3.7
Children under 18 years	1.4	1.0	1.2	1.0	1.3	1.2	1.3	1.4	1.3	1.5
Persons 65 years and over	(1)	(1)	(1)	(1)	(1)	(1)	(1)	(1)	(1)	(1)
Earners	1.6	0.5	0.6	0.8	1.0	1.2	1.4	1.5	1.7	2.0
Vehicles	2.0	0.8	0.8	1.1	1.2	1.3	1.6	1.8	2.1	2.5
Percent Distribution										
Male	47	35	31	37	35	40	41	49	49	52
Female	53	65	69	63	65	60	59	51	51	48
Percent Homeowner	62	27	20	27	31	31	48	54	65	82
With mortgage	52	15	9	14	14	20	37	42	55	75
Without mortgage	10	12	12	13	17	11	12	12	9	7
AVERAGE ANNUAL EXPENDITURES	57 668	23 258	20 277	22 154	26 810	30 428	38 266	42 908	51 002	84 052
Food	7 732	3 735	2 956	4 216	5 292	4 734	6 090	6 420	6 940	10 432
Food at home	4 542	2 569	2 262	3 321	3 823	3 214	3 918	3 997	4 106	5 695
Cereals and bakery products	638	361	307	438	549	430	499	566	579	816
Meats, poultry, fish, and eggs	1 003	698	557	901	770	787	957	858	900	1 209
Dairy products	489	253	219	336	397	329	386	410	420	645
Fruits and vegetables	824	418	385	507	693	521	740	712	739	1 059
Other food at home	1 588	838	795	1 139	1 414	1 147	1 336	1 451	1 467	1 966
Food away from home	3 191	1 166	693	895	1 469	1 520	2 172	2 423	2 834	4 736
Alcoholic Beverages	499	[2]69	[2]144	139	213	208	342	370	299	809
Housing	19 918	10 053	9 286	9 432	10 309	12 331	13 528	15 368	17 513	27 966
Shelter	11 959	6 360	5 715	5 681	6 041	7 602	8 137	9 227	10 590	16 702
Owned dwellings	7 760	2 200	1 076	1 037	1 320	1 943	3 613	4 658	6 454	13 070
Rented dwellings	3 702	4 154	4 628	4 630	4 647	5 559	4 355	4 365	3 909	2 670
Other lodging	496	[2]5	[2]11	[2]15	[2]74	100	169	204	227	962
Utilities, fuels, and public services	4 071	2 389	2 663	2 664	2 921	2 935	3 470	3 712	4 074	4 935
Household operations	1 527	479	305	309	395	548	636	834	940	2 666
Housekeeping supplies	659	359	232	360	350	507	389	500	494	954
Household furnishings and equipment	1 702	466	370	418	602	740	897	1 095	1 415	2 710
Apparel and Services	2 246	807	887	1 227	1 385	1 174	1 959	1 562	1 932	3 158
Transportation	9 845	4 487	2 786	2 826	4 064	5 009	7 342	7 630	9 717	13 877
Vehicle purchases (net outlay)	3 522	[2]2 127	[2]861	[2]243	[2]650	1 395	2 510	2 152	3 481	5 323
Gasoline and motor oil	3 265	1 450	1 191	1 610	1 941	2 201	2 693	3 078	3 305	4 142
Other vehicle expenses	2 548	728	595	880	1 306	1 228	1 940	2 143	2 655	3 508
Public and other transportation	510	182	139	93	167	185	198	257	277	905
Health Care	2 855	1 203	1 137	672	985	1 165	1 829	2 346	2 854	4 130
Health insurance	1 666	[2]614	592	333	418	685	1 036	1 472	1 768	2 384
Medical services	707	185	303	150	331	282	494	475	613	1 067
Drugs	370	334	222	130	182	165	242	315	379	504
Medical supplies	112	[2]71	[2]19	59	54	33	56	85	95	175
Entertainment	3 079	794	831	1 045	1 262	1 409	1 789	1 950	2 709	4 747
Personal Care Products and Services	715	244	289	304	326	476	500	545	603	1 021
Reading	96	30	49	20	26	44	47	53	87	152
Education	934	[2]521	136	88	217	306	400	519	532	1 652
Tobacco Products and Smoking Supplies	351	304	491	515	512	394	397	419	376	270
Miscellaneous	829	[2]173	401	572	542	620	401	817	761	1 112
Cash Contributions	1 519	468	540	418	584	720	765	1 107	1 398	2 307
Personal Insurance and Pensions	7 050	371	345	680	1 092	1 837	2 879	3 803	5 281	12 419
Life and other personal insurance	316	[2]59	[2]44	[2]48	62	105	122	162	208	560
Pensions and Social Security	6 734	312	301	632	1 030	1 733	2 757	3 641	5 073	11 859

[1]Value less than or equal to 0.05.
[2]Data are likely to have large sampling errors.

Table 11-22. Consumer Expenditures, Averages for Age Groups by Income Before Taxes: Reference Person 45 to 54 Years of Age, 2011–2012

(Number, dollar, percent.)

Item	Total	Complete reporting of income								
		Less than $5,000	$5,000 to $9,999	$10,000 to $14,999	$15,000 to $19,999	$20,000 to $29,999	$30,000 to $39,999	$40,000 to $49,999	$50,000 to $69,999	$70,000 and over
NUMBER OF CONSUMER UNITS (THOUSANDS)	24 722	765	700	1 150	885	2 042	2 139	2 123	3 674	11 243
CONSUMER UNIT CHARACTERISTICS										
Income Before Taxes	80 105	-14 295	7 961	12 732	17 806	24 911	34 732	44 691	59 775	134 810
Income After Taxes	77 040	-12 451	8 067	13 004	18 016	25 147	34 516	43 946	58 469	128 458
Age of Reference Person	50	50	50	50	50	50	50	49	50	50
Average Number in Consumer Unit										
All persons	2.8	1.8	1.8	1.9	2.2	2.4	2.5	2.6	2.7	3.2
Children under 18 years	0.6	0.4	0.3	0.4	0.5	0.6	0.5	0.6	0.6	0.8
Persons 65 years and over	0.1	(1)	(1)	(1)	20.1	0.1	0.1	0.1	0.1	0.1
Earners	1.7	0.6	0.6	0.5	0.8	1.1	1.5	1.6	1.8	2.1
Vehicles	2.3	1.2	1.0	1.1	1.2	1.4	1.7	2.1	2.3	2.9
Percent Distribution										
Male	47	44	45	40	46	44	40	46	43	51
Female	53	56	55	60	54	56	60	54	57	49
Percent Homeowner	72	38	40	31	43	49	57	68	75	89
With mortgage	53	20	15	14	20	26	37	48	57	73
Without mortgage	18	18	24	17	23	23	20	20	18	16
AVERAGE ANNUAL EXPENDITURES	60 069	30 877	20 980	21 278	24 559	30 214	34 373	42 068	50 494	88 485
Food	7 670	3 642	3 631	3 992	4 171	4 647	4 630	5 581	6 803	10 826
Food at home	4 564	2 319	2 788	2 851	3 033	3 095	3 239	3 528	4 300	6 012
Cereals and bakery products	622	341	404	363	439	411	427	505	584	817
Meats, poultry, fish, and eggs	1 006	493	691	762	678	719	790	815	879	1 300
Dairy products	486	244	307	286	331	324	326	353	448	655
Fruits and vegetables	837	474	503	469	532	545	589	625	801	1 115
Other food at home	1 612	767	885	971	1 053	1 097	1 107	1 230	1 587	2 124
Food away from home	3 106	1 323	843	1 141	1 139	1 553	1 391	2 053	2 504	4 814
Alcoholic Beverages	474	155	150	129	219	214	240	292	306	773
Housing	18 928	11 138	9 200	8 985	10 115	11 609	12 725	14 685	16 804	25 820
Shelter	11 177	7 303	5 810	5 620	5 798	6 785	7 565	8 213	9 649	15 312
Owned dwellings	7 699	2 543	2 298	1 431	1 937	2 670	3 513	4 939	6 534	12 094
Rented dwellings	2 647	4 107	3 463	4 123	3 825	3 954	3 897	2 988	2 747	1 681
Other lodging	831	2652	249	265	235	161	156	286	367	1 537
Utilities, fuels, and public services	4 311	2 442	2 403	2 375	2 837	3 213	3 502	3 965	4 196	5 327
Household operations	1 024	524	340	243	361	472	543	655	737	1 589
Housekeeping supplies	680	338	240	254	505	413	384	488	585	975
Household furnishings and equipment	1 736	531	407	494	614	727	731	1 363	1 636	2 618
Apparel and Services	2 010	1 277	773	646	895	1 236	940	1 408	1 477	3 055
Transportation	10 072	4 601	3 666	3 037	3 688	4 782	6 036	7 718	9 104	14 603
Vehicle purchases (net outlay)	3 079	21 529	21 299	2401	523	751	1 590	1 994	2 855	4 754
Gasoline and motor oil	3 345	1 429	1 340	1 359	1 741	2 286	2 512	2 927	3 328	4 365
Other vehicle expenses	3 015	1 321	880	1 101	1 307	1 561	1 654	2 566	2 554	4 400
Public and other transportation	633	322	148	175	118	185	281	231	366	1 084
Health Care	3 549	1 482	812	1 176	1 413	2 132	2 436	2 773	3 394	4 942
Health insurance	1 955	754	398	615	780	1 073	1 353	1 515	1 765	2 782
Medical services	917	365	182	275	250	537	683	706	1 003	1 245
Drugs	521	307	215	249	345	405	312	457	511	676
Medical supplies	156	256	217	38	38	117	88	95	115	239
Entertainment	3 110	1 542	1 002	944	997	1 456	1 777	2 025	2 791	4 630
Personal Care Products and Services	708	249	231	296	278	300	373	432	586	1 087
Reading	116	41	16	29	36	46	54	67	84	186
Education	2 151	1 312	2233	78	2115	311	573	776	873	4 015
Tobacco Products and Smoking Supplies	448	583	479	543	605	530	494	512	493	364
Miscellaneous	936	1 437	236	386	450	446	507	579	727	1 351
Cash Contributions	2 074	2 878	252	529	586	763	853	1 143	1 414	3 271
Personal Insurance and Pensions	7 823	540	398	509	992	1 740	2 733	4 077	5 639	13 561
Life and other personal insurance	423	2168	264	78	83	96	144	239	318	707
Pensions and Social Security	7 399	372	334	431	909	1 644	2 589	3 839	5 321	12 854

[1] Value less than or equal to 0.05.
[2] Data are likely to have large sampling errors.

Table 11-23. Consumer Expenditures, Averages for Age Groups by Income Before Taxes: Reference Person 55 to 64 Years of Age, 2011–2012

(Number, dollar, percent.)

Item	Total	Complete reporting of income								
		Less than $5,000	$5,000 to $9,999	$10,000 to $14,999	$15,000 to $19,999	$20,000 to $29,999	$30,000 to $39,999	$40,000 to $49,999	$50,000 to $69,999	$70,000 and over
NUMBER OF CONSUMER UNITS (THOUSANDS)	22 229	832	839	1 327	1 111	2 163	2 056	1 907	3 134	8 860
CONSUMER UNIT CHARACTERISTICS										
Income Before Taxes	76 536	-1 122	8 251	12 395	17 614	24 726	35 007	44 785	59 304	142 507
Income After Taxes	72 723	-1 598	8 330	12 268	17 819	24 517	34 540	43 801	57 511	133 976
Age of Reference Person	59.1	59.3	59.4	59.5	59.7	59.4	59.4	59.0	59.2	58.9
Average Number in Consumer Unit										
All persons	2.1	1.5	1.5	1.4	1.8	1.8	2.0	2.1	2.2	2.5
Children under 18 years	0.2	[1]0.1	0.1	[1]0.1	0.2	0.1	0.2	0.2	0.2	0.2
Persons 65 years and over	0.1	[1]0.1	([2])	[1]0.1	0.1	0.1	0.1	0.1	0.1	0.1
Earners	1.3	0.4	0.4	0.3	0.6	0.8	1.1	1.2	1.4	1.9
Vehicles	2.2	1.2	1.0	1.1	1.4	1.7	1.8	2.1	2.2	2.8
Percent Distribution										
Male	49	43	41	43	48	42	41	49	48	55
Female	51	57	59	57	52	58	59	51	52	45
Percent Homeowner	79	55	45	47	59	70	75	79	86	92
With mortgage	45	23	15	16	22	32	43	45	53	58
Without mortgage	34	32	30	31	38	38	32	34	33	34
AVERAGE ANNUAL EXPENDITURES	54 644	26 306	24 015	19 760	26 294	31 332	36 924	40 755	48 819	84 114
Food	6 662	4 112	4 446	2 844	3 938	3 939	5 079	4 969	6 169	9 721
Food at home	3 960	2 783	3 240	2 076	2 497	2 700	3 403	3 139	3 930	5 299
Cereals and bakery products	521	386	411	295	315	359	445	432	535	685
Meats, poultry, fish, and eggs	891	594	832	446	539	649	789	686	874	1 183
Dairy products	413	250	306	223	284	280	351	338	432	545
Fruits and vegetables	733	451	617	368	500	479	607	547	670	1 026
Other food at home	1 402	1 103	1 074	744	859	933	1 211	1 136	1 419	1 860
Food away from home	2 701	1 328	1 206	769	1 441	1 239	1 677	1 830	2 239	4 422
Alcoholic Beverages	481	166	317	89	165	183	239	274	383	851
Housing	17 209	10 592	8 412	8 166	9 630	12 089	13 392	14 122	15 617	24 359
Shelter	9 741	5 907	4 872	4 712	5 000	6 939	7 370	8 127	8 408	13 963
Owned dwellings	6 996	3 049	1 757	1 744	2 420	4 173	4 721	5 542	6 269	11 011
Rented dwellings	1 786	2 436	2 879	2 810	2 434	2 305	2 259	2 139	1 553	1 157
Other lodging	958	422	237	158	146	461	390	447	587	1 794
Utilities, fuels, and public services	4 022	2 625	2 289	2 276	2 954	3 219	3 613	3 605	4 024	5 092
Household operations	994	433	264	295	302	518	663	720	873	1 605
Housekeeping supplies	729	511	450	364	500	543	655	555	666	991
Household furnishings and equipment	1 724	1 115	537	520	874	870	1 092	1 116	1 647	2 708
Apparel and Services	1 671	896	982	476	845	802	1 305	864	1 435	2 691
Transportation	9 258	5 353	4 619	3 045	4 905	5 327	6 338	7 952	8 803	13 633
Vehicle purchases (net outlay)	2 923	[1]2 656	[1]2 219	152	1 352	1 400	1 773	2 233	2 635	4 516
Gasoline and motor oil	2 802	1 333	1 201	1 221	1 756	2 086	2 305	2 595	2 870	3 771
Other vehicle expenses	2 896	1 187	1 001	1 486	1 663	1 613	2 009	2 677	2 804	4 215
Public and other transportation	636	177	197	186	133	228	250	446	494	1 132
Health Care	4 216	1 748	1 401	1 928	2 415	3 167	2 935	3 722	4 371	5 893
Health insurance	2 234	914	653	1 052	1 118	1 565	1 617	2 013	2 586	3 056
Medical services	1 114	391	387	415	824	934	590	900	888	1 683
Drugs	707	362	319	386	438	584	645	703	753	890
Medical supplies	161	81	[1]42	76	34	84	84	105	144	265
Entertainment	2 841	891	1 143	1 208	1 417	1 625	1 885	1 974	2 423	4 478
Personal Care Products and Services	695	296	378	183	245	325	491	442	629	1 125
Reading	141	47	37	51	51	56	75	119	144	223
Education	995	[1]133	[1]343	[1]186	[1]131	137	380	479	358	2 058
Tobacco Products and Smoking Supplies	386	342	465	535	361	456	477	367	362	338
Miscellaneous	919	780	516	182	297	626	679	634	855	1 374
Cash Contributions	2 235	581	585	457	1 069	710	1 060	1 090	1 739	4 027
Personal Insurance and Pensions	6 935	368	370	409	825	1 890	2 589	3 746	5 530	13 342
Life and other personal insurance	525	138	125	159	152	550	235	242	419	861
Pensions and Social Security	6 410	230	246	250	673	1 340	2 353	3 504	5 111	12 480

[1]Data are likely to have large sampling errors.
[2]Value less than or equal to 0.05.

Table 11-24. Consumer Expenditures, Averages for Age Groups by Income Before Taxes: Reference Person 65 Years of Age and Over, 2011–2012

(Number, dollar, percent.)

Item	Total	Less than $5,000	$5,000 to $9,999	$10,000 to $14,999	$15,000 to $19,999	$20,000 to $29,999	$30,000 to $39,999	$40,000 to $49,999	$50,000 to $69,999	$70,000 and over
						Complete reporting of income				
NUMBER OF CONSUMER UNITS (THOUSANDS)	26 513	938	1 414	3 259	3 194	4 812	3 234	2 409	3 020	4 233
CONSUMER UNIT CHARACTERISTICS										
Income Before Taxes	43 990	-1 356	8 425	12 738	17 377	24 870	34 685	44 981	59 080	127 574
Income After Taxes	43 167	-1 834	8 357	12 663	17 357	24 771	34 307	44 543	58 387	123 766
Age of Reference Person	74.8	75.9	75.9	76.9	76.8	76.2	74.7	73.7	73.0	71.6
Average Number in Consumer Unit										
All persons	1.7	1.3	1.3	1.2	1.4	1.6	1.8	1.9	2.1	2.3
Children under 18 years	0.1	([1])	([1])	([1])	([1])	([1])	0.1	0.1	0.1	0.1
Persons 65 years and over	1.4	1.2	1.1	1.1	1.2	1.4	1.4	1.5	1.5	1.6
Earners	0.5	[2]0.1	[2]0.1	0.1	0.1	0.2	0.4	0.6	0.8	1.2
Vehicles	1.6	1.0	0.8	0.9	1.2	1.5	1.7	1.8	2.2	2.5
Percent Distribution										
Male	43	35	30	27	35	42	46	48	51	59
Female	57	65	70	73	65	58	54	52	49	41
Percent Homeowner	81	67	56	63	72	82	86	90	90	95
With mortgage	22	9	10	11	13	18	23	25	29	41
Without mortgage	58	57	45	51	59	64	62	65	61	54
AVERAGE ANNUAL EXPENDITURES	39 806	22 387	18 335	18 786	24 657	30 823	36 817	39 761	50 453	82 161
Food	5 107	3 887	2 839	2 745	3 379	4 052	4 762	5 088	6 573	9 203
Food at home	3 291	2 689	2 196	2 027	2 417	2 807	3 178	3 359	4 170	5 117
Cereals and bakery products	464	386	315	314	356	405	450	496	576	673
Meats, poultry, fish, and eggs	679	587	492	425	474	560	676	658	849	1 086
Dairy products	350	243	218	214	254	308	349	367	429	543
Fruits and vegetables	661	576	415	429	473	561	634	659	834	1 041
Other food at home	1 136	898	757	644	860	974	1 068	1 179	1 482	1 773
Food away from home	1 816	1 198	644	718	962	1 245	1 584	1 729	2 404	4 086
Alcoholic Beverages	326	149	85	59	98	192	274	283	480	874
Housing	13 771	9 481	7 692	7 899	9 919	11 317	13 344	14 263	15 778	25 380
Shelter	7 396	5 278	4 245	4 555	5 538	5 892	6 920	7 391	8 317	13 928
Owned dwellings	5 029	2 675	1 920	2 233	3 053	3 935	4 901	5 468	6 088	10 570
Rented dwellings	1 658	2 196	2 181	2 203	2 251	1 641	1 558	1 278	1 365	1 018
Other lodging	710	407	145	119	235	317	461	645	864	2 340
Utilities, fuels, and public services	3 411	2 460	2 258	2 276	2 718	3 168	3 422	3 743	4 050	5 025
Household operations	1 084	763	496	387	676	1 012	1 046	1 093	1 014	2 348
Housekeeping supplies	616	493	289	307	424	478	586	686	793	1 082
Household furnishings and equipment	1 263	486	403	374	563	766	1 370	1 349	1 604	2 998
Apparel and Services	1 074	257	631	586	505	650	832	1 086	1 519	2 409
Transportation	6 154	2 767	2 037	2 195	3 522	4 034	5 553	5 921	8 910	14 178
Vehicle purchases (net outlay)	1 927	[2]450	[2]228	354	843	921	1 358	1 425	2 999	5 949
Gasoline and motor oil	1 765	1 064	777	833	1 129	1 535	1 760	2 063	2 514	3 008
Other vehicle expenses	2 018	902	887	876	1 369	1 390	2 093	2 093	2 792	3 908
Public and other transportation	444	351	145	132	182	188	342	339	605	1 313
Health Care	4 948	2 519	2 301	2 577	3 316	4 710	5 330	5 781	6 426	7 847
Health insurance	3 132	1 741	1 509	1 631	2 200	3 139	3 481	3 656	3 992	4 656
Medical services	862	350	316	423	446	621	815	955	1 219	1 812
Drugs	757	349	380	426	529	822	861	945	949	980
Medical supplies	196	79	95	97	140	129	174	225	266	398
Entertainment	2 015	1 199	880	919	1 094	1 746	1 803	1 808	2 829	4 042
Personal Care Products and Services	568	269	266	269	336	428	483	618	681	1 218
Reading	149	85	65	55	82	116	146	146	222	303
Education	241	[2]109	[2]23	30	80	62	138	180	229	948
Tobacco Products and Smoking Supplies	202	132	148	133	168	212	227	231	235	245
Miscellaneous	829	380	436	337	450	1 109	716	819	772	1 527
Cash Contributions	2 424	989	803	716	1 345	1 678	2 108	2 028	3 350	6 065
Personal Insurance and Pensions	1 998	163	129	265	363	516	1 101	1 509	2 448	7 921
Life and other personal insurance	340	123	109	139	142	252	319	331	393	852
Pensions and Social Security	1 658	[2]41	[2]19	126	221	264	782	1 178	2 055	7 069

[1]Value less than or equal to 0.05.
[2]Data are likely to have large sampling errors.

CHAPTER 12: AMERICAN TIME USE SURVEY

HIGHLIGHTS

This chapter presents data from the American Time Use Survey (ATUS). The survey was introduced in the sixth edition of the *Handbook of U.S. Labor Statistics*. Its purpose is to collect data on the activities people do during the day and the amount of time they spend on each one.

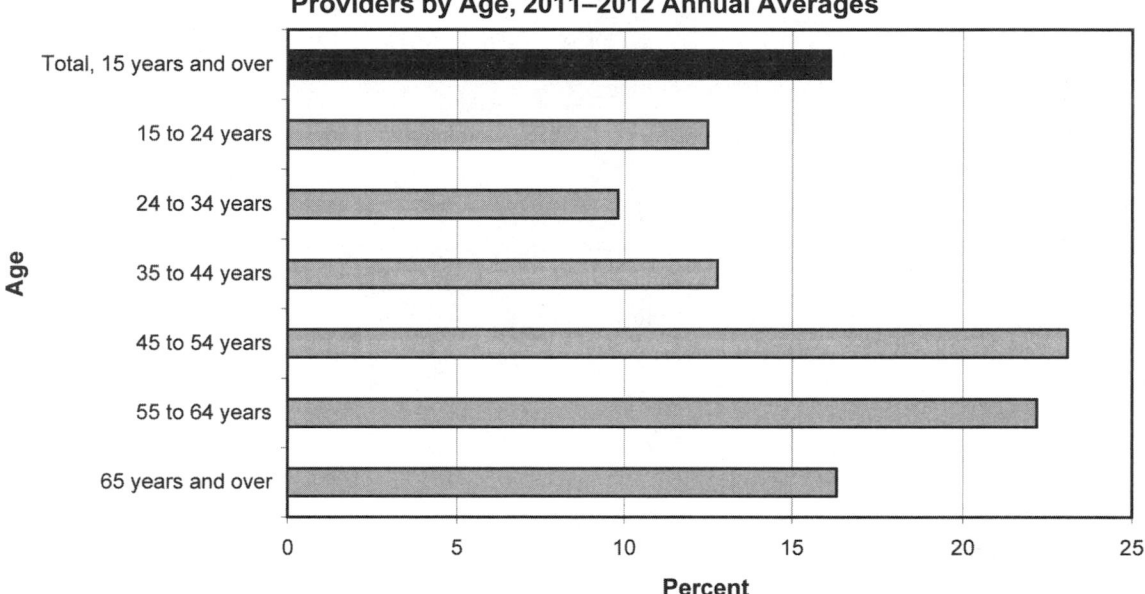

Figure 12-1. Percent Change in U.S. Population Who Were Eldercare Providers by Age, 2011–2012 Annual Averages

Note: Eldercare providers are those who in the previous 3 to 4 months cared for someone with a condition related to aging.

In 2012, 16.1 percent of the population were eldercare providers. Individuals aged 45 to 54 and 55 to 64 were the most likely to provide eldercare, while those ages 25 to 34 were least likely to provide eldercare. The majority of eldercare providers were women. (See Tables 12-8 and 12-9.)

OTHER HIGHLIGHTS

- On an average day, 82 percent of women and 65 percent of men spent some time doing household activities such as lawn care, cooking, and cleaning. (See Table 12-1.)

- Men worked 55 minutes more than women on days that they worked. This difference partly reflects women's greater likelihood of working part time. However, even among full-time workers men worked longer than women—8.5 hours compared with 7.9 hours. (See Table 12-3.)

- Multiple jobholders were far more likely to work at home than single job holders (34.4 percent compared with 22 percent). (See Table 12-5.)

- The more education a person attained, the greater the likelihood likely they worked at home. On the days that they worked, 38.4 percent of employed persons age 25 years and over with a bachelor's degree or higher did some work at home, compared with only 5.4 percent of those with less than a high school diploma. (See Table 12-5.)

NOTES AND DEFINITIONS

SURVEY METHODOLOGY

While the Bureau of Labor Statistics (BLS) has long produced statistics about the labor market, including information about employment, hours, and earnings, the American Time Use Survey (ATUS) marks the first time that a federal statistical agency has produced estimates on how Americans spend another critical resource—their time. Data collection for the ATUS began in January 2003. Sample cases for the survey are selected monthly, and interviews are conducted continuously throughout the year. In 2012, approximately 12,500 individuals were interviewed.

ATUS sample households are chosen from the households that have completed their eighth (final) interview for the Current Population Survey (CPS), the nation's monthly household labor force survey. (See Chapter 1 of this *Handbook* for a description of the CPS.) ATUS sample households are selected to ensure that estimates will be representative of the nation.

An individual age 15 years or older is randomly chosen from each sample household. This "designated person" takes part in a one-time telephone interview about his or her activities on the previous day (the "diary day").

All ATUS interviews are conducted using Computer Assisted Telephone Interviewing. Procedures are in place to collect information from the small number of households that did not provide a telephone number during the CPS interview.

CONCEPTS AND DEFINITIONS

Average day reflects an average distribution across all persons in the reference population and all days of the week. Average day measures for the entire population provide a mechanism for seeing the overall distribution of time allocation for society as a whole. The ATUS collects data about daily activities from all segments of the population age 15 and over, including persons who are employed and not employed. Many activities are not typically done on a daily basis, and some activities are only done by a subset of the population.

Average hours per day refers to time spent in a 24-hour day (between 4 a.m. on the diary day and 4 a.m. on the interview day) doing a specified activity.

Average hours per day, persons reporting the activity on the diary day is computed using responses only from those engaged in the particular activity on the diary day.

Average hours per day, population is computed using all responses from the sample population, including those from respondents who did not do the particular activity on their diary day. These estimates reflect the total number of respondents engaged in an activity and the total amount of time they spent on the activity.

Diary day is the day about which the designated person reports. For example, the diary day of a designated person interviewed on Tuesday would be Monday.

Household children refers to children under 18 years of age who reside in the household of the ATUS respondent. The children may be related to the respondent (such as their own children, grandchildren, nieces, nephews, brothers, or sisters) or not related (such as foster children or children of roommates). For secondary childcare calculations, respondents are asked about care of household children under 13 years of age.

EARNINGS

Usual weekly earnings represent the earnings of full-time wage and salary workers before taxes and other deductions and include any overtime pay, commissions, or tips usually received (at the main job in the case of multiple jobholders). Usual weekly earnings are only updated in ATUS for about a third of employed respondents—if the respondent changed jobs or employment status or if the CPS weekly earnings value was imputed. This means that the earnings information could be out of date because the CPS interview was done 2 to 5 months prior to the ATUS interview. Respondents are asked to identify the easiest way for them to report earnings (hourly, weekly, biweekly, twice monthly, annually, or other) and how much they usually earn in the reported time period. Earnings reported on a basis other than weekly are converted to a weekly equivalent. The term "usual" is as perceived by the respondent. If the respondent asks for a definition of usual, interviewers are instructed to define the term as more than half the weeks worked during the past 4 or 5 months.

Weekly earnings ranges refers to the ranges used to represent approximately 25 percent of full-time wage and salary workers. For example, 25 percent of full-time wage and salary workers with one job only had weekly earnings of $500 or less. These dollar values vary from year to year.

EMPLOYMENT STATUS

Employed persons are those who, at any time during the seven days prior to the interview: 1) did any work at all as paid employees, worked in their own business professions or on their own farms, or usually worked 15 hours or more an unpaid workers in family-operated enterprises; and 2) all those who were not working but had jobs or businesses from which they were temporarily absent due to illness, bad weather, vacation, childcare problems, labor-management disputes, maternity or paternity leave, job training, or other family or personal reasons, whether or not they were paid for the time off or were seeking other jobs.

Employed full time refers to workers who usually work 35 hours or more per week at all jobs combined.

Employed part time refers to workers who usually work fewer than 35 hours per week at all jobs combined.

Not employed indicates persons who are not employed if they do not meet the conditions for employment. Not employed workers include those classified as unemployed as well as those classified as not in the labor force (using CPS definitions).

The numbers of employed and not employed persons in this report do not correspond to published totals from the CPS. While the information on employment from the ATUS is useful for assessing work in the context of other daily activities, the employment data are not intended for analysis of current employment trends. Compared to the CPS and other estimates of employment, the ATUS estimates are based on a much smaller sample and are only available with a substantial lag.

MAJOR ACTIVITY CATEGORY DEFINITIONS

Caring for and helping household members refers to time spent doing activities to care for or help any child (under age 18) or adult in the household, regardless of relationship to the respondent or the physical or mental health status of the person being helped. Caring for and helping activities for household children and adults are coded separately in subcategories.

Caring for and helping non-household members includes time spent caring for and helping any child or adult who is not part of the respondent's household, regardless of the relationship to the respondent or the physical or mental health status of the person being helped.

Eating and drinking includes all time spent eating or drinking (except when identified by the respondent as part of a work or volunteer activity), whether alone, with others, at home, at a place of purchase, in transit, or somewhere else.

Educational activities include taking classes (including Internet and other distance-learning courses), doing research and homework, and taking care of administrative tasks, such as registering for classes or obtaining a school ID. For high

school students, before- and after-school extracurricular activities (except sports) also are classified as educational activities.

Household activities are those done by respondents to maintain their households. These include housework, cooking, yard care, pet care, vehicle maintenance and repair, and home maintenance, repair, decoration, and renovation. Food preparation is always classified as a household activity.

Leisure and sports includes sports, exercise, and recreation; socializing and communicating; and other leisure activities, such as watching television, reading, or attending entertainment events.

Organizational, civic, and religious activities captures time spent volunteering for or through an organization, performing civic obligations, and participating in religious and spiritual activities.

Other activities, not elsewhere classified includes security procedures related to traveling, traveling not associated with a specific activity category, ambiguous activities that could not be coded, or missing activities that were considered too private to report.

Personal care activities consist of sleeping, bathing, dressing, health-related self-care, and personal or private activities. Receiving unpaid personal care from others (for example, "my sister put polish on my nails") is also captured in this category.

Primary activity is the main activity of a respondent at a specified time.

Purchasing goods and service includes the purchase of consumer goods as well as the purchase or use of professional and personal care services, household services, and government services. Most purchases and rentals of consumer goods, regardless of mode or place of purchase or rental are classified in this category.

Secondary activity is an activity done at the same time as a primary activity. With the exception of the care of children under age 13, information on secondary activities is not systematically collected in the ATUS.

Telephone calls, mail, and email captures telephone communication and handling household or personal mail and email. Telephone and Internet purchases are classified in purchasing goods and services.

Working and work-related activities refers to time spent working, doing activities as part of one's job, engaging in income-generating activities (not as part of one's job), and job search activities. "Working" includes hours spent doing the specific tasks required of one's main or other job, regardless of location or time of day. Travel time related to working and work-related activities includes time spent commuting to and from one's job, as well as time spent traveling for work-related activities, generating income, and job searching.

SOURCES OF ADDITIONAL INFORMATION

Additional information, including expanded definitions and estimation methodology, is available from BLS news release USDL 13-1178, "American Time Use Survey—2012 Results," which is available on the BLS Web site at http://www.bls.gov/tus/.

Table 12-1. Average Hours Per Day Spent in Primary Activities[1] for the Total Population and for Persons Reporting the Activity on the Diary Day, by Activity Category and Sex, 2011 and 2012 Annual Averages

(Hours, percent.)

Activity	Hours per day, total population			Percent of population reporting the activity on the diary day			Hours per day for persons reporting the activity on the diary day		
	Both sexes	Men	Women	Both sexes	Men	Women	Both sexes	Men	Women
2011									
All Activities[2]	24.00	24.00	24.00	X	X	X	X	X	X
Personal care activities	9.49	9.25	9.72	100.0	100.0	100.0	9.49	9.25	9.73
Sleeping	8.71	8.62	8.80	99.9	99.9	99.9	8.72	8.63	8.81
Eating and drinking	1.24	1.27	1.21	95.9	96.5	95.3	1.29	1.32	1.27
Household activities	1.77	1.37	2.16	74.0	65.0	82.5	2.40	2.11	2.62
Housework	0.58	0.27	0.87	33.8	18.9	47.8	1.71	1.43	1.82
Food preparation and cleanup	0.56	0.31	0.79	53.4	40.1	66.0	1.04	0.76	1.20
Lawn and garden care	0.19	0.26	0.13	9.1	11.5	6.8	2.12	2.28	1.85
Household management	0.12	0.10	0.14	16.2	13.9	18.4	0.76	0.73	0.78
Purchasing goods and services	0.72	0.62	0.82	42.6	38.4	46.6	1.70	1.61	1.77
Consumer goods purchases	0.37	0.31	0.43	39.1	35.4	42.5	0.95	0.87	1.01
Professional and personal care services	0.07	0.05	0.10	7.2	5.3	9.0	1.02	0.85	1.11
Caring for and helping household members	0.51	0.33	0.67	24.4	19.5	29.1	2.08	1.70	2.31
Caring for and helping household children	0.39	0.24	0.54	20.8	15.7	25.6	1.90	1.54	2.10
Caring for and helping non-household members	0.21	0.19	0.22	11.7	10.9	12.5	1.77	1.75	1.80
Caring for and helping non-household adults	0.07	0.08	0.06	7.7	7.5	7.8	0.93	1.05	0.82
Working and work-related activities	3.57	4.23	2.95	44.6	50.4	39.2	7.99	8.39	7.52
Working	3.20	3.81	2.63	42.1	47.9	36.7	7.60	7.96	7.17
Educational activities	0.47	0.49	0.45	8.4	8.5	8.3	5.65	5.83	5.48
Attending class	0.28	0.30	0.25	5.4	5.7	5.1	5.12	5.31	4.93
Homework and research	0.15	0.14	0.16	5.7	5.7	5.7	2.65	2.55	2.74
Organizational, civic, and religious activities	0.35	0.30	0.40	14.0	11.7	16.2	2.53	2.59	2.49
Religious and spiritual activities	0.15	0.12	0.19	9.1	7.0	11.0	1.71	1.76	1.69
Volunteering (organizational and civic activities)	0.15	0.14	0.16	6.1	5.6	6.6	2.47	2.48	2.45
Leisure and sports	5.21	5.55	4.89	95.2	95.7	94.8	5.47	5.80	5.16
Socializing and communicating	0.70	0.63	0.77	35.6	32.3	38.8	1.97	1.95	1.98
Watching television	2.75	2.99	2.53	78.3	79.7	77.0	3.51	3.75	3.28
Participating in sports, exercise, and recreation	0.30	0.39	0.22	18.6	20.4	16.9	1.64	1.93	1.31
Telephone calls, mail, and e-mail	0.16	0.11	0.20	21.2	16.5	25.7	0.73	0.66	0.78
Other activities n.e.c.	0.29	0.29	0.30	16.5	15.4	17.6	1.78	1.88	1.69
2012									
All Activities[2]	24.00	24.00	24.00	X	X	X	X	X	X
Personal care activities	9.49	9.22	9.74	100.0	99.9	100.0	9.49	9.22	9.74
Sleeping	8.73	8.60	8.86	99.9	99.9	99.9	8.74	8.61	8.86
Eating and drinking	1.25	1.30	1.20	96.0	95.9	96.0	1.30	1.35	1.25
Household activities	1.74	1.29	2.17	73.7	64.5	82.3	2.36	1.99	2.63
Housework	0.60	0.28	0.90	34.6	19.8	48.4	1.73	1.40	1.86
Food preparation and cleanup	0.53	0.28	0.75	52.5	39.2	64.9	1.00	0.72	1.16
Lawn and garden care	0.18	0.25	0.12	9.8	11.7	8.0	1.87	2.11	1.53
Household management	0.13	0.10	0.15	16.3	13.6	18.8	0.78	0.77	0.79
Purchasing goods and services	0.72	0.60	0.84	41.4	37.2	45.3	1.74	1.60	1.85
Consumer goods purchases	0.35	0.27	0.43	37.5	34.0	40.8	0.94	0.80	1.05
Professional and personal care services	0.08	0.06	0.10	7.4	5.6	9.0	1.10	1.05	1.13
Caring for and helping household members	0.51	0.35	0.66	24.5	19.7	28.9	2.09	1.79	2.27
Caring for and helping household children	0.40	0.27	0.53	20.4	15.6	24.8	1.98	1.71	2.14
Caring for and helping non-household members	0.18	0.16	0.20	11.2	9.9	12.3	1.62	1.59	1.64
Caring for and helping non-household adults	0.06	0.06	0.05	7.3	7.0	7.5	0.80	0.91	0.70
Working and work-related activities	3.53	4.17	2.94	43.9	48.8	39.3	8.05	8.54	7.49
Working	3.19	3.74	2.67	41.8	46.5	37.4	7.63	8.05	7.13
Educational activities	0.50	0.53	0.47	8.5	8.8	8.2	5.87	6.01	5.73
Attending class	0.28	0.30	0.26	5.4	5.8	5.1	5.16	5.17	5.14
Homework and research	0.17	0.18	0.16	6.2	6.1	6.2	2.75	2.89	2.63
Organizational, civic, and religious activities	0.32	0.26	0.38	13.8	10.9	16.6	2.33	2.42	2.27
Religious and spiritual activities	0.15	0.12	0.18	9.0	6.7	11.1	1.66	1.72	1.63
Volunteering (organizational and civic activities)	0.13	0.11	0.15	6.0	5.0	7.0	2.13	2.21	2.08
Leisure and sports	5.37	5.79	4.97	96.2	96.9	95.6	5.58	5.98	5.20
Socializing and communicating	0.74	0.72	0.76	37.2	35.4	38.9	2.00	2.04	1.96
Watching television	2.83	3.07	2.61	80.1	80.9	79.3	3.54	3.80	3.29
Participating in sports, exercise, and recreation	0.32	0.41	0.24	19.3	21.7	17.0	1.67	1.90	1.39
Telephone calls, mail, and e-mail	0.16	0.11	0.20	19.8	15.7	23.6	0.78	0.70	0.84
Other activities n.e.c.	0.24	0.23	0.25	14.1	12.8	15.3	1.69	1.80	1.60

Note: Data refer to respondents age 15 years and over, unless otherwise specified.

n.e.c. = Not elsewhere classified.

[1]A primary activity is designated by a respondent as his or her main activity. Other activities done simultaneously are not included.
[2]All major activity categories include related travel time.
X = Not applicable.

Table 12-2. Average Hours Per Day Spent in Primary Activities[1] for the Total Population by Age, Sex, Race, Hispanic Origin, and Educational Attainment, 2012 Annual Averages

(Hours.)

Characteristic	Personal care activities	Eating and drinking	Household activities	Purchasing goods and services	Caring for and helping household members	Caring for and helping non-household members	Working and work-related activities	Educational activities	Organizational, civic, and religious activities	Leisure activities	Telephone calls, mail, and e-mail	Other activities n.e.c.
Both Sexes, 15 Years and Over	9.49	1.25	1.74	0.72	0.51	0.18	3.53	0.50	0.32	5.37	0.16	0.24
15 to 19 years	10.44	1.00	0.67	0.55	0.13	0.18	1.05	3.35	0.27	5.86	0.19	0.31
20 to 24 years	9.82	1.20	0.85	0.54	0.58	0.14	3.61	1.09	0.18	5.55	0.19	0.26
25 to 34 years	9.46	1.23	1.49	0.71	1.03	0.13	4.59	0.40	0.19	4.42	0.11	0.24
35 to 44 years	9.21	1.20	1.82	0.73	1.05	0.12	4.82	0.21	0.30	4.27	0.09	0.18
45 to 54 years	9.20	1.19	1.87	0.70	0.39	0.20	4.92	0.06	0.33	4.81	0.12	0.22
55 to 64 years	9.27	1.31	2.07	0.86	0.15	0.27	3.68	0.03	0.39	5.59	0.17	0.22
65 to 74 years	9.41	1.41	2.53	0.85	0.11	0.25	1.39	0.01	0.49	7.10	0.20	0.26
75 years and over	9.89	1.52	2.42	0.73	0.12	0.17	0.31	0.00	0.52	7.68	0.30	0.33
Men, 15 Years and Over	9.22	1.30	1.29	0.60	0.35	0.16	4.17	0.53	0.26	5.79	0.11	0.23
15 to 19 years	10.09	1.04	0.58	0.37	0.10	0.19	0.86	3.53	0.25	6.55	0.16	0.28
20 to 24 years	9.42	1.17	0.64	0.47	*	0.15	3.51	1.02	0.22	6.63	0.16	0.32
25 to 34 years	9.17	1.24	1.06	0.56	0.62	0.13	5.39	0.42	0.15	4.93	0.09	0.25
35 to 44 years	8.94	1.28	1.20	0.62	0.74	0.09	6.02	0.19	0.24	4.45	0.06	0.18
45 to 54 years	9.01	1.25	1.34	0.58	0.34	0.15	5.65	0.05	0.26	5.09	0.08	0.21
55 to 64 years	8.95	1.36	1.65	0.72	0.11	0.23	4.43	*	0.28	5.97	0.12	0.16
65 to 74 years	9.22	1.56	2.06	0.72	0.09	0.23	1.72	0.00	0.46	7.64	0.11	0.19
75 years and over	9.77	1.66	1.89	0.67	0.10	0.16	0.55	0.00	0.42	8.11	0.25	0.43
Women, 15 Years and Over	9.74	1.20	2.17	0.84	0.66	0.20	2.94	0.47	0.38	4.97	0.20	0.25
15 to 19 years	10.81	0.96	0.76	0.73	0.17	0.17	1.25	3.15	0.29	5.14	0.23	0.34
20 to 24 years	10.21	1.23	1.06	0.61	0.86	0.13	3.70	1.16	0.14	4.48	0.23	0.20
25 to 34 years	9.74	1.21	1.92	0.85	1.42	0.12	3.81	0.39	0.24	3.93	0.13	0.24
35 to 44 years	9.48	1.13	2.40	0.84	1.34	0.15	3.67	0.24	0.35	4.09	0.13	0.18
45 to 54 years	9.38	1.14	2.37	0.81	0.44	0.25	4.22	0.06	0.39	4.55	0.16	0.23
55 to 64 years	9.57	1.25	2.46	0.99	0.18	0.31	2.98	0.03	0.49	5.24	0.22	0.27
65 to 74 years	9.57	1.28	2.95	0.97	0.13	0.26	1.09	0.00	0.51	6.61	0.28	0.31
75 years and over	9.97	1.42	2.78	0.77	0.13	0.18	0.15	0.00	0.60	7.39	0.34	0.25
White, 15 Years and Over	9.43	1.27	1.82	0.72	0.51	0.19	3.59	0.49	0.30	5.30	0.15	0.23
Men	9.18	1.32	1.36	0.59	0.35	0.16	4.26	0.51	0.25	5.69	0.11	0.22
Women	9.67	1.23	2.26	0.84	0.66	0.21	2.96	0.46	0.36	4.94	0.19	0.23
Black, 15 Years and Over	9.83	0.92	1.32	0.82	0.44	0.18	3.01	0.45	0.46	6.06	0.20	0.30
Men	9.52	0.93	0.96	0.70	0.28	0.16	3.37	0.42	0.37	6.87	0.13	0.31
Women	10.09	0.92	1.62	0.92	0.57	0.19	2.71	0.48	0.53	5.40	0.27	0.30
Hispanic,[3] 15 Years and Over	9.83	1.18	1.79	0.67	0.68	0.15	3.51	0.77	0.29	4.76	0.11	0.27
Men	9.58	1.20	1.14	0.57	0.44	0.13	4.11	0.81	0.21	5.49	0.08	0.25
Women	10.07	1.15	2.43	0.78	0.93	0.17	2.90	0.73	0.37	4.03	0.14	0.30
Marital Status and Sex												
Married, spouse present	9.21	1.34	2.07	0.78	0.73	0.18	3.94	0.08	0.38	4.95	0.11	0.23
Men	8.97	1.39	1.51	0.67	0.54	0.14	4.79	0.05	0.33	5.30	0.08	0.23
Women	9.45	1.28	2.64	0.89	0.93	0.22	3.06	0.12	0.42	4.59	0.15	0.24
Other marital statuses	9.78	1.15	1.40	0.66	0.28	0.18	3.11	0.94	0.26	5.80	0.20	0.24
Men	9.50	1.19	1.03	0.51	0.14	0.18	3.45	1.08	0.18	6.36	0.15	0.24
Women	10.02	1.12	1.71	0.78	0.39	0.18	2.82	0.81	0.33	5.34	0.24	0.25
Educational Attainment, 25 Years and Over												
Less than a high school diploma	10.13	1.12	2.10	0.59	0.55	0.14	2.53	0.00	0.30	6.23	0.07	0.19
High school graduate, no college[4]	9.50	1.21	2.11	0.69	0.39	0.25	3.39	0.07	0.30	5.78	0.13	0.19
Some college or associate degree	9.27	1.23	1.95	0.82	0.56	0.18	3.84	0.20	0.36	5.17	0.17	0.26
Bachelor's degree and higher[5]	9.01	1.43	1.74	0.83	0.67	0.15	4.54	0.20	0.39	4.61	0.18	0.26

Note: 0.00 = Estimates are approximately zero.

[1]A primary activity is designated by a respondent as his or her main activity. Other activities done simultaneously are not included.
[2]All major activity categories include related travel time.
[3]May be of any race.
[4]Includes persons with a high school diploma or equivalent.
[5]Includes persons with bachelor's, master's, professional, and doctoral degrees.
* = Figure does not meet standards of reliability or quality.

Table 12-3. Average Hours Worked Per Day by Employed Persons on Weekdays and Weekends, by Selected Characteristics, 2012 Annual Averages

(Number, percent.)

Characteristic	Total employed (thousands)	Employed persons who worked on an average day			Employed persons who worked on an average weekday			Employed persons who worked on an average Saturday, Sunday, or holiday[1]		
		Number (thousands)	Percent of employed	Hours per day[2]	Number[3] (thousands)	Percent of employed	Hours per day[2]	Number[4] (thousands)	Percent of employed	Hours per day[2]
Both Sexes[5]	150 877	102 817	68.1	7.65	124 530	82.5	7.97	50 621	33.6	5.71
Full-time worker	114 136	83 117	72.8	8.22	101 844	89.2	8.60	38 813	34.0	5.86
Part-time worker	36 741	19 701	53.6	5.24	22 832	62.1	5.26	11 783	32.1	5.18
Men[5]	79 458	55 361	69.7	8.07	67 033	84.4	8.44	27 368	34.4	5.90
Full-time worker	66 470	48 759	73.4	8.46	59 467	89.5	8.87	23 541	35.4	6.02
Part-time worker	12 988	6 602	50.8	5.16	7 675	59.1	5.18	3 773	29.0	5.05
Women[5]	71 419	47 456	66.4	7.16	57 499	80.5	7.44	23 251	32.6	5.48
Full-time worker	47 666	34 358	72.1	7.87	42 378	88.9	8.21	15 265	32.0	5.61
Part-time worker	23 754	13 099	55.1	5.29	15 164	63.8	5.30	7 993	33.6	5.23
Multiple Job Holding Status										
Single job holder	138 106	92 250	66.8	7.65	113 179	82.0	7.95	42 361	30.7	5.74
Multiple job holder	12 771	10 567	82.7	7.60	11 328	88.7	8.19	8 559	67.0	5.55
Educational Attainment, 25 Years and Over										
Less than a high school diploma	9 879	6 563	66.4	7.76	8 099	82.0	8.05	3 337	33.8	6.30
High school graduate, no college[6]	36 749	24 589	66.9	7.97	30 220	82.2	8.15	10 893	29.6	6.76
Some college or associate degree	33 843	22 569	66.7	7.86	27 596	81.5	8.14	10 493	31.0	6.08
Bachelor's degree or higher[7]	49 670	36 252	73.0	7.57	44 128	88.8	8.09	16 996	34.2	4.21

Note: Data refer to persons age 15 years and over, unless otherwise specified.

[1]Holidays are New Year's Day, Easter, Memorial Day, the Fourth of July, Labor Day, Thanksgiving Day, and Christmas Day. In 2012, the telephone call center was closed the day after New Year's Day, so data were not collected about this holiday.
[2]Includes work at main and other job(s) and excludes travel related to work.
[3]Number was derived by multiplying the "total employed" by the percentage of employed persons who worked on an average weekday.
[4]Number was derived by multiplying the "total employed" by the percentage of employed persons who worked on an average Saturday, Sunday, or holiday.
[5]Includes workers whose hours vary.
[6]Includes persons with a high school diploma or equivalent.
[7]Includes persons with bachelor's, master's, professional, and doctoral degrees.

Table 12-4. Average Hours Worked Per Day at Main Job Only by Employed Persons on Weekdays and Weekend Days, by Selected Characteristics, 2012 Annual Averages

(Number, percent.)

Characteristic	Total employed (thousands)	Worked on an average day			Worked on an average weekday			Worked on an average Saturday, Sunday, or holiday[1]		
		Number (thousands)	Percent	Hours per day[2]	Number[3] (thousands)	Percent	Hours per day[2]	Number[4] (thousands)	Percent	Hours per day[2]
Class of Worker										
Wage and salary workers	139 487	93 584	67.1	7.65	114 995	82.4	7.94	42 631	30.6	5.74
Self-employed workers[5]	11 135	7 611	68.4	6.87	8 686	78.0	7.11	4 694	42.2	5.66
Occupation										
Management, business, and financial operations	23 190	16 964	73.2	7.86	20 835	89.8	8.38	7 751	33.4	4.53
Professional and related	36 444	24 962	68.5	7.31	30 225	82.9	7.68	11 265	30.9	4.72
Services	25 770	15 576	60.4	7.45	18 265	70.9	7.57	9 627	37.4	6.93
Sales and related	15 798	10 493	66.4	7.29	11 744	74.3	7.58	7 210	45.6	6.04
Office and administrative support	18 628	12 087	64.9	7.49	15 815	84.9	7.68	3 340	17.9	5.36
Farming, fishing, and forestry	*	*	*	6.92	*	*	6.94	*	*	6.86
Construction and extraction	6 802	4 653	68.4	7.74	5 940	87.3	8.00	1 680	24.7	5.60
Installation, maintenance, and repair	5 395	3 627	67.2	8.35	4 815	89.2	8.59	1 277	23.7	6.58
Production	8 159	5 593	68.6	7.97	7 208	88.3	8.14	1 954	23.9	6.57
Transportation and material moving	8 825	6 036	68.4	8.27	7 563	85.7	8.42	2 487	28.2	7.22
Earnings of Full-Time Wage and Salary Earners[6]										
$0 to $540	23 959	17 024	71.1	8.10	20 962	87.5	8.23	7 646	31.9	7.26
$541 to $810	23 397	15 694	67.1	8.20	20 606	88.1	8.37	5 989	25.6	7.02
$811 to $1,230	23 405	15 959	60.2	8.30	20 504	87.6	8.73	5 660	24.2	5.52
$1,231 and higher	23 554	17 968	76.3	8.31	21 688	92.1	8.96	7 959	33.8	3.60

Note: Data refer to persons age 15 years and over, unless otherwise specified.

[1]Holidays are New Year's Day, Easter, Memorial Day, the Fourth of July, Labor Day, Thanksgiving Day, and Christmas Day. In 2012, the telephone call center was closed the day after New Year's Day, so data were not collected about this holiday.
[2]Includes work at main job only and excludes travel related to work.
[3]Number was derived by multiplying the "total employed" by the percentage of employed persons who worked on an average weekday.
[4]Number was derived by multiplying the "total employed" by the percentage of employed persons who worked on an average Saturday, Sunday, or holiday.
[5]Includes self-employed workers whose businesses are unincorporated. Self-employed workers whose businesses are incorporated are classified as wage and salary workers.
[6]These values are based on usual weekly earnings. Each earnings range represents approximately 25 percent of full-time wage and salary workers who held only one job.
* = Figure does not meet standards for reliability or quality.

Table 12-5. Average Hours Worked Per Day at All Jobs by Employed Persons at Workplaces or at Home, by Selected Characteristics, 2012 Annual Averages

(Number, percent.)

Characteristic	Total employed (thousands)	Employed persons who reported working on an average day[1]								
		Number (thousands)	Percent	Average hours of work	Location of work[2]					
					Persons who reported working at their workplaces on an average day			Persons who reported working at home on an average day[3]		
					Number (thousands)	Percent	Average hours of work at workplace	Number (thousands)	Percent	Average hours of work at home
Full- and Part-Time Status and Sex										
Both sexes[4]	150 877	102 817	68.1	7.65	86 857	84.5	7.92	23 878	23.2	3.01
Full-time worker	114 136	83 117	72.8	8.22	72 115	86.8	8.35	18 502	22.3	3.19
Part-time worker	36 741	19 701	53.6	5.24	14 742	74.8	5.81	5 376	27.3	2.38
Men[4]	79 458	55 361	69.7	8.07	47 369	85.6	8.27	12 828	23.2	3.07
Full-time worker	66 470	48 759	73.4	8.46	42 695	87.6	8.56	10 828	22.2	3.12
Part-time worker	12 988	6 602	50.8	5.16	4 673	70.8	5.63	2 000	30.3	2.83
Women[4]	71 419	47 456	66.4	7.16	39 488	83.2	7.50	11 050	23.3	2.93
Full-time worker	47 666	34 358	72.1	7.87	29 419	85.6	8.05	7 674	22.3	3.30
Part-time worker	23 754	13 099	55.1	5.29	10 069	76.9	5.89	3 377	25.8	2.11
Multiple Job Holding Status										
Single job holder	138 106	92 250	66.8	7.65	78 770	85.4	7.92	20 242	21.9	3.02
Multiple job holder	12 771	10 567	82.7	7.60	8 087	76.5	7.91	3 636	34.4	2.96
Educational Attainment, 25 Years and Over										
Less than a high school diploma	9 879	6 563	66.4	7.76	6 141	93.6	7.90	357	5.4	3.18
High school graduate, no college[5]	36 749	24 589	66.9	7.97	22 285	90.6	8.04	3 118	12.7	3.56
Some college or associate degree	33 843	22 569	66.7	7.86	19 032	84.3	8.18	4 769	21.1	3.17
Bachelor's degree or higher[6]	49 670	36 252	73.0	7.57	28 069	77.4	7.98	13 914	38.4	2.87

Note: Data refer to persons age 15 years and over, unless otherwise specified.

[1]Includes work at main and other job(s) and excludes travel related to work.
[2]Respondents may have worked at more than one location.
[3]"Working at home" includes any time the respondent reported doing activities that were identified as "part of one's job"; this category is not restricted to persons whose usual workplace is their home.
[4]Includes workers whose hours vary.
[5]Includes persons with a high school diploma or equivalent.
[6]Includes persons with bachelor's, master's, professional, and doctoral degrees.

Table 12-6. Average Hours Worked Per Day at Main Job Only by Employed Persons at Workplaces or at Home, by Selected Characteristics, 2012 Annual Averages

(Number, percent.)

Characteristic	Total employed (thousands)	Employed persons who reported working on an average day[1]								
		Number (thousands)	Percent	Hours of work	Location of work[2]					
					Persons who reported working at their workplaces on an average day			Persons who reported working at home on an average day[3]		
					Number (thousands)	Percent	Hours of work at workplace	Number (thousands)	Percent	Hours of work at home
Class of Worker										
Wage and salary worker	139 487	93 584	67.1	7.65	81 764	87.4	7.91	18 428	19.7	2.58
Self-employed worker[4]	11 135	7 611	68.4	6.87	4 047	53.2	7.08	4 270	56.1	4.86
Occupation										
Management, business, and financial operations	23 190	16 964	73.2	7.86	13 107	77.3	8.19	6 028	35.5	3.70
Professional and related	36 444	24 962	68.5	7.31	19 248	77.1	7.85	9 226	37.0	2.58
Services	25 770	15 576	60.4	7.45	13 849	88.9	7.52	1 571	10.1	4.01
Sales and related	15 798	10 493	66.4	7.29	9 008	85.8	7.54	2 245	21.4	3.20
Office and administrative support	18 628	12 087	64.9	7.49	11 338	93.8	7.63	1 123	9.3	2.13
Farming, fishing, and forestry	*	*	*	6.92	*	*	8.71	*	*	3.12
Construction and extraction	6 802	4 653	68.4	7.74	4 139	89.0	7.92	743	16.0	2.50
Installation, maintenance, and repair	5 395	3 627	67.2	8.35	3 424	94.4	8.29	534	14.7	*
Production	8 159	5 593	68.6	7.97	5 439	97.2	8.08	348	6.2	*
Transportation and material moving	8 825	6 036	68.4	8.27	5 472	90.7	8.51	432	7.2	1.98
Earnings of Full-Time Wage and Salary Earners[5]										
$0 to $480	23 959	17 024	71.1	8.10	16 164	94.9	8.17	1 139	6.7	*
$481 to $730	23 397	15 694	67.1	8.20	14 894	94.9	8.20	1 381	8.8	2.36
$731 to $1,150	23 405	15 959	68.2	8.39	14 194	88.9	8.55	3 188	20.0	2.53
$1,151 and higher	23 554	17 968	76.3	8.31	14 872	82.8	8.59	6 075	33.8	2.92

Note: Data refer to persons age 15 years and over, unless otherwise specified.

[1]Includes work at main job only and excludes travel related to work.
[2]Respondents may have worked at more than one location.
[3]"Working at home" includes any time the respondent reported doing activities that were identified as "part of one's job"; this category is not restricted to persons whose usual workplace is their home.
[4]Includes self-employed workers whose businesses are unincorporated. Self-employed workers whose businesses are incorporated are classified as wage and salaryworkers.
[5]These values are based on usual weekly earnings. Each earnings range covers approximately 25 percent of full-time wage and salary workers.
* = Figure does not meet standards for reliability or quality.

Table 12-7. Average Hours Per Day Spent by Persons Age 18 Years and Over Caring for Household Children Under 18 Years, by Sex of Respondent, Age of Youngest Household Child, and Day, 2008–2012 Combined Annual Averages

(Number.)

Activity	Hours per day caring for household children								
	Total			Weekdays			Weekends and holidays		
	Both sexes	Men	Women	Both sexes	Men	Women	Both sexes	Men	Women
Persons in Households with Children Under 18 Years									
Caring for household children as a primary activity	1.33	0.91	1.69	1.42	0.92	1.85	1.13	0.89	1.32
Physical care	0.43	0.24	0.60	0.46	0.25	0.64	0.37	0.22	0.50
Education-related activities	0.10	0.06	0.14	0.13	0.08	0.18	0.03	0.02	0.04
Reading to/with children	0.04	0.03	0.04	0.04	0.03	0.05	0.03	0.02	0.04
Talking to/with children	0.05	0.03	0.06	0.05	0.03	0.07	0.03	0.02	0.04
Playing/doing hobbies with children	0.29	0.27	0.32	0.27	0.24	0.30	0.34	0.34	0.34
Looking after children	0.08	0.06	0.09	0.07	0.05	0.09	0.09	0.09	0.10
Attending children's events	0.06	0.05	0.07	0.05	0.04	0.06	0.08	0.08	0.09
Travel related to care of household children	0.17	0.12	0.22	0.21	0.14	0.27	0.09	0.07	0.10
Other childcare activities	0.11	0.06	0.15	0.13	0.07	0.18	0.06	0.03	0.07
Persons in Households with Youngest Child 6 to 17 Years									
Caring for household children as a primary activity	0.79	0.55	1.01	0.87	0.57	1.13	0.61	0.49	0.72
Physical care	0.15	0.08	0.20	0.17	0.09	0.23	0.10	0.05	0.13
Education-related activities	0.12	0.07	0.16	0.15	0.09	0.21	0.04	0.03	0.05
Reading to/with children	0.01	0.01	0.02	0.01	0.01	0.02	0.01	0.01	0.02
Talking to/with children	0.06	0.03	0.08	0.07	0.04	0.09	0.04	0.02	0.05
Playing/doing hobbies with children	0.07	0.09	0.06	0.06	0.08	0.05	0.10	0.11	0.08
Looking after children	0.05	0.04	0.06	0.04	0.03	0.06	0.06	0.05	0.07
Attending children's events	0.08	0.06	0.09	0.06	0.05	0.07	0.12	0.10	0.13
Travel related to care of household children	0.16	0.11	0.20	0.19	0.13	0.24	0.09	0.08	0.10
Other childcare activities	0.09	0.05	0.13	0.11	0.06	0.15	0.05	0.03	0.07
Persons in Households with Youngest Child Under 6 Years									
Caring for household children as a primary activity	1.98	1.37	2.47	2.08	1.36	2.66	1.74	1.39	2.03
Physical care	0.78	0.43	1.05	0.81	0.44	1.10	0.70	0.42	0.92
Education-related activities	0.09	0.05	0.11	0.11	0.07	0.15	0.02	0.01	0.03
Reading to/with children	0.06	0.05	0.07	0.06	0.05	0.07	0.05	0.04	0.06
Talking to/with children	0.03	0.02	0.04	0.03	0.02	0.04	0.02	0.01	0.03
Playing/doing hobbies with children	0.56	0.50	0.61	0.52	0.44	0.59	0.63	0.62	0.64
Looking after children	0.11	0.09	0.13	0.11	0.08	0.13	0.13	0.13	0.13
Attending children's events	0.04	0.03	0.04	0.03	0.02	0.05	0.05	0.06	0.04
Travel related to care of household children	0.19	0.13	0.24	0.24	0.15	0.30	0.08	0.06	0.09
Other childcare activities	0.13	0.07	0.18	0.16	0.09	0.22	0.06	0.03	0.08

Note: Universe includes respondents age 18 years and over living in households with children under 18 years of age, whether or not they provided childcare.

Table 12-8. Number and Percent of U.S. Population and Various Subpopulations Who Were Eldercare Providers, by Sex, 2011–2012 Annual Averages

(Number in thousands.)

Characteristic	Total			Men			Women		
	Total civilian noninstitu-tional population	Eldercare providers[1]		Total civilian noninstitu-tional population	Eldercare providers[1]		Total civilian noninstitu-tional population	Eldercare providers[1]	
		Number	Percent of population		Number	Percent of men		Number	Percent of women
Age									
Total, 15 years and over	245 521	39 564	16.1	118 933	17 500	14.7	126 588	22 064	17.4
15 to 24 years	42 553	5 330	12.5	21 579	2 569	11.9	20 975	2 761	13.2
25 to 34 years	41 170	4 050	9.8	20 484	2 035	9.9	20 686	2 015	9.7
35 to 44 years	39 570	5 060	12.8	19 431	2 301	11.8	20 140	2 758	13.7
45 to 54 years	43 773	10 106	23.1	21 397	4 267	19.9	22 377	5 839	26.1
55 to 64 years	37 656	8 366	22.2	18 110	3 517	19.4	19 546	4 849	24.8
65 years and over	40 797	6 652	16.3	17 932	2 810	15.7	22 865	3 842	16.8
Race and Hispanic or Latino Ethnicity[2,3]									
White	200 022	33 149	16.6	97 633	14 720	15.1	102 389	18 429	18.0
Black or African American	29 561	4 678	15.8	13 238	1 806	13.6	16 323	2 872	17.6
Hispanic or Latino ethnicity	36 452	3 792	10.4	18 534	1 943	10.5	17 919	1 849	10.3
Employment Status									
Employed	150 132	25 035	16.7	79 757	11 925	15.0	70 375	13 110	18.6
Full-time workers	114 946	18 680	16.3	66 967	9 893	14.8	47 979	8 788	18.3
Part-time workers	35 187	6 354	18.1	12 790	2 032	15.9	22 397	4 323	19.3
Not employed	95 389	14 529	15.2	39 176	5 575	14.2	56 213	8 954	15.9
Educational Attainment, 25 Years and Over									
Less than a high school diploma	22 828	2 056	9.0	11 565	1 177	10.2	11 263	879	7.8
High school graduates, no college	63 398	10 062	15.9	30 554	4 597	15.0	32 844	5 465	16.6
Some college or associate degree	50 922	9 552	18.8	22 977	3 579	15.6	27 945	5 973	21.4
Bachelor's degree and higher	65 819	12 564	19.1	32 258	5 577	17.3	33 561	6 987	20.8
Parent of Household Children Under 18 Years									
Parent of one or more household children	67 676	8 873	13.1	29 651	3 505	11.8	38 025	5 368	14.1
Parent of a household child age 6 to 17, none younger	35 758	6 000	16.8	16 201	2 403	14.8	19 557	3 597	18.4
Parent of a household child under age 6	31 918	2 873	9.0	13 450	1 102	8.2	18 468	1 771	9.6
Not a parent of a household child	177 845	30 691	17.3	89 282	13 995	15.7	88 564	16 696	18.9
Marital Status									
No spouse or unmarried partner present in household	108 829	15 939	14.6	49 895	6 616	13.3	58 934	9 323	15.8
Spouse or unmarried partner present in household	136 692	23 625	17.3	69 037	10 883	15.8	67 654	12 742	18.8

[1]Eldercare providers are those who in the previous 3 to 4 months cared for someone with a condition related to aging. Estimates were calculated for persons who cared for at least one person age 65 or over.
[2]Not all subcategories are shown.
[3]May be of any race.

Table 12-9. Number and Percent of Eldercare Providers by Sex and Selected Characteristics, 2011–2012 Annual Averages

(Number.)

Characteristic	Eldercare providers[1]					
	Total		Men		Women	
	Number	Percent	Number	Percent	Number	Percent
Parent of Household Children Under 18 Years of Age						
Total, 15 years and over	39 564	100.0	17 500	100.0	22 064	100.0
Parent of one or more household children	8 873	22.4	3 505	20.0	5 368	24.3
Parent of a household child age 6 to 17, none younger	6 000	15.2	2 403	13.7	3 597	16.3
Parent of a household child under age 6	2 873	7.3	1 102	6.3	1 771	8.0
Not a parent of a household child	30 691	77.6	13 995	80.0	16 696	75.7
Number of Care Recepients[2]						
Caring for one person	27 785	70.2	12 019	68.7	15 766	71.5
Caring for two persons	8 772	22.2	4 121	23.5	4 651	21.1
Caring for three or more persons	2 926	7.4	1 340	7.7	1 586	7.2
Relationship to Care Recipient						
Total, all eldercare providers	39 564	(3)	17 500	(3)	22 064	(3)
Caring for a spouse or unmarried partner[4]	1 893	4.8	766	4.4	1 127	5.1
Caring for a parent	16 804	42.5	7 004	40.0	9 799	44.4
Caring for a grandparent[5]	7 312	18.5	3 300	18.9	4 012	18.2
Caring for another related person	8 095	20.5	3 964	22.7	4 131	18.7
Caring for a friend or neighbor	7 491	18.9	3 419	19.5	4 072	18.5
Caring for someone else	2 859	7.2	1 302	7.4	1 557	7.1
Eldercare providers caring for one person only	27 785	100.0	12 019	100.0	15 766	100.0
Caring for a spouse or unmarried partner[4]	1 675	6.0	703	5.9	971	6.2
Caring for a parent	11 293	40.6	4 444	37.0	6 849	43.4
Caring for a grandparent[5]	4 883	17.6	2 183	18.2	2 699	17.1
Caring for another related person	4 808	17.3	2 307	19.2	2 501	15.9
Caring for a friend or neighbor	4 053	14.6	1 874	15.6	2 179	13.8
Caring for someone else	1 073	3.9	507	4.2	566	3.6
Age of Care Recipient						
Total, all eldercare providers	39 564	(3)	17 500	(3)	22 064	(3)
Caring for someone age 65 to 69	5 171	13.1	2 382	13.6	2 789	12.6
Caring for someone age 70 to 74	7 206	18.2	3 459	19.8	3 746	17.0
Caring for someone age 75 to 79	9 225	23.3	4 129	23.6	5 095	23.1
Caring for someone age 80 to 84	10 971	27.7	4 764	27.2	6 207	28.1
Caring for someone age 85 or older	14 530	36.7	6 195	35.4	8 335	37.8
Eldercare providers caring for one person only	27 785	100.0	12 019	100.0	15 766	100.0
Caring for someone age 65 to 69	2 839	10.2	1 191	9.9	1 648	10.5
Caring for someone age 70 to 74	3 647	13.1	1 655	13.8	1 992	12.6
Caring for someone age 75 to 79	5 045	18.2	2 121	17.6	2 924	18.5
Caring for someone age 80 to 84	6 347	22.8	2 865	23.8	3 482	22.1
Caring for someone age 85 or older	9 907	35.7	4 186	34.8	5 721	36.3
Care of Household or Nonhousehold Members						
Provided eldercare to household member(s) only	5 331	13.5	2 435	13.9	2 896	13.1
Provided eldercare to nonhousehold member(s) only	33 557	84.8	14 638	83.6	18 919	85.7
Provided eldercare to both household and nonhousehold person(s)	676	1.7	426	2.4	250	1.1
Frequency of Care[6]						
Provided care daily	7 771	19.6	3 190	18.2	4 581	20.8
Provided care several times a week	9 316	23.5	4 057	23.2	5 259	23.8
Provided care once a week	7 918	20.0	3 749	21.4	4 169	18.9
Provided care several times a month	7 557	19.1	3 163	18.1	4 393	19.9
Provided care once a month	5 040	12.7	2 490	14.2	2 550	11.6
Other	1 962	5.0	849	4.9	1 112	5.0
Duration of Care						
Provided care for less than 1 year	9 056	22.9	3 644	20.8	5 412	24.5
Provided care for 1 to 2 years	10 655	26.9	4 814	27.5	5 840	26.5
Provided care for 3 to 4 years	6 633	16.8	2 982	17.0	3 651	16.5
Provided care for 5 to 9 years	7 133	18.0	3 165	18.1	3 968	18.0
Provided care for 10 years or more	6 087	15.4	2 894	16.5	3 193	14.5

Note: Data refer to persons 15 years and over.

[1] Eldercare providers are those who in the previous 3 to 4 months cared for someone with a condition related to aging. Estimates were calculated for persons who cared for at least one person age 65 or over.
[2] Data do not sum to total because some persons did not respond to the question identifying the number of care recipients.
[3] Categories sum to more than 100 percent because some eldercare providers cared for more than one person.
[4] Care for a spouse or unmarried partner may be underreported.
[5] Persons caring for a grandparent with whom they lived are included in the category "Caring for another related person."
[6] Survey participants were asked how often they provided care in the past 3 to 4 months; this information was used to categorize them by frequency of care. Corresponding time and percent estimates were measured using information about care provided on the diary day.

Table 12-10. Percent of Eldercare Providers Who Provided Care and the Time They Provided This Care by Day of Week and Selected Characteristics, 2011–2012 Annual Averages

(Number.)

Characteristic	Number of eldercare providers	Percent of eldercare providers who provided care per day[1]			Average hours per day eldercare providers[1] spent providing care			Average hours per day eldercare providers[1] spent providing care on days they engaged in the activity		
		Total, all days	Weekdays	Weekends and holidays	Total, all days	Weekdays	Weekends and holidays	Total, all days	Weekdays	Weekends and holidays
Age										
Total, 15 years and over	39 564	23.0	21.9	25.7	0.74	0.71	0.83	3.22	3.23	3.21
15 to 24 years	5 330	15.4	15.4	15.2	0.19	0.21	0.15	1.25	*	*
25 to 34 years	4 050	12.9	8.8	20.1	0.38	*	0.66	2.99	*	3.27
35 to 44 years	5 060	20.5	20.0	21.6	0.50	0.47	0.57	2.45	2.36	2.63
45 to 54 years	10 106	22.3	22.4	22.0	0.73	0.74	0.71	3.27	3.29	3.22
55 to 64 years	8 366	26.0	22.9	33.6	0.90	0.80	1.13	3.45	3.51	3.35
65 years and over	6 652	34.7	33.6	37.3	1.41	1.38	1.48	4.07	4.11	3.98
Sex										
Men	17 500	20.8	18.8	25.8	0.60	0.51	0.80	2.86	2.74	3.08
Women	22 064	24.8	24.4	25.6	0.86	0.86	0.85	3.47	3.54	3.31
Race and Hispanic Origin[2]										
White	33 149	22.3	20.9	25.2	0.69	0.65	0.79	3.11	3.11	3.11
Black or African American	4 678	30.5	30.8	30.0	1.12	1.11	1.16	3.68	3.61	3.88
Hispanic or Latino ethnicity[3]	3 792	28.1	31.6	21.1	0.79	0.88	0.62	2.82	2.79	2.93
Employment Status										
Employed	25 035	19.1	17.5	22.8	0.45	0.39	0.59	2.34	2.21	2.57
Full-time workers	18 680	17.9	16.1	22.0	0.44	0.37	0.60	2.47	2.30	2.75
Part-time workers	6 354	22.6	21.4	25.4	0.46	0.43	0.52	2.03	2.02	2.06
Not employed	14 529	29.8	29.5	30.5	1.25	1.26	1.22	4.20	4.29	4.02
Educational Attainment, 25 Years and Over										
Less than a high school diploma	2 056	32.9	*	27.0	1.26	1.38	1.07	3.82	3.76	3.95
High school graduates, no college	10 062	25.1	23.2	29.4	0.82	0.77	0.93	3.26	3.32	3.16
Some college or associate degree	9 552	25.4	24.3	27.9	0.95	0.92	1.02	3.74	3.78	3.66
Bachelor's degree and higher	12 564	21.2	19.7	24.5	0.67	0.62	0.79	3.18	3.15	3.23
Percent of Household Children Under 18 Years										
Parent of one or more household children	8 873	17.4	16.9	18.5	0.53	0.51	0.59	3.07	3.01	3.18
Parent of a household child age 6 to 17, none younger	6 000	20.0	19.3	21.0	0.70	0.58	0.78	3.25	3.00	3.73
Parent of a household child under age 6	2 873	12.3	11.4	13.7	*	*	0.22	*	*	1.61
Not a parent of a household child	30 691	24.6	23.2	28.0	0.80	0.76	0.90	3.26	3.28	3.22
Marital Status										
No spouse or unmarried partner present in household	15 939	24.1	23.6	25.4	0.71	0.71	0.71	2.94	3.01	2.79
Spouse or unmarried partner present in household	23 625	22.3	20.6	25.9	0.76	0.70	0.90	3.43	3.40	3.48
Number of Care Recipients[4]										
Caring for one person	27 785	24.5	24.0	25.7	0.84	0.80	0.94	3.44	3.35	3.65
Caring for two persons	8 772	19.4	16.3	25.9	0.51	0.47	0.58	2.62	2.91	2.24
Caring for three or more persons	2 926	20.5	18.1	25.9	0.50	0.47	0.59	2.46	2.59	2.26
Relationship to Care Recipient										
Eldercare providers caring for one person only	27 785	24.5	24.0	25.7	0.84	0.80	0.94	3.44	3.35	3.65
Caring for a spouse or unmarried partner[5]	1 675	71.4	*	*	3.98	4.03	3.89	5.58	5.67	5.39
Caring for a parent	11 293	28.5	28.3	29.0	0.94	0.90	1.04	3.31	3.20	3.57
Caring for a grandparent[6]	4 883	13.2	13.2	13.3	0.25	*	0.26	1.91	*	1.99
Caring for another related person	4 808	20.3	18.1	25.1	0.64	0.51	*	3.13	2.84	3.58
Caring for a friend or neighbor	4 053	14.8	14.5	15.6	0.28	0.28	*	1.90	1.92	*
Age of Care Recipient										
Eldercare providers caring for one person only	27 785	24.5	24.0	25.7	0.84	0.80	0.94	3.44	3.35	3.65
Caring for someone age 65 to 69	2 839	23.6	24.2	22.4	0.52	*	0.53	2.20	*	2.38
Caring for someone age 70 to 74	3 647	22.4	19.6	29.0	0.79	0.75	0.86	3.51	3.85	2.98
Caring for someone age 75 to 79	5 045	25.5	25.6	25.2	0.88	0.87	0.91	3.46	3.41	3.60
Caring for someone age 80 to 84	6 347	25.3	26.5	22.4	0.83	0.86	0.74	3.26	3.25	3.28
Caring for someone age 85 or older	9 907	24.5	23.1	27.6	0.95	0.83	1.22	3.87	3.58	4.41

[1]Eldercare providers are those who in the previous 3 to 4 months cared for someone with a condition related to aging. Estimates were calculated for persons who cared for at least one person age 65 or over.
[2]Not all subcategories are shown.
[3]May be of any race.
[4]Data do not sum to total because some persons did not respond to the question identifying the number of care recipients.
[5]Care for a spouse or partner may be underreported.
[6]Refers only to persons caring for a grandparent who did not live with them. Persons caring for a grandparent with whom they lived are included in the category "Caring for another related person."
* = Figure does not meet standards of reliability or quality.

Table 12-10. Percent of Eldercare Providers Who Provided Care and the Time They Provided This Care by Day of Week and Selected Characteristics, 2011–2012 Annual Averages—*Continued*

(Number.)

Characteristic	Number of eldercare providers	Percent of eldercare providers who provided care per day[1]			Average hours per day eldercare providers[1] spent providing care			Average hours per day eldercare providers[1] spent providing care on days they engaged in the activity		
		Total, all days	Weekdays	Weekends and holidays	Total, all days	Weekdays	Weekends and holidays	Total, all days	Weekdays	Weekends and holidays
Care of Household or Nonhousehold Members										
Provided eldercare to household member(s) only	5 331	65.2	64.7	66.3	2.86	2.78	3.04	4.38	4.29	4.58
Provided eldercare to nonhousehold member(s) only	33 557	16.3	15.2	18.8	0.41	0.39	0.46	2.52	2.55	2.47
Frequency of Care[7]										
Provided care daily	7 771	64.4	63.3	67.0	2.64	2.57	2.80	4.10	4.06	4.18
Provided care several times a week	9 316	25.5	25.7	25.1	0.57	0.58	0.56	2.24	2.25	2.22
Provided care once a week	7 918	10.7	7.0	19.4	0.23	0.16	0.40	2.17	2.29	2.07
Provided care several times a month	7 557	7.9	7.4	8.9	0.14	0.13	0.17	1.77	1.69	1.93
Provided care once a month	5 040	2.2	1.8	3.3	0.05	*	0.09	2.36	*	*
Duration of Care[8]										
Provided care for less than 1 year	9 056	17.5	17.7	17.0	0.52	0.53	0.51	2.97	2.97	2.98
Provided care for 1 to 2 years	10 655	22.9	22.2	24.4	0.75	0.79	0.66	3.29	3.58	2.71
Provided care for 3 to 4 years	6 633	27.6	25.1	33.6	0.94	0.97	0.88	3.41	3.85	2.62
Provided care for 5 to 9 years	7 133	25.5	24.7	27.1	0.80	0.62	1.17	3.12	2.49	4.30
Provided care for 10 years or more	6 087	23.6	20.8	30.3	0.78	0.64	1.09	3.28	3.09	3.60

[1]Eldercare providers are those who in the previous 3 to 4 months cared for someone with a condition related to aging. Estimates were calculated for persons who cared for at least one person age 65 or over.
[7]Survey participants were asked how often they provided care in the past 3 to 4 months; this information was used to categorize them by frequency of care. Corresponding time and percent estimates were measured using information about care provided on the diary day.
[8]For persons who provided eldercare to more than one person, the duration of care is calculated based on the person for whom they had cared the longest.
* = Figure does not meet standards of reliability or quality.

Table 12-11. Time Spent Providing Eldercare and Percent of the Eldercare Population Engaging in Various Caregiving Activities, by Sex, 2011–2012 Annual Averages

(Percent.)

Characteristic	Eldercare time spent in selected activities, percent distribution			On days they provided care					
				Percent[1] who engaged in the activity			Average hours spent providing care		
	Total	Men	Women	Total	Men	Women	Total	Men	Women
Total, activities reported as care done for those age 65 and over	100.0	100.0	100.0	(1)	(1)	(1)	3.22	2.86	3.47
Eating and drinking	7.1	6.2	7.5	22.2	20.4	23.5	0.23	0.18	0.26
Household activities	20.9	19.2	21.9	38.2	34.0	41.1	0.67	0.55	0.76
Housework	6.3	4.2	7.5	11.5	8.3	13.6	0.20	0.12	0.26
Food preparation and cleanup	9.5	8.3	10.1	28.1	23.5	31.1	0.31	0.24	0.35
Lawn and garden care	1.9	2.7	1.5	3.5	4.1	3.1	0.06	0.08	0.05
Household management	1.2	0.9	1.4	5.8	4.8	6.6	0.04	0.03	0.05
Purchasing goods and services	4.2	4.3	4.1	14.5	13.7	15.0	0.13	0.12	0.14
Caring for and helping household members	6.4	6.1	6.5	19.0	18.2	19.6	0.21	0.17	0.23
Caring for household adults	5.3	4.8	5.6	15.7	15.0	16.2	0.17	0.14	0.19
Physical care for household adults	3.2	1.7	4.1	8.6	7.8	9.1	0.10	0.05	0.14
Providing medical care to household adults	0.7	0.8	0.7	7.0	7.1	6.9	0.02	0.02	0.02
Helping household adults	0.6	1.0	0.4	4.1	5.6	3.2	0.02	0.03	0.02
Caring for and helping nonhousehold members	10.1	9.1	10.6	24.7	21.0	27.2	0.33	0.26	0.37
Caring for nonhousehold adults	3.7	1.8	4.7	8.9	4.5	11.8	0.12	0.05	0.16
Physical care for nonhousehold adults	1.8	1.0	2.2	4.1	1.7	5.7	0.06	0.03	0.08
Providing medical care to nonhousehold adults	0.4	0.1	0.6	2.5	1.5	3.2	0.01	*	0.02
Helping nonhousehold adults	6.2	7.3	5.6	17.6	18.1	17.3	0.20	0.21	0.19
Housework, cooking, and shopping assistance for nonhousehold adults	2.3	1.8	2.5	6.1	6.3	5.9	0.07	0.05	0.09
House and lawn maintenance and repair assistance for nonhousehold adults	1.8	2.6	1.4	2.5	3.6	1.8	0.06	0.07	0.05
Picking up and dropping off nonhousehold adults	0.6	0.6	0.6	6.1	4.1	7.3	0.02	0.02	0.02
Working and work-related activities	4.4	5.4	3.9	3.7	4.0	3.6	0.14	0.16	0.13
Organizational, civic, and religious activities	2.4	1.9	2.7	4.4	3.4	5.1	0.08	0.05	0.09
Leisure and sports	33.7	38.5	31.0	35.8	35.2	36.2	1.09	1.10	1.07
Socializing and communicating	13.1	13.0	13.1	23.4	22.1	24.3	0.42	0.37	0.45
Watching TV	13.7	19.1	10.7	11.6	10.2	12.5	0.44	0.55	0.37
Participating in sports, exercise, and recreation	1.5	1.7	1.4	2.7	3.5	2.1	0.05	0.05	0.05
Telephone calls, mail, and e-mail	1.0	0.5	1.3	5.8	4.3	6.8	0.03	0.01	0.05
Traveling	8.1	7.0	8.7	27.1	25.8	27.9	0.26	0.20	0.30
Other activities, not elsewhere classified	1.8	1.7	1.8	5.4	4.0	6.3	0.06	*	0.06

[1]Percents sum to more than 100 percent because some eldercare providers did more than one care activity on days they provided care.
* = Figure does not meet standards of reliability or quality.

CHAPTER 13: INCOME IN THE UNITED STATES (CENSUS BUREAU)

This chapter presents data on income and earnings in the United States collected by the Census Bureau. Income, as distinguished from earnings, includes income from pensions, investments, and other sources and is measured as real income in 2012 dollars.

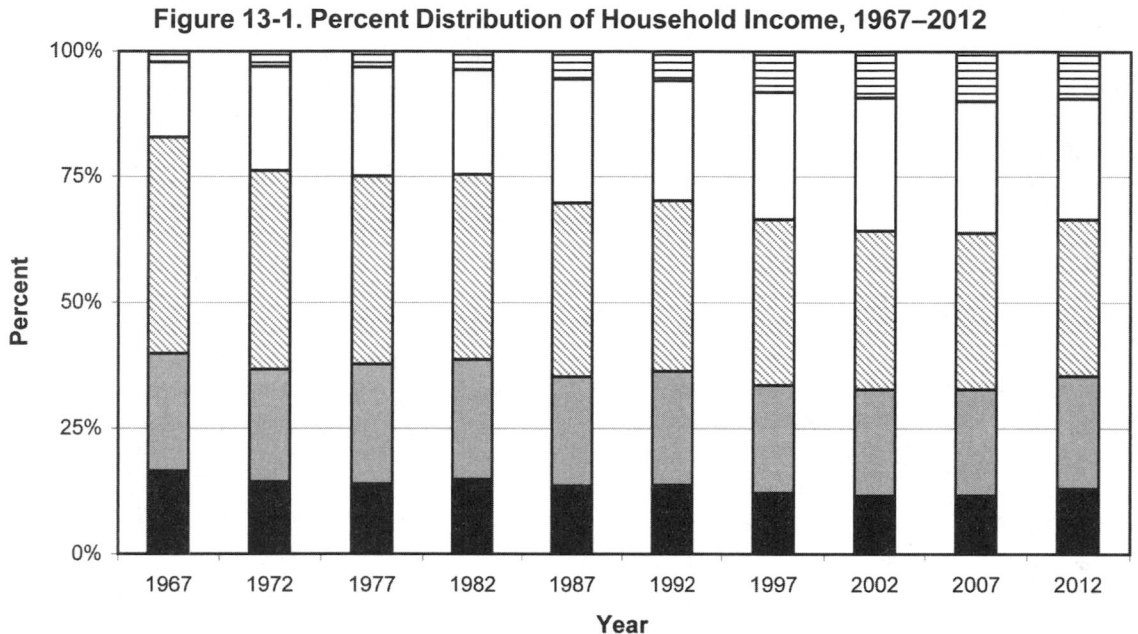

Figure 13-1. Percent Distribution of Household Income, 1967–2012

■ $0–$14,999 □ $15,000–$34,999 ▨ $35,000–$74,999 □ $75,000–$149,999 ▤ $150,000 and over

The proportion of households with income over $150,000 was lower in 2012 than in 2007. In 2007, 10.0 percent of all households had an income over $150,000 and 4.7 percent had an income over $200,000. By 2012, 9.5 percent of households had an income over $150,000 while 4.5 percent of households had an income over $200,000. (See Table 13-2.)

OTHER HIGHLIGHTS

- Median income varied by race and ethnic origin. In 2012, Asians had the highest median income at $68,636, followed by non-Hispanic Whites ($57,009), Hispanics ($39,005), and Blacks ($33,321). (See Table 13-1.)

- From 2011 to 2012, median income increased 3.2 percent in the West—higher than any other region. The West also has the highest median income in 2012. Median income increased 1.5 percent in the Midwest and 0.3 percent in the South, but declined 0.7 percent in the Northeast. (See Table 13-1.)

- The two-year average median household income was $51,059 in the United States in 2011–2012, a decrease from $51,496 in 2010–2011. It varied significantly by state. Median household income was the highest in Maryland ($71,076), followed by New Hampshire ($67,538) and Connecticut ($65,515). (See Table 13-5.)

- Median family income in the United States was $62,527 in 2012. Mississippi continued to have the lowest family income at $45,857. Maryland had the highest median family income at $85,985, followed by Connecticut ($85,254) and New Jersey ($84,442). (See Table 13-6.)

NOTES AND DEFINITIONS

COLLECTION AND COVERAGE

The data in Tables 13-1 through 13-5 are from the Annual Social and Economic Supplement (ASEC) to the 2012 Current Population Survey (CPS). The CPS ASEC provides timely estimates of household income and individual earnings, as well as the distribution of that income. The population represented is the civilian noninstitutionalized population living in the United States. Members of the Armed Forces living off post or with their families on post are included if at least one civilian adult lives in the household—hence, the CPS ASEC universe is slightly larger than the CPS universe, which does not include persons who are on active duty in the armed forces

The data in Tables 13-6 and 13-7 come from the American Community Survey (ACS). The ACS is an annual survey that covers the same type of information that had been collected every 10 years from the decennial census long form questionnaire. The ACS eliminated the need for a separate long form in the 2010 Census. The CPS ASEC and ACS surveys differ in the length and detail of its questionnaire, the number of households interviewed, the methodology used to collect and process the data, and, consequently, the income and poverty estimates produced.

The sample size of the ACS is much larger (approximately 3.5 million in 2012) compared to the sample size of the CPS ASEC (100,000). Although it is smaller, the CPS ASEC is a high-quality source of information due to its detailed questionnaire and experienced interviewing staff. Another notable difference between the two surveys is that the ACS is a mandatory, whereas the CPS ASEC is voluntary.

CONCEPTS AND DEFINITIONS

The *Gini index of income inequality* (also known as the Gini ratio, Gini coefficient, or index of income concentration) is a statistical measure that summarizes the dispersion of income across an entire income distribution. Values range from 0 to 1. A Gini value of 1 indicates "perfect" inequality; that is, one household has all the income and the rest have none. A value of zero indicates "perfect" equality, a situation in which all households have equal income.

Equivalence-adjusted income inequality is another way to measure income inequality. Equivalence adjusted income takes into consideration the number of people living in the household and how these people share resources and take advantage of economies of scale. For example, the household-income-based distribution treats income of $30,000 for a single-person household and a family household similarly, while the equivalence-adjusted income of $30,000 for a single-person household would be more than twice the equivalence-adjusted income of $30,000 for a family household with two adults and two children. The equivalence adjustment used here is based on a three-parameter scale that reflects:

1. On average, children consume less than adults.

2. As family size increases, expenses do not increase at the same rate.

3. The increase in expenses is larger for a first child of a single-parent family than the first child of a two-adult family.

ADDITIONAL INFORMATION

Additional information is available in the Census publication "Income, Poverty, and Health Insurance Coverage in the United States: 2012," on the Census Bureau Web site at http://www.census.gov/hhes/www/income/income.html.

Table 13-1. Income and Earnings Summary Measures, by Selected Characteristics, 2011 and 2012

(Numbers in thousands, dollars, percent; income in 2012 dollars.)

Characteristic	2011			2012			Percent change in real median income (2012 less 2011)	
		Median income (dollars)			Median income (dollars)			
	Number	Estimate	90 percent confidence interval[1] (+/-)	Number	Estimate	90 percent confidence interval[1] (+/-)	Estimate	90 percent confidence interval[1] (+/-)
ALL HOUSEHOLDS	121 084	51 100	422	122 459	51 017	343	0.0	0.86
Type of Households								
Family households	80 506	63 574	457	80 902	64 053	772	0.8	1.22
Married-couple	58 949	75 678	965	59 204	75 694	612	0.0	1.26
Female householder, no husband present	15 669	34 340	830	15 469	34 002	984	0.0	3.53
Male householder, no wife present	5 888	50 602	2 189	6 229	48 634	1 558	0.0	4.50
Nonfamily households	40 578	30 853	429	41 558	30 880	475	0.1	1.72
Female householder	21 383	26 024	528	21 810	26 016	586	0.0	2.55
Male householder	19 195	36 223	814	19 747	36 989	750	2.1	2.53
Race[2] and Hispanic Origin of Householder								
White	96 964	53 304	377	97 705	53 706	631	0.8	1.10
White, not Hispanic	83 573	56 570	551	83 792	57 009	591	0.8	1.13
Black	15 583	32 902	855	15 872	33 321	1 300	1.3	3.66
Asian	5 374	66 489	2 631	5 560	68 636	3 109	3.2	5.16
Hispanic[3]	14 939	39 430	919	15 589	39 005	879	0.0	2.64
Age of Householder								
Under 65 years	94 241	56 802	486	94 535	57 353	505	1.0	1.04
15 to 24 years	6 180	31 096	969	6 314	30 604	1 085	0.0	4.33
25 to 34 years	19 846	51 835	708	20 017	51 381	597	0.0	1.61
35 to 44 years	21 241	63 209	708	21 334	63 629	1 508	0.7	2.36
45 to 54 years	24 195	65 195	1 884	24 068	66 411	988	1.9	3.21
55 to 64 years	22 779	57 105	1 186	22 802	58 626	1 354	2.7	2.89
65 years and older	26 843	33 810	595	27 924	33 848	631	0.1	2.30
Nativity of Householder								
Native born	103 965	51 862	401	104 909	51 803	385	0.0	0.83
Foreign born	17 119	45 359	1 270	17 550	45 475	779	0.3	2.89
Naturalized citizen	8 874	53 010	1 184	9 192	53 015	1 934	0.0	3.68
Not a citizen	8 246	38 686	1 288	8 358	37 721	1 035	0.0	3.63
Disability Status of Householder								
Households with householder aged 18 to 64	94 050	56 846	487	94 360	57 389	514	1.0	1.05
With disability	8 793	25 951	1 152	8 830	25 974	967	0.1	5.43
Without disability	84 787	60 652	750	85 025	61 103	399	0.7	1.24
Region								
Northeast	21 774	54 989	1 498	22 125	54 627	1 601	0.0	3.31
Midwest	26 865	49 740	1 162	27 093	50 479	777	1.5	2.16
South	45 604	47 879	753	45 938	48 033	857	0.3	1.71
West	26 840	53 470	1 008	27 303	55 157	1 022	3.2	2.07
Residence								
Inside metropolitan statistical areas	101 526	52 651	441	102 784	52 988	717	0.6	1.26
Inside principal cities	40 616	44 481	1 109	41 152	45 902	795	3.2	2.37
Outside principal cities	60 910	58 474	772	61 631	58 780	930	0.5	1.51
Outside metropolitan statistical areas[4]	19 558	41 374	965	19 676	41 198	1 031	0.0	2.32
Earnings of Year-Round Full-Time Workers								
Men with earnings	57 993	49 209	796	59 009	49 398	768	0.4	1.84
Women with earnings	43 683	37 894	259	44 042	37 791	594	0.0	1.51
Disability Status								
Workers without disability, age 15 and older								
Men with earnings	55 655	49 506	793	56 551	49 806	719	0.6	1.82
Women with earnings	42 462	37 951	263	42 750	37 988	630	0.1	1.58
Workers with disability, age 15 and older								
Men with earnings	1 622	43 093	2 757	1 739	41 540	1 504	0.0	6.81
Women with earnings	1 152	34 882	2 690	1 229	33 790	2 468	0.0	10.85

[1]A 90-percent confidence interval is a measure of an estimate's variability. The larger the confidence interval in relation to the size of the estimate, the less reliable the estimate.
[2]Federal surveys now give respondents the option of reporting more than one race. Therefore, there are two basic ways of defining a race group. A group such as Asian may be defined as those who reported Asian and no other race (the race-alone or single-race concept) or as those who reported Asian regardless of whether they also reported another race (the race-alone-or-in-combination concept). This table shows data using the race-alone concept. The use of the single-race population does not imply that it is the preferred method of presenting or analyzing data; the Census Bureau uses a variety of approaches. Information on people who reported more than one race, such as White and American Indian and Alaska Native or Asian and Black or African American, is available from Census 2010 through American FactFinder. About 2.9 percent of respondents reported more than one race in Census 2010.
[3]May be of any race.
[4]The "outside metropolitan statistical areas" category includes both micropolitan statistical areas and territory outside of metropolitan and micropolitan statistical areas.

Table 13-2. Households, by Total Money Income, Race, and Hispanic Origin of Householder, 1967–2012

(Numbers in thousands, percent, dollars; income in 2012 CPI-U-RS adjusted dollars.)

Race and Hispanic origin of householder and year	Number	Percent distribution										Median income (dollars)		Mean income (dollars)	
		Total	Under $15,000	$15,000 to $24,999	$25,000 to $34,999	$35,000 to $49,999	$50,000 to $74,999	$75,000 to $99,999	$100,000 to $149,999	$150,000 to $199,999	$200,000 and over	Value	Standard error	Value	Standard error
All Races															
1967[1]	60 813	100.0	16.5	11.6	11.8	20.2	22.7	9.9	5.2	1.3	0.9	42 934	156	48 019	156
1968	62 214	100.0	15.1	11.4	11.9	18.8	23.7	11.3	5.9	1.1	0.8	44 785	162	50 667	162
1969	63 401	100.0	14.8	10.9	11.1	18.0	23.9	11.9	6.9	1.4	1.0	46 449	172	52 845	166
1970	64 778	100.0	15.0	10.9	11.4	17.5	23.8	11.8	7.1	1.5	1.0	46 089	169	52 775	169
1971[2]	66 676	100.0	15.0	11.6	11.2	17.2	23.6	11.8	7.2	1.4	1.0	45 641	177	52 491	167
1972[3]	68 251	100.0	14.4	11.3	11.0	16.4	23.0	12.6	8.2	1.9	1.2	47 596	182	55 395	172
1973	69 859	100.0	13.7	11.7	10.4	15.9	23.0	13.0	8.9	1.9	1.4	48 557	185	56 155	171
1974[4,5]	71 163	100.0	13.6	11.7	11.5	16.5	22.6	12.8	8.3	1.8	1.1	47 019	181	54 985	172
1975[5]	72 867	100.0	14.4	12.5	11.7	16.3	22.4	12.2	7.7	1.8	1.0	45 788	186	53 467	167
1976[6]	74 142	100.0	14.1	12.2	11.4	16.0	22.6	12.7	8.2	1.8	1.1	46 548	172	54 752	169
1977	76 030	100.0	13.9	12.4	11.4	15.3	22.0	13.0	8.8	1.9	1.3	46 842	176	55 567	169
1978	77 330	100.0	13.5	11.8	11.1	15.3	21.9	13.3	9.4	2.3	1.4	48 655	197	57 266	220
1979[7]	80 776	100.0	13.7	11.3	11.1	15.3	21.9	13.3	9.6	2.4	1.4	48 520	230	57 636	218
1980	82 368	100.0	14.1	11.8	11.7	15.3	21.7	12.7	9.3	2.1	1.3	46 985	241	55 881	204
1981	83 527	100.0	14.5	12.3	11.8	15.5	20.9	12.4	9.3	2.0	1.2	46 205	242	55 200	201
1982	83 918	100.0	14.8	12.0	11.8	15.7	20.9	11.9	9.1	2.3	1.4	46 082	208	55 535	206
1983	85 407	100.0	14.5	12.3	11.5	15.8	20.5	12.2	9.3	2.5	1.5	45 760	208	55 654	208
1984[8]	86 789	100.0	14.1	11.8	11.5	15.4	20.3	12.6	10.0	2.7	1.7	47 181	215	57 808	213
1985[9]	88 458	100.0	14.2	11.6	11.0	15.2	20.4	12.4	10.6	2.8	1.9	48 063	260	59 149	234
1986	89 479	100.0	13.9	11.0	10.8	14.7	20.1	12.8	11.2	3.2	2.2	49 764	258	61 482	250
1987[10]	91 124	100.0	13.5	11.0	10.7	14.6	19.8	13.1	11.6	3.3	2.3	50 389	238	62 664	257
1988	92 830	100.0	13.4	10.9	10.5	14.6	20.0	13.0	11.7	3.5	2.5	50 776	248	63 443	283
1989	93 347	100.0	12.6	10.8	10.5	14.6	19.9	13.3	11.9	3.7	2.7	51 681	284	65 295	284
1990	94 312	100.0	12.9	11.1	10.6	14.8	20.1	13.0	11.5	3.5	2.6	50 994	261	63 698	269
1991	95 669	100.0	13.4	11.6	10.6	15.2	19.3	12.5	11.4	3.5	2.3	49 529	238	62 347	256
1992[11]	96 426	100.0	13.7	12.0	10.6	14.9	18.9	12.9	11.1	3.4	2.5	49 122	232	62 277	261
1993[12]	97 107	100.0	13.7	11.7	11.0	14.7	18.5	12.6	11.3	3.7	2.8	48 884	228	64 824	351
1994[13]	98 990	100.0	13.2	12.1	10.5	14.7	18.3	12.5	11.5	3.9	3.1	49 429	225	66 081	355
1995[14]	99 627	100.0	12.5	11.6	10.5	14.7	19.2	12.5	12.0	3.9	3.1	50 978	295	67 228	368
1996	101 018	100.0	12.5	11.5	10.5	14.3	18.7	12.9	12.1	4.3	3.3	51 720	261	68 668	385
1997	102 528	100.0	12.1	11.0	10.4	14.2	18.6	12.8	12.6	4.4	3.8	52 784	244	70 880	397
1998	103 874	100.0	11.5	10.6	10.0	14.4	18.5	12.9	13.4	4.7	4.1	54 702	324	72 947	394
1999[15]	106 434	100.0	10.7	10.8	10.2	13.6	18.0	13.0	13.8	5.0	4.8	56 080	262	75 428	391
2000[16]	108 209	100.0	10.9	10.3	10.2	13.7	18.4	12.7	13.9	5.3	4.6	55 987	176	76 180	300
2001	109 297	100.0	11.2	10.7	10.0	14.0	18.0	13.0	13.5	4.9	4.7	54 766	167	75 491	301
2002	111 278	100.0	11.6	10.7	10.5	13.8	17.7	13.0	13.6	4.9	4.4	54 127	177	73 837	277
2003	112 000	100.0	12.1	11.0	9.9	13.9	17.6	12.4	13.5	5.1	4.5	54 079	235	73 741	270
2004[17]	113 343	100.0	12.1	10.9	10.2	14.1	17.6	12.6	13.0	5.2	4.4	53 891	238	73 501	277
2005	114 384	100.0	11.8	11.1	9.7	14.0	17.9	12.6	13.1	5.0	4.7	54 486	182	74 502	281
2006	116 011	100.0	11.6	10.3	10.6	13.7	18.0	12.1	13.5	5.3	4.9	54 892	236	75 810	293
2007	116 783	100.0	11.6	10.7	10.4	13.5	17.5	12.5	13.8	5.3	4.7	55 627	155	74 869	261
2008	117 181	100.0	12.1	11.1	10.5	13.7	17.7	12.3	13.1	5.1	4.5	53 644	146	72 968	258
2009[18]	117 538	100.0	12.1	11.1	10.7	13.8	17.8	11.9	12.9	5.1	4.5	53 285	228	72 767	260
2010[19]	119 927	100.0	12.9	11.5	10.8	13.4	17.6	11.6	12.8	4.9	4.4	51 892	342	70 970	379
2011	121 084	100.0	13.3	11.3	10.9	13.7	17.7	11.4	12.2	5.1	4.4	51 100	256	71 133	376
2012	122 459	100.0	13.0	11.7	10.7	13.6	17.5	11.7	12.5	5.0	4.5	51 017	209	71 274	421
White[20]															
1967[1]	54 188	100.0	15.1	10.8	11.4	20.6	23.8	10.5	5.5	1.4	1.0	44 774	162	49 775	168
1968	55 394	100.0	13.8	10.6	11.5	19.1	24.8	11.9	6.3	1.2	0.9	46 630	174	52 489	174
1969	56 248	100.0	13.6	10.1	10.6	18.1	24.9	12.7	7.4	1.5	1.1	48 476	177	54 805	183
1970	57 575	100.0	13.7	10.3	11.0	17.7	24.7	12.4	7.6	1.6	1.1	48 005	185	54 622	179
1971[2]	59 463	100.0	13.6	10.9	10.9	17.3	24.5	12.5	7.7	1.5	1.1	47 739	182	54 392	177
1972[3]	60 618	100.0	13.0	10.6	10.6	16.5	23.9	13.2	8.8	2.1	1.3	49 932	191	57 550	187
1973	61 965	100.0	12.4	11.0	10.1	15.9	23.7	13.7	9.5	2.1	1.6	50 889	194	58 326	185
1974[4,5]	62 984	100.0	12.2	11.1	11.1	16.6	23.5	13.4	8.9	2.0	1.2	49 173	185	57 022	185
1975[5]	64 392	100.0	12.8	12.0	11.5	16.4	23.2	12.9	8.2	1.9	1.1	47 883	175	55 442	182
1976[6]	65 353	100.0	12.5	11.5	11.2	16.0	23.3	13.4	8.8	2.0	1.2	48 760	202	56 858	183
1977	66 934	100.0	12.4	11.7	11.2	15.4	22.8	13.7	9.3	2.1	1.4	49 258	207	57 738	186
1978	68 028	100.0	11.9	11.3	10.9	15.4	22.6	14.0	9.9	2.5	1.5	50 580	223	59 388	239
1979[7]	70 766	100.0	12.1	10.7	10.8	15.4	22.6	13.9	10.2	2.6	1.6	50 872	242	59 909	239

[1]Implementation of a new Curent Population Survey (CPS) Annual Social and Economic Supplements (ASEC) processing system.
[2]Introduction of 1970 census sample design and population controls.
[3]Full implementation of 1970 census-based sample design.
[4]Implementation of a new CPS ASEC processing system. Questionnaire expanded to ask 11 income questions.
[5]Some of these estimates were derived using Pareto interpolation and may differ from published data that were derived using linear interpolation.
[6]First-year medians were derived using both Pareto and linear interpolation. Before this year, all medians were derived using linear interpolation.
[7]Implementation of 1980 census population controls. Questionnaire expanded to show 27 possible values from a list of 51 possible sources of income.
[8]Implementation of Hispanic population weighting controls and introduction of 1980 census-based sample design.
[9]Recording of amounts for earnings from longest job increased to $299,999. Full implementation of 1980 census-based sample design.
[10]Implementation of a new CPS ASEC processing system.
[11]Implementation of 1990 census population controls.
[12]Data collection method changed from paper and pencil to computer-assisted interviewing. In addition, the 1994 ASEC was revised to allow for the coding of different income amounts on selected questionnaire items. Limits either increased or decreased in the following categories: earnings limits increased to $999,999, Social Security limits increased to $49,999, Supplemental Security Income and public assistance limits increased to $24,999, veterans' benefits limits increased to $99,999, and child support and alimony limits decreased to $49,999.
[13]Introduction of 1990 census sample design.
[14]Full implementation of 1990 census-based sample design and metropolitan definitions, 7,000 household sample reduction, and revised editing of responses on race.
[15]Implementation of the 2000 census-based population controls.
[16]Implementation of a 28,000 household sample expansion.
[17]Data revised to reflect a correction to the weights in the 2005 ASEC.
[18]Median income is calculated using $2,500 intervals. Beginning with 2009 income data, the Census Bureau expanded the upper income intervals used to calculate medians to $250,000 or more.
[19]Implementation of 2010 census-based population controls.
[20]For 2001 and earlier years, the CPS allowed respondents to report only one race group.

Table 13-2. Households, by Total Money Income, Race, and Hispanic Origin of Householder, 1967–2012—*Continued*

(Numbers in thousands, percent, dollars; income in 2012 CPI-U-RS adjusted dollars.)

Race and Hispanic origin of householder and year	Number	Percent distribution											Median income (dollars)		Mean income (dollars)	
		Total	Under $15,000	$15,000 to $24,999	$25,000 to $34,999	$35,000 to $49,999	$50,000 to $74,999	$75,000 to $99,999	$100,000 to $149,999	$150,000 to $199,000	$200,000 and over	Value	Standard error	Value	Standard error
White[20]—*Continued*															
1980	71 872	100.0	12.4	11.2	11.5	15.5	22.5	13.3	9.9	2.3	1.4	49 569	255	58 136	223
1981	72 845	100.0	12.6	11.7	11.6	15.7	21.6	13.1	9.9	2.2	1.4	48 819	225	57 513	218
1982	73 182	100.0	13.0	11.4	11.6	15.9	21.6	12.6	9.8	2.5	1.6	48 243	219	57 824	226
1983	74 376	100.0	12.5	11.7	11.3	16.2	21.3	12.8	9.9	2.7	1.7	47 988	217	57 964	226
1984[8]	75 328	100.0	12.3	11.2	11.3	15.5	21.1	13.2	10.6	2.9	1.9	49 774	250	60 193	234
1985[9]	76 576	100.0	12.5	11.0	10.8	15.3	21.1	13.0	11.3	3.0	2.1	50 688	271	61 577	258
1986	77 284	100.0	12.1	10.5	10.7	14.7	20.7	13.5	11.9	3.5	2.4	52 319	254	64 042	274
1987[10]	78 519	100.0	11.5	10.4	10.6	14.7	20.6	13.8	12.3	3.6	2.5	53 090	267	65 342	282
1988	79 734	100.0	11.4	10.3	10.4	14.7	20.8	13.6	12.3	3.7	2.7	53 678	317	66 149	311
1989	80 163	100.0	10.7	10.4	10.4	14.7	20.4	14.0	12.6	4.0	3.0	54 363	265	68 014	315
1990	80 968	100.0	11.0	10.7	10.5	15.0	20.6	13.6	12.2	3.8	2.8	53 187	244	66 268	296
1991	81 675	100.0	11.4	11.2	10.5	15.4	19.8	13.2	12.1	3.7	2.6	51 902	252	64 979	283
1992[11]	81 795	100.0	11.6	11.5	10.5	15.1	19.5	13.6	11.9	3.6	2.7	51 645	250	65 089	290
1993[12]	82 387	100.0	11.7	11.3	10.8	14.8	19.2	13.3	12.0	3.9	3.1	51 574	300	67 729	391
1994[13]	83 737	100.0	11.4	11.7	10.4	14.8	18.8	13.1	12.2	4.2	3.4	52 132	293	68 993	401
1995[14]	84 511	100.0	10.9	11.1	10.5	14.7	19.5	13.1	12.6	4.2	3.4	53 506	280	69 907	405
1996	85 059	100.0	10.7	11.2	10.3	14.3	19.2	13.4	12.8	4.6	3.6	54 152	280	71 395	423
1997	86 106	100.0	10.5	10.7	10.2	14.2	18.9	13.3	13.4	4.7	4.2	55 590	352	74 033	451
1998	87 212	100.0	9.9	10.1	9.7	14.3	18.9	13.6	14.0	5.0	4.5	57 553	288	76 256	449
1999[15]	88 893	100.0	9.2	10.5	10.0	13.6	18.4	13.5	14.5	5.2	5.1	58 324	295	78 169	442
2000[16]	90 030	100.0	9.6	10.0	9.9	13.7	18.5	13.2	14.6	5.5	5.0	58 555	259	79 005	339
2001	90 682	100.0	9.8	10.5	9.7	13.8	18.2	13.4	14.2	5.3	5.1	57 735	271	78 479	337
White Alone[21]															
2002	91 645	100.0	10.2	10.2	10.2	13.5	18.1	13.5	14.3	5.2	4.7	57 544	234	76 790	313
2003	91 962	100.0	10.5	10.6	9.8	13.9	17.8	12.9	14.2	5.5	4.9	56 967	223	76 887	308
2004[17]	92 880	100.0	10.5	10.6	10.0	13.9	17.9	13.0	13.8	5.5	4.7	56 716	222	76 470	315
2005	93 588	100.0	10.2	10.6	9.6	14.1	18.1	13.2	13.8	5.3	5.1	57 106	249	77 581	321
2006	94 705	100.0	10.0	10.0	10.4	13.7	18.3	12.6	14.3	5.6	5.2	57 707	167	78 699	328
2007	95 112	100.0	10.0	10.4	10.2	13.4	17.8	12.9	14.5	5.6	5.1	57 712	171	77 884	297
2008	95 297	100.0	10.5	10.8	10.3	13.4	18.1	12.8	13.8	5.4	4.8	55 786	162	75 919	292
2009[18]	95 489	100.0	10.4	10.8	10.4	13.9	18.2	12.4	13.7	5.4	4.8	55 516	165	75 516	291
2010[19]	96 306	100.0	11.1	11.2	10.6	13.4	18.0	12.2	13.6	5.2	4.8	54 454	266	74 150	427
2011	96 964	100.0	11.4	10.8	10.8	13.9	18.1	11.9	12.9	5.5	4.7	53 304	230	74 333	431
2012	97 705	100.0	11.2	11.3	10.6	13.5	17.9	12.2	13.2	5.3	4.8	53 706	384	74 416	464
White, Not Hispanic[20]															
1972[3]	58 005	100.0	12.9	10.4	10.4	16.3	24.1	13.5	9.0	2.1	1.4	50 644	241	58 217	260
1973	59 236	100.0	12.3	10.8	9.8	15.8	23.7	14.0	9.8	2.2	1.6	51 338	240	58 978	249
1974[4,5]	60 164	100.0	12.1	10.8	10.9	16.5	23.6	13.7	9.2	2.0	1.3	49 593	244	57 664	252
1975[5]	61 533	100.0	12.6	11.7	11.3	16.3	23.4	13.2	8.4	2.0	1.1	48 244	256	56 121	272
1976[6]	62 365	100.0	12.2	11.3	11.0	15.9	23.5	13.6	9.1	2.1	1.3	49 754	290	57 588	257
1977	63 721	100.0	12.2	11.5	11.0	15.2	22.9	14.0	9.6	2.1	1.5	50 235	283	58 453	276
1978	64 836	100.0	11.7	11.1	10.7	15.2	22.7	14.2	10.2	2.6	1.6	51 533	271	60 089	258
1979[7]	67 203	100.0	11.9	10.6	10.6	15.3	22.8	14.2	10.4	2.6	1.6	51 588	286	60 602	265
1980	68 106	100.0	12.0	10.9	11.3	15.4	22.8	13.6	10.2	2.3	1.4	50 447	108	58 900	265
1981	68 996	100.0	12.3	11.5	11.5	15.6	21.8	13.3	10.2	2.3	1.4	49 524	252	58 237	242
1982	69 214	100.0	12.6	11.1	11.5	15.9	21.8	12.8	10.1	2.6	1.6	49 052	247	58 674	251
1983	69 648	100.0	12.0	11.4	11.2	16.1	21.5	13.0	10.2	2.8	1.8	49 222	248	59 487	254
1984[8]	70 586	100.0	11.8	10.9	11.1	15.5	21.3	13.4	11.0	3.0	2.0	50 807	282	61 239	274
1985[9]	71 540	100.0	11.9	10.6	10.6	15.2	21.3	13.3	11.6	3.1	2.2	51 827	265	62 776	285
1986	72 067	100.0	11.6	10.1	10.5	14.7	20.9	13.9	12.2	3.7	2.5	53 508	276	65 313	300
1987[10]	73 120	100.0	11.0	10.1	10.4	14.5	20.9	14.1	12.8	3.7	2.6	54 549	304	66 620	309
1988	74 067	100.0	10.8	10.0	10.2	14.5	20.9	14.0	12.8	3.9	2.8	55 157	325	67 500	317
1989	74 495	100.0	10.2	10.1	10.2	14.5	20.5	14.2	13.0	4.2	3.1	55 533	272	69 376	340
1990	75 035	100.0	10.5	10.3	10.3	14.8	20.7	13.9	12.6	4.0	2.9	54 403	254	67 736	307
1991	75 625	100.0	10.8	10.9	10.3	15.3	20.0	13.5	12.6	3.9	2.7	53 141	261	66 373	296
1992[11]	75 107	100.0	11.0	11.1	10.2	14.9	19.7	14.0	12.4	3.8	2.9	53 378	330	66 743	308
1993[12]	75 697	100.0	11.0	10.8	10.5	14.6	19.4	13.7	12.5	4.2	3.3	53 472	313	69 515	415
1994[13]	77 004	100.0	10.7	11.3	10.2	14.7	19.0	13.5	12.7	4.4	3.6	53 814	285	70 751	420

[3]Full implementation of 1970 census–based sample design.
[4]Implementation of a new CPS ASEC processing system. Questionnaire expanded to ask 11 income questions.
[5]Some of these estimates were derived using Pareto interpolation and may differ from published data that were derived using linear interpolation.
[6]First-year medians were derived using both Pareto and linear interpolation. Before this year, all medians were derived using linear interpolation.
[7]Implementation of 1980 census population controls. Questionnaire expanded to show 27 possible values from a list of 51 possible sources of income.
[8]Implementation of Hispanic population weighting controls and introduction of 1980 census–based sample design.
[9]Recording of amounts for earnings from longest job increased to $299,999. Full implementation of 1980 census–based sample design.
[10]Implementation of a new CPS ASEC processing system.
[11]Implementation of 1990 census population controls.
[12]Data collection method changed from paper and pencil to computer-assisted interviewing. In addition, the 1994 ASEC was revised to allow for the coding of different income amounts on selected questionnaire items. Limits either increased or decreased in the following categories: earnings limits increased to $999,999, Social Security limits increased to $49,999, Supplemental Security Income and public assistance limits increased to $24,999, veterans' benefits limits increased to $99,999, and child support and alimony limits decreased to $49,999.
[13]Introduction of 1990 census sample design.
[14]Full implementation of 1990 census–based sample design and metropolitan definitions, 7,000 household sample reduction, and revised editing of responses on race.
[15]Implementation of the 2000 census–based population controls.
[16]Implementation of a 28,000 household sample expansion.
[17]Data revised to reflect a correction to the weights in the 2005 ASEC.
[18]Median income is calculated using $2,500 intervals. Beginning with 2009 income data, the Census Bureau expanded the upper income intervals used to calculate medians to $250,000 or more.
[19]Implementation of 2010 census-based population controls.
[20]For 2001 and earlier years, the CPS allowed respondents to report only one race group.
[21]Beginning with the 2003 CPS, respondents were allowed to choose one or more races. White alone refers to people who reported White and did not report any other race category. The use of this single-race population does not imply that it is the preferred method of presenting or analyzing the data; the Census Bureau uses a variety of approaches. Information on people who reported more than one race, such as White and American Indian and Alaska Native or Asian and Black or African American, is available from Census 2010 through American FactFinder. About 2.9 percent of respondents reported more than one race in Census 2010.

Table 13-2. Households, by Total Money Income, Race, and Hispanic Origin of Householder, 1967–2012—*Continued*

(Numbers in thousands, percent, dollars; income in 2012 CPI-U-RS adjusted dollars.)

Race and Hispanic origin of householder and year	Number	Percent distribution										Median income (dollars)		Mean income (dollars)	
		Total	Under $15,000	$15,000 to $24,999	$25,000 to $34,999	$35,000 to $49,999	$50,000 to $74,999	$75,000 to $99,999	$100,000 to $149,999	$150,000 to $199,000	$200,000 and over	Value	Standard error	Value	Standard error
White, Not Hispanic[20]—Continued															
1995[14]	76 932	100.0	9.9	10.6	10.1	14.6	19.9	13.6	13.3	4.4	3.7	55 619	290	72 187	432
1996	77 240	100.0	10.0	10.6	9.9	14.2	19.4	13.9	13.4	4.8	3.8	56 521	388	73 554	...
1997	77 936	100.0	9.7	10.3	9.8	13.9	19.0	13.8	14.1	5.0	4.4	57 879	302	76 405	...
1998	78 577	100.0	9.2	9.7	9.4	13.9	19.1	14.0	14.7	5.3	4.8	59 701	343	78 698	481
1999[15]	79 819	100.0	8.8	10.0	9.6	13.3	18.4	13.8	15.2	5.5	5.5	60 849	384	80 732	478
2000[16]	80 527	100.0	9.3	9.5	9.5	13.3	18.4	13.4	15.2	5.9	5.4	60 831	244	81 409	365
2001	80 818	100.0	9.4	10.0	9.4	13.4	18.2	13.6	14.9	5.5	5.5	60 054	249	80 985	367
White Alone, Not Hispanic[21]															
2002	81 166	100.0	9.7	9.8	9.7	13.1	18.1	13.9	15.1	5.5	5.1	59 859	235	79 278	337
2003	81 148	100.0	10.0	10.1	9.4	13.4	17.9	13.2	14.9	5.9	5.3	59 646	288	79 758	338
2004[17]	81 628	100.0	10.0	10.2	9.6	13.4	17.8	13.5	14.6	5.9	5.1	59 454	272	79 326	345
2005	82 003	100.0	9.6	10.0	9.4	13.6	18.1	13.6	14.5	5.7	5.5	59 729	202	80 687	356
2006	82 675	100.0	9.4	9.5	9.9	13.3	18.2	13.0	15.0	6.0	5.7	59 700	214	81 704	361
2007	82 765	100.0	9.5	9.9	9.7	12.9	17.8	13.2	15.3	6.1	5.6	60 818	274	81 041	327
2008	82 884	100.0	9.8	10.3	9.7	13.0	18.2	13.3	14.6	5.8	5.3	59 218	240	79 023	323
2009[18]	83 158	100.0	9.7	10.3	9.9	13.6	18.3	12.8	14.4	5.8	5.2	58 299	299	78 402	320
2010[19]	83 314	100.0	10.3	10.8	10.1	13.1	18.0	12.5	14.4	5.6	5.3	57 351	470	77 226	484
2011	83 573	100.0	10.6	10.3	10.3	13.4	18.2	12.4	13.6	5.9	5.2	56 570	335	77 652	488
2012	83 792	100.0	10.3	10.7	10.1	13.2	18.0	12.6	14.0	5.8	5.3	57 009	359	77 843	515
Black[20]															
1967[1]	5 728	100.0	30.0	18.9	15.6	16.6	12.3	3.9	2.2	0.3	0.2	25 996	433	31 238	349
1968	5 870	100.0	27.1	19.2	15.8	16.4	13.8	5.1	2.2	0.3	0.0	27 497	399	33 489	353
1969	6 053	100.0	26.4	17.6	15.8	17.1	15.2	5.2	2.3	0.3	0.1	29 302	432	34 883	371
1970	6 180	100.0	27.1	16.6	15.4	16.0	15.7	5.9	2.8	0.4	0.2	29 219	401	35 678	385
1971[2]	6 578	100.0	27.8	17.4	14.4	16.3	15.3	5.8	2.6	0.3	0.1	28 199	420	34 943	359
1972[3]	6 809	100.0	27.1	17.4	13.9	16.0	15.1	7.1	2.6	0.4	0.3	29 145	437	36 817	393
1973	7 040	100.0	25.2	18.0	13.3	15.8	17.4	6.1	3.4	0.6	0.2	29 955	467	37 198	370
1974[4,5]	7 263	100.0	26.1	16.8	15.3	15.8	15.7	7.0	2.9	0.3	0.1	29 244	353	36 370	323
1975[5]	7 489	100.0	27.5	17.6	13.3	16.2	15.7	6.2	3.0	0.4	0.0	28 745	423	35 881	318
1976[6]	7 776	100.0	26.6	17.6	13.3	15.2	16.7	6.9	3.2	0.3	0.2	28 994	360	37 044	330
1977	7 977	100.0	26.2	18.7	14.0	14.6	15.4	6.8	3.7	0.4	0.3	29 068	390	37 244	331
1978	8 066	100.0	26.8	16.0	13.3	14.9	16.2	7.4	4.7	0.7	0.1	30 396	643	38 846	507
1979[7]	8 586	100.0	27.0	16.4	13.4	14.5	15.9	7.7	4.4	0.4	0.2	29 868	545	38 324	472
1980	8 847	100.0	28.0	17.2	13.8	14.0	15.2	7.2	3.9	0.6	0.2	28 557	539	37 063	456
1981	8 961	100.0	29.7	17.2	13.5	13.9	14.8	6.9	3.5	0.4	0.1	27 395	460	35 987	436
1982	8 916	100.0	29.6	16.9	13.0	14.4	15.5	6.8	3.1	0.4	0.2	27 342	439	35 975	450
1983	9 236	100.0	29.8	16.5	13.4	14.2	14.4	6.9	4.3	0.5	0.1	27 232	511	36 220	447
1984[8]	9 480	100.0	28.6	16.8	13.3	14.4	13.9	7.4	4.7	0.8	0.2	28 355	545	37 816	465
1985[9]	9 797	100.0	28.0	15.9	13.0	14.0	15.4	7.6	4.9	0.9	0.3	30 157	586	39 347	511
1986	9 922	100.0	28.7	14.8	12.3	14.5	15.1	7.7	5.2	1.2	0.5	30 142	592	40 440	550
1987[10]	10 192	100.0	28.7	14.8	12.4	14.8	14.3	7.9	5.1	1.3	0.6	30 302	580	40 915	563
1988	10 561	100.0	28.4	15.1	11.6	14.2	14.6	8.0	6.0	1.5	0.6	30 600	638	41 921	612
1989	10 486	100.0	26.9	14.3	11.8	14.3	16.0	8.1	6.5	1.5	0.5	32 331	658	42 901	583
1990	10 671	100.0	27.4	14.6	11.9	14.0	16.1	8.3	5.8	1.4	0.6	31 806	725	42 259	571
1991	11 083	100.0	28.9	14.5	11.5	14.3	15.9	7.6	5.4	1.4	0.5	30 920	649	41 173	538
1992[11]	11 269	100.0	28.6	15.7	11.4	14.6	14.8	8.0	5.1	1.2	0.6	30 072	614	40 807	553
1993[12]	11 281	100.0	27.7	15.2	12.7	14.3	14.2	7.6	6.0	1.4	0.8	30 564	604	42 606	707
1994[13]	11 655	100.0	26.1	15.4	11.8	14.3	14.9	8.4	6.5	1.7	1.0	32 214	599	44 826	643
1995[14]	11 577	100.0	24.5	15.3	11.8	15.0	16.4	8.0	6.8	1.4	0.9	33 500	571	45 479	778
1996	12 109	100.0	24.3	14.5	12.4	14.4	15.9	9.7	6.4	1.5	1.0	34 218	673	47 301	924
1997	12 474	100.0	22.9	14.1	12.5	15.2	16.7	9.4	6.6	1.8	1.0	35 731	615	47 018	675
1998	12 579	100.0	23.0	14.3	12.0	15.1	15.7	8.9	7.7	2.1	1.1	35 663	558	48 025	641
1999[15]	12 838	100.0	20.4	13.7	12.2	14.2	16.4	9.9	8.6	3.2	1.5	38 460	717	53 001	761
2000[16]	13 174	100.0	19.4	13.4	13.1	14.3	18.0	9.3	8.6	2.6	1.3	39 556	524	52 237	529
2001	13 315	100.0	20.7	13.6	12.0	15.3	16.8	10.1	8.1	2.0	1.3	38 220	450	50 902	537

[1]Implementation of a new Curent Population Survey (CPS) Annual Social and Economic Supplements (ASEC) processing system.
[2]Introduction of 1970 census sample design and population controls.
[3]Full implementation of 1970 census–based sample design.
[4]Implementation of a new CPS ASEC processing system. Questionnaire expanded to ask 11 income questions.
[5]Some of these estimates were derived using Pareto interpolation and may differ from published data that were derived using linear interpolation.
[6]First-year medians were derived using both Pareto and linear interpolation. Before this year, all medians were derived using linear interpolation.
[7]Implementation of 1980 census population controls. Questionnaire expanded to show 27 possible values from a list of 51 possible sources of income.
[8]Implementation of Hispanic population weighting controls and introduction of 1980 census–based sample design.
[9]Recording of amounts for earnings from longest job increased to $299,999. Full implementation of 1980 census–based sample design.
[10]Implementation of a new CPS ASEC processing system.
[11]Implementation of 1990 census population controls.
[12]Data collection method changed from paper and pencil to computer-assisted interviewing. In addition, the 1994 ASEC was revised to allow for the coding of different income amounts on selected questionnaire items. Limits either increased or decreased in the following categories: earnings limits increased to $999,999, Social Security limits increased to $49,999, Supplemental Security Income and public assistance limits increased to $24,999, veterans' benefits limits increased to $99,999, and child support and alimony limits decreased to $49,999.
[13]Introduction of 1990 census sample design.
[14]Full implementation of 1990 census–based sample design and metropolitan definitions, 7,000 household sample reduction, and revised editing of responses on race.
[15]Implementation of the 2000 census–based population controls.
[16]Implementation of a 28,000 household sample expansion.
[17]Data revised to reflect a correction to the weights in the 2005 ASEC.
[18]Median income is calculated using $2,500 intervals. Beginning with 2009 income data, the Census Bureau expanded the upper income intervals used to calculate medians to $250,000 or more.
[19]Implementation of 2010 census-based population controls.
[20]For 2001 and earlier years, the CPS allowed respondents to report only one race group.
[21]Beginning with the 2003 CPS, respondents were allowed to choose one or more races. White alone refers to people who reported White and did not report any other race category. The use of this single-race population does not imply that it is the preferred method of presenting or analyzing the data; the Census Bureau uses a variety of approaches. Information on people who reported more than one race, such as White and American Indian and Alaska Native or Asian and Black or African American, is available from Census 2010 through American FactFinder. About 2.9 percent of respondents reported more than one race in Census 2010.
. . . = Not available.

Table 13-2. Households, by Total Money Income, Race, and Hispanic Origin of Householder, 1967–2012—*Continued*

(Numbers in thousands, percent, dollars; income in 2012 CPI-U-RS adjusted dollars.)

Race and Hispanic origin of householder and year	Number	Percent distribution										Median income (dollars)		Mean income (dollars)	
		Total	Under $15,000	$15,000 to $24,999	$25,000 to $34,999	$35,000 to $49,999	$50,000 to $74,999	$75,000 to $99,999	$100,000 to $149,999	$150,000 to $199,999	$200,000 and over	Value	Standard error	Value	Standard error
Black Alone[22]															
2002	13 465	100.0	21.3	14.1	12.6	15.6	15.3	9.4	7.6	2.3	1.7	37 046	499	51 066	590
2003	13 629	100.0	22.2	14.2	11.9	14.8	16.3	9.0	8.1	2.2	1.3	37 010	482	50 101	537
2004[17]	13 809	100.0	22.8	13.6	12.2	15.9	15.0	9.8	7.2	2.2	1.5	36 583	380	49 392	535
2005	14 002	100.0	22.2	15.3	11.2	15.1	16.1	8.8	7.6	2.5	1.3	36 293	354	49 932	542
2006	14 354	100.0	22.0	13.4	13.1	14.7	16.1	8.7	7.9	2.3	1.8	36 406	274	51 391	635
2007	14 551	100.0	21.8	13.5	12.4	14.7	15.9	9.6	8.3	2.3	1.5	37 558	526	51 639	576
2008	14 595	100.0	22.0	13.6	12.8	15.7	16.0	8.6	7.7	2.3	1.4	36 491	470	49 623	531
2009[18]	14 730	100.0	22.3	14.4	13.5	14.5	15.5	9.0	7.2	2.3	1.4	34 880	422	49 291	562
2010[19]	15 265	100.0	24.6	14.2	12.6	14.3	15.2	8.4	7.1	2.1	1.4	33 830	525	47 344	659
2011	15 583	100.0	25.3	14.7	12.3	13.3	15.5	8.1	6.9	2.3	1.6	32 902	520	48 242	820
2012	15 872	100.0	24.0	15.5	12.0	14.3	15.0	8.5	7.3	2.1	1.5	33 321	790	47 737	753
Black Alone or in Combination															
2002	13 778	100.0	21.3	14.1	12.5	15.6	15.4	9.3	7.7	2.3	1.8	37 239	490	51 479	600
2003	13 969	100.0	22.1	14.2	12.0	14.7	16.3	9.1	8.1	2.2	1.4	37 065	466	50 332	533
2004[17]	14 151	100.0	22.6	13.5	12.1	15.8	15.2	9.8	7.3	2.2	1.5	36 753	337	49 546	526
2005	14 399	100.0	22.1	15.2	11.1	15.0	16.1	8.8	7.7	2.5	1.4	36 406	347	50 253	547
2006	14 709	100.0	21.8	13.3	13.0	14.8	16.2	8.6	8.0	2.4	1.8	36 592	271	51 808	635
2007	14 976	100.0	21.8	13.5	12.3	14.8	15.8	9.5	8.4	2.4	1.6	37 752	515	51 860	567
2008	15 056	100.0	21.8	13.6	12.8	15.7	15.9	8.6	7.8	2.4	1.4	36 626	468	49 779	520
2009[18]	15 212	100.0	22.2	14.3	13.4	14.5	15.6	9.0	7.2	2.3	1.5	35 058	447	49 542	552
2010[19]	15 909	100.0	24.4	14.3	12.8	14.3	15.0	8.5	7.2	2.2	1.5	33 863	495	47 915	660
2011	16 165	100.0	25.2	14.7	12.2	13.3	15.5	8.1	7.0	2.3	1.7	33 042	565	48 498	789
2012	16 559	100.0	23.8	15.3	12.0	14.3	14.9	8.5	7.5	2.1	1.5	33 718	798	48 160	738
Asian and Pacific Islander[20]															
1987[10]	. . .	100.0	11.0	10.9	8.9	11.3	17.9	13.6	17.3	6.1	3.0	62 309	2 316	. . .	. . .
1988	1 913	100.0	9.6	11.0	7.9	12.1	19.7	13.4	16.1	6.7	3.6	60 179	2 473	75 238	2 247
1989	1 988	100.0	9.3	8.2	7.7	12.4	20.2	15.4	16.1	4.9	5.9	64 547	1 745	80 241	2 335
1990	1 958	100.0	9.7	8.3	8.9	11.3	19.3	14.1	17.4	6.5	4.4	65 482	1 940	79 041	2 238
1991	2 094	100.0	11.1	8.8	9.5	12.7	18.3	13.9	15.0	6.4	4.3	59 925	1 933	76 085	2 243
1992[11]	2 262	100.0	11.2	10.0	8.5	11.8	19.7	13.0	16.1	5.4	4.3	60 611	1 749	75 120	2 065
1993[12]	2 233	100.0	13.2	9.5	8.8	12.0	14.7	14.4	17.8	5.3	4.3	60 003	2 951	78 618	3 165
1994[13]	2 040	100.0	10.8	10.1	7.2	13.1	17.5	14.4	15.5	6.0	5.3	62 020	2 350	80 527	2 869
1995[14]	2 777	100.0	11.8	9.4	6.7	12.8	19.9	13.6	14.7	6.1	5.1	60 759	1 524	82 621	3 333
1996	2 998	100.0	11.6	7.6	8.4	11.9	19.0	12.2	17.4	7.5	4.4	63 063	2 260	82 401	2 955
1997	3 125	100.0	10.6	8.0	7.5	11.7	19.2	14.4	16.6	6.9	5.1	64 543	1 794	84 000	2 603
1998	3 308	100.0	10.1	7.8	7.8	12.8	18.1	12.5	18.3	6.5	6.0	65 607	1 826	84 698	2 446
1999[15]	3 742	100.0	10.1	7.4	7.1	12.0	16.2	13.7	16.0	8.7	8.9	70 224	2 475	92 860	2 354
2000[16]	3 963	100.0	8.6	6.8	7.6	11.0	16.4	14.3	18.2	8.9	8.3	74 343	1 268	97 063	2 015
2001	4 071	100.0	9.4	7.1	8.0	12.2	17.1	13.3	17.0	7.9	7.8	69 560	1 660	94 882	2 240
Asian Alone[23]															
2002	3 917	100.0	9.3	7.6	8.4	12.1	17.3	12.7	17.8	7.8	7.0	67 167	1 175	89 401	1 743
2003	4 040	100.0	12.5	9.1	5.2	10.5	16.5	13.7	16.9	8.6	7.0	69 536	1 366	87 356	1 547
2004[17]	4 123	100.0	9.7	7.8	7.3	11.1	17.8	13.2	17.0	8.4	7.7	69 900	1 485	93 012	1 799
2005	4 273	100.0	10.4	7.7	6.5	9.6	18.2	12.6	18.1	7.6	9.3	71 855	837	94 204	1 662
2006	4 454	100.0	9.3	7.0	8.1	9.7	17.5	12.1	17.9	10.1	8.4	73 155	1 906	100 548	2 164
2007	4 494	100.0	9.7	7.6	7.5	10.5	15.8	13.2	18.6	9.2	8.1	73 202	1 534	94 148	1 661
2008	4 573	100.0	11.0	7.9	7.8	11.3	15.2	12.2	17.8	9.0	8.0	69 996	1 478	91 909	1 603
2009[18]	4 687	100.0	11.2	7.1	8.4	10.1	16.8	12.0	16.8	8.6	9.1	70 083	1 356	97 211	1 975
2010[19]	5 212	100.0	10.4	8.8	7.6	10.1	18.0	11.3	16.8	9.1	7.8	67 671	1 659	89 075	1 786
2011	5 374	100.0	10.5	8.6	8.2	11.1	17.0	13.1	17.4	6.9	7.1	66 489	1 600	87 433	2 116
2012	5 560	100.0	10.4	7.4	7.6	10.9	17.6	12.5	16.3	8.8	8.5	68 636	1 890	91 400	1 836
Asian Alone or in Combination															
2002	4 079	100.0	9.5	7.5	8.4	12.0	17.6	12.8	17.7	7.7	6.8	66 732	1 010	88 673	1 686
2003	4 235	100.0	12.4	9.1	5.5	10.5	16.6	13.8	16.8	8.5	6.8	68 991	1 538	86 656	1 491
2004[17]	4 346	100.0	9.7	7.7	7.3	11.2	17.9	13.4	16.8	8.5	7.4	69 833	1 408	92 543	1 747
2005	4 500	100.0	10.3	7.7	6.5	10.0	17.9	12.7	18.1	7.6	9.2	71 801	857	94 088	1 642
2006	4 664	100.0	9.3	6.9	8.0	9.9	17.7	12.3	18.0	10.0	8.1	72 770	1 841	99 677	2 086
2007	4 715	100.0	9.7	7.5	7.4	10.7	15.8	13.4	18.2	9.3	8.0	72 950	1 535	93 642	1 601
2008	4 805	100.0	10.9	7.9	7.7	11.5	15.2	12.3	17.8	8.8	8.0	69 922	1 507	92 056	1 586
2009[18]	4 940	100.0	11.3	7.1	8.4	10.4	16.5	12.0	16.7	8.5	9.1	69 659	1 536	96 461	1 895
2010[19]	5 550	100.0	10.2	8.9	7.9	10.5	17.9	11.4	16.7	8.8	7.7	66 900	1 543	88 157	1 693
2011	5 705	100.0	10.6	8.7	8.1	11.0	16.8	13.2	17.4	6.8	7.4	66 353	1 597	87 577	2 096
2012	5 872	100.0	10.2	7.4	7.6	11.2	17.7	12.3	16.3	8.8	8.5	68 182	1 737	91 703	1 894

[10]Implementation of a new CPS ASEC processing system.
[11]Implementation of 1990 census population controls.
[12]Data collection method changed from paper and pencil to computer-assisted interviewing. In addition, the 1994 ASEC was revised to allow for the coding of different income amounts on selected questionnaire items. Limits either increased or decreased in the following categories: earnings limits increased to $999,999, Social Security limits increased to $49,999, Supplemental Security Income and public assistance limits increased to $24,999, veterans' benefits limits increased to $99,999, and child support and alimony limits decreased to $49,999.
[13]Introduction of 1990 census sample design.
[14]Full implementation of 1990 census–based sample design and metropolitan definitions, 7,000 household sample reduction, and revised editing of responses on race.
[15]Implementation of the 2000 census–based population controls.
[16]Implementation of a 28,000 household sample expansion.
[17]Data revised to reflect a correction to the weights in the 2005 ASEC.
[18]Median income is calculated using $2,500 intervals. Beginning with 2009 income data, the Census Bureau expanded the upper income intervals used to calculate medians to $250,000 or more.
[19]Implementation of 2010 census-based population controls.
[20]For 2001 and earlier years, the CPS allowed respondents to report only one race group.
[22]Black alone refers to persons who reported Black and did not report any other race category.
[23]Asian alone refers to persons who reported Asian and did not report any other race category.
. . . = Not available.

Table 13-2. Households, by Total Money Income, Race, and Hispanic Origin of Householder, 1967–2012—*Continued*

(Numbers in thousands, percent, dollars; income in 2012 CPI-U-RS adjusted dollars.)

Race and Hispanic origin of householder and year	Number	Percent distribution										Median income (dollars)		Mean income (dollars)	
		Total	Under $15,000	$15,000 to $24,999	$25,000 to $34,999	$35,000 to $49,999	$50,000 to $74,999	$75,000 to $99,999	$100,000 to $149,999	$150,000 to $199,999	$200,000 and over	Value	Standard error	Value	Standard error
Hispanic[24]															
1972[3]	2 655	100.0	15.2	16.5	15.3	22.0	19.3	7.3	3.4	0.6	0.5	37 681	736	43 311	736
1973	2 722	100.0	14.6	16.3	15.2	18.7	22.6	7.7	4.1	0.4	0.3	37 619	855	43 707	711
1974[4,5]	2 897	100.0	15.5	16.6	15.3	18.8	21.2	7.4	4.1	0.6	0.4	37 399	819	43 324	705
1975[5]	2 948	100.0	18.4	17.4	15.5	18.2	19.6	6.9	3.1	0.5	0.4	34 399	761	40 837	726
1976[6]	3 081	100.0	19.1	16.7	14.6	18.3	19.4	7.7	3.5	0.5	0.2	35 111	749	41 491	675
1977	3 304	100.0	16.9	15.8	15.2	18.7	19.6	8.2	4.4	0.8	0.3	36 747	645	43 367	670
1978	3 291	100.0	16.3	15.2	14.4	18.4	20.6	9.3	4.8	1.0	0.3	38 122	924	45 031	911
1979[7]	3 684	100.0	16.6	14.6	14.5	17.7	20.2	9.1	5.7	1.1	0.6	38 442	1 108	46 512	934
1980	3 906	100.0	18.1	16.0	14.8	16.9	18.8	9.1	4.9	1.0	0.5	36 217	982	44 237	881
1981	3 980	100.0	17.9	15.9	13.6	18.3	18.9	9.1	5.0	0.9	0.4	37 063	1 015	44 507	850
1982	4 085	100.0	20.3	16.7	14.2	16.8	17.7	8.2	4.7	0.9	0.5	34 675	916	42 794	868
1983	4 326	100.0	20.9	16.1	13.4	17.6	17.4	8.4	4.9	1.0	0.3	34 851	883	42 438	815
1984[8]	4 883	100.0	20.5	14.6	14.5	15.4	18.7	9.1	5.5	1.1	0.5	35 766	897	44 474	867
1985[9]	5 213	100.0	20.2	16.7	12.7	16.3	17.6	8.9	6.0	1.1	0.5	35 541	830	44 410	722
1986	5 418	100.0	19.0	16.2	13.4	15.7	17.9	8.8	7.2	1.3	0.5	36 682	955	46 319	762
1987[10]	5 642	100.0	19.5	15.0	13.1	16.8	17.0	9.8	6.2	1.6	1.1	37 386	812	47 923	887
1988	5 910	100.0	19.5	14.3	12.9	16.4	18.4	9.4	6.3	1.9	1.0	37 970	962	48 478	1 028
1989	5 933	100.0	18.0	13.6	13.2	16.1	18.2	10.9	6.9	1.8	1.2	39 193	760	50 047	860
1990	6 220	100.0	17.9	15.8	12.8	16.4	19.0	9.1	6.4	1.6	0.9	38 029	780	47 637	785
1991	6 379	100.0	18.3	15.8	12.9	17.1	17.7	8.9	6.5	1.8	0.9	37 306	776	47 468	760
1992[11]	7 153	100.0	19.5	15.5	13.6	17.2	16.7	8.9	6.1	1.5	0.8	36 233	749	46 214	726
1993[12]	7 362	100.0	19.3	15.9	13.8	17.2	16.5	8.6	6.3	1.4	1.1	35 810	720	47 397	997
1994[13]	7 735	100.0	20.1	16.1	12.5	16.3	16.6	8.9	6.6	1.8	1.1	35 882	666	48 385	1 207
1995[14]	7 939	100.0	20.6	16.1	14.2	16.0	15.6	9.0	6.0	1.4	0.9	34 199	745	46 677	1 047
1996	8 225	100.0	18.3	16.5	14.1	15.7	17.0	8.8	6.5	1.8	1.3	36 293	704	49 553	1 147
1997	8 590	100.0	18.5	14.5	13.5	16.5	17.7	8.8	7.1	1.9	1.6	37 982	678	51 183	1 033
1998	9 060	100.0	16.8	14.1	12.7	17.8	17.4	9.6	7.9	2.0	1.7	39 853	768	53 851	1 145
1999[15]	9 579	100.0	13.6	14.6	13.6	16.8	18.2	10.2	9.1	2.2	1.8	42 368	616	55 658	988
2000[16]	10 034	100.0	12.9	13.7	12.7	16.8	19.5	10.9	9.0	2.4	2.1	44 224	637	58 637	844
2001	10 499	100.0	13.2	14.3	12.4	16.9	18.4	11.5	8.7	2.9	1.7	43 531	552	57 561	728
2002	11 339	100.0	13.6	13.5	14.1	16.8	18.0	10.9	8.6	2.5	2.0	42 250	615	57 290	766
2003	11 693	100.0	14.7	14.6	12.8	17.7	17.4	10.2	8.4	2.3	1.9	41 194	573	55 515	614
2004[17]	12 178	100.0	14.7	13.9	13.6	16.8	18.7	9.7	8.2	2.6	1.8	41 659	583	55 767	682
2005	12 519	100.0	14.3	14.7	11.7	17.7	18.6	10.2	8.3	2.5	2.1	42 302	420	55 441	557
2006	12 973	100.0	14.4	13.2	13.2	16.3	19.0	10.0	9.0	3.1	1.8	43 025	575	57 595	661
2007	13 339	100.0	14.3	13.5	13.5	16.4	18.1	11.1	8.7	2.6	1.8	42 833	576	56 286	592
2008	13 425	100.0	15.6	14.0	14.0	16.3	17.2	9.4	8.8	3.0	1.7	40 431	518	54 997	569
2009[18]	13 298	100.0	15.5	14.2	13.6	15.6	17.8	9.6	8.9	2.7	2.0	40 720	537	55 910	613
2010[19]	14 435	100.0	16.6	14.1	14.2	15.0	17.7	9.8	8.2	2.8	1.7	39 629	613	54 123	695
2011	14 939	100.0	16.3	14.4	13.9	16.6	17.3	9.1	7.8	2.8	1.7	39 430	558	53 446	606
2012	15 589	100.0	16.8	14.6	13.6	15.8	17.1	9.7	7.9	2.6	1.9	39 005	534	53 422	698

[3]Full implementation of 1970 census–based sample design.
[4]Implementation of a new CPS ASEC processing system. Questionnaire expanded to ask 11 income questions.
[5]Some of these estimates were derived using Pareto interpolation and may differ from published data that were derived using linear interpolation.
[6]First-year medians were derived using both Pareto and linear interpolation. Before this year, all medians were derived using linear interpolation.
[7]Implementation of 1980 census population controls. Questionnaire expanded to show 27 possible values from a list of 51 possible sources of income.
[8]Implementation of Hispanic population weighting controls and introduction of 1980 census–based sample design.
[9]Recording of amounts for earnings from longest job increased to $299,999. Full implementation of 1980 census–based sample design.
[10]Implementation of a new CPS ASEC processing system.
[11]Implementation of 1990 census population controls.
[12]Data collection method changed from paper and pencil to computer-assisted interviewing. In addition, the 1994 ASEC was revised to allow for the coding of different income amounts on selected questionnaire items. Limits either increased or decreased in the following categories: earnings limits increased to $999,999, Social Security limits increased to $49,999, Supplemental Security Income and public assistance limits increased to $24,999, veterans' benefits limits increased to $99,999, and child support and alimony limits decreased to $49,999.
[13]Introduction of 1990 census sample design.
[14]Full implementation of 1990 census–based sample design and metropolitan definitions, 7,000 household sample reduction, and revised editing of responses on race.
[15]Implementation of the 2000 census–based population controls.
[16]Implementation of a 28,000 household sample expansion.
[17]Data revised to reflect a correction to the weights in the 2005 ASEC.
[18]Median income is calculated using $2,500 intervals. Beginning with 2009 income data, the Census Bureau expanded the upper income intervals used to calculate medians to $250,000 or more.
[19]Implementation of 2010 census–based population controls.
[24]Because Hispanics may be of any race, data in this report for Hispanics overlap with data for racial groups. Hispanic origin was reported by 14.2 percent of White householders who reported only one race, 4.6 percent of Black householders who reported only one race, and 2.6 percent of Asian householders who reported only one race. Data users should exercise caution when interpreting aggregate results for the Hispanic population and for race groups, because these populations consist of many distinct groups that differ in socioeconomic characteristics, culture, and recentness of immigration. Data were first collected for Hispanics in 1972.

Table 13-3. Income Deficit or Surplus of Families and Unrelated Individuals by Poverty Status, 2012

(Numbers of families and unrelated individuals in thousands, deficits and surpluses in dollars.)

Characteristic	Total	Size of deficit or surplus								Average deficit or surplus (dollars)		Deficit or surplus per capita (dollars)	
		Under $1,000	$1,000 to $2,499	$2,500 to $4,999	$5,000 to $7,499	$7,500 to $9,999	$10,000 to $12,499	$12,500 to $14,499	$15,000 or more	Estimate	90 percent confidence interval[1] (+/-)	Estimate	90 percent confidence interval[1] (+/-)
Below Poverty Threshold, Deficit													
All families	9 520	633	926	1 470	1 281	1 040	959	873	2 339	9 785	172	2 806	52
Married-couple families	3 705	310	405	620	441	413	356	352	807	9 348	283	2 443	76
Families with a female householder, no husband present	4 793	234	392	682	684	531	515	448	1 307	10 361	232	3 112	74
Families with a male householder, no wife present	1 023	88	129	167	157	96	87	73	225	8 666	508	2 892	172
Unrelated individuals	12 558	1 009	2 197	2 571	1 419	1 207	4 154	–	–	6 542	99	6 542	99
Above Poverty Threshold, Surplus													
All families	71 423	652	986	1 786	1 850	1 994	1 956	2 079	60 120	73 357	890	23 852	293
Married-couple families	55 519	295	489	950	1 014	1 123	1 149	1 342	49 156	82 430	1 090	26 296	343
Families with a female householder, no husband present	10 696	263	377	602	597	629	577	519	7 132	38 676	1 326	13 289	475
Families with a male householder, no wife present	5 208	94	121	234	238	242	229	218	3 832	47 872	2 214	17 189	846
Unrelated individuals	43 628	1 513	1 944	3 140	2 840	2 900	2 421	2 303	26 566	33 186	740	33 186	740

[1]A 90 percent confidence interval is a measure of an estimate's variability. The larger the confidence interval in relation to the size of the estimate, the less reliable the estimate.
– = Quantity represents or rounds to zero.

Table 13-4. Income Distribution Measures Using Money Income and Equivalence-Adjusted Income, 2011 and 2012

(Percent distribution.)

Measure	2011				2012				Percent change (2011–2012)			
	Money income		Equivalence-adjusted income		Money income		Equivalence-adjusted income		Money income		Equivalence-adjusted income	
	Estimate	90 percent confidence interval[1] (+/-)	Estimate	90 percent confidence interval[1] (+/-)	Estimate	90 percent confidence interval[1] (+/-)	Estimate	90 percent confidence interval[1] (+/-)	Estimate	90 percent confidence interval[1] (+/-)	Estimate	90 percent confidence interval[1] (+/-)
Shares of Aggregate Income by Percentile												
Lowest quintile	3.2	0.05	3.4	0.05	3.2	0.05	3.4	0.06	–	1.82	-1.0	1.91
Second quintile	8.4	0.07	9.0	0.07	8.3	0.08	9.0	0.08	-0.6	1.17	-0.2	1.02
Middle quintile	14.3	0.10	14.8	0.10	14.4	0.12	14.8	0.12	0.4	0.94	0.5	0.87
Fourth quintile	23.0	0.14	22.8	0.14	23.0	0.16	22.9	0.17	0.2	0.82	0.4	0.84
Highest quintile	51.1	0.28	50.0	0.30	51.0	0.32	49.9	0.35	-0.1	0.76	-0.2	0.78
Top 5 percent	22.3	0.38	22.1	0.38	22.3	0.43	22.1	0.43	-0.2	2.39	-0.1	2.41
Summary Measures												
Gini index of income inequality	0.477	0.003	0.463	0.003	0.477	0.003	0.463	0.004	–	0.85	-0.10	0.87

[1]A 90-percent confidence interval is a measure of an estimate's variability. The larger the confidence interval in relation to the size of the estimate, the less reliable the estimate.
– = Quantity represents or rounds to zero.

Table 13-5. Two-Year Median Household Income by State, 2000–2012

(Income in 2012 CPI-U-RS adjusted dollars.)

State	2000–2001	2001–2002	2002–2003	2003–2004	2004–2005	2005–2006	2006–2007	2007–2008	2008–2009	2009–2010	2010–2011	2011–2012
UNITED STATES	55 377	54 447	54 103	53 986	54 189	54 689	55 260	54 636	53 465	52 513	51 496	51 059
Alabama	46 416	46 796	47 252	45 518	44 110	43 457	44 983	47 088	45 114	42 950	43 293	43 472
Alaska	72 429	70 876	66 035	65 824	66 335	64 993	67 004	68 999	67 092	63 254	59 775	61 140
Arizona	54 214	53 048	51 053	52 346	53 257	53 174	52 710	51 158	49 496	48 971	49 511	48 340
Arkansas	41 417	42 287	40 644	41 239	42 821	42 658	43 689	43 696	40 664	39 854	41 400	40 592
California	61 858	60 920	61 046	60 690	60 352	61 935	62 359	61 260	60 445	58 592	55 823	55 751
Colorado	64 192	62 851	61 992	62 101	60 596	61 382	65 568	66 349	62 431	61 479	61 643	58 555
Connecticut	68 041	68 663	68 379	67 799	66 912	68 956	71 048	70 004	69 200	69 160	68 142	65 515
Delaware	65 742	63 849	62 283	59 802	59 334	59 988	60 084	57 261	54 928	56 926	56 974	52 387
District of Columbia	54 178	51 629	53 050	54 526	52 868	54 062	55 721	57 759	58 084	59 573	58 178	60 826
Florida	49 522	47 883	48 592	48 964	49 918	51 289	51 364	49 274	48 342	47 566	46 227	46 060
Georgia	55 543	55 011	53 892	51 400	51 918	55 105	55 029	51 581	47 846	46 244	46 697	47 527
Hawaii	65 126	60 949	62 542	66 539	69 224	69 473	69 881	68 252	62 589	61 219	61 491	58 272
Idaho	49 872	48 866	50 517	53 410	52 939	52 293	53 547	52 518	50 322	49 736	49 000	48 186
Illinois	60 649	57 196	55 441	56 190	56 467	56 175	56 786	57 468	56 694	54 982	52 558	51 717
Indiana	53 428	52 378	52 677	52 209	50 683	50 811	52 130	51 080	48 519	47 974	46 982	45 766
Iowa	53 899	52 767	52 028	52 205	53 718	54 749	54 483	53 816	53 884	52 836	51 444	52 356
Kansas	54 229	54 053	54 808	52 570	49 674	50 653	52 790	52 381	49 462	48 056	47 805	48 557
Kentucky	49 102	48 385	46 516	44 699	43 225	44 065	44 327	43 785	44 776	44 455	41 988	40 888
Louisiana	42 087	43 310	42 618	43 057	44 039	42 674	43 651	43 970	45 413	44 801	41 448	40 296
Maine	48 586	47 260	46 685	48 286	50 949	51 819	52 508	51 701	50 607	50 538	50 603	49 945
Maryland	71 069	70 708	68 652	67 362	70 292	71 838	72 592	70 310	68 326	68 117	68 962	71 076
Massachusetts	65 053	65 699	63 622	63 423	64 559	64 447	63 876	64 534	63 942	63 551	64 402	64 146
Michigan	59 553	56 470	55 362	53 786	52 695	54 712	55 036	53 883	51 165	48 947	49 317	49 958
Minnesota	70 329	69 019	67 830	67 072	65 982	63 889	64 153	61 433	59 308	57 453	57 064	60 412
Mississippi	42 424	39 266	40 137	41 553	40 457	39 110	40 418	40 075	38 208	38 852	41 067	39 295
Missouri	56 871	54 104	54 615	52 927	50 889	50 662	50 856	50 021	50 651	50 105	47 490	48 247
Montana	42 684	43 063	43 521	41 929	42 581	45 348	47 577	47 046	44 518	43 384	42 295	43 104
Nebraska	56 113	55 590	54 760	54 062	54 795	55 596	54 641	54 276	53 594	54 062	56 035	54 487
Nevada	59 947	58 132	56 895	56 895	57 041	58 120	59 701	59 122	56 720	54 421	50 972	47 680
New Hampshire	67 237	68 589	69 989	69 217	68 042	68 797	72 703	72 702	69 611	69 323	68 714	67 538
New Jersey	67 175	68 394	69 807	68 580	70 861	76 018	72 256	68 325	69 493	67 460	64 976	65 167
New Mexico	44 875	44 107	44 540	45 959	46 949	45 696	47 352	47 009	45 754	47 080	45 195	43 142
New York	54 472	54 090	53 490	53 846	54 880	55 201	54 558	54 006	53 783	53 062	52 059	49 688
North Carolina	50 291	48 049	46 572	47 726	49 188	47 393	46 754	46 984	45 320	45 476	46 154	43 852
North Dakota	47 208	46 312	48 326	49 062	48 650	48 184	49 510	52 601	53 266	53 384	55 626	56 653
Ohio	55 737	54 335	54 405	53 334	52 163	52 130	53 322	52 212	49 582	48 652	46 952	44 978
Oklahoma	44 712	46 357	45 677	46 488	46 215	44 253	46 043	48 515	49 143	47 305	47 430	48 937
Oregon	55 097	53 440	52 667	50 907	50 884	52 783	54 629	55 397	53 860	52 886	52 946	52 189
Pennsylvania	56 325	55 328	53 920	53 607	54 035	54 831	54 422	54 227	53 191	51 118	50 916	51 428
Rhode Island	57 781	56 718	54 978	57 044	58 235	59 698	60 613	58 404	56 025	54 554	52 211	53 061
South Carolina	49 517	48 600	48 149	47 535	47 174	46 216	47 039	46 958	44 476	43 991	42 417	42 661
South Dakota	50 042	49 894	48 839	49 655	50 360	51 242	51 568	53 215	52 041	48 279	47 985	48 812
Tennessee	45 935	46 835	47 053	46 562	46 313	46 344	45 980	43 979	42 856	42 005	41 901	43 079
Texas	52 235	52 117	50 135	49 674	49 520	49 018	50 159	50 288	50 200	50 240	49 924	50 999
Utah	62 399	61 242	61 301	61 677	63 153	63 339	60 744	62 984	64 652	61 137	58 182	57 497
Vermont	52 849	53 893	54 444	55 770	58 584	59 416	55 838	53 277	55 039	57 440	55 921	54 264
Virginia	64 021	64 252	65 869	65 279	61 612	63 053	65 281	65 808	65 433	64 198	63 748	64 278
Washington	55 903	56 387	58 489	59 997	60 126	60 943	63 318	62 355	62 520	61 894	58 591	60 112
West Virginia	38 849	37 977	39 187	40 735	41 716	43 308	45 182	43 564	41 931	44 190	43 872	43 124
Wisconsin	59 464	58 698	58 175	56 677	54 053	55 691	57 826	55 692	54 724	53 888	53 085	53 112
Wyoming	52 176	51 131	51 939	54 155	53 889	53 083	53 775	55 429	56 523	55 473	55 310	56 580

Table 13-6. Median Family Income in the Past Twelve Months, by Number of Earners and State, 2012

(Income in 2012 inflation-adjusted dollars.)

State	Total	No earners	1 earner	2 earners	3 or more earners
UNITED STATES	62 527	30 996	44 754	82 601	100 585
Alabama	52 700	27 076	39 768	75 975	91 764
Alaska	80 219	35 499	53 489	98 516	120 533
Arizona	56 792	35 931	41 993	77 156	90 434
Arkansas	50 300	27 021	37 081	68 037	88 098
California	66 215	29 588	47 798	89 951	98 490
Colorado	71 083	37 204	50 242	86 686	99 785
Connecticut	85 254	35 159	60 403	105 599	121 636
Delaware	70 655	38 668	51 711	86 016	109 375
District of Columbia	82 268	20 167	45 793	135 293	137 318
Florida	54 777	34 362	41 334	74 156	88 388
Georgia	56 684	25 714	40 631	78 272	93 231
Hawaii	77 447	43 263	52 975	89 870	116 499
Idaho	54 483	31 661	40 303	67 202	83 485
Illinois	68 705	31 986	47 536	88 139	103 917
Indiana	58 596	32 383	41 250	76 091	93 813
Iowa	64 122	34 672	42 346	78 524	93 917
Kansas	62 955	34 506	43 793	79 012	94 198
Kentucky	53 012	24 668	40 633	74 977	92 045
Louisiana	54 059	23 540	38 639	79 837	98 071
Maine	58 689	30 697	40 560	75 225	95 368
Maryland	85 985	37 701	58 202	107 945	125 384
Massachusetts	82 977	29 916	55 794	104 558	122 734
Michigan	59 295	34 355	44 072	79 500	98 076
Minnesota	73 511	37 378	48 876	88 341	104 980
Mississippi	45 857	21 103	35 306	67 465	85 453
Missouri	57 274	31 044	40 994	74 157	95 390
Montana	59 706	37 012	40 419	70 447	86 757
Nebraska	63 442	34 118	41 866	75 402	89 109
Nevada	56 954	33 880	41 054	75 689	92 064
New Hampshire	78 524	35 440	52 588	93 417	112 999
New Jersey	84 442	34 979	60 317	107 293	127 535
New Mexico	51 449	26 958	38 914	73 151	89 881
New York	68 395	28 470	47 414	92 335	112 857
North Carolina	54 995	28 024	40 736	74 631	90 005
North Dakota	70 573	33 545	44 098	84 110	107 948
Ohio	60 088	30 707	43 057	79 303	99 557
Oklahoma	54 988	28 592	39 749	73 080	90 988
Oregon	59 476	35 940	44 779	77 330	89 547
Pennsylvania	65 109	30 698	47 119	84 137	103 802
Rhode Island	71 293	29 717	48 651	91 978	110 368
South Carolina	52 763	27 732	39 301	73 566	92 989
South Dakota	61 505	32 375	39 040	74 611	93 128
Tennessee	53 342	27 619	39 759	72 406	91 437
Texas	59 765	27 064	41 354	80 092	91 594
Utah	64 801	38 831	49 347	72 461	99 010
Vermont	66 047	32 631	43 772	80 413	98 626
Virginia	74 485	34 748	51 817	93 415	110 629
Washington	69 937	40 135	52 996	89 660	104 412
West Virginia	51 320	27 574	42 415	74 853	88 125
Wisconsin	65 154	35 429	43 958	81 052	97 994
Wyoming	68 827	34 994	51 116	81 326	106 905

Table 13-7. Median Family Income in the Past Twelve Months, by Size of Family and State, 2012

(Income in 2012 inflation-adjusted dollars.)

State	Total	2-person families	3-person families	4-person families	5-person families	6-person families	7-or-more-person families
UNITED STATES	62 527	56 646	63 543	76 049	70 403	64 478	65 086
Alabama	52 700	48 770	51 621	66 434	62 290	60 338	59 566
Alaska	80 219	76 118	82 377	85 581	86 013	71 307	80 000
Arizona	56 792	55 022	56 503	64 604	59 837	53 837	49 132
Arkansas	50 300	46 495	50 755	58 333	60 385	54 465	48 051
California	66 215	62 009	66 618	75 111	65 030	62 754	70 848
Colorado	71 083	65 701	71 138	83 330	73 383	72 545	62 476
Connecticut	85 254	72 761	86 254	104 670	100 693	96 033	99 499
Delaware	70 655	62 350	68 439	85 806	87 569	61 817	82 329
District of Columbia	82 268	89 233	68 715	101 582	71 018	75 980	79 164
Florida	54 777	51 839	53 952	63 196	60 475	58 402	56 179
Georgia	56 684	52 610	55 829	68 085	60 772	53 182	52 167
Hawaii	77 447	65 708	80 618	83 538	93 283	83 642	110 474
Idaho	54 483	51 105	52 366	59 971	60 546	65 512	68 306
Illinois	68 705	61 253	70 014	81 680	79 382	66 034	66 084
Indiana	58 596	51 926	61 021	71 113	67 766	65 582	60 021
Iowa	64 122	58 057	64 027	76 173	72 621	72 467	69 595
Kansas	62 955	57 502	65 394	72 453	72 541	64 118	59 060
Kentucky	53 012	47 788	53 639	67 839	62 498	58 207	51 908
Louisiana	54 059	49 078	53 768	68 890	64 281	60 363	53 757
Maine	58 689	53 979	61 702	72 841	66 548	53 551	46 895
Maryland	85 985	75 992	86 655	105 685	96 619	93 891	95 628
Massachusetts	82 977	69 569	84 269	105 299	102 213	96 574	108 926
Michigan	59 295	52 540	61 110	74 863	69 715	61 706	57 985
Minnesota	73 511	64 454	77 579	90 945	87 069	77 714	71 034
Mississippi	45 857	44 149	43 766	51 140	49 433	50 828	46 492
Missouri	57 274	51 421	57 468	72 230	65 715	65 044	62 978
Montana	59 706	55 715	60 107	69 954	67 812	60 109	59 806
Nebraska	63 442	59 564	61 380	73 402	72 847	71 094	65 197
Nevada	56 954	55 349	54 790	61 732	60 459	55 582	58 140
New Hampshire	78 524	67 408	82 656	97 499	96 497	80 779	89 806
New Jersey	84 442	70 150	85 575	103 946	102 202	98 164	94 377
New Mexico	51 449	49 538	50 548	55 184	52 363	59 727	54 162
New York	68 395	59 631	70 151	83 614	79 274	73 441	72 323
North Carolina	54 995	51 662	55 049	66 147	58 700	50 352	48 901
North Dakota	70 573	61 172	72 041	87 154	90 279	92 221	80 924
Ohio	60 088	53 075	60 679	76 381	71 373	67 929	60 827
Oklahoma	54 988	51 097	55 641	64 916	57 980	60 229	59 020
Oregon	59 476	55 568	60 693	70 812	60 879	61 658	66 925
Pennsylvania	65 109	55 872	70 092	81 961	80 084	73 170	67 879
Rhode Island	71 293	61 510	74 720	91 592	78 898	62 128	74 547
South Carolina	52 763	48 891	54 010	62 490	59 038	51 420	55 097
South Dakota	61 505	56 899	60 259	75 267	73 896	74 348	45 977
Tennessee	53 342	48 053	56 042	62 805	62 082	56 945	56 259
Texas	59 765	56 296	59 567	68 566	60 495	53 194	57 342
Utah	64 801	57 734	65 311	70 176	70 788	74 168	77 576
Vermont	66 047	60 346	67 388	79 128	79 667	59 817	74 052
Virginia	74 485	65 510	75 774	90 945	84 423	81 137	81 877
Washington	69 937	63 409	72 286	84 970	73 535	72 113	65 618
West Virginia	51 320	45 284	54 229	65 442	66 131	50 747	61 401
Wisconsin	65 154	57 903	67 808	80 198	78 232	63 858	62 549
Wyoming	68 827	65 237	70 319	76 120	69 867	72 301	67 815

CHAPTER 14: OCCUPATIONAL SAFETY AND HEALTH

HIGHLIGHTS

This chapter includes data on work-related illnesses and injuries and fatal work injuries from the Injuries, Illnesses, and Fatalities (IIF) program. Data are classified by industry and selected worker characteristics.

Figure 14-1. Incidence Rates of Nonfatal Occupational Injuries and Illnesses by Major Industry in the Private Sector, 2012

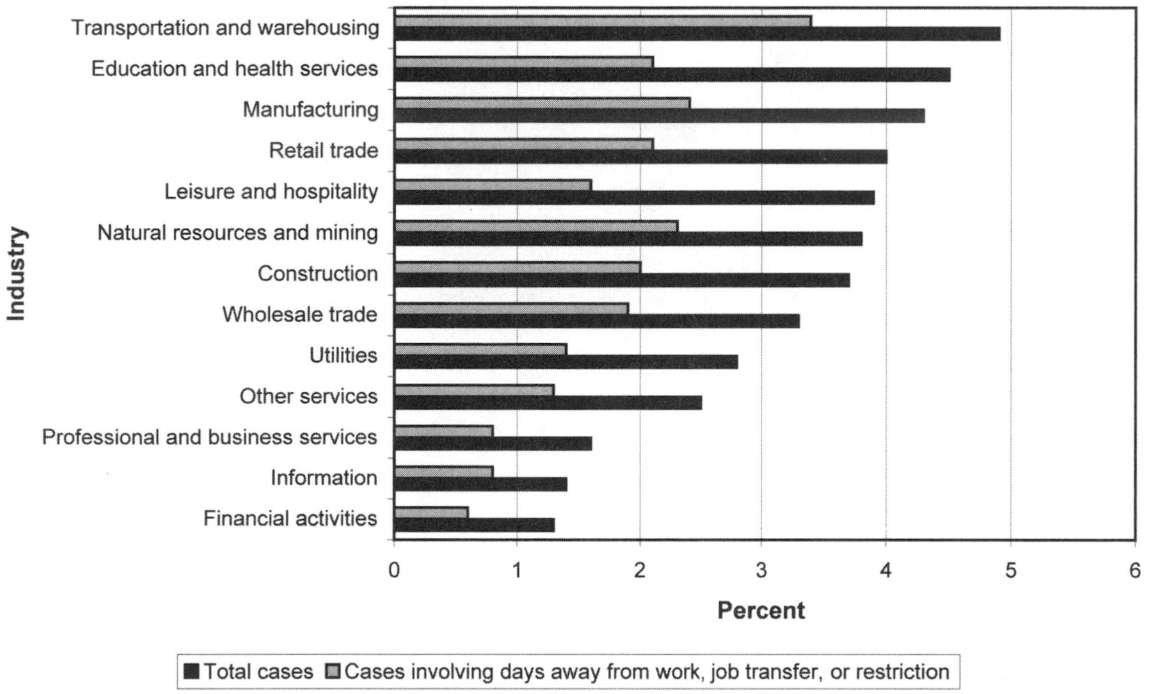

Transportation and warehousing continued to have the highest incidence rate of non-fatal occupational injuries and illnesses among all major industries at 4.9 per 100 full-time workers in 2012. Rates for injuries and illness requiring days away from work, job transfer, or restriction were much lower, ranging from 0.6 per 100 full-time workers in financial activities services to 3.4 per 100 full-time workers in transportation and warehousing. (See Table 14-1.)

OTHER HIGHLIGHTS

- The rate of nonfatal occupational injuries and illnesses for all workers in the private industry declined slightly to 3.4 cases per 100 full-time workers in 2012. It has declined throughout the past decade. (See Table 14-1.)

- Workers aged 45 to 54 years old had the highest number of nonfatal occupational injuries and illnesses, followed by those aged 25 to 34 years old. (See Table 14-6.)

- According to preliminary data, 4,383 workplace fatalities occurred in 2012, a decline of 6.6 percent from 2011. Men were far more likely than women to be killed on the job, accounting for nearly 92 percent of all fatalities. (See Table 14-9.)

- Motor vehicle operators had the highest number of fatalities among all occupations at 817, followed by construction trade workers at 577. (See Table 14-10.)

NOTES AND DEFINITIONS

COLLECTION AND COVERAGE

The Injuries, Illnesses, and Fatalities (IIF) program at the Bureau of Labor Statistics (BLS) provides annual reports on the number of workplace injuries, illnesses, and fatalities. BLS has reported annually on the number of work-related injuries, illnesses, and fatalities since 1972, after the Occupational Safety and Health Act of 1970 was passed.

NONFATAL OCCUPATIONAL INJURIES AND ILLNESSES

The Survey of Occupational Injuries and Illnesses is a federal-state program in which employer's reports are collected annually from over 230,000 private industry establishments and processed by state agencies cooperating with the BLS. Summary information regarding the number of injuries and illnesses is copied by these employers directly from their recordkeeping logs to the survey questionnaire. The questionnaire also asks for the number of employee hours worked (needed in the calculation of incidence rates) as well as its average employment (needed to verify the unit's employment-size class).

Occupational injury and illness data for coal, metal, and nonmetal mining and for railroad activities were provided by the Department of Labor's Mine Safety and Health Administration and the Department of Transportation's Federal Railroad Administration. The survey excludes all work-related fatalities as well as nonfatal work injuries and illnesses to the self-employed; to workers on farms with 10 or fewer employees; to private household workers; and, nationally, to federal, state, and local government workers.

Injuries and illnesses logged by employers conform with definitions and recordkeeping guidelines set by the Occupational Safety and Health Administration, U.S. Department of Labor. Under those guidelines, nonfatal cases are recordable if they are occupational illnesses or if they are occupational injuries which involve lost worktime, medical treatment other than first aid, restriction of work or motion, loss of consciousness, or transfer to another job. Employers keep counts of injuries separate from illnesses and also identify for each whether a case involved any days away from work or days of restricted work activity, or both, beyond the day of injury or onset of illness.

Occupational injuries, such as sprains, cuts, and fractures, account for the vast majority of all cases that employers log and report to the BLS survey. Occupational illnesses are new cases recognized, diagnosed, and reported during the year. Overwhelmingly, those reported are easier to directly relate to workplace activity (e.g., contact dermatitis or carpal tunnel

syndrome) than long-term latent illnesses, such as cancers. The latter illnesses are believed to be under-recorded and, thus, understated in the BLS survey.

CONCEPTS AND DEFINITIONS

Days away from work are cases that involve days away from work, days of restricted work activity, or both.

The data are presented in the form of *incidence rates*, defined as the number of injuries and illnesses or cases of days away from work per 100 full-time employees. The formula is (N/EH) x 200,000, where N is the number of injuries and illnesses or days away from work, EH is the total hours worked by all employees during the calendar year, and 200,000 represents the base for 100 full-time equivalent workers (working 40 hours per week, 50 weeks per year).

Median days away from work is a measure used to summarize the varying lengths of absences from work among the cases with days away from work. The median is the point at which half of the cases involved more days away from work and half involved less days away from work.

Occupational illness is an abnormal condition or disorder (other than one resulting from an occupational injury) caused by exposure to environmental factors associated with employment. It includes acute and chronic illnesses and diseases that may have been caused by inhalation, absorption, ingestion, or direct contact. Long-term latent illnesses can be difficult to relate to the workplace and are believed to be understated in this survey.

Occupational injury is any injury—such as a cut, fracture, sprain, or amputation—that results from a work accident or from exposure to an incident in the work environment

FATAL OCCUPATIONAL INJURIES

The Bureau of Labor Statistics (BLS) Census of Fatal Occupational Injuries (CFOI) produces comprehensive, accurate, and timely counts of fatal work injuries. CFOI is a federal-state cooperative program that has been implemented in all 50 states and the District of Columbia since 1992. To compile counts that are as complete as possible, the census uses multiple sources to identify, verify, and profile fatal worker injuries. Information about each workplace fatality—occupation and other worker characteristics, equipment involved, and circumstances of the event—is obtained by cross referencing the source records, such as death certificates, workers' compensation reports, and federal and state agency administrative reports. To ensure that fatalities are work-related, cases are substantiated with two or more independent source documents, or a source document and a follow-up questionnaire.

Data compiled by the CFOI program are issued annually for the preceding calendar year. These data are used by safety and health policy analysts and researchers to help prevent fatal work injuries by:

- informing workers of life threatening hazards associated with various jobs;

- promoting safer work practices through enhanced job safety training;

- assessing and improving workplace safety standards; and

- identifying new areas of safety research.

The National Safety Council has adopted the Census of Fatal Occupational Injuries figure, beginning with the 1992 data year, as the authoritative count for work related deaths in the United States.

SOURCES OF ADDITIONAL INFORMATION

For more extensive definitions and description of collection methods, see Chapter 9 in the *BLS Handbook of Methods* and the BLS news releases USDL 13-2257, "Nonfatal Occupational Injuries and Illnesses Requiring Days Away from Work, 2012"; USDL 13-2119, "Employee Reported Workplace Injuries and Illnesses–2012"; and USDL 13-1699, "National Census of Fatal Occupational Injuries in 2012 (Preliminary Results)," available on the BLS Web site at http://www.bls.gov/iif/.

Table 14-1. Incidence Rates[1] of Nonfatal Occupational Injuries and Illnesses, by Selected Industries and Case Types, 2012

(Number, rate per 100 full-time workers.)

Industry[2]	NAICS code[3]	Total recordable cases	Cases with days away from work, job transfer, or restriction			Other recordable cases
			Total recordable cases	Cases with days away from work[4]	Cases with job transfer or restriction	
PRIVATE INDUSTRY[5]		3.4	1.8	1.0	0.7	1.6
Goods-Producing[5]		4.1	2.3	1.2	1.1	1.8
Natural resources and mining[5,6]		3.8	2.3	1.4	0.9	1.5
Agriculture, forestry, fishing and hunting[5]	11	5.5	3.3	2.0	1.3	2.2
Crop production[5,7]	111	5.3	3.1	1.8	1.3	2.2
Animal production[5,7]	112	6.2	3.6	2.5	1.1	2.7
Forestry and logging	113	4.3	2.5	2.2	*	1.8
Support activities for agriculture and forestry	115	5.3	3.5	1.8	1.7	1.8
Mining[6]	21	2.1	1.3	0.9	0.4	0.8
Oil and gas extraction	211	1.5	0.8	0.7	0.1	0.7
Mining (except oil and gas)[8]	212	2.8	1.9	1.4	0.4	1.0
Support activities for mining	213	1.9	1.2	0.6	0.5	0.7
Construction	23	3.7	2.0	1.4	0.6	1.6
Construction of buildings	236	3.4	1.8	1.4	0.4	1.6
Heavy and civil engineering construction	237	3.2	1.7	1.1	0.6	1.5
Specialty trade contractors	238	3.9	2.2	1.5	0.6	1.7
Manufacturing	31-33	4.3	2.4	1.1	1.3	1.9
Food manufacturing	311	5.4	3.4	1.3	2.2	1.9
Beverage and tobacco product manufacturing	312	6.5	4.4	1.9	2.5	2.1
Textile mills	313	3.4	1.9	0.7	1.2	1.5
Textile product mills[7]	314	3.1	1.7	0.8	0.9	1.4
Apparel manufacturing[7]	315	2.2	1.2	0.6	0.6	1.0
Leather and allied product manufacturing	316	5.1	2.9	1.2	1.8	2.1
Wood product manufacturing	321	6.5	3.8	2.0	1.8	2.7
Paper manufacturing	322	3.0	1.7	0.8	0.9	1.3
Printing and related support activities	323	2.8	1.5	0.8	0.7	1.3
Petroleum and coal products manufacturing	324	1.5	0.9	0.5	0.4	0.6
Chemical manufacturing	325	2.3	1.4	0.7	0.7	0.9
Plastics and rubber products manufacturing[7]	326	5.0	2.8	1.3	1.5	2.2
Nonmetallic mineral product manufacturing	327	5.1	2.8	1.5	1.3	2.2
Primary metal manufacturing	331	6.2	3.5	1.6	1.9	2.7
Fabricated metal product manufacturing	332	5.7	2.9	1.5	1.3	2.8
Machinery manufacturing[7]	333	4.2	2.1	0.9	1.1	2.2
Computer and electronic product manufacturing	334	1.4	0.7	0.3	0.3	0.7
Electrical equipment, appliance, and component manufacturing	335	3.1	1.7	0.7	1.0	1.4
Transportation equipment manufacturing[7]	336	5.2	2.8	1.1	1.7	2.4
Furniture and related product manufacturing[7]	337	4.9	2.6	1.1	1.5	2.2
Miscellaneous manufacturing	339	2.8	1.5	0.7	0.8	1.4
Service-Providing		3.2	1.6	1.0	0.6	1.6
Trade, transportation, and utilities[9]		3.9	2.3	1.3	1.0	1.6
Wholesale trade		3.3	1.9	1.1	0.9	1.3
Merchant wholesalers, durable goods	423	2.9	1.6	0.9	0.7	1.3
Merchant wholesalers, nondurable goods	424	4.4	2.9	1.6	1.3	1.5
Wholesale electronic markets and agents and brokers	425	1.7	0.8	0.4	*	*
Retail trade	44-45	4.0	2.1	1.1	1.0	1.8
Motor vehicle and parts dealers	441	3.8	1.7	1.1	0.6	2.1
Furniture and home furnishings stores	442	3.8	2.4	1.4	1.0	1.3
Electronics and appliance stores	443	2.2	1.4	*	*	0.8
Building material and garden equipment and supplies dealers	444	5.2	3.4	1.7	1.7	1.8
Food and beverage stores	445	4.7	2.7	1.4	1.2	2.0
Health and personal care stores	446	2.1	0.7	0.6	0.1	1.4
Gasoline stations	447	2.3	1.1	0.7	0.4	1.2
Clothing and clothing accessories stores	448	2.3	0.9	0.6	0.3	1.4
Sporting goods, hobby, book, and music stores	451	2.8	1.3	0.7	0.6	1.6
General merchandise stores	452	5.3	2.9	1.2	1.7	2.4
Miscellaneous store retailers	453	3.6	1.7	0.9	0.9	1.9
Nonstore retailers	454	2.8	1.8	1.0	0.7	1.0

Note: Components may not sum to totals because of rounding.

[1] The incidence rates represent the number of injuries and illnesses per 100 full-time workers and were calculated as: (N/EH) x 200,000 (where N = number of injuries and illnesses; EH = total hours worked by all employees during the calendar year; 200,000 = base for 100 equivalent full-time workers working 40 hours per week, 50 weeks per year).
[2] Totals include data for industries not shown separately.
[3] North American Industry Classification System—United States, 2007.
[4] Days away from work cases include those that result in days away from work with or without job transfer or restriction.
[5] Excludes farms with fewer than 11 employees.
[6] Data for mining include establishments not governed by the Department of Labor's Mine Safety and Health Administration (MSHA) rules and reporting, such as those in oil and gas extraction and related support activities. Data for mining operators in coal, metal, and nonmetal mining are provided to BLS by MSHA. Independent mining contractors are excluded from the coal, metal, and nonmetal mining industries. These data do not reflect the changes the Occupational Safety and Health Administration (OSHA) made to its record-keeping requirements effective January 1, 2002; thus, estimates for these industries are not comparable to estimates in other industries.
[7] Industry scope changed in 2009.
[8] Data for mining operators in this industry are provided to BLS by MSHA. Independent mining contractors are excluded. These data do not reflect the changes OSHA made to its record-keeping requirements effective January 1, 2002; thus, estimates for these industries are not comparable to estimates in other industries.
[9] Data for employers in rail transportation are provided to BLS by the Department of Transportation's Federal Railroad Administration (FRA).
* = Figure does not meet standards of reliability or quality.

Table 14-1. Incidence Rates[1] of Nonfatal Occupational Injuries and Illnesses, by Selected Industries and Case Types, 2012—*Continued*

(Number, rate per 100 full-time workers.)

Industry[2]	NAICS code[3]	Total recordable cases	Cases with days away from work, job transfer, or restriction			Other recordable cases
			Total recordable cases	Cases with days away from work[4]	Cases with job transfer or restriction	
Service-Providing—*Continued*						
Transportation and warehousing[9]	48	4.9	3.4	2.2	1.1	1.5
Air transportation	481	7.4	5.5	4.3	1.2	1.9
Rail transportation[9]	482	1.8	1.3	1.1	0.1	0.5
Water transportation	483	2.2	1.8	1.6	0.2	0.4
Truck transportation	484	4.5	3.0	2.1	0.8	1.6
Transit and ground passenger transportation	485	5.1	3.4	2.5	0.9	1.8
Pipeline transportation	486	2.1	0.7	0.6	0.2	1.3
Scenic and sightseeing transportation	487	3.6	2.1	1.6	0.5	1.5
Support activities for transportation	488	3.7	2.5	1.6	0.9	1.2
Couriers and messengers	492	7.1	5.0	2.9	2.1	2.0
Warehousing and storage	493	5.5	3.9	1.8	2.1	1.5
Utilities	22	2.8	1.4	0.8	0.6	1.4
Information	51	1.4	0.8	0.6	0.2	0.6
Publishing industries (except Internet)		1.0	0.5	0.4	0.1	0.5
Motion picture and sound recording industries	512	1.6	0.5	0.3	0.2	1.1
Broadcasting (except Internet)	515	1.5	0.9	0.6	0.3	0.6
Telecommunications[7]	517	2.0	1.4	1.1	0.3	0.6
Data processing, hosting, and related services[7]	518	0.8	0.3	0.2	0.1	0.5
Other information services[7]	519	0.7	0.4	0.4	*	0.2
Financial activities	*	1.3	0.6	0.4	0.2	0.7
Finance and insurance		0.7	0.2	0.2	0.1	0.5
Monetary authorities–central bank	521	1.3	0.5	0.3	0.2	0.7
Credit intermediation and related activities	522	0.9	0.3	0.2	*	([10])
Securities, commodity contracts, and other financial investments and related activities	523	0.2	0.1	([10])	([10])	0.2
Insurance carriers and related activities	524	0.7	0.2	0.2	0.1	([10])
Funds, trusts, and other financial vehicles	525	0.8	0.4	0.3	*	([10])
Real estate and rental and leasing	53	2.9	1.6	1.0	0.6	1.3
Real estate	531	2.6	1.3	0.9	0.4	1.2
Rental and leasing services	532	3.8	2.4	1.3	1.1	1.4
Lessors of nonfinancial intangible assets (except copyrighted works)	533	0.6	0.2	0.1	*	0.4
Professional and business services	*	1.6	0.8	0.5	0.3	0.8
Professional, scientific, and technical services[7]		0.9	0.3	0.2	0.1	0.6
Management of companies and enterprises	55	1.1	0.5	0.3	0.2	0.6
Administrative and support and waste management and remediation services	56	2.8	1.6	1.1	0.5	1.2
Administrative and support services[7]	561	2.6	1.5	1.0	0.5	1.1
Waste management and remediation services	562	5.4	3.4	2.1	1.3	2.0
Education and health services	*	4.5	2.1	1.2	0.9	2.4
Educational services		1.9	0.8	0.6	0.3	1.1
Health care and social assistance	62	4.8	2.3	1.3	1.0	2.6
Ambulatory health care services	621	2.6	0.9	0.6	0.3	1.7
Hospitals	622	6.6	2.7	1.5	1.1	3.9
Nursing and residential care facilities	623	7.6	4.7	2.4	2.3	2.9
Social assistance	624	3.5	1.8	1.2	0.6	1.7
Leisure and hospitality	*	3.9	1.6	1.0	0.6	2.2
Arts, entertainment, and recreation		4.6	2.3	1.3	1.0	2.3
Performing arts, spectator sports, and related industries	711	5.5	2.8	1.6	*	2.7
Museums, historical sites, and similar institutions	712	4.4	2.0	1.2	0.8	2.4
Amusement, gambling, and recreation industries	713	4.3	2.2	1.2	1.0	2.1
Accommodation and food services	72	3.8	1.5	1.0	0.5	2.2
Accommodation	721	5.2	2.8	1.5	1.3	2.4
Food services and drinking places	722	3.4	1.2	0.9	0.3	2.2
Other services	*	2.5	1.3	0.9	0.4	1.2
Other services, except public administration		2.5	1.3	0.9	0.4	1.2
Repair and maintenance	811	3.0	1.6	1.3	0.3	1.4
Personal and laundry services	812	2.1	1.3	0.8	0.5	0.8
Religious, grantmaking, civic, professional, and similar organizations	813	2.3	1.0	0.6	0.4	1.3

Note: Components may not sum to totals because of rounding.

[1]The incidence rates represent the number of injuries and illnesses per 100 full-time workers and were calculated as: (N/EH) x 200,000 (where N = number of injuries and illnesses; EH = total hours worked by all employees during the calendar year; 200,000 = base for 100 equivalent full-time workers working 40 hours per week, 50 weeks per year).
[2]Totals include data for industries not shown separately.
[3]North American Industry Classification System—United States, 2007.
[4]Days away from work cases include those that result in days away from work with or without job transfer or restriction.
[7]Industry scope changed in 2009.
[9]Data for employers in rail transportation are provided to BLS by the Department of Transportation's Federal Railroad Administration (FRA).
[10]Data too small to be displayed.
* = Figure does not meet standards of reliability or quality.

Table 14-2. Incidence Rates[1] of Nonfatal Occupational Injuries and Illnesses, by Major Industry Sector, Employment Size, and Ownership, 2012

(Rate per 100 full-time workers.)

Industry sector	All establishments	Establishment employment size (workers)				
		1 to 10	11 to 49	50 to 249	250 to 999	1,000 or more
ALL INDUSTRIES INCLUDING STATE AND LOCAL GOVERNMENT[2]	3.7	1.7	3.2	4.3	4.0	4.4
Private Industry[2]	3.4	1.6	3.0	4.2	3.6	3.7
Goods Producing[2]	4.1	2.8	4.4	4.7	3.7	3.2
Natural resources and mining[2,3]	3.8	*	4.1	4.3	3.6	2.8
Construction	3.7	3.0	4.3	4.1	2.4	0.8
Manufacturing	4.3	2.4	4.7	5.0	3.9	3.4
Service Providing	3.2	1.4	2.8	4.0	3.5	3.9
Trade, transportation, and utilities[4]	4.0	1.8	3.5	4.8	4.8	4.4
Information	1.0	*	*	1.9	1.3	0.9
Financial activities	1.0	1.3	1.4	1.6	1.1	0.7
Professional and business services	2.0	1.2	1.9	1.8	1.4	0.9
Education and health services	5.0	1.1	2.8	5.4	5.3	5.5
Leisure and hospitality	4.0	1.4	3.1	4.9	5.7	5.3
Other services, except public administration	3.0	1.8	2.4	3.8	3.2	2.8
State and Local Government[2]	6.0	3.3	5.4	5.4	5.9	5.7
State government[2]	4.0	*	*	4.1	5.3	4.2
Local government[2]	6.0	*	*	5.7	6.2	6.6

[1]The incidence rates represent the number of injuries and illnesses per 100 full-time workers and were calculated as: (N/EH) x 200,000 (where N = number of injuries and illnesses; EH = total hours worked by all employees during the calendar year; 200,000 = base for 100 equivalent full-time workers working 40 hours per week, 50 weeks per year).
[2]Excludes farms with fewer than 11 employees.
[3]Data for mining include establishments not goverened by the Mine and Safety and Health Administration rules and reporting such as those in oil and gas extraction and related support activities.
[4]Data for employers in railroad transportation are provided to the Bureau of Labor Statistics (BLS) by the Federal Reserve Administration, U.S. Department of Transportation.
* = Figure does not meet standards of reliability or quality.

Table 14-3. Number of Cases and Incidence Rate[1] of Nonfatal Occupational Injuries and Illnesses for Industries with 100,000 or More Cases, 2012

(Number, rate per 100 full-time workers.)

Industry[2]	NAICS Code[3]	Total cases (thousands)	Incidence rate
ALL INDUSTRIES INCLUDING STATE AND LOCAL GOVERNMENT[4]		3 769.1	3.7
Elementary and secondary schools (local government)	6 111	251.1	5.2
General medical and surgical hospitals (private industry)	6 221	230.2	6.5
Food services and drinking places (private industry)	722	208.4	3.4
Specialty trade contractors (private industry)	621	123.5	2.6
Ambulatory health care services (private industry)	238	119.2	3.9
Administrative and support services (private industry)	452	118.5	5.3
Nursing care facilities (private industry)	561	108.8	2.6
General merchandise stores (private industry)	6 231	[5]100.2	7.9

[1]The incidence rates represent the number of injuries and illnesses per 100 full-time workers and were calculated as: (N/EH) x 200,000 (where N = number of injuries and illnesses; EH = total hours worked by all employees during the calendar year; 200,000 = base for 100 equivalent full-time workers working 40 hours per week, 50 weeks per year).
[2]Totals include data for industries not shown separately.
[3]North American Industry Classification System—United States, 2007 .
[4]Excludes farms with fewer than 11 employees.
[5]The point estimate for this industry exceeds 100,000 cases; however, the true number of cases may be less than 100,000 at the 95 percent confidence level.

Table 14-4. Incidence Rates[1] of Nonfatal Occupational Injuries and Illnesses, by Major Industry Sector, Category of Illness, and Ownership, 2012

(Rate per 100 full-time workers.)

Industry sector	Total cases	Skin diseases or disorders	Respiratory conditions	Poisonings	Hearing loss	All other illnesses
ALL INDUSTRIES INCLUDING STATE AND LOCAL GOVERNMENT[2]	20.2	3.2	1.9	0.3	2.1	12.7
Private Industry[2]	17.5	2.6	1.5	0.2	2.1	11.0
Goods Producing[2]	28.6	3.7	1.2	0.3	7.5	16.0
Natural resources and mining[2,3]	20.0	3.6	1.7	0.9	1.5	12.3
Construction	8.1	1.9	0.5	0.2	0.2	5.3
Manufacturing	38.6	4.4	1.5	0.2	11.5	21.0
Service Providing	14.5	2.3	1.6	0.2	0.7	9.7
Trade, transportation, and utilities[4]	13.9	1.6	*	0.1	1.8	8.7
Information	9.1	0.9	0.4	0.2	0.9	6.7
Financial activities	9.4	1.0	1.0	0.1	*	7.3
Professional and business services	8.7	1.8	1.0	0.3	0.2	5.5
Education and health services	25.9	4.2	2.6	0.3	0.1	18.7
Leisure and hospitality	12.7	3.2	1.5	0.2	0.1	7.8
Other services, except public administration	10.8	2.5	1.5	*	0.5	6.0
State and Local Government[2]	37.3	7.1	4.5	0.8	1.9	23.1
State government[2]	37.8	6.2	4.8	0.6	1.9	24.3
Local government[2]	37.2	7.5	4.4	0.9	1.8	22.6

[1]The incidence rates represent the number of injuries and illnesses per 100 full-time workers and were calculated as: (N/EH) x 200,000 (where N = number of injuries and illnesses; EH = total hours worked by all employees during the calendar year; 200,000 = base for 100 equivalent full-time workers working 40 hours per week, 50 weeks per year).
[2]Excludes farms with fewer than 11 employees.
[3]Data for mining include establishments not goverened by the Mine and Safety and Health Administration rules and reporting such as those in oil and gas extraction and related support activities.
[4]Data for employers in railroad transportation are provided to the Bureau of Labor Statistics (BLS) by the Federal Reserve Administration, U.S. Department of Transportation.
* = Figure does not meet standards of reliability or quality.

Table 14-5. Number of Cases of Nonfatal Occupational Injuries and Illnesses, by Major Industry Sector, Category of Illness, and Ownership, 2012

(Rate per 100 full-time workers.)

Industry sector	Total cases	Skin diseases or disorders	Respiratory conditions	Poisonings	Hearing loss	All other illnesses
ALL INDUSTRIES INCLUDING STATE AND LOCAL GOVERNMENT[1]	207.8	33.3	19.9	3.0	21.2	130.4
Private Industry[1]	154.8	23.2	13.5	1.9	18.5	97.7
Goods Producing[1]	53.1	6.8	2.3	0.5	14.0	29.6
Natural resources and mining[1,2]	3.5	0.6	0.3	0.2	0.3	2.2
Construction	4.1	0.9	0.3	0.1	0.1	2.6
Manufacturing	45.6	5.2	1.7	0.2	13.6	24.8
Service Providing	101.6	16.4	11.2	1.4	4.6	68.1
Trade, transportation, and utilities[3]	29.2	3.4	*	0.3	3.8	18.2
Information	2.2	0.2	0.1	(4)	0.2	1.6
Financial activities	6.3	0.7	0.7	0.1	*	4.9
Professional and business services	11.8	2.5	1.3	0.4	0.2	7.4
Education and health services	37.9	6.1	3.9	0.4	0.1	27.3
Leisure and hospitality	11.0	2.8	1.3	0.2	0.1	6.8
Other services, except public administration	3.1	0.7	0.4	*	0.1	1.7
State and Local Government[1]	53.0	10.1	6.4	1.1	2.6	32.7
State government[1]	15.1	2.5	1.9	0.2	0.8	9.7
Local government[1]	37.9	7.6	4.5	0.9	1.9	23.0

[1]Excludes farms with fewer than 11 employees.
[2]Data for mining include establishments not goverened by the Mine and Safety and Health Administration rules and reporting such as those in oil and gas extraction and related support activities.
[3]Data for employers in railroad transportation are provided to the Bureau of Labor Statistics (BLS) by the Federal Reserve Administration, U.S. Department of Transportation.
[4]Data too small to be displayed.
* = Figure does not meet standards of reliability or quality.

Table 14-6. Number of Nonfatal Occupational Injuries and Illnesses Involving Days Away from Work,[1] by Selected Worker Characteristics and Private Industry, 2012

(Number.)

Characteristic	Total private[2,3,4]	Goods-producing			
		All goods-producing	Natural resources and mining[2,3]	Construction	Manufacturing
TOTAL CASES	905 690	222 050	25 040	71 730	125 280
Sex					
Men	559 830	191 360	21 210	70 270	99 880
Women	342 640	30 550	3 810	1 400	25 350
Age					
14 to 15 years	120	*	*	*	*
16 to 19 years	21 170	3 120	660	670	1 790
20 to 24 years	89 590	20 060	2 730	6 280	11 060
25 to 34 years	202 200	52 740	7 090	20 000	25 650
35 to 44 years	195 270	52 250	5 320	17 910	29 020
45 to 54 years	219 150	55 490	5 030	18 040	32 410
55 to 64 years	136 880	31 240	3 040	7 280	20 920
65 years and over	27 260	3 510	490	520	2 510
Length of Service with Employer					
Less than 3 months	95 670	31 280	5 520	11 430	14 320
3 to 11 months	171 540	44 020	5 000	15 710	23 310
1 to 5 years	300 490	63 860	7 960	21 500	34 400
More than 5 years	325 220	80 790	5 940	22 610	52 240
Race and Hispanic Origin					
White only	362 480	108 210	5 530	40 330	62 350
Black only	70 710	12 400	510	2 590	9 300
Hispanic only[5]	118 940	41 770	10 580	11 200	20 000
Asian only	13 770	2 990	130	430	2 430
Native Hawaiian or Pacific Islander only	2 940	440	*	160	270
American Indian or Alaskan Native only	4 200	1 430	80	800	550
Hispanic[5] and other race	710	100	*	*	80
Multiple races	1 130	110	*	30	80
Not reported	330 830	54 600	8 210	16 170	30 220

Characteristic	Service-providing							
	All service-providing	Trade, transportation, and utilities[4]	Information	Financial activities	Professional and business services	Education and health services	Leisure and hospitality	Other services
TOTAL CASES	683 640	277 520	15 350	25 790	70 330	178 330	89 480	26 820
Sex								
Men	368 470	194 350	11 760	16 020	45 350	36 600	44 880	19 510
Women	312 090	80 230	3 590	9 770	24 960	141 640	44 570	7 320
Age								
14 to 15 years	110	30	*	*	*	50	30	*
16 to 19 years	18 050	6 820	120	170	1 050	2 400	6 550	940
20 to 24 years	69 520	27 410	1 020	3 030	6 420	14 200	13 810	3 630
25 to 34 years	149 470	54 690	3 310	5 940	19 200	38 500	21 690	6 130
35 to 44 years	143 010	59 400	3 800	5 640	14 470	38 210	16 060	5 430
45 to 54 years	163 660	72 010	3 920	5 650	16 210	44 260	16 520	5 090
55 to 64 years	105 650	43 020	2 450	4 500	9 390	32 710	9 390	4 190
65 years and over	23 750	9 500	320	610	2 600	6 110	3 400	1 200
Length of Service with Employer								
Less than 3 months	64 400	24 400	720	1 360	9 900	11 850	11 750	4 410
3 to 11 months	127 520	49 150	1 740	4 560	14 150	31 770	20 690	5 460
1 to 5 years	236 630	89 330	3 820	11 520	23 670	66 540	33 940	7 810
More than 5 years	244 430	108 380	8 700	8 130	21 750	66 690	21 770	9 010
Race and Hispanic Origin								
White only	254 270	99 890	4 140	8 920	25 840	72 700	29 500	13 270
Black only	58 310	15 640	770	2 620	5 280	24 810	7 690	1 500
Hispanic only[5]	77 170	23 110	830	3 000	14 850	13 320	18 170	3 890
Asian only	10 780	3 060	100	360	1 040	3 340	2 680	200
Native Hawaiian or Pacific Islander only	2 490	750	*	60	230	670	730	50
American Indian or Alaskan Native only	2 770	1 040	20	50	180	700	540	220
Hispanic[5] and other race	620	380	*	*	50	140	50	*
Multiple races	1 020	200	*	*	530	130	110	40
Not reported	276 230	133 460	9 490	10 780	22 320	62 510	30 040	7 650

Note: Components may not sum to totals because of rounding.

[1]Days away from work cases include those that result in days away from work with or without restricted work activity.
[2]Excludes farms with fewer than 11 employees.
[3]Data for mining include establishments not governed by the Department of Labor's Mine Safety and Health Administration (MSHA) rules and reporting, such as those in oil and gas extraction and related support activities. Data for mining operators in coal, metal, and nonmetal mining are provided to the Bureau of Labor Statistics (BLS) by MSHA. Independent mining contractors are excluded from the coal, metal, and nonmetal mining industries. These data do not reflect the changes the Occupational Safety and Health Administration (OSHA) made to its record-keeping requirements effective January 1, 2002; thus, estimates for these industries are not comparable to estimates in other industries.
[4]Data for employers in rail transportation are provided to BLS by the Federal Railroad Administration, U.S. Department of Transportation.
[5]May be of any race.
* = Figure does not meet standards of reliability or quality.

Table 14-7. Number, Incidence Rate,[1] and Median Days Away from Work[2] for Nonfatal Occupational Injuries and Illnesses Involving Days Away from Work[3] for Gender and Age Groups in Private Industry, State Government, and Local Government, 2012

(Number, rate.)

Characteristic	Total private, state, and local governments			Private industry[4,5,6]			State government[4,5,6]			Local government[4,5,6]		
	Number	Incidence rate	Median days away from work	Number	Incidence rate	Median days away from work	Number	Incidence rate	Median days away from work	Number	Incidence rate	Median days away from work
TOTAL CASES	1 153 980	112.4	9	905 690	102.3	8	66 950	167.7	10	181 340	177.8	9
Gender												
Male	702 250	122.6	10	559 830	109.5	10	36 150	219.0	11	106 270	235.0	10
Female	447 020	99.4	7	342 640	92.5	7	29 480	130.3	9	74 890	132.2	8
Age												
14–15	170	*	2	120	*	2	*	*	*	50	*	1
16–19	22 470	112.9	4	21 170	111.0	4	250	111.9	3	1 050	168.0	4
20–24	96 750	109.8	5	89 590	108.9	4	2 140	123.5	7	5 030	120.2	5
25–34	245 370	106.6	6	202 200	99.5	6	12 160	155.0	8	31 000	161.0	7
35–44	256 480	111.5	9	195 270	99.1	9	15 710	178.4	11	45 510	187.0	8
45–54	293 700	121.7	11	219 150	107.5	12	20 710	204.3	10	53 840	196.0	10
55–64	184 910	114.7	12	136 880	103.0	14	11 500	144.1	11	36 520	178.9	10
65 and over	34 320	89.2	14	27 260	82.8	14	1 610	108.6	11	5 450	133.3	13

[1]The incidence rates represent the number of injuries and illnesses per 100 full-time workers and were calculated as: (N/EH) x 200,000 (where N = number of injuries and illnesses; EH = total hours worked by all employees during the calendar year; 200,000 = base for 100 equivalent full-time workers working 40 hours per week, 50 weeks per year).
[2]Median days away from work is the measure used to summarize the varying lengths of absences from work among the cases with days away from work.
[3]Days away from work cases include those that result in days away from work with or without restricted work activity.
[4]Excludes farms with fewer than 11 employees.
[5]Data for mining include establishments not governed by the Mine Safety and Health Administration rules and reporting, such as those in Oil and Gas Extraction and related support activities.
[6]Data for employers in rail transportation are provided to BLS by the Federal Railroad Administration, U.S. Department of Transportation.
* = Figure does not meet standards of reliability or quality.

Table 14-8. Number, Percent Distribution, and Median Days Away from Work[1] for Nonfatal Occupational Injuries and Illnesses Involving Days Away from Work[2] for Race or Ethnic Origin and Length of Service in Private Industry, State Government, and Local Government, 2012

(Number, rate.)

Characteristic	Total private, state, and local governments			Private industry[3,4,5]			State government[3,4,5]			Local government[3,4,5]		
	Number	Percent	Median days away from work	Number	Percent	Median days away from work	Number	Percent	Median days away from work	Number	Percent	Median days away from work
TOTAL CASES	1 153 980	100.0	9	905 690	100.0	8	66 950	100.0	10	181 340	100.0	9
Race or Ethnic Origin												
White only	455 160	39.4	7	362 480	40.0	7	18 650	27.9	9	74 030	40.8	6
Black only	89 100	7.7	8	70 710	7.8	7	8 500	12.7	9	9 900	5.5	10
Hispanic or Latino only[6]	134 010	11.6	9	118 940	13.1	8	3 540	5.3	10	11 530	6.4	14
Asian only	15 770	1.4	7	13 770	1.5	7	550	0.8	3	1 450	0.8	40
Native Hawaiian or Pacific Islander only	3 500	0.3	8	2 940	0.3	6	240	0.4	22	330	0.2	24
American Indian or Alaskan Native only	5 100	0.4	7	4 200	0.5	6	160	0.2	11	740	0.4	7
Hispanic or Latino and other race[6]	990	0.1	5	710	0.1	1	*	*	*	270	0.1	66
Multi-race	1 280	0.1	4	1 130	0.1	4	70	0.1	4	80	(7)	16
Not reported	449 080	38.9	10	330 830	36.5	10	35 230	52.6	12	83 020	45.8	11
Length of Service with Employer												
Less than 3 months	102 260	8.9	6	95 670	10.6	6	1 580	2.4	7	5 010	2.8	4
3–11 months	185 830	16.1	7	171 540	18.9	7	4 210	6.3	7	10 070	5.6	6
1–5 years	357 460	31.0	8	300 490	33.2	7	16 120	24.1	9	40 850	22.5	9
More than 5 years	489 760	42.4	11	325 220	35.9	12	41 820	62.5	10	122 720	67.7	10

[1]Median days away from work is the measure used to summarize the varying lengths of absences from work among the cases with days away from work.
[2]Days away from work cases include those that result in days away from work with or without restricted work activity.
[3]Excludes farms with fewer than 11 employees.
[4]Data for mining include establishments not governed by the Mine Safety and Health Administration rules and reporting, such as those in Oil and Gas Extraction and related support activities.
[5]Data for employers in rail transportation are provided to BLS by the Federal Railroad Administration, U.S. Department of Transportation.
[6]May be of any race.
. . . = Not available.
[7]Data too small to be displayed.
* = Figure does not meet standards of reliability or quality.

Table 14-9. Fatal Occupational Injuries, by Selected Worker Characteristics and Selected Event or Exposure, Preliminary 2012

(Number, percent.)

Characteristic	Fatalities		Selected event or exposure[1] (percent of total for characteristic category)			
	Number	Percent	Homicides	Highway[2]	Falls	Struck by object
TOTAL	4 383	100	11	24	15	12
Employee Status						
Wage and salary workers[3]	3 396	77	10	27	15	11
Self-employed[4]	987	23	14	13	16	15
Sex						
Men	4 045	92	9	24	15	12
Women	338	8	29	21	16	4
Age[5]						
Under 16 years	19	(6)	...	5	...	16
16 to 17 years	9	(6)	...	33	11	...
18 to 19 years	58	1	12	24	12	12
20 to 24 years	275	6	11	25	7	11
25 to 34 years	703	16	14	23	11	9
35 to 44 years	792	18	12	25	13	11
45 to 54 years	1 102	25	10	25	17	10
55 to 64 years	869	20	9	23	17	13
65 years and over	552	13	6	22	23	16
Race and Hispanic Origin						
White	3 002	68	8	25	15	12
Black	446	10	22	26	9	9
Hispanic[7]	708	16	9	22	21	14
American Indian or Alaskan Native	34	1	...	15	9	15
Asian	137	3	36	12	18	5
Native Hawaiian or Pacific Islander	7	(6)	...	...	...	...
Multiple races	5	(6)	20	...	...	...
Other or not reported	44	1	20	23	14	...

Note: Totals for 2012 are preliminary. Totals for major categories may include subcategories not shown separately. Components may not sum to totals because of rounding.

[1]The figure shown is the percentage of the total fatalities for that demographic group.
[2]"Highway" includes deaths to vehicle occupants resulting from traffic incidents that occur on the public roadway, shoulder, or surrounding area. It excludes incidents occurring entirely off the roadway, such as in parking lots or on farms; incidents involving trains; and deaths of pedestrians or other non-passengers.
[3]May include volunteers and other workers receiving compensation.
[4]Includes self-employed workers, owners of unincorporated businesses and farms, paid and unpaid family workers, and members of partnerships; may also include owners of incorporated businesses.
[5]There were eight fatalities for which there was insufficient information to determine the age of the decedent.
[6]Less than or equal to 0.5 percent.
[7]May be of any race.
. . . = Not available.

Table 14-10. Fatal Occupational Injuries, by Occupation and Selected Event or Exposure, Preliminary 2012

(Number, percent.)

Occupation[1]	Fatalities		Selected event or exposure (percent of total for characteristic category)[2]			
	Number	Percent	Homicide	Highway[3]	Falls	Struck by object
TOTAL	4 383	100	11	24	15	12
Management	429	10	13	13	11	13
Top executives	30	1	10	33	...	...
Operations specialties managers	23	1	13	26	...	...
Other management	365	8	13	10	12	15
Business and financial operations	22	1	18	45	14	...
Computer and mathematical	8	(4)	12	...	...	...
Architecture and engineering	33	1	...	33	12	9
Engineers	22	1	...	32	...	...
Life, physical, and social science	19	(4)	11	32	...	...
Community and social services	37	1	38	22	...	...
Legal	8	(4)	...	...	...	...
Education, training, and library	24	1	...	...	25	...
Arts, design, entertainment, sports, and media	44	1	11	7	16	...
Entertainers and performers, sports and related workers	27	1	...	...	...	...
Health care practitioners and technical	49	1	...	31	14	...
Health diagnosing and treating practitioners	29	1	...	17	14	...
Health technologists and technicians	17	(4)	...	59	...	...
Health care support	10	(4)	...	40	30	...
Protective service	224	5	40	22	4	3
Fire fighting and prevention workers	18	(4)	11	33	6	...
Law enforcement workers	119	3	41	29	3	...
Other protective service workers	68	2	49	6	7	...
Food preparation and serving related	53	1	34	13	19	...
Supervisors, food preparation and serving workers	14	(4)	50	...	...	...
Building and grounds cleaning and maintenance	245	6	4	10	27	22
Building cleaning and pest control workers	49	1	16	16	29	...
Grounds maintenance workers	156	4	...	8	28	29
Personal care and service	64	1	33	14	8	...
Sales and related	216	5	51	12	11	2
Supervisors, sales workers	106	2	57	6	7	3
Retail sales workers	63	1	63	5	16	...
Sales representatives, services	10	(4)	...	30	30	...
Sales representatives, wholesale and manufacturing	15	(4)	...	60	...	...
Office and administrative support	82	2	23	24	16	5
Material recording, scheduling, dispatching, and distributing workers	47	1	11	30	15	6
Farming, fishing, and forestry	245	6	...	12	5	31
Agricultural workers	139	3	...	18	6	17
Fishing and hunting workers	34	1	...	3	6	...
Forest, conservation, and logging workers	64	1	...	...	5	75
Construction and extraction	838	19	1	13	35	10
Supervisors, construction and extraction workers	117	3	1	18	33	12
Construction trades workers	577	13	1	10	40	8
Extraction workers	86	2	...	26	15	22
Installation, maintenance, and repair	326	7	5	16	13	24
Vehicle and mobile equipment mechanics, installers, and repairers	104	2	6	12	3	46
Other installation, maintenance, and repair	179	4	3	15	18	13
Production	211	5	6	8	14	16
Supervisors, production workers	22	1	...	...	...	...
Metal workers and plastic workers	82	2	4	11	12	18
Transportation and material moving	1 150	26	6	50	6	9
Air transportation workers	71	2	...	...	...	...
Motor vehicle operators	817	19	7	67	5	6
Water transportation workers	13	(4)	...	...	...	...
Material moving workers	207	5	4	12	14	21
Military	43	1	7	7	...	...

Note: Totals for 2012 are preliminary. Totals for major categories may include subcategories not shown separately. Components may not sum to totals because of rounding. There were three fatalities for which there was insufficient information to determine a specific occupation classification.

[1]Based on the 2010 Standard Occupational Classification (SOC) system.
[2]The figure shown is the percentage of total fatalities for that occupation group.
[3]"Highway" includes deaths to vehicle occupants resulting from traffic incidents that occur on the public roadway, shoulder, or surrounding area. It excludes incidents occurring entirely off the roadway, such as in parking lots or on farms; incidents involving trains; and deaths of pedestrians or other non-passengers.
[4]Less than or equal to 0.5 percent.
. . . = Not available.

INDEX